THE LEGAL PROFESSION

ETHICS IN CONTEMPORARY PRACTICE

■ ■ ■

by

Ann Southworth
Professor of Law
University of California, Irvine, School of Law

Catherine L. Fisk
Chancellor's Professor of Law
University of California, Irvine, School of Law

AMERICAN CASEBOOK SERIES®

WEST
ACADEMIC
PUBLISHING

Mat #41666765

American Casebook Series is a trademark registered in the U.S. Patent and Trademark Office.

© 2014 LEG, Inc. d/b/a West Academic
    444 Cedar Street, Suite 700
    St. Paul, MN 55101
    1-877-888-1330

West, West Academic Publishing, and West Academic are trademarks of West Publishing Corporation, used under license.

Printed in the United States of America

ISBN: 978-1-62810-172-0

For John, Amy, and Ben.

AS

For Erwin, Jeff, Adam, Alex, Mara, and Kim.

CLF

ACKNOWLEDGMENTS

The basic premise of this book—that the study of lawyers' ethics should be thoroughly integrated with an in-depth examination of the profession's history, structure, regulation, and practice organizations—draws inspiration from other scholars and teachers too numerous to mention by name. It is an outgrowth of a rich and continuing conversation about what law schools should do to educate law students to become knowledgeable and reflective about the profession they are preparing to enter and their places within it. Our students, and the many lawyers and scholars who participated in our course over the past four years, have helped us immeasurably as we have worked to translate an abstract proposition about the interconnectedness of professional identity, legal institutions, and the varied forms of legal practice, into a set of teaching materials.

We are grateful to the many authors and publishers who have given us permission to reprint their copyrighted work. UC Irvine's law librarians and two of our students, Sasha Nichols and Aaron Benmark, provided superb research assistance. Rick Abel, Susan Carle, Scott Cummings, Bryant Garth, Clare Pastore, Cassandra Burke Robertson, and Carole Silver, as well as anonymous reviewers of earlier versions of this manuscript, gave us many excellent suggestions. Our assistant, Nicola McCoy, devoted countless hours to a multitude of tasks required to prepare this manuscript for publication.

In editing excerpts of articles, books, and cases, we have omitted some textual material without ellipses, and we have omitted most footnotes and citations without notation, in order to manage the book's length and promote its readability.

SUMMARY OF CONTENTS

PART II. THE ATTORNEY-CLIENT RELATIONSHIP

PART III. CONFIDENTIALITY

PART IV. CONFLICTS OF INTEREST

PART V. PROFESSIONALISM IN CONTEXT: A SURVEY OF PRACTICE SETTINGS/TYPES

SUBPART A. CRIMINAL PRACTICE

TABLE OF CONTENTS

PART II. THE ATTORNEY-CLIENT RELATIONSHIP

PART III. CONFIDENTIALITY

PART V. PROFESSIONALISM IN CONTEXT: A SURVEY OF PRACTICE SETTINGS/TYPES

SUBPART A. CRIMINAL PRACTICE

SUBPART B. LARGE ORGANIZATIONAL CLIENTS

SUBPART D. LAWYERS AND THE PRACTICE
OF DISPUTE RESOLUTION

SUBPART E. PUBLIC INTEREST PRACTICE

TABLE OF CASES

The principal cases are in bold type.

THE LEGAL PROFESSION
ETHICS IN CONTEMPORARY PRACTICE

PART I

AN INTRODUCTION TO THE AMERICAN LEGAL PROFESSION

. . .

This book is designed to help you prepare to chart successful, rewarding, and responsible careers in law. Drawing from various disciplines, including philosophy, economics, history, sociology, and psychology, it will teach you about the variety of practice settings in which lawyers work and the professional opportunities and challenges of each. It will also give you some of the tools you will need to resolve the legal and ethical issues that lawyers confront in practice and to navigate the enormous legal, cultural, and economic forces that are reshaping the legal profession.

One of the purposes of these materials is to help you decide what to do with your law degree and to appreciate the tradeoffs that various choices entail. To that end, we will systematically examine the different practice settings in which lawyers work, including prosecutors' offices, public defender organizations, small, medium, and large private firms, corporate counsel offices, nonprofit advocacy groups, legal aid, government agencies, and the judiciary. That information will help you assess the fit between various types of practices and your own character traits, values, strengths, and aspirations. Even if you have already decided how to use your law degree, this class will provide a valuable overview of the legal profession and an appreciation for the enormous range of things that lawyers do.

Like most books on professional responsibility, this one will teach you the Model Rules of Professional Conduct and other elements of the law that governs lawyers. We will consider gaps and ambiguity in that law and how lawyers respond (and should respond) to such legal uncertainty. However, our approach departs from some professional responsibility texts in emphasizing the relationship between lawyers' ethics and the practice contexts in which lawyers work. Lawyers' workplaces have been called arenas of professionalism, where lawyers' views about their roles and obligations take shape.[1] Those arenas are at least as important as

---

[1] Robert L. Nelson & David M. Trubek, *Arenas of Professionalism: The Professional Ideologies of Lawyers in Context*, in LAWYERS' IDEALS/LAWYERS' PRACTICES: TRANSFORMATIONS IN THE AMERICAN LEGAL PROFESSION 177–214 (Robert L. Nelson, David M. Trubek & Rayman L. Solomon eds. 1992).

rules of professional conduct, disciplinary committees, liability controls, and lawyers' individual consciences in determining how lawyers frame and resolve ethical conundrums. Therefore, we will study legal ethics in context, paying close attention to lawyers' work settings, institutional roles, and economic pressures.

As future leaders of the profession, you also need to understand issues and problems that confront the profession as a whole. Such issues include the legal services market and its regulation, the distribution of legal services, the profession's demographics and social structure, lawyers' roles in regulatory processes, and the implications of globalization for the legal profession. Whether you like it or not, friends and strangers alike will begin looking to you for commentary on the legal profession and its function in American society. You will be held to account for the public's general skepticism about lawyers. Responding to questions about the profession (and to lawyer jokes) will be easier once you have developed well-informed views about those issues. These materials will push you to decide which criticisms are justified, what policy responses are appropriate, and which sectors of the profession will win and lose under various reform proposals.

This book is divided into six units. Part I introduces the concept of a profession, the legal profession's history and demographics, the allocation of authority within the attorney-client relationship, competing conceptions of the lawyer's role, and other major concepts and themes that will arise throughout the course. Part II examines the attorney-client relationship. It looks at the formation of the relationship, the allocation of decision-making authority between attorney and client, and circumstances under which the lawyer may or must withdraw. It then surveys some of the law relating to the dealings between lawyers, their clients, and the clients of other lawyers. Part III focuses on the attorney-client privilege and the duty of confidentiality. We will consider justifications for confidentiality, the exceptions to privilege and confidentiality, and their applications to organizational clients. Part IV covers conflicts of interest—a general category of rules designed to ensure that lawyers serve clients loyally. Part V introduces you to the many different types of practice settings in which lawyers work and to issues of professionalism as they arise in those types of practice. Part VI addresses issues facing the entire profession, including access to justice, the profession's relationship to the market for legal services, diversity within the profession, competition for regulatory control, technology's influence on practice, globalization, lawyer satisfaction, and the legal profession's future.

A. THE ROLE OF THE LAWYER AND THE LEGAL PROFESSION

You've undoubtedly arrived at law school with some ideas about what you might want to do with a law degree. Perhaps there are causes you would like to advance, or maybe you think instead in terms of providing excellent service to particular types of clients. You also came here with a set of values, attributes, and political commitments that comprise your personal identity—perhaps tied in some way to where you come from, your social background, your parents' expectations, your prior experiences, religion, race, ethnicity, gender, and/or sexual orientation. At the same time, you're entering a profession with its own history and a set of institutions and practices that may be relevant to your search for an attractive future within it. In addition, your conduct as a lawyer will be constrained by various sources of law and regulation and by work-related pressures that you'll need to navigate. One of your challenges ahead lies in finding ways to reconcile your sense of justice and personal identity with your professional aspirations, legal duties, the norms in your workplace, and the expectations of clients and other participants in the legal system.

Nothing in law itself will tell you how to accomplish that. Indeed, the law will not answer many of the most critical questions that you'll confront as you seek a satisfying career in the legal profession—including what practice areas to pursue and what types of clients to represent, how to resolve tensions and sometimes outright conflicts between the pressures of practice and your moral compass, and when and how to express your personal identity in your professional life. One of the purposes of this book is to give you some of the information and tools you'll need to navigate a professional life that is consistent with your values and sense of self.

This Part introduces those issues and offers some perspectives on how you might address them. Chapter 1 introduces the role of the lawyer as a professional and considers why lawyers generally believe they should be bound by ethical rules that differ from those that govern the conduct of nonlawyers. Chapter 2 provides an overview of the profession's history, demographics and institutions, and explores what people mean when they refer to lawyers as a profession and to certain types of lawyer conduct as "professional" or "unprofessional." Chapter 3 examines and evaluates different conceptions of lawyers' roles—their responsibilities to clients, third parties, and the public. Chapter 4 considers whether and how a lawyer's background, experience, political values, and identity traits do or should influence a lawyer's professional life.

CHAPTER 1

THE ROLE OF THE LAWYER

■ ■ ■

A. INTRODUCTION TO THE ROLE OF THE LAWYER

Most lawyers share a fundamental belief that their role as lawyers legally and ethically obligates them to engage in some behavior that might not be permissible if they were acting in a capacity other than as a lawyer. That belief underlies a great deal of the law governing lawyers. More significant, many lawyers are guided in their daily work by the notion that a lawyer's role requires or prohibits certain types of behavior. The notion is reflected not just in the law governing lawyers (such as formal rules of legal ethics) but in the ways that lawyers relate to their clients and to third parties and in the implicit norms governing law offices. In this chapter we begin to consider the lawyer's role. In particular, we focus on the question of whether and how the legal and moral responsibilities of lawyers differ from those of non-lawyers. We begin with a problem based on a classic case about whether a lawyer's duties to her client compel her to keep confidential information that she would almost certainly feel morally obligated to disclose if she were acting in a capacity other than as a lawyer. We then read an excerpt of an influential article by a legal philosopher explaining and critiquing the idea that the lawyer's role allows lawyers to behave under different ethical norms than should govern non-lawyers.

B. ARE LEGAL ETHICS DIFFERENT FROM OTHER ETHICS?

Topic Overview

Why do lawyers believe they owe special duties to their clients that do not conform with ordinary ethics? Besides the rules of professional responsibility, what norms, market pressures, and other sources of guidance influence how lawyers behave in their role as lawyers? If you found yourself in the situation confronting each of the lawyers and clients in the case below, what would you do?

PROBLEM 1–1: THE CASE OF SPAULDING V. ZIMMERMAN, *263 MINN. 346 (MINNESOTA SUPREME COURT 1962)*[1]

David Spaulding, age 20, was injured in an automobile accident in 1956. The accident involved two cars at a rural crossroads late in the day. David was riding with five others on their way to the county fair. Their car was driven by Florian Ledermann, age 15, who was driving on a farm permit. Florian's sister, Elaine, was killed in the accident, and many others, including David, were seriously injured. In the other car, John Zimmerman, age 19, was driving himself and four friends and family members home from their jobs at the Zimmerman family's small business. Passengers in that car also died and were seriously injured. Because children of both the Ledermann and the Zimmerman families were injured and killed, the families were both plaintiffs and defendants in the litigation.

After the accident, David was examined by his family physician, Dr. James Cain, who diagnosed a severe chest injury with multiple rib and clavicle fractures and a concussion and hemorrhages of the brain. At Dr. Cain's suggestion, David was examined by Dr. John Pohl, an orthopedic specialist, who took X-rays of his chest. Dr. Pohl made a detailed report which stated, among other things: "The lung fields are clear. The heart and aorta are normal." The report did not indicate that David was suffering an aorta aneurysm, although in fact he was. At the suggestion of Dr. Pohl, David received a neurological examination by Dr. Paul Blake, who also did not find the aorta aneurysm.

In the meantime, at defendants' request, David was examined by Dr. Hewitt Hannah, a neurologist. It is customary in civil litigation involving claims for a plaintiff's personal injury for defendants to retain their own doctor to examine the plaintiff to assess the nature and extent of the injury. Dr. Hannah reported to attorneys for defendant Zimmerman that:

> "The one feature of the case which bothers me more than any other part of the case is the fact that this boy of 20 years of age has an aneurysm, which means a dilatation of the aorta and the arch of the aorta. Whether this came out of this accident I cannot say with any degree of certainty. Of course an aneurysm or dilatation of the aorta in a boy of this age is a serious matter as far as his life. This aneurysm may dilate further and it might rupture with further dilatation and this would cause his death.

> "It would be interesting also to know whether the X-ray of his lungs, taken immediately following the accident, shows this dilatation or

---

[1] The facts stated here and in the notes following Problem 1–1 are drawn from the Minnesota Supreme Court's opinion and from an article about the case written by two law professors who interviewed the surviving participants. Roger C. Cramton & Lori P. Knowles, *Professional Secrecy and Its Exceptions:* Spaulding v. Zimmerman *Revisited,* 83 MINN. L. REV. 63 (1998). *See also* Roger Cramton, Spaulding v. Zimmerman: *Confidentiality and its Exceptions, in* LEGAL ETHICS: LAW STORIES (Deborah L. Rhode & David Luban, eds., 2006).

not. If it was not present immediately following the accident and is now present, then we could be sure that it came out of the accident."

Neither David nor his father was aware that David had the aorta aneurysm. They believed that he was recovering from the injuries sustained in the accident. After the medical examinations, lawyers for David and for the defendants agreed that for $6,500 David and his father would settle all claims arising out of the accident.

After the parties agreed to settle the case, David's lawyer presented to the court a petition for approval of the settlement. The petition, which included affidavits from David's doctors, described David's injuries as found by Dr. Cain. The defendants did not present any evidence and, based on David's petition, the court approved the settlement and dismissed the case.

Two years later, David was examined again by Dr. Cain as part of a checkup required by the Army reserve. This time, Dr. Cain discovered the aorta aneurysm. He re-examined the X-rays which had been taken shortly after the accident and at this time discovered that they disclosed the beginning of the process which produced the aneurysm. He promptly sent David to another doctor who confirmed the finding of the aorta aneurysm and immediately performed surgery to repair it. The surgery saved David's life, but it caused him to lose the ability to speak.

Shortly thereafter, David filed a suit seeking to vacate the settlement and to reopen the case. David alleged that the aorta aneurysm was caused by the accident and, therefore, that his damages were greater than he had believed at the time the suit was settled.

The trial court vacated the settlement and the Minnesota Supreme Court affirmed. Their reasoning rested on three crucial points. First, the courts emphasized that the mistake concerning the existence of the aneurysm and, therefore, the extent of David's injuries was not mutual. For unknown reasons, David's lawyer failed to use the procedures available in civil litigation that enable each party to discover the facts known to the other party before the case goes to trial or is settled.

Second, the Minnesota Supreme Court said: "That defendants' counsel concealed the knowledge they had is not disputed. The issue is the character of the concealment. Was it done under circumstances that defendants must be charged with knowledge that plaintiff did not know of the injury? If so, an enriching advantage was gained for defendants at plaintiff's expense. There is no doubt of the good faith of both defendants' counsel. There is no doubt that during the course of the negotiations, when the parties were in an adversary relationship, no rule required or duty rested upon defendants or their representatives to disclose this knowledge."

Third, although the Minnesota Supreme Court determined that the defendants had no obligation to reveal their medical evidence to the plaintiffs in the absence of a request through the mechanisms of pretrial discovery, the court stated, "once the agreement to settle was reached, it is difficult to characterize the parties' relationship as adverse. At this point all parties were interested in securing court approval." The court then said that "to hold that the concealment was not of such character as to result in an unconscionable advantage over plaintiff's ignorance or mistake, would be to penalize innocence and incompetence and reward less than full performance of an officer of the court's duty to make full disclosure to the court when applying for approval in minor settlement proceedings." Yet the court also stated: "While no canon of ethics or legal obligation may have required them to inform plaintiff or his counsel with respect [to their medical evidence], or to advise the court therein, it did become obvious to them at the time, that the settlement then made did not contemplate or take into consideration the disability described."

NOTES ON SPAULDING V. ZIMMERMAN

1.   *What Would You Do?* If you knew someone was suffering a life-threatening condition and you knew that he did not know, would you consider yourself morally obligated to tell him to enable him to get medical care that might save his life? If you believe you would have a moral obligation to tell him, why (if at all) should a lawyer not have the same obligation? The most important question the *Spaulding* case asks you to consider is what aspects of the lawyer's role prompted the defendants' lawyers to say nothing to David Spaulding about his condition if, as non-lawyers, they would certainly have told him.

2.   *What Did David's Lawyer Do Wrong?* David Spaulding's lawyer owed David competent representation. Model Rule 1.1. Ordinarily, it would seem to be incompetent to settle a personal injury case without first obtaining the defense evidence about the extent of the plaintiff's injuries, and Dr. Hannah's report was available to David through a routine discovery request. David's lawyer was young and inexperienced, which may partly explain why he did not request a copy of Dr. Hannah's report. But the lawyer may also have feared that if he requested the defense doctor's report, the defense would request the reports of David's physicians, one of which recommended waiting to settle the case until the full extent of David's injuries became known. Apparently both families wanted to settle the case quickly, so David's lawyer may have feared that a court would not approve a settlement if David's doctor recommended waiting. If David's lawyer made a strategic calculation rather than an ignorant blunder in failing to request Dr. Hannah's report, would your decision about whether to allow David to reopen the case change? Why should clients be bound by the strategic (or simply stupid) choices of their lawyers?

3.   *What is Sound Advice?* Did counsel for the defendants serve their clients well? The two lawyers representing the Zimmerman defendants never informed their clients about David's aneurysm; they apparently made the decision not to disclose without consulting either the Zimmermans or the insurance company that was paying them. Although the duty of

confidentiality prohibited them from disclosing David's injury without a discovery request or client consent, nothing in the rule would have discouraged them from seeking consent to disclose or counseling the Zimmermans and the insurance company about the full range of options. Indeed, the rules of ethics encourage lawyers to keep clients informed (Model Rule 1.4) and to consult with clients in making important decisions (Model Rule 1.2). Why do you imagine the lawyers did not discuss disclosure of the aneurysm with their clients?

Some empirical literature suggests that lawyers wrongly tend to assume their clients are governed only by selfish concerns and prefer their own financial interests over the interests of others. But clients often want a helpful counselor and may be more concerned about the welfare of others than lawyers tend to think.[2]

4. ***Who Was the Client of the Defense Counsel?*** In accident cases like *Spaulding v. Zimmerman,* it is common for the defendant to be represented by a lawyer who is chosen and paid by the insurance company. The lawyer typically represents both the defendant-insured and the insurance company, and their interests are not always aligned. The Zimmermans, for example, might have wanted David to learn of the aneurysm, both because they cared about saving his life and because the damages would be paid by the insurance company and not by them personally. The insurance company's interests are perhaps more complex to determine. If one thinks of the company solely as an entity interested in minimizing its immediate financial liabilities, one can imagine it preferring that David not know. If one thinks of its reputation in the community, or of the wishes of the company's executives, employees and shareholders as people, one might imagine the insurance company would prefer that its lawyers tell David. If you can imagine why the insurance company would have preferred that David not learn about the aneurysm, can you imagine any reason why the Zimmerman family would wish him not to know? If the wishes of the Zimmermans and the insurance company conflict about whether to disclose, how should the lawyer act? There are other circumstances where the interests of two clients may come into conflict, such as where the lawyer represents both a corporation and one of its employees or executives. We consider the challenges of dual representation in Parts IV and V of this book.

5. ***Duty of Confidentiality.*** A rule of legal ethics in effect in Minnesota at the time these events occurred prohibited the defendants' lawyers from revealing David's condition to David or his counsel without either a discovery request or the defendants' consent. That is, without a discovery request or the consent of their clients, the defense lawyers were prohibited from disclosing David's injuries to him even if they thought it was necessary to save his life. Today, the role governing the duty of

---

[2] See Marvin Mindes, *Trickster, Hero, Helper: A Report on the Lawyer Image,* 1982 AM. B. FOUND. RES. J. 177.

confidentiality that lawyers owe to their clients in most jurisdictions has an exception that might allow the defendants' lawyers to disclose the aneurysm to David even if their clients did not consent. As we will see in Chapter 7, the rule in most states today permits a lawyer to disclose confidential information obtained in the course of representing a client when the lawyer "reasonably believes" disclosure is necessary "to prevent reasonably certain death or substantial bodily harm." Model Rule 1.6(b)(1).

6. ***Duty to Client, to Third Party, and to the Court.*** The Minnesota Supreme Court said that "during the course of the negotiations, when the parties were in an adversary relationship, no rule required or duty rested upon defendants or their representatives to disclose this knowledge." But the court's decision to re-open the case was premised on the view that the defense counsel did have a duty to disclose the information when the parties sought court approval of the settlement. As we will see, the rules of ethics impose greater duties of candor on lawyers vis-à-vis courts than they impose on lawyers' dealings with adversaries and third parties in negotiation and in litigation. That is, a lawyer is required to inform courts of some things they are not required to disclose to others. Some criticize this as a double standard that is justified by no policy other than the power that courts have over lawyers. We will consider in Chapter 25 whether there are justifications for requiring greater candor in lawyers' dealings with some people or entities than others.

7. ***Would You Argue the Defense Side?*** The young lawyer, Richard Pemberton, who argued the case for the Zimmermans in the Minnesota Supreme Court, later said he received the opportunity to argue it because one of the more senior lawyers in his firm found the case unpleasant. A supreme court argument is ordinarily a fun and prestigious assignment that a senior lawyer would not pass up. But many would find it difficult to defend the proposition that a lawyer may not disclose confidential information even to save someone's life. If you had been Richard Pemberton and had been assigned the case because a senior lawyer found it distasteful, would you take the case even if you found your client's position morally wrong? What would be the professional and personal advantages and disadvantages for the junior lawyer to handle the matter or to refuse to handle it?

8. ***Reconciling Law with Conscience.*** While the requirements of the rules of professional responsibility and the other law governing lawyers are extremely important to know and follow, for lawyers, as for everyone else, professional conduct should also be guided by conscience. In most circumstances, the law governing lawyers will be reconcilable with conscience, but that may not always be true. As Pemberton recalled:

> After twenty years in practice, I would like to think that I would have disclosed the aneurysm of the aorta as an act of humanity and without regard to the legalities involved, just as I surely would now. You might suggest to your students in the

course on professional responsibility that a pretty good rule for them to practice respecting professional conduct is to do the right thing.

9. ***Protecting Clients from Wrongful Lawyer Conduct.*** In very rare cases, a lawyer may conclude that her conscience compels her to do something that the law of professional responsibility prohibits, or vice versa. Some violations of legal rules, even if motivated by conscientious objection, can have grave consequences for the lawyer, including in some cases disbarment and criminal prosecution, and can harm clients. If the defense counsel had disclosed the aneurysm over the objection of their clients, should they be subject to professional discipline? Would your answer depend on whether you think the disclosure harmed their clients? Would it depend on whether the clients have other ways of protecting themselves from whatever harm their lawyers did to them, such as suing the lawyer for malpractice or firing the lawyer?

As we will see later in this book, powerful clients (like the insurance company in a case like *Spaulding*) often sway lawyers to act in what the client perceives to be its interests by the implicit or explicit threat to fire the lawyer or to withhold future business. The defense counsel's failure to consult with the Zimmermans about whether to inform David may have been motivated less by the lawyers' sense of what the rules of professional responsibility required than by what they believed the insurance company would want and by their unwillingness even to raise a delicate issue that might alienate a valuable client.

C. JUSTIFICATIONS FOR A DISTINCT FORM OF LEGAL ETHICS

As *Spaulding v. Zimmerman* illustrates, lawyers sometimes believe that their duties to their client may permit or require them to do things that they would not do except in their capacities as lawyers. Legal philosopher Richard Wasserstrom wrote the classic article exploring the philosophical justifications for role differentiation. As you see, Wasserstrom is critical of the idea that the professional role of lawyers permits or justifies behavior that would be considered unethical if engaged in by non-lawyers.

LAWYERS AS PROFESSIONALS: SOME MORAL ISSUES

Richard Wasserstrom
5 Human Rights 1 (1975)

[This paper examines a moral criticism of lawyers which, Wasserstrom notes, tends to be made by non-lawyers and to be rejected by lawyers.] The criticism is that the lawyer-client relationship renders the lawyer at best systematically amoral and at worst more than occasionally immoral in his or her dealings with the rest of mankind.

[T]he issue I propose to examine concerns the ways the professional-client relationship affects the professional's stance toward the world at large. The primary question that is presented is whether there is adequate justification for the kind of moral universe that comes to be inhabited by the lawyer as he or she goes through professional life. For at best the lawyer's world is a simplified moral world; often it is an amoral one; and more than occasionally, perhaps, an overtly immoral one.

[O]ne central feature of the professions in general and of law in particular is that there is a special, complicated relationship between the professional, and the client or patient. For each of the parties in this relationship, but especially for the professional, the behavior that is involved, is to a very significant degree, what I call role-differentiated behavior. And this is significant because it is the nature of role-differentiated behavior that it often makes it both appropriate and desirable for the person in a particular role to put to one side considerations of various sorts—and especially various moral considerations—that would otherwise be relevant if not decisive.

Being a parent is, in probably every human culture, to be involved in role-differentiated behavior. In our own culture, and once again in most, if not all, human cultures, as a parent one is entitled, if not obligated, to prefer the interests of one's own children over those of children generally. That is to say, it is regarded as appropriate for a parent to allocate excessive goods to his or her own children, even though other children may have substantially more pressing and genuine needs for these same items. If one were trying to decide what the right way was to distribute assets among a group of children all of whom were strangers to oneself, the relevant moral considerations would be very different from those that would be thought to obtain once one's own children were in the picture. In short, the role-differentiated character of the situation alters the relevant moral point of view enormously.

A similar situation is presented by the case of the scientist. For a number of years there has been debate and controversy within the scientific community over the question of whether scientists should participate in the development and elaboration of atomic theory, especially as those theoretical advances could then be translated into development of atomic weapons that would become a part of the arsenal of existing nation states. The dominant view, although it was not the unanimous one, in the scientific community was that the role of the scientist was to expand the limits of human knowledge. Atomic power was a force which had previously not been utilizable by human beings. The job of the scientist was, among other things, to develop ways and means by which that could now be done. And it was simply no part of one's role as a scientist to forego inquiry, or divert one's scientific explorations because of the fact that the fruits of the investigation could

2. **Within the Bounds of the Law.** Does this associate place sufficient emphasis on the "as long as they are lawful" limitation in the principle of neutrality?

* * *

The following exchange explores those questions. Stephen Pepper, who offers perhaps the best defense of the amoral conception of the lawyer's role in the excerpt below, uses another term to describe this conception; he calls it the "first-class citizenship model."

THE LAWYER'S AMORAL ETHICAL ROLE: A DEFENSE, A PROBLEM, AND SOME POSSIBILITIES

Stephen L. Pepper
1986 American Bar Foundation Research Journal 613

[In 1975] Richard Wasserstrom published a provocative paper focusing attention on the moral dimension of the lawyer-client relationship. Much of Wasserstrom's exposition concerned the role-differentiated morality of the lawyer-client relationship, what he referred to as the amoral professional role. Wasserstrom was critical, but "undecided," about the value of that role. This essay is a defense of the lawyer's amoral role.

The role of all professionals, observed Wasserstrom, "is to prefer . . . the interests of client or patient" over those of other individuals. "[W]here the attorney-client relationship exists, it is often appropriate and many times even obligatory for the attorney to do things that, all other things being equal, an ordinary person need not, and should not do." Once a lawyer has entered into the professional relationship with a client, the notion is that conduct by the lawyer in service to the client is judged by a different moral standard than the same conduct by a layperson. Through cross-examination, a lawyer may suggest to a jury that a witness is lying when the lawyer knows the witness is telling the truth. A lawyer may draft contracts or create a corporation for a client to enable the distribution and sale of cigarettes, Saturday Night Specials,* or pornography. A lawyer may draft a will for a client disinheriting children should they marry outside the faith. The traditional view is that if such conduct by the lawyer is lawful, then it is morally justifiable, even if the same conduct by a layperson is morally unacceptable and even if the client's goals or means are morally unacceptable. As long as what lawyer and client do is lawful, it is the client who is morally accountable, not the lawyer.

---

* [Eds: A Saturday Night Special was a cheap and easily obtainable handgun that was commonly used in violent crimes in the 1980s; debates about banning the sale of such handguns in the 1980s were similar to debates about whether to ban the sale of assault weapons today.]

The First Class Citizenship Model. The premise with which we begin is that law is a public good available to all. Society, through its "lawmakers"—legislatures, courts, administrative agencies, and so forth—has created various mechanisms to ease and enable the private attainment of individual or group goals. The corporate form of enterprise, the contract, the trust, the will, and access to civil court to gain the use of public force for the settlement of private grievance are all vehicles of empowerment for the individual or group; all are "law" created by the collectivity to be generally available for private use. In addition to these structuring mechanisms are vast amounts of law, knowledge of which is intended to be generally available and is empowering: landlord/tenant law, labor law, OSHA, Social Security—the list can be vastly extended. Access to both forms of law increases one's ability to successfully attain goals.

The second premise is a societal commitment to the principle of individual autonomy. This premise is founded on the belief that liberty and autonomy are a moral good, that free choice is better than constraint, that each of us wishes, to the extent possible, to make our own choices rather than to have them made for us. This belief is incorporated into our legal system, which accommodates individual autonomy by leaving as much room as possible for liberty and diversity. Leaving regulatory law aside for the moment, our law is designed (1) to allow the private structuring of affairs (contracts, corporations, wills, trusts, etc.) and (2) to define conduct that is intolerable. The latter sets a floor below which one cannot go, but leaves as much room as possible above that floor for individual decision making. Diversity and autonomy are preferred over "right" or "good" conduct.

The third step is that in a highly legalized society such as ours, autonomy is often dependent upon access to the law. And while access to law—to the creation and use of a corporation, to knowledge of how much overtime one has to pay or is entitled to receive—is formally available to all, in reality it is available only through a lawyer. Our law is usually not simple, usually not self-executing. For most people most of the time, meaningful access to the law requires the assistance of a lawyer. If the conduct which the lawyer facilitates is above the floor of the intolerable—is not unlawful—then this line of thought suggests that what the lawyer does is a social good.

For the lawyer to have moral responsibility for each act he or she facilitates, for the lawyer to have a moral obligation to refuse to facilitate that which the lawyer believes to be immoral, is to substitute lawyers' beliefs for individual autonomy and diversity. Such a screening submits each to the prior restraint of the judge/facilitator and to rule by an oligarchy of lawyers. If the conduct is sufficiently "bad," it would seem that it ought to be made explicitly unlawful. If it is not that bad, why subject the citizenry to the happenstance of the moral judgment of the particular lawyer to whom each has access? If making the conduct unlawful is too onerous because the law would be too vague, or it is too difficult to identify the conduct in advance, or there is not sufficient social or political concern, do we intend to delegate to the individual lawyer the authority for case-by-case legislation and policing?

A final significant value supporting the first-class citizenship model is that of equality. If law is a public good, access to which increases autonomy, then equality of access is important. For access to the law to be filtered unequally through the disparate moral views of each individual's lawyer does not appear to be justifiable. Even given the current and perhaps permanent fact of unequal access to the law, it does not make sense to compound that inequality with another. If access to a lawyer is achieved (through private allocation of one's means, public provision, or the lawyer's or profession's choice to provide it), should the extent of that access depend upon individual lawyer conscience? One of the unpleasant concomitants of the view that a lawyer should be morally responsible for all that she does is the resulting inequality: unfiltered access to the law is then available only to those who are legally sophisticated or to those able to educate themselves sufficiently for access to the law, while those less sophisticated—usually those less educated—are left with no access or with access that subjects their use of the law to the moral judgment and veto of the lawyer.

The Adversary System. Much writing on the amoral role of the lawyer has dealt with the layperson's common conception of what lawyers do: criminal defense. The amoral role is justified by the need of the "man in trouble" for a champion familiar with the law to aid him in facing the vast resources of the state bearing down on him, attempting to seize his most basic liberties and put him in jail. In this context, however, there is another champion, the prosecutor, with greater resources, opposing and balancing the lawyer's amorality. More important, there are a neutral judge and a jury whose roles are significantly less amoral than the advocate's. Critics of the lawyer's role have had a field day distinguishing this situation from civil litigation and from nonlitigation (what most lawyers are working on most of the time). The critics suggest that a role justified by the rather unusual context of the criminal justice system simply is not justified in the far more common lawyer roles. Where there is no judge responsible for applying the law from a neutral stance, where there is no lawyer protecting those who may be victimized or exploited by another person's use of "the law"—in these situations the critics of the amoral role argue that the lawyer must take on the neutral judge's role and screen access to and use of the law. Their point is that a role modeled on Perry Mason does not fit the lawyer working for Sears drafting form consumer contracts.

It is therefore significant that the justification for the lawyer's amoral role sketched above has not once mentioned the adversary system, has not been based on any premise involving an opposing lawyer or a neutral judge or jury.

Before moving on from the adversary system criticism, it is appropriate to note that the adversary system image of the lawyer as the champion against a hostile world—the hired gun—is not the proper image for the general role of the lawyer presented here (although it may be the proper image for the criminal defense lawyer). Rather, the image more concordant with the first-class citizenship model is that of the individual facing and needing to use a very large and very complicated machine (with lots of whirring gears and spinning data tapes) that he can't get to work. This is "the law" that confronts the individual in our society. It is theoretically there for his use, but he can't use it for his purposes without the aid of someone who has the correct wrenches, meters, and more esoteric tools, and knows how and where to use them. Or the image is that of someone who stands frustrated before a photocopier that won't copy (or someone whose car won't go) and needs a technician (or mechanic) to make it go. It is ordinarily not the technician's or mechanic's moral concern whether the content of what is about to be copied is morally good or bad, or for what purpose the customer intends to use the car.

The Problem of Legal Realism. Up to this point in the discussion, access to the law as the primary justification for the amoral professional role has been presented with relatively little focus on what "the law" refers to. The implication has been that the law is existent and determinable, that there is "something there" for the lawyer to find (or know) and communicate to the client. The "thereness" of the law is also the assumption underlying the commonly understood limit on the amoral role: the lawyer can only assist the client "within the bounds of the law." This accords with the usual understanding of the law from the lay or client point of view, but not from the lawyer's point of view. The dominant view of law inculcated in the law schools, which will be identified here as "legal realism," approaches law without conceiving of it as objectively "out there" to be discovered and applied. A relatively little explored problem is the dynamic between the amoral professional role and a skeptical attitude toward law.

By "legal realism" I mean a view of law which stresses its open-textured, vague nature over its precision; its manipulability over its certainty; and its instrumental possibilities over its normative content. From "positivism" modern legal education takes the notion of the separation of law and morality: in advising the client, the lawyer is concerned with the law as an "is," a fact of power and limitation, more than as an "ought." From "legal realism" it takes the notion of law as a prediction of what human officials will do, more than as an existent, objective, determinable limit or boundary on client behavior. From "process jurisprudence" it takes an emphasis on client goals and private structuring, an instrumental use of law that deemphasizes the determination of law through adjudication or the prediction of the outcome of adjudication. These three views of "the law" are mutually reinforcing rather than conflicting. To the extent that legal education inculcates these views, "the law" becomes a rather amorphous thing, dependent upon the client's situation, goals, and risk preferences. What is the interaction between this view of the law and the view of the lawyer as an amoral servant of the client whose assistance is limited only by "the law"?

The apt image is that of Holmes's "bad man." The modern lawyer is taught to look at the law as the "bad man" would, "who cares only for the material consequences." The lawyer discovers and conveys "the law" to his client from this perspective and then is told to limit his own assistance to the client based upon this same view of "the law." The modern view of contract law, for example, deemphasizes the normative obligation of promises and views breach of contract as a "right" that is subject to the "cost" of damages. Breach of contract is not criminal and, normally, fulfillment of a contractual obligation is not forced on a party (not "specifically enforced," in contract law terminology). The client who comes in with a more normative view of the obligation of contracts will be educated by the competent lawyer as to the "breach as cost" view of "the law." Similarly, modern tort law has emphasized allocation of the "costs" of accidents, as opposed to the more normative view of 19th- and early 20th-century negligence law. Thus, negligence law can be characterized as establishing a right to a nonconsensual taking from the injured party on the part of the tortfeasor, subject once again to the "cost" of damages. An industrial concern assessing and planning conduct which poses risks of personal injury or death to third parties will be guided by a lawyer following this view away from perceiving the imposition of unreasonable risk as a "wrong" and toward perceiving it as a potential cost.

From the perspective of fully informed access to the law, this modification of the client's view is good because it accords with the generally accepted understanding of the law among those who are closest to its use and administration—lawyers and judges. It is accurate; it is useful to the client. From the perspective of the ethical relationship between lawyer and client, it is far more problematic. If one combines the dominant "legal realism" understanding of law with the traditional amoral role of the lawyer, there is no moral input or constraint in the present model of the lawyer-client relationship. The client who consults a lawyer will be guided to maximize his autonomy through the tools of the law—tools designed and used to maximize freedom, not to provide a guide to good behavior. If one cannot rely on the client or an alternative social institution to provide that guide, to suggest a moral restraint on that which is legally available, then what the lawyer does may be evil: lawyers in the aggregate may consistently guide clients away from moral conduct and restraint.

Assume client consults lawyer concerning discharge of polluted water from a rural plant. Client wants to know what the law requires, respects "the law," and intends to comply. Removing ammonia from the plant's effluent is very expensive. The EPA limit is .050 grams of ammonia per liter of effluent, and the EPA has widely publicized this standard to relevant industries. In addition to this information, however, lawyer informs client that inspection in rural areas of the state is rare and that enforcement officials always issue a warning (give a second chance) prior to applying sanctions unless the violation is extreme. Moreover, lawyer also informs client that it is known informally that violations of .075 grams per liter or less are ignored because of a limited enforcement budget. In such a situation, lay ignorance of legal technicalities and the realities of enforcement would seem to lead toward more obedience of "the law" (the .050-gram limit). Access to an amoral, "legal realist" lawyer leads toward violation of "the law." Given the model elaborated above, unless the client comes equipped with strong moral guidance, there will be no pressure to obey the law as written. (Worse, if the client is a corporate manager, she may be bound by her own amoral professional role which perceives shareholder profit as its primary guide.)

<u>Potential Answers to the Problem of Legal Realism</u>. [Pepper offers several ideas about how to ameliorate the dilemma sketched above, including these.]

The first alternative is to accept the situation described above as either proper or unavoidable. To the extent that the pure "legal realist" view is the basis for conduct, law without enforcement is rendered meaningless. This in turn suggests the need for vast increases in resources devoted to law enforcement. Such a prospect is rather daunting in an era of insufficient government means. More important, the societal atmosphere likely to accompany such an emphasis on law enforcement is not pleasant to contemplate.

[Another] possibility emphasizes the utility of wide-ranging communication between lawyer and client. Instead of defining the client's goals in narrow material terms and approaching the law solely as means to or constraint on such goals, this view opens the relationship to moral input in two ways. First, the lawyer's full understanding of the situation, including the lawyer's moral understanding, can be communicated to the client. The professional role remains amoral in that the lawyer is still required to provide full access to the law for the client, but the dilemma sketched above is ameliorated by moral input from the lawyer which supplements access to the law. The autonomy of the client remains in that she is given access to all that the law allows, but the client's decisions are informed by the lawyer's moral judgment. The second way the dialogue model infuses a moral element into the lawyer-client relationship is from the side of the client. The current situation minimizes the client's moral input as well as the lawyer's. The client comes in with a human problem (family, business, corporate, etc.); the lawyer defines it in legal terms, usually including a legal goal and legal means to that goal, all perceived from the amoral legal realist stance. Both goal and means may well be defined by the client's interests as presumed by the lawyer: usually maximization of wealth or avoidance of incarceration. More communication drawn from the client by an open lawyer may substantially qualify those presumed goals as well as limit means.

This paper began with the example of the lawyer cross-examining a witness known to be truthful in such a way as to suggest to the jury that the witness might be lying. Dialogue with the client may educate the lawyer to the fact that the client does not want to win that way, that the lawyer is wrong in assuming that winning by all lawfully available means is the task the client intended for the lawyer. To the contrary, the client may want to have "the facts" judged by "the law" and may have no desire to win if the truth does not lead to that conclusion. Or the client may believe that exposing the truthful witness to the implied accusation of dishonesty is a moral wrong of sufficient import to prevent its use even to gain that to which he believes justice entitles him. The client may simply not want to win by immoral means. Or, looking at the dialogue with the moral input coming from the lawyer, if the lawyer is the one morally troubled by such a cross examination and the client is not, the lawyer's perception may engage or educate the client, or the client's overall regard for the lawyer may be sufficient for the client to agree that the tactic should not be used.

Two limits on the "moral dialogue" approach must be recognized. First, it is expensive. Such a dialogue requires time, and time is the lawyer's stock in trade. Either the client must be willing and able to pay for the expanded conversation at the lawyer's regular hourly rate, or the lawyer must be willing to accept a lower income. Second, client receptivity to the approach will vary with the context. The criminal defendant facing years in prison and represented by a public defender will be less open to the dialogue than will the corporate officer dealing with in-house counsel. Lawyers in some contexts may be simply unable to engage in dialogue with their clients; the larger the cultural and economic gap between lawyer and client, the less likely is meaningful moral dialogue. Thus, both limits suggest there will be a spectrum of the kinds of legal practice for which the moral dialogue ethic is suitable or possible.

Assuming a lawyer feels bound (either morally or under legally enforced professional ethics) to the amoral ethic, he or she may perceive in a particular situation a higher value that supports conduct contrary to the lawyer role. Conscientious objection always remains an alternative in such a situation: one can recognize the moral and legal validity of the amoral role, but choose not to follow it. If such conscientious objection is not limited to extreme cases, however, it is little different from the lawyer as policeman, judge, and/or deceiver. To the extent the lawyer allows moral considerations to trump professional obligation, his role is no longer amoral.

Conclusion: The Moral Autonomy of the Lawyer. Given this essay's stress on autonomy, it is fair to ask: Where in the amoral role is there a place for the lawyer's moral autonomy? Lawyers are far more intimately involved with and identified with their clients than grocers or landlords are with their customers and tenants. This causes much of the disquiet with the amoral role both within and without the profession. If the client chooses to be the "bad man," to do that which is lawful but morally wrong, does not the lawyer become a bad person, compelled by the amoral role to assist, yet intimately connected to and identified with the client's wrongdoing?

Part of the answer lies in the principle of professionalism sketched at the beginning of [this essay]. Because of the large advantages over the client built into the lawyer's professional role, and because of the disadvantages and vulnerability built into the client's role, the professional must subordinate his interest to the client's when there is a conflict. The lawyer is a good person in that he provides access to the law; in providing such access without moral screening, he serves the moral values of individual autonomy and equality. This ought to be enough, for the underlying professional ethic cautions that when there is a conflict between lawyer and client, the professional must remember that the raison d'etre for his role is service to the client.

The rest of the answer can be found in those limited areas in which the moral autonomy of the lawyer can function compatibly with the amoral professional ethic. Initially, the lawyer has the choice of whether or not to be a lawyer. It should be clear that this choice involves important moral consequences. Second, the lawyer has the choice of whether or not to accept a person as a client. Third, a large degree of moral autonomy can be exercised through the lawyer-client moral dialogue. Fourth, conscientious objection is an ever present option within the realm of the lawyer's moral autonomy. These four areas combined create a meaningful field for the exercise of the lawyer's moral autonomy.

The result, I believe is that the good lawyer can be a good person; not comfortable, but good.

NOTES ON PEPPER

1. ***Are Clients Entitled to Lawyers' Assistance for All Goals and Means That Are Not Illegal?*** Are you persuaded by Pepper's argument that, if conduct is sufficiently bad, it ought to be made explicitly unlawful, and that if it's not that bad, or if "making that conduct unlawful is too onerous," clients are entitled to legal assistance with their projects?

2. ***An Oligarchy of Lawyers?*** What do you think of Pepper's argument that encouraging lawyers to refuse to facilitate that which they believe to be immoral would subject clients to rule by an "oligarchy of lawyers"? Are lawyers likely to agree among themselves as to what projects are objectionable on moral grounds?

3. ***What Types of Clients Does Pepper Envision?*** Pepper paints a picture of the attorney-client relationship in which clients lack access to the machinery of law without help from lawyers and are therefore vulnerable to lawyers who would deny clients access to law based on the lawyers' moral objections. He also refers to "the disadvantages and vulnerability built into the client's role." What types of clients do you think Pepper envisions when he says that clients are vulnerable to lawyers in this way?

* * *

How would a lawyer who adopts the amoral conception of a lawyer's role handle each of the following problems?

PROBLEM 3–1

Your client is on trial for murder. A prosecution witness will testify that your client was at the scene of the crime at the relevant time. You know that the testimony is true because your client has conceded that to you in confidence, although your client insists he did not commit or witness the murder because he left before the killing occurred. You also know that the witness has a prior perjury conviction. If the client wants you to attempt to impeach the witness by drawing attention to the witness's prior perjury conviction, should you do so?

PROBLEM 3–2

XYZ Corporation manufactures an intrauterine contraceptive device that is alleged to have caused thousands of injuries to users, including infections that have led to sterility and death. Thousands of claims have been filed against XYZ corporation— some baseless and some meritorious. There is no question that the device has caused serious injuries to some consumers, but the manufacturer correctly notes that the injuries are sometimes exacerbated by certain types of sexual activity. The judge supervising the litigation has allowed inquiry into the plaintiffs' sexual history as long as the questions are "reasonably likely to lead to the discovery of admissible evidence." The manufacturer has noticed that aggressive questioning about a plaintiff's sexual practices in pretrial depositions tends to lead plaintiffs to settle early for small amounts. Is there anything wrong with the manufacturer's lawyer's practice during depositions of dwelling on a long, well-developed list of "dirty questions" that have proven successful in encouraging quick and modest settlements?[2]

PROBLEM 3–3

A tax lawyer has devised a new strategy to enable his clients to avoid paying taxes. He does not believe that the strategy should be allowed but thinks that there is a non-frivolous argument that it is legal. He also knows that the Internal Revenue Service lacks the resources to identify the strategy and take the matter to court. Should he suggest this strategy to his clients?[3]

PROBLEM 3–4

A client hires a lawyer to help him obtain a divorce from his wife. It quickly becomes apparent that the client wants the lawyer to assist him in doing his best to strip the wife of everything she has and inflict maximum pain on her, without regard for maintaining relationships within the family, protecting the interest of the children, or anything else. Should the lawyer agree to represent the client? If he does, should he accede to his client's wishes about the goals and strategy for accomplishing them?

PROBLEM 3–5

Lawyers for the U.S. Justice Department have been asked to advise the executive branch about the legality of waterboarding, an interrogation technique in which the detainee experiences a near-drowning experience. Administration officials would like to be able to use the technique because they believe that it will bolster their efforts to deter terrorism. Torture is clearly prohibited by an international treaty to which the United States is a party and by a U.S. statute. Whatever advice the lawyers give is unlikely to be tested in court, and the effect of the lawyers' advice will be to immunize from criminal prosecution any government employees who use the technique. May the lawyers draft a memo advising the Administration that waterboarding is legal if they believe that U.S. national security depends upon its use?[4]

---

[2] This example comes from litigation over injuries caused by the Dalkon Shield I.U.D. *See* SHELDON ENGELMAYER & ROBERT WAGMAN, LORD'S JUSTICE: ONE JUDGE'S BATTLE TO EXPOSE THE DEADLY DALKON SHIELD I.U.D. 87–90 (1985).

[3] This example is adapted from one included in WILLIAM H. SIMON, THE PRACTICE OF JUSTICE: A THEORY OF LAWYERS' ETHICS 142 (1998).

[4] We will examine the real case on which this problem is based, in all its complexity, in materials on counseling in government practice.

D. CRITIQUES OF THE AMORAL CONCEPTION

Moral philosopher and Professor David Luban takes strong exception to the amoral conception of the lawyer's role. He argues that lawyers are just as morally accountable for the choices they make as lawyers as they would be as ordinary citizens.

THE LYSISTRATIAN PREROGATIVE: A RESPONSE TO STEPHEN PEPPER

David Luban
1987 American Bar Foundation Research Journal 637

Abraham Lincoln once said to a client in his Springfield law practice:

> Yes, we can doubtless gain your case for you; we can set a whole neighborhood at loggerheads; we can distress a widowed mother and her six fatherless children and thereby get you six hundred dollars to which you seem to have a legal claim, but which rightfully belongs, it appears to me, as much to the woman and her children as it does to you. You must remember that some things legally right are not morally right. We shall not take your case, but will give you a little advice for which we will charge you nothing. You seem to be a sprightly, energetic man; we would advise you to try your hand at making six hundred dollars in some other way.

Lincoln seems to have taken "some things legally right are not morally right" to be an important truth. It shows that exercising one's legal rights is not always morally acceptable. Lincoln evidently concluded that helping someone exercise their legal rights is not always morally acceptable. And so, Lincoln rejected the lawyer's amoral ethical role.

Pepper disagrees with this line of thinking, arguing instead that "[t]he lawyer is a good person in that he provides access to the law." But some things legally right are not morally right, and so in any such argument we must ask how the rabbit of moral justification manages to come out of the hat. And the answer, I believe, is the one we all expected: rabbits don't come out of hats unless they have been put in the hats to begin with. Pepper, I believe, assumes that the morality is already in the law, that in an important sense anything legally right is morally right. That, however, cannot be.

The argument for the amoral role goes as follows: *First premise*: "law is intended to be a public good which increases autonomy." *Second Premise*: "autonomy [is] preferred over 'right' or 'good' conduct"; "increasing individual autonomy is morally good." *Third premise*: "in a highly legalized society such as ours, . . . access to the law . . . in reality . . . is available only through a lawyer." *Conclusion*: "what the lawyer does is a social good." "The lawyer is a good person in that he provides access to the law."

I deny the second premise, that individual autonomy is preferred over right or good conduct: it is the point at which the rabbit gets into the hat. Pepper appears to have blurred the crucial distinction between the desirability of people acting autonomously and the desirability of their autonomous act. It is good, desirable, for me to make my own decisions about whether to lie to you; it is bad, undesirable, for me to lie to you. It is good that people act autonomously, that they make their own choices about what to do; what they choose to do, however, need not be good. Pepper's second premise is plausible only when we focus exclusively on the first of each of these pairs of propositions; it loses its plausibility when we turn our attention to the second. Other things being equal, Pepper is right that "increasing individual autonomy is morally good," but when the exercise of autonomy results in an immoral action, other things aren't equal. You must remember that some things autonomously done are not morally right.

Pepper's subsequent argument is that since exercising autonomy is good, helping people exercise autonomy is good. Though this is true, it too is only half the story. The other half is that since doing bad things is bad, helping people do bad things is bad. The two factors must be weighed against each other, and this Pepper does not do.

Compare this case: The automobile, by making it easier to get around, increases human autonomy; hence, other things being equal, it is morally good to repair the car of someone who is unable by himself to get it to run. But such considerations can hardly be invoked to defend the morality of fixing the getaway car of an armed robber, assuming that you know in advance what the purpose of the car is. The moral wrong of assisting the robber outweighs the abstract moral goodness of augmenting the robber's autonomy.

Pepper admits that it "may be morally wrong to manufacture or distribute cigarettes or alcohol, or to disinherit one's children for marrying outside the faith, but the generality of such decisions are left in the private realm." That is true, but that doesn't imply that such exercises of autonomy are morally acceptable. On the contrary, it concedes that they are immoral. And this is simply to return to the distinction between the desirability of exercising autonomy and the undesirability of exercising it wrongly.

Pepper sees this. To make his argument work, he distinguishes between (merely) immoral conduct and intolerable conduct, and says that intolerable conduct "ought to be made explicitly unlawful"; at one point, indeed, he equates "not unlawful" conduct with conduct "above the floor of the intolerable." Using this distinction, he argues in effect that unlawful conduct is conduct the immorality of which does not outweigh the value of autonomous decision-making. If we didn't want people to make up their own minds about such conduct, we would make it illegal, and thus the fact that we haven't shows that we do not disapprove of it sufficiently to take the decision out of people's own hands.

The conclusion does not follow, however. There are many reasons for not prohibiting conduct besides the reason that we don't think it's bad enough to take it out of people's hands. We should not put into effect prohibitions that are unenforceable, or that are enforceable only at enormous cost, or through unacceptably or disproportionately invasive means. We should not prohibit immoral conduct if it would be too difficult to specify the conduct, or if the laws would of necessity be vague or either over or underinclusive, or if enforcement would destroy our liberties. All these are familiar and good reasons for refraining from prohibiting conduct that have nothing whatever to do with the intensity of our disapprobation of the conduct.

Pepper acknowledges this too, but resists its implication by posing this rhetorical question: "If making the conduct unlawful is too onerous because the law would be too vague, or it is too difficult to identify the conduct in advance, or there is not sufficient social or political concern, do we intend to delegate to the individual lawyer the authority for case-by-case legislation and policing?" I do not treat this question as rhetorical; I answer it "yes." The reason goes, I think, to the heart of my disagreement with Pepper.

What bothers Pepper the most, I believe, is the idea that lawyers should interpose themselves and their moral concerns as "filters" of what legally permissible projects clients should be able to undertake. His concern, in turn, appears to have two aspects to it, one specific to lawyers, the other more general: "Such a screening submits each to . . . rule by oligarchy of lawyers." More generally, it appears to me that Pepper objects to anyone, lawyer or not, interposing his or her scruples to filter the legally permissible projects of autonomous agents.

The first of these worries is illusory, for there is no oligarchy of lawyers, actual or potential, to worry about. An oligarchy is a group of people ruling in concert, whereas lawyers who refuse to execute projects to which they object on moral grounds will do so as individuals, without deliberating collectively with other lawyers.

The second worry is more interesting. Unlike Pepper, I am not troubled by the existence of informal filters of people's legally permissible projects. Far from seeing these as a threat to the rule of law, I regard them as essential to its very existence. We—people, that is—are tempted to a vast array of reprehensible conduct. Some of it can be and is tolerated; some of it we do not engage in because of our scruples; and some of it the law proscribes. But the law cannot proscribe all intolerable conduct, for human society would then be crushed flat by a monstrous, incomprehensible mass of law. And scruples—conscience, morality—will not take up all the slack. Instead, we rely to a vast extent on informal social pressure to keep us in check. When conscience is too faint, people worry about what other people will say, think, and do, and guide their behavior accordingly.

Imagine now what would happen if we could no longer count on this sort of motivation, so that we would have to enforce desirable behavior legally. When we begin to reflect on the sheer magnitude of altruistic behavior we take for granted in day-to-day life, we realize that society could not exist without the dense network of informal filters provided by other people.

Among those filters is noncooperation. Many nefarious schemes are aborted because an agent's associates or partners or friends or family or financial backers or employees will have nothing to do with them. My argument is that far from this being an objectionable state of affairs, neither society nor law could survive without such filters.

And, to conclude the argument, I do not see why a lawyer's decision not to assist a client in a scheme that the lawyer finds nefarious is any different from these other instances of social control through private noncooperation. It is no more an affront to the client's autonomy for the lawyer to refuse to assist in the scheme than it is for the client's wife to threaten to move out if he goes ahead with it. Indeed, the lawyer's autonomy allows him to exercise the "the "Lysistratian prerogative"—to withhold services from those of whose projects he disapproves, to decide not to go to bed with clients who want to "set a whole neighborhood at loggerheads."

Pepper wants to allow the lawyer's autonomy a narrower scope: to refrain from being a lawyer, to engage in moral dialogue with clients, to decline to represent a client, and in extreme cases to engage in conscientious objection against odious professional obligations. The last two of these together add up to the Lysistratian prerogative, except for Pepper's limitation of conscientious objection to extreme cases. He includes this limitation because he thinks that only extremely objectionable actions outweigh the value of enhancing client autonomy. I believe, however, that in almost every case of significant client immorality the good of helping the client realize his autonomy will be outweighed by the bad of the immoral action the client proposes.

The morally pernicious effect of "legal realism" is a splendid discovery of Pepper's. As we have seen, Pepper's defense assumes that the law itself reflects a society's moral beliefs and the relative intensities of its moral judgments. The legal realist, on the other hand, is a moral skeptic about the law, who has bathed its clauses in cynical acid until all encrustations of morality have been dissolved. The result, as Pepper notes, is that "there is no moral input or constraint in the present model of the lawyer-client relationship."

There are two versions of "legal realism": one, which I will call High Realism, is an important philosophy of law; the other, which I will call Low Realism, amounts to skepticism about law, and is no more a philosophy of law than "what's right is whatever you can get away with" is a philosophy of ethics. Low Realism is the claim that law is "a prediction of what human officials will do." High Realism is the claim that law is a prediction of what human officials will do *in their good faith efforts to interpret and enforce authoritative rules.* According to Low Realism, as long as the relevant officials will not sanction you, you have *by definition* committed no infraction of the law. Low Realism drains law of its normative content.

When we realize this, we realize that while the problem Pepper raises is of enormous practical importance, it arises only because Low Realism has come to be believed and lived by many lawyers.

I cannot, however, resist pointing out that the amoral ethical role Pepper defends contributes to the prevalence of Low Realism. When getting the client whatever he or she wants is conceived of as the lawyer's preponderant professional obligation, it is psychologically natural to reduce the dissonance between that obligation and legality by understanding the law as *whatever I can get officials to give my client.* Take the normative content out of the lawyer's role and the lawyer will feel impelled to take the normative content out of law as well and define it as victor's spoils pure and simple.

NOTES ON LUBAN'S CRITIQUE OF PEPPER

1.   *Lawyers as Informal Filters.* Is Luban right that there is nothing wrong with lawyers serving as an "informal filter" on people pursuing legally permissible projects? Does your answer depend at all on the type of client or the particular circumstances of the matter at hand?

2.   *High Realism v. Low Realism.* Which type of Realism do you think you're learning in law school—the High version or the Low?

* * *

Consider the following argument by Professor Andrew Kaufman, who asserts that both Pepper and Luban make important points but that neither is entirely convincing.

A Commentary on Pepper's
"The Lawyer's Amoral Ethical Role"

Andrew L. Kaufman
1986 American Bar Foundation Research Journal 651

My sense is that both sides of the argument over the moral accountability of lawyers have a good deal to teach practitioners—but that neither has the full answer.

In holding high the importance of autonomy, diversity, and equality, Professor Pepper links those goals with the notion that if proposed conduct has not been made unlawful, then at least generally the lawyer should help the client achieve his or her objective. Note that Professor Pepper does not make the lesser point that it is *permissible* for the lawyer to aid the client. He seems to be making the larger point that it is *wrong* for lawyers, except perhaps in exceptional cases, *to refuse to help their clients to achieve lawful ends.*

Professor Pepper [argues] that it is always, or almost always, morally good to help the client achieve an end that is not unlawful. It is one thing, however, to *play up* the autonomy and equality points in urging an amoral role for lawyers. It is quite another to *play down* the moral aspect of the reality that sometimes—for a variety of reasons having nothing to do with morality—conduct generally agreed to be immoral is not made unlawful.

For example, it is not unlawful for a wife to cut her husband out of her will without telling him, even though she knows that his will favors her, but I think that most of us would agree that there are many situations in which it would be immoral for her to do so. As a lawyer drafting the will, I would not be assuaged by the argument that I am facilitating the wife's first-class citizenship in doing so. Moral dialogue may not be enough in that kind of case. And if that example does not grab you, how about doing the legal work that sets the seller of Saturday Night Specials up in business and helps him to continue. Professor Pepper is not bothered by that one, at least not in the abstract. Is it unfair of me to ask how many dead people shot by guns sold by his client would begin to make him worry?

For me and for many lawyers, I suspect that there are enough situations where the moral constraints are such that they outweigh what Professor Pepper calls the first-class citizenship considerations that they cannot be called truly exceptional. I think that the ethic of professional responsibility should and does recognize that it is entirely appropriate for the lawyer to refuse the amoral role in a significant number of situations—not just in the matter of choice of client, but also in the performance of the actual tasks the client wishes the lawyer to do.

However, I part company with Professor Luban on the general thrust of his position as I have understood it. I believe that there is a great deal more scope for role-differentiated behavior than his position allows and that lawyers have to be very careful about overriding clients' wishes in the name of morality.

The issues we like to discuss under the heading of morality often turn out to be considerably less clear-cut in reality than we portray them in the classroom. Moral issues are often cloudy in the lawyer's office because in many, if not most, situations when people come to lawyers, it is very difficult for lawyers to get a strong sense of moral right and wrong because of one-sided, incomplete information about facts and especially about the consequences of particular actions.

And so the occasions on which lawyers may have a real moral choice to make in the advice they give—aside from the important initial choice they make about the kind of practice to which they aspire—may not be so numerous as the protagonists on this issue would have us believe. Likewise, there are other situations where it is perfectly appropriate for a lawyer with a strong moral position to recognize that there are other reasonable solutions to the moral dilemma and thus to defer to the client's differing moral judgment.

NOTES ON KAUFMAN

1. *A Middle Ground?* Are you convinced by Kaufman's argument for a middle ground in the debate between Pepper and Luban?

2. *Practice Type as a Moral Choice.* Notice that Kaufman insists that the "initial choice . . . about the kind of practice to which they aspire" is a moral choice. We will return to this issue in our examination of alternatives to the amoral conception of the lawyer's role.

E. ALTERNATIVES TO THE AMORAL CONCEPTION

If one finds the amoral conception of the lawyer's role unsatisfactory, what other possibilities are available? This section canvasses various alternatives.

1. **Against Role-Based Morality.** The strongest version of the argument against a role morality for lawyers that differs from non-professional morality comes from David Luban, author of the critique of Pepper excerpted above. He argues that lawyers should be guided and judged by the same types of moral considerations that apply to ordinary citizens. He makes a single exception for criminal defense work, because he believes that aggressive, client-centric advocacy is necessary to protect

the constitutional rights of defendants and to guard against abuses of governmental power.[5]

Deborah Rhode similarly argues that "[a]ttorneys should make decisions as advocates in the same way that morally reflective individuals make any ethical decision." Under her approach, lawyers "could not simply retreat into some fixed conception of role that denies personal accountability for public consequences or that unduly privileges clients' and lawyers' own interests":

> Client trust and confidentiality are entitled to weight, but they must be balanced against other equally important concerns. Lawyers also have responsibilities to prevent unnecessary harm to third parties, to promote a just and effective legal system, and to respect core values such as honesty, fairness, and good faith on which that system depends.[6]

2. **Contextual Alternatives.** William Simon has argued for what he calls the "Contextual View," according to which "Lawyers should take those actions that, considering the relevant circumstances of the particular case, seem likely to promote justice."[7] He carefully distinguishes his notion of justice from "ordinary morality":

> "Justice" here connotes the basic values of the legal system. Decisions about justice are not assertions of personal preferences, nor are they applications of ordinary morality. They are legal judgments grounded in the methods and sources of authority of the professional culture. I use "justice" interchangeably with "legal merit." The latter has the advantage of reminding us that we are concerned with the materials of conventional legal analysis. The former has the advantage of reminding us that these materials include many vaguely specified aspirational norms.

Simon's "Contextual View" requires consideration of the totality of circumstances, but it also directs the lawyer's attention to several types of recurring tensions at the heart of our legal system. One is the tension between substance and procedure that arises from the lawyer's understanding of the limitations on her judgment about the substantive merit of the matter, on the one hand, and the limitations of established procedures for deciding the matter, on the other hand. As a general rule, lawyers may reasonably assume that judges, juries, and officials overseeing administrative procedures are better positioned than individual lawyers to make reliable determinations about the merits of cases. However, where lawyers have reason to believe that the relevant

---

[5]   DAVID LUBAN, LAWYERS AND JUSTICE: AN ETHICAL STUDY (1988).

[6]   DEBORAH L. RHODE, IN THE INTERESTS OF JUSTICE 67 (2000).

[7]   WILLIAM H. SIMON, THE PRACTICE OF JUSTICE 138–39 (1998).

procedures are defective, they must take greater responsibility for ensuring a just outcome:

> Perhaps an adverse party or official lacks information or resources needed to initiate, pursue, or determine a claim. Or perhaps an official is corrupt, or politically intimidated, or incompetent. Or perhaps the relevant procedures are ill designed to resolve the matter. The basic response of the Contextual View to the substance-procedure tension is this: the more reliable the relevant procedures and institutions, the less direct responsibility the lawyer need assume for the substantive justice of the resolution; the less reliable the procedures and institutions, the more direct responsibility she needs to assume for substantive justice.

This attention to procedural context suggests that in situations where the checks and balances of adversary processes are not present, including, for example, in counseling private clients about legal compliance or government agencies about their conduct, the lawyer has a greater responsibility to ensure that outcomes are legally valid and just than in situations where processes are reliable.

Another type of tension noted by Simon is that between the form and purpose of rules. Simon argues that lawyers should take responsibility for ensuring that the rules they invoke are applied in a manner that takes into account their purposes. The amoral conception tends to allow the manipulation of form to defeat purpose, but the Contextual View allows such manipulation only where the purposes are problematic or unclear:

> The Contextual View responds to the Purpose-versus-Form tension with the following maxim: the clearer and more fundamental the relevant purposes, the more the lawyer should consider herself bound by them; the less clear and more problematic the relevant purposes, the more justified the lawyer is in treating the relevant norms formally [by which he means "understanding them to permit any client goal not plainly precluded by their language."]

Overall, Simon's approach requires lawyers to assess the particular circumstances of the case at hand and to exercise discretionary judgment to vindicate justice: "Lawyers should focus on the direct consequences of their actions and should try to vindicate justice in the particular case: not their private idiosyncratic notions of justice but notions of justice that can be defended in terms of legal authority and public values."

3. **The Citizen Lawyer.** Robert Gordon has argued that lawyers should strive to be "citizen lawyers" who not only seek to avoid subverting justice in their daily practices but also attempt to serve the public and to improve the operation of law and its administration. The following

excerpt sketches some attributes of this ideal type, which he concedes "has lately fallen out of favor."

THE CITIZEN LAWYER—A BRIEF INFORMAL HISTORY OF A MYTH WITH SOME BASIS IN REALITY

Robert W. Gordon
50 William & Mary Law Review 1169 (2009)

In advising clients contemplating litigation, the citizen lawyer takes into account the merits or justice of the claim. She seeks to dissuade plaintiffs from pursuing plainly meritless claims, and encourages defendants towards fair settlements and away from invalid defenses of just claims.

When involved in litigation, the citizen lawyer regards herself as an "officer of the court," that is, a trustee for the integrity and fair operation of the basic procedures of the adversary system, the rules of the game, and their underlying purposes. She fights aggressively for her client, but in ways respectful of the fair and effective operation of this framework. In discovery, she frames requests intended to elicit useful information rather than to harass and inflict costs, and responds to reasonable requests rather than obstructing or delaying. She claims privilege or work product protection only when she thinks a fair-minded judge would be likely to independently support the claim. In deciding how ferociously to attack the credibility of a witness on cross-examination, she tries to assess and take into account the likely truthfulness of the witness and the underlying merits of the case.

In advising clients outside litigation, the citizen lawyer is the "wise counselor," who sees her job as guiding the client to comply with the underlying spirit or purpose as well as the letter of laws and regulations to desist from unlawful conduct, and if needed, to do so with strong advice backed by the threat of withdrawal, and in extreme cases, of disclosure. If the client needs her help to resist or change unfavorable law, she makes the challenge public and transparent, to facilitate its authoritative resolution.

To generalize more broadly, the citizen lawyer identifies broadly with the institutions, goals, and procedures of the legal system, even though she may (and if she is conscientious, probably does) also think that aspects of the existing system are inefficient, oppressive, or fundamentally unjust. She feels a sense of proprietorship, or ownership in common, of the legal framework—that the law, considered aspirationally as well as conservatively, as a set of norms and principles rather than a collection of particular rules, is in her profession's special stewardship, to preserve and cultivate and reform so it can serve its best purposes. In some instances, it may be that unjust laws or bad interpretations of them are so entrenched in conventional legal practice that a lawyer could not deprive a client of the unjust advantages they confer without committing malpractice. In that case, the citizen lawyer works with law reform commissions, bar committees and task forces, legislative committees, and administrative agencies to reform laws to make them more just and efficient, regardless of whether the reforms would help or hurt their clienteles.

4.   **Fidelity to Law.** Bradley Wendel rejects the notion that lawyers' conduct should be guided by ordinary morality. He also denies that lawyers should take responsibility for serving the public interest or achieving justice. Legality, rather than morality, justice, or the public good, is his touchstone. He advocates for an approach that is similar to the amoral conception (which Wendel calls the "Standard Conception") but places much greater emphasis on what he calls "fidelity to law." Many types of lawyer conduct that Pepper says are permitted to facilitate "first-class citizenship" are unavailable under Wendel's approach because they are inconsistent with the lawyer's obligation to uphold the law.

LAWYERS AND FIDELITY TO LAW
W. Bradley Wendel (2010)

The Standard Conception of legal ethics consists of two principles of action for lawyers: Partisanship and Neutrality. Partisanship is generally understood as the maxim that a lawyer should act to vindicate the interests of clients. [But] the first aspect of a conception of legal ethics centered on fidelity to law [is] that the legal entitlements of clients, not client interests, ordinary moral considerations or abstract legal norms such as justice, should be the object of lawyers' concerns when acting in a representative capacity. When representing clients, lawyers must respect the scheme of rights and duties established by the law, and not seek to work around the law because either they or their clients believe the law to be unjust, inefficient, stupid, or simply inconvenient. The obligation of respect means that lawyers must treat the law as a reason for action as such, not merely a possible downside to be taken into account, planned around, or nullified in some way. This obligation applies even if it would be very much in the client's interests to obtain a result that is not supported by a plausible claim to a legal entitlement.

Critics of the Standard Conception often stigmatize freestanding role-based normative systems as narrowing the range of reasons that a professional may consider in deliberating about how to act. My claim is that the ideal of partisanship, properly understood, represents a commitment to the value of legality. Legality may be seen as narrower than morality in general, but as I will argue, it also represents a distinctive way for citizens to live together and treat each other with respect, as equals. Thus, rather than inhabiting a "simplified moral world," lawyers actually inhabit a world of demanding ethical obligations of fidelity to law. The Standard Conception, therefore, should be modified so that the Principle of Partisanship is understood as requiring lawyers representing clients to protect the legal entitlements of their clients, not merely to seek to advance their interests. Talking about obligations such as loyalty and partisanship is unobjectionable, as long as it is understood that the object of the lawyer's commitment is not obtaining whatever the client wants, but what the client is legally permitted to have. In this modification of the Standard Conception, which is grounded on the fidelity to law, lawyers still have obligations of loyalty and partisanship which run to clients, but which are constituted by the legal entitlements of clients. Legal ethics is therefore not primarily an excuse for immoral behavior but a higher duty incumbent upon occupants of a professional role.

Lawyers who represent clients act to protect legal entitlements by asserting them in litigated disputes or negotiations, counsel their clients on what the law permits, and structure their clients' affairs with reference to the law. As this term will be used here, a legal entitlement is a substantive or procedural right, created by the law, which establishes claim-rights (implying duties upon others), privileges to do things without interference, and powers to change the legal situation of others (e.g., by imposing contractual obligations). Entitlements may be created by courts, legislatures, administrative agencies, or by citizens themselves, using legal tools for private ordering, such as wills, trusts, contract, partnerships, and corporations. Substantive legal entitlements have the effect of defining the boundaries between the competing interests of citizens.

In addition to substantive entitlements, the law also establishes procedural entitlements, which regulate the manner in which substantive entitlements are investigated and adjudicated. For example, a lawsuit must be commenced with pleadings which are formally served using specified procedures. This process ensures that someone who is made a defendant in a lawsuit has notice of the claims being asserted against him, and an opportunity to defend himself. The rules of evidence also create procedural entitlements, which ensure that substantive rights and obligations are adjudicated in an orderly way, on the basis of admissible evidence only, and without unjustified interference with the rights of the litigants or of third parties. One of the fundamental principles structuring the law governing lawyers is that a lawyer's role is defined and bounded by the client's legal entitlements. To put it another way, the lawyer is an agent for a principal, the client, and as such can have no greater power than that possessed by the client. [W]hen a lawyer is acting in a representative capacity, her legal obligations are constrained by the client's legal entitlements. Acting on any other basis, such as ordinary moral reasons or the interests of clients, would exceed the lawful power of the lawyer as agents [sic].

A corollary of the principle that the client's legal entitlements structure the attorney-client relationship is that lawyers may not permissibly assist clients in legal wrongdoing. The lawyer disciplinary rules state that lawyers may not "counsel a client to engage, or assist a client, in conduct that the lawyer knows is criminal or fraudulent," and agency law provides that the lawyer retains inherent authority, which cannot be overridden at the instance of the client, to refuse to perform unlawful acts. Whatever lawyers do for their clients must be justified on the basis of their clients' lawful rights, permissions, and obligations.

This approach to legal ethics depends to a great extent on the determinacy of law. If the law differentiates individual or group interests or preferences from socially-established rights, there must be something about the process of law-making and law-application that enables lawyers to figure out when their clients are appealing to an actual legal entitlement, as opposed to merely asserting what they wish to be the case. Clients and lawyers sometimes talk as though the law can be made to mean pretty much anything a clever lawyer wants it to mean. I am not really worried about this caricatured version of legal realism here. A more serious objection is that the law cannot be made to mean anything at all, but even so, there is a range of reasonable interpretations that the law might bear, and it is an important aspect of legal ethics to determine what a lawyer should do within that zone of reasonableness.

There is a difference between trying to figure out what the law actually is, and acting in accordance with what one believes the law ought to be. Where the law is unclear, citizens and lawyers may be aiming at a moving target, they may see only through a glass darkly, or some other metaphor may better capture the idea that legal judgments are not always capable of being made with a great deal of precision. Nevertheless, it is possible to distinguish aiming at the law from trying to get around it (which requires, ironically, that one have the law fairly clearly in view, to know how to evade it)*. It is permissible, of course, to make arguments about what one believes the law ought to be, but these are formally different from statements about what the law actually permits or

---

* [Editors' Note: This footnote is Wendel's.] Compare Harry Frankfurt's distinction between lies and bullshit, in HARRY G. FRANKFURT, ON BULLSHIT (2005). Lying is necessarily parasitic upon belief in the existence and knowability of the truth. A liar seeks to persuade others of something that the liar believes not to be true. Bullshit, by contrast, is indifference to the truth. The lawyers who structured the transactions underlying the Enron collapse and the [U.S. Department of Justice Office of Legal Counsel (OLC)] lawyers who drafted the torture memos were engaged in lying, because they knew what the law was and sought to evade it. Those who claim that the law is radically indeterminate, including some defenders of the Enron and OLC lawyers, are bullshitting.

requires. This observation about this formal difference leads to a point about the institutional structure of litigation and non-litigation representation. Lawyers representing clients in litigated matters must have some leeway to assert arguable legal interpretations, leaving it up to opposing counsel to challenge these positions, and to the court to make a decision about the best interpretation of the law. However, litigation is a special case, in which lawyers share responsibility for other institutional actors for getting the law right. In counseling and transactional representation, by contrast, the lawyer is frequently the only actor who has any power to render a judgment about what the law permits. That is not to deny that there is a range of meanings that the law can reasonably be understood to bear—within that range, there is nothing wrong with the lawyer adopting a view that is consistent with her client's interests. At the same time, however, lawyers are not permitted to adopt positions outside the range of reasonable interpretations, simply because it would be advantageous to their clients if they did so.

Notes on Alternatives to Amoral Advocacy

1. **Strengths and Weaknesses of the Alternatives.** What are the strengths and weaknesses of these alternatives to amoral advocacy? Do you find any (or all) of them preferable to the amoral conception of the lawyer's role? If so, why?

2. **What Contextual Factors Might Matter?** Under Simon's "Contextual View," what kinds of factors might a lawyer consider in deciding how to respond to particular dilemmas? Might a partial list include the procedural context (litigation, counseling, transactional work), the interests of other affected parties, whether other affected interests are well represented, access to relevant information, and the purposes of the relevant laws and rules?

3. **Good Citizenship as a Business Asset.** There are obvious benefits for the legal system in lawyers' adherence to Gordon's conception of the citizen lawyer. Are there circumstances in which a lawyer's reputation for good citizenship might enhance her ability to attract clients? What types of clients might want to hire lawyer-citizens?

4. **Plausible and Reasonable Interpretations of Law.** What is the significance of Wendel's use of the term "plausible" in the last sentence of the first paragraph and "reasonable" in the last sentence of the final paragraph?

5. **The Problems.** How would a lawyer who adopted these various alternatives to the amoral conception resolve Problems 3–1 through 3–5? How would she resolve the problem regarding the discharge of polluted water from a rural plant in Pepper's essay?

6. **Simplicity and Ease of Application.** Are any of the alternative models as easy to apply as the amoral view? Are some more difficult to

follow than others? To the extent that these alternative models require lawyers to engage in more reflection than the amoral advocacy model, is that a strength or weakness of the alternatives?

F. IS CRIMINAL DEFENSE DIFFERENT?

One common feature of many alternatives to the amoral conception is that they tend to carve out criminal defense work for special treatment. There are various arguments about whether or when criminal defense is a special case in which amoral advocacy is permissible.

For example, David Luban, who takes a hard line against amoral advocacy in all other contexts, makes an exception for criminal defense work because he thinks aggressive advocacy is justified in order to protect individuals against a powerful institution—the state. However, he argues that brutal cross-examination of rape victims is off limits because rape involves another institution that presents a pervasive threat to individual well-being—"patriarchy—a network of cultural expectations and practices that engenders and encourages male sexual violence."[8]

Simon rejects the idea that critics of amoral advocacy should make a special exception for criminal defense. He agrees that criminal defense lawyers can appropriately defend clients they believe are guilty, insist that the prosecution prove every element beyond a reasonable doubt, and take advantage of the rights that the law gives defendants, including the right to exclude unlawfully obtained evidence. But he disagrees with the notion that criminal defense lawyers should enjoy wholesale permission to use deceptive tactics, such as presenting perjured testimony by defendants, or threatening to bring out embarrassing but irrelevant information about adverse witnesses. He argues that advocates for the deceptive and aggressive tactics in criminal defense tend to portray the state as Leviathan with unlimited resources, when in fact that's rarely the case, and to neglect the interests of crime victims and the worthy goal of deterring future crimes. He suggests that Luban's argument for prohibiting aggressive tactics in rape cases illustrates the larger point that "formal institutions [such as the state] are not the only important threats to liberty" and that "a wide and unspecifiable variety of social processes that are experienced as diffuse violence can do so as well." Nevertheless, Simon would allow aggressive tactics in particular cases involving procedural breakdowns that would lead to legal injustice or excessive or arbitrary punishment of the defendant.[9]

Wendel's approach, emphasizing fidelity to law, would allow the use of some tactics in criminal defense work that would be unjustified in most

---

[8] David Luban, *Partisanship, Betrayal and Autonomy in the Lawyer-Client Relationship: A Reply to Stephen Ellmann*, 90 COLUM. L. REV. 1004, 1027–29 (1990).

[9] WILLIAM H. SIMON, THE PRACTICE OF JUSTICE 170–194 (1998).

other practice settings. He argues that aggressive advocacy is permissible in criminal defense work because the defendant has a procedural legal entitlement to have the case against him proven beyond a reasonable doubt. Outside of the criminal defense context, he argues that deceptive tactics are much more difficult to defend, especially in counseling and transactional contexts, where there is no adversary process and no neutral adjudicator.[10]

NOTES ON CRIMINAL DEFENSE AS A SPECIAL CASE

1. *Is Criminal Defense Special?* Are you persuaded by arguments that criminal defense presents a special case that generally permits criminal defense lawyers to engage in tactics that would be immoral for other lawyers, or do you find Simon's critique of that view more compelling?

2. *Must One Choose?* If you're finding it difficult to choose among these conceptions of role, you are in good company. Many thoughtful observers (including your casebook authors) find it easy to reject the amoral conception as articulated by Pepper but more difficult to settle on an alternative that seems entirely satisfactory in every situation. Perhaps it's unnecessary to embrace any particular approach for all purposes. Consider this comment by Professor Andrew Kaufman:

> As I survey the field of professional responsibility today, I must confess to a feeling of nakedness. Everyone who is anyone has either created or adopted a model. For myself, I hold eclectic views on the theoretical issue that divides Professors Pepper and Luban—and indeed, the whole community of professional commentators. [W]hen the issue of role arises in a particular situation that does not fit into an area where there is a rule, I think that it is good that we lawyers are not always given a prepackaged answer. There is something to be said for our being forced to figure out for ourselves what action is called for by the facts of a particular situation, even it if is uncomfortable to have to work it out for ourselves.[11]

G. THE CHOICE OF CLIENTS AND CAUSES

As a matter of aspirational ideals, the American legal profession has long acknowledged that lawyers should assist in meeting the profession's duty to make legal services broadly available. The Comment to Model Rule 1.2 provides that "[l]egal representation should not be denied to people who are unable to afford legal services, or whose cause is controversial or the subject of popular disapproval." But in practice lawyers are generally free to pick and choose their clients and causes and to decline matters for weighty moral reasons or for the most pedestrian reasons, including the most common reason of all—the client's inability to

---

[10] W. BRADLEY WENDEL, LAWYERS AND FIDELITY TO LAW 191–93 (2010).

[11] Andrew L. Kaufman, *A Commentary on Pepper's "The Lawyer's Amoral Ethical Role"*, 1986 AM. B. FOUND. RES. J. 651, 655 (1986).

pay. Accordingly, many commentators think it appropriate to hold lawyers accountable for their decisions about whom to serve, notwithstanding that the comment to Rule 1.2 states that "representing a client does not constitute approval of the client's views or activities." According to this view, lawyers' freedom to decline to represent a client for moral reasons necessarily entails moral accountability for the clients that lawyers <u>do</u> choose to represent. An essay on the decision of a black lawyer affiliated with the ACLU to represent the Ku Klux Klan in resisting the state of Texas's attempt to subpoena the Klan's membership list endorses this logic:

> Once we accept [that a lawyer should not be compelled to represent a client because of his moral disagreement with that individual's views or objectives], it is no longer possible to contend that lawyers bear no moral responsibility for their decision to represent particular clients. If a lawyer has the moral right to refuse to accept a case, then the decision not to exercise this option—in other words, to agree to take the case—also carries moral significance.[12]

Monroe Freedman, a strong advocate for the amoral conception ("that the client is entitled to make the important decisions about the client's goals and the lawful means used to pursue those goals"), also insists that the lawyer's broad discretion to accept or reject a particular client means that it is a decision for which lawyers are properly held accountable.

Concluding that lawyers are morally accountable for their choice of clients, however, is not the same as saying that it is wrong to represent disreputable clients. Criminal defense lawyers, for example, do not necessarily approve of their clients or the conduct that is the basis for their clients' prosecution; instead, they typically justify their roles in terms of defending constitutional rights, checking police and prosecutorial power, and protecting defendants from unjustifiably harsh punishment. Similarly, civil libertarians sometimes represent clients they find abhorrent in order to advance principles they hold dear.

In assessing lawyers' accountability for representing unpopular clients, should it matter *why* the client is unpopular? Suppose the source of the unpopularity is that the client has engaged or is engaging in anti-social behavior that escapes law enforcement—e.g., promoting racial violence, bribing government officials, producing unreasonably dangerous products, defrauding consumers, polluting the environment, or disregarding safety regulations designed to protect workers. Should it matter whether the representation relates to past conduct or future

---

[12] David B. Wilkins, *Race, Ethics, and the First Amendment: Should a Black Lawyer Represent the Ku Klux Klan?*, 63 GEO. WASH. L. REV. 1030 (1995).

projects? Should it matter whether the representation is paid or pro bono, or whether the lawyer is "the last lawyer in town"?

Lawyers sometimes assert that it should be sufficient justification for representing an unpopular client that everyone deserves representation. Is that right—is that sufficient justification when there is no reason to believe that the client cannot find other counsel? David Wilkins has argued that "[t]he claim that 'this person deserves legal representation' is fundamentally different from the argument that 'I should provide that service.'" William Kunstler drew the same distinction in explaining why he would defend the World Trade Center bombers but not the Ku Klux Klan; "Everyone has a right to a lawyer, that's true. But they don't have a right to me."[13]

Questions about the morality of lawyers' representation of unpopular clients sometimes arise as to whole classes of clients, such as when people ask how criminal defense lawyers can represent defendants they know are guilty, or when people ask corporate litigators to explain how they justify representing tobacco companies and gun manufacturers. In 2007, Charles Stimson, Deputy Assistant Secretary of State for Detainee Affairs, considered such a question about the representation of Guantanamo detainees:

> Somebody asked, "Who are the lawyers around this country representing detainees down there?" And you know what, it's shocking. The major firms in this country are out there representing detainees, and I think quite honestly, when corporate CEOs see that these firms are representing the very terrorists who hit their bottom line back in 2001, these CEOs are going to make those law firms choose between representing terrorists or representing reputable firms.[14]

Such questions also arise as to lawyers' representation of particular clients in particular matters, as revealed in the following examples:

Bernard Madoff. Lawyer Ira Lee Sorkin represented Bernard L. Madoff, who pled guilty in 2009 to having operated a massive Ponzi scheme that defrauded investors of billions of dollars. According to a *New York Times* story at the time, Sorkin received many angry messages about his willingness to represent Madoff, including one so threatening that he referred it to the F.B.I. Sorkin explained that he understood the anger but that "to preserve a system that can protect the people who

---

[13] DEBORAH L. RHODE, IN THE INTERESTS OF JUSTICE 79 (2000).

[14] David Luban, *Lawfare and Legal Ethics in Guantanamo,* 60 STAN. L. REV. 1981 (2008) (quoting Stimson).

didn't do bad things, you have to represent people who did do bad things. That's the role we play.[15]

Philip Morris. During her years in private practice at the law firm of Davis Polk, Kirsten Rutnik, now U.S. Senator (N.Y.) Kirsten Gillibrand, represented tobacco giant Philip Morris in connection with the Department of Justice's efforts to obtain the company's research on the health effects of cigarette smoking and the connection between smoking and cancer. The Justice Department sought to obtain documentation of that research to prove that tobacco industry executives had lied about the dangers of smoking. A *New York Times* article on the matter asserted that Gillibrand "was involved in some of the most sensitive matters related to the defense of [Philip Morris]," including efforts to shield damaging company documents from public disclosure.[16]

John Demjanjuk. In 1993, Hofstra Law Professor Monroe Freedman published an article in the *Legal Times* critical of lawyer Michael Tigar's decision to represent John Demjanjuk, the man the Justice Department accused of being Ivan the Terrible of Treblinka, accessory to the murder of 850,000 Jews. Freedman argued that all lawyers should bear a "burden of justification" for the work they undertake and that Tigar should ask himself these questions: "Is John Demjanjuk the kind of client to whom you want to dedicate your training, your knowledge, your extraordinary skills? Did you go to law school to help a client who has committed mass murder of other human beings with poisonous gases? Of course, someone should, and will, represent him. But why you?" In a subsequent interview, Tigar called Freedman's notion that lawyers should bear a burden of justification for the clients they choose to represent a "pernicious" ethical standard. He explained that in representing Demjanjuk, he was seeking to hold the U.S. government to its own principles, a fitting way to honor victims of the Holocaust.[17]

The Defense of Marriage Act Case. In 2011, Republicans in the House of Representatives hired the law firm of King & Spalding to defend the constitutionality of the Defense of Marriage Act (DOMA), which prohibited federal recognition of same-sex marriages, after Attorney General Eric Holder announced that the Obama Administration would no longer defend the statute. Gay rights groups criticized King & Spalding, as did lawyers within the firm who objected on moral grounds to the position the client was taking and believed that the firm's handling of this

---

[15] Diana B. Henriques, *Madoff Lawyer Absorbs Part of the Rage*, N.Y. TIMES, Mar. 11, 2009, at B1.

[16] Raymond Hernandez & David Kocieniewski, *As New Lawyer, Senator Was Active in Tobacco's Defense*, N.Y. TIMES, Mar. 27, 2009, at A1.

[17] David Margolick, *At the Bar; The Demjanjuk Episode, Two Old Friends and Debate from Long Ago*, N.Y. TIMES, Oct. 15, 1993, at B18.

matter would interfere with its ability to recruit and retain gay lawyers. The firm eventually withdrew from the representation in June of 2011. A statement issued by the firm's chairman explained that the firm's process for vetting the matter prior to accepting it had been inadequate. Perhaps noteworthy in this respect, the contract between the law firm and the House contained a provision that prohibited any of the firm's lawyers and other employees from any engaging in any kind of advocacy "to alter or amend" DOMA.

When the firm decided to withdraw, Paul Clement, the former U.S. Solicitor General and King & Spalding partner who was handling the case, resigned the firm in protest. In explaining the move, Clement wrote: "I resign out of the firmly held belief that a representation should not be abandoned because the client's legal position is extremely unpopular in certain quarters. Defending unpopular clients is what lawyers do." Gay rights advocates responded strongly against Clement's suggestion that his representation of the G.O.P House members in this matter was analogous to the representation of indigents, political dissenters, or downtrodden criminal defendants. One observer argued, "No serious case can be made that an institution as powerful as Congress has a right to the services of the biggest law firms and the most credentialed lawyers. The Defense of Marriage Act is not unpopular, and while Congress may be indebted, it is not indigent."[18] The spokesman for a gay rights group said, "Mr. Clement's statement misses the point entirely. While it is sometimes appropriate for lawyers to represent unpopular clients when an important principle is at issue, here the only principle he wishes to defend is discrimination and second-class citizenship for gay Americans."[19] However, Attorney General Eric Holder defended Clement, saying that "[i]n taking on the representation—representing Congress in connection with DOMA, I think he is doing that which lawyers do when we're at our best."

Some observers thought while King & Spalding had no obligation to take the case, it should have continued to serve the client after having accepted the matter. Both the *New York Times* and the *Washington Post* published editorials condemning King & Spalding's withdrawal.[20] The Model Rules generally permit lawyers to withdraw from representing clients if withdrawal can be accomplished without harming the client and in a variety of other circumstances. See Model Rule 1.16.

---

[18] Dale Carpenter, *How the Law Accepted Gays*, N.Y. TIMES, Apr. 29, 2011, at A27.

[19] Michael D. Shear & John Schwartz, *Law Firm Won't Defend Marriage Act*, N.Y. TIMES, Apr. 26, 2011, at A1.

[20] *See The Duty of Counsel*, N.Y. TIMES, Apr. 28, 2011 at A24; *A Law Firm Caves to the Left's Hypocrisy*, WASH. POST, Apr. 28, 2011 at A24.

Which side do you think had the better of the argument about the propriety of the firm's decision to represent the House in this matter and its subsequent decision to withdraw?

After resigning from King & Spalding, Paul Clement joined Bancroft LLC, where he continued to handle the DOMA matter. (In January of 2013, the House and Bancroft agreed to raise the spending cap on attorneys' fees in the DOMA case from $2.75 million to $3 million.) The Supreme Court found the Defense of Marriage Act unconstitutional in June of 2013. *United States v. Windsor*, 133 S. Ct. 2675 (2013).

NOTES ON THE CHOICE OF CLIENTS AND CAUSES

1. ***What Would You Do?*** Would you have been willing to represent Bernie Madoff in his fraud prosecution, Phillip Morris in tobacco cases, John Demjanjuk in connection with charges that he was an accessory to murder of many thousands, or the House of Representatives in the DOMA case?

2. ***Fair to Judge?*** A *New York Times* article on Kirstin Gillibrand's role in the tobacco litigation quotes University of Chicago law professor Todd Henderson saying that it is unfair to assess lawyers by whom they represent: "Nobody would want to live in a world in which lawyers are judged by the clients they take." Do you agree?

3. ***Factors Relevant for an Individual Lawyer's Choice of Clients?*** If you were practicing on your own, what factors would you take into account in deciding what clients to serve? Would your answer depend on what particular projects and/or positions the clients wanted you to take on their behalf? How might financial considerations affect your decisions?

4. ***Criteria and Processes for Law Firms.*** If you were working as an associate in a private firm, what criteria and processes would you want your firm's management to use in choosing clients? If you were a senior partner in the same firm, do you think you would give the same answers? What arguments would you anticipate from those who disagree with you?

H. SUMMARY

This chapter considered whether lawyers are sometimes permitted, or required, to do on behalf of clients things that would otherwise be wrong to do. We analyzed one conception of role that many lawyers seem to adopt: the "amoral" conception of the lawyer's role, which says that lawyers are unaccountable for anything they do on behalf of clients so long as it is not illegal. We considered why many lawyers find that model attractive. We read Stephen Pepper's defense of the amoral conception, based on an argument that law is a public good that should be available to all, that lawyers are critical for access to the machinery of law, and therefore that it is good for lawyers to give clients unfiltered access to all that the law permits. We also explored several criticisms of Pepper's defense of the amoral role. We paid special attention to what Pepper calls "the problem of legal realism"—that when lawyers take an extremely skeptical view of the boundaries of law and adopt the amoral conception of their role, they may guide clients away from moral conduct and legal compliance. We considered Luban's outright rejection of role—differentiated morality and Kaufman's argument for a middle-ground—an approach that allows lawyers to refuse to assist clients where the moral choice is obvious but also to defer to clients when the moral implications of the client's ends and means are not so clear.

This chapter also examined various alternatives to the amoral conception of the lawyers' role—arguments against role morality except in criminal defense work, contextual alternatives, the "citizen lawyer" model, and a conception of role based in "fidelity to law"—and how each of these alternatives would apply to particular sets of facts. We also considered the related issue of lawyers' accountability for their decisions about what clients and causes to serve. We examined the propriety of representing unpopular clients and the kinds of factors that might be relevant to individuals and firm leaders who make decisions about whether to handle controversial clients and matters.

CHAPTER 4

EXPRESSIONS OF SELF IN LAWYERING

■ ■ ■

A. INTRODUCTION

How should one's background, experience, political values, and identity traits influence a lawyer's professional life? Is it desirable that elements of "self" should inform the kinds of careers one pursues as a lawyer, the types of clients and causes one represents, and how one goes about one's work? As you consider the role of the lawyer, consider which aspects of your identity motivate your decision to become a lawyer and how, if at all, you would expect any of your identity traits to influence your conception of your professional role.

There is a vast academic and legal press literature about the experiences of various social groups in the legal profession. We examine some of that literature, with particular emphasis on the demographics of the profession and institutional and other factors that explain the underrepresentation of some social groups, in Chapter 37. In this chapter, we focus on a specific topic: whether or how personal identity does or should influence a lawyer's professional behavior and conception of role. In the context of considering these issues, we also introduce some of the rich literature on the salience of particular identities—such as race, gender, religion, and sexual orientation.

B. SHOULD PERSONAL IDENTITY INFLUENCE PROFESSIONAL IDENTITY?

Topic Overview

How are aspects of a lawyer's identity relevant to his or her professional role? In what ways do or should race, ethnicity, gender, national origin, sexual orientation, social class, disability, religion, or other aspects of identity affect what lawyers choose to do in the profession and how they do it? Does professional identity require lawyers to downplay aspects of their personal identity, such as by dressing in a particular way, or avoiding referring to certain topics? Why do some lawyers find it important to express aspects of their identity in their professional work and others do not?

BEYOND "BLEACHED OUT" PROFESSIONALISM: DEFINING PROFESSIONAL RESPONSIBILITY FOR REAL PROFESSIONALS

David B. Wilkins
Ethics in Practice: Lawyers' Roles, Responsibilities, and Regulation
(Deborah Rhode ed., 2000)[1]

In the standard view, becoming a professional involves more than simply performing a specific job or assuming a certain social standing. Instead, it involves becoming a particular kind of person; a person who both sees the world and acts according to normative standards and conventions that are distinct from those that govern nonprofessionals. Through a complex process involving self-selection, professional education, collegial socialization, and the threat of professional discipline, individuals who enter into professions are presumed to adopt a new professional identity based on the unique norms and practices of their craft. This "professional self," in turn, subsumes all other aspects of a professional's identity—gender, race, ethnicity, religion—and becomes the sole legitimate basis for actions undertaken within the confines of his or her professional role. Bleached out professionalism, as I will refer to this standard account, is central to the dominant model of American legal ethics.

It is not surprising that bleached out professionalism has become a core professional ideal. Norms such as neutrality, objectivity, and predictability are central to American legal culture. Lawyers are the gatekeepers through which citizens gain access to these important legal goods. If the law is to treat individuals equally, the argument goes, then lawyers must not allow their nonprofessional commitments to interfere with their professional obligation to give their clients unfettered access to all that the law has to offer. A professional ideology that treats a lawyer's nonprofessional identity as relevant to her professional conduct appears to threaten this important role.

In addition to the benefits that bleached out professionalism offers to the consumers of legal services, it also appears to safeguard the interests of the women and men who become lawyers. The universalizing claims made on behalf of the professional self suggest that differences among those who become lawyers that might matter outside of the professional sphere are irrelevant when evaluating these individuals' professional practices. This "professional" status is particularly important for the profession's new entrants—Jews, women, blacks, and other racial and religious minorities. These traditional outsiders have a powerful stake in being viewed as lawyers simpliciter, freed by their professional status from the pervasive weight of negative identity-specific stereotypes.

---

[1]   © 2000 Oxford University Press, Inc. By permission of Oxford University Press, USA.

Finally, bleached out professionalism appears to uphold the legal system's core commitment to the fundamental equality of persons. Thus, the idea that a lawyer's gender, race, or religion is irrelevant to her professional role seems to flow directly from the broader claim that the legal rules and procedures that lawyers interpret and implement should also be unaffected by identity. The claim that "our constitution"—and, indeed, justice itself—is colorblind" (or "gender blind") is a bedrock principle of our legal order, and indeed of our public morality. Lawyers who either explicitly or implicitly call attention to issues involving race or gender—including their own racial or gender identity—seemingly undermine this ideal.

Historicizing Professionalism. Like every normative system, the current understanding of professional role was created at a particular time and a particular place. As many scholars have documented, this period was dominated by a handful of relatively homogeneous elite New York lawyers who wielded considerable influence over the creation of the modern professional ideal. Moreover, these founders acted in an era in which various forms of identity-based discrimination were an accepted part of the legal and moral landscape. These initial conditions cast a continuing shadow over current understandings of professionalism.

Many of today's professional ideals can be traced to particular aspects of the identities of the profession's founding fathers. For example, the elite lawyers who created the rules of professional conduct raised entry requirements and pushed for stringent restrictions on commercial practices such as advertising and solicitation as a means of distancing themselves from the new wave of immigrant lawyers who, out of necessity, relied on many of these practices.

The Persistence of Identity. Empirical and anecdotal research confirms that contingent features of a person's identity exert a strong influence over how that person perceives and is perceived by others. For example, in his pioneering work on careers and developmental relationships inside corporations, David Thomas reports that race and gender significantly influence conduct and perceptions within organizations. This influence takes many forms. Chief among them is the preference that senior mentors have for protégés who remind them of themselves. White men, as Thomas's work repeatedly demonstrates, feel more comfortable in working relationships with other white men. My own research on law firms suggests that, notwithstanding their professional training, lawyers are not immune to this tendency.

The Value of Identity Consciousness. Proponents of bleached out professionalism assume that identity consciousness is simply an impediment to efficient and ethical professional service. This view, however, ignores the extent to which identity-related issues have played a positive role for each of the three constituencies bleached out professionalism is designed to serve: clients, lawyers, and the legal system.

From the consumers' perspective, bleached out professionalism tends to discourage innovation in the delivery of professional services. Many of the most powerful critiques of current professional norms have been launched in the name of particular identities. [F]or example, the feminist critique of adversary ethics [has] been in the forefront of the alternative dispute resolution movement.

One can tell a similar story about the critique mounted by blacks and other minorities of traditional hiring and evaluation policies in large law firms. Many corporate clients increasingly see good reasons to value law firm diversity in circumstances where those who are resisting greater integration in the name of "professional" standards may not.

Acknowledging a greater role for identity-specific professional commitments can also help the legal profession fulfill its fundamental mandate of promoting social justice. Consider, for example, the evolving role that black lawyers have played in the struggle for racial justice in the United States. The legal campaign to end "separate but equal" was spearheaded by Charles Hamilton Houston, Thurgood Marshall, and an elite core of black lawyers. As vice dean of Howard Law School in the 1930s, Houston expressly taught his students that they had an obligation to use their legal talents to improve the status of the black community. Although this stance did not prevent Houston and his protégé Thurgood Marshall from forming valuable and enduring relationships with white lawyers, it was a direct call on black attorneys to carry their racial identity into their professional role.

Today, many of the brightest and best-educated black lawyers spend some or all of their careers working in large corporate law firms, in corporate legal departments, or otherwise servicing the needs of large corporations. At first blush, it appears that these lawyers will have little to do with helping African Americans achieve social justice. There is, however, another way to look at the connection between black corporate lawyers and the social justice concerns of the African American community. Although these women and men may never be as directly involved in the struggle for racial justice as their forebearers in the civil rights movement, they nevertheless have important opportunities to contribute to this cause. These contributions include challenging stereotypes about black intellectual inferiority; acting as "role models" for other African Americans; helping to open up additional opportunities for blacks in law and elsewhere; directing their own resources and the resources of their employers toward projects that will benefit the black community; using corporate practice as a springboard to gain political influence to assist black causes; and persuading their powerful clients to act in ways that are less harmful (and perhaps even beneficial) to the interests of the black community.

[B]lack lawyers have good grounds for rejecting the claims of bleached out professionalism apart from the concerns of social justice. For many blacks, having a strong sense of connections to the black community is an important source of strength and well-being in an otherwise hostile world. Bleached out professionalism suggests that these feelings must be confined to the "private" realm.

Connecting one's self-worth to the "recognition" of one's identity as a black (or as a woman, or as a Jew, or as a gay man) can be an essential step toward being treated as a whole human being, but it can also produce "scripts" about the proper way to be black (or a woman, or Jewish, or gay) that deny our individual humanity. And caring about the welfare and advancement of group members can either help to produce a more equitable society or contribute to the oppression of one group over another.

[I]t is apparent that certain kinds of identity consciousness, based on certain kinds of identity, are more likely than others to produce either positive or negative effects. Thus, the first kind of identity consciousness—noticing how identity affects you and the world—is, in our contemporary era, both the least problematic and the most applicable to all forms of identity. One can see the benefits of this first form of identity consciousness by comparing [Los Angeles District Attorney] Gil Garcetti's actions in the [high-profile murder trial of O.J. Simpson, a noted African-American athlete and movie actor who was charged with killing his wife and her friend] with [New York] Governor Pataki's in the Johnson case. [The Johnson case involved Robert Johnson, an elected black district attorney representing the Bronx. Johnson announced that he would refuse to seek the state's newly enacted death penalty in a highly publicized case involving three minority youths accused of shooting a white police officer, in part because he believed it would inevitably be applied in a racially discriminatory manner].

Garcetti took concerted steps to ensure that Simpson would be prosecuted in a jurisdiction where there were likely to be black jurors, by a prosecution team that included at least one prominent black lawyer. It is important to note that Garcetti would not have been able to take these important steps unless he had first "noticed" the manner in which race was likely to play an important role in the case. Although Garcetti, like virtually all of the other participants in the case, initially took the position that race was not an issue in the Simpson prosecution, this standard bleached out view was clearly false. Long before racism [of some LA police officers] or the racial composition of the jury surfaced as issues in the case, the simple fact that a black man was accused of murdering his white ex-wife and her handsome white friend ensured that race was likely to play an important role in how many participants in the process viewed the case. By coming to terms with this reality, Garcetti helped to produce a proceeding that would protect Simpson from unfair inferences based on the color of his skin.

Pataki's decision to replace Robert Johnson with a white attorney who was a committed death penalty hawk had the opposite effect. But by not "noticing" how race affects capital punishment cases, Pataki's actions arguably further entrenched existing racial divisions about the administration of capital punishment For reasons that have been well documented, black citizens have reason to believe that equal justice under law is often not achieved in practice. This is particularly true in cases involving the death penalty. There is substantial evidence that race does play an important role in whether prosecutors seek the death penalty and whether juries are likely to impose this punishment. Replacing a black district attorney who has expressly attempted to take this reality into account with a white lawyer who is a known death penalty hawk sends a powerful message to the black constituents of this district that their concerns about the discriminatory nature of capital punishment will not be heard.

By carefully examining the moral claims underlying various calls for identity consciousness, we can begin to separate those moves away from bleached out professionalism that are likely to promote fundamental fairness and those that are likely to detract from this goal. If lawyers were merely ordinary citizens seeking to act morally in the world, this analysis might be all that is needed. But lawyers are not simply citizens; they are professionals who have made an express commitment to uphold the rules of legal ethics and to safeguard the interests of both clients and citizens. The partial, but nevertheless important truth about bleached out professionalism outlined [above] underscores that these commitments carry significant moral weight. Therefore, in addition to examining the moral justifications for particular claims of identity consciousness, we must also address how recognizing even a legitimate claim might undermine values central to the lawyer's role.

NOTES ON WILKINS

1. **Possible Benefits of Identity Consciousness?** According to Wilkins, awareness of a lawyer's various identity traits plays a positive role for clients, lawyers, and the legal system. In what ways? In Wilkins' terms, which "moves away from bleached out professionalism are likely to promote fundamental fairness" and which will not?

2. *Will Identity Traits Influence Your Career?* Are you persuaded by his account? How, if at all, do you imagine your identity traits will play a role in your career?

C. HOW DOES PERSONAL IDENTITY INFLUENCE PROFESSIONAL ROLE?

Professor Wilkins asserts that "[e]mpirical and anecdotal research confirms that contingent features of a person's identity exert a strong influence over how that person perceives and is perceived by others." While few dispute some aspects of this claim and many find it obvious to describe how a person's race or gender influences how others perceive one in some circumstances, there is less consensus about whether or precisely how race, gender, national origin, religion, sexual orientation, disability, social class, or other traits or features of lawyers influence how they perform their professional role. Do white lawyers perform their professional role differently than black lawyers? If so, how?[2]

In the late 1970s and early 1980s, lawyers and scholars contemplated whether the entry of a significant number of women into the legal profession would transform the practice of law. Many hoped that women would not merely assimilate into the practice of law, but rather that their entry would transform the profession and the law. The challenge—and it proved to be a huge challenge—was exploring the intuition that women might differ from men in how they approached being a lawyer in a way that avoided oversimplification or assuming that all women are one way and all men are another.

A particularly influential school of thought on the question whether women would perform the role of lawyer differently than men do was inspired by Harvard educational psychologist Carol Gilligan, who published a 1982 book, *In A Different Voice: Psychological Theory and Women's Development*, which said that male and female children learned to use different forms of moral reasoning. The male model of reasoning, according to Gilligan, used abstracted, universalistic principles applied to problematic situations to create an "ethic of justice." The female model of moral reasoning, which Gilligan termed an "ethic of care," was more relational, connected, and contextual and focused on people and the substance of a problem, rather than on rules. Gilligan's work inspired some legal scholars to suggest that the differences Gilligan found in male and female moral reasoning also manifested in differences in male and female styles of lawyering, and that women as lawyers were more likely

---

[2] *See* KENNETH W. MACK, REPRESENTING THE RACE: THE CREATION OF THE CIVIL RIGHTS LAWYER (Harvard University Press, 2012).

to focus on relationships and men on rights and rules.[3] A huge literature in social theory and social sciences also explored the concept of masculinity. As applied to law, scholars considered whether, if gender is a significant factor in explaining how lawyers and other social actors behave, what feminine and masculine approaches to law might be, and whether the categories feminine and masculine made sense as applied to lawyers.

Lawyers and legal scholars recognized, of course, that generalizations about male and female (or masculine and feminine) styles of lawyering or professional identities were huge oversimplifications. Professor Naomi Cahn explained,

> As a practical matter, the research does not support essentialist categories of male and female that correlate with moral orientations. Specifically, Carol Gilligan's research does not provide a basis for universalization of the terms "male" and "female." Neither sex uses either of the moral orientations exclusively. Many men and most women actually combine aspects of each orientation in their thought processes. Although when they focus on one perspective, most men do choose a rights perspective, most women do not choose a care perspective. In studies only of men it is harder to perceive a care focus, and, thus it is less likely to appear as a significant factor; only by including women can we perceive the dimensions of an ethic of care. [Carol Gilligan] asked eighty educationally advantaged people to describe a moral conflict. Fifty-four of the participants focused on either an ethic of justice or care. Of these fifty-four, one third of the female respondents focused on justice, and one third focused on care; all but one of the men chose the justice perspective. While this shows that men are more likely to choose an ethic of rights, it does not show that women are more likely to choose an ethic of care. While it demonstrates the necessity of including women in order to appreciate the different themes, it also cautions us not to generalize that the different voice we have identified is feminine—that is, it describes many women, some men, and possibly the views of some members of other socially subordinate groups.[4]

As for what would characterize a female or male (or masculine or feminine) style of lawyering, Cahn said,

> the answer is that we do not really know; nor, perhaps, should we care. Instead, we should examine how people practice law,

---

[3]   See, e.g., Carrie Menkel-Meadow, *Portia in a Different Voice: Speculations on a Women's Lawyering Process*, 1 BERKELEY WOMEN'S L.J. 39 (1985); Carrie Menkel-Meadow, *Portia Redux: Another Look at Gender, Feminism, and Legal Ethics*, 2 VA. J. OF SOC. POL. & L. 75 (1994).

[4]   Naomi R. Cahn, *Styles of Lawyering*, 43 HASTINGS L.J. 1039, 1052 (1992).

what styles people use, and how these different styles affect attorney-client relationships, opposing counsel interactions, and court appearances. Some of what we observe may correlate with attributes that have been labeled male or female, even though both men and women may be using 'cross-gendered' styles. What is important is to recognize that many attributes of what has been labeled a 'female style of lawyering' could help improve the litigation process and that, in fact, many already have been implemented by men and women.

She concluded: "Feminist theory helps us critique existing lawyering methods, and develop and appreciate alternative methods of being a lawyer, but does not require us to label these new developments by gender."[5]

One systematic exploration of feminist methods of being a lawyer is the following. Note that Professor Bartlett attempts to avoid the essentialism problem by referring to feminist lawyers rather than female lawyers; both men and women can be feminists. But the entry of women into the profession was of course the catalyst to feminism as a legal method.

FEMINIST LEGAL METHODS
Katharine T. Bartlett
103 Harvard Law Review 829 (1990)

When feminists "do law," they do what other lawyers do: they examine the facts of a legal issue or dispute, they identify the essential features of those facts, they determine what legal principles should guide the resolution of the dispute, and they apply those principles to the facts. This process unfolds not in a linear, sequential, or strictly logical manner, but rather in a pragmatic, interactive manner. Facts determine which rules are appropriate, and rules determine which facts are relevant. In doing law, feminists like other lawyers use a full range of methods of legal reasoning—deduction, induction, analogy, and use of hypotheticals, policy, and other general principles.

In addition to these conventional methods of doing law, however, feminists use other methods. These methods, though not all unique to feminists, attempt to reveal features of a legal issue which more traditional methods tend to overlook or suppress:

Asking the Woman Question. Feminists across many disciplines regularly ask a question—a set of questions, really—known as "the woman question," which is designed to identify the gender implications of rules and practices which might otherwise appear to be neutral or

---

[5] *Id.* at 1068–1069.

objective. [H]ave women been left out of consideration? If so, in what way; how might that omission be corrected? What difference would it make to do so? In law, asking the woman question means examining how the law fails to take into account the experiences and values that seem more typical of women than of men, for whatever reason, or how existing legal standards and concepts might disadvantage women. The question assumes that some features of the law may be not only nonneutral in a general sense, but also "male" in a specific sense. The purpose of the woman question is to expose those features and how they operate, and to suggest how they might be corrected.

Once adopted as a method, asking the woman question is a method of critique as integral to legal analysis as determining the precedential value of a case, stating the facts, or applying law to facts. "Doing law" as a feminist means looking beneath the surface of law to identify the gender implications of rules and the assumptions underlying them and insisting upon applications of rules that do not perpetuate women's subordination. It means recognizing that the woman question always has potential relevance and that "tight" legal analysis never assumes gender neutrality.

Feminist Practical Reasoning. Some feminists have claimed that women approach the reasoning process differently than men do. In particular, they say that women are more sensitive to situation and context, that they resist universal principles and generalizations, especially those that do not fit their own experiences, and that they believe that "the practicalities of everyday life" should not be neglected for the sake of abstract justice. Whether these claims can be empirically sustained, this reasoning process has taken on normative significance for feminists, many of whom have argued that individualized factfinding is often superior to the application of bright-line rules, and that reasoning from context allows a greater respect for difference and for the perspectives of the powerless.

Practical reasoning approaches problems not as dichotomized conflicts, but as dilemmas with multiple perspectives, contradictions, and inconsistencies. These dilemmas, ideally, do not call for the choice of one principle over another, but rather "imaginative integrations and reconciliations," which require attention to particular context. Practical reasoning sees particular details not as annoying inconsistencies or irrelevant nuisances which impede the smooth logical application of fixed rules. Nor does it see particular facts as the *objects* of legal analysis, the inert material to which to apply the living law. Instead, new facts present opportunities for improved understandings and "integrations."

Consciousness Raising. Another feminist method for expanding perceptions is consciousness-raising. Consciousness-raising is an interactive and collaborative process of articulating one's experiences and making meaning of them with others who also articulate their experiences. Feminist consciousness-raising creates knowledge by exploring common experiences and patterns that emerge from shared tellings of life events. What were experienced as personal hurts individually suffered reveal themselves as a collective experience of oppression.

Consciousness-raising is a method of trial and error. When revealing an experience to others, a participant in consciousness-raising does not know whether others will recognize it. The process values risk-taking and vulnerability over caution and detachment. Honesty is valued above consistency, teamwork over self-sufficiency, and personal narrative over abstract analysis. The goal is individual and collective empowerment, not personal attack or conquest.

NOTES ON BARTLETT

1. ***Women and the Transformation of the Legal Profession.*** In what ways and to what extent do you believe that the entry of large numbers of women into the legal profession over the past several decades has changed the profession's structures and norms? What changes, if any, do you think are yet to come?

2. ***Gender, Legal Ethics, and the Role of the Lawyer.*** Scholars influenced by Gilligan's work on moral reasoning assert that women may have a different legal ethics than men. Do men and women have different styles of being lawyers or of approaching ethical dilemmas? If the distinction is not, in your view, between men and women, but instead between masculine and feminine styles, what are those styles?

3. ***Are There Feminist Legal Methods?*** In what respects, if any, do the three feminist legal methods discussed by Bartlett allow for the integration of personal identity into professional role? If they acknowledge the possibility of expression of self in a professional role, are they limited to gender identity, or are they applicable to any aspect of identity?

D. PERSONAL IDENTITY AS A SOURCE OF INSPIRATION IN PROFESSIONAL LIFE

Thus far in this chapter, we have considered whether personal identity should or does influence how lawyers perform their professional role. We now consider another aspect of those two questions: how might personal identity be a source of inspiration or guidance to lawyers?

Many aspects of one's personal experience or identity might be a source of inspiration. One obvious source of inspiration is religion.

RELIGIOUS LAWYERING IN A LIBERAL DEMOCRACY: A CHALLENGE AND AN INVITATION

Russell G. Pearce and Amelia J. Uelmen
55 Case Western Reserve Law Review 127 (2004)

Although one of us prays as a Jew and one of us prays as a Christian, our prayers express who we are and who we want to be. We aspire to weave God's law into our professional lives, and to discover God's own hand at work, sanctifying our world and our lives.

[R]eligious lawyering brings a positive contribution to advance the administration of justice without undermining the basic values of liberal democracy.

Associations of Catholic lawyers and Jewish lawyers, as well as chapters of the Christian Legal Society, have been gathering for decades. Many religious traditions include illustrious examples of lawyers who have integrated their religious values into their professional decisions. And certainly the ties between religious values and the legal profession's goals of public service, civility, and honesty were evident long before the 1990s.

In one sense, the religious lawyering movement builds upon and strengthens these long-standing community organizations and commitments. For example, it would be interesting to trace the extent to which efforts to integrate religious values into professional life have contributed to the growth of faith-based pro bono legal services to the poor. Religious lawyering may also strengthen lawyers in their resolve to set aside the necessary time for religious observance, even in the midst of the profession's pressing demands on their time.

But we posit that the religious lawyering project which has been germinating over the past decade asks for more—and presents a much deeper challenge for the legal profession. Unlike many previous "law and religion" discussions, the religious lawyering movement focuses less on the conceptual relationships and tensions between law and religion and how these play out in a democracy, and more on ways in which religious values and perspectives may provide a completely different structural framework for an approach to professional life.

As anthropologist Clifford Geertz has described, the core of religious perspective is "the conviction that the values one holds are grounded in the inherent structure of reality, that between the way one ought to live and the way things really are there is an unbreakable inner connection." Religious lawyering draws out the "unbreakable inner connection" between "the way things really are" and "the way one ought to live"—not only in a private "non-work" sphere, but also in professional life. On this basis religious lawyering insists that there should be room in the profession for such convictions about the "inherent structure of reality," and for lawyers then to integrate this perspective and to apply its substantive critiques and contributions to the issues which arise not just at the margins, but in the heart of ordinary day-to-day legal practice.

The religious lawyering movement suggests that this is a step to be taken not just within one's heart or the quiet of one's individual conscience. It insists that this is an appropriate topic for open conversation, dialogue and debate in law offices, in judges' chambers, in legislatures, and even in law schools.

The recent growth of the religious lawyering movement is, at least in part, a response to the legal profession's failure to offer lawyers a satisfactory way to understand their role and responsibilities. Religion offers religious lawyers a constructive framework within which they can respond to a host of questions that the professionalism rhetoric leaves unanswered. It not only offers answers to the more practical question of how to be a good lawyer and a good person, but also responds to deeper and more existential questions such as why try to be a good person in the first place. For many religious people, this larger overarching framework provides a moral anchor that enables them not only to resist temptations of greed and abuse of power, but also to situate their legal work within a sense of responsibility and service to the larger community. Although the answers will differ depending on the religion and the individual, there will be answers.

Religion also offers religious lawyers a way to transcend the dichotomy between the noble professional and the selfish business person. The notion of a calling or vocation, common to many religions, can make all work meaningful. As Martin Luther King, Jr. taught: "If it falls your lot to be a street sweeper, sweep streets like Michelangelo painted pictures, like Shakespeare wrote poetry, like Beethoven composed music; sweep streets so well that all the host of Heaven and earth will have to pause and say, "Here lived a great street sweeper, who swept his job well." What is true of street sweepers is equally true of lawyers.

Religious lawyering provides a robust framework for lawyers to explain why they are morally accountable for their service as the governing class and why they must incorporate personal integrity and consideration of the public good into client representation. This does not mean lawyers must abandon client advocacy. It does require, however, that lawyers recognize that their own decisions regarding client goals are always morally laden, thus pushing them to engage clients in conversation regarding the morality of their conduct.

Despite these benefits, religious lawyering faces three types of objections related to its effectiveness, fairness, and compatibility with liberal democracy.

1) Does religious lawyering really make a difference? The first objection is quite simple. Religious people are no more moral than anyone else. After all, recent headlines recount many examples of religiously devout business people and professionals who nonetheless have been caught in corporate scandals and other illegal conduct.

Our claim is not that religious people are inherently more moral. Rather, we argue that religious lawyering offers lawyers a reason to behave ethically at a time when persuasive reasons to accept moral accountability are hard to find. While no guarantee, it does offer religious lawyers a way to draw a substantial and consistent connection between their religious values and their professional decisions. People who find religion a compelling source of moral authority may find it an equally compelling source in their work as lawyers.

2) Is religious lawyering unfair to clients? Another objection arises from the fear that religious lawyers will impose their religious discourse and worldviews on clients. This brings to mind an incident in which an American Airlines pilot asked Christian passengers to raise their hands and suggested that the other passengers might want to speak to the Christians about their faith during the flight. Many thought that the pilot's suggestion was completely inappropriate and that it was extremely unfair for the pilot to proselytize his captive passengers.

Is a religious lawyer like that American Airlines pilot? Model Rule 2.1 provides that "in rendering advice, a lawyer may refer not only to law but to other considerations, such as moral, economic, social and political factors, that may be relevant to the client's situation." The Comment to the rule makes clear that "it is proper for a lawyer to refer to relevant moral and ethical considerations in giving advice." If the religious lawyer explains to the client the full range of options, including the moral implications of each, that seems to fall squarely within the rule and not to present a problem.

Even while permitted, discussion of religion with clients is often inappropriate. What is most bothersome about the American Airlines example is the pilot's abuse of his power in imposing his views on a literally captive audience of buckled-in passengers. While perhaps not captive to the same degree, in many practice contexts clients are often more vulnerable than their trusted lawyers. Like those American Airlines passengers who felt that the pilot was disrespectful, clients who wish to avoid proselytizing of any kind in their professional relationships should be able to do so.

3) Is religious lawyering dangerous for democracy? The third challenge to religious lawyering is the argument that it poses a danger to liberal democracy—our system of majority rule that protects individual and minority rights.

These fears appear to arise from two sources. First, in a country that is more than 75% Christian, Jews, Muslims, and people of other minority religions might very well worry that they will suffer unequal and unfair treatment if actors in our legal system make decisions based on religious identity. Moreover, non-believers may have an even greater fear of discrimination given that close to 87% of Americans identify themselves as believers. A second and related worry is that allowing more room for religion in the public square will inevitably lead to divisiveness and intolerance, adding further fuel to the fires of polarizing culture wars.

Despite these fears, religious lawyering does not offend our system of liberal democracy. The United States Constitution promotes liberal democracy by prohibiting the establishment of religion and protecting free exercise. While disagreeing about the particular contours of these provisions, most political theorists agree that in a liberal democracy, citizens should have the freedom to make political decisions based on religious convictions. Whether and how to express religious convictions in the public square, especially when one serves a public role, is of course the subject of intense controversy. But even assuming the disputed point that the lawyer-client relationship is part of the public square, this debate implicates how religious lawyers discuss their religion with their clients, not whether they can appropriately ground their approach to lawyering in their religion.

Even when religious lawyering is placed against the backdrop of American liberal democracy's protections and constraints, some may still fear discrimination and intolerance. It is understandable that minority groups fear majorities, whether religious or not. Nonetheless, as a practical matter, the United States continues as a liberal democracy only because the vast majority of religious Americans find liberal democratic values consonant with their religious values.

If a lawyer's religious approaches to lawyering generate discrimination and intolerance, the lawyer's conduct should be subject to professional and social critique, and discipline where appropriate, just as any other approach that is less than respectful of others. To the extent that religious approaches and perspectives are difficult for others to understand, religious lawyers should work harder to make themselves understood—as would be reasonable to ask of any attorney who fails to communicate her views effectively.

At a time when many believe that law is no longer a noble profession, many lawyers see no reason to devote time and energy to promoting the public good. Religious lawyering may offer a powerful antidote: a robust framework for lawyers to integrate into their professional lives their most deeply rooted values, perspectives and critiques, and persuasive reasons to improve the quality of justice and work for the common good. At its best, religious lawyering echoes Martin Luther King's advice to the street sweeper. How wonderful it would be, indeed, if we practiced law so well that the host of heaven and earth would pause to say, here lived great lawyers who did their job well.

NOTES ON PEARCE AND UELMEN

1. **Does Personal Identity Enrich the Lawyer's Conception of Professional Role?** Do you agree with Pearce and Uelmen that the rhetoric of professionalism does not answer a host of important questions that lawyers may have about their work lives—that the legal profession has "fail[ed] to offer lawyers a satisfactory way to understand their role and responsibilities"?

2. **Does Emphasis on Personal Identity Create Tension in a Pluralist Society?** To what extent might the desire of a deeply religious lawyer to find an expression of self in professional role create tension with other actors in a secular legal system on issues as to which religious and secular values differ? Do Pearce and Uelmen adequately answer such concerns? Is drawing inspiration from religion in a professional role more or less likely to create tension with other actors in a legal system than is expressing other aspects of one's identity in professional role? In other words, is religion different from race or national origin or other aspects of oneself with respect to how it inspires or guides lawyers?

3. **An Ethical Poverty in the Relationship Between Lawyer and Client?** Pearce and Uelmen's argument draws on views expressed by Thomas Shaffer, who rejects amoral advocacy on the ground that it promotes a morally defective relationship between the lawyer and client. He argues that lawyers are obliged to counsel clients about their obligations to community and not just their interests and rights.[6] We will consider his views more closely when we discuss conflicts of interest doctrine and how it relates to the practice of family law in Chapter 10.

* * *

Another account of the way in which a lawyer finds an expression of self in his professional role is the following story of the career of Harvard Law Professor William Rubenstein.

FROM THE CLOSET TO THE COURTROOM
Carlos Ball
Beacon Press 2010

Bill Rubenstein, the son of an accountant and a former schoolteacher, was born in 1960 and grew up in Squirrel Hill, a predominantly Jewish neighborhood in Pittsburgh. Although he knew that he was gay from a

---

[6] Thomas L. Shaffer, *The Unique, Novel, and Unsound Adversary Ethic*, 41 VAND. L. REV. 697 (1988).

young age, Rubenstein remained in the closet throughout his four years of college at Yale. In fact, it was not until the summer of 1982, a few months after he graduated from college, that Rubenstein first came out to a friend. That friend proceeded to warn him about a mysterious disease that seemed to be afflicting gay men in New York and San Francisco. Rubenstein had not heard about the illness and did not give the matter much thought. Shortly after arriving at Harvard in 1983 to pursue a law degree, Rubenstein joined the gay law student organization and came out to members of his study group, most of whom were straight men. Much to his relief, none of them seemed to care.

While Rubenstein was taking small yet determined steps to come out of the closet, AIDS was transforming itself from a relatively rare illness into a national epidemic of frightening proportions. The stigma that accompanied the spread of AIDS pushed some gay men back (or further) into the closet. But for Rubenstein, as for many LGBT people of his generation, AIDS had the opposite effect. As it became clear that the epidemic would soon have a devastating impact on thousands of gay men across the country, Rubenstein started feeling a growing sense of solidarity both with those who were becoming ill and with the partners and friends who were caring for them.

Rubenstein's education as a gay man took place primarily in the bars and cafés of Boston and Cambridge. There was not much to learn on the subject, however, from his law school classes, where the topic of homosexuality never arose. Perplexed by this silence, Rubenstein spent an evening at the Harvard law library looking for what legal books had to say about homosexuality. Despite searching for several hours, he found no discussion of homosexuality as a legal topic, much less any reference to actual lives led by lesbians and gay men. It was as if LGBT people, as far as the law was concerned, were invisible.

After receiving his law degree in 1986, Rubenstein moved to Washington, D.C., to clerk for a federal district judge. In his spare time, he volunteered for the Whitman-Walker Clinic—the largest AIDS service organization in the nation's capital—by drafting wills for its clients. On many early evenings after leaving the judge's chambers, Rubenstein stopped by the Clinic to pick up files containing interviews of gay men about their dying wishes. Most of these men had few assets, their bequests consisting of leaving small bank accounts, furniture, and pets to partners and friends. In his apartment at night, Rubenstein drafted wills based on these modest requests, dropping them off at the Clinic the following morning on his way back to work. He did not meet any of the men whose final wishes he transcribed into legal documents, though he frequently saw their names in the local gay newspaper's obituary pages. He also sometimes recognized their names stitched into the colorful patches of the AIDS quilt that was spread out like an ocean of grief on the Washington Mall.

By the middle of the 1980s, the AIDS epidemic had become the leading cause of death among twenty-five- to forty-four-year-olds in the United States. In doing so, it reversed, as one writer put it, "the natural order of life as the old buried the young and the young buried one another." Surrounded by so much death and dying, Rubenstein came to assume that the disease would kill him before he reached the age of thirty. With a perceived life expectancy of less than five years, he decided in 1987 to dedicate his professional life as a lawyer to doing whatever he could to help people with AIDS. As a result, he got a job with the ACLU's Lesbian and Gay Rights Project (as well as its recently created AIDS Project).

In his first year at the ACLU, Rubenstein represented a woman with AIDS quarantined by public health officials in South Carolina. The young lawyer filed a habeas corpus petition in federal court in Charleston, demanding that the government justify the continued detention of his client. The case was assigned to district court (now U.S. Court of Appeals) judge Karen Henderson, a Reagan appointee. When Rubenstein showed up in Judge Henderson's courtroom to argue the petition, he noticed that the furniture had been rearranged so that the quarantined woman and her lawyer would have to sit in the back of the courtroom. It seemed that the judge, apparently fearing that she might contract HIV from the mere presence of Rubenstein's client in the courtroom, wanted her as far away from the bench as possible. Rubenstein was forced to make his legal arguments from the back of the room, practically shouting in order to be heard. Perhaps not surprisingly, Judge Henderson denied the habeas corpus petition. Rubenstein then went across the street to the state courthouse and, with the assistance of a local lawyer, convinced a judge there to issue an order releasing his client from confinement.

In another instance, Rubenstein threatened to sue the state of Alabama when it refused to use Medicaid money to pay for AZT prescribed to individuals with AIDS. When confronted with the possibility of a lawsuit brought by the ACLU, the state relented and agreed to pay for the medication. The evening after state officials announced their change in policy, a group of Alabamians with AIDS gathered at a Birmingham apartment to celebrate the good news. From there, one of them called Rubenstein at his New York office to thank him for his help with the case. As Rubenstein spoke to the caller, and as he heard the celebratory din in the background, he felt pleased that he had been able to help his clients in a tangible way; as a direct result of his advocacy, after all, the state government had agreed to pay for their AIDS treatment. But he also suspected, as in fact would turn out to be the case, that every person with AIDS present in that Birmingham apartment that evening would be dead in a few years.

Death was an inescapable part of Rubenstein's early professional life as an attorney, and the young lawyer tried to deal with this awful reality as best he could. Rubenstein found some solace in the fact that the legal work he was doing was challenging and fascinating. There had never before in the United States been an epidemic quite like this one; the disease tested not only political and medical institutions but also legal ones. Although Rubenstein was aware that there were limits to what the law could accomplish, he also knew that it could be deployed in certain instances to benefit people with AIDS in tangible ways. There was also a creativeness to the AIDS activism of the late 1980s that motivated Rubenstein to keep fighting for his clients. AIDS activists during that time did everything from chaining themselves to drug companies' trucks to demonstrating with cardboard tombstones in front of government buildings to draping antigay senator Jesse Helms's house with a gigantic condom. There was a theatricality and an inventiveness to the political activism that Rubenstein found mesmerizing and captivating. In the end, Rubenstein felt proud to be manning the barricades, so to speak, with individuals, most of whom were quite young, who were committed to fighting until their last breaths to pressure, cajole, and embarrass those in power to treat the epidemic with the seriousness that it demanded. There was a dignity and pride in this perseverance that, despite the relentlessness of the disease, was inspiring.

NOTES ON BALL

1. ***Can You Choose an Identity or Does It Choose You?*** Bill Rubenstein enjoyed a successful career as a civil rights lawyer specializing in LGBT issues before becoming a law professor. In a memoir of his years as a student at Harvard Law School and his early career as a lawyer, Rubenstein notes the significance of his gay identity to his career choices. He also says the following about one of his faculty colleagues: "Professor Halley identifies herself as a member of the LGBT community in the law professors' directory—the first full member of the Harvard faculty to do so. Professor Halley's work, however, challenges the identity-based nature of social movements, investigating whether identity is not, ultimately, as imprisoning as it is liberating. In a unique demonstration that the personal is political, Professor Halley refers to herself as a 'gay man.'" Rubenstein remarked that twenty years after he graduated, Harvard Law School "finally has a faculty member willing to identify publicly as a gay man—and he's a woman."[7] What does Rubenstein mean by saying that a woman can choose to be a gay man?

---

[7] William B. Rubenstein, *My Harvard Law School*, 39 Harv. C.R.-C.L. L. Rev. 317 (2004). *See also* JANET HALLEY, SPLIT DECISIONS: HOW AND WHY TO TAKE A BREAK FROM FEMINISM (2006).

2. *Liberation or Constraint?* How would you reconcile the account of the life and career experience of Professor Rubenstein with Professor Halley's idea that identity can be "as imprisoning as it is liberating"? In what respects might finding expressions of self in one's legal work be liberating? In what respects might it be constraining?

E. SUMMARY

In this chapter we have considered three sets of questions about the role that personal identity traits play in a lawyer's role as a professional. We began with normative questions: Should lawyers aspire to express aspects of their personal identity in their work as lawyers? If so, when and why? If not, why not? Second, we considered descriptive questions: in what ways does personal identity influence how lawyers go about their work? Do aspects of one's identity lead one to approach ethical problems, or client relations, or legal reasoning, or any other aspect of a lawyer's work differently than others who do not share those identity traits? Third, we examined a mix of descriptive and normative issues on the particular question of whether lawyers find aspects of their personal lives to be a source of inspiration and meaning in their work, and whether the inspiration that some find in expressing their self in their work is alienating to others. We also raised questions about whether or to what extent identity traits define how people think of themselves and are perceived by others, either as a defining factor (e.g., women are different from men, or people generally think women are different from men) or as a tendency on a spectrum (e.g., gender identities as masculine and feminine tend to be associated with different behaviors, but there are wide variations in the way that people perform their identities and in the ways in which others perceive them).

As the context for our study of these three sets of questions, we considered examples of several of the most salient identity traits in contemporary American society: race, gender, religion, and sexual orientation. Other aspects of your sense of self may be more important to you than these, and we encourage you to reflect on whether that is so and why. Which identity traits will matter to you and to others who work with you? As you consider the notion that professional role is influenced by identity traits, consider the significance in your life of those that you choose, those that are ascribed by others, those that are more or less mutable, and those that may not be as salient to others as they are to you.

PART II

THE ATTORNEY-CLIENT RELATIONSHIP

∎ ∎ ∎

This Part focuses on the attorney-client relationship. Aspects of this relationship are covered throughout the book, as we have seen already in connection with our discussion of the meaning of professionalism in Chapter 2 and the role of the lawyer in Chapter 3. Lawyers owe many duties to clients and to the legal system, including duties of competence, diligence, confidentiality, and loyalty, and much of the law governing lawyers concerns how lawyers should manage competing obligations to clients, the public, third parties, and the legal system itself. In this part, we focus on other aspects of the attorney-client relationship, including beginning and ending attorney-client relationships, the allocation of decision-making authority between lawyers and clients, fee arrangements, transactions between lawyers and clients, protections for prospective clients, and restrictions on lawyers' interactions with represented parties.

These are important topics in the lives of every lawyer. They raise normative, legal, and empirical questions, and those questions are interrelated. How should the attorney-client relationship be structured? How do the rules of professional conduct, contract, and other sources of law constrain lawyer-client relationships? What authority do lawyers hold to make decisions relating to the representation? Should lawyers and clients be allowed to enter into whatever fee arrangements they can agree upon, or should the rules of professional conduct limit those arrangements? When, if ever, is it appropriate for lawyers to enter into business transactions or sexual relationships with clients? What duties do lawyers owe to clients who are represented by other lawyers? As we'll see, there are rules addressing all of these issues, and, with rare exceptions, those rules treat all lawyers and clients alike. But one's attitude about whether and to what extent regulation of the attorney-client relationship is necessary and appropriate may turn on empirical questions regarding how lawyer-client relationships actually operate in practice and especially on the power that clients wield to protect themselves in their interactions with lawyers in various types of circumstances. The answers to those empirical questions vary according to the many different types of practices in which lawyers engage.

In Chapter 5, on starting and ending attorney-client relationships and the allocation of decision-making authority between lawyers and clients, we focus on how lawyers should and do interact with their clients, as well as how the law defines the boundaries of lawyers' and clients' authority. We will also consider how differences in the particular circumstances of various types of practice and the power exercised by clients in those practice contexts influence who actually "calls the shots." In Chapter 6, we consider several rules designed to protect clients from lawyer overreaching, and we assess the consequences and wisdom of these rules.

CHAPTER 5

STARTING AND ENDING THE ATTORNEY-CLIENT RELATIONSHIP AND ALLOCATING AUTHORITY DURING IT

■ ■ ■

A. INTRODUCTION

For the most part, the division of authority between lawyers and clients is worked out between them through negotiation and deference. On the allocation of authority, as on most other aspects of law practice, lawyers are guided by the norms of their practice group, their own sense of appropriate behavior, the constraints imposed by the market for legal services, and their social relations with their clients. The Model Rules of Professional Conduct, however, impose some guidelines. Model Rule 1.2 specifies that the client decides upon "the objectives of representation." In particular, the client decides whether to file or to settle a civil suit, whether to plead guilty to criminal charges, and whether to appeal any matter. The lawyer decides on the means by which the client's objectives are to be pursued, including how to gather and use evidence and which legal arguments to make. Model Rule 1.2 requires lawyers to communicate with the client as to the means by which the client's objectives are to be pursued. Model Rule 1.4 further requires that lawyers regularly and reasonably communicate with their clients to enable the client to make informed decisions. Moreover, in criminal cases, under the Fifth Amendment to the U.S. Constitution, clients decide whether to assert or to waive their constitutional right to testify in their own criminal case and whether to appeal a criminal conviction. Under the Sixth Amendment, the defendant has a right to represent himself in his criminal trial. *Faretta v. California*, 422 U.S. 806 (1975).

This chapter examines how attorney-client relations are formed and how lawyers and clients share decision-making authority. It then considers when and whether lawyers' deference to the wishes of clients serves the interests of clients or the public. The chapter covers the constitutional standards and ethical rules about when lawyers must consult with and defer to their clients. The chapter concludes with the law governing termination of the attorney-client relationship.

B. STARTING THE ATTORNEY-CLIENT RELATIONSHIP

Most attorney-client relationships begin with a face-to-face meeting followed by a written or oral agreement. That contract, called the "retainer agreement," spells out the terms of the employment and fee arrangement. But lawyers sometimes are deemed to have attorney-client relationships in other, sometimes more ambiguous, circumstances. In *Togstad v. Vesely, Otto, Miller & Keefe*, 291 N.W.2d 686 (Minn. 1980), a court found an attorney-client relationship where the lawyer offered legal advice but turned down the client's case and never entered into a written agreement to represent the client. Another famous case, *Westinghouse Electric Corporation v. Kerr-McGee Corp.*, 580 F.2d 1311 (7th Cir. 1978), held that members of a trade group were clients of a law firm that represented the trade group, at least for purposes of the conflict of interest rules, when the trade group members provided sensitive confidential information to the firm.

Attorney-client relationships can exist without the payment of any fees by the client. Lawyers who represent clients pro bono owe those clients the same duties they owe to paying clients. When a lawyer is paid by one person to represent another, the person represented by the lawyer is the lawyer's client, and the lawyer may not allow the person who pays the fees to direct or influence the lawyer's performance of her duties on behalf of the client. Model Rule 5.4.

C. WHO CALLS THE SHOTS?

In this section, we consider various empirical studies that describe the allocation of authority in the lawyer-client relationship. We also identify what factors influence when and whether lawyers defer to client decisions about matters of strategy.

Empirical studies of lawyers in different practice settings have found wide variation in the extent to which lawyers direct their clients or cede control. In the first excerpt below, from a review of empirical research on lawyers' relationships with clients, Professor Lynn Mather explores economic and social factors that influence the relationship. Powerful clients who are paying the bills may demand more substantial influence over every aspect of the representation than the law requires. Where clients do not pay by the hour or where the lawyer handles small matters for a large number of clients who may not be repeat clients, the lawyer may exercise more control even than the law suggests the lawyer should. Following the Mather excerpt, different accounts drawn from empirical studies of particular practice settings explore how and why lawyers or clients effectively control the course of the representation. Following these descriptions, we examine some of the normative arguments about whether and when lawyers should defer to client preferences about the goals and means of lawyers' work.

In this section, we consider various empirical studies that describe the allocation of authority in the lawyer-client relationship. We also identify what factors influence when and whether lawyers defer to client decisions about matters of strategy.

WHAT DO CLIENTS WANT? WHAT DO LAWYERS DO?

Lynn Mather
52 Emory Law Journal 1065 (2003)

Lawyers' approaches to client representation vary considerably by areas of practice and type of client. Within specific legal fields lawyers generally share an understanding of the appropriateness and value of their particular way of working with their clients. Lawyers' decisions to control their clients or to cede control seem to be based less on formal legal principles and more on economic and social factors.

Just like other workers, lawyers appear to respond to economic incentives in the course of their work. Thus, client resources and fee structure influence lawyers' approach to representation. A single or flat case fee encourages private criminal defense attorneys to minimize time on a case and to dominate their clients. Personal injury lawyers, who are paid on a contingency fee, also benefit from a quick turnover of cases and tend to exercise considerable client control. By contrast, business lawyers, who bill by the hour, typically allow their clients to set the agenda and pace of work. Comparison of lawyers representing poverty and civil rights claims found that, with some exception, lawyers who were dependent upon their clients for their salaries generally expressed more deferential views than did lawyers whose payment came from other sources. Exceptions to these patterns in criminal practice or divorce work frequently came from clients with substantial resources. Clients with deep pockets could more easily resist their lawyers' control and, if they chose to, direct case strategies themselves.

The relationship between lawyer and client also explains why some lawyers exercise greater control over clients than others do. Lawyers in high volume practices, such as criminal defense or divorce work, do not depend on any particular client for a significant source of their income. This provides the lawyer with leverage to part ways with clients who resist her advice. On the other hand, corporate lawyers whose annual income depends heavily on one or two clients may have difficulty exerting substantial influence over them. As the saying goes, "you can't be a good lawyer with just one client." That is to say, professional independence and objectivity are threatened by a lawyer's economic reliance on her client. Furthermore, clients who are "repeat players," regularly using the courts, show less deference to their lawyers than "one shotters" who use the courts infrequently. But repeat player clients who regularly work with the same lawyers over time willingly cede control to them and rely on them for advice.

How lawyers represent their clients also depends upon the organizational context of lawyers' work. Law firms and other legal organizations develop shared cultures or house norms that profoundly affect how a lawyer practices, including her approach to clients. Informal communities of legal practice develop around certain legal specialties (e.g., divorce, personal injury) and in small towns and cities where lawyers repeatedly work with one another. Thus, particular norms of client representation develop and influence lawyers in those communities to behave accordingly in order to maintain their reputations.

Variation in the characteristics of individual clients sheds further light on why lawyers choose different professional roles. Lawyers who exercised considerable client control often referred to the characteristics of their clients to justify or explain the need for the attorney's influence. Criminal defense lawyers commented on their clients' lack of intelligence; divorce lawyers emphasized their clients' emotional instability and self-absorption; and legal services attorneys pointed to their clients' lack of sophistication. On the other hand, corporate lawyers pointed to their business clients' extensive knowledge and sophistication to justify a collaborative style or attorney deference to client. Other factors might also explain differences in the degree of independent judgment and influence lawyers exercise over clients. These include: the nature of the problem and the available legal remedies; the type of legal work performed (e.g., litigation, transactional, organization, counseling, etc.); the degree of uncertainty and the clients' willingness to accept risk; political goals for lawyers and client; and any external controls over lawyer-client interactions (e.g., governmental regulation, ethics supervision within a law firm or company, appellate processes, or insurance systems).

* * *

Mather's empirical study of lawyers found that corporate clients exert substantial control over both the objectives and the minute details of their lawyers' work. In the following excerpt, Professor David Wilkins elaborates on the ways in which the market for large firm legal services enables corporate clients to control the attorney-client relationship.

DO CLIENTS HAVE ETHICAL OBLIGATIONS TO LAWYERS?
SOME LESSONS FROM THE DIVERSITY WARS

David B. Wilkins
11 Georgetown Journal of Legal Ethics 855 (1998)

Corporations traditionally found it efficient to invest in long-term relationships with a full-service outside firm that acted as both "diagnostician" of the client's legal needs and as reliable "referring agents" (often to another member of the same law firm) to ensure that the client's problems were handled correctly. These long term relationships, in turn, created economic disincentives to lawyer-switching that gave lawyers de facto power over even the largest corporate clients.

[T]oday's corporate clients have found ways to reduce the major information asymmetries [that formerly characterized most attorney-client relationships]. The mechanism by which clients have closed the knowledge gap is simple. Instead of relying on outside firms to meet their diagnostic and referral needs, corporations are increasingly internalizing these functions by building sophisticated and extensive in-house legal staffs. The result is a dramatic reduction in the switching costs facing clients and an elimination of lawyers' market power.

Corporate clients are making aggressive use of their new-found leverage. Corporations now routinely shop for lawyers, often holding so-called "beauty contests" in which firms from around the country compete for the right to do some important piece of corporate business. In order to "win" these contests, firms must be willing to reduce their normal fees and to consent to exacting supervision over virtually every aspect of the services they perform. Even if they meet these new requirements, law firm partners know that the business will be taken away (or that they will not receive additional work) if in-house lawyers become dissatisfied with either the quality or the price of the firm's work.

These market developments turn [the] assumption [of client vulnerability to lawyer domination] on its head. Not only do corporate clients have the power to prevent delicts committed by their lawyers, they also have the leverage to pressure firms into engaging in strategic behavior on their behalf, or at a minimum, into failing to police the corporation's own strategic conduct.

* * *

There is also a difference in lawyer styles, even within practices in which clients are not paying the bills and often are not sophisticated enough or do not have enough resources to control their lawyers. The following empirical study of civil rights and poverty lawyers in Chicago found differences in the nature and extent of client control:

LAWYER-CLIENT DECISION-MAKING IN CIVIL RIGHTS AND POVERTY PRACTICE: AN EMPIRICAL STUDY OF LAWYERS' NORMS

Ann Southworth
9 Georgetown Journal of Legal Ethics 1101 (1996)

One of the purposes of this study was to gather empirical data bearing on a charge that has dogged civil rights and poverty lawyers for several decades: that they assume too much control in their relationships with clients. From the left, critics have argued that lawyer oppression thoroughly pervades professional conventions and language and that lawyers may be unable to avoid dominating their clients through conscious effort. From the right, critics have argued that legal services and poverty lawyers manipulate clients to further their own political agendas and to advance their own careers.

The research reported here suggests that, even among the relatively small number of lawyers in Chicago who work on civil rights and urban poverty issues, lawyers' views about the proper allocation of decision-making roles between lawyer and client vary substantially by the types of practice settings in which they work. Most legal services lawyers reported that they played significant roles in decisions affecting their clients and that they sometimes chose strategies without consulting clients. These lawyers commonly explained that their clients were unsophisticated and that they relied on lawyers as experts who could tell them what to do. Many also emphasized that their clients had no real alternatives to the strategies their lawyers recommended. Lawyers who worked for law school clinics said that they generally devised strategies on their own or with other lawyers and community leaders, and some of them worked without clients. Lawyers in advocacy organizations also reported that they played substantial roles in choosing strategies and that they often decided what positions to take based on their own research or experience. Lawyers in civil rights firms participated aggressively in choosing strategies, but most of them emphasized that they consulted with clients about all important decisions. Lawyers in grass-roots organizations asserted that allowing clients to make decisions was an end in itself; it was an essential element of their plans for empowering their clients. Business lawyers who worked for community groups and minority entrepreneurs said that they advised clients liberally about how to run their operations and to structure transactions, but they expressed the most deferential views about their roles in decisions affecting their clients' interests.

[Professor Southworth then offered some speculations, based on her interview data, on the factors influencing how legal services and civil rights lawyers share decision-making responsibility with their clients.]

Lawyers who were dependent upon their clients for their salaries generally expressed more deferential views than did lawyers whose payment came from other sources, although there were notable exceptions to this general pattern.

Lawyers who worked for legal services, law school clinics, and advocacy organizations were less financially dependent on their clients than were other lawyers in the sample, and these lawyers generally reported that they played substantial roles in decisions regarding strategy.

Civil rights attorneys were more financially dependent on their clients, and they expressed notably more deferential views than their counterparts in legal services, law school clinics, and advocacy organizations. While a few of these lawyers performed some of their work pro bono, more often they worked on a contingency arrangement or hoped to recover attorneys' fees under a fee-shifting statute. Clients did not pay these lawyers directly, but clients could walk away and thus defeat the attorneys' fee prospects if their lawyers displeased them.

These data suggesting some correlation between attorney-client interactions and sources of payment generally are consistent with John Heinz and Edward Laumann's account of professional power. In their comprehensive study of the social structure of the Chicago bar, Heinz and Laumann concluded that differences in professional control among the lawyers in their sample were attributable primarily to differences in the market power and sophistication of their clients. They found that civil rights lawyers enjoyed more professional autonomy or "freedom of action" than any other of thirty types of practices included in their study, in large part because their clients were less powerful. In trying to explain why lawyers generally exercise less control in their relationships with clients than doctors do in their relationships with patients, Heinz and Laumann observed that many clients, particularly corporate clients, hold substantial market power, whereas consumers of medical services generally are unorganized. They concluded that the autonomy of lawyers who serve individuals and small businesses, including civil rights lawyers, "may more closely approximate the doctor's degree of independence from client control" because these lawyers rely on particular clients much less than corporate lawyers do. They further noted that "most legal matters are primarily concerned with money," while medical risks are more difficult to quantify, and therefore, clients are more likely than patients to impose budgets on the professionals who serve them

However, this "control of the purse strings" account of professional power does not so neatly explain the views of the lawyers who worked for grass-roots organizations and business lawyers. Lawyers for grass-roots organizations expressed some of the most deferential views in the group, but the funding for their salaries came primarily from foundations and government rather than from clients. Many of these grass-roots lawyers developed long-term relationships with client organizations that may have expected considerable deference from their lawyers. Moreover, they seemed ideologically committed to giving clients control, and they may have recruited lawyers who shared that goal. Business lawyers sometimes received fees for their work, but more often they performed their work pro bono. Yet these lawyers, too, expressed some of the most deferential views of all lawyers in the sample. Perhaps business lawyers deferred to clients who did not pay because they were accustomed to deferring to paying clients who were well-organized, powerful consumers of legal services.

Lawyers who worked for poor, unemployed clients generally reported that they made decisions for their clients more often than lawyers who worked for more highly educated, financially stable, and sophisticated clients.

Lawyers who worked with their clients on ongoing projects generally displayed more deferential views than lawyers who represented their clients in isolated encounters with the legal system. Civil rights lawyers, lawyers for grass-roots organizations, and business lawyers, more often than other lawyers in the sample, had worked with their clients before, and they reported giving clients substantial control.

There also may be some relationship among the types of services that lawyers performed, the types of practice settings in which they worked, and their willingness to defer to clients. Lawyers in legal services, law school clinics, and advocacy organizations focused primarily on litigation, and these lawyers more than attorneys in other practice settings said that they made decisions for clients. Perhaps litigation, more than organizing or transactional work, lends itself to claims that lawyer expertise should trump clients' judgment about strategy.

NOTES ON MATHER, WILKINS AND SOUTHWORTH

1. *Identify and Assess the Empirical Accounts of Lawyer-Client Relationships.* According to Mather, Wilkins, and Southworth, what factors influence the allocation of decision-making control between lawyers and clients? Are you persuaded by their accounts?

2. *What Role Does Law Play in Influencing This Aspect of Lawyer Behavior?* Outside the role of indigent criminal defense counsel (as illustrated by *Jones v. Barnes* and *United States v. Kaczynski*, the two cases excerpted below), issues about the division of authority between lawyers and clients are rarely litigated. Why do you suppose that is? Should law play a greater role than it does (perhaps in the form of bar disciplinary committees

enforcing Model Rules 1.2 and 1.4), or is this something best left to the market and social sanctions?

D. HOW SHOULD DECISION-MAKING BE ALLOCATED?

In this section, we move from *descriptive* claims about attorney-client decision-making to *normative* claims about how lawyers *should* share authority with their clients. We consider whether normative claims rest on descriptive assumptions, whether the arguments for more or less client control are persuasive for all clients, all matters, and all practice settings, and whether the concerns of persons other than lawyers and clients should be relevant in deciding whether lawyers should defer to client wishes.

In the previous section, we examined as a *descriptive* matter what the rules of professional conduct require of lawyers and how economic, social, and practical considerations affect the allocation of power in the relationship. But the relationship between lawyer and client should also be considered from a *normative* perspective: how *should* decision-making authority be allocated between lawyer and client and how should lawyers handle the discretion that the law gives them? A lively debate among ethicists and scholars of the legal profession has focused on the justification for lawyer control of the client and vice versa. The debate is often muddied by conflicting empirical claims about whether attorney domination of client is the most pervasive or significant problem or whether client domination of attorney is. Conflicting notions about the actual nature of the attorney-client relationship lead to different normative conclusions about how much lawyers should defer to clients. After first reading an excerpt of the classic Wasserstrom article on the lawyer-client relationship which we first encountered in Chapter 1, we will examine some of the principal arguments about when and why lawyers should defer to client wishes and when and why they should not.

Consider whether normative claims rest on descriptive assumptions, whether the arguments for more or less client control are persuasive for all clients, all matters, and all practice settings, and whether the concerns of persons other than lawyers and clients should be relevant in deciding whether lawyers should defer to client wishes.

LAWYERS AS PROFESSIONALS: SOME MORAL ISSUES

Richard Wasserstrom
5 Human Rights 1 (1975)

One pervasive feature of the relationship between any professional and the client is that it is in some sense a relationship of inequality. This relationship of inequality is intrinsic to the existence of professionalism.

To begin with, there is the fact that one characteristic of professions is that the professional is the possessor of expert knowledge of a sort not readily or easily attainable by members of the community at large. The consequence is that the client is in a poor position effectively to evaluate how well or badly the professional performs. In the professions, the professional does not look primarily to the client to evaluate the professional's work. In addition, because the matters for which professional assistance is sought usually involve things of great personal concern to the client, it is the received wisdom within the professions that the client lacks the perspective necessary to pursue in a satisfactory way his or her own best interests, and that the client requires a detached, disinterested representative to look after his or her interests.

Finally, to be a professional is to have been acculturated in a certain way. It is to have satisfactorily passed through a lengthy and allegedly difficult period of study and training. It is to have done something hard. Something that not everyone can do. It is hard, I think, if not impossible, for a person to emerge from professional training and participate in a profession without the belief that he or she is a special kind of person, both different from and somewhat better than those nonprofessional members of the social order. It is equally hard for the other members of society not to hold an analogous view of the professionals. And these beliefs surely contribute, too, to the dominant role played by a professional in any professional-client relationship.

[The criticism of professionals I want to consider] might begin by conceding, at least for purposes of argument, that some inequality may be inevitable in any professional-client relationship. But it sees the relationship between the professional and the client as typically flawed in a more fundamental way, as involving far more than the kind of relatively benign inequality delineated above. This criticism focuses upon the fact that the professional often, if not systematically, interacts with the client in both a manipulative and a paternalistic fashion. The point is not that the professional is merely dominant within the relationship. Rather, it is that from the professional's point of view the client is seen and responded to more like an object than a human being, and more like a child than an adult.

Desirable change could be brought about in part by a sustained effort to simplify legal language and to make the legal processes less mysterious and more directly available to lay persons.

The more fundamental changes, though, would, I think, have to await an explicit effort to alter the ways in which lawyers are educated and acculturated to view themselves, their clients, and the relationships that ought to exist between them.

* * *

Client-Centered Lawyering. Wasserstrom's normative critique of the lawyer is not merely that the lawyer dominates the client but that, in doing so, the lawyer treats the client "more like an object than a human being, and more like a child than an adult." This critique of lawyers has been amplified by scholars who advocate "client-centered" lawyering.[1] The model of client-centered lawyering characterizes the attorney as a responsive, nonjudgmental, empathetic helper and leaves both priority-setting and decision-making to the client. Much of the client-centered lawyering literature has focused on clinical legal education and on poverty law practice in which the lawyer (or law student in a clinic) represents individuals (rather than organizations) and the individuals tend to be significantly poorer, less educated, and less socially privileged than the lawyer. The literature on client-centered lawyering argues that litigation in the adversary system encourages attorneys to make strategic decisions and fails to recognize the client's interest in participating in strategic planning; the proponents of the model believe that client involvement in every aspect of the representation will promote the autonomy and growth of the client and will ameliorate the harmful social effects of class, gender, and racial differences between lawyers and clients.

When the Client is an Organization. Another powerful normative critique of the conventional division of authority between lawyers and clients imagines a different type of client and, in some respects, a different type of lawyer. When the client is an organization, some scholars have argued, it is important to attend to the ways in which lawyers decide who within the client organization "speaks for" the client. Professors Susan Koniak and George Cohen argue that the most troubling ethical questions about the lawyer-client relationship arise not, as Wasserstrom imagined, when the client is an individual and the lawyer's superior education and social power enables lawyer domination, but rather "when

---

[1] *See, e.g.,* DAVID A. BINDER, *ET AL.,* LAWYERS AS COUNSELORS: A CLIENT-CENTERED APPROACH (West 1991).

clients are entities and the law governing these clients and the lawyer's relationship to them is contested."[2] They continue:

> The traditional approach to legal ethics assumes that the "bounds of the law" [within which lawyers are said to owe clients a duty of zealous advocacy] are known and focuses on the fact that these boundaries permit much undesirable behavior. From this perspective, the moral dilemma for the lawyer is the conflict between promoting the client's interests within these known bounds and protecting the interests of society against client behavior that is lawful, but harmful. But the premise underlying this dilemma is often false. Uncertainty is inherent in law, if only because lawmakers cannot identify and address all possible problems in advance. Thus, the meaning of a legal rule in a particular situation almost always demands a conscious act of interpretation, the creation of a story about the rule. In counseling clients, lawyers must do more than read legal rules; they must use the stories embodied in court opinions, legislative debates and executive agency pronouncements to assess their client's proposed or past conduct.

But, as Koniak and Cohen point out, much of the work that lawyers do involves the representation of entities or groups, as opposed to individuals. A number of notable instances of lawyer participation in client misconduct, including Watergate and massive frauds by savings and loans in the 1980s, did not involve lawyers who dominated their clients but, instead, lawyers who either willingly assisted or were arguably dominated by their clients. In some cases, lawyers were complicit in client wrongdoing, in part because they were dependent on a relationship with a single person within the client entity. Koniak and Cohen assert that when a client is an organization, and when the law is unclear about who within the organization speaks for the client, it makes little sense to speak of the lawyer dominating the client or vice versa. In such cases they point out, the lawyer and, sometimes, certain people within the client organization have a great deal of discretion to determine what the client's interests are. They can use that discretion to pursue their own interests at the expense of the interests of other people within the client organization. Koniak and Cohen also point out that the problem of excessive discretion to pursue some people's interests in the name of pursuing the client's interest is compounded when the substantive law governing the transaction is unclear. In such circumstances, the lawyer and some within the client entity may be able to engage in behavior that may be inimical to the interests of others within the entity or to the interests of the public at large.

---

[2] Susan P. Koniak & George M. Cohen, *In Hell There Will Be Lawyers Without Clients or Law*, 30 HOFSTRA L. REV. 129 (2001).

The phenomenon of organizational client domination of lawyers to pursue illegal or socially harmful ends prompted Professor David Wilkins to propose, in a section of the article excerpted above and in other work, that legal ethics should imagine clients owing ethical obligations to lawyers in addition to the duties lawyers owe clients. Wilkins asserted that the relationship between a corporate client and its law firm should be imagined as a joint venture, in which "[c]orporate clients have an ethical obligation to impose only those demands on their joint venture partners that are reasonably necessary to achieve the corporation's legitimate objectives from the representation. Corporate clients have a right to pressure lawyers to deliver quality legal services at fair prices. This does not imply, however, that these sophisticated purchasing agents are entitled to exploit their market power for capricious reasons or for reasons that have nothing to do with the legitimate objectives of the representation." Moreover, Wilkins continued, "corporations have an ethical obligation not to tempt, deceive, or coerce firms into participating in conduct that the corporation knows to be unlawful or unethical, or that is designed to procure a corporate advantage that the client knows it is not legally entitled to receive."[3] We will consider this issue further depth in Chapter 18 when we examine the lawyer's obligations as a counselor to a corporate client.

NOTES ON NORMATIVE DEBATES ABOUT
LAWYER-CLIENT DECISION-MAKING

1. *When Do Lawyers Dominate Clients?* Consider the empirical claim underlying Wasserstrom's argument about attorney-client interactions. Which attorney-client relationships do you think it accurately describes and which does it not?

2. *When Do Clients Dominate Lawyers?* Mather, Southworth, Wilkins, and Koniak and Cohen observe that there is wide variation among lawyers and clients as to whether the lawyer controls or is controlled by the client. Their work and that of other scholars suggests that lawyers who represent large organizations, especially wealthy and powerful ones, are often exceedingly deferential to the wishes of the clients in determining both objectives and strategies in the representation. If, unlike the situation Wasserstrom supposes, the client is powerful and sophisticated about the law, does Wasserstrom's criticism of the professional relationship disappear? Are there other criticisms you might make of the relationship in such a case?

3. *Who Speaks for the Client?* According to Koniak and Cohen, sometimes the law is clear about who within an organization gets to decide

---

[3]   David B. Wilkins, *Do Clients Have Ethical Obligations to Lawyers? Some Lessons from the Diversity Wars*, 11 GEO. J. OF LEGAL ETHICS 855 (1998). *See also* David B. Wilkins, *Team of Rivals? Toward a New Model of the Corporate Attorney-Client Relationship*, 78 FORDHAM L. REV. 2067 (2010).

on what the organization will do (as in the case of some corporations with clear lines of authority), but often it is not clear (as where a lawyer represents partnerships or small corporations with officers and directors who disagree). What difference should it make in thinking about the allocation of authority in lawyer-client relationships whether the client is an organization rather than a person? When the law is unclear about who within the client organization speaks for the entity, why do you suppose it would be difficult to say whether the lawyer dominates the client or vice versa? Does Wilkins propose an approach that will help lawyers sort out these problems?

4. ***When Is Client-Centered Lawyering Desirable?*** Consider the normative claims Wasserstrom and Wilkins make in light of the literature on client-centered lawyering. What factors *should* influence a lawyer's judgment about when and how to confer with a client and when and why to defer to a client's choice? Should it matter whether the subject of the representation is a transaction, or advising a client about what the law requires, as opposed to litigation? Should it matter whether the case is civil or criminal? Should it matter whether the lawyer has been retained by the client or appointed by the court or the public defender's office? Should it matter whether there is a difference of opinion among people within the client entity about their goals and interests?

5. ***When Does the Client Know Best?*** Client-centered lawyering can be particularly challenging for lawyers when the lawyer believes that the client is making an unwise but not illegal or immoral decision. What considerations should inform a lawyer's decision about whether to defer to a client's preferences in such a situation? Consider (a) the difference between representing an individual or an organization, (b) the effect of the client's decision on third parties; (c) whether the client is sophisticated or unsophisticated about the law, business, or other considerations pertinent to the matter; and (d) any other factors that should influence a lawyer's judgment about whether to defer to a client.

PROBLEM 5–1

A lawyer working in a publicly-funded legal services clinic represents a victim of domestic violence. The lawyer has obtained a court order requiring the client's husband to stay away from her, and the husband has repeatedly violated the order and continues to come to the family home threatening violence to the client. The lawyer urges the client to ask the court to hold the husband in contempt for violating the order, which will result in the husband being put in jail. The client refuses to allow the lawyer to enforce the order. She says that if her husband is put in jail he will lose his job and she needs him to keep working so that he can provide some money for their children. The lawyer knows that the husband has been highly irregular about giving any money to the client, and the lawyer also suspects that the client is susceptible to psychological manipulation by the husband. The lawyer fears that the husband may ultimately kill or seriously harm the client if he continues to have contact with her. On the other hand, the husband does provide some money for the children and the client is nearly destitute. If the lawyer strongly believes in client-centered lawyering, what should the lawyer do?

E. LAW GOVERNING THE ALLOCATION OF AUTHORITY

Although issues about division of authority between lawyer and client are rarely litigated (because powerful clients can threaten to fire their lawyer if the lawyer refuses the client's direction and vulnerable clients may neither know of their rights nor be able to institute litigation to enforce them), there is some law setting minimum standards to which lawyers must adhere in sharing authority with their clients. Under the Fifth Amendment to the U.S. Constitution, clients decide whether to assert or to waive their constitutional right to testify in their own criminal case and whether to appeal a criminal conviction. Under the Sixth Amendment, the defendant has a right to represent himself in his criminal trial. *Faretta v. California*, 422 U.S. 806 (1975). Two Model Rules are especially pertinent. Model Rule 1.2 specifies that the client decides upon "the objectives of representation." The lawyer decides on the means by which the client's objectives are to be pursued, including how to gather and use evidence and which legal arguments to make. And, generally, the lawyer is the one who speaks and is spoken to, orally and in writing, in tribunals.

Model Rule 1.2: The Allocation of Authority Between Client and Lawyer

A lawyer shall abide by a client's decisions concerning the objectives of representation and shall consult with the client about the means by which they are to be pursued.

Objectives include whether to initiate a civil suit, whether to settle, and whether to appeal.

In a criminal case, objectives include how to plead (innocent, guilty, or no contest), whether to waive a right to a jury trial, and whether the client will testify.

Model Rule 1.2 requires lawyers to communicate with the client as to the means by which the client's objectives are to be pursued. Model Rule 1.4 further requires that lawyers regularly and reasonably communicate with their clients to enable the client to make informed decisions.

Model Rule 1.4: The Duty to Communicate

A lawyer shall: (1) promptly inform the client of any decision or circumstance with respect to which the client's informed consent is required and explain the matter to the extent necessary to permit the client to make informed decisions; (2) reasonably consult with the client about the means by which the client's objectives are to be accomplished; (3) keep the client reasonably informed about the status of the matter; and (4) promptly comply with reasonable requests for information.

Even in the classic case in which a lawyer represents an individual, the question of who ought to decide which issues is not without difficulty, as illustrated in the leading Supreme Court decision on the issue.

JONES V. BARNES
Supreme Court of the United States
463 U.S. 745 (1983)

CHIEF JUSTICE BURGER delivered the opinion of the Court.

In 1976, Richard Butts was robbed at knifepoint by four men in the lobby of an apartment building. Butts informed a Housing Authority detective that he recognized one of his assailants as a person known to him as "Froggy." The following day the detective arrested respondent David Barnes, who is known as "Froggy." The jury convicted respondent of first- and second- degree robbery and second-degree assault.

The Appellate Division [New York's appellate court] assigned Michael Melinger to represent respondent on appeal. Respondent sent Melinger a letter listing several claims that he felt should be raised. Respondent [sent Melinger] a copy of a *pro se* brief he had written. In a return letter, Melinger accepted some but rejected most of the suggested claims, stating that they would not aid respondent in obtaining a new trial and that they could not be raised on appeal because they were not based on evidence in the record. Melinger then listed seven potential claims of error that he was considering including in his brief, and invited respondent's "reflections and suggestions" with regard to those seven issues. The record does not reveal any response to this letter.

Melinger's brief to the Appellate Division concentrated on three of the seven points he had raised in his letter to respondent. In addition, Melinger submitted respondent's own *pro se* brief. Thereafter, respondent filed two more *pro se* briefs, raising three more of the seven issues Melinger had identified.

At oral argument, Melinger argued the three points presented in his own brief, but not the arguments raised in the *pro se* briefs. [The appellate court affirmed Barnes's conviction.]

On August 8, 1978, respondent filed a *pro se* petition for a writ of habeas corpus. Respondent raised five claims of error, including ineffective assistance of trial [and appellate] counsel.

A divided panel of the Court of Appeals held that when "the appellant requests that [his attorney] raise additional colorable points [on appeal], counsel *must argue the additional points to the full extent of his professional ability*." In the view of the majority, this conclusion followed from *Anders v. California*, 386 U.S. 738 (1967). In *Anders*, this Court held that an appointed attorney must advocate his client's cause vigorously and may not withdraw from a nonfrivolous appeal. The Court of Appeals majority held that, since *Anders* bars counsel from abandoning a nonfrivolous appeal, it also bars counsel from abandoning a nonfrivolous issue on appeal.

The court concluded that Melinger had not met the above standard in that he had failed to press at least two nonfrivolous claims. We reverse.

There is, of course, no constitutional right to an appeal, but the Court [has] held that if an appeal is open to those who can pay for it, an appeal must be provided for an indigent. It is also recognized that the accused has the ultimate authority to make certain fundamental decisions regarding the case, as to whether to plead guilty, waive a jury, testify in his or her own behalf, or take an appeal. In addition, we have held that, with some limitations, a defendant may elect to act as his or her own advocate, *Faretta v. California,* 422 U.S. 806 (1975). Neither *Anders* nor any other decision of this Court suggests, however, that the indigent defendant has a constitutional right to compel appointed counsel to press nonfrivolous points requested by the client, if counsel, as a matter of professional judgment, decides not to present those points.

This Court, in holding that a state must provide counsel for an indigent appellant on his first appeal as of right, recognized the superior ability of trained counsel in the "examination into the record, research of the law, and marshalling of arguments on [the appellant's] behalf." Yet by promulgating a *per se* rule that the client, not the professional advocate, must be allowed to decide what issues are to be pressed, the Court of Appeals seriously undermines the ability of counsel to present the client's case in accord with counsel's professional evaluation.

Experienced advocates since time beyond memory have emphasized the importance of winnowing out weaker arguments on appeal and focusing on one central issue if possible, or at most on a few key issues.

There can hardly be any question about the importance of having the appellate advocate examine the record with a view to selecting the most promising issues for review. This has assumed a greater importance in an era when oral argument is strictly limited in most courts—often to as little as 15 minutes—and when page limits on briefs are widely imposed.[6] Even in a court that imposes no time or page limits, however, the new *per se* rule laid down by the Court of Appeals is contrary to all experience and logic. A brief that raises every colorable issue runs the risk of burying good arguments in a verbal mound made up of strong and weak contentions.

This Court's decision in *Anders*, far from giving support to the new *per se* rule announced by the Court of Appeals, is to the contrary. *Anders* recognized that the role of the advocate "requires that he support his client's appeal to the best of his ability." Here the appointed counsel did just that. For judges to second-guess reasonable professional judgments and impose on appointed counsel a duty to raise every "colorable" claim suggested by a client would disserve the very goal of vigorous and effective advocacy that underlies *Anders*.

JUSTICE BRENNAN, with whom JUSTICE MARSHALL joins, dissenting.

The Sixth Amendment provides that "[in] all criminal prosecutions, the accused shall enjoy the right to have the *Assistance* of Counsel for his defence" (emphasis added). I find myself in fundamental disagreement with the Court over what a right to "the assistance of counsel" means. The import of words like "assistance" and "counsel" seems inconsistent with a regime under which counsel appointed by the State to represent a criminal defendant can refuse to raise issues with arguable merit on appeal when his client, after hearing his assessment of the case and his advice, has directed him to raise them.

I believe the right to "the assistance of counsel" carries with it a right, personal to the defendant, to make that decision, against the advice of counsel if he chooses.

If all the Sixth Amendment protected was the State's interest in substantial justice, it would not include such a right. However, in *Faretta*, we decisively rejected that view of the Constitution. *Faretta* establishes that the right to counsel is more than a right to have one's case presented competently and effectively. It is predicated on the view that the function of counsel under the Sixth Amendment is to protect the dignity and autonomy of a person on trial by assisting him in making choices that are his to make, not to make choices for him, although counsel may be better able to decide which tactics will be most effective for the defendant. *Anders* also reflects that view. Even when appointed counsel believes an appeal has no merit, he must furnish his client a brief covering all

---

6   The ABA Model Rules of Professional Conduct provide: "A lawyer shall abide by a client's decisions concerning the objectives of representation . . . and shall consult with the client as to the means by which they are to be pursued. . . . In a criminal case, the lawyer shall abide by the client's decision, . . . *as to a plea to be entered, whether to waive jury trial and whether the client will testify.*" [MODEL RULES OF PROF'L CONDUCT R. 1.2(a) (2013)]

arguable grounds for appeal so that the client may raise any points that he chooses.

The right to counsel as *Faretta* and *Anders* conceive it is not an all-or-nothing right, under which a defendant must choose between forgoing the assistance of counsel altogether or relinquishing control over every aspect of his case beyond its most basic structure (*i.e.*, how to plead, whether to present a defense, whether to appeal). A defendant's interest in his case clearly extends to other matters. He may want to press the argument that he is innocent, even if other stratagems are more likely to result in the dismissal of charges or in a reduction of punishment. He may want to insist on certain arguments for political reasons. He may want to protect third parties. [T]he proper role of counsel is to assist him in these efforts, insofar as that is possible consistent with the lawyer's conscience, the law, and his duties to the court.

[T]he Court argues that good appellate advocacy demands selectivity among arguments. That is certainly true—the Court's advice is good. It ought to be taken to heart by every lawyer called upon to argue an appeal in this or any other court, and by his client. It should take little or no persuasion to get a wise client to understand that, if staying out of prison is what he values most, he should encourage his lawyer to raise only his two or three best arguments on appeal, and he should defer to his lawyer's advice as to which are the best arguments. The Constitution, however, does not require clients to be wise, and other policies should be weighed in the balance as well.

It is no secret that indigent clients often mistrust the lawyers appointed to represent them. There are many reasons for this, some perhaps unavoidable even under perfect conditions—differences in education, disposition, and socio-economic class—and some that should (but may not always) be zealously avoided. A lawyer and his client do not always have the same interests. Even with paying clients, a lawyer may have a strong interest in having judges and prosecutors think well of him, and, if he is working for a flat fee—a common arrangement for criminal defense attorneys—or if his fees for court appointments are lower than he would receive for other work, he has an obvious financial incentive to conclude cases on his criminal docket swiftly. Good lawyers undoubtedly recognize these temptations and resist them, and they endeavor to convince their clients that they will. It would be naive, however, to suggest that they always succeed in either task. A constitutional rule that encourages lawyers to disregard their clients' wishes without compelling need can only exacerbate the clients' suspicion of their lawyers.

The role of the defense lawyer should be above all to function as the instrument and defender of the client's autonomy and dignity in all phases of the criminal process.

I cannot accept the notion that lawyers are one of the punishments a person receives merely for being accused of a crime.

NOTES ON JONES V. BARNES

1.   *Why Is the Constitution Relevant Only in Cases of Appointed Defense Counsel?* The Court in *Jones v. Barnes* analyzes the attorney-client relationship under the U.S. Constitution because criminal defendants who are too poor to hire their own lawyers have a constitutional right to be represented by lawyers appointed by and paid by the state. Therefore, the criminal defense lawyer's behavior is governed by the Constitution because the Constitution regulates the conduct of state government actors (including appointed criminal defense counsel). When an individual hires and pays for her own lawyer, the Constitution does not regulate the lawyer's behavior. However, the rule the Court adopts under the Constitution regarding lawyer-client allocation of responsibility in *Jones v. Barnes* is consistent with the standard that Model Rule 1.2 imposes on all lawyers, both those who are paid by the government and those who are paid by private clients.

2.   *The Objectives-Means Test.* Under Model Rule 1.2 and the ruling in *Jones v. Barnes*, what decisions does the client make in a criminal case?

3.   *What Is an Objective?* Can you imagine a situation in which the decision about which arguments to present on appeal is an "objective" rather than a means to achieve an objective? Is the decision about which evidence to present at trial always a means to an objective? Is the distinction in Model Rule 1.2 between "objectives" and "means" sound? Can you think of a better approach?

4.   *Assessing the Objectives-Means Test.* What are the arguments for allocating to lawyers authority over tactical decisions or the means to achieve an objective? What are the arguments for allocating some of those decisions to clients? Which of the arguments you identify in answers to those questions suggest that the Model Rules or the Constitution should allocate more control to clients and which arguments suggest that lawyers should share more authority than the law requires?

5.   *Should the Lawyer's Own Interests Matter?* To what extent should the lawyer's concerns about his own reputation, credibility, or values affect decisions about strategy when the lawyer and client disagree? Does the law give sufficient weight to those concerns in allocating decision-making authority between lawyers and clients?

PROBLEM 5–2

Arnie, a divorce lawyer, meets with Lydia, a new client whose husband is seeking a divorce. Lydia is a 40-year-old stay-at-home mother of young children. She has consulted Arnie because her original lawyer had qualms about the settlement and urged Lydia to talk to Arnie about it.

Lydia tells Arnie she does not want a fight: "I just don't want it to get into an ugly, pitched battle with name calling and recriminations."

After listening to Lydia's account of why her husband seeks a divorce, Arnie tells Lydia that her husband surely has another woman. He urges Lydia to be more aggressive in protecting her economic interests. Lydia insists there is not another woman. Arnie responds: "For your husband, divorce is a fiscal inconvenience. But for you, this can be the most important financial decision that you'll ever make in your life."

At the conclusion of their meeting, Lydia is wavering. Without Lydia's knowledge, Arnie then hires a private detective to follow the husband. The investigator takes several photographs of Lydia's husband and the other woman in very compromising positions.

Arnie arranges to meet with Lydia, who informs him at the start that she has decided to accept the settlement offer. "In the long run, there are more important things than money," she insists. "I don't want to lose respect for him, and I don't want the children to, either." Tapping the envelope containing the photos, Arnie muses that he will just put the "investigation" of her "husband's affairs, financial, otherwise," on hold. Predictably curious, Lydia asks to look in the envelope. Arnie warns Lydia that "it may be painful." She looks, and she is devastated.

Lydia and Arnie then meet with husband and his lawyer. Arnie never shows the photos to the husband or his lawyer, but says that he is quite sure the husband is having an affair. The husband's lawyer points out that marital infidelity is legally irrelevant to the spousal or child support obligations at divorce. Arnie says that the husband would nevertheless surely prefer that information about his private life not become public knowledge. He then uses other, financial, information the investigator obtained to force the husband to increase his offer considerably.

After the meeting ends with Lydia and the husband signing the settlement agreement, Arnie is pleased with himself, but Lydia is crying uncontrollably. She tells Arnie: "I think what you did was despicable. I'll never be able to look at him again with any kind of respect or affection." For Arnie, she says, it was "all so easy . . . Just get the money. I lost my life, my children lost a family. And there's no amount of money that would compensate for that." Arnie asks Lydia if she wants to return the money. She does not.

Did Arnie exceed his authority when he connived to override his client's stated wishes in order to secure the money he truly believed she would later regret not having? Should he have requested Lydia's authorization before hiring a detective to follow her husband? Did he give sufficient respect to Lydia's declaration that "there are more important things than money"?[4]

---

[4] This problem is drawn from Stephen Gillers, *Popular Legal Culture: Taking L.A. Law More Seriously*, 98 YALE L.J. 1607, 1612–14 (1989). Professor Gillers, in turn, was describing an episode of the television show *L.A. Law*.

UNITED STATES V. KACZYNSKI

United States Court of Appeals for the Ninth Circuit
239 F.3d 1108 (2001)

[Theodore Kaczynski, a former mathematics professor at the University of California at Berkeley, was arrested in a remote Montana cabin in 1996. Kaczynski, whom the FBI dubbed the "Unabomber," had, over a period of nearly 20 years, carried out a campaign of mailing bombs to people whom he considered part of the "industrial-technological system," including computer scientists, geneticists, behavioral psychologists, and public-relations executives. Kaczynski's devices killed three people and injured many others. The FBI found Kaczynski after he published a manifesto in the *New York Times* and *Washington Post* which he called "Industrial Society and Its Future" and articulated his "dream . . . of a green and pleasant land liberated from the curse of technological proliferation." David Kaczynski read the manifesto and suspected that its author was his brother, who had isolated himself from society 25 years before. David reluctantly decided to inform the FBI of his suspicions, although he sought assurances that the government would not seek the death penalty and expressed his belief that his brother was mentally ill. On the basis of information provided by David, the FBI arrested Kaczynski and, despite David's anguished opposition, the government announced its intent to seek the death penalty.

Following Kaczynski's indictment, Federal Defenders Quin Denvir and Judy Clarke were appointed to represent him. Kaczynski and his lawyers had a fundamental disagreement about strategy. The lawyers believed that the only defense that might avoid the death penalty was that Kaczynski was mentally ill. Kaczynski made clear that a defense based on mental illness was unacceptable to him.

Between late November and January 5, when the trial was set to begin, Kaczynski informed the court that he had a conflict with his attorneys over the presentation of a mental status defense and was considering whether he wanted Tony Serra, a San Francisco lawyer whom he believed would not employ a mental state defense, to represent him. Although at one point he said the conflict with his lawyers was resolved, the day the trial was to begin Kaczynski asked for new counsel or to represent himself. The district court refused to allow Serra to take over because of the delay it would cause and ruled that Clarke and Denvir could control the defense and present evidence of his mental condition over Kaczynski's objection. Shortly thereafter, the district judge learned from the U.S. Marshals office that Kaczynski had attempted suicide. Accordingly, the court postponed the trial and ordered a competency examination, to be completed before ruling on Kaczynski's request to represent himself. A court-appointed psychiatrist examined Kaczynski and concluded that he was competent.

After the trial court denied Kaczynski's request to represent himself, Kaczynski pleaded guilty in exchange for the government's agreement not to seek the death penalty. Kaczynski was sentenced to four consecutive life sentences, plus 30 years imprisonment. Kaczynski then brought this action seeking to vacate his guilty plea on the ground that he had not voluntarily made the plea because he had been forced into it by his lawyers.]

RYMER, CIRCUIT JUDGE:

Kaczynski contends that his plea was involuntary because he was improperly denied his *Faretta* right, or because he had a constitutional right to prevent his counsel from presenting mental state evidence. Even if neither deprivation suffices, still the plea was involuntary in his view because it was induced by the threat of a mental state defense that Kaczynski would have found unendurable.

[A] plea must be voluntary to be constitutional. A plea is voluntary if it represents a voluntary and intelligent choice among the alternative courses of action open to the defendant. A plea of guilty entered by one fully aware of the direct consequences must stand unless induced by threats, misrepresentation (including unfulfilled or unfulfillable promises), or perhaps by promises that are by their nature improper.

The [trial] court noted that Kaczynski specifically referred to the disagreement with his attorneys about a mental status defense, but did not suggest in any way that he believed this disagreement affected the voluntariness of his plea. Further, the court found that Kaczynski showed no signs of anxiety or distress when he stated that he was voluntarily entering into the plea; that nothing about his demeanor indicated he endured any coercion; that he admitted the charges with no sign of reservation; and that his sworn plea statements were "lucid, articulate, and utterly inconsistent with his present claim that he did not voluntarily plead guilty."

Kaczynski was clearly aware of the consequences of his plea (and does not contend otherwise). The decision to plead guilty in exchange for the government's giving up its intent to seek the death penalty and to continue prosecuting him was rational given overwhelming evidence that he committed the Unabomb crimes and did so with substantial planning and premeditation, lack of remorse, and severe and irreparable harm.

However, we held in *United States v. Hernandez*, 203 F.3d 614 (2000), that wrongly denying a defendant's request to represent himself forces him to choose between pleading guilty and submitting to a trial *the very structure* of which would be unconstitutional. Therefore, we must consider whether Kaczynski's plea was rendered involuntary on account of a wrongful refusal to grant his request for self-representation.

Kaczynski argues that he was coerced into pleading guilty by his counsel's insistence on a mental state defense, that his counsel deceived him in order to gain his cooperation with some such defense, and that he was induced to plead guilty by a choice (being unable to represent himself or to proceed without the mental state defense) that was constitutionally offensive.

Even if Kaczynski were misled by his counsel about the degree to which evidence of his mental state would be adduced in the guilt phase, he learned for sure what their plans were on January 4 when they previewed their opening statement for him and he does not allege, nor does the record show, that they in any way threatened or misled him with respect to the plea or its consequences. Kaczynski hypothesizes that counsel may have used mental state evidence as a threat to pressure him into an unconditional plea bargain as a means of saving him from the risk of a death sentence, but admits that this is speculative and that no proof for it is possible. He points out that "the accused has the ultimate authority to make certain fundamental decisions regarding the case, as to whether to plead guilty, waive a jury, testify in his or her own behalf, or take an appeal," *Jones v. Barnes,* 463 U.S. 745, 751 (1983), and argues that evidence about mental status is of the same order of magnitude. The government, on the other hand, submits that it is equally clear that appointed counsel, and not his client, is in charge of the choice of trial tactics and the theory of defense. We need not decide where along this spectrum control of a mental defense short of insanity lies, because Kaczynski agreed that his counsel could control presentation of evidence and witnesses to be called (including expert witnesses and members of his family who would testify that he was mentally ill) in order to put on a full case of mitigation at the penalty phase. Thus, as the district court found, Kaczynski's claim that his plea was involuntary due to his aversion to being portrayed as mentally ill is inconsistent with his willingness to be so portrayed for purposes of avoiding the death penalty. This leaves only the pressure that Kaczynski personally felt on account of his wish to avoid the public disclosure of evidence about his mental state sooner rather than later. We agree with the district court that this does not transform his plea into an involuntary act.

REINHARDT, CIRCUIT JUDGE, dissenting:

The case of Ted Kaczynski not only brings together a host of legal issues basic to our system of justice, it also presents a compelling individual problem: what should be the fate of a man, undoubtedly learned and brilliant, who determines, on the basis of a pattern of reasoning that can only be described as perverse, that in order to save society he must commit a series of horrendous crimes? What is the proper response of the legal system when such an individual demands that he be allowed to offer those perverse theories to a jury as his only defense in a capital case—a defense that obviously has no legal merit and certainly has no chance of success? What should the response be when he also insists on serving as his own lawyer, not for the purpose of pursuing a proper legal defense, but in order to ensure that no evidence will be presented that exposes the nature and extent of his mental problems? The district judge faced these questions and, understandably, blinked. He quite clearly did so out of compassionate and humanitarian concerns. Nevertheless, in denying Kaczynski's request to represent himself, the district court unquestionably failed to follow the law.

[I]t is easy to appreciate why, as one commentator has suggested, "[t]he judicial system breathed a collective sigh of relief when the Unabomber pled guilty." Indeed, all the players in this unfortunate drama—all except Kaczynski, that is—had reason to celebrate Kaczynski's unconditional guilty plea. His attorneys had achieved their principal and worthy objective by preventing his execution. The government had been spared the awkwardness of pitting three experienced prosecutors against an untrained, and mentally unsound, defendant, and conducting an execution following a trial that lacked the fundamental elements of due process at best, and was farcical at worst. Judge Burrell had narrowly avoided having to preside over such a debacle and to impose a death penalty he would have considered improper in the absence of a fair trial. It is no wonder that today's majority is not eager to disturb so delicate a balance

The problem with this "happy" solution, of course, is that it violates the core principle of *Faretta v. California*—that a defendant who objects to his counsel's strategic choices has the option of going to trial alone.

NOTES ON U.S. V. KACZYNSKI

1. **When the Lawyer Believes the Client Cannot Make a Reasoned Decision.** Model Rule 1.14 recognizes that the proper allocation of decision-making between lawyer and client might differ "[w]hen a client's capacity to make adequately considered decisions in connection with a representation is diminished, whether because of minority, mental impairment or for some other reason." The rule instructs the lawyer to maintain a normal client-lawyer relationship "as far as reasonably possible." But when the lawyer "reasonably believes" that such a client "is at risk of substantial physical, financial or other harm unless action is taken and cannot adequately act in the client's own interest," the lawyer may take "reasonably necessary protective action, including consulting with individuals or entities that have the ability to take action to protect the

client and, in appropriate cases, seeking the appointment of a guardian ad litem, conservator, or guardian" who has legal power to make the decisions that the client is not competent to make. How would Model Rule 1.14 apply to *U.S. v. Kaczynski*?

2.   ***What Was the Right Thing to Do?*** Did the defense lawyers do the right thing in *U.S. v. Kaczynski*? Should their views on the morality of the death penalty affect how we assess whether they did the right thing?

3.   ***What Did Model Rule 1.2 Require?*** Did defense counsel violate Model Rule 1.2? Was presentation of evidence about Kaczynski's mental status a means or an objective? If a client considers something an objective and a lawyer considers it a means, how should the legal system resolve the dispute between them?

4.   ***What Did Model Rule 1.4 Require?*** Even if presenting mental status evidence was a strategy decision for the lawyers rather than an objective for the client to decide, did defense counsel violate Model Rule 1.4 by failing to consult with Kaczynski? Is there any justification for whatever failures Denvir and Clarke committed in consulting with Kaczynski about strategy?

5.   ***How Are Disputes Over Strategy Resolved When Clients Pay the Lawyers' Fees?*** If David Barnes or Theodore Kaczynski had hired and paid for their own lawyers, how do you imagine they and their lawyers would have resolved disputes over which arguments and evidence to present? Should your imagined answer to that question have any bearing on how the constitutional rights at issue in those cases are resolved?

F.   ENDING THE ATTORNEY-CLIENT RELATIONSHIP

Lawyer client relationships typically end when the work on the matter has been completed. The relationship may end before the representation has concluded if either the client fires the lawyer or the lawyer withdraws. The Model Rules allow clients to fire lawyers "at any time, with or without cause," although the client is obligated to pay for the services the lawyer performed prior to the termination. Model Rule 1.16 Comment [4]. A client represented by court-appointed counsel must obtain court approval to fire his lawyer and, as illustrated in the Kaczynski case, courts will allow such clients to fire their appointed counsel if there is reason and if doing so is not a tactic to delay a trial.

Model Rule 1.16: Terminating Representation

A lawyer *must* withdraw from representing a client if the client fires the lawyer, if the lawyer's physical or mental condition materially impairs the lawyer's ability to represent the client, or if the representation will violate law.

A lawyer *may* withdraw from representation if

- withdrawal can be accomplished without material adverse effect on the interests of the client,

- the client persists in a course of action that the lawyer reasonably believes is criminal or fraudulent,

- the client has used the lawyer's services to perpetrate a crime or fraud,

- the client insists upon taking action that the lawyer considers repugnant

- the client fails to fulfill an obligation to the lawyer and the lawyer has given notice that the lawyer will withdraw if the obligation is not fulfilled

- the representation will result in an unreasonable financial burden on the lawyer or has been rendered unreasonably difficult by the client, or

- other good cause for withdrawal exists.

If the representation is in a matter pending before a tribunal, a lawyer must give notice to and secure permission from a tribunal when terminating a representation.

When terminating representation, a lawyer must take steps to protect the client's interests, including by giving reasonable advance notice to the client, allowing time for employment of substitute counsel, and returning papers to the client.

G. SUMMARY

In most circumstances, the division of authority between lawyers and clients is worked out between them through negotiation and deference. Empirical studies show that lawyers' approaches to sharing authority with their clients vary considerably by areas of practice and type of client and that lawyers' decisions to control their clients or to cede control seem to be based less on formal legal principles than on economic and social factors. Some normative theories about the lawyer-client relationship, particularly the *client-centered lawyering model*, urge that lawyers should accord substantial authority to the client to determine the goals and the processes of the representation. But some scholars have cautioned that too much deference to client demands can be problematic, particularly where clients seek to involve lawyers in wrongdoing.

The legal standard, imposed both by Model Rule 1.2, and by the U.S. Constitution when a lawyer is appointed by the government, is that the client decides the *objectives* of the representation and the lawyer decides the *means* by which those objectives are to be pursued. Although certain decisions clearly fall within the category of objectives—such as whether to settle a civil case or to plead guilty in a criminal case—the line between means and objectives can be unclear. The lawyer is obligated by Model Rule 1.4 to consult with a client about the means by which objectives are to be pursued. The proper allocation of decision-making between lawyer and client may differ when a client's capacity to make adequately considered decisions is diminished, although Model Rule 1.14 instructs the lawyer to maintain a normal client-lawyer relationship as far as reasonably possible. We considered generally whether the law governing lawyers strikes the right balance between client control and lawyer discretion.

Finally, we examined the standards under which lawyers must and may terminate the attorney-client relationship.

CHAPTER 6

PROTECTIONS AGAINST LAWYER OVERREACHING

■ ■ ■

A. INTRODUCTION

One of the fundamental duties owed by lawyers to clients is a duty of loyalty. The particulars of this general obligation include a variety of duties we will cover in more detail later in this book. One such duty is to avoid conflicts of interest with current clients—situations in which the lawyer's own interests or the lawyer's obligations to others jeopardize the lawyer's ability to provide competent client service. In essence, the duty of loyalty requires the lawyer to put the client's interests above her own, at least to some extent. In this chapter, we explore circumstances in which a lawyer's own interests may come into conflict with the client's. In Chapters 10–12, we will cover other aspects of conflicts of interest relating primarily to conflicts between multiple clients.

We now turn to a set of provisions designed to promote the integrity of the lawyer-client relationship and to protect clients from lawyer overreaching. There are several general Model Rules that spell out fundamental duties that lawyers owe to all clients, including the duty of competence (Rule 1.1) and diligence (Rule 1.3). As we'll see in Chapter 10, the basic conflict of interest rule, Rule 1.7, prohibits a lawyer from undertaking or continuing a representation of a client if there is a significant risk that the representation will be materially limited by the lawyer's responsibilities to another client, a third person, or the lawyer's *own* interests. Here we focus on several other more specific provisions that define boundaries of the attorney-client relationship.

This chapter begins by examining one of the most fundamental ways in which lawyers' and clients' interests may conflict— in the lawyers' fee arrangements. We then consider restrictions on lawyer-client transactions, sexual relationships with clients, interactions with prospective clients, and communications with represented parties.

B. FEES

Most types of lawyers' fees are handled by agreement between lawyers and client. The most common types of fee arrangements are: 1)

139

an hourly fee, 2) a flat fee, and 3) a contingent fee, whereby a lawyer takes a certain amount or a proportion of the recovery if the client prevails and nothing if the client loses. Lawyers also sometimes combine elements of these different fee types. In Part V, we will examine a variety of questions regarding particular types of attorneys' fees, ethical issues relating to fees, and how different types of fee arrangements relate to different types of practices.

In all types of fee arrangements, there are tensions between the interests of lawyers and clients, as Susan Shapiro observes in her study of conflicts of interest in private practice:

> No matter how lawyers fund their practice conflicts of interest necessarily follow. Those paid by the hour have an incentive to over-prepare, protract their services, or do unnecessary work. Those who are on salary that does not reflect caseload, who are paid a preset fee, or who estimate the fee up front and agree not to exceed it by a given amount have an incentive to shirk. Those funded by contingency fees, whose compensation reflects a fixed percentage of civil damage awards or settlements, allocate effort where it is likely to lead to greatest or most immediate reward, neglecting those with small injuries or those that are costly to prove. Compensation arrangements of all kinds necessarily pit the interests of the client against those of the lawyer, though perhaps in different ways and at different junctures in the representation. There is no way around it.[1]

Although attorneys' fees are governed primarily by ordinary contract law, they are also limited by rules of professional conduct. Model Rule 1.5(a) provides that lawyers' fees must not be "unreasonable", and it specifies certain factors that should be considered in determining reasonableness. Rule 1.5 also contains several other restrictions on attorneys' fees. Part (b) provides that a lawyer must communicate to the client the scope of the representation and the fees and expenses for which the client will be responsible. Part (c) provides that contingent fee agreements must be in writing, and Part (d) prohibits contingent fee arrangements in certain types of matters— namely domestic relations and criminal defense. Part (e) limits referral fees, which are fees charged by one lawyer for referring a matter to another lawyer. We will consider contingent fees and referral fees more closely in Chapter 23, which examines the practices of plaintiffs' lawyers. In this chapter, we focus primarily on Rule 1.5's requirement that attorneys' fees must not be "unreasonable".

---

[1] SUSAN SHAPIRO, TANGLED LOYALTIES: CONFLICT OF INTEREST IN LEGAL PRACTICE 242 (2002).

Model Rule 1.5. Fees

A lawyer shall not charge or collect unreasonable fees. Factors to be considered in determining the reasonableness of fees include:

- The time and labor required, the novelty and difficulty of the questions involved, and the skill required to perform the service properly

- The likelihood that handling the matter will preclude the lawyer from taking other work

- The fee customarily charged in the locality for similar services

- The amount involved and results obtained

- Time limitations imposed by the client or circumstances

- The nature and length of the professional relationship with the client

- The experience, reputation and ability of the lawyer

- Whether the fee is fixed or contingent

Rule 1.5 does not establish a clear rule for deciding when a fee agreement would establish an unreasonable fee; it identifies a number of factors for consideration but does not specify at what point the facts relevant to any of the factors, or several in combination, would render a fee unreasonable. Decisions by bar disciplinary committees and courts about what constitutes an unreasonable fee are not entirely consistent.

1. *What Is an Excessive Fee?* Consider the following cases and holdings.

In In the Matter of Fordham, 423 Mass. 481, 668 N.E.2d 816 (1996), the Massachusetts Supreme Judicial Court interpreted the Model Code counterpart to Rule 1.5, which prohibited "excessive" fees, and upheld a sanction for a lawyer who successfully handled a drunk driving case but charged over $50,000 in hourly fees for the work. The lawyer was an accomplished litigator with little experience with criminal matters. He pursued a novel theory for suppressing the breathalyzer results, and he filed four pretrial motions. At trial, the judge found the defendant not guilty of driving under the influence. In a decision upholding sanctions against the attorney, the court found that the number of hours that the lawyer had spent on the case (and thus the amount of fees charged) substantially exceeded what would be charged for similar services by a prudent experienced lawyer in the locality. It found that, although the case was difficult and the breathalyzer argument creative, the time spent on the case was out of proportion to the case's difficulty. It also found that the lawyer's lack of experience with this type of case did not justify the high fee because a client "should not be expected to pay for the education of a lawyer."

In *Tarver v. State Bar*, 37 Cal. 3d 122 (1984), the California Supreme Court upheld sanctions against a lawyer who had claimed a fee of $55,000 in an age discrimination action in which the client had been reinstated and awarded $31,000 in back wages. The court found that the claimed fee, which was almost twice the amount of the actual award of monetary damages to his client, was "unconscionable."

In *Brobeck, Phleger & Harrison v. Telex Corp.*, 602 F.2d 866 (9th Cir. 1979), the Ninth Circuit approved the enforcement of a contingency fee agreement between the Brobeck law firm and its client, Telex Corporation, whereby Telex was obligated to pay Brobeck $1 million when Telex settled the case, despite the fact that Brobeck's only work in the case had been to file a petition for certiorari in the Supreme Court. The court noted that this was "not a case where one party took advantage of another's ignorance, exerted superior bargaining power, or disguised unfair terms in small print." The court noted that Telex was a sophisticated multi-million dollar corporation, represented by able counsel, and had sought out the best representation it could find. Although the fee was "clearly high", the court found that Telex had received substantial value for Brobeck's services.

Can you reconcile these holdings? If so, how? Is one common thread among them the client's sophistication and ability to understand and anticipate the possible consequences of the fee arrangement?

2. *What Public Policies Are Served?* When, if ever, should courts decline to enforce contract provisions regarding attorneys' fees on the ground that they are excessive or unreasonable? What public policy goals do restrictions on the amount of attorneys' fees advance? Are limits on the freedom of lawyers and clients to contract for lawyer services justified by the clients' vulnerability or the effects of these arrangements on lawyers' incentives and/or their impact on broader social arrangements?

3. *One Standard for All Lawyers?* Are the unreasonableness limitation and the multi-factor test used to give content to that standard sufficiently attentive to differences among types of lawyers' practices and the types of clients served? Should the same standards govern lawyers who handle drunk driving cases and those who handle litigation and/or transactions for multi-million dollar corporations? Do the existing standards give these very different types of lawyers enough guidance about what constitutes an unreasonable fee?

C. LAWYER-CLIENT TRANSACTIONS

Lawyers and clients occasionally enter into business transactions with each other. For example, a lawyer who represents a developer in real estate transactions might acquire a part ownership of a building or parcel of land that the client is developing. Or a lawyer who represents a fledgling company might purchase (or accept payment of fees in the form of) shares of stock in the company. In each of these situations, there is reason to be concerned that the lawyer might favor her own interests at the expense of the client's.

Rule 1.8 establishes several specific limitations on lawyers' interactions with clients, including restrictions on business transactions with clients. In all business transactions between lawyers and clients, the terms must be fair and reasonable, clients must be adequately informed, and they must consent in writing. In addition, there are specific prohibitions on the types of deals lawyers can make with clients. Until a representation is concluded, lawyers cannot enter into an agreement with a client whereby the lawyer obtains the literary or media rights to a portrayal of the client or the matter. Lawyers may not accept compensation from anyone other than the client unless the client consents and there is no interference with the lawyer's independent judgment on behalf of the client. Other specific prohibitions apply to loans from lawyers to clients, gifts from clients to lawyers, and some types of ownership interests in the subject matter of litigation. Here we will consider only the general requirement that terms of business transactions must be reasonable and fully disclosed, and the prohibition on lawyer acquisition of literary and media rights.

Lawyer-Client Transactions

- A lawyer shall not enter into a business transaction with a client unless the terms are fair and reasonable and are fully disclosed to the client and the client gives written informed consent. (Model Rule 1.8(a)).

- Prior to the conclusion of representation of a client, a lawyer shall not make or negotiate an agreement giving the lawyer literary or media rights to a portrayal or account based in substantial part on information relating to the representation. (Model Rule 1.8(d)).

What are the legitimate reasons for lawyers and clients to enter into business transactions? What are the risks to clients? Do Rule 1.8's requirements that business transactions be "fair and reasonable" and fully disclosed to clients adequately protect clients? Would it be preferable to impose a flat prohibition on any transactions with clients? What would be the costs of a flat prohibition?

PROBLEM 6–1

Several entrepreneurs seek Lawyer's assistance in launching a high-tech start-up. The entrepreneurs are short on cash. Therefore, they propose paying the lawyer for her time by giving her 3 percent of company's stock. Is this arrangement permissible under Rule 1.8? Suppose that the business is a huge success and eventually is worth $100 million. The lawyer, who has held her stock, now owns shares worth $3 million. Would this arrangement violate Rule 1.5's prohibition on unreasonable fees?[2]

Literary or Media Rights. In addition to general limitations on business transactions between the lawyer and client, Rule 1.8 also contains a specific prohibition on entering into an agreement prior to the end of the representation that gives the lawyer the literary or movie rights to a client's story, if those rights are "based in substantial part on information relating to the representation." The purpose of this provision is that what makes for a good story does not necessarily serve the client's interests well. Imagine, for example, circumstances in which a criminal defense lawyer concludes that the movie rights to a case might be worth substantially more if a client received a death sentence than they would be if the client received a long prison term. Similarly, a book about a client's civil case might sell better if it involved miserable drama and suffering for the client and other participants in the litigation than it would if the representation proceeded smoothly for all concerned.

The prohibition on negotiating with a client for rights to a client's story is not limited to criminal defense work. Consider the following case involving a prosecutor's negotiation of a contract for a book about a case he was prosecuting:

CAMM V. STATE

Indiana Court of Appeals
957 N.E.2d 205 (2011)

BAKER, JUDGE:

Appellant-defendant David R. Camm argues that the trial court erred when it found that the prosecutor's now cancelled literary contract did not constitute clear and convincing evidence of an actual conflict of

---

[2] This problem is based loosely on *Passante v. McWilliam*, 62 Cal. Rptr. 2d 298 (Cal. Ct. App. 4th 1997). In *Passante,* the lawyer arranged for a $100,000 loan for his client, a fledgling baseball manufacturing company. The company's directors accepted the loan and orally agreed among themselves that the lawyer should receive three percent of the company's stock in gratitude for the lawyer's help. Years later, after the company's value had grown substantially, the lawyer asked for his stock and the company refused. The lawyer sued, and a jury returned a $33 million verdict for the lawyer. The trial judge set aside the verdict, largely because he concluded that the lawyer had violated his ethical duty by failing to advise his client that it should consult with another lawyer before giving him three percent of its stock. The appellate court affirmed the trial court's decision.

interest. Concluding that prosecutor's literary contract created an irreversible, actual conflict of interest with his duty to the people of the state of Indiana, we find that the trial court erred when it denied Camm's petition.

Camm now faces his third trial and second retrial for allegedly shooting and killing his wife, seven-year-old son, and five-year-old daughter at the family home in Georgetown. In the prior two trials, Camm was convicted of all three murders, but the convictions were overturned on appeal.

A panel of this court reversed Camm's convictions from the first trial after finding the State's evidence of Camm's extramarital affairs prejudicial. The panel then remanded for retrial. Following the retrial, our Supreme Court reversed Camm's convictions after determining that the trial court had committed reversible error when it admitted hearsay evidence and speculative evidence that Camm had molested his daughter. But, our Supreme Court found that the evidence presented at the second trial was sufficient to support the convictions and, therefore, remanded the case for retrial.

Keith Henderson is the Floyd County Prosecutor and served as prosecutor for Camm's second trial. At midday on March 3, 2006, hours before the jury reached a verdict in the second trial, Literary Agency East, Ltd. sent Henderson's wife an email together with a literary representation agreement to find a publisher for a book Henderson intended to write about the Camm case. On March 10, 2006, Henderson signed the agreement. On March 28, 2006, the trial court sentenced Camm to life without parole.

Frank Weimann served as Henderson's agent. Henderson, with his initial co-author Steve Dougherty, wrote a sixty-page proposal for his forthcoming book about the Camm case, which Weimann sent to several publishers. On June 3, 2009, Weimann negotiated a publishing agreement with Berkley Penguin Group (Penguin) for Henderson's book, tentatively titled, "Sacred Trust: Deadly Betrayal." Henderson and his new co-author, Damon DiMarco, each received an advance of $1,700 and agreed to deliver a manuscript to the publisher by August 1, 2009.

After our Supreme Court reversed Camm's conviction following the second trial, Penguin decided to delay any decision to move forward with the book until our Supreme Court ruled on the State's petition for rehearing. On July 30, 2009, Henderson sent an email to Weimann raising several concerns should the State's petition for rehearing be denied. In that email, he wrote the following:

> Frank, as you know Camm was reversed. On Monday,
> the State filed for reconsideration. I should know within 60

days or so the Court's decision. If the reversal stands, I will make a decision on whether or not to bring him to trial for the third time. If there is a third trial, I anticipate it occurring spring to summer of 2010.

I am committed to writing the book as is Damon. A tremendous amount of work has been done to this point. It's a great story that needs to be told. However, the book cannot come out prior to the completion of a potential third trial. It would jeopardize the case, potentially getting me removed from the case due to certain disclosure and opinions we are writing in the book. This cannot happen. In addition, as you and Damon have discussed, this is now a bigger story.

At a minimum, I want the publisher to acknowledge and agree to a pushed back time frame that allows me to do my job and not jeopardize justice for Kim, Brad, and Jill [the shooting victims]. They may be thinking that already, I simply need the acknowledgment. After that, I would like for you to push for something more out of the contract either on the front end or the back. That issue I will leave for your judgments and persuasion skills.

Finally is the issue of the advance check. I am concerned that by cashing the check, I and Damon are acquiescing to the publisher's time frame in the agreement notwithstanding the problems I cited above. If the worst case scenario occurs and the publisher wants to put a book on the shelf prior to the completion of a potential third trial, I would have no choice but to void the contract and hopefully start over after completion.

Weimann communicated Henderson's concerns to Penguin. Penguin believed that the best solution to avoid compromising Henderson was for him and his co-author to return the advance checks and cancel the contract. It also suggested that they could "always start over again after the completion of the legal process."

Henderson and Penguin cancelled the contract in September 2009. He and his co-author subsequently returned their advance checks. Penguin never received a copy of a manuscript for the proposed book. No agreement exists between Henderson and Penguin to produce a book about the Camm case in the future.

On November 30, 2009, our Supreme Court denied the State's petition for rehearing, and, the next day, Henderson refiled the murder charges against Camm. Later that same day, Camm filed a verified petition for appointment of special prosecutor seeking the removal of Henderson as prosecutor. On December 2, 2009, Henderson issued a press release responding to Camm's petition for a special prosecutor in which he stated that the publishing agreement he had for a book about the Camm case had been cancelled after the second trial was reversed. He also stated that he was "more convinced now than ever that when this matter is completed, the unedited version of events needs to be told." In a December 3, 2009, press release, he announced that he would retry Camm and reiterated his statements from the prior day's press release. Henderson also filed with the trial court a response stating "that the agreement to publish a full account of the investigation and trials . . . was conditioned on the affirmation by the Supreme [Court] with full understanding that the agreement would be terminated in the event of reversal" and that "upon receiving notice of reversal of this case by the Indiana Supreme Court, the agreement to publish an account of the investigation and trial was immediately terminated by the prosecutor."

The trial court held a hearing on the petition. Camm called Dean Norman Lefstein, a professor of law and Dean Emeritus at Indiana University School of Law, to testify on his behalf. Dean Lefstein has an extensive background in legal ethics scholarship. Dean Lefstein testified that Henderson's actions evinced a conflict of interest under the Indiana Rules of Professional Conduct and the American Bar Association's Standards for Criminal Justice. Particularly, Dean Lefstein testified that Henderson's actions are a conflict of interest under Indiana *Rules 1.7* (conflict of interest current client) and *1.8(d)* (conflict of interest, literary rights.)

On January 7, 2011, the trial court issued an order denying Camm's petition for a special prosecutor. It found Henderson was no longer a party to any agreement to author a book about the Camm case, but he might pursue such a deal in the future. It also found that a manuscript for the book exists but that Henderson claims not to have seen it nor does he possess the book as it is the product of his co-author. In light of these findings, the trial court concluded:

> The defense had presented "some evidence" of a "potential conflict" but there has been no showing that the prosecutor's past book agreement has affected his prosecution of the case for the people of the State of Indiana. For example, even though the case has now been reversed twice and the prosecutor has chosen to proceed to trial for a third time, that decision has not been shown to be against the State's interests by "clear and convincing" evidence as even our own Supreme Court held that there is sufficient evidence for a jury to find the defendant guilty at trial.

The trial court acknowledged that it had heard evidence of how the book agreement could affect Henderson's loyalties and decision but had heard no evidence that the agreement had affected those loyalties or decisions. Additionally, the trial court noted that it has no authority to determine whether Henderson had committed any ethical violations.

On January 20, 2011, Camm filed a motion to certify the trial court's order for interlocutory appeal, which the trial court granted. Camm, without objection from the State, requested that this court accept jurisdiction. On March 11, 2011, we accepted jurisdiction. Camm now appeals.

Camm argues that the trial court erred when it denied his petition to disqualify Henderson and appoint a special prosecutor. More specifically, Camm contends that an actual conflict of interest exists because, when Henderson signed the literary contract, he irreversibly divided his loyalties between his personal interests in his book and his duties as a prosecutor for the people of the State of Indiana.

The Indiana Rules of Professional Conduct are instructive as to whether a prosecutor's interest in literary rights constitutes a conflict of interest. *Rule 1.8(d)* Conflict of Interest: Current Clients: Specific Rules provides:

> Prior to the conclusion of representation of a client, a lawyer shall not make or negotiate an agreement giving the lawyer literary or media rights to a portrayal or account based in substantial part on information relating to representation.

Comment [9] to the rule states that the purpose behind such prohibition is that "measures suitable in the representation of the client may detract from the publication value of an account of the representation." In the case of a prosecutor, the concern is, among others, that a prosecutor may conduct the prosecution in such a way that does not serve the ends of justice or weakens the public confidence in the fairness of the trial. At oral argument, the State admitted that, were a literary contract in place today, Henderson would have an actual conflict of interest.

The trial court held that the cancellation of the contract weighs against finding an actual conflict of interest, and, likewise, the State argues that the cancellation of the contract precludes this court from finding that an actual conflict of interest exists. Notwithstanding the State's contention, this is a bell that cannot be unrung. Henderson signed a contract to author and publish a book about the Camm case prior to Camm's third retrial, and, in doing so, he permanently compromised his ability to advocate on behalf of the people of the State of Indiana in this trial.

Our decision today does not rest solely on whether or not there was a contract in place. Henderson has established a personal agenda to both write this book and ensure that Camm is prosecuted. Henderson's own words are evidence of that agenda. In his email to his literary agent following reversal, Henderson stated: "I am committed to writing the book as is Damon. A tremendous amount of work has been done to this point. It's a great story that needs to be told. . . . In addition, as you and Damon have discussed, this is now a bigger story." And, in a statement to the media, Henderson wrote that he was "more convinced now than ever that when this matter is completed, the unedited version of events needs to be told."

As prosecutor, Henderson should not have a personal interest in this case separate from his professional role as prosecutor. In other words, Henderson cannot be both committed to writing a book about the Camm case and serve as prosecutor. Such a personal interest creates an actual conflict of interest with his duties as prosecutor.

In light of the facts of this case, Camm has shown clear and convincing evidence of an actual conflict of interest. By entering into a literary contract based in substantial part on information relating to [this] case, the prosecutor has created a personal interest that is in conflict with his duties as the People's representative. This conflict has and will undercut his ability to represent their interest in a just and fair trial due to issues created by him that did previously not exist. Cancellation of the contract does little to obviate Henderson's personal interest; and the public trust in the integrity of the judicial process requires us to resolve any serious doubt in favor of disqualification.

We reverse and remand for the appointment of a special prosecutor and for further proceedings consistent with this opinion.

NOTES ON CAMM V. STATE

1.   ***What Is the Threat?*** What exactly is the conflict involved in this case between the prosecutor's personal interests and his duties to his client? Doesn't simply doing the prosecutor's job well in this case make for a good story? What might we fear about how the book contract could interfere with the prosecutors' fulfillment of his duties?

2.   ***Should the Rule Be More Restrictive, or Less?*** Does Rule 1.8(d) go far enough in limiting lawyers' ability to negotiate agreements for literary and media rights to an account based in substantial part on information relating to a representation? Should the rule prohibit entering into such agreements even after the representation has ended?

On the other hand, some critics say that the rule is too restrictive—that it should allow a criminal defendant to transfer rights media rights to a lawyer in exchange for legal representation. In *Maxwell v. Superior Court of California*, 639 P.2d 248 (Cal. 1982), the California Supreme Court held that the defendant's constitutional right to counsel required that he be allowed to trade his story for representation so long as he did so knowingly, voluntarily and following full disclosure of the risks and benefits. But the applicable California ethics rule, unlike Rule 1.8, did not include Rule 1.8's flat prohibition on contracts for media rights. In a jurisdiction in which Rule 1.8 applies, it is unclear whether such an arrangement would be allowed.

As you evaluate the proper scope of Rule 1.8(d), consider the retainer agreement in the *Maxwell* case, which contained the following disclosure provision:

> "IT IS HEREBY DISCLOSED BY THE LAWYERS TO MAXWELL that the provisions of this agreement may create a conflict of interest between Maxwell and the Lawyers, and that the provisions of this agreement may give to the Lawyers a monetary interest adverse to the interests of Maxwell. This conflict of interest may manifest itself in many ways including but not limited to the following: [P] a. The Lawyers may have an interest to create publicity which would increase the money which they might get as a result of this agreement, even if this publicity hurt Maxwell's defense. [P] b. The Lawyers may have an interest not to raise certain defenses which would questions the sanity or mental capacity of Maxwell because to raise these defenses might make this agreement between the Lawyers and Maxwell void or voidable by Maxwell. [P] c. The Lawyers may have an interest in having Maxwell be convicted and even sentenced to death so that there would be increased publicity which might mean that the Lawyers would get more money as a result of this agreement. [P] d. The Lawyers may have other interests which are adverse to Maxwell's interests as a result of this agreement. The Lawyers affirm that they will not be influenced in any way by any interest which may be adverse to that of Maxwell. The Lawyers will raise every defense which they, in their best judgment based upon their experience feel is warranted by the evidence and information at their disposal and which, taking into consideration the flow of trial and trial tactics, is in Maxwell's best interests. The Lawyers will conduct all aspects of the defense of Maxwell as would a reasonably competent attorney acting as a diligent, conscientious advocate."

Does reading this provision give you any qualms about an approach that relies on client consent to remedy conflicts between lawyers and clients when clients trade media rights for representation?

D. SEXUAL RELATIONSHIPS WITH CLIENTS

Rule 1.8(j) bans a lawyer from engaging in sexual relations with a client unless the sexual relationship existed before the attorney-client relationship began. The rule was adopted in response to accumulating complaints about the manipulation and sexual exploitation of emotionally vulnerable clients, particularly in divorce matters.

The rule applies to organizational clients as well as individual clients. The comment to Rule 1.8 explains that both inside and outside counsel for an organization are prohibited from having a sexual relationship with a "constituent of the organization who supervises, directs or regularly consults with that lawyer concerning the organization's legal matters." Rule 1.8 cmt. [19].

Does it make sense to have a per se ban on sexual relationships with clients but not on business relationships with clients? Do organizational clients need the protection provided by Rule 1.8? Does application of the Rule to lawyers who serve large organizations unduly restrict lawyers' freedom of association, or is it a reasonable limitation on the freedom that takes into account the countervailing benefits of preserving a boundary between a lawyer's professional and personal concerns?

E. PROSPECTIVE CLIENTS

Prospective clients who consult lawyers but do not ultimately become their clients sometimes reveal confidential information that could be harmful to the prospective clients if used against them in subsequent matters. Rule 1.18 gives prospective clients some protection, though not as much protection as "real" clients receive.

Model Rule 1.18: Duties to Prospective Clients

- A lawyer who has learned confidential information from a prospective client may not reveal that information.

- A lawyer may not represent a client with interests materially adverse to those of a prospective client "in the same or substantially related matter" if the lawyer received information from a prospective client that could be significantly harmful to that person in the matter.

Rule 1.18 provides that even when no lawyer-client relationship follows a consultation with a client about the possibility of undertaking work for him or her, a lawyer who has learned confidential information from the prospective client shall not reveal that information. The rule also provides that a lawyer may not represent a client with interests materially adverse to those of prospective client "in the same or substantially related matter" if the lawyer received information from a prospective client that could be significantly harmful to that person in the matter. However, such a conflict is not imputed to other lawyers in the same firm; if a lawyer is disqualified because she received confidential information from a prospective client, other lawyers in the firm nevertheless are permitted to represent the current client if both the current and prospective clients give informed consent, or the lawyer who received the confidential information from the prospective client took steps to ensure that he did not acquire more than the necessary information to determine whether the firm could undertake the representation, the disqualified lawyer is screened from any participation in the matter, and written notice of the conflict is given to the prospective client. We will discuss the imputation doctrine in Chapter 12.

PROBLEM 6–2

Lawyer One has just been retained by Wife, who wants Lawyer One's help in divorcing Husband. The next day, Husband approaches Lawyer Two in the same firm to ask him to represent Husband in seeking a divorce from Wife. Before Lawyer Two can do anything to stop him, Husband reveals that he has been having an affair but doesn't want Wife to know about it because she would probably try to use his infidelity as leverage against him when he seeks to obtain sole custody of their daughter. May Lawyer One continue to represent Wife?

F. COMMUNICATING WITH REPRESENTED PARTIES

The "no-contact" rule prohibits a lawyer from communicating with another lawyer's client. The rule requires lawyers who wish to communicate with represented persons to do so through the clients' lawyers rather than directly. It allows for direct communication between a lawyer and another lawyer's client only with the other lawyer's consent; consent of the represented client is not sufficient under the rule.

Model Rule 4.2: Communicating with Person Represented by Counsel

- In representing a client, a lawyer may not communicate about the subject of the representation with a person the lawyer knows to be represented by another lawyer in the matter, unless the lawyer has the consent of the other lawyer or is authorized by law or court order.

Defenders of the rule prohibiting lawyers from contacting another lawyer's client justify it as one of a series of rules designed to protect the attorney-client relationship from outside interference. In particular, they say that the no-contact rule protects clients who might otherwise be fooled into relinquishing rights and revealing confidential information to opposing counsel.[3] Critics argue that the rule is overbroad—that a flat

---

[3]   *See, e.g.,* Restatement of the Law Governing Lawyers § 158, cmt b.

ban on communications with represented persons is unnecessary to protect clients from lawyer over-reaching. They insist that if the rule is designed to protect clients' interests, rather than lawyers' priorities, clients should have the power to waive the requirement. Critics also note that, by requiring every communication involving a lawyer and someone else's client to be funneled through another lawyer, Rule 4.2 needlessly drives up legal fees.

Do you find the justifications for the no-contact rule compelling? As you consider this question about the policies and interests served by the no-contact rule, keep in mind that the rule prevents a lawyer from contacting a represented client even when that client initiates the communication. It also applies even if the lawyer knows that the other lawyer is violating his duties to a client. In *The Verdict*, a movie based on a real medical malpractice case, the plaintiff's lawyer fails to communicate to his client a settlement offer from the liability insurer for the hospital and doctors, and the offer expires. The rule prohibiting the defendant from communicating directly with the plaintiff appears to have disserved the plaintiff in that instance. Is there anything a defendant's counsel could do in such circumstances to get around the problem without violating the no-contact rule? Notice that the no-contact rule does not prohibit clients from communicating with one another.

The rule is relatively straightforward in its ordinary application to individual clients in civil litigation, although new social media are creating interesting new questions. A recent ethics opinion from the San Diego County Bar Association addressed the question of whether sending a Facebook "friend request" to a represented party violates California's version of the no-contact rule. One member of the ethics committee that drafted the opinion said: "Lawyers are making very wide use of social media, and we wanted to test the proposition that lawyers could use social media to reach out to parties that are represented. Is that a legitimate form of the kind of broad investigation that lawyers engage in using the Internet?" The opinion concluded that it was not—that lawyers who try to friend opposing parties as an investigative tool are attempting to deceive them.[4]

Some of the most controversial aspects of the rule relate to its application to contacts with employees of organizational clients and to public and private investigative activities that precede litigation.

Application of the No-Contact Rule to Communications with Constituents of an Organizational Client. Suppose a client alleges job discrimination. May the lawyer for this prospective plaintiff interview any of the client's co-workers? Her supervisor? If the plaintiff's lawyer cannot contact any of the likely defendant's employees, such as the

---

[4]   Cynthia Foster, *Ethics Opinion Tackles 'Friend' Requests*, THE RECORDER, June 22, 2011.

plaintiff's co-workers, supervisor, or any others who might have knowledge of what occurred, how is the plaintiff to gather the facts necessary to allege a case of employment discrimination? Under the Federal Rules of Civil Procedure and the state law equivalents, lawyers must make reasonable inquiry into the facts and law before filing a lawsuit and must allege the facts establishing a cause of action with a certain degree of particularity. If they fail to do so, the complaint will be dismissed and sanctions may be imposed.

The following case addresses the question of how the rule applies to communications with constituents of an organizational client in the context of informal investigation prior to litigation.

HOBART CORPORATION V. WASTE MANAGEMENT OF OHIO, INC.

2012 WL 996525 (S.D. Ohio 2012)

Background. Plaintiffs' Second Amended Complaint asserts claims against Defendant Dayton Power & Light Co. [DP&L] (and others). The claims arise from allegations of hazardous waste disposal at the South Dayton Dump and Landfill Site (the Site) in Moraine, Ohio. Plaintiffs allege, in part, "Defendant DP&L arranged for the disposal of wastes at the Site, including waste containing hazardous substances from its facilities and operation located in and around Dayton. DP&L contributed to Contamination at the Site through its disposal of wastes that included hazardous substances at the Site. . . ." DP&L denies this allegation.

The parties' present dispute concerns Plaintiffs' desire (and subpoena) to depose a current DP&L employee Charles L. Fields. DP&L opposes the proposed deposition as a sanction for ethical misconduct committed, DP&L asserts, by one of Plaintiffs' attorneys, Leslie G. Wolfe, Esq. DP&L contends that attorney Wolfe violated Rule 4.2 of the Ohio Rule of Professional Conduct by contacting and communicating ex parte with Mr. Fields—a current DP&L employee—about factual matters at issue in this case. Plaintiffs perceive no ethical violation and seek to compel Mr. Fields' deposition.

Remarkably, Mr. Fields has been a DP&L employee since 1962. His present job title is "AC Network Splicer 2" apparently in DP&L's electrical construction department. In the past, DP&L employed him as a truck driver.

DP&L relies on Mr. Fields' affidavit. Mr. Fields states that a former DP&L employee, Jim Tharpe, phoned him. Mr. Fields had known Mr. Tharpe when they both worked at DP&L. Mr. Tharpe told Mr. Fields about the present case and predicted that Mr. Fields would probably receive a call from attorney Wolfe. Mr. Fields continues:

7.   In early 2007, after my telephone conversation with Mr. Tharpe, I received two telephone calls from Leslie Wolfe, who identified herself as an attorney representing parties in a lawsuit against DP&L involving the cleanup of the South Dayton Dump.

8.   In the first telephone call with Ms. Wolfe, she introduced herself and asked if she could call me back to discuss my personal experiences with the South Dayton Dump. I indicated that she could call me back. During the first call, Ms. Wolfe did not ask me any specific questions about the South Dayton Dump.

9.   In second telephone call with Ms. Wolfe, she asked me if I was an employee of DP&L, and I indicated that I was still employed at DP&L. I do not recall Ms. Wolfe asking me whether I was represented by legal counsel.

Plaintiffs, presumably through attorney Wolfe, represent in their Brief, "One of the attorneys for Plaintiffs contacted Mr. Fields, identified herself as counsel for Plaintiffs in this action, and asked whether Mr. Fields was represented and, if not, whether he consent[ed] to speak to her concerning his past duties as a truck driver for DP&L. Mr. Fields confirmed that he was not represented by counsel and agreed to answer questions about his activities as a truck driver for DP&L."

Returning to Mr. Fields' affidavit, he explains:

10.   During the second telephone call with Ms. Wolfe, she asked me questions about my experiences and knowledge of the South Dayton Dump, including whether I ever hauled any fly ash or other waste to the South Dayton Dump when I worked at DP&L's Longworth Steam Station facility in the 1960's. I answered Ms. Wolfe's questions.

11.   During the second telephone call with Ms. Wolfe, she told me that she would have to issue a subpoena to me . . . .

A subpoena followed.

[A]fter initial scheduling hiccups, [t]he parties agreed to proceed with the deposition.

The current disagreement began with a letter [in which] DP&L's counsel objected "to the subpoena served upon its employee, and our client, Charles Fields." DP&L's counsel also wrote, "The purpose of this objection is to provide notice that we intend to seek to suspend Mr. Field[s'] deposition in order to pursue appropriate remedies for a potential violation of Rule. 4.2 of the Ohio Rules of Professional Conduct by Plaintiffs' counsel. . . ."

Discussion. The pertinent Ohio Rule of Professional Conduct states:

Rule 4.2: Communication with Person Represented by Counsel:

> In representing a client, a lawyer shall not communicate about the representation with a person the lawyer *knows* to be represented by another lawyer in the matter, unless the lawyer has the consent of the other lawyer or is authorized to do so by law or a court order.

The main Rule 4.2 issue in the parties' present dispute concerns whether attorney Wolfe knew Mr. Fields was represented by DP&L's attorneys when she communicated with him ex parte.

Comment 7 following Rule 4.2 sheds light on how and when such knowledge arises. Comment 7 explains in part (emphasis added):

> In the case of a represented organization, the rule prohibits communications with a constituent of the organization, who supervises, directs, or regularly consults with the organization's lawyer concerning the matter or has authority to obligate the organization with respect to the matter **or whose act or omission in connection with the matter may be imputed to the organization for purposes of civil . . . liability . . .**

As to the purpose of Rule 4.2, *Wasmer v. Ohio Dept. of Rehabilitation and Corrections* explains:

> As the courts have consistently held, the purpose of a prohibition against ex parte communications such as that embodied in Rule 4.2 is to protect an organization from improper disclosures of attorney-client communications or untoward intrusions into the attorney-client relationship in the context of an organization's ability to prosecute and defend litigation. It is not designed to protect an organization against disclosure of facts which may be prejudicial to its litigation position. The purposes of the rule are best served when it prohibits communication with those employees closely identified with the organization in the dispute, those employees empowered to make litigation decisions, and those employees whose acts or omissions are at issue in the case.

2007 WL 593564 (S.D. Ohio 2007).

Plaintiffs point out that during the Wolfe/Fields communications, Mr. Fields indicated that "he had no supervisory or managerial responsibilities at DP&L." DP&L does not specifically assert that Mr. Fields has ever held supervisory or managerial duties while employed by DP&L. The record also lacks probative evidence indicating that Mr.

Fields falls within the initial groups of current employees comment 7 describes. He was not (1) a supervisor, director, or DP&L constituent who regularly consulted with DP&L's lawyers concerning this case, or (2) a DP&L constituent holding the authority to obligate DP&L in this case.

The parties' dispute thus boils down to whether attorney Wolfe violated Rule 4.2 by communicating ex parte with Mr. Fields because he was a DP&L constituent "whose act or omission in connection with the matter may be imputed to the organization for purposes of civil . . liability."

DP&L argues that attorney Wolfe's ex parte contact with Mr. Fields violated Rule 4.2 because he was such a person—again, a constituent "whose act or omission in connection with the matter may be imputed to the organization for purposes of civil . . . liability." DP&L emphasizes that Mr. Fields was not an observer to potentially hazardous waste dumping at the Site; he was an actor—a DP&L-employed truck driver—who recalls driving DP&L's fly ash to the Site.

Plaintiffs contend that Rule 4.2 did not prohibit attorney Wolfe's ex parte contact with Mr. Fields because his factual recollections of hauling waste to the Site cannot be imputed to DP&L. They assert that Mr. Fields "made no statement which could be offered against DP&L as an admission. He was strictly a truck driver with factual information regarding the delivery of materials to the South Dayton Dump Site."

Plaintiffs' contentions overlook or minimize the impact Mr. Fields' potential testimony might have on DP&L's liability. His potential testimony—if fully credited and based on the present record—would reveal that he drove DP&L's fly ash and other waste materials to the South Dayton Site for disposal during the 1960s. Such testimony would tend to support Plaintiffs' allegations, in their Second Amended Complaint, that "DP&L contributed to Contamination at the Site through its disposal of wastes that included hazardous substances at the Site"; and "DPL was a regular customer at the Site, and had its own . . . access to the Site for disposal of waste materials, including wastes containing hazardous substances." In other words, DP&L is indubitably correct to assert that Plaintiffs "hope to impute his [Mr. Fields'] acts to DP&L in order to establish the central issue in this case: Whether DP&L disposed of hazardous substances in the Dump Site. Indeed, Mr. Fields' affidavit places him within the group of current employees *Rule 4.2*, comment 7 shields from ex parte communications—those "whose act or omission in connection with the matter may be imputed to the organization for purposes of civil or criminal liability."

Plaintiffs contend, citing *Paulson v. Plainfield Trucking, Inc.*, 210 F.R.D. 654, 657–58 (D. Minn. 2002), "Rule 4.2 clearly permits *ex parte* interviews of current employees who are 'mere witnesses' to an event for which the organization is being sued." But, based on the present record, Mr. Fields was more than an observer of alleged disposal of hazardous waste by DP&L at the Site. He participated in the alleged hazardous disposal, or under attorney Wolfe's brief description, he "formerly drove DP&L's fly ash from several of its power generating stations to the South Dayton Dump site." To this extent, *Paulson's* "mere witness" language does not apply to Mr. Fields.

Although the above points towards the conclusion that attorney Wolfe ran aground on Rule 4.2 when she spoke ex parte to Mr. Fields, the issue of whether attorney Wolfe violated Rule 4.2 by contacting and speaking ex parte with Mr. Fields remains a close question. Too much remains unclear. The record can be reasonably read as indicating that attorney Wolfe did not have sufficient evidence to know with certainty that Mr. Fields was involved with disposal of hazardous waste materials at the Site until she spoke with him. Before that time, her information about Mr. Fields derived from only one other source—Mr. Tharpe. The record is presently silent about the source of Mr. Tharpe's information about Mr. Fields. Was Mr. Tharpe reporting his own personal knowledge about Mr. Fields' activities? Was he reporting what Mr. Fields, or someone else, had told him about Mr. Fields' activities? Mr. Fields's affidavit does not address these questions. And he provides scant information about the extensiveness of attorney Wolfe's second conversation with him. He merely explains that attorney Wolfe asked him "questions about [his] experiences and knowledge of the South Dayton Dump, including whether [he] ever hauled fly ash or other waste to the South Dayton Dump when I worked at DP&L's Longworth Steam Station facility in the 1960's. [He] answered Ms. Wolfe's questions." Did she ask two questions, ten questions, fifty questions? Did she probe the extent of Mr. Fields' purported activities or personal knowledge? Or, did she merely confirm that Mr. Fields is a current DP&L employee "whose acts or omissions are at issue in the case," and once learning this, did she immediately terminate her questions and seek to depose him with DP&L's counsel? The record at present is simply inadequate to answer such questions with accuracy.

And these questions are significant [because] Rule 4.2's purpose of preventing untoward intrusions into the attorney-client relationship in the context of an organization's ability to prosecute and defend litigation, is tempered by the warning that Rule 4.2 is not designed to protect an organization against disclosure of facts which may be prejudicial to its litigation position. It must be recalled that RPC 4.2 is an *ethical* rule, not a rule through which corporations gain the ability to control the flow of information to opposing parties.

Regardless of how any or all of the above matters play out in the present case, the record does not support the issuance of the protective order DPL seeks. Even assuming, arguendo, that attorney Wolfe violated Rule 4.2 by communicating ex parte with Mr. Fields, the appropriate sanction should not preclude his deposition.

NOTES ON HOBART CORPORATION V. WASTE MANAGEMENT OF OHIO, INC.

1. ***Which Constituents?*** What current employees may a lawyer contact, according to *Hobart Corporation v. Waste Management of Ohio, Inc.* (and paragraph 7 of the Comment to Rule 4.2)?

2. ***Former Constituents.*** Could plaintiffs have interviewed Mr. Fields if he had retired several years before the plaintiffs filed this lawsuit? Of course, Mr. Field's acts or omissions while employed by the company could still be imputed to the organization for purposes of civil or criminal liability even after he retired. Nevertheless, Comment 7 to Rule 4.2 provides that "consent of the organization is not required for communication with a former constituent."

3. ***Communications with Unrepresented Persons.*** Rule 4.3 provides that "in dealing with a person who is not represented by counsel, a lawyer shall not state or imply that the lawyer is disinterested." What policies does this rule serve? What is the relationship between Rules 4.2 and 4.3? That is, does any employee of an organizational client whom a lawyer is permitted to contact under Rule 4.2 and who is not represented by other counsel, constitute an unrepresented person within the meaning of Rule 4.3?

4. ***Application of the No-Contact Rule to Prosecutors.*** A great deal of controversy between bar groups and prosecutors revolves around the question of the scope of Rule 4.2's application to criminal investigations and prosecutions. When a prosecutor is supervising an investigation of an ongoing crime such as a fraud or some other complex business crime in which the suspects may be represented by counsel during the crime and the investigation, a literal application of Rule 4.2 might prevent the prosecutor or any law enforcement official acting at her direction from speaking with (or even secretly wiretapping) anyone in the organization or anyone else represented by counsel. It is generally agreed that the no-contact rule applies once a represented defendant has been formally charged. But does the rule also prevent communications with a represented defendant at the investigatory, pre-indictment phase? At what point does a proceeding become sufficiently concrete to constitute a "matter" as to which the client is represented within the meaning of Rule 4.2?

Most of the decisions that have addressed this point have held that pre-indictment investigation by prosecutors and their agents is not subject to the no-contact rule. However, a few contrary decisions in the white collar context have worried prosecutors, who say that applying the rule to pre-indictment investigations gives special treatment to defendants who have retained a lawyer prior to the criminal investigation—namely, professional criminals and those involved in organized crime. Prosecutors generally have taken the position that contacts occurring in undercover investigations fit within the "authorized by law" exception to the Rule. In 2002, following a tussle between the U.S. Department of Justice, Congress, and the ABA over the rule and its application through state ethics code to federal prosecutors, the ABA amended the comment (par. 5) to Rule 4.2 to clarify that "communications authorized by law may include investigative activities of lawyers representing governmental entities, directly or through investigative agents, prior to the commencement of criminal or civil enforcement proceedings."

G. SUMMARY

This chapter has explored a variety of protections against lawyer over-reaching. It examined limitations on attorneys' fees and restrictions on transactions between lawyers and clients, including those involving literary or media rights and sexual relationships. We also considered duties owed by lawyers to prospective clients, as well as restrictions on lawyer's communications with represented parties. With respect to each of these limitations, we examined the policies underlying the rules and noted the differential impact of the rules on various types of clients and lawyers.

PART III

CONFIDENTIALITY

■ ■ ■

CHAPTER 7

INTRODUCTION TO THE ATTORNEY-CLIENT PRIVILEGE AND THE DUTY OF CONFIDENTIALITY

■ ■ ■

A. INTRODUCTION

One of the most longstanding and fundamental features of the attorney-client relationship is the lawyer's obligation to guard the client's confidences. The lawyer's duty of confidentiality is encoded in two distinct but overlapping bodies of law: the attorney-client privilege and the broader duty of confidentiality. The attorney-client privilege is a longstanding rule of evidence prohibiting courts and other tribunals from forcing a lawyer or a client to reveal client communications. The duty of confidentiality is a general principle of more recent vintage that requires lawyers to guard the confidentiality of all information relating to the representation of a client. The duty of confidentiality is encoded in Model Rule 1.6, which provides that a "lawyer shall not reveal information relating to the representation of a client unless the client gives informed consent, the disclosure is impliedly authorized in order to carry out the representation" or disclosure is permitted by one of seven specifically enumerated exceptions, including to prevent reasonably certain death or substantial bodily harm, to prevent clients from committing crimes or frauds using the lawyer's services or to rectify the harms caused by such crimes or frauds, to obtain legal advice, or to comply with law or court order. We will cover the scope of Rule 1.6 and the exceptions to it in detail in Chapter 9. For now, simply focus on the general rule and how it differs from the attorney-client privilege.[1]

---

[1] In your civil procedure course, you may have learned about another sort of privilege, the work-product doctrine. The work-product rule is applicable to pretrial discovery in civil cases. *See* Fed. R. Civ. P. 26(b)(3). It provides a qualified exemption from discovery for materials prepared "in anticipation of litigation" by the party or the party's attorney, and a more stringent exemption for such materials that reveal "the mental impressions, conclusions, opinions, or legal theories of an attorney." *See also* Hickman v. Taylor, 329 U.S. 495 (1947). The nuances of the work-product doctrine are generally considered an aspect of civil discovery, not part of the lawyer's general ethical duties to guard the confidentiality of client information and communications.

> **Topic Overview and Chapter Structure**
>
> This chapter first examines the general considerations behind the attorney-client privilege and the duty of confidentiality. Then it covers the contours of the attorney-client privilege. It concludes by looking at what lawyers must do to avoid waiving the protections of the privilege. (Chapter 8 examines how the attorney-client privilege applies when clients are organizations. That chapter also covers exceptions to the attorney-client privilege that apply to both individual and organizational clients. Chapter 9 covers the duty of confidentiality.)

The principal justification for the strong duty of confidentiality is instrumental: society benefits when people obtain good legal advice to conform their conduct to law and to enable the adversary system to function. Confidentiality is necessary for clients to trust lawyers enough to be truthful, and clients must be truthful in order for lawyers to provide sound advice. In some cases, the lawyer's obligation to guard the confidentiality of client communications and other information serves to protect the Fifth Amendment right against self-incrimination (because it prevents the government from forcing a lawyer to reveal what the client would have a right not to reveal) and the Sixth Amendment right to effective assistance of counsel. Lawyers sometimes also assert that confidentiality is intrinsically beneficial to lawyers because it spares lawyers the indignity of being expected or required to tattle on clients. On the other hand, confidentiality imposes costs on society, as it is a barrier to the discovery of truth. Moreover, behind the shelter of secrecy, clients sometimes get away with wrongdoing about which lawyers are aware and which they may be in a position to prevent. And confidentiality can provide lawyers with an excuse not to reveal wrongful conduct and prevent harms to others. Much of the law governing the scope of the lawyer's duty of confidentiality reflects a tension between these competing considerations.

Attorney-Client Privilege and the Duty of Confidentiality Compared. Students often confuse attorney-client privilege and confidentiality, but it is important to keep them separate because they apply in different contexts, and the requirements of and exceptions to each are distinct. The attorney-client privilege is an evidentiary rule that prohibits a *tribunal* from *compelling* a lawyer or client to reveal confidential communications between the lawyer and client. The duty of confidentiality covers more information than the attorney-client privilege and also prohibits voluntary disclosure. The attorney-client privilege applies to a narrower category of information (communications only) and it protects only against disclosure compelled by a tribunal. One reason the distinction matters is that there are more exceptions to the duty of confidentiality than there are to the privilege. As we will see in the materials that follow, the privilege applies to fewer forms of information and in narrower circumstances, but it has fewer exceptions. The duty of confidentiality applies to all information lawyers possess, so long as it relates to the representation of a client, and it applies in all circumstances (including casual conversations, not just to efforts by tribunals to compel disclosure), but there are more circumstances in which lawyers are nevertheless permitted to reveal confidential information.

The Attorney-Client Privilege

The attorney-client **privilege** is a **rule of evidence** that protects *communications* made in *confidence* between client and lawyer **relating to the provision of legal advice** against *compelled* **disclosure by a** *tribunal*.

Model Rule 1.6: The Duty of Confidentiality

The **ethical duty of confidentiality** prevents lawyers from *voluntarily* disclosing *any confidential information relating to the representation* of a client **except with client** *consent* or where **disclosure is** *impliedly authorized* to carry out the representation, or where disclosure is **permitted by one of the Rule's** *exceptions*.

The following chart illustrates the differences between the attorney-client privilege and the duty of confidentiality under Model Rule 1.6:

	Attorney-Client Privilege	Duty of Confidentiality
Nature & Source of Rule	Evidentiary rule developed by courts	Ethics rule developed by bar
Effect	Prevents pretrial discovery and/or testimony in courts and tribunals	Applies to lawyers' activities in all settings
Scope	Communication between attorney & client for purpose of providing legal assistance with expectation of confidentiality	All "information relating to the representation"

	Attorney-Client Privilege	Duty of Confidentiality
Waiver	Intentional or inadvertent waiver by client or by lawyer eliminates privilege	Client's revelation of confidential information does not affect lawyer's duty to keep information confidential

The duty of confidentiality is much broader than the attorney-client privilege; the privilege is only a rule of evidence having to do with the power of a tribunal to compel disclosure of communications, whereas the duty of confidentiality is a general principle governing the lawyer's obligation to clients. The privilege is part of the larger duty of confidentiality, and the relationship between the two may be illustrated as follows:

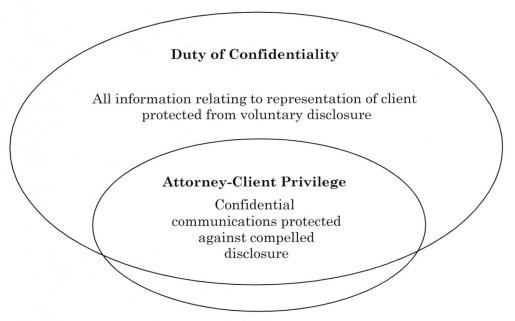

The law of privilege and confidentiality has a huge impact on how lawyers do their work. It restricts the ability of lawyers to talk about cases with others. Lawyers must take care to guard the security of their offices, their paper files, and their electronic data. Pretrial discovery of facts is complicated by the need to review every document and statement for claims of privilege. The duty of confidentiality underlies the law of conflicts of interest which, as we will see in Part IV, restricts the job mobility of lawyers and limits clients' choice of lawyers.

B. GENERAL CONSIDERATIONS BEHIND CONFIDENTIALITY AND ATTORNEY-CLIENT PRIVILEGE

PROBLEM 7–1: THE 26-YEAR-OLD SECRET AND THE ISSUE OF WRONGFUL CONVICTION

In 1982, two men shot a security guard at a McDonald's restaurant in Chicago. A second security guard was wounded in the shooting and identified two men as the shooters: Edgar Hope and Alton Logan. Hope told his lawyer, a Cook County public defender named Marc Miller, that he had committed the McDonald's shooting not with Logan, but with another man, Andrew Wilson. In fact, Hope told Miller that he had never seen Logan before. He said: "You need to tell his lawyer he represents an innocent man." Hope told Miller to check the word on the street and he would find that Wilson was "the guy who guards my back." Miller did and confirmed his client's account. A few days after police arrested Hope and Logan, they arrested Wilson for shooting two Chicago police officers. Two public defenders, Jamie Kunz and Dale Coventry, were appointed to represent Wilson for the police shooting, a crime that carried the death penalty. Miller told Kunz that Hope had implicated Wilson as the shooter in the McDonald's case. Kunz and Coventry went to visit Wilson in jail and confronted him with the allegation. Wilson, they recalled, seemed unabashed and even somewhat gleeful in confessing he had shot the security guard in the McDonald's.

Kunz and Coventry now faced a serious dilemma. Their client had confessed to a murder for which he hadn't been charged and for which an innocent man was being prosecuted. The problem was that Wilson told them in confidence. Kunz and Coventry believed their client would be sentenced to death if he were convicted for shooting the police officers. They twice asked if he would permit them to reveal his confession to the security guard killing after his death, and twice he agreed. Wilson was originally sentenced to death, but his sentence was changed to life in prison without possibility of parole after he asserted that police had tortured him to secure his confession.

So Kunz and Coventry wrote and swore to an affidavit, which they signed, along with Marc Miller, recounting Hope's and Wilson's confidential statements to them. Coventry sealed the affidavit in an envelope and locked it in a metal box which he hid under a bed in his home. Kunz and Coventry hoped to use the affidavit to help Logan. They asked ethics commissions, lawyers, and the bar association for advice about whether they could reveal the secret, and everyone told them they could not. They planned that if Logan was sentenced to death, they would appeal to the governor to commute his sentence. But Logan received a sentence of life in prison. So Coventry kept the affidavit in a sealed envelope in a locked metal box in his home. Meanwhile, Alton Logan had heard that Wilson had confessed, and when Logan got new a new lawyer for a retrial, he asked his new lawyer to talk to Miller. Miller told Logan's new lawyer that Logan was innocent but that there was nothing more he could do. Logan confronted Wilson in prison and asked him to tell the truth, but Wilson just smiled and walked away.

After 26 years, Wilson died in prison. When Kunz heard that Wilson had died, he called Coventry and told him the news. Coventry opened the box and unsealed the envelope. In a hearing to exonerate Logan and with the judge's permission, the affidavit was read aloud. Kunz, Coventry and Miller testified about the affidavit, about Wilson's confession, and about Hope's statement. Although the State of Illinois initially insisted it would retry Logan, eventually charges against him were dismissed and Logan was released, after having served 26 years for a crime he did not commit.

At the end Kunz said: "I am anguished and always have been over the sad injustice of Alton Logan's conviction. Should I do the right thing by Alton Logan and put my client's neck in the noose or not? It's clear where my responsibility lies and my responsibility lies with my client."[2]

NOTES ON PROBLEM 7–1

1. ***Arguments For and Against the Duty of Confidentiality.*** Both the law of attorney-client privilege and the professional responsibility rules of most states prohibit lawyers from ever disclosing a confidential client communication like that made by Wilson without client consent, even to save an innocent person from the death penalty or from serving decades in prison for a crime he did not commit.[3] While an exception to the duty of confidentiality allows disclosure to prevent reasonably certain death or substantial bodily harm, that exception does not override the attorney-client privilege which in many jurisdictions does not have an exception to allow disclosure of a communication such as Wilson's. What are the justifications for such a rule? What are the arguments against it?

2. ***Contemplating Civil Disobedience.*** The question whether the law allows a lawyer to disclose client confidences in situations like that faced by Kunz and Coventry is not the only consideration for lawyers, who may (like anyone else) contemplate violating the law when they believe it is

---

[2] This account of the case of Alton Logan is drawn from Sharon Cohen, *A 26-Year-Old Secret Could Free Inmate*, www.news.aol.com; Center on Wrongful Convictions, Northwestern University Law School, *available at* http://www.law.northwestern.edu/legalclinic/wrongful convictions/exonerations/il/alton-logan.html. Peter A. Joy & Kevin C. McMunigal, *Confidentiality and Wrongful Incarceration*, 23 CRIM. JUST. 46 (2008).

[3] *See* James E. Moliterno, *Rectifying Wrongful Convictions: May a Lawyer Reveal Her Client's Confidences to Rectify the Wrongful Conviction of Another?*, 38 HASTINGS CONST. L.Q. 811, 821–23 (2011) (two state ethics codes expressly allow lawyers to disclose client confidences, but other state ethics codes do not and may even prevent lawyers from disclosing without client consent); Peter A. Joy & Kevin C. McMunigal, *Confidentiality and Wrongful Incarceration*, 23 CRIM. JUST. 46 (2008) (citing several state cases holding that attorney-client privilege prohibits lawyers from revealing client confidences to exonerate a wrongly convicted person).

justified by some higher moral imperative. Of course, a crucial element of civil disobedience is being prepared to face punishment for violation of law. Punishments lawyers might face in this circumstance could range from a relatively mild censure from the bar to disbarment. If you were in Kunz and Coventry's situation, what would you do? Should it matter how likely it is that revealing the confidence will actually prompt the court to set aside the conviction? If Kunz and Coventry had revealed the confidence, should the Illinois Bar institute disciplinary proceedings against them? What discipline would be appropriate? What should the Cook County Public Defender do about lawyers who violate their client's confidence to save the life of an innocent convict?

3. ***The Death of the Client.*** In the Alton Logan case, the lawyers persuaded the client to consent to disclosure of his confession after his death. If he had not consented to disclosure after his death, however, the lawyers might have been obligated to keep his secret forever. In hard cases, courts sometimes have struggled to decide whether the death of the client should terminate the attorney-client privilege (see below *Privilege After the Death of the Client*). The duty of confidentiality always survives the client's death. See Rule 1.6 cmt. [par.20] ("The duty of confidentiality continues after the client-lawyer relationship has terminated"); Restatement (Third) of the Law Governing Lawyers § 111 cmt. C, at 8 ("The duty [of confidentiality] extends beyond the end of the representation and beyond the death of the client"). What interests are served by keeping Wilson's secret after he is dead while Logan still lives in prison? Consider the case of Lee Hunt, in Problem 7–2.

PROBLEM 7–2

Imagine you are newly assigned by the state attorney general to examine the conviction of Lee Hunt, who was sentenced in 1986 to life in prison for the murders of two people whom Hunt and a co-defendant, Jerry Cashwell, allegedly shot in a drug deal gone awry. Hunt was a marijuana dealer. Gene Williford, an associate of Hunt's who received immunity, testified that Hunt had told him that he intended to teach one of the victims a lesson for stealing drugs. Williford also testified that he dropped Hunt off at the murder scene and that he later picked up Hunt and Cashwell, who both appeared to be wearing bloody clothing. Williford, however, did not witness the killings and never claimed that Hunt had admitted to them. Hunt's mother and aunt said that he was at home with them that night. A prison informant, who received a plea deal on separate charges, testified that Hunt told him some details about the murders, including that the victims were "killed over drug money." A third person testified that he received a box of bullets from Cashwell after the killings. An FBI analysis matched bullets from that box to the crime-scene bullets, but in 2005, the bureau ended its reliance on bullet-lead-matching after experts concluded that matching a crime-scene bullet to another bullet was scientifically invalid.

After Jerry Cashwell died in prison in 2003, Staples Hughes, the public defender who represented Cashwell, came forward to declare that his client had told him that he committed the murders alone and that Hunt was not involved. Hughes said he waited until his client died because he believed that attorney-client privilege precluded him from disclosing his client's admission. Hughes said that shortly after Cashwell's arrest, his client provided him with a detailed confession and Cashwell consistently said for two decades that he committed the murders alone. Shortly before he died, Cashwell said that he felt bad about what happened to Hunt.

Experts now agree that the bullet-matching evidence is unreliable. Williford and the prison informant are both dead. A lawyer for Hunt has sought to vacate Hunt's conviction based on Hughes' affidavit about Cashwell's confession, and the judge has referred Hughes to the state bar for discipline for breaching the duty of confidentiality. What should the state's position be both about the conviction and about discipline for Hughes?[4]

PROBLEM 7–3: THE BURIED BODIES CASE

Frank Armani and Francis Belge were appointed to defend Robert Garrow on murder charges. Garrow confessed to them that he had committed prior rapes and two other unsolved murders and he told them where to find the bodies of those victims. Armani and Belge found the bodies where Garrow had said and attempted to use the information in plea negotiations with the prosecutor; they offered to provide information about the unsolved murders in exchange for favorable treatment on the murder charges Garrow faced. The plea negotiations proved fruitless. Garrow went to trial and the jury convicted him of murder. Garrow later escaped from prison. Police asked Armani for information that might help recapture Garrow. Armani recalled that Garrow had once told him how he had eluded police in the past, and based on that, the police found Garrow. Armani was willing to tell police what Garrow had said about prior escapes because, during Garrow's trial, Garrow had greeted Armani's daughter by name when she came to the courtroom to watch her father in trial. Armani asked his daughter how she knew Garrow, and she replied that she didn't, which led Armani to believe that Garrow had been stalking her.

When it became known that Belge and Armani had information about the unsolved murders but refused to reveal the location of the bodies, public sentiment turned strongly against them. They were indicted for violating two provisions of state law requiring anyone knowing of a death without medical attendance to report the death to the authorities and

---

[4] John Solomon, *The End of a Failed Technique—But Not of a Prison Sentence*, WASH. POST, Nov. 18, 2007, *available at* http://www.washingtonpost.com/wp-dyn/content/article/2007/11/17/AR2007111701641.html?sid=ST2007111701983; Robert P. Mosteller, *The Special Threat of Informants to the Innocent Who Are Not Innocents: Producing "First Drafts," Recording Incentives, and Taking a Fresh Look at the Evidence*, 6 OHIO ST. J. CRIM. L. 519 (2009).

requiring a decent burial of the dead. *People v. Belge*, 372 N.Y.S.2d 798 (1975); *People v. Belge*, 376 N.Y.S.2d 771 (1975) (indictment dismissed).

NOTES ON PROBLEMS 7–2 AND 7–3

1. ***The Reliability of Lawyer Testimony About Client Communications.*** If one reason for allowing lawyers to reveal client confidences after the death of the client is that the client will not suffer and the innocent person may be exonerated, a countervailing concern might be that no one is left alive to test the reliability of the lawyer's account of what the client said. In Problem 7–2, none of the witnesses who testified in Lee Hunt's trial is alive. How should a prosecutor or a judge evaluate the reliability of the evidence of guilt or innocence?

2. ***Can Lawyers and Clients Use Confidentiality and Privilege for Tactical Advantage?*** Did Armani and Belge violate the duty of confidentiality by offering to reveal the location of the bodies in the plea negotiations but refusing to do so when the negotiations failed? (For purposes of answering this and the remaining questions in these notes, assume that the Model Rules, rather than the rules in place at the time, New York's Code of Professional Responsibility, applied.) Assume that their client authorized disclosure only if it would secure a favorable plea deal. Absent client consent, is a disclosure for tactical purposes one that is "impliedly authorized in order to carry out the representation" within the meaning of Model Rule 1.6(a)? Should there be any limit on how lawyers and clients can seek tactical advantage through disclosing information?

3. ***Should Attorneys Be Prosecuted for Keeping Confidences or Disciplined for Revealing Them?*** Does criminal prosecution of lawyers for refusing to reveal the information violate the attorney-client privilege? The New York court dismissed the indictment against the lawyers. In dismissing the indictment against Belge, the court found that his duty to protect his client's confidences exempted him from the obligation to comply with New York laws requiring reports of death and decent burial of the dead. Should the state bar discipline Hunt's lawyer in Problem 7–2 for breaching attorney-client privilege?

4. ***The Justifications for Confidentiality.*** Compare the justifications for permitting defense counsel to disclose (a) the location of the buried bodies, (b) Garrow's possible hiding place, and (c) information that would free a wrongfully convicted person from prison. Which disclosures should be permitted? Which should not?

THE EMPIRICAL BASIS FOR
PROTECTING CONFIDENTIALITY

Topic Overview

The confidentiality of client communications and information is usually justified by the argument that confidentiality is necessary to induce clients to provide full and frank information to their lawyers and to enable lawyers to be candid and thorough in return. If clients and lawyers knew that what they say could be used by their adversary in litigation, the argument goes, they would not be honest or would withhold damaging information or advice. According to this argument, confidentiality benefits society at large because if clients obtain good legal advice they are more likely to comply with the law. Thus, although confidentiality is a barrier to learning the truth, it is justified as being instrumentally necessary to encourage people to comply with the law, which benefits society in the long term more than society is harmed by lawyers hiding the truth.

As you read the cases and materials in the next three chapters, pay close attention to the use of these sorts of instrumental justifications for confidentiality and privilege, and ask yourself whether the empirical assumptions underlying these instrumental justifications are well-founded.

The confidentiality of client communications and information is usually justified by the argument that confidentiality is necessary to induce clients to provide full and frank information to their lawyers and to enable lawyers to be candid and thorough in return. Confidentiality is also thought to be justified in criminal cases for the same reason that the constitution provides a Fifth Amendment right against self-incrimination and a Sixth Amendment right to counsel: enabling clients to communicate in confidence with their lawyers protects against abuses of government power.

Empirical support for the instrumental justification of confidentiality is scarce. Anecdotally, criminal defense lawyers note that some clients will not tell their lawyers the full truth regardless of the privilege, and others will tell confidential facts to anyone who will listen. Academic studies of confidentiality in different practice sectors have found that many clients do not know about the attorney's duty of confidentiality, or do not understand how broadly it applies or the exceptions to it. Some studies show that many lawyers do not inform their clients of the scope of the privilege (and, particularly, of the scope of the exceptions). And one study found that only 30% of former clients reported giving information to lawyers that they would not have given without confidentiality and only half predicted they would withhold information from lawyers without confidentiality.[5]

The link between confidentiality and legal compliance is even more questionable. Comment [2] to Rule 1.6 asserts that "almost without exception, clients come to lawyers in order to determine their rights and what is, in the complex of law and regulations deemed to be legal and correct," and that "almost all clients follow advice given, and the law is upheld." But one need not be a cynic to question the notion that clients almost always seek advice in order to learn how to follow the law. Indeed, Daniel Fischel, former Dean of the University of Chicago Law School, has argued that confidentiality rules either have no effect on compliance or tend to *decrease* the level of legal compliance because legal advice sometimes has the effect of enabling clients to find ways to evade legal requirements.[6] Indeed, Fischel asserts that the "legal profession, not clients or society as a whole, is the primary beneficiary of confidentiality rules" because confidentiality serves primarily to increase the demand for legal services. Unfortunately, there is no strong empirical evidence available upon which to base claims that confidentiality either promotes or discourages compliance with the law.

Keep the instrumental justification for the attorney-client privilege and duty of confidentiality in mind as we consider the details about these two bodies of law below. Ask yourself whether clients would be candid with their lawyers absent confidentiality, whether confidentiality tends to promote legal compliance or reduce it, and whether the exceptions to confidentiality serve the interests of lawyers or clients or courts. Notwithstanding the rhetoric about the value of confidentiality, the protection is not absolute. Thus, focus on whether social utility of recognizing a new application or exception would undermine trust between lawyers and clients more than the existing exceptions already do and whether, in any case, the benefits of any expansion of the exceptions would outweigh the costs.

C. ELEMENTS OF THE
ATTORNEY-CLIENT PRIVILEGE

The attorney-client privilege protects communications made in confidence between client and lawyer relating to the provision of legal

---

[5]   Fred C. Zacharias, *Rethinking Confidentiality*, 74 IOWA L. REV. 351, 380–83 (1989). See also Leslie C. Levin, *Testing the Radical Experiment: A Study of Lawyer Responses to Clients Who Intend to Harm Others*, 47 RUTGERS L. REV. 81 (1994); Eric Slater & Anita Sorenson, *Corporate Legal Ethics—An Empirical Study: the Model Rules, the Code of Professional Responsibility, and Counsel's Continuing Struggle Between Theory and Practice*, 8 J. CORP. L. 601 (1983); Note, *Functional Overlap Between the Lawyer and Other Professionals: Its Implications for the Privileged Communications Doctrine*, 71 YALE L.J. 1226 (1962).

[6]   Daniel R. Fischel, *Lawyers and Confidentiality*, 65 U. CHI. L. REV. 1 (1998).

advice against compelled disclosure by a tribunal. Each element of the privilege is important.

Elements of Attorney-Client Privilege

- Communications (not facts)
- Made in confidence
- Between attorney and client and their agents
- Relating to the provision legal advice
- Protected against compelled disclosure by a tribunal

---

1. COMMUNICATIONS

The privilege covers only *communications*, whether they are oral, written, or even silent or a gesture (such as a nod or a shrug). The attorney client privilege applies to efforts by courts and tribunals to compel a lawyer to testify (or to produce documentary evidence) revealing a client's communication. Thus, if a tribunal issues an order (known as a subpoena) to a lawyer and/or client demanding them to testify about their communications or correspondence or to provide copies of the correspondence, the lawyer and/or client can invoke the privilege and refuse to testify or to provide the documents. If a client tells a lawyer something, what the client said is privileged ("I buried a body in my yard") and a court may not force the lawyer to reveal what the client said. Similarly, if the lawyer asked the client "Do you know where the body is?" and the client shrugged in response, the lawyer cannot be compelled to reveal that the client shrugged. However, the lawyer can be compelled to testify about noncommunicative facts about the client (for example, about whether the client resides at a particular address).

The privilege does not protect the underlying facts from disclosure. If the police seek a search warrant for the client's yard, the underlying fact (that a body is buried in the yard) is not privileged and therefore the client and his lawyer may not resist the issuance of the warrant on the ground that it will reveal the fact. Similarly, in a civil suit to recover damages for the wrongful death, the victim's family's lawyer may ask the client whether he buried the body in the yard and the client cannot decline to answer on the grounds of attorney-client privilege. (The client may be entitled to refuse to answer on other grounds.) But the lawyer can refuse to answer the question because a truthful answer would require the lawyer to reveal a privileged communication.

The privilege protects only communications, not things. Thus, if a client gives copies of his tax returns to his lawyer along with bank statements showing the client received income in excess of what he declared on his tax returns, a court can compel the lawyer to produce the tax returns and bank statements in an action against the client for tax evasion. However, if the client wrote a letter to the lawyer to accompany the tax returns and bank statements, the letter would be privileged from disclosure. The fact that a lawyer represents a client is ordinarily not privileged, even if the fact of representation may tend to communicate. A lawyer running for elected office, for example, cannot assert attorney-client privilege to prevent his opponent in the election from revealing that he once represented a controversial client. A lawyer who is known to represent members of a notorious gang cannot prevent the FBI from discovering the names of his clients. In addition, the amount of legal fees a lawyer was paid and who paid them are also not generally privileged.

PROBLEM 7–4

A driver hit and killed a pedestrian and fled the scene. The driver seeks your advice and says he would like to turn himself in. You think the police and prosecutors would like to avoid the expense and difficulty of finding the driver and might be willing to negotiate a more favorable plea arrangement in exchange for the driver voluntarily turning himself in. You suggest this to the prosecutor, who refuses and promptly seeks to subpoena you to reveal the identity of your client. Can you resist? *See Baird v. Koerner*, 279 F.2d 623 (9th Cir. 1960) (lawyer cannot be forced to reveal names of client who anonymously, through the lawyer, offered to pay delinquent taxes because it would effectively reveal the communication in which the client revealed that he owed taxes); Restatement (Third) of the Law Governing Lawyers § 69 (in rare cases, the fact of representation may reveal communications, and may be privileged).

2. CONFIDENTIAL COMMUNICATIONS BY AND TO WHOM?

Although originally the privilege protected communications only by clients, today it protects communications by lawyers as well. Courts concluded that the same incentives for candid communication and legal advice apply to lawyers' communications as to clients'. The privilege also covers communications by or to the agents of clients and lawyers. We will consider the scope of the privilege in the context of organizational clients below. For the moment, it suffices to note that the purpose of extending the privilege to communications by or to agents is the same as for granting the privilege to clients and lawyers themselves: it facilitates communication and the provision of legal advice. Thus, a communication by the secretary, bookkeeper, accountant, or literary agent of an individual client to the secretary, paralegal, or associate of a lawyer is protected as an attorney-client communication.

The reason why it matters whether a party to a communication is an agent of the client or the lawyer is related to the requirement that communications must occur in circumstances in which the client and the lawyer reasonably expect confidentiality. If a client confesses to a murder in a crowded elevator in which her lawyer and ten other people hear the confession, the communication is not privileged.

PROBLEM 7–5

Consider a communication between an individual client and her lawyer that occurs in a room in which the client's best friend and the lawyer's summer associate are the only two other people present. Absent some reason to believe that the client's friend is her agent for purposes of obtaining legal advice, the presence of the friend will prevent the communication from being privileged because it destroys the expectation of confidentiality. What about the summer associate? What about a law student who was there only for a day to shadow her lawyer mentor?

3. FOR THE PURPOSE OF OBTAINING LEGAL ADVICE

Not every communication with a lawyer is privileged. The crucial question is whether the communication was for the purpose of obtaining or providing legal advice. Casual conversation is not privileged if it is not in connection with obtaining legal advice. And if a lawyer is not acting as a lawyer, but instead as a business advisor, the communications are not privileged. But, conversely, it is not necessary that the lawyer have been formally retained. Creation of a formal attorney-client relationship is not determinative of whether a person communicated with a lawyer to obtain legal advice. It is important for lawyers to be clear when they are acting as a lawyer rather than in some other capacity.

PROBLEM 7–6

After a short, mildly successful career as an actor, Alicia became a lawyer. She remains well connected to her old friends in the entertainment business and hopes to build a practice representing actors and writers as a talent agent. A talent agent proposes clients for jobs, negotiates with producers over the terms of employment, and, occasionally, drafts clients' contracts. Some talent agents are lawyers, but many are not. What arguments can you make about whether some or all of Alicia's conversations with her clients are privileged?

4. COMPELLED DISCLOSURE BY A TRIBUNAL

The attorney-client privilege is a rule of evidence. Like all other rules of evidence, it governs what use may be made of evidence in tribunals. And, like all other rules of evidence, it is enforced only by tribunals. The attorney-client privilege does not prevent a lawyer from voluntarily revealing a confidential communication in casual conversation or to a government agency. The duty of confidentiality (covered below in Chapter 9), however, does.

PROBLEM 7–7

You are negotiating a lease for a client. Another party to the transaction asks what is the most your client is willing to pay. You say you'd rather not answer, and the other party becomes irritated and accuses you of bad faith in negotiations. Seeking to mollify the person, can you explain that the attorney-client privilege prevents you from disclosing what your client told you about his bottom line position?[7]

5. PRIVILEGE IS THE CLIENT'S

The attorney-client privilege exists for the benefit of clients, not lawyers. Although the lawyer has a duty to guard the confidentiality of communications, if the client wishes to disclose a privileged communication, the lawyer cannot stop him (even if, for example, the communication is embarrassing to the lawyer).

6. PRIVILEGE AFTER THE DEATH OF THE CLIENT

As we saw in Problems 7–1 and 7–2, the duty of confidentiality continues after the death of the client and, generally, so does the attorney-client privilege. If the purpose of the privilege is to induce client candor, one could imagine some clients being concerned about protecting their own reputation or that of their family and friends even after their death. Yet, it also seems intuitively appealing that if the communication remains of interest after the client's death, the interests of the living should outweigh the interests of the dead and the privilege should therefore terminate at the client's death. A number of cases presenting wrenching dilemmas have attempted to delineate when the privilege terminates after the death of the client. These cases are worth considering perhaps less for learning the minutiae of the law and more for what they reveal about the purposes of the attorney-client privilege.

In _Swidler & Berlin v. United States_, 524 U.S. 399 (1998), the Supreme Court held the attorney-client privilege survives the death of the client in a case arising out of the Office of Independent Counsel's investigation of the investments of President Clinton and Hillary Rodham Clinton in an Arkansas real estate venture known as Whitewater. The Independent Counsel investigation expanded to include alleged improprieties in the termination of some White House travel office employees and, eventually, to the President's personal relationship with a

---

7   The answer is no, because no tribunal is attempting to compel disclosure. However, the duty of confidentiality does cover confidential information about your client's position, although you could reveal it if either your client consents or you reasonably believe it is impliedly authorized by your client in order to get the lease.

White House intern. The Independent Counsel sought to obtain notes of conversations between a White House lawyer Vincent Foster and Foster's own lawyer when Foster sought legal advice concerning the Independent Counsel's investigation of the firing of the travel agents. Foster committed suicide shortly after consulting his lawyer. The appeals court held that the privilege did not survive Foster's death, noting that courts sometimes allow lawyers to testify about what their deceased clients said about the meaning of a will that the lawyer drafted. (This is the so-called "testamentary exception.") The court of appeals ruled that the interest in determining whether a crime occurred outweighed the policies justifying the privilege, and opined that clients might not care enough about their reputation after death to make them reluctant to confide in their lawyers for fear of what the lawyer would say after they die. The Supreme Court reversed. The Court reasoned that the arguments against the survival of the privilege, at least on the facts of the Foster case, were speculative because too little is known about whether posthumous termination of the privilege would diminish a client's willingness to confide in the lawyer. In a concurring opinion, Justice O'Connor, joined by Justices Scalia and Thomas, stated that "a criminal defendant's right to exculpatory evidence or a compelling law enforcement need for information may, where the testimony is not available from other sources, override a client's posthumous interest in confidentiality."

What are the arguments for allowing a lawyer to testify about a deceased client's intent in drafting a will? Are they more or less compelling than allowing lawyers to testify about deceased clients' confessions to a crime for which another had been convicted? And what about confidences that might be relevant to the investigation of Bill (and Hillary) Clinton for a dubious real estate investment, for alleged misconduct in firing White House employees, and, in the case of Bill Clinton, for alleged sexual harassment of a White House intern? Do you believe that the possibility of posthumous revelation of confidences would make clients reluctant to talk to lawyers? If you find the O'Connor approach in the Foster case appealing, how would you define the scope of the exception? What is a "compelling law enforcement need" for privileged information?

PROBLEM 7–8

Macumber was being tried for two murders. His lawyer attempted to call as witnesses two lawyers who had represented a man who had been convicted of another murder that occurred in the same vicinity as the two murders of which Macumber was accused. Their client had confessed, before his death, to the two murders for which Macumber was being tried. The two lawyers sought and received an ethics opinion from the Arizona State Bar that they could disclose their client's confession to the defense, to the prosecution, and to the court in Macumber's case. The Arizona Supreme Court held that the trial court properly excluded their testimony, but did not provide reasons. *State of Arizona v. Macumber*, 544 P.2d 1084 (Ariz. 1976). What reasons can you supply for excluding the lawyers' testimony or for allowing it?

PROBLEM 7–9

Charles Stuart was suspected in the deaths of Carol Stuart and Christopher Stuart. Charles spoke for two hours with his lawyer and, the next day, committed suicide. The prosecution wished to compel the lawyer to testify before the grand jury about Charles' conversation with him. The Massachusetts Supreme Judicial Court refused to allow the testimony. *Matter of John Doe Grand Jury Investigation*, 562 N.E.2d 69 (Mass. 1990). Why do you suppose other members of the Stuart family would or would not want the lawyer to testify about what Charles said? Should it matter whether the dead person had an incentive to make a false confession? Should admissibility turn on whether the lawyer for the dead person has an incentive to lie about the alleged confession? Should nature of the relationship between the client and the victims matter? Should the court consider the wishes of the survivors of either the victims or the alleged perpetrator(s)?

PROBLEM 7–10

Miller suffered arsenic poisoning after visiting a bowling alley, but he recovered. A few days later, while he was at home under the care of his wife, Miller died of arsenic poisoning. Police found evidence that Miller's wife was having an affair with Willard, who had given Miller a glass of beer at the bowling alley. After Miller's death, Willard consulted a lawyer. Several days later, Willard committed suicide, leaving a will naming his wife as the beneficiary. In an investigation of Mrs. Miller for the murder of her husband, the state moved for an order requiring Willard's lawyer to testify about what Willard had said to him about the Miller case. Should the lawyer be forced to testify? *In re Miller*, 584 S.E.2d 772 (N.C. 2003), held that attorney-client privilege survives death of client but the North Carolina Supreme Court remanded the case to the trial court with instructions to require the lawyer to write an affidavit, which would be read by the trial court but no one else, describing Willard's communications with his lawyer. The trial court should determine whether the communications "relate to the interests, rights, activities, motives, liabilities, or plans of some third party, the disclosure of which would not tend to harm the client," and whether the client communicated with the attorney "for a proper purpose." The court explained:

> While communications concerning the client's own criminal culpability and his defense is certainly privileged, it is difficult to fathom how any communications relating to a third party's criminal

activity, concealment thereof or obstruction of justice could fall within such category, when disclosure thereof would not tend to harm the client. The concept of "proper purpose" relates not only to whether the communications involve the client's future illegal activity, obstruction of justice or activity directly or indirectly aiding a third party in some illegal activity, but it also relates only to communications that would properly benefit the client as opposed to a third party.

Because Willard is dead, in what ways could he be harmed by revealing what he said about Mrs. Miller poisoning her husband? Should it matter whether the Miller children or other survivors could sue Willard's estate for damages for his involvement in the attempt to poison Mr. Miller at the bowling alley?

NOTES ON THE ELEMENTS OF THE ATTORNEY-CLIENT PRIVILEGE

1. *An Absolute or a Qualified Privilege?* Do the policies underlying the attorney-client privilege justify an absolute privilege? Why not instead qualify the privilege so that it could be overridden in cases of compelling need for the information? If you believe the privilege should be overridden in cases of compelling need, how would you define which needs are compelling?

2. *The Terrorism Exception.* After September 11, 2001, the United States Department of Justice changed its policy about attorney-client privilege for prison inmates suspected of being terrorists. A new regulation governing federal prisons provides that if a federal law enforcement or intelligence agency has "reasonable suspicion" that "a particular inmate may use communications with attorneys or their agents to further or facilitate acts of terrorism, the Director, Bureau of Prisons, shall provide appropriate procedures for the monitoring or review of communications between that inmate and attorneys or attorneys' agents who are traditionally covered by the attorney-client privilege." The regulation requires written notice to the inmate and attorneys involved that all communications between them will be monitored and are not protected by the attorney-client privilege. 28 C.F.R. § 501.3(d). Is this regulation a desirable incursion on the attorney-client privilege? Would your analysis differ as to the portion of the same regulation that allows secret taping without notification to the lawyer or the inmate upon approval of a federal judge?

3. *What Is a Compelling Need for Disclosure?* Is exoneration of an innocent person convicted of a crime sufficiently compelling to create an exception to the attorney-client privilege? Is prevention of a future crime a compelling need? How likely must it be that the revelation of the confidential communication will exonerate a person or prevent a crime before a court may order disclosure?

D. WAIVER OF ATTORNEY-CLIENT PRIVILEGE

If a client or a lawyer acting on behalf of a client reveals a privileged communication to third parties, the privilege is waived as to that communication. The privilege may also be waived as to communications relating to it. For example, if a client reveals an attorney's email to her, the email from the client to which the attorney responded may lose its privilege. One of the most frequently litigated issues about the attorney-client privilege is whether some actions of either the client or the lawyer resulted in a waiver of the privilege and, if so, how broadly the waiver extends. If the client deliberately chooses to reveal to others what she told her lawyer, the client waives the privilege. Because the privilege is a barrier to uncovering the truth, it is easy to see why courts have been reluctant to allow litigants to assert privilege to selectively control which aspects of the truth will be revealed on the same subject matter.

Three important but distinct issues often arise in the analysis of waiver. One is whether a waiver of the privilege as to some aspects of a communication or series of communications waives the privilege as to the rest of the communication or, more broadly, waives the privilege as to all documents or communications concerning the same subject matter. The second is whether the waiver of the privilege in one forum or vis-à-vis one litigant waives the privilege in other fora or in disputes with other litigants. The third is whether an inadvertent disclosure waives the privilege.

Waiver of Attorney-Client Privilege

- **Waiver**: if a client or lawyer acting on behalf of a client reveals a privileged communication, the privilege is waived as to that communication.

- **Deliberate partial waiver**: deliberate disclosure of some of a client's communications waives privilege regarding other communications relating to same matter.

- **Deliberate limited waiver**: deliberate disclosure of communications in one proceeding or to one entity waives the privilege vis a vis other proceedings or entities regarding an undisclosed communication on the same matter or the same communication if the communications concern the same subject matter and ought in fairness to be considered together.

- **Inadvertent waiver:** inadvertent disclosure of privileged communication does not waive privilege if the lawyer made reasonable efforts to prevent inadvertent disclosure and to rectify the error by notifying others of privileged status and seeking to recover it.

Deliberate partial waiver. Suppose the client consults a lawyer for assistance in selling her house. If the Internal Revenue Service prosecutes the client for failing to pay taxes on the proceeds of the sale, and the client resists payment of penalties on the ground that she relied on advice of counsel that the income was not taxable, the client waives the privilege about the tax advice. Now imagine that the buyer of the house sues the client for fraud in the sale and seeks information about what the client told the lawyer for purposes of proving that the client knowingly misled her about a defect in the house. Disclosure of some information in the client's communications with the lawyer may waive the privilege as to all the information in the advice regarding the transaction, especially if a court concludes that the failure to pay tax is part of the same scheme as the fraud on the buyer.

The issue of partial waiver arose in the litigation against tobacco companies over whether they misled consumers about the harmful properties of cigarettes. Tobacco companies, acting through their lawyers, had commissioned scientific studies of the effects of nicotine and other substances in their products. The tobacco company lawyers released to the public those studies showing mild or no negative health effects and withheld those studies showing harmful effects. Because the results of the studies were communicated by clients to lawyers for purposes of legal advice about litigation and regulatory proceedings, the communications regarding the studies were arguably covered by attorney-client privilege.

Some courts concluded that disclosure of some of the studies waived privilege as to other studies, reasoning that the lawyers and clients intended to mislead adversaries and the court about the facts.[8]

Deliberate limited waiver. Disclosure of privileged documents to some entities for some purposes while attempting to retain privilege as to other uses is known as limited waiver. The Department of Justice and other prosecutors often seek to induce companies that are being investigated for white collar crime and other alleged legal violations to provide the government with all documents relating to the companies' internal investigations of the matter in exchange for a promise of leniency in prosecution or sentencing. Some companies give privileged documents to the criminal prosecutor or regulatory agency in an effort to persuade the government to refrain from instituting any criminal or civil proceeding. Courts have disagreed over whether revealing the documents to the government waives the privilege against later use of the documents in litigation brought by non-governmental plaintiffs.[9] Federal Rule of Evidence 502, which governs attorney-client privilege in federal courts, was amended in 2008 to provide that "When the disclosure is made in a federal proceeding or to a federal office or agency and waives the attorney-client privilege, the waiver extends to an undisclosed communication or information in a federal or state proceeding only if: (1) the waiver is intentional; (2) the disclosed and undisclosed communications or information concern the same subject matter; and (3) they ought in fairness to be considered together."

Inadvertent waiver. A third frequently litigated issue about attorney-client privilege is whether inadvertent disclosure of privileged communications waives the privilege. Lawyers have accidentally left privileged documents in plain view on a table at a deposition or in court, have accidentally included privileged documents in boxes of materials delivered to opposing parties in pretrial discovery, and have accidentally sent a privileged document to the wrong fax number or the wrong email address. Courts have disagreed about whether inadvertent disclosure constitutes a waiver. Most courts find no waiver if the lawyer made reasonable efforts to prevent inadvertent disclosure and to rectify the error by notifying others of privileged status and seeking to recover it. As

---

[8] *See, e.g.*, Michael V. Ciresi, Roberta B. Walburn, & Tara D. Sutton, *Decades of Deceit: Document Discovery in the Minnesota Tobacco Litigation*, 25 WM. MITCHELL L. REV. 477, 499, 508 (1999) (describing the long-running effort of the Minnesota Attorney General and lawyers representing plaintiffs injured by tobacco products to force tobacco companies to produce evidence showing they knew of risks of tobacco); Alison Frankel, *Stubbing Out the Privilege*, AM. LAW., June 1998; Rex Bossert, *A Splintered Privilege: Two Judges Have Taken Exception to Tobacco's Confidentiality Claims*, NAT'L L.J., Apr. 7, 1997, at A1.

[9] *Compare* Diversified Indus. v. Meredith, 572 F.2d 596 (8th Cir. 1977) (en banc) (privilege not waived), *with In re* Columbia/HCA Healthcare Corp. Billing Practices Litig., 293 F.3d 289 (6th Cir. 2002), *and In re* Qwest Commc'ns Int'l, Inc., 450 F.3d 1179 (10th Cir. 2006) (privilege waived).

a consequence, many lawyers include in every email message and fax cover sheet a statement advising that if an email or fax message containing privileged material is sent to the wrong recipient, the recipient should delete the message and any attachments and notify the sender immediately. The 2008 amendment to Federal Rule of Evidence 502 allows litigants to "claw-back" inadvertently disclosed documents if they took "reasonable steps to prevent disclosure" and "promptly took reasonable steps to rectify the error." Can you see why lawyers' email messages now routinely contain advisories about privilege?

E. SUMMARY

Crucial aspects of the attorney-client relationship are the lawyer's duty to guard the confidentiality of all information concerning the client under Model Rule 1.6 and the evidentiary privilege against compelled disclosure of attorney-client communication. Subject to exceptions we will cover in Chapter 9, Model Rule 1.6 prohibits a lawyer from revealing, except where compelled by law, as necessary to carry out the representation, or with client consent, *all* confidential information relating to the representation of a client. The attorney-client privilege is narrower in scope; it protects only against compelled disclosure by a tribunal, and it covers only communications between lawyer and client. Although the privilege applies only to tribunal-compelled disclosure, because the protections of the privilege are waived by disclosure, attorneys consider it important to treat confidential communications with care in order to avoid waiving the privilege.

Model Rule 1.6 and the attorney-client privilege erect a barrier to the discovery of the truth that lawyers consider to be justified by the need to promote complete and honest disclosure by clients in order to provide effective legal advice. But critics of the law of confidentiality question whether confidentiality is in fact necessary to promote client candor. Some doubt whether clients indeed use confidentiality in order to comply with law and instead think lawyers and clients often use confidentiality strategically to enable sophisticated clients to violate law and to save attorneys from having to report illegal conduct of which they are aware and which prompt reporting could prevent.

CHAPTER 8

THE ATTORNEY-CLIENT PRIVILEGE OF ORGANIZATIONAL CLIENTS AND EXCEPTIONS TO THE PRIVILEGE

■ ■ ■

A. INTRODUCTION

In this chapter, we examine some major controversies over the scope of the attorney-client privilege. We begin by studying how the privilege applies to organizations. Although the law is settled that organizational clients are entitled to the attorney-client privilege just as individual clients are, the justifications for extending the privilege to organizations are not obvious. If the principal justification for creating the privilege is to encourage clients to seek legal advice in order to conform their conduct to law, and to be candid with their lawyers when doing so, consider whether corporations would be hesitant to obtain legal advice if there were no privilege, and whether corporate employees who speak to the corporation's lawyer would be candid without the privilege, or even with it. The issue of organizational privilege is particularly complicated as a practical matter when, as is often the case, a lawyer represents both an organization and one or more of its employees. In such cases, the interests of the organization and the employee may not be completely aligned, particularly if the corporation is accused of wrongdoing in which the employee is alleged to have played a part, and the question who can invoke the privilege becomes difficult. At the end of the chapter we consider the exceptions to the attorney-client privilege.

B. THE ATTORNEY-CLIENT PRIVILEGE OF ORGANIZATIONS

The Organization as a Client and the Attorney-Client Privilege

A lawyer employed or retained by an organization represents the organization. Unless the lawyer for an organization agrees to represent a constituent of the organization (such as an employee, officer, director, or shareholder), the lawyer represents only the organization and not the constituent.

When a constituent of an organization communicates in confidence with the organization's lawyer concerning matters within the scope of the constituent's duties, the communication is protected by Model Rule 1.6 (governing confidentiality) and by the organization's attorney-client privilege.

Unless the lawyer for the organization represents both the organization and the constituent, the constituent cannot prevent communications between the constituent and the lawyer from being used or revealed by the organization or the lawyer. If the organization is the client, the duty of confidentiality and the attorney-client privilege apply to the organization, not the constituent.

When a client is an organization, including a corporation, a question arises about which organizational employees' communications count as the client's. The Model Rule states that the privilege is the client's, and the client is "the organization acting through its duly authorized constituents." Model Rule 1.13(a). But the rule does not say whose communications count as the client's when the client is a corporation. The following case addresses that issue.

UPJOHN CO. V. UNITED STATES
United States Supreme Court
449 U.S. 383 (1981)

JUSTICE REHNQUIST delivered the opinion of the Court:

Upjohn Co. manufactures and sells pharmaceuticals here and abroad. In January 1976 independent accountants conducting an audit of one of Upjohn's foreign subsidiaries discovered that the subsidiary made payments to or for the benefit of foreign government officials in order to secure government business. The accountants so informed Mr. Gerard Thomas, Upjohn's Vice President and General Counsel. It was decided that the company would conduct an internal investigation of what were termed "questionable payments." As part of this investigation the attorneys prepared a letter containing a questionnaire which was sent to "All Foreign General and Area Managers" over the Chairman's signature.

The letter [and questionnaire noted] recent disclosures that several American companies made "possibly illegal" payments to foreign government officials and emphasized that the management needed full information concerning any such payments made by Upjohn. The letter indicated that [Upjohn's attorneys had decided] "to conduct an investigation for the purpose of determining the nature and magnitude of any payments made by the Upjohn Company or any of its subsidiaries to any employee or official of a foreign government." The questionnaire sought detailed information concerning such payments.

[T]he Internal Revenue Service began an investigation to determine the tax consequences of the payments. The Service issued a summons demanding production of "All files relative to the investigation conducted under the supervision of Gerard Thomas to identify payments to employees of foreign governments and any political contributions made by the Upjohn Company or any of its affiliates since January 1, 1971 and to determine whether any funds of the Upjohn Company had been improperly accounted for on the corporate books during the same period."

The company declined to produce the documents on the grounds that they were protected from disclosure by the attorney-client privilege.

The attorney-client privilege is the oldest of the privileges for confidential communications known to the common law. Its purpose is to encourage full and frank communication between attorneys and their clients and thereby promote broader public interests in the observance of law and administration of justice. The privilege recognizes that sound legal advice or advocacy serves public ends and that such advice or advocacy depends upon the lawyer's being fully informed by the client.

The Court of Appeals [held that, when the client is a corporation, the attorney-client privilege applied only to communications with the "control group" of the corporation. The Court of Appeals reasoned that,] the client was an inanimate entity and only the senior management, guiding and integrating the several operations, can be said to possess an identity analogous to the corporation as a whole.

Such a view, we think, overlooks the fact that the privilege exists to protect not only the giving of professional advice to those who can act on it but also the giving of information to the lawyer to enable him to give sound and informed advice. The first step in the resolution of any legal problem is ascertaining the factual background and sifting through the facts with an eye to the legally relevant.

In the case of the individual client the provider of information and the person who acts on the lawyer's advice are one and the same. In the corporate context, however, it will frequently be employees beyond the control group as defined by the court below—officers and agents responsible for directing the company's actions in response to legal advice—who will possess the information needed by the corporation's lawyers. Middle-level—and indeed lower-level—employees can, by actions within the scope of their employment, embroil the corporation in serious legal difficulties, and it is only natural that these employees would have the relevant information needed by corporate counsel if he is adequately to advise the client with respect to such actual or potential difficulties.

The control group test adopted by the court below thus frustrates the very purpose of the privilege by discouraging the communication of relevant information by employees of the client to attorneys seeking to render legal advice to the client corporation. The attorney's advice will also frequently be more significant to noncontrol group members than to those who officially sanction the advice, and the control group test makes it more difficult to convey full and frank legal advice to the employees who will put into effect the client corporation's policy.

The narrow scope given the attorney-client privilege by the court below not only makes it difficult for corporate attorneys to formulate sound advice when their client is faced with a specific legal problem but also threatens to limit the valuable efforts of corporate counsel to ensure their client's compliance with the law. In light of the vast and complicated array of regulatory legislation confronting the modern corporation, corporations, unlike most individuals, constantly go to lawyers to find out how to obey the law.[2]

The communications at issue were made by Upjohn employees[3] to counsel for Upjohn acting as such, at the direction of corporate superiors in order to secure legal advice from counsel. Information, not available from upper-echelon management, was needed to supply a basis for legal advice concerning compliance with securities and tax laws, foreign laws, currency regulations, duties to shareholders, and potential litigation in each of these areas. The communications concerned matters within the scope of the employees' corporate duties, and the employees themselves were sufficiently aware that they were being questioned in order that the corporation could obtain legal advice.

---

[2] The Government argues that the risk of civil or criminal liability suffices to ensure that corporations will seek legal advice in the absence of the protection of the privilege. This response ignores the fact that the depth and quality of any investigations, to ensure compliance with the law would suffer, even were they undertaken. The response also proves too much, since it applies to all communications covered by the privilege: an individual trying to comply with the law or faced with a legal problem also has strong incentive to disclose information to his lawyer, yet the common law has recognized the value of the privilege in further facilitating communications.

[3] Seven of the eighty-six employees interviewed by counsel had terminated their employment with Upjohn at the time of the interview. Petitioners argue that the privilege should nonetheless apply to communications by these former employees concerning activities during their period of employment. Neither the District Court nor the Court of Appeals had occasion to address this issue, and we decline to decide it without the benefit of treatment below.

The Court of Appeals declined to extend the attorney-client privilege beyond the limits of the control group test for fear that doing so would entail severe burdens on discovery and create a broad "zone of silence" over corporate affairs. Application of the attorney-client privilege to communications such as those involved here, however, puts the adversary in no worse position than if the communications had never taken place. The privilege only protects disclosure of communications; it does not protect disclosure of the underlying facts by those who communicated with the attorney.

Here the Government was free to question the employees who communicated with Thomas and outside counsel. Upjohn has provided the IRS with a list of such employees, and the IRS has already interviewed some 25 of them. While it would probably be more convenient for the Government to secure the results of petitioner's internal investigation by simply subpoenaing the questionnaires and notes taken by petitioner's attorneys, such considerations of convenience do not overcome the policies served by the attorney-client privilege. As Justice Jackson noted in his concurring opinion in *Hickman v. Taylor*, 329 U.S. 495 (1947), "Discovery was hardly intended to enable a learned profession to perform its functions on wits borrowed from the adversary."

NOTES ON UPJOHN

1. ***Justifications for Extending the Privilege to Organizations.*** Why should corporations be entitled to the attorney-client privilege? Are you persuaded by the justification offered by the Court and its response to the argument in the Court's footnote 2?

2. ***The Control Group Test vs. the Scope of Employment Test.*** What justifications does the Court offer for its broad interpretation of the corporate attorney-client privilege? What are the advantages and disadvantages of the broad privilege adopted by the Court in *Upjohn* as compared to the narrower control group rule it rejected? Would a narrower rule change the way that employees behave? Would it change the way lawyers for the corporation behave?

3. ***Former Employees?*** As explained in the Court's footnote 3, several of the people questioned by Upjohn's general counsel were no longer employees of the company at the time of the interview. The Court did not decide whether the attorney-client privilege would extend to their communications, although a number of courts have held that communications with the client's former employees are privileged. *See Admiral Ins. Co. v. United States*, 881 F.2d 1486 (9th Cir. 1989). What are the arguments for and against extending the corporation's privilege to communications with former employees? Note that the Court identifies the scope of the privilege in the employees' statements as covering their activities during their period of employment. If the Court's principal

justification for the privilege is that it will enable corporations to comply with the law prospectively, how will communications of *former* employees concerning their past actions serve that goal?

C. PRIVILEGE AND THE PROBLEM OF DUAL REPRESENTATION

Topic Overview

Subject to conflict of interest rules we will cover in Part IV, a lawyer who represents an organization may undertake to represent a constituent of the organization as well. If the lawyer represents both, then both clients can have some control over the use of confidential communications and information. If the lawyer represents only the organization, however, the lawyer should advise constituents with whom she speaks that the client is the organization and that the communications or other confidential information the constituent provides to the lawyer may be used or revealed at the option of the organization, including for purposes that will harm the constituent. The issues of confidentiality, privilege and dual representation are complex and difficult for lawyers who need to build relationships of trust and candor with the client's officers and employees but who must also act in the interest of the organization, not necessarily in the interest of the officers and employees.

When employees of a corporation communicate with company lawyers, the corporation (which is the client) is entitled to claim or to waive the privilege as to their communications. The corporation could also decide, based on the employees' answers, to fire the employees, to report them to the government for criminal prosecution, or to take whatever other action against them that it deems appropriate. Given that, what advice would you offer to an employee who is asked to discuss possible corporate wrongdoing with the corporation's lawyers? What impact, if any, should the employees' interests and incentives have on the scope of the corporate attorney-client privilege?

Model Rule 1.13(f) imposes obligations on a corporation's lawyer investigating suspected wrongdoing by a corporate employee. Indeed, Rule 1.13(f) applies whenever the employee's and the organization's interest might be adverse and where the employee might not recognize the adversity. The lawyer must warn any organizational client employee when the client's interests are adverse to the employee's interest and remind the employee that the lawyer represents the organization, not the employee with whom the lawyer wants to talk about the suspected wrongdoing. This is sometimes known as an *Upjohn* warning.

Confidentiality and Conflicting Interests in Organizations

A lawyer employed or retained by an organization represents the organization acting through its duly authorized constituents. (MR 1.13)

In dealing with an organization's directors, officers, employees, members, shareholders or other constituents, a lawyer shall explain the identity of the client when the lawyer knows or reasonably should know that the organization's interests are adverse to those of the constituents with whom the lawyer is dealing. (MR 1.13(f))

What effect do you imagine compliance with MR 1.13(f) will have on the willingness of an employee to speak candidly with counsel for the corporation? Should your answer to that question have any bearing on whether the attorney-client privilege should extend to all corporate employees acting within the scope of their employment as determined in *Upjohn*?

These questions are addressed in the following case. To understand the case, it helps to understand the nature of stock options. To divide ownership of a company, the company will sell shares, also called stock. A person who owns shares in a company can sell those shares to other people or back to the company at the market price. A stock option is an option to buy stock in a company at a future date (the vesting date) at a set price (the strike price or exercise price), and are valuable to the extent that the strike price is less than the market price. A number of companies compensate their executives handsomely, some say extravagantly, in a combination of cash and stock options. Stock options are not, by themselves, an objectionable form of compensation, as they provide incentives to increase the value of the company—and the value of stock—through wise management and innovation. But senior executives at many companies, including Broadcom (as we see in the case that follows), negotiated for valuation systems for the options that made their options worth more simply by changing the date on which they were deemed to have been granted in order to maximize the difference between the price the employee must pay to purchase the stock from the company and the price at which the employee can sell it. If the strike price is very low, the option is more valuable. This practice was known as backdating. The executive and the company would agree to treat the stock options as if they had been granted on a date when the share price, and thus the strike price, was at its lowest during a given period in order to maximize the difference between the strike price and the current market price. Backdating was not itself illegal, provided that the benefit to the employees is recorded on the corporate books as a non-cash compensation expense to the corporation.[1]

UNITED STATES V. RUEHLE

United States Court of Appeals for the Ninth Circuit
583 F.3d 600 (9th Cir. 2009)

In March 2006, the *Wall Street Journal* published the first of a series of articles called "The Perfect Payday," which suggested that a number of public companies were backdating stock options granted to their employees. Shortly thereafter, in mid-May 2006, an investor rights group publicly identified Broadcom as one of the corporations that appeared to have engaged in backdating. As a result of the media attention and in anticipation of an inquiry from the Securities and Exchange Commission ("SEC"), Broadcom's Board of Directors and company management decided to bring in outside counsel to commence an internal review [which it called the "Equity Review"] of the company's current and past stock option granting practices. [William J.] Ruehle, as Broadcom's CFO, was among those intimately involved in that decision from the outset. On May 18, 2006, Broadcom's Audit Committee engaged Irell [& Manella], a private law firm with which it had longstanding ties, to conduct the Equity Review by investigating the propriety of the measurement dates utilized by Broadcom in its option granting process and identifying those grants which failed to meet the measurement date requirements of generally accepted accounting principles. Irell immediately commenced its review, which entailed collecting corporate documents and records and conducting interviews with past and current Broadcom employees.

Broadcom representatives, including Ruehle, met with Irell lawyers on May 24 and 25, 2006, to discuss the scope of the Equity Review. It was agreed that Irell would report the results of its inquiries to the Audit Committee. It was also decided that the Board would not appoint a panel of independent, outside directors to oversee the Equity Review. On May 26, 2006, a formal meeting of the Audit Committee was convened. Ruehle and other senior Broadcom executives, several members of the Board, and Irell lawyers were among those present. During the hour-long meeting, Irell partner David Siegel explained the nature of typical "backdating" investigations and discussed the status of Irell's internal review, including the necessary involvement of Broadcom's outside independent auditors, Ernst & Young LLP, who would have to review and opine on the accuracy of the company's audited financial statements and regulatory filings. Siegel also cautioned "that Irell can handle issues related to the proper accounting for option grants but that if an issue of self-dealing or

---

[1]   Charles Forelle and James Bandler, *The Perfect Payday—Some CEOs Reap Millions by Landing Stock Options When They Are Most Valuable; Luck—or Something Else?*, WALL ST. J., Mar. 18, 2006, at A1.

management or Board integrity arose, a special committee of independent directors would need to be appointed and special independent counsel engaged to conduct that inquiry." The Audit Committee and other representatives of Broadcom made clear that the intent was to turn over the information obtained through the Equity Review to the auditors, to fully cooperate with government regulators, and, if necessary, to self-report any problems with Broadcom's financial statements.

As many within Broadcom had anticipated, civil lawsuits soon followed the media reports about the company's back-dating of stock options. [The suits] alleged wrongdoing in relation to Broadcom's stock option granting practices; both suits named Broadcom and also personally named Ruehle, among other Broadcom officers and directors, as an individual defendant.

[Irell lawyers had a number of conversations with Ruehle during June 2006 about Broadcom's stock option granting practices and his role as the company's CFO. Irell attorneys testified that they provided Ruehle a so-called *Upjohn* or corporate *Miranda* warning informing him that the corporate lawyers do not represent the individual employee; that anything said by the employee to the lawyers will be protected by the company's attorney-client privilege subject to waiver of the privilege in the sole discretion of the company; and that the individual may wish to consult with his own attorney if he has any concerns about his own potential legal exposure. Ruehle testified that he did not recall receiving any such warnings. The district court disbelieved the Irell lawyers who took no notes nor memorialized their conversation on this issue in writing, and it apparently credited Ruehle's testimony that no such warnings were given. The court of appeals accepted the district court's finding on this. Nevertheless, the court of appeals remarked that Ruehle never indicated to the lawyers that he was seeking legal advice in his individual capacity. This suit concerns statements Ruehle made to the Irell lawyers about his role in the backdating scandal that Broadcom directed Irell to disclose to Broadcom's outside auditors, Ernst & Young, as well as to the Securities and Exchange Commission ("SEC") and the United States Attorney's Office (the "Government"). Prior to making these disclosures, Irell never obtained Mr. Ruehle's consent.]

In late June 2006, Irell advised Ruehle to secure independent counsel with respect to the investigations and the pending civil suits. Ruehle retained the law firm Wilson Sonsini Goodrich & Rosati to represent him individually. Nevertheless, Ruehle remained heavily involved in the company's internal review and he was privy to Irell's reports to the Audit Committee of its findings and ultimately the disclosures of the information gathered by Irell to Ernst & Young.

[The district court held that "Ruehle reasonably believed that the Irell lawyers were meeting with him as his personal lawyers, not just Broadcom's lawyers. Mr. Ruehle had a legitimate expectation that whatever he said to the Irell lawyers would be maintained in confidence. He was never told, nor did he ever contemplate, that his statements to the Irell lawyers would be disclosed to third parties, especially not the Government in connection with criminal charges against him. Irell had no right to disclose Mr. Ruehle's statements, and Irell breached its duty of loyalty when it did so. Accordingly, the Court must suppress all evidence reflecting Mr. Ruehle's statements to the Irell lawyers regarding stock option granting practices at Broadcom." The court of appeals reversed.]

Ruehle's statements to the Irell attorneys were not "made in confidence" but rather for the purpose of disclosure to the outside auditors. That he might regret those statements after later learning of the subsequent corporate disclosure to law enforcement officials is not material to the privilege determination as of June 2006.

The notion that Ruehle spoke with Irell attorneys Heitz and Lefler with the reasonable belief that his statements were confidential is unsupported by the record. Of particular significance is what was said in the meetings he attended prior to June 1, 2006, with Irell attorneys, company management, and the Audit Committee, as acknowledged in Ruehle's own testimony. He frankly admitted that he understood the fruits of Irell's searching inquiries would be disclosed to Ernst & Young in order to convince the independent auditors of the integrity of Broadcom's financial statements to the public, or to take appropriate accounting measures to rectify any misleading reports.

Ruehle was no ordinary Broadcom employee. He served as the public company's CFO—the senior corporate executive charged with primary responsibility for Broadcom's financial affairs. This was a sophisticated corporate enterprise with billions of dollars in sales worldwide, aided by accountants, lawyers, and advisors entrusted with meeting a multitude of regulatory obligations. The duties undertaken by Ruehle broadly encompassed not only accurately and completely reporting the company's historical and current stock option granting practices, but also Broadcom's strict compliance with reporting and record keeping requirements imposed through the Securities Exchange Act of 1934 and the Sarbanes-Oxley Act of 2002, among many other federal and state rules and regulations. As the head of finance, Ruehle cannot now credibly claim ignorance of the general disclosure requirements imposed on a publicly traded company with respect to its outside auditors or the need to truthfully report corporate information to the SEC.

Ruehle was also intimately involved in all aspects of the Equity Review, including the planning, investigatory, and disclosure stages.

Ruehle was a full participant in the initial May 2006 meetings with the Irell attorneys where the scope of representation and the details of the Equity Review were decided and agreed upon, even before convening the formal Audit Committee meeting. From the outset, it was settled and made widely known to senior management that Broadcom intended to fully cooperate with the SEC and the auditors. Ruehle, as the primary contact with Ernst & Young over the years, personally introduced the Irell attorneys to the team of outside auditors. Thereafter, he repeatedly met with the Audit Committee, senior management, the Irell attorneys, and the auditors, and remained fully apprised throughout the summer of 2006 of the status of Irell's investigation and the flow of information.

In his testimony at the evidentiary hearing, Ruehle acknowledged the broad nature of the planned third-party disclosure, noting that Irell was directed, to his knowledge, to freely share "all factual information" gleaned through the Equity Review—whether "good, bad, or ugly."

As Ruehle anticipated when he met with the Irell attorneys in June 2006, the information obtained through the Equity Review, including his input, was passed on to Ernst & Young. He never raised any anxiety about the possible disclosure over what he now claims was intended to be confidential and thus privileged information. Ruehle had ample opportunity to raise any concern he might have harbored. Ruehle not only attended meetings where the Audit Committee directed Irell to disclose to Ernst & Young the fruits of the Equity Review, he was also present at meetings where disclosures to the auditors actually occurred. He did not object. Even after engaging independent counsel to apprise him of his legal rights, Ruehle never claimed that he thought his statements to Irell during the Equity Review, later shared with the auditors, were confidential—until the specter of criminal liability arose in 2008.

Ruehle contends that, notwithstanding his obligation to fully cooperate in Broadcom's internal review, he would not have provided information as part of the Equity Review had he known it could be used in support of a criminal investigation or an SEC enforcement action. The district court [found that] Mr. Ruehle never understood that Irell might disclose statements adverse to Mr. Ruehle's interests to the Government for use in a criminal case against him.

This analysis misses the mark. The salient point from a privilege perspective is that Ruehle readily admits his understanding that all factual information would be communicated to third parties, which undermines his claim of confidentiality to support invoking the privilege. Ruehle's subjective shock and surprise about the subsequent usage of the information he knew would be disclosed to third-party auditors—e.g., information subsequently shared with securities regulators and the

Justice Department now used to support a criminal investigation and his prosecution—is frankly of no consequence here.

Ruehle's argument runs squarely into the settled rule that any voluntary disclosure of information to a third party waives the attorney-client privilege, regardless of whether such disclosure later turns out to be harmful.

NOTES ON RUEHLE

1. ***Sorting Out the Issues.*** *Ruehle* addresses several important issues and resolves them in a manner on which reasonable minds differ (as one would expect, given that the court of appeals reversed a thoughtful district court opinion). It is important to disentangle several issues:

(a) Who Is the Client? Who was/were Irell's client(s) at the time Ruehle spoke to the Irell attorneys? The district court found that Irell represented Ruehle as well as Broadcom, or at least that Ruehle reasonably believed they did. The Ninth Circuit did not overturn that finding, but did state that Ruehle never told Irell that he believed the firm was representing him in his individual capacity. If it was clear that Irell represented only Broadcom, Ruehle would have no basis in law for believing that his statements were privileged as to him. If Irell represented Ruehle as well as Broadcom at the time Ruehle spoke to the Irell lawyers, could he reasonably expect the communications would be privileged and confidential? If it was not clear whether Irell represented Ruehle, what should Irell have done to clarify matters? See Model Rule 1.13(f).

If the Irell lawyers had given Ruehle the *Upjohn* warning as required by Rule 1.13(f), what do you suppose Ruehle would have done?

The Ninth Circuit emphasizes that Ruehle understood at the time he spoke to Irell that the information he provided would be revealed to Ernst & Young, Broadcom's outside auditors, and therefore that the information would be disclosed by Ernst & Young publicly as part of Broadcom's required disclosures to the Securities Exchange Commission and prospective investors. Does that shed light on who the Ninth Circuit believed Irell was representing at the time?

(b) Privilege and Agents of the Lawyer and Client. Statements by or to agents of either the client or the lawyer, or both, are privileged even though they are not, strictly speaking, between just the lawyer and the client. The court holds that Ruehle's statements were not privileged because Ruehle knew they would be revealed to the Audit Committee, including Ernst & Young, a major accounting firm that Broadcom had retained as its independent auditor. The court assumes that everyone expected the Audit Committee to reveal the statements to investors and others because Audit Committees customarily do. If Ernst & Young were hired by either Broadcom or Irell to assist in evaluating the backdating, and it were not clear whether Broadcom intended that Ernst & Young would reveal the information publicly, the fact that the statements were revealed to them would not necessarily mean they are not confidential or that the privilege as to them is waived. What other facts would you need to know about to whom Irell or Broadcom intended the Audit Committee and Ernst & Young to reveal Ruehle's statements in order to determine whether the privilege applies? The court states: "The Audit Committee and other representatives of Broadcom made clear that the intent was to turn over the information obtained through the Equity Review to the auditors, to fully cooperate with government regulators, and, if necessary, to self-report any problems with Broadcom's financial statements." Would your analysis of the privilege change if Broadcom made it clear that it intended the Audit Committee *not* to reveal the information to the government or the public?

(c) *Confidentiality vs. Waiver.* Because the statements were to be revealed to Ernst & Young, the court states both that Ruehle did not reasonably expect the statements to be confidential and that he waived the privilege. Technically, those are two separate issues. If a client makes an easily audible statement to her lawyer in a crowded elevator, the privilege never attaches to the communication because the communication was not confidential when it was made. If a client tells something to a lawyer in confidence but anticipates later making the statement public, the communication is privileged until the client repeats it publicly, which waives the privilege. In some situations, like *Ruehle,* the distinction between a communication never being privileged and a privilege being waived may be difficult to discern on the facts and, in any event, may not matter. In other situations, however, the distinction may matter. For example, if a client makes two statements on unrelated matters in confidence anticipating later revealing one of the statements, the client may be able to argue that it waived the privilege only as to the matter that was revealed, not as to the matter about which nothing was revealed.

2. *Subsequent Disputes Between Two Clients Jointly Represented.* The problem of the scope of the privilege in instances of dual representation of an organizational client and an employee of the organization is related to the problem of the privilege and joint representation of any two clients. When a lawyer represents two clients jointly in the same or related matters (for example, joint venturers in setting up a business, or both Ruehle and Broadcom in the backdating matter), each separate client's privileged communications, although shared with the other client(s), remain privileged with respect to the rest of the world. That means that one co-client cannot waive the privilege of the other with respect to third parties and the act of sharing confidences within the group does not waive the privilege. However, the co-clients cannot invoke the privilege against each other in subsequent litigation between them. Thus, if Broadcom sued Ruehle for fraud, or Ruehle sued Broadcom for

wrongful termination of his employment, neither could prevent the other from using Ruehle's privileged statements in litigation.

3. ***Remedies for Violations of the Duty to Warn.*** In *Ruehle*, the district court found that the Irell lawyers did not provide the *Upjohn* warning required under Model Rule 1.13(f) and the California Rules of Professional Conduct informing Ruehle about whom they represented. If that finding is correct, the Irell lawyers breached their duty. Unfortunately for the employee who makes compromising statements to a lawyer, even though a lawyer breaches a duty in failing to warn, the employee probably has no effective remedy.

D. EXCEPTIONS TO THE ATTORNEY-CLIENT PRIVILEGE

1. CRIME/FRAUD EXCEPTION

If a client consults a lawyer for advice about how to accomplish a future crime or fraud, the communication is not privileged. On the other hand, if the client consults about a past crime or fraud, the communication is privileged. The crucial distinction is between communications made in furtherance of a crime or fraud (unprivileged) and those made to mount a defense to a past crime or fraud (privileged).

PROBLEM 8–1

Consider again the U.S. Department of Justice regulation governing prison inmates suspected of terrorism. The regulation states that its purpose is "deterring future acts that could result in death or serious bodily injury to persons, or substantial damage to property that would entail the risk of death or serious bodily injury to persons." It also states that communications between inmates and attorneys "are not protected by the attorney-client privilege if they would facilitate criminal acts or a conspiracy to commit criminal acts." This aspect of the regulation reflects the rule that communications are not privileged when they are made in furtherance of a crime.

PROBLEM 8–2

For a number of years you have been the personal lawyer to a prominent and long-serving member of Congress, Representative R. Like everyone else around Washington, D.C., you know generally about Representative R's successful fundraising for his successful re-election campaigns and you know his personal fortune has become considerable since he entered Congress. You have heard rumors about how Representative R's well-heeled corporate and individual supporters benefitted from loopholes or special provisions Representative R inserted into legislation.

(a)   One day Rep. R called you to inform you that he had heard that he was the subject of a criminal investigation by the Public Integrity Section of the Department of Justice which prosecutes cases of public corruption. He asked you and your law firm to represent him during the investigation. You agreed. You begin reviewing R's documents and talking with the DOJ about the matter to determine what they know and what they are investigating. You discover they know a great deal and Representative R has good reason to fear indictment on a large number of serious public corruption charges. You inform R of this and the charges he faces. The next day R calls you and asks: "Can you tell me which countries do not have an extradition treaty with the United States allowing extradition to the United States for a person in the country who is charged with the crimes you told me I face?" Should you answer his question?

(b)   Assume you responded to Rep. R's question about treaties by saying that you would have to look into it. You did some quick legal research and determined that aiding someone to escape from a jurisdiction where criminal charges are pending may be a crime. You also learned which countries do not have extradition treaties with the United States. You didn't return R's call. Unbeknownst to you and to R, the FBI had tapped R's phone and recorded the conversation in which he asked you about extradition treaties. The Department of Justice has now subpoenaed you to testify about what you responded to R. Must you testify?

(c)   Assume that you do not now and never did represent R. You receive a phone call from your law school classmate who is a relatively new member of Rep. R's staff. She says that she has grown increasingly uncomfortable with R's fundraising practices and, in particular, with the possibility that some campaign contributions may be finding their way into Rep. R's personal finances and with the possibility that Rep. R may be taking bribes. She seeks your advice about whether or how, short of quitting her job, she could extricate herself from any responsibility for handling contributions and responding to donor requests for favors. Should you answer her question and, if you do, are your communications with her privileged?

2.   DISPUTES BETWEEN LAWYER AND CLIENT

The privilege does not apply to communications relevant to any dispute between a lawyer and client. Thus, if the client sues the lawyer for malpractice asserting that the lawyer gave bad advice that led to the client being sued for a violation of law, the communications concerning the disputed advice will not be privileged. In the Broadcom backdating case, for example, if Broadcom sued Irell for malpractice asserting that Irell gave Broadcom poor advice about the legality of and accounting for the stock options, Broadcom would waive its claim to privilege in its communications with Irell about the backdating. Similarly, if Irell sued Broadcom for failure to pay attorneys' fees, their communications relevant to the services Irell performed for Broadcom would not be privileged.

3. OTHER EXCEPTIONS

Courts occasionally find other exceptions to the attorney-client privilege. One such exception exists when a court believes that a party and his or her lawyer have deliberately misled the court. Another exists in some jurisdictions to allow lawyers to reveal privileged communications to prevent harms to third parties.

E. SUMMARY

When the client is an organization, the duty of confidentiality and the attorney-client privilege run to the organization, not to the organization's officers, employees, directors, or shareholders. Nevertheless, when an organization's employee or other constituent communicates with the organization's lawyer about a matter within the employee's scope of employment and concerning the lawyer's representation, the communication or information is covered by the organization's attorney-client privilege and by the ethical duty of confidentiality. Because the privilege is the client's not the employee's, the client may use or disclose that information or communication as it wishes, including by firing the employee or reporting him to the government for criminal prosecution. As a consequence, Model Rule 1.13(f) obliges the lawyer for an organization to give an Upjohn warning to an organizational client's constituent when the lawyer knows or reasonably should know that the organization's interests are adverse to those of the constituent with whom the lawyer is dealing. The duty to warn can present a delicate situation for a lawyer who wishes to secure the cooperation and candor of all corporate employees in order to gather information necessary to represent the organization.

When the lawyer represents both the organization and the constituent, however, each separate client's privileged communications may be disclosed to the jointly represented clients but not to third parties. Neither jointly-represented client can waive the privilege on behalf of the other, although they cannot invoke the privilege in subsequent litigation between them.

Important exceptions to the privilege exist for communications made in furtherance of a crime or fraud and for communications relevant to a dispute between and lawyer and client.

Chapter 9

The Duty of Confidentiality

■ ■ ■

A. INTRODUCTION

In this chapter we look at the duty that the rules of professional conduct impose on every lawyer to guard the confidentiality of all information relating to the representation. The information covered by the duty is broad, and the exceptions are relatively broad as well. The duty of confidentiality has tremendous significance in the daily lives of lawyers as it constrains where and how they confer with clients and third parties, how they research the facts of cases and other matters, and even how they manage their offices and their paper and electronic data storage. It affects lawyers' careers, as it underlies the law of conflict of interest which, as we will see in Part IV, restricts the ability of lawyers to switch jobs or to take on certain clients. And, as we saw in *Spaulding v. Zimmerman* in Chapter 1, in the stories of Alton Logan, Lee Hunt and the lawyers Armani and Belge in Chapter 7, and as we will see in this chapter, the duty of confidentiality has a significant impact on the public and third parties. It prompts or sometimes requires lawyers to keep secret information that ordinarily they would disclose, which can have most grievous consequences.

B. ELEMENTS OF THE DUTY OF CONFIDENTIALITY

Model Rule 1.6: Confidentiality of Information

(a) A lawyer shall not reveal information relating to the representation of a client unless the client gives informed consent, the disclosure is impliedly authorized to carry out the representation or the disclosure is permitted by paragraph (b).

(b) A lawyer may reveal information relating to the representation of a client to the extent the lawyer reasonably believes necessary:

   (1) to prevent reasonably certain death or substantial bodily harm;

   (2) to prevent the client from committing a crime or fraud that is reasonably certain to result in substantial injury to the financial interests or property of another and in

---

furtherance of which the client has used or is using the lawyer's services;

(3) to prevent, mitigate or rectify substantial injury to the financial interest or property of another that is reasonably certain to result or has resulted from the client's commission of a crime or fraud in furtherance of which the client has used the lawyer's services;

(4) to secure legal advice about the lawyer's compliance with these Rules;

(5) to establish a claim or defense on behalf of the lawyer in a controversy between the lawyer and the client, to establish a defense to a criminal charge or civil claim against the lawyer based upon conduct in which the client was involved, or to respond to allegations in any proceeding concerning the lawyer's representation of the client;

(6) to comply with other law or a court order; or

(7) to detect and resolve conflicts of interest.

The duty of confidentiality applies in a wide range of circumstances in which the attorney-client privilege does not. It applies to all information a lawyer acquires from all sources in the course of and relating to the representation, not just communications with clients. It prohibits voluntary disclosure by the lawyer, including in casual conversation, and it prohibits a lawyer from using confidential information to the disadvantage of a current, former, or prospective client even if the lawyer does not disclose the information. But it does not allow a lawyer to resist disclosure when compelled by law or court order. The attorney-client privilege, in contrast, applies *only* to disclosure compelled by a tribunal. But where the privilege applies, it requires lawyers to resist disclosures that would otherwise be mandated by law or court order. Unlike the attorney-client privilege, the duty of confidentiality applies even where the information is known to nonprivileged third persons; the duty ceases only when the information becomes generally known. Unlike the attorney-client privilege, which was created by courts as a matter of common law and is enforced by courts through the exclusion of evidence, the duty of confidentiality is a rule of professional conduct created and codified by the bar, and it is enforced by the bar through disciplinary proceedings.

Because everything a lawyer learns in the course of a representation is covered by the duty of confidentiality if it is related to the representation, Model Rule 1.6(a) includes an obviously necessary provision allowing disclosure when it is "impliedly authorized in order to carry out the representation." Without such a provision, lawyers would be able to say or do little on behalf of clients because many statements a lawyer makes reveal confidential information. For example, a lawyer negotiating a deal on behalf of her corporate client is impliedly authorized to reveal confidential information about the client's business to the extent necessary to secure favorable terms in the transaction. A lawyer negotiating a plea agreement is impliedly authorized to reveal confidential information about the client's background or circumstances in order to secure leniency.

As with the attorney-client privilege, attorneys may use or disclose confidential information with the informed consent of clients. Consent is informed only if the lawyer has advised the client of the proposed course of action along with its risks, benefits, and reasonable alternatives. Thus, a lawyer representing a client charged with a murder may, with the client's consent, reveal to the prosecution that the client was, at the time of the murder, in the arms of his best friend's wife. Because of the breadth of the information covered, most of the conceptual work done by Model Rule 1.6 lies in the seven enumerated exceptions to the rule.

C. EXCEPTIONS TO THE DUTY OF CONFIDENTIALITY

Each one of the several exceptions to Model Rule 1.6 begins with the qualification that the lawyer "may" disclose the confidential information only "to the extent that" the lawyer "reasonably believes" disclosure is "necessary" to prevent the harm specified in each exception. This qualifying language is important. First, the lawyer retains the option *not* to disclose (except where a court orders or law compels disclosure). Second, lawyers must not disclose more than is necessary; where partial disclosure will head off the problem, partial disclosure is all that may be made. Third, the lawyer must be "reasonable" in believing that disclosure is necessary, which means the lawyer should deliberate about the disclosure, and perhaps seek legal advice and/or do factual or legal research. And, finally, the disclosure must be *necessary* to prevent the harm, not just one plausible way of preventing it.

1. PREVENTION OF DEATH OR SUBSTANTIAL BODILY HARM

As you learned in the opening pages of this book, Model Rule 1.6(b)(1) now allows lawyers to reveal confidential information to the extent the lawyer "reasonably believes necessary to prevent reasonably certain death or substantial bodily harm."

Re-read Problem 1–1 in Chapter 1, which is an account of the famous case about confidentiality and the role of the lawyer, *Spaulding v. Zimmerman*, 116 N.W.2d 704 (Minn. 1962).

NOTES ON SPAULDING V. ZIMMERMAN

1. ***The History of and Variations on the Death or Injury Exception to Confidentiality.*** At the time of *Spaulding*, the ethics rules of Minnesota, like those of most states, did not allow an exception for lawyers to reveal confidential information to prevent death or substantial bodily injury. The Model Rules first recognized such an exception in 1983, but a few states still do not have exceptions as broad as Model Rule 1.6(b)(1). For example, California allows disclosure of confidential information only "to the extent that the [lawyer] reasonably believes the disclosure is necessary to prevent a criminal act that the [lawyer] reasonably believes is likely to result in death of, or substantial bodily harm to, an individual." Calif. Rule of Professional Conduct 3–100(B). Would a lawyer confronted with the situation of *Spaulding v. Zimmerman* in California be permitted to disclose to David that he was suffering from an aortal aneurysm?

2. ***The Scope of the Death or Substantial Bodily Injury Exception.*** The lawyer's discretion to disclose under the Model Rule 1.6(b)(1) exception to prevent "reasonably certain death or substantial bodily harm" is limited by the requirement that death be "reasonably certain" and that bodily harm be both "reasonably certain" and "substantial." Consider what these terms mean:

(a) Were the harms David faced from the aneurysm "reasonably certain"? Note that he lived for another two years with the condition before it was discovered during the military service physical. But note also that the surgery that repaired his aorta caused him to lose the capacity to speak.

(b) You represent an employee who has been fired from his job. Your client is irate and has threatened to return to his former workplace with a gun and shoot as many people as he can. What would you need to do in order to determine whether the client is making an idle threat or whether he in fact has the ability and the willingness to shoot his former co-workers? At what point would you be permitted by Model Rule 1.6(b)(1) to reveal his statements?

3. ***Assessing the Scope of the Exception.*** Why should the lawyer's permission to disclose be so narrowly limited?

4. ***Comparing Lawyers to Other Professionals.*** Note that lawyers are unusual among professionals in having discretion to decide whether to disclose confidences in order to prevent harms to third persons. Teachers and others who have responsibility for the care of children are required by law in many states to report suspected child abuse. The legal liability of Pennsylvania State University for the failure to report incidents of child

sexual assault by Jerry Sandusky, a member of the senior coaching staff of the football team, turned on a duty under Pennsylvania law to report such incidents.[1] Psychotherapists are under a duty in some jurisdictions to report patients who make credible threats to kill or injure others, as illustrated following the mass shooting in a movie theatre in Aurora, Colorado by a disturbed former graduate student who had been a patient of a psychotherapist.[2] Why should lawyers have discretion whether to report credible threats of harm by their clients when other professionals are required to do so?

5. ***Civil Disobedience.*** The narrow scope of the exception to prevent death or injury may be a case where the lawyer's moral compass points in a different direction than do the norms of the practice community or the rules of professional responsibility. As we saw about the lawyers in *Spaulding v. Zimmerman*, whatever moral intuitions people may have about when to breach a confidence to avoid harm to a third party, the professional acculturation of lawyers tends to make them more likely to guard client confidences than nonlawyers may think desirable. In circumstances in which the narrow scope of the exception to confidentiality for the prevention of death or injury prohibits lawyers from revealing a confidence to avert a harm to a third party, should the lawyer engage in civil disobedience to the rules of professional responsibility?

2. CLIENT CRIMES AND FRAUDS

Topic Overview

This section examines the exception to the duty of confidentiality for lawyer involvement in client crimes and frauds. As we study the relationship between confidentiality and lawyer involvement in client wrongdoing, consider not only what the law is, but also why this has been such a vexing issue for the bar, why lawyers are tempted to facilitate client fraud, whether and why the duty of confidentiality seems to be a barrier to the transparency that might prevent such problems or nip them in the bud, and what both the organized bar and law firms could do to address the problem.

---

[1] *See* Richard Pérez-Peña, *In Report, Failures Throughout Penn State*, N.Y. TIMES, July 13, 2012, at B12 (noting internal investigation found Penn State officials may have violated Pennsylvania law requiring certain officials to report suspected child abuse to state authorities).

[2] *See* Jack Healy, *Files Offer Glimpse Into Shooting Suspect*, N.Y. TIMES, Sept. 29, 2012, at A15 (noting that psychiatrist who saw the alleged shooter once several weeks before the shooting contacted police, which she did only because she was "very concerned" about him).

Model Rule 1.6(b) Exceptions for Client Crimes and Frauds in Which Lawyer's Services Are Used

A lawyer may confidential information to the extent the lawyer reasonably believes necessary

(b)(2)   to prevent the client from committing a crime or fraud that is reasonably certain to result in substantial injury to the financial interests or property of another and in furtherance of which the client has used or is using the lawyer's services; or

(b)(3)   to prevent, mitigate or rectify substantial injury to the financial interests or property of another that is reasonably certain to result or has resulted from the client's commission of a crime or fraud in furtherance of which the client has used the lawyer's services.

Subsection (b)(2) refers to future crimes or frauds and (b)(3) refers to past crimes or frauds.

Every few years, a new scandal involving massive frauds bursts into the headlines of the legal news. Sometimes lawyers were obviously involved and sometimes the role of lawyers is unclear. But in any case of a massive business fraud, lawyers were probably somewhere because large-scale business transactions invariably require the assistance of lawyers. And in almost every case, one of the most hard-fought issues in the subsequent civil and criminal litigation concerns the scope of the lawyers' duty to preserve the confidentiality of information and communications about the fraud and whether the confidentiality protections will have the effect of insulating both the clients and their lawyers from accountability for fraudulent and criminal behavior. The scope of some of these scandals was huge, and the involvement of lawyers was pervasive, yet the state bar discipline of the lawyers was comparatively small. The absence of vigorous bar discipline in some cases of spectacular client fraud raises significant questions about how society should best regulate lawyer misconduct and what role lawyer confidentiality has played in facilitating these examples of business misconduct.

To outside observers, the organized bar's insistence on broad confidentiality protections is particularly dispiriting when the protections may insulate the lawyers' own illegal conduct, or, at a minimum, their willingness to turn a blind eye toward large-scale fraudulent activity in which legal advice played a crucial part. The bar has long condemned criminal or fraudulent behavior by lawyers. Model Rule 1.2 prohibits lawyers from "assist[ing] a client in conduct the lawyer knows is criminal or fraudulent," and Model Rule 8.4 defines professional misconduct to include the commission of "a criminal act that reflects adversely on the lawyer's honesty, trustworthiness or fitness as a lawyer in other respects" and engaging in "conduct involving dishonesty, fraud, deceit or misrepresentation." The bar now recognizes exceptions both to attorney-client privilege and to the duty of confidentiality for lawyer involvement in client crimes or frauds. Model Rule 1.6(b)(2) and (b)(3). Yet, as critics point out with some justification, the bar's efforts to punish elite lawyers for their involvement in client frauds have been anemic while its insistence on the values of confidentiality in these cases has been rather more robust.

As noted above in Chapter 7 on attorney-client privilege, if a client consults a lawyer for advice about how to accomplish a future crime or fraud, the communications relating to that request for advice are not privileged. On the other hand, if the client consults about a past crime or fraud, the communication is privileged. The crucial distinction is between communications made in furtherance of a crime or fraud (unprivileged) and those made to mount a defense to a past crime or fraud (privileged).

A similar exception exists to the duty of confidentiality. Model Rule 1.6(b) articulates two related exceptions allowing lawyers to reveal confidential information "to the extent the lawyer reasonably believes necessary"

"(2) to prevent the client from committing a crime or fraud that is reasonably certain to result in substantial injury to the financial interests or property of another and in furtherance of which the client has used or is using the lawyer's services; [or]

"(3) to prevent, mitigate or rectify substantial injury to the financial interests or property of another that is reasonably certain to result or has resulted from the client's commission of a crime or fraud in furtherance of which the client has used the lawyer's services."

Subsection (b)(2) refers to future crimes or frauds and (b)(3) refers to past crimes or frauds. Both exceptions allow disclosure only if the client has used or is using the lawyer's services to achieve the crime or fraud. The requirement that the lawyers' services be involved before the lawyer is allowed to reveal the confidence is important and controversial. If a lawyer learns of a past or planned client fraud or crime but has not provided services to enable it, the lawyer may withdraw from representing the client but the lawyer cannot, under Model Rule 1.6(b)(2) or (3), warn the intended victims to prevent it or to enable them to mitigate their losses. The lawyer may not even do what is known as "noisy withdrawal," which is to withdraw from representing the client and suggest in so doing that there is reason for the client's other lawyers or business partners to be wary.

Model Rule 1.6 subsections (b)(2) and (b)(3) were adopted by the ABA in 2003 after news of corporate accounting scandals at Enron, Worldcom and other companies had dominated the headlines for months. It had become quite clear that lawyers, particularly lawyers at large elite firms that tend to represent Fortune 100 companies, had been deeply involved in the corporate frauds and crimes. Until then, the ABA had consistently insisted that lawyers should not disclose client frauds. In 2002, Sarbanes-Oxley required the SEC to adopt minimum standards of conduct for securities lawyers. The SEC's first set of proposals included provisions that would have required lawyers to withdraw when the client was engaging in fraud or other serious violations of law, to notify the SEC of their withdrawal, and to disaffirm work submitted to the SEC that related to the client wrongdoing. In 2003, while the SEC's proposals were pending, the ABA adopted the new exceptions to Rule 1.6 now codified in subsections (b)(2) and (b)(3).

Not every state has adopted a version of Model Rule 1.6(b)(2) and (b)(3). Many have, and indeed all but eight states and the District of Columbia adopted rules allowing lawyers to disclose client frauds in which their services have been used before the ABA finally did in 2003. Model Rule 1.6(b)(2) and (b)(3) give the lawyer discretion whether to report the fraud. Some states, including Florida, New Jersey, Virginia, and Wisconsin *require* lawyers to disclose frauds. Hawaii and Ohio require lawyers to disclose confidences to rectify a client's crime or fraud in which the lawyer's services were used. A handful of states (Alabama, California, the District of Columbia, Kentucky, Missouri, Montana, Nebraska and Rhode Island) forbid lawyers to disclose confidences to prevent future crimes unless the crime threatens death or substantial bodily injury. For example, California allows disclosure of confidential information only "to prevent a criminal act" that is "likely to result in death" or substantial bodily injury. California Rule of Professional Conduct 3–100. It does not allow disclosure of crimes that will cause only financial harm and does not allow disclosure of civil wrongs.

It is extremely important to note, however, that the contours of the ethics rules may not be the most important factor lawyers consider in deciding how to handle a client who appears to be engaged in fraud. Lawyers will typically be far more concerned with being sued civilly or prosecuted criminally for their own participation in the fraud than they are with bar discipline. The reason is simple: state bars have rarely instituted disciplinary proceedings against lawyers in large firms, even in the face of significant evidence that lawyers were involved in client frauds. But elite lawyers and large firms have been criminally prosecuted and sued civilly and have paid substantial sums to settle fraud litigation.

PROBLEM 9–1: THE BURIED BODIES CASE (AGAIN)

Consider again the Armani and Belge case in Chapter 7. Would any of the exceptions to confidentiality apply to either Garrow's confessions about the prior rapes and murders and the locations of the bodies or to Garrow's description of how he eluded capture by the police in the past? Was Armani legally justified in revealing what Garrow said about escape from police? If not, was he nevertheless morally justified? On what basis?

PROBLEM 9–2: O.P.M.

O.P.M. was a computer leasing firm whose business model was to purchase computers and lease them to other companies. They used the existing leases as collateral for loans, and used the loan proceeds to purchase more computers for future leases. O.P.M. (which stood for Other People's Money) gained market share by maintaining low prices on the leases, but the low-priced leases meant that the leases were not sufficiently valuable to serve as collateral for the size of the future loans that O.P.M. wanted. So the two O.P.M. partners forged documentation of the leases to make it appear that the leases were for larger amounts than they were. O.P.M.'s outside counsel, the law firm Singer Hutner, negotiated the loans and processed the paperwork. Consider their obligations at two different points in time:

a.   In the beginning, the Singer Hutner lawyers did not know that the loans they were negotiating and the paperwork they were processing to obtain those loans were based on fraudulent leases. O.P.M.'s accountant discovered that the company's partners had forged the lease papers that had been given to the lawyers and informed the lawyers. What should the lawyers have done?

b.   The lawyers continued to process new loans, in part because O.P.M. was the law firm's major client and in part in reliance on advice of a legal ethics expert who told them that the lawyers could not reveal the past frauds and had no responsibility to police their client to be sure that it was not committing more frauds. (This advice was based on the Code of Professional Responsibility, the relevant authority in New York at the time, rather than the Model Rules.) After processing millions of dollars of new loans, an O.P.M. partner confessed to the lawyer that O.P.M. had continued to forge the leases. Singer Hutner withdrew from representing O.P.M. What, if anything, should they have said to the lawyers who replaced them about their reasons for withdrawing? What else should they have done?

At the time this episode occurred, the lawyers were governed by the Code of Professional Conduct, which contained confidentiality provisions that were different than the confidentiality provisions of the Model Rules. In particular, the Code did not contain the exceptions now found in Model Rule 1.6(b)(2) and (b)(3) allowing lawyers to reveal confidential information to prevent future client frauds or crimes or to rectify the effects of past crimes or frauds in furtherance of which the client used the lawyer's service. If something like O.P.M. were to happen today, what would the lawyers be permitted to say or do at the time they first discovered the frauds? What could they say later when they withdrew from representation and handed the matter over to successor counsel? When the Singer Hutner lawyers withdrew, they said nothing about the fraud to their successors, and the successor law firm continued to close loans for O.P.M. Millions of dollars in loans negotiated by the successor lawyers were also fraudulent.

The lawyers for O.P.M. received three distinct pieces of advice from their ethics counsel: (1) they could not reveal the client's frauds; (2) they had no duty to police the client's future transactions to ensure that no future lease was fraudulent; and (3) the firm was not required to withdraw because it had no information suggesting that O.P.M. would continue the frauds. As you can see, Model Rule 1.6 now would allow the lawyers to reveal the past frauds. Should the lawyers have done more than take the client's word that the future leases were not fraudulent? This is not a question of confidentiality, but instead is a question of avoiding assisting the client in the commission of fraud. What are the risks to lawyers who fail to make any effort to determine whether the client is continuing to commit fraud? The O.P.M. partners were convicted of crimes and sentenced to prison and the lawyers paid at least ten million dollars to settle a suit brought against them by defrauded lenders. What could the new lawyers have done to protect themselves from becoming involved in the client's fraudulent activities?

3. DISPUTES BETWEEN LAWYER AND CLIENT

As with the attorney client privilege, Model Rule 1.6 has an exception allowing lawyers to disclose confidential information to protect lawyers in disputes with their clients. This exception to the duty of confidentiality is surprisingly broad, given the reluctance of the bar to allow disclosures to protect third parties. A lawyer may disclose confidential information "to the extent the lawyer believes reasonably necessary to establish a claim or defense on behalf of the lawyer in a controversy between the lawyer and the client, to establish a defense to a criminal charge or civil claim against the lawyer based upon conduct in which the client was involved, or to respond to allegations in any proceeding concerning the lawyer's representation of the client." Model Rule 1.6(b)(5).

Notice that unlike the similar exception to the attorney-client privilege, this exception is not limited to disputes between the lawyer and the client, where the client may be said to have waived confidentiality by either suing the lawyer for malpractice or not paying his legal bill and inviting the lawyer to sue him. This allows disclosure in those circumstances but goes farther and allows lawyers to disclose confidences in any litigation instituted by a third person "based upon conduct in which the client was involved." Rule 1.6(b)(5) even allows the lawyer simply to "respond to allegations in any proceeding concerning the lawyer's representation of the client." The lawyer, in other words, is free to protect his or her own reputation or financial interests by revealing confidential client information. Cynics about lawyers assert that the breadth of this exception, particularly in contrast to the narrowness of the other exceptions that allow disclosure to protect third parties, reflects no greater policy purpose than simply lawyers' desire to protect their own self-interest at the expense of clients and their ability to get away with it because it is lawyers, after all, who draft the rules of professional conduct. Can you identify policies justifying the exception to respond to the cynics? Can you identify the operative terms in the language of Model Rule 1.6(b)(5) and argue how they should be interpreted in order to address some of the concerns raised by the cynics?

4. SECURING LEGAL ETHICS ADVICE AND CONFLICTS CHECKS

When lawyers are in doubt about their legal obligations, including their obligations under the rules of professional conduct, they should obtain legal advice. Model Rule 1.6(b)(4) is an exception to the duty of confidentiality that allows lawyers to reveal confidential information "to the extent the lawyer reasonably believes necessary to secure legal advice about the lawyer's compliance with [the Model] Rules." The attorney-client privilege contains a similar but slightly narrower exception providing that a lawyer does not waive the privilege if she discloses confidential communication for the purpose of obtaining legal advice, but in the case of privileged communications lawyers are supposed to avoid actually disclosing the communication and instead to ask for advice by use of hypothetical questions. For example, the public defenders who represented Wilson, the man who confessed the murder for which Alton Logan was wrongly convicted, could disclose to the lawyers whom they consulted for ethical advice that they represented a man who had confessed to a murder for which another man had been convicted. But, because they were obliged not to disclose the actual confession, they should frame their request for advice in general or hypothetical terms such as: "Suppose a lawyer represented a person serving a life sentence for one crime and that client confessed to a crime for which another was convicted. What, if anything, may a lawyer disclose to the prosecution, the judge, and the lawyer for the innocent man? Under what circumstances may the lawyer disclose it?"

Model Rule 1.6(b)(7) allows lawyers to reveal confidential information as necessary to detect whether the lawyer's change of employment or the change in law firm composition has resulted in a conflict of interest. (As will be seen in Part IV, when lawyers come and go from law offices they may create conflicts of interest between the interests of the clients.)

5. COMPLIANCE WITH OTHER LAW OR COURT ORDER

Model Rule 1.6(b)(6) allows lawyers to reveal confidential information to the extent the lawyer reasonably believes necessary "to comply with other law or a court order." Comment [12] to Rule 1.6 suggests that not every law that would appear to require disclosure of confidential information supersedes the lawyer's duty of confidentiality, but the Model Rules do not attempt to define when laws trump the lawyer's duty under Rule 1.6. Comment [15] further requires lawyers to make efforts to obtain an authoritative ruling that disclosure is in fact required by law and to consult with the client before disclosing. Beyond court orders, other laws that may require lawyers to reveal confidences include laws prohibiting securities fraud or requiring reporting of certain financial or other information.

6. OTHER EXCEPTIONS TO CONFIDENTIALITY

A few exceptions to confidentiality are found in rules other than Model Rule 1.6 and are covered in detail elsewhere in this book. For example, under Model Rule 3.3 a lawyer has a duty of candor toward a tribunal that creates an exception to confidentiality when it is necessary to avoid making false statements to the court. Rule 3.3 also requires lawyers to take reasonable remedial measures to correct false statements after, for example, a client lies to the court, including if necessary revealing information that would be confidential under Rule 1.6. This rule is covered in Chapter 13.

Similarly, under Model Rule 1.13, a lawyer representing an organization may be permitted to reveal confidences when misconduct of agents of the organization may injure the organization and the highest decision-making body within the organization has refused to take appropriate corrective action. This rule is covered in Chapters 18 and 19.

Model Rule 4.1 provides that a lawyer shall not fail to disclose a material fact "when disclosure is necessary to avoid assisting a criminal act by a client, unless disclosure is prohibited by Rule 1.6." That provision requires disclosure in many client fraud situations. This rule is covered in Chapters 14 and 25.

COMPARING THE EXCEPTIONS TO CONFIDENTIALITY AND TO ATTORNEY-CLIENT PRIVILEGE

Exception	Attorney-Client Privilege	Duty of Confidentiality
Crime-Fraud	Communications in furtherance of crimes or fraud are not privileged	Model Rule 1.6(b)(2): Lawyer may disclose information to prevent the client from committing a crime or fraud that is reasonably certain to result in substantial injury to the financial interests or property of another and in furtherance of which the client has used or is using the lawyer's services Model Rule 1.6(b)(3): Lawyer may disclose information to prevent, mitigate or rectify substantial injury to the financial interest or property of another that is reasonably certain to result or has resulted from the client's commission of a crime or fraud in furtherance of which the client has used the lawyer's services
Prevention of death or substantial bodily injury	In a very few jurisdictions, there is an exception to privilege to allow lawyers to reveal information	Model Rule 1.6(b)(1): To prevent reasonably certain death or substantial bodily harm

Exception	Attorney-Client Privilege	Duty of Confidentiality
Prevention of misleading tribunal	Use of privilege to mislead a court constitutes "fraud on the tribunal" and results in loss of privilege as necessary to avoid deception	Model Rule 3.3: If a lawyer, client, or witness called by lawyer has offered material evidence and the lawyer comes to know of its falsity, the lawyer shall take reasonable remedial measures, including, if necessary, disclosure to tribunal
Disputes between attorney and Client	Privilege is waived as to communications necessary to resolve disputes between attorney & client (e.g. malpractice, nonpayment of fees)	MR 1.6(b)(5): Lawyer may reveal information to establish a claim or defense on behalf of the lawyer in a controversy between the lawyer and the client, to establish a defense to a criminal charge or civil claim against the lawyer based upon conduct in which the client was involved, or to respond to allegations in any proceeding concerning the lawyer's representation of the client

Exception	Attorney-Client Privilege	Duty of Confidentiality
Disputes between two clients jointly represented	Either client can prevent the other from revealing privileged communications to third parties, but neither party can invoke privilege against the other in subsequent disputes between them	Restatement § 60 Comment *l* presumes that confidential information will be shared between co-clients and restricts the ability of lawyers to jointly represent clients when one insists on not sharing information with another
To allow lawyer to obtain legal ethics advice	No exception. But lawyers can seek ethics or other legal advice by asking hypothetical questions that do not reveal the confidential communications.	Model Rule 1.6(b)(4): To secure legal advice about the lawyer's compliance with these Rules
To comply with law or court order	No exception.	Model Rule 1.6(b)(6): To comply with other law or a court order

D. CONFIDENTIALITY AND LAWYER-CLIENT DISAGREEMENTS OVER STRATEGY

We saw above that a lawyer may reveal confidential information with the informed consent of the client or where revelation is impliedly authorized by the representation. We also saw that a client may limit the scope of implied authorization by express direction. What happens if a client refuses consent and explicitly limits the ability of a lawyer to reveal information that the lawyer believes should be revealed for the client's benefit? As explained in Chapter 5, Model Rule 1.2(a) provides that the lawyer ordinarily decides the tactics of the representation, although the lawyer should confer with the client, and the client decides the objectives. How should they resolve disputes over tactics when the client directs the lawyer not to reveal information protected by Model Rule 1.6? Is the attorney bound by the client's decision to withhold confidential information to his own detriment? This is the dilemma of the classic country ballad, "Long Black Veil"

> Ten years ago on a cool dark night
> There was someone killed 'neath the town hall light
> There were few at the scene and they all did agree
> That the man who ran looked a lot like me

> The judge said "Son, what is your alibi?
> If you were somewhere else then you won't have to die"
> I spoke not a word although it meant my life
> I had been in the arms of my best friend's wife

> She walks these hills in a long black veil
> She visits my grave where the night winds wail

> Nobody knows, no and nobody sees
> Nobody knows but me[3]

Imagine you are the lawyer representing the defendant in the Long Black Veil case. (In the song, the defendant apparently is not represented by counsel, perhaps because the song was written before the Supreme Court decided *Gideon v. Wainwright* establishing the right to counsel in criminal cases or perhaps just because it makes a better song if the accused has no lawyer.) Should you call the best friend's wife as a witness to testify about the client's alibi over your client's objection? What weight, if any, should be given to the interests of third parties, such as the best friend and the wife and their children, or the spouse and family of the defendant?

Of course, as in any case of lawyer-client disagreement over strategy, the lawyer may seek to withdraw. As explained in Chapter 5, Model Rule 1.16 provides that a lawyer may withdraw from representing a client if withdrawal can be accomplished without material adverse effect on the client or if the client insists upon taking action that the lawyer considers repugnant or with which the lawyer has a fundamental disagreement. When the representation involves appearing before a tribunal, a lawyer may not be permitted to withdraw immediately. Courts often will not allow a lawyer to withdraw during or shortly before a trial or other important proceeding in litigation. It is at these crucial points, of course, where disagreements over strategy are likely to surface and to be most intense.

---

[3] LEFTY FRIZZELL, LONG BLACK VEIL (Columbia Records 1959). Originally recorded by Lefty Frizzell in 1959 with songwriting credited to Danny Dill & Marijohn Wilkin.

NOTES ON LAWYER-CLIENT DISAGREEMENTS
OVER CONFIDENTIALITY

1. ***The Divorce Lawyer.*** Recall from Chapter 5 the divorce lawyer who hires a private investigator to uncover proof of the husband's infidelity and thereby overcomes his client's reluctance to risk enmity with her soon-to-be-ex-husband by demanding more money as a settlement at divorce. If the client insisted that the lawyer not reveal evidence of the tryst to her husband's attorney in the divorce settlement negotiations, may the lawyer do so over the client's objection?

2. ***The Unabomber Case.*** Recall the Unabomber case from Chapter 5. Ted Kaczynski insisted he had agreed to undergo psychiatric evaluation only because his lawyers promised him they would not disclose the results of the examinations to the prosecution, the court, or the public. His lawyers did so anyway. Assume he is correct about the facts. Did Denvir and Clarke violate Model Rule 1.6(a)? Consider whether the disclosure was "impliedly authorized in order to carry out the representation" and whether they had informed client consent to disclosure. If neither of those applies, then the disclosure would be prohibited unless one of the seven exceptions in Rule 1.6(b) applies. Does any of them apply?

E. SUMMARY

The duty of confidentiality applies to all information a lawyer acquires from all sources in the course of representation. It prohibits voluntary disclosure by the lawyer, including in casual conversation. But it does *not* allow a lawyer to resist disclosure when compelled by law or court order. The attorney-client privilege, in contrast, applies *only* to communications and *only* to disclosure compelled by a tribunal. But where the privilege applies, it requires lawyers to resist disclosures that would otherwise be mandated by law or court order. Unlike the attorney-client privilege, the duty of confidentiality applies even where the information is known to nonprivileged third persons; the duty ceases only when the information becomes generally known.

Model Rule 1.6(a) allows disclosure of confidential information when it is "impliedly authorized in order to carry out the representation." And, as with privilege, the lawyer may disclose confidential information with client consent.

The breadth of the duty of confidentiality invites other exceptions as well. Under Model Rule 1.6(b), a lawyer may reveal information to the extent the lawyer reasonably believes necessary

- to prevent reasonably certain death or substantial bodily injury (this exception does not exist as broadly under some state ethics rules, including California's)

- to prevent the client from committing future a crime or fraud that is reasonably certain to result in substantial injury to the financial interests or property of another and in furtherance of which the client has used the lawyer's services

- to prevent, mitigate, or rectify substantial financial or property harms that is reasonably certain to result or has resulted from the client's past crime or fraud in furtherance of which the client used the lawyer's services

- in disputes between the lawyer and client, including to respond to allegations in any proceeding concerning the lawyer's representation of the client

- to secure ethics advice or to determine whether the lawyer has a conflict of interest.

In addition, under other rules, a lawyer may or must reveal confidential information.

- A lawyer must take reasonable remedial measures, including if necessary disclosure of confidential information, if the lawyer, the lawyer's client, or a witness offered by the lawyer makes a false statement of material fact to a tribunal. Model Rule 3.3(a)(3).

- A lawyer representing an organization may be permitted to reveal confidential information when misconduct of officers, employees, or other constituents of the organization may injure the organization and the highest decision-making body within the organization has refused to take appropriate corrective action. Model Rule 1.13.

- A lawyer shall not fail to disclose a material fact when disclosure is necessary to avoid assisting a criminal act by a client, unless disclosure is prohibited by Rule 1.6. Model Rule 4.1.

PART IV

CONFLICTS OF INTEREST

■ ■ ■

This part of your materials addresses situations in which tension between the client's interests and some competing interest or concern might tempt a lawyer to violate his duties to serve a client loyally and protect confidential information. Those competing interests might involve another current or former client, or the lawyer's own interests, or those of his partners, family or friends. The conflict of interest rules that we study in this Part are designed to guard against incentives that might lead a lawyer to disregard duties to clients.

Imagine an independently wealthy lawyer who has no need to earn an income, no family ties or close friends, no political or ideological convictions, no demands on his time outside his practice, no partners, and just one client, an individual, whom the lawyer will represent pro bono. This lawyer has no interest in finding new clients, developing social ties, taking on partners, earning a living, or changing jobs.[1] His only ambition is to serve his only client well. That lawyer would exemplify disinterestedness and would have no reason to be concerned about running afoul of the bar's conflicts of interest rules. He would also be a rare lawyer indeed.

Unlike the imaginary lawyer just described, most lawyers in the real world operate in a complex web of social and professional relationships and intersecting financial and political interests. For most lawyers, therefore, navigating conflicts of interest is an everyday fact of life. Lawyers in all types of practice are subject to conflict of interest rules designed to promote loyal service to clients and protection of client confidences. Conflict of interest issues take many different forms and arise in an astounding variety of scenarios. The basic concept is that lawyers should not represent conflicting interests without the consent of all affected clients. The doctrine of vicarious or imputed disqualification generally provides that if one lawyer has a conflict so do all other lawyers in the same firm. This doctrine means that if a conflict of interest prevents Lawyer A from representing a client, Lawyer B in the same firm also is unable to represent the client in most circumstances.

---

[1] This hypothetical lawyer is based on the "young orphan, Lawrence Lexman" in SUSAN SHAPIRO, TANGLED LOYALTIES: CONFLICTS OF INTEREST IN LEGAL PRACTICE 54–55 (2002).

The law is this area is complex and challenging, but it is also highly relevant and critical to most lawyers' daily practices. Deciding whether a representation can begin or continue often matters greatly to clients, as well as to the lawyers and firms involved. Failing to avoid or resolve a conflict can lead to catastrophic consequences for firms and individuals— disqualification of the lawyer and the law firm from representing a client, forfeiture of fees paid for services already rendered, loss of a client, bar discipline, malpractice liability, and even, in extreme cases, prison. On the other hand, there are good reasons why lawyers and clients are sometimes reluctant to obey conflict rules. Loyal service to one client often means frustrating another client or prospective client. Conflict rules limit clients' freedom to choose their lawyers and to enjoy efficiencies that go with continuing with a representation rather than hiring new counsel. From the lawyer's perspective, the rules can interfere with efforts to build a practice because they impose limitations on which clients a lawyer can serve. The doctrine of vicarious disqualification also fosters conflict within firms over which lawyers' clients will be served and which will need to seek counsel elsewhere. Moreover, clients and lawyers who seek to enforce conflict of interest standards do not always do so for high-minded reasons.

Some conditions of modern practice have made conflict of interest issues more relevant and challenging than ever. As the average size of the organizations in which lawyers practice has increased, so has the influence of the imputation rules, which can affect hundreds and sometimes even thousands of other lawyers in the same firm as the disqualified lawyer. Keeping track of all clients and identifying and resolving conflicts is an enormous job in most large firms. Deciding how to resolve conflicts generates internal discord in firms, as partners vie to keep their own clients happy and to acquire new ones. The increased mobility of lawyers complicates that task because, as lawyers come and go, they sometimes carry conflicts with them to their new jobs and colleagues. Increased specialization has accentuated those problems; clients often prefer lawyers with substantial experience in particular substantive areas, but that experience often comes through representing clients who might be on the opposite side of a previously represented client in a subsequent litigation or transactional matter. The consolidation of American industry requires firms to track relationships among affiliated enterprises to assess whether conflicts prohibit them from representing a client. Although the ABA has taken position that a lawyer who represents an organization does not by virtue of that representation necessarily represent affiliated organizations (Rule 1.7, Comment 34), related organizations are sometimes so interrelated that they are treated as one organization for purposes of the conflict of interest rules.

As explained in Part I, disciplinary agencies acting under the supervision of state supreme courts hold primary responsibility for enforcing the rules of professional conduct. That is as true of the conflict of interest rules as it is of other ethics rules. As a practical matter, however, the conflict of interest rules are enforced in litigation primarily through motions to disqualify opposing counsel. While litigants sometimes file motions to disqualify in good faith, disqualification motions are also used tactically to deprive opponents of their choice of lawyers and to impose additional costs on them—costs involved in hiring new lawyers and bringing them up to speed. Judges' suspicions about the motivations underlying disqualification motions have led courts to separate the question of whether there is a violation of conflict of interest rules from the issue of whether disqualification is an appropriate remedy, so that not every violation of the conflict of interest rules leads to disqualification.

This Part is organized into three chapters. The first (Chapter 10) focuses on concurrent representation issues, which involve primarily whether a lawyer can represent two or more clients simultaneously. The second (Chapter 11) considers conflicts issues involving former clients—whether a lawyer's past representation of a client should prevent her from subsequently representing a different client. The third (Chapter 12) addresses imputed disqualification and its exceptions.

CHAPTER 10

CONCURRENT CONFLICTS

■ ■ ■

A. INTRODUCTION

This chapter focuses on concurrent (or "simultaneous") conflicts between present clients. We will consider the standards for analyzing concurrent conflicts—that is, what constitutes a concurrent conflict and when such conflicts are "consentable," meaning that the lawyer may proceed despite the conflict if he gains consent from the clients. We will also consider some real life concerns that sometimes lead lawyers to violate those standards.

This chapter reviews the basic standard that applies to concurrent conflicts. It then considers how that standard applies to organizations that have affiliated entities and when, if ever, lawyers and clients can agree to waive conflicts in advance. We also explore how the rule applies to particular practice situations: criminal defense, the representation of multiple parties to a transaction, joint representation of an organization and its employees, estate planning, the representation of insurance companies and those they insure, and class actions. Finally, we consider when lawyers may take legal positions in one matter that are contrary to legal positions taken on behalf of clients in another unrelated matter.

B. THE BASIC STANDARD

Model Rule 1.7 describes how a lawyer should analyze conflicts between two or more current clients.

Model Rule 1.7: Concurrent Conflicts:

Model Rule 1.7 provides that a lawyer is prohibited from representing a client if one of two types of conflicts exists:

- the client's interests are "directly adverse" to those of another client, or

- there is a "significant risk" that a representation will be "materially limited" by a lawyer's obligation to another client.[1]

If either of these types of conflicts exists, the lawyer may proceed only if each affected client gives informed consent. The lawyer is not permitted to seek such client consent in circumstances where the conflict is particularly problematic.

Under Rule 1.10(a) on imputed disqualification, if one lawyer is prohibited from representing a client, all lawyers in the same firm are prohibited from representing that client. (We will explore this rule and its exceptions in Chapter 12.)

Direct Adversity. What is direct adversity under Rule 1.7(a)(1)? The quintessential example is litigating against a current client. If a Lawyer who represents Client A in one matter also represents Client B in a lawsuit against Client A, the representation of Client B against Client A is "directly adverse" to the interests of a current client, even if the two pieces of litigation are completely unrelated. So, for example, if Lawyer is representing Client A in a suit against A's former employer, Lawyer's simultaneous representation of Client B in a suit against Client A for assault would be directly adverse to Client A. Direct adversity can also arise in transactional and counseling matters. Lawyer's representation of Client B in negotiations with Client A to purchase a piece of land from A, while simultaneously advising Client A on tax matters, would be directly adverse to Client A, even though the two matters are completely different.

"Significant Risk" that Representation Will Be "Materially Limited". Even if there is no direct adversity, a concurrent conflict exists if there is a "significant risk" that the representation of one client would be "materially limited" by a lawyer's responsibility to another client. For example, a lawyer representing two co-defendants in civil litigation might have trouble competently and diligently representing one client's position if it is based on a recollection of events or a legal defense that is inconsistent with the testimony or defense that another client will offer. Similarly, a lawyer who is asked to advise multiple individuals seeking to

---

[1] As you saw in Chapter 6, Rule 1.7 also applies where there is a significant risk that the representation will be "materially limited" by a lawyer's own interests.

form a joint venture might find it difficult to advocate all positions that each of the individuals might wish to take because of the lawyer's duties to the others.

"Consentable" Conflicts. If there is a conflict under Rule 1.7(a), the lawyer must determine whether the conflict is "consentable," meaning that the clients can agree to have the lawyer represent them notwithstanding the conflict. The lawyer may not seek client consent to the conflict if he does not reasonably believe that he can provide competent and diligent representation to each client or if proceeding with the representation would involve asserting a claim by one client against another in the same proceeding or would otherwise be illegal. If the conflict is consentable and both clients give informed consent, the conflict is considered cured. If the conflict cannot be cured with client consent, the lawyer must decline the representation. If the representation has already begun, the lawyer must withdraw from at least one of the representations, and may have to withdraw from both.

The following case illustrates how Rule 1.7 applies in civil litigation.

IN RE PETITION FOR DISCIPLINARY ACTION AGAINST CHRISTOPHER THOMAS KALLA

Supreme Court of Minnesota
811 N.W.2d 576 (2012)

PER CURIAM.

The Director of the Office of Lawyers Professional Responsibility served and filed a petition for discipline in September 2010 alleging that Christopher Kalla engaged in a conflict of interest prohibited by the Minnesota Rules of Professional Conduct. Following a hearing, a referee concluded that Kalla had engaged in a conflict of interest and recommended that Kalla be publicly reprimanded and receive supervised probation for two years.

The conflict of interest at issue arose from Kalla's representation of two clients, whom we refer to as "Client A" and "Client B." In 2006, Client A borrowed money from an individual lender ("the Lender") to use as a down payment for the purchase of a home. The loan was secured by a mortgage on the real property. The mortgage was arranged by Future Mortgage, a company owned by Client B. Client B, who was also a real estate agent, assisted Client A with the purchase of her home and connected Client A to the Lender. When Client A later tried to refinance her loans, her mortgage broker identified potential legal problems with the Lender's loan and referred Client A to Kalla for legal assistance.

Kalla reviewed Client A's loan from the Lender and reached the conclusion that the loan was usurious [meaning that the interest rate exceeded legal limits]. In October 2007, Kalla filed a lawsuit on Client A's behalf, seeking to invalidate the loan and mortgage. During his investigation of Client A's claim, Kalla discovered that Client B had also borrowed money from the Lender and advised Client B about the potential usury issues with the Lender's loans.

The Lender filed an answer and counterclaim to the lawsuit, in which he identified Future Mortgage as the broker of the loan to Client A. The answer and counterclaim therefore identified Client B and Future Mortgage as key players in the lawsuit. Thereafter, Kalla undertook representation of Client B, filing a usury lawsuit on behalf of Client B against the Lender. Kalla did not inform Client B before he undertook her representation that Client B or her company, Future Mortgage, were in any way implicated in Client A's lawsuit.

The Lender filed a third-party complaint [a claim filed by a defendant against someone who is not already in the case] in Client A's lawsuit naming Client B and Future Mortgage as defendants. Prior to serving the third-party complaint, the Lender's attorney talked to Kalla about the problem for Kalla in representing both Clients A and B, who would be on opposing sides of the case after the third-party complaint was served. After receiving the Lender's third-party complaint, Kalla asked both clients to sign conflict-of-interest waivers. Client A signed the waiver but Client B did not. Kalla continued to represent both clients without a signed conflict-of-interest waiver from Client B. Minnesota Rule of Professional Conduct 1.7 prohibits concurrent conflicts of interest. The rule explains that concurrent conflicts can arise in two situations. The first is when "the representation of one client will be directly adverse to another client." Minn. R. Prof. Conduct 1.7(a)(1). The second is when "there is a significant risk that the representation of one or more clients will be materially limited by the lawyer's responsibilities to another client, a former client or a third person, or by a personal interest of the lawyer." Minn. R. Prof. Conduct 1.7(a)(2). We need not decide whether representing a plaintiff and a third-party defendant in the same lawsuit presents a situation of direct adversity because we hold that Kalla's representation of Clients A and B posed a significant risk that the dual representation would materially limit his representation of each client in violation of Rule 1.7(a)(2).

Kalla was representing Client A, the plaintiff in a usury lawsuit, at the same time he was representing Client B, a third-party defendant in the same lawsuit. This put Kalla in a situation where advocating for Client A would potentially harm Client B. Kalla's ability to fully advocate for both clients was materially limited by Kalla's dual representation. This concurrent conflict of interest was technically waivable under subpart (b) of Rule 1.7. However, waiver only excuses the conflict if "each affected client gives informed consent, confirmed in writing." Minn. R.

Prof. Conduct 1.7(b)(4). Kalla never obtained written consent from Client B to represent both clients; thus the conflict was not waived. Therefore, Kalla's representation of Clients A and B without Client B's informed consent violated Rule 1.7(a)(2).

Based on Kalla's misconduct and aggravating circumstances, the referee recommended that Kalla be publicly reprimanded and be placed on two years of supervised probation. Given the record before us, we see no reason to deviate from the referee's recommendation, which we hereby adopt.

NOTES ON IN RE KALLA

1. *Direct Adversity v. Significant Risk of Material Limitation.* Does this case involve "directly adverse" representation or a "significant risk" that the representation of one client will be "materially limited" by the lawyer's responsibilities to another client? Under Rule 1.7, does it matter?

2. *What Was Kalla Thinking?* What factors do you think might help explain how Kalla got himself into such trouble?

PROBLEM 10–1

Lawyer represents Monster Developer (MD) in its efforts to acquire city approval to build a stadium and related hotel and restaurant facilities in the surrounding areas. Rural Landowner (RL) has approached Lawyer to ask her to represent RL in an unrelated suit against MD for having sold RL land with major environmental contamination that was not disclosed at the time of sale. May Lawyer handle this matter for RL? If not, may Lawyer's partner take the matter?

C. RELATED ENTITIES

Kalla involved the application of Rule 1.7 to one lawyer in a small practice serving primarily individual clients. But the rule also applies to lawyers in large firms, whose clients are primarily large organizations, many of which are complex entities with numerous affiliates. The following case considers when a corporate client's affiliate is a current client for purposes of Rule 1.7.

This case also addresses the use and interpretation of "advance" or "prospective" waivers—essentially contracts to waive future conflicts. In this case, the waiver was included in an "engagement agreement," which is a letter outlining the agreement between the attorney and client regarding the scope of work, fees, and other terms of the representation. Advance waivers are the subject of the next section of this chapter.

GSI COMMERCE SOLUTIONS, INC. V. BABYCENTER, L.L.C.

United States Court of Appeals for the Second Circuit
618 F.3d 204 (2d Cir. 2010)

WINTER, CIRCUIT JUDGE:

GSI Commerce Solutions, Inc. appeals from Judge Rakoff's order granting a motion by BabyCenter, LLC, a wholly-owned subsidiary of Johnson & Johnson, Inc. ("J&J"), to disqualify Blank Rome, LLP, as GSI's counsel. The court concluded that the doctrine forbidding concurrent representation without consent applies because the relationship between BabyCenter and J&J, which Blank Rome represents in other matters, is so close that the two are essentially one client for disqualification purposes. The district court therefore disqualified Blank Rome from representing GSI in the instant matter because the law firm had not obtained consent from J&J.

J&J entered into an Engagement Agreement with Blank Rome in 2004. The agreement, contained in a letter to J&J, describes the scope of Blank Rome's representation as limited to compliance matters involving J&J and J&J affiliates "in connection with [European Union legislation that regulated the processing of personal data]." The bulk of the agreement concerns two provisions purporting to waive certain conflicts of interest. The first provision addresses Blank Rome's concurrent representation of Kimberly-Clark in a specific patent matter "adverse to [J&J's] corporate affiliate, McNeil PPC, Inc." The second provision seeks a prospective waiver of all conflicts arising out of Blank Rome's representation of Kimberly-Clark in patent matters adverse to J&J and affiliates.

Blank Rome also attached a standard Addendum, which provides in relevant part:

> Unless otherwise agreed to in writing or we specifically undertake such additional representation at your request, we represent only the client named in the engagement letter and not its affiliates, subsidiaries, partners, joint venturers, employees, directors, officers, shareholders, members, owners, agencies, departments or divisions. If our engagement is limited to a specific matter or transaction, and we are not engaged to represent you in other matters, our attorney-client relationship will terminate upon the completion of our services with respect to such matter or transaction whether or not we send you a letter to confirm the termination of our representation.

Pursuant to this Engagement Agreement, Blank Rome advised J&J on a variety of privacy matters, much of which was related to J&J affiliates. In particular, Jennifer Daniels, a partner at Blank Rome, provided affiliates with privacy-related services, including the preparation of policies and procedures, guidance documents, and training materials. In 2006, Ms. Daniels represented BabyCenter in a privacy-related matter. Blank Rome did not, however, advise J&J with regard to the E-Commerce Services Agreement between BabyCenter and GSI, which is the subject of the current litigation. It also appears that Blank Rome received no confidential information relevant to that agreement during its representation of J&J or, separately, BabyCenter.

We have not previously considered whether, and under what circumstances, representation adverse to a client's corporate affiliate implicates the duty of loyalty owed to the client. However, the issue has been addressed by the ABA and also has been discussed extensively in other courts. The ABA's Model Rules of Professional Conduct provide that a "lawyer who represents a corporation or other organization does not, by virtue of that representation, necessarily represent any constituent or affiliated organization, such as a parent or subsidiary." Model Rule 1.7 cmt. 34. However, an attorney may not accept representation adverse to a client affiliate if "circumstances are such that the affiliate should also be considered a client of the lawyer." *Id.* Many courts have reached the conclusion that the bar to concurrent representation applies if a firm's representation adverse to a client's corporate affiliate reasonably diminishes the level of confidence and trust in counsel held by the client. Put another way, these courts focus on the reasonableness of the client's belief that counsel cannot maintain the duty of undivided loyalty it owes a client in one matter while simultaneously opposing that client's corporate affiliate in another.

We agree that representation adverse to a client's affiliate can, in certain circumstances, conflict with the lawyer's duty of loyalty owed to a client. The factors relevant to whether a corporate affiliate conflict exists are of a general nature. Courts have generally focused on: (i) the degree of operational commonality between affiliated entities, and (ii) the extent to which one depends financially on the other. Courts have also focused on the extent to which the affiliated entities rely on or otherwise share common personnel such as managers, officers, and directors. In this respect, courts have emphasized the extent to which affiliated entities share responsibility for both the provision and management of legal services. This focus on shared or dependent control over legal and management issues reflects the view that neither management nor in-house legal counsel should, without their consent, have to place their trust in outside counsel in one matter while opposing the same counsel in another. As to financial interdependence, several courts have considered the extent to which an adverse outcome in the matter at issue would result in substantial and measurable loss to the client or its affiliate. Courts have also inquired into the entities' ownership structure.

[T]he record here establishes such substantial operational commonalty between BabyCenter and J&J that the district court's decision to treat the two entities as one client was easily within its ample discretion. First, BabyCenter substantially relies on J&J for accounting, audit, cash management, employee benefits, finance, human resources, information technology, insurance, payroll, and travel services and systems. Second, both entities rely on the same in-house legal department to handle their legal affairs. The member of J&J's in-house legal department who serves as "board lawyer" for BabyCenter helped to negotiate the E-Commerce Agreement between BabyCenter and GSI that is the subject of the present dispute. Moreover, J&J's legal department has been involved in the dispute between GSI and BabyCenter since it first arose, participating in mediation efforts and securing outside counsel for BabyCenter. Finally, BabyCenter is a wholly-owned subsidiary of J&J, and there is at least some overlap in management control.

When considered together, these factors show that the relationship between the two entities is exceedingly close. That showing in turn substantiates the view that Blank Rome, by representing GSI in this matter, reasonably diminishes the level of confidence and trust in counsel held by J&J.

GSI argues that, with the Engagement Letter, J&J and Blank Rome dispositively waived the corporate affiliate conflict. We agree that a law firm may ordinarily accept representation involving a corporate affiliate conflict if the client expressly consents.

However, Blank Rome failed to obtain J&J's consent to the instant corporate affiliate conflict. Although certain provisions of the Engagement Agreement may constitute a waiver by J&J of certain corporate affiliate conflicts, they do not waive the conflict at issue here. [B]ecause the instant matter does not fall into the narrow category of cases waived [in the Engagement Letter], Blank Rome did not contract around the corporate affiliate conflict at issue here.

GSI argues that the Engagement Agreement gives Blank Rome carte blanche to accept representation adverse to J&J affiliates that are not separately Blank Rome clients. This argument relies entirely on the clause that states: "Unless otherwise agreed to in writing or we specifically undertake such additional representation at your request, we represent only the client named in the engagement letter and not its affiliates, subsidiaries, partners, joint venturers, employees, directors, officers, shareholders, members, owners, agencies, departments, or divisions."

We are unpersuaded. The waiver provisions unambiguously state that the contemplated conflicts arise out of Blank Rome's representation of J&J and third-parties in matters adverse to J&J affiliates, and not out of some separate representation of those affiliates. GSI's construction of the Addendum also fails. If the broadly-worded, standard language of the Addendum actually waives all corporate affiliate conflicts, then there is no possible purpose served by the nonstandard waiver provisions waiving only certain corporate affiliate conflicts. Adopting GSI's construction of the Addendum as waiving all such conflicts would render the more specific and more limited waiver provisions meaningless. Because GSI's construction of the broadly-worded, standard language of the Addendum would strip the remainder of the Engagement Agreement of any meaning, it violates basic canons of construction of contract law.

Having concluded that Blank Rome's representation of GSI implicates the duty of loyalty owed to J&J, and having further concluded that Blank Rome did not contract around that duty, the question remains whether GSI can meet its heavy burden that representation of GSI should nonetheless be allowed. As to this question, we find that GSI has failed to adduce any evidence showing that such representation will not result in an actual or apparent conflict in loyalties.

For the foregoing reasons, we affirm.

NOTES ON GSI COMMERCE SOLUTIONS, INC. V. BABYCENTER, L.L.C.

1. ***Conflicts Rules Apply to All Types of Matters—Not Just Litigation.*** Blank Rome's ongoing representation of J&J and its affiliates involved primarily advising on privacy matters, while the matter as to which J&J sought to disqualify Blank Rome lawyers from representing GSI involved arbitration. As you study the conflict of interest rules, keep in mind that they apply equally to lawyers' representation of clients in a variety of roles, including litigation, counseling, arbitration, and transactional matters.

2. ***What Policies Served Here?*** Notice that there was no overlap among the Blank Rome lawyers who represented J&J and its affiliates and the Blank Rome lawyers who represented GSI in its dispute with BabyCenter. Moreover, Blank Rome lawyers received no confidential information relevant to the agreement between GSI and BabyCenter during its representation of J&J or BabyCenter. Under these circumstances, what policies are served by disqualifying Blank Rome from representing GSI?

3. ***Tracking and Monitoring Conflicts.*** Try to imagine the logistical difficulty involved in tracking conflicts of interest in large firms with thousands of corporate clients, many of which are complex entities with numerous affiliates. Large firms rely on computer programs to help them track and monitor conflicts, but the task remains immense even with the benefit of such technology.

PROBLEM 10–2

Lawyer One works in Large Law Firm and is currently handling intellectual property matters for Corporation, a major media conglomerate based in New York. One of Corporation's subsidiaries, a local radio station in Miami, recently fired one of its popular talk show hosts. The former host wants to hire one of Lawyer One's partners, Lawyer Two, who works in Large Law Firm's Miami office, to handle his employment dispute with the radio station. May Lawyer Two take the matter?

D. ADVANCE WAIVERS

In *GSI Commerce Solutions, Inc. v. BabyCenter LLC*, the retainer agreement between Blank Rome and J&J included an advance waiver of conflicts involving the representation of Kimberly-Clark in patent matters related to J&J. The court's decision did not turn on that provision because the conflict did not involve the representation of Kimberly-Clark. But we include the language here so that you can see what an advance waiver looks like:

> We believe that if, in the future, our firm were requested by Kimberly-Clark to represent it in patent matters related to Johnson & Johnson or its affiliates or subsidiaries, our representation of Johnson & Johnson [on European Union data protection matters] and in other unrelated matters and our present and future representation of Kimberly-Clark would not adversely affect our relationship with either client. . . .

> Specifically, this letter seeks confirmation that, should our representation of Kimberly-Clark in connection with patent-related proceedings involve Johnson & Johnson, or any other entity related to Johnson & Johnson, Johnson & Johnson consents, and will not object, to our continuing representation of Kimberly-Clark in connection with these proceedings. . . .

Why Do Lawyers and Clients Use Advance Waivers? Why might lawyers sometimes seek advance waivers rather than waiting until a conflict arises to seek consent? Why would a client ever sign an advance waiver? The justification typically offered for advance waivers is that they address the reluctance a lawyer might otherwise feel about representing a client that might later seek to disqualify the lawyer from continuing to represent a long-standing client or from securing future business. Advance waivers can help clarify the lawyer's and client's expectations in advance of the representation. On the other hand, overly-broad advance waivers may reflect overreaching by lawyers, especially in circumstances where the waivers are drafted by the same lawyers whose representation the client seeks.

Are Advance Waivers Enforceable? Under what circumstances should advance waivers be enforceable? Courts have generally been skeptical about enforcing advance waivers. However, Rule 1.7, Comment 22, permits them under certain conditions. It says that the effectiveness of an advance waiver should be determined "by the extent to which the client reasonably understands the material risks that the waiver entails." It suggests two conditions for the enforceability of an advance waiver: that the client be "an experienced user of the legal services involved" and that the client consent to "a particular type of conflict with which the client is already familiar." The comment also suggests that consent is more likely to be effective if the client is represented by other counsel in negotiating the waiver.

Can you imagine any reasons why a lawyer might be reluctant to advise a client to hire another lawyer to negotiate and draft the advance waiver?

The "Hot Potato" Doctrine. When a lawyer or law firm would like to undertake a new representation but encounters a conflict with a current client that has not signed a valid advance waiver and is now unwilling to waive the conflict, may the lawyer escape the conflict by simply dropping the current client in order to serve the new one? (As we'll see in Chapter 11, the rules on duties to former clients with respect to conflicts of interest are more permissive than those for current clients.) The Model Rules do not speak to this issue, but the courts have created the "hot potato" doctrine, which forbids withdrawal for the purpose of representing the new (usually more remunerative) client. The *Restatement* endorses the hot potato rule, stating that "[a] premature withdrawal violates the lawyer's obligation of loyalty to the existing client and can constitute a breach of the client-lawyer contract of employment." Restatement (Third) of the Law Governing Lawyers, § 132, Cmt. C.

PROBLEM 10–3

Lawyer, who practices in a medium-sized firm in a Midwestern city, regularly handles litigation matters for Big Company, the largest employer in the region. Although she is not currently representing Big Company on any cases, she hopes that Big Company will bring her more work soon. Meanwhile, Little Guy, a small local business that occasionally tangles with Big Company over zoning issues, would like to retain Lawyer to handle a real estate purchase that is likely to require many months to complete. Lawyer would very much like to take the matter, but she fears that accepting the matter for Little Guy might prevent her from also handling litigation that Big Company might bring to her soon. May Lawyer ask Little Guy to sign an advance waiver as to any future conflicts regarding her representation of Big Company so that she can represent both Big Company and Little Guy simultaneously?

Alternatively, may Lawyer drop Little Guy as a client if, while Lawyer is working on the real estate transaction for Little Guy, Big Company brings Lawyer a case that would otherwise create a concurrent conflict with Little Guy?

* * *

Common Situations in Which Concurrent Conflicts Arise. The concurrent conflict rules come into play in all sorts of situations—far too many to canvass here. Just a few examples of contexts where these issues are especially likely to arise include the joint representation of criminal co-defendants, multiple parties to a transaction, family members in estate planning, an organization and its employees, insurers and those they insure, and members of a plaintiff class. Differences in the power and sophistication of parties jointly represented, and obvious divergences in their interests, can make joint representation in all these situations highly problematic. Perhaps in an ideal world, all these clients would hire their own lawyers to ensure lawyers' single-minded devotion to their interests. But insisting on separate counsel sometimes means sacrificing the significant cost-savings and information pooling advantages that can result from sharing lawyers. Therefore, lawyers, clients, and regulators continue to wrestle with trade-offs involved in deciding what counts as a conflict of interest and what constitutes valid client consent in these situations.

E. CRIMINAL DEFENSE

In criminal matters, co-defendants might sometimes wish to be represented by a single lawyer to save costs and to promote cooperation. But the stakes involved in the selection of counsel can be very high. Co-defendants might be differently situated in terms of their culpability, available defenses, the likelihood of conviction, punishment, and willingness to deal with prosecutors (and/or prosecutors' willingness to deal with them).

Although the joint representation of criminal co-defendants is common in some communities, all of the relevant rules, case law, and expert commentary strongly discourage the practice. The Model Rules take the position that "[t]he potential for a conflict of interest in representing multiple defendants in a criminal case is so grave" that ordinarily lawyers should decline such representation. MR 1.7, Comment 23.

The joint representation of criminal defendants also sometimes raises constitutional concerns. A defendant represented by a lawyer who has a conflict may challenge his conviction on the ground that it violates his

Sixth Amendment right to counsel.[2] In *Holloway v. Arkansas*, 435 U.S. 475 (1978), the Supreme Court held that a defendant's Sixth Amendment right to counsel was violated when a trial judge rejected a criminal defense lawyer's timely objection to representing three co-defendants, and the Court overturned the resulting conviction.

Although defendants generally are permitted to waive conflicts created by their lawyer's representation of a co-defendant in the same case, concerns about conflicts of interest sometimes lead trial judges to disqualify counsel over defendants' objections, even where the defendants are willing to waive the conflict. In *Wheat v. U.S.*, 486 U.S. 153 (1988), the Court found no Sixth Amendment violation where the trial judge concluded that disqualification was necessary to avoid a conflict and protect the integrity of a criminal trial. (But see *State v. Smith*, 761 N.W.2d 63 (2009), in which the Supreme Court of Iowa found a Sixth Amendment violation where the trial court insisted on separate counsel despite defendant's knowing waiver of the conflict where there was no serious likelihood that a conflict would arise.)

What would be the costs and benefits of simply allowing co-defendants to decide whether to waive conflicts in order to be jointly represented by one lawyer? Should the permissibility of waiver depend on how serious the conflict is, whether the defendant would be entitled to have separate counsel appointed by the state, and whether the lawyer has some prior relationship with one of the defendants or some other reason to favor one over the other? What kinds of information might be relevant in determining whether the waiver is truly informed?

Would you favor a flat ban on multiple representation of criminal defendants? What would be the drawbacks of such a rule?

PROBLEM 10–4

Co-defendants A and B have been charged with armed robbery, a felony. They are both represented by Lawyer. The prosecutor believes that A planned the crime and was the only one carrying a weapon. The prosecutor offers to accept B's guilty plea to a misdemeanor if B will testify against A. Can Lawyer continue to represent both A and B if both clients consent to the joint representation?

* * *

Are the defendant's interests the only ones implicated by conflicts of interest by defendant's counsel? Consider the following well-publicized criminal case against John Edwards, a Democratic presidential candidate in 2004 and 2008, and the prosecutor's role in identifying and

---

[2]   The Sixth Amendment to the U.S. Constitution provides: "In all criminal prosecutions, the accused shall enjoy the right . . . to have the Assistance of Counsel for his defense." U.S. CONST. amend. VI.

drawing the court's attention to a possible conflict of interest for defense counsel.

JOHN EDWARDS' LAWYER FACES CONFLICTS QUESTION
The BLT: The Blog of Legal Times[4]
October 10, 2011

[Lawyer] Abbe Lowell has been in demand lately, so much so that a judge in former presidential candidate John Edwards' criminal case may hold a hearing to ensure Lowell can represent Edwards conflict-free.

Edwards, a Democrat, is facing a six-count federal indictment. Justice Department prosecutors say that he received more than $900,000 in illegal campaign contributions from two wealthy donors, including the late Dallas plaintiffs' lawyer Fred Baron.

While the case was under investigation, Lowell represented Baron's widow, Lisa Blue, and Edwards' former campaign pollster, Harrison Hickman. But two months ago, after it became clear the case is likely headed to trial, Edwards hired Lowell as his lead attorney. That creates potential conflicts of interest because prosecutors may call Blue and Hickman as witnesses, according to a new court motion from prosecutors asking for a hearing.

Moreover, while representing Blue and Hickman, Lowell contacted Edwards' mistress, Rielle Hunter, to gather information about the case.

The potential conflicts may not be a problem. Blue, Hickman and Edwards are all OK with Lowell representing Edwards, and Lowell "is not in possession of any client confidences of Ms. Blue or Mr. Hickman," according to the prosecutors' motion. But it's still something that [the judge] should hold a hearing on, the prosecutors wrote.

"The government emphasizes at the outset that we are in no way suggesting that Mr. Lowell has engaged in any improper conduct. Nevertheless, his prior representation of Ms. Blue and Mr. Hickman presents distinct possibilities of potential conflicts that, in the government's view, necessitate this court's inquiry at a hearing and, potentially, proper advisement of the defendant, to ensure that any proffered waiver is knowing, intelligent, and voluntary," says the motion.

The motion cites two examples [of cases in which attorneys were] disqualified from cases in which they earlier represented witnesses, notwithstanding the defendants having waived the issue. Prosecutors write that Edwards' case is different from those two because Blue and Hickman are less-important witnesses. "We bring these cases to the

---

4   *John Edwards' Lawyer Faces Conflicts Question*, THE BLT: THE BLOG OF LEGAL TIMES (Oct. 10, 2011, 12:55 PM), http://legaltimes.typepad.com/blt/2011/10/john-edwards-lawyer-abbe-lowell-faces-conflicts-question.html.

court's attention only to emphasize the importance of this type of potential conflict," they say.

Lowell, in an e-mailed statement, said: "We have discussed this issue with the government to its satisfaction; its inquiry to make a record is appropriate; and we will respond in a court filing."

NOTES ON THE JOHN EDWARDS CASE

1. ***Potential v. Actual Conflicts—How Serious?*** How likely is it that the potential conflict of interest identified in the prosecutors' motion will materialize into an actual conflict? How serious is the potential conflict?

2. ***Prosecutors' Motivations.*** Why do you think the prosecutors filed the motion seeking a court ruling on the potential conflict of interest in this case?

F.　PARTIES TO A TRANSACTION

Suppose that several entrepreneurs want to create a business together. They are short on cash and want to save money by sharing the cost of hiring a lawyer. They would like to hire you to represent them in working out the details and drafting all necessary documents. May you do it? To take an even more dramatic and common example, suppose both a buyer and a seller of property seek to hire one lawyer to handle the transaction. Is that permitted? Is it wise?

This scenario is governed by Rule 1.7. Recall that the rule provides that if there is "direct adversity" or a "material limitation" conflict, the lawyer must assess whether she can competently and diligently represent each affected client and, if so, she must also obtain the consent of the affected clients. At a minimum, as part of the informed consent process, the lawyer must advise the clients about the possible risks of joint representation, including the likelihood that she will have to withdraw from representing any of the clients if a dispute arises among them. In very simple transactions in which it is highly unlikely that the parties will have a disagreement over the terms of the deal (as might occasionally be true with the sale/purchase of a house), joint representation may be permissible, though it is risky. In complex transactions, such as negotiating and drafting documents to buy or sell a business, joint representation is almost certainly unwise.

In her comprehensive study of conflict of interest in the private practice of law in Illinois, Susan Shapiro found that most of the lawyers she interviewed would not agree to represent two parties to a transaction. Those who refused generally cited three reasons:

> They argue, first, that there is no such thing as a fair or friendly deal, a truly neutral legal agreement, or a mechanism for

balancing loyalty . . . Second, with ongoing clients, law firms often have confidential information about the parties that could be used to the advantage or disadvantage of another. . . . [T]hird, . . . deals go sour all the time; something inevitably goes wrong or becomes adversarial, and the law firm is blamed for favoring one client over another.

One of the lawyers whom Shapiro interviewed described why he would not agree to represent two parties to a transaction:

> [Client A] was about to combine with [Client B]. They were going to rent space from them; they were going to use their facilities; they were going to use their personnel. I didn't think that I could do a fair job of representing both of them because there was too much—as I viewed it—there was too much potential for conflict. "How much should they charge? Should it be higher; should it be lower? How much worth of clerical help will they get? How much time would they get? What kind of priorities would they have?" I don't think I could have resolved that between the two of them. And so I told [Client B] to seek independent counsel.[3]

PROBLEM 10–5

Three prospective clients come to Lawyer for assistance in launching a start-up high tech company. Client A has a great new smart-phone app. Client B has managerial experience and would serve as the company's CEO. Client C would provide most of the financing to get the project started. May Lawyer represent all three clients in creating business? If so, under what circumstances?

G. JOINT REPRESENTATION OF AN ORGANIZATION AND ITS EMPLOYEES

A lawyer for an organization sometimes faces the question of whether she may represent one or more employees of the organization while also representing the organization itself with respect to the same subject matter. For example, an organization might be accused of misconduct, such as fraud, and an individual who participated in the decisions that amounted to the fraud might also be accused of wrongdoing.

Why might an employee find it advantageous to be represented by the company's attorney? What are the risks?

If it appears that the organization and the employee are likely to point fingers at one another, joint representation is impossible. If, however, the organization and employee will assert the same defense,

---

[3]   SUSAN SHAPIRO, TANGLED LOYALTIES: CONFLICT OF INTEREST IN LEGAL PRACTICE 68–69 (2002).

joint representation may be permitted with both clients' informed consent. Joint representation may be attractive to the employee because the organization typically pays the legal fees, but it is also sometimes perilous because the organization is in a better position than the employee to provide future legal business, and therefore the lawyer might be tempted to favor the employer if the employer's and employee's interests eventually diverge.

PROBLEM 10–6

Lawyer has been retained to represent Amazing Airlines in a suit by the families of passengers killed in a crash. Lawyer is about the interview the pilot of plane, who miraculously survived. May lawyer offer to represent the pilot as well as Amazing Airlines? If so, under what conditions?

H. ESTATE AND BUSINESS PLANNING FOR FAMILIES

Estate Planning. Lawyers commonly represent couples who wish to have one lawyer draft their wills. In her study of conflicts of interest in private practice, Susan Shapiro observed that, until quite recently, estate planning lawyers "never questioned" the propriety of representing both spouses in estate planning. But professional associations and malpractice insurers are beginning to draw lawyers' attention to the problems that can result. Several of the lawyers interviewed by Shapiro offered examples of the types of dilemmas that sometimes arise:

> Obviously, on the whole, the more nuclear the family is . . . the more "Ozzie and Harriet" the family is, the less likelihood there is for conflict. That is to say, both husband and wife are parents of the same children, and more often than not, they have the same goals and ends and attitudes in mind. Even then, there is the potential for conflict. . . . Well, this nuclear family has assets—whose name might the assets be registered in when they come to see you? Quite often, they're in joint tenancy. Estate planning oftentimes requires that the couple break up their joint tenancies. Now the question is: okay, fine, whose name do we register it in and how might that—theoretically—develop in the future? That is to say, you put the house in your wife's name and then you get divorced, where are you now?

> You represent the husband, okay? The husband runs a business and the husband and wife come in, want a will. And you go through the litany with them. The husband calls back later and says, "I'd like to make a little change in the will. And I want to take a little less from my wife and give it to [. . .]" whatever, girlfriend, what not. The problem is, who do you

represent? You have situations where you've got to do something. You should have an obligation—I think—to at least disclose the change to the wife, because she is also a client at this point. I don't know how that situation would end up getting resolved.[4]

Should conflict of interest rules be applied more flexibly to the joint representation of family members than to the joint representation of unrelated clients? What are the competing considerations?

PROBLEM 10–7

Husband and Wife come to Lawyer, a trust and estates lawyer, seeking assistance in drafting their wills. After the initial meeting, during which Husband and Wife appear to be in complete agreement about what their wills should say, Husband contacts Lawyer separately to say that he would like to provide for a child he fathered long ago, before he and Wife married. He also emphasizes that he doesn't want Wife to know about the provision because it might cause needless conflict in their marriage. May Lawyer continue to represent both Husband and Wife? If not, may he continue to represent either of them?

Tax and Other Business Matters for a Family. Conflicts can also arise where members of a family use the same lawyer for matters other than estate planning. In the following case, a lawyer got into serious trouble by handling various tax and business matters for several family members whose interests may have seemed congruent initially but ultimately came into conflict.

IN THE MATTER OF THE DISCIPLINARY PROCEEDING AGAINST LARRY A. BOTIMER

Supreme Court of Washington
166 Wash.2d 759 (2009)

OWENS, J.:

The Washington State Bar Association accused attorney Larry Botimer of violating several provisions of the Rules of Professional Conduct (RPCs) regarding his representation and legal services provided to Ruth Reinking (Ruth), including failure to obtain informed consent in writing to a conflict of interest and improper disclosure of client confidences. The Disciplinary Board agreed that the recommendation of the hearing officer for a six-month suspension was appropriate.

Botimer served for several years as a tax preparer and tax advisor to Ruth and other members of the Reinking family, including Ruth's son Jan Reinking (Jan) and his wife Janet Reinking (Janet). Botimer assisted

---

4   *Id.*

Ruth with decisions related to her ownership stake in Magnolia Health Care Center, Inc., a nursing home facility. [After Ruth retired from the business, she continued to own it, but she leased it to Jan and Janet]. Botimer prepared tax returns for Magnolia. He also assisted Ruth with business matters related to another care facility, ACC, run by her other son, James Reinking (James). Controversy arose when James would not recognize that Ruth and/or Jan had an ownership stake in ACC. Botimer assisted Jan and Ruth in negotiations with James regarding potential solutions.

Botimer did not obtain conflict waivers in the course of his assistance of the various members of the Reinking family. Further, he did not discuss the advantages and disadvantages of joint representation. Botimer did not use a written client engagement agreement or any other method to obtain consent in writing to the conflict.

Ruth, Jan, and Janet decided to close Magnolia and sell the property in August 2000. The proceeds of this sale were to go to the three family members, with Jan and Janet expecting half. Apparently, Botimer also requested that his fees be paid out of these proceeds. Upon the sale, Ruth did not share the proceeds with Jan, Janet, or Botimer. Instead, she used the proceeds to satisfy her loan guarantees to ACC.

In 2002, Botimer terminated his representation of Ruth with a letter stating that "her failure to cooperate with him, refusal to follow his advice and failure to pay for [his] legal services" led to his decision. [The letter also informed Ruth that Botimer was sending correspondence to the IRS to inform the agency "that [Ruth's tax] returns do not contain a true record of [her] taxable income." Botimer followed through and sent the letter to the IRS informing the agency of Ruth's failure to correctly state her income.]

To resolve disputes stemming from the sale of Magnolia, Jan and Janet sued Ruth, James, and ACC in 2004 on theories of conversion [the unlawful taking or use of someone's property], fraudulent misrepresentation, breach of contract, and others. Jan and Janet sought damages of $530,951.30, which represented one-half of the proceeds from the Magnolia property. Botimer cooperated with Jan and Janet's attorney in the lawsuit, and provided him with three declarations to use in pretrial proceedings. Ruth did not give her consent to these disclosures, and no court ordered this revelation of Ruth's client information.

Botimer argues that there was no manifest conflict of interest, and even if there was, it was merely a potential conflict. Under former RPC 1.7(b)(2), an attorney faced with a concurrent conflict of interest may continue in joint representation, but only upon obtaining informed consent in writing from each affected client. The hearing officer found no such consent and concluded that Botimer violated former RPC 1.7(b). Substantial evidence supports the hearing officer's conclusion that Botimer maintained a conflict of interest without consent by his clients.

The hearing officer found conflict inherent in Ruth and Jan's various business arrangements. Ruth and Jan were lessor and lessee of the Magnolia real property, and Botimer assisted both of them in this venture. Botimer also assisted Ruth on estate planning matters, while advising Jan as a potential beneficiary of Ruth's estate. Also, when advising on a possible restructuring of ACC, a potential conflict arose in the context of Botimer's representation of Ruth and Jan. Substantial evidence exists on the record to support these findings and conclusions.

The need to obtain informed consent in writing arises when there exists a "likelihood that a difference in interests will eventuate" that may "materially interfere with the lawyer's independent professional judgment." Rule 1.7 cmt. 8. Botimer never obtained consent from Ruth, Jan, or Janet for multiple representation and does not now dispute this fact.

[The court also found that Botimer had violated his confidentiality duties by disclosing Ruth's confidences to counsel for Jan and Janet and to the IRS.]

Botimer's entanglements in the Reinking family's tax and business affairs created the potential for conflict of interest. Because he failed to obtain the necessary waivers, Botimer violated former RPC 1.7. Further, Botimer did not satisfy former RPC 1.6 when he failed to protect his client confidences up to the limit of applicable law. We accept the Board's recommendation of a six-month suspension.

NOTES ON IN RE BOTIMER

1. *Potential v. Actual Conflicts.* At the time Botimer first began providing tax preparation and advising services to Ruth Reinking and her family, what do you suppose was the state of relationships within the Reinking family? Can you identify a point at which Botimer surely should have recognized that he could not represent all members of the family even if no disagreements among them had been apparent at the start?

2. *Relationships Between Conflicts and Confidentiality Concerns.* Notice that Botimer's six-month suspension from practice was based on his breach of confidentiality as well as his violation of the conflict of interest rule. Concerns about confidentiality and conflicts are often intertwined. What is the connection between the two violations in this case?

3. *Values Served By Joint Representation of Family Members.* Is it always problematic for a single lawyer to represent multiple family members who seek the lawyer's assistance in arranging their financial affairs or engaging in estate planning? What values are served by joint

representation in these situations that might not be as relevant in the representation of unrelated clients?

4. *Who Is the Client?* Thomas Shaffer has argued that in the most common type of estate planning matters—a married couple seeking a lawyer's assistance in drafting their wills—the lawyer's client is a family rather than two (married) individuals. He asserts that a view of legal ethics that treats families as "a collection of interests and rights that begin and end in radical individuality" is "corrupting" and "untruthful" because it "leaves the family out of the account."[5] Do you agree? If he is right, what are the implications for how lawyers should handle disagreements that arise within the family during the course the representation?

5. *Families v. Corporations.* Would it be any less plausible to treat the family as the client in some estate planning matters than it is to treat the corporation as the client in other contexts? Are there relevant differences between corporations and families that bear on how lawyers should deal with internal conflict within these two types of collective entities?

6. *"Counsel for the Situation".* During Louis Brandeis's Senate confirmation hearing for his appointment to the U.S. Supreme Court, opponents charged that he had repeatedly engaged in ethical violations by representing multiple parties with conflicting interests. In one such matter, James T. Lennox, the owner of a tannery business on the brink of insolvency, consulted Brandeis for help. Brandeis recommended that Lennox appoint Brandeis's partner, George Nutter, as trustee to whom Lennox should assign his business assets for the benefit of creditors and thereby persuade creditors not to push the business into bankruptcy. Nutter was appointed trustee, but things did not go well; Lennox's father was found to be hiding firm assets, Lennox himself was uncooperative, and Nutter eventually took the firm into bankruptcy upon the petition of creditors. Lennox claimed to be surprised to discover that Brandeis and Nutter were not representing him but were instead serving his creditors, and Lennox hired another lawyer to represent him in the bankruptcy proceedings. At Brandeis's confirmation hearing, Lennox's new lawyer described his confrontation with Brandeis about the propriety of advising Lennox to assign his business assets to Nutter as trustee:

> He said to me, in substance, "I did not agree to act for Mr. Lennox when he came to me. When a man is bankrupt and cannot pay his debts, . . . he finds himself with a trust, imposed upon him by law, to see that all his property is distributed honestly and fairly and equitably among all his creditors. . . . Such was Mr. Lennox's situation when he came to me, and he consulted me merely as the trustee for his creditors, as to how best to discharge that trust, and I advised him in that way. I did not

---

[5] Thomas L. Shaffer, *The Legal Ethics of Radical Individualism*, 65 TEX. L. REV. 963 (1987).

intend to act personally for Mr. Lennox, nor did I agree to." "Yes," I said, "but you advised him to make the assignment. For whom were you counsel when you advised him to do that, if not for the Lennoxes?" He said, "I should say that I was counsel for the situation."[6]

The phrase, "counsel for the situation," is now commonly used as shorthand for the view that lawyers sometimes should seek to harmonize competing interests and reach accommodations that preserve relationships rather than strive to maximize individual clients' self-interest. While that certainly is not the prevailing view of lawyers' roles in most practice contexts, some version of this understanding of the lawyer's responsibilities is not uncommon among lawyers for small businesses, school boards, and local civic and charitable organizations, where discerning who has authority to speak for the entity can be vexing and where lawyers may need to help groups resolve internal conflicts in order to accomplish their purposes. In the large organizational client sector, lawyers who serve on the legal staffs of corporations with multiple divisions and layers, and lawyers for governmental agencies that are embroiled in disagreements over policy, often find themselves mediating among various constituencies that claim to speak for the organizational client.[7] We will return to these issues in Part V.

I. INSURANCE COMPANIES AND INSUREDS

When an insured person is sued for an event covered by the policy, the policy usually provides that the insurance company will provide a lawyer to defend the insured and pay any damages up to the amount specified in the policy. When an attorney is paid by an insurance company to handle a matter for the insured, who is the client? The Restatement of the Law Governing Lawyers § 134 says that the insured is always the client, but by contract or state law, the insurer is sometimes also a client. If a claim will be covered completely by the insurance policy, there may be no conflict between the interests of the insured and the insurer. What happens, though, if the lawyer learns something that would suggest that the insurer could contest the coverage—e.g., that the insured violated the terms of the policy? What happens if the insured and insurer disagree about discretionary work or expenses in litigation that might affect whether an award will exceed the policy limits? What happens if the insurer wants to settle but the insured does not? In all these situations, there may be conflicts of interest that make it impossible for the lawyer to represent both the insurer and insurer.

---

[6]   Clyde Spillenger, *Elusive Advocate: Reconsidering Brandeis as People's Lawyer*, 105 YALE L.J. 1445 (1996).

[7]   See GEOFFREY C. HAZARD, JR., ETHICS IN THE PRACTICE OF LAW 61–62 (1978).

Recall that in *Spaulding v. Zimmerman*, discussed in Chapter 1, we speculated that the wishes of the insurance company might have diverged from those of the individual defendants with respect to confidential information about Spaulding's medical condition; if defense counsel had consulted both the individual defendants and the insurer, they might have discovered that the individual defendants were more willing than the insurance company to divulge Spaulding's aneurism. The *Spaulding* scenario also illustrates why such conflicts of interest matter. Since insurance defense counsel earn their livelihood from repeat business from insurers, they might be tempted to take direction from insurance companies when the interests of insurers and insured clients conflict.

J. CLASS ACTIONS

A plaintiff class action is a form of a lawsuit in which a large group of people collectively bring a claim to court. In a class action, one or several named plaintiffs sue on behalf of a proposed class, and the suit may proceed as a class action only if the group can show that they have suffered a common injury or injuries. But the interests of the members of a plaintiff class action seldom are exactly the same. In cases involving thousands of plaintiffs seeking monetary or injunctive relief through a class action lawsuit, there often are differences among class members in the type and degree of their concerns and desired remedies.

By its very nature, the class action device demonstrates that our legal system does not always insist that every individual client must receive counsel with undivided loyalty. In very large class actions, it would be impractical to confer with each class member to explain potential conflicts and obtain informed consent. On the other hand, it is clearly improper for a lawyer to proceed with a class action if the clients' concerns and desired remedies are more conflicting than common. Rules of civil procedure provide some safeguards designed to protect the interests of individual class members, but significant discretion remains with lawyers to determine whether they can adequately represent all members of a plaintiff class.

We will discuss the relationship between class actions and conflict of interest doctrine, and some particular instances involving the tension between these two bodies of law, in Chapter 30.

K. POSITIONAL CONFLICTS

May a lawyer make a legal argument in one matter that is contrary to a legal position taken on behalf of another client in another matter without obtaining client consent? Lawyers are generally free to take positions on issues of law that are contrary to the interests of their clients. Indeed, some lawyers believe that being prepared to argue opposing sides of legal issues is the essence of what it means to be a lawyer. Sometimes, however, "positional conflicts" (sometimes called issue conflicts) may rise to the level of prohibited conflicts. Comment 24 to Rule 1.7 states:

> Ordinarily a lawyer may take inconsistent legal positions in different tribunals at different times on behalf of different clients. The mere fact that advocating a legal position on behalf of one client might create precedent adverse to the interests of a client represented by a lawyer in an unrelated matter does not create a conflict of interest. A conflict of interest exists, however, if there is a significant risk that a lawyer's action on behalf of one client will materially limit the lawyer's effectiveness in representing another client in a different case; for example, when a decision favoring one client will create a precedent likely to seriously weaken the position taken on behalf of the other client. Factors relevant in determining whether the clients need to be advised of the risk include: where the cases are pending, whether the issue is substantive or procedural, the temporal relationship between the matters, the significance of the issue to the immediate and long-term interests of the clients involved and the clients' reasonable expectations in retaining the lawyer. If there is a significant risk of material limitation, then absent informed consent of the affected clients, the lawyer must refuse one of the representations or withdraw from one or both matters.

The Supreme Court of Delaware found such a disqualifying positional conflict in *Williams v. State*, 805 A.2d 880 (2002). Defendant was sentenced to death after a jury recommended, by a vote of 10–2, that he be so sentenced. Defendant's counsel, Bernard O'Donnell, filed a motion to withdraw from representing the defendant on appeal and for a substitute counsel to be appointed. He asserted that defendant could argue on appeal that the trial court erred when it concluded that it was required to give "great weight" to the jury's recommendation in favor of the death penalty—a position directly contrary to a position he was advocating on behalf of a different client in another capital murder appeal pending also before the Delaware Supreme Court. O'Donnell expressed concern that his representation of both clients on this issue would create the risk that an unfavorable precedent would be created for one client or the other. The Court agreed, finding that under the circumstances, O'Donnell faced a disqualifying conflict of interest within the meaning of Del. Law. R. Prof. Conduct 1.7(b), and that withdrawal and substitution of counsel was proper.

Williams v. State presents a clear example of an impermissible positional conflict, but lawyers face many much more ambiguous situations in the real world, where the positions that lawyers take on behalf of one client might conflict with positions taken on behalf of another current client but where the harm is not immediate or direct. As a practical matter, lawyers for powerful clients tend to steer clear of positional clients—not because they worry about enforcement of vague standards such as the one articulated in the comment to Rule 1.7 but because they fear irritating existing and prospective clients, who might take their business elsewhere. One lawyer interviewed by Shapiro described how his firm had become less able to take conflicting positions on legal issues as it had become more successful in gaining large institutional clients. He said that his firm's tradition had been that "[w]e're cowboys—whoever wants to hire us to shoot, that's what we do," but that issue conflicts were beginning to change the firm's culture:

> [A]s we represent larger and larger institutions, corporations, we are more identified with the establishment. And, therefore, anti-establishment types of lawsuits are bad for us. For example, taking a high-profile case before the United States Supreme Court in favor of punitive damages—that's very much against the interests of most of our clients. [T]o have the constitutionality of punitive damages sustained by the United States Supreme Court is very bad for [that corporation] and all the manufacturers. They don't like it. Certain rules relating to expert witnesses; the more loose the rules are as to who's an expert and on what subject, that's bad for defendants—and we represent defendants. So that would be a bad institutional issue. Telling corporations they can't cut down trees is bad. Well, you lose clients, I mean, you just lose clients. That's the thing that's vexing us. It won't be the Wild West anymore. It'll be sad. . . . It's reality.

Another lawyer in Shapiro's study said:

> We will not try to advance certain theories in a tax court, because we know that there will be adverse reaction—I mean, adverse impact—on lots of clients. In the antitrust area, we wouldn't, probably, like to challenge too many mergers, because we do a lot of mergers and acquisitions. We might not like to go in and try to make new law in the antitrust area to expand the reach of the antitrust laws, because it would impact, probably, a lot more clients than the one that we're helping. The same way in the securities law. You wouldn't want to necessarily try to make new law that would be adverse to, quote, "corporate America"—just because it's cutting off your nose. I mean,

everybody sits up and says, "You mean, [this firm] is representing that guy in this stupid case?"[8]

This tendency to avoid taking positions that might harm the long-term interests of clients or prospective clients, even where they do not constitute impermissible conflicts, helps explain trends toward the specialization of private practice. Firms that cater to large institutional clients tend not to represent clients on both sides of recurring types of disputes involving repeat players—between organized labor and management, lenders and borrowers, brokers and investors, franchisers and franchisees, insurance companies and insureds, etc. Firms that serve primarily individuals and small businesses are less likely to worry about positional or issue conflicts because their clients are more likely to be one-time clients who lack the clout to demand that their lawyers avoid positional conflicts. Moreover, lawyers in small firms often cannot afford to specialize in taking one side or the other in such recurring disputes.

Related issues arise when a lawyer's work on behalf of one client might disadvantage another client in business competition even though it would not involve taking a position adverse to the client (a "business" conflict), or where a current client would disapprove of a position that a lawyer might take on behalf of another client (an "ideological" conflict). Neither of these is a true conflict prohibited by the Model Rules. But both can affect a lawyer's relationships with clients, and so they are real issues in terms of the business of practicing law.

Law firms that develop expertise in an area often attract clients from the same industries. Of course, the lawyers handling the work for those clients must avoid conflicts involving those clients and protect the clients' confidential information. Beyond that, however, there are often serious client relations issues to manage, some based on a lurking concern that the client's confidential information will somehow reach competitors. One lawyer interviewed by Shapiro explains:

[I]f you do a lot of work for a company in one particular technical area, they might not want you to represent competitors, even if there is no conflict with respect to a certain matter, because we've become very educated in their technology and in their trade secrets and their confidential information. I've had clients that have been concerned that, if you represent a competitor— even though the subject matter isn't a conflict in the technical sense—if you learn about their technology, there's a chance that some of the information—through you—will kind of seep through. Some clients are very concerned about that; some aren't concerned at all. But it's something you have to always be

---

[8] SUSAN P. SHAPIRO, TANGLED LOYALTIES: CONFLICT OF INTEREST IN LEGAL PRACTICE (2002).

cognizant of, depending on what you're doing. If you have a client that's a major enough client—important enough—that feels a concern over this, you probably [. . .] Well, we certainly have passed up work that would create more of a client relationship problem than an ethical conflict.[9]

Some clients are worried less about the potential leakage of confidential information than about a general question of loyalty:

> We have had a client for some time. One of our partners is approached with the possibility of representing a competitor of this client. There is no ethical conflict. We could undertake the representation of both without violating the ethical rules. But the existing client may be keen to be represented by a law firm that doesn't represent any competitor. Some clients are pretty sophisticated and it doesn't bother them. But big sophisticated companies can also be the most jealous. Indeed, some corporations will try to retain all the expert law firms in the area to impede their competitors.

Ideological conflicts arise when law firms take positions that offend beliefs and values held by important existing or prospective clients. These conflicts tend to arise in connection with pro bono work involving highly charged social and cultural issues—e.g., abortion, gay rights, gun control, and the death penalty. Firms are rarely obliged to decline such pro bono cases to comply with ethics rules; these conflicts are not about loyalty to clients or observing fiduciary responsibilities. Rather, as Susan Shapiro has argued, they are about "the raw power of clients to influence the substantive agendas of their lawyers."[10]

In Part VI, we will delve more deeply into how business and ideological conflicts sometimes interfere with law firms' willingness to participate in pro bono service for those unable to pay, to represent clients whose interests collide with more powerful players, and to participate in efforts to improve the law and the legal system.

PROBLEM 10–8

Lawyer works for Large Law Firm, which represents many national banks. He has been asked by a local legal aid clinic to handle a pro bono matter on behalf of an elderly woman who lost her home in the recent housing crisis because she agreed to onerous mortgage terms that she did not understand and ultimately couldn't manage. She has a meritorious argument that the lender did not adequately disclose the terms of the mortgage and violated federal laws designed to protect borrowers from overreaching by lenders. The lender is not a client of Large Law Firm.

---

[9]　*Id.* at 141–42.

[10]　*Id.* at 168.

Nevertheless, Lawyer's partners object to having Lawyer handle the pro bono matter because they worry that the firm's banking clients will be offended by Lawyer's participation in the case and will take their business elsewhere. Does Lawyer have a "real" conflict? Does he have other reasons for concern?

L. SUMMARY

This chapter explored one large category of conflicts of interest—those involving concurrent (or simultaneous) conflicts between the interests of present clients. We examined the basic standard that applies to such conflicts, how the standard applies to related entities, and when such conflicts can be waived in advance by the client. We also considered some contexts in which concurrent conflicts commonly arise—in criminal defense, the representation of multiple parties to a transaction, estate planning, joint representation of an organization and its employees in litigation, insurance defense, and class actions. We also considered positional conflicts, in which the lawyer takes a legal position in one matter that conflicts with a position she takes on behalf of another client in an unrelated matter. With respect to all of these issues, we explored what values these concurrent conflict of interest rules are designed to serve, how they affect lawyers' and clients' incentives, and how they relate to and tend to shape lawyers' practices.

CHAPTER 11

CONFLICTS INVOLVING FORMER CLIENTS

■ ■ ■

A. INTRODUCTION

This chapter addresses conflicts that involve taking positions adverse to a former client (sometimes called "successive conflicts"). Recall that Rule 1.7, a rule designed to protect the interests of current clients, forbids a lawyer from accepting any representation that will be directly adverse to a current client, or any representation where there is a significant risk that the lawyer's representation of one client will be materially limited by a lawyer's responsibilities to another client, unless the lawyer reasonably believes that she can provide competent and diligent representation to each client and the clients consent. Rule 1.9 spells out the duties that lawyers owe to former clients. Those duties are in some respects narrower than the duties owed to current clients, and they emphasize confidentiality more than loyalty. Under Rule 1.9, if matters are not the "same or substantially related," the lawyer may proceed to represent a person against a former client even without consulting the former client. Remember, however, that whether or not a lawyer is allowed to handle a matter against a former client, a lawyer may not reveal information relating to the representation of a former client or use confidential information to the disadvantage or a former client. Rule 1.9(c).

In this chapter, we first consider the standard laid out in Rule 1.9(a). We then explore what it means for two matters to be the same or substantially related. Finally, we address the question of when a current client becomes a former client, such that the less restrictive conflict of interest rules for former clients apply.

B. THE BASIC STANDARD

Model Rule 1.9: Conflicts Involving Former Clients

A lawyer may not work on behalf of a new client if the work involves "the same or a substantially related matter" as a former representation and the new client's interests are "materially adverse to the interests of the former client" unless the former client gives informed consent in writing.

The following case illustrates the basic standard governing conflicts involving former clients.

IN THE MATTER OF DISCIPLINARY PROCEEDINGS AGAINST NIKOLA P. KOSTICH

Supreme Court of Wisconsin
330 Wis.2d 378 (2010)

PER CURIAM.

The facts giving rise to this disciplinary matter are as follows. In 1965, when G.K. was 13 years old and in eighth grade at St. Patrick's School in Milwaukee, Wisconsin, he was repeatedly sexually molested by Sister Norma Giannini ("Giannini"), a Catholic nun who was his teacher, the principal of the school, and a friend of the family.

In late 1996 or early 1997 G.K. met with Attorney Nikola Kostich to explore the possibility of bringing a civil action against Giannini. G.K. shared highly confidential information with Kostich including specific information regarding the sexual assaults. Kostich explained that there might be a statute of limitations issue and stated he would research that issue and get back to G.K. The parties discussed attorney fees but no retainer agreement was signed.

G.K. also authorized Kostich to obtain medical records from G.K.'s therapist. After the initial meeting Kostich sought additional details about the abuse and obtained G.K.'s therapy records. In August 1997, after a second meeting with G.K., Kostich advised G.K. that he would not take the case because he believed the statute of limitations precluded a civil suit.

In 2006, after learning that Giannini's departure from the state of Wisconsin in 1969–1970 meant a criminal charge might still be viable, G.K. contacted the police regarding the sexual assaults. In December 2006 Giannini was charged with two counts of indecent behavior with a child, a Class C felony, in Wisconsin. The criminal charges concerned the sexual assaults upon G.K. and one other student at St. Patrick's School.

On January 9, 2007, Kostich appeared as attorney of record on behalf of Giannini along with another attorney from Chicago. Giannini entered a not guilty plea and the matter was scheduled for trial.

When G.K. learned that Kostich was representing Giannini, he contacted Kostich and objected to the representation on the basis of what he believed to be Kostich's prior representation of him on the same matter. Kostich denied that he had any conflict of interest in representing Giannini and refused to terminate his representation of Giannini.

G.K. filed a grievance against Kostich with the Office of Lawyer Regulation. Kostich responded to the grievance in a letter dated March 9, 2007, denying that he had ever represented GK or that there was any conflict. He continued to represent Giannini. Giannini subsequently entered no contest pleas to both charges.

The referee made a number of factual findings, ultimately finding that Kostich did represent G.K. and concluding there was a clear conflict of interest with respect to Kostich's representation of Giannini. These findings included the fact that Kostich knew that G.K.—identified as a victim by Giannini and in the criminal complaint—was the same individual Kostich met with to discuss a possible civil case against Giannini. Kostich had received G.K.'s therapy records both when initially investigating the matter and then later as part of the discovery materials obtained from the district attorney in the Giannini criminal matter. The police reports detailing the Giannini abuse investigation also indicated that G.K. referred to Kostich as his attorney.

Kostich testified that he reviewed the supreme court rules regarding conflicts of interest and determined there was no conflict. He did not consider it necessary to obtain written permission from G.K. to represent Giannini. The referee observed that Kostich believed he met with G.K. out of professional courtesy and that was it. He did, however, acknowledge that he considered retaining another attorney if it became necessary to cross-examine G.K. in the Giannini criminal proceeding.

The requirements of SCR 20:1.9 pertain to situations involving a conflict of interest with a former client. SCR 20:1.9(a) provides:

> A lawyer who has formerly represented a client in a matter shall not thereafter represent another person in the same or a substantially related matter in which that person's interests are materially adverse to the interests of the former client unless the former client gives informed consent, confirmed in a writing signed by the client.

Kostich contended that he did not represent G.K. Kostich noted that no retainer agreement was signed, no authorizations were signed at his office, no file was created on behalf of G.K., and no notes were taken during the initial meeting with G.K.

Whether an attorney-client relationship is created depends upon the intent of the parties and is a question of fact. An attorney-client relationship is not formed simply because one of the parties knows that the other is an attorney. Such knowledge, however, coupled with legal advice being sought and provided, ordinarily is enough to establish the relationship. Moreover, the existence of a lawyer/client relationship is determined principally by the reasonable expectations of the person seeking the lawyer's advice.

G.K. reasonably believed that there was an attorney-client relationship with Kostich when he shared highly confidential information about childhood sexual assaults and other sensitive mental health information with Kostich for the purpose of pursuing litigation against Giannini.

We agree with the referee's finding that G.K. was a former client of Kostich. As noted, SCR 20:1.9(a) provides that an attorney may not represent one client whose interests are materially adverse to the interests of a former client if the representation involves a matter that is the same or substantially related to the nature of the prior representation of the former client unless the former client consents in writing.

Kostich's former relationship with G.K. and his subsequent representation of Giannini were both adverse and substantially related. G.K. sought legal advice from Kostich regarding assaults committed by Giannini and whether he could pursue litigation against Giannini. Kostich then undertook to defend Giannini in a criminal matter in which she was prosecuted for the same assaults on G.K. There is no dispute that Kostich received G.K.'s therapy records sometime in 1997 or that Kostich later received substantially the same records as part of the discovery materials in the criminal case against Giannini. *See* ABA Model Rules of Prof'l Conduct R. 1.9 cmt. ("When a lawyer has been directly involved in a specific transaction, subsequent representation of other clients with materially adverse interests in that transaction *clearly is prohibited*." (Emphasis added).)

Kostich certainly did not obtain G.K.'s consent to the later representation of Giannini. Indeed, when G.K. learned that Kostich was going to represent Giannini in the criminal charges arising from the assaults, G.K. contacted Kostich and voiced his objection to the representation, and Kostich refused to step down as Giannini's attorney.

Thus, the record evidence amply supports the referee's conclusion that by representing Giannini on criminal charges in which G.K. was the victim, after G.K. had consulted with Kostich about bringing a civil action against Giannini for the same sexual assaults that were the subject of the criminal proceedings, Kostich acted contrary to former and current SCR 20:1.9(a).

NOTES ON KOSTICH

1. ***Formation of the Attorney-Client Relationship—Reasonable Expectations of the Person Seeking the Lawyer's Advice.*** The Supreme Court of Wisconsin found that G.K. was Kostich's client even though he had not entered into a retainer agreement or signed any papers. The standard articulated by the court is one that is broadly applicable: "[T]he existence of a lawyer/client relationship is determined principally by the reasonable expectations of the person seeking the lawyer's advice." Similarly, in a famous case, *Westinghouse Electric Corp. v. Kerr-McGee Corp.*, 580 F.2d 1311 (7th Cir. 1978), the court held that a trade association's members, which transmitted confidential information to the association's lawyers, reasonably believed that they did so in the context of a fiduciary relationship and therefore were entitled to the protection of conflict of interest rules. Lawyers must constantly be alert to the possibility that conflicts rules may come into play in situations where they did not intend to establish an attorney-client relationship.

2. ***What Is a Matter?*** What is a "matter" for purposes of the conflicts rules? A matter is anything that is the subject of the representation. It could be litigating or arbitrating an existing dispute, such as G.K.'s civil lawsuit against Giannini. It could be handling a transaction, such a sale of a business or purchase of land. It could be advising a client on legal compliance issues, such as Blank Rome's counseling on privacy matters for Johnson & Johnson and BabyCenter in *GSI Commerce Solutions, Inc. v. BabyCenter LLC* in Chapter 10.

C. THE SUBSTANTIAL RELATIONSHIP TEST

In *Kostich*, the court found that Kostich's defense of Giannini in the criminal matter would involve representing interests materially adverse to the interests of his prior client, G.K., because Kostich would be defending his former client's opponent. It also found that these representations in the civil and criminal matters involved the same underlying allegations of sexual assault. But matters need not be so closely intertwined as they were in *Kostich* in order to fall within Rule 1.9(a)'s prohibition. Consider the following case, which illustrates how courts determine whether two more distinct matters are nevertheless "substantially related".

R & D MULLER, LTD. V. FONTAINE'S
AUCTION GALLERY, LLC

74 Mass. App. Ct. 906 (2009)

The plaintiff, R & D Muller, Ltd., appeals from the allowance of the defendants' motion to disqualify the plaintiff's attorneys, Cain, Hibbard, Myers & Cook. At issue is whether Cain Hibbard's prior representation of defendants John and Dina Fontaine is substantially related to the current litigation.

The plaintiff brought the present suit against a number of defendants, including the Fontaines and certain companies and trusts established by them, to recover damages sustained as a result of an auction gone awry. American Investment Properties, Inc. (AIP), consigned a 1,500-ounce solid gold statue of Mickey Mouse, called "Celebration Mickey," for auction by Albany Auction Gallery and two of the Fontaine business entities—Fontaine's Auction Gallery, LLC, and Dina's Antiques, Inc. When the auction was held, the high bidder, Roger Jakubowski, was allowed to leave with "Celebration Mickey" without paying for it. AIP then assigned its interest in "Celebration Mickey" and any associated claims to the plaintiff, which expended nearly $300,000 to retrieve the statue. Seeking to recover these costs, the plaintiff sued the defendants, asserting various theories of recovery, including breach of contract, breach of fiduciary duty, and negligence.

Of particular pertinence to the disqualification issue, one count of the complaint seeks to "pierce the corporate veil" so as to impose liability upon the Fontaines individually on account of the actions and omissions of Dina's Antiques, Inc., and Fontaine's Auction Gallery, LLC. In support of that claim, the plaintiff alleges that "Defendant Auction Gallery and Defendant Dina's Antiques failed to secure corporate formalities, or had nonfunctioning offices or directors, or failed to maintain corporate records." The plaintiff also alleges that there was confused intermingling of assets and roles among the Fontaine business entities.

Affidavits and exhibits submitted in support of the motion to disqualify establish that, between 1980 and 1990, Cain Hibbard had represented the Fontaines on personal and business matters. Among other things, in 1987, Cain Hibbard helped Dina Fontaine (Dina) incorporate Dina's Antiques, Inc., and advised her on the proper maintenance of corporate formalities. Two years later, on March 14, 1989, Cain Hibbard sent Dina a letter reminding her of the necessity of maintaining the corporate records of Dina's Antiques, Inc., so that they reflected the current state of the corporation accurately. The letter also advised Dina that "these records are necessary to support the corporation's role as a separate entity, and they help to maintain a barrier against personal liability."

On this record, the motion judge did not abuse his discretion in concluding that Cain Hibbard should be disqualified. The relevant provision of the Massachusetts Rules of Professional Conduct states: "A lawyer who has formerly represented a client in a matter shall not thereafter represent another person in the same or a substantially related matter in which that person's interests are materially adverse to the interests of the former client unless the former client consents after consultation." Mass.R.Prof.C. 1.9(a). This rule applies where the current representation is adverse to the interests of the former client, and the matters of the two representations are substantially related. It is undisputed that Cain Hibbard's representation of the plaintiff is adverse to its former clients; only the second element is contested. Prohibition of successive representation arises from the attorney's duty . . . to preserve his client's confidences and secrets. Thus, if the previous representation exposed counsel to confidential information that could be used against the client in the present litigation, the two matters will be deemed "substantially related."

Here, the judge determined that, even though considerable time had passed since Cain Hibbard represented the Fontaines, the attorneys had been exposed to confidential information that could be used to the Fontaines' disadvantage in the present case. The plaintiff's claim is grounded in the principle that, despite the general rule that a corporation and its stockholders are separate legal entities, one corporation, or a person controlling it, may become liable for the acts or torts of an affiliate or a subsidiary under common control where additional facts permit the conclusion that an agency or similar relationship exists between the entities. Among the several factors a court may consider to determine whether such a relationship exists is nonobservance of corporate formalities.

The correspondence Cain Hibbard sent to Dina indicates that the firm had advised her and Dina's Antiques with respect to observing corporate formalities, in part to help "maintain a barrier against personal liability," and had provided her with backdated corporate resolutions to facilitate her belated compliance. In these circumstances, the judge could conclude in his discretion that Cain Hibbard had been exposed to confidential information germane to the present dispute and that the current and former matters are substantially related for purposes of rule 1.9(a).

NOTES ON R & D MULLER, LTD. V. FONTAINE'S AUCTION GALLERY, LLC

1. ***More on What the Substantial Relationship Test Covers.*** The court determined that while representing the Fontaines on personal and business matters, Cain Hibbard had been exposed to confidential information

that could be used against them in plaintiff's current suit against the Fontaines. One of the topics of Cain Hibbard's representation of the Fontaines—their compliance with corporate formalities necessary to shield them from personal liability—was a critical issue in the current suit against the Fontaines.

But it is not always necessary for the party moving for disqualification to show such a close subject matter connection between two matters in order to demonstrate that they are substantially related. Nor is it necessary to show that the lawyer against whom the disqualification motion is brought actually acquired confidential information that could be used to the client's detriment. Model Rule 1.9, Comment 3, provides that matters are substantially related "if they involve the same transaction or legal dispute *or if there otherwise is a substantial risk that confidential factual information as would normally have been obtained in the prior representation would materially advance the client's position in the subsequent matter.*" In other words, if the matters are such that one would expect the lawyer to have acquired relevant confidential information in the first representation that could be used to the client's detriment in the subsequent representation, the matters are substantially related for purposes of this rule.

2.   ***Substantial Risk of Acquiring Relevant Confidential Information.*** The party moving for disqualification under Rule 1.9(a) need not demonstrate that confidential information was actually transmitted to the lawyer in the previous representation; it is enough to show that there is a substantial risk that such information normally would have been obtained. The rationale for this formulation of the rule is that requiring clients to disclose confidences in order to show that the confidences are threatened by the lawyer's role in the subsequent matter would defeat the goal of preserving the confidences.

3.   ***Don't Focus on Subject Matter Labels.*** Keep in mind that matters sometimes may be "substantially related" even though the subject matter of the two matters is quite different. For example, suppose that a lawyer who represented a business person in connection with his business affairs is subsequently approached by the business person's former spouse to represent her in seeking increased child support. The subject matter categories of the two representations –business planning and family law—are distinct, but some of the confidential information that the attorney is likely to have acquired in the first representation, including information about the business person's assets, could be highly relevant in an action by his former spouse.

4.   ***Screening.*** Screening is the process of shielding a lawyer from participation in a matter or access to confidential information relating to a matter. Screens (also sometimes called "Chinese Walls") are measures taken to ensure that the lawyer has no access to client documents, does not talk with other lawyers in the firm about the matter, and earns no fees from the matter. Screens generally do not prevent the imputation of conflicts by one

lawyer to other lawyers in a firm. In most states, the rules of professional conduct provide that screens may be used to cure the imputation of conflicts of interest within a firm only in very limited circumstances. We will study those situations in Chapter 12.

Even where screens will not prevent imputed conflicts, however, firms sometimes use them to reassure clients that are willing to waive an imputed conflict that their confidential information will be protected, and screens sometimes are one of the conditions of the waiver. Firms also sometimes impose screens where there is no real conflict of interest that would prevent the representation but where a screen would give comfort to the client. So, for example, a law firm might voluntarily impose screens in order to attract business from economic competitors.

* * *

Applying what you've learned about the standard for judging conflicts involving former clients under Rule 1.9(a), how would you resolve the following problems?

PROBLEM 11–1

Lawyer drafts a will for a client who wishes to disinherit her daughter. Thereafter, daughter seeks to hire Lawyer to challenge the validity of the same will. May Lawyer handle the matter for daughter?

PROBLEM 11–2

Lawyer represented Regional Manufacturer in litigation brought by the Environmental Protection Agency (EPA) over environmental violations. The case settled after Regional Manufacturer agreed to pay major fines. One of Regional Manufacturer's former executives now seeks to hire Lawyer to handle a lawsuit against his former employer. He alleges that he was wrongfully fired in connection with his role in pressing Regional Manufacturer to remedy the environmental problems that were the basis for the EPA's lawsuit against Regional Manufacturer. May lawyer handle the matter?

PROBLEM 11–3

Lawyer represented High Tech in its negotiations with major retailers to sell a new device that promises to revolutionize how consumers use smart phones. One of High Tech's major competitors now seeks to hire Lawyer to handle its intellectual property work. May Lawyer accept this work from High Tech's competitor without High Tech's consent?

D. WHEN DOES A CURRENT CLIENT BECOME A FORMER CLIENT?

As you've seen, the standard for concurrent representation is stricter than the one for conflicts involving former clients. Therefore, it's often important to know whether a representation is current, and thus governed by the rules governing concurrent conflicts, or has ended, and therefore is subject to the successive conflict of interest standards. The following case addresses that issue and illustrates how much can turn on the distinction between present and past representations.

BANNING RANCH CONSERVANCY V. THE SUPERIOR COURT OF ORANGE COUNTY

193 Cal. App. 4th 903 (2011)

Petitioner Banning Ranch Conservancy is a nonprofit public benefit corporation dedicated to preserving Banning Ranch, a 400-acre coastal property, as open space. The Conservancy has objected to the plans by real party in interest City of Newport Beach to build a four-lane divided highway on this land, and critically commented about adverse impacts during the environmental review process under the California Environmental Quality Act (CEQA). In 2010, the Conservancy, represented by the law firm of Shute, Mihaly & Weinberger (the Shute firm), filed the underlying CEQA litigation to challenge the project approval. In August 2010, the City filed a motion to disqualify the Shute firm based on alleged conflicts of interest. The City had two different theories: First, the City claimed to be the firm's *former* client on at least eight different matters, all of which were closed some five to 10 years ago. Second, the City claimed to be the Shute firm's *current* client based on two identically worded letter agreements, drafted and signed in 2005.

The 2005 agreements provide that the Shute firm would provide legal services to the City, on an "as-requested" basis, in connection with "public trust matters of concern to [the City]." The agreements, however, conditioned such representation on the Shute firm's confirmation of its "ability to take on the matter." The City's supporting declarations showed the 2005 agreements never had been terminated.

In opposing the disqualification motion, the Shute firm declared that it prepared the 2005 agreements in conjunction with the City's request for representation regarding proposed mooring permit regulations. The Shute firm performed a total of 1.2 hours of work on this matter, and sent the City its final invoice in July 2005. The Shute firm continued doing some minor legal work on another matter, but that matter concluded in early 2006. Other than the initial matter concerning mooring permit regulations, the City never requested that the Shute firm undertake any other legal work pursuant to the 2005 letter agreements.

No attorney from the Shute firm has since communicated with any of the City's attorneys, staff, or council members regarding any legal matter other than in conjunction with the underlying lawsuit. By contrast, the City since has hired at least 10 different law firms other than the Shute firm to represent it on CEQA matters since 2006.

Attorney Amy Bricker, who was assigned by the Shute firm to work on the underlying suit, declared she performed a conflicts check before agreeing to represent the Conservancy, and spoke extensively with the two partners at the Shute firm who were most familiar with its prior work with the City. She confirmed that "none of the prior matters bore any substantial relationship to the [instant] litigation." For example, the John Wayne Airport litigation involved airport noise. The Balboa Village Improvement Project, which ended in 2004, involved a challenge to a project by an arbor society seeking to protect certain ficus trees. The Shute firm declared there were no substantial relationships between any of the prior matters and its current work for the Conservancy.

On September 9, 2010, the trial court held a hearing on the City's motion. The court granted the motion to disqualify, determining that the City remained the Shute firm's current client. "The Court finds that [the Shute firm] is also counsel for [the] City pursuant to the terms of two ongoing retainer agreements ... Both agreements are executed by [the Shute firm] and [the City] ... [The Shute firm] provides no evidence that either of the retainer agreements was terminated, and the agreements do not provide that it would expire under their own terms."

The trial court recognized that the matter was not a "slam dunk." Obviously there are important interests—very important interests on both sides, which the court has given due consideration to, and has balanced.

Disqualification motions implicate competing considerations. On the one hand, these include clients' rights to be represented by their preferred counsel and deterring costly and time-consuming gamesmanship by the other side. The client has an interest in competent representation by an attorney of his or her choice and perhaps, the interest in avoiding inconvenience and duplicative expense in replacing counsel already thoroughly familiar with the case. Balanced against these are attorneys' duties of loyalty and confidentiality and maintaining public confidence in the integrity of the legal process.

There are different disqualification standards for attorneys who have conflicts with former clients and those who have conflicts with current clients. As to conflicts involving successive representation with former clients, courts look to whether there is a "substantial relationship" between the subjects of the current and the earlier proceedings. In contrast, there is a more stringent standard when an attorney simultaneously represents two current clients with conflicting interests. Disqualification, as the parties agree, is *mandatory* in such circumstances even though the simultaneous matters may have nothing in common. Something seems radically out of place if a lawyer sues one of the lawyer's own present clients in behalf of another client. Even if the representations have nothing to do with each other, so that no confidential information is apparently jeopardized, the client who is sued can obviously claim that the lawyer's sense of loyalty is askew.

We separately analyze each scenario, and conclude the trial court abused its discretion in disqualifying the Shute firm from representing the Conservancy.

The prohibition against simultaneous representations of adverse clients has been analogized to the biblical injunction against serving two masters. Until litigation comes to an end, clients rightfully rely upon their attorneys' undivided allegiance and faithful, devoted service. The rule is designed to preclude attorneys from being placed in the position of choosing between conflicting duties, or reconciling conflicting interests.

There is no evidence from which a current attorney-client relationship can be inferred or implied from a course of dealings between the Shute firm and the City. The City does not claim that it is being currently represented by the Shute firm on any outstanding matter. Indeed, the underlying facts establish, without dispute, that the Shute firm has not represented the City on any specific matter since 2006, and has not since communicated with the Shute firm on any legal issue.

Instead, the City contends, and the trial court agreed, the simultaneous representation arises because of the express provisions of the 2005 agreements alone. According to the City, the "two Legal Retainer Agreements between the City and Shute Mihaly are best described as on-going, prospective legal retainer agreements."

None of the language in the 2005 agreements is reasonably susceptible to the suggested interpretation that the City remains a current client of the Shute firm. We concur with the Conservancy's characterization of these agreements as providing a "general framework . . . under which potential future representation could occur should the City request and [the Shute firm] accept, work on any particular matter." As the Conservancy explains, the 2005 agreements were designed to expedite the Shute firm's future relationships with City, but "did not create an attorney-client relationship absent an actual request, and acceptance, for representation on a particular matter."

The trial court erroneously equated these framework retainer agreements with "classic" retainer agreements. The latter type of retainer agreements (which also may be called "general" or "true" retainer agreements) involve clients who pay an engagement retainer fee to secure ongoing legal representation for a specified period of time.*

No such commitments are contained in the 2005 agreements. The Shute firm did not receive any engagement retainer fee, and the Shute firm made no commitments for future legal representation. To the contrary, in section 3, the Shute firm said only that it would have to "confirm the Firm's ability to take on the matter." The 2005 agreements are not classic retainer agreements, and do not create a contractual ongoing attorney-client relationship in the absence of a specific request by the City and an equally specific acceptance by the Shute firm.

The trial court did not disqualify the Shute firm from representing the Conservancy based on its past representation of the City in other matters. Although the Shute firm previously represented the City on numerous legal matters (primarily relating to issues concerning the John Wayne Airport and the adaptive reuse of the former El Toro Marine Corps Air Station), none of these cases bore any substantial relation to the current litigation brought by the Conservancy against the City. Under California law, a law firm is subject to disqualification based upon its prior representation under the following circumstances: If there is a substantial relationship between the subject of the current representation and the subject of the former representation, the attorney's access to privileged and confidential information in the former representation is presumed and disqualification of the attorney from the current representation is mandatory in order to preserve the former client's confidences. *Fremont Indemnity Co. v. Fremont General Corp.*, 143 Cal.App.4th 50 (2006)).

The City cites the Shute firm's "national recognition as a leading environmental and land use law firm . . . ," and the "special insight" the firm's attorneys have gained into the City's approach to land use matters through its prior representation of the City in past decades. According to the city manager, "the City's approach to CEQA, the CEQA Guidelines and the California Coastal Act was created in part based upon the advice and counsel the City received from Shute Mihaly in the form of confidential documents protected by the attorney-client privilege."

Merely knowing of a former client's general business practices or litigation philosophy is an insufficient basis for disqualification based upon prior representation. In *Fremont*, the Court of Appeal reversed a

---

* [Eds: As the court explained, "Classic retainer agreements, in essence, are option agreements: in exchange for the payment of an engagement retainer fee, the attorneys commit themselves to take on future legal work, regardless of inconvenience, client relations or workload constraints. Lawyers make two present sacrifices at the time of signing a general retainer agreement: they reallocate their time so that they can stand ready to serve the general retainer client to the exclusion of other clients and they give up their right to be hired by persons with interests that conflict with the general retainer client, thus again foregoing potential income."]

disqualification order where the law firm's former representation was unrelated to the current dispute, and where there was no reason to believe the firm acquired material confidential information during the course of the prior representation. Because the record did not support a substantial relationship sufficient to give rise to an inference that the firm acquired material confidential information, the *Fremont* court found an abuse of discretion.

As *Fremont* and other cases hold, former representation alone does not give rise to a lifetime prohibition against future representation of an opposing party. Without evidence of a substantial relationship between the former and present representations, the City has failed to satisfy well-settled requirements. Accordingly, the Conservancy is able to retain its choice of counsel.

NOTES ON BANNING RANCH CONSERVANCY v. SUPERIOR COURT

1. *Differences in Standards for Concurrent and Successive Conflicts and How Those Differences Affect Lawyers' and Clients' Incentives.* How are differences between the standards for concurrent and successive conflicts likely to affect the behavior of lawyers and clients? Might the discrepancy between the standards sometimes tempt clients to claim that lawyers still represent them when, in fact, the representation has ended? Do lawyers sometimes face a contrary incentive to assert that a representation has ended—or to end it by dropping the client—in order to benefit from the more liberal successive conflict standards? (Recall the "hot potato" rule, discussed in Chapter 10).

2. *Advantages and Disadvantages of Ambiguity Regarding When an Attorney-Client Relationship Ends.* Some firms make a practice of sending letters at the close of a matter indicating that the attorney-client relationship has ended, but that practice is not universal. Why do you suppose some lawyers and firms prefer to leave unclear whether the end of a particular matter marks the end of the attorney-client relationship? What are the costs of such ambiguity?

Consider the following observations by a lawyer in Susan Shapiro's study:

> A lawyer likes to think that, if he did a good job, that client's going to come back if they have another problem. . . . A lawyer's reluctant to say, "It's a former client." I'm hoping they're going to send me more business, because I did such a good job for them.

> One of our partners brought in a deal from [a large national insurance company]

—never represented them before. . . . Now he did that deal. He hoped to get more deals. He was told he was going to get more deals. Is that a former client when that deal was over? Is it a current client? When does it become a former client? Do you think that anyone in their right mind is going to now send a letter to that client saying, "It was a pleasure working for you. We don't work for you anymore. We consider our relationship terminated. Very truly yours?" No. They might send a letter— which I would recommend sending,—saying, "It's been a pleasure handling this deal. We look forward to working with you again."— whatever. But the concept of termination of the relationship in that situation is very difficult from a practical standpoint.

PROBLEM 11–4

Lawyer's firm has occasionally handled Big Company's employment matters, and it periodically sends Big Company newsletters on current legal issues and invites members of Big Company's management team to attend seminars sponsored by the firm. Even Bigger Business just contacted Lawyer to ask whether he would handle a huge antitrust lawsuit that Even Bigger Business plans to file against Big Company. Can Lawyer take the case?

E. SUMMARY

This chapter has focused on the question of when lawyers may represent a new client against a former client. It examined the basic standard set forth in Rule 1.9(a) and explored what it means for matters to be the "same or substantially related". Since conflict of interest rules for the protection of former clients are more permissive than those for current clients, we also considered how one distinguishes between current and former clients. Throughout these materials, we have paid close attention to how the conflict of interest rules influence lawyer-client interactions and how they relate to the business of practicing law.

CHAPTER 12

IMPUTED CONFLICTS

■ ■ ■

A. INTRODUCTION

The doctrine of imputed (sometimes called "vicarious") disqualification attributes the conflicts of one lawyer to all other lawyers in the same firm. The concept is simple; if one lawyer has a conflict of interest that prevents him from representing a client, all other lawyers in that firm are disqualified as well. For example, if one lawyer is handling a contract dispute on behalf of a business against one of its suppliers, no lawyer in the firm may represent the supplier in that action. The representation of the supplier would be directly adverse to a current client, and the disqualification of one lawyer is imputed to all lawyers in the firm. Similarly, if a lawyer cannot represent a new client against a former client in a matter because the new matter would be substantially related to one in which the lawyer represented the former client, that lawyer's partners and associates are similarly disqualified from undertaking the representation.

The basic premise of imputed disqualification is that lawyers who practice together are "one lawyer" for purposes of the rules governing loyalty to clients. The rationale is that lawyers in a firm have access to each other's files, consult with one another, and share incentives. The imputation rule applies to firms large and small, however geographically dispersed, and whether or not lawyers actually have access to protected information about each other's clients.

The principle of imputation generally applies while lawyers are associated in the same firm. Special rules apply when the disqualification is based on a personal interest of the disqualified lawyer, when the disqualified lawyer switches firms, and when the disqualified lawyer is a former government lawyer. As with other types of conflicts, imputed conflicts may be waived by the affected clients.

This chapter begins by examining the basic doctrine of imputation and then explores situations in which imputation does not apply.

B. THE BASIC RULE

Model Rule 1.10: Imputation of Conflicts of Interest

- Rule 1.10(a) provides that lawyers in a firm many not represent a client when any one of them practicing alone would be prohibited from doing so by Rules 1.7 (governing concurrent conflicts) or 1.9 (governing conflicts involving former clients).

The imputation rule rests on the legal fiction that all lawyers in one firm are "one lawyer." Is there any practical basis for the notion that a threat to one lawyer's loyalty to a client or commitment to confidentiality also affects the behavior or incentives of other lawyers in the same firm? In small firms, the assumption that lawyers might learn confidential client information about each other's clients through conversation at the water cooler seems plausible. In very large firms, the idea that every lawyer actually acquires the confidences of all the firm's clients is more questionable, but technology has made it at least *possible* for lawyers in these firms to share information with one another instantaneously. Moreover, lawyers who practice in the same firm, whether large or small, share many professional and financial interests, and where the lawyer's professional and financial interests suggest that her loyalty to the client will be impaired, her colleagues' loyalty might be similarly affected. Advocates of strong imputation rules also note that, whether or not the first and second dangers are real, clients and the public might lose confidence in the system if the firm of a disqualified lawyer were allowed to proceed.

You've already seen the principle of imputation in action in several of the cases you read in Chapters 10 and 11: *GSI Commerce Solutions, Inc. v. BabyCenter, LLC, R&D Muller, Ltd. v. Fontaine's Auction Gallery* (the Celebration Mickey case)*,* and *Banning Ranch Conservancy v. Superior Court.* In all these cases, the alleged conflicts did not involve *the same* lawyers representing clients with adverse interests; rather, they involved lawyers who worked together in the same firm and who were therefore treated as one lawyer under the imputation doctrine. Since the imputation principle is straightforward and by now familiar, we do not include another case to illustrate how it works.

C. WHEN IMPUTATION DOES NOT APPLY

We now consider some circumstances when the imputation doctrine does not apply. As with other areas of legal ethics regulations, the rules on imputation vary by jurisdiction. We focus here primarily on the Model Rules and the situations that they carve out for special treatment.

Conflicts Are Not Imputed to Other Lawyers in the Same Firm When:

- The prohibition is based on a personal interest of the disqualified lawyer and does not present a significant risk of impairing the representation of the client by the firm's remaining lawyers (Model Rule 1.10(a)(1))

- A lawyer moves to a new firm and has no material confidential information about a client represented by her prior firm (Model Rule 1.9(b))

- The disqualified lawyer leaves the firm and no lawyer remaining in the firm has material confidential information about the matter (Model Rule 1.10(b))

- The disqualified lawyer is a former government lawyer, in which case screening is allowed to prevent imputation

- Imputed conflicts may be waived by the client (Model Rule 1.10c)

---

1. ***Prohibitions Based on Personal Interests of the Disqualified Lawyer.*** One major exception to imputation arises when the prohibition is based on a personal interest of the disqualified lawyer and does not present a significant risk of materially limiting the representation of the client by the firm's remaining lawyers. Model Rule 1.10(a)(1). So, for example, if a lawyer is disqualified from representing a person because the lawyer's opinions, values, or commitments would make it difficult to do a good job in representing that person—e.g., because the client fired one of her friends, because she holds political views that are sharply at odds with the client's mission, or because the lawyer has a personal relationship with one of the client's competitors—other lawyers in her firm are not necessarily disqualified by operation of imputation.

2. ***Lawyers Who Move Between Firms.*** Several other exceptions to imputation address issues relating to how the combination of lawyer mobility and imputed disqualification affects law firms. If the conflicts of a lawyer's former firm always followed that lawyer to her new firm, and if a firm were forever saddled with the conflicts of lawyers who left a firm, lawyers' ability to change jobs would be substantially restricted. A special set of provisions have been developed to handle these situations. We treat them here as exceptions to imputation, but they might also be viewed as special rules consistent with the idea that imputation should apply only while lawyers are associated in the same firm.

- **When a Lawyer Moves to a New Firm and Has No Confidential Information About the Prior Firm's Former Client—Model Rule 1.9(b).** This provision limits the extent to which conflicts of a lawyer's former firm are attributed to the lawyer who moves to a new firm. It allows a lawyer who moves from one firm to another to demonstrate that his former firm's conflict should not be imputed to him because he did not receive confidential information about his prior firm's client. For example, suppose that Arnie worked for Jackson & Jules, and, while he was there, other lawyers in his firm (not Arnie) defended Client A in an antitrust case. Arnie subsequently joins Babcock & Baron and is asked to sue Client A on behalf of Client B in a patent infringement action. Even if the antitrust and patent infringement actions were deemed to be substantially related, Arnie could represent Client B in the suit against Client A as long as he did not acquire confidential information relating to the antitrust matter from Client A while working for Jackson & Jules. This rule is particularly relevant and important for junior lawyers who often switch firms early in their careers and whose job prospects might be seriously impaired if all conflicts of their former employers were imputed to them.

- **When a Lawyer with a Conflict Leaves a Firm—Model Rule 1.10(b).** Rule 1.10(b) permits a firm to represent a person with interests directly adverse to those of a client represented by a lawyer formerly associated with the firm in the same or substantially related matter if no lawyer remaining in the firm has material confidential information. This provision codifies a holding in *Novo Terapeutisk Laboratorium A/S v. Baxter Travenol Laboratories, Inc.*, 607 F.2d 186 (7th Cir. 1979) (en banc), in which a partner who had confidential information about a potential lawsuit by Novo against Baxter took Baxter as a client with him when he joined a new firm. Novo later retained the partner's former firm to sue Baxter, and Baxter moved to disqualify the firm. The Court rejected the argument for disqualification in the absence of any allegation that the partner had shared Baxter's confidences about Novo's potential suit with his former partners before leaving the firm. This exception allows a firm to avoid an imputed conflict by ending its relationship with a disqualified lawyer.

- **Lateral Hiring with Screens.** A final, highly controversial exception adopted by the ABA House of Delegates in 2009 provides that where a lawyer hired laterally from another firm is personally disqualified under Rule 1.9, the new law firm should not necessarily be prevented from proceeding with the representation as long as the new lawyer is screened from participation in the matter, receives no part of the fee, and written notice is given to any affected client. Rule 1.10(a)(2). As discussed briefly above in Chapter 11, screening is the process of isolating a lawyer from any participation in the matter through procedures designed to protect the client's confidential information and ensure that the screened lawyer earns no part of the fee from the matter. About half the states have not adopted any version of this exception.

3. ***Former Government Lawyers.*** The bar and courts have developed different conflict of interest rules, and different imputation standards, for former government lawyers who enter private practice after government service. With respect to imputation, the rule for former government lawyers is more permissive; it allows screening to avoid imputation.[1] The rationale for the more lenient imputation rule for former government lawyers is that it is necessary to attract qualified lawyers into public service by ensuring that they will not subsequently find it difficult to find jobs in private practice.

4. ***Waiver.*** An imputed conflict may also be waived by the affected client. Model Rule 1.10(c).

* * *

The following case rejects the most controversial of the exceptions to imputation provided for in the Model Rules—Rule 1.10(a)(2)'s provision allowing for screening of newly hired laterals. It also explores some problems with the operation of ethical screens.

BELTRAN V. AVON PRODUCTS, INC.
U.S. District Court, Central District of California
2012 WL 2108667

MR 1.9(b)(1, 2)
comment 3
1.10(a)(2)

CORMAC J. CARNEY, DISTRICT JUDGE

Plaintiff Marina Beltran brought this nationwide putative class action against cosmetic company Avon Products, Inc., alleging that Avon defrauded American consumers by marketing and advertising its products as being free of animal testing when, in fact, it tested on animals. Plaintiff is represented by the law firms of Eagan Avenatti, LLP and the X-Law Group, P.C. Avon's lead counsel is Dennis S. Ellis with the law firm of Paul Hastings, LLP. Shortly after Plaintiff filed suit, Avon

---

[1] Rule 1.11 provides that when a former government lawyer is disqualified, no other lawyer in the firm with which that lawyer is associated may undertake or continue the representation unless the disqualified lawyer is screened from participation in the matter and written notice is promptly given to the affected government agency.

moved to disqualify both firms representing Plaintiff under California Rule of Professional Conduct 3–310(E) on the grounds that Jason M. Frank, a partner with Eagan Avenatti, previously represented Avon in a products liability case and two consumer class actions when he was an attorney at Paul Hastings from 2001 to 2007. Mr. Frank spent over 300 hours working on Avon matters, for which Avon was billed over $100,000. Mr. Frank is not currently part of Plaintiff's litigation team. Given Mr. Frank's prior representations of the company, Avon argues that Mr. Frank has actual knowledge of adverse confidential information. Avon argues that such knowledge is also presumed because the former and present Avon matters are substantially related. Avon further argues that although Mr. Frank is not counsel of record for Plaintiff, his conflict of interest is imputed to his firm as well as to the X-Law Group, such that both firms must be vicariously disqualified.

Mr. Frank has been a partner at Eagan Avenatti since February 2009. Before joining Eagan Avenatti, Mr. Frank was employed at Paul Hastings as a summer associate, associate, and eventually partner from 1996 to 2009, with the exception of a two-year period between June 1999 and February 2001 when he worked at another firm. Mr. Frank and Mr. Ellis, a partner at Paul Hastings and Avon's current lead counsel on this matter, have been colleagues and friends for over 15 years. Avon has been a client of Paul Hastings for approximately 20 years. Since 2001, Mr. Ellis has represented Avon in several matters and has served as Paul Hastings' "Relationship Partner" for Avon since 2004. During his tenure at Paul Hastings, Mr. Frank worked with Mr. Ellis on several matters and shared the same legal assistant from 2001 to 2009.

Specifically, while at Paul Hastings, Mr. Frank worked on the following three cases involving Avon as the defendant. First, in 2001, Paul Hastings represented Avon in *Beck v. Avon Products, Inc.*, a products liability action. The plaintiff in *Beck* alleged that she suffered facial injuries following her use of Avon's ANEW All-In-One Perfecting Complex, SPF 15. Mr. Ellis was the senior associate on the *Beck* case. The plaintiff in *Beck* took over 20 corporate depositions of Avon on various aspects of Avon's business, from product manufacturing to testing and marketing. Mr. Frank's main tasks included, among other things, preparing oppositions to motions to compel second corporate depositions; traveling to Northern California with Mr. Ellis to argue the motions before a discovery referee; drafting an opposition to the discovery referee rulings; and strategizing on settlement. Mr. Frank worked a total of 143.5 hours on the case, and Avon was billed $41,615 for his work. Second, in 2003, Paul Hastings represented Avon in *Blakemore v. Avon Products, Inc.*, a consumer class action by Avon's Independent Sales Representatives, alleging that Avon shipped its Independent Sales Representatives products they did not order. In *Blakemore*, Mr. Ellis served as the senior associate. Mr. Frank's primary tasks included, among other things, discussing discovery strategies with Mr. Ellis and Mr. Steinbrecher [another senior lawyer on the case]; drafting a motion to strike the complaint; and conferencing with the litigation team on various pretrial motions, research issues, and appeal. Mr. Frank worked a total of 70.5 hours, and Avon was billed $14,250 for his work. Third, in 2005, Paul Hastings represented Avon in *Scheuffler v. Avon Products, Inc.*, another consumer class action. In *Scheuffler*, the plaintiff alleged that Avon had defrauded the general public by misleadingly advertising and marketing certain products as having "anti-aging benefits." Mr. Ellis was the lead partner on the case, and Mr. Frank worked under him as the senior associate on the matter from February 2005 to April 2007. Mr. Frank was primarily responsible for the day-to-day case management. Mr. Frank's tasks included conferring with the litigation team regarding Avon's defense strategy; corresponding with Avon regarding case development; drafting demurrer and motion to strike papers; conducting research for motions; helping prepare Avon's document retention notice; and arguing on behalf of Avon at the demurrer hearing, among others. Mr. Frank worked a total of 121.75 hours, and Avon was billed $50,710 for his work.

Motion to Disqualify Plaintiffs' Counsel. On February 28, 2012, after initially reaching out to Mr. Ellis, Mr. Frank informed his friend and former colleague that Eagan Avenatti would be filing suit against Avon. On the same day, Plaintiff filed her Complaint. Shortly thereafter, Avon retained Paul Hastings to handle this case. On March 12, 2012, Mr. Ellis telephoned Mr. Frank and advised him that Avon intended to seek disqualification of Plaintiff's counsel.

Avon moves to disqualify Plaintiff's counsel, Eagan Avenatti and the X-Law Group, on two independent grounds. First, Avon argues that Mr. Frank has acquired material, confidential information from his former representations of Avon in the *Beck*, *Blakemore*, and *Scheuffler* matters in violation of California Rule of Professional Conduct 3–310(E). Second, Avon argues that Mr. Frank's acquisition of confidential information is presumed under California's "substantial relationship" test given the extent of Mr. Frank's involvement in the prior Avon matters and the implication of similar factual and legal issues. Although Mr. Frank is not part of Plaintiff's litigation team, Avon further argues that knowledge acquired by Mr. Frank must be imputed to Eagan Avenatii as well as the X-Law Group, and that an ethical wall is neither legally sufficient nor proper under the circumstances to overcome Mr. Frank's conflict of interest.

In her opposition, Plaintiff contends that both grounds for disqualification fail. Plaintiff argues that Avon has not provided sufficient evidence that Mr. Frank possesses material, confidential information.

Plaintiff further contends that Avon has not satisfied its burden of showing a substantial relationship between the *Beck*, *Blakemore*, and *Scheuffler* matters and the instant action as none of the former cases involve claims related to animal testing. Plaintiff further argues that even if Mr. Frank acquired confidential information, a sufficient and timely ethical wall was implemented that would obviate the need to disqualify Eagan Avenatti. Finally, even if the disqualification of Eagan Avenatti were warranted, Plaintiff argues that there is no clear authority requiring the vicarious disqualification of Eagan Avenatti's co-counsel the X-Law Group.

In successive representation cases, disqualification of counsel is warranted under two situations: (1) the attorney in fact has adverse confidential information or (2) the attorney's acquisition of confidential information is presumed because the prior and present cases are substantially related. In the first scenario, the former client may seek to disqualify a former attorney from representing an adverse party by showing the former attorney actually possesses confidential information adverse to the former client. However, it is well-established that proof of actual possession of confidential information is not necessary to disqualify the former attorney. Rather, under the second scenario for disqualification, it is enough that the attorney is acting adversely to the former client and a "substantial relationship" exists between the subjects of the current and former engagements. Where a substantial relationship between the successive representations is established, access to confidential information by the attorney in the course of the first representation is *presumed* and disqualification of the attorney's representation of the second client is mandatory.

There is sufficient evidence that Mr. Frank has acquired material, confidential information from his prior representations of Avon in the *Beck*, *Blakemore*, and *Scheuffler* matters. Mr. Ellis, who worked closely with and supervised Mr. Frank in the previous Avon actions, submitted a sworn declaration that Mr. Frank acquired adverse confidential information regarding Avon's business, corporate witnesses, legal strategies, product testing protocols, and marketing and advertising practices. Mr. Frank states, "with a hundred percent certainty," that he does not know and has never possessed any confidential information about Avon that would be relevant to the present lawsuit. Mr. Frank's representations of his involvement in the previous Avon matters are simply implausible in light of the scope and extent of his contributions to Avon's defense of those cases, which spanned the course of six years and totaled 336 hours for over $100,000. Despite Mr. Frank's efforts to minimize his role on the previous Avon matters, Mr. Frank's time entries and Avon's supporting declarations provide ample evidence to the Court that Mr. Frank's involvement in the prior Avon matters was substantial and exposed him to confidences that were not part of the public record. Mr. Frank's possession of confidential information is also presumed because his prior representations of Avon are substantially related to the present case. A "substantial relationship" exists when the evidence before the trial court supports a rational conclusion that information material to the evaluation, prosecution, settlement or accomplishment of the former representation given its factual and legal issues is also material to the evaluation, prosecution, settlement or accomplishment of the current representation given its factual and legal issues. Here, there is abundant evidence that supports a rational conclusion that information material to the prior Avon matters is also material to the present lawsuit.

Although none of the prior Avon cases specifically involved claims that Avon purportedly misrepresented that it did not test on animals, identity of claims [is] not required. The Beck products liability action implicated Avon's testing protocols, which is also relevant and material to the instant case while both *Blakemore* and *Scheuffler* dealt with consumer class actions. Scheuffler also involved claims that Avon defrauded American consumers through false advertising and misrepresentation of its products. As in *Scheuffler*, the present case involves legal claims for false advertising and unfair competition. Finally, as discussed above, Mr. Frank's work in the prior Avon matters are substantive and wide-ranging. Through his representation of Avon, there is—at the very least—a "reasonable possibility" that he acquired confidential information regarding Avon's business and marketing practices, its litigation and settlement strategies, and its testing protocols that are not publicly available and, if imparted to Plaintiff, would confer a significant advantage to Plaintiff in this lawsuit.

Although Mr. Frank is not part of Plaintiff's litigation team, his conflict of interest is imputed to his law firm Eagan Avenatti. Normally, an attorney's conflict is imputed to the law firm as a whole on the rationale that attorneys, working together and practicing law in a professional association, share each other's, and their clients' confidential information. Nevertheless, Plaintiff claims that disqualification is not warranted because an ethical wall was immediately imposed to cordon off Mr. Frank from the instant case after Mr. Frank spoke with Mr. Ellis on March 12, 2012. As a matter of law, however, an ethical wall is insufficient to overcome the possession of confidential information by the segregated attorney, except in very limited situations involving former government attorneys now in private practice. Even if an ethical wall were legally sufficient, it was untimely because it was not imposed until March 12, 2012, two weeks after Plaintiff filed her complaint against Avon. Nor did Plaintiff's counsel send written notice to Avon regarding the implementation of an ethical wall. The effectiveness of an ethical wall is further compromised by the close proximity of attorneys working together in one office at Eagan Avenatti, which consists of less than ten attorneys, and by Mr. Frank's co-representation of parties with Mr. Avenatti and Mr. Sims in several concurrent class actions. The Court also notes that Mr. Frank has already actively participated in the current litigation by speaking with Mr. Ellis about the case and the instant motion (as early as February 28, 2012), submitting a declaration in support of Plaintiff's opposition to the disqualification motion, reviewing Avon's motion, and even seeking to participate telephonically at the May 21, 2012 hearing. Mr. Frank's behavior casts doubt as to whether an ethical wall can be successfully implemented and maintained in this case.

The Court also finds that, although there is no direct California authority regarding vicarious disqualification of an associated law firm, disqualification of the X-Law Group is warranted under the circumstances of this case. The X-Law Group consists of four attorneys, two of whom have already collaborated with Eagan Avenatti in the filing of the complaint against Avon in *Estee Lauder* and this case. It is also reasonable to assume that the two law firms engaged in fairly extensive discussions about the case and Plaintiff's litigation strategy before filing their complaint and prior to the erection of an wall ethical segregating Mr. Frank from the case. Even if the X-Law Group did not, in fact, acquire confidential information, their involvement in the case would taint the appearance of probity and fairness of the proceedings.

In a motion to disqualify, it is also proper to consider such factors as whether disqualification would result in prejudice to the nonmoving party. Here, the Court finds that prejudice to Plaintiff is minimal given the early stage of the litigation. Avon's motion to disqualify Plaintiff's counsel does not appear to be tactically motivated and granting it will not unduly prejudice Plaintiff.

For the foregoing reasons, Avon's motion to disqualify is GRANTED. The law firms of Eagan Avenatti and the X-Law Group are both disqualified from representing Plaintiff in the present lawsuit.

NOTES ON BELTRAN V. AVON PRODUCTS, INC.

1. *California's Rule Compared to MR 1.9.* The court's finding that Jason Frank had a disqualifying conflict was based not on Model Rule 1.9 but rather on California's Rule—Rule 3–310E, which provides that a lawyer "shall not, without the informed written consent of the client or former client, accept employment adverse to the client or former client where, by reason of the representation of the client or former client, the member has obtained confidential information material to the employment." The *Beltran* court found not only that Frank had actually acquired confidential information relevant to Plaintiff's action, but also that Frank's acquisition of material confidential information could be presumed because there was a "substantial relationship" between the prior matters in which he had

represented Avon and the current suit. California is in the process of considering a new conflicts rule that is essentially the same as Model Rule 1.9.

2.   ***Should Screens Be Permitted to Cure Imputed Conflicts?*** When, if ever, do you think "screens" should be allowed to cure imputed conflicts of interest? Does this case suggest some reasons why many jurisdictions have rejected screening as a cure for imputed conflicts relating to the lateral hiring of disqualified lawyers?

3.   ***Relevant Experience and the Acquisition of Confidential Information.*** Do you think there might have been any connection between the experience that made Mr. Frank an especially attractive hire for Eagan Avenatti and the arguments that Avon made about why Eagan Avenatti should be disqualified from representing plaintiffs in this lawsuit?

4.   ***Broad and Narrow Framing.*** Disqualification in successive conflicts cases sometimes turns on how broadly or narrowly the court defines the category of confidential information that would normally have been obtained in the prior representation. Notice how the court described the categories of confidential information Mr. Frank would have been exposed to while at Paul Hastings that would be relevant in subsequent suits against Avon: Avon's business and marketing practices, its litigation and settlement strategies, and its testing protocols. Characterizing the material confidential information this broadly means that disqualification would be appropriate in situations where the factual and legal issues of the former and current litigation are very different.

5.   ***Co-Counsel Disqualified.*** Judge Carney's decision to disqualify not only Eagan Avenatti but also an associated law firm with which it was working, the X-Law Group, was the first such ruling in California. But the Second Circuit issued a similar ruling in *Fund of Funds, Ltd. v. Arthur Andersen & Co.*, 567 F.2d 225, 233 (2d Cir. 1977), which disqualified a firm that was associated with the disqualified firm because allowing the associated firm to proceed with the representation would be "allowing [the conflicted firm] to violate by indirection those very strictures it cannot directly contravene." Do you think that this extension of imputation to other associated law firms is good policy?

* * *

Applying what you've learned about the imputation doctrine, how would you resolve the following problems?

PROBLEM 12–1

Lawyer 1 is handling litigation on behalf of Client One out of his firm's Los Angeles office. Lawyer 2, in the same firm's Dubai office, would like to handle a negotiation on behalf of Client Two against Client One in a matter that is unrelated to the litigation that Lawyer 1 is handling for

Client One. May Lawyer 2 handle the negotiation by Client Two against Client One?

PROBLEM 12–2

Partner represents Silicon Valley Wonder in a patent infringement action against Major Conglomerate. Senior Associate leaves the firm to join another firm and soon after arriving at the new firm is asked to work on a piece of intellectual property litigation against Silicon Valley Wonder. While at his former firm, Senior Associate never worked on the patent infringement action for Silicon Valley Wonder and did not acquire any confidential information about the client. May Senior Associate now work on the litigation against Silicon Valley Wonder?

PROBLEM 12–3

Assume that the facts are the same as in the first sentence of Problem 12–2—that is, that Partner represents Silicon Valley Wonder in a patent infringement action against Major Conglomerate. Soon after the litigation ends, Partner leaves the firm to join another firm, and he takes with him the two other lawyers who worked on the litigation, along with all files pertaining to the litigation. If no lawyer remaining in Partner's former firm has any confidential information about Silicon Valley Wonder, could that firm handle subsequent intellectual property litigation against Silicon Valley Wonder?

PROBLEM 12–4

Assume that the facts are the same as in Problem 12–2 except that Senior Associate acquired confidential information about Silicon Valley Wonder while at his former firm. May other lawyers at Senior Associate's new firm handle the lawsuit against Silicon Valley Wonder if Senior Associate is screened?

D. SUMMARY

This chapter examined the doctrine of imputation and the rationale for the doctrine. It also explored circumstances when imputation does not apply. The rules attempt to balance several policies that are in tension with one another—one the one hand, allowing lawyers considerable freedom to move between employers and to do so without transmitting conflicts to all other lawyers with whom they associate along the way, while, on the other hand, ensuring that lawyers' loyal service to clients is not compromised and that clients' confidential information is adequately protected.

PART V

PROFESSIONALISM IN CONTEXT: A SURVEY OF PRACTICE SETTINGS/TYPES

■ ■ ■

INTRODUCTION

We devote this Part to a survey of the many different types of practice settings in which lawyers work and the issues of professionalism that arise in those various types of practice. We first consider lawyers who work as either prosecutors or defense lawyers in the criminal process. We then examine attorneys who serve large organizational clients while working at large firms, in corporations, and in government. Next, we consider lawyers who serve primarily individual and small business clients from solo practices and small firms. Boutique firms, which straddle the two hemispheres of practice, also appear in this survey. We then study lawyers who work as mediators, arbitrators, and judges, as well as those who work in legal aid programs and public interest organizations. For each of these practice types, the reading materials examine what the practices look like, the ethical issues that are most salient in each, and some of the relevant law that governs lawyers. We will also consider materials from other disciplines that lend useful perspectives on how these practices operate and the forces that tend to shape lawyers' behavior in each setting.

SUBPART A

CRIMINAL PRACTICE

■ ■ ■

No area of practice offers a richer array of issues regarding the role of the lawyer than the criminal justice system. Many of the most acute ethical dilemmas lawyers face occur in criminal defense or criminal prosecution. Many of the proudest achievements of the American bar and American law are reflected in the role of criminal lawyers. Many of its most abject failures are found here too. In this segment, we consider the big issues about lawyers' conduct in criminal justice, an aspect of the American legal system in which lawyers play a more central role than any other.

We begin in Chapter 13 by examining the lawyer's role in criminal defense. In Chapter 14, we study the role of the prosecutor.

CHAPTER 13

CRIMINAL DEFENSE PRACTICE

■ ■ ■

A. INTRODUCTION

Criminal defense practice is not one practice setting but many varied ones. But there are characteristics of criminal defense practice that are common to all. Contrary to popular perception, only a small part of the job of most criminal defense lawyers consists of trials. Most criminal defense lawyers spend most of their time prior to trial, investigating the facts, litigating over which evidence may properly be considered proof of guilt, and negotiating the terms on which clients would be willing to enter a plea to a criminal charge. While all criminal defense lawyers occasionally try cases and some do so frequently, the popular perception that the criminal defense lawyer is always and only a well-resourced and clever courtroom tactician is a misconception. Some lawyers spend significant time and money investigating a case prior to trial; others have relatively little time or money to investigate a case prior to negotiating a plea agreement or trying the case. Only a small segment of the criminal defense bar has the resources to conduct the most thorough investigation and to mount the cleverest defense. Many criminal defense lawyers represent a very large number of impoverished clients in a high-volume practice in which the overwhelming majority of clients will plead guilty to a crime. The various kinds of criminal defense work have different kinds of rewards and satisfactions, and the ethical issues that lawyers confront vary radically depending on the nature of the practice.

The overwhelming majority of people charged with crimes are poor. In 1996, the most recent year for which federal Bureau of Justice Statistics are available, 82 percent of felony defendants in state courts were indigent, as were 66 percent of federal felony defendants in 1998.[1] Ninety-five percent of criminal defendants are charged in state courts. Because the vast majority of criminal defendants are too poor to hire their own lawyers, they are represented by lawyers whom they neither choose nor pay for; the representation they receive from appointed counsel varies from superb to abysmal. Criminal defendants without much personal wealth but who are not poor enough to qualify for representation by the

---

[1] Caroline Wolf Harlow, *Bureau of Justice Statistics Special Report: Defense Counsel in Criminal Cases*, U.S. DEPT. OF JUSTICE, BUREAU OF JUSTICE STATISTICS (Nov. 2000), http://bjs.ojp.usdoj.gov/index.cfm?ty=pbdetail&iid=772.

public defender or court-appointed counsel typically hire lawyers in solo practice and small firms; lawyers in such practices handle criminal defense matters ranging from misdemeanors to the most serious felonies.

At the other end of the spectrum, a segment of lawyers in private practice, in both large and small firms, specialize in criminal defense for wealthy individuals and companies suspected or accused of crimes. Lawyers in that specialty, known as white-collar criminal defense because the crimes often involve business wrongdoing, typically spend a great deal of time and money during the investigative stage before criminal charges are filed, advising clients about whether or how proposed transactions may risk criminal investigation, and attempting to persuade the law enforcement agency and prosecutors that no crime was committed or that criminal prosecution is unwarranted for some other reason. As one leading study of white collar criminal defense practice observed, the white collar criminal defense attorney "is usually called in by the client to conduct a defense before the government investigation is completed and in some cases even before it begins. The defense attorney employs his own investigators, who are experts in accounting and finance, as well as a staff of legal researchers. He learns thoroughly the details of the case, usually having a greater ability to do this than the government investigator and prosecutor. This attorney, in distinct contrast to the attorney handling street crime, has a number of opportunities to argue the innocence of his client before the government makes a decision to issue an indictment. But above, all, and this is the central theme of the white-collar criminal defense function, the defense attorney works to keep potential evidence out of government reach by controlling access to information."[2]

The same ethical rules apply to all lawyers, including all criminal defense lawyers. In addition, the ABA has promulgated standards for lawyers engaged in particular types of practice, and lawyers also rely on these standards for guidance and courts or disciplinary agencies sometimes look to them in determining whether a lawyer's conduct has fallen below the minimum standard. One such set of standards, the ABA Standards for Criminal Justice, governs criminal prosecution and defense practice.[3]

Among the fundamental rules governing all lawyers is Model Rule 1.1, which requires all lawyers to "provide competent representation to a client." Competent representation "requires the legal knowledge, skill, thoroughness and preparation reasonably necessary for the representation." Model Rule 1.3 requires a lawyer act with "reasonable diligence and promptness" in representing a client. For lawyers with

---

[2] *See* KENNETH MANN, DEFENDING WHITE COLLAR CRIME: A PORTRAIT OF ATTORNEYS AT WORK 5 (1985).

[3] http://www.americanbar.org/groups/criminal_justice/standards.html.

reasonable case loads and adequate resources, the requirements of competence and diligence present no problem. Although lawyers in all practice settings occasionally fail to meet the minimum standards of competence and diligence, we address these two rules here because indigent criminal defense is poorly funded in some jurisdictions, and critics charge that paltry pay, scarce resources for investigators, forensic experts, and other services necessary to investigate a case and mount a defense, and crushing caseloads lead some criminal defense lawyers to provide poor quality representation.[4]

Model Rules 1.1 and 1.3: The Lawyer's Duties of Competence and Diligence

- A lawyer must provide competent representation to a client. Competent representation requires the legal knowledge, skill, thoroughness and preparation reasonably necessary for the representation.

- A lawyer must act with reasonable diligence and promptness in representing a client.

- A lawyer's workload must be controlled so that each matter can be handled competently.

Competent representation for all lawyers is ensured first and foremost by workplace training and supervision. Senior lawyers in an office train junior lawyers about what is expected and how to perform the job well. A second important source of regulation of lawyer competence is the market: clients seek out skilled lawyers, as reflected in reputation and results in past cases. A third important source of regulation of lawyer competence is the threat of liability for malpractice. Most lawyers who can afford it purchase insurance policies to cover the threat of being sued by a client for malpractice. Malpractice insurers therefore also play a role in ensuring minimum lawyer competence by requiring certain office procedures (like a calendaring system), as a condition of issuing an insurance policy and by charging a price for insurance that reflects the experience of the lawyer. Finally, the organized bar attempts to regulate lawyer competence through the threat of discipline either by the state bar (which can suspend or revoke a lawyer's license to practice law) or by the tribunals in which lawyers appear (every court can suspend or revoke a lawyer's privilege to appear in that court). (The law of malpractice and the processes of bar discipline are covered in Chapter 36.)

---

[4] *See, e.g.,* Benjamin H. Barton & Stephan Bibas, *Triaging Appointed Counsel Funding and Pro Se Access to Justice,* 160 U. PENN. L. REV. 967 (2012); STANDING COMM. ON LEGAL AID & INDIGENT DEFENDANTS, AM. BAR ASS'N, GIDEON'S BROKEN PROMISE: AMERICA'S CONTINUING QUEST FOR EQUAL JUSTICE 9–10 (2004).

When a lawyer has a huge caseload and few resources to conduct factual and legal research, however, it may be difficult to decide, as a matter of law or practical moral judgment, whether representation is reasonably competent and diligent. The Comments to the Model Rules do not acknowledge the problem of scarce resources. Competence "includes inquiry into and analysis of the factual and legal elements of the problem, and use of methods and procedures meeting the standards of competent practitioners. It also includes adequate preparation." Model Rule 1.1 Comment [5]. The Comment allows that the required preparation is determined "in part by what is at stake; major litigation and complex transactions ordinarily require more extensive treatment than matters of lesser complexity and consequence." In criminal defense when a client may face a long prison sentence, the matter is certainly of great consequence. How should an overworked lawyer manage? Comment [2] to Model Rule 1.3 insists that "A lawyer's work load must be controlled so that each matter can be handled competently." Yet the Comment does not indicate who will control that workload, and the shortage of lawyers available for indigent criminal defense in some jurisdictions make compliance with the rule difficult if not impossible.

Plea Bargains

A plea bargain is an agreement in which the defendant agrees to plead guilty to a crime, usually in exchange for a prosecutor's recommendation with regard to a more lenient sentence than is possible or sometimes in exchange for dropping some of the charges.

Plea bargaining is extremely common in both state and federal criminal systems. The negotiation of plea agreements is a major part of the job of every prosecutor and criminal defense lawyer. Over 90 percent of federal criminal convictions were secured by a guilty plea in 2009, as were 95 percent of state felony convictions in the nation's 75 largest counties in 2006. Prosecutors prepare their case and propose a plea deal. Defense lawyers present exculpating or mitigating evidence during the negotiations, and then decide whether to recommend that the client accept whatever deal the lawyer ultimately persuades the prosecutor to make. The role of defense counsel may be quite different depending on the case. Plea negotiation can be an elaborate and carefully managed process in cases, such as white collar criminal matters, in which the defense has abundant resources and proof of the crime involves a great deal of complex documentary evidence and testimony. In street crime cases against individual defendants where the evidence of guilt is clear and straightforward and the defendant does not have the money to pay a lawyer to conduct exhaustive negotiations over the plea, the plea negotiation may be a relatively short process in which the prosecutor offers to accept a plea to certain charges and to recommend a particular sentence and the defendant may accept it without much more than urging leniency based on assertions about the defendant's character or circumstances.

Although plea bargaining is common in the U.S., it is not without controversy. Defenders of the system see it as essential to conserve scarce resources and an unproblematic way to handle the vast majority of cases in which there is no serious doubt about the defendant's factual guilt. Critics believe it allows prosecutors to extort confessions from innocent defendants who are too risk averse (or whose lawyers are ill-prepared) to go to trial and risk a long sentence.

Because criminal defense practice differs dramatically depending on whether the client has the resources to mount a full-scale defense beginning at the pre-indictment stage of the process, the ethical issues that are most salient depend on the type of practice. We will therefore consider two segments of the practice separately. We begin with the challenges facing indigent criminal defense lawyers. Then we will turn to the issues of ethics in trial advocacy and client counseling that apply to all lawyers but that are particularly relevant in cases in which the lawyer and client have the resources to mount a full-scale defense through the trial.

B. UNDERSTANDING INDIGENT CRIMINAL DEFENSE

In this section, we first read two of the leading empirical studies describing the job of the public defender in a major American city. Both are by sociologists who conducted extensive and in-depth interviews with lawyers in the public defender's office of Cook County, Illinois, located in Chicago. While these studies reveal a great deal about the job of a state public defender in an urban area, and especially one in which critics believe the funding may not be adequate to the demands of the caseload, not every finding of the study could be generalized to cover the job of public defenders in smaller cities or in offices where the funding is adequate to manage the caseload.

Topic Overview

The arena in which a lawyer practices is a powerful influence on her conception of her role, her working relationships with clients, other lawyers, and third parties, and her approach to legal and ethical problems. Criminal defense practice varies radically between urban public defenders, who represent large numbers of impoverished persons in a high-volume practice that involves negotiating guilty pleas and seeking social services for clients and their families, and corporate or white collar criminal defense lawyers in large firms, who often devote substantial resources to the pre-indictment investigation of a single, complex case.

The shortage of resources for the defense of indigent persons is a pervasive problem in many areas of the United States and raises significant and difficult questions for the legal profession about the quality of justice and the meaning of the constitutional right to effective assistance of counsel.

REINTERPRETING THE ZEALOUS ADVOCATE: MULTIPLE INTERMEDIARY ROLES OF THE CRIMINAL DEFENSE ATTORNEY

Nicole Martorano Van Cleve
In Lawyers in Practice: Ethical Decision Making in Context
(Leslie C. Levin & Lynn Mather, eds., University of Chicago Press, 2012)[5]

The main Cook County Criminal Courthouse is the biggest and busiest felony courthouse in the United States. The 36 Criminal Division judges hear more than 28,000 felony cases [annually], half of which are nonviolent, drug-related charges. At any one time, these judges have about 275 pending cases on their dockets. The defendants awaiting trial are decidedly male, minority, and poor. The Cook County Public Defender's Office represents between 22,000 and 23,000 indigent defendants each year. These individuals are determined by a judge to be too poor to secure private defense counsel. The vast majority are pretrial detainees unable to make bond. Compounding these disadvantages, many inmates suffer from drug addiction, mental illness, or both.

Adjacent to the main criminal court is a jail complex that houses 10,000 criminally accused defendants. More than two-thirds of the jail population meets the criteria for drug dependency or abuse. In addition, the Cook County Jail holds so many inmates with serious mental illness that it is one of the largest providers of psychiatric care in the country.

Defense attorneys conceptualize their work as being structured by two central challenges: (1) defendant-based challenges fueled by addiction, poverty, and/or mental illness; and (2) system-based challenges that compromise the quality and character of justice. System-based challenges include limitations in treatment resources and cultural norms that stigmatize zealous advocacy within the courtroom workgroup. Regardless of the lawyers' inclination to be client-centered in their approach to decision making, defense attorneys are acutely aware that they are representing defendants with co-occurring problems like poverty, addiction, and mental illness and there may be more than just their client's freedom at stake. Many defendants stand to be deported, lose custody of their children, or forfeit their jobs or benefits because of the possibility of felony conviction. Yet, system-based challenges confound defense lawyers' obligations and decisions. Defense attorneys describe a criminal justice system that is woefully underfunded. Treatment options are particularly limited.

Cook County criminal defense attorneys identify two distinct types of advocacy in criminal defense—"zealous trial advocacy" or "zealous treatment advocacy." Trial advocacy addresses the client's legal needs while treatment advocacy addresses the client's rehabilitative needs and social challenges.

For many defense attorneys, justice is not based on an acquittal or reduction of charge but on understanding and responding to the clients' needs—both legal and extralegal. For example, through his public defender, one defendant made an appeal to the judge to seek a longer intensive probation with drug treatment rather than a shorter term in the state penitentiary. As the defendant appealed in open court, "I need to change and be there for my six children. I want this longer sentence for the drug program. I need the structure in my life."

Criminal defense lawyers find themselves widening the scope of the practice of law into areas traditionally viewed as "social work." This is particularly true when the client is battling addiction or mental illness and the "word of the client" is not reliable. In these instances, like a social worker, the attorney must reach out to other resources, family networks, and specialists to investigate and piece together the best interest of the client and help define his rehabilitative and/or adjudicative goals.

Given the inadequacies of the system [of mental health and drug treatment for offenders] and the intolerance of prosecutors and some judges [to arguments that a defendant's criminal behavior was influenced by drug or mental health problems], defense attorneys are placed in a precarious ethical position when they advocate for treatment. While their client may desperately need social services and/or treatment, many attorneys try to "save" their clients from the system itself—hiding the client's mental health issues or addiction. The best they can do is minimize time for their client.

In advocating for their clients, defense attorneys must navigate and adjust to the court culture itself—anticipating how their strategies and tactics will be received by their prosecutor and judge. Cook County is characterized by a horizontal representation system in which public defenders and prosecutors are assigned to a single courtroom as consistent members of a courtroom workgroup. Over time, they become friends, and their biggest concern is to be sure not to hurt each other too much. In Cook County, public defenders described this organizational arrangement as exerting strong incentives to assume a cooperative posture—as well as harsh penalties for seeming adversarial. Some public defenders discussed a relative "power imbalance" between them and the prosecutor and judge. Public defenders were careful "not to annoy them, or otherwise their clients would receive poor deals in the plea bargaining process."

Prosecutors often classified which defense attorneys were "good" or "bad" based on whether the attorney was able to "control" her client into pleading guilty. Defense attorneys who pursue "too many" motions and trials often find that their reputations suffer as a result. Some defense attorneys described a court culture of prosecutors and judges that often punished defendants for the zealous actions of their attorneys.

THE PUBLIC DEFENDER: THE PRACTICE OF LAW IN THE SHADOWS OF REPUTE

Lisa J. McIntyre
University of Chicago Press, 1987[6]

When I asked current public defenders what had surprised them about the job, almost all responded by saying that one of their biggest surprises (and disappointments) had been the lack of respect. Although some public defenders believe that many judges are prosecution minded, they seem to regard this as inevitable, if not entirely fair. What the lawyers find less easy to accept is that judges often treat them as second-class lawyers.

If something is going to hurt a client's case, the lawyers said, they must object. Over and over I was told that when a judge refuses to let you argue a motion that is important to your case, you must object; when the judge allows into evidence what you believe to be incompetent or improper material you must object: "There are times when you have got to say, 'Come on, judge.' You have to do that sometimes and of course it's scary. Now I have been scared, and I've backed down sometimes when I

---

shouldn't have. But I go back in there the next day and start all over again, because I will have gone home that night and chewed myself out for backing down." But when a judge's treatment of a lawyer merely reflects a disregard of the lawyer's dignity, the lawyers feel that to fight back will hurt their client: "Everything you do is going to affect your client, you know? If I'm being a jerk, or if I'm taking myself too seriously, I've got a client who's going to suffer. As opposed to sometimes, if I can shuffle or tap-dance a little bit, if I get my client to walk out with no criminal record, or time served, or whatever. And it never bothered me to do that. [Pause] Well, as I'm getting older perhaps it is starting to bother me a little bit."

Ironically, it is the clients who tend to be among the most dismissive of the lawyers' claims to respect. Two-thirds of the former public defenders interviewed agreed with the statement, "My clients often seemed to doubt my ability as a lawyer just because I was a public defender."

In theory, professional competency belies the need for supervision, and, in fact, supervisors in the public defender's office are treated as if they are redundant. "The way this office is run, you're pretty much on your own. There is a supervisory structure, but mainly there is nobody looking over your shoulder, no one evaluating, no one correcting you, no one giving you feedback on what you do."

The myth of competency embraces public defenders from the moment that they are appointed to the office. [P]ublic defenders work as a company of equals. Even when supervision or teaching and the like do occur, they are carefully done in a way that nurtures the myth and allows it to go unchallenged. Similarly, the lack of general policy identified by these lawyers suggests that, as far as they are concerned, the organization's hand rarely intrudes into their professional autonomy.

All of the current public defenders with whom I spoke and nearly all (93 percent) of the former assistants interviewed in my research agreed that people "constantly" ask public defenders, "How can you defend those people?" The overwhelming majority (97 percent) of former public defenders interviewed agreed that they had believed that they were putting their legal skills to good use by working as public defenders. Only five (8 percent) said that they would not join the office if they had it to do over again.

How can you defend people whom you know are guilty? Public defenders usually respond in a manner that is more weary than indignant: "Oh God, *that* question! How do you represent someone you know is guilty? So you go through all the things. You know, 'he's not guilty until he's proven guilty, until he's been proved guilty beyond a reasonable doubt.' I think everyone deserves the best possible defense, the most fair trial he can get. It's a guarantee of the Constitution, no more, no less."

Under some circumstances, mere empathy with the client's situation permits lawyers to feel justified when defending someone whom they know is factually guilty. "Look, kids get into trouble, some kids get into serious trouble. I can understand that. In juvenile court, our job isn't to punish, the result is supposed to be in the best interests of the minor. Here you've got to keep them with their family and give them all the services you can so they don't do this again."

But the alien character especially of the crimes that their clients are alleged to have committed often mean that "you have to care more about your clients' rights than you can usually care about your clients." On the surface, what a defense lawyer does is simply protect the client's rights. But many lawyers transform the nature of the battle. They are not fighting for the freedom of the client per se but to keep the system honest: "It doesn't mean that I want to get everybody off. It means that I try to make sure the state's attorneys meet up to their obligations, which means that the only way they can prove someone is guilty is beyond a reasonable doubt, with competent evidence. If they can't do that, then my client deserves to go home." They do not defend simply because their clients have rights but because they believe that those rights have been, are, or will be ignored by others in the criminal justice system.

Public defenders do feel as if they are often mugged—by the legal system. There is a lot of real and passionate anger: "Some people said I'd become cynical after a while. Well, I might be more cynical about some things, but I don't think I have really changed my attitude. If anything, I might have become a little more gung ho. You see that there really is an awful lot of injustice. It becomes very real and it's scary. I find myself becoming very angry in this job, all the time."

Public defenders are quick to admit that they usually do not ask their clients whether they are guilty or innocent. [When asked why, one responded:] "Because in the first place, it is irrelevant. It's not my role to decide whether they are guilty—in our sense of the term guilt. [I]t is my role to fashion a defense and to be creative. If the person says to me 'This is how I did it,' it's pretty hard for me to come around and try to do something for them. In general, I fence around with some of my questions. I ask them about an alibi or something like that. But the more I think they are guilty, the less I will ask."

Public defenders do not begin their relationship with a client by asking awkward questions because once the client admits guilt, it limits what the public defender can ethically do. Being honest, ethical and "scrupled" in a system that many of them believe is corrupt is very important to the lawyers with whom I spoke.

Public defenders try not to go into a trial with cases that cannot be won. Unfortunately, most of their cases are of this type—loser (or "dead-bang loser") cases, cut-and-dried situations in which the client was caught red-handed and "the state has everything but a videotape of the crime." In large part, being competent is being able to convince a client that it is not in his or her best interests to insist on a trial that cannot be won.

Ask any public defender "What was your worst case?" and chances are you will hear about a case that was a loser. Understanding the nature of a loser case is crucial, for embedded in the concept—and in the distinctions that lawyers make between losers and other sorts of cases—is the clue to what makes public defenders tick. "The worst case is where the state has an overwhelming amount of evidence and there is nothing you can do with it. It's a case where you get beat up in court. And that is just no fun."

The opposite of a loser case is not necessarily a winner. It is a fun case, which in turn must be distinguished from a boring case:

> I don't like armed robberies because they are boring. There are only one or two issues—either the guy did it or he didn't—and that doesn't make for very interesting work. The case I am trying right now is a murder that is really a lot of fun. Listen to me! "A murder is a lot of fun." How can I say that? [Laugh] It's a murder of a baby, and here I am with my two little kids and you would think that I would feel terrible about that, wouldn't you? But it's an interesting case because the facts are such that they [the state] don't really have much evidence in the case—a lot of people could have done it. It's all circumstantial evidence. That's fun. It's something for me to get excited about and get into, whereas a lot of cases—there are just no issues and that makes them boring.

Talcott Parsons once commented: "The fact that the case can tried by a standard procedure relieves [the attorney] of some pressure of commitment to the case of his client. He can feel that, if he does his best then having assured his client's case of a fair trial, he is relieved of the responsibility for an unfavorable verdict." One of the attorneys with whom I spoke seemed to confirm Parsons's hypothesis: "There is a certain consolation of going to trial with a loser case. If I lose, what the hell. I gave it my best shot. If I lose, *it was a loser*. If I win, it's amazing."

Most of the attorneys, however, were not so sanguine and could not detach themselves from the outcomes of their cases so easily. Even losing a loser case, most of them said, is incredibly hard on the attorney. The attorneys are not much comforted by the fact that the client was guilty— or probably guilty, anyway. "There was a case, not too long ago, that I really came to believe that they had no evidence on my man, and I fought very hard for him. We lost, and I felt very bad about that. Afterward, he just fell apart, started screaming at me back in the lockup. We had this big fight. And I yelled at him, 'You know, I really put myself on the line, too, and I did everything I could for you, and what are you doing yelling at me? Cause I really believed, and I worked hard.' And then I misspoke myself, because I said, 'And I really believed that you didn't do this.' And he said, 'Would it make you feel any better if I told you that I did do it?' [Laugh] I said, 'I don't want to know; don't tell me!' I still don't want to know, and that's how it is."

Lawyers hate to lose because, although reason tells them that a case is a loser, sentiment says that justice favors not the stronger case but the better lawyer. What makes losing any case, even a loser, so bad is their belief that, in the hands of a *good* attorney, there is really no such thing as a dead-bang loser case.

The stress of being on trial and the pain of losing are compounded on those rare occasions when the lawyer believes the defendant is innocent. For this reason, although the lawyers will say, "I don't care if he's guilty or innocent," their claim to neutrality is often a lie. When they say, "I don't care if my client is guilty," what they usually mean is, "I prefer my clients to be guilty."

Losing is one of the costs of being an attorney; losing a lot (I was told) is one of the costs of being a public defender.

Perhaps the most important way in which they cope with losing is knowing that they do not always lose. When I asked one attorney "How do you keep going when you lose?" he said: "Always remembering that there is a flip side of that—you feel great when you win. There is no feeling like that. And *that* wouldn't feel as good if it weren't so hard to win.

Failure is something with which every professional must cope. But implicit in the question, "How can you defend those people?" is the idea that public defenders ought to have trouble coping with winning. The lawyers are protected by the fact that they rarely win cases for clients who are horrible criminals. But however rarely it occurs, the possibility of winning big someday and then having your client kill again exists in the future of every defense lawyer. Often it seemed that one of the things that helps the lawyer not to feel too bad about winning is one of the things that makes it so hard to lose—that is, their relationship with the client. Most of the lawyers said that usually, especially when they go to trial, they end up liking their clients. In most cases, the lawyers spoke with some affection about their "guys."

There is in any human being a soul you can reach. [Pause] Now I use language like this hesitantly, you know; people usually look at you like you're crazy when you talk like this. But if you are willing to take the risk and open up your heart and reach into their hearts, you will reach it.

You need to do that for yourself. You need to do that, too, because if you are going to try the case for either a judge or a jury, you have to make that person human. They are someone. And that is what costs. 'Cause every time you do that, you are giving something of yourself away. You get something, sure, but you give away a lot.

NOTES ON THE ROLE OF THE PUBLIC DEFENDER

1. *Understanding the Role of the Public Defender.* How do the lawyers in these two studies describe their role? What value do they perceive in their work? Which aspects of their descriptions of their job do you think would be generalizable to any lawyer appointed to represent an indigent person accused of a crime, and which do you think are a function of practice in a large city or in an office in which the resources are inadequate to manage the case load?

2. *"How Can You Defend Those People?"* Why do the lawyers in the McIntyre study seem "weary" rather than "indignant" about being asked to explain why they defend people who are (or may be) guilty of a crime? What value is there in defending people who have (or may have) committed crimes? To what extent do you think a lack of social consensus about the value of representing those accused of crime influences the respect for criminal defense lawyers and the funding for indigent criminal defense?

3. *Scarce Resources.* How does the scarcity of resources—for hiring enough lawyers and investigators, for drug or mental health treatment, or for operating the court system—affect the way that these public defenders see their role? What ethical dilemmas arise because of the scarcity of resources and the huge caseloads for judges, public defenders, and prosecutors? In public defender offices with adequate resources, such as the federal and some state public defender services such as the one described in the Ogletree excerpt below, lawyers describe the rewards and challenges of indigent criminal defense differently (and generally much more positively) than the lawyers in these two studies. And, in contrast to these two studies of Cook County, in many regions the office of the public defender attracts talented lawyers who relish the challenge of a fast-paced trial practice and the rewards of advocacy on behalf of those accused of crime.

4. *Respect.* The public defenders in McIntyre's study identify lack of respect from clients, other lawyers, and judges as a major source of frustration in their job. What accounts for that lack of respect? What are the consequences—for public defenders, for the legal profession, and for the criminal justice system—of the lack of respect for the work of indigent criminal defense lawyers?

C. THE RIGHT TO EFFECTIVE ASSISTANCE OF COUNSEL

One of the most momentous United States Supreme Court decisions affecting the legal profession was *Gideon v. Wainwright*, 372 U.S. 335 (1963), which created a constitutional right to counsel for individuals charged with a crime that could result in imprisonment. Although the Court held that those too poor to afford a lawyer are entitled to have one appointed at government expense, the Court left it up to governments to fund the provision of lawyers. As we will see, there is wide variation among counties, states, and the federal government in how the *Gideon* obligation is funded and administered. In this section, we look first at the constitutional law governing appointed criminal defense lawyers. We then survey some of the challenges in implementing the right to counsel. Finally, we look at a body of constitutional law that has developed in large part because the quality of representation provided by some appointed criminal defense is sometimes very poor. That law attempts to decide when the criminal defendant has received such ineffective assistance of counsel as to violate the constitutional right to counsel.

1. THE CONSTITUTIONAL LAW GOVERNING APPOINTED CRIMINAL DEFENSE LAWYERS

Many aspects of the attorney-client relationship are worked out privately by agreement between the lawyer and the client. To the extent the relationship is governed by law, it is governed by the contract between the lawyer and client, by the rules of professional responsibility adopted by the state in which the lawyer practices, and by the tribunals in which the lawyer appears in the course of the representation. However, when an indigent individual is charged with a crime that could result in imprisonment or an indigent juvenile is charged with any crime, the Supreme Court held in *Gideon v. Wainwright*, 372 U.S. 335 (1963), and later cases that states are required to provide an attorney at government expense. The source of the right to counsel in *Gideon* is the Sixth Amendment to the U.S. Constitution, which provides that "in all criminal prosecutions, the accused shall enjoy the right . . . to have the assistance of counsel for his defense." In that circumstance, because the government is choosing and paying for the lawyer, the Constitution regulates the relationship. As we will see, however, the level of competence demanded of indigent criminal defense lawyers by the Constitution as the courts have interpreted it is fairly minimal. (See below *Ineffective Assistance of Counsel*.)

2. THE CHALLENGES OF IMPLEMENTING *GIDEON*

All 50 states, the District of Columbia, and the federal government have created separate systems to comply with the Sixth Amendment right to counsel for indigent criminal defense. Jurisdictions have adopted one of two systems, or sometimes a combination of both, to discharge their responsibility under *Gideon*. A majority have established public defender offices as a government-funded and administered office staffed by lawyers and investigators who specialize in indigent criminal defense. Some rely on private lawyers appointed by the court to handle indigent criminal defense. Public defenders' offices are the counterpart of the prosecutors' offices in each jurisdiction. The federal government has created an Office of the Federal Defender in the majority of the 94 federal districts across the country to represent indigent persons accused of federal crimes; in a minority of districts, private lawyers appointed by the court provide defense of the indigent. States use a combination of public defenders and private lawyers. Some states pass on the responsibility for establishing and funding indigent criminal defense to county governments, most of which are limited in their ability to raise revenue through taxes. Some counties provide indigent defense cheaply by using flat fee contracts under which local lawyers are paid a set amount to defend those in need of counsel. Such flat fee agreements create incentives for lawyers to spend as little time and money as possible working on a case. For example, a federal court overturned a death sentence in Texas on the grounds that the defense lawyer, who had been paid only $11 per hour, had provided ineffective assistance and "the justice system got only what it paid for."[7] A leading expert on the administration of the death penalty in southern states reported that in one case a lawyer defending a capital case in Alabama was paid $4 per hour and another received $5 per hour.[8]

The availability and quality of appointed counsel varies widely from state to state and even among counties in a single state. Although the Supreme Court requires counsel be appointed to represent those who cannot afford to hire their own lawyers, the Court has no power to order governments to appropriate funds to pay for the enforcement of constitutional rights, and the money that states and counties spend varies. The Federal Defenders and some county public defenders offices are generally excellent, staffed with talented criminal defense lawyers and investigators who provide outstanding representation. The Public Defender Service in the District of Columbia, the only local defender funded by Congress, is widely considered to provide superb

---

[7] Martinez-Macias v. Collins, 979 F.2d 1067 (5th Cir. 1992); *see also* STANDING COMM. ON LEGAL AID & INDIGENT DEFENDANTS, AM. BAR ASS'N, GIDEON'S BROKEN PROMISE: AMERICA'S CONTINUING QUEST FOR EQUAL JUSTICE 9–10 (2004) (collecting examples of underpaid criminal defense lawyers in many jurisdictions).

[8] Stephen B. Bright, *Counsel for the Poor: The Death Sentence Not for the Worst Crime But for the Worst Lawyer*, 103 YALE L.J. 1835 (1993) (collecting examples).

representation. It is one of the only public defender offices in the country "that consistently meets nationally recognized standards for indigent defense, including safeguards to protect its lawyers from judicial or political pressures, a commitment to providing investigative services, and a one-of-a-kind caseload management system that ensures lawyers never have so many clients that they cannot ethically represent each of them."[9] In jurisdictions with well-funded offices, the job of public defender is highly sought-after by young lawyers and also by lawyers with considerable experience. In some areas, however, as noted in the excerpt below, the money the county spends for indigent criminal defense is grossly inadequate and the quality of the defense provided in some cases is very poor.

In many jurisdictions, legislatures have increased the number of crimes and the length of sentences but cut the budget for indigent criminal defense. As a result, public defenders must juggle ever-larger case loads. Although the National Advisory Commission on Criminal Justice Standards recommends that attorneys handle no more than 150 felony cases a year, according to one study, in the five years preceding 2009, the average public defender case load in Miami-Dade County jumped from 367 felonies per year in 2006 to 500 per year in 2009, even though the public defender's office budget was cut 12.6 percent.[10] Over a third of people charged with misdemeanors in state and federal courts are represented by no lawyer at all because the constitutional right to counsel applies only where the defendant faces incarceration.[11]

THE RIGHT TO COUNSEL IN CRIMINAL CASES, A NATIONAL CRISIS
Mary Sue Backus & Paul Marcus
57 Hastings Law Journal 1031 (2005–2006)

In a case of mistaken identity, Henry Earl Clark of Dallas was charged with a drug offense in Tyler, Texas. After his arrest, it took six weeks in jail before he was assigned a lawyer, as he was too poor to afford one on his own. It took seven more weeks after the appointment of the lawyer, until the case was dismissed, for it to become obvious that the police had arrested the wrong man. While in jail, Clark asked for quick action, writing, "I [need to] get out of this godforsaken jail, get back to my job . . . I am not a drug user or dealer. I am a tax-paying American."

---

[9] Bob Kemper, *Gideon: Right to Counsel? Landmark Decision Falls Short of Promise,* WASH. LAW., Sept. 2009, at 25–26.

[10] THE CONSTITUTION PROJECT, JUSTICE DENIED: AMERICA'S CONTINUING NEGLECT OF OUR CONSTITUTIONAL RIGHT TO COUNSEL (Apr. 2009).

[11] Caroline Wolf Harlow, *Bureau of Justice Statistics Special Report: Defense Counsel in Criminal Cases,* U.S. DEPT. OF JUSTICE, BUREAU OF JUSTICE STATISTICS (Nov. 2000), http://bjs.ojp.usdoj.gov/index.cfm?ty=pbdetail&iid=772.

During this time, he lost his job and his car, which was auctioned. After Clark was released, he spent several months in a homeless shelter.

Sixteen-year-old Denise Lockett was retarded and pregnant. Her baby died when she delivered it in a toilet in her home in a South Georgia housing project. Although an autopsy found no indication that the baby's death had been caused by any intentional act, the prosecutor charged Lockett with first-degree murder. Her appointed lawyer had a contract to handle all the county's criminal cases, about 300 cases in a year, for a flat fee. He performed this work on top of that required by his private practice with paying clients. The lawyer conducted no investigation of the facts, introduced no evidence of his client's mental retardation or of the autopsy findings, and told her to plead guilty to manslaughter. She was sentenced to twenty years in prison. Tony Humphries was charged with jumping a subway turnstile in Atlanta to evade a $1.75 fare. He sat in jail for fifty-four days, far longer than the sentence he would have received if convicted, before a lawyer was appointed, at a cost to the taxpayers of $2330. A mother in Louisiana recently addressed a state legislative committee:

> My son Corey is a defendant in Calcasieu Parish, facing adult charges. He has been incarcerated for three months with no contact from court-appointed counsel. Corey and I have tried for three months to get a name and phone number of the appointed attorney. No one in the system can tell us exactly who the court-appointed attorney is. The court told us his public defender will be the same one he had for a juvenile adjudication. The court-appointed counsel told me he does not represent my son. The court clerk's office cannot help me or my son. We are navigating the system alone.

> Eight weeks ago we filed a motion for bond reduction. We have heard nothing—not even a letter of acknowledgement from the court that it received our motion. Without a lawyer to advocate on Corey's behalf, we are defenseless. How many more months will go by without contact from a lawyer? How many more months will go by without investigation into the case?

The Chief Public Defender of Fairfax County, Virginia (metropolitan Washington, D.C.) resigned in July 2005, after just ten months in the position. She said that even with legislative reforms in Virginia her office had so many clients and so few lawyers that the attorneys simply could not adequately represent the defendants at trials and on appeal. [In 2004], the twenty lawyers in the office defended more than 8000 clients.

The challenges facing defenders, including overwhelming caseloads, lack of supervision and training, inadequate compensation and resources, and political pressure, all raise significant ethical issues for defense attorneys, prosecutors, and judges. Although professional standards for defenders are clear, systemic deficiencies push defenders to compromise their efforts on behalf of clients. These questionable compromises undermine ethical standards and, in turn, contribute to the denigration of the legal profession and the criminal justice system. Judges, prosecutors, lawyer disciplinary bodies, and defenders themselves are loath to call attention to these ethical failings. There is a huge chasm between what ethics rules demand and how lawyers actually represent indigent defendants.

Ethically a lawyer is required to serve her clients with competence and diligence. The lawyer must be thorough, adequately prepared, and a zealous advocate on behalf of the client's interests. Regular communication is expected in order to keep the client reasonably informed and to respond to the client's reasonable requests for information. In addition, a lawyer is required to consult with the client regarding how the lawyer will pursue important objectives and to explain matters to clients so that they may make informed decisions.

In practice, the average lawyer working in an overburdened public defender office, or as an appointed or contract attorney whose compensation is so anemic that the hourly wage barely covers overhead expenses, may do none of these things. The problem arises, for instance, with a lawyer carrying a misdemeanor caseload three times the size of the national recommended standards, who meets a client for the first time just before court is called into session. That attorney simply does not have the time or the resources to investigate, prepare, or communicate adequately with the client so that the client can make an informed decision and the attorney can advocate zealously for his client's best interests. Even where the matters are not complex, sheer volume can preclude anything other than an assembly line approach, which falls far short of professional standards. Such is the case for the two contract defenders in Allen County, Indiana, who were assigned 2668 misdemeanor cases last year. Each attorney makes less than $2000 a month and maintains a private practice on the side. Not surprisingly, the overwhelming majority of defendants plead guilty; only twelve went to trial in a year.

Calling the practice unethical, chief public defenders in two jurisdictions, Broward County, Florida and St. Louis, Missouri, recently refused to continue the "meet 'em and greet 'em and plead 'em" approach. In Broward County, public defenders will no longer be allowed to recommend plea agreements to clients at arraignments or first hearings unless the attorney has met with the defendant, established a relationship and has an opportunity to properly assess the case, the client and any plea offer. The change was made in acknowledgment that the prior practice of recommending a plea, often portrayed as a one time offer that would worsen over time, at a lawyer's first encounter with a client with almost no information about the case fails to meet ethical standards. Such an approach makes it nearly impossible to determine whether a plea is in a defendant's best interest or to fulfill the duty to explain the matter sufficiently for the client to make an informed decision. For this reason, the ABA Criminal Justice Standards require independent investigation: "Under no circumstances should defense counsel recommend to a defendant acceptance of a plea unless appropriate investigation and study of the case has been completed, including an analysis of controlling law and the evidence likely to be introduced at trial." Similarly, in St. Louis the chief defender characterized representation of certain misdemeanor defendants as "unethical, unprofessional and unconstitutional." As a result, he instituted a policy of no longer automatically representing defendants the first time they appear in court after having been arrested on misdemeanor charges. The chief defender concluded that it was not possible to "render constitutional, ethical and professional assistance of counsel upon walking into court with no discovery, no opportunity for investigation and no opportunity to counsel the accused. Both of these jurisdictions have simply recognized that, despite caseload pressures, ethics rules require more of defense attorneys than encouraging their clients to accept the prosecution's plea offers.

The ethical dilemmas are not limited to misdemeanor court, however. They may arise wherever caseload pressures make it impossible for defenders to devote sufficient time to each case. Noting the trend of increasing caseloads without corresponding increases in resources, a legislative audit of the public defender agency in Alaska explicitly acknowledged a "heightened concern for professional ethics violations." And, although the state expressed a willingness to defend its legal professionals against claims of such violations, the report candidly advised that "each attorney must weigh his/her ever increasing caseload and the demands from the public, against the potential of violating the professional code of ethics, resulting in disciplinary action." That is a rather stark and appalling warning that ethical violations may be inherent in the job of public defender.

Alaska is not alone in raising the alarm. The recent ABA report assessing the status of *Gideon's* mandate across the nation reached a similar conclusion. It found that "defense lawyers throughout the country are violating these ethical rules by failing to provide competent, diligent, continuous, and conflict-free representation." As disturbing as it is to suggest that ethical violations are commonplace, it is even more alarming that courts and disciplinary authorities routinely overlook these breaches of professional rules of conduct. The likelihood of any individual defender being subjected to discipline for violation of the minimum levels of competence or zealousness is small. Most disciplinary agencies seem reluctant to bring charges against defenders whose conduct breaches ethical rules, perhaps because it seems unfair to blame an individual attorney when the failings are more a function of systemic inadequacies. The reluctance to sanction defenders of the indigent may also reflect the concern that sanctions could discourage other lawyers from accepting cases of indigent defendants. Such a result would exacerbate the problem of an already short supply of attorneys willing to take on this type of work.

Another possible enforcement mechanism, malpractice actions by defendants, is likely to be as unavailing as recourse to lawyer disciplinary bodies has been. Many states require that a plaintiff must first succeed in obtaining post-conviction relief for ineffective assistance of counsel before bringing a malpractice claim. Moreover, some courts, including some that require post-conviction relief, have held that the plaintiff must effectively demonstrate her actual innocence, not just that she would have been acquitted save for the attorney's negligence.

Prosecutors and judges must also bear some responsibility in maintaining ethical standards within the criminal justice system, and the roles of both warrant further exploration. The prosecutorial ideal of seeking to "do justice," rather than just pursuing conviction of those who are arrested, has long established roots in our legal tradition. Despite their duty to seek justice, there are prosecutors who zealously pursue their role as a representative of the government's interest in conviction, often to the exclusion of other interests. Indeed, some prosecutors are more likely to exploit defense incompetence than to take steps to guard against it. For example, there are prosecutors who encourage quick guilty pleas as a way of clearing their dockets and maintaining high conviction rates with low costs. Most authorities hold that prosecutorial intervention in the face of ethical violations by defense counsel is only required if there is a constitutional violation, not if the performance of defense counsel is simply lacking. Indeed, reporting of substandard behavior of defense counsel by the prosecutor must be undertaken with care. There is a substantial concern that if the standards were too lax as to when a prosecutor could report a defense attorney for ethical violations, the procedure would become another litigation tactic.

The role of judges in both monitoring and correcting ethical abuses by defense counsel is also worthy of further attention. Although judges have strong incentives to encourage the quick resolution of cases and to sidestep the issue of the effectiveness of defense counsel in order to move the docket along, judges are uniquely situated to prevent ethical violations. In appointing counsel, monitoring pretrial activities and evaluating counsel's preparedness, observing courtroom performance and participating in plea bargaining negotiations, the judge must be cognizant that it is the judge, not counsel, who has the ultimate responsibility for the conduct of a fair and lawful trial. Regardless of the potential role prosecutors and judges might play in supporting ethical norms in the criminal justice system, defense attorneys themselves have a strict ethical obligation to control their workload in order to ensure that they can deliver competent representation. Some courts have recognized the ethical conflict inherent in carrying an excessive caseload and meeting the professional obligations of competence and diligence. They support attorneys' efforts to manage their workload by either declining appointments or withdrawing from representation. The Eastern District of Pennsylvania has suggested that if a public defender is overburdened, he may at any time decline an appointment, and should decline to accept an appointment if the defender is not in a position to properly defend an action. Similarly, the California Court of Appeal stated, "when a public defender reels under a staggering workload, he should proceed to place the situation before the judge, who upon a satisfactory showing can relieve him, and order the employment of private counsel at public expense. Courts have occasionally done just that. For example, the Florida District Court of Appeals has upheld a trial court order allowing a public defender to withdraw from representation in six felony cases because of an excessive caseload.

NOTES ON THE CONSTITUTIONAL RIGHT TO COUNSEL

1. **Considering the Options.** What options face an individual public defender who has too many cases to handle? What are the advantages and disadvantages of the strategies described by Backus and Marcus?

2. **Why Are Resources Scarce?** Why is the issue of too many cases and too few resources a problem in some jurisdictions? If it is such a significant problem, why do legislatures not simply solve it by appropriating more money to fund criminal defenders?

3. **Enforcing the Right to Competent Counsel.** Why do you suppose judges have not been more insistent (or effective) in calling for improved representation for indigent criminal defendants?

3. INEFFECTIVE ASSISTANCE OF COUNSEL

In a series of cases, the Supreme Court has interpreted the Sixth Amendment not simply to protect the right to have a lawyer but the right to *effective* assistance of counsel. In *Strickland v. Washington*, 466 U.S. 668, 687, 695 (1984), the Court held that a defendant may have his conviction overturned and receive a new trial if he can prove (1) that his lawyer "made errors so serious that counsel was not functioning" as an any reasonable lawyer would and (2) that, but for the errors, "the fact finder would have a reasonable doubt respecting guilt." The Supreme Court extended the protections of the Sixth Amendment to the plea bargaining stage. *Padilla v. Kentucky*, 559 U.S. 356, 130 S. Ct. 1473

(2010) (failure to inform client of the immigration consequences of pleading guilty to a crime is ineffective assistance); *Missouri v. Frye*, 132 S. Ct. 1399 (2012) (failure to inform defendant that prosecution offered a plea agreement is ineffective assistance). The extension of the right to effective assistance at the plea bargaining stage is crucial because 97 percent of federal convictions and 94 percent of state convictions are the result of guilty pleas.[12]

Courts have made it difficult for defendants to set aside convictions on the ground of ineffective assistance of counsel. They have declined to find ineffective assistance when defense counsel was drunk, asleep, or absent from the courtroom during crucial parts of the prosecution's case. *See Tippens v. Walker*, 77 F.3d 682, 687 (2d Cir. 1996) (articulating a test for how much sleeping during trial renders counsel ineffective); *Burdine v. Johnson*, 262 F.3d 336 (5th Cir. 2001) (split en banc court rules that counsel's sleeping during portions of a death penalty trial is presumptively prejudicial to the defense). Courts have done so either because they have determined that the lawyer's failures did not fall below the prevailing standards of acceptable conduct or because, even if it did (as the dissent reasoned in the *Burdine* case involving the lawyer who slept through some portions of the trial), they found that counsel's errors did not prejudice the defense.

The Supreme Court has held that some total failures on counsel's part constituted ineffective assistance. Thus, in *Wiggins v. Smith*, 539 U.S. 510 (2003), the Court held that a lawyer's failure to investigate the existence of mitigating evidence in a death penalty case was ineffective assistance when an investigation would have revealed that the defendant suffered extreme childhood neglect and physical and sexual abuse which affected his mental and emotional capacity and health. Similarly, in *Rompilla v. Beard*, 545 U.S. 374 (2005), the Court set aside a death sentence after determining that the defendant's lawyers failed to conduct an investigation into the defendant's criminal record even after the prosecutor informed them that it intended to use the criminal record to prove the aggravating factors necessary to impose a death sentence.

Other total failures of counsel, however, have not been ineffective assistance. Defense counsel's complete failure to prepare a case for mitigation in a death penalty case was held to be a reasonable strategic decision, notwithstanding the fact that counsel knew of evidence suggesting the possibility that mitigating evidence might be available (in

---

[12] *See* Dept. of Justice, Bureau of Justice Statistics, *Sourcebook of Criminal Justice Statistics Online, Table 5.22.2009*, U. OF ALBANY, SOURCEBOOK OF CRIMINAL JUSTICE STATISTICS (May 22, 2009), http://www.albany.edu/sourcebook/pdf/t5222009.pdf; Sean Rosenmerkel, Matthew Durose, & Donald Farole, Jr., *Felony Sentences in State Courts, 2006—Statistical Tables*, DEPT. OF JUSTICE, BUREAU OF JUSTICE STATISTICS 1 (last updated Nov. 2010), http://bjs.ojp.usdoj.gov/content/pub/pdf/fssc06st.pdf; Padilla v. Kentucky, 130 S. Ct. 1473, 1485–86 (2010) (recognizing pleas account for nearly 95% of all criminal convictions).

that case, that defendant had spent time in a state hospital for emotionally handicapped children and a psychologist had recommended confining him in a mental institution). *Cullen v. Pinholster*, 131 S. Ct. 1388 (2011).

The Sixth Amendment is not a solution to the problems of competent indigent criminal defense. The remedy for a violation of the defendant's Sixth Amendment right to effective assistance of counsel is not that the defendant will be acquitted. Rather, the most the defendant will get is a new trial, and not necessarily with an excellent lawyer. When the ineffective assistance prejudiced the defendant's decision whether to accept a plea bargain, the court must require the prosecution to re-offer the plea and the judge will have discretion whether to impose a new (and lighter) sentence based on the plea or to leave the sentence the same.

D. THE REWARDS AND CHALLENGES OF CRIMINAL DEFENSE PRACTICE

The bleak accounts offered by Van Cleve and McIntyre of the nature of work in the Cook County public defender's office and the chronic underfunding of indigent criminal defense in some jurisdictions may leave you wondering why anyone would want to be a criminal defense lawyer, especially a public defender. In many jurisdictions, the public defender's office is adequately staffed and funded and the job is highly sought after by elite lawyers. All criminal defense lawyers, however, sometimes are asked, especially by nonlawyers, "how can you represent someone whom you know is guilty of a horrible crime?" The following excerpt explores the way in which one young public defender (now a professor at Harvard Law School) found satisfaction in being a public defender and the role that working in the highly-regarded and well-resourced Public Defender Service of the District of Columbia played in his thinking.

BEYOND JUSTIFICATIONS: SEEKING MOTIVATIONS TO SUSTAIN PUBLIC DEFENDERS

Charles J. Ogletree, Jr.
106 Harvard Law Review 1239 (1993)

Often, in attaining a client's end—typically that of avoiding conviction—public defenders do many things that would commonly be considered immoral. Public defenders defend clients who they know are guilty, seek to suppress relevant evidence, fail to reveal incriminating facts, and make truthful witnesses appear to be liars. If defenders do their jobs well, their work undoubtedly achieves results in the courtroom that may or may not reflect the truth.

Theorists of the ethical dimension of lawyering have struggled to endow this form of representation with moral coherence. Some theorists conclude that, in her role as public defender, a lawyer is not implicated in the guilt or immorality of her clients. Provided that she acts within the bounds of the law, she bears no responsibility for the choices and actions of her clients. The guilt or innocence of the client and the nature of the crime are extraneous. [This justification can be called "role-morality."] In addition to "role-morality," two other theories have been advanced to justify zealous advocacy on the part of the public defender: "client-centered" and "systemic" justifications. Commentators who espouse "client-centered justifications" maintain that zealous advocacy is necessary to promote the social and moral good of the client. "Systemic justifications" focus not on the interests of the various actors within the adversary system, but on the adversary system itself. Systemic justifications of zealous advocacy are premised on the underlying structure of the adversary system. This structure requires an advocate for each of the parties, an impartial judge, and in the criminal context, the right to have a jury determine, after hearing all evidence, where the "truth" lies.

My goal in this Article, however, is to move beyond defending and attacking these justifications. I seek to show that even the most compelling justification fails to motivate public defenders to do their jobs with energy and enthusiasm. Regardless of their theoretical or logical merits, these abstract justifications simply do not inspire or excite; and, for the public defender who has become disillusioned or dispirited, they do not offer a source of renewed vitality or commitment.

[After a lengthy analysis of the three justifications for criminal defense practice outlined above, Professor Ogletree uses the example of a personal tragedy he experienced while working as a public defender to explore why public defenders believe their professional work advances justice. He describes how his faith in the justice of criminal defense was shaken when his beloved sister Barbara, a police officer, was stabbed to death in her living room by an unknown assailant.]

My determination to track down my sister's murderer and secure his conviction led me to adopt an outlook that was in many ways incompatible with the justifications I had consistently used to defend my profession. As a public defender, I firmly believed in the necessity of putting the state to the test at trial, and just as importantly, of severely constraining the behavior of police in pursuit of criminal suspects. I now saw only the harm that could result from constitutional restrictions on a police officer's ability to search for evidence and suspects. When it came to my sister's murder, I did not want any procedural safeguards for the criminal. I wanted the state to use all evidence, obtained by any means whatsoever, to convict her attacker. I wanted the satisfaction of knowing that the person responsible for her death would be brought to justice. I wanted retribution.

As I experienced this unsettling contradiction between my abstract beliefs and my reaction to Barbara's murder, I began to reconsider my role as a public defender. I imagined the assailant's trial and contemplated the posture that his defense lawyer might take. I began to fear that the killer's attorney might be someone like me, zealously committed to challenging the state's case—someone intent on acquittal, regardless of the crime with which his client is charged and the strength of the evidence against his client. I feared that such a defense lawyer might expose a previously unknown dark side of Barbara's life, or through obfuscation, innuendo, and distortion, create a dark side to her life.

Imagining the role the defense attorney would play at the trial of Barbara's killer forced me to face squarely the real consequences suffered by victims and their families as a direct result of the zealous advocacy of clever defense lawyers. I had to consider how victims feel about lawyers like myself, lawyers who secure dismissals on technicalities, or who seek to raise sufficient doubt for a jury to find the client not guilty, even in the face of strong evidence against the accused.

[Professor Ogletree contemplated resigning from his job, but ultimately decided not to.] I concluded that I could still approach my work with the same conviction that I had always brought to it. In reaching this decision, I asked myself what Barbara would have done in a similar situation. I tried to imagine how Barbara would have responded if a police officer had killed me without cause. I knew she would have been angry, devastated, and hurt, and she would have expected the officer to be punished. Yet Barbara's commitment to victims in the criminal justice system probably would have led her to continue her work with the same pride and professionalism as before.

Shortly thereafter, the Deputy Director of the Criminal Justice Act Office requested that I take a case. He asked me to represent a defendant charged with felony murder, with an underlying felony of rape. The facts of the case struck a resonant chord. A young black woman had been found dead; she had been raped and then strangled with her own stockings. About twenty feet from the victim's body, the police had discovered a man's wallet containing the identification of the defendant, Craig Strong. Strong had recently been paroled from prison, where he had been serving a life sentence for rape. Prior to his conviction he had been acquitted of two previous rape charges; all three of the earlier rapes had occurred in the same area as the crime scene, a mere two blocks from Strong's house.

After learning these background facts, I went to visit Strong. When I saw him in the cell block, it was clear to me that he was frightened. He did not know what would happen to him that day or thereafter. In telling me about his life, his family, and his fears, Strong revealed that his father had been murdered when Strong was young, and that he had no positive male role models as he grew up. He did not know whether anyone would represent him, or how his family would react to his arrest. As awful as his crime was, I could see that he wanted someone—anyone—to say, "I'm on your side."

Despite my sister's recent murder, I accepted the case. Though I had made my decision, I continued to reexamine my commitment to zealous representation of indigent defendants in general, and of Craig Strong in particular. I was concerned that my feelings about my sister's murder might interfere somehow with my ability to represent Strong, especially in light of the fact that her assailant had not been caught. Might I subconsciously harbor unacknowledged resentments that would lead me to be underzealous in Strong's defense? Might I over-identify with the victim's family, and therefore be unworthy of my client's trust? I was aware of instances in which lawyers decided not to represent clients for undisclosed personal reasons. Nothing in the Model Code, however, explicitly addressed potential internal conflicts of the sort I was confronting.

I decided to tell Strong about Barbara's murder. I described the potential conflict and explained that he had the right to seek new counsel if he doubted my ability to represent him. We went before the judge, who also knew of my sister's murder, and the judge offered Strong the opportunity to seek new counsel. Strong confirmed that he wanted me to represent him, and the judge expressed no misgivings about that decision.

[Professor Ogletree then describes his efforts to secure Strong's acquittal, first by unsuccessfully seeking to suppress physical evidence linking Strong to the crime because the police had failed to obtain a search warrant, and then, at trial, by careful preparation and vigorous cross-examination of witnesses.] During this time, I visited him regularly in jail, talked to him on the phone almost every day, and took pains to keep him apprised of our efforts. I sent him letters and copies of all motions and briefs filed on his behalf. I also visited his family. Strong lived with his mother, his sister, a niece, and a nephew. His mother was a proud woman who tried to hide her pain upon hearing that her son had again been arrested. She wanted the best for her son, and she could not bring herself to believe that he had again been accused of rape, let alone that he may have killed his victim.

[Professor Ogletree describes his misgivings, and that of his co-counsel, as they thought about the possibility that Strong might be acquitted and released from jail. Strong was convicted on all counts and faced a likely sentence of life in prison. Professor Ogletree then considered what he learned from his experience and how it sheds light on the motivations of lawyers who provide indigent criminal defense.]

One need not experience personally the pain of violent crime to need a sustaining motivation in order to continue working as a public defender. Virtually all public defenders fight a daily battle against burnout and the creeping erosion of confidence that inevitably accompany defending acts we cannot condone and protecting those who are the source of so much harm and grief. This slow, daily erosion differs from my own personal motivational crisis only in that mine was more sudden and sharp in its onslaught. Whether the process unfolds subtly or suddenly, all defenders must confront the disturbing consequences of their zealous representation of guilty clients.

The phenomenon of burnout is one of the most powerful and widely experienced forces that causes public defenders to lose interest in their work, or to abandon criminal defense practice altogether. Former public defenders typically attribute burnout to the psychological impact of confronting hundreds of crimes, victims, and criminals on a daily basis. Moreover, the better the defender is, the more frequently she must face the consequences of getting favorable results, even for guilty clients.

Public defenders typically explain their choice of vocation in terms of abstract justifications [such as] their ardent belief in the constitutional values that the public defender upholds. At some point, however, abstract theoretical justifications fall short in the face of reality. For example, defenders who are motivated by a belief that no individual is guilty until proven so, soon find that such moral indeterminacy does not comport with their daily experiences. Public defenders know that frequently their clients are guilty beyond any reasonable doubt.

In looking back on my experience with Craig Strong, I believe that my empathy for Strong became one of the primary sustaining motivations for continuing zealously to defend him in spite of the pain of my sister's murder. I viewed Strong as a person and as a friend, and thus I was able to disassociate him from the person who had murdered my sister. I did not blame him, nor did I resent him because I had been victimized by crime. Instead, I viewed Strong as a victim as well. However, my sense of his victimization differed from traditional justifications for criminal defense practice in that it was not based on generalizations about criminals or pity for him. Instead, my empathy was based on my ability to relate to him as a person and to develop a friendship with him. I viewed Strong as a man whom the police had surprised in a warrantless arrest; someone from whom the police had seized incriminating evidence without a search warrant. I did not think about what he had done, nor did I feel responsible for what he might do if released. I knew that at that moment I was my client's only friend, and that my friend wanted to go home.

My view of empathy has significant implications for the character of the lawyer-client relationship. My relationships with clients were rarely limited to the provision of conventional legal services. I did not draw rigid lines between my professional practice and my private life. My relationship with my clients approximated a true friendship. I did for my clients all that I would do for a friend. I took phone calls at all hours, helped clients find jobs, and even interceded in domestic conflicts. I attended my clients' weddings and their funerals. When clients were sent to prison, I maintained contact with their families. Because I viewed my clients as friends, I did not merely feel justified in doing all I could for them; I felt a strong desire to do so.

I realize that empathy alone did not sustain me. I also felt various motivations that centered around how I envisioned myself and my task. I describe these motivations under the rubric of "heroism." I saw myself as a kind of "hero" of the oppressed, the one who fights against all odds, a sort of Robin Hood figure who can conquer what others cannot and who does not always have to conform to the moral rules society reserves for others. One element of this "hero" mentality, of course, is the thrill of winning. Certainly, many public defenders are driven in part by a desire to win; at PDS, for example, lawyers with excellent track records of acquittals were regarded with awe. For the public defender, there is glory in the "David versus Goliath" challenge of fighting the state, and the battle of wits that characterizes the courtroom drama only adds to the thrill of the trial. Even the phrase we commonly used to describe a successful defense—"stealing" the case from the prosecution—invoked the image of Robin Hood stealing from the rich and powerful to give to the helpless and weak. Indeed, some people become criminal defenders because they love the challenge, are competitive by nature, and have unusual personal curiosity. They like the idea of representing the underdog, where the scales are tipped against them, the prosecutor has all the resources, and they have virtually none.

The daily realities of the PDS office pose challenges to both empathy and heroism as motivations. Even the most empathetic public defender will find her commitment sorely challenged by the persistence of defendants who commit violent crimes repeatedly. Moreover, as an empathetic person, she may find that she has empathy for not just the defendant but also for the victim, and perhaps even for future victims whose safety would be threatened by the defendant's release. In the face of such feelings, empathy for one's client may prove difficult to sustain. Likewise, while the Robin Hood ideal will add a certain thrill to the job of public defender, the luster soon fades as the defender confronts the practical realities of the job—the daily drudgery of paperwork and the less-than-glamorous settings of the public defender's office, the criminal court, and the jail.

Empathy and heroism also may prove counterproductive when taken to the extreme. They may cause the public defender to lose sight of the external moral limitations on her conduct. Empathic feelings, for example, can result in over-identification with the client. Without the benefit of critical distance, a defender may be tempted to overstep ethical boundaries in her zeal to help her client. The same result can occur when a lawyer becomes overly enamored of the "heroic" role—the hero of the oppressed, after all, does not have to play by society's rules. For example, an overly empathetic or heroic attorney may be inclined to present a perjurious witness if this course of action is likely to win the case. Another potential danger of empathy is that it can lead to problematic allocation of resources. The empathic role I have described demands that the public defender devote substantial time and effort to every client. In a situation of extremely limited attorney resources, hours spent in the service of one client necessarily come at the expense of another equally needy criminal defendant.

Heroism can lead to similar problems. The heroic defender views herself as the champion of her client against the oppressive system. To her, each case is an epic battle against an inhumane established order. To beat the system when the odds are stacked against her, the attorney must pour an inordinate amount of scarce resources into each case. Again, this is time that she could spend representing others.

Of course, the resource allocation problems I have identified cannot be attributed solely to the use of empathy and heroism as motivations. These problems arise in all public interest work, and no satisfactory answer is readily apparent. In a society where access to legal representation is largely dependent on wealth, the poor inevitably have restricted access to attorney services. One solution to the problem I have posed would be to increase the aggregate amount of time available to indigent clients by providing more attorneys and a wider distribution of subsidized legal services. Unfortunately, this solution is as unrealistic as it is obvious; an increase in the availability of legal services is precluded by a lack of funding and compounded by a shortage of attorneys interested in legal aid.

The office at which I worked upon graduation from law school, the District of Columbia Public Defender Service, used a variety of techniques to [develop empathy among public defenders]. In our six-week orientation program, and throughout our tenure, PDS reminded defenders that most clients would be poor, uneducated, and from single-parent families, and that a family history of drug abuse would be common. We were taught to view the client as a victim someone who had endured suffering and deprivation, and who would continue to suffer without our assistance. It was argued that there was a direct relationship between the client's social background and his present status. It was not enough to understand this connection in the abstract. We were encouraged to immerse ourselves in the reality of each client's life, to get to know him, his background, his family and friends.

The office did not advise its attorneys to adopt my style of representation. It did not instruct defenders to accept late-night phone calls from clients or to counsel them about nonlegal problems. Indeed, many lawyers preferred not to become involved to this degree with their clients. Attorneys were encouraged to develop their own ways of empathizing with clients. The office also made it possible for lawyers adequately to attend to their clients (and for lawyers like me to devote the time necessary to foster close relationships with clients) by limiting attorneys' caseloads. The attorneys handle no more than 50 to 60 criminal cases or 40 juvenile cases at one time. The low caseloads allow PDS attorneys to devote a significant amount of time to each individual client. Such representation is both individualized and continuous.

This continuous representation extends beyond the litigation setting. The office's Offender Rehabilitation Division (ORD) provides community-based social services for defendants and their families, develops rehabilitation programs, and provides studies of the defendant's background for use at sentencing. Because they are working in an office that helps clients with employment, educational opportunities, and family support, PDS lawyers need not feel as though they are merely setting clients free to commit further criminal acts. To the extent that rehabilitative or supportive services can remedy the problems that have caused the client to become involved with the criminal justice system, those services will be provided. Rather than focusing narrowly on the short-term goal of acquittal (although that certainly is the primary objective), the office helps clients in a comprehensive sense.

The culture at PDS also trumpeted heroism as a motivation for defenders. The office culture stressed the value of winning. Attorneys developed reputations based on their success at trial. To emphasize the value of winning, the office kept a blackboard that recorded the progress of all of the trial proceedings of our attorneys. The entire office would join in the celebration of every acquittal won by a PDS attorney. Like players on a team, PDS attorneys often attended court proceedings to provide moral support and encouragement to colleagues during trial, as if to cheer them on to victory. Attorneys who won at trial also received tangible rewards such as promotions to supervisory positions within the office. New lawyers always sought out the successful senior attorneys for opportunities to serve as junior counsel on their cases.

Not only did PDS reward heroism, but it also worked to help lawyers realize the heroic ideal. In addition to providing all new lawyers with comprehensive training before they represented their first client, the office provided senior attorneys with periodic supplemental training. New lawyers represented juveniles in bench trials before moving to adult felony cases and jury trials. Furthermore, supervisors and colleagues provided invaluable feedback and support to attorneys on their cases. Lawyers routinely rehearsed their opening statements and closing arguments in front of at least two supervisors before going to court. In all of these ways, the office stressed the importance of attaining excellence in one's profession and of providing each client with the best possible defense.

NOTES ON THE REWARDS AND CHALLENGES OF INDIGENT CRIMINAL DEFENSE

1. ***What Are the Satisfactions of Criminal Defense Practice?*** We have examined in some detail the challenges of indigent criminal defense practice in a world of scarce resources. But the job also has many rewards. What are the common themes in the Van Cleve, McIntyre, and Ogletree descriptions of the ways that public defenders describe their role and the challenges and satisfactions of the job? What are the differences among them?

2. ***What Is the Relationship Between Money, Prestige, and the Intrinsic Rewards of Law Practice?*** The Public Defender Service of the District of Columbia, where Professor Ogletree worked, is one of the most prestigious indigent criminal defense offices in the country. It attracts young lawyers with sterling credentials, provides excellent training, and some of its alumni take jobs as law professors and in law practices in other elite settings. In addition, as noted above, the PDS receives funding directly from Congress and is comparatively better funded than many public defender's offices (perhaps in part because it does not have to rely on local tax revenues). How do the prestige of the PDS and the adequacy of its resources affect how PDS lawyers there regard their role? Is it reasonable to imagine that a massive infusion of resources into indigent criminal defense would address the problems identified in other readings in this chapter? Which problems would it not address?

3. ***What Should Motivate Lawyers?*** What do you find appealing, or problematic, in Ogletree's account of empathy and heroism as motivations for indigent criminal defense lawyers?

4. ***Another Reflection on Representing Those Accused of Crime.*** How would the Ogletree account differ, as a narrative or as an essay on the role of criminal defense counsel, if Strong had been acquitted and had later been accused of another rape? Would your willingness to accept an appointment to represent someone accused of a crime depend on whether you believed the accused was innocent? Are there crimes for which you could not defend someone? Do your answers to those questions influence your views about the right to effective assistance of counsel in those cases?

E. ETHICAL ISSUES IN TRIAL ADVOCACY: LYING CLIENTS AND HONEST AND COACHED WITNESSES

As we saw in the materials on the lawyer's role in Chapter 3, many think that the strongest case for the desirability of lawyers acting as amoral advocates may be made in the criminal defense context. Defense of those accused of crimes presents perhaps the purest case, in our adversary system, where the lawyer's diligent advocacy to protect the client from the considerable power of the state aligns with the lawyer's "special responsibility for the quality of justice." Preamble to Model Rules, par. 1. Almost every lawyer agrees that even a defendant who is guilty of a heinous crime is entitled to a competent defense in order that the government's considerable power to accuse, to investigate, and to incarcerate not be abused. The Model Rules explicitly recognize the propriety of representing a criminal defendant whom the lawyer knows is guilty. Model Rule 3.1, which prohibits lawyers from bringing or defending a proceeding "unless there is a basis in law and fact for doing so," says that a "lawyer for a defendant in a criminal proceeding, may nevertheless so defend the proceeding as to require that every element of the case be established." Comment [3] to Rule 3.1 elaborates that the lawyer's duty under the rule is "subordinate to federal or state constitutional law that entitles a defendant in a criminal matter to the assistance of counsel in presenting a claim or contention that otherwise would be prohibited by this Rule." In other words, because the burden of proof is on the government in a criminal case to prove guilt beyond a reasonable doubt, a lawyer may ethically defend one whom she knows to be guilty as a way of forcing the government to sustain its burden of proof.

Model Rule 3.1: Meritorious Claims and Defenses

A lawyer shall not bring or defend a proceeding, or assert or controvert an issue, unless there is a basis in law and in fact for doing so that is not frivolous, which includes a good faith argument for an extension, modification, or reversal of existing law.

A lawyer for the defendant in a criminal proceeding may nevertheless so defend the proceeding as to require that every element of the case be established.

Yet the morality of a decision to represent a person accused of a heinous crime is not always an easy question, particularly when the lawyer believes the client may be guilty. We saw this in Chapter 3, in the well-known debate in the legal press between law professor and criminal defense lawyer Michael Tigar and law professor Monroe Freedman over the ethics of Tigar's representation of John Demjanjuk, who had been accused of killing hundreds of Jews at the Treblinka concentration camp during WWII. As we saw, evidence had come to light that Demjanjuk was not a guard at Treblinka, although he may have been an equally murderous guard at the Sobibor camp where tens of thousands of French Jews perished in 1942. Professor Freedman criticized Tigar's decision to represent Demjanjuk: "Is John Demjanjuk the kind of client to whom you want to dedicate your training, your knowledge, and your extraordinary skills as a lawyer? Did you go to law school to help a client who has committed mass murder of other human beings with poisonous gases? Of course, someone should, and will, represent him. But why you, old friend?"[13]

Tigar defended his choice to represent Demjanjuk, insisting that the government had suppressed evidence and that his client's guilt must be proved. He explained: "We must remember the Holocaust, and we should pursue and punish its perpetrators. We dishonor that memory and besmirch the pursuit if we fail to accord those accused of Holocaust crimes the same measure of legality and due process that we would give to anyone accused of wrongdoing. Precisely because a charge of culpable participation in the Holocaust is so damning, the method of judging whether such a charge is true should be above reproach."[14]

As a lawyer, how will you judge the ethics of choices about whom to represent?

One may be skeptical about whether zealous criminal defense advocacy always furthers justice. The prosecution is not always more powerful than the defendant. Some criminal defendants, including corporations and executives accused of large-scale financial crimes, may have more resources than the prosecutors and may use their resources to secure acquittals or lenient plea agreements. The government does not have infinite resources to prosecute crime; overcoming zealous criminal defense requires the government to expend resources on criminal prosecution that might also be spent on education or environmental protection. Regardless of the wealth of a defendant, some fear securing an acquittal if the accused later commits another horrible crime. Third parties (including crime victims) have a stake in seeing that justice is done, although that does not necessarily equate with conviction of the accused. In sum, the justice of zealous criminal advocacy and whether amoral advocacy is justifiable even in the context of criminal defense are not beyond dispute.

---

[13] Monroe Freedman, *Must You Be the Devil's Advocate?*, LEGAL TIMES, Aug. 23, 1993.

[14] Michael E. Tigar, *Setting the Record Straight on the Defense of John Demjanjuk*, LEGAL TIMES, Sept. 6, 1993.

Even if one is convinced that amoral advocacy is justified in the context of criminal defense, there are still instances in which the criminal defense lawyer's loyalty to the client may be in tension with the lawyer's duties as an officer of the court. In this segment, we examine ethical issues in advocacy. They arise most commonly in the context of criminal defense, although they are not unique to it. First we examine the problem of the lying client: If a client whom the lawyer suspects may be guilty wishes to testify (perhaps falsely) in his own defense, what should the lawyer do? In this context, we also examine the related question of what sorts of witness preparation are permissible. Second, we examine the problem of the truthful witness: What is acceptable in cross-examining a witness whom defense counsel suspects has testified truthfully? Third, we examine the issue of counseling the destruction of or failure to retain evidence, in the context of pre-indictment criminal investigations. (The issue also arises in civil contexts.) While it is clearly illegal to destroy evidence (or for a lawyer to advise its destruction) when the client is a known target of a criminal investigation, companies and individuals are not required to retain forever every document they ever possess. If it is not clear where ordinary disposal of old files crosses into illegal obstruction of justice, when it is permissible for a lawyer to advise a client that it may discard possibly incriminating information?

1. THE LYING CLIENT

Although Model Rule 3.1 allows lawyers to seek acquittal of those whom they suspect or know to be guilty, there are limits on what lawyers can do toward that end. One limit has to do with whether the lawyer can allow a client to testify falsely at trial. Few issues in legal ethics have attracted more attention than the dilemma facing a criminal defense lawyer whose client wishes to invoke her constitutional right to testify in her own defense when the lawyer believes the client may testify falsely. The issue is important not because it arises frequently in practice; experienced practitioners insist it does not. Rather, it is important because it presents a stark conflict between the lawyer's duty of confidentiality to the client and duty of candor to the tribunal. The duty of confidentiality prohibits a lawyer to reveal "information relating to the representation of a client." Model Rule 1.6. The purpose of the rule is to encourage clients to confide in their lawyers in order to build the trust necessary to enable the lawyer to gather all the pertinent information and to represent the client effectively. The rule has few exceptions, and in some states, there is no exception even to allow lawyers to reveal confidences necessary to save a life or to free a wrongly convicted prisoner. Model Rule 1.6 does not contain (at least expressly) an exception to allow a lawyer to reveal that her client intends to commit perjury.

The lawyer's duty of candor to a tribunal is equally strong. Model Rule 3.3 prohibits lawyers from offering "evidence that the lawyer knows to be false." Rule 3.3 specifically requires that if "a lawyer, the lawyer's client, or a witness called by the lawyer, has offered material evidence and the lawyer comes to know of its falsity, the lawyer shall take reasonable remedial measures, including, if necessary, disclosure to the tribunal." The Rule goes on to state that a lawyer "may refuse to offer evidence, *other than the testimony of a defendant in a criminal matter*, that the lawyer reasonably believes is false." Comment [9] to Rule 3.3 provides: "Because of the special protections historically provided criminal defendants, however, this Rule does not permit a lawyer to refuse to offer the testimony of such a client where the lawyer reasonably believes but does not know that the testimony will be false. Unless the lawyer knows the testimony will be false, the lawyer must honor the client's decision to testify." The reason for the exception is that the defendant has a constitutional right to testify in his or her own criminal case. Rule 3.3 is not the only law prohibiting the knowing presentation of false testimony. A lawyer who knowingly facilitates a witness to testify falsely may be guilty of the crime of suborning perjury.

Model Rule 3.3: The Lawyer's Duty of Candor Toward the Tribunal

A lawyer shall not knowingly

- Make a false statement of fact or law to a tribunal or fail to correct a false statement of material fact or law previously made to the tribunal by the lawyer.

- Offer evidence that the lawyer knows to be false. If a lawyer, the lawyer's client, or a witness called by the lawyer has offered material evidence and the lawyer comes to know of its falsity, the lawyer shall take reasonable remedial measures, including, if necessary, disclosure to the tribunal.

- These duties apply to all lawyers, including defense counsel in criminal cases.

A lawyer may refuse to offer evidence, other than the testimony of a defendant in a criminal case, that the lawyer reasonably believes is false. This rule does not permit a lawyer to refuse to offer the testimony of a client who is the defendant in a criminal case where the lawyer reasonably believes but does not know that the testimony will be false. Unless the lawyer knows the testimony will be false, the lawyer must honor the client's decision to testify.

Lawyers have a duty both to avoid knowingly facilitating prospective perjury and to take remedial measures to address false testimony afterward once the lawyer learns of its falsity. The remedial obligation imposed by Model Rule 3.3 puts the lawyer in a difficult situation because she may harm her own reputation, jeopardize the case, and harm her client by revealing the falsity, especially if the client committed perjury. Because of the delicacy of the situation, Comment [10] to Model Rule 3.3 suggests a number of steps the lawyer should take. First, the lawyer should remonstrate with the client confidentially and seek the client's cooperation in correction of the false statements. If that fails, the Comment says the advocate "must take further remedial action," including withdrawal from the representation if it is permitted. But if withdrawal will not undo the effect of the false evidence, the lawyer "must make such disclosure to the tribunal as is reasonably necessary to remedy the situation, even if doing so requires the lawyer to reveal information that otherwise would be protected by Rule 1.6."

Model Rule 3.3: The Lawyer's Duty to Remedy the Use of False Evidence

If a lawyer has offered evidence to a tribunal that the lawyer comes to know is false, the lawyer must take reasonable remedial actions:

- The lawyer must first remonstrate confidentially with the client to persuade the client to withdraw or correct the false evidence. If that fails, the lawyer must take further remedial action.

- The lawyer may withdraw. If withdrawal is not permitted or will not undo the effect of the false evidence, the lawyer must make such disclosure as is reasonably necessary to remedy the situation.

- The obligation to disclose applies even if doing so requires the lawyer to reveal confidential information that would otherwise be protected from disclosure under Model Rule 1.6.

The Supreme Court held that a lawyer does not render ineffective assistance of counsel if he threatens to withdraw if the client commits perjury. *Nix v. Whiteside*, 475 U.S. 157 (1986). But the Court has never created a rule for what the lawyer should do. (The U.S. Supreme Court does not establish ethical rules governing lawyers, except those who appear before it. State supreme courts promulgate ethical rules for all lawyers admitted to practice in their state.) The following case explores the options facing a lawyer whose client proposes to testify falsely.

PEOPLE V. JOHNSON

California Court of Appeal 1998
62 Cal. App. 4th 608

KREMER, PRESIDING JUSTICE.

Anthony L. Johnson was convicted of numerous violent sexual offenses, kidnappings and robberies. He was sentenced to 5 consecutive life terms plus 440 years. On appeal, he contends he was denied his right to testify in his own defense. We conclude the court erred in denying Johnson his constitutional right to testify but find the error harmless beyond a reasonable doubt.

At trial, after the prosecution had completed its case-in-chief, defense counsel requested and was granted an in camera hearing. Defense counsel told the court he had "an ethical conflict" with Johnson about Johnson's desire to take the stand and testify. Defense counsel explained, "I cannot disclose to the court privileged communications relating to that, but I'm in a position where I am not willing to call Mr. Johnson as a witness despite his desire to testify." In response to the court's question, Johnson indicated defense counsel had accurately described the situation. [The court decided that Johnson would not be called as a witness and Johnson did not testify at his trial.]

Under the early common law, interested parties, including persons accused of committing a crime, were disqualified from presenting sworn testimony. This disqualification of parties from presenting sworn testimony was clearly established by the end of the 16th century in civil cases on the basis the party's testimony was untrustworthy. By the mid-19th century, parties and interested witnesses in civil cases were allowed to give sworn testimony in England and in most states in this country. The elimination of the disqualification was based primarily on an argument that a witness's motive for lying should go to the weight, not the admissibility, of testimony. Criminal defendants, however, were still deemed incompetent to testify. The two main arguments against permitting criminal defendants to testify were: (1) criminal defendants were so likely to commit perjury to avoid conviction that their testimony was inherently untrustworthy and (2) permitting criminal defendants to testify would erode the constitutional right to remain silent and the presumption of innocence because suspicion would fall on the defendant who failed to testify.

[In the 20th century, most states changed their law and held that criminal defendants were competent to testify.] In 1987, the United States Supreme Court explicitly held a criminal defendant had a constitutional right to testify on his own behalf.

A problem arises, as in this case, where the defendant asserts his right to testify and his attorney knows or suspects the defendant will give perjured testimony. A conflict then arises between the defendant's constitutional right to testify (and his Sixth Amendment right to the assistance of counsel) and the attorney's ethical obligation not to present perjured testimony. Attorneys have long been prohibited by the attorney rules of professional conduct from participating in the presentation of perjured testimony. [The court then surveyed California's and other ethical rules, including Model Rule 3.3, prohibiting counsel from offering perjured testimony.]

There has been much scholarly discussion of what an attorney should do when faced with a client who intends to commit perjury. We examine various options.

1. *Full Cooperation with Presenting Defendant's Testimony even when Defendant Intends to Commit Perjury*

Professor Freedman argues an attorney should fully cooperate with putting on his client's testimony even when the client intends to commit perjury. (See Freedman, Professional Responsibility of the Criminal Defense Lawyer: The Three Hardest Questions (1966) 64 MICH. L. REV. 1469.) Professor Freedman argues the importance of client confidentiality and, as well, the attorney's duty to provide effective representation by gathering all necessary information are more important than an attorney's duty to be candid with the court. Therefore, Professor Freedman argues defense counsel must sometimes permit his client to commit perjury and be prepared to argue the client's perjurious testimony to the jury.

No court has endorsed this view. Freedman's approach has also been much criticized by the legal commentators because it conflicts with legal ethics rules prohibiting an attorney from knowingly participating in presenting perjured testimony as well as rules requiring an attorney to disclose a client's intention to commit a crime.

2. *Persuading the Client Not to Commit Perjury*

All the legal commentators agree that when faced with a client who indicates he will commit perjury, an attorney should first attempt to persuade the client to testify truthfully. The United States Supreme Court has held an attorney acted consistently with professional rules of ethics and did not deny the defendant the right to effective assistance of counsel by persuading the defendant not to commit perjury. *Nix v. Whiteside*, 475 U.S. 157, 169 (1986).

The persuasion solution, when it succeeds, is the ideal solution since it involves neither the presentation of perjured testimony nor disclosure of client confidences. Yet, it does not answer the question of what should be done when the client insists on testifying falsely despite his attorney's best efforts to dissuade him.

3. *Withdrawal from Representation*

The Model Rules provide an attorney should make a motion to withdraw from representation when the representation will result in a violation of law or rules of professional conduct. (Model Rules, rule 1.16(a)(1).

This approach, while it protects the attorney's interest in not presenting perjured testimony, does not solve the problem. The court may deny the motion to withdraw. Even if the motion to withdraw is granted, the problem remains. That approach could trigger an endless cycle of defense continuances and motions to withdraw as the accused informs each new attorney of the intent to testify falsely. Or the accused may be less candid with his new attorney by keeping his perjurious intent to himself, thereby facilitating the presentation of false testimony.

4. *Disclosure to the Court*

Another alternative is that the attorney should disclose the perjury to the court. Initially, we note that some of the other proposed solutions involve some disclosure, i.e., implicit in solutions of making a motion to withdraw or having the defendant testify in a narrative manner is, at least, an implicit disclosure to the court that the attorney believes the defendant may commit perjury. Disclosure has been criticized because it compromises the attorney's ethical duty to keep client communications confidential and results in a significant conflict of interest between the attorney and his client if the attorney discloses to the court that the defendant has perjured himself. Additionally, until the defendant actually takes the stand and testifies falsely, there is always a chance the defendant will change his mind and testify truthfully. Finally, disclosure is only a partial solution. If the disclosure occurs before the defendant has taken the stand, the disclosure will require some additional action, i.e., a decision as to whether the defendant's statement is, in fact, false and a further decision whether the defendant will be permitted to testify and in what form and manner. Disclosure before the defendant testifies could result in a mini-trial on the perjury issue before the defendant has had the opportunity to take the stand and testify truthfully.

5. *The Narrative Approach*

Under the narrative approach, the attorney calls the defendant to the witness stand but does not engage in the usual question and answer exchange. Instead, the attorney permits the defendant to testify in a free narrative manner. In closing arguments, the attorney does not rely on any of the defendant's false testimony. In the early 1970's, the American Bar Association adopted the narrative approach in its Project on Standards for Criminal Justice, Standards Relating to the Defense Function. Standard 7.7.

The narrative approach has been criticized on the basis the attorney participates in committing a fraud on the court. The narrative approach has also been criticized as communicating to the jury that the defendant is committing perjury. One court has stated, "This procedure could hardly have failed to convey to the jury the impression that the defendant's counsel attached little significance or credibility to the testimony of the witness, or that the defendant and his counsel were at odds. Prejudice to the defendant's case by this trial tactic was inevitable." (*State v. Robinson* (1976) 290 N.C. 56, 67.) Another commentator has stated: "by telegraphing her own belief in the inveracity of the accused, the defendant's lawyer arguably violates the ethical prohibitions against counsel serving as a witness and against expressing a personal opinion about the client's 'credibility . . . or . . . guilt or innocence'

6. *Refusing to Permit the Defendant to Testify*

The opposite extreme from Professor Freedman's solution of full cooperation by the attorney in presenting the defendant's testimony is a refusal to permit the defendant to testify at all. This solution is justified by the theory that an attorney has an ethical obligation not to participate in the presentation of perjured testimony and the defendant has no right to commit perjury. Preclusion of the testimony as a solution has been criticized because it essentially substitutes defense counsel for the jury as the judge of witness credibility; it puts the determination of whether the defendant is telling the truth or a lie into the hands of defense counsel. (See Rifkin, *The Criminal Defendant's Right to Testify: The Right to Be Seen But Not Heard* (1989) 21 COLUM. HUM. RTS. L. REV. 253, 272.) Further, under this approach, a determination is made that the defendant will commit perjury before he has even taken the witness stand. Finally, this approach, while safeguarding the attorney's ethical obligations not to participate in presenting perjured testimony, results in a complete denial of the defendant's right to testify.

7. *The Narrative Approach Represents the Best Accommodation of the Competing Interests*

None of the approaches to a client's stated intention to commit perjury is perfect. Of the various approaches, we believe the narrative approach represents the best accommodation of the competing interests of the defendant's right to testify and the attorney's obligation not to participate in the presentation of perjured testimony since it allows the defendant to tell the jury, in his own words, his version of what occurred, a right which has been described as fundamental, and allows the attorney to play a passive role. In contrast, the two extremes—fully cooperating with the defendant's testimony and refusing to present the defendant's testimony—involve no accommodation of the conflicting interests; the first gives no consideration to the attorney's ethical obligations, the second gives none to the defendant's right to testify. The other intermediate solutions—persuasion, withdrawal and disclosure—often result in no solution, i.e., the defendant is not persuaded, the withdrawal leads to an endless chain of withdrawals and disclosure compromises client confidentiality and typically requires further action.

NOTES ON THE LYING CLIENT

1. *What Is the Best Approach to Client Perjury?* States differ in what they require when a lawyer knows her client will testify falsely. While California, as you see from *People v. Johnson*, allows narrative testimony, Oregon requires the lawyer to withdraw. *In re A.,* 276 Or. 225 (1976). Model 3.3 Comment [7] does not approve the narrative approach. It also prohibits Option 1 as outlined in People v. Johnson. That is, it prohibits lawyers assisting clients to testify falsely. Model Rule 3.3 does not explicitly explain what a lawyer should do to prevent prospective perjury. In cases where the client has already testified falsely, Rule 3.3 requires lawyers to first try Option 2 (remonstrating with client), then Option 3 (withdrawal), and only then to use Option 4 (disclosure to court). Which of the approaches to the problem of client perjury do you find preferable?

2. *When Does a Lawyer Know?* When does a lawyer know that her client proposes to lie under oath? Comment [8] to Model Rule 3.3 says: "The prohibition against offering false evidence only applies if the lawyer knows that the evidence is false. A lawyer's reasonable belief that the evidence is false does not preclude its presentation to the trier of fact. A lawyer's knowledge that the evidence is false, however, can be inferred from the circumstances. Thus, although a lawyer should resolve doubts about the veracity of testimony or other evidence in favor of the client, the lawyer cannot ignore an obvious falsehood." Does this provide enough guidance for lawyers to distinguish between what they know, what they suspect, and what they don't "know" but what is an "obvious falsehood"?

3. *What a Lawyer Knows and What a Lawyer Should Know.* As you decide whether Model Rule 3.3 provides adequate guidance to lawyers, consider the facts of *Nix v. Whiteside*, 475 U.S. 157 (1986): Whiteside went to visit a man named Love in his apartment and the two got into an argument. Love directed his girlfriend to get his "piece" and then reached under his pillow. Whiteside then stabbed Love in the chest, killing him. Whiteside told his lawyer that he had stabbed Love as he was pulling a pistol from underneath the pillow, but added that he had not actually seen a gun although he believed Love had one. The police did not find a gun at the scene and none of the witnesses to the stabbing reported seeing one. About a week before trial, during preparation for his testimony, Whiteside told his lawyers that he had seen something "metallic" in Love's hand. When asked about it, Whiteside said: "In Howard Cook's case there was a gun. If I don't say I saw a gun, I'm dead." The lawyer told Whiteside that the testimony would be perjury and that in any event it was unnecessary to prove Love had a gun

because Whiteside needed only to prove that he reasonably believed he was in danger. If Whiteside insists on taking the stand to testify, does his lawyer have sufficient reason to believe that Whiteside will testify falsely?

* * *

2. THE COACHED WITNESS

A related problem, common in both civil and criminal trials, is what lawyers can and cannot do in preparing a witness to testify. This problem arises much more often in lawyers' practice than does the relatively unusual problem of client perjury. Model Rule 3.4 prohibits a lawyer to falsify evidence, or to "counsel or assist a witness to testify falsely." It also prohibits lawyers to "unlawfully obstruct another party's access to evidence," which could include counseling a witness not to testify fully and truthfully.

Model Rule 3.4

A lawyer shall not

- Unlawfully obstruct another party's access to evidence

- Falsify evidence, counsel or assist a witness to testify falsely

---

Consider some examples:

PROBLEM 13–1: ANATOMY OF A MURDER

An accused murderer is about to meet with his lawyer for the first time. At the outset of the interview, the lawyer informs his client that the law of the state recognizes only four legal defenses to murder, and describes them. The defendant apparently concludes that his best bet is to rely on temporary insanity—one of the four possible defenses his lawyer just described—and he describes the facts in a way that suggests he was suffering from temporary insanity at the time of the killing. (This figures in a 1958 novel, *Anatomy of a Murder*, by Robert Traver, a pseudonym of Michigan Supreme Court Justice John Voelker. The novel was made into a 1958 movie, also called *Anatomy of a Murder*, starring Jimmy Stewart.)

PROBLEM 13–2: IMPROVING A WITNESS'S DELIVERY

An anesthesiologist is charged with criminal negligence in connection with the death of a patient. While preparing to testify at his trial, the defendant initially responded to his lawyers' practice questions in a cold, detached, clinical manner. His lawyers encouraged the doctor to adopt a warmer tone, to display more emotion, and to refer to the decedent by her first name rather than as the patient. In his testimony, the doctor followed their advice and employed his attorneys' characterizations almost verbatim to describe events. In considering the propriety of the lawyers' advice, should it matter whether the doctor is not fluent in English and he memorizes his lawyers' characterizations of the facts in order to make himself clear and avoid having to testify through a translator?

PROBLEM 13–3: PREPARING A WITNESS TO CONFRONT ADVERSE EVIDENCE

In preparing a witness (not a defendant) to testify at a trial in which the corporation for which she works and some of its officers are charged with fraud and other financial crimes, a defense lawyer shows the witness a document, signed by the witness, which flatly contradicts a response that the witness has just given to a question. The lawyer and the witness discuss the document and try to figure out a way to reconcile the inconsistency.

PROBLEM 13–4: COACHING A WITNESS NOT TO VOLUNTEER OR SPECULATE

In preparing witnesses to testify in the trial of the corporation and its officers for fraud, defense counsel take great pains to prepare questions designed to make certain that the witnesses do not reveal anything beyond what the questions specifically request. The lawyers admonish the witnesses to be truthful but also not to "volunteer" anything beyond what the lawyers and the witnesses have discussed in answer to the questions.

PROBLEM 13–5: ADVISING A WITNESS ABOUT THE LAW BEFORE ASKING ABOUT THE FACTS

In preparing the plaintiff to testify in a negligence case, his lawyer discusses damages available in negligence claims. Fearing that the plaintiff may be embarrassed to bring it up, the lawyer reminds him that loss of sexual desire or function is a compensable element of damages if it was caused by the defendant's actions.

PROBLEM 13–6: ADVISING A WITNESS ABOUT WHAT OTHER WITNESSES SAY

During preparation for trial, a witness expresses uncertainty as to her ability to identify the accused assailant. The prosecutor thereupon informs her, truthfully, that the defendant has also been identified by the other victim. (What if the prosecutor neglected to mention that the other victim was uncertain about the identification of the assailant?)

Lawyers disagree about the permissible boundaries of witness preparation. Some condemn most of the techniques noted above, especially informing the defendant of the law before asking him about the facts and telling one eyewitness that others have identified the defendant as the assailant (especially if others have not). Others have defended most of them, although the *Anatomy of a Murder* style of coaching and misleading a witness about what other witnesses recall are highly controversial.[15] As we saw, Model Rule 3.4(b) provides that a lawyer "shall not falsify evidence, counsel or assist a witness to testify falsely." A draft would have prohibited lawyers from providing advice that they could "reasonably foresee will aid a client in giving false testimony." That rule has not been adopted. Would you favor its adoption? Which of the examples in Problems 13–1 through 13–6 above do you find most troublesome? Which, if any, are prohibited by Model Rule 3.4(b)? Which would be prohibited if the modification were adopted?

* * *

3.   THE HONEST WITNESS

While encouraging or allowing witnesses to give false testimony is clearly unethical and can also be the crime of suborning perjury, another way in which lawyers can thwart the search for the truth is by skillful cross-examination of a truthful witness. Cross-examining a witness who comes across as sympathetic to the jury is one of the most difficult to master and prized courtroom techniques. Lawyers tend to regard impeaching the honest witness with a mixture of awe and ambivalence. The Model Rules do not explicitly address it. Many lawyers believe that it is not morally permissible to impeach the testimony of a witness the lawyer knows is testifying truthfully, and their position finds some support in Model Rule 3.4(b), which prohibits a lawyer to "falsify evidence, counsel or assist a witness to testify falsely." By extension, one might argue, it should not be permissible to try to show that a truthful witness is not to be believed. Is there a meaningful difference between offering false testimony and trying to prove that truthful testimony false? Model Rule 4.4 provides that "a lawyer shall not use means that have no substantial purpose other than to embarrass, delay, or burden a third person." While one might argue that impeaching the truthful witness who is not a party to the litigation is embarrassing to the witness, if one accepts that winning the case on behalf of the client is a "substantial purpose," the cross-examination is not a violation of the rule.

The ABA Standards for Criminal Defense provide that "defense counsel's belief or knowledge that a witness is telling the truth does not preclude cross-examination." The standard also provides, however, that "[t]he interrogation of all witnesses should be conducted fairly, objectively, and with due regard for the dignity and legitimate privacy of the witness, and without seeking to intimidate or humiliate the witness unnecessarily." ABA Criminal Defense Function Standard 4–7.6.

---

[15] See Hal R. Lieberman, *Be Aware of Ethical Witness Preparation Rules*, N.Y.L.J., May 25, 2000, at 29; Dennis Suplee & Diana Donaldson, *A Defense of Reconstructing Reality: Witness Preparation Helps Litigants Have Confidence in Inherently Frail Memories*, LEGAL INTELLIGENCER, Mar. 2, 2010.

As a practical matter, lawyers do not often believe they confront the hard ethical question about impeaching a truthful witness because they often are unsure whether the witness is indeed telling the truth and can easily convince themselves that the witness is not. One of the most famous examples of cross-examining an arguably honest witness occurred in a criminal prosecution of two owners of the Triangle Shirtwaist Company after a 1911 fire in their New York City factory killed 146 immigrant women sweatshop workers. The owners were indicted on manslaughter charges based on a New York state law providing that factory doors "shall not be locked, bolted or fastened during working hours." The doors to the factory were bolted shut. As a result, the workers were trapped in the building and either burned or leapt from the windows to their death. The prosecution's final witness, Kate Alterman, testified that she was an employee in the factory and was there when the fire broke out. She testified that as she was at the window ready to jump, she saw a co-worker named Rose Schwartz struggle unsuccessfully to open a door before she was engulfed in flames. On cross-examination, the defense counsel, Max Steuer, asked the witness all she did and saw on the ninth floor of the factory the moment she first saw the fire. The witness repeated her story using the exact same words she had used when testifying on direct examination. After asking her questions on another topic, Steuer again asked Alterman to describe what she had seen and done, and again she used the same words to narrate the events. Steuer asked her whether she had omitted a word. Alterman began to move her lips to narrate the events again, and when she reached the point where she omitted the word, she said "Yes, I made a mistake; I left that word out." Steuer then repeated the exercise twice more, and twice more she recited the same story verbatim. The two factory owners were acquitted. As one commentator said in lauding Steuer's cross-examination, "Historians say the acquittal was due to the trial judge's narrow charge to the jury. But Steuer's brilliant cross-examination of the People's star witness must have had more than a little to do with the result."[16]

Critics of Steuer's technique insist it is wrong to assume that Alterman's testimony was perjured. "To equate Kate Alterman's possibly rehearsed testimony with premeditated dishonesty represents an enormous leap of faith and completely ignores the socioeconomic and historic context of that testimony. The women who testified at the trial spoke little English. Approximately half of them spoke no English at all, and many of those who did were illiterate. They had barely survived a traumatic fire in which many of their friends and co-workers had burned to death. The notorious conditions under which they had worked in this

---

[16]　Daniel J. Kornstein, *A Tragic Fire—A Great Cross-Examination*, N.Y.L.J., Mar. 28, 1986, at 2.

country provided no basis for them to believe that their own words could sway the power structure the legal system represented."[17]

NOTES ON CROSS-EXAMINING A TRUTHFUL WITNESS

1. *Distinguishing the Tactic from the Result.* Did Steuer do something morally wrong in cross-examining Alterman? If so, what was it? Would it matter whether he knew that Alterman was telling the truth? Telling the truth about what? If the factory owners had been convicted of the charges in the Triangle Shirtwaist fire, would your views about the permissibility of the cross-examination change? Is there a difference between the propriety of what Steuer did and the propriety of preparing the doctor to testify in Problem 13–2 above?

2. *When Is Cross-Examination Permissible?* Under what circumstances and in what ways is it acceptable to impeach the testimony of a truthful witness? The Restatement Third of the Law Governing Lawyers § 106, Comment c, asserts: "A particularly difficult problem is presented when a lawyer has an opportunity to cross-examine a witness with respect to testimony that the lawyer knows to be truthful, including harsh implied criticism of the witness's testimony, character, or capacity for truth-telling. Even if legally permissible, a lawyer would presumably do so only where that would not cause the lawyer to lose credibility with the tribunal or alienate the fact-finder. Moreover, a lawyer is never required to conduct such examination, and the lawyer may withdraw if the lawyer's client insists on such a course of action in a setting in which the lawyer considers it imprudent or repugnant." If the lawyer and client disagree about the strategic benefits of impeaching the testimony of a witness or the lawyer considers it repugnant to do so, withdrawal in the middle of a trial or a deposition is probably not a realistic option. Model Rule 1.16(b)(4) allows a lawyer to withdraw if "the client insists upon taking action that the lawyer considers repugnant or with which the lawyer has fundamental disagreement," but permission of the tribunal may be required. Even if withdrawal would be permitted by the court (which it may not be in the middle of trial), unless the lawyer in question is quite senior, insisting on withdrawing may be regarded by his or her superiors as tantamount to resigning from the firm or law office.

The failure of the Model Rules to stake out a clear and straightforward position on impeaching the testimony of a truthful witness may be explained by the difficulty of distinguishing when it is appropriate from when it is not. For example, should it matter whether the lawyer harbors doubt about the witness's truthfulness? If so, must the lawyer believe that the witness is lying (or innocently mistaken) about everything, or just some things? How would we know when the lawyer knows the witness is lying and when the lawyer is simply trying to gain a tactical advantage? What kinds of impeachment are permissible? If you conclude that Steuer's cross-examination of Alterman was

---

[17] Ann Ruben & Emily Ruben, *Letter to the Editor*, N. Y. L.J., Apr. 14, 1986, at 2.

morally wrong, is it because it is always or only sometimes wrong to point out that a witness's testimony has been rehearsed? Could you draft a rule that prohibits inappropriate impeachment of a witness?

F. ETHICAL ISSUES IN COUNSELING AND LITIGATION: RETENTION AND DESTRUCTION OF DOCUMENTS

One of the most common temptations to lawyer misconduct arises in the handling of documents and digital data during or in anticipation of litigation. While we address document retention policies here because the law and ethics of destroying documents arises commonly in criminal investigations of organizations, document retention and destruction is an issue for almost any lawyer advising a large organizational client.

In civil disputes, and in anticipation of criminal or government-initiated civil investigations, lawyers must review evidence in possession of their client to determine what must be provided to an adversary in civil pretrial discovery or to government investigators or retained for their future examination. Every few years, a scandal bursts into the news involving lawyers—often with sterling credentials practicing in elite firms—who get into serious trouble because they counseled clients to destroy documents (or advised that destruction was permissible) or themselves hid documents. Different aspects of the ethical and practical issues confronting lawyers in handling client documents will be discussed at many places in this book. Here we discuss one facet of the larger issue: when a lawyer represents a client who is or may soon become the target of a criminal investigation, what advice can the lawyer give the client regarding the retention or destruction of documents?

The issue arises commonly, although not exclusively, in the representation of corporations and other entities. Most large corporations and many small ones have formal policies governing which documents and electronic records should be retained and which should be destroyed. These document retention policies, as they are commonly known, really are document destruction policies, for they direct information technology departments and all others within the corporation when computer drives can be wiped, when old hard disks and removable electronic storage devices can be incinerated, wiped, or recycled, and when paper documents can be sent to the shredder or put in the recycling bin. As one lawyer said, "[s]uch policies are justified by the desire to reduce storage costs. But they are also sometimes justified by the desire to eliminate the cost and burden that a firm would have to bear in a regulatory investigation or litigation were it required to produce huge amounts of information not necessary for the conduct of the firm's ongoing business."[18] The challenge is drawing the line between the circumstances when destruction of documents is permissible (even if it is motivated by the desire to reduce the costs and burdens for firms that are subject to regulatory investigation or civil or criminal litigation) and those when it constitutes obstruction of justice.

Model Rule 3.4 provides that a lawyer shall not "unlawfully obstruct another party's access to evidence or unlawfully alter, destroy or conceal a document or other material having potential evidentiary value. A lawyer shall not counsel or assist another person to do any such act." In addition, destruction of documents and other evidence can constitute obstruction of justice or spoliation of evidence, both of which are crimes under federal and state law.

Document Destruction and the Obstruction of Justice

- **Model Rule 3.4(a)** provides that a lawyer shall not unlawfully obstruct another party's access to evidence or unlawfully alter, destroy or conceal a document or other material having potential evidentiary value. A lawyer shall not counsel or assist another person to do any such act.

- **18 U.S.C. § 1512** makes it a federal crime to knowingly and corruptly persuade another person to withhold documents from an official proceeding, but one who persuades another to shred documents under a document retention policy does not commit a crime if he does not have in contemplation any particular official proceeding in which those documents might be material.

- A provision of the Sarbanes-Oxley Act, **18 U.S.C. § 1519**, makes it a federal crime to knowingly alter, destroy, mutilate, conceal, or falsify any record, document, or tangible object with the intent to impede, obstruct, or influence the investigation or proper administration of any matter within the jurisdiction of any department or agency of the United States. Unlike 18 U.S.C. § 1812, the statute does not explicitly require that a government investigation be pending or that a lawyer who advises the adoption of a document retention policy knows of some particular government inquiry.

---

[18] Lewis Liman, *Exploring the Nexus Requirement In Obstruction of Justice Prosecutions*, N.Y.L.J., Nov. 16, 2011, at 7.

A famous example of the dangers of document destruction policies concerns the once-great accounting firm Arthur Andersen. The firm had worked as an independent public auditor for the Houston-based energy trading company Enron. Andersen had certified Enron's accounting of its profits and losses for purposes of investors. (Independent public accounting is legally required for corporations that sell securities to the public in order to prevent the companies from misleading investors about the value of the company.) Enron's accounting was creative to the point of fraudulent, as the company's clever executives had devised a number of ways to structure transactions that made it appear that its losses were profits. It "imploded in a wave of accounting scandals," just as one of its vice presidents, Sherron Watkins, had predicted that it would. As it was collapsing, a number of criminal investigations were commenced against the corporation, its top executives, and its accounting firm, Andersen.

Shortly after the *Wall Street Journal* published an article in August 2001 suggesting improprieties at Enron, Andersen formed an Enron "crisis response team." Nancy Temple, an in-house lawyer at Andersen, designated the Enron matter internally as a "government/regulatory investigation" and emailed Andersen's lead partner in Houston that he should "remind" the Enron team "of our documentation and retention policy." In October, Enron announced a $1 billion charge to earnings, a statement that the firm was less profitable than it had previously reported. The Securities Exchange Commission, which regulates the stock market and has the power to criminally prosecute companies for fraud and other dishonesty in the sale of securities to the public, informed Enron that it had opened an informal investigation. Nevertheless, Temple and the Houston partner continued to remind Andersen employees of the company's document retention policy. Andersen employees began shredding paper documents and deleting electronic files relating to the work the firm had done for Enron and continued until the SEC opened a formal investigation and served a subpoena on Andersen requiring that they provide the SEC with all documents relating to their work for Enron.

The government indicted Andersen under 18 U.S.C. § 1512, which makes it illegal to "knowingly" and "corruptly persuad[e] another person . . . with intent to . . . cause" that person to "withhold" documents from an "official proceeding." After its destruction of documents and the subsequent indictment became public, Andersen lost most of its clients and went out of business. The jury convicted Andersen, but the Supreme Court ultimately reversed the conviction on the ground that the jury had not been properly instructed about legal requirements of "knowing" and "corrupt" persuasion when a lawyer advises a client to destroy documents. *Arthur Andersen LLP v. United States*, 544 U.S. 696 (2005). The Court stated that corporate document retention policies are common and are not themselves illegal. Moreover, in some instances a lawyer's advice to withhold information from the government is not wrong, as when a lawyer advises a client to invoke the Fifth Amendment privilege against self-incrimination or invokes the attorney-client privilege protecting disclosure of any confidential communication between an attorney and her client. The Court explained that the statute did not require that an official proceeding be pending at the time the advice is given to destroy documents, but that the statute is not violated by "someone who persuades others to shred documents under a document retention policy when he does not have in contemplation any particular official proceeding in which those documents might be material." 544 U.S. at 708.

In the Enron collapse, as in the bankruptcies of a number of other formerly profitable corporations that had engaged in dubious accounting, thousands of employees lost their jobs. Investors, including company employees whose entire retirement incomes were invested in falsely overvalued company stock, lost huge amounts of money. Responding to public outrage over corporate manipulation of stock value, Congress enacted the Sarbanes-Oxley Act to increase regulation and disclosure requirements for companies. Sarbanes-Oxley imposes a number of disclosure requirements on lawyers that we will cover later in this book. With respect to the responsibilities of lawyers and clients for retention of documents, Sarbanes-Oxley created a new federal crime. The statute makes it a felony to knowingly alter, destroy, conceal, or falsify "any record, document, or tangible object with the intent to impede, obstruct, or influence the investigation or proper administration of any matter within the jurisdiction of any department or agency of the United States." 18 U.S.C. § 1519. Our large regulatory state places many business activities "within the jurisdiction of a department or agency of the United States." The statute does not explicitly require that a government investigation must be pending in order to trigger criminal responsibility if someone "destroys . . . any record, document, or tangible object." Moreover, if one intent of a document destruction policy is to prevent, as a general matter, the company from having to produce its voluminous records in the event of some unspecified government agency investigation, it would appear that section 1519 now renders such policies risky. Hence, some lawyers now advise clients to take appropriate steps to preserve documents and to suspend document destruction policies when credible evidence of some unlawful conduct comes to light, even if no governmental inquiry is in sight.[19]

---

[19] See David Howard, *In House Counsel Increasingly Seek Advice on Document Preservation*, CORP. COUNS., Mar. 30, 2005; Beryl Howell, *The Slippery Slope from Spoliation to Obstruction*, N.Y.L.J., July 27, 2006, at 21.

NOTES ON DOCUMENT RETENTION POLICIES

1. ***The Pros and Cons of Document Retention Policies.*** What are the costs to the firm and to the government or any civil litigant who may sue the firm, if the firm preserves too much data and documentary evidence rather than too little?

2. ***Criminal Intent and Obstruction of Justice.*** Can you solve the problem that troubled the Court in *Andersen* and Congress in Sarbanes-Oxley: what intent must a lawyer or client have in destroying documents to justify treating it as a crime? What are the costs and benefits of defining the required criminal intent too broadly as opposed to too narrowly?

PROBLEM 13–7: ADVISING A CORPORATION ON A DOCUMENT RETENTION POLICY

You are outside counsel to a company that manufactures plastics. Your client does not have a document retention policy. Six months ago, when you first began to represent the company, you recommended that the company adopt a document retention policy and offered to draft a standard policy providing for the destruction of most documents more than two years old. You know that many companies have such policies. The company's CEO said he would look into it but the matter was dropped as the client decided to cut its legal bills in response to a drop in profits in the last quarter. Recently, an environmental organization and a news organization have issued reports of high levels of carcinogens in the air, dirt, and water surrounding your client's manufacturing plant. They also have gathered demographic data showing a much higher incidence of cancer in the surrounding neighborhood than in the county as a whole. No litigation has been filed and you are unaware of any regulatory or criminal proceedings having been instituted. The chief safety officer of the company has come to see you with a box of documents and a computer disk drive full of internal company memoranda and other documents from five to ten years old showing that the company knew that its processes caused a leak of certain known carcinogens into the air and, perhaps, the dirt and water, surrounding the plant. After reviewing the information with the chief safety officer, you advise that he should retain the documents pending further research and investigation by you. You conduct some research and determine that the emissions violate a number of state and federal environmental laws. When you deliver the results of your research to the client's CEO, he says that he has decided to adopt the document retention policy you proposed. What should you consider in formulating your response to the situation? What would you say to the chief safety officer and to the CEO?

G. SUMMARY

This chapter has focused on criminal practice. Because the vast majority of people charged with crimes are poor, we began by studying lawyers who represent the indigent. Although there is a constitutional right to effective assistance of counsel in any criminal case in which the defendant faces a prison sentence, the funding to implement the constitutional right is inadequate in some jurisdictions, and some appointed criminal defense lawyers therefore struggle to provide adequate representation. Courts have been very reluctant to find that even serious lapses of competence violate the right to counsel, perhaps in part because courts lack meaningful ability to provide the funds to enable lawyers to do a better job and in part because of a belief that overturning a conviction is not an appropriate remedy for the problem.

Most lawyers agree that, because the burden of proof is on the government in a criminal case to prove guilt beyond a reasonable doubt, a lawyer may ethically defend one whom she knows to be guilty as a way of forcing the government to sustain its burden of proof. The hard ethical issues concern how far a criminal defense lawyer may go in discharging her obligation to defend the accused. Although a defendant has a constitutional right to testify in his own defense, criminal defense lawyers are prohibited from helping a client to testify falsely. There is less agreement about the law and ethics of permitting the defendant to do so without the lawyer's assistance.

The more common set of difficult ethical issues in both criminal defense and civil litigation concern when a lawyer's assistance to a client suspected or accused of a crime or other wrongdoing crosses the line from zealous advocacy to violating duties to the opposing party or to the court. Preparing witnesses to testify may violate Model Rule 3.4 or even constitute suborning perjury if the lawyer encourages a witness to testify falsely. Cross-examination designed to impeach the credibility of a witness whom the lawyer knows to be telling the truth probably violates no Model Rule, but some lawyers consider it immoral. The most common ethical issue that pits the lawyer's duties to client against the lawyer's duties of candor to opposing parties and to tribunals arises in both civil and criminal practice; it concerns the retention and destruction of documents. Many lawyers advise companies on the adoption and administration of document retention policies, which typically provide for destruction of certain documents after a specified period of time. While such policies are lawful, in the context of a criminal investigation the implementation of such a policy may be illegal for the lawyer and client and a violation of Model Rule 3.4 for the lawyer.

CHAPTER 14

CRIMINAL PROSECUTION

■ ■ ■

A. INTRODUCTION

Federal, state, and local governments employ thousands of lawyers as criminal prosecutors. Criminal prosecutors are chosen in three ways. In the state criminal system, a District Attorney in each county is typically elected by the people. In addition, many state attorneys general are elected in statewide elections. In the federal system, the Attorney General of the United States and the U.S. Attorney in each federal district are appointed by the President and confirmed by the Senate. The thousands of prosecutors who work for the state attorneys general, county district attorneys, city attorneys, the U.S. Department of Justice in Washington, D.C., and the US Attorneys in each federal district are hired under civil service rules, and thus typically do not serve just at the pleasure of one who is elected or who is appointed by the executive.

Work as a prosecutor is varied. Like most lawyers, they do the majority of their work out of court. Prosecutors supervise ongoing criminal investigations, working with police and other investigators to interview witnesses and to seek and review documentary and physical evidence. Once they have compiled evidence, prosecutors decide whom to charge with what crimes. Within each district attorney's or U.S. Attorney's office, there are procedures to enable more senior lawyers to oversee the investigations, charging decisions, trial work, plea bargaining, and the other work assigned to the more junior lawyers in order to ensure uniformity of policy. There is some independent review (either by the grand jury or by a judge) of the sufficiency of the evidence to support a charge, but the review is extremely deferential to the prosecutor. Prosecutors spend a great deal of time negotiating plea bargains with defense counsel, as the overwhelming majority of criminal cases are resolved by a guilty plea. Prosecutors appear in court in the pretrial process to litigate motions to suppress evidence or to deny bail. And, of course, prosecutors try cases and defend convictions on appeal.

Like most lawyers, prosecutors often specialize. Specialties include street crime like drug dealing, robberies or gang-related violence, white collar crime, including financial, banking, or securities fraud, or crimes against children.

Prosecutors occupy a unique role with unique ethical responsibilities. For that reason, there is a Model Rule (3.8) devoted exclusively to the role of the prosecutor. Prosecutors exercise extraordinary power. They have access to all the investigatory resources of the government. They have the power, subject to some judicial oversight, to order people and their property to be searched, to order people arrested and held prior to trial, and to compel reluctant third parties to testify. Prosecutors have substantial power to determine what sentences people will serve because about 95 percent of those charged plead guilty[1] and both federal and state criminal law have sentencing rules that limit judges' discretion to depart from the sentence recommended in the statute. The crime charged determines the crime to which a defendant may plead and the sentence that will be imposed.

Prosecutors exercise significant discretion with little transparency. There is some accountability, although it is generally within the office rather than to the public in any meaningful sense, as it is rare for a president to ask for the resignation of a U.S. Attorney or for the voters to turn an elected DA out of office. Prosecutors have judicially unreviewable discretion to decide whom to investigate, whom to charge, which crimes to charge, whom to call as a witness, whether to dismiss charges, and what sentence to recommend or to accept in exchange for a guilty plea.[2] Like most government lawyers, a prosecutor's client is the people or the government. The absence of a traditional client enables prosecutors to take a broad view of what justice requires in a particular case, but it also means that no one outside the bureaucracy of the federal or state Department of Justice or law enforcement community effectively constrains how prosecutors exercise their power.[3] As we will see in later chapters, prosecutors are not the only lawyers whose client is sufficiently amorphous to raise issues of accountability; most government lawyers, as well as lawyers who bring class actions, or who represent causes, movements, or loose organizations, also operate without strong client constraints.

While some standards do govern the exercise of discretion in the prosecutorial role, and office policies are often very detailed, there is little enforceable law that constrains prosecutors' discretion. Prosecutors are only rarely disciplined by the bar and are absolutely immune from civil liability for the exercise of their prosecutorial judgment, even for egregious breaches of duty. *Imbler v. Pachtman*, 424 U.S. 409 (1976). Prosecutors are subject to judicial discipline, but judges rarely impose it.

---

[1]   Ronald F. Wright, *Trial Distortion and the End of Innocence in Federal Criminal Justice*, 154 U. PA. L. REV. 79, 90 (2005).

[2]   Bruce Green & Fred Zacharias, *Prosecutorial Neutrality*, 2004 WIS. L. REV. 837, 840–42.

[3]   Fred C. Zacharias, *Structuring the Ethics of Prosecutorial Trial Practice: Can Prosecutors Do Justice?*, 44 VAND. L. REV. 45 (1991).

Criminal convictions may be overturned for prosecutorial misconduct, but courts are reluctant to do so.

The prosecutor's duty to seek justice exists in some tension with the prosecutor's role as an adversary in the criminal justice system, which is one of the most adversarial sectors of the American legal system. Whatever one's views about the extent to which a criminal defense lawyer may ethically act as a zealous advocate, including by obtaining acquittal of a person whom the lawyer knows to be factually guilty, many believe a prosecutor's role as an advocate should be tempered by an obligation to ensure that only the guilty are convicted. The difficulty is in the details. Particularly in matters such as pretrial disclosure of evidence, which occurs without judicial supervision in both criminal and civil litigation, many lawyers (not only prosecutors) are tempted to slight their obligations to their adversary. Some prosecutors' failure to disclose exculpatory evidence, especially when combined with poor quality defense counsel, leads to wrongful convictions, although people disagree about the extent of the problem.

Chapter Organization

This chapter begins with an overview of the law governing the prosecutorial role. It then considers four of the most significant issues about the prosecutorial role. First is whether law and norms are effective in balancing justice and effectiveness in law enforcement in the context of the problem of wrongful convictions. The chapter next looks at prosecutorial power and discretion in charging crimes and in plea bargaining. Then we consider the prosecutor's responsibilities to disclose exculpatory information to the defense prior to trial. The final topic concerns what all lawyers, but especially prosecutors, can say to the press.

B. THE LAW GOVERNING THE PROSECUTORIAL ROLE

Prosecutors serve a dual role as advocates seeking conviction and as officers of justice. As Comment [1] to Model Rule 3.8 says, a "prosecutor has the responsibility of a minister of justice and not simply that of an advocate." The Supreme Court famously described the role of federal prosecutors in *Berger v. United States*, 295 U.S. 78 (1935): "The United States Attorney is the representative not of an ordinary party to a controversy, but of a sovereignty whose obligation to govern impartially is as compelling as its obligation to govern at all; and whose interest, therefore, in a criminal prosecution is not that it shall win a case, but that justice shall be done. As such, he is in a peculiar and very definite sense the servant of the law, the twofold aim of which is that guilt shall not escape or innocence suffer."

The Role of the Prosecutor

The prosecutor has the responsibility of a minister of justice and not simply that of an advocate. She has a duty to seek justice, not merely to convict. The government's interest in a criminal prosecution is not that it shall win a case, but that justice shall be done.

The actions of prosecutors are governed by the United States Constitution and, in the case of state prosecutors, the constitution of the state. One principal federal constitutional provision regulating prosecutors' behavior is the Fifth Amendment, which provides that "No person shall be held to answer for a capital, or otherwise infamous crime, unless on a presentment or indictment of a Grand Jury" nor "shall be compelled in any criminal case to be a witness against himself, nor be deprived of life, liberty, or property, without due process of law." Another is the Sixth Amendment, which provides "In all criminal prosecutions, the accused shall enjoy the right to a speedy and public trial, by an impartial jury of the State and district wherein the crime shall have been committed," and the right "to be informed of the nature and cause of the accusation; to be confronted with the witnesses against him; to have compulsory process for obtaining witnesses in his favor, and to have the assistance of counsel for his defense." An elaborate body of law has developed under the Fifth and Sixth Amendments governing the criminal process; that law is typically covered in detail in law school courses on criminal procedure. A significant aspect of the constitutional role of prosecutors is the prosecutor's constitutional duty under the due process clause of the Fifth Amendment to disclose exculpatory information to the defense under *Brady v. Maryland*, 373 U.S. 83 (1963). (Part III of this book examines the duty of confidentiality and attorney-client privilege, which, as applied to the duty of criminal defense lawyers, implicate the Fifth Amendment right against self-incrimination and the Sixth Amendment right to effective assistance of counsel.)

In addition to the ethical duties of all lawyers—such as diligence, competence, preparation, candor to the tribunal, and fairness to opposing counsel—prosecutors have specific obligations. Model Rule 3.8 provides that a prosecutor should prosecute only when there is probable cause, make reasonable efforts to ensure that the accused has been advised of the right to counsel and has been given a reasonable opportunity to obtain counsel, disclose exculpatory information to the defense, and take measures to overturn wrongful convictions.

Model Rule 3.8: Special Responsibilities of a Prosecutor

- Refrain from prosecuting a charge not supported by probable cause

- Make reasonable effort to assure that the accused has been advised of the right to counsel and has a reasonable opportunity to obtain counsel

- Not seek to obtain from an unrepresented defendant a waiver of important rights

- Disclose exculpatory and mitigating evidence

- Refrain from extrajudicial comments that have a substantial likelihood of heightening public condemnation of the accused

- Seek to remedy wrongful convictions, including by disclosing new, credible, and material evidence of innocence to the convicted person and to an appropriate court.

The ABA has promulgated standards governing prosecutors. American Bar Association Standards for Criminal Justice, Prosecution Function and Defense Function (3d ed. 1993).[4] The purposes of the Standards are to give guidance, where appropriate, beyond the minimum requirements of the law and, in some cases, to influence the development of the law.[5] Standard 3–1.2 generally defines the prosecutor's role as "an administrator of justice, an advocate, and an officer of the court; the prosecutor must exercise sound discretion in the performance of his or her functions." The Standard famously insists that the "duty of the prosecutor is to seek justice; not merely to convict."

The ABA is in the process of revising the Standards for Criminal Justice; a new version is expected to be submitted for final approval by the ABA's House of Delegates in 2014. A proposed revision to Standard 3–1.2 defines the prosecutor's function slightly more expansively than the existing Standard by adding the following new subsections:

> (b) The primary duty of the prosecutor is to seek justice within the bounds of the law. The prosecutor serves the public interest and must act to protect the innocent, convict the guilty, and consider the interests of victims. The prosecutor's obligation to enforce the law while exercising sound discretion

---

[4] http://www.americanbar.org/content/dam/aba/publications/criminal_justice_standards/prosecution_defense_function.authcheckdam.pdf.

[5] Bruce A. Green, *Foreword: Developing Standards of Conduct for Prosecutors and Criminal Defense Lawyers*, 62 HASTINGS L.J. 1093, 1103 (2011) (discussing the 2009–2011 process for revising the standards).

includes honoring the constitutional and legal rights of suspects and defendants.

(d) The prosecutor is not merely a legal advocate for conviction or imprisonment in criminal cases. The prosecutor should be knowledgeable about, and consider, alternatives to prosecution or conviction that may be applicable in individual cases. The prosecutor's office should be available to assist other groups in the law enforcement community and the community at large, in addressing problems that lead to, or result from, criminal activity.

What do you think will be accomplished by defining the prosecutor's job as proposed by revised Standard 3–1.2?

Prosecutors are absolutely immune from civil liability for exercises of their prosecutorial judgment, regardless of their motives or the legality of their conduct, *Imbler v. Pachtman,* 424 U.S. 409 (1976), or even for their decisions in managing their office, *Van de Kamp v. Goldstein*, 555 U.S. 335 (2009). Therefore, for example, a prosecutor is absolutely immune from liability for damages even for an offense as egregious as knowingly using perjured witness testimony.[6] Prosecutors enjoy only qualified immunity for conduct they undertake when they act as police officers or give legal advice to police officers in connection with investigating crimes. *Burns v. Reed,* 500 U.S. 478 (1991) (prosecutor who advised police that they could interrogate a suspect under hypnosis entitled only to qualified immunity). Qualified immunity means that they cannot be held liable for their conduct except for actions that no reasonable prosecutor would believe to be legal. What policies are supported by granting prosecutors absolute immunity from suit, both for their judgments as lawyers and for the management of their office? What policies support granting prosecutors, like police officers, qualified immunity for their investigative functions?

Prosecutorial Immunity

Prosecutors are **absolutely immune** from suit for all conduct they undertake while exercising their **role as lawyers**. They have **qualified immunity** from suit, meaning they cannot be held liable except for conduct that **no reasonable prosecutor would believe to be legal**, for conduct they undertake while **acting as police officers or while advising police officers** in investigating crimes.

---

[6] *See, e.g.,* Fields v. Wharrie, 740 F.3d 1107 (7th Cir. 2014) (in a case brought by an exonerated defendant seeking damages for having served 25 years on death row, a prosecutor is absolutely immune from liability for knowingly introducing perjured witness testimony, but is not immune from liability for actions during investigation of case before trial in which prosecutor induced the witness to commit perjury).

Although discipline of prosecutors, either by courts or by the bar, is relatively rare, and prosecutors are generally immune to civil liability for their conduct, the most common form of penalty for prosecutorial misconduct is to suppress evidence, dismiss charges against the defendant, or overturn a conviction.

C. WRONGFUL CONVICTIONS

Topic Overview

Nothing draws into sharper relief questions about the role of the prosecutor than the conviction of innocent people. If a prosecutor is imagined only as a zealous advocate for one side of an adversary proceeding, perhaps the prosecutor has no greater duty to avoid convicting the innocent than any other lawyer has to avoid winning a case that he should lose. But prosecutors have a duty to seek justice, and the difficult questions are how to reconcile a prosecutor's duty to seek justice with the prosecutor's role as an adversary in the most adversarial aspect of the American legal system.

Although it is difficult to determine precisely how frequently wrongful convictions occur, some believe the problem is serious. As of 2011, more than 270 people had been exonerated through DNA testing, and hundreds of others have been exonerated through evidence other than DNA testing.[7] Of course, these cases represent a tiny fraction of the tens of thousands of persons who are convicted of crimes; it is difficult to know whether wrongful conviction is an extreme rarity (as many believe) or is more common (as others believe). A study of forensic evidence in sexual assault convictions in Virginia between 1973 and 1987 found that the convicted offender could be ruled out as a source of evidence, suggesting exoneration, in 8 to 18 percent of cases.[8] Studies of wrongful convictions identify a number of reasons why innocent defendants are convicted, including mistaken eyewitness accounts (in 75 percent of cases in which the defendant is exonerated), false confessions induced after prolonged interrogation (16 percent of cases), perjured testimony by co-defendants or other criminal defendants who exchange testimony implicating the defendant for leniency in their own cases (21 percent of cases), and flawed forensic evidence (half of cases).[9] It is difficult to determine how often prosecutorial misconduct contributed to a wrongful conviction, although one study concluded that prosecutorial misconduct

---

[7] *Looking Back, Looking Ahead*, THE INNOCENCE PROJECT IN PRINT (Innocence Project/Benjamin N. Cardozo Sch. of Law, New York, NY) Summer 2011, at 3.

[8] JOHN ROMAN, POST-CONVICTION DNA TESTING AND WRONGFUL CONVICTION 506 (Urban Inst., June 2012).

[9] BRANDON GARRETT, CONVICTING THE INNOCENT (2011) (study based on files of first 250 DNA exonerations).

led to wrongful convictions in eighteen percent of the cases in which a defendant was exonerated.[10]

What responsibility should prosecutors bear to prevent wrongful convictions? If the prosecutor's role is to be a zealous advocate for conviction and if that conception of role imagines that it is the defense's job to prevent conviction, blame for the prevalence of false convictions may be laid primarily on inadequate defense counsel, inept or dishonest police, bungled handling of evidence, confused eyewitnesses, or jurors who are too easily swayed by argument rather than evidence. In this vision of the role, the honest prosecutor does justice by pressing as hard as the rules permit to seek convictions in every case in which there is sufficient evidence to convince the prosecutor of the defendant's guilt (more on this below), and it is the job of the other players in the criminal justice and adversary system—judge, jury, defense attorneys, crime labs, witnesses, and police—to ensure that only the guilty are convicted.

If, however, the prosecutor's role is envisioned as a "minister of justice" (in the words of the Model Rule) who must "seek justice, not merely convict" (in the words of the ABA Standard), the prosecutor has an independent duty to ensure that only the guilty are convicted, even if she must step back from her role as an advocate. In this conception of role, the prosecutor cannot count on the adversary system to produce truth, but instead must ensure that truth is revealed regardless of whether witnesses, defense counsel, judge, and jury are doing their jobs.[11] Indeed, the more prosecutors suspect that defense counsel are not doing their job, the less appropriate it is for the prosecutor to serve as a zealous advocate for conviction.

Yet for lawyers trained to believe that the adversary system is the best vehicle for finding truth and that the criminal trial is the paragon of the adversary process, the question of when and how the prosecutor should temper her advocacy for conviction with affirmative steps to ensure that justice is done is a difficult one both in theory and in daily practice. The law and ethical norms governing prosecutors offer only general guidance.

Model Rule 3.8 requires prosecutors to take steps to rectify false convictions.

---

[10] EMILY M. WEST, COURT FINDINGS OF PROSECUTORIAL MISCONDUCT CLAIMS IN POST-CONVICTION APPEALS AND CIVIL SUITS AMONG THE FIRST 255 DNA EXONERATION CASES 1 (Innocence Project 2010) (reporting studies of cases alleging prosecutorial misconduct in which the defendant was later exonerated; finding that courts found prosecutorial misconduct led to 18 percent of convictions).

[11] Bennett Gershman, *The Prosecutor's Duty to Truth*, 14 GEO. J. LEGAL ETHICS 309 (2001) (discussing the literature and arguments on whether the prosecutor has an independent duty to truth or can instead rely on adversary system to produce the truth, and concluding that the prosecutor has a duty to produce the truth).

Model Rule 3.8 Requires Prosecutors to Address Wrongful Convictions:

When a prosecutor knows of new, credible and material evidence creating a reasonable likelihood that a convicted defendant did not commit an offense of which the defendant was convicted, the prosecutor shall:

(1) promptly disclose that evidence to an appropriate court or authority, and

(2) if the conviction was obtained in the prosecutor's jurisdiction, the prosecutor must promptly disclose that evidence to the defendant unless a court authorizes delay, and undertake further investigation, or make reasonable efforts to cause an investigation, to determine whether the defendant was convicted of an offense that the defendant did not commit.

When a prosecutor knows of clear and convincing evidence establishing that a defendant in the prosecutor's jurisdiction was convicted of an offense that the defendant did not commit, the prosecutor shall seek to remedy the conviction.

Note that Rule 3.8 imposes a duty to rectify false convictions *after* they have happened. Why do you suppose the ABA did not impose a duty to prevent false convictions beforehand? A proposed new ABA Standard 3–4.5 imposes a slightly more rigorous duty: "A prosecutor's office should not file or maintain charges if it believes the defendant is innocent, no matter what the state of the evidence." Do you believe the proposed new Standard would address the problem of wrongful convictions?

Prosecutors vary in their approach to claims that persons in their jurisdiction may have been, or will be, convicted of crimes they did not commit. Some prosecutors recognize wrongful convictions as a problem and their offices have formal policies and procedures to prevent and correct wrongful convictions. Some earnestly believe that innocent people are never convicted in cases filed in their office and do not see any pressing need to examine the cases they have won or the processes in their office. Anecdotal evidence has shown that some prosecutors who have convicted innocent people have been reluctant to consider evidence strongly suggesting or proving that an innocent person was convicted.[12] An example of a prosecutor's reluctance to consider the possibility of wrongful conviction is the case of *Van de Kamp v. Goldstein*, 555 U.S. 335 (2009).

---

[12] See Daniel S. Medwed, *The Zeal Deal: Prosecutorial Resistance to Post-Conviction Claims of Innocence,* 84 B.U. L. REV. 125 (2004).

Thomas Goldstein was an engineering student when the Long Beach Police Department arrested him for the shooting of John McGinest, in 1979. Mr. Goldstein had no criminal record and no history of violence. There was no evidence that he owned a firearm or that he had ever had any contact with the victim. Several eyewitnesses described the possible perpetrator. Most descriptions bore no resemblance to Mr. Goldstein. Mr. Goldstein was a suspect because he lived near where the shooting occurred and was at home the night of the murder. Police obtained one eyewitness identification after showing the man a photo of Goldstein and describing him as the perpetrator.

After Goldstein was in custody, the police placed a well-known jailhouse informant named Eddie Fink, a heroin addict and career felon, in Goldstein's cell. Fink had repeatedly testified to jailhouse confessions in return for favorable dispositions of his own criminal charges. After one night in Goldstein's cell, Fink reported to the police that Goldstein, a complete stranger to him, had confessed. Goldstein, however, had told everyone else that he was innocent.

Fink testified to the confession at Goldstein's trial. Fink also swore that the Los Angeles District Attorney had not traded any benefits for his testimony against Goldstein and that he had never received any such benefits in the past. These were both lies. Fink had struck numerous deals over the course of a decade with the Long Beach Police and the Los Angeles District Attorney in exchange for his testimony. The District Attorney's Office had secured Fink's testimony against Mr. Goldstein with a promise to reduce Fink's sentence on a pending theft charge from 16 months to less than two months. Goldstein's trial counsel could not expose Fink as a liar because the prosecution did not disclose the deals. (This violated the prosecutor's constitutional obligation to disclose exculpatory evidence to the defense.) Goldstein was convicted and sentenced to life in prison.

A decade later, a Los Angeles County civil grand jury issued a report asserting that the Los Angeles District Attorney's Office and various police departments within its jurisdiction coached jailhouse informants to elicit (and sometimes fabricate) confessions from criminal defendants. After that, the eyewitness who had identified Goldstein recanted his testimony.

Although the only two pieces of evidence against Goldstein were discredited, the prosecution still refused to dismiss charges against him. Even after two courts determined that Goldstein was innocent and ordered him released, the government delayed his release for a few months while prosecutors considered whether there was a way to prove his guilt.[13]

NOTES ON WRONGFUL CONVICTIONS

1. ***Understanding How Prosecutors Think About Wrongful Convictions.*** What legitimate and illegitimate factors might influence some prosecutors to refuse to concede, or only very grudgingly concede, that they may be seeking to convict, or have convicted, the wrong person? How often do you think lawyers believe their case is shaky once they have spent substantial time on it? How often do you think lawyers believe that the result they obtained in a case was the wrong result?

2. ***Prosecutors and the Police.*** How skeptical of police should we expect prosecutors to be? If a prosecutor suspects that the evidence presented by police officers is unreliable, or that the police have not provided exculpatory evidence to the prosecutor, what should the prosecutor do? What pressures might a prosecutor feel about challenging the reliability of police investigation, given that prosecutors routinely rely on and work with police officers?

3. ***Considering Incentives.*** When is an acquittal at trial or a decision to drop charges evidence that justice was done rather than that the prosecutor in charge of the case made a mistake? In many settings, people tend to focus on what they can quantify, and it is particularly common to evaluate employees based on objective and easily quantifiable measures that serve as a proxy for the harder to measure qualities of skill and diligence. If the common practice of counting and rewarding convictions based on verdicts or guilty pleas is thought to create incentives for prosecutors to disregard the possibility that a defendant might be innocent, what other measure of success would reward and incentivize skill and hard work? Are there other institutional reforms in prosecutors' offices that would make wrongful convictions less likely to occur?

4. ***Jail House Snitches and Other Forms of Unreliable Evidence.*** In the Goldstein case, the assistant DA apparently did not know that Fink was a well-known jailhouse snitch. Although Fink had provided testimony against several other cellmates in exchange for favorable treatment in his own many prior cases, there was no centralized record in the DA's office about witnesses and the deals they had previously struck in exchange for testimony. Moreover, there is no evidence that the assistant DA who tried the case knew that the police had gotten the eyewitness identification only by showing the witness a photograph of Goldstein and telling him that Goldstein was the perpetrator. Although, as we will see below in the discussion of prosecutors' duties to disclose exculpatory information to defense counsel, both the constitution and ethics rules hold prosecutors responsible for

---

[13] Henry Weinstein, *Man Wrongly Imprisoned for 24 Years Files Civil Rights Suit*, L.A. TIMES, Dec. 1, 2004; Henry Weinstein, *Justice Triumphs—Finally*, L.A. TIMES, Dec. 12, 2004.

knowing and disclosing exculpatory information in the files of *all* law enforcement agencies, there are practical barriers to prosecutors knowing about evidence possessed by the police or other agencies. Thomas Goldstein filed civil litigation after being released from prison seeking to hold prosecutors responsible for negligence in failing to train deputy district attorneys or to maintain a system whereby prosecutors could learn about the deals witnesses had struck. The Supreme Court held that prosecutors' absolute immunity from suit covered the administrative management of the evidence, not just their prosecutorial decisions in filing charges or advocacy. *Van de Kamp v. Goldstein*, 555 U.S. 335 (2009).

5. ***How Do You Change Someone's Mind?*** What might explain the reluctance of new DAs to take a hard look at the case once informed about the possible or likely falsity of the evidence against Goldstein 20 years later? If all or most of the evidence and witnesses are no longer available, how is a prosecutor to evaluate the reliability of a conviction? The problems facing a prosecutor may differ when the exonerating evidence is based on DNA, although even there prosecutors may doubt the reliability of DNA evidence when other evidence pointed toward guilt. In some rape and murder cases, for example, once DNA evidence proved that the semen or biological material on or near the victim did not come from the defendant, prosecutors have nevertheless insisted that the conviction should stand because the defendant might have killed the victim and another man had sex with the victim. Defense counsel derisively call this the "unindicted co-ejaculator" theory.[14] Why does a theory that seems patently ridiculous to some defense counsel seem plausible to some prosecutors?

6. ***Institutional Reforms to Detect or Prevent Wrongful Convictions.*** What institutional reforms might prosecutors' offices adopt in order to counteract the resistance of some prosecutors to conceding that past convictions might be erroneous? A newly-elected district attorney in Dallas, Texas established an autonomous division within his office charged with responsibility for investigating claims of wrongful conviction. The unit, staffed by two prosecutors, an investigator and a paralegal, works with innocence projects in New York and Texas as well as defense lawyers, and has helped exonerate over a dozen wrongfully convicted men. Similar divisions have been established in other prosecutors' offices.[15] One prosecutor criticized the establishment of such divisions, insisting that his office ensures the integrity of convictions before filing any case and by scrutinizing the use of DNA evidence. Under what circumstances are the pretrial and trial process sufficient to ensure the integrity of convictions, as the prosecutor suggests? If the trial process alone is insufficient, what should be done? If independent conviction integrity divisions are established, how should they be structured and staffed in order to maximize their effectiveness?

---

[14] Andrew Martin, *The Prosecution's Case Against DNA*, N. Y. TIMES, November 25, 2011.

[15] Molly Hennessy-Fiske, *Dallas County District Attorney a Hero to the Wrongfully Convicted,* L.A. TIMES, May 8, 2012, at A1.

7. ***Bar Discipline?*** Might the incentives and culture within prosecutors' offices change if bar disciplinary authorities increased their efforts to enforce the general duty of competence under Model Rule 1.1 and the specific duties of prosecutors under Model Rule 3.8? Professors Fred Zacharias and Bruce Green argued that prosecutors should be disciplined if a series of actions in a case create an unreasonable risk of obtaining a wrongful conviction, even though individually each of those actions would not be wrongful.[16] As an example, they listed eight tactics that, when used together, create an unreasonable risk of a wrongful conviction in a hypothetical case involving corporate fraud: "(a) securing an accomplice's cooperation by offering immunity; (2) falsely informing the accomplice that the evidence overwhelmingly suggests the employee attended a meeting where the fraud was discussed; (3) reminding the accomplice that the immunity agreement requires him to cooperate fully; (4) obtaining the accomplice's testimony that the employee attended the meeting, even though the accomplice's lawyer expresses doubts about the accomplice's credibility on this point; (5) failing to seek evidence that would contradict the account; (6) ignoring the absence of evidence corroborating the accomplice's account; (7) failing to disclose the expression of doubt by the accomplice's attorney, on the theory that it was not evidence and was made in the course of plea negotiations; and (8) presenting the accomplice's testimony in evidence at the employee's trial." Considered separately, which of these tactics are permissible and which violate the law? Why might the combination of these tactics create an unreasonable risk of a false conviction, even though individually none of them is typically the basis for bar discipline and some are permissible? What do you consider the advantages and disadvantages of this proposal? What other strategies for the training, management, or oversight of prosecutors do you think would reduce the incidence of wrongful convictions?

D. PROSECUTORIAL DISCRETION IN CHARGING

Prosecutors have wide discretion that is not subject to judicial review in deciding which cases to investigate, which suspects to charge, what crimes to charge, and whether to offer a plea bargain and, if so, on what terms. Prosecutorial discretion is one of the most significant aspects of the lawyer's role. In this section, we examine the nature of prosecutorial discretion and three ethical and practical issues about charging: (1) the tension between the allowing prosecutors and judges discretion to consider the specifics of context while ensuring consistency and uniformity; (2) how prosecutors should handle cases in which the evidence of guilt is less than overwhelming; and (3) how prosecutors should handle cases in which there may be reasons not to prosecute or to be lenient even where there is abundant evidence of guilt.

---

[16] Fred C. Zacharias & Bruce Green, *The Duty to Avoid Wrongful Convictions: A Thought Experiment in the Regulation of Prosecutors*, 89 B.U. L. Rev. 1 (2009).

PROSECUTORIAL DISCRETION IN THE POST-*BOOKER* WORLD

Norman C. Bay

37 McGeorge Law Review 549 (2006)

When a matter is referred to the prosecutor, she must first decide if it should be investigated. If the prosecutor chooses to decline prosecution, that declination is unreviewable. A prosecutor deciding to pursue the matter can often direct the investigation. Who should law enforcement agents interview? Which leads should be pursued? Should places be searched and evidence seized? If so, which places and what evidence? Is a warrant necessary, or is there an applicable exception to the warrant requirement? Would electronic surveillance be helpful? If so, can a warrant be obtained? What forensic analysis needs to be done?

At some point, the prosecutor may proceed to the grand jury. Absent a waiver by the defendant, the grand jury must indict all felony cases.[*] The prosecutor can determine what evidence the grand jury will hear and which witnesses should be subpoenaed to the grand jury. Once a witness is brought to the grand jury, counsel is excluded; nor is a judge present. The prosecutor can also ask the grand jury to issue subpoenas to compel the production of certain types of evidence, from documents to physical evidence. Thus, the prosecutor guides the grand jury's broad investigative powers.

If charges are warranted, the prosecutor now has the discretion to select the charges that the grand jury will be asked to consider. In the ordinary case, so long as the prosecutor has probable cause to believe that the accused committed an offense defined by statute, the decision whether or not to prosecute, and what charge to file or bring before a grand jury, generally rests entirely in her discretion.

Assuming the grand jury returns an indictment, the prosecutor now has the discretion to move for the defendant's pretrial detention if the defendant poses a danger to the community or a flight risk. Even if the defendant is not detained pretrial, the prosecutor can request that certain conditions of release be imposed.

If the parties enter into plea negotiations, the prosecutor wields the discretion to control the terms of an offer. The prosecutor also has the power to determine if she wishes to work with a potential cooperating defendant. Cooperation may be particularly important for defendants otherwise facing lengthy prison sentences, especially a mandatory minimum penalty under the drug laws. Once the cooperation is complete, the prosecutor has the power to inform the court of the defendant's

---

[*] [Eds: In the federal system, a grand jury indictment is required unless it is waived by the defendant. Many states do not use the grand jury system and instead require prosecutors to file an "information" with the court showing that there is probable cause to prosecute the defendant for the crimes specified in the information.]

helpfulness. Obviously, an enthusiastic letter from the prosecutor may prove decisive to a sentencing judge.

If the case goes to trial, the prosecutor develops a theory of her case and the strategy for implementing it. She decides which witnesses to call and what evidence to present; she alone determines what the opening statement will be, as well as the closing argument and rebuttal.

Prosecutorial discretion arises again if the jury convicts the defendant. If the defendant was released pre-trial, the prosecutor may now move for his detention. At sentencing, the prosecutor may ask that a particular sentence be imposed. As part of that allocution, she may oppose the defendant's attempt to obtain a more lenient sentence and argue for a more severe sentence based upon the circumstances of the case.

Post-sentencing, the prosecutor still retains a considerable amount of discretion. Among other things, the prosecutor has the discretion to decide whether or not to appeal the sentence imposed by the court. She may also file a Rule 35 motion to reduce the sentence if the defendant cooperates post-sentencing and provides substantial assistance. While the Bureau of Prisons bears ultimate responsibility for the placement of prisoners, the prosecutor may contact the Bureau to share her views on where the defendant should be incarcerated. The prosecutor's views will be solicited at some later date if the defendant seeks executive clemency, whether a pardon or commutation of sentence.

* * *

1. THE TENSION BETWEEN UNIFORMITY AND DISCRETION

In the 1980s and 1990s, Congress and many state legislatures imposed mandatory minimum sentences to ensure that everyone convicted of the same crime received the same sentence. Such laws eliminated the discretion of judges in sentencing, but prosecutors retained discretion to charge crimes with greater or lesser sentences. In the same period, many legislatures enacted enhanced penalties for recidivists; some of these laws were enacted in the wake of horrible murders committed by men who had recently been released from prison and were intended to punish harshly those who had proven unable or unwilling to refrain from crime. Whatever the reasons for determinate sentencing laws and enhanced penalties for recidivists, they have had the perhaps unintended consequence of enhancing the power of prosecutors to decide what sentences defendants will serve by deciding what crime to charge. For example, a prosecutor could charge a person arrested with drugs and a gun with a relatively minor crime of drug possession, punishable by a year in prison or a fine, or major crimes including sale of drugs, and possession of drugs with the use of a weapon, punishable by many years in prison.

To the extent that determinate sentencing regimes are intended to treat like cases alike, they have failed in many jurisdictions because different prosecutors have different philosophies about which crimes to charge. For example, in some counties, the district attorney rarely if ever seeks the death penalty, while the same murder committed in the next county might prompt a capital charge. In California, there was wide variation among counties as to when district attorneys would invoke the Three Strikes law to seek a 25-to-life sentence for a minor third offense like shoplifting.[17] (In 2012, California modified the Three Strikes law to prohibit 25-to-life sentences for minor nonviolent offenses in most cases.) Prosecutors differ in determining whether firing multiple shots at a car or committing multiple sexual acts in a single sexual assault constitute multiple separate crimes or one.[18]

Studies have suggested that the exercise of discretion may be influenced by bias. In *McCleskey v. Kemp*, 481 U.S. 279 (1987), for example, the Supreme Court confronted evidence that in Georgia the death penalty was inflicted more often on black defendants and killers of white victims than on white defendants and killers of black victims. The Court rejected the contention that the racial disparity in death sentences violated the constitution. In the years since *McCleskey*, scholars have continued to compile evidence that criminal laws are enforced more often and more harshly against men of color than against whites.[19]

Under *McCleskey* and other cases, it is nearly impossible for any individual defendant to challenge his prosecution or sentence as the product of systemic or individual bias. What institutional mechanisms might be implemented to make prosecutors and police more attentive to the possibility that their individual or collective decisions about arrest, charging, and prosecution are having a disparate impact on the basis of race or other illegitimate factors? One scholar proposed the use of "racial impact studies" and criminal justice racial and ethnic task forces as a way to raise awareness of the existence of racial bias.[20] Studies of the results of many such initiatives in different states found that "they overlook the

---

[17] *See* FRANKLIN E. ZIMRING, ET AL., PUNISHMENT AND DEMOCRACY (2001) (analyzing disparities in sentences under California's Three-Strikes law).

[18] *See, e.g.*, Jeffrey M. Chemerinsky, *Counting Offenses*, 58 DUKE L.J. 709 (2009) (gathering cases and analyzing when multiple acts committed in the course of one criminal episode constitute separate crimes).

[19] Jeffrey Fagan & Mukul Bakhshi, *New Frameworks for Racial Equality in Criminal Law*, 39 COLUM. HUM. RTS. L. REV. 1 (2007) (surveying literature showing racial disparities in prosecution's request for death sentences and in imposition of death sentences when victim is white and defendant is black, and also racial disparities other crimes and sentences in many states).

[20] Angela J. Davis, *Racial Fairness in the Criminal Justice System: the Role of the Prosecutor*, 39 COLUM. HUM. RTS. L. REV. 202 (2007).

most glaring causes of disparity and the most promising measures to reduce them."[21] What would make state efforts to reduce racial disparities in criminal justice more effective?

One way to address disparities among prosecutors in charging decisions is by adopting a uniform policy that is applied to every prosecutor within the jurisdiction. At the state level, obtaining such uniformity would require some form of legislation, because district attorneys are typically elected at the county level and thus enjoy some autonomy in setting policy. The U.S Attorney's Manual, which is issued by the U.S. Department of Justice and governs every U.S. Attorney's office in all 94 federal districts across the United States, in theory can produce national uniformity in federal charging. As amended in 2003 by Attorney General John Ashcroft, it states the following policy regarding charging:

> § 9–27.300 Selecting Charges—Charging Most Serious Offenses
>
> [O]nce the decision to prosecute has been made, the attorney for the government should charge, or should recommend that the grand jury charge, the most serious offense that is consistent with the nature of the defendant's conduct, and that is likely to result in a sustainable conviction. The "most serious" offense is generally that which yields the highest range under the sentencing guidelines.
>
> To ensure consistency and accountability, charging and plea agreement decisions must be made at an appropriate level of responsibility and documented with an appropriate record of the factors applied.

This section of the U.S. Attorneys' Manual also states, however, that the selection of charges be based on

> an individualized assessment of the extent to which particular charges fit the specific circumstances of the case, are consistent with the purposes of the Federal criminal code, and maximize the impact of Federal resources on crime. Thus, for example, in determining 'the most serious offense that is consistent with the nature of the defendant's conduct that is likely to result in a sustainable conviction," it is appropriate that the attorney for the government consider, inter alia, such factors as whether the penalty is proportional to the seriousness of the defendant's conduct, and whether the charge achieves such purposes of the

---

[21] Jesse J. Norris, *State Efforts to Reduce Racial Disparities in Criminal Justice: Empirical Analysis and Recommendations for Action*, 47 GONZ. L. REV. 493 (2012).

criminal law as punishment, protection of the public, specific and general deterrence, and rehabilitation.[22]

In addition, through various memoranda issued by the Attorney General, U.S. Attorney's offices are instructed to consider additional factors that can lead to greater lenience. (And, of course, such memos can be used to urge prosecutors to seek harsher punishments as well.) For example, in an August 2013 memo, Attorney General Eric Holder instructed prosecutors not to charge nonviolent defendants without a criminal history or ties to drug trafficking organizations with any offense involving an amount of illegal drugs that would trigger the mandatory minimum sentence.[23] The Manual allows prosecutors to consider resource constraints in deciding which offenses to charge or what plea agreement to offer. If proving the most serious offense will require expenditure of more resources, or demanding a plea to the most serious offense will prompt a defendant to insist on going to trial, prosecutors may charge or seek a plea to less serious offenses. In view of the possible tension between these provisions, do you imagine the Manual has been effective in producing uniformity? What are the arguments for and against requiring charging of the most serious readily provable offense? If uniformity is to be desired and yet you oppose choosing the most serious readily provable offense, what alternative would you propose?

What are the arguments for and against leaving charging and plea bargaining decisions to the discretion of individual prosecutors or to particular prosecutors' offices? Note that the U.S. Attorneys' Manual requires charging decisions to be "made at an appropriate level of responsibility and documented with an appropriate record of the factors applied."

* * *

2.   PROSECUTORIAL DISCRETION AND THE SUFFICIENCY OF EVIDENCE

The Model Rules and the ABA Standards require that prosecutors have sufficient evidence of guilt before initiating a prosecution. Model Rule 3.8(a) provides that the prosecutor shall "refrain from prosecuting a charge that the prosecutor knows is not supported by probable cause." The ABA Standard Relating to the Administration of Criminal Justice, The Prosecution Function, Standard 3–3.9 provides:

---

[22]   United States Attorneys' Manual, Chapter 9–27.300, Office of the U.S. Attorneys, Dep't of Justice (2002), *available at* http://www.justice.gov/usao/eousa/foia_reading_room/usam/title9/27mcrm.htm#9-27.300.

[23]   Memorandum to the U.S. Attorneys & Assistant Attorneys General for the Criminal Div. (Aug. 12, 2013), *available at* http://www.justice.gov/oip/docs/ag-memo-department-policypon-charging-mandatory-minimum-sentences-recidivist-enhancements-in-certain-drugcases.pdf.

(a) A prosecutor should not institute, or cause to be instituted, or permit the continued pendency of criminal charges when the prosecutor knows that the charges are not supported by probable cause. A prosecutor should not institute, cause to be instituted, or permit the continued pendency of criminal charges in the absence of sufficient admissible evidence to support a conviction.

(b) The prosecutor is not obliged to present all charges which the evidence might support. The prosecutor may in some circumstances and for good cause consistent with the public interest decline to prosecute, notwithstanding that sufficient evidence may exist which would support a conviction. Illustrative of the factors which the prosecutor may properly consider in exercising his or her discretion are:

     (i)   the prosecutor's reasonable doubt that the accused is in fact guilty;

     (ii)   the extent of the harm caused by the offense;

     (iii) the disproportion of the authorized punishment in relation to the particular offense or the offender;

     (iv) possible improper motives of the complainant;

     (v)   reluctance of the victim to testify;

     (vi) cooperation of the accused in the apprehension or conviction of others; and

     (vii) availability and likelihood of prosecution by another jurisdiction

(c) A prosecutor should not be compelled by his or her supervisor to prosecute a case in which he or she has a reasonable doubt about the guilt of the accused.

(d) In making the decision to prosecute, the prosecutor should give no weight to the personal or political advantages or disadvantages which might be involved or to a desire to enhance his or her record of convictions.

Both Model Rule 3.8 and the Standard state that a prosecutor should not bring charges not supported by "probable cause." But the standard of proof required to convict a defendant is evidence "beyond a reasonable doubt," which is a much higher standard than probable cause. Standard 3–3.9(a) alludes to the difference by saying in the first sentence that a prosecutor should not bring or continue to press charges not supported by probable cause and, in the second sentence, by saying that a prosecutor should not bring or continue to press charges not supported by "sufficient admissible evidence to support a conviction." At what point in the pretrial or trial process should a prosecutor decide that he should have more than probable cause? Why do Model Rule 3.8 and the ABA Standards leave unanswered so many questions about how prosecutors should exercise their discretion? Consider the following case.

PROBLEM 14–1

You are a young prosecutor preparing for trial in a robbery case. The police have prepared a file showing the following. The defendant, a twenty-year-old black man, was accused of robbing at gunpoint a seventy-seven-year-old white man outside an apartment building. The file states that the complainant identified the defendant from an array of photographs and later picked him out from a lineup containing two other persons, one of whom was a police officer known to the complainant. The file contains no other evidence.

The defendant's criminal record reveals he has been getting into trouble since he dropped out of high school three years ago. He has been arrested several times, but the charges have been dismissed. He was convicted of robbery two years ago and served three months in jail. Several days after he came home, the police picked him up again in connection with the present robbery. He has been in jail for the past year awaiting trial.

The file shows that the complainant's initial description of the defendant—that the assailant was a young black man about five feet four inches tall—differed from the defendant's actual height of six feet two inches. You interviewed the complainant and found him to be an intelligent man who gave a convincing account of the event. You went to the vestibule where the crime occurred; it was well-lit, which suggests the complainant's identification was accurate. You talked to the janitor who had initially called the police and to several tenants but learned nothing useful. The defendant's lawyer says the client is innocent, but he has no alibi—he says he was home alone watching TV at the time of the robbery. The defendant took a lie detector test; the polygraph examiner said the defendant is telling the truth about his innocence. You asked the complainant to return to your office for another interview. You asked him to look at an array of twenty photographs of young black males; the array included two photographs of the defendant. The complainant selected a photograph of someone else and insisted he was sure that was the robber. You assembled another array, also with two photos of the defendant, and asked him to do it again. Again the complainant picked out someone else. Should you proceed to trial?[24]

* * *

---

[24] This problem is drawn from Bennett L. Gershman, *The Prosecutor's Duty to Truth*, 14 GEO. J. LEGAL ETHICS 309 (2001).

3. PROSECUTORIAL DISCRETION IN CHARGING DECISIONS BASED ON SOCIAL POLICY

What factors should a prosecutor consider in deciding whom to charge and for which crimes even when the prosecutor has evidence of guilt sufficient to convict? ABA Standard 3–3.1(b) on the Function of the Prosecutor provides: "A prosecutor should not invidiously discriminate against or in favor of any person on the basis of race, religion, sex, sexual preference, or ethnicity in exercising discretion to investigate or to prosecute. A prosecutor should not use other improper considerations in exercising such discretion." Besides avoiding invidious discrimination, what factors should be relevant or irrelevant to the charging decision? How much social engineering should prosecutors attempt to do in their decisions about criminal prosecution? Is it appropriate for them to consider whether prosecution will achieve beneficial effects for the defendant or the community, or will harm a defendant's life prospects?

As viewers of television crime dramas know, prosecutors sometimes charge low-level participants in a gang, a drug distribution network, or the Mafia with serious crimes in order to force them to cooperate in identifying and testifying against the high-level people in the criminal network. What are the problems with allowing prosecutors to threaten severe criminal penalties to induce cooperation? Is the answer to the objection that the legislature authorized severe penalties so the prosecutor bears no moral responsibility for using all the tools at her disposal? If you do not find that argument persuasive, is there any justification for the tactic? If so, are you troubled by its application in the problem below?

PROBLEM 14–2

The police have arrested a 15-year-old boy who they suspect has been recruited by a local gang to serve as a courier in drug deals. The boy has no prior criminal record and has been a solid student, although lately his grades have fallen, he quit the marching band, and his school attendance has been spotty. The boy had a modest quantity of drugs in his possession at the time he was arrested, but he insisted that the drugs were not his—that someone slipped them in his backpack without his knowledge, and he took and passed a drug test to prove it. The police believe the boy's older cousin and next-door neighbor are active gang members and high-volume drug dealers. The police suspect the boy could provide abundant information about the gang and would be a compelling witness whose testimony could help secure the convictions of several gang members. The boy has refused to talk to the police. The police urge you to charge him with a crime in order to have leverage to force him to testify against the gang members who, they say, have terrorized the neighborhood and have forced kids like the boy to get involved in drug dealing.

Ordinarily, you would not prosecute a first-time offender for possession of drugs, and you would hate to ruin this kid's life, including his chances at college and a job, by saddling him with a criminal record at this young age. Your office routinely declines to prosecute the students at the nearby elite liberal arts college for drug sales and possessions of the type and amount of drugs possessed by the boy. Your supervisor has explained that policy by saying she feels that the drug problem at the college is small, most of the kids will get clean if left to grow up, and the harm that criminal prosecution would cause for the students is great. On the other hand, the boy's confession and the drug test suggest the drugs were not for personal consumption. The police find the boy's story that he did not know he had the drugs incredible, as he ran from the police when they asked to speak to him. They are convinced he is involved in drug dealing, which carries a much more serious penalty than simple possession. You would like to do something to stop the boy from sliding into the gang and drug dealing. Should you charge the boy with any crime, or the more serious crime, in order to get him to testify against higher-level people in the gang?

E. PROSECUTORS AND PLEA BARGAINING

As noted above in Chapter 13, plea bargaining is extremely common in both state and federal criminal systems. Over 90 percent of federal criminal convictions were secured by a guilty plea in 2009, as were 95 percent of state felony convictions in the nation's 75 largest counties in 2006.[25] Critics insist that the proliferation of long mandatory minimum sentences enables prosecutors to overcharge and to force innocent defendants to plead guilty to avoid extremely long sentences and/or incarceration in jails and prisons that cannot guarantee prisoners' safety.[26] On the other hand, some scholars argue that plea bargaining is not more likely than trial to convict innocent people, and may be less likely to do so. Yet even these scholars found evidence of innocent defendants pleading guilty; the debate is over the extent of the problem.[27] While prosecutors insist that plea bargaining saves resources when there is no serious doubt about guilt, critics insist that prosecutors tend to settle their weakest cases by guilty plea to boost their conviction rate and to avoid potentially embarrassing losses in some cases and also to manage a heavy caseload without adequate scrutiny of the quality and accuracy of the police work that went into identifying and arresting the suspect.[28]

---

[25] *Federal Justice Statistics, 2009*, BUREAU OF JUSTICE STATISTICS, U.S. DEP'T OF JUSTICE 12, Table 9 (2011), *available at* http://bjs.ojp.usdoj.gov/content/pub/pdf/fjs09.pdf; *Felony Defendants in Large Urban Counties, 2006*, BUREAU OF JUSTICE STATISTICS, U.S. DEP'T OF JUSTICE (2010), *available at* http://bjs.ojp.usdoj.gov/content/pub/pdf/fdluc06.pdf.

[26] The literature on plea bargaining is vast. *See, e.g.*, Stephanos Bibas, *Plea Bargaining Outside the Shadow of Trial*, 117 HARV. L. REV. 2463 (2004) (surveying the literature and criticizing certain aspects of plea bargaining).

[27] Oren Gazal-Ayal & Avishalom Tor, *The Innocence Effect*, 62 DUKE L.J. 339 (2012).

[28] Stephen J. Schulhofer, *A Wake-Up Call from the Plea-Bargaining Trenches*, 19 LAW & SOC. INQUIRY 135, 137 (1994).

The absence of trials makes the nature and extent of any problem of wrongful convictions based on guilty pleas invisible to the public and to the judiciary.[29]

Particular controversy surrounds plea bargaining in capital cases. Although many people find it hard to believe that a defendant would plead guilty to a murder he or she did not commit, a number of defendants have, in part because they lacked resources to mount a defense, their lawyer doubted their claims of innocence, and the prosecution offered to recommend a sentence other than death. As scholars have observed, police and prosecutors feel a particular pressure to solve murder cases, which compounds the risk of error at every stage of the investigation and trial.[30]

As noted in Chapter 13, the Supreme Court held that ineffective assistance of defense counsel during plea bargaining may be grounds to vacate the conviction and set aside the plea. *Padilla v. Kentucky*, 559 U.S. 356, 130 S. Ct. 1473 (2010) (failure to inform client of the immigration consequences of pleading guilty to a crime is ineffective assistance); *Missouri v. Frye*, 132 S. Ct. 1399 (2012) (failure to inform defendant that prosecution offered a plea agreement is ineffective assistance). ABA Standard 3–4.1(c) on the Function of the Prosecutor provides that a "prosecutor should not knowingly make false statements or representations as to fact or law in the course of plea discussions with defense counsel or the accused." Model Rule 4.1 also provides that a lawyer "shall not knowingly make a false statement of material fact or law." To procure a plea deal by a knowingly misrepresenting a material fact violates Rule 4.1.

PROBLEM 14–3

A defendant is charged with passing a forged check in the amount of $88, a crime punishable by two to ten years in prison. The prosecutor offers a plea agreement: if the defendant will plead guilty to the crime, the prosecutor will recommend a five-year sentence. If the defendant does not accept the plea agreement, however, the prosecutor threatens to return to the grand jury and seek to have the defendant indicted under the state's recidivist sentencing statute. Because the defendant was convicted, ten years previously at age 18, of statutory rape of his 15-year-old girlfriend, and five years ago of possession of a small amount of an illegal narcotic, the defendant is eligible to be considered a "career criminal" under the state statute and be punished by life in prison.

---

[29] *See* John G. Douglass, *Fatal Attraction: The Uneasy Courtship of Brady and Plea Bargaining*, 20 EMORY L.J. 439, 489 (2001) (noting the controversy over the prevalence of pleas by innocent defendants).

[30] *See* Samuel R. Gross, *The Risks of Death: Why Erroneous Convictions are Common in Capital Cases*, 44 BUFF. L. REV. 469 (1996).

NOTES ON PROBLEM 14–3

1. *When, if Ever, Is Plea Bargaining Unethical?* Are there ethical issues in allowing this form of threat to induce a defendant to plead? Would it matter if the defendant is innocent of the charge of passing the forged check? The Supreme Court held in *Bordenkircher v. Hayes*, 434 U.S. 357 (1978), on facts similar to the problem above, that a prosecutor does not violate due process by threatening to seek a life sentence under a recidivist statute if a defendant declined a plea agreement for a recommended five-year sentence. That it does not violate the constitutional guarantee of due process, however, does not resolve the question whether the practice is ethical. Do you think the prosecutor's approach to the plea deal is ethical?

2. *What Are the Limits of Discretion in Charging or Dropping Charges to Induce a Plea?* If you have ethical qualms about allowing prosecutors to threaten to charge crimes carrying longer sentences if the defendant refuses a plea agreement, do you have the same ethical qualms about allowing prosecutors to agree to drop charges carrying longer sentences if the defendant pleads guilty to a charge carrying a lesser sentence?

F. DISCLOSURE OBLIGATIONS

In *Brady v. Maryland*, 373 U.S. 83, 87 (1963), the Supreme Court established that prosecutors have a duty to disclose material exculpatory information to defense counsel upon request. The Court held "the suppression by the prosecution of evidence favorable to an accused upon request violates due process where the evidence is material either to guilt or to punishment, irrespective of the good faith or bad faith of the prosecution." In subsequent cases, the Court has expanded *Brady* obligations, providing the accused with greater access to evidence. In *United States v. Bagley*, 473 U.S. 667, 675–76 (1985), the Court held that prosecutors must disclose not only exculpatory evidence (that negates guilt, supports an affirmative defense such as self-defense or duress, or diminishes the severity of the crime or the sentence) but also impeaching evidence (that undermines the government's case). Prosecutors must disclose exculpatory evidence even if they do not find the information credible or have other contradictory information. Impeachment evidence that must be disclosed includes evidence that might cast doubt on the credibility of government witnesses, including information regarding a witness's prior convictions, biases, or self-interest, such as inducements used to motivate a witness to testify on behalf of the government.

Some states have adopted statutes that impose more expansive disclosure duties on prosecutors. Several states use a variation of Model Rule of Professional Conduct 3.8(d) as a standard.[31] Model Rule 3.8(d)

---

[31] Ellen Yaroshefsky, *Prosecutorial Disclosure Obligations*, 62 HASTINGS L.J. 1321, 1326 (2011); Daniel S. Medwed, *Brady's Bunch of Flaws*, 67 WASH. & LEE L. REV. 1533, 1538–39, 1557 (2010).

requires that prosecutors "make timely disclosure to the defense of all evidence or information known to the prosecutor that tends to negate the guilt of the accused or mitigates the offense."

Other states and localities have adopted "open file" discovery policies, which generally require prosecutors to disclose all nonprivileged information gathered in a case to the defense "as early as possible." There are wide variations among them in which files they make available. Some invite defense counsel to view all information gathered in a case. Others give the defense substantial, but not total, access. In all open file systems, exceptions exist for witness safety or the protection of confidential informants.

The Prosecutor's Disclosure Obligations

Under **Brady v. Maryland** and later cases, prosecutors **must disclose** to the defense evidence that tends to **negate guilt, support an affirmative defense, or diminish the severity of the crime or sentence,** as well as evidence that **impeaches the credibility of government witnesses**.

Prosecutors have a duty learn about and **disclose evidence known to all government agents**, including the police.

The disclosure must be made in a **"timely"** manner. Although the constitution is not violated if the prosecutor fails to disclose impeachment evidence prior to a plea bargain. Model Rule 3.8 may require disclosure of all evidence before a plea bargain.

In jurisdictions that have adopted **"open file" discovery** either by law or as a matter of prosecutorial office policy, prosecutors must disclose all evidence known to the government.

The ABA Standards for Criminal Justice, The Prosecution Function, also require disclosure by the prosecutor:

Standard 3–3.6 Quality and Scope of Evidence Before Grand Jury

(b) No prosecutor should knowingly fail to disclose to the grand jury evidence which tends to negate guilt or mitigate the offense.

(c) A prosecutor should recommend that the grand jury not indict if he or she believes the evidence presented does not warrant an indictment under governing law.

Standard 3–3.11 Disclosure of Evidence by the Prosecutor

(a) A prosecutor should not intentionally fail to make timely disclosure to the defense, at the earliest feasible opportunity, of the existence of all evidence or information which tends to negate the guilt of the accused or mitigate the offense charged or which would tend to reduce the punishment of the accused.

(b) A prosecutor should not fail to make a reasonably diligent effort to comply with a legally proper discovery request.

(c) A prosecutor should not intentionally avoid pursuit of evidence because he or she believes it will damage the prosecution's case or aid the accused.

Despite constitutional and statutory disclosure requirements, disclosure violations occur. Some believe prosecutorial failure to disclose is epidemic, while others contend disclosure violations are only episodic.[32] Studies conducted by academics and journalists offer conflicting assessments as to the frequency with which *Brady* violations occur. A 1998 analysis of 1,500 allegations of prosecutorial misconduct over the previous ten years found "hundreds" of instances in which prosecutors intentionally concealed exculpatory or impeachment evidence.[33] A 2011 survey of federal judges found that thirty percent of respondents had encountered at least one prosecutorial disclosure violation in the preceding five years.[34] The U.S. Department of Justice, however, found only fifteen disclosure violations between 2000 and 2009.[35]

Critics suggest *Brady* violations occur because prosecutors who commit them believe that they will not be caught (the defense rarely knows when evidence is withheld), and when they are caught they will not be punished, nor will a guilty verdict be overturned.[36] Indeed, prosecutors are rarely punished when disclosure violations are uncovered. A 1987 study of published compilations of state disciplinary decisions and surveys returned by professional disciplinary representatives in forty-one states since *Brady* was decided in 1963 found only nine cases "in which discipline was even considered."[37] Thirty-five states reported that no formal complaints had been filed for *Brady*-type misconduct. A follow-up study in 1997 found only seven

---

[32] Bennett L. Gershman, *Litigating Brady v. Maryland: Games Prosecutors Play*, 57 CASE WESTERN RESERVE L. REV. 531 (2007) (epidemic); Cynthia E. Jones, *A Reason to Doubt: The Suppression of Evidence and the Inference of Innocence*, 100 J. CRIM. L. & CRIMINOLOGY 415, 435–36 (2010) (episodic).

[33] Bill Moushey, *Discovery Violations Have Made Evidence-Gathering a Shell Game*, PITTSBURGH POST-GAZETTE, Nov. 24, 1998, at A1.

[34] Fed. Judicial Ctr., A Summary Of Responses To A National Survey Of Rule 16 Of The Federal Rules Of Criminal Procedure And Disclosure Practices In Criminal Cases 8 (2011).

[35] Mike Scarcela, *DOJ Outlines Changes after Stevens Case*, LEGAL TIMES, Oct. 19, 2009.

[36] *See* Alafair S. Burke, *Improving Prosecutorial Decision Making: Some Lessons of Cognitive Science*, 47 WM. & MARY L. REV. 1587 (2006); Alafair S. Burke, *Revisiting Prosecutorial Disclosure*, 84 IND. L.J. 481 (2009); Daniel S. Medwed, *Brady's Bunch of Flaws*, 67 WASH. & LEE L. REV. 1533, 1538–39, 1557 (2010).

[37] Richard A. Rosen, *Disciplinary Sanctions Against Prosecutors for Brady Violations: A Paper Tiger*, 65 N.C. L. REV. 693, 718–19, 731–32 (1987).

bar disciplinary proceedings had been initiated against prosecutors for disclosure violations between 1987 and 1997; the prosecutors received discipline ranging from a reprimand to a six-month suspension.[38] A survey by the California Commission on the Fair Administration of Justice found 53 cases between 1997 and 2007 in which prosecutorial misconduct resulted in a reversal of the conviction; the California State Bar did not investigate or discipline any prosecutors.[39] A 2011 survey of federal trial judges reported that judges rarely hold prosecutors in contempt or report them to Department of Justice's Office of Professional Responsibility (OPR) or the state bar.[40] Instead, the two most frequently reported responses to disclosure violations were ordering immediate disclosure of the evidence and granting a continuance. One study found a reversal rate of less than twelve percent in cases with *Brady* violations.[41]

Brady violations also occur because some prosecutors find it difficult to fair-mindedly examine the evidence in their possession and determine what must be disclosed. An Assistant U.S. Attorney was charged in 2007 with illegally withholding evidence to secure convictions in a terrorism case in Detroit, but he was acquitted.[42] He may have believed so strongly in the guilt of the defendants and felt such pressure to convict suspected terrorists that he engaged in conduct that warranted charging him with a crime. In 2006, Durham, North Carolina District Attorney Michael Nifong withheld crime laboratory and other evidence in a case in which the public believed three Duke University athletes had raped an African-American woman. (Nifong was later disbarred for his misconduct, but he is one of the very few prosecutors ever to be disciplined for disclosure violations.)[43] A prosecutor does not violate *Brady* if exculpatory evidence is immaterial and, even if it is material, the failure to disclose it will not be the basis for overturning a verdict unless the defendant proves the

---

[38] Joseph R. Weeks, *No Wrong Without a Remedy: The Effective Enforcement of the Duty of Prosecutors to Disclose Exculpatory Evidence*, 22 OKLA. CITY U. L. REV. 833, 881 (1997).

[39] CALIFORNIA COMMISSION ON THE FAIR ADMINISTRATION OF JUSTICE, REPORT AND RECOMMENDATIONS ON REPORTING MISCONDUCT, at 3–5 (2007).

[40] Fed. Judicial Ctr., A Summary of Responses to a National Survey of Rule 16 of the Federal Rules of Criminal Procedure and Disclosure Practices in Criminal Cases, 29 (Feb. 2011). A study of state judges reached the same conclusion: judges are more likely to order disclosure and grant a continuance than to discipline prosecutors or overturn convictions. Ken Armstrong and Maurice Possle, *The Verdict: Dishonor*, CHI. TRIB., Jan. 10, 1999, at 1C.

[41] Burke, *Revisiting Prosecutorial Disclosure*, 84 IND. L.J. at 490 n.54.

[42] Mike Scarcella, *17 Prosecutors Behaving Badly*, NAT'L L.J., Dec. 21, 2009.

[43] Indeed, equally if not more egregious violations in two prior North Carolina cases in which defendants were sentenced to death and later exonerated resulted in no discipline of prosecutors in one case and only a reprimand in the other. Amir Efrati, *It's Rare for Prosecutors to Get the Book Thrown Back at Them*, WALL ST. J., Apr. 16, 2009, at A11; Robert P. Mosteller, *Exculpatory Evidence, Ethics, and the Road to the Disbarment of Mike Nifong: The Critical Importance of Full Open-File Discovery*, 15 GEO. MASON L. REV. 257 (2008); N.C. State Bar v. Brewer, 644 S.E.2d 573 (N.C. Ct. App. 2007) (upholding the dismissal on statute of limitations grounds of disciplinary charges against prosecutors who hid exculpatory evidence in a capital case).

failure to disclose changed the outcome of the proceeding. *United States v. Bagley*, 473 U.S. 667, 682 (1985). Such a standard requires prosecutors to assess pre-verdict what will change the result, and to overcome their own cognitive biases that lead them to forget the existence of or undervalue the significance of exculpatory evidence.

Brady and state ethics codes leave some uncertainty about the time at which exculpatory material must be disclosed. Although the *Brady* obligation theoretically spans the entire lifespan of the case, "from arraignment to Death row," and Model Rule 3.8(d) requires "timely disclosure," courts tend to be vague about exactly what "timely" means. Disclosure must be made in sufficient time to permit defendant to make effective use of that evidence at trial. But since courts only have occasion to enforce the rule after it has been violated, they tend to frame violations in counterfactual terms as "the point at which a reasonable probability will exist that the outcome would have been different if an earlier disclosure had been made." *United States v. Coppa*, 267 F.3d 132 (2d Cir. 2001). Some states require disclosure a certain number of days after request by defense counsel or within a certain number of days before trial.[44] Prosecutors believe that early disclosure can pose risks. A defendant who learns the names of witnesses may attempt to intimidate them, and even a defendant who would not dream of intimidating a witness may try to script the testimony of his or her own witnesses in response.

Under the Constitution, the Supreme Court ruled that *Brady* is not violated by the prosecution's failure to reveal impeachment evidence before a plea bargain. *United States v. Ruiz*, 536 U.S. 622, 631, 633 (2002). The Court reasoned that Brady is a trial right and that requiring the prosecution to reveal impeachment evidence would not advance the government's and the defendant's shared interests in efficient administration of justice and in facilitating guilty pleas from defendants who are factually guilty. The Court has not ruled on whether the Constitution compels disclosure of exculpatory (as opposed to impeachment) evidence in plea bargaining. What are the arguments for treating the two kinds of evidence the same or differently?

The ethical rules governing disclosure of impeachment and exculpatory evidence may require more of prosecutors than does the Constitution. Model Rule 3.8(d) requires prosecutors to make "timely disclosure to the defense of all evidence or information known to the prosecutor that tends to negate the guilt of the accused or mitigates the offense." Can you make the arguments for or against the proposition that "timely" means disclosure prior to entry of a guilty plea? Can you make the arguments for or against treating exculpatory information differently

---

[44]   Yaroshefsky, *Prosecutorial Disclosure Obligations*, 62 HASTINGS L.J. at 1337–1338.

than impeachment evidence, under the standard requiring disclosure of information "that tends to negate the guilt of the accused or mitigates the offense"? The ABA has issued a Formal Opinion insisting that timely disclosure under Rule 3.8(d) means prior to plea proceedings, which in many cases means prior to arraignment. ABA Formal Op. 09–454.

Open file discovery is not without flaws. Prosecutors fear it enables defendants to intimidate witnesses and fabricate their defense to rebut the evidence against them. Defense lawyers fear it enables prosecutors in complex cases to bury the defense in a mountain of inscrutable material. In the trial against former Enron executive Jeff Skilling, for example, prosecutors provided eighty million pages of documents to the defense.[45] A lower court in Skilling's case suggested that an attempt to bury exculpatory evidence in a mountain of irrelevant evidence may itself be a *Brady* violation.[46] The Supreme Court has not addressed whether overdisclosure is ever a *Brady* violation, but suggested in another case that it is not necessarily one. *Strickler v. Greene*, 527 U.S. 263, 283 n.23 (2004) ("We certainly do not criticize the prosecution's use of the open file policy").

Another difficulty with disclosure concerns evidence in the files of law enforcement agents other than the prosecutors. Prosecutors have a duty to learn of and disclose evidence known to all government agents, including the police, *Kyles v. Whitley,* 514 U.S. 419, 437 (1995). Yet, prosecutors may not know or have ready access to everything in every law enforcement agency file. Compulsory disclosure of evidence in police files may endanger witnesses or damage ongoing investigations. Generally, courts have held that a prosecutor does not violate *Brady* by not disclosing exculpatory evidence if the defense knew of the evidence and could have obtained it from a source other than the prosecutor.[47]

1.　BRADY VIOLATIONS IN STREET CRIME CASES: THE CASE OF *CONNICK V. THOMPSON*

The case of John Thompson, who spent eighteen years in prison (fourteen on death row) for a crime he did not commit, brought to light the problem of *Brady* violations in the run-of-the-mill street crime cases that dominate the dockets of local district attorneys. *Connick v. Thompson*, 131 S.Ct. 1350, 1356 (2011). *See also State v. Thompson*, 825 So. 2d 552 (La. Ct. App. 2002). In 1985 the Orleans Parish District Attorney's Office charged Thompson with the murder of Raymond

---

[45]　Medwed, *Brady's Bunch of Flaws*, 67 WASH. & LEE L. REV. at 1536–1537.

[46]　United States v. Skilling, 554 F.3d 529, 576 (5th Cir. 2009); Joel Cohen & Danielle Alfonzo Walsman, *Ethics and Criminal Practice*, N.Y. L. J. Sept. 4, 2009.

[47]　WAYNE R. LaFAVE, ET AL., CRIMINAL PROCEDURE § 24.3(b) (3d ed. 2011).

Liuzza, Jr. News coverage of the murder led three victims of an unrelated robbery to identify Thompson as their attacker.

> As part of the robbery investigation, a crime scene technician took from one of the [robbery] victims' pants a swatch of fabric stained with the robber's blood. Approximately one week before Thompson's armed robbery trial, the swatch was sent to the crime laboratory. Two days before the trial, assistant district attorney Bruce Whittaker received the crime lab's report, which stated that the perpetrator had blood type B. There is no evidence that the prosecutors ever had Thompson's blood tested or that they knew what his blood type was. Whittaker claimed he placed the report on assistant district attorney James Williams' desk, but Williams denied seeing it. The report was never disclosed to Thompson's counsel. The prosecutors did not mention the swatch or the crime lab report at trial, and the jury convicted Thompson of attempted armed robbery. A few weeks later, Williams and special prosecutor Eric Dubelier tried Thompson for the Liuzza murder. Because of the armed robbery conviction, Thompson chose not to testify in his own defense. He was convicted and sentenced to death. In late April 1999, Thompson's private investigator discovered the crime lab report from the armed robbery investigation in the files of the New Orleans Police Crime Laboratory. Thompson was tested and found to have blood type O, proving that the blood on the swatch was not his. Thompson's attorneys presented this evidence to the district attorney's office, which, in turn, moved to stay the execution and vacate Thompson's armed robbery conviction. The Louisiana Court of Appeals then reversed Thompson's murder conviction, concluding that the armed robbery conviction unconstitutionally deprived Thompson of his right to testify in his own defense at the murder trial. In 2003, the district attorney's office retried Thompson for Liuzza's murder. The jury found him not guilty.

Connick, 131 S.Ct. at 1356–57. Thompson sued the Orleans Parish District Attorney's Office and the DA, Harry Connick, alleging that the suppression of exculpatory evidence at his trial had been caused by Connick's deliberate indifference to an obvious need to train the prosecutors in his office. The trial court found Connick liable under 42 U.S.C. § 1983 for a violation of Thompson's constitutional rights. On appeal, the Fifth Circuit affirmed, but the Supreme Court reversed in 2011. *Connick v. Thompson*, 131 S.Ct. 1350, 1356 (2011).

NOTES ON CONNICK V. THOMPSON

1. ***Why Ignore or Avoid Finding Exculpatory Evidence?*** Why do you suppose the assistant DA Whittaker, who first received the crime lab report showing the blood type on the fabric swatch, did not ask to have Thompson's blood type tested? Why do you suppose he did not follow up with Williams to be sure that Williams received the report and handed it over to Thompson's lawyers? If Williams did indeed receive the report from Whittaker, why do you suppose he ignored it and did not provide it to the defense?

2. ***Institutional Reform.*** What institutional reforms would be effective in ensuring that exculpatory evidence is routinely provided to defense lawyers?

2. BRADY VIOLATIONS IN HIGH-PROFILE WHITE COLLAR CASES: THE CASE OF *UNITED STATES V. STEVENS*

Beginning in early 2003, the U.S. Department of Justice and the Federal Bureau of Investigation ("FBI") began investigating Ted Stevens, a long-time Republican U.S. Senator from Alaska, for potential violations of Senate rules in failing to report gifts he received. The investigation focused on Stevens' relationship with Bill Allen, the chief executive and part owner of VECO, an Alaskan oil exploration and drilling company. In July 2008, a grand jury indicted Senator Stevens for failing to report gifts, concealing receipt of things of value, using his official position and his Senate office to benefit those who had given him gifts, and knowingly making false statements on Senate financial disclosure forms.[48]

After the trial had begun in Washington, Senator Stevens' defense team alleged that prosecutors withheld exculpatory evidence. The DOJ's Office of Professional Responsibility (OPR) launched an investigation into allegations of *Brady* violations before the trial had ended.[49] After the jury convicted Senator Stevens on all counts but before he was sentenced, FBI Special Agent Chad Joy filed a whistleblower statement with the court alleging misconduct on behalf of several prosecutors and investigators involved in the case. Over the next several months, Judge Sullivan asked prosecutors for documents that Special Agent Joy claimed could exculpate Senator Stevens.[50] As it became clearer to the DOJ that prosecutors involved in the case may have withheld exculpatory evidence, Attorney General Eric Holder dropped all charges against Stevens, and Judge

---

[48] Dept. of Justice, Office of Professional Responsibility, No. 08–231, Investigation of Allegations of Prosecutorial Misconduct in *United States v. Theodore F. Stevens* (2010), 1–2.

[49] *Id.*, at 17–18; Report to Hon. Emmet G. Sullivan at 49–63, In re Special Proceedings (2009) (Misc. No. 09–0198).

[50] Transcript of Motion Hearing at 6, U.S. v Stevens (2009) (No. 08–231); Erika Bolstad, *Stevens Judge Orders Inquiry*, ANCHORAGE DAILY NEWS, Apr. 8, 2009, at A1.

Sullivan set aside the jury's verdict.[51] Judge Sullivan initiated criminal contempt proceedings against several of the prosecutors and took the highly unusual step of appointing his own independent investigator, Henry Schuelke, to determine whether there was a basis to prosecute members of the prosecution team for violating court orders and obstructing justice.[52]

In the wake of the Stevens trial, Attorney General Holder appointed a working group to propose changes in how federal prosecutors handle discovery. In January 2010, the group released three memoranda creating new procedures and a step-by-step guide for prosecutors working through the discovery process. Each U.S. Attorney's Office and the central DOJ must have a "discovery coordinator" to provide annual training to prosecutors and to serve as on-location advisors. Each office must establish a discovery policy that reflects local, district, and national discovery requirements.[53]

In the spring of 2012, both the Department of Justice Office of Professional Responsibility (OPR) and Judge Sullivan's independent investigator, Schuelke, released their reports on the Stevens prosecutors. Joseph Bottini and James Goeke, Assistant U.S. Attorneys in Alaska, were found to have "engaged in professional misconduct by acting in reckless disregard of their disclosure obligations" and to have withheld and concealed significant exculpatory information.[54] One was suspended without pay for 40 days and the other for 15 days. The OPR determined that supervising prosecutors involved in the Stevens prosecution did not violate any laws or rules, but did chastise the team several times for poor supervision of various aspects of the investigation and prosecution. Schuelke decided not to pursue criminal charges against any of the DOJ attorneys involved in the investigation and prosecution.

In the wake of the reports, Schuelke, defense lawyers, and some members of Congress have pushed for changes to discovery rules.[55] Congress considered, but has not enacted, "The Fairness in Disclosure of Evidence Act of 2012," which would require prosecutors to disclose evidence

---

[51] U.S. v Theodore F. Stevens, No. 08–CR–231, 2009, WL 6525926 at 1 (2nd. Cir. Apr. 7, 2009); Evan Perez, *Judge Orders Probe of Prosecutors*, WALL ST.J., Apr. 8, 2009, at A4.

[52] Transcript of Motion Hearing at 3, U.S. v. Stevens (2009) (No. 08–231); Joe Palazzolo and Mike Scarcela, *Judge Dismisses Case Against Stevens*, LEGAL INTELLIGENCER, Apr. 8, 2009.

[53] Memorandum from David W. Ogden, Deputy Attorney General, Issuance of Guidance and Summary of Actions Taken in Response to the Report of the Department of Justice Criminal Discovery and Case Management Working Group (Jan. 4, 2010); Guidance for Prosecutors Regarding Criminal Discovery (Jan. 4, 2010); Requirement for Office Discovery Policies in Criminal Matters (Jan. 4, 2010).

[54] DEPT. OF JUSTICE, INVESTIGATION OF ALLEGATIONS OF PROSECUTORIAL MISCONDUCT IN *UNITED STATES V. THEODORE F. STEVENS*, 26, 513.

[55] Mike Scarcella, *Federal Discovery Reform Sought in Wake of Botched Stevens Case*, DAILY BUS. REV., Apr. 2, 2012; Mark A. Srere et al., *The Prosecutorial Misconduct Report in U.S. v. Stevens and the Fairness in Evidence Disclosure Act of 2012: Two Strong Steps Toward Open File Discovery*, U.S.L.W., May 8, 2012.

that "may reasonably appear to be favorable to the defendant . . . without delay after arraignment and before the entry of any guilty plea."[56] The DOJ, however, cautioned against adopting the proposed legislation because it "would upset the careful balance of interests at stake in criminal cases, cause significant harm to victims, witnesses, and law enforcement efforts, and generate substantial and unnecessary litigation that would divert scarce judicial and prosecutorial resources."[57]

The aftermath of the Stevens prosecution is a dismal story for the lawyers involved. Most of them avoided discipline and all avoided criminal prosecution, but it was an especially awful experience for Nicholas Marsh, a young Justice Department lawyer who spent four years building the cases that resulted in convictions of several people involved in the Stevens incident. As the internal investigation of misconduct dragged on for months and years, the senior lawyers were able to remain prosecutors by transferring from the Washington, D.C. headquarters of the Department of Justice to U.S. Attorneys offices, while he was exiled to a position he considered the end of his career. Believing his career was ruined and that he had been scapegoated for the transgressions of his supervisors, Marsh became severely depressed and ultimately committed suicide. He was 37 years old.[58]

NOTES ON THE STEVENS CASE

1. ***Changing the Win-at-All-Costs Mindset.*** If a win at all costs mentality explains the prosecutors' failures in the Stevens case, what is the most effective strategy to address that problem?

2. ***What Would You Advise?*** Knowing what you know now, if Nicholas Marsh had been your friend, what advice would you have given him if he came to you and explained that he thought his team was not fully complying with its disclosure obligations but that he might jeopardize his own career if he rocked the boat? What if instead he was in charge of producing exculpatory and impeachment evidence to the defense and debated whether to provide more rather than less information?

3. ***The Politics of Political Cases.*** The Department of Justice (headed by an Attorney General appointed by a Democratic President) gave a high profile to its decision to dismiss the charges against Stevens, and some speculated it was an effort to convince the legal community that the Department was above politics and was determined to reform its ranks. As will be seen in Chapter 20, some believe DOJ's reputation was tarnished because it had become unduly politicized during the presidency of George W.

---

[56] Fairness in Evidence Discovery Act of 2012, S. 2197, 112th Cong. (2012), §§ 2(a)(1) and 2(c)(1).

[57] Statement for the Record, Dept. of Justice, Comm. on the Judiciary, U.S. Senate, Hearing on the Special Counsel's report on the Prosecution of Senator Ted Stevens (Mar. 28, 2012), 1, 5.

[58] Jeffrey Toobin, *Casualties of Justice*, NEW YORKER, Jan. 3, 2011, at 39.

Bush. Democratic Attorney General Holder may have been eager to prove that the DOJ was once again above politics by pushing hard against prosecutors who had gone after a Republican Senator. It was too late to save Stevens' political career, of course, and Stevens had little time to feel vindicated; he died in a plane crash not long after.

Yet critics remain concerned that another case of an allegedly politicized prosecution of a Democrat did not get the scrutiny it deserved because it might be seen as Democrats going after Republicans for bringing corruption cases against Democrats. The Republican U.S. Attorney in Alabama appointed by George W. Bush, Laura Canary, initiated a prosecution of Don Siegelman, the Democratic governor of Alabama, asserting that campaign contributions were bribes. The investigation ultimately cost Siegelman re-election, and, although one jury verdict was overturned on the grounds of misconduct, he was eventually convicted of corruption. Some insisted that the prosecution was politically motivated because U.S. Attorney Laura Canary was married to a leading Republican political activist in Alabama and was closely connected to Karl Rove and to the man who eventually replaced Siegelman as Alabama's governor. The intrigue grew thicker in the wake of disclosures of improper contacts between the prosecutors and jurors in Siegelman's re-trial, conversations between Canary and Karl Rove suggesting Canary should "go after" Siegelman, and the failure of the DOJ to act on evidence of prosecutorial misconduct provided in 2007 by a whistleblower in the Alabama U.S. Attorney's office. The intrigue grew thicker still when it appeared that the DOJ had failed to investigate allegations of similar gifts made to leading Republican elected officials in Alabama, including Jeff Sessions (formerly Alabama Attorney General and now U.S. Senator).[59]

As revealed in both the Stevens and Siegelman cases, criminal prosecutions of elected officials for corruption pose challenges to prevent misconduct motivated either by a win-at-all-costs mentality or by a desire to target politicians of the opposing party. Is there any reason to believe that investigations of prosecutorial misconduct are more or less immune to political pressure than are any other investigations? What should the Department of Justice and state prosecutors do to minimize the risk both that criminal investigations will be motivated by or influenced by political considerations and that investigations of prosecutorial misconduct will similarly be influenced by politics?[60]

---

[59] Adam Zagorin, *More Allegations of Misconduct in Alabama Governor Case*, TIME MAGAZINE, Nov. 14, 2008, *available at http://www.time.com/time/nation/article/0,8599, 1858991,00.html*; Adam Nagorin, *Selective Justice in Alabama?* TIME MAGAZINE, Oct. 7, 2007, *available at* http://www.time.com/nation/article/0,8599,1668220-11,00.html.

[60] *See* Anthony S. Barkow & Beth George, *Prosecuting the Political Defendants*, 44 GEORGIA L. REV. 953 (2010) (proposing reforms to the way that DOJ handles prosecutions of political defendants); Richard E. Myers, II, *Who Watches the Watchers in Public Corruption Cases?* 2012 U. CHI. LEG. FORUM 13 (discussing the challenges of regulating the prosecution of public corruption).

3. THE DUTY TO DO JUSTICE

PROSECUTORIAL DISCRETION AT THE CORE: THE GOOD PROSECUTOR MEETS BRADY

Janet C. Hoeffel
109 Penn State Law Review 1133 (2005)

The professional codes are clear about one aspect of the [prosecutor's obligation] to do justice. It is the prosecutor's ethical duty to make timely disclosure to the defense all evidence or information known to the prosecutor that tends to negate the guilt of the accused or mitigates the offense. Therefore, the good "ethical" prosecutor discloses this evidence. A former prosecutor-turned-judge calls it the "ouch test": "If a prosecutor is looking at [his or her] case and says 'Ouch, that hurts,' that means it should be turned over to the defense. Basically, anything that hurts the prosecution's case is arguably favorable to the defense." Or, in the words of an Assistant United States Attorney, "when you are looking at [disclosure obligations under] *Brady*, if you have to think about whether it should be disclosed, it probably needs to be disclosed."

Scholars hope and expect most prosecutors will think and operate in accordance with these principles. This expectation is skewed by the fact that many of the legal scholars writing in the area of prosecutorial discretion are former Assistant United States Attorneys ("AUSA"s). It is enormously important to point out that neither an AUSA nor a former AUSA-turned-academic is an average prosecutor. The typical AUSA has graduated from a good law school near the top of his class. Federal prosecutors are an elite group with enormous prestige. The young Assistant receives training, has a supervisor, and has an army of federal agents at his disposal. It does not take long for him to realize the incredible power of his position.

Hence, the federal prosecutor has a vested interest in seeing himself as just. Gifted with all of the prestige and power of the office, if forced to describe himself or his colleagues, he must say he is worthy of the power. He must show that the public can trust him, or he will be forced to cede his discretion.

The federal prosecutor may in fact be in a position to show some ethical restraint to his prosecutorial zeal. The run-of-the-mill federal case is a victimless drug or weapons charge that has been sealed up tightly by federal law enforcement before it reaches his desk. Most of the cases are slam-dunk convictions. He may need not stretch to the limit every exercise of discretion and every rule favorable to the prosecution in order to gain a conviction. Hence, it may be that some federal prosecutors occasionally serve the role of an "ethical" prosecutor, but this image, I submit, is far from reality.

I have a different vision of the good prosecutor because in my eight years as a criminal defense attorney, I met many prosecutors in different jurisdictions, and I never met the "ethical" prosecutor, in the sense envisioned by the ethics code.

Most crimes are handled by local prosecutors, who hail from a very different place than federal prosecutors. The typical state prosecution is much messier than a federal prosecution. The police work is sloppier, the resources are limited, and the case loads are heavy. In many of the crimes, victims push for prosecution, the press follows every homicide or rape, and the boss needs a high record of convictions for re-election. The typical local prosecutor does not have the luxury, the time, or the inclination to draw his sense of power from exercising discretion in favor of the defendant. He will only be noticed, climb the career ladder, or become a member of elected office himself if he racks up the convictions.

The local prosecutor has plenty of power: power to pursue or dismiss charges, power to offer pleas and immunity, power of superior information, power of reputation, and power of lording it over the guilty, the pitiful, and the shamed. I never met a prosecutor who did not love the power he was able to cultivate. I have come to believe it is a matter of human nature rather than a despicable display: no rational human being can resist the temptation to enjoy and pursue this power. And it is not like the power of teacher over student, where the teacher may be inclined to show mercy toward the student. Rather, the prosecutor is placed in an adversarial process, in which he must pursue his side with adversarial zeal if the process is to work as designed. He has little problem mustering this zeal because he, the public, and the courts believe he wears the white hat. The combination of power and white hat justice form the intoxicating milieu of the prosecutor's office.

The prosecutor does not even think about "doing justice" in the sense the ethics professors envision. What prosecutor would not believe he is doing justice by fulfilling his concomitant duty to be a zealous advocate? Isn't the whole idea of becoming a prosecutor to put the bad guys behind bars and keep the public safe? And didn't the prosecutor sign up for an adversarial system of justice? Once the adversarial process has begun, we should fully expect the normal, human, and good prosecutor to have the single-minded goal of winning the case for the prosecution. That is the prosecutor our system of justice cultivates and encourages.

PROBLEM 14–4

Olmedo Hidalgo and David Lemus were convicted of shooting Marcus Peterson, the bouncer of a New York nightclub, in 1990. They were sentenced to 25 years to life. At their trial, several bouncers identified them as the assailants and Lemus's ex-girlfriend testified that he confessed to her that he shot Peterson. A decade later, a former member of a gang confessed that he and a friend had shot Peterson. The DA's office opened an investigation in 2003 to examine the case. Daniel Bibb, a 21-year veteran of the office, was assigned to conduct it.

Bibb spent almost two years tracking down new witnesses and evidence. After he and two detectives had conducted 50 interviews in more than a dozen states and found witnesses the police had missed, Bibb concluded that the defendants were innocent. Lawyers for Hidalgo and Lemus persuaded a court to order an evidentiary hearing on the question whether the men were innocent. The evidentiary hearing is a pivotal moment in a wrongful conviction case, for it is the opportunity for the lawyers for the defendants to present the new evidence. Bibb informed his supervisors at the DA's office that he believed the new evidence he had gathered showed the defendants were innocent. Bibb's supervisors instructed him to go into the evidentiary hearing, present the government's case that the verdicts were correct, and let the judge decide. Bibb believed that to do so would violate his duty as a prosecutor to do justice.

So he prepared for the hearing in collaboration with defense counsel to persuade the new witnesses to testify to the evidence that had convinced him that Hidalgo and Lemus were innocent. He hunted down the witnesses again—many were former gang members or were in the witness protection program or in prison—and persuaded them to agree to testify. He helped the defense lawyers plan their examination of the witnesses. He told the witnesses what questions to expect during the defense examination and during his own cross-examination. When he cross-examined witnesses who had extensive criminal records that could have been used to impeach their testimony, he declined to vigorously impeach them. When the testimony at the hearing ended, Bibb persuaded his supervisors to dismiss the charges against Hidalgo. But his supervisors insisted that Lemus was guilty. Bibb refused to have anything further to do with the hearing. Another DA wrote the post-hearing brief. And when the trial judge ordered a new trial for Lemus (rather than ordering his release), Bibb resigned as a DA. The DA's office tried Lemus again and the jury acquitted him.[61]

NOTES ON THE DUTY TO DO JUSTICE

1. *What Should a Lawyer Do in an Adversary System?* Did Daniel Bibb do the right thing in working with the defense to present the case that he believed was true? Should it matter whether you know enough about the evidence to know in fact whether Hidalgo and Lemus were innocent? Is or should there be a difference in how we think about Bibb's conduct in cooperating with the defense depending on whether he were working on the trial that convicted Hidalgo and Lemus originally or the

---

[61] The problem is drawn from Benjamin Weiser, *Doubting Case, A Prosecutor Helped the Defense*, N.Y. TIMES (June 23, 2008), and Robert Morgenthau, Letter to the Editor, N.Y. TIMES (June 24, 2008).

evidentiary hearing that was conducted to determine whether to set aside their convictions?

2.   ***What Is the Prosecutor's Duty of Loyalty and to Whom Is It Owed?*** Did Bibb betray his duty of loyalty to his client? Who was his client?

3.   ***Insubordination or Doing Justice?*** Did Bibb violate obligations he owed to his supervisors, including the elected DA? Who should ultimately decide how to handle a case—the assistant DA who knows the case well or the elected DA who is more directly accountable to the people? Once his supervisors refused to take his advice to ask the court to vacate the convictions at the start of the hearing, should he have either followed their instructions or refused to participate in the hearing? The elected DA insisted later that Bibb could not easily have been replaced by another lawyer because Bibb was the one who knew the case and the new evidence thoroughly.

4.   ***What Were Bibb's Alternatives?*** If his supervisors refused to let him withdraw from the case, join the defense motion to vacate the conviction, or litigate the hearing as he thought best, what should Bibb have done?

G. PRESS COVERAGE OF CRIMINAL TRIALS

Two Model Rules regulate what lawyers can say to the public and the media about ongoing trials. Model Rule 3.6 regulates extrajudicial statements made by all lawyers participating in any kind of trial, not just criminal trials. It has particular salience in criminal trials, however, because of the typically greater media interest in criminal trials than in ordinary civil trials. Model Rule 3.8(f) also prohibits prosecutors from making certain extrajudicial statements and also requires prosecutors to make reasonable efforts to ensure that other people working with them in law enforcement do not make statements that prosecutors would be prohibited from making.

Public Statements about Trials

Model Rule 3.6:

A lawyer participating in an investigation or litigation shall not make a public extrajudicial statement that the lawyer knows or should know will have a substantial likelihood of materially prejudicing an adjudicative proceeding.

There are a number of exceptions. A lawyer is allowed to state:

- the claim, offense or defense involved and, except when prohibited by law, the identity of the persons involved;

- information contained in a public record;

- that an investigation of a matter is in progress or the result of any step in the litigation;

- a request for assistance in obtaining evidence and information;

- a warning of danger concerning the behavior of a person involved; and

- in a criminal case, in addition to the above, the lawyer may state the identity, residence, occupation and family status of the accused; information necessary to aid in apprehension of that person; and the fact, time and place of arrest.

- A lawyer may make a statement that a reasonable lawyer would believe is required to protect a client from the substantial undue prejudicial effect of recent publicity not initiated by the lawyer or the lawyer's client. A statement made pursuant to this paragraph shall be limited to such information as is necessary to mitigate the recent adverse publicity.

Model Rule 3.8(f):

Except for statements that are necessary to inform the public of the nature and extent of the prosecutor's action and that serve a legitimate law enforcement purpose, prosecutors shall refrain from making extrajudicial comments that have a substantial likelihood of heightening public condemnation of the accused.

Prosecutors shall exercise reasonable care to prevent investigators, law enforcement personnel, or other persons assisting or associated with the prosecutor in a criminal case from making statements that the prosecutor would be prohibited from making under Rule 3.6 or 3.8(f).

ABA Standard on The Prosecution Function 3–1.4 takes a more general approach, providing that "a prosecutor should not make or authorize the making of an extrajudicial statement that a reasonable person would expect to be disseminated by means of public communication if the prosecutor knows or reasonably should know that it will have a substantial likelihood of prejudicing a criminal proceeding." In addition, Standard 3—5.10 cautions that a "prosecutor should not make public comments critical of a verdict." A proposed revised Standard (renumbered 3–1.7) governing statements to the media goes farther to condemn prosecutors making a statement that will "have a substantial likelihood of prejudicing a criminal proceeding or unnecessarily heightening public condemnation of the accused, except for statements that are necessary to inform the public of the nature and extent of the prosecutor's or law enforcement actions and which serves a legitimate law enforcement purpose." Further, the new standard would prohibit secret or anonymous leaks of non-public information to the media, on or off the record. The revised Standard also appears to address "perp" walks and other similar activities: "Absent a legitimate and compelling law enforcement purpose, the prosecutor should not 'stage' or assist law enforcement in staging, real or fictional events that address specific cases or investigations solely for the media, nor should the prosecutor invite media presence during investigative actions without careful consideration of the interests of all involved, including suspects, defendants, and the public. However, a prosecutor may reasonably accommodate media requests for access to public information and events."

In considering the appropriate scope and content of press statements about pending cases, recall the values underlying the free speech protection of the Constitution. The public has an interest in knowing about government actions, including criminal prosecutions, but defendants have a right to a fair trial that can be harmed by excessive pretrial publicity. Whatever the speech rights of prosecutors (who, as government employees, have no First Amendment right to speak publicly about their work), defense lawyers and lawyers do have First Amendment rights to speak, but those rights can be balanced against other rights, such as the defendant's right to a fair trial. The First Amendment protection of attorney speech is unclear because there have been few Supreme Court cases directly about it. Attorneys do not relinquish their speech rights when they acquire a license to practice law, but the Court has also recognized that attorneys are officers of the court and their speech can be restricted, at least when there is a substantial likelihood of materially prejudicing an adjudicatory proceeding.[62]

NOTES ON THE PROSECUTOR'S RESPONSIBILITIES IN DEALING WITH THE PRESS

1. ***The Policy.*** What competing policies underlie the rules regulating what prosecutors and other lawyers can say to the press and to the public?

2. ***Understanding Prosecutor's Motivations for Speaking to the Press.*** What legitimate and illegitimate reasons would motivate a prosecutor (or law enforcement agents) to discuss a case with the public or the press?

3. ***State of Mind.*** In assessing whether a prosecutor has violated Rule 3.8(f) by making a statement that has a "substantial likelihood of heightening public condemnation of the accused," should the prosecutor's intent in making the statement be relevant? For example, suppose a prosecutor running for re-election announces at the indictment of an alleged child molester that "Pedophilia is a scourge in our society. I intend to use the full power of my office to find and punish those who prey on children. This case is one step in that direction." Does that statement violate Rule 3.8(f)?

4. ***Practical Considerations.*** What practical considerations should prosecutors bear in mind when speaking to the press in a high-profile case? Why would a prosecutor want to make a public statement about the investigation or the indictment? Why might a prosecutor be wise to refrain? Most debate over media statements have focused on the harm they can do to suspects and to the jury pool, but media statements can also affect the way prosecutors see their own case.

5. ***Specific Rules vs. General Standards.*** What are the comparative advantages of specifically listing prohibited and allowed statements in Rule 3.6 and 3.8(f) as opposed to generally prohibiting prejudicial statements as in the ABA Standard?

6. ***Institutional Reforms.*** What institutional practices in law offices and, perhaps, in the media or by the bar, would minimize the risk of violations of Model Rules 3.6 and 3.8(f) and the Standard governing publicity and press statements?

---

[62] Gentile v. State Bar of Nevada, 501 U.S. 1030 (1991).

7. *Why Is Discipline So Rare?* Prosecutors are seldom disciplined for press statements even when the statements are clear violations of ethics rules. Are there any good reasons for disciplinary committees to be reluctant to initiate proceedings against prosecutors for pretrial publicity?

PROBLEM 14–5

Governor Rod Blagojevich of Illinois was prosecuted for corruption. Among the charges were that, in exchange for campaign contributions, the governor offered an appointment to the U.S. Senate seat vacated when Barack Obama was elected President. The lead prosecutor in the case commented to the press when announcing the charges against Blagojevich that the governor had gone on a "political corruption crime spree"; that his conduct "would make Lincoln roll over in his grave"; that "the breadth of corruption laid out in these charges is staggering" and that Blagojevich "put a 'for sale' sign on the naming of a United States senator."

Do the prosecutor's statements violate Model Rules 3.6 or 3.8(f)? Do they violate either the current ABA Standard or the proposed one? What harms, if any, are caused by prosecutors making such statements at a press conference announcing the filing of charges or the return of an indictment? Is there a difference between making such comments at the pre-trial stage (where the evidence has not yet been ruled admissible or subjected to cross-examination) and making them to the media after a trial?

PROBLEM 14–6

Dominique Strauss-Kahn, a managing director of the International Monetary Fund and a prominent French politician who was expected to run for the presidency of France, was arrested and charged in New York City for attempted rape of a New York hotel maid. On his way to a first court appearance, police escorted him in hand-cuffs past a phalanx of cameras; photos of the so-called "perp walk" appeared in the media worldwide. In the days following the arrest, police leaked lurid details of the allegations against him. His lawyers did not initially speak to the press, although in due course a number of stories questioning the reliability of the complainant's story emerged. Eventually, the complainant too was pilloried in the press, with news stories suggesting she had fabricated the whole thing in order to extort money from him. The charges against Strauss-Kahn were eventually dropped, although not until stories about him and allegations of prior incidents of sexual assault had been published. He did not run for President of France. Both his reputation and that of the maid who accused him of assault were severely damaged by the pre-trial publicity.

The prosecutors insist that the police provided information to the press and staged the procession of Strauss-Kahn to the court appearance in hand-cuffs without any involvement or knowledge of prosecutors. Did the prosecutors nevertheless violate Model Rule 3.8(f), which requires prosecutors to "exercise reasonable care to prevent investigators, law enforcement personnel, employees or other persons assisting or associated with the prosecutor in a criminal case from making an extrajudicial statement that the prosecutor would be prohibited from making?" What aspects, if any, of the handling of the Strauss-Kahn matter violate Model Rules 3.6 and 3.8(f)? Does the approach proposed by the revised Standard 3–1.7 strike the right balance?

PROBLEM 14–7

In March 2006, Duke University lacrosse players hired a nude dancer to perform at a team party. Later that night, the dancer accused three players of raping her. Mike Nifong, the Durham, North Carolina District Attorney, was running for re-election. The sensational media attention prompted him to speak to the press about what he believed the evidence would show as a way of demonstrating the seriousness with which he would take allegations of criminal conduct by university students. Nifong said that he was convinced a rape had occurred, and denounced the players' conduct as "reprehensible" and like a "cross burning." He said that the nurse who had examined the dancer at the hospital found that her condition was consistent with having suffered a sexual assault. Nifong also said, about the status of DNA tests of samples taken from the dancer, the house where the party occurred, and some suspects, that "there are many questions people are asking that they would not be asking if they saw the results." He also criticized the players for refusing to speak to the police on the advice of counsel.[63] Which of Nifong's statements violate Model Rule 3.6 or 3.8(f)? In assessing this, consider whether it should matter whether his statements were truthful, whether they stated matters that were already in the public record, or whether they responded to public comments already made by the defense.

H. SUMMARY

Prosecutors occupy a unique and powerful role with unique responsibilities in the American legal system. They have access to all the investigatory resources of government, and they decide, with little judicial oversight, whom to investigate and charge with crime. Model Rule 3.8 imposes special duties on prosecutors, including a duty to ensure that adequate evidence supports any charges, to disclose exculpatory

---

[63] The prosecution of the players collapsed when the evidence from the crime lab failed to show that any student had raped the woman, the woman was unable to identify her alleged assailants, DNA testing of the rape kit revealed DNA from four unidentified males (not lacrosse players) in the dancer's body, and other evidence showed that at least one of the students who had been charged was not at the party at the time of the alleged attack. Although Problem 14–7 focuses on Nifong's public statements to the press, many commentators considered his failure to disclose this exculpatory evidence to the defense to be the more egregious ethical violation. *See* R. Michael Cassidy, *The Prosecutor and the Press: Lessons (Not) Learned from the Nifong Debacle,* 71 LAW & CONTEMP. PROBS. 67 (2008); Robert P. Mosteller, *Exculpatory Evidence, Ethics, and the Road to the Disbarment of Mike Nifong, The Critical Importance of Full Open-File Discovery,* 15 GEO. MASON L. REV. 257 (2008); North Carolina State Bar v. Nifong, Amended Findings of Fact, Conclusions of Law, and Order of Discipline, available at *http://www.ncbar.com/discipline/printorder.asp?id=505.*

information to the defense, to ensure the accused has been given a right to counsel, and to rectify wrongful convictions. More generally, prosecutors have a duty to seek justice, not merely to seek convictions. Although bureaucratic policies, such as the U.S. Attorneys' Manual, constrain the exercise of their discretion, little external law is enforced against prosecutors, as they are absolutely immune from civil liability for their conduct as lawyers and are rarely subject to bar discipline.

The prosecutor's duty to seek justice exists in tension with the prosecutor's role as an adversary in the highly adversarial American criminal justice system. The tension in the prosecutor's role is particularly acute in the prosecutor's obligation under *Brady v. Maryland* and Model Rule 3.8(d) to disclose in a timely manner evidence known to the prosecutor or to other law enforcement agents to the defense before trial. Although timely disclosure of exculpatory, mitigating and impeachment evidence is required, not all laws require disclosure of impeachment evidence before a plea bargain. Failure to disclose exculpatory evidence to the defense is a leading cause of wrongful convictions. No consensus exists about what institutional reforms within prosecutors' offices would most effectively address the problem of wrongful convictions, but Model Rule 3.8 does impose upon prosecutors a duty to investigate and seek to rectify wrongful convictions.

All lawyers have a duty under Model Rule 3.6 to avoid public statements that have a substantial likelihood of materially prejudicing a trial or adjudicative proceeding. In addition, Model Rule 3.8(f) imposes additional requirements on prosecutors. A prosecutor is permitted to make statements necessary to inform the public of the nature and extent of the prosecutor's action and to make statements that serve a legitimate law enforcement purpose. Prosecutors may not make extrajudicial comments that have a substantial likelihood of heightening public condemnation of the accused. Rule 3.8 also imposes on prosecutors a duty to exercise reasonable care that police and others working with prosecutors do not say what the prosecutors themselves cannot.

SUBPART B

LARGE ORGANIZATIONAL CLIENTS

■ ■ ■

INTRODUCTION

This unit focuses on lawyers who serve large organizational clients. Those lawyers work primarily in three practice settings: big law firms, in-house legal positions in corporations, and government. Several features of these practice areas do not fit the portrait of law practice reflected in the ethics rules. First, the rules generally portray clients as individuals, not large organizations, but lawyers who represent organizations face distinctive challenges that relate to the question of who speaks for the client. Second, the rules focus on the rights and obligations of individual lawyers who practice on their own or in small firms and pay little attention to how lawyers function in large firms, in-house legal departments, and government. Lawyers in these work settings tend to work in teams; individual decision-making in these institutions is typically enmeshed in larger governance processes. Third, the ethics rules tend to portray clients as vulnerable individuals, but organizational clients typically are not vulnerable—or at least not in the same ways as individual clients sometimes can be.[165]

WHO IS THE CLIENT WHEN THE CLIENT IS AN ORGANIZATION?

You've already seen that lawyers owe clients many duties, including the duty to communicate with the client (Rule 1.4), to exercise independent professional judgment and give candid advice (Rule 2.1), and to keep the client's confidences (Rule 1.6). But when a lawyer represents an entity rather than an individual, how does the lawyer fulfill those duties? In the chapters on confidentiality, you saw some of the difficulties of applying the attorney-client privilege and the duty of confidentiality to organizations. Regarding the duty to communicate with the client and to exercise independent judgment and give candid advice, with *whom* should the lawyer talk and to whom should he render candid advice? Rule 1.13, the only ethics rule that focuses on representing organizational clients, simplifies matters—at least in theory—by treating organizations as

---

[165] For a fuller discussion of these and other assumptions underlying the ethics rules and their inconsistency with the conditions of modern law practice, *see* David B. Wilkins, *Everyday Practice is the Troubling Case: Confronting Context in Legal Ethics*, in EVERYDAY PRACTICES AND TROUBLE CASES 68 (Sarat et al., eds. 1998).

though they were individual clients. But implementing that single client conception in the representation of organizations can be problematic.

The Basic Rule—Model Rule 1.13(a)

A lawyer who represents an organization represents the organization acting through its "duly authorized constituents."

Ordinarily a Lawyer Takes Direction from "Duly Authorized Constituents". In circumstances when organizations are working well, it may not be particularly challenging for the lawyer to decide who has authority to speak for the client and with whom the lawyer should communicate. Model Rule 1.13(a) establishes the basic rule about how the client is defined. It states that the lawyer represents the organization as a legal entity, acting through its "constituents," such as officers, directors, employees, shareholders, etc. The organization is a fictional person that can function only through constituents (individuals) empowered to act on its behalf. Those individuals owe duties to the organization, and so the lawyer's and those individuals' incentives should run in the same direction. Ordinarily, therefore, the lawyer takes guidance from the person or persons designated by the organization's authority structure to interact with the lawyer.

The Lawyer's Dilemma When Lines of Authority Are Unclear and/or Constituents Disagree. Sometimes the lines of authority within an organization are unclear, and then it becomes more difficult for the lawyer to determine how to interact with the organization's constituents. Moreover, internal disagreements sometimes arise within the client organization. When that happens, the interests and conduct of the constituents with whom the lawyer ordinarily interacts and the interests of the entity may diverge, and things then become tricky. It can be especially difficult for the lawyer to distinguish between the interests of the entity and those of its constituents when those constituents are the people with whom the lawyer interacts day-to-day and also the ones who hold the power to hire and fire the lawyer.

Reporting Up the Ladder When Constituents Are Violating Duties to the Organization. Another problem for the lawyer for an organization arises when constituents of the organization are violating their legal duties to the entity and/or engaging in illegal conduct that might be imputed to the organization. Rule 1.13(b) requires a lawyer in those circumstances to take action to protect the organization's interests. It further states that unless the lawyer reasonably believes that it is not necessary in the best interest of the organization to do so, the lawyer "shall refer the matter to higher authority in the organization, including, if warranted by the circumstances, to the highest authority that can act on behalf of the organization as determined by applicable law." This obligation to take the matter up the organizational hierarchy is sometimes called the "up the ladder" reporting requirement. If the highest authority that can act on behalf of the organization, usually the board of directors, fails to remedy the illegality and the lawyer "reasonably believes that the violation is reasonably certain to result in substantial injury to the organization," the rule gives the lawyer permission, but no obligation, to reveal confidential information "to the extent the lawyer reasonably believes necessary to prevent substantial injury to the organization." (Rule 1.13(c).)

Model Rule 1.13(b) and (c): When Constituents Are Violating Law or Legal Obligation to the Organization

- If a lawyer for an organization knows that an officer, employee or other person associated with the organization is violating a legal obligation to the organization or engaging in a legal violation relating to the representation that is likely to injure the organization, the lawyer must act to protect the organization's interests.

- Unless the lawyer reasonably believes it is not in the organization's best interest to do so, the lawyer shall take the issue up the organizational ladder.

- If the highest authority that can act for the organization fails to remedy the problem, the lawyer may reveal confidential information to the extent the lawyer reasonably believes necessary to protect the organization from substantial injury.

The Rule's Limitations. Notice some of the limitations of the provision requiring lawyers to report up the organizational ladder. It applies only when the lawyer "knows" of ongoing activity or future activity that is a violation. The definitional section of the Model Rules (Rule 1.0) indicates that "knows" means actual knowledge, although knowledge can be inferred from circumstances. The duty to report up the ladder applies only when the misconduct relates to the representation. Thus, if a lawyer in an outside firm is hired to handle an organization's employment dispute and stumbles upon evidence that the organization is engaging in environmental violations, she has no obligation under this provision to take the issue up the organizational ladder. Finally, the violation must be one that "is likely to result in substantial injury to the organization." Likely injury to third parties or constituents of the organization does not necessarily meet this requirement. Even where the trigger requirement is not met, however, the comment to Rule 1.13 indicates that the lawyer may take important matters up the ladder in order to fulfill her duties to the organization: "Even in circumstances where a lawyer is not obligated by Rule 1.13 to proceed, a lawyer may bring to the attention of an organizational client, including its highest authority, matters that the lawyer reasonably believes to be of sufficient importance to warrant doing so in the best interest of the organization."

The Current and Old Versions of Rule 1.13 Compared. The current version of Rule 1.13 requires considerably more of the lawyer than the prior version did. Under the previous version of the rule, a lawyer who discovered illegal conduct that threatened substantial harm to the organization had permission, but no obligation, to take the matter up the organizational hierarchy. And if the lawyer went to the highest authority and that authority refused to stop the illegal conduct, the lawyer's only option was to resign; the rule did not permit the lawyer to blow the whistle to protect the organization. In 2003, following several well-publicized corporate scandals in which lawyers were in a position to stop corporate fraud but failed do so, the ABA modified Rules 1.6 and 1.13 to give lawyers permission (in Rule 1.6(b) and (c)) and more responsibility (Rule 1.13(b) & (c)) to respond to illegal conduct by organizational constituents. The ABA's stricter rules followed the SEC's adoption of regulations implementing the Sarbanes-Oxley Act. Those regulations impose an up-the-ladder reporting requirement on lawyers who advise clients in the preparation of documents that foreseeably may become part of submissions to the SEC and who become aware of a material violation of securities law.[166]

As we'll see, lawyers who think that Rule 1.13 defines the extent of their obligations and the limits of their liability while representing organizational clients are sorely mistaken. Lawyers convicted of aiding and abetting crimes in connection with corporate and governmental scandals of the past few decades, have learned that lesson the hard way.

LAWYERS' INDIVIDUAL RESPONSIBILITY WHILE WORKING IN LARGE ORGANIZATIONS

The focus of the ethics rules on the rights and obligations of individual lawyers likely reflects the fact that, until recently, the vast majority of American lawyers worked in solo practice or in informal collaboration with several other lawyers. It is unsurprising, therefore, that the rules emphasize lawyers' individual deliberation and decision-making and implicitly suggest that even lawyers who work in organizations are largely free of external review and constraint. But decision-making becomes more complex when lawyers work in organizations. As David Luban has observed, "loyalties become tangled, and personal responsibility is diffused," "bucks are passed and guilty knowledge bypassed," and "[c]hains of command not only tie people's

---

[166] Part 205—Standards of Professional Conduct for Attorneys Appearing and Practicing Before the Commission in the Representation of an Issuer, 17 C.F.R. Part 205 (2003).

hands, they fetter their minds and consciences as well."[167] Particularly worrisome for a junior lawyer is the prospect that a boss might pressure the junior lawyer to engage in misconduct or that the junior lawyer will lose the ability to discern right from wrong.

The Rules contain two provisions that pay particular attention to the circumstances of junior and supervisory lawyers in organizations. Model Rule 5.2 addresses the ethical responsibility of the junior lawyer, stating that "[a] lawyer is bound by the Rules of Professional Conduct notwithstanding that the lawyer acted at the direction of another person." The only exemption to full formal accountability for a junior lawyer's deference to a senior lawyer applies when the subordinate lawyer acts "in accordance with a supervisory lawyer's reasonable resolution of an arguable question of professional duty." Rule 5.2(b). Rule 5.1 addresses the responsibilities of partners and other senior lawyers, charging them with a duty to ensure that the firm has policies designed to assure compliance with the rules. The same rule also makes senior lawyers responsible for junior lawyers' violations of the rules if the senior lawyers order or ratify the conduct or know of it at a time when its consequences can be avoided or mitigated and fail to take action.

Although these rules establish certain duties of lawyers who work in organizations, they do not fully account for important sources of supervision, control, and influence on individual lawyer decision-making within organizations. While many of these sources of control and influence are entirely benign—and tend to reinforce individual lawyers' best instincts about how to behave—it is also true that lawyers who work in large organizations sometimes find it challenging to reconcile individual conscience with their felt responsibilities and loyalties. The fragmentation of knowledge and accountability within large organizations sometimes adds to the complexity of exercising professional judgment and acting on it.

CLIENT VULNERABILITY

The image of an individual client vulnerable to the power of the state and his lawyer does not square well with the experiences of lawyers who represent organizational clients. These clients do not fit the paradigm of the criminal defendant whose freedom or even life might be taken away by the state. When the client is the government, the image of the lawyer as the champion of the individual against the state seems particularly inapt because the government lawyer's client is the state, or some subunit thereof—an agency, department or commission. Most corporations are highly sophisticated consumers of legal services, provided either in-house (by lawyers employed directly by the corporation) or by lawyers in an outside firm, and they are capable of discerning what services they need,

---

[167] DAVID LUBAN, LEGAL ETHICS AND HUMAN DIGNITY 237 (2007).

shopping for competitive pricing, and sanctioning lawyers who disappoint them by filing malpractice actions and withholding future business. Indeed, as we'll see, sometimes the experience of lawyers for organizational clients stands the image of client vulnerability on its head. Lawyers can find themselves susceptible to being drawn into grave trouble through misconduct by the organization's constituents, and they may feel vulnerable to the power of clients to punish their lawyers for refusing to go along.

CHAPTER 15

LARGE LAW FIRMS

∎ ∎ ∎

A. INTRODUCTION

The following materials explore the large firm practice setting: how large law firms have changed over the past several decades, the current practices and cultures of these institutions, and their implications for lawyers, clients, and the public. Although many more lawyers work in solo and small firm settings than in large firms, the number of lawyers in large firms is still substantial. Lawyers in firms of 51 or more lawyers comprise roughly 20 percent of all American lawyers in private practice today.[1] The largest 350 U.S. firms, all of which have more than one hundred attorneys, collectively employ over 146,000 lawyers.[2] Moreover, large law firms have enormous influence within the legal profession, American society, and the global economy. Understanding the history of these institutions, their operations, and the dramatic changes they have undergone over the past few decades, is important for understanding the American legal profession as a whole.

This chapter considers the origins and structure of large law firms, how they have changed over time, their internal labor markets, and the experience of large firm associates. It also examines the values of large firm lawyers, their relationships with clients, several scandals involving large firm lawyers, and the future of large firms.

B. THE LARGE LAW FIRM: ORIGINS, STRUCTURE, AND CHANGE

Large law firms serve primarily corporate clients, offering transactional, counseling, and litigation services and a broad range of legal expertise. Big firms typically are divided into departments—e.g., litigation, real estate, securities, banking, tax, etc.—and their lawyers' expertise is highly specialized. The firms are hierarchical, composed of working groups containing junior and senior lawyers. Many large firms include two tiers of partners: equity partners, who share in the firm's

---

[1]   American Bar Foundation, The Lawyer Statistical Report (2012).

[2]   *The NLJ 350 Regional Report: The Top U.S. and International Markets*, NAT'L L. J., June 16, 2014, http://www.nationallawjournal.com/id=1402583484262/The-NLJ-350-Regional-Report-The-Top-US-and-International-Markets?slreturn=20140621142330.

profits, and non-equity partners, who are primarily salaried employees. Firms also employ a variety of other lawyers, including associates and lawyers who are "of counsel" to the firm. The latter title applies to lawyers with a variety of statuses, including permanent associates, lawyers with secure part-time arrangements, and retired partners who nevertheless remain available for consultation by the firm and its clients.

The large law firm and its distinctive practice style emerged around the turn of the twentieth century. The New York firm of Cravath, Swaine & Moore is widely credited with having pioneered the model, which is still the basic template for big private firms. Under the "Cravath system," firms hired lawyers directly out of prestigious law schools, and senior lawyers then supervised and reviewed these new lawyers during a prolonged apprenticeship of six to ten years. The firm then either promoted these associates to partnership or shepherded them into legal jobs outside the firm.

The Golden Age. A so-called "Golden Age" for large law firms was the 1950s and 1960s, as described in the following excerpt:

THE TRANSFORMATION OF THE BIG LAW FIRM

Marc Galanter and Thomas Palay
In Lawyers' Ideals/Lawyers' Practices: Transformations in the American Legal
Profession 31–62 (R. Nelson, D. Trubek & R. Solomon, eds., 1992)[3]

Before the Second World War the big firm had become the dominant kind of law practice. It was the kind of lawyering consumed by the major economic actors. It commanded the highest prestige. It attracted many of the most highly talented entrants to the profession. It was regarded as the "state of the art," embodying the highest technical standards. In the postwar years this dominance was solidified.

This golden age of the big firm, the late 1950s and the early 1960s, was a time of stable relations with clients, of steady but manageable growth, of comfortable assurance that an equally bright future lay ahead—which is not to say that its inhabitants did not look back fondly to an earlier time when professionalism was unalloyed.

New York firms loom disproportionately large in studies of the golden age. New York City was home to a much larger share of big-firm practice then than it is now. In the early 1960s, there were twenty-one firms in New York with fifty or more lawyers and only seventeen firms of that size in the rest of the country. A few years earlier, the largest firm in New York (and the country) was Shearman & Sterling & Wright with thirty-five partners and ninety associates. Three other Wall Street firms had

---

over a hundred lawyers. The twentieth-largest firm in New York had fifty lawyers.

Firms were built by "promotion to partnership." Lateral hiring was almost unheard of, and big firms did not hire from one another. Partners might leave and firms might split up, but it didn't happen very often.

Hiring of top law graduates soon after their graduation was one of the building blocks of the big firm. Most hiring was from a handful of law schools, and walk-in interviews during the Christmas break were the norm. Starting salaries at the largest New York firms were uniform—$4000 in 1953, rising to $7500 in 1963. The "going rate" was fixed at a luncheon, attended by managing partners of prominent firms, held annually for this purpose.

Historically, the big firms had confined hiring to white Christian males. Few African-Americans and women had the educational admission tickets to contend for these jobs. But there were numerous Jews who did and, with a few exceptions, they too were excluded. This exclusion began to break down slowly after the Second World War. Jewish associates were hired, and some moved up the ladder to partner. The lowering of barriers to Jews was part of a general lessening of social exclusiveness. In 1957, 28 percent of the partners in the eighteen firms studied by Erwin Smigel were listed in the Social Register. [The Social Register is a directory of names and addresses of prominent American families who form the social elite; listing in it has historically been limited to members of "polite society," or those with "old money".] By 1968, the percentage had dropped to 20 percent. But African-Americans and other minorities of color were still hardly visible in the world of big law firms. In 1956 there were approximately eighteen women working in large New York firms— something less than one percent of the total complement of lawyers.

Only a small minority of those hired as associates achieved partnership. Of 454 associates hired by the Cravath firm between 1906 and 1948, only 36 (just under 8 percent) were made partners. Cravath may have been the most selective but it was not that different from other firms.

The time it took to become a partner varied from firm to firm and associate to associate. For the New York lawyers becoming partners around 1960 the average time seems to have been just under ten years. Outside New York the time to partnership was closer to seven years. Throughout the 1960s the time to partnership dropped.

One of the basic elements of the structure of the big firm is the up or out rule that prescribes that after a probationary period, the young lawyer will either be admitted to the partnership or will leave the firm. Many firms had an explicit up or out rule, but there was at work a competing and powerful norm that it was not nice to fire a lawyer.

Termination tended to be drawn out and disguised. For associates who did not make partner, firms undertook outplacement, recommending them for jobs with client corporations and with smaller firms. Ties might be maintained as the firm referred legal work to them or they served as outside counsel to the corporation.

Partners were chosen by proficiency, hard work, and ability to relate to clients. In many cases there was some consideration of the candidate's ability to attract business. Achieving partnership, the "strongest reward," meant not only status but security and assurance of further advancement. There was certainly pressure to keep up with one's peers, but competition between partners was restrained.

The work of the big firm was primarily office work in corporate law, securities, banking, and tax with some estate work for wealthy clients. Divorces, automobile accidents, and minor real estate matters would be farmed out or referred to other lawyers. Litigation was not prestigious, and it was not seen as a money-maker. Where big firms were involved in litigation, it was typically on the side of the defendant. Big firms usually represented dominant actors who could structure transactions to get what they wanted; it was the other side that had to seek the help of courts to disturb the status quo. Disdain of litigation reflected the prevailing attitude among the corporate establishment that it was not quite nice to sue. Relations with clients tended to be enduring. Corporations had strong ties to "their" law firms.

Large firms elsewhere were constructed along the same "promotion to partnership" lines, but tended to operate a bit differently. Firms outside New York tended to be more recently founded. There was also less departmentalization, specialization, and supervision. The organization was less formal, with fewer rules about meetings, training, conflicts of interest, and so on. The turnover of associates was lower, and there was less up or out pressure. Partnership was also easier to attain and came earlier. Outside New York, firms were less highly leveraged. [Leverage is the ratio of associates to partners.]

For big firms, circa 1960 was a time of prosperity, stable relations with clients, steady but manageable growth, and a comfortable assumption that this kind of law practice was a permanent fixture of American life. Big law firms enjoyed an enviable autonomy. They were relatively independent vis-à-vis their clients; they exercised considerable control over how they did their work; and they were infused with a sense of being in control.

NOTES ON GALANTER & PALAY

1. ***Golden? For Whom?*** In what sense were the 1950s and 1960s a "golden age" for big law firms? What were the attractive and unattractive features of this era? For whom?

2. ***Relations with Clients.*** What were the most notable aspects of large law firms' relationships with clients during this period?

3. ***Hiring and Promotion.*** What were the most notable features of large law firms' hiring and promotion practices for attorneys during this period?

Changes Since the 1950s. Large law firms have changed significantly since the so-called "Golden Age." Perhaps the most striking changes relate to their increased size and geographic reach. In the 1950s, there were 38 law firms in the United States with more than 50 lawyers, most of them in New York City.[4] In 2011, there were 20 firms worldwide with over 1500 lawyers, and all of the 100 largest firms had over 500.[5] In 1960, big firms were clearly identified with particular localities; it was unusual for a firm to have a branch office.[6] By 1991, American firms had opened branch offices in 31 different foreign cities.[7] Today, over 10 percent of lawyers in the 250 largest U.S. firms work in overseas offices.[8] As we'll see in Part VI, large U.S. law firms increasingly compete with large global law firms based in other countries.

Large firms have also changed markedly in their relationships with clients and in-house counsel and their hiring and promotion practices. The following excerpt summarizes some of the most notable of these changes in the legal services industry from the 1970s to 1990:

> Starting in the 1970s, lateral movement became more frequent, soon developing into a systematic means of enlarging the specialties and localities a firm could service and acquiring rainmakers who might bring with them or attract new clients. Eventually the flow of lateral movement widened out from individual lawyers, to whole departments and groups within firms, and finally to whole firms. Mass defections and mergers became common, enabling firms in one stroke to add new departments and expand to new locations.

---

[4]   ERWIN O. SMIGEL, THE WALL STREET LAWYER 58 (1964).

[5]   *The 2012 Global 100: Most Attorneys*, Am. Law., Sept. 28, 2012, http://www.american lawyer.com/PubArticleTAL.jsp?id=1202571229481.

[6]   ERWIN O. SMIGEL, THE WALL STREET LAWYER 207 (1964).

[7]   Richard L. Abel, *Transnational Law Practice*, 44 CASE W. RES. L. REV. 737, 834–836 (1994).

[8]   *Analysis of the Legal Profession and Law Firms* (as of 2007), Harv. L. Sch. Program on Legal Prof., http://www.law.harvard.edu/programs/plp/pages/statistics.php#wlw (last visited Nov. 7, 2011).

As firms get larger, the task of maintaining an adequate flow of business becomes more precarious, and firms become more prone to splitting up or failing. Firms are more vulnerable to defections by valued clients or by the lawyers to whom those clients are attached. Size multiplies the possibility of conflicts of interests, and the resulting tension between partners who tend old clients and those who propose new ones can often lead to a breakaway. Surrounded by other firms attempting to grow by attracting partners with special skills or desirable clients, firms are vulnerable to the loss of crucial assets.

Contemporaneous with the growth of big law firms, in-house corporate law departments grew in size, budget, functions, authority, and aggressiveness. This change has resulted in a marked increase in the portion of the corporation's routine legal work conducted in-house. The relation of corporate law departments to outside counsel has shifted from comprehensive and enduring retainer relationships toward less exclusive and more task-specific ad hoc engagements. In their relationship with outside law firms, today's enlarged corporate legal departments impose budgetary restraints, exert more control over cases, demand periodic reports, and engage in comparison shopping among firms.

At the same time that business clients retracted much routine work into their corporate law departments, they experienced a great surge of litigation and other risk-prone, high-stakes transactions. Suddenly, the corporate work of large outside firms shifted from its historic emphasis on office practice back toward the litigation from which the large firm had turned away in its infancy. The new aggressiveness of in-house counsel, the breakdown of retainer relationships, and the shift to discrete transactions have made conditions more competitive. The practice of law has become more openly commercial and profit-oriented, "more like a business." Firms rationalize their operations and engage professional managers and consultants; firm leaders worry about billable hours, profit centers, and marketing strategies. "Eat what you kill" compensation formulas emphasize rewards for productivity and business-getting over "equal shares" or seniority.

The need to find new business leads to aggressive marketing. Some firms take on marketing directors, a position unknown even in 1980. Others place increased emphasis on "rainmaking" by more of the firm's lawyers, providing those lawyers responsible for bringing in business with a new ascendency over their colleagues. [T]he time required for promotion to partner has lengthened, firms have become more highly leveraged—that is, the ratio of associates to partners has risen, and the chances of becoming a partner are perceived to have decreased.[9]

The following excerpt addresses how changes in the corporate legal services industry since the Golden Age have affected trust and loyalty among lawyers, as well as lifestyle concerns, within those institutions.

THE CHANGE AGENDA: TOURNAMENT WITHOUT END
Marc S. Galanter and William D. Henderson
American Lawyer, Dec. 1, 2008

Several key economic conditions of the so-called Golden Age no longer prevail. The bite of group opinion weakens with increased size, dispersion, and diversity; the power to sanction is undercut by mobility. A larger professional and public arena gives greater scope and incentive to express professional eminence in a monetary metric. As a result, large corporate law firms operate in an atmosphere of internal and external competition that has no historical antecedent. [There has been] a wide-scale adaptation to major structural changes in the marketplace, including the globalization of corporate clients, the bureaucratization of corporate legal departments, the lower cost and greater availability of information, and erosion of cohesive firm culture due to sheer size and geographic dispersion. But it is an adaptation that confers disproportionate power on the most single-minded pursuers of the bottom line.

This sea change is evident in the harried workplace endured by equity partners, who already hold the proverbial brass ring. [M]any of these partners would gladly trade a portion of their earnings for a shorter workweek, greater job security, more interesting work, the opportunity to mentor (or be mentored), do more pro bono work, or take a long, uninterrupted vacation. Yet, these aspirations are virtually impossible to negotiate when rainmaking partners located in multiple offices through the world are free to exit at any time with clients in tow. This outcome is dictated not by an absence of professional ideals but a widening and intractable collective action problem that undermines the requisite conditions for the embodiment of those ideals.

For the vast majority of modern large law firms, economics rather than culture are the glue that holds the firm together. Indeed, the distinguishing feature of the [prevailing culture of large law firms] is a constant focus on the real or imagined marginal product of each lawyer in the firm—associates, of counsel, sundry off-track attorneys, and equity

---

[9]   Marc S. Galanter & Thomas Palay, *Why the Big Get Bigger: The Promotion-to-Partner Tournament and the Growth of Large Law Firms*, 76 VA. L. REV. 747 (1990).

and non-equity partners. Although this system is remarkably effective at maximizing the financial return on (at least some) human capital, it simultaneously undermines or hinders other values cherished by the profession.

The contemporary market for corporate legal services bears little resemblance to the comfortable regional guilds of the 1950s, 1960s, and 1970s. For example, law firms often expand geographically so that important clients have the benefit of "one-stop shopping." Yet, staffing a financially self-sufficient branch office often relies upon the recruitment of lateral partners. According to our analysis of over 14,000 lawyers who lateraled into a corporate law partnership (mostly Am Law 200) between 2000 and 2005, a stunning 96.8 percent moved between offices in the same metropolitan area. As firms move into each other's backyards to better compete nationally and internationally, the competition for lateral talent plays out in a very localized way.

Geographic expansion carries cultural costs that most law firm managers have tended to underestimate. When a partnership encompasses several hundred lawyers in a dozen widely spaced offices pieced together by mergers and lateral hires, it is very difficult to sustain (much less create from whole cloth) an organizational ethos in which partners are willing to make sacrifices for the long-term welfare of the firm. Too few lawyers trust that they will be around (or kept around) to reap the larger rewards.

Many law firms may have inadvertently reached a tipping point that is triggered by innate human limitations. Drawing upon his research on primates, the British anthropologist and evolutionary biologist Robin Dunbar posited that "there is a cognitive limit to the number of individuals with whom any one person can maintain stable relationships, that this limit is a direct function of relative neocortex size, and that this in turn limits group size." For humans, the "Dunbar number" is 150.

How does a geographically dispersed law firm with 300 partners and 500 associates (most of whom avidly read the Above the Law blog) negotiate a more sustainable business model [and a more attractive lifestyle for lawyers working within large firms]? The economic power within the firm lies with potentially mobile rainmaking partners who are loath to subsidize the lifestyles of lower-earning colleagues whom they barely know.

NOTES ON CHANGES IN LARGE LAW FIRMS SINCE THE GOLDEN AGE

1. **What Changed and Why?** How have large law firms changed since the 1950s? What have been the major drivers of change?

2. ***Who Cares?*** Why should anyone other than the lawyers employed by large firms care about the more competitive atmosphere in these institutions? Are there any possible benefits or adverse consequences of those changes for clients? For the public?

3. ***Diversity.*** One of the major changes in large firms not captured in these excerpts is their increased diversity since the 1960s—the large influx into this sector by Jews, Catholics, women, and racial and ethnic minorities. The hiring practices that excluded these categories of lawyers have been abandoned. That is not to say, however, that the composition of lawyers in large law firms reflects the demographics of the profession as a whole. We will examine how women and racial, ethnic, and religious minorities have fared in large law firms very briefly in the next section and then again in Part VI.

C. THE INTERNAL LABOR MARKET: THE PROMOTION-TO-PARTNERSHIP TOURNAMENT

The following three excerpts explore the structure and internal labor markets of large law firms—why some lawyers join firms rather than operating as solo practitioners and how the promotion to partnership "tournament" in large firms works. The first excerpt describes the law firm as a mechanism for sharing human capital and the "promotion-to-partnership tournament" as a means of providing mutual assurances to partners and associates that their expectations will be met. The second excerpt critiques the notion that the tournament actually functions as the authors of the first article suggest. In particular, it challenges the idea that the promotion-to-partnership tournament operates in a completely meritocratic way to reward partnership to those who are most able. The third excerpt describes recent changes in large firms' personnel practices that have transformed a one-time tournament—for promotion to partnership—into something more closely resembling an unending competition. It explores how lawyers who join large law firms today face an ongoing struggle to retain clients and maintain their positions in the firms' hierarchies.

WHY THE BIG GET BIGGER: THE PROMOTION-TO-PARTNER TOURNAMENT AND THE GROWTH OF LARGE LAW FIRMS

Marc S. Galanter & Thomas M. Palay
76 Virginia Law Review 747 (1990)

To understand why attorneys organize their firms as they do, we must explain why they associate in the first place. Attorneys may enter into cooperative associations for various reasons, but we are interested in those combinations based upon an exchange of human capital for labor. An attorney, like any other producer, combines labor with the capital she has accumulated over time. Unlike an automobile manufacturer, most of a lawyer's capital consists of human assets. Her human capital combines four types of assets: her pre-law-school endowment of intelligence, skills, and general education; her legal education and experience-dependent skills; her professional reputation; and her relationships with her clients.

An attorney may find herself with surplus human capital as a result of the constraints on her personal supply of labor, which is ultimately fixed by the working hours in the day. Her reputation or expertise, for instance, may increase the demand for her services, but she simply does not have the additional hours to accept more work.

Imagine a sole practitioner, *P,* who has shareable surplus human capital. She would like to lend or rent these assets to *A,* an attorney with little human capital of his own, but a full complement of labor. For convenience, one can think of *P* as a "partner" and *A* as an "associate." *P* might contract with *A* to produce an output, using his labor and her capital, which one of them then would sell to a client. If *A* resells the product, typically he would pay *P* a "rent" equal, in theory, to the marginal product of the capital, keeping the remainder for himself both as a "wage" and as a return on his own assets. If *P* markets the product to the client, as is typically the case, she would pay *A* the marginal product of his labor and capital, retaining the remainder—minus overhead and other support costs—as compensation for her capital.

Contracting with anyone, even an attorney, while conceptually straightforward, often presents difficulties in practice. Assume for convenience that *P,* the lawyer with surplus capital, retains control over the output. The contract requires enforcement, monitoring, or adaptation as conditions change. We refer to the institutional arrangement for conducting these activities as a governance mechanism. Attorneys tend to use internal organization—the firm—to govern the sharing of their human capital.

In a world without transaction costs, there is no a priori reason a law firm must result from contracting among attorneys. We interact, however, in an economy replete with transaction costs. Parties to complex, long-term contracts, like those necessary to lend human capital, face a variety of impediments to smooth exchanges. The parties must create a governance structure to monitor behavior, to adapt the agreement to changed circumstances, and to ensure that the parties actually perform agreed-upon exchanges.

Long-term agreements render the parties vulnerable to the opportunistic conduct of their trading opposites. *P,* as the lender of human capital, has three potential concerns. First, *A* might "grab" assets *P* lends to him. For instance, *A* might depart with a client in tow. Second, the prospect of *A*'s prematurely "leaving," or at least threatening to leave, with firm-specific skills and information for which P has paid, but not amortized fully, may trouble P. While the investments are generally worthless to A if he leaves, P's inability to recover the unamortized portion of her investments in A makes her vulnerable to his departure. Third, A might "shirk," that is, either fail to make the expected (and already paid-for) human-capital investments that A must make to further P's interests, or fail to employ borrowed assets to their full potential, thereby depriving P of her expected returns.

A, too, has concerns about potential opportunistic conduct. He needs assurance that P will fairly compensate him for his labor and for any human capital he brings to or develops on P's behalf. Where part of A's compensation involves a possibility of promotion to an ownership interest in P's business, A also seeks assurance that if he meets implicit conditions, P actually will promote him. In theory, P should be able to devise a contract specifying that A will receive rewards based on his productivity. For the contract to be effective, however, both parties must be able to obtain inexpensive and reliable indicators of A's effort or output, or at a minimum, both parties must have identical information about A's productivity. Otherwise, both parties cannot verify compliance with the contract terms. But monitoring output in the provision of legal services to clients is difficult and costly.

Both sides, therefore, make increased expenditures ex ante to protect themselves against the possibility that the other party will attempt to exploit its ex post bargaining advantage. These expenditures take the form of governance mechanisms that are bilateral and unique to the parties. The firm in general (and the law firm in particular), is one such specialized governance structure.

First, to assure the partners that they will receive the proper return on the investments they make—whether those investments are in client relationships, reputation, or the skills they impart to associates—the firm must induce associates not to grab or leave prematurely. The firm wants to ensure that the associate has an incentive to remain with the firm until it fully amortizes those investments. Deferring payment of some percentage of the associate's salary creates part of that incentive. Those who do not steal or leave prematurely receive the deferred salary in varying forms of promotion and bonuses.

While deferred compensation partially alleviates problems related to grabbing and leaving, partners still must find some method of motivating associates not to shirk. To provide both the necessary assurances and incentives for maximum effort, the big law firm typically ties the payment of its deferred bonus to the outcome of what we call the "promotion-to-partner tournament." For a fixed period of time (six to ten years), the firm pays salaries to associates who neither grab nor leave. At each successive stage in the hierarchy part of the associate's salary increase includes a deferred bonus for non-opportunistic behavior in the earlier years. In addition, during this period the firm implicitly tells its associates that it constantly evaluates them for a "super-bonus," paid in the form of promotion to partner. The firm evaluates associates on their production of two goods important to the firm's future welfare: high quality legal work and their own human capital. An associate's final standing in the tournament, measured subjectively not mechanistically, therefore will depend upon the size and quality of his "bundle" of both goods. After the fixed period of time has expired, the firm ranks the players in a particular class and declares the top [X] percent the winners.

NOTES ON GALANTER & PALAY

1. ***What Is the Promotion-to-Partnership Tournament?*** What are the essential features of the promotion-to-partnership tournament as described by Galanter & Palay? How does it work? What problems does it solve?

2. ***Is Large Firm Growth Inevitable?*** In parts of this article not included here, the authors asserted that their tournament theory explained why large firms have grown since the 1970s (thus the title of the piece, "Why the Big Get Bigger"). They suggested that continued expansion of large firms was an inevitable by-product of the promotion-to-partnership tournament— that because firms need to commit to granting a fixed number of partnerships in order to ensure that associates will work hard and not "shirk" or leave, they have an internal "growth engine." Critics argued that this theory paid too little attention to the relationship between firm growth and the market for corporate legal services; if demand for corporate legal services falls, law firms cannot continue to add and promote associates at a steady or growing rate. The authors have since revised their theory to acknowledge the importance of business cycles and their relationship to large firms' hiring and promotion practices.[10]

* * *

The following article by Professors Wilkins and Gulati challenges the notion that the promotion-to-partner tournament operates meritocratically to reward the best attorneys with partnerships.

---

[10] Marc Galanter & William Henderson, *The Elastic Tournament: A Second Transformation of the Big Law Firm*, 60 STAN. L. REV. 1867 (2008).

RECONCEIVING THE TOURNAMENT OF LAWYERS: TRACKING, SEEDING, AND INFORMATION CONTROL IN THE INTERNAL LABOR MARKETS OF ELITE LAW FIRMS

David B. Wilkins & G. Mitu Gulati
84 Virginia Law Review 1581 (1998)

A plausible model of the internal labor markets of elite firms must account for the fact that these institutions must resolve two separate, albeit interrelated, problems: monitoring and training. We argue that firms have responded to this dual challenge by adopting a complex incentive system designed to motivate every associate to work hard with relatively little supervision, while at the same time ensuring that the firm has a sufficient number of trained associates to satisfy its staffing and partnership needs. The promotion-to-partner tournament is one, but only one, part of this complex system. Instead, law firms employ a multiple incentive system that, paradoxically, incorporates practices typically found in the kind of "real" tournaments upon which tournament theory is loosely based but that are not included in the standard economic model. Contrary to standard economic theory, lawyers in these institutions compete in a "multi-round" tournament, which includes practices such as "tracking," "seeding," and "information control" typically found in sporting events and other kinds of formal competitions.

Not Everyone Is Competing. It is impossible to spend time talking to law students about their career goals without coming to the conclusion that many of the young women and men who join large law firms have no intention of staying long enough to become partners. The fact that some significant percentage of entering associates do not see themselves as participating in the tournament creates two important problems for firms. First, firms must find other ways to motivate those associates who do not intend to compete in the race to make partner. Second, firms must develop ways of identifying those associates who are interested in winning the tournament.

The Playing Field Is Not Level. Large law firms produce two categories of work that must be done by associates. The first category consists of work that provides valuable training in the skills and dispositions of lawyering. Training work also enables an associate to develop strong relationships with particular partners. This relational capital is crucial to an associate's partnership chances. Associates depend on their partner-mentors to give them good work (and to protect them from bad assignments), to pass on important client relationships, and ultimately to push for their promotion among their fellow partners. Without strong advocates in the partnership, an associate's chances of winning the tournament are substantially diminished.

[Large law firms also] produce a substantial amount of "paperwork." Examples of paperwork range from writing, answering, and supervising discovery requests, to proofreading and making slight modifications to pre-existing corporate documents, to writing legal memos to the file or for review by senior associates, to faxing important documents to the client. Paperwork is unlikely to develop the kind of higher order skills and judgment that partners look for when evaluating associates for partnership. Nor does this work typically result in an associate developing relational capital, since partners rarely have much contact with those who are only doing paperwork and tend to notice these unlucky associates only when something goes wrong.

Individual Umpires Have a Stake in Who Wins the Tournament. Partners are players with vested interests, as opposed to neutral decision-makers, because partnership no longer means tenure. With tenure and lockstep compensation, existing partners face relatively few threats to their privileged positions. This security, in theory, frees partners from self-interest and enables them to vote to promote the best qualified associates. When one takes away tenure and makes compensation variable, partners inevitably begin asking questions such as: "If we make this person partner, will he someday vote to have my compensation reduced, or worse, to have me fired?" As such, individual partners are likely to have interests that are at least in tension, and potentially at odds, with the interests of the firm as a whole.

[P]artners have an incentive to ration time spent on training and to invest only in those associates who are most likely to provide direct benefit to their practices (i.e., the one or two associates for whom an individual partner can provide a steady stream of billable assignments). Individual partners have strong incentives to favor their own protégés over the arguably better qualified protégés of others. In the early years, senior partners need junior partners who will do their work (without trying to steal their clients) while the senior lawyers go out to look for additional business. In later years, senior partners depend on their protégés to support them when the senior lawyers are no longer able to protect their own interests in the partnership. Given these realities, we should expect tournament winners to be selected as much on the basis of politics as on firm efficiency.

Choosing the Best Representatives, Not the Best Performers. In the standard tournament model, winners are selected solely on the basis of their past contributions to the firm. This selection criterion makes sense because the point of the tournament is to induce employees to exert high levels of effort and care at their current jobs by promising that those who perform the best will be rewarded in the future. In order for this commitment to be credible, however, the firm must clearly signal that tournament rewards will be given on the basis of past performance and not on the basis of the firm's prediction about future performance in the higher level job. [B]ut at the time the firm chooses tournament winners, it has already acquired all the benefits of the employee's work during the probationary period. As a result, it has the incentive to award tournament prizes on the basis of what is in the firm's best interest in the future, to wit, selecting employees that the firm believes will perform better at the higher level job regardless of how these employees performed as juniors. From the associate's perspective, the fact that partnership is more of a prediction about the future than a reward for past service makes it difficult to evaluate the fairness of the firm's partnership choices.

Who's on First? Galanter and Palay assert that the promotion-to-partner tournament solves the mutual monitoring problems of associates and partners by making the rules of the game visible to all parties. If firms were structured as simple economic tournaments, one would expect to see firms do everything possible to make the partnership process an open book so that associates (and law students) could see that the process was indeed a fair one in which those who performed best were promoted.

[P]artnership decisions at these firms are explicitly structured to be a black box, i.e., to provide as little external visibility as possible. Associates have little or no information about what goes on at partnership or committee meetings, and the partnerships at these firms do not see disclosing the details of these meetings as a way to increase efficiency.

The Tournament Reconceived: Why This Is Not Your Father's Partnership Tournament. There is one group of associates for whom the prospect of making partner is their primary motivation: senior associates in their last few years before partnership. With respect to these lawyers, there does appear to be a tournament at work. Several aspects of the competition among senior associates resemble the assumptions underlying standard tournament theory. First, given that associates rationally believe that their lateral job prospects diminish in the few years before partnership (on the assumption that they are leaving because they are not "good enough" to make partner), associates without a strong commitment to winning the tournament are likely to leave before they get to this stage. Moreover, by year six or seven, a senior associate has invested heavily in developing firm-specific human capital, an investment that is not fully reflected in his or her current compensation. The only way to recoup this investment fully is to win the jump in compensation that comes with winning the partnership prize. Finally, senior associates know that there are only a finite number of partnership slots; a number, in most cases, that is smaller than the number of senior associates remaining in the pool, and that will vary depending on the state of the market for legal services at the time the partnership decision is made. Senior associates have, in all likelihood, developed significant amounts of both human and relational capital, and are therefore competing on a roughly level playing field. Each of these contestants has also acquired at least one important partner-mentor who, because she has invested in the associate's training, has a strong incentive to monitor other partners to ensure that her protégé associate is treated fairly in the evaluation process.

These conditions, i.e., closely matched contestants [and] assurances of fairness mirror those present in sports settings and other contests that are structured as tournaments. Under these conditions, a tournament structure may efficiently induce extra effort by contestants (in this case, senior associates) in the last stages of the competition.

The fact that senior associates, at this final stage, are locked in a competition that resembles a tournament, however, does not mean that junior associates are participating in a similar structure. [I]t is in the best interest of these institutions if these scarce goods end up being concentrated in the small pool of senior associates from which the firm will ultimately make its selection.

Tracking. Firms create a multi-round tournament by the manner in which they distribute and evaluate training work. Associates who do well on their initial training assignments are given preferential access to additional training opportunities. Those junior associates who successfully complete a number of such assignments move up to become senior associates, giving them even greater access to training opportunities, and, equally important, helping them build strong relationships with partners. [O]nce associates are firmly on the training track, they are likely to be further protected in the evaluation process.

Through tracking, firms strengthen the commitments of associates whom they want to stay. Associates who continue to get good work are more likely to be happy and to stay at the firm. At the same time, those associates who consistently receive only paperwork are likely to realize that their partnership chances are limited and leave voluntarily (as soon as they have earned enough money or obtained enough general training for an in-house or other job). Firms benefit from these "voluntary" departures in two ways. First, at a human level, firing someone is not easy. Second, at the institutional level, "voluntary" departures make it easier for firms to tell both remaining associates and law students that the odds for those who "really want" to become partners are substantially better than the naked statistics showing the percentage of each entering class that actually obtains this goal would lead one to believe.

Seeding: Theoretically, firms could rely exclusively on [tracking associates in multiple rounds of competition] before deciding which associates to put on the training track. This process, however, is not what we observe. Instead, some associates are "seeded" directly onto the training track. These favored associates immediately get assigned projects with the potential for creating high levels of firm-specific and relational capital, e.g., assignments with lots of client and partner contact.

The project assignment process at law firms resembles the seeding model. Many—perhaps most—associates obtain their initial work assignments on the basis of some combination of their expressed preferences and random selection. There are other associates, however, whose fortunes are left less to chance. Law firms have an incentive to protect those recruits whom the firm believes to be especially valuable. If initial assignments are left to chance, a highly prized associate—for example, a former Supreme Court clerk—might get discouraged and leave the firm (or stop investing in winning the tournament) because he receives a bad initial assignment or believes that in order to succeed, he must outperform all of the other associates in his class. One way to prevent this from happening is to seed the especially valuable candidates by giving them immediate access to the training track.

Although firms have the same incentives as U.S. Open officials to protect their best players, firms have considerably less information than tennis officials to develop their initial rankings. [B]ecause the elite firms hire new associates who have never practiced law, these institutions must base their initial rankings largely on predictions based on the associate's law school, clerkship, law review membership, and law school performance. These easily observable signals only loosely correlate with actual lawyering skills. [T]he best students do not always make the best associates, let alone the best partners. Although firms could uncover more detailed information about potential candidates—for example, by conducting in-depth substantive interviews, calling law professors, or closely analyzing a candidate's writing skills—collecting this kind of additional information is expensive and the results are difficult to evaluate. Despite the low correlation between the signals used by firms to seed and the skills needed to be either an associate or a partner, firms still have an incentive to use these signals to seed associates. Regardless of whether they have a high correlation with job skills, signals such as law school status and grades are both "visible" and "rankable" to two communities that are of pivotal importance to elite firms: clients and law students.

Information Management. Tournament theory assumes that it is in the firm's interest to make the rules of the game transparent to all concerned. However, it is clear that firms have strong incentives to manage the flow of information to associates and law students in order to maximize the system's overall incentive effects.

Information management systems exist in some tournaments. For example, in certain debate tournaments, teams are not told whether they have won or lost their preliminary rounds until after all of these rounds have been completed. Similarly, until recently, in soccer only the referee knew exactly how much time was left in the game. By withholding this information, tournament officials hope to induce maximum effort by all participants. Elite firms utilize a similar information control policy. [F]irms pursue a "black box" approach in which associates are provided only a vague idea about the criteria for making partner and almost no information about how these criteria are applied in particular cases. Notwithstanding the fact that junior associates are formally reviewed at least once a year, most of these lawyers have relatively little information about their partnership chances. Moreover, to the extent that associates are told about their own performance, they are rarely given information about the performance of their peers. [F]irms tend to keep the evaluations of associates in their first few years vague and generally upbeat.

NOTES ON WILKINS & GULATI

1.   *Partners' Incentives.* According to Wilkins and Gulati, how do the incentives of law firm partners differ from partners' incentives as described in Galanter & Palay's account of the promotion-to-partnership tournament?

2.   *Tracking, Seeding and Information Control.* According to Wilkins and Gulati, how "tracking," "seeding," and "information control" affect the careers of associates in large law firms?

3.   *Who Wins and Who Loses?* If Wilkins and Gulati are correct about how the promotion to partnership tournament actually works in most large law firms, what are the implications for who wins and who loses?

4.   *Why Elite?* In this article, Wilkins & Gulati use the terms "large law firm" and "elite law firm" interchangeably. One sees a similar equation of size and eliteness in some other materials on the legal profession.[11] Why do you suppose many lawyers and commentators associate large firms with elite practice? What does elite mean in this context?

* * *

The following article describes changes in hiring and promotion practices in large law firms since 1990, when Galanter & Palay's "promotion-to-partnership tournament" article was published. It explains how the structure of firms has changed, from the inverted funnel shape of early firms (with large numbers of associates channeled through to the partnership decision,

---

[11] *See, e.g.,* Derek Muller, *Ranking of Law Schools By Elite Employment Outcomes,* available at http://excessofdemocracy.com/blog/2013/12/ranking-law-schools-by-elite-employment-outcomes (defining elite employment to mean jobs in firms of one hundred or more and federal court clerkships); Above the Law, *Quality Jobs Score,* available at http://abovethelaw.com/careers/2014-law-school-rankings/#methodology (defining "quality jobs" as positions with the largest 250 firms and federal court clerkships).

after which partners remained until they died or retired), to a "core and mantle" structure, in which a core of owner-partners ("equity partners") is surrounded by a much larger mantle of employed lawyers. The mantle includes not only associates who aspire to become partners, but also non-equity partners, who do not share in the firm's profits, and other salaried lawyers.

THE CHANGE AGENDA: TOURNAMENT WITHOUT END

Marc S. Galanter and William D. Henderson
American Lawyer, Dec. 1, 2008

Over the last three decades, most large law firms have modified the tournament structure in a number of ways. The typical result is a firm that bears a funhouse mirror resemblance to the inverted funnel of the classical tournament firm. We refer to this new model as the "core and mantle" firm. There is a now an inner core of equity partners swathed in an outer mantle made up of senior nonpartners under an array of titles, such as nonequity partner, of counsel, special counsel, staff attorney, senior attorney, and permanent associate. In recent years, the mantle appears to be growing much faster than the core. For example, in fiscal year 2007, the number of equity partners working for Am Law 200 firms grew by 2.2 percent (26,949 to 27,550), while the nonequity partner ranks grew by 10.2 percent (13,608 to 14,995).

The core and mantle model accommodates heavy lateral traffic between competing law firms. In a complete turnabout from the mid-century "Golden Age," lateral movement between firms is now routine. According to our analysis of data assembled by American Lawyer research, between 2000 and 2005 over 13,000 lateral partners joined, left, or moved between Am Law 200 firms.

Within the firm, lawyers work longer to make equity partner; thereafter, they work in the shadow of possible de-equitization.* Thus, the key feature of the core and mantle model is perpetual competition within the law firm to achieve, enlarge, and maintain one's equity status. In other words, the promotion-to-partnership tournament has been transformed into a perpetual tournament. The only finish line is retirement or death.

NOTES ON GALANTER & HENDERSON

1.   **Core and Mantle.** What changes in the structure of large law firms do Galanter & Henderson describe? What are the changes in personnel

---

*   [Eds.] De-equitization is a process by which an equity partner, who is a part owner of the equity of the law firm, is involuntarily divested of his/her ownership interest and becomes instead an employee of the firm.

practices that correspond with a shift in large firm structure over the past three decades from an inverted funnel to a core and mantle?

    2.   ***Implications for Lawyers' Careers?*** If Galanter and Henderson have accurately described the structure of today's large firms, what are the implications of that structure for the careers of large firm lawyers?

    3.   ***Firm Culture.*** If Galanter & Henderson are right that "perpetual competition" is the "key feature of the core and mantle model," how would you expect that unending competition to affect the internal culture of large firms?

D. THE EXPERIENCE OF LARGE FIRM ASSOCIATES

This following article explores the experiences and expectations of young lawyers in large firms and the characteristics of those who stay long enough to be considered for partnership.

EXPLORING INEQUALITY IN THE CORPORATE LAW FIRM APPRENTICESHIP: DOING THE TIME, FINDING THE LOVE

Bryant G. Garth and Joyce Sterling
22 Georgetown Journal of Legal Ethics 1361 (2009)

This article began as an investigation into the reasons that women and minorities seem disproportionately not to "fit" in large law firm settings and stay on to become partners. Its goal was to add a qualitative component to the raw data collected as part of the After the J.D. Project. Drawing on more than sixty-six interviews with lawyers in their third to sixth years of private practice, our particular aim was to see what factors contribute to the persistence of the inequalities that commentators expected to disappear long ago. On the basis of the interviews, we can indeed point to a number of examples demonstrating a lack of fit from the perspective of lawyers beginning their careers. The story suggested by the interviews, however, is more complex.

Our findings and approach in this article can be introduced through the career of a lawyer who at the time of the interview was five years into the partnership track of a leading Washington, D.C. litigation firm. Now, according to his firm's web site, he is a partner. Although the first in his family to attend college, and with a capacity for hard work that may have stemmed from that social position, he came from a solid middle class background and attended elite post-secondary schools capped by a federal clerkship. He began his career as a practitioner at the firm, and he reported three years ago that "I never thought I would be a big firm lawyer." He had expected instead to "burn out quickly." He liked the people in the firm, however—"the best part of the job is the people I work with." He also found strong mentors who advised and helped him, for example, to "try a case in [a particular] area." He did flirt with the law teaching market but did not find a suitable position. In short, he was not at all wedded to the large law firm or particularly focused on partnership. The main reason he was still there, he reported, was that, "nothing has driven me away." He had no children at the time of the interview, and his wife was a governmental attorney well acquainted with the work regime of a large law firm. He carefully noted, in addition, that he and his wife made sure that they were not "locked into" the big firm lifestyle of the high roller. Nevertheless, he stayed at the firm. From his perspective, he did not participate and compete in a seven or eight year "tournament of lawyers" seeking partnership. Instead, he did his apprenticeship and almost by accident ended up as a partner.

The story provides support for two complementary but also potentially competing narratives about the path of associates in large law firms. The relationship between the narratives is complex. One is the narrative of the path from associates to partners. From the perspective of the example just given, the accident that favored the partnership move depended on a number of factors that are not randomly distributed in the lawyer population. These factors, not surprisingly, tend to favor men over women, whites over minorities, and elite graduates over non-elite graduates. Minorities and women are not likely to survive the attrition process so essential to the corporate law firm partnership system.

This narrative recognizes that lawyers starting careers in corporate law firms need to find ways to put in very long hours for a substantial period of years. There are two key elements of that survival. One element is "finding the love" or support necessary to successfully fulfill the obligations of the apprenticeship. Put simply, they are more likely to be able to continue the work if they get support from others inside and outside of the firm—including junior and senior associates and partners. The other aspect of "finding the love" emerges from supportive spouses, family, and peers. One problem with the situation of minorities and women in large law firms is that these firms were built by and for white males with wives at home. Those who do not blend in terms of ethnicity, race, and gender face one set of obstacles; those without home support face another. Success comes most easily to those who feel welcome and comfortable at work and have a warm and supportive home outside of work.

The second element necessary to a successful corporate apprenticeship is "doing the time." Lawyers starting their careers in corporate law firms need to find ways to put in very long hours for a substantial period of time. "Doing the time" requires the patience and commitment to put in the time necessary to compete for and attain partnership. "Doing the time" may require lawyers to work weekends, spend late nights, and travel on assignments. In an earlier article, one of the current authors suggested that the law firm as currently organized fits Lewis Coser's definition of a "greedy institution." A greedy institution makes total claims on its members. Large corporate law firms command total loyalty and commitment and implicitly assume that lawyers will have someone at home to care for the personal aspects of life.

The second narrative is about the reproduction of the legal elite and more generally social class in the United States. Historically, the lawyers who gained the prestigious partnership positions were from the most elite law schools, which historically and currently draw mainly from relatively advantaged social groups. Individuals who gained entry into the leading law schools would join the ranks of the associates at the large corporate law firms, and out of that pool would come a new generation of partners. Those who did not become partners would be placed at boutique firms or would become in-house counsel of businesses with strong relationships with the particular corporate firms. In this manner a network of lawyers from similar backgrounds and schools secured the leading legal positions in the corporate law firms and the businesses with which they dealt. The status of the positions was reinforced partly by relatively high salaries, but also by the fact that they were occupied by individuals validated with degrees from the most prestigious schools.

Our interviews, we shall see, suggest a potential disconnect in the story of the reproduction of the elite dominated by the most prestigious law schools. The corporate law firms now hire associates from a much wider pool of law schools than in the past. A disproportionately large portion of the associates come from the most prestigious schools, but many other schools with students from relatively less advantaged backgrounds are also represented. One might posit that those who become partner will naturally tend to come from the most elite schools, partly because of the relative numbers, partly because they presumably have more talent as represented by their undergraduate grades and LSATs, and partly because they will be likely to fit in with the existing partners with similar backgrounds.

We will suggest, however, that the corporate law firm apprenticeship is increasingly becoming disconnected from the competition for partnership. In particular, the preliminary evidence suggests that the most elite law graduates will translate the prestige that comes from three or so years at a corporate law firm into a highly valued position *elsewhere* in the legal profession or business world. They will not stay around to build the bonds that might pull them into the partnership ranks.

This second narrative, therefore, co-exists unevenly with the first one. Women and minorities who were long excluded from the elite partnership positions at the corporate law firms continue to be unlikely to stay and make their way to a partnership position. But those who used to dominate the corporate law firm partnerships may also be unlikely to stay. It is certainly possible that existing partners could find some way to recruit a new generation from among the most prestigious schools—at least, as our example suggests, from those who are among the hungrier graduates at those schools. But it also appears that the emerging pattern for the most prestigious law graduates is to leave before playing the game for partnership. Our data suggest that those from the less prestigious schools and the less advantaged social backgrounds may take a disproportionate number of the corporate law partnerships.

To compare the two narratives, the corporate law firm apprenticeship may reproduce privilege *in the legal profession* as those who go through it move into prestigious and powerful positions that are mostly outside the corporate law firms, but the corporate law firms themselves may be losing some of their ability to reproduce the elite credentials of their traditional partnership stock. This outcome may not be a problem, and indeed it may be a welcome development. The problem, or more precisely the contradiction, is that the corporate law firms have historically used the prestige value of their partners' law degrees as a key aspect of their credibility as leaders of the profession and the provision of professional services.

I. <u>The Large Law Firm Apprenticeship</u>. Many beginning lawyers experience their work in a corporate law firm as an apprenticeship expected to last three years or so. Law students in elite settings are socialized to believe that the appropriate way to begin their careers as lawyers is to work very hard for a decent period of time at a large law firm. One self-assured lawyer contemplating moving into the government stated, for example, that he was "looking" for a new position since he had "done the three year thing at a firm." Another lawyer noted specifically that, "Being an associate is like being a resident. You do it for five years and then you think about your life." An Hispanic lawyer with South American roots working in a major Chicago firm stated simply, "OK well you know . . . let's take a stab at [the corporate law firm]," but not with the "goal of I'm going to be a partner." It is, in the words of another, "a stamp on the early portion of your career."

It is of course hard work, but, according to a lawyer who departed a top New York City firm after doing the apprenticeship, it is something that ought to be done at this stage of the career. Even though he "worked all those hours . . . for the first three years," he suggested, "you know three years is not a long time in your life." As many others, he was prepared to give up those years.

The process of socialization toward the apprenticeship in corporate law firms has been traced in studies of law schools, including popular works and works by social scientists. Sometimes the findings are presented as if there is some concerted effort within the law schools to move idealistic legal talent toward the service of large corporations, but it is more accurate to say that law students learn by many routes that there are hierarchies in the legal profession just as there are hierarchies in law schools, and that the "right" way to continue on the fast track is to start at a large corporate law firm. As Christa McGill showed in her research into cultural aspects of different law schools, the socialization process varies according to the eliteness of the school and its perceived institutional mission. Those lacking the opportunity to work in corporate law firms are likely also not to understand why anyone would want to put in those hours working for corporations for three years—no matter the potential compensation. One of our interviewees from a school where it would be very difficult to gain access to an elite corporate firm said that, "I had originally thought I wanted to go with a large law firm. . . . [but] I realized it was not a good fit . . . I wanted to enjoy having a life outside of the law. The law is not my life." In addition to the lawyers at the relatively elite schools, it is not unusual for pockets of students at non-elite schools, such as, for example, the members of the Law Review, to adopt the very same feeling about the importance of securing an apprenticeship in a large corporate law firm. They sustain each other in the assumption that their status in law school means they ought to do the corporate law apprenticeship.

This period of at least the first two or three years tends not to promote much planning or reflection among the lawyers. It is striking how many of the new corporate lawyers asked about their plans for the future made remarks that suggested a relative lack of planning. A lawyer five years into a large D.C. firm says, "I haven't" any plans. Another at a prestigious L.A. law firm says simply that he is "not very goal-oriented." A lawyer at a major Chicago firm said that he is "not a big goal setter or planner." A woman at a large firm also in L.A. said about her short term goals: "I have no clue." She planned to be an associate for four or five years, not do anything "wrong" to preclude partnership, but also certainly not focus on partnership. A male associate at one of the most prestigious D.C. firms said about his future: "[I have] some vague ideas, but I wouldn't say any concrete goals."

Instead of planning for the future, these lawyers tend to take on faith that what they are doing will serve them well in whatever they do. Relatively few of the interviewees even commented on the importance of their apprenticeship in the corporate law firm. Those who commented certainly understood that the apprenticeship was part of what most considered the fast-track for legal careers. One lawyer without elite credentials who found a spot at a large Chicago firm did see what she had achieved: "everything I can learn here helps me here and would also help [me] anywhere else." Another referred to future "avenues of employment" opened by the corporate law firm apprenticeship. As stated by an Asian graduate in San Francisco, "they always tell you in law school, go to the highest point and then you can always go down." A lawyer from a non-elite school who found himself in a position a year into practice at a small firm taken over by a major national firm, decided to move and was able to secure a position at a top New York firm. He reported that he made his choice of firms because, "I figured it would be a good, gold star to have on my resume for a few years."

That faith in the utility of the apprenticeship allows lawyers to work very hard, doing work that is often drudgery. An elite law graduate at one of the most prestigious Wall Street firms noted that he worked until 8:30 or 9:00 most nights, but he also might work until midnight in a particular week in addition to a typical four or five hours on Sunday. He stated that he was, "willing to make the sacrifices to [his] personal life" and that the associates all built a norm of strenuous work. He said that the "associates know who's working hard and who's not working hard," and that he did not want to be a "slacker." A similar but more upbeat characterization of the hours by a Wall Street associate was, "when I was single it was just like, it was kind of fun." According to an Asian woman from a large urban law school working at a large San Francisco firm, "I kind of know my job is to make life easy for partners," and "because I'm a younger associate I want to get in as many hours as I can . . . to prove myself." An associate racking up prodigious hours for a leading D.C. firm said, "It's up to you to make it interesting perhaps or to perhaps work harder at it."

It took an Arab-American with a top law degree a while to recognize the reality and adapt: "My first year I hated it a lot," he reported, and "I never knew what time I could go home." He came "to appreciate that it's part of the job" stating, "Oh, yeah, okay, so this is my job, so deal with it." A woman doing real estate at an elite Los Angeles firm stated simply, "My job is a lowly job of sifting documents around and reviewing them," but she characterized the work as "fun." Associates in litigation similarly celebrate very small achievements. For example, a Chicago lawyer stated that, "overall I've been extremely happy here . . . learning to litigate," referring to participation in client contact depositions and relatively simple hearings in some smaller cases that the firm had. A less sanguine interpretation of an early litigation apprenticeship by a woman in the Silicon Valley was that she "basically spent a year reviewing documents" and writing some research memos.

Many others in litigation noted the satisfaction they get from pro bono representation. A lawyer at one of the top Los Angeles firms stated that, "you get to run the case on your own, and you get to court." A similarly positioned African-American D.C. lawyer highlighted the "real litigation experience" that comes from pro bono as contrasted with the regular work of associates. One Asian woman in a litigation-oriented firm in Los Angeles even asserted that she consciously did considerable pro bono representation in order "to get trial experience." The large law firms provide good pro bono opportunities that can ameliorate the drudgery, provide client contact, and build skills, especially in litigation. It is interesting, however, to contrast the observations of those in less prestigious litigation settings. In those settings the lawyers are really seeing action in trials by sitting as first or second chair.

Among those in the corporate law firms, in short, we find a very common identity and perspective. It is found in essential respects across the board among the different racial and ethnic groups and among men and women. They are putting in the time, building their resume, and learning some skills along with a large dose of drudgery. Few expect to stay and become partner. The general attitude toward partnership, however, is more complex than a simple plan and expectation to leave. Statements from respondents suggest a vague openness to partnership, such as the tentative expression by a woman at a large Chicago firm that she "thinks" she could go for partner. A lawyer at a prestigious D.C. firm admits likewise that his "assessment of partnership prospects" is relevant to his decision whether to leave the firm. The lawyer discussed in the beginning of this article, we discovered through a computer search, had indeed made partner. It may be recalled that he had expected to "burn out quickly," but apparently, he had enough openness to accept the partnership when it was offered. A recently named partner of a national firm in its New York City office intimated when we interviewed him that partnership would be a nice accomplishment, but he also talked of moving to a smaller firm closer to where he lived because, "It's not worth it if I miss my kid growing up." Apparently he has also been caught up by the lure of "the brass ring."

II. The Mutual Support Structure for Associates. We have seen how associates enact the role that they picked up in law school. They put in the time and do the work to get through the corporate law firm apprenticeship. There are factors that emerge from the interviews that help that survival process.

One key aspect of support for the corporate law firm apprenticeship is simply the fact of classmates and friends working in the same situation. When an entire cohort is in the same situation, it makes more sense to the participants. A woman with a degree from an elite law school working in a large L.A. firm stated, for example, "most of my friends work as hard as I do." An African American at a large Chicago firm stated similarly that "all your friends are working too." A woman working in New York City whose husband was also a lawyer said, "I would meet my friends for drinks or dinner at ten" and that her "husband did the same thing." This peer impact could also occur within a firm, for example, the D.C. lawyer who reported five to seven close friends within his peer group at the firm, and a New York City lawyer who has "three or four" associates "that spend a lot of time talking about these issues" of careers.

There is a natural progression that leads to the almost inevitable departure of associates after three years or so. They sense that they have served their apprenticeship. They are both reminded and encouraged to move by the steady departures they witness among their cohort at the firm, their classmates, and their friends. These departures also shrink the support that helped to sustain them through the long hours and late evenings that are typical of associates' lives. The expected time horizon ends and much of the support structure collapses. The question then becomes which of the lawyers socialized to do the large law firm apprenticeship and move on will be the "outliers" who stay for the partnership tournament.

Those who stay around past three or four years tend to go against what seems to be the normal pattern of attrition. We see that the partnership tournament in some form may then engulf those who remain. But the "tournament" looks very different if we ask the most important question, which is who in these firms will be in a position to be one of the few survivors that turns his or her attention to partnership.

We have presented the self-reinforcing process that leads so many talented law graduates both to enter corporate practice and to move out prior to serious consideration for partnership. We know from the results of the process that women and minorities tend not to be there at the time of that serious consideration. They are disproportionately underrepresented in the partnership ranks despite what are often relatively positive numbers in the ranks of the beginning associates. Surveys from American Lawyer Media and NALP constantly reinforce the fact that women are hired as associates in the top firms, with 250 people and over, in equal proportions to their male counterparts. However, the proportion of partners that are women or minorities has remained stagnant for almost two decades.

Reproducing Elite? A Post-Script. We noted at the outset that corporate law firms were not only white male and protestant organizations, but they also were dominated by graduates of the most elite schools. Graduates of the most elite schools still start their careers at large law firms, especially the most prominent and profitable ones, in higher percentages than do graduates of other schools. Graduates of elite schools, in addition, are more likely to come from privileged backgrounds than are graduates from schools lower in the law school pecking order.

It is more difficult from our interviews to see how the relatively privileged fare in terms of attrition. Will the law firms, we asked earlier, find ways to ensure that enough of the graduates of the most elite schools will stay around for the partnership competition to ensure that they will keep what they might believe is a critical mass of such graduates and the symbolic value that comes from that presence? If so, does that mean both that the most elite graduates and those with the most privileged backgrounds who tend to graduate from those schools will disproportionately stay through the apprenticeship and beyond? It could be that more of their friends sustain them for longer, for example, or that they more easily form the kinds of relationships—marrying the firm—conducive to partnership.

Our qualitative data are inconclusive, but there are some hints that large law firm success in terms of partnership may not favor the privileged. Those from privilege may not feel the attraction of staying on the path to potential partnership, especially as the time to partnership continues to grow, and they also have a sense that they will land on their feet if they change positions. They are likely to be less hungry perhaps than those who fought their way into the corporate law firms. The partnership is also less attractive since it no longer is a ticket to a somewhat less-pressured elite status. Any impact from this unwillingness to stay in the apprenticeship would be compounded by the fact that the most elite law graduates are likely to work initially at the firms with the lowest partnership rates and accordingly the most demanding and stressful working conditions.

There is some evidence that the associates in our interview pool who stay late in their apprenticeship and potentially could become partners are those from relatively less privileged backgrounds and typically not the most elite schools. Those who are hungriest and who fought their way into large law firms are perhaps more averse to leaving and more willing to do what it takes to position themselves for the prestige and economic reward that goes with partnership. They may also have spouses or family that share that hunger. [Our interviews provide] some support for the idea that those who come up through the ranks will not only be disproportionately male and white, but also disproportionately from among the relatively less privileged among those law graduates able to enter these firms.

NOTES ON GARTH & STERLING

1. **Who Stays and Leaves?** This research tends to confirm to Wilkins & Gulati's observation, based on anecdotal evidence, that "not everyone is competing" in the promotion to partnership tournament. What does this research suggest about the characteristics of those who drop out and those who stay to compete?

2. **The Large Firm Apprenticeship.** According to Garth & Sterling's account, what do associates believe they gain through an apprenticeship in a large law firm? Why, according to this account, do many associates with elite credentials leave before being considered for promotion to partnership? Why

would associates who seem well-positioned to achieve partnership decide to leave after just a few years?

3. ***Implications for Large Law Firm Recruiting.*** The authors note that large law firms currently sit "at the top of the professional hierarchy"? (Recall that Heinz & Laumann's findings were consistent with this claim.) If large firms lose their ability to attract elite law graduates, are they likely to remain at the top of the profession's prestige hierarchy? Do you think they already have begun to lose ground?

E. WHO IS THE CLIENT OF A CORPORATE LAWYER?

The following excerpt explores how "who is the client?" questions arise for lawyers who represent corporations—the client type most common for lawyers in large law firms. It explores why corporate lawyers sometimes may find it difficult to act on the knowledge that the corporation, rather than any of its constituents, is the lawyer's client.

WHO IS THE CLIENT? THE CORPORATE LAWYER'S DILEMMA
Ralph Jonas
39 Hastings Law Journal 617 (1988)

It is axiomatic that a corporation is a distinct, discrete legal entity that exists separate and apart from its officers, agents, directors, and shareholders. It is almost equally axiomatic that a lawyer who is retained to represent a corporation owes his allegiance solely to that legal entity, and not to the corporation's officers, directors, and shareholders.

These simple predicates, however, mask a morass. A corporation is a legal fiction. Its independent existence has been created out of statutory "whole cloth." Only by reason of legislative fiat has this "entity" been separated from its owners and its managers.

Therefore, we have the perverse situation in which the lawyer who represents a publicly held corporation is selected and retained by, and reports to and may be fired by, the principal officers and directors of the corporation—*who are not his clients.* Moreover, the shareholders of a corporation, who, collectively, are the owners of the mythical beast, typically do not participate in the process by which the lawyer is selected, retained, or fired.

In the corporate arena, the lawyer lives in an "Alice in Wonderland" world. The client to which he owes undivided loyalty, fealty, and allegiance cannot speak to him except through voices that may have interests adverse to his client. He is hired and may be fired by people who may or may not have interests diametrically opposed to those of his client. And finally, his client is itself an illusion—a fictional "person" that exists or expires at the whim of its shareholders, whom the lawyer does not represent.

It is not surprising, therefore, that to a great extent lawyers simply do not concern themselves with these ethical considerations, or if they do, become so frustrated in their application that they throw up their hands in despair.

NOTES ON JONAS

1. **What's So Hard About Representing Corporations?** Recall that Rule 1.13 is designed to address the problem identified by Jonas here. It defines the corporation as the client of the corporate lawyer and specifies when and how the lawyer should respond to evidence that corporate constituencies are engaging in conduct that is likely to harm the corporation. Does this excerpt suggest reasons why corporate lawyers may find this rule challenging to implement and why they may sometimes be reluctant to follow its requirements?

2. **What's Corporate Scandal Got to Do with It?** Jonas describes an essential difficulty with important ethical implications for lawyers who represent corporations. The client is a legal fiction with no ability to communicate or make decisions except through the acts of its officers, directors, employees, and shareholders; the people with whom the corporate lawyers must interact every day in order to serve the client organization are not the client. Indeed, the interests of those individuals with whom the lawyer regularly communicates sometimes conflict with the client's interests. Nevertheless, those very people make decisions about which lawyers to hire and fire. Does this "Alice in Wonderland" world that the corporate lawyer inhabits help explain some situations in which lawyers become embroiled in corporate wrongdoing?

As you read Part G of this chapter on corporate fraud and Chapter 19 on various corporate scandals of the past several decades in which in-house lawyers have been implicated, consider the possible relevance of Jonas's analysis.

F. LARGE FIRM LAWYERS' VALUES AND RELATIONSHIPS WITH CLIENTS

Here we examine the attitudes and values of lawyers who practice in large law firms. How do they view their relationships with clients? Do they seek to influence their corporate clients' positions on important issues affecting the public or third parties? How often do they disagree with what the client seeks to accomplish or the means the client wishes to use to achieve its ends? When those situations arise, how do they respond?

This section surveys some of the available research on those questions.

IDEOLOGY, PRACTICE, AND PROFESSIONAL AUTONOMY: SOCIAL VALUES AND CLIENT RELATIONSHIPS IN THE LARGE LAW FIRM

Robert L. Nelson
37 Stanford Law Review 503 (1985)

My central thesis is that lawyers in large firms adhere to an ideology of autonomy in their perceptions of both the role of legal institutions in society and the role of lawyers vis-à-vis clients, but that this ideology has little bearing on their practice. In the realm of practice, these lawyers enthusiastically attempt to maximize the interests of clients and rarely experience serious disagreement with the broader implications of a client's proposed course of conduct. The dominance of client interests in the practical activities of lawyers contradicts the view that large-firm lawyers serve a mediating function in the legal system. The lawyers of elite firms may well take progressive stands on certain issues within the profession, may lead efforts at legal rationalization, and may exhibit a liberal orientation on general political questions, but the direction of their law reform activities and their approach to the issues that arise in ordinary practice ultimately are determined by the positions of their clients.

The principal database for the present analysis consists of structured interviews with a random sample of 224 lawyers [from four Chicago firms], stratified proportionally by seniority. In addition, in-depth interviews were conducted with 61 "elites" who sat on their respective firms' governing committees or who were recognized leaders of a workgroup or department.

I chose to ask three questions about the relationships of lawyers to clients. First, I sought to measure the respondent's perception of the breadth of the lawyer's role. A commonly mentioned concern is that specialization in large firms has narrowed the lawyer's view of her normative role, that she may no longer see it as her responsibility to gain an overview of her client's affairs or to give clients more than technical legal advice. A second and related question dealt with lawyers' opportunities to give nonlegal advice. And third, I asked whether the lawyers had "ever refused an assignment or potential work because it was contrary to your personal values." This construction was intended to include matters that violated the code of professional ethics, as well as other values not codified.

Large-firm lawyers adhere to a broad conception of their role vis-à-vis clients. More than three-quarters of the sample (76%) responded that it was appropriate to act as the conscience of a client when the opportunity presented itself. Virtually the same majority (75%) responded that they had the opportunity to give nonlegal advice to clients, but there are significant differences by field and partnership status. Litigation presents practitioners with fewer opportunities for giving nonlegal advice.

By far the leading reason for giving nonlegal advice (mentioned by 43.8% of respondents) is that a business decision is involved. The majority of other responses have a pragmatic ring as well: that the client asked for advice (14.2%), that the field of law required it as part of the practice (24.9%), that matters required personal investment decisions (11.2%), or that the client needed personal advice (19.5%). Very few of the responses suggest broader moral or social concerns.

[H]ow often do they have conflicts with clients over the propriety or morality of client positions? Only 16.22% of the sample ever refused an assignment or potential work, and one-third of these 36 respondents had done so twice. [H]alf of the coded refusals were in response to violations of professional ethics, such as ongoing criminal conduct by clients, conflicts of interest, and the use of the law to harass other parties. [R]oughly one-half of the other refusals implicated personal values, with several respondents refusing to defend clients against certain types of accusations. Reflecting their seniority, partners were more than twice as likely as associates (28% to 11%) to have refused an assignment.

What can we infer from the finding that less than a quarter of the practitioners in this sample have encountered a conflict with personal values, and that half of the situations where lawyers refused work did not involve the subtleties of the public interest but were instead rather obvious violations of professional rules? Three broad explanations can be offered for this pattern. First, the vast majority of tasks that lawyers in these firms perform turn on technical matters involving parties of roughly equal status and resources. In preparing a securities offering, in arranging a leveraged leasing transaction, or in planning an estate, lawyers are not called on to deal with questions of good and evil (beyond considerations of simple honesty). Even in hotly contested matters, such as the hostile acquisition of a corporation or antitrust litigation, the contest is not between "good guys" and "bad guys." During the course of pretesting the values questions, one associate chuckled at the moral tone of the items. His comment was something like: "Are you kidding? My work [big case litigation] doesn't raise questions of conscience, it's just a fight over which big corporation is going to get a bigger chunk of the pie." The social questions of our time simply do not come up frequently in large-firm practice.

Second, even though the social values of my sample may be somewhat more liberal than those of business elites, the attitudes of lawyers and clients are not widely divergent. Operating with the same basic values as their clients, these lawyers will often interpret the social implications of a course of action in much the same way that their clients do. The similarity of values between lawyer and client is reinforced by the career choices of lawyers. Clearly there are some types of practice that involve rather explicit choices about which side a lawyer will take, for instance, between labor and management in labor relations, and between plaintiffs and defendants in several areas of litigation. Most of these choices are made when a lawyer chooses the law firm or other setting in which she will practice. Once this choice is made, lawyers are left with a limited set of case-by-case, client-by-client judgments about refusing assignments.

Third, it may be that professional training and experience teach lawyers to transform potentially troubling questions of values into matters of technique and strategy. [Norwegian sociologist Vilhelm] Aubert suggests that this is one of the primary functions of lawyers and that it may contribute to the resolution of disputes between embittered adversaries. But this tendency also may undercut the ability and inclination of lawyers to mediate conflicts or act as normative agents.

* * *

THE ELASTIC TOURNAMENT: A SECOND TRANSFORMATION OF THE BIG LAW FIRM

Marc Galanter & William Henderson
60 Stanford Law Review 1867 (2008)

Throughout the twentieth century, the elite corporate bar has perpetuated the lore that its organizations and individual members adhere to strict standards of professionalism rather than the morals of the marketplace. This image is reinforced within the popular culture by the tort reform movement, which casts plaintiffs' lawyers as greedy and unprincipled. Solo and small firm lawyers are also perennially overrepresented in state bar disciplinary proceedings because of higher levels of client complaints and alleged ethics violations. Conversely, as observed by Lisa Lerman, "[s]ome of the wealthiest American lawyers—partners in large firms—have enjoyed a widespread assumption that their ethical standards are impeccable."

In a seminal study on lawyer ethics conducted during the early 1960s, lawyer and sociologist Jerome Carlin provided compelling empirical evidence that large firm lawyers were much more likely to comport with the bar's formal and informal ethics regime. Drawing upon interviews with lawyers, legal ethics texts, and published opinions of committees on professional ethics, Carlin's research team devised a detailed questionnaire that set forth a wide array of ethical conflicts in contexts involving a lawyer's obligations to clients, colleagues, or the administration of justice. The questionnaire was then administered via interview to a representative sample of 800 lawyers in private practice in the central business core of New York City. One of the major findings of Carlin's study was that large firm lawyers were much more likely to conform to, and internalize, the bar's formal and informal code of ethics.

Yet, as Carlin unpacked his findings, he observed that the different rates of ethical violation and conformity were not the product of firm size per se, but [varied] with the presence or absence of ethical stressors that were strongly correlated with different clientele and practice settings. In general, lawyers in the largest New York City firms enjoyed the largest incomes, the most stable base of clients, the fewest appearances in state courts (which were the most rife with corruption), less pressure from clients to violate the law, and the time and resources to participate in elite bar associations. Thus, inspecting all the data, Carlin concluded, "[l]arge-firm lawyers . . . have low rates of violation because they are largely insulated from client and court-agency pressures, while small-firm lawyers and individual practitioners have high rates of violation because they are most exposed to these situational inducements to violate."

A lot has changed in the forty years since Carlin published his study. The large firm lawyers studied by Carlin enjoyed enduring client relationships. According to a 1959 Conference Board survey of 286 manufacturing companies, "three fourths of them retain outside counsel on a continuing basis. . . . Companies more frequently report that 'present outside counsel have been with us for many, many years,' or that 'we are satisfied with the performance of our outside counsel and have never given any thought to hiring another.'" Only a few years after the publication of Carlin's study, another commentator on Wall Street law firms observed that the large commercial and investment banks were the "epitome of the locked-in client" because of the vast specialized knowledge that had accumulated within by the firms' large banking departments. One Wall Street partner estimated that client turnover during the 1960s, in dollar volume, was "5 per cent a year, mostly in one-shot litigation."

Ironically, Carlin's descriptions of the pressures surrounding small firm lawyers in the 1960s seem to apply aptly to today's large law firm marketplace.

> The lower the status of the lawyer's clientele, the more precarious and insecure his practice. Lawyers with low-status clients tend to have an unstable clientele; that is, they have a higher rate of [client] turnover . . . The small businessman is more likely than a large corporation to shop around and switch

attorneys: he may be on the lookout for a less expensive, sharper, and more compatible lawyer. This type of client is also more likely to divide his legal business among several lawyers . . . Lawyers with low-status clients also report more competition from other lawyers in obtaining clients, and that they have been hurt by such competition.

John Conley and Scott Baker recently observed, "the Wall Street elite now occupy that circle of hell that Carlin had reserved for the most desperate of solo practitioners."

In [a] recent qualitative empirical study of ten large law firms, many factors contributed to the climate of insecurity.[85] Partners reported that "firms no longer 'own' the work they do because" a competitor is always working to lure the client away. Because the firm can no longer predictably hand off clients as older partners retire, younger lawyers are less likely to develop strong loyalties to the firm, which further undermines the project of developing firm-specific capital. Firm management evaluates the profitability of partners and practice groups by focusing on hours billed and fee collection (i.e., "realization"), which, in turn, fosters competition within the firm for marketing expenditures, equity partnership seats, and new hires. Similarly, the conflict of interest checks are a frequent source of tension because individual lawyers or practice groups could be forced to turn away lucrative business. Even if an individual partner manages to cement a strong business relationship with a corporate general counsel, that security could be disrupted by higher firm-imposed billing rates that the client is unwilling to pay. Further, the specter of de-equitization hangs over all lawyers who are slow to adapt. "Large firms view good lawyers as expendable."

Several commentators have argued that market power is a necessary precondition of professional values, including adherence to the formal ethical norms of the bar. According to Erwin Smigel's sociological account of large Wall Street law firms of the 1960s, large law firms flourished economically because their clients were paying a premium for expert and autonomous advice. "Independent legal opinion is perhaps the commodity they offer, and the primary commodity for which they are paid." Even if Smigel accurately described the client-firm relationship of the late 1950s and early 1960s, now there is broad consensus that the vast majority of corporate clients hire outside counsel to obtain a specific, cost-effective result. Not surprisingly, as extensive qualitative field work has revealed, the ethical norm that is most widely embraced by large firm lawyers is the very one that reduces the strains in the lawyer-client relationship: zealous advocacy.

---

[85] See Kimberly Kirkland, *Ethics in Large Law Firms: The Principle of Pragmatism*, 35 U. MEM. L. REV. 631 (2005).

Under the elastic tournament's regime of mobility, the structural implications for outside counsel are virtually impossible to ignore. In the pages of *The American Lawyer*, one large firm partner, who temporarily served as a client's in-house counsel, offered two golden rules to solidify their client relationships: "[m]ake inside counsel's lives easier" and "[m]ake inside counsel look good in front of their clients, colleagues, superiors, and subordinates." In some instances, the outside lawyer is hired to reinforce to company executives the position staked out by the general counsel, and if he or she wants to be hired again, "it behoove[s] him [or her] not to offer a contrary opinion." In this highly atomized economic climate, it is likely that ethical gray zones will get resolved in the client's favor, and insecure lawyers will be less likely to acknowledge any black or white.

Let us be clear, however, that our discussion oversimplifies the history, culture, and governance of a wide array of large firms. In our discussions with lawyers, we have run across examples of large law firms that continue to share-risk and inspire investment in the collective enterprise of the firm. Ethical lapses were regarded as threats to a hallowed firm reputation and the trust of longtime colleagues. But this ethos becomes harder to maintain (and virtually impossible to create or restore) in larger, geographically dispersed firms that are perpetually competing for clients and entry-level associates.

NOTES ON NELSON AND GALANTER & HENDERSON

1. ***How Do These Lawyers Define Professionalism?*** If the descriptions of large firm lawyers' values and practices in the Nelson and the Galanter & Henderson excerpts are correct, how would you describe the prevailing conception(s) of professionalism held by lawyers in large law firms?

2. ***Implications of These Trends for Lawyer Independence.*** How do the trends described by Galanter & Henderson contribute to an environment in which individual lawyers within large firms are likely to find it difficult to follow professional and ethical principles that are "at odds with the client's objectives"? How do they relate to the various conceptions of the lawyer's role examined in Chapters 3?

3. ***Implications for Self-Regulation.*** To the extent that lawyers come to see their work for corporate clients simply as a series of self-interest-maximizing market transactions that tend to go more easily if the lawyer does not attempt to offer independent advice and instead focuses primarily on making inside counsel and executives look good, should the public value the work of lawyers? Should it respect the notion that the legal profession should be allowed to regulate itself without outside interference?

4. ***"Padding Hours".*** The study by Lisa Lerman noted in the Galanter & Henderson excerpt examined billing fraud by prominent lawyers

in large elite law firms. The practice she examined involves "padding hours"—exaggerating the amount of time spent on projects and thereby cheating clients.

Lerman's research turned up no such cases involving large firm lawyers prior to 1989 and thirty-six such cases thereafter—a pattern she attributes to the "rising dominance of income generation as the central goal" of large firm practice. She also noted that most of the law firms at which the lawyers involved in these billing scandals worked billed clients by the hour, set high annual targets for billable hours, and used the number of hours billed per year as a primary criterion for evaluating and compensating lawyers. She suggested that these policies invite misconduct:

> As long as lawyers are making records of how long they work on particular matters, and the time recorded translates into dollars billed, there is an incentive to record more time than was actually worked, and/or to do unnecessary work in order to bill for it. Many lawyers, of course, would not inflate their hours or their work, but those whose moral compass is less focused will do so. By setting annual billable hour targets for lawyers, law firms may invite— perhaps almost require—dishonest recordation of time. The incentive to overbill already present as a result of hourly billing and as a result of the annual targets is intensified by [the practice of using the number of hours billed per year as a primary criterion to evaluate and compensate lawyers].[12]

Does Lerman underestimate the possibility that lawyers can work very hard without engaging in deception? Does she place too much blame on law firms' policies and too little on the individuals who engage in overbilling?

Additional factors that contribute to bill padding in large firms include firms' failures to monitor billing practices. In fact, in several high profile incidents, lawyers who have reported billing fraud within their firms have been either ignored or penalized.[13] Moreover, in some types of matters, such as bankruptcy, neither the lawyers nor clients have an incentive to keep fees under control because those costs are ultimately borne by others. In bankruptcy proceedings, creditors foot the bill for lawyers' fees.[14]

---

[12] Lisa G. Lerman, *Blue-Chip Bilking: Regulation of Billing and Expense Fraud By Lawyers*, 12 GEO. J. LEGAL ETHICS 205, 294–95 (1999).

[13] See Bohatch v. Butler & Binion, 977 S.W.2d 543 (1998)(a lawyer who reported what she believed was billing fraud by one of her partners was dismissed from the partnership); see also Nathan Koppel, *Lawyer Charge Opens Window on Bill Padding*, WALL ST. J., Aug. 30, 2006 (reporting on an incident in which a junior partner at Holland & Knight LLP believed that the partner in charge of billing had inflated the junior partner's hours; the junior partner reported the incident and thereafter left the firm because he was dissatisfied that the firm had not taken action against the billing partner).

[14] See Andy Peters, *Eight Firms to Share $30M in Delta Bankruptcy Legal Fees*, DAILY REPORT, June 7, 2006.

G. LARGE FIRMS AND CORPORATE MISCONDUCT

We now explore some of the pressures that may contribute to misconduct in this realm of practice. In a wave of scandals of the past several decades, lawyers in large firms appear to have facilitated wrongdoing by their corporate and banking clients. As you contemplate the following three such episodes, try to imagine why the lawyers behaved as they did and what they might have done differently.

Kaye, Scholer and the Lincoln Savings and Loan Debacle. In the 1980s and 1990s, long before the financial crisis relating to the housing bubble, there was a crisis in the savings and loan ("thrift" or "S&L") industry; over one thousand savings and loan associations failed during that period. The bailout from that debacle cost American taxpayers hundreds of billions of dollars. S&Ls lent money to homeowners with long pay-back periods (usually 30 years) but acquired the money used to make those loans from short-term depositors to whom they paid interest. Deposits in S&Ls were federally insured, meaning that if the S&L lacked sufficient assets to pay depositors who wished to withdraw their funds, the depositor could collect from the government's Federal Deposit Insurance Corporation (FDIC). In return for FDIC protection, S&Ls were subject to extensive regulations and regular examinations designed to ensure that they did not take excessive risks that would ultimately be borne by the American taxpayer. When interest rates increased during the 1970s, the S&Ls were caught in a squeeze. Partial deregulation of S&Ls allowed thrifts to make riskier investments, and some engaged in fraudulent deals to stay above water.

Lincoln Savings and Loan, based in Irvine, California, was one of the most notorious institutions involved in the savings and loan crisis of the 1980s. Its owner/operator, Charles Keating, was known for his aggressive management of Lincoln and his political influence acquired through large campaign contributions. (The "Keating Five" lobbying scandal involved five U.S. Senators who received major campaign contributions from Keating and intervened on his behalf to ward off regulators and ease regulations that had made it difficult for Lincoln to continue making risky investments with taxpayer-insured dollars.) Lincoln engaged in a series of prohibited risky investments and fraudulent transactions to remain solvent and hide its true financial condition from regulators. The Office of Thrift Supervision (OTS), the agency charged with periodically examining S&L books to ensure their compliance with thrift regulations, sought access to Lincoln's records as part of its oversight responsibilities. Lincoln hired Jones Day, and later (when Jones Day was not sufficiently aggressive in fending off OTS inquiries) Kaye Scholer to represent it in connection with its interactions with bank examiners. The Kaye Scholer lawyer who took primary responsibility for the matter was Peter Fishbein—the same Peter Fishbein who succeeded the Singer Hutner lawyers in the O.P.M. scandal described in Chapter 9 (the duty of confidentiality).

Kaye Scholer lawyers treated the matter like adverse litigation rather than a bank examination. The firm directed examiners—who were legally entitled to full access to the thrift's records—to channel all inquiries through the firm and not to communicate directly with Lincoln personnel. In its dealing with the regulators, Kaye Scholer also made a series of statements about Lincoln's underwriting practices and transactions that directly contradicted statements contained in Kaye Scholer's own memos. Those memos became available to the government when Lincoln finally collapsed and was taken over by the Resolution Trust Corporation (a governmental organization) as receiver.

In 1992, the Resolution Trust Corporation, charged with paying depositors from taxpayer funds and from proceeds from settlements made with those who allegedly assisted Lincoln in its schemes, brought charges against Kaye Scholer and three of its partners. It sought restitution of losses of at least $275 million. The agency also issued a "freeze" order designed to prevent the law firm's assets from being dissipated. Within a week, the firm settled the matter for $41 million without contesting the charges or admitting or denying the allegations.[15]

Enron. The collapse of the huge Houston-based energy company, Enron Corporation, in 2001 involved one of the largest corporate frauds of modern times. It resulted in many criminal prosecutions against Enron's officers and suits by shareholders against secondary actors, including several prominent law firms. The fraudulent scheme at issue was Enron's use of "special purpose entities" (SPEs) to hide losses and make the company look more profitable than it was. These SPEs were nominally independent of Enron but were in fact created for the purpose of hiding losses. Enron's in-house counsel and at least two outside firms played important roles in structuring and documenting the transactions. A report issued by the court-appointed bankruptcy examiner found that Enron's counsel were centrally involved in structuring the SPEs and reviewing company disclosures concerning them.[16] In some instances, the report attributed the lawyers' failure to prevent or disclose the fraud to their lack of understanding of the transactions involved, while in other instances the report called it willful blindness.

A report of the New York City Bar Association concluded that Enron's lawyers, including lawyers in its primary outside law firm, Vinson & Elkins, were in a position to have questioned various aspects of management's conduct and that, while some did so, none brought their

---

[15] For a fuller discussion of this matter, see In the *Matter of Kaye, Scholer, Fierman, Hays & Handler: A Symposium on Government Regulation, Lawyers' Ethics, and the Rule of Law*, 66 S. CAL. L. REV. 977 (1993).

[16] In re Enron Corp., Final Report of Neal Batson, Court-Appointed Examiner, Appendix C.

concerns to Enron's board of directors.[17] The report emphasized the obligations of outside counsel to ask whatever questions were necessary to ensure that their services were not being used to improperly remove debt from the company's financial reports, as well as their duty to candidly advise the client on legal and other risks posed by a transaction or disclosure.[18] In trying to explain why lawyers failed to fulfill those duties, the report noted the trend toward "limited, piecemeal representations by outside firms," which means that no one outside firm has a complete understanding of a client's business and the general context of the transactions that he or she is structuring and documenting. It also noted that "[t]here is an increased risk, in this legal environment, that lawyers may unwittingly facilitate a client's misconduct, or lose the opportunity to counsel against it," and that this risk is magnified by the increasingly competitive nature of the profession:

> Both partners and clients are less tied to a given firm than was typical until roughly the 1980s. Today a partner's compensation may importantly depend on retaining a significant client, and a firm's profitability may depend on its ability to retain its partners with "portable business." At the same time, most public companies are no longer tied to a single law firm, a relationship that gave the firm a sturdy platform from which to render unwelcome advice. Today, public companies unhappy with the advice or service of one firm can and do readily switch their business to other firms. This competitive environment creates pressures on outside counsel to avoid confronting clients about questionable transactions or accounting treatments in order to maintain the client relationship.[19]

It may also be worth noting that Enron was Vinson & Elkins's largest client at the time of the events that led to the criminal prosecutions and civil suits.

Refco. In 2007, Joseph Collins, a partner in the large law firm of Mayer Brown, was charged with helping to hide the debts of his client, Refco, a futures and commodities broker that went public and collapsed in 2005. At the time, it was the fifth largest bankruptcy in U.S. history. Collins was accused of helping Refco's executives manipulate its balance sheet by drafting loan agreements that temporarily transferred Refco's losses from its books at the year's end to a related party controlled by the company's chairman and CEO, thereby creating the impression that

---

[17] As noted in the introduction to Part VA, Rule 1.13's up-the-ladder reporting provisions have become much more stringent since the time of the Enron debacle.

[18] New York City Bar, Report of the Task Force on the Lawyer's Role in Corporate Governance 25–26, 114–118 (2006).

[19] Report of the Task Force on the Lawyer's Role in Corporate Governance, November 2006, pp. 112–14.

Refco was a profitable company and defrauding shareholders. According to the indictment, Collins and other Mayer Brown lawyers played an indispensable role in facilitating the fraudulent scheme to hide $2.4 billion of debt from auditors and investors by preparing the documents that concealed the company's debt. In 2009, a jury convicted Collins on five securities fraud counts, and he was sentenced to seven years in prison. In January of 2012, the U.S. Court of Appeals for the Second Circuit overturned his conviction and ruled that he was entitled to a new trial because the judge had improper discussions with a juror outside the presence of Mr. Collins's lawyers.[20] However, on November 16, 2012, he was again convicted—of conspiracy, securities fraud, and wire fraud, and in July 2013 he was sentenced to a year in prison.[21]

During the trial, Collins testified that he was a victim of the Refco fraud, that Refco officials had lied to him, and that he was unaware that his client was engaging in fraud. He said that he relied on the numbers the client gave him, delegated the drafting of the documents to a Mayer Brown associate who worked for him, and spent little time on the transactions: "I didn't personally spend a lot of time. I delegated them . . . I didn't structure them. I didn't negotiate them. I didn't talk to customers about them. They just didn't require much of my time." He added, "I do many transactions for many clients and I can't possibly keep in mind everything" that happens. "I don't have that information. I can't compile it and I can't remember it." He also testified that his client lied to him about the purpose of the loans. [22]

It's hard to know exactly what Collins knew about the Refco fraud. One reading of the evidence suggests that he unknowingly facilitated the perpetuation of a massive fraud. But why didn't Collins and the associates who worked with him ask questions that would have uncovered the scandal? After all, his client had a history of unlawful activity. Since 1983, regulators had cited Refco more than 140 times for various misdeeds, including siphoning money from client accounts.[23]

As we ponder this question, it may be worth noting that Refco was Collins's biggest client; according to the indictment, his work for Refco generated $40 million in fees from 1997 to 2005[24] and accounted for more

---

[20] See Peter Lattman, *Conviction Overturned for an Ex-Refco Lawyer*, N.Y. TIMES, January 10, 2012.

[21] Mark Hamblett, *Ex-Mayer Brown Partner Convicted at Retrial*, N.Y. L. J., Nov. 19, 2012; Patricia Hurtado, *Ex-Refco Lawyer Gets Year for Aiding $2.4 Billion Fraud*, BLOOMBERG.COM, July 15, 2013.

[22] Mark Hamblett, *Collins Takes the Stand to Defend His Role as Attorney for Refco*, N.Y. L. J., June 19, 2009, p. 1.

[23] Susan Beck, *Target Practice*, AM. LAW, Nov. 1, 2008, p. 84, 87; *see also* Sung Hui Kim, *Naked Self-Interest? Why the Legal Profession Resists Gatekeeping*, 63 FLA. L. REV. 129, 130 (2011) ("Collins's claim that he just didn't know [about the fraud] remains troubling in light of Refco's long rap sheet of rogue transactions and prior criminal prosecutions.").

[24] United States v. Collins, 07–01170 (S.D. N.Y.), Indictment p. 2.

than half his time on matters for the company.[25] Collins had a clean reputation at Mayer Brown; one of his former partners described him as "the Richie Cunningham of Mayer Brown."[26] But not all of his former partners accepted the notion that he had no reason to know that his client was engaging in fraud. One said that Collins should have been asking more questions: "It's hard for me to understand how anyone could work on loan documents and not ask, 'what is the purpose behind this loan?' When you're doing a financing, knowing the use of proceeds is important to understand whether the loan is illegal." One journalist speculated that "Mayer Brown's eat-what-you-kill culture arguably led to lapses in judgment that that, in the end, hurt the clients and the firm." (Three civil suits relating the Refco's collapse were also filed against Mayer Brown.)[27] The judge who sentenced Collins after his first trial said, "I don't believe that Mr. Collins committed these crimes for greed or money because he would have been paid through his firm; I think this is a case of excessive loyalty to his client."[28]

NOTES ON THE CASE STUDIES

1.   ***Why Did These Episodes Occur?*** What do you think might explain the lawyers' conduct in each of these incidents? What might the lawyers in each of these situations have done differently?

2.   ***The Lawyer's Role?*** Recall from Chapter 3 that some have argued that lawyers' conception of role should vary by the procedural context in which they operate. How should the lawyer for a client engaged in a bank examination view his role? Kaye Scholer and its defenders asserted that Kaye Scholer's tactics were justified by the firm's role as litigation counsel for Lincoln. But most commentators took the view that Kaye Scholer lawyers were not justified in behaving as aggressive advocates in a context in which the client had affirmative disclosure obligations as an insured, regulated thrift. OTS argued that Kaye Scholer acquired its client's disclosure duties by virtue of having taken control of the examination process and "interposing" itself between its client and the regulators. OTS further argued that Kaye Scholer violated its professional duties under Model Rules 1.2(d), 3.3 and 4.1 by making misrepresentations about Lincoln's investments and underwriting standards, knowingly transmitting misleading material prepared by Lincoln to OTS, and doctoring files to obscure underwriting failures. Most commentators agreed that Kaye Scholer could not intentionally deceive regulators without violating its obligation under Rule 1.2 and 4.1 to avoid assisting the client in fraudulent conduct.[29]

---

[25]   Hamblett, N.Y.L.J., June 19, 2009.

[26]   [Eds. Richie Cunningham was the exceedingly wholesome character played by Ron Howard in the television sitcom Happy Days, 1974–1984.]

[27]   Susan Beck, *Target Practice*, AM. LAW., Nov. 1, 2008, p. 84.

[28]   Mark Hamblet, *Ex-Mayer Partner Gets 7 Years Over Refco*, N.Y. L. J., Jan. 15, 2010.

[29]   *See, From the Trenches and Towers,* 23 LAW & SOC. INQUIRY 243-271 (1998).

3. ***Common Features.*** Notice some of the similarities between the Vinson &Elkins/Enron and Collins/Refco matters. In both, the client was the lawyers' major client, in both cases the lawyers insisted they didn't know that they were facilitating fraud, and in both the lawyers were documenting transactions whose purposes they did not understand.

4. ***Who Is the Client (Yet Again)?*** Regarding the lawyers' conduct in Enron, consider the remark by one Vinson & Elkins lawyer: "When clients ask us [if they can do something] our job is to . . . figure out if there is a legally appropriate way to do it. That's what we do. And so does every other law firm in America."[30] Is the job of the lawyer to "figure out if there is a legally appropriate way to do" whatever the client asks? What does "legally appropriate" mean? Who does this Vinson & Elkins lawyer appear to view as his client?

William Simon offered this comment on the above quote by the Vinson & Elkins lawyer: "That V&E could see its participation in the Enron deceptions as a matter of loyalty to its client bespeaks deep confusion that seems to arise from a failure to treat seriously the meaning of organizational representation."[31] Do you agree? What factors other than deep confusion might explain the role of outside lawyers in these corporate scandals?

5. ***Willful Blindness.*** Can lawyers avoid responsibility for client fraud by avoiding knowledge about their clients' business? How should lawyers handle clients that deliberately keep them in the dark? Should lawyers refuse to work for clients who do not give them sufficient information to ensure that they are not facilitating fraud?

Although the Model Rules sometimes require actual knowledge of client misconduct to trigger lawyers' responsibilities, such knowledge can be inferred from the circumstances. (Rule 1.0(f)) In the context of work for organizations, the comment to Rule 1.13 warns that "a lawyer cannot ignore the obvious." Moreover, in a number of cases, courts have found lawyers liable for securities law violations where they consciously avoided knowing that a client's conduct was fraudulent.[32] Lawyers who fail to investigate when they suspect that their clients are engaging in misconduct not only jeopardize their own reputations but also risk criminal and civil liability for facilitating the deception.

H. THE FUTURE OF THE LARGE FIRM

Is the big firm model sustainable? What does the future hold for large law firms and the lawyers who work for them?

---

[30] Patty Waldmeir, *Inside Track: Don't Blame the Lawyers for Enron*, FINANCIAL TIMES, Feb. 21, 2002.

[31] William H. Simon, *After Confidentiality: Rethinking the Professional Responsibilities of the Business Lawyer*, 75 FORDHAM L. REV. 1453, 1464, 1467 (2006).

[32] For a list of collected cases illustrating this point, *see* Rebecca Roiphe, *The Ethics of Willful Ignorance*, 24 GEO. J. LEGAL ETHICS 187 (2010).

In 2010, Professor Larry Ribstein published an article entitled "The Death of Big Law," in which he argued that the large firm business model is unworkable.[33] Noting that many large firms had recently dissolved, gone bankrupt, or significantly downsized, he asserted that these events reflect more than just a shrinking economy—that they indicate that the basic business model of the large U.S. firm is defective and requires fundamental restructuring. According to Ribstein, client demand for cheaper and more sophisticated legal services, and intensified competition in the global legal services market, threaten the large law firm's stability. He predicted that the dominant role that major law firms have enjoyed in the legal services market will end and that "big law" will devolve into smaller and less hierarchical firms.

The following commentary on the same topic offers a slightly less dire prediction.

BIG BUT BRITTLE: ECONOMIC PERSPECTIVES ON THE FUTURE OF THE LAW FIRM IN THE NEW ECONOMY
Bernard A. Burk & David McGowan
2011 Columbia Business Law Review 1

Fundamental changes are indeed afoot. Although rumors of the "Death of Big Law" have been greatly exaggerated, it is leading a much more interesting and challenging life. We believe, however, that the recent economic downturn is not the root cause of those challenges. The recession simply laid bare economic forces that have been building for some time, and compelled greater responsiveness to those forces. These phenomena will drive significant evolution in the structure and practices of the large, elite law firm, but they do not threaten the viability of the large law firm as such.

In the summer of 2007, the *American Lawyer*, extrapolating from business as usual, estimated that the Am Law 200 law firms alone would hire 10,000 entry-level associates to begin in the fall of 2008. We all know what happened next: the housing bubble burst. Capital markets seized; numerous investment and commercial banks either failed, collapsed into a more solvent acquirer, or sought government-funded life-support. Demand for high-end legal services plummeted as transactional activity slowed to a crawl. Falling corporate revenues and budgets forced client companies to avoid or curtail all but the most essential legal work, and to reassess the cost and staffing of any work that was unavoidable. Naturally these events had profound effects on the law firms that served these clients.

Large law firms shed personnel in unprecedented numbers. In addition to laying off existing employees, firms also drastically cut new

---

[33] Larry E. Ribstein, *The Death of Big Law*, 2010 WIS. L. REV. 749 (2010).

associate hiring. In 2009 and 2010, numerous firms rescinded existing employment offers or "deferred" new hires' start dates 3 to 12 months or more.

A number of firms are also adjusting their rules for advancement. Until recently, the vast majority of large firms paid associates' salaries, and often their bonuses as well, in a strictly seniority-based "lockstep" system. A number of firms are experimenting with abandoning lockstep in favor of a "tiered" system that ties advancement to demonstrated professional experience, achievement, or (more inchoately) "merit."

Traditional pricing has come under greater scrutiny. Though many large firms announced increases in their "rack" (i.e., standard) rates in early 2009 and again in early 2010, those increases were generally more modest than prior years', and discounting appears rampant. In addition, "creative" billing arrangements, such as flat fees, volume discounts, contingent fees, and "success fees" (discounted fees with enhancements for defined levels of success in the engagement), are the watchword of the day.

The lower-priced, lower-overhead boutique enjoyed a resurgence as small groups of partners left BigLaw to set up more nimble and flexible specialty shops. From October 2008 through September 2009, 114 Am Law 200 partners left their firms to start or join small practices, up from 70 the year before.

Are new trends emerging from, or being revealed by, the sudden and drastic changes the economy has visited on us? Is that fundamental change in business model coming? Will firms' hands be forced by economic pressures beyond their control?

As Yogi Berra (or was it Neils Bohr?) said, predictions are hard, especially about the future. With all appropriate trepidation and humility, then, we offer the following [predictions about what we can expect in the market for corporate legal services as the recession recedes.]

Disaggregation of legal services, and the price competition that causes and results from it, will accelerate. Corporate clients are not going to become any less sophisticated, and will in increasing numbers scour their legal work for tasks that can be routinized, commoditized, and conveniently handed to low-cost providers or handled more economically in-house. Technology will continue to lower the cost of coordinating with economically-priced, appropriately skilled workers wherever in the world they may be found. Downsourcing, insourcing, and outsourcing will become more prevalent as clients insist on them, and elite law firms do what is necessary to remain competitive.

The number of highly compensated, partnership-track associate positions at large firms will fall. Legal process and similar routinized and commodified work will less and less support elite-firm associates' rates. As such work is pushed down and out at large firms, fewer conventional partnership-track associates will be needed to staff it.

The number of well-compensated, indefinite-term nonpartnership positions at large law firms will increase. Slowing the decrease in leverage resulting from reduced hiring and retention of associates, indefinite-term nonpartner attorney positions (variously denominated nonequity partners, senior associates, counsel, or the like) will continue to increase. These positions will increasingly be offered in lieu of partnership to highly qualified technical specialists, former "service partners," and other skilled and experienced practitioners who are useful in supporting the firm's practice. These personnel will be generously compensated, will have some standing within the firm, and will have some level of opportunity to become equity partners if they develop significant business of their own.

The number of staff and spot-contract positions at large law firms, compensated at levels comparable to nonattorney staff and limited to legal process and other routine work, will increase (to the extent they are not replaced by technological substitutes). Aside from the classes of well-compensated nonpartners (associates, nonequity partners, counsel), a separate class of staff and contract attorneys will develop at many firms. Their work will be limited to routinized and commodified work such as legal process, and possibly the kinds of routine legal work large companies (and some law firms) are increasingly outsourcing abroad. These are becoming the assembly-line jobs of the twenty-first century: tedious, repetitive, rushed, and pressured by emphasis on quantity over quality, and even subject to ergonomic and repetitive stress injuries. Such workers may begin to organize to protect themselves.

The fewer conventional associate positions that remain available at large firms will in some respects be more professionally rewarding than the greater number available before the recession. As repetitive and commodified work becomes a smaller part of the typical associate workload, associates may get greater access to more challenging and responsible tasks; and as the number of partnership-track associates falls, they also may get more access to supervision and training. As it always has, however, the job will still typically involve a fair complement of drudgery, long hours, stress, and relatively poor chances of promotion. The typical "elastic tournament" partner probably won't get markedly more pleasant to work for either. But at least associates may end up doing more of something that more closely resembles traditional law practice, and gaining more useful professional skills and experience in the process than many have in recent years.

Equity partnerships will grow more slowly, and be more rigorously limited to those demonstrating success in business generation and control. Because the highly leveraged work that tends to provide law firms the greatest profit margins will be under continuing cost and price pressure, margins will erode and higher-margin work will become more scarce. Relentless pruning of partnerships through de-equitizations and dismissals will continue, further focusing profits and power in an increasingly narrow equity "core" reached only through control of substantial amounts of profitable law business. After this shakeout, many equity partnerships will continue to grow (or begin to grow again), by both lateral acquisition and internal promotion, but generally only of persons selected for their ability to attract and control law business and thus enhance the partnership's internal referral network.

After the recession-induced shakeout, overall growth in the number of well-compensated lawyer positions at larger firms will continue, but more slowly. In the near term, the shakeouts and reorganizations that the recession and the economic forces described above will continue to produce will cause many firms to shrink, or grow only slowly— particularly as measured by the census of more highly-compensated partners, associates, and indefinite-term nonpartners (excluding the growing underclass of legal process providers who are paid at levels comparable to nonlawyer staff).

Lateral mobility will remain a significant force and BigLaw will remain brittle. Partnerships will continue to try and increase profits per partner (and the returns from their internal referral networks) by seeking new partners with relational capital, leading to profitability greater than the partnership's current mean. They will tend to splinter off partners with lower margins and profitability. Partners whose current practice environment is less complementary to their relational capital, or who otherwise perceive a better environment elsewhere, will also move.

Segmentation between a small cadre of "super-elite" firms and a larger group of "semi-elite" firms will become more pronounced. Because some practice specialties generally tend to be more profitable than others, these trends suggest increasing concentration in a more limited array of practices, at least nearer the top of the profitability scale. This process will continue to press the nascent stratification between "super-elite" and "semi-elite" firms emerging in the data.

High-margin specialty boutiques will remain a significant part of the competitive landscape. As technology allows small firms to enjoy scale economies, some may be able to achieve margins that approach the margins of large firms in similar market segments. Boutiques will remain a recognizable part of high-margin practice in the future as some portion of elite-firm lawyers leave profitable large firms to trade some amount of money for smaller scale, lower overhead, greater intimacy, and a more direct hand on the tiller.

One thing this discussion should make clear is that the large American law firm is not dying. The basic conditions that have driven increasing demand for sophisticated legal services for many decades remain in place. The legalized nature of society, business, and wealth-creation in this country has not materially changed, and governmental intervention in any number of areas (including the healthcare, energy, and financial services industries, among others) suggests more of the same for years to come. As the economy recovers, there will be plenty for high-end specialists to do in contexts and with stakes that will continue to support some degree of premium pricing. The same forces that drew elite lawyers together into larger and larger aggregations also remain in place, and while such phenomena as the erosion of firm-specific capital will continue to impart a certain brittleness to the form, there is no reason to believe that centripetal forces will not, on balance, remain paramount at least up to sizes at least as large as some of the larger firms today.

By the same token, however, the large law firm is evolving. The suddenness and extremity of the current recession exposed a number of incongruities that had been developing in the large-firm business model over the last ten to twenty years, and the correction of those incongruities is now concertedly underway. Important changes are emerging as a result, the course of some of which we guess at above. But none of them should spawn revolutionary rather than evolutionary development in the way that complex and sophisticated legal services are produced and delivered.

We are confident that the economic forces we identify are salient ones and must be part of any cogent understanding of legal labor markets. We do not praise or endorse a great many of the trends we observe, or the events they are catalyzing. Many of them have sown disruption, disappointment, and loss in the lives of honest, hardworking people. Many other trends—particularly those that characterize the twenty-first century "elastic tournament" environment—have rendered the lives of the lawyers that live with them impoverished socially and emotionally, bleaker and more isolated. As other commentators have also observed, these are not the result of narcissism, venality, or sociopathy in the elite bar; they are normal and predictable human and institutional responses to changes in technology and markets over which the Bar has no control. But if we wish to improve the lot of those who are suffering the brunt of these developments, we must acknowledge and respect the forces that created them, and fashion remedies that swim with the tide of economic change rather than rail against it.

NOTES ON BURK & McGOWAN

1. ***The Forces of Change.*** What forces do Burk & McGowan identify as important features of the changed landscape in which large law firms now compete for business? How are those forces affecting how large law firms operate? What further consequences do the authors predict? Are the authors' predictions plausible?

2. ***Dewey & LeBoeuf's Collapse.*** In 2012, Dewey & LeBoeuf LLP, a global law firm headquartered in New York City, declared bankruptcy. At the time of the bankruptcy filing, the firm employed over 1000 lawyers in 26 offices around the world. Many factors likely contributed to the firm's collapse, including a weak economy, large debts, excessive multi-year compensation guarantees for some partners, and mistakes committed by the firm's senior managers. When rumors began to surface about the firm's financial difficulties, the partnership unraveled quickly, as lawyers headed for the doors to pursue lateral opportunities in other law firms.[34] The rapid disintegration of Dewey &LeBoeuf illustrates Burk & McGowan's observation that mega-firms are "brittle"—vulnerable to splinting apart suddenly when the firm's only major assets, its lawyers, begin to leave in significant numbers.

3. ***What's to Like and Dislike?*** Based on all you have learned thus far about large law firms, what do you find attractive and unattractive about this practice setting? Do you think that the future of practice in these institutions is likely to be more or less attractive than the present? Why?

I. SUMMARY

This chapter has examined the history of large law firms and enormous changes they have undergone since the 1950s. Those changes include huge increases in firm size, greater diversity in the lawyers hired by large firms, less stable relationships with corporate clients, more lateral movement by lawyers between firms, and ongoing struggle by lawyers within firms to maintain their status within the firm hierarchy. We also examined large law firms' hiring and promotion practices and how recent changes in the structure of large firms have affected the careers and experiences of large firm lawyers, including young associates. We next explored the professional autonomy, values, and ethics of lawyers who work in large law firms. We considered how large firm lawyers tend to view their roles and responsibilities, and how current conditions in this practice realm might relate to patterns of lawyer misconduct. We examined several specific examples in which large firm lawyers have become embroiled in corporate scandals and what lessons

---

[34] *See* Peter Lattman, *Dewey & LaBoeuf Files for Bankruptcy*, N.Y. TIMES, May 28, 2012; James B. Stewart, *The Collapse: How a Top Legal Firm Destroyed Itself*, NEW YORKER, Oct. 13, 2013.

might be learned from those episodes. Finally, we speculated about what the future holds for large law firms and the lawyers they employ.

CHAPTER 16

SUPERVISORY/SUBORDINATE
RELATIONSHIPS

■ ■ ■

A. INTRODUCTION

This chapter considers how lawyers' individual decision-making is affected by their participation in practice teams and how the diffusion of responsibility in organizational practice tends to make attorney behavior in organizations difficult to monitor and regulate. It pays special attention to the situation of junior lawyers who sometimes may feel pressure to overlook or engage in misconduct.

As discussed in the introduction to Part V.B, the Model Rules may not adequately account for important sources of supervision, control, and influence over individual lawyer decision-making within organizations. Recall that two rules focus on the responsibilities of junior and supervisory lawyers in organizations. Model Rule 5.2 provides that "[a] lawyer is bound by the Rules of Professional Conduct notwithstanding that the lawyer acted at the direction of another person," although the junior lawyer may defer to a senior lawyer when the junior lawyer acts "in accordance with a supervisory lawyer's reasonable resolution of an arguable question of professional duty." Rule 5.1 charges partners and other senior lawyers with responsibility to ensure that the firm has policies that promote compliance with the rules. Rule 5.1 also makes a senior lawyer responsible for a junior lawyer's violation of the rules if the senior lawyer orders or ratifies the conduct or knows of it at a time when its consequences can be avoided or mitigated and fails to take action. Both of these rules focus primarily on the responsibilities of individual lawyers rather than the groups and organizations in which they practice.

A Subordinate Lawyer's Responsibility

- Rule 5.2: A lawyer is bound by the rules of professional conduct even if she acts at the direction of another person, but a junior lawyer may defer to a senior lawyer's reasonable resolution of an arguable question of professional duty.

Supervisory Lawyers' Responsibility

- Rule 5.1:

  - Partners and other lawyers with managerial authority are responsible for ensuring that the firm has policies to promote compliance with the rules of professional conduct.

  - A lawyer with supervisory authority over another lawyer should ensure that the other lawyer conforms to the ethics rules.

A senior lawyer is responsible for a junior lawyer's violation of the rules if the senior lawyer orders or ratifies the conduct or is a partner or has comparable managerial authority over the other lawyer and knows of the conduct at a time when its consequences can be avoided or mitigated but fails to take reasonable remedial measures.

The materials in this chapter explore how lawyers' participation in supervisory and subordinate relationships affects their behavior, and it examines the implications for lawyers' ethics and regulation. We first consider a well-known case in which a prominent senior lawyer engaged in misconduct that not only ruined his career but also imperiled the future of the junior lawyer with whom he worked. We then review social psychology research that may help us understand what happened in this instance and what lessons it holds for lawyers who work in organizations and on teams. Finally, we consider whether the individualistic approach to professional responsibility reflected in the Model Rules is an adequate way to regulate lawyers who work in organizations and whether imposing discipline at the level of the firm might be a useful supplement to individual sanctions in some cases.

B. THE *BERKEY PHOTO V. KODAK* INCIDENT

One of the most infamous examples of lawyer misconduct in litigation arose in an antitrust case brought by a small photograph developing company, Berkey Photo, against the then-huge camera, film, and photographic technology company, Eastman Kodak. Kodak was represented by the respected New York firm of Donovan Leisure Newton & Irvine. Mahlon Perkins, a senior Donovan Leisure partner working on the case, withheld critical documents that had been called for in discovery. He thereafter lied about the documents to the federal judge presiding over the case, contending that the documents had been destroyed. Perkins eventually confessed to the judge that he had withheld the documents and had committed perjury. He served a month in jail following his conviction for contempt of court. Joseph Fortenberry, a senior associate working on the matter with Perkins, was aware that Perkins was lying and tried to warn him by reminding Perkins that the documents were in his briefcase. But Perkins ignored him, and Fortenberry did not take any additional measures to notify the judge or to ensure that Berkey Photo received the documents. Fortenberry was passed over for partnership shortly after the matter came to light. (Donovan Leisure partners later claimed that the partnership decision had nothing to do with Fortenberry's role in the scandal and had been made two months before the Perkins matter came to light. Nevertheless, Fortenberry reportedly was not hired by any law firm to which he applied for a job.[1])

Why do you suppose Fortenberry did not take action? As a matter of law, what were Fortenberry's responsibilities under Rules 3.3, 3.4 and 5.2? Suppose that Fortenberry had told another senior partner about the incident before Perkins confessed his perjury to the judge in the case. What responsibilities would Rule 5.1 then impose on the senior partner and his firm?

Does the outcome for Fortenberry have any bearing on your views about how he should have responded when he discovered that Perkins was lying?

C. SOCIAL SCIENCE RESEARCH ON OBEDIENCE AND CONFORMITY

The following two excerpts describe some social science research on how individual decision-making is affected by participation in groups. One of the excerpts describes a famous study on obedience, and the other summarizes research on conformity. The authors focus primarily on the implications of this research for the behavior of lawyers in private firms, but it is broadly relevant to all lawyers who work in teams.

---

[1]   *See* James B. Stewart, Jr., *Kodak and Donovan Leisure: The Untold Story*, Am. Lawyer, Jan. 1983, at 24, 62.

THE ETHICS OF WRONGFUL OBEDIENCE

David L. Luban

Legal Ethics and Human Dignity 237 (Oxford University Press 2007)[2]

One of the best-known and most painful examples of [lawyers' wrongful obedience] was the Berkey-Kodak antitrust litigation in 1977, a bitterly contested private antitrust action brought by Berkey Photo against the giant of the industry. In the heat of adversarial combat, Mahlon Perkins, an admired senior litigator for the large New York law firm representing Kodak, snapped. For no apparent reason, he lied to his opponent to conceal documents from discovery, then perjured himself before a federal judge to cover up the lie. Eventually he owned up, resigned from his firm, and served a month in prison. Perhaps this sounds like an instance of chickens coming home to roost for a Rambo litigator. But by all accounts, Perkins was an upright and courtly man, the diametrical opposite of a Rambo litigator.[3]

Joseph Fortenberry, the associate working for him, knew that Perkins was perjuring himself and whispered a warning to him; but when Perkins ignored the warning, Fortenberry did nothing further to correct his misstatements. "What happened," recalls another associate, "was that he saw Perkins lie and really couldn't believe it. And he just had no idea what to do. I mean, he . . . kept thinking there must be a reason. Besides, what do you do? The guy was his boss and a great guy!"[4]

Notice the range of explanations here. First, the appeal to hierarchy: the guy was his boss. Second, to personal loyalty: the guy was a great guy. Third, to helplessness: Fortenberry had no idea what to do. Fourth, Fortenberry couldn't believe it. He kept thinking there must be a reason. The last is an explanation of a different sort, suggesting that Fortenberry's own ethical judgment was undermined by the situation he found himself in.

As a matter of fact, the same may be said of Perkins. He wasn't the lead partner in the litigation; he belonged to a team headed by a newcomer to the firm, an intense, driven, focused, and controlling lawyer, who (though he was entirely ethical) put pressure on himself and pressure on those around him. In a situation of supreme stress, Perkins's judgment simply failed him.

In Berkey-Kodak, neither Perkins nor Fortenberry received an explicit order to break the rules, but sometimes lawyers do. (And in Berkey-Kodak, Perkins's behavior, ignoring Fortenberry's whispered warnings, amounts to a tacit instruction to Fortenberry to say nothing.)

---

[2] © 2007 by Oxford University Press, Inc. By permission of Oxford University Press, USA.

[3] For an extended account, see JAMES B. STEWART, THE PARTNERS: INSIDE AMERICA'S MOST POWERFUL LAW FIRMS 327–65 (1983).

[4] Steven Brill, *When a Lawyer Lies,* ESQUIRE 23–24 (Dec. 19, 1979).

What guidance do the ethics rules give when this happens? ABA Model Rule 5.2(a) denies the defense of superior orders to a subordinate lawyer ordered to behave unethically, but Rule 5.2(b) states that a subordinate may defer to "a supervisory lawyer's reasonable resolution of an arguable question of professional duty." The problem is that the pressures on subordinate lawyers may lead them to misjudge when a question of professional duty is arguable and when the supervisor's resolution of it is reasonable. Remember that Fortenberry "kept thinking there must be a reason" when he heard Perkins perjure himself before a federal judge. This was not even close to an arguable question, and there is nothing reasonable about perjury—but the very fact that it was Fortenberry's respected supervisor who committed it undermined his own confidence that he understood what was reasonable and what was not. When that happens, Rule 5.2(b) will seem more salient to an associate than the bright-line prohibition on wrongful obedience that the first half of the rule articulates.

The Milgram obedience experiments. I want to see what we can learn about wrongful obedience from the most celebrated effort to study it empirically, Stanley Milgram's experiments conducted at Yale. Even though these experiments are very well known, it is useful to review the details of what Milgram did and what he discovered.

Imagine, then, that you answer Milgram's newspaper advertisement, offering $20 if you volunteer for a one-hour psychology experiment. When you enter the room, you meet the experimenter, dressed in a gray lab coat, and a second volunteer, a pleasant, bespectacled middle-aged man. What you don't know is that the second volunteer is in reality a confederate of the experimenter.

The experimenter explains that the two volunteers will be participating in a study of the effect of punishment on memory and learning. One of you, the learner, will memorize word-pairs; the other, the teacher, will punish the learner with steadily increasing electrical shocks each time he makes a mistake. A volunteer, rather than the experimenter, must administer the shocks because one aim of the experiment is to investigate punishments administered by very different kinds of people. The experimenter leads you to the shock-generator, a formidable-looking machine with thirty switches, marked from 15 volts to 450. Above the voltages, labels are printed. They range from "Slight Shock" (15–60 volts) through "Danger: Severe Shock" (375–420 volts); they culminate in an ominous-looking red label reading "XXX" above 435 and 450 volts. Both volunteers experience a 45-volt shack. Then they draw lots to determine their role. The drawing is rigged so that you become the teacher. The learner mentions that he has a mild heart problem and the experimenter replies rather nonresponsively that the shocks will cause no permanent tissue damage. The learner is strapped into the hot seat and the experiment gets under way.

The learner begins making mistakes, and as you escalate the shocks he grunts in pain. Eventually he complains about the pain, and at 150 volts he announces in some agitation that he wishes to stop the experiment. You look inquiringly at the man in the gray coat, but he says only, "The experiment requires that you continue." As you turn up the juice, the learner begins screaming. Finally, he shouts out that he will answer no more questions. Unflapped, the experimenter instructs you to treat silences as wrong answers. You ask him who will take responsibility if the learner is injured, and he states that he will. You continue.

As the experiment proceeds, the agitated learner announces that his heart is starting to bother him. Again, you protest, and again the man in the lab coat replies, "The experiment requires that you continue." At 330 volts, the screams stop. The learner falls ominously silent, and remains silent until the bitter end.

But it never actually gets to the bitter end, does it? You may be excused for thinking so. In a follow-up study, groups of people heard the Milgram experiment described without being told the results. They were asked to guess how many people would comply all the way to 450 volts, and to predict whether they themselves would. People typically guessed that at most one teacher out of a thousand would comply—and no one believed that they themselves would.

In reality, 63 percent of subjects complied all the way to 450 volts. Moreover, this is a robust result: it holds in groups of women as well as men, and experimenters obtained comparable results in Holland, Spain, Italy, Australia, South Africa, Germany, and Jordan; indeed, the Jordanian experimenters replicated the 65 percent result not only among adults but among seven-year-olds. Originally, Milgram had intended to run his experiments in Germany, to try to understand how so many Germans could participate in the Holocaust; his American experiments were merely for the purpose of perfecting his procedures. After the American dry run, however, Milgram remarked: "I found so much obedience, I hardly saw the need of taking the experiment to Germany."

In my view, we should regard the radical underestimates of subjects' willingness to inflict excruciating shocks on an innocent person as a finding just as important and interesting as the 65 percent compliance rate itself. The Milgram experiments demonstrate not only that in the right circumstances we are quite prone to destructive obedience, but also that we don't believe this about ourselves or about our neighbors—nor do we condone it. Corroborating this final conclusion, subjects in another experiment had the Milgram set-up described to them, and were shown the photograph of a college student who had supposedly participated in the experiment as a "teacher." They were asked to rate the student in the photograph (weak/strong, warm/cold, likable/not likable), based on appearance. Unsurprisingly, the ratings varied drastically depending on what level of shock the student had supposedly proceeded to—the higher the shock, the weaker, colder, and less likable the subject. The natural explanation of the "likability" finding is that subjects found the teacher unattractive to the degree that they found behavior unattractive—from which it follows that they disapproved of her compliance.

In short, Milgram demonstrates that each of us ought to believe three things about ourselves: that we strongly disapprove of destructive obedience; that we think we would never engage in it; and that the odds are almost two to one that we are fooling ourselves to think we would never engage in it.

Milgram was flabbergasted by his findings. He and other researchers ran dozens of variations on the experiment, which I won't describe, although I'll mention some of them shortly. His battery of experiments, which lasted for years and ultimately involved more than 1,000 subjects, stands even today as the most imaginative, ambitious, and controversial research effort ever undertaken by social psychologists.

The Milgram experiments place moral norms in conflict. One is what I will call the performance principle: the norm of doing your job properly, which in hierarchical work-settings includes the norm of following instructions. The other is the no-harm principle: the prohibition on torturing, harming, and killing innocent people. In the abstract, we might think, only a sadist or a fascist would subordinate the no-harm principle to the performance principle. But the Milgram experiments seem to show that what we think in the abstract is dead wrong. Two out of three people you pass in the street would electrocute you if a laboratory technician ordered them to.

The question is why.

[T]he key to understanding Milgram compliance lies in features of the experimental situation. The feature I wish to focus on is the slippery-slope character of the electrical shocks. The teacher moves up the scale of shocks by 15-volt increments, and reaches the 450-volt level only at the thirtieth shock. Among other things, this means that the subjects never directly confront the question "Should I administer a 330-volt shock to the learner?" The question is "Should I administer a 330-volt shock to the learner given that I've just administered a 315-volt shock?" It seems clear that the latter question is much harder to answer. As Milgram himself points out, to conclude that administering the 330-volt shock would be wrong is to admit that the 315-volt shock was probably wrong, and perhaps all the shocks were wrong.

Cognitive dissonance theory teaches that when our actions conflict with our self-concept, our beliefs and attitudes change until the conflict is removed. We are all pro se defense lawyers in the court of conscience. Cognitive dissonance theory suggests that when I have given the learner a series of electrical shocks, I simply won't view giving the next shock as a wrongful act, because I won't admit to myself that the previous shocks were wrong.

Let me examine this line of thought in more detail. Moral decision-making requires more than adhering to sound principles, such as the no-harm principle. It also requires good judgment, by which I mean knowing which actions violate a moral principle and which do not. Every lawyer understands the difference between good principles and good judgment—it is the difference between knowing a rule of law and being able to apply it to particular cases. As Kant first pointed out, you can't teach good judgment through general rules, because we already need judgment to know how rules apply. Judgment is always and irredeemably particular.

Let's assume that most of Milgram's subjects do accept the no-harm principle, and agree in the abstract that it outweighs the performance principle—again, the responses of audiences hearing the Milgram experiments described strongly suggest that this is so. The subjects still need good judgment to know at what point the electrical shocks violate the no-harm principle. Virtually no one thinks that the slight tingle of a 15-volt shock violates the no-harm principle: if it did, medical researchers would violate the no-harm principle every time they take blood samples from volunteers. Unsurprisingly, only two of Milgram's thousand subjects refused to give any shocks at all.

But how can 30 volts violate the no-harm principle if 15 volts didn't? And if a 30-volt shock doesn't violate the no-harm principle, neither does a shock of 45 volts.

Of course we know that slippery-slope arguments like this are unsound. At some point, the single grains of sand really do add up to a heap, and at some point shocking the learner really should shock the conscience as well. But it takes good judgment to know where that point lies. Unfortunately, cognitive dissonance generates enormous psychic pressure to deny that our previous obedience may have violated a fundamental moral principle. That denial requires us to gerrymander the boundaries of the no-harm principle so that the shocks we have already delivered don't violate it. However, once we knead and pummel the no-harm principle, it becomes virtually impossible to judge that the next shock, only imperceptibly more intense, crosses the border from the permissible to the forbidden. By luring us into higher and higher level shocks, one micro-step at a time, the Milgram experiments gradually and subtly disarm our ability to distinguish right from wrong. Milgram's subjects never need to lose, even for a second, their faith in the no-harm principle. Instead, they lose their capacity to recognize that administering an agonizing electrical shock violates it.

What I am offering here is a corruption of judgment explanation of the Milgram experiments. The road to hell turns out to be a slippery slope, and the travelers on it really do have good intentions—they "merely" suffer from bad judgment.

Explaining Berkey-Kodak through corruption-of-judgment theory. With these thoughts in mind, let me return to the Berkey-Kodak case and see what light the corruption-of-judgment theory may shed on it. The theory suggests that we should find the partner's and associate's misdeeds at the end of a slippery slope, beginning with lawful adversarial deception and culminating with lies, perjury, and wrongful obedience. Following this lead, one fact leaps out at us: the misdeeds occurred during a high-stakes discovery process.

Every litigator knows that discovery is one of the most contentious parts of civil litigation. Civil discovery is like a game of Battleship. One side calls out its shots—it files discovery requests—and the other side must announce when a shot scores a hit. It makes that announcement by turning over a document. There are two big differences. First, unlike Battleship, it isn't always clear when a shot has scored a hit. Lawyers get to argue about whether their document really falls within the scope of the request. They can argue that the request was too broad, or too narrow, or that the document is privileged, or is attorney work-product. Second, unlike Battleship, lawyers don't always get to peek at the opponent's card after the game. When the opponent concludes that a shot missed her battleship, she makes the decision ex parte—she doesn't have to announce it to her adversary, who may never learn that a smoking-gun document (the battleship) was withheld based on an eminently debatable legal judgment.

Every litigation associate goes through a rite of passage: she finds a document that seemingly lies squarely within the scope of a legitimate discovery request, but her supervisor tells her to devise an argument for excluding it. As long as the argument isn't frivolous there is nothing improper about this, but it marks the first step on to the slippery slope. For better or for worse, a certain kind of innocence is lost. It is the moment when withholding information despite an adversary's legitimate request starts to feel like zealous advocacy rather than deception. It is the moment when the no- deception principle encoded in Model Rule 8.4(c)— "It is professional misconduct for a lawyer to engage in conduct involving dishonesty, fraud, deceit or misrepresentation"—gets gerrymandered away from its plain meaning. But, like any other piece of elastic, the no-deception principle loses its grip if it is stretched too often. Soon, if the lawyer isn't very careful, every damaging request seems too broad or too narrow; every smoking-gun document is either work-product or privileged; no adversary ever has a right to "our" documents. At that point the fatal question is not far away: Is lying really so bad when it is the only way to protect "our" documents from an adversary who has no right to them? If legitimate advocacy marks the beginning of this particular slippery slope, Berkey-Kodak lies at its end.

UNETHICAL OBEDIENCE BY SUBORDINATE ATTORNEYS: LESSONS FROM SOCIAL PSYCHOLOGY

Andrew M. Perlman
36 Hofstra Law Review 451 (2007)

Consider the plight of a lawyer—fresh out of law school with crushing loan debt and few job offers—who accepts a position at a medium-sized firm. A partner asks the young lawyer to review a client's documents to determine what needs to be produced in discovery. In the stack, the associate finds a "smoking gun" that is clearly within the scope of discovery and spells disaster for the client's case. The associate reports the document to the partner, who without explanation tells the associate not to produce it. The associate asks the partner a few questions and quickly drops the subject when the partner tells the associate to get back to work.

We would like to believe that the young lawyer has the courage to ensure that the partner ultimately produces the document. We might hope, or expect, that the lawyer will report the issue to the firm's ethics counsel, if the firm is big enough to have one, or consult with other lawyers in the firm, assuming that she has developed the necessary relationships with her colleagues despite her junior status.

In fact, research in the area of social psychology suggests that, in some contexts, a subordinate lawyer will often comply with unethical instructions of this sort. These studies demonstrate that we ascribe too much weight to personality traits like honesty, and that contextual factors have far more to do with human behavior than most people recognize. Social psychologists have called this tendency to overemphasize individual personality differences and underestimate the power of the situation "the fundamental attribution error." Indeed, a number of experiments have amply demonstrated that situational forces are often more powerful predictors of human behavior than dispositional traits like honesty.

The importance of context is apparent from a number of experiments related to conformity, the most celebrated of which is a 1955 study by Solomon Asch.

Asch wanted to determine how often a group member would express independent judgment despite the unanimous, but obviously mistaken, contrary opinions of the rest of the group. To make this determination, Asch designed a study involving two cards.

In one version of the study, the experimenter told the subject that he was about to participate in a vision test and asked the subject to sit at a table with four other individuals who were secretly working with the experimenter.

All five people were shown the two cards and asked to identify which line in the card on the right (A, B, or C) was the same length as the line shown in the card on the left. Each person was asked his opinion individually and answered out loud, with the subject of the experiment going near the end. After each person had answered, a new set of cards was produced, and the participants were once again asked their opinions.

During the initial rounds, all of the confederates chose the obviously right answer. Not surprisingly, under this condition, the subject also chose the right answer.

In some subsequent rounds, however, Asch tested the subject's willingness to conform by prearranging for the confederates to choose the same wrong answer. Even though the four confederates were obviously mistaken, subjects of the experiment nevertheless provided the same wrong answer as the confederates 35.1% of the time, with 70% of subjects providing the wrong answer at least once during the experiment.

Most importantly, Asch found that the introduction of certain variables dramatically affected conformity levels. For example, Asch found that conformity fell quickly as the confederate group size dropped from three (31.8% of the answers were wrong) to two (13.6% were wrong) to one (3.6% were wrong), but did not increase much in groups larger than seven (maxing out at about 37%). Moreover, conformity fell by more than 50% in most variations of the experiment when one of the confederates dissented from the group opinion.

Not surprisingly, other studies have shown that conformity levels increase when (as is true in the law) the answer is more ambiguous. For example, in studies pre-dating Asch's, Muzafer Sherif placed a subject in a dark room and asked the person to look at a projected spot of light and guess how far it moved. Notably, the light did not move at all, but only appeared to move due to an optical illusion called the autokinetic effect. The precise extent of the perceived movement was thus impossible for subjects to determine objectively.

In one variation of the experiment, a subject gave individual assessments and was subsequently put in a room with a confederate, whose opinion intentionally varied from the subject's. As expected, the subject's assessments quickly came into line with the confederate's or (when the subject was placed in a group) with the group's. Thus, Sherif found that questions with ambiguous answers tended to produce more conformity, because people were understandably less certain of their original assessments.

The Asch and Sherif studies offer compelling evidence—also supported by more recent experiments—that a group member's opinion is easily affected by the group's overall judgment. Critically, the studies also reveal that this effect varies considerably, depending on situational variables, such as the level of ambiguity in the assigned task, the number of people in the group, the status of the person in the group (e.g., high status people feel more comfortable offering a contrasting view), and the existence of dissenters. The situation, in short, has a powerful effect on human behavior.

The basic point of these studies is that manipulations of the immediate social situation can overwhelm in importance the type of individual differences in personal traits or dispositions that people normally think of as being determinative of social behavior. As a result, subtle features of [the] situation prompt ordinary members of our society to behave extraordinarily.

Recall that numerous factors contribute to conformity, including the size of the group, the level of unanimity, the ambiguity of the issues involved, group cohesiveness, the strength of an individual's commitment to the group, the person's status in the group, and basic individual tendencies, such as the desire to be right and to be liked.

Many of these factors frequently exist in law practice. For instance, lawyers often have to tackle problems that contain many ambiguities of law and fact. Even questions that, at first, seem to have well-settled answers are often susceptible to an analysis that can make the answers seem unclear. Indeed, law students are trained to perform this particular art of legal jiu jitsu.

Given the uncertainty of many legal answers and lawyers' expertise in identifying (or manufacturing) those uncertainties, lawyers are especially susceptible to the forces of conformity. For example, the subordinate in the initial discovery hypothetical may review the discovery rules and find language that could theoretically (though implausibly) support the partner's position, particularly if she perceives that other lawyers at the firm are engaging in similar behavior. Thus, despite her initial belief about the document's discoverability, she might begin to believe that her original view was either a product of inexperience or a failure to appreciate fully all of the nuances about how discovery works in practice. She might consequently come to think that her initial view was wrong, even though it was quite clearly right. And if the document's discoverability fell into an area that was even slightly grey instead of black and white, the tendency to conform would be even greater.

The hierarchical structure of lawyering also makes conformity more likely. Studies suggest that strong conformity forces exist even in "arbitrarily constructed groups . . . that hold no long-term power to reward conformity or punish dissent." Lawyers, however, work in groups that are not arbitrarily constructed and actually do hold long-term power to reward conformity or punish dissent. Attorneys typically work in settings where other group members, such as senior partners or corporate executives (e.g., in-house counsel jobs), control the professional fates of subordinates, a condition that increases the likelihood of conformity. So, for example, the young lawyer in the initial hypothetical would feel a powerful, though perhaps unconscious, urge to conform, especially given that she had trouble finding a job and faced significant financial burdens.

Social status also affects conformity. There is evidence that people with more social prestige feel more comfortable deviating from the prevailing opinion. By contrast, a person with a lower status, such as the junior law firm associate in the hypothetical, will be more likely to conform to protect her more vulnerable position.

Unanimity also encourages conformity, and unanimity is common among lawyers who are working together on the same legal matter. Studies have shown that zealous advocacy tends to make lawyers believe that the objectively "correct" answer to a legal problem is the one that just so happens to benefit the client. This tendency causes teams of lawyers to agree on many issues, making it even more difficult for dissenting voices to be heard. So in the discovery example, the absence of a dissenting voice would make the subordinate more likely to assume that her initial position was incorrect or, at the very least, not worth pursuing.

The point here is not that lawyers will always conform to the views of superiors or colleagues. Plenty of lawyers express their own beliefs, even under very difficult circumstances. The claim is that powerful social forces exist in many law practice settings that make conformity more likely than most people would expect.

NOTES ON RESEARCH ON OBEDIENCE AND CONFORMITY

1. *How Much Do These Theories Explain?* Do Luban's corruption of judgment theory and Perlman's arguments about the power of pressure to conform adequately explain Fortenberry's conduct? In other words, do obedience and conformity norms fully account for how junior lawyers respond to ethical dilemmas that they confront in practice? What other factors might you expect to influence how junior lawyers behave? In the hypothetical at the heart of Perlman's piece, what role, if any, might you expect the junior

lawyer's lack of alternative job prospects and his personal financial situation play in his deliberations about how to respond?

2.   ***Rules 5.1 and 5.2.*** How would Rules 5.1 and 5.2 apply to Perkins and Fortenberry in the Berkey Photo incident? Do Rules 5.1 and 5.2 strike the right balance between holding lawyers responsible for their individual behavior and taking into account of the need for lawyers who work in teams to respond to the situations they confront in a coordinated way?

3.   ***The Threat of Bar Discipline v. Obedience Norms.*** Why wouldn't the threat of bar discipline for violations of Rule 5.2 always overcome a junior lawyer's tendency to obey a supervisor's decision (explicit or implicit) when the supervisor's resolution of the ethical dilemma is unreasonable? Might the answer lie in the fact that much misconduct never comes to light and that, even when it does, disciplinary sanctions are rare?

As we'll see in the materials on bar discipline, a very small percentage of the complaints that go to the state bar result in any kind of discipline or even investigation. Moreover, lawyers in large firms are especially unlikely to be sanctioned. We will explore some possible reasons for this discrepancy in the rates of discipline for large firm lawyers and lawyers in small and solo practice when we examine the disciplinary system in Chapter 36.

D. DISCIPLINE FOR LAW FIRMS?

If, as we've just seen, individual lawyer behavior is sometimes strongly influenced by their participation in teams and their roles in organizations, should our systems for regulating professional conduct reach firms and not just individual lawyers? Notice that the two Model Rules that address supervisory and subordinate relationships among lawyers—Rules 5.1 and 5.2—still focus primarily on *individual* lawyer conduct. Disciplinary sanctions for violations of these rules fall on the *individuals* involved, not on the groups or organizations in which they practice.

The following case illustrates the difficulty that sometimes arises in assigning individual blame in circumstances where lawyers work in teams. It also provides one example of how standards of professional responsibility are imposed and enforced by the tribunals before which lawyers practice, and not just through bar disciplinary processes. In this case, the court looked to the Federal Rules of Civil Procedure for limits on "discovery abuse"—the tactical misuse of the discovery process to deny opponents access to relevant information.

Qualcomm v. Broadcom. In *Qualcomm Inc. v. Broadcom Corp.,* 2008 WL 66932 (S.D. Cal. 2008), a federal magistrate judge awarded $8.5 million in sanctions against Qualcomm and additional sanctions against six of Qualcomm's outside counsel for failing to produce hundreds of thousands of documents that Broadcom had requested in discovery.[5] (Those sanctions were based on Fed. R. Civ. P. 26 and 37, which authorize courts to punish parties and attorneys who fail to comply with discovery obligations and court orders.) The magistrate judge found that the sanctioned attorneys had failed to conduct a reasonable inquiry into the adequacy of Qualcomm's document production and had ignored warning signals that the document search was not thorough and that the document production was incomplete. The most junior of the "Qualcomm Six," Adam Bier, had been assigned the task of preparing one of the trial witnesses, and while doing so he learned of an email message that was clearly called for in discovery and should have been turned over to Broadcom. The magistrate judge found that the discovery of this email put Bier and the five other lawyers on notice that many other highly relevant documents had not been produced and that Qualcomm's previous document searches had been inadequate. In addition to imposing sanctions against Qualcomm and its attorneys, the magistrate judge also referred the sanctioned lawyers to the California State Bar for possible discipline:

> [T]he Sanctioned Attorneys assisted Qualcomm in committing this incredible discovery violation by intentionally hiding or recklessly ignoring relevant documents, ignoring or rejecting numerous warning signs that Qualcomm's document search was inadequate, and blindly accepting Qualcomm's unsupported assurances that its document search was adequate. The Sanctioned Attorneys then used the lack of evidence to repeatedly and forcefully make false statements and arguments to the court and jury. As such, the Sanctioned Attorneys violated their discovery obligations and also may have violated their ethical duties. To address the potential ethical violations, the Court refers the Sanctioned Attorneys to The State Bar of California for an appropriate investigation and possible imposition of sanctions.

The district court, which had the power to review the findings of the federal magistrate judge, vacated the sanctions order and remanded the matter to the magistrate judge to allow the sanctioned lawyers to defend their conduct, using otherwise privileged documents as necessary, under the self-defense exception to the attorney-client privilege.

On remand, the magistrate judge declined to impose sanctions against any of the outside lawyers. *Qualcomm Inc. v. Broadcom Corp.*, 2010 WL 1336937 (S.D. Cal. 2010). Although she stated that there was

---

[5]   In the United States federal courts, magistrate judges are appointed to assist United States district court judges in the performance of their duties. Magistrate judges are appointed by a majority vote of the federal district judges of a particular district and serve terms of eight years if full-time, or four years if part-time, and may be reappointed.

"still no doubt in this Court's mind that this massive discovery failure resulted from significant mistakes, oversights, and miscommunication on the part of both outside counsel and Qualcomm employees," she found that the evidence was insufficient to establish that any of the lawyers had acted in bad faith, and therefore she concluded that sanctions were inappropriate. (A finding of bad faith was relevant to the award of sanctions under the Federal Rules of Civil Procedure.) In reaching this conclusion, the magistrate judge cited evidence of "an incredible breakdown in communication" and lack of meaningful communication "that permeated all of the relationships (amongst Qualcomm employees, between Qualcomm employees and outside legal counsel, and amongst outside counsel)." She noted the failure of outside counsel to meet with the relevant Qualcomm employees to ensure appropriate document collection and to obtain the information required to understand how Qualcomm's computer system was organized. She observed that no attorney took supervisory responsibility for ensuring that responsive documents were produced and that there was no clear agreement among the participants regarding how the document collection and production would proceed. She further found that there was inadequate follow-up in response to contradictory evidence about where relevant documents might be found. She stated that she was "dismayed" that "none of the involved attorneys considered the larger discovery picture"—that the existence of the "new" documents indicated that the prior document collection had been inadequate and that still "no one suggested that any follow-up discovery investigation be conducted." Still, since she found no bad faith by any of the outside attorneys, she declined to award sanctions.

The state bar took no action on the disciplinary referrals. The following blog entry described what happened to the most junior lawyer of the "Qualcomm Six" while the sanctions order was pending:

> [When] sanctions were levied, the attorneys were referred to the state bar for investigation, and Bier's career hit a rough patch.
>
> "We'd love to send you to the hiring partner down the hall, but we can't touch you," Bier says he was told more than once by law firms who interviewed him. "We have lots of Fortune 500 clients; they're all freaking out about e-discovery."
>
> Fortunately for Bier and his former colleagues, the sanctions entered by the magistrate judge were ultimately vacated.
>
> As for Adam Bier, he still isn't sure how he—a very junior associate at the time of the original events, a "baby lawyer" just a few months into private practice—got mixed up in the whole mess. Understandably, in view of the nightmare he experienced,

he has traded in litigation for a transactional practice. A few years ago, he started his own practice . . .

So far, so good—in fact, he said his main problem these days is that his business is getting overwhelming. It's a good problem to have.[6]

NOTES ON QUALCOMM V. BROADCOM

1. ***No Bad Faith v. Responsible Conduct.*** Does the magistrate's finding that none of the Qualcomm Six acted in bad faith mean that they behaved appropriately?

2. ***The Limited Reach of Standards That Turn on Individual Responsibility.*** Does this case suggest a problem with disciplinary standards that require a finding of misbehavior by particular individuals?

3. ***How Can Junior Lawyers Protect Themselves?*** This matter seems to have ended reasonably well for Adam Bier, but it might not have. As a young lawyer just starting out in practice, what strategies might you adopt to ensure that you don't find yourself on the wrong side of ethics issues like those faced by Joseph Fortenberry and Adam Bier?

* * *

Proposals for Disciplinary Action Against Law Firms as Well as Lawyers. As we've seen earlier in this chapter, in summaries of research on obedience and conformity and in our examination of several episodes involving lawyers' interactions while working in teams, lawyers' participation in groups sometimes significantly shapes their conduct. And yet the Model Rules that address supervisory and subordinate relationships among lawyers—Rules 5.1 and 5.2—focus primarily on *individual* lawyer conduct and responsibility. Moreover, when lawyers violate these rules, the disciplinary sanctions fall on the *individuals* involved, not on the groups or organizations in which they practice.

Should disciplinary agencies have authority to discipline law firms as well as well individual lawyers? Consider the following argument in favor of such an approach.

PROFESSIONAL DISCIPLINE FOR LAW FIRMS?
Ted Schneyer
77 Cornell Law Review 1 (1992)

Law practice in the United States is regulated in many ways, but most comprehensively through a specialized system that metes out professional discipline to those who violate the rules of legal ethics.

---

[6] Christopher Danzig, *Dispatch from Amelia Island: When Clients Attack*, ABOVE THE LAW, Sept. 9, 2011.

Disciplinary agencies have always taken individual lawyers as their targets. They have never proceeded against law firms either directly, for breaching ethics rules addressed to them, or vicariously, for the wrongdoing of firm lawyers in the course of their work. The traditional focus on individuals has probably resulted from the system's jurisdictional tie to licensing, which the state requires only for individuals, and from the system's development at a time when solo practice was the norm.

Legal practice, however, has changed. While as late as 1951, sixty percent of the bar practiced alone, two-thirds now work in law firms and other organizations; in addition, more lawyers in private practice now work in firms than as sole practitioners. Law firms themselves have also changed [by becoming much larger and more highly leveraged]. The proportionally larger number of inexperienced lawyers within firms has heightened the need for supervision.

As law firms have grown, firm governance has become more complex. A few large firms may still govern themselves the old-fashioned ways— either as a patriarchy ruled by a single senior partner or as a loose collection of nearly independent practitioners. But most firms now recognize the limits of individual partner control in the face of extensive personal liability for firm malpractice and have adopted a variety of bureaucratic controls to limit their exposure: policy manuals, formal rules, committees, specialized departments, and centralized management.

As law firms grow, the potential harm they can inflict on clients, third parties, and the legal process grows as well. At the same time, the law firm, at least the larger firm, is ripening into an institution that presents new opportunities for bureaucratically controlling the technical and ethical quality of law practice. Indeed, the large firm may now be ready to perform the control or monitoring function for its lawyers that the hospital [or HMO] performs for the medical profession.

So far, however, those who make disciplinary policy have taken little notice of these developments. True, the Model Rules of Professional Conduct notes that "the ethical atmosphere of a firm can influence the conduct of its members." The Model Rules also make clear that supervisory lawyers are responsible for monitoring their subordinates. But the ABA, the state supreme courts that adopt the ABA codes, and the agencies that assist the courts in disciplinary enforcement have yet to confront the infrequency of disciplinary proceedings against lawyers in firms.

Proceedings against lawyers in large or even medium-sized firms are very rare. Yet, judging from the frequency with which larger firms and their lawyers are the targets of civil suits, motions to disqualify, and sanctions under the rules of civil procedure, disciplinable offenses occur with some regularity in those firms. Some observers attribute the paucity of disciplinary actions against larger-firm lawyers to an informal immunity from disciplinary scrutiny that those lawyers, as the most prestigious segment of the bar, supposedly enjoy. Others point out that the types of misconduct that most often generate grievances and disciplinary sanctions—neglect of cases and misappropriation of client property, respectively—occur much more often in small practices than in larger firms. Still others cite the reactive nature of disciplinary enforcement; the authorities do not normally investigate until clients (or, occasionally, nonclients) complain about a lawyer's conduct. On this theory, the businesses that predominate on the client lists of large firms rarely report complaints against their lawyers. Unlike the "one shot" individuals whom sole practitioners tend to represent, regular business clients may not view the disciplinary process as a "governance mechanism" for their relations with lawyers, and may instead rely on their ability to take their business elsewhere to protect them.

These factors may help to explain the infrequency of disciplinary proceedings against large-firm lawyers, but additional explanations, so far neglected, have important implications for disciplinary policy. These explanations stem from the nature of group practice. First, even when a firm has clearly committed wrongdoing, courts may have difficulty, as an evidentiary matter, in assigning blame to particular lawyers, each of whom has an incentive to shift responsibility for an ethical breach onto others in the firm. Many, perhaps most, of the tasks performed in large firms are assigned to teams. Teaming not only encourages lawyers to take ethical risks they would not take individually, but also obscures responsibility, which makes it difficult for both complainants and disciplinary authorities to determine which lawyers committed a wrongful act.

Second, even when courts and disciplinary agencies can link professional misconduct to one or more lawyers in a firm as an evidentiary matter, they may be reluctant to sanction those lawyers for fear of making them scapegoats for others in the firm who would have taken the same actions in order to further the firm's interests.

Third and most important, a law firm's organization, policies, and operating procedures constitute an "ethical infrastructure" that cuts across particular lawyers and tasks. Large law firms are typically complex organizations. Consequently, their infrastructures may have at least as much to do with causing and avoiding unjustified harm as do the individual values and practice skills of their lawyers. [The article here cites several examples of ethical lapses in large firms.] But who was—and who was not—responsible for the arguable failure of these firms to develop the appropriate infrastructure? In such matters, the locus of individual responsibility seems inherently unclear, in part because it is difficult to attribute omissions to specific individuals in a group. Even a firm with a well-defined management structure does not delegate the duty to make firm policy and maintain an appropriate infrastructure solely to management. To varying degrees this remains every partner's business—and sometimes, as a result, no one's. In no aspect of law firm work is teaming, and thus collective responsibility, more important than in the development of firm structure, policy, and procedures.

Given the evidentiary problems of pinning professional misconduct on one or more members of a lawyering team, the reluctance to scapegoat some lawyers for sins potentially shared by others in their firm, and especially the importance of a law firm's ethical infrastructure and the diffuse responsibility for creating and maintaining that infrastructure, a disciplinary regime that targets only individual lawyers in an era of large law firms is no longer sufficient. Sanctions against firms are needed as well.

While there has been little attention to these points in the field of lawyer discipline, scholars and policymakers have given considerable attention to analogous matters. Commentators have considered the significance of bureaucratic or structural variables in accounting for corporate crime; the pros and cons of making corporations, and not just their agents, liable for crimes committed in the furtherance of organizational interests; and the appropriate mix of criminal sanctions for organizational offenders.

The criminal sanctions that are recognized as appropriate for convicted corporations can easily be converted into a sensible scheme of disciplinary sanctions for law firms.

NOTES ON LAW FIRM DISCIPLINE

1. *Law Firm Discipline Remains Rare.* As of today, only two states—New York and New Jersey—have adopted ethics rules permitting firms as well as individuals to be disciplined, and those two states have rarely used that authority. A proposal to include a provision allowing for the discipline of law firms in the Model Rules as part of the Ethics 2000 revisions was removed before the proposed rules were sent to the ABA House of Delegates for approval. Opponents of the proposed revision successfully argued that law firm discipline is unnecessary because bar disciplinary committees can effectively deter misconduct by sanctioning the individuals involved. Critics of the proposed rule also argued that the primary sanctions available to disciplinary committees—disbarment, suspension of law licenses, reprimands, and modest fines—are designed to regulate individual conduct and are not well-suited for shaping the behavior of institutions.[7] But

---

[7]   Am. Bar. Ass'n, Ctr. For Prof'l Responsibility, Testimony of Robert A. Creamer, Joseph R. Lundy, and Brian J. Redding, Attorneys' Liability Assurance Society, Inc. to the American Bar

proponents of the rule change countered that firm discipline could work if monetary sanctions were sufficiently large—that firms would take collective responsibility for attorney conduct if the financial costs of failing to do so were substantial. Some advocates for firm discipline argued in favor of an additional requirement that firms designate an internal compliance specialist.[8]

2. *How Might Firm Discipline Influence Lawyers' Individual and Collective Behavior?* Critics of the current approach to lawyer regulation argue that the policies and procedures of the firms in which lawyers practice are an essential element of effective oversight and regulation of the legal profession. They argue that the current approach, which stresses individual responsibility, neglects the importance of law firms' policies and procedures. In the excerpt above, for example, Schneyer asserts that the prospect of professional discipline for firms would encourage law firms to develop an "ethical infrastructure" that deters lawyer misconduct. Others have argued that firms' policies and procedures, both formal and informal, play "an active and increasingly important role in lawyer socialization and the day-to-day interpretation of professional regulation."[9] According to this view, law firms' internal controls—such as conflicts screening procedures, mechanisms for reporting ethical issues, formal billing guidelines, peer review, policies for protecting client confidentiality, responding to client misconduct, and the like—are at least as important as the bar's disciplinary process in discouraging lawyer misconduct and promoting ethical behavior.[10]

3. *Firms Are Still Subject to Other Types of Liability for Lawyer Misconduct.* Although most jurisdictions have no rules of professional conduct that allow for firm discipline, law firms are still vulnerable to harm attributable to the misconduct of their lawyers. Prosecutors occasionally charge law firms for criminal violations, and firms may also face civil suits and malpractice claims for their lawyers' misdeeds. In 2006, for example, Milberg Weiss was criminally indicted for secret, illegal payments made by some of the firm's partners to induce clients to become named plaintiffs in class action lawsuits.[11] The development and marketing of dubious tax shelters by a partner in the firm of Jenkens & Gilchrist resulted in a government investigation, a $108 million settlement of a class action by former clients, and, ultimately, the firm's demise.[12] Since the mid-1980s,

---

Association Ethics 2000 Commission (Feb. 15, 2001), available at http://www.abanet.org/cpr/e2k/e2k-witness_lundy.html.

[8] Elizabeth Chambliss & David Wilkins, *A New Framework for Law Firm Discipline*, 16 GEO. J. LEGAL ETHICS 335 (2003).

[9] Chambliss & Wilkins, 16 GEO. J. LEGAL ETHICS 335, at 338.

[10] *Id.*

[11] *See* Martha Neil, *Milberg Weiss in the Hot Seat: Should Law Firms Ever Be Indicted?* ABA J., Dec. 25, 2006.

[12] Paul Davies et al., *Law Firm's Work on Tax Shelters Leads to Demise*, WALL ST. J., Mar. 30, 2007, at A1.

there have been dozens of verdicts and settlements exceeding $20 million in malpractice claims against major firms, and many more in the $3–19 million range.[13] Thus, law firms have reason to be concerned about how their lawyers' misconduct can inflict harm on the institution through criminal sanctions, civil lawsuits, malpractice liability, and reputational damage. Not surprisingly, therefore, many law firms have created ethics committees and/or designated ethics specialists and appointed general counsel, with responsibility for resolving problems and developing policies to promote professional responsibility.

E. SUMMARY

In this chapter, we explored regulatory and ethical issues surrounding the conduct of lawyers who work in teams. We identified two Model Rules that address the responsibilities of junior lawyers and their supervisors. We then examined social science research on how behavior tends to be influenced by individuals' participation in groups, and we considered several incidents involving lawyers' failure to take responsibility for legal compliance while working in teams. We examined possible limitations of the current approach to lawyer regulation, which focuses primarily on individual lawyer responsibility, and possible benefits of alternative approaches. Finally, we addressed how the procedures and policies of lawyers' workplaces may influence how lawyers behave.

---

[13] Professional Services Group, Aon Risk Services, at http://www.aon.com/risk-services/professional-services/loss-prevention.jsp (last visited July 2, 2013).

CHAPTER 17

A LARGE FIRM LAWYER'S DOWNFALL

∎ ∎ ∎

A. INTRODUCTION

This chapter is devoted entirely to a case study. It focuses on the downfall of John Gellene, a brilliant and hardworking Wall Street lawyer who lost his license to practice law and was sentenced to 15 months in prison following his failure to disclose that he and his law firm were representing two parties with conflicts of interest in a bankruptcy proceeding. Taking into account all you've learned thus far about conflicts of interest, the organization and culture of large law firms, and supervisory/subordinate relationships, try to make sense of what happened to this lawyer.

The first part of this chapter is a case, *United States v. Gellene*, in which the Seventh Circuit affirmed Gellene's conviction and prison sentence. Following the case is an account that provides some background on Gellene's personal history, his career, and his interactions with the New York State bar, his firm partners, and various courts. As you read these materials, try to assess whether Gellene is simply a flawed character who has only himself to blame for his troubles, or whether other people and institutions also bear some responsibility for this sorry incident.

B. THE STORY OF JOHN GELLENE

UNITED STATES V. GELLENE
182 F.3d 578 (7th Cir. 1999)

RIPPLE, CIRCUIT JUDGE.

John G. Gellene, a partner at the law firm of Milbank Tweed Hadley & McCloy ("Milbank") in New York, represented the Bucyrus-Erie Company ("Bucyrus") in its Chapter 11 bankruptcy. Mr. Gellene filed in the bankruptcy court a sworn declaration that was to include all of his firm's connections to the debtor, creditors, and any other parties in interest. The declaration failed to list the senior secured creditor and related parties. Mr. Gellene was charged with two counts of knowingly and fraudulently making a false material declaration in the Bucyrus bankruptcy case, in violation of 18 U.S.C. § 152, and one count of using a document while under oath, knowing that it contained a false material declaration, in violation of 18 U.S.C. § 1623. Although Mr. Gellene admitted that he had used bad judgment in concluding that the representations did not need to be disclosed, he asserted that he had no fraudulent intent. After a six-day trial, on March 3, 1998, the jury returned guilty verdicts against Mr. Gellene on all three counts. Mr. Gellene was sentenced to 15 months of imprisonment on each count, to run concurrently, and was fined $15,000.

I. Background

Bucyrus, a manufacturer of mining equipment based in South Milwaukee, Wisconsin, had retained Milbank to represent it in general corporate matters in the 1980s. Between 1988 and 1992, Bucyrus' financial transactions, including a leveraged buy-out, left the company with more than $200 million in debt. During that time, the head of Milbank's Mergers and Acquisitions Department, Lawrence Lederman, managed the Bucyrus account. In 1993, Lederman brought in Mr. Gellene, a bankruptcy attorney at Milbank, to work on the financial restructuring of Bucyrus.

At that time, the major parties with an interest in Bucyrus included Goldman Sachs & Co., Bucyrus' largest equity shareholder, which held 49% of the Bucyrus stock; Jackson National Life Insurance Company ("JNL"), Bucyrus' largest creditor, which held approximately $60 million in unsecured notes; and South Street Funds, a group of investment entities, which held approximately $35 million in senior secured notes and leasehold interests. South Street Funds was managed and directed by Greycliff Partners, an investment entity which consisted of financial advisers Mikael Salovaara and Alfred Eckert, former employees of Goldman Sachs.

On February 18, 1994, Bucyrus filed its Chapter 11 bankruptcy petition in the Eastern District of Wisconsin. Because the legal representation of a debtor is subject to court approval, Bucyrus submitted an application requesting that Milbank be appointed to represent it in the bankruptcy. Pursuant to Bankruptcy Rule 2014, the application included the required sworn declaration disclosing "any connection" that Milbank had with "the Debtors, their creditors, or any other party in interest." Mr. Gellene, Milbank's lead attorney in the Bucyrus bankruptcy, under oath disclosed that his firm had previously represented Goldman Sachs and JNL in "unrelated" matters and would continue to represent Goldman Sachs in non-Bucyrus proceedings. Mr. Gellene did not disclose any of Milbank's representations of South Street, Greycliff Partners or Salovaara.

The United States Trustee and JNL filed objections to Mr. Gellene's Rule 2014 declaration. They sought additional information regarding

Milbank's representation of Goldman Sachs and questioned whether there was a sufficient conflict of interest to bar Milbank's retention as counsel for the debtor.

On March 23, 1994, the bankruptcy court conducted a hearing on the issue. It requested that Mr. Gellene submit a second declaration containing more detail about possible conflicts of interest.[4] The court specifically commented: "If you represent them [Goldman Sachs] in other matters, then I think it's important to state precisely what arrangements have been made internally to separate what you're doing in this matter with the recommendation in other matters."

On March 28, 1994, Mr. Gellene signed a second sworn Rule 2014 statement providing details about Milbank's representation of Goldman Sachs and the "Chinese wall" that the firm planned to put in place. It also disclosed its prior representation of two other creditors, Cowen & Co. and Mitsubishi International. The declaration then stated:

> Besides the representations disclosed in my declaration dated February 18, 1994, after due inquiry I am unaware of any other current representation by Milbank of an equity security holder or institutional creditor of [Bucyrus].

Mr. Gellene again did not disclose any representation by Milbank of South Street, Greycliff Partners or Salovaara. However, at the time of both declarations, Milbank was doing their legal work, including the representation of Salovaara when his partner, Alfred Eckert, sued him.[5]

At Milbank, one partner recognized that there might be a conflict of interest between Milbank's representation of Salovaara in the Salovaara-Eckert dispute and its representation of Bucyrus in its bankruptcy proceedings. At a meeting on December 22, 1993, with Mr. Gellene, Lederman and Milbank partner Toni Lichstein, all of whom were working on the Bucyrus bankruptcy and the Salovaara-Eckert dispute, Lichstein raised the possibility of conflict. Both Lederman and Mr. Gellene stated it was not a problem. Lichstein raised the issue again in March 1994 after she, representing Salovaara, had attended a South Street investors' meeting at which South Street's investment in Bucyrus was discussed. At

---

[4] The bankruptcy court also told Mr. Gellene: "New York is different from Milwaukee . . . Professional things like conflicts [of interest] are taken very, very seriously. And for better or worse you're stuck in Wisconsin."

[5] In November 1993, after Salovaara's partner Alfred Eckert decided to pursue employment elsewhere, Salovaara threatened and ultimately took legal action against him. Milbank served as Salovaara's attorney through June of 1994, although a New Jersey firm was listed as the counsel of record in the initial litigation. The dispute between Salovaara and Eckert involved control of South Street and Greycliff; it was still ongoing in 1998. On December 9, 1993, during the Salovaara-Eckert dispute, Mr. Gellene and other Milbank lawyers began representing South Street and Greycliff in an acquisition of a $15 million note and claim in the Colorado bankruptcy of George Gillett. Mr. Gellene was the Milbank partner in charge of the matter. In fact, Mr. Gellene billed work on this project the same day that he signed his second declaration in the Bucyrus case.

that time, Mr. Gellene responded that Salovaara was not a creditor of Bucyrus and that all disclosure obligations had been satisfied. However, Lederman suggested that, if Lichstein had further concerns, Salovaara should obtain other counsel. After that, Milbank's representation of Salovaara in his dispute with Eckert slowed and eventually ended. By December 1994, Lederman had resigned his representation of South Street/Greycliff and had written off the billings generated in a tangential matter, a Colorado bankruptcy (about $16,000), and in the Salovaara-Eckert dispute (more than $300,000). Mr. Gellene also wrote off $13,000 in fees and expenses on the Bucyrus bankruptcy billings. Mr. Gellene never informed anyone at Bucyrus of the other Milbank representations.

Meanwhile, the Bucyrus bankruptcy creditors' committee worked through the summer and fall of 1994 to see if it could formulate a plan that would satisfy the major creditors. By late fall, a compromise was reached and all the parties to the Bucyrus bankruptcy agreed to the new plan of reorganization.

Thereafter, Milbank filed a petition requesting compensation for its work on the bankruptcy case. In November 1995, a hearing was held on Milbank's application for more than $2 million in legal fees and expenses. The United States Trustee and JNL both opposed the application. Mr. Gellene was lead attorney for Milbank at those hearings. However, when he testified in support of his firm's request for fees, Milbank partner David Gelfand was the attorney who put on Mr. Gellene's testimony. Gelfand presented Mr. Gellene's sworn declarations to him on the stand. Mr. Gellene testified that the supplemental Rule 2014 declaration had disclosed Milbank's relationship with Goldman Sachs and thus that the court had been fully aware of that relationship. However, Mr. Gellene did not testify that his firm had represented and was continuing to represent South Street and Greycliff. The United States Trustee did not learn of that representation until the late fall of 1996. The court ultimately awarded Milbank approximately $1.8 million in fees and expenses.[9]

In late 1996, JNL discovered that Milbank had represented Salovaara in his dispute with Eckert at the same time it was representing Bucyrus. JNL then filed a motion in the bankruptcy court in December 1996 seeking disgorgement of Milbank's fees. Mr. Gellene did not respond to the motion. On February 24, 1997, when his partners became aware of the motion and asked him about it, Mr. Gellene responded falsely that the answer was due in a few days. Mr. Gellene even altered the JNL filing to conceal the date it had been signed. When that deception was uncovered, however, Mr. Gellene admitted to Lichstein and Gelfand that he had lied about the response due date.

---

[9]   Based on Mr. Gellene's false statements, the bankruptcy court subsequently directed Milbank to return the $1.8 million to the bankruptcy estate.

In March 1997, Mr. Gellene filed a third declaration with the bankruptcy court. In it, he explained that he had made an error in legal judgment by omitting Milbank's representations of South Street and of Salovaara and took "full personal responsibility for failing to disclose these matters to the court."

On December 9, 1997, a federal grand jury returned a three-count indictment against Mr. Gellene, charging him with two counts of bankruptcy fraud and with one count of perjury. It alleged that Mr. Gellene had lied three times in the course of a bankruptcy case: twice when he filed the Rule 2014 declarations knowing that they were false and once when he used the supplemental declaration, while under oath at a bankruptcy hearing, knowing that it contained a false material declaration.

At Mr. Gellene's trial, the government produced evidence of other false representations by the defendant, evidence that was admitted under Rule 404(b) of the Federal Rules of Evidence. The first concerned Mr. Gellene's bar status. He joined the New York State Bar in 1990; however, between 1981 and 1990 he represented himself to be a member of that bar in court filings and in legal publications. Mr. Gellene also represented himself to be a member of the federal bar in the Southern District of New York, both by repeatedly appearing in that court and by claiming that membership when applying for membership in the Eastern District of Wisconsin to represent Bucyrus in its bankruptcy proceedings.

The second category of evidence admitted at trial concerned Milbank's relationship with Lotus Cab Company: Mr. Gellene had included his charges to the cab company in the itemized expenses of the Milbank fee request but had failed to disclose to the court the ownership interest of some law firm partners in that company. The third false representation admitted at Mr. Gellene's trial under Rule 404(b) was made to the Colorado bankruptcy court. After South Street, Milbank's client, failed to produce discovery documents in the bankruptcy case of George Gillett, the bankruptcy court dismissed the South Street claim. Mr. Gellene moved for reconsideration; he stated that the delay in producing the documents was caused by the winding-up of South Street and by the ongoing dispute between Eckert, the managing partner of South Street, and the Funds' portfolio advisor, Greycliff Partners, regarding control of the funds. At Mr. Gellene's trial, however, Eckert testified that Mr. Gellene's explanation was not true and that he had produced the documents shortly after Mr. Gellene had requested them—which was after the deadline for production of the documents.

Mr. Gellene testified as the only defense witness at his trial. He stated that he began work at Milbank in 1980 and developed a bankruptcy practice. He testified that Lederman gave him the Bucyrus work and the South Street/Greycliff representation. He also admitted being aware in December 1993 of his firm's representation of Salovaara in the Eckert dispute. He testified that he failed to disclose these representations in the Bucyrus bankruptcy because he did not consider Salovaara to be a creditor, did not distinguish South Street/Greycliff from Salovaara, and thus did not think the representations needed to be disclosed. He also testified that the matters involving Salovaara, South Street and Greycliff were unrelated to the Bucyrus matter and that an agreement with Salovaara had already been reached. He called these conclusions "bad judgment" and "stupid, but not criminal." The jury did not agree; it convicted him on all three counts.

II. Discussion

A. Bankruptcy Fraud under 18 U.S.C. § 152(3). At trial, the district court instructed the jury on the elements of bankruptcy fraud and specifically instructed that "[a] statement is fraudulent if known to be untrue and made with intent to deceive." Mr. Gellene submits that the court's definition of "fraudulent" as "with intent to deceive" is erroneous. In his view, the statute requires that the statement be made not simply with the intent to deceive but with the intent to defraud. He further claims that, because the government misapprehended the statutory requirement, it failed to present evidence that he made his declarations with an intent to defraud because it believed it needed to prove merely an intent to deceive. He submits that the distinction between the two terms is significant: To deceive is to cause to believe the false or to mislead; to defraud is to deprive of some right, interest or property by deceit. Therefore, under § 152 of the Bankruptcy Code, he contends, the defendant must have a specific intent to alter or to impact the distribution of a debtor's assets and not merely to impact the integrity of the legal system, as the government argued.

We cannot accept Mr. Gellene's narrowly circumscribed definition of "intent to defraud" or "fraudulently." Mr. Gellene would limit exclusively the statute's scope to false statements that deprive the debtor of his property or the bankruptcy estate of its assets. In our view, such a parsimonious interpretation was not intended by Congress.

First, the plain wording of the statute suggests no such limited scope. Rather, the plain wording of the statute punishes making a false statement "knowingly and fraudulently." The common understanding of the term "fraudulently" includes the intent to deceive. Indeed, our case law has long acknowledged a broader scope for the statutory language than Mr. Gellene suggests. We have held that the section is designed to reach statements made with intent to defraud the bankruptcy court. Section 152 has long been recognized as the Congress' attempt to criminalize all the possible methods by which a debtor or any other person may attempt to defeat the intent and effect of the Bankruptcy Code and that the expansive scope of the statute reaches beyond the wrongful sequestration of a debtor's property and also encompasses the knowing and fraudulent making of false oaths or declarations in the context of a bankruptcy proceeding.

Thus, whether the deception at issue is aimed at thwarting the bankruptcy court or the parties to the bankruptcy, § 152 is designed to protect the integrity of the administration of a bankruptcy case. As one commentator has put it:

> The orientation of title 11 toward debtors' rehabilitation and equitable distribution to creditors relies heavily upon the participants' honesty. When honesty is absent, the goals of the civil side of the system become more expensive and more elusive. To protect the civil system, bankruptcy crimes are not concerned with individual loss or even whether certain acts caused anyone particularized harm. Instead, the statutes establishing the federal bankruptcy crimes seek to prevent and redress abuses of the bankruptcy system. Thus, most of the crimes do not require that the acts proscribed be material in the grand scheme of things, that the defendant benefit in any way nor that any creditor be injured.

Mr. Gellene's narrow reading of the statute leads him to take a narrow view of the provision's materiality requirement. In his view, the statute criminalizes only fraud that is intended to frustrate the equitable distribution of assets in the bankruptcy estate. As counsel explained at oral argument, the fraud ought to be considered material only when it is related to the estate's assets, to pecuniary and property distribution issues. Under this narrow interpretation, his failure to divulge his representation of a major secured creditor of the debtor was not material, he asserts, because it was not intended to impact on the equitable distribution of assets in the bankruptcy.

We agree that § 152 requires that materiality be an element of the crime of bankruptcy fraud and, indeed, we have incorporated such a requirement in our analysis of § 152 fraud. That material matter about which the misrepresentation was made could of course be the debtor's business transactions, the debtor's estate assets, the discovery of those assets, or the history of the debtor's financial transactions. However, we have never accepted Mr. Gellene's view that only misrepresentations that relate to the assets of the bankruptcy estate are material.

We have no doubt that a misstatement in a Rule 2014 statement by an attorney about other affiliations constitutes a material misstatement. The Bankruptcy Code requires that attorneys who seek to be employed as counsel for a debtor apply for the bankruptcy court's approval of that employment. Bankruptcy Rule 2014 requires the potential attorney for the debtor to set forth under oath any "connections with the debtor, creditors, [and] any other party in interest." Fed. R. Bankr.P. 2014(a). The disclosure requirements apply to all professionals and are not discretionary. The professionals cannot pick and choose which connections are irrelevant or trivial. Counsel who fail to disclose timely and completely their connections proceed at their own risk because failure to disclose is sufficient grounds to revoke an employment order and deny compensation.

We now consider whether there was sufficient evidence of Mr. Gellene's guilt. We therefore must determine, after viewing the evidence in the light most favorable to the government, whether a rational trier of fact could have found the essential elements of the offense of bankruptcy fraud beyond a reasonable doubt.

Our review of the record verifies that the government established Mr. Gellene's knowledge of his duty to disclose. It set forth Mr. Gellene's expertise in bankruptcy and the bankruptcy court's statements alerting him to the importance of full disclosures. Mr. Gellene was fully apprised of the importance of the information that had been excluded. He had been questioned by his law partner, Toni Lichstein, several times about whether there might be a conflict of interest and whether all necessary disclosures had been made. Yet Mr. Gellene continued to withhold the information over a two-year period; he simultaneously worked on the Bucyrus bankruptcy and represented South Street, Greycliff and Salovaara without informing his client Bucyrus of the other representations.

In addition to the direct evidence of Mr. Gellene's intentional fraudulent omission of information from the Rule 2014 applications, the government offered evidence that he had committed deceptions on the bankruptcy court and other courts with respect to (1) his failure to disclose his law firm partners' interest in the Lotus Cab Company, from whom he had submitted a bill; (2) his failure to file documents in a Colorado bankruptcy court; and (3) the status of his bar memberships. Moreover, Mr. Gellene himself testified regarding his mental state; therefore, the jury had an opportunity to judge in detail his innocent explanations regarding his conduct. After viewing the evidence in the light most favorable to the government, we conclude that there was evidence from which a jury reasonably could have found beyond a reasonable doubt that Mr. Gellene knowingly and fraudulently made two false material declarations in the Bucyrus bankruptcy case.

B. Perjury under 18 U.S.C. § 1623. Mr. Gellene was convicted on Count 3 of using a document, while under oath, knowing that it contained a material falsehood, in violation of 18 U.S.C. § 1623.

At the fee hearing, Mr. Gellene testified on direct examination that he previously had disclosed to the bankruptcy court Milbank's representation of Goldman Sachs; in the course of his testimony, he referred to the two sworn declarations as exhibits to establish that disclosure. The second declaration in particular demonstrated that Milbank had divulged its relationship with Goldman Sachs and had put in place a "Chinese wall" to keep separate the Goldman Sachs legal representation and the Bucyrus bankruptcy work. That second declaration then made this concluding statement, alleged to be false in Count 3:

> Besides the representations disclosed in my declaration dated February 18, 1994, after due inquiry, I am unaware of any other current representation by Milbank of an equity security holder or institutional creditor of the Debtors.

However, when Mr. Gellene drafted this Rule 2014 disclosure statement (around March 28, 1994) and when he used it at the fee hearing (November 29, 1995), he and his firm were actively representing South Street and Greycliff. Notably, Milbank's representation of those entities was not known at the time of the fee hearing to anyone involved in the Bucyrus bankruptcy.

Mr. Gellene challenges his conviction on several grounds. First, he claims that the evidence was not sufficient to prove his guilt beyond a reasonable doubt because his testimony at the fee hearing did not constitute a knowing "use" of a "false material" document. Second, he asserts (for the first time on appeal) that, because the document was literally true, his statement based on the declaration cannot form the basis for a perjury conviction. And, third, he submits that the district court should have granted the motion for judgment of acquittal. We shall address the first two contentions in some detail and, in the course of our analysis, also discuss the sufficiency of the evidence.

The false swearing statute, as the government seeks to apply it here, requires the "use" of a false statement. Mr. Gellene claims that his testimony at the fee hearing was entirely and historically accurate. In his view, the focus of the inquiry was on another paragraph of his March 1994 declaration, the paragraph that disclosed his relationship with Goldman Sachs. Mr. Gellene contends that he did not "use" the paragraph mentioned in the indictment because he never referred to that paragraph or used that paragraph to bolster his testimony; the inquiry was limited to Milbank's relationship with Goldman Sachs, and he made no mention at the fee hearing of the paragraph set forth in the indictment.

We cannot accept this argument. The thrust of JNL's challenge to the fee petition was a challenge to Milbank's divided loyalty. Although its allegation was limited to Milbank's association with Goldman Sachs, a fair interpretation of the record—and one the jury was certainly entitled to accept—was that JNL's foundational concern was that Milbank's divided loyalties might jeopardize the position of the creditors. The statement at issue in the indictment informed, and assured, the bankruptcy court that, beyond the area of acknowledged concern (Milbank's relationship with Goldman Sachs), there were no other areas of representation of which Mr. Gellene was aware. The statement conveyed the message that, once he met JNL's concern about Goldman Sachs, there was no other cause for concern about Milbank's divided loyalties and the fee petition could be approved.

We believe that the district court was correct in its determination that Mr. Gellene "used" the designated paragraph of the supplemental statement in his 2014 application during his testimony. His reference to— and his reliance upon—the application allowed him to demonstrate not only that he had disclosed the representation of Goldman Sachs but also that he had examined other possible areas of concern and had determined that there were no other similar representations that warranted the court's scrutiny before awarding fees.

The jury was entitled to believe that the statement was designed to lull the bankruptcy court and the parties into believing that there were no other Milbank relationships deserving of scrutiny before the award of fees. The jury was entitled to conclude that the sequence of events established that Mr. Gellene had knowingly used the document to convey such an impression to the bankruptcy court. Indeed, Mr. Gellene stated prior to the hearing that he intended to use the declarations in response to JNL's allegation that Milbank had conflicts of interest. David Gelfand, who examined Mr. Gellene at that hearing, later testified that Mr. Gellene had chosen to proffer his sworn declarations as exhibits and had orchestrated the subsequent questioning of his own sworn testimony. According to Gelfand, the purpose in presenting the documents was to establish that Milbank was entitled to the $2 million in fees because all potential conflicts had been disclosed and considered by the bankruptcy court. There is no question that his proffer of the statement constituted use of a material document under § 1623.

The record permitted the jury to conclude that Mr. Gellene knowingly introduced the false document in order to gain approval of Milbank's $2 million fee request. Evaluating the testimony presented to it, the jury was entitled to conclude that Mr. Gellene had virtually bragged about the forthrightness of Milbank's disclosure of its representation of Goldman Sachs, all the while knowing that no one involved in the bankruptcy proceedings was aware of Milbank's undisclosed representations of South Street and the other entities. It was not until the next year that the falsity of that disclosure information was discovered. Only then could the United States Trustee seek return of the fees and an order of sanctions against Milbank.

Accordingly, we believe that sufficient evidence existed for the district court to find that materiality has been established.

During the course of trial, the court admitted evidence that Mr. Gellene had misrepresented his status as a member of the bar when applying to become a member of the bar of the Eastern District of Wisconsin: He stated that he was a member of the bar of the Southern District of New York and had been a member since 1981, but in fact he has never been a member of that bar, despite repeated appearances in that court over the years. In addition, Mr. Gellene practiced law in New York State between 1981 and 1990 without ever joining that bar. During that time, he represented himself to be a member of the New York bar in legal publications and court filings. The court also admitted evidence of (1) Mr. Gellene's misrepresentation to the Colorado bankruptcy court concerning his failure to produce discovery documents, and (2) Mr. Gellene's misrepresentation to the Wisconsin bankruptcy court in this case concerning his law firm's relationship with Lotus Cab Company.

Mr. Gellene explained that he had passed the bar but had neglected to complete the requisite paperwork to be licensed. He also admitted that he did not tell his law firm that he was not a member of the bar and, as a result, practiced law for almost nine years without a proper license. Nevertheless, he contends that the government sought to admit this irrelevant evidence to prove his propensity to make misrepresentations, thereby allowing the jury to infer that he must have been untruthful and even must have fraudulently intended the charged conduct. In his view, stating that he was a licensed attorney when he only had passed the bar exam, although not commendable conduct, is not equivalent to the state of mind involved with providing false testimony as to a material issue under litigation.

In admitting the evidence, the district court reasoned that, by denying that he had the requisite fraudulent intent for the charged crimes, Mr. Gellene had made intent an issue in the case; therefore, the court concluded, the government was entitled to rebut that contention with evidence of other bad acts that tended to undermine the defendant's innocent explanations for his act. Concerning Mr. Gellene's bar status, the court determined that there was clear evidence of (1) his knowledge that he was not a member of the New York state bar and (2) "his continuing intent for a period of almost nine years to deceive anyone who would have an interest [in] believing that indeed he was a member of the New York bar." The court then determined that this intent to deceive concerning his bar status was similar to his intent to defraud, to deceive and to perjure himself under Counts 1, 2 and 3 of the indictment. It noted

Mr. Gellene's status as an officer of the court—in the bankruptcy court in Milwaukee, a federal court in New York, a bankruptcy court in Denver, or elsewhere—and then found that his conduct in those courts was similar and "appropriate to consider on the very narrow issue of this defendant's intent in his candor with the United States Bankruptcy Court in the Eastern District of Wisconsin."

We cannot say that the district court abused its discretion in admitting the evidence. The district court was correct in its determination that Mr. Gellene had placed his intent in issue. It was clear from the parties' opening statements that the facts were basically not in dispute and that the focus of the trial would be on the intention underlying Mr. Gellene's conduct. On this record, we also think that the district court was entitled to conclude that Mr. Gellene's false representations regarding his bar status and his other misrepresentations were similar enough in nature to the charged offenses to be relevant. Both the charged conduct and these other misrepresentations involve intentional misrepresentations before a court. The evidence admitted by the district court, like the offenses of conviction, tended to show intentional dishonesty, absence of mistake, and a cavalier disregard for the truth in his dealings with tribunals. For instance, Mr. Gellene's intentional deception in falsely representing to various courts (including the United States District Court for the Eastern District of Wisconsin) that he was a member of the bars of other courts, when he was not, is not dissimilar to his intentional deception in falsely representing to the bankruptcy court that he had no connection with other parties in interest in the bankruptcy, when in fact he was representing the major secured creditor. Certainly, his attempt to treat the earlier conduct as de minimis, trivial, a matter of neglect, a matter of embarrassment but not a knowing deception—when the circumstances evince knowing deception—is similar to the dishonesty reflected in his filings of the two fraudulent disclosure statements and the perjurious statement he made subsequent to the filing of those documents in order to win the requested $2 million fee award.

Even when such evidence has a slight tendency to show Mr. Gellene's propensity to commit wrongs, its predominant effect pertained to the legitimate purpose of proving [the defendant's] intent. We note, moreover, that the district court instructed the jury that Mr. Gellene was "not on trial for any act or conduct not alleged in the indictment" and that the jury was allowed to consider "evidence of acts of the defendant other than those charged in the indictment . . . only on the question of the defendant's intent." Jury Instructions at 4, 9. Given these limiting instructions, we cannot say that the danger of prejudice outweighed the probity of the evidence. The district court did not abuse its discretion in admitting evidence of Mr. Gellene's false representations and omissions concerning his bar status with respect to the "narrow issue" of his intent.

III. Conclusion

For the foregoing reasons, we affirm the judgment of the district court.

Affirmed.

* * *

C. BACKGROUND ON THE CASE

[Purchase and read carefully Milton C. Regan, Jr., "Bankrupt in Milwaukee: A Cautionary Tale," in LEGAL ETHICS STORIES 203–32 (2006)]

NOTES ON GELLENE

1.   ***What Happened and Why?*** What went wrong? How do you account for Gellene's conduct in this case? Is this simply a story of a flawed individual succumbing to temptation? Is Milbank's organizational culture partly to blame? Did any larger social and/or economic forces play important roles in this episode?

2.   ***Was the Relevant Law Clear Enough?*** What law applied to the lawyers' conduct in this matter, and what purposes is that law designed to serve? Did it provide adequate guidance to the individuals involved? Would any changes in the applicable law have generated better outcomes?

3.   ***Lessons for Law Firms.*** What lessons does this case study offer for Milbank Tweed (and other similarly situated large law firms)? Should they have adopted better systems for identifying and monitoring conflicts of interest and ensuring that the affected lawyers resolved them appropriately? Should they have responded more quickly to evidence that Gellene was sloppy about filing bar applications and meeting deadlines? Should they have insisted that he seek the help he needed to manage his workload? Should they have fired him immediately at the first hint that he would lie to get himself out of trouble?

D. SUMMARY

This chapter has explored a case study involving a young and talented lawyer in a large firm who violated various basic standards of professional conduct and thereafter was disbarred and imprisoned. We examined the legal violations and other types of deception he committed. We also considered whether the institutional context in which he practiced and the culture of his firm might have played a significant part in this episode. Finally, we reflected on what the firm, and particular partners within the firm, might have done to avert this outcome.

CHAPTER 18

COUNSELING

■ ■ ■

A. INTRODUCTION

This chapter focuses exclusively on the counseling role. In the materials that follow, we pay particular attention to counseling corporate clients, but the questions raised in these materials are broadly relevant to lawyers' advising of other types of clients, including governmental entities, nonprofit groups, small businesses, and individual clients.

Litigators' behavior receives a reasonable amount of scrutiny from opposing counsel, judges, and the press, and the publicity surrounding high-profile litigation makes it accessible and reasonably well-understood by the public. Lawyers' work in the counseling and regulatory compliance realm occurs largely behind closed doors, without external oversight or judicial scrutiny, and this activity is much less well-understood by the general public. But lawyers' counseling may be at least as consequential as the work of litigators because it shapes clients' decisions about future behavior in important ways. For individual clients, counseling sometimes affects how clients treat relatives, employees, neighbors, business partners, and affected strangers. In the context of corporate counseling, lawyers influence how clients deal with regulators, competitors, accountants and other service providers, employees, and consumers. In all types of practices, lawyers in their counseling roles often affect whether and to what extent clients comply with the law. Thus, important public policies and private interests often depend on decisions that clients make in consultation with their lawyers.

This chapter identifies the Model Rules provisions on counseling and then addresses three primary questions. First, how does counseling differ from advocacy and why is zealous advocacy widely viewed as an inappropriate model for lawyers' counseling work? Second, what types of information and advice should a lawyer convey while counseling a client? When, if ever, should her advice include information about government enforcement practices, and when should it address non-legal matters, such as economic or moral concerns? We will then explore the challenges that lawyers sometimes face in providing independent advice to clients, and we will pay special attention to the pressures that outside counsel to corporations sometimes encounter. In Chapter 19, we will consider counseling by in-house lawyers, and we will examine counseling by government lawyers in Chapter 20.

B. MODEL RULES ON COUNSELING

Counseling

- Rule 2.1 provides that a lawyer who serves as a counselor must exercise independent professional judgment and render candid advice. The lawyer's advice may properly refer to non-legal considerations that may be relevant to the client's situation.

- Rule 1.2(d) provides that a lawyer shall not counsel a client to engage in conduct that the lawyer knows is criminal or fraudulent or assist a client in such conduct.

Model Rule 2.1 requires lawyers who serve as advisors to exercise independent professional judgment and give candid advice. The Comment offers guidance about the content of these requirements:

> A client is entitled to straightforward advice expressing the lawyer's honest assessment. Legal advice often involves unpleasant facts and alternatives that a client may be disinclined to confront. In presenting advice, a lawyer endeavors to sustain the client's morale and may put advice in as acceptable a form as honesty permits. However, a lawyer should not be deterred from giving candid advice by the prospect that the advice will be unpalatable to the client.

The Rule also provides that "[i]n rendering advice, a lawyer may refer not only to law but to other considerations such as moral, economic, social and political factors that may be relevant to the client's situation." The Comment explains that "advice couched in narrow legal terms may be of little value to a client, especially where practical considerations, such as costs or effects on other people, are predominant": "Purely technical legal advice, therefore, can sometimes be inadequate." The Comment also states that lawyers may appropriately refer to moral and ethical considerations in giving advice: "Although a lawyer is not a moral advisor as such, moral and ethical considerations impinge upon most legal questions and may decisively influence how the law will be applied."

In addition, Rule 1.2(d) provides that "a lawyer shall not counsel a client to engage, or assist a client, in conduct that the lawyer knows is criminal or fraudulent." And, of course, Rule 1.13 is broadly applicable to the representation of organizations, including corporations, in counseling as well as litigation. Recall that Rule 1.13 provides that a lawyer retained by an organization represents the entity acting through its constituents, and that a lawyer who discovers that an officer or employee is engaged in activity that is a violation of a legal obligation to the organization, or a violation of law that might be imputed to the organization, and that is likely to result in substantial injury to the organization, must act in the best interest of the organization. That generally means that the lawyer must take the matter up the organizational hierarchy.

C. COUNSELING VERSUS ADVOCACY

How does counseling differ from advocacy, and why is the distinction important? The Model Rules do not address this question directly, but the following classic statement on the distinction and its significance is often cited:

PROFESSIONAL RESPONSIBILITY: REPORT OF THE JOINT CONFERENCE
Lon L. Fuller and John D. Randall
44 ABA Journal 1159 (1958)

The Lawyer's Role as Counselor. Vital as is the lawyer's role in adjudication, it should not be thought that it is only as an advocate pleading in open court that he contributes to the administration of the law. The most effective realization of the law's aims often takes place in the attorney's office, where litigation is forestalled by anticipating its outcome, where the lawyer's quiet counsel takes the place of public force. Contrary to popular belief, the compliance with the law thus brought about is not generally lip-serving and narrow, for by reminding him of its long-run costs the lawyer often deters his client from a course of conduct technically permissible under existing law, though inconsistent with its underlying spirit and purpose.

Although the lawyer serves the administration of justice indispensably both as advocate and as office counselor, the demands imposed on him by these two roles must be sharply distinguished. The man who has been called into court to answer for his own actions is entitled to a fair hearing. Partisan advocacy plays its essential part in such a hearing, and the lawyer pleading his client's case may properly present it in the most favorable light. A similar resolution of doubts in one direction becomes inappropriate when the lawyer acts as counselor. The reasons that justify and even require partisan advocacy in the trial of a cause do not grant any license to the lawyer to participate as legal adviser in a line of conduct that is immoral, unfair, or of doubtful legality. In saving himself from this unworthy involvement, the lawyer cannot be guided solely by an unreflective inner sense of good faith; he must be at pains to preserve a sufficient detachment from his client's interests so that he remains capable of a sound and objective appraisal of the propriety of what his client proposes to do.

NOTES ON FULLER & RANDALL

1. *Counseling v. Litigating.* How do lawyers' responsibilities in counseling differ from their responsibilities in litigation, according to Fuller and Randall? Do you agree with their view that the duties of lawyers in these two roles must be "sharply distinguished"?

2. *Procedural Context.* According to Fuller and Randall, how do differences in the duties of litigators and counselors relate to differences in the procedural context of their work?

D. WHAT TYPES OF ADVICE SHOULD COUNSELING INCLUDE?

What should be the content of lawyer's advice to clients? Should it include discussion of matters that are not strictly legal? If so, under what circumstances?

As the comment to Rule 2.1 notes, lawyers generally hold no special expertise in matters of business, economics, and morality, but legal issues are often inextricably bound up with non-legal matters. Providing narrow legal advice in such circumstances may not serve clients well. Indeed, some commentators have argued that lawyers who fail to counsel their clients about non-legal considerations when those other factors are intertwined with legal issues disserve their clients. Monroe Freedman, for example, has argued that lawyers frustrate client autonomy when they decline to discuss non-legal considerations with their clients and simply "assum[e] that the client wants . . . to maximize his material or tactical position in every way that is legally permissible, regardless of non-legal considerations."[1] (Recall *Spaulding v. Zimmerman.*) Professors Hazard and Hodes have noted that in some circumstances non-legal considerations are so pervasive that "no pure legal choice exists."[2] Others have argued that lawyers' non-legal counseling is sometimes important to help clients understand the full implications of their decisions.[3] Of course, the extent to which lawyers can and should raise non-legal considerations may depend on the lawyer's and client representative's comfort level with one another. If the client is an organization, it may also depend on the

---

[1]   MONROE H. FREEDMAN & ABBE SMITH, UNDERSTANDING LAWYERS' ETHICS (2d ed. 2002).

[2]   GEOFFREY C. HAZARD, JR. & WILLIAM HODES, THE LAW OF LAWYERING § 23.3, at 23–4.1 (3d ed. 2004).

[3]   *See* Robert A. Kagan & Robert Eli Rosen, *On the Social Significance of Large Law Firm Practice,* 37 STAN. L. REV. 399, 438-39 (1985) ("Corporate managers, operating under time pressure and intra-corporate rivalries, sometimes fail to consider the full economic and moral implications of their decisions. In such cases, lawyers might speak for the true' economic interests of the corporation, as against the perceptions of particular managers.").

lawyer's experience and seniority and the client representative's status within the organization.[4] In the corporate client counseling context, lawyers who offer advice that touches on moral issues may be more likely to be effective if they frame their advice in terms of risk and reputational concerns rather than ethics. Professor Robert Gordon, whose article on corporate counseling appears below, has noted that "most lawyers, or at least lawyers for big, powerful companies, will phrase negative advice as prudential rather than moralistic, supporting their recommendations with reasons that sound much more like statements of technical rules or empirical predictions of risks and results than political or moral judgments."[5]

When, if ever, should a lawyer give a client information that the client might use to violate the law? For example, is it legitimate for the lawyer to give the client information about the likelihood that the law will be enforced? Does your answer depend on what type of law it is, or on any other considerations?

COUNSELING AT THE LIMITS OF THE LAW: AN EXERCISE IN THE JURISPRUDENCE AND ETHICS OF LAWYERING

Stephen L. Pepper
104 Yale Law Journal 1545 (1995)

The client often wants or needs to understand what the law is in order to evaluate options and make decisions about his or her life, and the most common function of lawyers (across specializations and areas of practice) is to provide that knowledge. Knowledge of the law, however, is an instrument that can be used to follow the law or to avoid it. When the lawyer is in a situation in which the client may well use the relevant knowledge of the law to violate the law or avoid its norms, what ought the lawyer to do?

Assume an Environmental Protection Agency water pollution regulation, widely publicized to relevant industries, prohibiting discharge of ammonia at amounts greater than .050 grams per liter of effluent. The client owns a rural plant that discharges ammonia in its effluent, the removal of which would be very expensive. The lawyer knows from informal sources that: (1) violations of .075 grams per liter or less are ignored because of a limited enforcement budget; and (2) EPA inspection in rural areas is rare, and in such areas enforcement officials usually issue a warning prior to applying sanctions unless the violation is extreme (more than 1.5 grams per liter). Is it appropriate for the lawyer

---

[4]   Larry O. Natt Gantt, II, *More Than Lawyers: The Legal and Ethical Implications of Counseling Clients on Nonlegal Considerations*, 18 GEO. J. LEGAL ETHICS 365 (2005).

[5]   *See* Robert W. Gordon, *The Independence of Lawyers*, 68 B. U. L. REV. 1, 28 (1988).

to educate the client concerning these enforcement-related facts even though it may motivate the client to violate the .050 gram limit?

A second, well-known example is the client who wants to file a tax return reporting a favorable outcome based upon an arguable interpretation of the law. The lawyer is confident the IRS would challenge the client's return if it became aware of this interpretation and would be highly likely to succeed in the event of litigation. If that were to occur, the penalties would likely be only the tax due plus interest. The lawyer knows that in the past the audit rate for this type of return has been less than two percent, and knows that this fact is likely to lead this client to take the dubious position on her return. Ought the lawyer to communicate this information to the client?

If the law becomes generally perceived as merely indicating a potential cost, a penalty that one is free to incur and to discount by the probability of its enforcement, then structuring our common life together through law becomes vastly more difficult and requires vastly more resources. For example, consider the last two situations, environmental regulation and tax. To the extent the client is led to perceive enforcement as a part of law, or, one might say, led to reduce law to the probability of enforcement, the power and effectiveness of the law as written, of the law as norm, has been reduced. Such a conflation of law with enforcement may be the untoward result of legal advice to the client under this "legal realist" view of the law. And the recently dominant jurisprudential trend in the law schools—law and economics—substantially reinforces this effect of legal realism by perceiving legal limits and rules as just another "cost," and clients as "profit maximizers," simply Holmes' "bad man"[*] dressed in modern clothes.

I present below a series of distinctions that might assist a lawyer in deciding what information about the law to give to the client, and what not to give. [Pepper then identifies various factors that might inform the lawyer's decision about whether to give the client the information about enforcement practices.]

[With respect to the water pollution hypothetical, Pepper offers the following possible basis for deciding whether or not to provide the information.]

It is possible that a disparity between a written rule and the way it is enforced is intended government policy, and thus amounts to a *de facto* amendment of the law by a governmental actor with the power to make such a change. On the other hand, it is also possible that the lax

---

[*] [Eds. This refers to Oliver Wendell Holmes's view that law should be defined as a prediction of how courts will behave. In his paper, "The Path of the Law," Holmes argued that bad men care simply about staying out of jail and avoiding paying damages.]

enforcement is not a matter of policy, but rather results from unintended circumstances such as budget limits, incompetence, or happenstance.

Imagine two possible reasons why enforcement inspections might be rare in rural areas. First, it might be that rural water tends to be significantly cleaner than urban water (at least in regard to ammonia) and that pollution, if it is occurring, is far less likely to be harmful in the rural environment than in the urban environment. Multiple sites discharging the same pollutant are also far less likely. These facts may have been known when discharge limits for the particular effluent were promulgated, but more detailed regulation defining "urban" as opposed to "rural" and articulating differential limits for the two types of area, or otherwise more accurately calibrating the limit to the environmental context, may not have been feasible. The agency thus may have framed the limit with the most typical area and the most serious harms in mind, with the intention of exercising regulatory discretion to fine tune the regulation to different areas and conditions. The regulation was promulgated with knowledge that it was intended more for urban areas than rural, and the enforcement disparity known to the lawyer might well be part of the regulator's policy. Alternatively, the .05 gram ammonia limit may be the regulator's best judgment as to the amount sufficiently likely to cause significant harm regardless of the presence of other effluents or multiple sites. The less frequent testing in rural areas may be attributed solely to insufficient funds for enforcement, and the fact that it is less expensive to test in the urban areas.

In the first situation, it is meaningful to say that the .05 limit is not "really" the legal limit in rural areas. The source of law—the regulatory agency—has intentionally made the law-as-enforced different from the law-as-written for reasons related to its legal mission. Since the harm the agency is to prevent is unlikely to occur in the rural area, even over the .05 limit, the agency has tailored the law through enforcement decisions. When, however, lax enforcement is based simply upon cost, incompetence, or inadvertence, rather than substantive reasons, [advising the client about enforcement practices undermines the "real" legal limit].

If the lawyer knows the reasons for a significant differential between the law-as-written and the law-as-enforced, then the "law/enforcement" distinction might be used in deciding what information to convey to the client. Frequently, however, the lawyer does not know.

NOTES ON PEPPER

1. *Counseling About Non-Legal Considerations.* Do you agree with the notion, reflected in the comment to Model Rule 2.1, that lawyers sometimes should counsel clients not only about purely legal matters but also about other types of closely related concerns that are inextricably bound up

with legal considerations? From what sources of knowledge and authority should lawyers draw in advising clients about non-legal matters?

2. *When Is It Ethical to Advise Clients About Regulatory Enforcement Practices?* Do you find Pepper's argument helpful in distinguishing between circumstances when it is ethically permissible to advise clients about regulatory enforcement practices and when it is not? How often do you think lawyers will be in a position to know whether lax enforcement is the result of "policy" judgments and when it is simply a consequence lack of resources, incompetence, or mistake?

3. *Corporate Counseling.* What special challenges does the duty to advise present when the client is a corporation?

PROBLEM 18–1

A. You are outside counsel for a major utility, a publicly traded corporation. An engineer employed by the company approaches you to express concern that a small amount of reactor coolant water has been leaking through one or more of the thousands of tubes inside the two steam generators for one of the utility's nuclear reactors. He is unsure whether the situation presents a danger to the public. If the reactor has to be shut down and the system repaired, the utility will face huge expense and lost revenues. The utility is required by federal statute to report to the Nuclear Regulatory Commission (NRC), the agency that oversees all U.S. nuclear facilities, any safety issues that could jeopardize the lives or health of citizens.

How should you respond to the information that the engineer has given you? (Re-read Model Rule 1.13 if you do not recall its details.)

B. You decide to raise the issue with the utility's top executives. They express the view that the safety risk is negligible and that the cost of making the repairs is prohibitive. They tell you to drop the matter. Should you or must you take steps to ensure that the corporate board considers the issue?

C. You know that the budget for the NRC has been trimmed substantially over the past few years, and therefore mandatory inspections are infrequent. Moreover, you think that even if the NRC were to conduct an inspection of the reactors, it is unlikely that it would detect the leak absent prompting from someone inside the utility because the agency simply does not have the resources to conduct the kind of extensive inspection that would be necessary to discover the leak. You also have learned that the NRC has recently begun to focus its regulatory enforcement efforts on utilities with a prior history of violations, which your client does not have. Should you tell your client what you know about the NRC's resources and enforcement practices?

E. CORPORATE COUNSELING

The last few decades have seen a spate of major corporate scandals in which lawyers have been implicated. The attention of the media and politicians has focused primarily on corporate officers and accounting firms, while the role of lawyers has received much less notice. On the rare occasion when the spotlight shifts to lawyers' involvement, the question tends to be whether lawyers should have blown the whistle on corporate illegality. That is a weighty question, of course, and we explored it briefly in the materials on confidentiality. (Recall the discussion of the O.P.M. debacle in Chapter 9.) But it is important to consider more broadly what role lawyers should play in averting the client's participation in such wrongdoing, especially when the lawyer's assistance is integral to its accomplishment. What steps should lawyers take to prevent the client from engaging in misconduct—or at least to ensure that lawyers play no part in assisting any such illegality?

The remaining materials in this chapter address that question.

A NEW ROLE FOR LAWYERS? THE CORPORATE COUNSELOR AFTER ENRON
Robert W. Gordon
35 Connecticut Law Review 1185 (2003)

Lawyers seem to have played a relatively minor part in the theater of deception and self-dealing that has led to the collapse of Enron Corp. ("Enron") and other corporate titans of the 1990s. [But] it is clear that the advice both in-house lawyers and outside law firms gave to the managers of Enron and other companies like it was instrumental in enabling those managers to cream off huge profits for themselves while bringing economic ruin to investors, employees, and the taxpaying public. Although the lawyers were not principally responsible for these acts of waste and fraud, their advice was a contributing (and often necessary) cause of those acts. Such fraud could not have been carried out without the lawyers' active approval, passive acquiescence, or failure to inquire and investigate.

How are we to understand why the lawyers acted as they did? Observers from outside the profession, and even some from within the profession, are tempted to say that the lawyers were simply weak and corrupt, or, for those who prefer to talk this way, that the lawyers were rational economic actors. They want the client's business, in an intensely competitive market, and so they will wish to approve anything senior management of the client firm asks, averting their eyes from signs of trouble and their noses from the smell of fish.

But this is the amoral rational calculator's perspective, and professionals in high-status jobs at respectable blue-chip institutions do not like to think of themselves as amoral maximizers. Like human beings everywhere who want to enjoy self-respect and the esteem of others, they tell stories about how what they do is all right, even admirable; however, some of the stories that the lawyers would like to tell were not available in this situation.

Law as the Enemy: Libertarian Antinomianism. In recent years many lawyers have taken on the values of and completely identified with their business clients, some of whom see law as an enemy or a pesky nuisance. I call this the viewpoint of the libertarian antinomian, because it rests on an express contempt for, and disapproval of, law and regulation. Tax law, products liability tort law, drug law, health and safety law, environmental law, employment discrimination law, toxic waste cleanup law, foreign corrupt payments law, SEC disclosure regulation, and the like are all shackles on risk-taking initiative. They interfere with maximizing profits, and anything that does that must be bad.

Law as Neutral Constraint: The Lawyer as Risk-Manager. This viewpoint is much like the first, but without the negative normative spin. Adverse legal consequences are not an evil, they are just a fact. In this view, law is simply a source of "risk" to the business firm; it is the lawyers' task to assess and, to the extent possible, reduce it. These lawyers do not feel a moral imperative, as libertarians do, to defy or undercut the law; but neither do they feel one to comply.

These two story-lines were not available in the case of Enron, for the obvious reasons that managers were looting the companies for their own benefit while concealing debts and losses from workers and investors. When the lawyers and accountants outwitted the pesky regulators—who, had they known what was happening, might have put a stop to it—they were not helping heroic outlaws add value to the economy and society by defying timid convention, but enabling, if not abetting, frauds and thieves. Nor were the professionals objectively, if amorally, assessing risks and weighing benefits against costs of efficient breach. It seems not to have occurred to them that outsiders might find out that the many-sided transactions with special entities were not actually earning any real returns, but merely concealing debts and losses, and that when that happened, Enron's stock price would tumble, and with it, all the houses of cards secured by that stock. The company they advised is now facing at least seventy-seven lawsuits as a result of its conduct. At best, the lawyers were closing their eyes to the risk of disaster; at worst, they were helping to bring it on.

The lawyers have been relying instead on different stories, somewhat in conflict with one another.

"We Din' Know Nothin'": The Lawyer as Myopic or Limited-Function Bureaucrat. These are claims that the lawyers were not at fault because their role was limited: We didn't know, we weren't informed; the accountants said the numbers were okay; management made the decisions; our representation was restricted to problems on the face of the documents or to information submitted to us.

Many of these claims of innocent ignorance now look pretty dubious. Some of the outside law firms in fact worked closely with Andersen accountants in structuring many of the transactions. Sometimes lawyers made notes that they needed further information or managers' or the board's approval to certify a deal, but signed opinions and proxy statements even if they never got it. Sometimes they expressed doubts about the deals. In the end, the doubting lawyers never pressed the issues.

Some of their claims of limited knowledge are plausible, however, because Enron never trusted any one set of lawyers with extensive information about its operations—it spread legal work out to over 100 law firms. If one firm balked at approving a deal, Enron managers would go across town to another, more compliant firm. It is this layering of authority, fragmentation of responsibility, and decentralization that has made it possible for the chairman, CEO and board of directors of Enron, as well as the lawyers, to claim that they did not know much about what was going on in their own company. One question for lawyers—as well as for senior managers and board members—is whether they can conscientiously and ethically do their jobs and exercise their functions as fiduciaries in organizations structured to diffuse responsibility and prevent their access to the big picture.

The Lawyer as Advocate. The classic defense of the corporate lawyer's role, both most often advanced and held in reserve if other defenses fail, is of course that we are advocates, whose duty is zealous representation of clients. We are not like auditors, who have duties to the public; our duties are only to our clients. Our job is to help them pursue their interests and put the best construction on their conduct that the law and facts will support without intolerable strain, so as to enable them to pursue any arguably-legal ends by any arguably-legal means. The paradigmatic exercise of the adversary-advocate's role is the criminal defense lawyer's; and the role is a noble role, both because it furthers the client's freedom of action and protects his rights against an overbearing state, and because it facilitates the proper determination of his claims and defenses.

<u>Inadequacy of the Excuses</u>. The Enron and similar scandals illustrate the limits of all these standard stories as adequate accounts of the corporate lawyer's proper role.

Despite their increasing popularity among practicing and some academic lawyers, the profession surely has to reject out of hand libertarian-antinomian and neutral-risk-assessment theories of its appropriate role and ethics. Both construe the client's interests and autonomously-chosen goals as supreme goods, and law as a set of obstacles that the lawyer helps to clear out of the way. The antinomian ranges the lawyer alongside his client as an opponent of law, someone who sees law as merely an imposition and a nuisance. The lawyer as risk-assessor also views legal norms, rules, institutions, and procedures in a wholly alienated fashion from the outside, as a source of opportunity and risk to his client.

Some might dispute whether even ordinary citizens of a liberal-democratic republic may, consistent with their enjoyment of its privileges and protections, legitimately adopt such a hostile or alienated attitude toward its laws. People who participate in self-rule through the representatives they elect—constrained by the constitutional limits their ancestors have adopted in conventions or by amendments—and whose lives are mostly benefited from the restraints law puts on private predation and public oppression, should generally internalize the norms and purposes of their legal system and voluntarily respect and obey even the laws they do not particularly like.

[U]nless people internalize the norms and respect the general obligation to obey the law, they will tend to violate it when they can get away with it. That is a recipe for anarchy, because all law depends on voluntary compliance, on my willingness to keep my hands off of your property even when nobody can see me stealing it, and to report my taxable income honestly even though I know only one percent of returns are audited. Societies whose leaders and institutions have conditioned their members into contempt for law and its norms and purposes are plagued by theft, fraud, crime, unenforceable contracts, uncollectible taxes, valueless currencies, and general civil strife. Evidently, this does not mean that society will fall apart unless everyone feels that they must obey every law all the time. In all societies, people obey some laws instinctually, some willingly, and others grudgingly; and they ignore or routinely violate others that they think do not matter all that much. But a general disposition in most people to respect the laws and the purposes behind them really does seem to be a precondition to peaceful, prosperous, cooperative, and orderly social life, which is why good societies put a lot of effort into socializing their citizens into dispositions of general law-abidingness.

However one comes out on this broader argument does not, it seems to me, really much affect the question at issue here: Whether lawyers representing *public corporations* may confront the legal system as alienated outsiders, determined to work around it and minimize its effects to the extent it gets in the way of the client's projects. To this the right answer ought to be, unequivocally, no.

People who defend corporations' taking a "bad man's" approach to law sometimes seem to suggest that business entities should have special privileges—more leeway than individual persons—to game and evade regulations they do not like, because, as engines of growth, job-creation, innovation, and shareholder wealth, they are heroic actors on the social scene, a breed of Nietzschean supermen, beyond good and evil. The taxes, regulations, and liabilities that government pygmies and plaintiffs' lawyers keep trying to impose on them, on the other hand, are often foolish and inefficient, the product of ignorant populism or envy or special-interest rent-seeking. This attitude plays well in boom periods, but it sounds a lot less convincing when defrauded and impoverished employees and investors are licking the wounds from their losses and looking to more, not less, regulation to protect them in the future. Anyway, it is basically an incoherent position. A strong state and effective legal system are preconditions, not obstructions, to successful capitalism, ones capable of legislating and enforcing an adequate infrastructure of ground-rules creating stable currencies, defining and enforcing property rights, contracts, and rules for the transparent and fair operation of markets, and deterring frauds, thefts, torts, discrimination, abuses of labor and harms to competition, health, safety, and the environment.

Of course, the laws in force are not always those businesses would prefer, nor are regulations anywhere near optimally efficient. But though businessmen running large public corporations love to grumble about the SEC, the EPA, and OSHA—and products-liability class-action suits—they are hardly in a position to claim that they are like Jim Crow southern blacks, or vagrants picked up and accused of crimes: powerless outcasts and victims. Big American business firms are not discrete and insular minorities. They have exceptional access to influence in legislatures, administrative agencies, and the courts through government advisory commissions, trade associations, lobbies, and lawyers.

Indeed, it is precisely because of their exceptional power to collectivize and command resources and employees, and to influence governments, that American legal tradition and popular opinion have usually concluded that corporations need to be more, and not less, constrained by law than ordinary citizens. If corporations cheat on or evade their taxes, the treasury loses billions; if corporations bribe politicians or officials, whole governments may be corrupted; and if corporations ignore environmental restraints, entire ecosystems may be wiped out. When it became clear that the financial statements of Enron, WorldCom, Tyco, Adelphia, and Global Crossing* could no longer be trusted, investors fled the markets en masse.

It may be that a natural person cannot be compelled to internalize the values promoted by law, or to feel an obligation to obey the law, without violating his or her dignity or freedom of conscience. But a company has no soul to coerce, dignity to offend, or natural freedom to restrain. Nor can it be schooled by parents, educators, and peers into a general disposition toward sociability or law-abidingness. It can only have the character that its managers, contracts, and organizational incentives and the legal system build into it. It is a creature of law made to serve limited social purposes. Since we are free to construct the character of these artificial persons, we should construct them for legal purposes as good citizens, persons who have internalized the public values expressed in law and the obligation to obey even laws they do not like, for the sake of the privileges of the law that generally benefits them as well as the rest of us.

Nothing in this conception prevents the good corporate citizen from challenging taxes and laws he thinks are unfairly or improperly applied to him; or trying to change them through political action. But it does foreclose the amoralist's argument, that the corporation should be free to ignore, subvert, or nullify the laws because the value it contributes to society justifies its obeying the higher-law imperatives of profit-seeking and shareholder-wealth-creation. If the artificial person is constructed as a good and law-abiding person, it follows that the manager who ignores or tries to nullify the valid objectives of law and regulation is not acting as a responsible or faithful agent of his principal, the good corporate citizen.

If the corporation should be constructed and presumed to have the interests of a good, law-respecting, citizen, so should its lawyers (even more so). Lawyers are not simply agents of clients—they are also licensed fiduciaries of the legal system, "part of a judicial system charged with upholding the law," to use the ABA's words. They do not have, as the dissenting citizen does, the option of taking up a position outside the legal order, rejecting the norms and public purposes of the legal system and limiting themselves to a grudging and alienated outward compliance with such of its rules as they think they cannot safely or profitably violate when their interest or inclination is to do so. The lawyer is, by vocation, committed to the law.

Now, of course, the "norms and purposes and public values" of law are not something fixed and definite and certain; rather, they are

---

* [Eds. These were companies that appeared in the late 1990s to be quite profitable until they suddenly failed under circumstances suggesting that corporate officials had overstated their profitability and understated their liabilities.]

contested and dynamic and alterable—by, among other people, corporate clients and their lawyers. But there is a difference between trying to game and manipulate a system as a resistance movement or alienated outsider would, and to engage in a committed and good faith struggle within the system to influence it to fulfill what a good faith interpreter would construe as its best values and purposes.

Applying these general standards to many of the Enron transactions seems in some ways pretty simple. The purpose of the securities laws is to make public companies' financial condition transparent to investors. Agents of Enron had an interest in making their finances opaque, in order to boost the stock price of the company and with it their compensation in options, and to conceal the management fees they were paying themselves. They asked lawyers to manipulate the rules so that they would appear to be disclosing without actually disclosing. The lawyers obliged—and by so doing effectively thwarted the valid purposes of the laws.

How about the claims that the lawyers did not know the extent of the company's misrepresentations and frauds, relied on information given them by accountants or managers, saw only small pieces of the puzzle, and took on assignments validly narrowed and specialized in scope? These claims would really have to be analyzed in detail, case by case, to see if they are any good; and I do not find many of them very convincing. But I would make some general points about these claims.

One is that, although lawyers may take on an assignment that limits the scope of their representation or asks them to accept some facts as given, they may not agree to such limits as will preclude them from competent and ethical representation. They should not, for example, agree to write an opinion certifying the legality of a deal to third parties if they have some reason to be suspicious of the facts or numbers reported to them, without doing some digging to ensure that the facts are accurate. Nor should they give assurances that certain facts are true if they have no independent means of verifying them. If the client's agents are given unrestricted discretion to limit the scope of the lawyer's work, it becomes all too easy for them to use lawyers to paint a gloss of respectability (sprinkle holy water, as it were) on dubious transactions. Lawyers like to say that they have to assume and hope that their clients are not lying to them. But they should not passively cooperate in a corporate strategy to attach a respectable law firm's name to a scam, even if they are not dead certain that it is a scam.

More generally, the ways in which many corporations structure their legal services operate to prevent their receiving appropriately independent law-respecting advice. The practice of spreading fragments of business around to different outside firms, and different lawyers' offices within the company, makes it easy for managers to shop around for compliant lawyers, thus inducing races to the bottom, in which law firms or in-house counsel determined to give independent and conservative advice either lose out to their cross-town rivals or gradually acquiesce in the corrosion of their standards. It also eliminates responsibility, since no set of lawyers ever knows enough about the business decisions to know the likely purpose or effect of their advice, and how it fits into the company's plans as a whole. The lawyers could not sit down with managers and directly press them for information about the purposes and underlying facts of the transactions they were being asked to bless. And for the most part they did not try to do so.

The most important lessons of Enron, et al., for lawyers are the additional clouds of doubt they cast on the most common defense of the corporate lawyer's role, and the one most often invoked by the profession in the current debates over reform. That is the corporate lawyer as adversary-advocate.

This idea that the role of the corporate lawyer is really just like the role of the criminal defense lawyer has been criticized so often and so effectively that it always surprises me to see the idea still walking around, hale and hearty, as if nobody had ever laid a glove on it. I will quickly run through some of the strong objections to the analogy and then add another objection: The bar's standard construction of the corporate lawyer's role is deficient in part because it does not take the analogy seriously enough.

The most obvious objection is that legal advice given outside of adversary proceedings is not subject to any of the constraints of such proceedings. The reasons that the lawyer is given so much latitude to fight for his client in court is that the proceedings are open and public, effective mechanisms such as compelled discovery and testimony exist to bring to light suppressed inconvenient facts and make them known to adversaries and adjudicators, adversaries are present to challenge the advocate's arguments of law and his witnesses' and documents' view of facts, and there is an impartial umpire or judge to rule on their sufficiency and validity. Absent any of these bothersome conditions, lawyers can stretch the rules and facts very extravagantly in their clients' favor without risking contradiction by adversaries, or the annoyed reactions of judges or regulators to far-fetched positions.

In the trial setting, aggressive advocacy (at least in theory) supposedly operates to bring out the truth, by testing one-sided proof and argument against counter-proof and counter-argument. Ideally, it facilitates decisions of the legal validity of the parties' claims on the merits. Outside of such settings, one-sided advocacy is more likely to help parties overstep the line to violate the law, and to do so in such ways as are likely to evade detection and sanction, and thus frustrate the purposes of law and regulation.

The advocacy ideology regularly and persistently confuses the managers, who ask for lawyers' advice, with the lawyers' actual client, the corporate entity. Admittedly, much corporate-law doctrine makes this easy for them because it is excessively permissive in allowing lawyers to treat the incumbent managers who consult them as the entity. At least until the adoption last year of the Sarbanes-Oxley's Act's "up the ladder" reporting requirement, the bar's ethical rules also facilitated this conflation of the corporate client with management, by waffling over whether corporate counsel who becomes aware that a corporate agent has engaged in conduct that is a "violation of law" and is "likely to result in substantial injury to the organization" must report the misconduct up to or, if necessary, even beyond the board of directors. But the general principle is clear: A corporate agent acting unlawfully no longer represents the corporation, and the corporation's lawyer therefore owes him no loyalty, and no duty of zealous representation. On the contrary, if his illegal acts are harming the actual client, the lawyer should not help him out at all. And that, obviously, is a huge difference between representing a company and representing the criminally accused.

The point I want to add to these standard, but valuable, points is a simple one. Corporate lawyers could actually learn something useful from the role of the criminal defense lawyer. And that is that the adversary-advocate's role—like that of all lawyers—is in large part a public role, designed to fulfill public purposes: The ascertainment of truth and the doing of justice; the protection of the autonomy, dignity and rights of witnesses and especially of the accused; and the monitoring and disciplining of police and prosecutorial conduct. The defense lawyer is not merely or even mostly a private agent of his client, whose function is to zealously further the client's interest (which is usually to evade just punishment for his past conduct, or continue to engage in it in the future). He is assigned a specialized role in a public process in which his zealous advocacy is instrumental to the service of various public objectives. He is encouraged to make the best possible arguments for suppressing unlawfully seized evidence, not for the purpose of furthering his client's interest in freedom or getting away with crimes, but to protect third parties who are not his clients, i.e., other citizens whose freedom and security will be put at risk unless police misconduct is deterred. He is allowed to present a very one-sided, partial, and selective version of the evidence favoring the defense, in part because resourceful adversaries can poke holes in his story and present a counter-story, but even more to fulfill a public purpose—that of keeping prosecutors up to the mark, making sure they know that they have to put together a defense-proof case, deterring them from indicting where they do not have the evidence.

Defense counsel's zeal is restricted precisely at the points where it might help the client at the risk of damage to the performance of his public functions and the integrity of the procedural framework that those functions are designed to serve. He may not, for example, lie to judges, suppress or manufacture real evidence, pose questions on cross-examination that he has no basis in fact for asking, or suborn or knowingly put on perjured testimony.

If you extend this analysis of the public functions of the defense bar to the corporate bar, what might you conclude? That, like the defense lawyer's, the corporate lawyer's role has to be constructed so that it serves and does not disserve its public functions as well as its private ones. I have explained the public benefits of allowing defense lawyers to suppress unlawfully seized evidence, or to refrain from volunteering inconvenient facts pointing to their clients' guilt. But what are the benefits of allowing lawyers to conceal—or hide in a maze of fine print—facts from regulators and investors that would be highly relevant to determining what the companies' real earnings were, or whether its tax shelters had some economic purpose beyond avoidance, or that managers were setting up side deals paying themselves and their cronies huge bonuses? What is the virtue of allowing lawyers to pull the wool over the eyes of the understaffed bureaucrats who monitor their transactions and try to enforce the laws? Even if all of these schemes should turn out to be (at least arguably) technically legal, what values of overall human happiness, individual self-fulfillment, or economic efficiency are served by helping clients promote them? The autonomy of clients generally is a good thing, to be sure; but there is no virtue per se in action, any old action, that is freely chosen, if it is likely to bring destruction in its wake—including, in these examples, harm to the real clients themselves, not their incumbent managements but the long-term corporate entities and their constituent stake-holders.

The real lesson from the defense lawyer's or advocate's role is simply that the lawyer is, in addition to being a private agent of his clients, a public agent of the legal system, whose job is to help clients steer their way through the maze of the law, to bring clients' conduct and behavior into conformity with the law—to get the client as much as possible of what the client wants without damaging the framework of the law. He may not act in furtherance of his client's interest in ways that ultimately frustrate, sabotage, or nullify the public purposes of the laws—or that injure the interests of clients, which are hypothetically constructed, as all public corporations should be, as good citizens who internalize legal norms and wish to act in furtherance of the public values they express.

NOTES ON GORDON

1. *Evaluating Conceptions of the Corporate Counselor's Role.* What are the various conceptions of the corporate counselor's role that Gordon identifies and rejects? Why does he find each of them defective? Do you agree with his critiques?

2. *The Corporate Lawyer's Public Function.* What public functions does a criminal defense lawyer serve? What public functions does a corporate counselor serve? Does your answer to the latter question depend on how the lawyer conducts himself in that role?

3. *Corporations as Good Citizens?* Do you agree with Gordon that lawyers who counsel corporations should construct the character of their clients for legal purposes as "good citizens who have internalized the public values expressed in law and the obligation to obey even laws they do not like"?

4. *Can Lawyers Practice Competently and Ethically When Clients Leave Them in the Dark?* Corporate clients sometimes keep lawyers involved in decision-making and in a position to detect misconduct and to influence the client toward legal compliance. But what happens when the client, such as Enron, disaggregates its work across many firms so that no one set of lawyers is entrusted with extensive information about the client's operations? Do you agree with Gordon that lawyers whose clients decline to give them the information they need to assess the legality of the client's objectives cannot practice competently and ethically and so should decline to represent such clients?

PROBLEM 18–2

You are a partner in a large firm. One of your firm's major clients is Major Conglomerate, a technology company that sells products around the world. An executive in charge of sales in Latin America calls you to discuss a question. He explains that, as a condition of getting access to certain Latin American markets, his sales people are routinely asked to make small payments to local officials. He explains that he understands that such payments are probably not entirely proper but that they are essential for enabling his sales staff to meet the company's earnings targets for the year. He also emphasizes that his own job rides on meeting sales targets in Latin America. You explain that such payments violate a federal statute that prohibits various corrupt practices, including making bribes overseas, and that Major Conglomerate could be hit with heavy fines if the bribes were to come to light. You also explain that whatever bad publicity surrounded such a scandal could irretrievably harm the company's image. The manager of sales thanks you for your advice and hangs up. Several weeks later, you contact him to make sure that you have answered all of his questions and that he has resolved the situation appropriately. He does not return your calls. How should you respond?

F. INDEPENDENCE IN CORPORATE COUNSELING

The next two excerpts consider the consequences for corporate clients and lawyers when lawyers decline to offer independent advice to corporate management. Consider first William Allen's argument that professional independence is vital for serving corporate clients well and finding satisfaction in one's work as a business lawyer. The second excerpt, by David Wilkins, argues that excessive deference, which he calls the "agency model," leaves lawyers highly vulnerable to the misdeeds of powerful corporate clients.

CORPORATE GOVERNANCE AND A BUSINESS LAWYER'S DUTY OF INDEPENDENCE
William T. Allen
38 Suffolk University Law Review 1 (2004)

[W]hat arguments can support the happy thought that lawyers who subject their work for business clients to the discipline of their own independent review, will, if all other factors are held constant, tend to give more useful advice to their clients? Business clients are repeat players in most of the important contexts in which they have significant legal problems. They have ongoing relationships with government regulators, customers, suppliers, partners, joint-venturers, capital markets, etc. These relationships and the firm's reputation are valuable assets. Every action or dispute that affects the future of these relationships is likely to be optimally resolved only when appropriate weight is given to that fact. The zealous advocate can get in the way of a productive long-term relationship.

A legal counsel who views herself as an independent professional adds utility by helping her client see the reasonable limits of ambient legal ambiguity so that mutual satisfaction from important relationships can be achieved. An independent counselor never abandons a commitment to substantive legality. She will therefore ask what client action would most advantageously conform the client's activity to the principles underlying the relevant legal rule and protect future utility from the legal relationship at risk. The zealous advocate, on the other hand, asks whether there is any colorable argument that can be made to support an advantageous action. This approach—call it a litigator's stance—is shared, for example, by the accountant who invents abusive tax shelters, the lawyer who satisfies the aggressive opinion shopper, or the corporate lawyer who is willing to follow accounting technicality to call a loan a sale. This kind of advice may be an unavoidable stance in the one-shot litigation context, but it is dangerous to a business client in other settings.

In many instances, zealous advocacy attitudes will destroy or at least threaten states of mind that allow client firms to make relationship specific investments that produce value over time. To a substantial extent, large business corporations function on trust as well as on crisply defined legal rights. Trust is a valuable asset that emerges from a perception of shared norms of fair dealing, from patterns of prior fair practice, and from an expectation of future interactions. The diffusion of a zealous advocate mentality within a business firm, for example, would certainly erode trust and, in the long run, generate large increases in the costs of operating the firm. The detriments to the firm's relations with outside parties are not fundamentally different.

Think about what the zealous advocacy mentality might do in the context of a corporate crisis. In light of the Federal Organizational Sentencing Guidelines,* every large firm, from securities firms to chemical companies, must now be intensely concerned, not with stout resistance to law under every colorable theory clever counsel can imagine, but with compliance with regulatory law, with candor, and with voluntary remediation of violations. But corporate crises are not unique settings in which independent legal counseling will be valuable. In a business world in which all parties believed that their dealings were governed by the standards of zealous advocacy representation, sharply higher costs could be expected all over the place: in regulatory interactions, in commercial dispute resolution, and even in public product markets. Imagine, for example, the consequences of a zealous advocacy response to a product tampering scare.

Thus, except for the unfortunate pathologies that will arise in the one-shot litigation context, the world offers plenty of evidence that, for business clients, there is greater long-term value in legal services provided by lawyers whose zealous and loyal representation is constrained by a fundamental commitment to the finer ideals of the profession.

If the advice of talented lawyers with a developed sense of their own responsibilities as members of the bar will give more effective advice, why

---

* [Eds. Note: In 1991, the United States Sentencing Commission issued guidelines for federal judges imposing sentences on organizational defendants. These guidelines impose harsh penalties upon organizations whose employees or other agents commit federal crimes. The guidelines encourage organizations to develop "effective programs to prevent and detect violations of law," and identify seven "types of steps" that an effective program should include. Where organizations demonstrate an effort to implement the seven steps, judges impose lower sanctions. Revisions to the guidelines that took effect in 2004 contain new, heightened requirements for companies to try to detect and prevent violations of law and to establish an ethical culture. Those revisions require businesses to: (1) ensure that the organization "has an effective compliance and ethics program"; "evaluate periodically the effectiveness of the organization's compliance and ethics program"; and "periodically assess the risk of criminal conduct and take appropriate steps to design, implement, or modify each requirement to reduce the risk of criminal conduct identified through this process." See Ethics Resource Center, *Federal Sentencing Guidelines*, http://www.ethics.org/resource/federal-sentencing-guidelines.]

do we observe great demand for zealous advocacy-inspired business advice? The problem lies largely in the "agency problem." The client of a corporate lawyer is the corporation, but the voice of the client is a human agent for the corporation. These officers inevitably have a shorter time horizon than the organization considered as a whole, and they have a set of incentives that are imperfectly matched with those of the firm. This disjunction in incentives is most obvious when we look at the incentive pay structures of senior management, but it is far more pervasive than that. Thus, while some business clients may sometimes appear to seek out lawyers without a commitment to independent professional judgment, not all corporations do, and it is plausible that those that seek aggressive or accommodating lawyers are not accurately expressing the best choice for the corporation.

Different and important reasons to keep alive the self-critical capacity that an independent attorney possesses concern the personal satisfactions drawn from our lives as lawyers.

The model of an independent professional comes closer than the dominant zealous advocacy model to actually describing the greatest lawyers of this or earlier ages. Consider, for example, the case of Louis D. Brandeis. I refer not to the great Justice Brandeis but to the earlier, spectacularly successful practitioner. Brandeis' life in the law reminds us that a great business lawyer need not act as a tool of any private interest that seeks his assistance. Brandeis was committed in his work to advancing the common good of the parties and the public good. Controversially, he sometimes acted as "counsel for the situation." He undertook to counsel his clients, not to act as a mere implement in their hands. He refused to have his professional skills used in ways or for ends that he, as a citizen interested in the common good, could not endorse. Brandeis is especially eminent, of course, but the model he followed was one adopted by other great lawyers. Whether at the head of great Wall Street firms, or as trusted long-term advisors on Main Street, the role of independent counselor, not zealous advocate, is the role in which those who practice today are most likely to add value to their clients and to achieve the deeper satisfaction that seems absent from the lives of many lawyers.

Lawyers should be able to derive from their work in representing others some sense that they are contributing to the achievement of the deeper purposes of the justice system. We are too greatly invested in our professional lives to permit ourselves to merely be clever amoral agents. Certainly, we are not law enforcement officials; we serve a different role. But if we are to find our professional lives satisfying, our role as zealous advocates and loyal facilitators of legal transactions must be consistent with our role as independent professionals and moral actors dedicated to the achievement of the higher goals of the legal system. This role gives dignity and a sense of deeper meaning to our work as business lawyers.

The recognition, or more correctly, the hope, that we will be better and more satisfied lawyers if we act as self-consciously independent but loyal business lawyers will not, of course, simplify our lives. The life of a self-consciously independent lawyer will be more difficult and more ambiguous than that of the zealous advocate. But today we can offer the observation that the corporate board, energized by new expectations and more aggressive law enforcement, is more likely than ever before to be supportive of such a lawyer.

There is no easy rule book for working out the complexity that professional life presents. In this respect professional life is no different from any other aspect of our lives. But there is no hiding from complexity if we are to engage life fully and responsibly. Coherence is possible but simple clarity is often a delusion.

NOTES ON ALLEN

1. **Does Lawyer Independence Benefit Clients?** According to Professor Allen, how do clients benefit when lawyers give them independent advice rather than telling them what they want to hear? In what ways does a "zealous advocacy mentality" harm corporate clients?

2. **Reputation for Integrity as a Business Asset.** Some commentators have observed that a lawyer's reputation for integrity may serve clients who wish to signal to outsiders the legality and respectability of the company's past or future conduct.[6] Does that claim seem plausible to you?

3. **The Agency Problem.** In Allen's view, what is the "agency problem" that sometimes fuels demand for "zealous advocacy-inspired business advice"? Does Rule 1.13 resolve this agency problem?

4. **Benefits for Lawyers?** According to Allen, how do business lawyers benefit in terms of personal satisfaction when they offer independent advice? Are there other types of potential benefits for lawyers?

TEAM OF RIVALS? TOWARD A NEW MODEL OF THE CORPORATE ATTORNEY-CLIENT RELATIONSHIP
David B. Wilkins
78 Fordham Law Review 2067 (2010)

There is arguably no more quoted, or in the minds of many lawyers beloved, understanding of the duties owed by an advocate to his or her client than Brougham's legendary speech in defense of Queen Caroline. Speaking on the floor of the House of Lords in 1820, Lord Brougham

---

[6] *See, e.g.*, Robert Gordon, *The Independence of Lawyers*, 68 B. U. L. REV. 1 (1988).

eloquently stated what many still believe to be the essence of the lawyer's role:

> An advocate, in the discharge of his duty, knows but one person in all the world, and that person is his client. To save that client by all means and expedients, and at all hazards and costs to other persons, and, amongst them, to himself, is his first and only duty; and in performing this duty he must not regard the alarm, the torments, the destruction which he may bring upon others. Separating the duty of a patriot from that of an advocate, he must go on reckless of the consequences, though it should be his unhappy fate to involve his country in confusion.*

For almost two centuries, these words have stood as the embodiment of the ideal of zealous advocacy that lawyers owe to their clients. But of late, there have also been many who have questioned whether such an extreme standard of partisanship—ignoring the "alarm," "torment," and "destruction" of others—is the proper standard for lawyers to take in all circumstances. Specifically, I and others have argued that whatever the value of Brougham's conception in the context in which he made his famous claim—i.e., the representation of an individual criminal defendant facing the unchecked power of the King in circumstances where the defendant's head was quite literally on the line—this understanding has much less to recommend it when we consider how corporate lawyers ought to conceive of their duties, particularly in the area of regulatory compliance.

Today, these concerns are especially salient. As the spotlight of blame shines its accusatory light on the cast of characters involved in the current economic meltdown, it is only a matter of time before the inside and outside lawyers who represented the banks and other financial institutions we are currently bailing out will be called upon to take their turn in the dock. When they do, it is unlikely enforcement officials or the public will have much sympathy for an ethic that appears to command lawyers for these powerful clients to proceed "reckless of the consequences" even if it means casting "the country in confusion"—let alone bankruptcy. Given the current mood, there may be little the bar can do to avoid this "unhappy fate" this time around. But as we prepare to enter into a brave new world in which all corporate actors—lawyers included—will almost certainly face increased scrutiny, I want to suggest that the profession and those we purport to serve would do well to consider whether there is something more fundamentally wrong with applying Brougham's conception of the lawyer's role to the corporate context than the conflation of the standards of advocacy appropriate to

---

* [Eds.: Lord Brougham's speech occurred in his defense of Queen Caroline, estranged wife of King George IV, on charges of adultery and in connection with a bill aimed at dissolving the marriage and stripping Caroline of her royal title.]

the criminal context with those that should govern in civil or regulatory matters.

At the heart of Brougham's understanding of the lawyer's role stands a simple but powerful assumption: that the attorney-client relationship is essentially one of agency. Of course a lawyer "knows but one person in all the world" and is required to promote that person's interests "by all means and expedients and at all hazards and costs to other persons," even "to himself," Brougham would likely say. These are simply the duties that an agent owes to his or her principal. Lawyers are doing no more—and should be entitled to do no less—than others who are engaged by principals to protect their interests and pursue their goals

For all of its intuitive appeal, the agency model is no longer a helpful template for understanding the relationship between corporations and their outside firms.

A principal-agent model serves only to entrench the ability of powerful corporate-principals to impose their will on increasingly vulnerable lawyer-agents. Indeed, current market conditions have largely turned the traditional justification for the agency model on its head. By withholding information and manipulating incentives, sophisticated corporate clients now have the power to pressure their lawyers into taking risky or unethical actions that threaten to throw their law firms "into confusion" in the form of legal peril or financial ruin. "Innocent" lawyers who do not want to participate in such actions have no recourse other than to resign—or be fired. At the same time, "guilty" lawyers who have no interest in standing up to client pressure are given a pass on the ground that they are not responsible for the ends of the representation and are required to follow the client's direction so long as it is technically within the letter of the law. A model of the attorney-client relationship that recognizes that both clients and lawyers have reciprocal obligations of disclosure, forbearance, and fair dealing provides a better foundation for dealing with these increasingly important problems.

Market conditions in the last decades of the 20th century made it increasingly difficult for lawyers to play this gatekeeping role. [T]he agency model has contributed to this decline. By characterizing the relationship between corporate lawyers and their clients as fundamentally one of agency, the standard account systematically marginalizes, and indeed delegitimizes, a lawyer's allegiance to this broader public role. Rather than being viewed as "trusted advisors" who help to shape their clients' objectives in ways that ultimately serve both the clients' and the public's long-term goals, lawyers who seek to influence client ends are chastised as "moral policemen" who constrain their clients' "first class citizenship" by "arrogating to themselves" decision-making authority that should belong exclusively to their client-principals. The result has been an increasing tendency among even the most public-regarding segments of the corporate bar to embrace what Robert Gordon calls "schizoid lawyering" in which practitioners confine their public commitments to their own (increasingly scarce) private time, while accepting uncritically the instructions of their private clients unmediated by any attention to public ends.

Moreover, the agency model of the lawyer's role assumes that all ethical obligations flow from the lawyer-agent to the client-principal. Clients have only rights, not obligations. To be sure, these rights may be limited by a lawyer's correlative obligations to the legal framework and, on occasion, even by the lawyer's own interest in remaining an upright person while earning a satisfactory living. As important and as controversial as these limitations may be, however, they do not disturb the basic framework in which clients have no obligations, save for their duty to pay for the services they receive.

[Wilkins then proceeds to spell out his idea for a set of reciprocal relations between lawyers and clients that would involve lawyers more directly in ensuring clients' legal compliance and would leave them less vulnerable to client wrongdoing. He argues that the relationship between large and sophisticated corporate clients and their increasingly large and sophisticated outside counsel is better conceptualized as a new kind of strategic alliance or partnership than as the typical agent-principal relationship envisioned by Brougham. He cites some examples of major corporations that have recently reduced the number of outside firms they use and involved those outside counsel much more extensively in the corporation's operation and ongoing efforts to promote legal compliance.]

NOTES ON WILKINS

1. **Relations Between In-House Counsel and Outside Firms.** Recall what you learned in Chapter 15 about the changed relationship between in-house counsel and outside law firms over the past several decades. How might the decreased power of outside lawyers relative to in-house counsel have made lawyers in law firms less willing to offer independent advice to their clients?

2. **Lawyer Vulnerability and Corporate Scandals.** Is Professor Wilkins right to suggest that corporate lawyers' involvement in various corporate scandals of the past few decades is partly a consequence of their vulnerability to client demands under an agency conception of the attorney-client relationship? As you consider this question, recall the facts of the O.P.M., Lincoln Savings/Kaye Scholer, Enron, and Refco scandals described in Chapter 15.

3. **How Can Lawyers Protect Themselves?** What freedom and/or responsibility do the Model Rules currently give corporate lawyers to protect themselves from client misconduct? To what extent do the Model Rules

permit or require lawyers to choose their clients carefully, withdraw when they suspect mischief (Rule 1.16(b)), reveal confidential information to prevent or minimize injury caused by criminal or fraudulent conduct in which their services have been used (Rule 1.6(b)(2) & (3)), and exercise the "up the ladder" and "reporting out" provisions under Rule 1.13(b) & (c)?

G. SUMMARY

This chapter considered the distinction between counseling and advocacy and why differences in the procedural context in which counseling and advocacy occurs might affect lawyers' responsibilities in these two types of work. We examined what counseling should include, and we addressed whether it is ever appropriate for lawyers to give clients information they might use to evade the law, including information about law enforcement practices. We explored corporate counseling and how lawyers should handle situations in which they discover that a corporation's constituents are engaging in illegal conduct. Finally, we considered the concept of lawyer independence and how independence in corporate counseling relates to the interests of lawyers and clients.

CHAPTER 19

IN-HOUSE COUNSEL

■ ■ ■

A. INTRODUCTION

In-house lawyers, who are employed directly by their corporate clients, play an important role in the operation of major businesses. They generally hold responsibility for providing basic legal advice, selecting and monitoring outside attorneys, and preventing legal problems. Their duties have changed significantly since the 1960s, when in house counsel were often viewed as inferior lawyers who could not make it in the competition for big firm partnerships. Beginning in the 1970s, corporations began to find it more efficient to handle routine and recurring matters in-house rather than to pay high fees for outside counsel. Corporations increasingly looked to outside firms to handle specialized matters only on a transaction-specific basis, meaning that they hired outside counsel to handle particular cases and transactions rather than whole categories of needs. Meanwhile, the general counsel (the most senior in-house lawyer) acquired new status as the manager of all of the corporation's legal services, with responsibility for hiring outside counsel, controlling the costs of legal services purchased from outside law firms, and ensuring that the corporation complies with the law.

The chapter has five sections. The first examines the various functions of inside counsel, inside counsel's relationship with outside counsel, and the allocation of responsibilities between them. The second considers the question of professional independence—the extent to which inside counsel can and should guide their clients toward legal compliance and how that occurs. The third section examines a series of scandals in which in-house lawyers have been involved, as well as commentary on whether and how lawyers might have averted these disastrous episodes. The fourth section explores the roles of in-house counsel post-Enron. Finally, we consider the views of an experienced former general counsel of a major corporation about what it takes to be an effective in-house lawyer.

B. WHAT DO INSIDE COUNSEL DO?

In-house lawyers are called upon to handle a variety of law-related tasks within the corporation. Some, for example, may be primarily responsible for drafting contracts relating to the company's operations, while others are responsible for ensuring that the company complies with all relevant law relating to its hiring, firing, and ongoing relations with employees, environmental regulations, tax and regulatory filings, and technology licensing. In-house lawyers typically also handle the corporation's real estate matters. They often develop risk-management policies and educate other employees to avoid legal troubles. They are sometimes responsible for litigating basic matters, and they generally oversee higher stakes cases that the corporation farms out to law firms. Some in-house lawyers are generalists, while others specialize. The lead inside lawyer is the General Counsel, who usually is part of the corporation's senior management team.

The first excerpt reports findings from a study based on 86 interviews with in-house counsel, legally trained executives, and non-lawyer managers in 46 large corporations and financial institutions in Northern California, Chicago, and New York. The authors found that in-house counsel played three primary roles: "cops" (also sometimes called "gatekeepers"), who ensure that the company complies with the law; "counsel", who advise the company; and "entrepreneurs", who market legal advice as a means of helping the company meet its financial goals. Lawyers might play each of these roles exclusively, or they might wear different hats depending on the circumstances.

Cops, Counsel, and Entrepreneurs: Constructing the Role of Inside Counsel in Large Corporations
Robert L. Nelson and Laura Beth Nielsen
34 Law & Society Review 457 (2000)

It is useful in beginning to examine the roles of inside counsel to construct a set of categories that captures the range of lawyering styles in corporations. Our analysis of the interviews suggested that lawyers played three ideal typical roles: some spoke of their role as narrowly legal, some spoke of mixing legal and business advice, and some emphasized entrepreneurial or profit-generating uses of law. Bearing in mind that the ways lawyers describe their tasks are complex and sometimes contested by others in the organization, we attempted to devise a conceptual scheme that would allow us to classify individual lawyers by role type [as cops, counsel, and entrepreneurs].

Cops. When corporate counsel are playing the "cop" role, they are primarily concerned with policing the conduct of their business clients. (In many interviews, the corporate counsel refer to various businesspeople and business units within their corporation as their "clients," even though technically both lawyers and the business personnel are employees of the same organization.) They interact with business people almost exclusively through legal gatekeeping functions, such as approving contracts, imposing and implementing compliance programs, and responding to legal questions. Cops are less willing [than in-house lawyers in other roles] to offer non-legal advice, even when they have the opportunity.

The vice president for legal affairs for a major chemical firm exemplified the role of lawyer as cop. He was hired for the position from outside the corporation after a distinguished career in government and private practice. He interpreted his hiring as an effort by the corporation to bring in someone who would be independent within the corporate environment.

> I think that the thought is when you get somebody who has an independent stature, apart from his or her position in the corporation, that the person is also more likely to be independent and give you that independent professional judgment that is so essential.

Even though he was a member of the corporation's Board of Directors and the corporation's Executive Committee, he characterized his work "principally as a lawyer." A theme that consistently emerged in this interview, despite some discussion of lawyers attempting to act as part of the management team in the various subsidiaries of the corporation, was the need for lawyers to say no.

> I mean there are [business] people who want to do something and they just simply can't do it, they can't understand why, and then I say, "Well, that's just the way the law is."

And later, after recounting such an incident, he said,

> So, the businessmen had quite a lot of trouble with that, and I don't blame them; I do too. I have to say, "That's the law. You can't do it"; I would never say they can't do anything. I can't forbid it. I can say, "If you do it, you run the risk and you're going to go to prison; you don't have any defense. You've been advised you are in violation of the law."

Counsel. The role that corporate lawyers most often play is the counsel. Legal gatekeeping plays an important part in inserting these lawyers into business activities, but it is not the only basis on which they relate to management. Counsel most often confine their advice to legal questions and legitimate their suggestions or demands based on legal knowledge. Yet the counsel role implies a broader relationship with business actors that affords counsel an opportunity to make suggestions based on business, ethical, and situational concerns.

Our exemplar of this type, a general counsel in a bank, described this mixture of legal and business functions.

Forty percent of my time is spent managing the legal position, . . . 20% of my time is as the bank's chief compliance officer: dealing with regulators, overviewing the auditing process within the bank, [overseeing] training done by the legal division . . . Another 30% of my time is as consigliere of executive and senior management: I am the counselor; I am the guy who is asked to draft letters; to advise on particular issues, which can overlap with the first two primarily because it relates to the regulators . . . The remaining 10% of my time I practice law.

Q. The consigliere role, you distinguish that from the law practice?

A. Yes, because when I think of practicing law . . . it's more taking a particular legal problem and finding out what the law is, and then applying the law to the facts . . . That's not what I do most of the time when I am dealing with senior management. . . The law has very little to do with it. An example would be, the regulators have found what they believe to be a regulatory violation. Well, I've got either a member of my staff or outside counsel who confer with me on whether it is or isn't. That's practicing law. My consigliere role is how I am going to interface between the executive management and the regulators to convince the regulators that it's not [a violation]. And that has nothing really to do with the law. It's negotiating; it's common sense; . . . it's how it's communicated.

This corporate counsel clearly goes beyond merely giving legal advice, although it appears that it is the law and potential legal problems that bring him into business decisions.

I believe that it's my role to make the decision and to make sure the business person goes along with it. Now that's contrary to everything I'd say on the outside or any general counsel would say, because we'd say, "It's not our role to make business decisions." We lay out the risks and the alternatives to our clients and then they make an informed business decision. Well, if they are making an informed business decision, in my mind there is only one decision they can make, the one I want them to make or I think they ought to make—because that's my job. I don't conceive it to be just laying out the risks, but I have to know enough about the company and enough about the situations and circumstances to weigh those risks . . . If I think they are doing something that is legal, that is stupid, it's my job to say to them, "That's stupid," or to convince them in such a way that they come around to my point of view, thinking it's their point of view. So there are some people that I've had to use that deceptive type of process on more than others.

Our ideal typical counsel appears to be quite broadly involved in important managerial decisions; he draws on both legal and other forms of knowledge, and, according to his own account, he is highly influential.

Entrepreneurs. Although the ideal typical "counsel" is still primarily concerned with the legal aspects of business, entrepreneurs emphasize business values in their work. Entrepreneurial lawyers say law is not merely a necessary complement to corporate functions, law can itself be a source of profits, an instrument to be used aggressively in the marketplace, or the mechanism through which major transactions are executed. Our exemplar of the entrepreneur is the general counsel of a holding company, not yet 40 years old at the time of the interview, with a law degree from Harvard. He had been a securities specialist in a large corporate law firm before moving to his corporate employer, where he had worked his way up from being an inside transactional lawyer to general counsel of several subsidiaries, until reaching one of the top two law positions in the corporation. He became most animated in the interview when talking about the size of the "deals" he had put together, such as taking various subsidiaries public, the "phenomenal multiple" they had achieved in an especially large public offering, and the major acquisitions he had worked on for the corporation. His role, and that of many of the lawyers in the corporation, went well beyond giving legal advice.

> The chairman and the chief financial officer consult me, as part of the strategic planning process that we go on. On matters outside of the legal function, I think probably because of the credibility I've gained in representing them over the last ten years in a variety of contexts, they've never expected, and we don't expect, our attorneys to limit their advice and input to pure legal advice. The client here has never found that to be the most valuable type of relationship. There are some clients that certainly expect the lawyers to limit their input to legal advice, but those folks have not succeeded well and don't represent the mainstream of our business management.

This informant, and at least some of the other lawyers in his corporation, present themselves as offering advice "beyond the legal function," in large part because the executives of the corporation expect him to do so. These comments demonstrate that lawyers' roles in the corporation are not fixed choices among discrete categories, but evolve according to the needs of business.

Our entrepreneurial general counsel offered a telling contrast between his approach to his job and that of another general counsel in the corporation, a lawyer who was more senior than our informant, whom our informant had reported to prior to assuming a parallel position in the corporation. Our informant described why he thought he would eventually rise above his former superior.

> I knew his background; his background was litigation and anti-trust. I never believed he was an effective business counselor to the Board of Directors. That wasn't his style, his style was to manage contentious issues. That probably is why he and I succeeded so well together, because that's what I like to do the least. Anything that's negative, the criminal investigations that we've had, anti-trust litigation . . . If I never had to deal with them, the better. I was more interested in what I consider the positive side: raising money, buying companies, selling companies. I mean, at the end of the day your client was happy, or at least knew why the deal wasn't done . . . And Bill's background also was that he was personally kind of the conscience of the company in its formative years, when it was going from mom's and dad's and entrepreneurs into [a] professionally managed [firm]. And it's a role he was personally suited for, but it made him quite unpopular . . . He was the guy who had always played the devil's advocate . . . As the company's evolved and gotten older and become more professionally managed at the operating level, that role hasn't been that necessary; it wasn't one that I desired. [A senior executive] told me that Bill was never considered a candidate for corporate secretary . . . [even though] it was natural for that position to have gone to Bill . . . I was always very positive in my outlook, in my ability to succeed . . . And frankly I expect . . . who could possibly run this company in perhaps 15 or 20 years if it [isn't] me?

From these comments, it appears that Bill is a "cop" who was more influential in the corporation in an earlier era, when it "needed" a corporate conscience. According to our informant, the need for that role has diminished as the management of the corporation has become more professionalized. He attributes his own rise to influence to his ability to be a business counselor. Indeed, he expects to run the company some day in the future.

What is the motivating force in our informant's career?—his interest in making money and growing the company. He describes himself as part of the second-generation management of the corporation.

> I think the [senior management] group is extremely motivated by financial returns. Certainly the professional challenges are there too. The ability to take the business the next step, to take it from 10 [billion in revenues] to 20 [billion], which is very

doable given the marketplace opportunities ... It's a huge challenge. It's very exciting.

When we asked him how strongly he identified with the corporation, he made it clear that what he loved about it was the financial opportunities that it presented, rather than the functions it served.

What was so attractive to me about [the corporation] was, it was a fabulous venture capital firm, or a fabulous merchant banking firm. We had access, in fact we still do have access, to tremendous amounts of capital. We could stop growing the basic X business today, stop investing in X facilities, and the cash flow would be so tremendous that we would have to either go buy some other business ... or buy our own stock back, in which case I'll make a fortune because the stock price will go up. What excites me about any of these opportunities ... is the financial dynamic.

This entrepreneur derives great personal meaning from the contemporary managerial conception of the corporation: it is, above all, a financial institution. Our informant used his legal expertise to gain entree to the world of corporate finance. He continues to hold the title of General Counsel, which denotes continuing legal responsibilities. Yet it is clear that business objectives, rather than legal accomplishments, motivate his work.

NOTES ON NELSON & NIELSEN

1. *What Are the Roles?* According to Nelson & Nielsen, what are the different roles that in-house counsel play? What exactly does a lawyer in each of these roles—cop, counsel, or entrepreneur—do for the corporation? Which of these role types is mostly likely to serve the corporation's interests? Does your answer depend upon the situation?

2. *Playing Multiple Roles.* Notice that Nelson & Nielsen are not claiming that individual in-house lawyers necessarily play just one of these roles. They might instead pursue different lawyering styles at different times, depending on the circumstances.

3. *What Are the Personality Traits of Lawyers in These Positions?* What characteristics would you expect to be most important for lawyers in each of these roles? Which of these roles would fit your own personality and aptitudes best?

* * *

Inside Counsel's Relationship with Outside Counsel. As noted in the materials on large firms, inside counsel have gained substantial power vis-à-vis outside counsel during the past three decades. Inside counsel once handled primarily routine and low-stakes work within the corporation, while outside counsel served as the corporation's true legal advisors. But inside counsel—and especially the lead in-house lawyer, the general counsel—now play much more powerful roles. The general counsel, not the senior partner in the law firm, is often the primary counselor for the CEO and the board on law, ethics, and risk.[1] In addition, inside counsel also decide what work will stay inside, what work will go to outside firms, and which firms will be hired to handle the outsourced work. That transformation in the role of inside counsel has gone hand-in-hand with their increased role in management. According to a recent study by Deloitte, the number of in-house attorneys who are members of the senior management/executive team rose from 47 percent in 2005 to 62 percent in 2010. The same study concluded that general counsel hold a wider set of responsibilities than they did five years ago and that they are now more likely to be the first source of advice for senior management when serious legal or regulatory issues arise. Almost three-quarters of the 877 interviewed lawyers upon which the report was based said that the general counsel has greater influence in a business environment than a partner in a large law firm, compared with 35 percent who said that corporate counsel were more influential five years before.[2] One former general counsel of a major corporation has argued that these changes represent "a dramatic shift in power from outside private firms to inside law departments," which has contributed to a "dramatic[ ]" improvement in the quality of general counsel over the past two decades.[3]

Trends toward increased power in the hands of inside counsel vis-à-vis outside firms appear to have accelerated in the wake of the economic recession, as general counsel have forced private firms to compete for business and control costs. A 2010 report produced by the international law firm Eversheds, based on a survey of 130 general counsel and 80 law firm partners around the globe, concluded that general counsel had acquired substantially greater status and influence in the post-recession world.[4]

C. IN-HOUSE COUNSEL AND PROFESSIONAL INDEPENDENCE

One persistent question about in-house counsel has been whether they are able to exercise independent judgment. The traditional view has been that in-house counsel's economic and psychological dependence on

---

[1] *See* Ben W. Heineman, Jr. *The Rise of the General Counsel*, HARV. BUS. REV., Sept. 27, 2012.

[2] DELOITTE GLOBAL CORPORATE COUNSEL REPORT 2011: HOW THE GAME IS CHANGING (2011).

[3] Ben W. Heineman, Jr., *The Rise of the General Counsel*, HARV. BUS. REV., Sept. 27, 2012.

[4] Amy Miller, *Report: GCs Have More Power in Post-Recession World*, LAW.COM, Apr. 1, 2010.

her sole "client"—her employer—prevents her from monitoring her client's conduct and offering unwelcome advice. According to this view, pressure to perform as a "team player" undermines autonomy and interferes with the in-house lawyer's ability to protect the corporation from illegality.

The following excerpt focuses on the difficulty that in-house counsel sometimes face when they find themselves deprived of information they need to perform their jobs.

MORAL MAZES: THE WORLD OF CORPORATE MANAGERS
Robert Jackall
Oxford University Press 122–123 (1988)

Drawing lines when information is scarce becomes doubly ambiguous, a problem that often emerges in shaping relationships with one's colleagues. For instance, Black, a lawyer at Covenant Corporation, received a call from a chemical plant manager who had just been served with an order from the local fire department to build retaining dikes around several storage tanks for toxic chemicals so that firemen would not be in danger of being drenched with the substance should the tanks burst if there were a fire at the plant. The plant manager indicated that meeting the order would cause him to miss his numbers badly that year and he wondered aloud if the fire chief might, for a consideration, be persuaded to forget the whole thing. Black pointed out that he could not countenance even a discussion of bribery; the plant manager laughed and said that he was only joking and would think things over and get back to Black in a few weeks. Black never heard from the plant manager about this issue again; when they met on different occasions after that, the conversation was always framed around other subjects. Black did inquire discreetly and found out that no dikes had been built; the plant manager had apparently gone shopping for a more flexible legal opinion. Should he, Black wondered, pursue the matter or in the absence of any firm evidence just let things drop, particularly since others, for their own purposes, could misconstrue the fact that he had not acted on his earlier marginal knowledge? Feeling that one is in the dark can be somewhat unnerving.

More unnerving, however, is the feeling that one is being kept in the dark. Reed, another lawyer at Covenant, was working on the legal issues of a chemical dumpsite that Alchemy Inc. [a subsidiary of Covenant] had sold. He suddenly received a call from a former employee who had been having trouble with the company on his pension payments; this man told Reed that unless things were straightened out in a hurry, he planned to talk to federal officials about all the pesticides buried in the site. This was alarming news. Reed had no documentation about pesticides in the site; if Alchemy had buried pesticides there, a whole new set of regulations might apply to the situation and to Covenant as the former owner. Reed went to the chemical company's director of personnel to get the former employee's file but was unable to obtain it. Reed's boss agreed to help, but still the director of personnel refused to release the file. After repeated calls, Reed was told that the file had been lost. Reed went back to his boss and inquired whether it might be prudent for Covenant to repurchase the site to keep it under control. This was deemed a good idea. However, the asking price for the site was now three times what Covenant had sold it for. Everyone, of course, got hesitant; another lawyer became involved and began working closely with Reed's boss on the issue. Gradually, Reed found himself excluded from discussions about the problem and unable to obtain information that he felt was important to his work. His anxiety was heightened because he felt he · was involved in a matter of some legal gravity. But, like much else in the corporation, this problem disappeared in the night. Eventually, Reed was assigned to other cases and he knew that the doors to the issue were closed, locked, and bolted.

NOTES ON JACKALL

1. *What Do the Rules Require and/or Allow?* Both Black and Reed find themselves in the dark about legal problems at Covenant. Do Rules 1.2(a) and (d), 1.3, 1.6, 1.13, and 1.16 provide adequate guidance for lawyers caught in these difficult situations? What do the rules require of the lawyers and what discretion do they allow?

2. *What Should Black and Reed Do?* How would you respond in the situations facing Black and Reed? What are the personal and professional risks to these lawyers if they do nothing? What are the risks if they pursue the matters? As you consider these questions, recall the materials in Chapter 16 on supervisory/subordinate relationships and junior lawyers' responsibilities under Rule 5.2.

* * *

Consider the findings on lawyer independence in Nelson & Nielsen's study of inside counsel in the late 1990s:

COPS, COUNSEL, AND ENTREPRENEURS: CONSTRUCTING THE ROLE OF INSIDE COUNSEL IN LARGE CORPORATIONS
Robert L. Nelson and Laura Beth Nielsen
34 Law & Society Review 457 (2000)

The Gatekeeping Function: Pervasive but Circumscribed. When the corporate attorney acts as a gatekeeper, he or she monitors legal compliance and serves as a final hurdle or "gate" through which business ideas must pass prior to implementation. The ability to "trump" a business decision has been identified by researchers as a source of contention and confusion for both lawyers and their business clients from the earliest studies. Cops and counsel continue to confront such tensions.

One lawyer put it this way:

> When individuals in the organization come to me and say, "will you help me execute my deal?" if I come across to them or the lawyers on my staff come across to them as cops, they are not going to come to us. They are . . . either going to go elsewhere or operate in the dark without lawyers.

This lawyer identifies two possible negative outcomes of behaving too much like a cop. The business people will simply go without legal advice, or they will engage in an intra-organizational version of "forum shopping," bringing their problems to the lawyer in the company who is least likely to challenge the business-person's project.

Lawyers and business executives recognize that without some level of autonomy, counsel would not be able to guard the corporation from unwise legal risks. The interviews have a somewhat schizophrenic character in this respect. Lawyers indicated that they have the autonomy required to act independently and to be "deal-stoppers," but several claimed that their companies are "very ethical." When they observed clear cases of legal problems, informants were sure that their company would do everything required to ensure legal compliance. When questioned, almost every attorney could imagine a situation in which he or she would go over the head of management to become a deal-stopper, but few could recall situations in which they had actually done so. It seemed to us that if our respondents found themselves in a John Grisham-like tale of corporate intrigue, they would know how to get help. Most day-to-day business activity does not rise to this level, however.

Yet some attorneys acknowledged that their autonomy is constrained by the need to "get the deal done." Although their "official" role is to advise on legal risks, the business-people would prefer it if the lawyers gave only business-friendly legal advice. One lawyer explained, "Every business manager says they want honesty. They don't mean it, none of them mean it." In fact, this lawyer said that in his corporation, "it's a no-no to say no." According to this informant, inside lawyers are caught between their obligation to the law and their obligation to the company. This struggle for autonomy can have implications for lawyers' careers. The same lawyer said, "I will be honest, to the best of my ability . . . if my boss doesn't like it then let him get rid of me. Which almost happened a few years ago."

Another general counsel indicated that to whom lawyers report was very significant to him. He said that

> Lawyers . . . report to the General Counsel, they do not report to business. That was a deliberate decision. I mean, that might even become, for me, a "resignation" kind of decision, but I don't think there's any prospect of it turning into that kind of issue.

But I feel strongly about that—it's my job to protect their independence.

Apparently this general counsel would oppose decentralizing the legal function by placing lawyers under the authority of business units. Attorneys in centralized departments sometimes have difficulty learning what is happening throughout the corporation. An attorney who practiced in a centralized legal department complained that sometimes he had to "hunt down and chase and spy on [the business executives] in order to try to keep them in line."

Deploying lawyers in a decentralized structure, by housing them in functional units such as Human Resources or Engineering, allows lawyers to "stop [legally questionable] things earlier and know about those things earlier." Yet nesting attorneys in functional divisions exposes them to more intense pressure to agree with their business colleagues rather than offer objective legal advice.

No matter how much a lawyer may wish to be the moral compass of the organization and provide expert legal advice all the time, there are practical constraints on his or her ability to do so. The practical constraints most often mentioned by our respondents were lack of resources and profit pressures. One lawyer spoke of the bind between providing quality legal advice and keeping the costs associated with the legal department within a range that is acceptable to the businesspeople. She said,

> There simply aren't enough lawyers. There's enormous pressure to control costs and yet there's an inconsistent pressure . . . They have simultaneously said, "You've got to control expenses and you can't hire and in fact, you have to cut . . . " So you know that you're not doing the job all that well. You know you don't have enough people; you know you can't get any more.

Inside counsel, like their business peers, are under intense pressure to meet business objectives. The lawyers working in these conditions are, like the business professionals with whom they work, held responsible for the bottom line of their division. One attorney explained that the "bottom line results are really what make or break [a career] . . . the bottom line—success—is how everybody is judged." Another lawyer conceded that his responsibility is to the stockholder and that his job is first and foremost "to make sure that investment grows." These constraints and pressures affect all three types of inside counsel. They render the gatekeeping functions, and indeed other advisory functions, more difficult to perform.

Obviously some of our respondents interpose legal opinions that frustrate the plans of the business executives. Even the attorneys who claim to have the power to be deal-stoppers admit that they must use this power judiciously, however. Half of the lawyers in our sample acknowledge that, most of the time, the businesspeople in the company make the final determination regarding whether to assume a legal risk. The lawyer's role is reduced to informing business executives about the legal risks associated with different actions.

The blending of law and business makes it sometimes difficult for one to establish exactly who is making final decisions regarding business matters. Who makes the final decision is a function of the nature of the issue at hand, the personalities of the people involved, and the complexity of the legal matter involved. One lawyer explained it this way:

> Our job is to assess risks, and it's the businessperson's job to make decisions about risks, what risks they are willing to assume. Now, having said that, I also think of it as my job to make sure that the decision about what risks to assume is being made at the appropriate level. So, if somebody was prepared to assume a risk which I felt was inappropriate, I would say, "I don't think this is a decision for you to make. I need to talk to your boss."

In these comments the lawyer reveals a recognition of the distinction between business decisions and legal decisions, a preference to make only "legal" decisions, and a desire for the businessperson to make the "business" decisions. Nonetheless, the lawyer retains the power to ensure that the business decisions are being handled appropriately.

Corporate counsel who participate in the top management of their companies are different in this respect, however. Ten of 11 respondents who were part of the corporate or divisional management (91%) indicated that they made the final decision about whether to incur a legal risk, whereas only 35% of other lawyers claimed to make the final decision about legal risk. If all questions of legal risk percolated to a legal officer in top management, lawyers would be making such judgments. The clear impression from the interviews, however, is that not all questions go up the legal chain of command. Moreover, corporate counsel in top management contain the same proportions of cops, counsel, and entrepreneurs as the entire sample. They appear, therefore, to confront the same tensions as other lawyers in balancing gatekeeping and entrepreneurial roles.

<u>Views Across the Law/Business Divide: A Mixture of Suspicion and Appreciation</u>. Lawyers' attitudes about the businesspeople in their organization may affect how these lawyers approach their work. Several informants reported altering the legal advice they provide according to how they think business executives view them, as well as how they assess business executives' knowledge of the law and business ethics. Inside counsel often noted the legal sophistication of higher levels of management.

Yet a substantial minority of informants criticized businesspeople for poor business judgment and for failing to understand basic legal principles. For example, one inside counsel complained that "the low-I.Q. club is well-represented" among the businesspeople in his department. More substantively, he said that certain businesspeople are "so in love with [a particular] project, [that they] would do anything to get the deal done. They would compromise the integrity of the bank." Another lawyer expressed a similar sentiment when he said that at least some of the businesspeople "just want to get their deal done and get their bonus," without regard to "basic integrity, documentation, follow-through, responsibility, and accountability." Less insidious, but no less problematic, a number of lawyers indicated that the businesspeople were simply ignorant regarding the importance of the law and lawyers within the organization. One lawyer complained of businesspeople who are "bumpkins . . . who literally tell you they want to violate the law." Inside counsel also occasionally were critical of the way management works. They complained that the corporate culture was little more than nonsense, that businesspeople were often slow to make decisions and to take action.

Conversely, lawyers recognize that businesspeople do not always think highly of lawyers' roles within the company. Inside counsel report that businesspeople "do not really want to have them around," think of them as a "necessary evil," "don't associate lawyers with creative solutions," and do not view them as "team players." More than one-third of inside counsel suggested that they encountered a negative view of lawyers in the corporation. Despite these negative images, many attorneys believe that their work is appreciated by at least some of their clients.

All three types of inside counsel [the cop, counsel, and entrepreneur] must deal with tensions between lawyers and non-lawyers, although they appear to use different strategies with respect to such tensions. Attorneys as cops are less likely than counsels or entrepreneurs to soft-pedal their advice. They risk being characterized as inflexible, or worse. In at least one instance a "cop" was characterized by a manager as "not very smart . . . in a meeting this guy is like two pages behind, metaphorically." Counsel attempt to minimize conflicts with business people. Entrepreneurs market the law to nonlawyers.

Blending Law and Business. In a sense, all the lawyer roles we identify blend legal and business objectives. When a lawyer acts as a cop, he or she serves business by ensuring that the company meets its legal obligations. When a lawyer acts as a counsel, he or she tries to find legal means for doing business. When a lawyer acts as entrepreneur, his or her service to business is more obvious because the lawyer's goals and the businessperson's goals are the same—only the expertise is different. Here we discuss two ways in which inside lawyers explicitly pay deference to business objectives in practice: in their substantive legal advice and in the marketing of law to business.

Although much of the discussion here and elsewhere concerns the social control functions of law within corporations, much of what corporate lawyers do as they ply their substantive expertise is to invent ways to make (or save) money for corporations. Lawyers for corporations constantly use their legal expertise to advance the corporation's financial interests. Much of this activity involves the rather mundane application of existing law. But in large corporations that command huge resources and sophisticated legal talent, inside lawyers are constantly pushing to expand law and legal practices to generate new sources of corporate growth or to gain a new edge in economic competition.

[I]n order to ensure that business professionals will continue to consult them, lawyers try to make their advice more palatable to businesspeople. This marketing of the legal function is a response to a perceived threat. Many respondents indicated that there is a danger that the Legal Department may come to be viewed as expendable. The very existence of the Legal Department depends on lawyers' ability to change their image in the corporation.

As one lawyer-entrepreneur explained, "We need to make [the business executives] feel as though, by and large, our overall outlook is to try to help them accomplish the things they are trying to do, and, by and large, that's true and it's fine." Another informant cited with pride the fact that the lawyers of his division "have the best reputation in [the company] because we are so close to the businesspeople in getting the deal done." Another lawyer, who told us he convinces managers in his functional department to use his expertise, said, "I just want to be value-added; I want to be helpful. Mostly that's a pretty easy sell." This attorney indicated that he not only has to convince the business executives to use his services but also accomplishes this goal by using the business language of "value added." Other general counsel related that they were trying to change how their departments were perceived in their respective corporations. "I think there was a sense a couple of years ago that the lawyers . . . just weren't players. I'm trying to make it players." Another said,

> [A] significant part of our department was conceived, or seen, by the business people as a barrier to getting the job done, something to be gotten around, or past, or through, or whatever, and . . . we really needed to do some work to reestablish ourselves as counselors or partners.

Lawyers are now eager to be seen as part of the company, rather than as obstacles to getting things done. To do so, it appears that inside counsel are themselves interested in discounting their gatekeeping function in corporate affairs.

NOTES ON NELSON & NIELSEN

1. *Are In-House Counsel Less Independent?* As a general matter, are in-house lawyers likely to exercise more or less independence from clients than outside counsel? What factors, other than practice setting, are likely to influence corporate lawyers' ethical autonomy?

2. *Can Team Players Be Independent?* If, as Nelson & Nielsen suggest, many in-house counsel feel the need to prove themselves to be team players rather than nay-sayers, what are the implications for the in-house lawyer's professional independence? Is it possible to reconcile team participation and professional independence?

3. *In-House Counsel and Corporate Scandal.* Might there be some connection between the attitudes that Nelson & Nielsen describe and some of the corporate scandals noted in Chapter 15 (involving both outside and inside lawyers) and the additional ones noted below?

PROBLEM 19–1

Reread Problem 18–1 in Chapter 18. How would your responses vary, if at all, if you were in-house counsel rather than outside counsel? Would the relevant law be different? Are there any other differences in the situation of in-house counsel that might make it easier, more difficult, or in any other respect unlike the situation confronted by outside counsel?

D. CORPORATE SCANDALS AND THE ROLE OF IN-HOUSE COUNSEL

Here we consider a series of episodes in which in-house counsel were implicated in corporate scandals. In all of these incidents, there was plenty of blame to go around. We do not mean to suggest that the in-house counsel were the primary culprits. But in each of these incidents, in-house lawyers appear to have participated in, or failed to prevent, misbehavior that led to major damage to the company's earnings and/or reputation, as well as harm to the company's employees, stockholders, and others. As you read these stories, consider what in-house counsel might have done differently.

The Hewlett Packard Pretexting Scandal. On September 5, 2006, *Newsweek* revealed that Hewlett-Packard (HP), at the request of HP's chairwoman, Patricia Dunn, had hired a team of security experts to investigate board members and several journalists to identify the source of a leak of confidential information about HP's long-term business strategies. The security experts, in turn, used a spying technique known as pretexting, which involved using investigators impersonating HP board members and journalists in order to obtain their phone records. After the pretexting came to light, HP's general counsel, Ann Baskins, resigned, just hours before she was scheduled to appear as a witness before a U.S. House of Representatives committee that was investigating the spying scandal. The following article analyzes Baskins's role.

SAW NO EVIL

Sue Reisinger
Corporate Counsel (Online), Jan. 1, 2007[5]

Ann Baskins stood on September 28 before a congressional committee investigating the Hewlett-Packard Company spying scandal. Just hours earlier she had made the painful decision to resign as general counsel of the giant computer company. Standing before the committee, she held her right hand in the air and swore to tell the truth. Then, on the first question, Baskins exercised her Fifth Amendment right to remain silent and refused to tell anything.

While Baskins sat quietly, former HP chairwoman Patricia Dunn and CEO Mark Hurd told the committee that Baskins was to blame for the mess. They said that she had given them bad legal advice, and that she knew about and permitted the use of "pretexting"—using false pretenses to obtain personal information about others. Even Baskins's longtime friend and HP's outside counsel, Larry Sonsini of Wilson Sonsini Goodrich & Rosati, told Congress: "I think the record has become quite clear that who was in charge [of the spying] was the HP internal legal department. They took the responsibility on, rightly or wrongly."

So far, that was the public low for Baskins's career. In private, the due bills keep rolling in. By mid-November, Baskins and Palo Alto-based HP were facing investigations by the California attorney general's office, the U.S. attorney in San Francisco, the Federal Bureau of Investigation, the Federal Communications Commission, and the Securities and Exchange Commission. (As yet, Baskins has not been charged with any crimes.)

At least one of five shareholder suits against HP accuses Baskins of insider trading [the illegal practice of trading a company's stock using nonpublic information] and damaging the corporation. There are potential invasion of privacy suits from individuals whose phone records were stolen. And two phone companies have sued the detective agencies used in the pretexting; one of the suits also names as defendants "unidentified companies" and individuals that conspired with the agency to do the pretexting.

By some measure, Baskins has dodged the worst of the fallout. HP ousted Dunn and Kevin Hunsaker, the senior counsel in Baskins's office who oversaw the spying efforts. The California attorney general has indicted the pair, along with three private investigators, on four criminal counts related to the spying. The AG alleges that Dunn and Hunsaker personally provided home and cell phone numbers to the private investigators. All five defendants pled not guilty and await trial. If convicted on all counts, they each face a maximum of 12 years in prison and $55,000 in fines.

Little has been written about Baskins's role in the spying efforts, but an in-depth analysis of more than 1,500 pages of documents, as well as interviews with people close to the investigation, offers insights into how she let the spying probe spin out of control. The records, which include HP e-mails and interviews conducted by lawyers at Palo Alto-based Wilson Sonsini as part of the company's internal investigation, were made public by the House committee.

In the end, the HP scandal comes down to this: The spying probe became a runaway train. And Ann Baskins was the person in the best position to recognize the danger and stop it. But she didn't. In fact, the records show that from June 2005 to April 2006, Baskins raised legal questions about the tactics at least six times. But she never pushed for a definitive answer about whether the methods used were, in fact, lawful. Or, more importantly, whether they were unwise and dangerous to the company. In retrospect she could have, and should have, shut down the throttle on this train long before it crashed.

"Part of your responsibility as general counsel is to ask hard questions about whether conduct is just technically legal, or arguably illegal, or beyond the fringes of fraud," says Deborah Rhode, a professor of legal ethics and professional responsibility at Stanford Law School. "She was in the best position to see it and stop it."

Even Baskins concedes that she should have done more. Her attorney, K. Lee Blalack II, says Baskins would not comment for this story. But Blalack says that Baskins fully recognizes that instead of solely focusing on whether the investigation was legal, Baskins also should have questioned whether it was ethical. "She regrets that she did not do so," says Blalack, a partner in the Washington, D.C., office of O'Melveny & Myers.

According to those close to her, it wasn't like Baskins to fail to ask the right questions. She had deftly managed the legal issues that arose in HP's $8 billion spin-off of Agilent Technologies, Inc., in 1999. And she won praise in 2002 for her handling of the controversial $22 billion merger with Compaq Computer Corporation, including the sensitive civil suit brought by the heirs of HP's founders, who tried to block the deal.

Baskins was both a survivor of corporate politics and the very model of a good company soldier. Even during the congressional hearing, Dunn praised Baskins's commitment to the tech giant, adding, "Ann Baskins bleeds Hewlett-Packard blue ink."

A 1980 graduate of University of California, Los Angeles School of Law, Baskins spent only about a year in private practice. She joined HP in 1982 and slowly worked her way up the ranks. She was named vice president and corporate secretary in 1999 and general counsel in early 2000.

Philadelphia attorney Michael Holston, a longtime friend of Baskins, whose firm Morgan, Lewis & Bockius was brought in by HP execs to investigate the spying probe, calls Baskins "a terrific lawyer who did a great job for HP for nearly 25 years. And she is a woman of the highest ethical standards."

But the praise isn't universal. A former HP in-house lawyer, who requested anonymity because the attorney started a new job, is not surprised that the GC didn't step in to stop the spying. "Baskins was indecisive and disconnected as a manager," says the attorney, who declined to elaborate.

The beginning of the end for Baskins, 51, came in February of 2005, when Dunn and her allies on the board forced out then-CEO and chairwoman Carleton "Carly" Fiorina. The directors chose Dunn to chair the board. On April 1 Hurd became CEO, but someone had leaked news of his appointment to the press a few days earlier. An irate Dunn hired a Boston-based private investigator named Ron DeLia to search for the leaker. (The California attorney general later accused Dunn of providing DeLia with the home, office, and cell phone numbers of various HP directors and managers.) Records show that Dunn initiated those first spying efforts—without Baskins's knowledge—on April 19. Dunn named the spy probe Project Kona because she was vacationing in Hawaii at the time. (Neither Dunn nor her lawyer, James Brosnahan, a senior partner at Morrison & Foerster in San Francisco, returned calls for this story. DeLia also declined to comment through his attorney, John Williams, of Manchester, Williams & Seibert in San Jose.)

Why did Dunn act on her own at first? Records suggest she may have done so because HP's internal corporate politics were roiling. Dunn suspected everyone, including Baskins, as a possible leaker. And Baskins noted in the Wilson Sonsini interviews that her working relationship with Dunn and the board was "strained" by all the distrust at that time.

Dunn brought Baskins into the loop two months later. On June 14, according to e-mails and congressional testimony, DeLia e-mailed a seven-page report to Dunn that discussed the phone record searches and used the word "pretexting." Dunn forwarded a copy to Baskins the same day. This e-mail is the earliest mention of Baskins's involvement in any document that has so far been made public.

Dunn told DeLia that Baskins would join them in a teleconference call the next day to discuss the report. During that June 15 call, DeLia told the two women that telephone records were obtained by ruse from a telecommunications carrier, and he explained the word "pretexting" to them, according to the complaint filed by the attorney general's office. Baskins made sketchy, handwritten notes referring to "pretexting."

According to an affidavit attached to the AG's complaint, "DeLia recalled that Baskins was curious about pretexting and concerned about its legality, and had asked DeLia whether it was lawful. DeLia replied that he was aware of no laws that made pretexting illegal, and was aware of no criminal prosecutions for such activities." Asked in later interviews why she didn't challenge the pretexting when she first learned it involved acts of deceit, Baskins said that Dunn hadn't asked for her opinion. Her relationship with Dunn was such, Baskins added, that "you answered what you were asked" and no more.

E-mails show that pretexting continued through August 2005. That's when Anthony "Tony" Gentilucci, the manager of HP Global Security investigations and a member of the spy team, reported that the probe still could not find the leaker. But his final report offered helpful suggestions for future spying efforts. He advised engaging "HP legal [department in order] to invoke the attorney-client privilege"; assigning an attorney to direct the investigation; and conducting all future briefings "verbally and keeping written work product to a minimum." With that advice, Baskins put the issue behind her—or so she thought.

A new leak occurred in January 2006. A story on CNET Networks, Inc., a technology news service, reported confidential information about a potential HP acquisition. At Hurd's and Dunn's urging, Baskins quickly launched a new spy probe, dubbed Kona II. Baskins assigned Hunsaker, a six-year HP veteran and her senior counsel, to run it. He reported back to Baskins every other day, and to Dunn and Baskins together once a week, according to records. On January 23, Hunsaker e-mailed HP security that he was heading the new leak probe, at Baskins's request, "in order to protect the attorney-client privilege in the event there is litigation or a government inquiry of some sort."

Baskins also asked Hunsaker to further explore the legality of pretexting. This was the second opportunity, after initially learning about the technique from DeLia six months earlier, that Baskins had to demand in-depth research by an expert in criminal law. But that didn't happen. Instead, on January 30 Hunsaker sent the now-infamous e-mail to Gentilucci, asking, "How does Ron [DeLia] get cell and home phone records? Is it all aboveboard?"

Gentilucci replied that ruses are common in investigations. He said pretexting has been used in a number of probes, and "has not been challenged," although phone company employees could be held liable. His e-mail concluded: "I think it's on the edge, but aboveboard."

Hunsaker responded with four words that have haunted him ever since: "I shouldn't have asked." Then Hunsaker, in an e-mail, sought DeLia's assurances about the spying tactics. Again DeLia, as he had done in Kona I, insisted in e-mails that pretexting was lawful.

Michael Pancer, Hunsaker's attorney, says Baskins did nothing illegal here, and neither did his client. Pancer, a solo practitioner in San Diego, says Hunsaker would not comment for this story. But Pancer defends pretexting. "This [board leak] was a serious problem, and Kevin's ethical duty was to take every legal step necessary to help his client," Pancer says.

In interviews with the Wilson Sonsini lawyers, Hunsaker explained how, at Baskins's urging, he researched the issue of pretexting. He said he did about an hour's worth of online reading. If he had looked at the Web sites of the Federal Trade Commission or Federal Communications Commission—and there is no record that he did—Hunsaker would have seen that those agencies have a serious problem with pretexting and consider it illegal. In fact, the FTC at the time was investigating five private eye companies for pretexting. FTC lawyers sued the five companies for "unfair and deceptive practices" in May. In addition, more than ten states, as well as Congress, were considering specific legislation to outlaw pretexting. Several states have since made pretexting a crime.

Hunsaker admitted in the Wilson Sonsini interviews that he knew about a Verizon Communications Inc. privacy suit against an online company for pretexting. Actually, Verizon had filed two such privacy suits in 2005 against pretexters, and that fact also was available online. There is no record that anyone at HP thought to call the GC of Verizon or any other phone company to ask them about pretexting. Ironically, the president of Verizon is Lawrence Babbio, Jr., who sits on HP's board of directors. But no one asked Babbio for his thoughts on pretexting. (Hunsaker would later say they did not pretext Babbio's phone records.)

So, steeped in blissful ignorance, the HP spy team kept on pretexting until February 7, when the method faced its only real challenge. That's when two HP security employees, who were members of Hunsaker's spy team, saw some of the detailed phone records being collected. Former law enforcement officers, they went to their supervisor and questioned the legality and ethics of obtaining personal phone records. The supervisor confronted Hunsaker, who promised to relay their concerns to the "executives sponsoring this investigation" before proceeding or using the data. There is no record available of whether Hunsaker kept his promise.

Whether spurred by her own doubts or others', Baskins in early February ordered Hunsaker to undertake "a full process check" on the investigation, including the legality of its methods. This was yet another chance to ask the tough questions and to demand an outside counsel's opinion. Instead, she again turned to Hunsaker, who again merely asked DeLia to reassure them on the law.

To answer the question this time, DeLia, according to his Wilson Sonsini interview, turned to his outside attorney, John Kiernan, with whom he shared office space. Kiernan told DeLia that pretexting was not a crime. The attorney, a partner at Boston-based Bonner Kiernan Trebach & Crociata, wouldn't comment for this story. But in the Wilson Sonsini interviews, Kiernan said that neither HP nor DeLia had ever hired him to research the issue. He had based his quick comments to DeLia on a study done a year earlier by a law student who was clerking in his office. The clerk, Valerie Kloecker, is now an associate with Kiernan's firm and also wouldn't comment.

But on the basis of Kiernan's snap opinion, DeLia e-mailed Hunsaker, saying that "right now" (February 2006) there were no state or federal laws prohibiting pretexting. DeLia's e-mail went on to say there "is a risk of litigation." And added: "Note: the Federal Trade Commission has jurisdiction."

There is no record available to show whether Hunsaker relayed this "risk of litigation" to Baskins, or whether he bothered to check with the FTC. Apparently satisfied with whatever Hunsaker did tell her, Baskins let the probe continue.

On March 10 Hunsaker sent an 18-page draft report to Dunn, Baskins, and Hurd. It connected board member George "Jay" Keyworth II to the leaks, and said the investigation was still ongoing. It did not mention the word "pretexting," but said on page three that "the investigation team obtained, reviewed, and analyzed HP and third-party phone records to identify calls made to or from reporters or other individuals of interest." A footnote added: "It should be noted that, with respect to non-HP phone records, the investigation team utilized a lawful investigative methodology commonly utilized by entities such as law firms and licensed security firms in the United States to obtain such records."

Shortly before Dunn and Baskins were to discuss the report with Hurd at a March 15 meeting in Los Angeles, Baskins apparently grew uneasy. She asked Hunsaker to talk with outside counsel about pretexting in case Hurd had questions. Again, Baskins had a chance to demand a written opinion from an outside criminal lawyer. But once more, she relied on Hunsaker, who asked Gentilucci to call DeLia's lawyer, Kiernan.

This time Kiernan had a paralegal respond to HP. The paralegal gave Gentilucci an "update in which she said she could not find additional lawsuits or criminal charges to indicate that pretexting was (had become) illegal." Hunsaker reported back to Baskins that he had confirmed the legality of pretexting with outside counsel.

On March 15 Baskins and Dunn told Hurd that the probe concluded that Keyworth, a noted physicist, was the leaker. Before they confronted Keyworth, the executives decided to consult Larry Sonsini, who would later tell Congress that he was asked in mid-April only to look at "the sufficiency of evidence." Sonsini said he wasn't asked for, and didn't offer, any opinion about pretexting at this time.

E-mails between Baskins, Dunn, and Hunsaker indicate that Baskins shared Sonsini's comments with them during an April 15 conference call. The records do not indicate what Sonsini said, but two incidents the following week suggest that Baskins was growing more cautious.

First, Hunsaker was moved out of HP's legal department to become director of ethics. His lawyer, Pancer, calls it a promotion for his hard work. In an e-mail to his spy team, Hunsaker says simply that he's "no longer a member of the HP legal department." His new title was "director of ethics and SBC [standards of business conduct] compliance," and he would report to a senior vice president in marketing.

In the other incident that hints at Baskins's fears, she asked Hunsaker once again to discuss the legality of pretexting, this time in a memo. On April 24 Hunsaker e-mailed a one-page copy of his note to Gentilucci and DeLia. The e-mail says it was prepared "per Ann Baskins' specific request."

The note explains that the phone records were obtained using pretexting. To confirm the legality of pretexting, the memo cites three efforts. First, Hunsaker "conducted some preliminary legal research and determined that [pretexting] is not unlawful." Second, DeLia contacted the agency he subcontracted to do the pretexting, and the company said its methods "were not unlawful." Third, Gentilucci contacted attorney John Kiernan, whose firm "had conducted extensive research on this issue, and that the practice of pretexting . . . is not unlawful."

Hunsaker concludes: "As a result, the investigation team is confident that all phone records information . . . was obtained in a lawful manner." After reading this memo, was Baskins as confident? If not, she could have tried to derail this runaway train a final time before the report went to the board. But she didn't.

At HP's May 18 board meeting, the directors were told that Keyworth was the leaker. When the board voted 6 to 3 to ask Keyworth to resign, director Thomas Perkins angrily quit in protest. Throughout June and July, Perkins, a high-profile Silicon Valley venture capitalist, challenged the legality of the investigation and demanded answers from Baskins and Sonsini. Sonsini replied with his now oft-quoted e-mail: "I am sure Ann Baskins looked into the legality of every step of the inquiry and was satisfied that it was conducted properly."

That wasn't enough for Perkins, who made the entire mess public in late July. He told the attorney general's office, the SEC, and others about the investigation, including the pretexting. He also told the SEC he objected to how HP had portrayed his resignation in an 8–K filing.

Now facing a public outcry, HP in August asked Sonsini's firm to conduct an internal "investigation of the investigation." Partners Steven Schatz and David Berger conducted phone interviews of the participants—including four separate interviews with Baskins, and seven with Hunsaker. (Schatz said that no one at the law firm would comment for this story.) Baskins was allowed to sit in on several of the interviews, and even to participate in Kiernan's interview.

By the time the interviews were finished in late August, Baskins had to know she was in trouble. In her interviews with the lawyers, she was often evasive. For example, when asked about a July 2005 meeting on Kona I, Baskins "reported that her calendar does not show any meeting in mid-July of 2005." Baskins used a lot of "I don't recall" answers, and contradicted herself several times in different interviews, especially about her knowledge of pretexting and about her role in Kona I and Kona II.

The Wilson Sonsini report on August 30 concluded that "all persons involved" acted in good faith, but that "certain errors in judgment were made." While the use of pretexting at the time "was not generally unlawful," the report said the subcontractors may have used Social Security numbers while pretexting, "which more likely than not violates federal law." The report did not fault Baskins or Hurd, who "reasonably relied" on Hunsaker's assurances.

But Baskins still wasn't off the hook. The scandal snowballed through September, and HP hired another outside law firm, Morgan Lewis, to do a second internal investigation. The company also filed a new document with the SEC, outlining the spy probe and admitting that it had spied on at least two HP employees, seven members of its board, nine reporters, and their relatives.

That's when the dominoes started falling. Morgan Lewis came up with undisclosed, and what Hurd called "disturbing," findings about the spying operation. Dunn immediately resigned. Gentilucci and Hunsaker were also forced out. Baskins offered her resignation, but Hurd at first refused it.

Then the law enforcers and regulators opened their investigations. And Congress got into the act by demanding that Baskins and others at HP appear before the House subcommittee. The subcommittee had introduced a bill making pretexting a federal crime in January, and used HP to make its point for passage on national TV.

Baskins flew to the hearing on an HP corporate jet, along with her second attorney, Cristina Arguedas, a partner in Arguedas, Cassman & Headley in Berkeley. At the time, Baskins's lawyers were urging her to take the Fifth Amendment and not testify. But Baskins knew that the general counsel of HP could not refuse to answer Congress's questions and still keep her job.

Early on September 28 Baskins made the agonizing decision to resign and not testify. In a letter to the congressional committee, Baskins's lawyers wrote, "Given the current environment, Ms. Baskins simply has no choice" but to refuse to testify. (Baskins left the company with a $3.6 million severance package.)

Baskins may not be criminally liable for her role in Kona II. But some legal experts say that her ethical decisions were not beyond reproach. One critic is Rhode, the Stanford law professor, who looks at the psychology of what she calls "a moral meltdown." Rhode points out that this wasn't misconduct spurred by greed or self-dealing. In Baskins's case, she was reacting to what she viewed as unethical behavior—a board member's leak—and probably felt that she had a right to do whatever necessary to track down the leaker. "These [Baskins, et al.] were individuals who felt they were morally justified," according to Rhode.

One GC who has overseen investigations for his Fortune 500 media company says that beyond the legal and the ethical issues, Baskins failed to ask the crucial question: "How will all this affect the company if it shows up on page one of The New York Times?"

In Baskins's defense, Blalack argues that she was supervising more than 250 lawyers, and more than 600 employees globally. Under those circumstances, Blalack says, Baskins often had to rely on assurances from her subordinates. "Ms. Baskins asked for and received multiple assurances [from Hunsaker] that these investigative techniques were lawful," he insists.

In the end, Baskins's downfall came because of what she decided not to see. Susan Hackett, senior vice president and general counsel of the Association of Corporate Counsel, argues that it is unfair to expect GCs "to see around corners." But the unfortunate truth is, when it came to the legality of spying, Baskins had blinders on.

NOTES ON HP PRETEXTING SCANDAL

1.   ***Ethical (v. Legal) Considerations.*** Bart Schwartz, a former federal prosecutor hired by HP to analyze HP's practices after the pretexting scandal broke, told a *New York Times* reporter that he was struck by the lack of consideration given to ethical considerations in the board's efforts to investigate press leaks: "Doing it legally should not be the test; that is a given," he said. "You have to ask what is appropriate and what is ethical."[6]

2.   ***Discretion to Advise About Non-Legal Considerations.*** How might greater attention to ethics as well as law have informed how Baskins approached her responsibilities as HP's general counsel? Would she have served her client better if she had exercised more of the discretion that Rule 2.1 gives lawyers to advise not just about law but also about related concerns? Recall that the Comment [2] notes that "purely legal advice can sometimes be inadequate. It is proper for a lawyer to refer to relevant moral and ethical considerations in giving advice."

3.   ***A Junior Lawyer Takes the Fall.*** Notice that Hunsaker was forced out of HP, while Baskins left with a $3.6 million severance package. According to an in-house lawyer who practices in northern California (a friend of the authors of this textbook), the HP pretexting scandal generated a new term to describe situations in which a junior lawyer takes the blame for mistakes for which senior lawyers may also be responsible; it's sometimes called getting "Hunsakered."

* * *

Stock Options Backdating at Apple.[7] In 2001, Apple granted then-chief executive Steve Jobs and other members of the executive team, including Apple's then-General Counsel Nancy Heinen, options to purchase shares of Apple stock. Rather than set the strike price (the fixed price at which the owner of the option can purchase stock) at the closing price of the stock on the date of each grant, the options were backdated. Options backdating is the practice of altering the date a stock option was

---

[6]   See Damon Darlin, *Adviser Urges H.P. to Focus on Ethics Over Legalities*, N.Y.TIMES, Oct. 4, 2006.

[7]   This case study is drawn from extensive journalist coverage and the pleadings, including these sources: Amended Complaint, Securities and Exchange Commission v. Nancy R. Heinen and Fred D. Anderson, (2007) (No. C–07–2214 (JF)), 2007 WL 1908786; Steve Stecklow & Nick Wingfield, *U.S. Scrutinizes Grant to Jobs—Focus in Apple Case Is Cast on the Roles of 3 Ex-Officials*, WALL ST. J., Jan. 12, 2007, A3; Justin Scheck, *Apple Quietly Canned Lawyer Who Backdated*, LEGAL INTELLIGENCER, Jan. 9, 2007; Press Release, Apple, Apple's Special Committee Reports Findings of Stock Option Investigation (Oct. 4, 2006) (http://www.apple.com/pr/library/2006/10/04Apples-Special-Committee-Reports-Findings-of-Stock-Option-Investigation.html); John Markoff & Eric Dash, *Apple Panel on Options Backs Chief*, N.Y. TIMES, Dec. 30, 2006, at 1; Justin Scheck & Nick Wingfield, *Criminal Probe of Apple Options is Ended*, WALL ST. J., July 10, 2008, B3; Pamela A. MacLean, *Backdating Probes Lead to Changes*, NAT'L L.J., June 9, 2008; Order Granting Motion for Final Approval of Class Action Settlement; Granting Motion for Attorneys' Fees and Expenses; And Granting in Part Objector Pezzati's Motion for Attorneys' Fees and Incentive Award, *In re* Apple Inc. Securities Litigation (2011) (No. 5:06–CV–05208–JF), 2011 WL 1877988.

granted to an earlier date, usually a date when the price was lower. In the typical stock options backdating scenario, a company examines the company's historical stock market closing prices, picks a day when the company's stock price had dropped to a low or near-low point, and pretends that the options were awarded on that date. By setting the strike price below the market price, the company incurs a cost equal to the difference between the market price and the strike price, which also dilutes the values of the shares held by the public. To be legal, backdating must be clearly communicated to shareholders and properly reflected in earnings and tax calculations. The practice of backdating stock options without reporting and accounting for them properly had become widespread in the tech industry in the late 1990s.

Prior to 2002 and the enactment of the Sarbanes-Oxley Act, companies did not have to report the granting of stock options to the SEC until the end of the fiscal year. This lax reporting requirement meant that corporate boards could easily falsify dates on documents with little chance of being caught. (Changes in SEC reporting requirements under Sarbanes-Oxley require corporations to report stock option grants two business days after the options are granted, making backdating much more difficult.)[8] In March 2006, the *Wall Street Journal* and Professor Erik Lie of the University of Iowa analyzed stock options grants to top executives at several corporations between 1995 and 2002. They examined various stock options grants to executives and how much the stock price rose in the twenty days following the grant. Professor Lie hypothesized that a pattern of sharp stock appreciation after grant dates is an indication of backdating; by chance alone, grants ought to be followed by a mix of rises and declines in stock performance. They found instead a remarkable number of instances where companies granted stock options to executives immediately before a sharp increase in their stocks. [9]

In the wake of the *Wall Street Journal* report, the SEC and the Department of Justice ("DOJ") began investigating stock option grants before 2002, while companies affected by the options probe, including Apple and Broadcom, secured legal representation. Reports by the *New York Times* and the *Wall Street Journal* indicate that by July 2006, at least sixty companies had been targeted for investigation by the SEC and DOJ for stock options violations. Apple conducted an internal investigation and eventually released a statement acknowledging "serious concerns regarding the actions of two former officers in connection with the accounting, recording and reporting of stock option grants." Apple admitted in its SEC filings for October 2006 "that stock option grants made on 15 dates between 1997 and 2002 appear to have grant dates that

---

[8]   15 U.S.C § 78p(a)(2)(c) (2010).

[9]   Charles Forelle & James Bandler, *The Perfect Payday*, WALL ST. J., Mar. 18, 2006.

precede the approval of those grants." Apple restated its financial performance and reported an $84 million loss related to the backdating. Heinen abruptly left Apple shortly before the company admitted to improper handling of executive stock option dating.

Apple and its executives faced an array of lawsuits. In 2007, the SEC filed a civil lawsuit against Heinen and the former chief financial officer Fred Anderson for securities fraud. The SEC alleged that Heinen and Anderson participated in backdating the options and concealing the backdating. The complaint also alleged that Heinen personally benefitted by receiving options on 400,000 shares of Apple stock through one of the backdated grants. Anderson immediately settled with the SEC for $3.5 million, but Heinen denied all allegations of wrongdoing and fought the claims. (One of her criminal defense lawyers was Cristina Arguedas, who had previously represented Hewlett-Packard General Counsel Ann Baskins in connection with the pretexting scandal.) After a year of investigations and on the eve of testimony being given by Jobs, Heinen settled with the SEC for $2.2 million—the $1.6 million in "ill-gotten gains," $400,000 in interest on those gains, and a $200,000 fine. In the settlement agreement, Heinen agreed to a five-year ban against serving as an officer or director of any public company and a three-year suspension from practicing before the SEC. At roughly the same time Heinen settled with the SEC, the DOJ ended its criminal investigation without bringing charges against Heinen, Anderson, or anyone else involved in the assigning of options. Several months later, Apple executives, including Heinen, settled a class action lawsuit brought by shareholders.

A NOTE ON BACKDATING AT APPLE

1. ***What Explains Heinen's Conduct?*** What do you think might explain Heinen's alleged role in the backdating of stock options at Apple as described in the government's complaint? Was it personal greed? Fear of her boss? A casual attitude about falsifying documents? Too little experience with corporate governance and securities law? A lack of appreciation for how backdating stock options related to the public policy underlying securities law—to provide investors with complete and truthful information about public corporations' finances?

2. ***GCs Take the Fall?*** Many Silicon Valley companies experienced high turnover in the general counsel ranks in the wake of the backdating scandal. A 2008 survey of 38 Silicon Valley companies that had to restate financial results because of backdating found that only three GCs at the 30 companies that had general counsel at the time of the scandal still remained in their positions. Fourteen GC were direct casualties of the scandal; four were charged by the government, and ten either took the blame or resigned or were fired. Some observers suggested that technology companies unfairly

blamed their GCs for the backdating mess and took swift action against them in order to appease the SEC.[10]

* * *

Bribery at Walmart.[11] On April 22, 2012, the *New York Times* broke a story about a "vast" bribery scheme by Walmart in Mexico and a subsequent "hush-up" by Walmart's Bentonville headquarters. While a deeper investigation of the facts will be necessary before firm conclusions can be drawn about what occurred and what the long-term consequences will be, this episode already provides telling examples of alternative courses of action that in-house counsel can take when confronted with alleged corporate wrong doing.

Walmart became an international retail presence when it opened its first store outside Mexico City in 1991. By 2012, Walmart, through its international division Walmart International, operated 5,651 stores and employed 780,000 people in 26 countries. Key to such rapid expansion was the work of attorneys at Walmart headquarters in Bentonville, Arkansas and attorneys at the various international subsidiaries of Walmart, such as Walmart de Mexico, also known as Walmex. These attorneys helped secure permits necessary to fuel the expansion. But these attorneys—especially the ones located in Bentonville—had to ensure that employees in the vast international operations conformed to business regulations, including the Foreign Corrupt Practices Act ("FCPA"), which prohibits bribing foreign government officials.[12] Through Walmart International, Walmart expanded its presence in Mexico during the late 1990s and early 2000s. By 2012, one in five Walmart stores world-wide was located in Mexico. Eduardo Castro-Wright, who became chief executive of Walmex in 2002, played a large role in the growth of Walmex, setting aggressive growth goals and opening new stores quickly so that competitors would not have time to react.

According to the *New York Times,* bribes paid by Sergio Cicero Zapata, a Walmex attorney in charge of obtaining construction permits, also played a large role in Walmex's expansion. During his nearly 10-year tenure at Walmex, Cicero allegedly paid over $24 million in bribes to "gestors" who funneled bribes to government officials. Bribes paid by Cicero were used to change zoning laws and to make environmental

---

[10] Zusha Elinson, *GCs Get Optioned Out Over Backdating*, RECORDER, April 18, 2008.

[11] This account is based primarily on the following sources: David Barstow, *Vast Mexico Bribery Case Hushed Up by Wal-Mart After Top-Level Struggle*, N.Y. TIMES, Apr. 22, 2012; Peter J. Henning, *Weighing the Legal Ramifications of the Wal-Mart Bribery Case*, N.Y. TIMES, Apr. 23, 2012; Sue Reisinger, *Will Wal-Mart Regret Not Disclosing Its Bribery Investigation Sooner?*, CORP. COUNSEL, Apr. 24, 2012; Mark Tuohey et al., *An In-House Counsel Corporate Corruption Playbook*, CORP. COUNSEL, Apr. 26, 2012; Elizabeth Harris, *After Bribery Scandal, High-Level Departures at Walmart*, N.Y. TIMES, June 4, 2014.

[12] Foreign Corrupt Practices Act of 1977, Pub. L. No. 95–213, 91 Stat. 1494 (codified as amended at 15 USC §§ 78dd-1 to -3 (2000)).

objections disappear. In Walmex's effort to outpace its competition, the bribes quickened the pace at which Walmex could build new stores. Cicero explained in an interview with investigators that with the bribes "[w]hat we were buying was time."

Cicero told investigators that his orders to bribe officials came from the highest levels of Walmart de Mexico. Initially, Cicero paid two gestors—both attorneys—to funnel bribes to government officials. The gestors submitted invoices with brief, vaguely worded descriptions of their services. One code, for example, indicated a bribe to speed up a permit. Others described bribes to obtain confidential information or eliminate fines. At the end of each month, Castro-Wright and other executives at Walmex received a detailed report of all of such payments performed, and Walmex employees would then "purify" the payments in the company's records so that they appeared as simple legal fees. An internal audit reviewed by Walmart de Mexico executives in March 2004 raised red flags about the gestor payments. But rather than end the payments, Castro-Wright fired the auditor and instructed Jose Luis Rodriguezmacedo Rivera, Walmex's general counsel, to tell Cicero to diversify the list of gestors he used.

According to Cicero, he continued to bribe officials until he resigned in September 2004. Cicero said he was under orders to do whatever was necessary to obtain permits. But dealing with "greedy" bureaucrats and demanding corporate executives loaded Cicero with "pressure and stress." When the general counsel position for Walmex opened in 2004 and Cicero was passed over, Cicero was angry and bitter.

In September 2005, Cicero informed Maritza Munich, the general counsel of Walmart International, of " 'irregularities' authorized 'by the highest levels' at Walmart de Mexico." Munich was familiar with the corrupt practices of some business leaders and bureaucrats in Latin America. Before her brief tenure at Walmart, she served as general counsel in various departments with Procter & Gamble over a twelve-year period in Latin America. Once at Walmart she pushed the Walmart board to adopt a strict anticorruption policy. After receiving Cicero's email, Munich moved quickly to investigate. Within a few days, she hired a Harvard trained lawyer based in Mexico City named Juan Francisco Torres-Linda to debrief Cicero. Later that fall, Munich compiled memos recounting what Cicero told Torres-Linda and sent them to executives at Walmart in Bentonville. Walmart executives, including the general counsel Thomas A. Mars, initially turned to Willkie Farr & Gallagher to investigate the accusations. Willkie proposed a full investigation to scrutinize any payments to government officials and interviews with every person who might know about payoffs, including implicated members of WalMex's board.

Walmart executives opted for a more cursory inquiry—a "preliminary inquiry" conducted by the company's Corporate Investigations Unit ("CIU"). Munich objected to this approach, noting in an email that the investigation would be "at the direction of the same company officer who is the target of several of the allegations." Equally problematic in her view, CIU was understaffed and incapable of properly handling such an inquiry. Nevertheless, the CIU confirmed all of Cicero's allegations and noted that "[t]here is reasonable suspicion to believe that Mexican and USA laws have been violated."

Rather than pursue a deeper investigation recommended by the CIU, Walmart executives, including Mars, assigned responsibility for the investigation to Rodriguezmacedo, one of the executives under investigation.

Dissatisfied by the approach taken by Walmart executives, Munich communicated her reservations to Walmart executives and tendered her resignation. Her resignation letter stated her view that "Given the serious nature of the allegations, and the need to preserve the integrity of the investigation, it would seem more prudent to develop a follow-up plan of action, independent of Walmex management participation." She added that "The bribery of government officials is a criminal offense in Mexico."

Within a few weeks, Rodriguezmacedo completed his investigation. Despite the fact that Rodriguezmacedo was implicated in the conduct he was investigating, he concluded in a six page report that "[t]here is no evidence or clear indication of bribes paid to Mexican government authorities with the purpose of wrongfully securing any licenses or permits." The CIU responded to Rodriguezmacedo's report by pointing out the numerous inconsistencies in the report and advising executives in writing that it was "lacking." Walmart executives nevertheless accepted the report and closed the investigation in May 2006.

The U.S. Department of Justice is investigating whether Walmart paid bribes in Mexico to obtain new stores there in violation of the FCPA and whether executives covered up an internal inquiry into the payments. The government is also investigating accusations of bribery by Walmart in Brazil, China and India.[13]

* * *

Several days after the story about Walmart bribes in Mexico broke, Ben Heineman, former general counsel of GE, filed the following column:

---

[13] *Wal-Mart's Foreign Bribery Investigation Expands to India*, N.Y.Times, Nov. 15, 2012.

WAL-MART BRIBERY CASE RAISES
FUNDAMENTAL GOVERNANCE ISSUES

Benjamin W. Heineman, Jr.

Harv. L. Forum Corp. Gov. & Fin. Reg., April 28, 2012

Wal-Mart appeared to commit virtually every governance sin in its handling of the Mexican bribery case, if the long, carefully reported *New York Times story* is true.* The current Wal-Mart board of directors must get to the bottom of the bribery scheme in Mexico and the possible suppression by senior Wal-Mart leaders in Bentonville, Arkansas (the company's global headquarters) of a full investigation.

In addition, the board must also review—and fix as necessary—the numerous company internal governing systems, processes and procedures that appear to have been non-existent or to have failed.

<u>Culture of Silence</u>. Most corporate scandals are perpetuated by a culture of silence. Here there appears to have been no integrity hotline or whistleblower system that worked, because the alleged bribery scheme went on for years without anyone reporting it to an independent company ombudsperson (and some employees were clearly aware of it). Moreover, the Mexican business leaders hid the bribery scheme from the global Wal-Mart leadership in the U.S. And, as far as one can tell based on the allegations so far, the Wal-Mart leaders in the U.S., when they learned of the allegations in some detail, hid the matter from the Wal-Mart board of directors. Wal-Mart appears to have operated like a compartmentalized criminal enterprise rather than a lawful global company.

<u>General Counsel and Key Finance Officials as Partners, Not Guardians</u>. The general counsel and chief auditor in Mexico appear to have knuckled under to the demands of an ambitious country CEO with no legal and moral compass by helping to direct and hide the bribery scheme. Similarly, when the investigation was returned to Mexico by top Wal-Mart leaders in the U.S., the Mexican general counsel appears to have killed it with a false report after no further inquiry. Likewise, in the U.S., the Wal-Mart general counsel did not support the Wal-Mart international counsel—the heroine of the piece—who received the whistleblower's initial report and sought to have an independent, thorough investigation. The company's general counsel instead succumbed to the demands of top management in Bentonville who wanted to sweep the problem under the rug. The company's general counsel sent the investigative files back to the Mexican general counsel who had clearly been named as a central figure in the bribery scheme.

I have written many times that the hardest part of the GC and CFO jobs (and of inside legal and finance staffs) is to reconcile the tension

---

*   [Eds. note: We use Walmart's current spelling in this text, but some sources, including Heineman's article, include the hyphen that appeared in the company's logo through 2008.]

between being partner to the business leaders and guardians of the corporation. This appears to be one of the most striking cases where top legal and finance officials were oblivious to their fundamental integrity role and "partnered" with business leaders who were complicit at worse and totally obtuse at best.

NOTES ON WALMART BRIBERY

1. **Subsequent Developments.** On December 19, 2012, the *New York Times* published an in-depth story about particular bribes paid by Walmart de Mexico to secure permits to build stores in Mexico. The account, based on interviews with government officials and 15 hours of interviews with Sergio Cicero Zapata, asserts that the bribes were not just a response to "a corrupt culture that insisted on bribes as the cost of doing business":

> Rather, Wal-Mart de Mexico was an aggressive and creative corrupter, offering large payoffs to get what the law otherwise prohibited. It used bribes to subvert democratic governance—public votes, open debates, transparent procedures. It used bribes to circumvent regulatory safeguards that protect Mexican citizens from unsafe constructions. It used bribes to outflank rivals.[14]

As of late 2012, the Justice Department and SEC were investigating possible violations of the Foreign Corrupt Practices Act.[15] Walmart has also been hit with shareholder lawsuits from several major pension funds and attempts to unseat some of the corporate directors with ties to the bribery issue.[16]

2. **Variations in the Behavior of Walmart Lawyers.** Notice that Heineman concludes that there were important differences in the culpability of the various in-house lawyers at Walmart. He singles out one lawyer—"the heroine"—for praise because she voiced and acted on her concerns. He asserts that the other lawyers involved failed in their duties by succumbing to pressure to ignore, and, in some cases, by helping to hide, the bribery. Assuming that allegations summarized here are true, do you share Heineman's view that most of the Walmart lawyers involved in this episode fundamentally failed to fulfill their duties to the corporation? What explains why one lawyer spoke out and acted on her concerns while others did not? In retrospect, what might a corporate general counsel or senior executive do to create an environment in which lawyers take their legal and ethical obligations more seriously?

* * *

---

[14] David Barstow & Alejandra Xanic, *The Bribery Aisle: How Wal-Mart Used Payoffs to Get Its Way in Mexico*, N.Y.TIMES, Dec. 18, 2012.

[15] Stephanie Clifford & David Barstow, *Wal-Mart Inquiry Reflects Alarm on Corruption*, N.Y. TIMES, Nov. 15, 2012.

[16] Stephanie Clifford, *More Dissent is Expected Over a Wal-Mart Scandal*, N.Y.TIMES, June 6, 2013.

Enron's In-House Lawyers. Recall the Enron scandal, briefly described in Chapter 15. The Court Appointed Examiner for Enron noted numerous situations in which Enron's in-house lawyers failed to analyze and advise Enron management or its board of directors about issues relating to the use of special purpose entities to hide debt and thus to make the company appear to be more profitable than it was. The Examiner noted that it "appeared some of these attorneys considered officers to be their clients when, in fact, the attorneys owed duties to Enron." He further observed that "some of these attorneys saw their role in very narrow terms, as an implementer, not a counselor. That is, rather than conscientiously raising known issues for further analysis by a more senior officer or the Enron Board or refusing to participate in transactions that raised such issues, these lawyers seemed to focus only on how to address a narrow question or simply to implement a decision (or document a transaction)."[17]

Does the Examiner's account of the failings by Enron's in-house lawyers sound familiar? In what ways are the problematic behaviors identified by the Examiner for Enron similar to problematic conduct identified in the HP, Apple and Walmart episodes described above?

NOTES ON THE SCANDALS

1. *What Can We Learn?* What general lessons can be drawn for in-house counsel from these four scandals? To what extent can we attribute disappointing behavior by in-house lawyers in connection with these scandals to a lack of moral courage? To an excessively narrow view of their roles? To what extent can we attribute it to the difficulty of acting on the knowledge that the entity, rather than particular officers and managers, is the client? Consider William Simon's observation about the attitude of some of Enron's outside lawyers: "To suggest that a corporate lawyer's duty to her client requires her to do her best to effectuate a manager's request to find a lawful way to withhold information from the shareholders is to suggest that the manager is the client. Every corporate lawyer knows that the manager is not the client. Yet, most corporate lawyers think and talk much of the time as if the manager were the client. Moreover, few corporate lawyers have a coherent idea of what a corporate client could be other than the manager." [18]

2. *GM Ignition Switch Scandal.* As this book goes to print, GM faces investigations into its handling of faulty ignition switches in some of its vehicles—a defect that caused some Chevrolet Cobalts and other GM models to lose engine power and deactivate air bags. GM has acknowledged that the problem was linked to thirteen fatal crashes and that some mid-level employees knew of the defect for many years before GM issued the recall.[19]

---

[17] *In re Enron Corp.*, Final Report of Neal Batson, Court-Appointed Examiner, at 115.

[18] William Simon, *Legal Ethics After Confidentiality*, 75 FORDHAM L. REV. 1453 (2006).

[19] Bill Vlasic, *Inquiries at General Motors Are Said to Focus on Its Legal Unit*, N.Y. TIMES, May 17, 2014.

One of the issues under investigation is whether GM's lawyers played a role in delaying the recall and hiding information about the defects from regulators and families of crash victims.[20] GM's in-house lawyers reached a number of secret settlements of lawsuits over fatal accidents involving vehicles with defective ignitions before the recall on January 31, 2014.[21] In testimony at Senate hearings in April of 2014, GM's chief executive, Mary Barra, was asked to explain how GM's legal department could have known about the defects but failed to ensure that top management were aware of the problem. She testified that within GM "there were silos" and that information could be known by the legal team but not communicated to other parts of the business.[22] If, as alleged, GM in-house lawyers knew of the ignition switch defect for a significant time period during which GM's top management were unaware of the problem, what would it suggest about how the lawyers viewed their responsibilities?

3.　***What Should the In-House Lawyers Have Done Differently? Did the Relevant Law Provide Adequate Guidance and Leverage?*** How might in-house counsel in each of these episodes have behaved differently? Did the relevant law give them the guidance and leverage they needed to navigate these situations? If not, what changes in the law or rules might have given them the tools they required to prevent the fiascos in which their companies became embroiled, or at least to ensure that the lawyers were not themselves implicated?

E.　THE ROLE OF IN-HOUSE COUNSEL POST-ENRON

New regulatory controls and other reforms imposed in the wake of Enron and related scandals have given lawyers more responsibility and, perhaps, additional leverage to promote legal compliance by their corporate clients. As noted in the introduction to Part V.B, regulations adopted pursuant to Sarbanes-Oxley have imposed an up-the-ladder reporting requirement on lawyers who advise clients in the preparation of documents that foreseeably might become part of submissions to the SEC.[23] One of those regulations requires an attorney who becomes aware of evidence of a material violation of securities law to report it to the chief legal officer, who must in turn investigate, make sure that the company responds appropriately, and report back to the attorney who made the initial report. If the lawyer who made the initial report does not receive a

---

[20] Sue Reisinger, *GM In-House Lawyers Pulled Into Ignition Switch Probe*, CORP. COUNSEL, Apr. 7, 2014.

[21] Bill Vlasic, *Inquiries at General Motors Are Said to Focus on Its Legal Unit*, N.Y. TIMES, May 17, 2014.

[22] Sue Reisinger, *GM In-House Lawyers Pulled Into Ignition Switch Probe*, CORP. COUNSEL, Apr. 7, 2014.

[23] See 17 C.F.R. § 205.2(e) (2009) (mandating up-the-ladder reporting if there is "credible evidence, based upon which it would be unreasonable . . . for a prudent and competent attorney not to conclude that it is reasonably likely that a material violation has occurred".)

satisfactory response, she must take the issue up the ladder again and report the evidence to the company's board of directors.[24] Lawyers who violate the rule are subject to civil sanctions and penalties by the SEC.

Some companies have also given in-house lawyers greater authority within the corporation and beefed up compliance protocols. There has been a trend in recent years toward making the general counsel part of the senior management team. Modest evidence also suggests that at least some corporations are making legal compliance a higher priority. When a new general counsel took over Tyco following a series of ethics scandals that nearly destroyed the company, the legal team created a series of training programs designed to help employees and management appreciate the difference between what is legal and not and the importance of obtaining legal advice in close cases.[25] Walmart has significantly bolstered its compliance controls in the past few years. According to a *New York Times* story on the evidence of bribery in India, China and Brazil, Walmart has so far spent $35 million on a compliance program that began in spring 2011, and has more than 300 outside lawyers and accountants working on it.[26] (It is worth noting in this context that organizational sentencing guidelines adopted in 1991 and discussed in the next excerpt reduce sentences for corporations found guilty of criminal conduct—sometimes by as much as 95 percent—if they can demonstrate that they had in place an effective compliance program.)

It remains to be seen whether such changes—in general counsel's stature within corporations and in companies' implementation of compliance protocols—is just window-dressing or will instead actually reduce the frequency of the kinds of major corporate scandals that have so routinely made headlines during the past few decades. It is also uncertain how those changes in the regulatory climate have affected in-house counsel's influence.

Recent Research on In-House Counsel's Role. Recall that Nelson & Nielsen's research on corporate counsel, based on interviews conducted in the 1990s, concluded that in-house counsel generally deferred to corporate management.[27] While all lawyers in that study claimed to have sufficient authority to stop illegal transactions from proceeding, they also said that it was generally the prerogative of

---

[24] Alternatively, the company can set up a "Qualified Legal Compliance Committee" (QLCC) of independent board members, and the reporting attorney and chief legal officer can discharge their duties by reporting to the QLCC.

[25] David B. Wilkins, *Team of Rivals? Toward a New Model of the Corporate Attorney-Client Relationship*, 78 FORDHAM L. REV. 2067, 2118 (2010).

[26] Stephanie Cilfford & David Barstow, *Wal-Mart Inquiry Reflects Alarm on Corruption*, N.Y. TIMES, Nov. 15, 2012, A1.

[27] Robert L. Nelson & Laura Beth Nielsen, *Cops, Counsel, and Entrepreneurs: Constructing the Role of Inside Counsel in Large Corporations*, 34 LAW & SOC'Y REV. 457, 486–87 (2000).

management, not the lawyers, to determine whether the corporation should assume legal risk.

How might recent legislative initiatives designed to reform corporate governance and increase the transparency of corporate disclosures have influenced the power and authority of in-house lawyers? Might they have changed the in-house lawyer's role?

The following excerpt reports preliminary findings from interviews with ten general counsel from large corporations in 2007. The research suggests a greater willingness by these GCs to "assert jurisdiction over questions of legal risk" and to claim "broad gatekeeping duties" than did the lawyers in Nelson & Nielsen's research from the late 1990s.

GENERAL COUNSEL IN THE AGE OF COMPLIANCE: PRELIMINARY FINDINGS AND NEW RESEARCH QUESTIONS

Tanina Rostain
21 Georgetown Journal of Legal Ethics 465, 473–89 (2008)

During the last two decades legal demands on corporations have both increased and shifted focus. Beginning with the enactment of the Organizational Sentencing Guidelines in 1991, corporations have had incentives to create programs intended to disseminate compliance functions throughout the organization. These functions include the promulgation of codes of behavior, the institution of training programs, the identification of internal compliance personnel and the creation of procedures and controls to insure company-wide compliance with legal mandates. The emphasis on compliance pervades every sphere of corporate regulation, including environmental protection, occupational health, health care regulation, anti-terrorism legislation, and employment discrimination.

This paper uses a small pilot study of general counsel at Fortune 1000 companies. Approximately 60 general counsel at operating companies in a range of Fortune 1000 companies in different industries were invited by letter to participate in the pilot. Ten general counsel agreed to participate in the initial round of interviews, which took approximately one hour each. Most of the data collected focused on how respondents understood their gatekeeping roles.

Preliminary Data: General Counsel as Super Cops. Contrary to [previous research, including] Nelson and Nielsen's findings, the lawyers interviewed in this study articulated a robust account of their jurisdiction over questions of legal risk. Respondents were unanimous in insisting that responsibility for determining the appropriate level of risk to be undertaken by their companies lay with them.

In most cases, their authority was formalized in the reporting relations of their organizations: The large majority of respondents reported directly to the Chief Executive Officer or Chair of the Board. Even in the minority of instances when general counsel reported directly to the Chief Financial Officer, they insisted that they had easy access to the highest officials of the company and often brought disagreements with their direct superiors to them. The GC's occupied positions of power within the managerial hierarchy and were expected to play a significant role in monitoring compliance within the organization. Formal reporting lines, however, did not define the parameters of their authority. The majority of GC's, who reported to the CEO or Chair, used their direct access as a venue to raise issues of concern. Those who did not report directly to the CEO or Chair insisted that informality at the top levels of their companies facilitated communication with the CEO and Board on such matters.

Respondents in this study spoke with one voice about their gate-keeping functions, which they characterized in very strong terms. All were confident of their capacity to stop deals that they believed posed significant legal risks to the company. The GC of a Fortune 100 company used a variety of metaphors to explain his role. He noted that the business team plays "offense" while the legal department plays "defense." He also described his department as being "part of the team" while also "providing adult supervision." So far as he could recall, this GC had never had to go above a manager to prevent conduct he believed was illegal. Issuing a threat (implicitly or explicitly) was sufficient to deter managers from such conduct. (The typical response, according to this GC, was a heated speech from the manager in question about the excesses of regulators or Congress. The issue would then be dropped.)

Another GC could not recall an instance involving potentially illegal conduct when he had not been supported by the CEO. All the general counsel interviewed were emphatic that their opinions were heeded when it came to potentially illegal conduct. Raising the specter of illegality was usually enough to end the conversation.

Respondents claimed that it was easy to persuade managers to "do the right thing" because their companies had a deep culture of compliance. It is difficult to determine, however, whether these were self-serving statements made in the context of the interview, or whether these GC's deployed similar rhetorical devices in conversation with other executives to influence their behavior. Most of the GC's who responded to this study worked for traditional blue chip companies, none of which had a known history of legal problems or significant risk taking. Consistent with their claims about corporate culture, several respondents insisted that reputational considerations were often as important as legal ones. For a number of the respondents, the capacity to exercise influence also appeared to be a matter of personality. On the whole, they were very self-assured and expressed their views forcefully and with conviction, useful character traits when dealing with potentially recalcitrant executives.

Team Players and Cops. [M]ost respondents described their role as simultaneously being members of the business team while also preventing serious wrongdoing. The GC of a computer parts wholesaler observed:

> Our mission here as a legal team is to provide practical solutions to the highest priority problems in the business, so we view ourselves as having to provide solutions. Now, that doesn't mean that we're absolutely "yes men" and that they can do anything. Because we're not a highly regulated industry, there are very few things that we wind up doing that are going to be serious violations of a criminal or legal stature. If that's not the case, then all we're trying to do is help the team negotiate a business deal.

In the same vein, the GC of a fast food company made clear that his employer expected his department to be gatekeepers and team players at the same time. "I hope that we're thought of as part of the team up to a point . . . And 'up to the point' is [managers] understand also to some extent we are gatekeepers." Another GC, who worked for a designer clothing company spoke of the importance of having "good rapport" with other managers while avoiding being "a pushover." "You have to tell people when they are overstepping the bounds and doing something questionable."

Distinguishing Among Legal Risks. The fact that these GC's described themselves as strong gatekeepers does not mean that they treated all legal risks alike. Indeed, their capacity to differentiate among types of legal risks made it possible to function as cops and team players at the same time. An important function was distinguishing more significant legal risks, which fell within their decisional purview, and less important legal risks that they left to managers to decide.

The respondents distinguished between activities that they considered to be clearly illegal and conduct raising other types of legal risks. The GC of the computer parts wholesaler described the difference between the risks that he left to managers to decide and those that were his exclusive responsibility. As an example of the first, he described the occasional request from managers to include provisions to indemnify particular customers in connection with certain sales. From his point of view, indemnification made no sense as an economic or legal matter, but he often deferred to managers on this issue.

> At the end of the day, if the business team comes to me and says "for this particular set of clients, we're willing to take that risk

and here's the mitigating factors" . . . I try to set up a process by which they can prove to the executive team they've really thought through this, this is why we're doing it.

With other legal risks, this GC was clear that his department's role was to say "no." As an example, he described the situation where a customer wanted provisions in a contract that could be construed as fraudulent. A second common example came from the antitrust context: A manager who was quoted a competitor's price by a buyer wanted to contact the competitor to verify it. This lawyer was clear that in these situations, which were apparently not uncommon, he was firm that the conduct violated the law. As he put it, "[w]hen I make those statements that's pretty much [it]. People move on."

Expanded Gatekeeping Jurisdiction. Several general counsel saw themselves as having an expansive gatekeeping role, which involved invoking reputational and other concerns in corporate decision making. A GC who worked for a consumer goods manufacturer explained how she approached legal risk in dealings with areas of uncertainty:

> If the law is less than clear, or if the fact pattern isn't clear, then it is a matter of risk assessment. And one of the things that—and I am a firm believer—if it is a matter of assessing the risk, the lawyer's job is to give the best description or explanation of the risk and how it might impact the company and then ultimately it is a business decision.

She saw lawyers as especially well-suited to appreciate "the full risk picture." As she noted,

> business people might say oh well that is never going to happen. But lawyers know there is a chance it might happen and it could happen to you, and what is the likelihood of something happening versus if it happened, you know what is the consequence. It is sort of the multiplication of the two and so it is not just the fact that the likelihood is low, but if the consequence is enormous you do not want to be there.

This GC did not hesitate to offer her "personal assessment," which tracked her concerns about reputational risks to the company:

> I mean as a professional these are the pros and cons, but my personal opinion is, I wouldn't do this or, yes, okay, but you have to understand what the risk is and one of the elements of that risk assessment for us anyway, because we are primarily a consumer company, is reputation. So even though something is legal, the question is do you want to see it on the front page of the paper? And, how's it going to tarnish our reputation as a consumer company if this is what people read about us?

Applying a similar approach, the GC of a food processing company explained that legal risks were not the first issues he wanted the lawyers working for him to consider. According to this GC, he instructed them to ask themselves three questions, starting with whether the conduct was ethical—His test was whether he wanted it to appear in the *Wall Street Journal*—and then whether it was consistent with the company's core values. If action passed these two tests, then the last question was whether it was legal.

The Line Between "Legal" and "Business" Issues. Several general counsel were asked whether they believed it was appropriate to give their client business advice. One emphasized that thought he and the members of his department were very much a part of the business team, he did not "hold himself out as a business expert." His department's job was to "define the legal parameters in the question and be clear about what is legal advice and what isn't." In a similar vein, the GC of a major bottling company described his job as "I'll show you where the potholes are in the road and help you steer around them, but I am not going to be the one driving down the road. I shouldn't be the one driving down the road."

At a later point in the interview, however, this same GC recognized that in his position the line between business and legal advice often blurred. One of his major responsibilities was providing legal services around the development of new bottling centers. As he explained,

> [questions about] the organizational structure and real estate whether or not we're going to enter into a cooperative arrangement with four or five bottlers to build that plant . . . what's the structure going to look like, what form of organization, does it want to be an LLC, a joint venture, a corporation, who are the members, who do you govern the organization, all these things are very much the threshold is do we do it or not from a business proposition and I'm kind of the lead for whether we do it or not.

The positions of this GC are not internally inconsistent, nor are they inconsistent with the view of the previous GC quoted. The first emphasized the importance of staying within his specialized expertise. As he saw it, his authority to advise the company stemmed from his legal knowledge. The second GC, while recognizing the difference between law and business, was aware that a number of business decisions were imbued with legal considerations. In neither case did the lawyers stray into purely business advice.

In a variety of ways, the lawyers in this sample portrayed their authority inside the corporation as deriving from their legal knowledge and gatekeeping responsibilities. All suggested that their effectiveness as general counsel was a result of their capacity to distinguish among various legal risks. While all used the terminology of "legal risk," they did not treat legal risk as commensurable or subject to cost/benefit analysis. Unlike purely financial risks, legal risks came in different types, which it was their job to categorize. Clearly illegal conduct was off the table. Questionable conduct had to be negotiated. The GC's deployed a variety of techniques, including invoking reputational and ethical considerations to persuade their peers, proposing different, less risky ways to structure transactions, or leaving the issue to management to decide after providing a full discussion of the risks involved.

It is not surprising to discover that lawyers treat risks stemming from the rescission of a contract and non-compliance with state advertising laws on the one hand, and the violation of securities laws and criminal statutes on the other, as involving different types of considerations. In discussion of lawyers' roles inside the corporation, however, this characteristic of legal analysis is often obscured by the focus on the language of risk and risk management, which suggests that such risks occur on a single continuum. In contrast to earlier studies, which concluded that corporate counsel more often than not deferred to management, the lawyers in this sample saw line drawing as an integral part of their expertise. Even if they frequently deferred to management on low-level risks, they were the ultimate arbiters of which risks were negotiable and which were not. Their expertise in assessing different risks served as a basis for their assertion of professional power within their organizations.

Flavors of Compliance. Beginning with the enactment of the Organizational Sentencing Guidelines in 1991, the incentives for corporations to create internal compliance mechanisms in every sphere of corporate activity has grown.

In these pilot interviews, there was insufficient time to address how compliance functions were distributed among corporate lawyers and managers. When the subject did come up, most general counsel explained that they played a significant role in overseeing certain compliance functions, in particular ethics, while leaving others, such as human resources, occupational health and safety and financial compliance, to other specialists.

Wherever compliance was situated and whatever reporting structure was adopted around it, all the general counsel interviewed about the topic emphasized that they had played a significant role in institutionalizing compliance mechanisms and were invested in having systems that functioned properly.

Enter SOX. Most of the GC's interviewed contended that [the Sarbanes-Oxley Act (SOX)] had not provoked major changes in corporate governance at their companies. According to the respondents, their boards had independent directors and assertive audit committees before the statute's enactment. All the GC's questioned believed, however, that the statute had a more subtle positive effect on the involvement of directors.

The GC who earlier complained about the millions of dollars of compliance costs also noted that the statute's provisions addressing corporate governance had "caused a dialogue" and encouraged directors to become more informed about their responsibilities. In the same vein, the GC of a consumer goods manufacturer described how the statute made directors feel a greater sense of responsibility.

For one GC, the benefits of the statute went beyond process and reached the substantive decision making at the director and senior managerial level. This GC, who characterized SOX as "by far the most potentially distracting of the things we do that are regulatory," emphasized that the statute caused directors and senior managers to think twice about taking legally aggressive positions: "[T]he positive aspects . . . are an attention [at the top] to not trying to play the game too hard" or "thinking about pushing the envelopes before you push them."

In addition to influencing the behavior of directors, a number of general counsel reported that SOX had strengthened their capacity to shape board and managerial decision making around compliance issues. For several, the statute has been an opportunity to enhance the expert stature of the legal department. As one GC explained, after the statute it was imperative to hire lawyers with strong intellectual skills who were "well-versed in SOX."

The most far-reaching effect of the statute on the authority of GC's, however, likely derived from its new and increased criminal penalties. These provisions, coupled with an enforcement focus on wrongdoing at the top, had made directors and senior managers much more concerned about avoiding conduct that might be construed as illegal. As the GC of a medical device company emphasized,

> [Directors and senior managers] are afraid of going to jail. It is very effective in that way, in my view. It is almost to the point where you have to bend over backwards not to be shrill. And when you play the compliance card, make sure you mean it because you are going to stop these guys in their tracks . . . Once you say compliance, you are very, very empowered. The thing about Sarbanes-Oxley that I don't like . . . I think it is overkill in a variety of areas, but the power . . . to mandate a culture of compliance is very strong.

Making a similar point, another GC explained that he once or twice resorted to carrying handcuffs into a board meeting to "get attention."

Several GC's insisted that their empowerment as gatekeepers inside their companies predated the statute, but believed SOX served as an important resource for less experienced GC's who needed to assert authority over the corporation's legal compliance functions.

Although most general counsel initially claimed that SOX had not fundamentally changed board behavior at their companies, their responses suggest that the statute has had a subtle and wide spread influence on directors' approach to serving on boards and serves as resource for general counsel to draw on to assert their authority within the corporation.

NOTES ON ROSTAIN

1. *Compare the Findings.* Rostain's findings are strikingly different from those of Nelson and Nielsen, who found that in-house counsel generally were "subservient to managerial prerogatives":

> We find that inside lawyers work hard to avoid conflicts with business executives; they typically leave the final call on acceptable levels of legal risk to the businesspersons involved; and managers can exercise control over which lawyers work on their matters and thus influence the very style of lawyering employed inside the corporation.

> In some sense this is an unsurprising, commonplace observation. Despite claims of professional autonomy, corporate lawyers— whether in law firms or in corporate counsel's offices—have been reported to be closely aligned with client interests throughout the twentieth century, though arguing that inside counsel possessed considerable autonomy within the corporate structure, also tended to document the strong identification of corporate counsel with their employers and the rather severe tensions they experienced when their legal advice contradicted an executive's proposed course of action.

> In another sense our finding is significant because subordination to management continues in the contemporary period, despite profound changes in the structural position of inside counsel, in the presence of law in the corporate environment and the ideology of management itself. Inside counsel have gained power relative to their peers in outside law firms, but this apparently has not resulted in a fundamentally different role within the corporation. Law almost certainly has become a more salient concern for American business as a result of increased exposure to litigation, the rise of regulatory structures in the 1970s, and the increasing reliance on legal expertise in corporate governance, financing, and transactions. It appears that lawyers are indeed involved in many corporate functions, yet they report similar sorts of pressure to

conform to executives' preferences as the lawyers that [researchers] described from the 1960s and late 1970s. One significant reason may be the changed ideology of corporate management and a general corporate climate that devalues legal regulation. The inside counsel we interviewed reported dealing with extremely aggressive business executives who are interested in maximizing short-term results and cutting corporate costs. This managerial style is the hallmark of contemporary conceptions of the corporation. Staff functions such as the law are under pressure to reduce costs and reduce the drag on the velocity of business transactions. Hence our lawyer informants have attempted to craft a new image within the corporation in which lawyers are team players, rather than cops. Inside counsel have not abandoned their roles as monitors of corporate legality and analysts of legal risk, but they have adopted the current idiom of corporate management as they play those roles. Corporate lawyers, like the management they serve, attempt to be lean and mean.[28]

Is it possible to reconcile the different findings of these two studies? If so, how?

2. ***Reasons for Caution?*** Do you think that Rostain's thesis—that SOX has strengthened in-house counsel's influence and their capacity to shape board and managerial decision making around compliance issues—is unduly optimistic? Do you think it might reflect the particular (perhaps biased or unrepresentative) perspectives of the general counsel who agreed to be interviewed? Remember that this article is based on interviews with just ten general counsel. The larger study from which these preliminary findings draw is still underway. Stay tuned.

F.   WHAT DOES IT TAKE TO BE AN EFFECTIVE GENERAL COUNSEL?

In the following excerpt, Ben Heineman, former general counsel of GE, argues that the modern general counsel should function as "a lawyer-statesman"—"an acute lawyer, a wise counselor, and a company leader" who assists the corporation to achieve a fundamental fusion of "high performance with high integrity." In the first part of the article, Heineman discusses the general counsel's primary responsibilities. He then reflects on the challenges that in-house lawyers face in trying to ensure corporate compliance and in providing independent advice to the corporation while also functioning as employees whose jobs depend on maintaining favor with the corporation's officers and directors.

---

[28] Robert L. Nelson & Laura Beth Nielsen, *Cops, Counsel, and Entrepreneurs: Constructing the Role of Inside Counsel in Large Corporations*, 34 LAW & SOC'Y REV. 457, 486–87 (2000).

THE GENERAL COUNSEL AS LAWYER-STATESMAN: A BLUE PAPER*

Ben W. Heineman, Jr.

The General Counsel and the legal team must be creative, affirmative partners to business leaders in using their broad skills to accomplish the corporation's high performance objectives. The General Counsel should be at the table with the CEO on the broad array of performance issues: key operational initiatives, economic risk assessment and mitigation, major transactions, new strategic directions (new products, new markets, new geographies), important template contracts, resolution of major disputes (through mediation or arbitration if possible), and major accounting decisions. The fundamental task is to establish critical facts, define applicable legal principles, identify areas of risk and generate options for accomplishing performance goals while minimizing legal, ethical or reputation risk.

The General Counsel must be a leader in building an integrity infrastructure that embeds formal requirement (law and finance) and the company's ethical rules into business operations. This task requires an understanding of the enormously complex web of law and regulation at national, state and local level in nations all across the globe. Each business process (finance, sales, marketing, engineering) in each business unit in each country must be mapped to understand where requirements intersect—then those points of intersection must be risk-assessed with appropriate risk mitigation systems integrated into the business processes. The broad purposes of the integrity infrastructure are to prevent legal and ethical misses, to detect misses as soon as possible and then to respond quickly and effectively.

The General Counsel must play a lead role in defining and adopting ethical standards—beyond what the formal rules require—which bind the corporation across the globe. Great corporations often impose rules upon themselves: no bribery (even when not prohibited), building new facilities to world, not local law, standards; engaging in ethical sourcing so that third parties avoid child or prison labor and provide safe and healthy working conditions. The General Counsel has a key role in these decisions which go beyond asking "is it legal" to asking "is it right." The chief lawyer helps generate issues (by, for example, systematically reviewing claims on the corporation by various stakeholders); determining which ones require in depth analysis; conducting that analysis under an "enlightened self-interest" standard which understands that "costs" are also "investments," that "benefits" may be expressed in strictly financial

---

* Paper prepared for the Harvard Law School Program on the Legal Profession, available at http://www.law.harvard.edu/programs/plp/pdf/General_Counsel_as_Lawyer-Statesman.pdf.

terms but may also require judgment, and that the proper "accounting period" may be years, not just the next quarter.

The General Counsel must help develop early warning systems which allow the corporation to stay ahead of emerging global trends and expectations relating to formal rules, ethical standards, public policy and important country and geopolitical risk. These early warning systems are systematic: careful compilation of information from a variety of sources (cases, legislative proposals, commentary, NGO agendas); regular meetings to determine which issues require analysis; and then decisions about whether pro-actively to change policies and practices far in advance of when the company might be forced to do so.

The General Counsel must play a lead role in fostering employee awareness, knowledge and commitment to a high performance with high integrity culture. Employees must understand their basic obligations; must do the right thing under those duties; must live the core company values; and must understand enough about the technical rules to seek advice when in "gray areas." It is the task of the General Counsel, working with other key corporate staff, to create education and training materials on business and society issues which are as engaging as the education in business disciplines. This involves tracking, training and testing employees in high risk jobs; creating meaningful case-based learning; being candid about company failures; and integrating integrity training with business training.

The General Counsel must develop systems which give employees at all levels "voice" to express concerns about the corporation's adherence to law, ethics and values. Based on nearly 20 years in one of the world's most complex business enterprises, I believe that integrity is greatly advanced when employees are encouraged (indeed required) to report concerns without fear of retaliation. The General Counsel has a vital role in developing different forums for "voice" to be heard: through bottoms-up compliance reviews that start on the shop floor; through a powerful independent, internal audit staff doing compliance reviews; through candid communications from lawyers in the businesses to the General Counsel; and, most importantly, through a company "ombuds" system. The General Counsel (and the CFO) must treat all concerns promptly with dignity and respect and follow the facts wherever they lead—up, down or sideways. Employee trust in the integrity of the processes is key to a successful ombuds system that detects and deters.

The Partner-Guardian Tension and the Lawyer-Statesman Role. Although the role of General Counsel has been transformed in recent years, one dimension remains the same: the reliance on a good relationship with the CEO. And, at the core of that relationship, is what I term "the partner-guardian" tension. Indeed, in many recent scandals

546 PROFESSIONALISM IN CONTEXT PT. V

(from Enron-like accounting fraud to improper options back-dating to the credit crisis), General Counsel have failed as guardians. They were either excluded from decisions or failed to ask broad, probing questions about dubious actions.

Although the General Counsel must be a strong business partner for the CEO and other business leaders (to help the company but also to grain credibility), he or she must, at the same time, be guardian of the company (whom the General Counsel actually represents). This guardian role can involve slowing decisions down until facts are gathered and analysis completed—and, on occasion, it can involve saying "no" if no legitimate actions are possible. I do not believe that the choice for General Counsel (and inside lawyers generally) is to [become] a "yes person" for business leaders and be legally and ethically compromised or to be conservative, inveterate "naysayer" ultimately excluded from core corporate activity and decisions. Being at the table to assess facts, law, ethics, risk and options—to help find an appropriate way to accomplish business goals—is essential.

Certain conditions inside the company must be met before a General Counsel can resolve the tension and aspire to be a lawyer statesman. Most importantly, the board of directors and the CEO must understand and approve the broad role for General Counsel I have outlined here. The CEO must also support the General Counsel in hiring the outstanding, independent lawyers for key inside positions. This is not to say lawyers make critical decisions for the company: their primary job is to give the business leaders a range of legitimate options with different degrees of risk and explain pros and cons. Only after acute analysis, integrating all relevant perspectives, should they make recommendations. And, unless the action is unlawful, General Counsels, having spoken their piece, should defer to the CEO's discretion.

But the General Counsel must go into the position prepared to resign if asked to condone or do something clearly illegal or highly unethical or if excluded from major decisions. With a good CEO and a good Board, this will not happen, although there can be friction as hard decisions may yield tough conversations. With a bad CEO and a good Board, the General Counsel may be able to negotiate an honorable withdrawal. With a bad CEO and a bad board, the General Counsel obviously may simply have to quit—but with proper diligence before accepting the job this risk should be minimized.

NOTES ON HEINEMAN

1. *What, If Anything, Has Changed?* In what specific ways do the lawyers' roles as described by Rostain and Heineman differ from the roles played by most of the lawyers described in Nelson & Nielsen's research and in the scandals summarized in the previous section?

2. ***What Does It Take to Be an Effective In-House Lawyer?*** What conditions and lawyer traits are necessary in order for general counsel (and other in-house lawyers) to ensure that the company complies with the law and that they successfully guard the company's reputation while also working well with the company's management?

G. SUMMARY

This chapter explored the function of in-house counsel, relationships between in-house and outside lawyers, and the allocation of responsibility between them. It considered the extent to which in-house counsel can exercise independent judgment and ways in which the in-house lawyer's position as a full-time employee of the client can both facilitate and hinder the lawyer's ability to guide the client on legal compliance issues. It also examined the roles of in-house lawyers in several recent corporate scandals, and it invited you to contemplate what the lawyers involved in these episodes might have done to avert these outcomes. We also considered whether and how new corporate regulatory controls and other reforms introduced in the wake of Enron may have influenced the responsibility and authority of in-house lawyers. Finally, we explored the conditions necessary for in-house lawyers to be effective guardians of corporate compliance and integrity.

CHAPTER 20

GOVERNMENT LAWYERS

■ ■ ■

A. INTRODUCTION

Approximately 8 percent of American lawyers work in government (excluding the judiciary): roughly one-third each in federal, state and local government.[1] The work of government lawyers includes litigation, advising, and transactional work in a wide variety of substantive areas. We have studied two types of government lawyer (public defenders and prosecutors) in Chapters 13 and 14. Here we focus on all other lawyers representing government. While we focus mainly on lawyers who are employed full-time as government employees, lawyers in private practice are retained by governments to handle transactions or litigation, just as law firms are retained by other organizational clients. In addition, some governments hire lawyers in private practice to act essentially as the government's in-house counsel and to advise on every aspect of the government's work in the same manner as would a lawyer elected or appointed to serve as a city or county attorney or as in-house counsel for an agency, commission, or department.

At the federal and state level, the government lawyer typically operates in a complex environment in which separation of powers principles coexist with hierarchy within the legislative and executive branches. Elected officials may rightfully believe that they have some sort of mandate to pursue the policy agendas on which they campaigned, but they also are constrained by various sources of law, including laws enacted or enforced by other branches of government pursuing different agendas. Government lawyers sometimes face challenging questions of accountability to the electorate and to the rule of law when advising on whether and how the elected and appointed officials can pursue their policy agendas consistent with existing law. The challenges are sometimes compounded for lawyers for local governments who represent multiple agencies and officials within the municipal entity simultaneously.

---

[1] AMERICAN BAR ASSOCIATION, LAWYER DEMOGRAPHICS (2012), *supra* chapter 2; Harvard Law School Program on the Legal Profession, "Analysis of the Legal Profession and Law Firms (as of 2007)," http://www.law.harvard.edu/programs/plp/pages/statistics.php#wlw.

Topic Overview

Government lawyers confront a broad range of practical and ethical challenges, but here we consider three questions that we've seen in different forms in other practice contexts. First, who is the client of the government lawyer? Second, how should the government lawyer approach her counseling duties? And third, how do conflicts of interest principles apply in this setting?

B. WHO IS THE CLIENT OF THE GOVERNMENT LAWYER?

In Chapters 15–19 on lawyers in large law firms and in-house counsel positions, we noted that the client of the corporate lawyer is the corporation itself rather than any of the constituents. That abstract notion can be difficult to implement in practice, but at least there is some agreement in theory about who the client is. For some government lawyers, there is less agreement even in theory, in part because government typically does not have the kind of hierarchical and strictly defined authority structure that exists in most corporations. Our notion about who authoritatively speaks for the people on every issue is less clear than our notion of who speaks for a corporation. Who, then, is the client of the government lawyer?

Model Rule 1.13—Organization as Client

A lawyer employed or retained by an organization represents the organization acting through its duly authorized constituents.

The duty defined in this Rule applies to governmental organizations. Defining precisely the identity of the client and prescribing the resulting obligations of their lawyers may be more difficult in the government context. The client may be a specific agency, or a branch of government, or the government as a whole. A government lawyer may have authority under applicable law to question the conduct of government officials more extensively than that of a lawyer for a private organization in similar circumstances, and a different balance may be appropriate between maintaining confidentiality and assuring that the wrongful act is prevented or rectified.

Model Rule 1.13, the rule that guides lawyers who represent organizations as clients, does not attempt to identify the government lawyer's client except to note that "the duty defined in this Rule applies to governmental organizations." Although Rule 1.13 applies by its terms to all lawyers who serve organizational clients, it seems to contemplate its application to corporate clients more than governmental ones. The analogy to corporate representation is imperfect for many government lawyers because the lines of authority in government work are typically more complex than they are in corporate representation, the purposes of government more amorphous than the purposes of corporations, and the interests of the "ultimate" client of the government lawyer (citizens) are more diverse those of the ultimate client of the corporate lawyer (shareholders).[2] The Comment [9] to Rule 1.13 acknowledges these difficulties, noting that "defining precisely the identity of the client and prescribing the resulting obligations of such lawyer may be more difficult in the government context and is a matter beyond the scope of these Rules."

There is surprisingly little consensus, or even discussion among commentators, about how the government lawyer should define the client. At the federal level, the most commonly expressed rule of thumb is that a lawyer working with the executive branch represents the United States in the form of that branch.[3] Lawyers who work for city governments, which typically are organized on something closer to a corporate model than separation of powers principles, are often understood to represent the municipal entity as a whole. These approaches accommodate several principles that are in tension with one another. On the one hand, they acknowledge that the lawyer serves an institution whose legitimacy depends on being responsive to democratic, political processes, and that the lawyer therefore should give considerable deference to elected officials and their appointees. On the other hand, they recognize that the personal interests and political ambitions of individual government officials, as well as their short-sighted and narrow concerns, can interfere with their authority to speak for the public. Many have suggested that government attorneys hold an especially strong duty to uphold the law and to adhere to high standards of candor and integrity, reflecting their ultimate accountability to the public.[4]

Obviously, the government lawyer's client is not the individual agency head or elected official in his personal capacity, just as the corporate lawyer's client is not the individual who serves as the CEO. That is, the lawyer does not serve the personal interests of the person who happens to hold a government position. At the other end of the spectrum of possibilities, some have suggested that the government

---

[2] GEOFFREY C. HAZARD, JR., SUSAN P. KONIAK, ROGER C. CRAMTON, GEORGE M. COHEN, W. BRADLEY WENDEL, THE LAW AND ETHICS OF LAWYERING 580 (5th ed. 2010).

[3] *See* HAZARD, KONIAK, CRAMTON, COHEN & WENDEL at 582; Michael S. Paulsen, *Who 'Owns' the Government Attorney's Attorney-Client Privilege?*, 83 MINN. L. REV. 473 (1998).

[4] *See, e.g., In re Lindsey*, 148 F.3d 1100, 1008 (D.C. Cir. 1998)('Unlike a private practitioner, the loyalties of a government lawyer . . . cannot and must not lie solely with his or her client agency"); *Grey Panthers v. Schweiker*, 716 F.2d 23, 33 (D.C. Cir. 1983)(a government lawyer's client "is not only the agency they represent but also the public at large").

lawyer's client is the public or the "public interest."[5] One critic of the view that the client of the government lawyers is the "public interest" has argued that this notion is "incoherent" and anti-democratic:

> It is commonplace that there are as many ideas of the "public interest" as there are people who think about the subject. The idea that government attorneys serve some higher purpose fails to place the attorney within a structure of democratic government. Although the public interest as a reified concept may not be ascertainable, the Constitution establishes procedures for approximating that ideal through election, appointment, confirmation, and legislation. Nothing systemic empowers government lawyers to substitute their individual conceptions of the good for the priorities and objectives established through these governmental processes.[6]

Another observer, while agreeing that the U.S. Attorney General ultimately represents the American people, has questioned what guidance that axiom gives to the government lawyer: "Can one meet with [the American people] on a Tuesday morning in a conference room? Can one get them on a conference call to determine their desired ends and their preferred means to achieve them?"[7]

Client identity questions can become especially vexing for government lawyers working at the state and local levels. As we'll see, these lawyers often are charged with responsibility for representing multiple agencies and officials that occasionally come into conflict with one another. Determining how to proceed in those circumstances can be challenging and politically fraught.

NOTES ON THE CLIENT OF THE GOVERNMENT LAWYER

1. *Why Does It Matter for Government Lawyers to Identify Their Client?* Every lawyer who represents a large organization must consider who her client is. Why might government lawyers face particular difficulty in identifying their client, and why is it particularly important that they do so?

2. *Differences Among Government Clients.* The structure of government and the lawyer's specific role within government may lead to a

---

[5]   *See* Jesselyn Radack, *Tortured Legal Ethics: The Role of the Government Advisor in the War on Terrorism*, 77 U. COLO. L. REV. 1, 1 (2006) (arguing that government lawyers should adopt the "public interest" approach to lawyering, rather than the "agency" approach); Patricia M. Wald, *"For the United States": Government Lawyers in Court*, 61 LAW & CONTEMP. PROBS. 107 110 (1998) (arguing that the government lawyer's client is "not simply the individual whose particular fate is being litigated but also the U.S. citizenry at large, a client whose ultimate objective is that justice be done").

[6]   Geoffrey Miller, *Government Lawyers' Ethics in a System of Checks and Balances*, 54 U. CHI. L. REV. 1293 (1987).

[7]   *See* William R. Dailey, *Who is the Attorney General's Client?*, 87 NOTRE DAME L. REV. 1113, 1121–22 (2012).

variety of answers to the question of who is the government lawyer's client. A lawyer who advises a state environmental protection agency, for example, may have a clear and stable sense that her client is the agency. A lawyer who handles appeals on behalf of all or many agencies may think his client is whichever agency is a litigant except when the position that one agency wishes the lawyer to take conflicts with the policy or position of another agency. But when a lawyer occupies a slightly more generalist position, such as the Office of Legal Counsel of the U.S. Department of Justice, the identity of the client may be difficult to discern, as in the following case study.

C. THE GOVERNMENT LAWYER AS COUNSELOR

As in other practice settings, much of the most consequential work of government lawyers takes the form of counseling rather than litigating. Government lawyers' advice to officials is often confidential and leads public officials to make decisions that never become public. Moreover, lawyers' interpretations of law typically are not tested in court. While this is true of all client counseling by lawyers, the role of the government lawyer as counselor raises issues that counseling private clients does not because when the government acts on the advice of counsel its actions effectively become the law unless or until they are tested in court. Even when government lawyers' interpretations of law reach the courts, judges sometimes decline to rule on them, because of separation of powers concerns, sovereign immunity, or because judges view the legal interpretations as political questions that deserve judicial deference. Thus, much of the legal advice that government lawyers provide has the practical effect of binding law.

Some of the most highly controversial recent incidents involving legal counseling by government lawyers arose in connection with the "war on terror." We focus here on the conduct of lawyers in the Office of Legal Counsel (OLC), the section of the United States Department of Justice charged with advising the President about the legality of proposed policies and action.

1. A CASE STUDY: THE TORTURE MEMOS

Shortly after 9/11, Assistant Attorney General Jay Bybee and his chief deputy John Yoo, on behalf of OLC, wrote a series of memoranda regarding the George W. Bush administration's use of tactics to combat terrorism and to deal with detainees. The most infamous of these memos, excerpted below, was written in 2002 but remained secret for almost two years, until it was anonymously leaked to the *Washington Post* in the summer of 2004, shortly after it was revealed that U.S. personnel guarding a prison in Abu Ghraib tortured, raped, and killed several Iraqi prisoners. The incidents at Abu Ghraib provoked a national and international outcry over American abuse of detainees. The OLC opinion memos argued that the United States was not limited by prohibitions on torture contained in international conventions and that the President was free to order what the administration referred to as "enhanced interrogation" (which critics deemed torture) of detainees. Administration officials relied on this and other related OLC memoranda to authorize the use of a variety of tactics, including waterboarding, sleep deprivation, stress positions, and cramped confinement. The OLC memos played an important role in paving the way for the use of these techniques because they had the effect of protecting officials from criminal liability. Jack Goldsmith, the head of OLC who succeeded Bybee and soon thereafter withdrew and repudiated several of the OLC opinions on the use of enhanced interrogation techniques, noted: "It is practically impossible to prosecute someone who relied in good faith on an OLC opinion."[8]

As you read the following excerpts of the most notorious of the OLC memos, try to imagine how the authors understood their roles and how they might have been influenced by the particular circumstances under which they were asked to provide an opinion.

MEMORANDUM FROM JAY S. BYBEE TO ALBERTO GONZALEZ
(Office of Legal Counsel, U.S. Department of Justice, August 1, 2002)

You have asked for our Office's views regarding the standards of conduct under the Convention Against Torture as implemented by Sections 2340–2340A of title 18 of the United States Code. We conclude that for an act to constitute torture as defined in Section 2340, it must inflict pain that is difficult to endure. Physical pain amounting to torture must be equivalent in intensity to the pain accompanying serious physical injury, such as organ failure, impairment of bodily function, or even death. For purely mental pain or suffering to amount to torture under Section 2340, it must result in significant psychological harm of significant duration, e.g., lasting for months or even years.

"Severe Pain or Suffering". The key statutory phrase in the definition of torture is the statement that acts amount to torture if they cause "severe physical or mental pain or suffering." Section 2340 makes plain that the infliction of pain or suffering per se, whether it is physical or mental, is insufficient to amount to torture. Instead, the text provides that pain or suffering must be "severe." The statute does not, however, define the term "severe." "In the absence of such a definition, we construe a statutory term in accordance with its ordinary or natural meaning." FDIC v. Meyer, 510 U.S. 471, 476 (1994). The dictionary defines "severe" as "[u]nsparing in exaction, punishment, or censure" or "[I]nflicting discomfort or pain hard to endure; sharp; afflictive; distressing; violent;

---

[8]   JACK GOLDSMITH, THE TERROR PRESIDENCY: LAW AND JUDGMENT INSIDE THE BUSH PRESIDENCY 96 (2007).

extreme; as severe pain, anguish, torture." Thus, the adjective "severe" conveys that the pain or suffering must be of such a high level of intensity that the pain is difficult for the subject to endure.

Congress's use of the phrase "severe pain" elsewhere in the United States Code can shed more light on its meaning. See, e.g., West Va. Univ. Hosps., Inc. v. Casey, 499 U.S. 83, 100 (1991) ("[W]e construe [a statutory term] to contain that permissible meaning which fits most logically and comfortably into the body of both previously and subsequently enacted law."). Significantly, the phrase "severe pain" appears in statutes defining an emergency medical condition for the purpose of providing health benefits. These statutes define an emergency condition as one "manifesting itself by acute symptoms of sufficient severity (including severe pain) such that a prudent lay person, who possesses an average knowledge of health and medicine, could reasonably expect the absence of immediate medical attention to result in—placing the health of the individual . . . (i) in serious jeopardy, (ii) serious impairment to bodily functions, or (iii) serious dysfunction of any bodily organ or part." Id. § 1395w-22(d)(3)(B). Although these statutes address a substantially different subject from Section 2340, they are nonetheless helpful for understanding what constitutes severe physical pain. They treat severe pain as an indicator of ailments that are likely to result in permanent and serious physical damage in the absence of immediate medical treatment. Such damage must rise to the level of death, organ failure, or the permanent impairment of a significant body function. These statutes suggest that "severe pain," as used in Section 2340, must rise to a similarly high level—the level that would ordinarily be associated with a sufficiently serious physical condition or injury such as death, organ failure, or serious impairment of body functions—in order to constitute torture.

"Prolonged Mental Harm". As an initial matter, Section 2340(2) requires that the severe mental pain must be evidenced by "prolonged mental harm." To prolong is to "lengthen in time" or to "extend the duration of, to draw out." Webster's Third New International Dictionary 1815 (1988); Webster's New International Dictionary 1980 (2d ed. 1935). Accordingly, "prolong" adds a temporal dimension to the harm to the individual, namely, that the harm must be one that is endured over some period of time. Put another way, the acts giving rise to the harm must cause some lasting, though not necessarily permanent, damage. For example, the mental strain experienced by an individual during a lengthy and intense interrogation—such as one that state or local police might conduct upon a criminal suspect—would not violate Section 2340(2). On the other hand, the development of a mental disorder such as posttraumatic stress disorder, which can last months or even years, or even chronic depression, which also can last for a considerable period of time if untreated, might satisfy the prolonged harm requirement.

A defendant must specifically intend to cause prolonged mental harm for the defendant to have committed torture. It could be argued that a defendant needs to have specific intent only to commit the predicate acts that give rise to prolonged mental harm. Under that view, so long as the defendant specifically intended to, for example, threaten a victim with imminent death, he would have had sufficient mens rea for a conviction. According to this view, it would be further necessary for a conviction to show only that the victim factually suffered prolonged mental harm, rather than that the defendant intended to cause it. We believe that this approach is contrary to the text of the statute. The statute requires that the defendant specifically intend to inflict severe mental pain or suffering.

The President's Commander-in-Chief Power. Even if an interrogation method arguably were to violate Section 2340A, the statute would be unconstitutional if it impermissibly encroached on the President's constitutional power to conduct a military campaign. As Commander-in-Chief, the President has the constitutional authority to order interrogations of enemy combatants to gain intelligence information concerning the military plans of the enemy. The demands of the Commander-in-Chief power are especially pronounced in the middle of a war in which the nation has already suffered a direct attack. In such a case, the information gained from interrogations may prevent future attacks by foreign enemies. Any effort to apply Section 2340A in a manner that interferes with the President's direction of such core war matters as the detention and interrogation of enemy combatants thus would be unconstitutional.

Defenses. In the foregoing parts of this memorandum, we have demonstrated that the ban on torture in Section 2340A is limited to only the most extreme forms of physical and mental harm. We have also demonstrated that Section 2340A, as applied to interrogations of enemy combatants ordered by the President pursuant to his Commander-in-Chief power would be unconstitutional. Even if an interrogation method, however, might arguably cross the line drawn in Section 2340, and application of the statute was not held to be an unconstitutional infringement of the President's Commander-in-Chief authority, we believe that under the current circumstances certain justification defenses might be available that would potentially eliminate criminal liability. Standard criminal law defenses of necessity and self-defense could justify interrogation methods needed to elicit information to prevent a direct and imminent threat to the United States and its citizens.

Necessity. We believe that a defense of necessity could be raised, under the current circumstances, to an allegation of a Section 2340A violation.

The necessity defense may prove especially relevant in the current circumstances. On September 11, 2001, al Qaeda launched a surprise covert attack on civilian targets in the United States that led to the deaths of thousands and losses in the billions of dollars. According to public and governmental reports, al Qaeda has other sleeper cells within the United States that may be planning similar attacks. Indeed, al Qaeda plans apparently include efforts to develop and deploy chemical, biological and nuclear weapons of mass destruction. Under these circumstances, a detainee may possess information that could enable the United States to prevent attacks that potentially could equal or surpass the September 11 attacks in their magnitude. Clearly, any harm that might occur during an interrogation would pale to insignificance compared to the harm avoided by preventing such an attack, which could take hundreds or thousands of lives.

Under this calculus, two factors will help indicate when the necessity defense could appropriately be invoked. First, the more certain that government officials are that a particular individual has information needed to prevent an attack, the more necessary interrogation will be. Second, the more likely it appears to be that a terrorist attack is likely to occur, and the greater the amount of damage expected from such an attack, the more that an interrogation to get information would become necessary. Of course, the strength of the necessity defense depends on the circumstances that prevail, and the knowledge of the government actors involved, when the interrogation is conducted. While every interrogation that might violate Section 2340A does not trigger a necessity defense, we can say that certain circumstances could support such a defense.

* * *

This opinion has been widely condemned on a variety of grounds.

Some critics argued that the lawyers had no business engaging in lawyerly analysis of whether the legal authorities permitted torture—that they should have immediately condemned the proposed techniques on moral grounds.

Other critics argued that the memo's failing was that it was incompetent and disingenuous—it misstated the law, failed to grapple with relevant precedent, and buried contrary authority in the appendix. These critics generally emphasized the distinction between advocacy and counseling and the lawyer's duty to give independent, candid advice in the latter role. (See Model Rule 2.1) Some of these critics also emphasized the special context in which OLC lawyers operate—that "advice" delivered by OLC is not *just* advice but also has the effect of law itself because OLC opinions provide a "golden shield" against criminal liability for those who rely on them. Thus, the effect of the opinion was to enable government actors to engage in criminal behavior without being accountable for their actions. One such critic, journalist Anthony Lewis, observed that "[t]he memo reads like the advice of a mob lawyer to a mafia don on how to skirt the law and stay out of prison. Avoiding prosecution is literally a theme of the memorandum."[9]

John Yoo has made very clear that he stands by the memos. He did not (and still does not) think it was his job "to provide moral answers"; it was, instead, "to interpret the law so that people who make policy know the rules of the game."[10] Jay Bybee has also defended his part in signing the memos, although he has expressed some misgivings about the quality of the analysis and explanations.[11]

NOTES ON THE TORTURE MEMOS

1. ***Should Government Lawyers Consider the Morality of Government Actions?*** Should the OLC lawyers who drafted this opinion have taken the morality of torture into account in the opinion? If so, how?

2. ***Should Government Lawyers Consider the Public Interest?*** Did the OLC lawyers have a special obligation to consider the public interest while advising the governmental client about the legality of the proposed interrogation techniques? If so, how would they go about discerning what is in the public interest in this case? How should the lawyer resolve the tension between national security and human rights?

3. ***What Is the Purpose of This Memo?*** Notice that much of the memo focuses on what is required to prove that "a defendant" engaged in criminal conduct, the necessary proof of mens rea, and available defenses. What is the significance of the choice to refer to the government official conducting interrogation as a "defendant"? Does that raise questions about whether the primary purpose of the memo was to advise the government about whether certain interrogation techniques were legal or instead to assess whether individuals engaged in those techniques could be convicted of a crime?

4. ***Who Is the Client?*** Whose interests are served by the OLC memorandum of August 1, 2002? President George W. Bush? The Office of the President of the United States? The Department of Defense? The United

---

9   Anthony Lewis, *Making Torture Legal*, N.Y. REV. BOOKS, July 15, 2004.

10   "Frontline Interview With John Yoo," Oct. 18, 2005, available at http://www.pbs.org/wgbh/pages/frontline/torture/interviews/yoo.html.

11   *See* Neil A. Lewis, *Official Defends Signing Interrogation Memo*, N.Y. TIMES, Apr. 29, 2009 (noting that he still believes that "the conclusions were legally correct" but that he would clarify and sharpen the analysis if he had it to do again).

States? Those conducting the interrogation? Should the lawyer's expectation about who will rely on an OLC opinion affect who he regards as the client?

5. **What Is Good Advice?** Does the memo adequately consider arguments on the other side? Does it read like an advice memo, analyzing the issues in a thorough and fair-minded way, or more like a brief, arguing one side of the issue?

6. **Should Context Matter?** By many accounts, the atmosphere in Washington at the time OLC was asked to provide this opinion was extraordinarily tense. Many thought it likely that terrorists were planning another major attack. Should those circumstances have influenced the contents of OLC's opinion? How, or to what extent, should lawyers avoid such influence? Do their ethical duties require them to avoid it?

* * *

The next two excerpts reflect the debate about the legal and ethical merits of these memos. The first, a column by two University of Chicago law professors, supports Yoo's position; it challenges the notion that OLC lawyers should have tackled the moral as well as legal issues relating to the use of torture, and it rejects the claim that the opinion is incompetent. The second excerpt, by Bradley Wendel, agrees on the former point but disagrees with the latter.

A "Torture" Memo and its Tortuous Critics
Eric Posner and Adrian Vermeule
Wall Street Journal, July 6, 2004, A22

Recent weeks have seen a public furor over a Justice Department memorandum that attempted to define the legal term "torture," as used in federal statutes and treaties, and that pointed to constitutional questions that would arise if statutory prohibitions on torture conflict with the president's powers as commander in chief. An article in the *New York Times* quoted legal academics who criticized the memorandum's authors for professional incompetence, and for violating longstanding norms of professional practice and integrity in the Justice Department's Office of Legal Counsel (OLC). Neither charge is justified.

The academic critics have puffed up an intramural methodological disagreement among constitutional lawyers into a test of professional competence. Although we disagree with some of the memo's conclusions, its arguments fall squarely within the OLC's longstanding jurisprudence, stretching across many administrations of different parties, which emphasizes an expansive reading of presidential power.

[T]he memorandum's arguments are standard lawyerly fare, routine stuff. The definition of torture is narrow simply because, the memorandum claims, the relevant statutory texts and their drafting histories themselves build in a series of narrowing limitations, including a requirement of "specific intent." The academic critics disagree, but there is no foul play here.

As for the constitutional arguments, [e]veryone, including even the most strident of the academic critics, agrees that Congress may not, by statute, abrogate the president's commander-in-chief power, any more than it could prohibit the president from issuing pardons. The only dispute is whether the choice of interrogation methods should be deemed within the president's power, as the memo concludes. That conclusion may be right or wrong—and we, too, would have preferred more analysis of this point—but it falls well within the bounds of professionally respectable argument.

The Justice Department memorandum came out of the OLC, whose jurisprudence has traditionally been highly pro-executive. Not everyone likes OLC's traditional jurisprudence, or its awkward role as both defender and adviser of the executive branch; but former officials who claim that the OLC's function is solely to supply "disinterested" advice, or that it serves as a "conscience" for the government, are providing a sentimental, distorted and self-serving picture of a complex reality.

Th[e] conventional view [of presidential power] has been challenged in recent years by a dynamic generation of younger scholars who argue for an expansive conception of presidential power over foreign affairs, relative to Congress. Among this rising generation are legal scholars who have recently held office in the Justice Department, including John Yoo at Berkeley. The memorandum thus focuses not on restrictive Supreme Court precedents, but on the constitutional text, the structure of foreign affairs powers and the history of presidential power in wartime. [T]he academic critics' complaints [about the memo] have intellectually partisan overtones.

The critics also argue that the Justice Department lawyers behaved immorally by justifying torture. Although it is true that they did not, in their memorandum, tell their political superiors that torture was immoral or foolish or politically unwise, they were not asked for moral or political advice; they were asked about the legal limits on interrogation. They provided reasonable legal advice and no more, trusting that their political superiors would make the right call. Legal ethics classes will debate for years to come whether Justice's lawyers had a moral duty to provide moral advice (which would surely have been ignored) or to resign in protest.

For our part, we find it hard to understand why people think that the legal technicians in the Justice Department are likely to have more insight into the morality of torture than their political superiors or even the man on the street. But whatever one's views on the use of torture on the battlefield, the memorandum is not "incompetent" or "abominable" or any more "one-sided" than anything else that the Justice Department has produced for its political masters.

LEGAL ETHICS AND THE SEPARATION OF LAW AND MORALS
W. Bradley Wendel
91 Cornell Law Review 67 (2005)

Spectacular scandals involving lawyers are certainly nothing new. Wrongdoing by lawyers brought about or exacerbated the Watergate crisis, the savings and loan collapse, the corporate accounting fiasco that brought the 1990s tech stock boom to a crashing halt, and innumerable less prominent harms. But for sheer audacity and shock value, it is hard to top the attempt by elite United States government lawyers to evade domestic and international legal prohibitions on torture. The Bush administration was faced with an urgent question regarding the limits to impose on the interrogation techniques used by military, FBI, CIA, and other government agents and civilian contractors. Officials in the Department of Defense (DOD) and advisers to the President naturally turned to lawyers to interpret and apply the domestic and international legal norms governing the treatment of prisoners.

[The August 1, 2002 OLC memo] is not legal analysis of which anyone could be proud. The overwhelming response by experts in criminal, international, constitutional, and military law was that the legal analysis in the government memos was so faulty that the lawyers' advice was incompetent. Indeed, after the news media disclosed the memos, the Bush administration immediately distanced itself from the analysis, disavowing the memos as "abstract," "over-broad," and even irrelevant, in some instances, to the policy decisions actually made by high government officials.

What accounts for the poor quality of legal reasoning displayed by the memos? It is difficult to credit the explanation that the authors themselves were incompetent, since they worked for agencies—such as the OLC—which traditionally employ some of the very best legal talent in the country. Rather, the explanation is that the process of providing legal advice was so badly flawed, and the lawyers working on the memos were so fixated on working around legal restrictions on the administration's actions, that the legal analysis became hopelessly distorted.

The story of the legal analysis of torture begins with the invasion of Afghanistan following the September 11th terrorist attacks, which resulted in the capture of numerous prisoners suspected of affiliation with the Taliban or al-Qaeda. [T]he capture of high-ranking al-Qaeda members such as Abu Zubaida, Mohamed al-Kahtani, and Khalid Sheikh Mohammed raised the possibility that American officials may have custody of individuals with extremely valuable "actionable intelligence," in the lingo of military intelligence officials.

Intelligence personnel naturally made it a high priority to get these detainees to talk. Because many suspected militants had proven to be skilled at resisting traditional, noncoercive interrogation techniques such as promises of leniency in exchange for cooperation, American officials sought advice to see whether it would be legally permissible to use certain coercive techniques on "high value" captives. Specifically, CIA officials wanted to know whether their field agents would be subject to criminal prosecution for using physically painful interrogation methods such as "waterboarding," in which a detainee is strapped to a board and submerged until he experiences a sensation of drowning. Alternatively, the Agency sought guidance on the legality of techniques that do not require direct physical contact, such as depriving prisoners of sleep, forcing them to stand for extended periods of time or to assume stressful positions, bombarding them with lights or sound (including, bizarrely, repeating the Meow Mix cat food jingle for hours on end), and leaving them shackled for hours.

It appears that the CIA was perfectly willing to take off the gloves, so to speak, but was concerned with protecting its agents from future prosecution. The administration had already signaled its willingness to get as tough as necessary in order to prevent terrorist attacks. White House Counsel Alberto Gonzales repeatedly instructed lawyers to try to be as "forward-leaning" as possible when considering how much latitude to give interrogators dealing with suspected terrorists. Officials at various detention centers in the far-flung Gulag archipelago created by the administration had also indicated their cavalier attitude toward restrictions on their treatment of prisoners. Although it is not the case that security officials were willing to do anything at all during interrogations—no one has suggested threatening the families of suspected terrorists, for instance—it is nevertheless apparent that some American officials in the field had a strong interest in pushing the boundaries of acceptable interrogation techniques.

Administration officials sought legal advice on the applicability of any other domestic and international legal norms that would restrict the questioning of detainees captured in Afghanistan. Most troublesome were the 1984 Convention Against Torture and the federal legislation implementing it. The Convention and the federal statute are both stated in terms of "torture," suggesting that they do not prohibit something coercive but less than torture, like inhuman or degrading conduct. Lawyers in the OLC therefore sought to construe the operative term, torture, as narrowly as possible. Torture is defined in the statute as an "act specifically intended to inflict severe physical or mental pain or suffering," and severe pain and suffering is further defined as the prolonged harm caused by one of several enumerated acts. By focusing on the specific-intent requirement and the element of severe pain or suffering, the lawyers created an implausibly restrictive definition of torture: "The victim must experience intense pain or suffering of the kind that is equivalent to the pain that would be associated with serious physical injury so severe that death, organ failure, or permanent damage resulting in a loss of significant body function will likely result." Despite the plain meaning of the statutory language to the contrary, burning detainees with cigarettes, administering electric shocks to their genitals, hanging them by the wrists, submerging them in water to simulate drowning, beating them, and sexually humiliating them would not be deemed "torture" under this definition.

The lawyers drew support for this narrow definition from an unlikely source, namely several federal statutes defining an "emergency condition" for the purpose of obtaining health care benefits. Not only do these statutes have nothing to do with torture, but the syntax of the statutory text shows that the OLC lawyers got the interpretation backwards. For example, one statute defines an emergency condition as one manifesting itself by acute symptoms of sufficient severity (including severe pain) such that a prudent layperson could reasonably expect the absence of immediate medical attention to result in serious impairment to bodily functions, or serious dysfunction of any bodily organ or part. The statute is plainly not setting out a definition of severe pain in terms of organ failure or dysfunction, but using severe pain as one symptom among many—including organ failure or dysfunction. The lawyers also downplayed cases arising under statutes in more closely analogous contexts, such as the Torture Victim Protection Act (TVPA). The TVPA also defines torture in terms of severe pain and suffering and has acquired a sizeable body of case law interpreting the severity standard. The memo did cite the TVPA, but labors to distinguish cases tending to show that severe pain can result from acts that do not necessarily threaten permanent organ failure or dysfunction. Other cases demonstrate that the courts are willing to treat individual acts as torture; the OLC lawyers, however, buried these cases in an appendix to the memo.

If anything, the OLC lawyers did an even worse job of analyzing the available defenses to a criminal prosecution for violating the federal statute implementing the Torture Convention. The memo's conclusion, that the standard criminal law defense of necessity could justify what would otherwise be prohibited torture, fails both by virtue of the specific principles of interpretation applicable in the area of international humanitarian law and by ordinary criminal law standards. For one thing, the Torture Convention itself contains a clear nonderogation provision, which provides that "no exceptional circumstances whatsoever, whether a state of war or any other public emergency, may be invoked as a justification of torture."

As for domestic criminal law on necessity, there is no acknowledgment anywhere in the memo of the extremely rare circumstances under which necessity can successfully be invoked as a defense. Dudley and Stevens were sentenced to death for killing and eating the cabin boy,* and a criminal law treatise cites numerous cases similarly rejecting the necessity defense. One could imagine, though, circumstances in which a court might apply the necessity defense to justify conduct that would otherwise be criminal. Suppose an Air Force commander was communicating with the pilot of an armed F-16 fighter, which had intercepted a civilian airliner that had gone seriously off course and failed to respond to repeated attempts to contact it by radio. If the commander knew with certainty that the plane was American Airlines Flight 11, with Mohammed Atta at the controls, bound for the North Tower of the World Trade Center, it would be difficult to envision a court not permitting the officer to assert the defense of necessity in response to prosecution for ordering the destruction of the airplane.

The memo's analysis is so vague and open-ended, however, that it is difficult to find the logical stopping point. The authors seem to have in mind a case like the Air Force commander, but they do not limit their analysis to that case. The fault in the reasoning lies in the careless extension of the ticking-bomb hypothetical to the far more mundane scenarios actually confronting investigators, in which there are no background facts to suggest a substantial likelihood that a given detainee is likely to have critical, time-sensitive information.

There is nothing necessarily wrong with advancing creative arguments as long as they are clearly identified as such, with weaknesses and counterarguments candidly noted. But an interpretation that one could not advance with some measure of pride and satisfaction in front of an impartial, respected lawyer or judge is an erroneous interpretation. A lawyer violates her obligation of fidelity toward the law by basing advice or structuring a transaction on the basis of such a reading of the law. In addition, a lawyer who does not flag creative and aggressive arguments as such violates her fiduciary duty to her client by providing purportedly neutral advice without the caveat that the lawyer's interpretation may not accurately represent the applicable law.

My argument is not that a lawyer must always offer the most conservative legal advice or, metaphorically, handle the law with kid gloves. There are many mechanisms within the law for pushing the

---

* [Eds: *Regina v. Dudley and Stephens* is an old English case (14 Q.B.D. 273 (Queen's Bench Division 1884)) in which Dudley and Stephens killed and ate a fellow young seaman (Parker) to save themselves from starvation while all three were marooned in a lifeboat after a shipwreck. They were found guilty of murder.]

boundaries or seeking change. In the context of litigation, lawyers are permitted to take aggressive stances toward the law, subject to the requirements that the position not be frivolous, that any contrary authority be disclosed, and that the lawyer make no misstatements of law or fact. Some measure of aggressiveness is permissible in litigation because of the checking mechanisms built into the adversary system, such as an impartial referee, rules of evidence and procedure, and, of course, a well-prepared adversary. Similarly, certain kinds of administrative proceedings are accompanied by procedural checks to insure against the corrosive effect of excessive lawyer creativity. In transactional representation, however, these checks and balances are absent, and the lawyer in effect assumes the role of judge and legislator with respect to her client's legal entitlements. If a government lawyer says, for example, that the President has the authority as Commander-in-Chief to suspend the obligations of the United States under various international treaties, then for the purposes of that act, the lawyer's advice is the law. If the lawyer's advice is erroneous, the consequences for the government could be disastrous. Secrecy, combined with an aggressively "forward-leaning" stance toward the law, essentially creates an unaccountable legislature within the executive branch. Rather than assisting the client to comply with the law, the government lawyers in this case simply abandoned the ideal of compliance altogether in favor of their own, custom-built legal system.

At bottom, the vice of the torture memos is the ethical solipsism of lawyers who sincerely believed they were right, despite the weight of legal authority against their position. Academic defenders of the administration cite the works of "dynamic young constitutional scholars" whose views are better than those that have carried the day in the Supreme Court, Congress, and the forum of international treaty negotiation. No matter how brilliant these scholars are, their views are not the law. They have not been adopted by society, pursuant to fair procedures, as a resolution of the moral issue. Lawyers functioning in a representative capacity have no greater power to act on the basis of an all-things-considered moral judgment than do their clients. If clients are bound by the law, then lawyers are bound to advise them on the basis of the law, not on the basis of the lawyer's own judgment about what the best "forward-leaning" social policy would look like.

NOTES ON THE DEBATE OVER THE TORTURE MEMOS

1. *"Standard Lawyerly Stuff" v. "Ethical Solipsism."* What is the nature of the disagreement between Professors Posner and Vermeule, on the one hand, and Wendel, on the other? On what points do these commentators agree?

2. *"Merely Plausible" v. "Honest Appraisal."* In the fall of 2004, nineteen former OLC lawyers published *Principles to Guide the Office of Legal Counsel*, a document they described as their understanding of "the best practices of OLC" drawn from the longstanding practices of the Attorney General and the Office of Legal Counsel across time and administrations. The first of these principles was that:

> When providing legal advice to guide contemplated executive branch action, OLC should provide an accurate and honest appraisal of applicable law, even if that advice will constrain the administration's pursuit of desired policies. The advocacy model of lawyering, in which lawyers craft merely plausible legal arguments to support their clients' desired actions, inadequately promotes the President's constitutional obligation to ensure the legality of executive action.[12]

Would this principle essentially mean that executive branch lawyers should be held to the standard of Model Rule 2.1? Would that be good policy?

3. *Are Structural Changes Necessary to Ensure Independence?* Can government lawyers realistically be expected to offer independent advice while under pressure from politically powerful superiors and embroiled in intense situations such as those that confronted the lawyers who drafted the torture memos? Norman Spaulding has argued that structural changes are needed to better ensure that OLC lawyers give independent advice. He proposes that formal opinions issued by the Office of Legal Counsel should be made public, subject to very narrow exceptions.[13] Would you favor that requirement?

4. *Drone Strike Memos.* OLC wrote nine memos in or since 2010 asserting that the United States government could target and kill American citizens and other nationals using unmanned aerial drones. The United States has used drone strikes to kill large numbers of suspected militants, some of whom were U.S. citizens, and a number of noncombatants have been killed as collateral damage. Although the memos have never been released to the public because the Obama Administration claims they contain classified information, the Justice Department did prepare a white paper summarizing the legal arguments that it believed justified targeted killings, and the white paper was leaked to the public. The test summarized in the white paper for the targeted killing of an American citizen has been described as "marvelously abstract" and as being "like Swiss cheese" in its vagueness.[14] Scholars have disagreed about the legality of targeted killings by drone strikes, although debate about the legality is hampered by a lack of clarity as to how the program operates and what standards are used to determine the

---

[12] *Guidelines for the President's Legal Advisors*, 81 IND. L. J. 1345 (2005).

[13] Norman W. Spaulding, *Professional Independence in the Office of the Attorney General*, 60 STAN. L. REV. 1931 (2008).

[14] Eugene R. Fidell, *Drones and Democracy: A Legal Question but Also One of Policy*, DER SPIEGEL ONLINE, Feb. 8, 2013.

permissibility of killing.[15] The secrecy surrounding the targeted killing program and the legal justifications for it have drawn criticism from members of Congress who were denied access to the memos, from former Obama Administration officials, and from former Bush Administration officials, including John Yoo.[16] If the legal standard is either unknown or is very vague and if its application is entirely secret, have government lawyers done enough to ensure the legality of the government's policy? What is the appropriate mechanism to balance needs for secrecy while ensuring accountability of the government lawyers who authorize such uses of force and the officials who carry them out?

5. ***Were the Torture Memos Professional Misconduct?*** The Department of Justice's Office of Professional Responsibility (OPR) investigated the conduct of John Yoo and Jay Bybee over a period of several years. It concluded that John Yoo had committed "intentional professional misconduct when he violated his duty to exercise independent legal judgment and render thorough, objective and candid legal advice," and that Jay Bybee had committed "professional misconduct when he acted in reckless disregard of his duty to exercise independent legal judgment and render thorough, objective, and candid legal advice."[17] But Associate Deputy Attorney General David Margolis rejected OPR's findings, concluding that while Yoo and Bybee had used "flawed" legal reasoning and "poor judgment," they were not guilty of professional misconduct. Under Department of Justice rules, poor judgment does not constitute professional misconduct and would not trigger a referral to state bar associations for disciplinary action. Margolis also rejected the harsher sanctions recommended by OPR.[18]

D. CONFLICTS OF INTEREST
IN GOVERNMENT PRACTICE

Topic Overview

Should concurrent conflict of interest rules apply strictly to lawyers who serve state and local governmental entities? In many states and municipalities, the Attorney General, District Attorney, and City Attorney are elected, have a separate office, and may be from a different political party than the executive. Political and ethical conflicts arise because state and local agencies may not have their own lawyers and rely on lawyers who represent multiple agencies and entities.

---

[15] Michael Hirsh & Kristin Roberts, *What's In the Secret Drone Memos*, NAT'L L. J., Feb. 22, 2013; Robert P. Barnidge, Jr., *A Qualified Defense of American Drone Attacks in Northwest Pakistan Under International Humanitarian Law*, 30 B.U. INT'L L.J. 409 (2012) (concluding attacks are legal).

[16] Scott Shane, *Ex-Lawyer in State Department Criticizes Drone Secrecy*, N.Y. TIMES, May 8, 2013; John Yoo, *The Real Problem With Obama's Drone Memo*, WALL. ST. J., Feb. 9, 2013.

[17] Department of Justice, Office of Professional Responsibility Report, July 29, 2009, at 260.

[18] Memorandum for the Attorney General/Deputy Attorney General, from David Margolis, Associate Deputy Attorney General, January 5, 2010.

When a government lawyer is responsible for representing multiple local or state agencies and entities, what happens when there is conflict among those agencies and entities? What happens, for example, when city or county agencies come into opposition to one another? The possibilities for conflict are many: a government agency responsible for investigating and remedying fair employment practices might determine that another agency unlawfully discriminated in hiring, promoting or disciplining a government employee; an environmental protection agency might decide that a redevelopment agency's proposed construction project violates environmental laws. Is the City Attorney barred from representing either of the agencies against the other? Literal application of Rule 1.7 would automatically preclude representing and being adverse to a client, at least without meeting the material limitation test and consent requirement of Rule 1.7(a). The question considered in this section is whether the same principles should apply to the government lawyer, and, if so, under what circumstances.

Model Rule 1.7

A lawyer shall not represent a client if the representation will be directly adverse to another client or if there is a significant risk that the representation of one or more clients will be materially limited by the lawyer's responsibilities to another client unless the lawyer reasonably believes he will be able to provide competent representation to both and each affected client gives written informed consent.

Model Rule 1.11 is a special rule governing conflicts of interest for former and current government officers and employees. It focuses primarily on lawyers moving between government and private sector employment. In general terms, Rule 1.11 prohibits current and former government lawyers from representing clients in private practice or being involved as lawyers in government service "in matters in which the lawyer participated personally and substantially" while in the previous employment. To enable lawyers to move easily between government and the private sector, it takes a more relaxed approach to conflicts than is allowed by Model Rule 1.9, by disqualifying former government lawyers only from working on matters in which "the lawyer participated personally and substantially as a public officer or employee." MR 1.11(a). Notice that Model Rule 1.11(a) bars lawyers from accepting private employment in a matter in which they participated personally and substantially as government lawyers even if their representation would not be adverse to their former employer. This prohibition is broader than the general standard in Model Rule 1.9 for conflicts in successive representation, which applies only if the representation would be materially adverse to the interests of a former client. What is the justification for this difference? The Comment [3] explains that the purpose is not only to protect the former client but also "to prevent the lawyer from exploiting public office for the advantage of another client."

Rule 1.11 also prohibits the former government lawyer who acquired confidential information about a person while in government from thereafter representing a private client whose interests are adverse to that person in a matter in which the information could be used to the material disadvantage of that person. MR 1.11(c).

As applied to lawyers currently serving in government, Rule 1.11(d) states that Rules 1.7 (governing concurrent conflicts) and 1.9 (governing successive conflicts) apply "except as other law may otherwise expressly permit." The usual imputation principle of Rule 1.10 does not apply to former government lawyers and instead Rule 1.11(b) permits the former government lawyer to be screened and written notice to be given to the government.

1. A CASE STUDY: THE LOS ANGELES POLICE DEPARTMENT

The application of conflicts rules to a city attorney came to prominence in the early 1990s in Los Angeles when city officials tried to fire the LA Police Chief, Daryl Gates. Gates had been a controversial figure for some years because of the paramilitary style of policing he adopted. Many believed that Gates encouraged use of excessive force against suspects, especially people of color. Longstanding concerns about police brutality boiled over when a bystander videotaped LAPD officers brutally beating an unarmed black man, Rodney King, in a city street in March 1991. LA Mayor Tom Bradley called on Gates to resign, but Gates refused. The LA Police Commission, a civilian oversight board appointed by the mayor and confirmed by the city council, also tried to remove Gates. The 15 members of the LA City Council, however, were not all in favor of removing Gates. The Mayor and the City Council members are separately elected and, in the early 1990s, shared authority over the LAPD. The Los Angeles City Attorney, who is also elected, is responsible (along with his or her staff) for providing legal advice to all Los Angeles elected and appointed officials, departments and agencies. Everyone involved in the Gates imbroglio sought advice from the City Attorney's office, which created an interesting conflict of interest situation, as described below.

CITY ATTY. ROLE RAISES CONFLICT OF INTEREST ISSUE

H. Connell
L.A. Times, April 9, 1991

A potential conflict of interest by the Los Angeles city attorney's office—which has given legal advice to opposing factions in the Daryl F. Gates controversy—was raised as a central legal issue Monday in the court battle over the police chief's reinstatement.

City Atty. James K. Hahn's office told the Police Commission that it had the legal authority to place Gates on leave and, within days, advised the City Council on a legal maneuver to reverse the action, documents and interviews show. "There appears to exist ample legal authority, in both law and practice, to support the imposition of an involuntary administrative leave on the chief of police," Hahn's office advised the Police Commission in a confidential March 27 legal opinion.

Commissioners said they relied on the city attorney's advice when they ordered Gates to take a 60-day paid leave, pending completion of an investigation of the Rodney G. King beating.

In a closed session the next day, the [LA city] council asked Hahn and several of his office's lawyers for advice on legal steps it was considering taking to reinstate Gates. One of the council's tactics—settling a lawsuit that Gates was expected to file—was approved by the council. Gates filed the suit against the city. A Superior Court judge refused to immediately approve the settlement and instead ordered the Police Commission to return Gates to his job until an April 25 hearing.

As part of their argument against the settlement, attorneys for the commissioners and civil rights groups alleged that Hahn had a conflict of interest that should invalidate the settlement.

Hahn has a "gross, unlawful three-cornered conflict of interest, which precludes his serving either the legitimate interests of the city or the public interests," said Pete L. Haviland, an attorney for several civil rights groups trying to block the settlement.

Hahn's office denied there was a conflict in its advice to the Police Commission and City Council because both panels are part of the same legal entity—the city of Los Angeles.

Erwin Chemerinsky, USC law professor and an expert on legal ethics, said Hahn's office appeared to have a conflict of interest. "A lawyer can't represent adverse interests in a single matter," he said, adding that "the question of how to deal with Daryl Gates at this time is a single question." "Once (Hahn) advised the commission, he was the lawyer for the commission," Chemerinsky said. "He shouldn't be then helping the council undo what the commission did on the basis of his legal advice."

James Ham, former chairman of the Los Angeles County Bar Assn.'s ethics committee, said the Police Commission could have a "persuasive" argument that the city attorney erred. "They have a legal basis for complaining," Ham said. "They have a conflict issue that is legitimate." Ham and Chemerinsky said it would have been preferable for Hahn to disqualify his office from giving advice to both the commission and council.

Police Commission President Dan Garcia said he was "very upset" by the dual role of the city attorney's office. "They are selectively representing the Police Commission and the City Council at various times as they see fit," he said. Garcia said the decision to place Gates on leave was based on the memorandum from the city attorney's office. He said he was advised by the city attorney's office that it would have to disqualify itself from the Gates matter because of conflicts in representing competing branches of city government. Hahn's office denies this.

Mike Qualls, Hahn's spokesman, said the city attorney has only one client—the city of Los Angeles—and the power to settle lawsuits rests with the City Council.

Council members said they were shown legal opinions and given verbal advice by the city attorney Friday. Council President John Ferraro said the city attorney's staff answered questions and assured council members that what they were doing was legal.

Qualls said the city attorney has remained neutral in the dispute between the commission and the council and there was nothing contradictory in the legal advice provided to the two panels. He said the only potential conflict of interest would have been representing the city in an adversarial case against Gates, whose department it also represents in numerous lawsuits.

Qualls said that potential conflict was removed when the council decided to settle the lawsuit with Gates. Assistant City Atty. Merkin said it is not unusual for the city attorney to settle legal disputes between city departments. That, he said, was what the city attorney did in the Gates case.

Politically, Hahn, a potential rival of Mayor Tom Bradley in the 1993 elections, could be at odds with a core of his political constituency—the city's black community, which has been aggressive in seeking Gates' ouster.

NO CONFLICT BECAUSE THERE'S ONLY ONE CLIENT

Burt Pines*
Los Angeles Times, Apr. 30, 1991

The city attorney can properly advise several municipal agencies at once, as it is doing in the Gates matter.

The recent clash between the Los Angeles City Council and the Police Commission over the aborted attempt to place Police Chief Daryl Gates on administrative leave has provoked a number of questions about the role of the city attorney in interdepartmental conflicts.

Some have asked, "How could the city attorney advise the commission one day on the subject of administrative leave for the chief and, the next day, advise the council that it had the power to settle a lawsuit reinstating him?" "Why did the city attorney represent the City Council instead of the commission?" "Doesn't the city attorney have an inherent conflict of interest?"

Although the circumstances of this case are unusually dramatic, the issue of whom the city attorney represents is not new. It came up often during my term as city attorney. In 1978, I issued a memorandum that clarified the position of the office: "The civil branch of the Los Angeles city attorney's office represents only one client, namely, the City of Los Angeles." This analysis found, and continues to find, ample support in the law.

This precept is fundamental to understanding why the city attorney does not have a conflict of interest in advising various city departments that may sharply disagree with one another at any particular time. These departments are not separate legal entities but simply administrative arms of the city, a municipal corporation. Only that corporation is the city attorney's client. Only that municipal corporation is a legal entity, able to sue or be sued.

Conflicts between city departments involving an interpretation of law have traditionally been resolved by the city attorney's office. For example, in 1972, City Attorney Roger Arnebergh settled a jurisdictional dispute between the Department of Water and Power and the Department of Public Works over the distribution of reclaimed water. In 1975, I advised that the Department of Airports was not required to pay relocation assistance in amounts determined by the Board of Public Works. In 1982, City Attorney Ira Reiner resolved a conflict between the city controller and the Harbor Department regarding the propriety of certain entertainment expenses.

---

* [Eds: Burt Pines was Los Angeles City Attorney from 1973 to 1981.]

The city attorney is able to resolve these interdepartmental squabbles precisely because his client is the municipal corporation, not the individual officer or department involved.

Indeed, it would be unwise for city departments to have separate counsel. Aside from the 18 elected officials, Los Angeles has more than 30 separate departments or commissions. Internal conflicts occur on a daily basis. If each of these officials, departments and commissions had his or its own counsel, the cost would be astronomical. And the dependence of such attorneys on the appointing authority for their job security would compound the problem. They would invariably view themselves as advocates for their particular client's viewpoint, thereby sacrificing the objectivity and impartiality of an elected city attorney. The authority of the city attorney to settle legal disputes among different arms of city government would also be lost.

The city's reliance on an elected city attorney is sound. No structural changes are required. Of course, a conflict of interest may arise in a particular case from time to time that would disqualify the city attorney from acting, as in any law firm, whether public or private. While it is imperative that the city attorney be attentive to such potential conflicts, the conflicts do not, however, arise from the mere fact that two city departments are at odds.

The city attorney's office bears a heavy responsibility because it is the only law office for the city. The real key to its effectiveness lies in its continued ability to deliver excellent legal services, without the distraction of interdepartmental partisanship, and with the credibility that flows from independence, objectivity and integrity.

NOTES ON LOS ANGELES CITY ATTORNEY MATTER

1. *Was There a Conflict of Interest?* What is the disagreement among the commentators in these two excerpts about whether the Los Angeles City Attorney faced a conflict of interest in the Gates matter? Does saying that there is only one client, the City of Los Angeles, resolve the conflict to your satisfaction?

2. *Who Is the Client?* Recall that Model Rule 1.13 provides that when the client is an organization, the lawyer "represents the organization acting through its duly authorized constituents." The California Rules of Professional Conduct contain a similar provision, that "the client is the organization itself, acting through its highest authorized officer, employee, body, or constituent overseeing the particular engagement." Rule 3–600(A). Do these rules provide sufficient guidance in deciding who is the client in the Gates matter?

3. *Electoral Structure and Conflicts of Interest.* What is the significance in the analysis of the conflict of interest issue that the members

of the City Council, the Mayor, and the City Attorney were each separately elected and that the members of the Police Commission were appointed by the Mayor with the advice and consent of the City Council? If the City Attorney were appointed by the Mayor, as the United States Attorney General is appointed by the President, would your analysis of the conflict issue change? The Los Angeles City Charter authorized the Police Commission to remove Gates, and it also authorized the City Council to approve all settlements of litigation involving the City. Thus, each was, in the language of the Rule governing conflicts, the "highest authorized body . . . overseeing the particular engagement," but they disagreed.

4. *Power and Accountability.* After the LAPD-Gates matter, the City of Los Angeles redrafted its City Charter (the governing document that serves the same function for the city that a constitution serves for federal state governments). In that process, the Mayor urged that the new charter should narrow the City Attorney's authority to resolve legal disputes among different branches of government in situations like the LAPD-Gates matter. The Mayor criticized what he characterized as the City Attorney's view that its office is "the place for strategic decision making authority" and argued that the City Attorney should be appointed by the Mayor. A separately-elected City Attorney, the Mayor said, "places the City Attorney in the role of a policy maker when what is needed by the City of Los Angeles is legal representation. The City Attorney is not a third branch of government. The role of an attorney is <u>not</u> to sit as a de facto judicial branch or policy maker, arbitrating disputes or weighing the merits of competing policy choices." For his part, the City Attorney argued that an "elected City Attorney, through his or her independence, has the ability to rise above the political pressures which come to bear when departments and officers within the City have disputes with one another."[19] Which do you think is the better view?[20]

* * *

2. HIRING OUTSIDE COUNSEL AND MOTIONS TO DISQUALIFY GOVERNMENT LAWYERS

Conflicts of interest involving government lawyers are sometimes handled by retaining outside counsel to handle particular matters. Ordinarily, an office within the government has final decision-making authority on all requests to hire outside counsel, including when the request is based on a conflict of interest of the government lawyers. That happened in the following case. But what happens if the government lawyers who were advising two government agencies that become

---

[19] Letter from Richard J. Riordan to Members of the Los Angeles Elected Charter Reform Commission, July 20, 1998; Letter from James K. Hahn to Members of the Los Angeles Elected Charter Commission, June 24, 1998.

[20] Although the revised city charter enhanced mayoral control over a number of issues, it preserved the City Attorney as a separately elected office.

adversaries in litigation continue to represent one agency after the other has hired outside counsel? This is an issue of successive conflicts.

Rule 1.9—Duties to Former Clients

A lawyer who has formerly represented a client in a matter shall not thereafter represent another person in the same or a substantially related matter in which that person's interests are materially adverse to the interests of the former client unless the former client gives informed written consent.

As you read the following case, consider when and why a conflict of interest should justify an agency hiring outside counsel. Consider also whether the government lawyers should be disqualified from representing either of the government agencies that the lawyers formerly advised once the agencies become adversaries in litigation or otherwise.

CIVIL SERVICE COMMISSION V. SUPERIOR COURT

California Court of Appeal
163 Cal. App.3d 70 (1985)

WIENER, ACTING PRESIDING JUSTICE.

The difficult and sensitive question in this case is whether ethical considerations require disqualifying the County Counsel as attorney for the County of San Diego (County) in the pending litigation between the County and the Civil Service Commission of the County of San Diego (Commission).

[T]he functions of government make it necessary for some public agencies within a governmental body to be accorded a considerable degree of independence vis-à-vis that body. The Commission is such an agency. It is charged with administering the County's personnel system, in the context of which it is empowered to investigate complaints filed by county employees regarding personnel actions taken by various county agencies, and to make rulings based on those investigations. Needless to say, an adverse Commission ruling is not always warmly embraced by the affected county agency.

The present case arises out of two such complaints—one filed by Ardelia McClure and one filed by William Chapman—and the consequent investigations. Both employees held positions with the County's Department of Social Services, (Department) and complained of assignment and classification actions taken by the Department to implement budget cut-backs. As is true with respect to nearly all Commission actions, Commission members and staff working on the McClure and Chapman investigations freely consulted with the office of County Counsel for advice on legal matters. These consultations included discussions with County Counsel Lloyd Harmon and Deputy County Counsel Ralph Shadwell. At the time of the investigations, Shadwell was also the principal legal counsel for the Department of Social Services, whose actions the Commission was investigating. The topics of discussion included the extent of the Commission's authority to remedy any perceived violation of the County's personnel regulations. The Commission kept County Counsel apprised of the status of the investigation and the Commission deliberations with respect to the appropriate remedy.

Based on its investigations, the Commission ordered reinstatement of the affected employees, who had been demoted or laid off, and ordered back pay compensation. Disagreeing with the two rulings, the County filed suit in October 1983 against the Commission seeking judicial review of the Commission's action.

The County is and has been represented by the office of County Counsel. The Commission has obtained independent counsel. Based on County Counsel's prior advisory role to the Commission on these matters, the Commission unsuccessfully moved to disqualify County Counsel on the grounds of a conflict of interest.

We are thus faced with the question whether a public attorney who has advised a quasi-independent public agency with respect to a given matter may, consistent with his professional and ethical obligations, later represent other governmental entities suing the quasi-independent agency over the same matter.

[I]n the usual situation, we would expect that a conflict between or among county agencies would be resolved by the Board of Supervisors. Here, however, the conflict between the Department of Social Services and the Commission cannot be resolved in the usual manner because the County Charter gives the Commission authority independent of the County's normal hierarchical structure. The Board of Supervisors has been forced to sue the Commission in an attempt to overturn its rulings.

We are able to accept the general proposition that a public attorney's advising of a constituent public agency does not give rise to an attorney-client relationship separate and distinct from the attorney's relationship to the overall governmental entity of which the agency is a part. Nonetheless we believe an exception must be recognized when the agency lawfully functions independently of the overall entity. Where an attorney advises or represents a public agency with respect to a matter as to which the agency possesses independent authority, such that a dispute over the matter may result in litigation between the agency and the overall entity, a distinct attorney-client relationship with the agency is created.

Here, County Counsel was advising both the Commission and the affected county agencies at the time of the McClure and Chapman investigations. In fact, the same attorney was assigned to advise both the Commission and the Department of Social Services. To the extent that County Counsel is ever permitted to place himself in such a position in the first place, it is clear if the situation escalates to litigation, he cannot remain as counsel for one of his clients in opposition to the other.[5]

If the Commission is afforded access to independent legal advice, however, there is no reason County Counsel may not continue to vigorously represent the County even when such representation results in litigation against the Commission. We need not and do not decide whether the Commission, appropriately informed and advised in a given case, could validly waive the conflict at the advisory stage.

[W]e do not mean to suggest that government attorneys must necessarily be treated identically with attorneys in private practice. But neither are they immune from conflict problems similar to those which confront the private bar.

NOTES ON DISQUALIFICATION OF GOVERNMENT LAWYERS

1. ***Is Government Different?*** Should concurrent conflicts of interest rules apply strictly to lawyers who serve state and local governmental entities? When a government lawyer is responsible for representing multiple local or state agencies and entities, how should that lawyer respond when a dispute develops among the agencies and entities? When is it appropriate to hire outside counsel? When should a government lawyer be disqualified from continuing to represent one agency when he or she previously advised both that agency and another agency that has become its adversary? Should cost play any role in deciding what standards should apply?

2. ***What Is an Alternative Approach to Conflicts of Interest?*** If you do not advocate strict application of the concurrent conflict of interest rules to government lawyers, what standards do you think should apply? What rule or standard does the court use in *Civil Service Commission v. Superior Court*? Does the court's approach offer sufficient guidance for a situation like the Daryl Gates controversy?

---

[5] The County suggests that a "screening system" which divides County Counsel's office between an Advisory and a Litigation Division makes disqualification of the County Counsel unnecessary. The problem here is not so much in screening the litigators from the advisors but rather in screening attorneys representing the Commission from attorneys representing the County. County Counsel seems not to have perceived the conflict inherent at every stage of the proceedings—advisory and litigation—between the Commission and the County. Moreover, the "screening" process has been suggested only in very limited circumstances where an attorney, disqualified from participation in a case as a result of his prior employment, is "sealed off" from the rest of his new firm in order to avoid disqualification of that firm. Here, the Commission's relationship with County Counsel is not limited to a single attorney who previously represented the Commission while employed by another law firm. The Commission's ongoing relationship with the entire office of County Counsel, including Mr. Harmon himself, makes any attempted screening device inappropriate.

3. ***Model Rule 1.11 and Other Conflicts Rules.*** Rule 1.11(d)(1) provides that, "except as law may otherwise expressly permit," the government lawyer is bound by Model Rules 1.7 and 1.9.

PROBLEM 20–1

Two Large City police officers, Smith and Jones, shot a homeless woman, Bonnie Mitchell, on a city sidewalk. Officers Smith and Jones said they believed she lunged at them with a knife. Media coverage of the event quoted a bystander saying that she did not have a knife. The Large City Charter creates the office of the City Attorney to represent the City in legal proceedings and states that the City Attorney's client is Large City. The Charter also creates the Large City Police Commission, which oversees the Large City Police Department. The Police Commission is empowered to review the use of deadly force by police officers and, if it determines the use of force was not within policy, the police officers who kill a suspect are subject to discipline and criminal prosecution.

Alice Alvarez is an attorney in the City Attorney's office who advises the Police Commission. After Smith and Jones testified at a Police Commission hearing on the Mitchell shooting that they believed she was trying to stab them, the Commission, upon the advice of Alvarez, found the shooting to be within policy. Several weeks later, Officer Jones comes to see Alvarez in her office and says that he lied to the Police Commission. He says that Mitchell did not have a knife and that Officer Smith shot her after an angry argument in which Mitchell refused to remove her possessions from the sidewalk and was verbally abusive to Smith and Jones.

Meanwhile, Mitchell's children filed a civil suit against Large City and against Officers Smith and Jones seeking damages for her wrongful death. Large City and the officers are represented by Zachary Zelinsky, a lawyer in the City Attorney's office whose specialty is defending the city in civil rights and police abuse cases. Under the City Charter, the City Council decides whether to settle any litigation against the city, and Zelinsky has recommended that the City Council not settle the Mitchell suit.

Someone leaked to the *Large City Times* a story that one of the officers has said that Mitchell was not armed. Civil rights activists are quoted in the *Times* story speculating that the City Attorney may be trying to silence Alvarez because the City Attorney is the leading candidate to be elected District Attorney for the county in which Large City is located and he enjoys strong support from the police officers' union. The election is to occur in four weeks.

Alice Alvarez has sought your advice about what she should do.

Alternatively, assume you are counsel to a special task force appointed by the Large City Major to investigate the conduct of the City Attorney's office in the handling of the Mitchell matter. What should you advise?

E. SUMMARY

In this chapter we considered three issues: (1) Who is the client of the government lawyer? (2) How should the government lawyer approach her counseling duties? (3) How do conflicts of interest principles apply in this setting? With some ill-defined exceptions, the same rules apply to government lawyers as to others, including Rule 1.13 regarding the organizational client, Rule 2.1 on the duty to provide independent and candid advice, and Rules 1.7 and 1.9 regarding conflicts of interest. Rule 1.11 provides some special conflict of interest rules for former and current government lawyers. The size and complexity of government and the often diffuse nature of authority and electoral accountability often make it challenging for government lawyers to identify the client, to provide advice that serves the client's interest, and to determine when conflicts among government agencies should be regarded as conflicts of interest requiring separate counsel.

SUBPART C

INDIVIDUAL AND SMALL BUSINESS CLIENTS

■ ■ ■

In this section, we examine the sectors of the legal profession that serve primarily individuals and small businesses. Most of these lawyers work in solo and small firm practices. Within solo and small firm practice, however, there are wide variations in lawyers' social backgrounds, the types of clients they represent and work they do, and how they find clients and manage their practice. We begin our examination of these sectors with an overview of solo and small firm practice in Chapter 21. In Chapter 22, we examine advertising and solicitation, because those types of marketing are common in solo and small firm practice and have attracted substantial regulation, litigation, and controversy within the profession. In Chapter 23, we explore the plaintiffs' bar, with particular focus on the variety, status hierarchies, and referral networks within the sector of the profession that represents plaintiffs, individuals, and small businesses. In Chapter 24, we study boutique firms, many of which resemble large law firms in that they represent large organizational clients, but resemble small firms in their size and personnel practices and often specialize in particular subject areas.

CHAPTER 21

SOLO AND SMALL FIRM PRACTICE

■ ■ ■

A. INTRODUCTION

The largest single sector of law practice consists of lawyers who practice alone or in small firms. There are significant differences among solo and small firm practitioners in different regions and different practice types. As we will see in in this chapter and in Chapter 24, some small firm practitioners have elite credentials and represent large organizational clients, but many do not. This chapter focuses primarily on solo and small firm lawyers who represent individuals and small businesses; Chapter 24 examines the sector of small firm practice commonly known as "boutique" practice in which lawyers identify themselves as engaging in a similar quality and sophistication of practice as at large firms.

We begin with a sample of scholarly and journalistic descriptions of solo and small firm practice. The first part of the chapter illustrates the huge variety among types of solo and small firm practice, with particular attention to the differences in the way that these lawyers enter the practice, find clients, and manage their work lives. We also note the differences between rural, suburban, and urban practice, and different subject matter specialties. We will then examine some of the major ethical issues that are most salient to solo and small firm practitioners, many of which stem from cash flow problems that plague many small businesses. We will explore reasons why solo and small firm lawyers are more likely to face bar discipline than are lawyers in large firms and consider what, if anything, should be done about it.

B. PORTRAITS OF SOLO AND SMALL FIRM PRACTICE

Solo practitioners constituted three-fifths of the bar in 1948. Now they are 50 percent of lawyers in private practice, or about 38 percent of the bar. They are the largest single practice setting among American lawyers.[1] Small firms (five or fewer lawyers) account for another 10 percent of the profession, bringing solo and small firm practice to over half of lawyers in private practice and about 40 percent of the bar. Solo

---

[1] THE LAWYER STATISTICAL REPORT, AMERICAN BAR FOUNDATION (2012).

and small firm practice reflects the diversity of the American profession, but immigrants and people from modest socioeconomic backgrounds long predominated, in part because of the considerable barriers to entry to large firm, corporate, and government legal practice. The early-twentieth century waves of immigration from Ireland and Southern and Eastern Europe triggered a nativist alarm, especially among well-to-do whites in the urban areas where immigrants settled. The elite bar, composed primarily of Protestant corporate lawyers, attempted to curb the business-getting conduct of ethnic urban solo and small firm lawyers who practiced in areas such as personal injury and criminal law. The elites wrote ethics rules that proscribed client-getting activities such as solicitation and regulated contingent fee practices. In this and other ways, the organized bar "conveyed the impression that these ethnic lawyers—who struggled for clients—were less ethical than other lawyers."[2] Understanding this background sheds light on ways in which the rules of professional conduct have reflected social power and generated conflict within the profession over conceptions of professionalism.

In this segment, we explore the reality behind these stereotypes about solo and small firm practice. The first excerpt is from the leading study of the practice setting, a 1996 book based on lengthy interviews with solo and small firm lawyers in the greater New York City area. It portrays some of the distinctive qualities of the metropolitan solo and small firm practice sector and those who practice in it.

THE BUSINESS OF PRACTICING LAW: THE WORK LIVES OF SOLO AND SMALL-FIRM ATTORNEYS

Carroll Seron
Temple University Press, 1996[3]

Getting Started. There were two fairly typical career trajectories. One group began by working for the government. An equally notable group began as associates or employees of solo or small-firm practitioners. Less typical was the small group who began their careers in major Wall Street firms.

Attorneys described three fairly distinct though not mutually exclusive strategies of coping with the initiation rites of professionalization. Some cultivated an informal network of attorneys and court officials on whom they could call to ask questions, copy legal forms, or clarify court procedures. Some learned by watching other

---

2 Leslie Levin, *The Ethical World of Solo and Small Law Firm Practitioners*, 41 HOUSTON L. REV. 309 (2004).

3 © 1996 by Temple University. All Rights Reserved.

lawyers and then trying out what they saw. A minority of attorneys learned through mentors.

The entrepreneurial lawyers began their careers with a crystal-clear sense of what they wanted—and eventually got. Many reported having worked as investigators for insurance companies, where they realized that this was one area where a "poor boy" could make a living. The desire for autonomy runs throughout the work lives of these attorneys. Others knew that they did *not* want to work in a large firm. Daniel Levine "didn't want to be a cog in a wheel," and Renaud White thought "corporate law seemed awfully dull!"

A small group of women reported that they modified their expectations about work because of children or other family obligations.

Cash flow, an uncertain client base, a vulnerability to the ups and downs of the market, and the very nature of legal work explain why most of these attorneys do not feel financially secure.

Getting Clients. Richard Leavitt enjoyed the benefits of his father's earlier labors to build a legal practice in a remote community of Westchester County. When he joined his dad, he did what any aspiring lawyer must do to meet people: "You join what I call the animal clubs. You join the Elks. In my case, it was the Jaycees and the B'nai B'rith and the local Democratic Party and the local political party. I headed up the town's United Way." Most of these attorneys overwhelmingly agree that, with time, the single most important source of new clients is referrals from former clients. Most pointed out that referrals from professional colleagues—other lawyers, real estate agents, accountants or bankers—though neither as typical nor as important a source as client referrals are another important source of business.

Victor Cutolo said that friends and family are a big but "unfortunate" source of business because "they're a pain; they feel they can call you any time and it's very hard to be candid." It can also be difficult to bill friends who "always call you up for advice. It is always cheap!" One group of men, however, have turned family and friends into a positive client-getting resource. These men reported that work has come through local sports activities, high school friends who now own business, or special interest clubs.

The typical experimenter [with client getting] is a practitioner who begins with a core of referrals and builds a client base through professional networks and local activities, coupled with various forays into advertising or solicitation. Whether these attorneys place ads in local or citywide newspapers, develop brochures, or advertise on television, their efforts tend to be reluctant and haphazard.

As to newspaper advertising, Joseph Fitzsimmons, a solo practitioner and former lawyer at Jacoby and Meyers, said, "I don't' have the money for it! I'm not saying it's a bad way to obtain clients, but unless you have $25,000 a year minimum for an advertising budget, you're just throwing your money away."

Non-advertising newspaper coverage, however, may be a source of business. Eliot Klein, a Manhattan lawyer, had some cases with "substantial verdicts, over a million, two million dollars, and the local paper where I live had written them up. It was a very nice spread, and I called them and I complimented them on what they had written and that it was very nice." Nora Charles-Cox tries to get her name known in the community through her efforts on "public service type of things." For instance, she said, "I recently spoke at the YWCA. I was asked to speak on a panel, and that was covered really heavily by the press. I've had several shows that I've been involved in that have run on cable and several things on the radio."

The vast majority of experimenters feel that television advertising crosses the social divide between professional and unprofessional solicitation. Victor Cutolo asked, "Can you really take anything seriously that you see on TV?" Some pointed out that they do not advertise on television because of what their colleagues will think or because of potential damage to their reputation.

[Other lawyers described slight variations in their marketing practices.] Alan Fine has a highly specialized and limited practice, focusing on immigration. About 15 years ago, he was asked to write a weekly column on current immigration issues for the largest Korean newspaper in the United States. [Anticipating major change in federal immigration law enacted in 1986], he accepted the invitation and has been writing the column ever since. [He also does television and radio programs frequently], speaking for fifteen minutes and then taking calls on the air. His television and radio style is "like a type of documentary." He also produces "a lot of brochures," which he hands out when he does lectures.

Although Denise Dewey began by saying, "I don't advertise" and "it is just not my way of doing business," a different picture began to unfold as she indicated that there had been some articles about her cases in the *Post* and the *Daily News*.

Organizing Practices. Most of these attorneys [characterized the majority of their practices as] "routine in the sense that they involve things I've done before," and observ[ed] that their professional practices do not entail very much legal research. Rather, it is the "people side" of the law that complicates their work and makes each case different.

For partners in small, traditional law firms, friendship—if not family—is the concept that captures the essential dynamic of their organization. The majority of these partnerships are between men of approximately the same age, many of whom met at other firms or in school, or shared office space and decided to start a firm together. Typically, partners explain, their agreement is verbal. By contrast, an associate in a small firm is an employee—somewhat marginal, isolated, or cut off from the partners. A partnership "track"—the essential building block of the corporate law firm—does not exist in most small-firm practices. Although associates *may* become partners, there are no cues, no time frames, no ground rules, no clear expectations. Associates also reported that they are not quite sure how or if they are formally evaluated.

The process of hiring associates reveals the embeddedness of small firms in a local community. Most typically, partners reported, they look for attorneys with some work experience; they try to avoid hiring a recent law school graduate unless the individual worked for them while in school. They also prefer someone from the immediate area; the rationale is that they have watched the person function in court or in the local district attorney's office; they "know" his or her reputation.

Some attorneys, opting for even more independence than collegiality allows, work on their own. Seymour Kaplowitz of Manhattan summed it up: "The advantages are easy enough. You're your own boss. You make your own hours; you take the time that you need to devote to the projects that you want. You're not harassed in the sense that someone is looking over your shoulder, and you don't have to report to anyone." The relative isolation, the "frenetic" nature of solo practice, and, in some instances, the disrespect from peers are keenly felt, to be sure, but these factors do not outweigh the advantages.

Entrepreneurial legal practice is service oriented, but as in other postindustrial organizations a concern with service emphasizes efficiency and cost rather than process and quality. As a managing attorney at a local Jacoby and Meyers office put it, in weighing the relative importance of entrepreneurial and legal skills, the former is "more important" because the latter can "always be bought." Or, when asked what clients want from an attorney, Michael Fitzgerald, an associate at a storefront firm on Long Island, said that for "most clients, it's a toss-up [between] whether it's fast and cheap or cheap and fast!" Denise Dewey explained that working with clients is "all communication and salesmanship."

Overwhelmingly, the men and women who part company with the entrepreneurs agree that qualities such as the "personal touch," "communication," and a willingness to cultivate a "bedside manner" are their most important professional skills in working with clients. Carol

Shapiro, who has been practicing law for about 15 years, commented, "I haven't yet had a client who, you know, was looking for Clarence Darrow. I think they obviously want adequate and competent representation. But they *also* need people who are good listeners."

[W]hen attorneys describe what clients want in a lawyer, it is some variation on a demand for *their time.* Most of these practitioners imply that an entrepreneurial concern to be fast and cheap must be balanced by the demands to be responsive and caring.

NOTES ON SERON

1. *Variations in the Demographics of Solo and Small Firm Practice.* Because of the geographic focus of Seron's study, and the years in which it was conducted, the lawyers whom she interviewed were predominantly (but not exclusively) white, and many were immigrants or children of immigrants from Eastern and Southern Europe. If the study were replicated in greater New York City or other areas today, it would find the population of lawyers to be different. What impact, if any, do you think that might have on the findings? If the study were conducted in the area in which you live now or have lived in the past, what do you imagine it might find?

2. *The Path to Solo or Small Firm Practice.* What are the reasons given by lawyers in Seron's study for choosing solo or small firm practice?

3. *Marketing.* Should any of the marketing practices used by solo and small firm lawyers in Professor Seron's study be prohibited? If so, why? (We will return to this question when we examine the law governing lawyer advertising and solicitation in Chapter 22.)

* * *

In the following excerpt, based on interviews with 71 lawyers specializing in immigration law in New York City in 2006, Leslie Levin explores some of the characteristics of a relatively new type of urban practice.

SPECIALTY BARS AS A SITE OF PROFESSIONALISM: THE IMMIGRATION BAR EXAMPLE

Leslie Levin
8 University of St. Thomas Law Journal 194 (2011)

There appear to be some significant commonalities among members of the New York City immigration bar. One-third of the lawyers in the study are immigrants and almost one-third of the U.S.-born lawyers have at least one foreign-born parent. Some others had a strong connection with the immigrant experience. Most of the lawyers in the study did not attend elite law schools. Many are drawn to the work because of a desire to help others. A solo lawyer who was born in India explained:

I am in this legal profession not only because there's the power, prestige and money in this profession, but I get an opportunity to serve people in the community also—immigration is one area where you can serve—you can really serve needy people, all right? In all other areas like say real estate, it's basically financial gain to your clients, but in immigration law area it's a lifelong gain to your client—that's one reason.

Immigration is comprised of several sub-specialties. Business immigration lawyers perform the work that must be done for organizations to sponsor a foreign national to enter and work legally in the United States. Most immigration lawyers who do not focus primarily on business immigration do at least some family-based immigration work. Family-based immigration lawyers represent foreign nationals who seek legal status based on their familial relationship to someone who is already legally residing in the United States. Some immigration lawyers also handle asylum claims or deportation defense work, the latter of which involves removal proceedings brought against individuals based on criminal convictions or against persons who lack authorization to be in the United States.

Many immigration lawyers work in solo and small firms (two to five lawyers). Even business immigration lawyers who work in this setting may represent large corporate clients. Immigration lawyers also work in larger boutique immigration firms, typically of less than twenty lawyers, although the largest immigration firm, Fragomen LLP, had sixty-three lawyers in its New York City office and 250 lawyers world-wide at the time of the study. A small number of large corporate law firms (over 100 lawyers) employ a few business immigration lawyers, primarily as a way to service their existing corporate clients.

Business immigration lawyers often work from offices in midtown Manhattan or in White Plains, New York. A few work from home. Since they do not go to immigration court or routinely attend hearings, proximity to federal buildings is not essential. They may work in relative isolation from other immigration lawyers. In contrast, the offices of many lawyers who do other types of immigration work are clustered in a few office buildings on lower Broadway in Manhattan, close to 26 Federal Plaza, where the immigration courts, the United States Citizenship and Immigration Services' (USCIS) New York City district office, and most of the other immigration enforcement offices are located. Alternatively, those who have family-based or asylum practices work near the immigrant communities they service.

The nature of immigration practice may help create an environment conducive to a strong feeling of community among immigration lawyers. Immigration lawyers, unlike many other lawyers, do not negotiate or litigate against one another. Instead, their opponent is the Government, which may stand in the way of their clients' efforts to legally live or work in the United States. These lawyers are competitors for business, but the competition does not negate the feeling of community. One experienced lawyer explained why:

> [W]e're not generally in an adversarial situation with each other. I mean, there is competitiveness . . . I would like that big client; they would like that big client. Some are more cutthroat than others, in terms of that. But we're non-adversarial . . . [W]e're not in court on opposite sides of the table, and I guess because we are helping. [T]he main focus of my practice is business immigration, and you know, that's less helping than when— when I'm representing a French banker, it's less helping and nurturing than [when] I'm helping a housekeeper from Jamaica come here and make a better life for her children, which I do, too. And then the cases that are even more are when you're dealing with humanitarian issues, and helping issues. So that's still the roots of it.

More than two-thirds of the lawyers in the study had taken no immigration law course or clinic during law school. (Almost all who had done so had graduated from law school within the past dozen years.) Only 40% of the lawyers reported that they received some systematic training in the workplace in how to practice immigration law. As a result, many immigration lawyers in the study had to teach themselves how to practice immigration law. Several lawyers reported that early in their careers, they relied on mentors, materials, or seminars [provided by the American Immigration Lawyers Association (AILA), which is the largest immigration lawyers' specialty bar] to learn how to practice immigration law. This was especially likely if the lawyer worked in an office with no other experienced immigration lawyers. One solo lawyer who was relatively new to immigration practice explained his learning process: "I sort of did it on my own, and took some seminars . . . And then I keep reading a lot. AILA has a lot of publications, also, that are like tips, particular to how you handle Immigration officers, and what to do, or not to do—things like that. Those are, I think, are very helpful, for learning."

It is no accident that new lawyers turn to AILA to learn how to practice law. AILA deliberately seeks to train new immigration lawyers.

Not all immigration lawyers are good lawyers. In fact, some lawyers in the sample were openly critical of many of the lawyers who practice immigration law—including other AILA members. But in the view of many of the interviewed lawyers, a lawyer cannot even begin to be a good immigration lawyer unless he or she belongs to AILA. As one noted, "AILA represents, [I] . . . wouldn't say all of the immigration lawyers, but probably most good immigration lawyers belong to AILA." Closely connected to the conception of being a "good lawyer" is staying up to date with the law.

The fact that solo and small firm practitioners predominate in the immigration field may also create the conditions for a successful and collegial specialty bar. Generally speaking, lawyers in larger firms may rely heavily on office colleagues for information and for their understanding of professional norms. But many immigration lawyers are the only ones in their firms or office-sharing arrangements who practice immigration law. For such lawyers, AILA helps to provide collegial support not otherwise readily available. Indeed, membership in AILA seemed especially important for lawyers who worked on their own.

Although many immigration lawyers believe that their bar is unique, it shares certain similarities with other practice specialties in which solo and small firm lawyers predominate. Notably, personal injury lawyers generally do not oppose one another in court, and they share a common enemy: insurance companies. Personal injury lawyers also belong to a very collegial specialty bar association, the American Association for Justice, in which there is a great deal of information sharing. Criminal defense lawyers, like immigration lawyers, work in a system they consider unfair and they share a common opponent: the Government. Criminal defense attorneys also have a well-established specialty bar, the [National Association of Criminal Defense Lawyers (NACDL)], which provides services similar to AILA.

* * *

The following vignettes round out Seron's and Levin's portraits of solo and small firm practice by showing different paths which lawyers have recently taken into the practice setting and how lawyers in these practices today describe the rewards and challenges of their work. Unlike the Seron and Levin studies, most of these vignettes are drawn from news stories and are accounts of the experience of just a few lawyers.

Solo and Small Practice After Big Firm Practice. Some solo practitioners graduate from elite law schools and/or practice in elite large firms before leaving to find more autonomy and closer connections to their clients than they can find in a large firm representing large corporate clients. The following vignettes illustrate the phenomenon.

When Clair Harrington finished a three-year stint as a clerk for the Virginia Supreme Court, she had a plum job waiting for her at a big New York City law firm. But Harrington—who graduated high in her class at St. John's University School of Law—told the firm, Cahill Gordon & Reindel, that she wasn't interested. Instead, she joined Meyer, Goergen & Marrs, a firm of fewer than 10 lawyers in Richmond, Va.

Harrington had spent a law school summer working for the 250-lawyer New York firm. She knew what to expect and decided she wanted something else. Though the salary was smaller, she says, the quality of life of a small firm in a small city made the choice easy. "A really common complaint I heard from associates that summer was that they had three or four years' experience, and they still weren't even allowed to take their own depositions, much less appear in court," says Harrington.

At the Richmond firm, Harrington started out in litigation, and she was handling her own trials within three months. Eventually, she moved to the transactional side and found her niche in small-business lending. She was asked to become a partner after four years.

Harrington also likes having greater autonomy to handle her caseload. "I don't have to report to multiple tiers of managers, each with their own agenda. I like not being micromanaged," she says.

Amy Kleinpeter knows what Harrington means about the realities of big-firm management. Kleinpeter, who graduated from the University of Southern California Law School in the top 15 percent of her class, spent her first year as a lawyer at the Los Angeles office of Squire Sanders & Dempsey, which has about 800 lawyers in offices around the world. "I was bored out of my mind. I made great money, but I spent too much of it on Amazon. There are only so many hours a day I can do document review," says Kleinpeter. She also noticed that some of the partners she most admired at the big firm didn't have much control over their practices, even after 10, 20 or 30 years at the firm. "The people making decisions up through the layers of committees and managing partners often don't even know the people they oversee—even those who have been at the firm for decades. It's just too big," she says.

So Kleinpeter interviewed with a much smaller firm, Doumanian & Associates in Glendale, Calif., with only a handful of associates. Though she took a pay cut of almost two-thirds of her former salary, Kleinpeter was thrilled to have the chance to get into court and to deal with clients.

Kleinpeter stayed with the smaller firm for three years before deciding to go to an even smaller firm. In July, she opened a solo practice in Pasadena. "Sometimes it's scary, but I like it so much better than when I was at the big firm feeling like I never got to do anything worthwhile," she says.

Harrington says she has noticed that certain personalities seem drawn to smaller firms: entrepreneurial types and those who prefer control of their work environment over a large salary. "It's about the relationship between effort and benefit. In a smaller firm, that relationship is much more obvious. It's just that simple."[4]

Solo Practice and Recession. As Seron documented, solo and small firm practices are vulnerable to business trends and to the sudden loss of clients. Moreover, although some lawyers choose solo practice for the autonomy, many hang out a shingle as a matter of economic necessity: either they cannot find a firm job upon graduating from law school or they worked at a firm and were laid off during an economic downturn for the firm or for the economy. The effect of the enormous recession of 2008–2011 on solo and small firm practitioners varied by practice setting, of course, but it hit some practitioners hard, as illustrated in the following account.

Before the Recession [of 2008–2011], Andrea Goldman, 50, had a "fairly solid" client base handling construction, business and real estate disputes in Newton, Mass. But the economic downturn forced Goldman, a solo since 2000, to realize that her bread and butter—construction—was unprofitable both for her and her clients.

"Homeowners invest money in projects and then need to hire new contractors to complete the job or make repairs when problems develop," she explains. "They then seek my advice and are usually so strapped for cash that they either can't afford to pay me or I'm forced to litigate on a tight budget."

Even if Goldman could get a judgment against a contractor, collecting was well-nigh impossible. "I ended up turning most queries away after spending a considerable amount of time on the phone discussing the homeowner's issue."

Goldman would like to represent more contractors than homeowners, but that's been a difficult sell. "I'm not going to get huge companies; they'll go with the big firms downtown" in Boston, she says. "But a lot of the people I meet are too small to have repeat legal business."

In addition, many small contractors are so independent, it's a battle just to get them to realize they need an attorney,

---

[4]   Margaret Graham Tebo, *Living Large at a Smaller Size: Top-Tier Law Grads and Big-Firm Hot Shots Take Their Smarts to Smaller Practices*, ABA J., Jan. 2007, at 26.

followed by another battle to get them to realize they need Goldman.

Goldman's marketing activities would make many other solos dizzy. She runs the Home Contractor vs. Homeowner blog, writes, does seminars, belongs to the Builders Association of Greater Boston, and has signed up as a mediator or arbitrator for numerous organizations. She's also launching a consortium of construction attorneys that will serve as a referral service for the construction industry.[5]

Family-Friendly Solo Practice. As Seron's study showed, many lawyers choose solo practice because they believe it will give them greater control over their hours than they could have at a large firm. Some lawyers like the idea of solo practice, especially running a solo practice out of their home, so that they can be more available to their children.

"Both physically and psychologically, the comfort of being in my own space helps my productivity," says [Danielle G.] Van Ess, 34, now the mother of three girls. [Van Ess does estate planning, adoptions, and residential real estate work.] "I can change the heat, make coffee at any time and tend to my baby privately. I always hear people complaining about how they spilled coffee on their clothes on the way to work and are uncomfortable all day. If that happens to me, I can just run upstairs." [A Northford, Connecticut-based lawyer Susan Cartier] Liebel, who launched a home-based practice out of her bedroom in 1995, [said of her decision to practice at home:] "The people I have talked to want freedom to make choices that work for their families."

Isolation is [a] consideration for home-based workers, and [home-based solo practitioners say] finding ways to engage with the outside world is essential. Scheduling lunch appointments with colleagues and using public spaces (like a courthouse or law school library) to perform research are two of their strategies for staying connected.

[T]he home-based office was a no-brainer financially for Van Ess, who used the money she would have spent on rent for technology and to hire a team of virtual assistants. But her decision to work from home was also rooted in the psychological benefit that the cozy setting provides for her clients, many of whom are initially intimidated by the idea of seeking legal advice.

---

[5]   G.M. Filisko, *Turnaround: Solos Seek Advice to Survive a Struggling Economy*, ABA J. (Mar. 2010), at 51.

It works, Van Ess says, because she thinks of clients as guests, noting that many hug her on the way out. And when she goes to her clients' homes to conduct closings or to execute final documents, they get to return her gesture of hospitality. "It becomes very friendly instead of a sterile, buttoned-up kind of meeting," she says.[6]

Note the connection between the type of work and clients Van Ess represents and her decision to locate her practice in her home and to describe her clients as guests. Consider whether other types of work and other types of client would be equally adaptable to a home-based practice.

Rural Solo Practice. Most studies of the legal profession in the last half-century have focused on urban or suburban lawyers. While this is unremarkable for many reasons, including the increasing urbanization of the United States, small town lawyers still exist. Their practices are in many ways similar to any other solo or small firm practice, but the leading study of the rural bar, published by Donald Landon in 1990, found a number of differences between the urban or metropolitan and rural bars.[7] Landon found the rural bar in Missouri that he studied was relatively homogeneous racially, ethnically, and religiously because the rural communities he studied were homogeneous. He observed a close consensus on values among the lawyers and zealous partisanship in advocacy to be muted because the social context discouraged rural lawyers from some of the zealous and conflictual advocacy that is tolerated or encouraged in larger urban areas.[8] He also found the rural Missouri bar to be minimally stratified, with many lawyers' practices sharing a similar mix of clients. According to Landon, the status hierarchy was not based on who the lawyer represented, because lawyers represented a similar mix of clients, but rather on how lucrative the lawyer's practice was. The stigma that urban large firm lawyers attach to solo and small firm practitioners and to their entrepreneurial client-getting efforts did not exist; there were no large firms in small towns and *all* lawyers needed to be entrepreneurial in the same ways. Whereas "[t]he city entrepreneur adapts to the urban setting by a heavy reliance on brokers for business" "the rural entrepreneur relies on reputation."[9] The small town lawyers in Landon's study were less likely to specialize, as there were not enough clients in a single classification to enable a practice limited to a particular subject area.

---

[6]   Becky Beaupre Gillespie & Hollee Schwartz Temple, *Making the Home Work: It Takes More Than Space to Find Home Office Success* ABA J., July 2010, at 30.

[7]   DONALD D. LANDON, COUNTRY LAWYERS: THE IMPACT OF CONTEXT ON PROFESSIONAL PRACTICE (1990).

[8]   *Id.* at 146.

[9]   *Id.* at 149.

The types of matters that predominate differ from one rural area to another; the bar in a resort community will have different clients and types of cases than the bar in a farming community. While at one point a rural practice would limit a lawyer's access to information (particularly if the nearest county or university law library was distant and/or not well stocked), the Internet has changed that.

The following vignettes explore how lawyers have recently attempted to establish practices in two different rural areas. Remember, neither of these is a rigorous study of a representative sample of lawyers.

Situated halfway between Wichita, Kan., and Tulsa, Okla., lies the town of Sedan. With a population of roughly 1,200, Sedan is the largest city in Chautauqua County.

The January 2009 ad, placed by a local real estate broker in the *Journal of the Kansas Bar Association*, was at once plaintive and blunt: "We, the people of Sedan, Kan., have a dire need for an attorney. Chautauqua County has one remaining attorney, who is looking forward to retirement." The call attracted the attention of G. Thomas Harris, 65, who 18 months earlier had closed his general law practice in Richmond, Mo., 250 miles from Sedan. Harris opened a new law office across the street from Sedan's courthouse. Handling family law, estate planning, real estate law, criminal law, administrative law and personal injury matters, Harris, a grandfather of six, felt himself drawn to Sedan's relaxed setting.

Tiana McElroy hadn't seen the bar journal ad. But having grown up in northeast Kansas, and having worked in several small Kansas towns, McElroy thought Sedan would be a perfect complement to her office in nearby Coffeyville. "I went to law school because I wanted to make a difference," she says. And she decided Sedan was the kind of place where she could. Upon opening her Sedan office, McElroy placed a newspaper ad, giving her location as, simply, "between the Norgan's Sedan barber shop and Tom McCann's restaurant." She planned to charge clients $125 an hour but, given the recession, she decided to charge $80. Typical of a small-town practice, many Sedan residents stopped by McElroy's office just to talk.

Rural attorneys discover that they enjoy helping neighbors, owning their own cases and, for some, watching their practices flow with farming seasons.

Kansas has only 5.8 lawyers per 10,000 residents. The only states with fewer lawyers per capita are Arkansas (5.3) and North Dakota (4.4). But supply and demand is only one small part of the calculus connected with the rural and small-town practice. [One] seldom sees lawyers up and move from, say, Manhattan to Montana if there's no prior connection. "Most business comes from people who know, like and trust you. If you have no connections in a community where everyone knows everyone else, you've constructed other obstacles."

While generalized practices are the norm for lawyers in one-horse towns, experts insist that specialized lawyers can similarly thrive in rural areas. According to Harris, when a small-town lawyer provides good service, word spreads quickly and "you will end up with a lot of clients" no matter what your area of expertise. He advises opening an office in a visible location near the courthouse and participating in the community through the chamber of commerce and service clubs like Rotary. Join your local bar association's e-mail discussion list and participate. And if your bar doesn't have one, start one, he adds.

Surprisingly, establishing an office is not necessarily cheaper in rural areas given possible long drives to court and high-priced office space in towns with few corporate buildings. Phone, cell and Internet service can be pricey in sparsely populated areas. At the same time, [w]ith technology, a lawyer doesn't necessarily need the overhead of an office.

But after opening her Sedan office, McElroy only managed to pick up a handful of clients. "I think it's the economy," she says. "If people had more resources, I think they would have contacted me. I just couldn't hold out." McElroy closed her office in Sedan. She still has her Coffeyville office and is retooling her business model to make it work financially. "I also travel to Elk County [Howard, Kan.], which is pretty small. Really, most areas around here are small," she says. "Most attorneys in the area, of which there are not many, travel to other counties to represent people. That is what I do."

Sixty miles southeast of Minneapolis, Mazeppa is a prototypical American farm town of fewer than 1,000 residents, where visitors are just as likely to see tractors driving down the road as cars.

On his small Mazeppa farm, lawyer Bruce Cameron keeps chickens, geese and horses, raises hay and butchers animals for food. "A [farming] hobbyist compared to neighbors," Cameron is transitioning from his work as a senior programmer at a Mayo Clinic research lab to serving as a full-time solo attorney for Mazeppa farmers. With lawyering as his second career, Cameron is "still so green, I squeak."

He went to law school with dreams of being an IP lawyer but, he says, "not being in the top 10 percent of the class, being a second-career student and a 40-something competing with 20-somethings" put a damper on those plans. At the same time, his mentor, a solo practitioner in nearby Rochester, Minn., told Cameron that his own biggest mistake was not going solo right out of law school.

Meanwhile, whenever he chatted with his neighbors about his post-graduation plans, the conversation inevitably ended with Cameron hearing, "We could really use an attorney around here," he recalls. "With one little firm in a town north of me, my community was an underserved population. There's not a lot of competition."

He opened his doors at the beginning of the year, expecting to primarily handle wills and trusts, family law, bankruptcy and real estate matters. He bills clients $125 an hour, and he'll take on some small matters for a flat fee. Because his neighbors often tell him he'll be hired when "the second crop of hay is done," Cameron plans "to swing with the seasons." Cameron, who blogs about his solo practice at rurallawyer.com, worked out of his car and home at first, but eventually opened an actual office. "I had planned to meet my clients in their homes, but I did a market survey and found that the majority of people thought that having an office was more convenient," Cameron explains. "They go into town, see their bank, their feed dealer. Seeing a lawyer in town is convenient because they're already out. Also, farms are multigenerational and some people don't want their kids and grand-kids knowing their business. People also felt that if I was coming to them, they couldn't afford me."

Regarding his unorthodox career choice, Cameron quips, "I'm hoping it's a good idea once the abject terror wears off." In a more serious vein, he adds, "Out here, this is my community. I can serve it, I can make a profit doing it. It's exciting, scary, terrifying. On the other hand, it just felt right to do it."[10]

NOTES ON PATHS TO SOLO OR SMALL FIRM PRACTICE

1. ***Getting Started, Getting Clients, and Organizing the Practice.*** The Seron excerpt focused on three aspects of solo and small firm practice: getting started, getting clients, and organizing the practice. How do the lawyers in these excerpts approach these three fundamental aspects of law practice?

---

[10] Leslie A. Gordon, *Green Achers: The Lure of BigLaw and Big Cities May Stir Some. But for a Certain Solo Breed, the Small Town is the Place to Be,* ABA J., Nov. 2009, at 42.

2. ***Rewards and Challenges of Solo and Small Firm Practice.*** These studies and vignettes identify a number of features of solo or small firm practice that you may find appealing and some that may seem daunting. What are the major rewards and challenges of the practices? Which accounts of the practice do you find most plausible and which ones do you suspect may not reflect the realities of such practices in the area in which you live today?

3. ***The Economic Challenges of Small Businesses.*** A number of the lawyers in the vignettes identified autonomy and the ability to attain a reasonable work-life balance as the attractions of solo practice. And, yet, a number of the accounts of solo practice also identified the struggle to get clients and the razor-thin profit margins as the most significant challenges of the practice. Is there a tension between these two visions of solo practice? Notice the lawyers in the stories above whose practices were struggling, or who were sufficiently new that it was unclear at the time of the article whether they would survive financially. As we examine the following materials on ethical issues in solo and small firm practice, consider whether the financial pressures facing small law practices, which are of course shared with other small businesses, present unique challenges for lawyers because the ethical obligations they owe their clients may be more stringent than the ethical obligations other small business owners owe their clients.

C. ETHICAL ISSUES IN SOLO AND SMALL FIRM PRACTICE

Lawyers in solo and small firm practice are thought by some to be less competent and generally less ethical than lawyers in the large organizational client hemisphere. That perception may partly reflect pure animus of elites against the ethnic groups who tended to dominate the small firm sector in urban areas in the early and mid-twentieth century. It may also reflect a tendency of urbanites to dismiss rural areas as less sophisticated. But that perception may also have some basis in phenomena other than ethnic or regional bias. Jerome Carlin's classic study of solo practitioners found that the pressures of running a marginal practice did lead to ethical violations.[11] Lawyers in solo and very small firm practice are more likely than lawyers in large firms or government to be the subject of bar discipline. Is that because they commit more ethical violations? If so, are the ethical violations of solo lawyers attributable to personal traits of the lawyers or to the economic pressures of running a small business? Solo and small firm lawyers who are strapped for cash may be tempted to borrow from client accounts to make ends meet. Large well-established firms are rarely so short of cash, or so cut off from the ability to borrow from a bank, that they feel tempted to borrow money from client accounts in order to pay their secretaries' salary or their rent.

---

[11] JEROME E. CARLIN, LAWYERS ON THEIR OWN: THE SOLO PRACTITIONER IN AN URBAN SETTING (1994 rev. ed., originally published 1962), chapter 4.

In the materials that follow, we explore the ethical issues most salient in solo and small firm practice. In the process, we address some of the questions about the reasons for the disparity in bar discipline based on practice sector.

THE ETHICAL WORLD OF SOLO AND SMALL LAW FIRM PRACTITIONERS
Leslie C. Levin
41 Houston Law Review 309 (2004)

Solo and small firm lawyers are disciplined at a far greater rate than other lawyers. For example, in California, 78% of disciplinary cases prosecuted and completed in 2000–2001 were against solo practitioners, even though they represented only 23% of the lawyers practicing in that state. Similarly, 34% of Texas lawyers are solo practitioners, yet they receive 67% of all public sanctions. When Texas lawyers who practice in firms of two to five lawyers are added with solo practitioners, they make up 59% of all practicing lawyers yet they receive over 98% of all public discipline. Much of the discipline imposed on lawyers is for failure to communicate with clients and neglect of client matters.

Of course, the fact that solo and small firm practitioners receive a disproportionate amount of discipline does not, in itself, prove that these lawyers are less ethical than their colleagues who work in other practice settings. Individual clients with personal plight problems may be more likely than corporate clients to file discipline complaints against their lawyers. This may occur because individuals of moderate means have fewer mechanisms for redress when their lawyers engage in wrongdoing than do corporate clients. In addition, individuals are more likely to be emotionally invested in their personal plight matters or more adversely affected by their outcomes. It may be easier for under-financed discipline systems to successfully prosecute cases against solo or small firm practitioners—who have fewer resources to defend against these complaints—than it is to pursue large firm lawyers who may be able to hide behind the conduct of others. Finally, bias within the disciplinary system may account for a disproportionate amount of discipline being imposed on solo and small firm practitioners.

The discipline statistics provide only part of the picture, because many ethical issues arise in practice that are undetected by clients—who are the primary source of disciplinary complaints—or by the discipline system. In some cases, lawyers themselves do not know that bar rules have been violated. Even when complaints are made to disciplinary bodies, many violations of ethical rules are diverted outside the discipline system or are routinely underenforced. In order to get a better sense of the ethical world of these lawyers, it is therefore necessary to look beyond the statistics and more broadly into their practices and ethical decision-making.

In an effort to learn more about the ethical world and ethical decision-making of solo and small firm practitioners, I asked forty-one lawyers in the New York City metropolitan area about their professional development, office practices, and work experiences. I wanted to explore how lawyers who work on their own—or in very small practice settings—learn professional norms and go about resolving ethical questions.

The lawyers' practices ranged from the traditional solo or small firm "personal plight" practice to sophisticated transactional or corporate litigation practices. Most of the lawyers in the sample practiced in the areas of family law, personal injury, real estate, commercial work, workers' compensation, and trusts and estates. However, some of the other areas of practice included banking, criminal law, common carrier law, education law, intellectual property, and securities. Six lawyers in this group predominantly represented large corporations, sophisticated investors, or governmental entities such as school districts.

Although the lawyers practiced in a variety of physical settings, had significantly different types of clientele, and very different areas of expertise, many of them agreed that the tremendous pressure to bring in clients, along with cash flow, are the biggest challenges of working in a solo or small firm practice.

Specialization. Forty years ago most lawyers practiced in solo and small firm practices, and it was not unusual for those lawyers to maintain general practices in which they did real estate closings, personal injury cases, wills, and small corporate transactions. As the practice of law has become more complex and technology has increased the speed at which law is practiced, it has become both easier and harder for solo and small firm practitioners to keep up with changes in the law and to perform their work in a competent fashion. As a threshold matter, the ability of these lawyers to provide competent representation is affected by decisions they make about the number of areas in which they practice law, the number and types of clients they take on, their willingness to reach out to colleagues for assistance, and their diligence in staying abreast of changes in the law.

While some lawyers reported that when they started out in practice they did "everything," a number of them eventually made decisions about how many substantive areas of law they could handle competently, and most decided to limit their practices to a few substantive areas.

[O]ne third of the solo and small firm lawyers I interviewed were true general practitioners who regularly practiced in four or more areas. Most of them were male and worked outside of Manhattan. One important motivation for not limiting their work to a single practice area appears to be economic. Some lawyers who do not specialize are also motivated by the desire to provide "cradle to grave" service to their clients who rely on them heavily for advice.

The comments of a few of the lawyers I interviewed indicated that the pull to provide a range of legal services can be especially strong when the lawyer is rooted in the ethnic community or when the lawyer feels that she is a trusted family lawyer.

Advice Networks. For lawyers in solo and small firm practices, part of the key to performing competently is their ability to draw on the knowledge and judgment of other lawyers. Many of the lawyers I interviewed reported that they routinely reached out with questions that arose in practice, not only to other attorneys with whom they were formally affiliated, but also to suite mates and to attorneys outside their offices. Many lawyers reported having a group of attorneys—ranging in size from three to twelve lawyers—to whom they would reach out with questions. The group of attorneys to whom a lawyer reaches out when the lawyer has a question in practice is referred to here as the lawyer's advice network.

These lawyers rely on advice networks early in their careers to learn how to practice law, and they typically look first to lawyers with whom they are formally affiliated, to suite mates and to lawyer friends. As they become more experienced, many of them still rely on those networks for questions of judgment, when they want to learn about a judge or an adversary, or when they face legal questions they have not previously confronted.

Staying Up-to-Date on the Law. Most of the solo and small firm lawyers I interviewed believed that they were able to stay up-to-date on the law in the areas in which they practiced. More than half of them reported reading the *New York Law Journal*, the local daily legal newspaper, on a regular basis. The lawyers who specialized also often read a variety of trade and specialized legal materials because they felt it was essential to their representation of their clients. General practitioners relied heavily on written materials distributed by bar associations and on CLE courses, which are mandatory in New York, to stay current on the law in the areas in which they practiced.

Perception and Frequency of Ethical Challenges. Lawyers face ethical issues—in the broadest sense of the term—on a daily basis. Yet when asked about the "ethical issues" they encountered in their practice, the lawyers I interviewed rarely paused to ask what was meant by this deliberately ambiguous term. The lawyers' responses suggested that they usually interpreted the question to mean compliance with formal rules of professional conduct; only a handful of them interpreted it to include broader moral questions of right and wrong. More significantly, many of the lawyers I interviewed did not appear to think much about the ethical issues they encountered in their day-to-day work lives.

Of course, the reports by lawyers that they did not encounter many ethical issues in their practices does not mean that they did not actually confront ethical issues with some frequency. While a small number of the lawyers recognized that they constantly face ethical issues such as whether they represent their clients adequately, the responses of many of the lawyers I interviewed suggested that they simply did not think very much about legal ethics or that they did not consider the issues they confronted in moral or ethical terms.

The "Bad" Client.　The lawyers identified a wide array of ethical issues they encountered, but one of the most common ethical challenges encountered by solo and small firm practitioners was the problem of a client who wished to engage in some form of fraud. One attorney stated, "I've had clients ask me to change documents, change dates, change amounts, and I have had people ask me to do that. And you gotta be like, whoa." As another lawyer explained, "It's definitely clients who want to do stuff."

Some lawyers who frequently encountered clients who wished to engage in unethical conduct attributed this phenomenon to the nature of their practice specialty rather than to the size of their practice. For example, a lawyer who specialized in estate planning noted that many of his clients were in cash businesses and therefore "I'm constantly confronted with what my client is going to report." He observed, "Basically, my clients are hiring me to do things that are unethical." For this reason, "If you want to be a lawyer and you want to practice [tax] law, sometimes you have to bend the law."

Matrimonial lawyers reported that clients often sought to underreport their income on financial disclosure statements; real estate and commercial lawyers said that money "under the table" in purchase and sale transactions was common; and personal injury lawyers reported clients who faked the cause of their injury or who would ask about staying out of work longer than necessary to improve their chances of recovering a larger amount of money. These situations present some of the most serious ethical challenges for lawyers, as well as some of the greatest personal risks, because of the potential civil or criminal liability if they help their clients engage in fraud.

[S]ome solo and small firm lawyers reported that they had declined to represent certain clients for ethical reasons. The ability to turn away business is, however, a luxury reserved for lawyers who have developed economically successful law practices. As one successful estates lawyer explained, "Once you've been at this game for a while, I guess once you've amassed a couple of dollars, it's a lot easier to say no to a client than to take it on."

Office Management Problems. One common view of solo and small firm lawyers is that they often face problems arising from poor law office management, ranging from taking on too many matters, to poor filing and calendaring systems, to an inadequate understanding of the economics of law practice. These problems can directly contribute to neglect of client matters and failure to communicate with clients, which are among the most common reasons for lawyer discipline. Contrary to the conventional view, however, most of the lawyers I spoke with reported that they had control over their caseloads and calendaring and filing systems. Only a small number indicated that these were recurrent problems in their practices. [L]ife events can sometimes cause even a well-run practice to become temporarily unmanageable for lawyers, especially when they are working on their own. One of the solo practitioners I interviewed described how serious surgery had made it extremely difficult for him to keep his practice going while he was recovering, especially because he had no secretary. Another solo attorney described how a client had threatened to file a grievance against her because she had failed to promptly handle a client matter after the unexpected death of the lawyer's husband. In these cases the lack of a partner, associate, or paralegal made the task of handling client matters diligently virtually impossible for periods of time, even for the most conscientious lawyers.

The office arrangements and affiliations described by the lawyers I interviewed presented potential—yet mostly unrecognized—conflict of interest problems. Most of the lawyers I interviewed had no formal system for checking conflicts of interest among their clients, relying on an "in your head" method when new clients sought representation.

Resolving Ethical Problems in Practice. [T]he lawyers I interviewed learned informal bar norms through their communities of practice, starting with observations of other lawyers and conversations within their law offices. Indeed, their office-sharing arrangements often create rich social environments from which they learn a great deal during their early years in practice.

Although many of the early lessons are acquired through listening and passive observation, when new lawyers confronted serious ethical issues such as client fraud, some of them talked about reaching out to mentors or advice networks for guidance. For example, one lawyer told the story of running down the hall to consult with her partner, who was also her father-in-law, when she suspected that a long-time firm client had manufactured a personal injury claim. A solo practitioner explained that he was about to call a lawyer in his advice network to talk about a client who wanted to testify falsely at an upcoming criminal trial. Not surprisingly, sometimes the advice the lawyers received conformed with formal bar rules and sometimes it did not.

It appears that the conclusions that these lawyers reach the first few times they confront a particular ethical problem may provide a template of sorts that is used throughout their legal careers absent an extraordinary event, such as a disciplinary complaint, that may cause them to reconsider their practices. For example, some older lawyers described a stock response to ethical issues that was developed by watching a mentor or employer during their early years in practice. One lawyer described his response to what he said was the weekly problem of workers' compensation clients who were interested in defrauding insurance carriers: "My policy, which I inherited from my father, is basically to throw them out immediately, and I do. They always manage to find someone that will represent them but we won't."

Although it is possible that the lawyers' own personal morality also affects their responses to this issue, at least some of the lawyers I interviewed indicated that their personal morality did not play much of a role in their responses to this problem. Indeed, one young lawyer who self-described herself as a "good person" and who claimed, "if something doesn't feel right, I'm not going to do it," routinely looked the other way when cash was passed under the table in real estate transactions. Regardless of how lawyers arrive at their initial determination of how to handle an ethical challenge, the responses of the lawyers I interviewed suggest that once the "answer" to particular ethical issues is determined, it often continues to guide the lawyer in practice.

Psychological Processes and Ethical Decision-Making. What I found striking is that the lawyers I interviewed rarely spoke of lessons learned in law school when they described their ethical decision-making. Instead, they seemed to form their conclusions about how to resolve certain ethical questions during their early years in practice. Colleagues and mentors often affected their decision-making when first confronted with ethical issues. Their early conclusions appear to stay with these lawyers as they move through practice. Once these lawyers become more experienced, they do not seem to reconsider ethical questions they have previously addressed.

Lessons from social psychology help explain these observations. The psychological pressure on individuals to conform to the behavior of a group can be powerful. Although solo and small firm practitioners view themselves as "independent," these lawyers often operate within—and are influenced by—a rich social environment comprised of suite mates and members of their advice networks. Social psychologists have found that a group is more effective at inducing conformity if (1) it consists of experts; (2) the members are important to the individual; or (3) the members are comparable to the actor in some way. Certainly within collegial office-sharing arrangements or tightly-knit legal communities or practice specialties, many young lawyers would view the other lawyers with whom they come in contact as experts, as "important" colleagues, mentors, sources of referrals, or, at a minimum, as comparable to the young lawyer in some ways. Therefore, it would not be surprising that the psychological pressure to conform to certain types of behaviors would be powerful in this context. Whether the psychological pressure to conform to certain behaviors in large firm practice is equally strong is unclear.

The Perception of Formal Rules and Discipline.   The lawyers I interviewed view certain formal bar rules and the lawyer discipline system with open skepticism. Historically, solo and small firm lawyers have felt that some of the formal rules were written to limit their business-getting opportunities and they may be, to some degree, correct. These lawyers also harbor a concern that solo and small firm attorneys are unfairly targeted for discipline more often than lawyers who practice in other settings.

When skepticism about formal rules is coupled with concerns about the fairness of the discipline system, the likelihood of lawyer compliance with formal rules is further reduced. [S]ome of the lawyers I interviewed believe that bias arises not only in the disproportionate prosecution of solo and small firm practitioners, but also in the types of matters prosecuted and in the discipline actually imposed. Under-enforcement of formal bar rules that are clear and specific may also contribute to this perception. A few of the lawyers I interviewed questioned why prosecutors rarely face lawyer discipline or why large firm lawyers are rarely disciplined for clearly impermissible conduct. Of course, discipline sanctions may be imposed on these lawyers more often than other lawyers realize because the discipline may be private. But when the perception persists that the rules are not enforced—or that they are selectively enforced—this can lead to disrespect of formal bar rules and cynicism about the efficacy and purpose of the discipline system.

NOTES ON LEVIN

1.   ***What Accounts for the Disparity in Rates of Discipline?*** Why do you think lawyers in solo and small firm practice are disciplined at much higher rates than lawyers in other types of practice?

2.   ***Are Solo Practitioners Disciplined Too Much or Large Firm Lawyers Too Little, or Neither?*** How would we know whether the problem in the disparity of rates of discipline, if there is one, is that solo practitioners are disciplined too much or that the bar hasn't done enough to regulate incompetent or unscrupulous lawyers in other practice settings? What is the relationship between ethics rules and bar regulatory processes, on the one

hand, and the social structure and politics of the American legal profession, on the other?

3. ***Ethical Norms and the First Job.*** Seron and, especially, Levin identified the first job out of law school as being very important in teaching skills and norms. Do you think the first job is more or less significant for small firm and solo practitioners as compared to other lawyers? Is the phenomenon something that the bar should focus on in its efforts to ensure that lawyers are competent and ethical?

4. ***Should the Bar Prohibit Solo Practice?*** Professor Richard Abel, an eminent scholar of the legal profession, has proposed that lawyers be prohibited from practicing entirely solo. That is, every lawyer should be required to affiliate with at least one other lawyer in order to protect both the lawyers and their clients from the sort of problems identified by Seron and Levin. What do you think of that proposal? Does Levin suggest that informal affiliation may already be occurring? How might the bar build on the informal affiliations to protect lawyers and clients from the hazards of truly solo practice?

* * *

PROBLEM 21–1

If you were on a state or local bar association committee tasked to improve the ethics compliance of solo and very small firm practitioners, what changes would you propose? What obstacles would you foresee to the adoption of your proposals? Consider at least the following specific rule violations: (a) failure to communicate with clients (Model Rule 1.4); (b) incompetence (Model Rule 1.1); and (c) commingling the client's funds with the lawyer's funds (Model Rule 1.15). On this last point, note that one of the most common bases on which lawyers are disciplined or disbarred is for violations of the prohibition on commingling funds. Most lawyers disciplined for such violations practice solo or in small firms. Read Model Rule 1.15 and the Comment to it carefully and consider whether the problem is difficulty of understanding the rule or the temptation to violate it.

D. SUMMARY

In this chapter, we studied the nature of solo and small firm practice and some of the major ethical challenges lawyers face in this practice setting. Urban, suburban, and rural solo and small firm practice differ, and the ethnic and religious heterogeneity that has long characterized the sector in urban areas is less in some rural areas. We examined the ethical decision-making of solo and small firm practitioners and identified the rule violations for which they are most likely to be disciplined. We considered the reasons why they are more likely to face bar discipline than are lawyers in large firms. We concluded by considering proposals to improve ethics rules compliance in this sector.

CHAPTER 22

ADVERTISING AND SOLICITATION

■ ■ ■

A. INTRODUCTION

Controversies surrounding lawyer advertising and solicitation deeply divide the bar. Most lawyers in private practice, or the firms in which they practice, take measures to ensure that prospective clients are aware of their services. But the methods that lawyers use to market their services vary greatly, and different conceptions of "professionalism" attach to these different practices. The forms of advertising and solicitation used by some lawyers who represent individuals and small businesses are a constant source of complaint by other lawyers, who argue that such methods are undignified and harm the overall reputation of the bar. Even within the hemisphere of the bar representing individuals and small businesses, attitudes vary. Lawyers who are still developing their reputations sometimes depend on advertising to attract clients. That is also true of lawyers who specialize in class actions, whose potential members may not share social ties with the lawyers or each other. Lawyers with high positions in referral networks do not need to advertise because they can depend on other lawyers to send them a steady stream of clients.

Marketing takes much different form in the big firm sector. Large firm lawyers tend not to advertise on billboards, radio, television, or bus-stop benches, and they do not distribute flyers or contact accident victims. But large firms often distribute newsletters on legal topics to key clients and prospective clients and hold seminars to display their lawyers' expertise. They typically employ public relations and marketing experts who ensure that the achievements of the firm and its lawyers receive publicity. They facilitate the placement of profiles of their leading partners in business publications and generally seek to maintain a high profile in relevant markets. Large firm lawyers also engage in "client development"—a form of solicitation—by showcasing their expertise in meetings with prospective clients, and by socializing with them over meals and sports events.

Advertising and solicitation practices are closely intertwined, and the bar's efforts to regulate these practices are interrelated. We nevertheless deal with them separately in this chapter because the organized bar and the courts are more tolerant of advertising than of solicitation. With respect to both advertising and solicitation, as well as new forms of marketing through the Internet and social media, we consider the use, importance, and acceptance of the practices in different sectors of the bar. We also examine the relevant law, which includes U.S. Supreme Court decisions on the constitutional boundaries of lawyer advertising and solicitation regulations, as well relevant provisions of the Model Rules and several state variations. This chapter addresses advertising first, followed by in-person solicitation, and then marketing through the Internet and social media.

B. ADVERTISING

Lawyer advertising was common in the nineteenth century, when handbills and newspaper advertisements were the prevailing methods of reaching prospective clients. Many respected lawyers, including Abraham Lincoln and David Hoffman (author of one of the earliest ethics codes), advertised their services.[1] At the beginning of the twentieth century, however, bar leaders began to target commercial practices, such as advertising and solicitation. The ABA's 1908 Canons of Ethics adopted a broad prohibition on lawyer advertising, reflecting the elite bar's view that advertising was crass, undignified, and incompatible with a vision of professionalism according to which clients should find lawyers without any need for lawyers to seek them out. That essentially remained the bar's position until 1977, when the U.S. Supreme Court ruled that lawyers have a First Amendment right to engage in truthful advertising. From 1908 until 1977, all kinds of lawyers' promotional efforts received close scrutiny by the organized bar—from the size of signs marking law office doors to lawyers' use of business cards, stationery letterhead, and greeting cards.

In the late 1960s, various groups within and outside of the profession began to mobilize to challenge prohibitions on lawyer advertising. Consumer advocates, with support from the Federal Trade Commission and Department of Justice, argued that consumers benefit from the information contained in advertising. Lawyers associated with the movement to expand the availability of legal services to the poor sought to develop new modes of delivering legal services more cheaply, and they claimed that advertising was essential for establishing high volume, low margin practices.

---

[1]   See LORI B. ANDREWS, BIRTH OF A SALESMAN: LAWYER ADVERTISING AND SOLICITATION 1 (1980).

In *Bates v. State Bar of Arizona*,[2] the Supreme Court struck down Arizona's ban on newspaper or other media advertising by lawyers in a case involving a lawyer disciplined for placing a newspaper ad offering "legal services at very reasonable prices." The decision emphasized not only lawyers' free speech rights but also potential advantages to consumers, who might gain useful information from lawyer advertisements and who might benefit from lower prices resulting from greater competition in the legal services market. By the time the Supreme Court considered *Bates*, similar challenges were pending in ten jurisdictions.[3] One of those challenges was brought by the founders of the Los Angeles franchise law firm of Jacoby & Meyers, seeking a ruling that it could use marketing practices that were essential to its business model of providing standardized fees for basic legal services.[4]

Debates within the bar over lawyer advertising continue to reflect differences in the interests of the various sectors of the profession and the clientele they serve. Professor Geoffrey Hazard has argued that "[p]eople of means and education" have no need for advertisements because they know when to consult a lawyer and have the social connections to find one:

> For those of us in the middle and upper income and educated class, lawyer advertising is superfluous. Worse, it offends our sense of worth, dignity and self-esteem. We are competent and reliable, and self-contained and professionally modest. Lawyer advertising is loud, pushy, and undignified, and there is no reason for it.[5]

For clients in this category, a lawyer's reputation is sufficient to create the connection. Hazard argues, however, that for low-income people, reputation may not serve that connecting function, and advertising then becomes critical:

> Lawyer advertising is for low income people what lawyer "reputation" is for middle and upper income people: A means of bringing to mind the need to seek a lawyer and the name of a specific lawyer to turn to.[6]

---

[2]　433 U.S. 350 (1977).

[3]　See William Hornsby, *Clashes of Class and Cash: Battles from the 150 Years War To Govern Client Development*, 37 ARIZ. ST. L.J. 255, 264–65 n.44 (2005).

[4]　See *About Southern California Office, Jacoby & Meyers Law Offices*, http://www.jacoby meyers.com/southern-california-office.html (last visited Dec. 9, 2012) (for its "grand opening," the clinic invited a consumer group to hold an open house at its offices, located in a San Fernando Valley shopping center, and sought news coverage, which led to trouble with the California bar on the ground that the clinic was engaging in prohibited advertising).

[5]　Geoffrey C. Hazard, *Comment on Proposed Arizona Advertising Rule* (July 2, 1991) (quoted in Van O'Steen, *Bates v. State Bar of Arizona: The Personal Account of a Party and the Consumer Benefits of Lawyer Advertising*," ARIZ. ST. L. J., Summer 2005.)

[6]　*Id.*

One of the lawyers who brought the challenge in *Bates v. State Bar of Arizona* has similarly highlighted class divisions reflected in disagreements over lawyer advertising: "For those in lower income and less well-connected classes, advertising is fresh information about serious legal needs that people may have right now. Stifling lawyer advertising is class legislation in the name of professional dignity."[7] During several decades following *Bates*, the Supreme Court struck down a series of prohibitions on truthful advertising and written solicitation, while identifying some types of permitted regulation. For example, in *In re R.M.J.*,[8] the Court struck down a ban on professional announcements distributed to prospective clients but held that the bar could require that any such communications be marked as an "advertisement" to ensure that clients were not misled. *Zauderer v. Office of Disciplinary Counsel*[9] held that the First Amendment protected the use of a newspaper ad containing a drawing of the Dalkon Shield contraceptive device and advising readers that the law firm was suing on behalf of women injured by the device. *Zauderer* dismissed the idea that upholding the dignity of the profession was a substantial governmental interest:

> [W]e are unsure that the State's desire that attorneys maintain their dignity in their communications with the public is an interest substantial enough to justify the abridgment of their First Amendment rights. [T]he mere possibility that some members of the population might find advertising embarrassing or offensive cannot justify suppressing it. The same must hold true for advertising that some members of the bar might find beneath their dignity.

As we will see in the materials on solicitation, however, the Supreme Court has since endorsed the idea that a governmental interest in upholding the public's respect for the profession might justify some types of regulation.

Today, the Model Rules permit most truthful advertising. Rule 7.1 provides that "[a] lawyer shall not make a false or misleading communication about the lawyer or the lawyer's services. A communication is false or misleading if it contains a material misrepresentation of fact or law, or omits a fact necessary to make the statement considered as a whole not materially misleading." Rule 7.2(a) provides that lawyers "may advertise services through written, recorded or electronic communication, including public media," subject to Rule 7.1 and Rule 7.3, which restricts direct contact with prospective clients. (We

---

[7]   Van O'Steen, *Bates v. State Bar of Arizona: The Personal Account of a Party and the Consumer Benefits of Lawyer Advertising*, ARIZ. ST. L. J., Summer 2005.

[8]   455 U.S. 191 (1982).

[9]   471 U.S. 626 (1985).

explore Rule 7.3 below in the section on solicitation). Rule 7.4 limits what lawyers can say about their fields of practice and specialization.

First Amendment Limits on the Regulation of Lawyer Advertising

- In *Bates v. State Bar of Arizona* (1977), the Supreme Court held that an Arizona ban on newspaper or other media advertising violated the First Amendment.

Model Rules on Advertising

- **Rule 7.1** provides that a lawyer shall not make a false or misleading communication about the lawyer or the lawyer's services.

- **Rule 7.2(a)** provides that a lawyer may advertise services through written, recorded or electronic communication, including public media, but all such communications are subject to certain restrictions, including Rule 7.3, which governs direct contact with prospective clients.

Although it is now clear that flat bans on written advertising are constitutionally impermissible, significant uncertainty remains about what types of regulation still pass constitutional muster. The Model Rules establish fairly clear guidance about what is allowed, but many states have departed from the Model Rules' advertising provisions, and some have adopted much more restrictive regulations. Some states have attempted to ban particular advertising techniques on the ground that they may be misleading. Among the techniques that some states have banned are client testimonials, celebrity endorsements, the use of actors or models portraying clients, jingles, monikers (such as "Heavy Hitters"), and particular types of unverifiable representations regarding quality and results.

Many advocates for greater restrictions on lawyer advertising argue that some ads convey no helpful information to consumers and are just so crass and undignified that they tarnish the reputation of the profession. Consider some of these "noteworthy" advertisements that have appeared since *Bates*:

- An ad announcing a "HOLIDAY SPECIAL . . . Get that spouse of yours some'in he or she's been wantin' for a long time . . . A Deeeevorce . . . $150 Bucks . . . Happy Holidays."

- An advertisement advising readers that the law firm settles most claims quickly and "$ucce$$fully" and that where settlement doesn't succeed, the firm aggressively sues opponents. Prospective clients should call the firm at 1-800-SUE-THEM.

- An ad featuring a female model in a bikini and boxing gloves with the slogan "Protect yourself at all times."

- A television commercial featuring the lawyer, Ken Hur, the founder of a firm ("the Legal Clinic") in Madison, Wisconsin, dressed in a prison uniform, being escorted by guards to the electric chair. When guards ask if he has any last words, he answers: "I should have called the Legal Clinic."

- Lawyers with an admiralty practice marketed their services to sailors and fisherman by distributing condoms in packages shaped like oversized matchbooks marked with their name, phone number, and slogan: "Saving Seamen the Old-Fashioned Way."[10]

- A huge billboard in a night club district in Chicago featuring a woman in lingerie on one side of the billboard and a bare-chested man on the other, with the name of a law firm in the middle, followed by "Life is Short, Get a Divorce."[11]

- An ad offering a deal on divorce work: "Buy one divorce, get the next one half off. End the misery today!"[12]

Would you advocate banning any of these advertisements? If so, on what grounds?

Some advocates of greater restrictions on lawyer advertising frame their arguments, not in terms of dignity or taste, or protecting consumers from misleading ads, but rather in terms of maintaining public confidence in the fairness of the justice system. Would such concerns justify a prohibition on advertisements in which plaintiffs' personal injury lawyers portray themselves as pit bulls with spiked collars? Or a television ad in which an attorney portrays himself as a childhood "bully" who is now putting his bullying skills to use in "successfully shaking down the big insurance companies to help clients like you"?[13] Vincent Buzard, past president of the New York State Bar Association and creator of the task force that drafted new rules adopted in New York in 2007, has argued that "[i]nappropriate lawyer advertising causes the public and the legal system problems because it convinces people to believe that the legal system is some kind of lottery—the idea of 'come to us and you'll be wealthy.'" Opponents of restrictions on lawyer advertising tend to argue that justifications based in maintaining public confidence in the integrity of the legal system are insufficiently weighty to support advertising

---

[10] The first five of these examples come from William Hornsby, *Clashes of Classes*, ARIZ. STATE L. J. 255, 265–66 (2005).

[11] *See* Dirk Johnson, *Look at This Ad But Don't Get Any Ideas*, N.Y. TIMES, May 13, 2007.

[12] *Divorce Lawyer Has a Buy One, Get One Half Off Deal*, HUFFINGTON POST, August 26, 2013.

[13] *See* Ad for Attorney Jeff Zarzynski, http://www.youtube.com/embed/AlarMN5SCs4.

restrictions. A small firm lawyer who opposed the New York rules argued that advertising restrictions "tie[ ] our hands in terms of being able to tell prospective clients who we are."[14]

Over the past several decades, there has been a good deal of litigation over the constitutionality of various types of lawyer advertising regulations. The Supreme Court has upheld state bans on radio and television advertisements that employ emotional appeals, dramatizations, or celebrity endorsements. The Florida Supreme Court allowed the Florida Bar to prevent a law firm from using the image of a pit bull in its advertisements and 1-800-PIT-BULL as its telephone number, finding that "an advertising device that connotes combativeness and viciousness without providing accurate and objectively verifiable factual information falls outside the protections of the First Amendment.[15] In 2006, the New Jersey Supreme Court upheld a bar ruling that prohibited attorneys from mentioning a lawyer's designation as a "Super Lawyer" or one of the "Best Lawyers in America" by a commercial rating service in advertisements,[16] but in 2009 the court vacated the ruling, citing concerns about its constitutionality.[17] (It is not uncommon for large elite firms to prominently note their lawyers' listing in "Super Lawyers" and "Best Lawyers" rankings on their web pages.[18]) In 2011, a Florida federal district court struck down rules that were among the strictest in the country—prohibiting lawyers from using a broad range of common advertising techniques—jingles, certain slogans deemed "manipulative" and background noises.[19]

Another recent challenge focused on New York's newly enacted advertising rules, which barred portrayals of fictitious law firms, certain types of client testimonials, attention-getting techniques unrelated to attorney competence, and trade names or nicknames that implied an ability to get results. The lawyers whose advertisements were the subject of this challenge, Alexander, Alexander & Catalano, used a variety of such advertising gimmicks. In one television commercial, James Alexander and his partner portrayed themselves as giants looming over

---

[14] Dick Dahl, *New York Weighs Tough New Lawyer Advertising Rules*, LAWYERS WEEKLY USA, Aug. 14, 2006.

[15] The Florida Bar v. Pape, 918 So.2d 240 (Fla. 2005), reh'g granted (2006), cert. denied, 547 U.S. 1041 (2006).

[16] *See* Kris W. Scibiorski & Dana E. Sullivan, *Super Lawyers; Call yourself one and you're in super trouble*, N. J. LAWYER, July 24, 2006.

[17] *In re Opinion 39*, 197 N.J. 66 (2008).

[18] *See e.g., Cravath Ranked in New York Super Lawyer*, Nov. 23, 2011, at http://www. cravath.com/Cravath-Ranked-in-New-York-Super-Lawyers-11-23-2011/; "More Sidley Austin Lawyers Named in the 'Top 100 Washington D.C. Area Super Lawyers 2011' Than Any Other Firm," http://www.sidley.com/More-Sidley-Austin-Lawyers-Named-in-the-Top-100-Washington-DC-Area-Super-Lawyers-2011-Than-Any-Other-Firm-05-27-2011/.

[19] *See* Brian Baxter, *Judge Finds Certain Florida Bar Rules on Attorney Ads Too Vague*, AM. L. DAILY, Oct. 4, 2011.

local buildings and running so quickly to a client's house that they appear as blurs on the screen. They leaped onto roofs (to battle injustice in high places?) and provided advice about an insurance claim to space aliens.[20] The firm's ads also frequently included the firm's slogan, "heavy hitters," and phrases like "think big" and "we'll give you a big helping hand."

As you read the Second Circuit's opinion, consider the justifications offered for New York's restrictions on lawyer advertisements. Which justifications are persuasive to you and which are not? Are these justifications equally compelling in all sectors of the legal services market?

ALEXANDER, ALEXANDER & CATALANO LLC v. CAHILL
598 F.3d 79 (2d Cir. 2010)

CALABRESI, J:

New York adopted new rules prohibiting certain types of attorney advertising and solicitation, which were to take effect February 1, 2007. Plaintiffs challenged these provisions as violating the First Amendment.

<u>Background</u>. The Plaintiffs-Appellees-Cross-Appellants ("Plaintiffs") are an individual (James Alexander), a law firm (Alexander & Catalano), and a not-for-profit consumer rights organization (Public Citizen). Alexander is the managing partner of Alexander & Catalano, a personal injury law firm with offices in Syracuse and Rochester. Alexander & Catalano use various broadcast and print media to advertise. Prior to the adoption of New York's new attorney advertising rules, the firm's commercials often contained jingles and special effects, including wisps of smoke and blue electrical currents surrounding the firm's name. Firm advertisements also featured dramatizations, comical scenes, and special effects. To date, no disciplinary actions have been brought against the firm or its lawyers based on firm advertising. The new rules, however, caused the firm to halt its advertisements for fear of such action.

A press release explained that the new rules were designed to protect consumers "against inappropriate solicitations or potentially misleading ads, as well as overly aggressive marketing," and to "benefit the bar by ensuring that the image of the legal profession is maintained at the highest possible level."

We consider below a subset of these final rules:

N.Y. Comp. Codes R. & Regs., tit. 22, § 1200.0(c):

---

[20] See Nathan Koppel, *Objection! Funny Legal Ads Draw Censure: Sharks, Pit Bulls Out In Florida; UFO Clients Get the Ax in Syracuse*, http://online.wsj.com/article/SB1202342297339 49051.html.

(c) An advertisement shall not: (1) include an endorsement of, or testimonial about, a lawyer or law firm from a client with respect to a matter that is still pending; . . . (3) include the portrayal of a judge, the portrayal of a fictitious law firm, the use of a fictitious name to refer to lawyers not associated together in a law firm, or otherwise imply that lawyers are associated in a law firm if that is not the case; . . . (5) rely on techniques to obtain attention that demonstrate a clear and intentional lack of relevance to the selection of counsel, including the portrayal of lawyers exhibiting characteristics clearly unrelated to legal competence; . . . (7) utilize a nickname, moniker, motto or trade name that implies an ability to obtain results in a matter. . . .

<u>Discussion</u>. The Supreme Court has established a four-part inquiry for determining whether regulations of commercial speech are consistent with the First Amendment:

[1] whether the expression is protected by the First Amendment. For commercial speech to come within that provision, it at least must concern lawful activity and not be misleading. Next, we ask [2] whether the asserted governmental interest is substantial. If both inquiries yield positive answers, we must determine [3] whether the regulation directly advances the governmental interest asserted, and [4] whether it is not more extensive than is necessary to serve that interest. *Central Hudson Gas & Elec. Corp. v. Pub. Serv. Comm'n of N.Y.*

<u>The Disputed Provisions Regulate Commercial Speech Protected by the First Amendment</u>. Defendants argue strenuously to us that New York's content-based restrictions regulate speech that is not entitled to First Amendment protection at all.

The Supreme Court first recognized attorney advertising as within the scope of protected speech in *Bates v. State Bar of Arizona.*, in which the Court invalidated a ban on price advertising. The Court found that states cannot ban truthful advertising about what services the lawyer provides at specified prices. In so doing, the Court reserved the question of whether similar protection would extend to advertising claims as to the quality of services [that] are not susceptible of measurement or verification.

[T]he content-based restrictions in the disputed provisions regulate commercial speech protected by the First Amendment. The speech that Defendants' content-based restrictions seeks to regulate—that which is irrelevant, unverifiable, and non-informational—is not inherently false, deceptive, or misleading. Defendants' own press release described its proposed rules as protecting consumers against "*potentially* misleading ads." This is insufficient to place these restrictions beyond the scope of First Amendment scrutiny.

Central Hudson and the Content-Based Regulations.

Substantial Interest. Under the second prong of *Central Hudson*, the State must identify a substantial interest in support of its regulation[s]. Defendants proffered a state interest in "prohibiting attorney advertisements from containing deceptive or misleading content." The report by the New York State Bar Association's Task Force on Lawyer Advertising, which the State considered in formulating its new rules, identified protecting the public "by prohibiting advertising and solicitation practices that disseminate false or misleading information" as one of its key concerns. This state interest is substantial—indeed, states have a generally unfettered right to prohibit inherently or actually misleading commercial speech. The disputed regulations therefore survive the second prong of the *Central Hudson* analysis.

Materially Advance. The penultimate prong of the *Central Hudson* test requires that a regulation impinging upon commercial expression directly advance the state interest involved. The state's burden with respect to this prong is not satisfied by mere speculation or conjecture; rather, a governmental body seeking to sustain a restriction on commercial speech must demonstrate that the harms it recites are real and that its restrictions will in fact alleviate them to a material degree.

[The court found that defendants had failed to produce evidence that consumers have been misled by the types of promotional devices barred by the disputed provisions. It found that client testimonials are not inherently misleading, especially when they include a disclaimer emphasizing that past results to not necessarily indicate future performance. Regarding the prohibition of "techniques to obtain attention that demonstrate a clear and intentional lack of relevance to the selection of counsel, including the portrayal of lawyers exhibiting characteristics clearly unrelated to legal competence," the court found that defendants had produced no evidence that the techniques it sought to prevent seemed likely to mislead prospective clients.]

The sorts of gimmicks that this rule appears designed to reach— such as Alexander & Catalano's wisps of smoke, blue electrical currents, and special effects—do not actually seem likely to mislead. It is true that Alexander and his partner are not giants towering above local buildings; they cannot run to a client's house so quickly that they appear as blurs; and they do not actually provide legal assistance to space aliens. But given the prevalence of these and other kinds of special effects in advertising and entertainment, we cannot seriously believe—purely as a matter of "common sense"—that ordinary individuals are likely to be misled into thinking that these advertisements depict true characteristics. Indeed, some of these gimmicks, while seemingly irrelevant, may actually serve "important communicative functions: [they] attract [ ] the attention of the audience to the advertiser's message, and [they] may also serve to impart information directly." *Zauderer.* Plaintiffs assert that they use attention-getting techniques to "communicate ideas in an easy-to-understand form, to attract viewer interest, to give emphasis, and to make information more memorable." Defendants provide no evidence to the contrary; nor do they provide evidence that consumers have, in fact, been misled by these or similar advertisements."

Narrowly Tailored. The final prong of *Central Hudson* asks whether the "fit" between the goals identified (the state's interests) and the means chosen to advance these goals is reasonable; the fit need not be perfect. [L]aws restricting commercial speech need only be tailored in a *reasonable manner* to serve a substantial state interest in order to survive First Amendment scrutiny. Nonetheless, restrictions upon [potentially deceptive speech] may be no broader than reasonably necessary to prevent the deception. [A] state may not impose a prophylactic ban on potentially misleading speech merely to spare itself the trouble of distinguishing the truthful from the false, the helpful from the misleading, and the harmless from the harmful.

On this basis, even if we were to find that all of the disputed restrictions survived scrutiny under *Central Hudson's* third prong, each would fail the final inquiry because each wholly prohibits a category of advertising speech that is *potentially* misleading, but is not inherently or actually misleading in all cases. Because these advertising techniques are no more than potentially misleading, the categorical nature of New York's prohibitions would alone be enough to render the prohibitions invalid.

NOTES ON ALEXANDER, ALEXANDER & CATALANO LLC V. CAHILL

1. ***Are the Ads Really Misleading?*** Do you think that any serious argument can be made that the advertising techniques used by Alexander, Alexander and Catalano are likely to mislead consumers?

2. ***Which Lawyer Ads Receive First Amendment Protection?*** Return to the examples of lawyer advertising in the passage preceding the *Alexander* case. Which would be constitutionally protected from state regulation under the Second Circuit's analysis? Do you agree that they should be protected from regulation?

C. SOLICITATION

Solicitation of potential clients has long been regarded by the elite bar as demeaning to the profession, in part because it was associated with "stirring up litigation." Prohibitions on barratry (instigating quarrels and frivolous litigation) and champerty (an agreement to finance and carry the lawsuit in return for a percentage of the recovery) date to medieval times in England. But solicitation was largely unregulated in the United States throughout the nineteenth century. In the early twentieth century, prominent leaders of the legal profession targeted lawyers who, in their "eager quest for lucre," undermined the profession's nobler purposes.[21] Canon 27 of the ABA Canons of Professional Ethics provided that "[t]he most worthy and effective advertisement possible, even for a young lawyer, is the establishment of a well-merited reputation for professional capacity and fidelity to trust. This cannot be forced, but must be the outcome of character and conduct. [S]olicitation of business by circulars or advertisements, or by personal communications, or interviews not warranted by personal relations, is unprofessional." Jerold Auerbach describes how the bar's adoption of prohibitions on solicitation affected different strata of the legal profession:

> [A prohibition on solicitation] rewarded the lawyer whose law-firm partners and social contacts made advertising unnecessary at the same time that it attributed inferior character and unethical behavior to attorneys who could not afford to sit passively in their offices awaiting clients; it thus penalized both them and their potential clients, who might not know whether they had a valid legal claim or where, if they did, to obtain legal assistance. The canon prohibiting solicitation discriminated against those in personal injury practice, who bore the pejorative label "ambulance chasers."
>
> "Ambulance chasing" was never precisely defined. As a term of art it ostracized plaintiffs' lawyers who, representing outsiders to the economic system, solicited certain types of business. Once fee-hungry ambulance chasers were isolated, they would be excluded from professional respectability by a series of discriminatory ethical judgments. Their methods of solicitation were condemned, but nothing was said about company claim agents who visited hospitalized workers to urge a quick and inexpensive settlement.[22]

Individuals and organizations representing poor and middle class people, as well as racial and ethnic minorities, were frequently denounced by bar leaders as unprofessional and unethical. State bar disciplinary authorities often targeted such advocates for discipline for prohibited

---

[21] 29 A.B.A. Rep. 601–02 (1906) (quoted in Alexander Schwab, *In Defense of Ambulance Chasing: A Critique of Model Rule of Professional Conduct 7.3*, 29 YALE L. & POLY' REV. 603, 609 (2011)).

[22] JEROLD S. AUERBACH, UNEQUAL JUSTICE: LAWYERS AND SOCIAL CHANGE IN MODERN AMERICA 41–50 (1976).

solicitation.[23] For example, southern states attempted to prevent the NAACP from bringing litigation challenging segregation in schools and places of public accommodation by preventing NAACP lawyers from soliciting discrimination victims to serve as plaintiffs. (As discussed below, see *In re Primus,* the U.S. Supreme Court struck down one of those restrictions as applied to the NAACP.)

The governing rule in most jurisdictions today is Rule 7.3. It provides that "[a] lawyer shall not by in-person, live telephone or real-time electronic contact solicit professional employment from a prospective client when a significant motive for the lawyer's doing so is the lawyer's pecuniary gain, unless the person contacted is a lawyer or has a family, close personal, or prior professional relationship with the lawyer. (Rule 7.3(a)). It also prohibits soliciting employment from a prospective client if the client has made it known that he or she does not wish to be solicited (Rule 7.3(b)), and it includes a requirement that all communications targeted to a prospective client known to be in need of legal services in a particular matter must include the words "advertising material" on the outside envelope, and at the beginning and ending of any recorded or electronic communication (Rule 7.3(c)).

What policies underlie Rule 7.3's prohibition of certain types of solicitations? Are those justifications compelling, and, if so, are they compelling in all practice contexts to which Rule 7.3 applies?

1.   IN-PERSON SOLICITATION

The constitutional boundaries on the regulation of lawyers' in-person solicitation were set forth in companion cases decided on the same day in 1978: *Ohralik v. Ohio State Bar Association* and *In re Primus.*

OHRALIK V. OHIO STATE BAR ASSOCIATION
United States Supreme Court
436 U.S. 447 (1978)

MR. JUSTICE POWELL delivered the opinion of the Court.

In *Bates v. State Bar of Arizona,* this Court held that truthful advertising of "routine" legal services is protected by the First and Fourteenth Amendments against blanket prohibition by a State. The Court expressly reserved the question of the permissible scope of regulation of in-person solicitation of clients. Today we answer part of the question so reserved, and hold that the State—or the Bar acting with state authorization—constitutionally may discipline a lawyer for

---

[23] Susan D. Carle, *Race, Class, and Legal Ethics in the Early NAACP (1910–1920),* LAW & HIST. REV., Jan. 15, 2002, at 97.

soliciting clients in person, for pecuniary gain, under circumstances likely to pose dangers that the State has a right to prevent.

Appellant, a member of the Ohio Bar, lives in Montville, Ohio. On February 13, 1974, while picking up his mail at the Montville Post Office, appellant learned from the postmaster's brother about an automobile accident that had taken place on February 2 in which Carol McClintock, a young woman with whom appellant was casually acquainted, had been injured. Appellant made a telephone call to Ms. McClintock's parents, who informed him that their daughter was in the hospital. Appellant suggested that he might visit Carol in the hospital. Mrs. McClintock assented to the idea, but requested that appellant first stop by at her home.

During appellant's visit with the McClintocks, they explained that their daughter had been driving the family automobile on a local road when she was hit by an uninsured motorist. Both Carol and her passenger, Wanda Lou Holbert, were injured and hospitalized. In response to the McClintocks' expression of apprehension that they might be sued by Holbert, appellant explained that Ohio's guest statute would preclude such a suit. When appellant suggested to the McClintocks that they hire a lawyer, Mrs. McClintock retorted that such a decision would be up to Carol, who was 18 years old and would be the beneficiary of a successful claim.

Appellant proceeded to the hospital, where he found Carol lying in traction in her room. After a brief conversation about her condition, appellant told Carol he would represent her and asked her to sign an agreement. Carol said she would have to discuss the matter with her parents. She did not sign the agreement, but asked appellant to have her parents come to see her. Appellant also attempted to see Wanda Lou Holbert, but learned that she had just been released from the hospital. He then departed for another visit with the McClintocks.

On his way appellant detoured to the scene of the accident, where he took a set of photographs. He also picked up a tape recorder, which he concealed under his raincoat before arriving at the McClintocks' residence. Once there, he re-examined their automobile insurance policy, discussed with them the law applicable to passengers, and explained the consequences of the fact that the driver who struck Carol's car was an uninsured motorist. Appellant discovered that the McClintocks' insurance policy would provide benefits of up to $12,500 each for Carol and Wanda Lou under an uninsured-motorist clause. Mrs. McClintock acknowledged that both Carol and Wanda Lou could sue for their injuries, but recounted to appellant that "Wanda swore up and down she would not do it." The McClintocks also told appellant that Carol had phoned to say that appellant could "go ahead" with her representation. Two days later appellant returned to Carol's hospital room to have her sign a contract, which provided that he would receive one-third of her recovery.

In the meantime, appellant obtained Wanda Lou's name and address from the McClintocks after telling them he wanted to ask her some questions about the accident. He then visited Wanda Lou at her home, without having been invited. He again concealed his tape recorder and recorded most of the conversation with Wanda Lou. After a brief, unproductive inquiry about the facts of the accident, appellant told Wanda Lou that he was representing Carol and that he had a "little tip" for Wanda Lou: the McClintocks' insurance policy contained an uninsured-motorist clause which might provide her with a recovery of up to $12,500. The young woman, who was 18 years of age and not a high school graduate at the time, replied to appellant's query about whether she was going to file a claim by stating that she really did not understand what was going on. Appellant offered to represent her, also, for a contingent fee of one-third of any recovery, and Wanda Lou stated "O.K."

In explaining the contingent-fee arrangement, appellant told Wanda Lou that his representation would not "cost [her] anything" because she would receive two-thirds of the recovery if appellant were successful in representing her but would not "have to pay [him] anything" otherwise.

Wanda's mother attempted to repudiate her daughter's oral assent the following day, when appellant called on the telephone to speak to Wanda. Mrs. Holbert informed appellant that she and her daughter did not want to sue anyone or to have appellant represent them, and that if they decided to sue they would consult their own lawyer. Appellant insisted that Wanda had entered into a binding agreement. A month later Wanda confirmed in writing that she wanted neither to sue nor to be represented by appellant. She requested that appellant notify the insurance company that he was not her lawyer, as the company would not release a check to her until he did so. Carol also eventually discharged appellant. Although another lawyer represented her in concluding a settlement with the insurance company, she paid appellant one-third of her recovery in settlement of his lawsuit against her for breach of contract.

After a hearing, the Board found that appellant had violated Disciplinary Rules (DR) 2–103(A) and 2–104(A) of the Ohio Code of Professional Responsibility. The Board rejected appellant's defense that his conduct was protected under the First and Fourteenth Amendments. The Supreme Court of Ohio adopted the findings of the Board, reiterated that appellant's conduct was not constitutionally protected, and increased the sanction of a public reprimand recommended by the Board to indefinite suspension.

The solicitation of business by a lawyer through direct, in-person communication with the prospective client has long been viewed as inconsistent with the profession's ideal of the attorney-client relationship and as posing a significant potential for harm to the prospective client. It has been proscribed by the organized Bar for many years.

Appellant contends that his solicitation of the two young women as clients is indistinguishable, for purposes of constitutional analysis, from the advertisement in *Bates*. Like that advertisement, his meetings with the prospective clients apprised them of their legal rights and of the availability of a lawyer to pursue their claims. But in-person solicitation of professional employment by a lawyer does not stand on a par with truthful advertising about the availability and terms of routine legal services, let alone with forms of speech more traditionally within the concern of the First Amendment.

Unlike a public advertisement, which simply provides information and leaves the recipient free to act upon it or not, in-person solicitation may exert pressure and often demands an immediate response, without providing an opportunity for comparison or reflection. The aim and effect of in-person solicitation may be to provide a one-sided presentation and to encourage speedy and perhaps uninformed decision-making; there is no opportunity for intervention or counter-education by agencies of the Bar, supervisory authorities, or persons close to the solicited individual. In-person solicitation is as likely as not to discourage persons needing counsel from engaging in a critical comparison of the availability, nature, and prices of legal services; it actually may disserve the individual and societal interest, identified in *Bates*, in facilitating informed and reliable decision-making.

It also is argued that in-person solicitation may provide the solicited individual with information about his or her legal rights and remedies. In this case, appellant gave Wanda Lou a "tip" about the prospect of recovery based on the uninsured-motorist clause in the McClintocks' insurance policy, and he explained that clause and Ohio's guest statute to Carol McClintock's parents. But neither of the Disciplinary Rules here at issue prohibited appellant from communicating information to these young women about their legal rights and the prospects of obtaining a monetary recovery, or from recommending that they obtain counsel. DR 2–104(A) merely prohibited him from using the information as bait with which to obtain an agreement to represent them for a fee. The Rule does not prohibit a lawyer from giving unsolicited legal advice; it proscribes the acceptance of employment resulting from such advice.

Appellant does not contend, and on the facts of this case could not contend, that his approaches to the two young women involved political expression or an exercise of associational freedom. A lawyer's procurement of remunerative employment is a subject only marginally affected with First Amendment concerns. It falls within the State's proper sphere of economic and professional regulation. While entitled to some constitutional protection, appellant's conduct is subject to regulation in furtherance of important state interests.

Appellant has conceded that the State has a legitimate and indeed "compelling" interest in preventing those aspects of solicitation that involve fraud, undue influence, intimidation, overreaching, and other forms of "vexatious conduct." The Rules prohibiting solicitation are prophylactic measures whose objective is the prevention of harm before it occurs. The Rules were applied in this case to discipline a lawyer for soliciting employment for pecuniary gain under circumstances likely to result in the adverse consequences the State seeks to avert. In such a situation, which is inherently conducive to overreaching and other forms of misconduct, the State has a strong interest in adopting and enforcing rules of conduct designed to protect the public from harmful solicitation by lawyers whom it has licensed.

The State's perception of the potential for harm in circumstances such as those presented in this case is well founded. The detrimental aspects of face-to-face selling even of ordinary consumer products have been recognized and addressed by the Federal Trade Commission, and it hardly need be said that the potential for overreaching is significantly greater when a lawyer, a professional trained in the art of persuasion, personally solicits an unsophisticated, injured, or distressed lay person. Such an individual may place his trust in a lawyer, regardless of the latter's qualifications or the individual's actual need for legal representation, simply in response to persuasion under circumstances conducive to uninformed acquiescence. Although it is argued that personal solicitation is valuable because it may apprise a victim of misfortune of his legal rights, the very plight of that person not only makes him more vulnerable to influence but also may make advice all the more intrusive. Thus, under these adverse conditions the overtures of an uninvited lawyer may distress the solicited individual simply because of their obtrusiveness and the invasion of the individual's privacy, even when no other harm materializes. Under such circumstances, it is not unreasonable for the State to presume that in-person solicitation by lawyers more often than not will be injurious to the person solicited.

Mr. Justice Marshall, concurring in part and concurring in the judgments.

The circumstances in which appellant Ohralik initially approached his two clients provide classic examples of "ambulance chasing," fraught with obvious potential for misrepresentation and overreaching. Ohralik, an experienced lawyer in practice for over 25 years, approached two 18-

year-old women shortly after they had been in a traumatic car accident. One was in traction in a hospital room; the other hand just been released following nearly two weeks of hospital care. Both were in pain and may have been on medication; neither had more than a high school education. Certainly these facts alone would have cautioned hesitation in pressing one's employment on either of these women; any lawyer of ordinary prudence should have carefully considered whether the person was in an appropriate condition to make a decision about legal counsel. But appellant not only foisted himself upon these clients; he acted in gross disregard for their privacy by covertly recording, without their consent or knowledge, his conversations with Wanda Lou Holbert and Carol McClintock's family. This conduct, which appellant has never disputed, is itself completely inconsistent with an attorney's fiduciary obligation fairly and fully to disclose to clients his activities affecting their interests. And appellant's unethical conduct was further compounded by his pursuing Wanda Lou Holbert, when her interests were clearly in potential conflict with those of his prior-retained client, Carol McClintock.

What is objectionable about Ohralik's behavior here is not so much that he solicited business for himself, but rather the circumstances in which he performed that solicitation and the means by which he accomplished it. Appropriately, the Court's actual holding in *Ohralik* is a limited one: that the solicitation of business, under circumstances—such as those found in this record—presenting substantial dangers of harm to society or the client independent of the solicitation itself, may constitutionally be prohibited by the State. In this much of the Court's opinion in *Ohralik*, I join fully.

[But] notwithstanding the injurious aspects of Ohralik's conduct, even his case illustrates the potentially useful, information-providing aspects of attorney solicitation: Motivated by the desire for pecuniary gain, but informed with the special training and knowledge of an attorney, Ohralik advised both his clients (apparently correctly) that, although they had been injured by an uninsured motorist, they could nonetheless recover on the McClintocks' insurance policy. The provision of such information about legal rights and remedies is an important function, even where the rights and remedies are of a private and commercial nature involving no constitutional or political overtones.

In view of the similar functions performed by advertising and solicitation by attorneys, I find somewhat disturbing the Court's suggestion that in-person solicitation of business, though entitled to some degree of constitutional protection as "commercial speech," is entitled to less protection under the First Amendment than is "the kind of advertising approved in *Bates.*" The First Amendment informational interests served by solicitation, whether or not it occurs in a purely commercial context, are substantial, and they are entitled to as much protection as the interests we found to be protected in *Bates*.

Not only do prohibitions on solicitation interfere with the free flow of information protected by the First Amendment, but by origin and in practice they operate in a discriminatory manner. As we have noted, these constraints developed as rules of "etiquette" and came to rest on the notion that a lawyer's reputation in his community would spread by word of mouth and bring business to the worthy lawyer. The social model on which this conception depends is that of the small, cohesive, and homogeneous community; the anachronistic nature of this model has long been recognized. If ever this conception were more generally true, it is now valid only with respect to those persons who move in the relatively elite social and educational circles in which knowledge about legal problems, legal remedies, and lawyers is widely shared.

The impact of the non-solicitation rules, moreover, is discriminatory with respect to the suppliers as well as the consumers of legal services. Just as the persons who suffer most from lack of knowledge about lawyers' availability belong to the less privileged classes of society, so the Disciplinary Rules against solicitation fall most heavily on those attorneys engaged in a single-practitioner or small-partnership form of practice—attorneys who typically earn less than their fellow practitioners in larger, corporate-oriented firms. Indeed, some scholars have suggested that the rules against solicitation were developed by the professional bar to keep recently immigrated lawyers, who gravitated toward the smaller, personal injury practice, from effective entry into the profession. See J. Auerbach, *Unequal Justice* 42–62, 126–129 (1976). In light of this history, I am less inclined than the majority appears to be to weigh favorably in the balance of the State's interests here the longevity of the ban on attorney solicitation.

NOTES ON OHRALIK

1. ***What Harms and Benefits Did Ohralik's Solicitation Produce?*** What harms did Carol and Wanda suffer, and what benefits did they obtain, as a result of Ohralik's effort to solicit them as clients?

2. ***What Exactly Is the Problem?*** Is the problematic behavior in this case the solicitation of business? Was the lawyer's pecuniary motive the problem? Or was it rather solicitation under the particular circumstances of this case and using the particular methods that Ohralik employed—his clandestine audio recordings, his pursuit of both Carol and Wanda as clients when there was a potential conflict between their interests, the pressure he imposed on Carol to sign a retainer agreement, and his later suit against Carol for breach of contract when she tried to fire him? Could you draw a clear line between problematic and acceptable solicitation?

IN RE PRIMUS
United States Supreme Court
436 U.S. 412 (1978)

MR. JUSTICE POWELL delivered the opinion of the Court.

Appellant, Edna Smith Primus, is a lawyer practicing in Columbia, S. C. During the period in question, she was associated with the "Carolina Community Law Firm," and was an officer of and cooperating lawyer with the Columbia branch of the American Civil Liberties Union (ACLU). She received no compensation for her work on behalf of the ACLU, but was paid a retainer as a legal consultant for the South Carolina Council on Human Relations (Council), a nonprofit organization with offices in Columbia.

During the summer of 1973, local and national newspapers reported that pregnant mothers on public assistance in Aiken County, S. C., were being sterilized or threatened with sterilization as a condition of the continued receipt of medical assistance under the Medicaid program. Concerned by this development, Gary Allen, an Aiken businessman and officer of a local organization serving indigents, called the Council requesting that one of its representatives come to Aiken to address some of the women who had been sterilized. At the Council's behest, appellant, who had not known Allen previously, called him and arranged a meeting in his office in July 1973. Among those attending was Mary Etta Williams, who had been sterilized by Dr. Clovis H. Pierce after the birth of her third child. Williams and her grandmother attended the meeting because Allen, an old family friend, had invited them and because Williams wanted "[to] see what it was all about . . ." At the meeting, appellant advised those present, including Williams and the other women who had been sterilized by Dr. Pierce, of their legal rights and suggested the possibility of a lawsuit.

Early in August 1973 the ACLU informed appellant that it was willing to provide representation for Aiken mothers who had been sterilized. Appellant testified that after being advised by Allen that Williams wished to institute suit against Dr. Pierce, she decided to inform Williams of the ACLU's offer of free legal representation.

[The letter from Primus to Williams stated:

Dear Mrs. Williams:

You will probably remember me from talking with you at Mr. Allen's office in July about the sterilization performed on you. The American Civil Liberties Union would like to file a lawsuit on your behalf for money against the doctor who performed the operation. We will be coming to Aiken in the near future and would like to explain what is involved so you can understand what is going on.

Now I have a question to ask of you. Would you object to talking to a women's magazine about the situation in Aiken? The magazine is doing a feature story on the whole sterilization problem and wants to talk to you and others in South Carolina. If you don't mind doing this, call me *collect* at 254–8151 on Friday before 5:00, if you receive this letter in time. Or call me on Tuesday morning (after Labor Day) *collect.*

I want to assure you that this interview is being done to show what is happening to women against their wishes, and is not being done to harm you in any way. But I want you to decide, so call me collect and let me know of your decision. This practice must stop.

About the lawsuit, if you are interested, let me know, and I'll let you know when we will come down to talk to you about it. We will be coming to talk to Mrs. Waters at the same time; she has already asked the American Civil Liberties Union to file a suit on her behalf.

Sincerely,

Edna Smith
Attorney-at-law]

Shortly after receiving appellant's letter, the centerpiece of this litigation—Williams visited Dr. Pierce to discuss the progress of her third child who was ill. At the doctor's office, she encountered his lawyer and at the latter's request signed a release of liability in the doctor's favor. Williams showed appellant's letter to the doctor and his lawyer, and they retained a copy. She then called appellant from the doctor's office and announced her intention not to sue. There was no further communication between appellant and Williams.

The Board of Commissioners on Grievances and Discipline of the Supreme Court of South Carolina (Board) filed a formal complaint with the Board, charging that appellant had engaged in "solicitation in violation of the Canons of Ethics" by sending the August 30, 1973, letter to Williams. The Supreme Court of South Carolina entered an order which adopted verbatim the findings and conclusions of the panel report and increased the sanction to a public reprimand. We now reverse.

Unlike the situation in *Ohralik,* appellant's act of solicitation took the form of a letter to a woman with whom appellant had discussed the possibility of seeking redress for an allegedly unconstitutional sterilization. This was not in-person solicitation for pecuniary gain. Appellant was communicating an offer of free assistance by attorneys associated with the ACLU, not an offer predicated on entitlement to a share of any monetary recovery. And her actions were undertaken to express personal political beliefs and to advance the civil-liberties objectives of the ACLU, rather than to derive financial gain.

In *NAACP v. Button,* [we] held that "the activities of the NAACP, its affiliates and legal staff are modes of expression and association protected by the First and Fourteenth Amendments which Virginia may not prohibit, under its power to regulate the legal profession, as improper solicitation of legal business." The solicitation of prospective litigants for the purpose of furthering the civil-rights objectives of the organization and its members was held to come within the right to engage in association for the advancement of beliefs and ideas.

The record [in this case] does not support the state court's effort to draw a meaningful distinction between the ACLU and the NAACP. From all that appears, the ACLU and its local chapters, much like the NAACP and its local affiliates in *Button,* "[engage] in extensive educational and lobbying activities" and "also [devote] much of [their] funds and energies to an extensive program of assisting certain kinds of litigation on behalf of [their] declared purposes." The court below acknowledged that the ACLU has engaged in the defense of unpopular causes and unpopular defendants and has represented individuals in litigation that has defined the scope of constitutional protection in areas such as political dissent, juvenile rights, prisoners' rights, military law, amnesty, and privacy. For the ACLU, as for the NAACP, "litigation is not a technique of resolving private differences"; it is "a form of political expression" and "political association."

We find equally unpersuasive any suggestion that the level of constitutional scrutiny in this case should be lowered because of a possible benefit to the ACLU. The discipline administered to appellant was premised solely on the possibility of financial benefit to the organization, rather than any possibility of pecuniary gain to herself, her associates, or the lawyers representing the plaintiffs in the *Walker* v. *Pierce* litigation. It is conceded that appellant received no compensation for any of the activities in question. It is also undisputed that neither the ACLU nor any lawyer associated with it would have shared in any monetary recovery by the plaintiffs.

Contrary to appellee's suggestion, the ACLU's policy of requesting an award of counsel fees does not take this case outside of the protection of *Button.* Although the Court in *Button* did not consider whether the NAACP seeks counsel fees, such requests are often made by that organization. In any event, in a case of this kind there are differences between counsel fees awarded by a court and traditional fee-paying arrangements which militate against a presumption that ACLU sponsorship of litigation is motivated by considerations of pecuniary gain rather than by its widely recognized goal of vindicating civil liberties. Counsel fees are awarded in the discretion of the court; awards are not drawn from the plaintiff's recovery, and are usually premised on a successful outcome; and the amounts awarded often may not correspond to fees generally obtainable in private litigation. Moreover, under prevailing law during the events in question, an award of counsel fees in federal litigation was available only in limited circumstances. And even if there had been an award during the period in question, it would have gone to the central fund of the ACLU. Although such benefit to the organization may increase with the maintenance of successful litigation, the same situation obtains with voluntary contributions and foundation support, which also may rise with ACLU victories in important areas of the law. That possibility, standing alone, offers no basis for equating the work of lawyers associated with the ACLU or the NAACP with that of a group that exists for the primary purpose of financial gain through the recovery of counsel fees.

Appellant's letter of August 30, 1973, to Mrs. Williams thus comes within the generous zone of First Amendment protection reserved for associational freedoms.

Where political expression or association is at issue, this Court has not tolerated the degree of imprecision that often characterizes government regulation of the conduct of commercial affairs. The approach we adopt today in *Ohralik,* that the State may proscribe in-person solicitation for pecuniary gain under circumstances likely to result in adverse consequences, cannot be applied to appellant's activity on behalf of the ACLU. Although a showing of potential danger may suffice in the former context, appellant may not be disciplined unless her activity in fact involved the type of misconduct at which South Carolina's broad prohibition is said to be directed.

The record does not support appellee's contention that undue influence, overreaching, misrepresentation, or invasion of privacy actually occurred in this case. Appellant's letter of August 30, 1973, followed up the earlier meeting—one concededly protected by the First and Fourteenth Amendments—by notifying Williams that the ACLU would be interested in supporting possible litigation. The letter imparted additional information material to making an informed decision about whether to authorize litigation, and permitted Williams an opportunity, which she exercised, for arriving at a deliberate decision. The letter was not facially misleading; indeed, it offered "to explain what is involved so you can understand what is going on." The transmittal of this letter—as contrasted with in-person solicitation—involved no appreciable invasion of privacy; nor did it afford any significant opportunity for overreaching or coercion. Moreover, the fact that there was a written communication lessens substantially the difficulty of policing solicitation practices that do offend valid rules of professional conduct

The State is free to fashion reasonable restrictions with respect to the time, place, and manner of solicitation by members of its Bar. The State's special interest in regulating members of a profession it licenses, and who serve as officers of its courts, amply justifies the application of narrowly drawn rules to proscribe solicitation that in fact is misleading, overbearing, or involves other features of deception or improper influence. As we decide today in *Ohralik*, a State also may forbid in-person solicitation for pecuniary gain under circumstances likely to result in these evils. And a State may insist that lawyers not solicit on behalf of lay organizations that exert control over the actual conduct of any ensuing litigation.

[The separate opinion of Justice Marshall, concurring in part and concurring in the judgment, was published in the report of the *Ohralik* case excerpted above.]

MR. JUSTICE REHNQUIST, dissenting.

In this case and the companion case of *Ohralik* v. *Ohio State Bar Assn.,* the Court tells its own tale of two lawyers: One tale ends happily for the lawyer and one does not. If we were given the latitude of novelists in deciding between happy and unhappy endings for the heroes and villains of our tales, I might well join in the Court's disposition of both cases. But under our federal system it is for the States to decide which lawyers shall be admitted to the Bar and remain there; this Court may interfere only if the State's decision is rendered impermissible by the United States Constitution. We can, of course, develop a jurisprudence of epithets and slogans in this area, in which "ambulance chasers" suffer one fate and "civil liberties lawyers" another. But I remain unpersuaded by the Court's opinions in these two cases that there is a principled basis for concluding that the First and Fourteenth Amendments forbid South Carolina from disciplining Primus here, but permit Ohio to discipline Ohralik in the companion case. I believe that both South Carolina and Ohio acted within the limits prescribed by those Amendments, and I would therefore affirm the judgment in each case.

In distinguishing between Primus' protected solicitation and Ohralik's unprotected solicitation, the Court lamely declares: "We have not discarded the 'common-sense' distinction between speech proposing a commercial transaction, which occurs in an area traditionally subject to government regulation, and other varieties of speech." If Albert Ohralik, like Edna Primus, viewed litigation " 'not [as] a technique of resolving private differences,' " but as " 'a form of political expression' and 'political association,' " for all that appears he would be restored to his right to practice. And we may be sure that the next lawyer in Ohralik's shoes who is disciplined for similar conduct will come here cloaked in the prescribed mantle of "political association" to assure that insurance companies do not take unfair advantage of policyholders.

This absence of any principled distinction between the two cases is made all the more unfortunate by the radical difference in scrutiny brought to bear upon state regulation in each area. Where solicitation proposes merely a commercial transaction, the Court recognizes "the need for prophylactic regulation in furtherance of the State's interest in protecting the lay public." On the other hand, in some circumstances (at least in those identical to the instant case) "[where] political expression or association is at issue," a member of the Bar "may not be disciplined unless her activity in fact [involves] the type of misconduct at which South Carolina's broad prohibition is said to be directed."

I do not believe that any State will be able to determine with confidence the area in which it may regulate prophylactically and the area in which it may regulate only upon a specific showing of harm.

A State may rightly fear that members of its Bar have powers of persuasion not possessed by laymen, and it may also fear that such persuasion may be as potent in writing as it is in person. Such persuasion may draw an unsophisticated layman into litigation contrary to his own best interests, and it may force other citizens of South Carolina to defend against baseless litigation which would not otherwise have been brought. I cannot agree that a State must prove such harmful consequences in each case simply because an organization such as the ACLU or the NAACP is involved.

I cannot share the Court's confidence that the danger of such consequences is minimized simply because a lawyer proceeds from political conviction rather than for pecuniary gain. A State may reasonably fear that a lawyer's desire to resolve substantial civil liberties questions, may occasionally take precedence over his duty to advance the interests of his client. It is even more reasonable to fear that a lawyer in such circumstances will be inclined to pursue both culpable and blameless defendants to the last ditch in order to achieve his ideological goals. Although individual litigants, including the ACLU, may be free to use the courts for such purposes, South Carolina is likewise free to restrict the activities of the members of its Bar who attempt to persuade them to do so.

NOTES ON IN RE PRIMUS

1. *A Double Standard?* If the South Carolina bar was concerned about the overreaching by lawyers with respect to prospective litigants, why would it permit Dr. Pierce's lawyer to seek Ms. Williams's waiver of liability for the doctor's treatment of her but prohibit an ACLU lawyer from offering to represent her?

2. ***Why Doesn't* Bates *Control?*** On what basis did the Court in *Ohralik* and *Primus* find that the constitutionality of restrictions on in-person solicitation was not answered by the Court's decision in *Bates*?

3. ***Should the Standard Turn on the Lawyer's Motivation?*** Is the distinction between pecuniary motives and all other types of motives a sound basis for differentiating between permissible and impermissible types of in-person solicitation? Is there a better alternative?

4. ***Compare the Reasoning of Justices Marshall and Rehnquist.*** Both Justice Marshall in *Ohralik* and Justice Rehnquist in *Primus* rejected the distinction between pecuniary and other types of motives as unprincipled and ill-advised, but they did so for very different reasons. How would you characterize the primary differences between their perspectives?

First Amendment Limitations on the Regulation of Lawyer Solicitation:

- In ***Ohralik v. Ohio State Bar*** **(1978),** the Supreme Court held that Ohio could discipline a lawyer who approached accident victims, urged them to hire him, and secretly recorded their conversations. The *Ohralik* Court distinguished *Bates* on the ground that in-person solicitation of accident victims entails a greater potential for lawyer overreaching than truthful advertising directed to the general public.

- ***In re Primus*** (1978), decided on the same day as *Ohralik,* found that the First Amendment protected a lawyer for the ACLU who offered free representation to prospective clients in a case challenging their involuntary sterilization. The Court emphasized that the lawyer's motivation was political rather than financial.

Model Rule 7.3(a) adopts the distinction drawn in *Ohralik* and *Primus* between pecuniary and other motives. How should a disciplinary committee considering an alleged violation of Rule 7.3 discern the lawyer's motivations? Could it fairly rely primarily on what the committee knows about the objectives of the lawyer's employer, as the court did in *Primus*, or the type of practice setting in which the lawyer worked? Some research suggests that even ideologically driven lawyers often have mixed motives: many are concerned about making a living (pecuniary objectives) as well as advancing principles and the interests of their clients.[24] At what point do the motivations of such lawyers become

---

[24] *See* Scott Cummings and Ann Southworth, *Between Profit and Principle: The Private Public Interest Law Firm*, in PRIVATE LAWYERS AND THE PUBLIC INTEREST: THE EVOLVING ROLE OF PRO BONO IN THE LEGAL PROFESSION (Robert Granfield & Lynn Mather eds. 2009); Ann Southworth, *Professional Identity and Political Commitment Among Lawyers for Conservative*

sufficiently pecuniary that their efforts to identify clients whose cases advance principles that the lawyers seek to advance run afoul of Rule 7.3?

Model Rule Provisions on Lawyer Solicitation

- **Rule 7.3(a)** provides that a lawyer shall not by in-person, live telephone or real-time electronic contact solicit employment when a significant motive for doing so is pecuniary gain, unless the person contacted is a lawyer or has a family, close person, or prior professional relationship with the lawyer.

- **Rule 7.3(b)** provides that a lawyer may not solicit employment from a prospective client who has made it known that he does not wish to be contacted.

Have courts and bar committees been focusing on the right question? Rather than emphasizing the lawyer's motivation, should they instead focus on circumstances likely to result in coercion or undue influence? Some have argued that in-person solicitation should be protected where those worrisome conditions are not present, even if the lawyer is motivated by commercial concerns. Recall Justice Marshall's concurrence in *Ohralik*, in which he argued that the state may prohibit solicitation only under circumstances such as those that existed in that case— circumstances suggesting that the prospective client would feel pressured and coerced and presenting the prospect of "substantial harm to society or the client."

Would Rule 7.3 be constitutional as applied to a sophisticated business client? There are no reported instances of large firm lawyers being prosecuted for improper solicitation—for example, by taking prospective business clients out to lunch or on golf outings. Yet those practices seem to fall squarely within Rule 7.3's prohibition because the motivations for such practices are quite obviously "pecuniary"—tied to the lawyers' interest in attracting business to enhance the firm's profitability and their own standing within the firm.

In *Edenfeld v. Fane*,[25] an accountant challenged a Florida ban on in-person solicitation by accountants, and the U.S. Supreme Court invalidated the ban. The court distinguished *Ohralik* on the ground that the clients were sophisticated consumers of accounting services and that the meeting with prospective clients took place in circumstances unlikely to make the clients feel pressured: "while clients in *Ohralik* were approached at a moment of high stress and vulnerability, the clients in

---

Causes, in THE WORLDS CAUSE LAWYERS MAKE: STRUCTURE AND AGENCY IN LEGAL PRACTICE (Austin Sarat & Stuart Scheingold eds. 2005).

[25] 507 U.S. 761 (1993).

this case are meeting in their own offices, at a time of their own choosing." The Court added that "[t]he typical client of a CPA is far less susceptible to manipulation than the young accident victim in *Ohralik*. [The] prospective clients are sophisticated and experienced business executives who understand well the services that a CPA offers." According to those aspects of the Supreme Court's reasoning in *Edenfeld*, it seems likely that applying the solicitation ban to sophisticated clients of lawyers might be found unconstitutional. However, the *Edenfeld* Court observed that "Unlike a lawyer, a CPA is not a professional trained in the art of persuasion. A CPA training emphasizes independence and objectivity, not advocacy . . ." This leaves open whether the Court might distinguish between accountants and lawyers on the ground that lawyers' superior advocacy skills make them more threatening to the interests of unwitting clients.

2.   TARGETED COMMUNICATIONS

In *Shapero v. Kentucky Bar Association*,[26] the U.S. Supreme Court found that the First Amendment prevented Kentucky from prohibiting lawyers from sending truthful letters to potential clients known to face particular legal problems. The *Shapero* Court noted that "[l]ike print advertising, targeted, direct mail solicitation generally poses much less risk of over-reaching or undue influence than does in-person solicitation." It noted that "both types of written solicitation convey information about legal services [by means that are] more conducive to reflection and the exercise of choice on the part of the consumer than is personal solicitation by an attorney."

In *Florida Bar v. Went For It, Inc.*,[27] the U.S. Supreme Court upheld a rule prohibiting lawyers from contacting accident victims or their families by mail for 30 days after an accident. Justice O'Connor's majority opinion upheld Florida's restriction. It found that Florida had a substantial interest in protecting potential clients' privacy and in "maintaining the professionalism of the members of the bar." In finding that the regulation materially advanced those interests, the Court relied on the Florida bar's survey of public attitudes toward the legal profession, which indicated direct solicitation within 30 days of an accident invaded privacy interests and diminished the public image of lawyers: "The regulation, then, is an effort to protect the flagging reputation of Florida lawyers by preventing them from engaging in conduct that the Bar maintains is universally regarded as deplorable and beneath common decency because of its intrusion upon the special vulnerability and private grief of victims or their families." The Court distinguished *Shapero* on three grounds: 1) that Florida had identified an interest—

---

[26]   486 U.S. 466 (1988).

[27]   515 U.S. 618 (1995).

preventing lawyers' invasion of clients' privacy—not relied upon by Kentucky in *Shapero*; 2) that the restriction was for a limited period of time (30 days); and 3) that Florida had assembled evidence demonstrating harm caused by targeted mail.

Since the decision in *Went for It*, other states have adopted 30-day solicitation bans similar to Florida's,[28] while several states have considered such bans and rejected them. Do you support these rules? What are the costs of such bans? Is protecting the bar's image a sufficient justification for limiting lawyers' truthful speech? Does it make sense to institute these bans as to attorneys but not as to insurance company personnel, who often try to investigate and settle claims soon after an accident?

First Amendment Limitations on the Regulation of Targeted Mail

- In *Shapero v. Kentucky Bar Association* **(1988)**, a divided Court invalidated a rule that barred lawyers from sending letters targeted to potential clients known to need legal services. It found that letters do not involve the same coercive force as the personal presence of a trained advocate.

- But in *Florida Bar v. Went for It* **(1995)**, the Court upheld a 30-day ban on mail targeted to accident victims, finding that the rule was justified in order to protect the reputation of the legal profession.

Model Rule 7.3(c)

- provides that all communications soliciting employment from a prospective client who is known to be in need of legal services in a particular matter must include the words "Advertising Material" on the outside envelope and at the beginning and ending of any recorded or electronic communication unless the recipient is a lawyer, a member of the lawyer's family, or someone with whom the lawyer has a prior professional relationship.

D. THE INTERNET AND SOCIAL MEDIA

The Internet presents a host of issues relating to lawyer advertising and solicitation. Notice that Rules 7.2 and 7.3 now refer explicitly to

---

[28] *See* Alexander v. Cahill, 598 F.3d 79 (2d Cir. 2010) (upholding New York's new 30-day ban on contacting accident victims and noting that Connecticut, Arizona, Georgia, Louisiana, Missouri, and Tennessee have similar bans). Indiana and Kentucky have also adopted such rules.

"electronic communication" and "real-time electronic contact." However, these rules leave many open questions about lawyers' use of the Internet and social media to interact with prospective clients. How should regulators deal with web pages, chat rooms, blogs, listservs, and social and professional networking sites? The ABA Ethics 20/20 Commission has studied and sought comments on these issues, but it has not yet issued formal guidance on many of them.[29] As the reporter for the Working Group on the Implications of New Technologies has noted, "[i]t is unclear what constraints there are. The law is still very much in its infancy."[30]

Law firm web pages have become ubiquitous, and bar disciplinary authorities generally do not even try to monitor the truth of the material posted on these websites. Even the most staid large firms maintain web pages that contain effusive claims about the law firms' expertise and commitment to representing clients' interests. The website for Cravath, Swaine & Moore, for example, states that "Cravath has been known as one of the premier U.S. law firms for nearly two centuries" and that its lawyers "are recognized around the world for their commitment to the representation of our clients' interests." Cravath's home page touts the firm's rankings by several commercial rating services, its handling of high-profile litigation and transactions, and its recent senior hires. The website for Russ Brown Motorcycle Attorney, a firm that seeks to serve motorcycle riders nationwide, is more adventuresome.[31] Its home page highlights the firm's $19.4 million jury verdict in an accident injury case, as well as Russ Brown's induction into the Stirgis Motorcycle Hall of Fame, and it contains links to video advertisements for the firm's services (some using the slogan, "If you go down, call Russ Brown") and client testimonials. The site also invites prospective clients to live chat with a firm representative, and it contains links to Russ Brown's blogs, tweets, and social networking sites.

Constitutional protection for lawyer advertising differs from that for in-person solicitation, and therefore it is useful to consider whether these various types of practices made possible through the Internet are more like advertising or solicitation. Most firms' web pages are more like advertisements than in-person solicitation in the sense that they do not involve real-time interaction. (Many of these websites invite prospective clients to contact the firm by telephone or email, but they generally do not allow for real-time interaction.) What about chat rooms and blogs—Are they more like advertising or in-person solicitation? Chat rooms

---

[29] *See* ABA Commission on Ethics 20/20 Working Group on the Implications of New Technologies, Issue Paper Concerning Lawyers' Use of Internet Based Client Development Tools, Sept. 20, 2010.

[30] *See* Steven Seidenberg, *For Lawyers, the Appeal of Social Media Is Obvious. It's Also Dangerous*, ABA J., Feb. 2011.

[31] Available at http://www.russbrown.com/motorcycle-lawyer-media.html.

sometimes involve real-time interaction with prospective clients, and, in that sense, they seem more analogous to in-person solicitation than advertising. But interaction via the Internet involves more physical distance between clients and lawyers and may permit more reflection than is typical of many in-person encounters. Some jurisdictions have found lawyers' participation in chat rooms impermissible,[32] while others have concluded that chat room solicitation is not always prohibited.[33] Blogs arguably fall between websites and chat rooms in terms of the public policy concerns that drive the regulation of lawyers' advertising and solicitation.[34]

Chat rooms and social media sites also present special challenges relating to the requirement that lawyers' communications must not be false or misleading. Lawyers have less control over the content of those forms of communication than they do over face-to-face conversation, advertising, mail, and email. When other participants in these fora post misleading or exaggerated claims, Rule 7.1 seems to impose an obligation on the attorney to remedy the errors in some circumstances. That provision would seem to apply to LinkedIn and other social media that allow users to "recommend" others and praise their work. Lawyers who use Twitter to publicize their work may be subject to advertising restrictions. In jurisdictions that require that advertisements include disclosures and disclaimers, there may be no room left in a 140 character tweet to say anything meaningful.[35]

Should lawyers be allowed to offer their services on deal-of-day websites such as Groupon? Critics of this practice have raised a variety of objections, including longstanding arguments that advertising discounted legal services is undignified and potentially misleading. But three state bar associations—South Carolina, North Carolina, and New York—have now concluded that lawyers' participation in daily-deal sites may be acceptable.[36] The New York bar opinion emphasized, however, that lawyers must ensure that their representations about discounts are truthful: "The offered discount must not be illusionary, but must represent an actual discount from an established fee for the named

---

[32] *See, e.g.,* Florida Advertising Opinion A–00–1 (2000); Michigan Informal Ethics Opinion RI–276 (1996); Utah Ethics Opinion 97–10 (1997);Virginia Advertising Opinion A–0110 (1998); West Virginia Ethics Opinion 98–03 (1998).

[33] *See, e.g.,* Arizona Ethics Opinion 97–04 (1997); California Formal Ethics Opinion 2004–166.

[34] *See* David L. Hudson, Jr., *Virginia Supreme Court Holds That Advertising Rules May Be Applied to a Lawyer's Blog,* ABA J., Nov. 1, 2013 (commenting on Virginia Supreme Court decision holding that a lawyer's blog could be subject to disclaimer requirement).

[35] See Michael E. Lackey Jr. & Joseph P. Minta, *Lawyers and Social Media: The Legal Ethics of Tweeting, Facebooking and Blogging,* 28 TAURO L. REV. 149 (2012).

[36] Stephanie Francis Ward, *Coupon, You're On: Three Opinions Say Lawyers May Participate in Daily-Deal Websites,* 98 A.B.A.J. 24 (May 2012).

service. Otherwise the advertisement would be misleading."[37] (Deal-of-the-day websites have also raised concerns about splitting fees with nonlawyers, which is prohibited by Rule 5.4, covered in Part VI, but South Carolina, North Carolina and New York found the fee arrangements permissible.) The ABA has concluded that lawyers may offer legal services through deal-of-the-day or group coupon marketing programs so long as they comply with the Model Rules' requirements to avoid false or misleading statements and conflicts of interest.[38]

Finally, when lawyers use the Internet to market their services, the question arises as to which states have jurisdiction over those lawyers and which states' rules apply. As we will see in Chapter 34, email and the Internet have made it much easier for lawyers to practice law across state lines, which raises issues about the state-based system of bar discipline. Among those issues are whether a state has the power to regulate the digital advertising and solicitation of a lawyer who resides or maintains her office in another state where the Internet communication would be permissible. We will consider these questions of jurisdiction and choice of law in Part VI.

E. SUMMARY

In this chapter, we have examined the regulation of lawyers' efforts to attract clients. We considered the history of such regulation, its relationship to the social history of the bar, and how various types of marketing restrictions affect different strata of the profession. We studied cases establishing First Amendment limitations on the regulation of lawyers' advertisements and solicitation of clients, and several Model Rules that address lawyer advertising and solicitation. Finally, we considered issues raised by the Internet and social and professional networking sites and the considerable uncertainty that prevails in this new realm of lawyers' marketing activity.

---

[37] Id. (citing New York Opinion 897).

[38] ABA Formal Opinion 465: Lawyers' Use of Deal-of-the-Day Marketing Programs (October 21, 2013).

CHAPTER 23

PLAINTIFFS' PRACTICE

■ ■ ■

A. INTRODUCTION

The sector of the bar that specializes in representing plaintiffs is varied and also stratified, with some types of practices being more profitable and prestigious than others. The demographics and stratification of this sector have implications for the regulation of lawyers and for a number of contemporary debates about the desirability of changing the law governing torts, class actions, and attorneys' fees.

While large corporations occasionally sue each other and are represented by large firms as plaintiffs, they are frequently sued by employees, consumers, and other individuals or small businesses. Litigators at large firms are more likely to represent defendants, and litigators at small firms often specialize in representing plaintiffs. There are major differences in sophistication, complexity, remuneration, and business generation among practices specializing in representing plaintiffs. This chapter begins with a look at how plaintiffs' lawyers' professional identity is shaped in relation to their position on substantive law, the way they find clients and organize their practices, and their perception of how the public views the law. The chapter then examines the regulation of referral networks and attorneys' fees, in sectors in which clients typically cannot afford to pay their lawyers in advance or by the hour, and, therefore, rely on contingency fee agreements and on statutes authorizing the court to order the losing defendant to pay a prevailing plaintiff's attorneys' fees.

B. THE STRUCTURE OF THE PLAINTIFFS' BAR AND STRATIFICATION WITHIN IT

As we saw in Chapter 2, class, race and ethnic divisions are quite visible within the American legal profession and have been for many years. Until the mid- to late-twentieth century, corporate firms would not hire Jews or people of color, and some would not hire Catholics. As a result, large law firms in the major cities were segregated on the basis of race, ethnicity, and religion. Well into the twentieth century, in the major cities in the northeast and upper-midwest, plaintiffs' lawyers, like many lawyers in solo and small firm practice, were predominantly from working class families and often were from Irish or Eastern or Southern European immigrant families and were often Catholics or Jews. (Few academic studies of the bar have focused on southern and western states, so we know less about the demographics of the bar there.) Even today, lawyers serving large corporations tend to have attended elite universities, which draw disproportionately from privileged communities, while lawyers serving individuals and small businesses are more likely to come from working class and lower middle class backgrounds and to have attended state university law schools or local law schools.

The way that socioeconomic class and ethnicity have affected the careers of lawyers and contributed to the particular patterns of stratification in the bar generally, and among plaintiffs' lawyers, is the subject of the excerpt that follows. Although the article is relatively recent, the world of urban lawyers generally has changed since the events described in the study. Large law firms have abandoned their refusal to hire Catholics, Jews, and people of color, which has opened career opportunities. In addition, immigration from all parts of the world is changing the demographics of the bar.

PHILIP CORBOY AND THE CONSTRUCTION OF THE PLAINTIFFS' PERSONAL INJURY BAR

Sara Parikh and Bryant Garth
30 Law & Social Inquiry 269 (2005)

Philip Corboy has been at the top of the personal injury bar in Chicago for most of the period after World War II. He has the recognition of his peers, who know him as the "dean" of the personal injury bar in Chicago. He also has long-standing connections to the Democratic Party in Chicago and elsewhere, and a long list of philanthropic activities.

More generally, Corboy personifies the characteristics of elite personal injury lawyers in Chicago today. The elite tend to be Catholic or Jewish males who come from modest backgrounds and attend local law schools. They are at the top of a referral chain that channels the biggest cases to them and their firms, and they reinforce their position through their ability and willingness to bring high-risk cases to juries. In their professional lives they demonstrate their commitment to the collective through professional leadership, political activism, local philanthropy, and mentoring young lawyers like themselves who follow in their footsteps. In this article we examine how these came to be the defining traits of elite plaintiffs' lawyers in Chicago.

At the same time, Corboy's story provides a means to explore the sociological development of this major "subprofession"—the plaintiffs' bar. Their courtroom successes, professional and political activities, and local philanthropy all reinforce the stature of the elite within the plaintiffs' bar. This has translated into a substantial upgrading in the general social status of this segment of the personal injury bar.

In the period after World War II, the legal profession appeared to a young lawyer like Corboy to be dominated by and for the corporate bar, which recruited almost exclusively from a WASP establishment legitimated with degrees from Ivy League schools. Corporate lawyers controlled the bar associations and played civic roles that reinforced their professional status. Catholics or Jews or the graduates of local law schools, doubly penalized for their working-class or immigrant backgrounds, had limited access to the corporate elite. Lacking this access, they typically followed a different track.

[In an interview, Corboy recounted that his grandparents immigrated from Ireland; his parents graduated only from high school. After military service, Corboy graduated from Loyola Law School of Chicago as valedictorian in 1948, but found that Chicago firms refused to even interview young men like him. He said the] corporate bar "did not come on campus. They did not interview. I don't know how you got [a job with them], because I didn't get one. I think they chose people who were from prestige law schools who were on the law review and all that. The same way they do today."

[Corboy explained that his uncle got him a job interview at the City of Chicago Corporation Counsel's office, where he got his first job as a lawyer.]

Encouraged by his boss, Corboy became a precinct captain in the 49th ward in Chicago. He also ran for president of the Young Democrats of Cook County, losing in his first effort but succeeding the following year.

Legal careers within the political machine provided an alternative track to the one available to the corporate bar. The predominantly Irish Catholic political system in Chicago produced politicians, U.S. attorneys, municipal corporation counsel, state's attorneys, and public defenders, and there were places in the judiciary to reward those who provided service in the other positions. The products of the system, as Corboy himself noted, were "shaped" and "matured" by the "pristine political system." He added, "When I started the practice of law, all judges came through the political system." The judiciary's background meant that they "understood people. That understanding of people made them very, very good judges." The Chicago plaintiffs' bar has its roots in this local political environment.

James Dooley was another Irish Catholic graduate of Loyola. Dooley was building a reputation in the emerging field of personal injury. At the time, according to Corboy, there were "two types of lawyers that handled personal injury cases. Those who acquire business and are either called litigation lawyers or they're just called personal injury lawyers; they don't try cases." Then there were those like Dooley, who "tried cases." [Corboy went to work for Dooley.]

Dooley did not recruit from the corporate bar or the elite schools. Those with elite credentials still thought of personal injury lawyers as ambulance chasers with poor standards of professional ethics. Personal injury lawyers did not occupy prominent positions in professional organizations or have a reputation for trial craft. Dooley, Corboy could see, was working to distance himself and others like him who "tried cases" from the ambulance chasers and case processors.

The Dooley strategy was to gain respect for their craft as attorneys who tried cases. While a law practice focused on advice and negotiation had the highest prestige in the corporate bar at the time, the quest for professional respectability among personal injury lawyers militated in favor of investment in pure law—litigation—that would separate these lawyers from the taint of ambulance chasing and case processing. Dooley's activities also included an extensive appellate practice seeking to expand tort law on behalf of plaintiffs. Dooley invested in scholarship, authoring a three-volume treatise, Modern Tort Law (1977). Dooley in these ways built his reputation for trial and doctrinal expertise and not incidentally helped promote liberalization in tort law. He continued to practice as a leading plaintiffs' lawyer until he was elected to the Illinois Supreme Court in 1976.

Under Dooley's tutelage, Corboy invested heavily in the practice of trying cases. Corboy learned the importance both of trial craft and of the organizations that would celebrate it. Corboy also learned from Dooley how to prosper without the overt taint of ambulance chasing. Dooley followed a professional strategy to get business—through referrals from other lawyers. With this experience under his belt, Corboy left Dooley's firm in 1952 to start his own practice. At the time, it was standard practice for a young personal injury attorney to learn the trade under an established player, then leave to build his own practice.

Though it was common for younger lawyers to leave their mentors, this apprenticeship model had a strong element of paternalism. Dooley and Corboy maintained their relationship until Dooley's death. Dooley provided Corboy with early financial support, guidance, and advice on his cases, and encouraged his continued involvement in professional activities. Having seen how Dooley got business, when he went out on his own, he networked aggressively with other lawyers to generate business.

The referral system ensures that the higher value cases will, as a general rule, work their way up through the hierarchy of the plaintiffs' bar, thereby reinforcing the stratification in the profession and the dominance of the prevailing elite. [P]ersonal injury lawyers work hard to develop and maintain these referral relationships, and having a referral-based business is a sign of prestige in the personal injury bar. Corboy reflected that "I think there is a feeling of accomplishment when another lawyer recognizes your specialty . . . I like getting business from lawyers who think I'm competent." Another high-end plaintiffs' lawyer commented: "Having a good, strong referral base means that you don't have to do the other things that most attorneys desiring respect would want to avoid: advertising, chasing, having to work really hard to get cases."

The 1960s were watershed years for the plaintiffs' bar. They were able to improve their reputation with a combination of trial craft and professional bar activity, and they improved their economic position through legislative lobbying and legal arguments made to judges like themselves. The timing was right. They were in tune with the spirit of the socially activist state and indeed relatively moderate as a group in relation to the civil rights struggles and antiwar efforts.

The Illinois courts and legislature broadened the playing field of possible defendants in product liability, medical malpractice, and construction injury disputes. Changes in discovery rules also made it easier for plaintiffs' attorneys to build their cases. Elite plaintiff and defense lawyers helped to define the rules that governed their growing field. Certainly there were differences in perspective, but there was a shared sense that the law and practice of personal injury was developing in a positive fashion. The growing success in the courtroom fed further success in the appellate courts.

The attack on the plaintiffs' bar did not begin with corporate America. As litigation picked up for a number of reasons, attention began to focus more on the personal injury sector. The major challenge began through the writings of two academics, Robert Keeton and Jeffrey O'Connell, who promoted no-fault automobile insurance as an efficient way to bring compensation to accident victims. Liberal Democrats led by Michael Dukakis in Massachusetts, along with a few insurance companies, also lined up behind no-fault. The relatively liberal impetus for this activity underscores the fact that plaintiffs' lawyers—despite their proximity in background to the Chicago Democratic Party—had operated by emphasizing professionalism, especially skill in litigation and bar service—and a consensus in favor of compensation for victims. Their political connections remained quite local as well, and they had not invested much in the legal academy. They now confronted a group of policy and academic professionals who sought to take them out of the picture at a time when personal injury lawyers depended largely on automobile accidents. Reflecting on this time, one local plaintiffs' lawyer said that "no-fault would have ended the auto accident business and put all of the Irish and Jewish lawyers out of business."

In addition to the no-fault automobile insurance movement, the medical community also mobilized against the tort system in the 1970s. In 1976, the Illinois legislature passed the Medical Malpractice Reform Act, which, among other things, imposed a $500,000 cap on compensatory damages in medical malpractice disputes. [L]eading Illinois plaintiffs' lawyers used a litigation strategy to challenge the new legislation The Illinois Supreme Court again sided with the plaintiffs, invalidating the statute as unconstitutional.

In the face of no-fault and other emerging tort reform movements, accordingly, plaintiffs' lawyers made a concerted effort to establish ties to state legislators. The elite plaintiffs' lawyers in this way became major and sustained players in politics as a result of no-fault and its aftermath. They also became linked more directly to the Democratic Party. In the fight against no-fault, itself the product of academics and liberal politicians, some Republican defense lawyers also played important roles. Yet this plaintiff-defense alliance was short-lived. The plaintiffs' bar ultimately invested not in a bipartisan professional strategy above politics but rather in the Democratic relationships that were already built into their careers and their personal histories. They sought to protect their clients and their practices increasingly through the Democratic Party at the local and national level. They shifted from a concentration on professional respectability to one that combined efforts to build professional status with intense political partisanship.

Today, in fact, the very close ties to the Democratic Party are as much a part of the identity of the plaintiffs' bar as their commitment to professional bar activity, trial craft, and the referral system that channels the largest cases to the elite of the subprofession.

Plaintiffs' lawyers today do not have to reach out to establish contacts; they are sought after for their financial resources, for input on judicial candidates, and the like. In the words of Corboy, "Two senators called yesterday. One was from the State of Illinois. He was asking me my opinion of people who have been recommended for federal judgeships. There was another who wanted money from the State of Massachusetts." Another elite plaintiffs' lawyer noted, "I mean it's relentless. Relentless. And, you know, people think that plaintiffs' lawyers are just rolling in money. They call us every day. People running for Congress. People running for state rep. And nationally. Not just the president. You know, the attorney general in Iowa. The plaintiffs' bar, we get hit a lot." Professional responsibility within this subprofession, in short, now includes an obligation to give generously to the Democratic Party—which now embraces the plaintiffs' bar as well. To make the obvious point seen in national politics today, there are very strong personal and policy divisions now between the Republicans and the Democrats on the question of tort reform—an issue that energizes each side's stock of major contributors.

While Dooley had limited his activities to the plaintiffs' bar, Corboy became active in general bar associations as well, particularly the Chicago Bar Association. Corboy and others could see that they needed to gain recognition in the general bar associations long dominated by the corporate bar.

Corboy also followed the professional model of the corporate bar by building a philanthropic presence in the community. By the 1980s Corboy was already well known as a local philanthropist, with scholarship and fellowship programs at high schools and colleges across the city. Most of these scholarship programs are designed to help individuals get access to education—consistent with Corboy's own background and commitment to young law clerks who have worked during school.

By the 1970s, Corboy already began growing the next generation of plaintiffs' lawyers in Chicago. In his hiring practices and his mentoring philosophy, we can see just how Corboy reproduced a profession of lawyers much like himself. In his words, "I like people who have to work in order to get their education. And, if they've worked then they know how to juggle, they know how to study, and they know how to get things done."

The brand of professionalism embraced by the personal injury bar also highlights the modest personal characteristics (working-class background) of the successful plaintiffs' lawyer rather than the prestige of his or her degrees. Plaintiffs' lawyers draw upon their modest beginnings in their public rhetoric and in their appeal to juries. Stories of working-class men who now serve the underdog are ubiquitous in the rhetoric and self-concept of plaintiffs' lawyers. This rhetoric, along with their personal histories, distinguishes plaintiffs' lawyers from their corporate counterparts. It is part of their unique brand of professionalism.

Perhaps most illustrative of how far the plaintiffs' bar has come in just 50 years is its prominence in the national scene. One example is how the plaintiffs' bar quickly mobilized in response to the terrorist attacks of September 11, 2001. Shortly after the attacks, Congress pondered granting immunity to the airlines in order to protect the industry. In the process, Congress sought counsel from the plaintiffs' bar, who argued on behalf of the September 11 Victim Compensation Fund in lieu of lawsuits against the airlines. ATLA leaders called for a moratorium on lawsuits resulting from the attacks, and most plaintiffs' lawyers demonstrated restraint. The ABA then created a Task Force on Terrorism and the Law that, among other things, reviewed and advised the government on the development and administration of the September 11 Victim Compensation Fund. The mobilization and cooperation of the plaintiffs' bar was critical to the voluntary moratorium on lawsuits and the success of the fund. The plaintiffs' bar is sufficiently cohesive to hold in check those who might be tempted to take advantage of the disaster to reap financial gain but jeopardize the hard-earned respectability of this subprofession.

David Wilkins's study of black Chicago lawyers reveals striking parallels between the development of the plaintiffs' bar in the second half of the 20th century, and the evolution of the black bar in that same time period. For example, originally excluded from mainstream professional associations that were dominated by the white Protestant corporate elite, both plaintiffs' lawyers and black lawyers responded by establishing their own professional associations. Early on, both groups essentially operated in "parallel worlds" alongside mainstream professional associations that were dominated by the corporate elite. Eventually, both groups began to make headway into mainstream professional associations. Today, general bar associations are no longer the exclusive domains of the corporate elite. Instead, many formerly excluded groups—including plaintiffs' lawyers, black lawyers, and women lawyers—now play an active role in these associations and are represented in the leadership of these organizations.

In both groups, we also see a heavy reliance on social networks, within a relatively small subgroup, for career building and for advancing the interests of the collective. As the plaintiffs' bar relies heavily on referral networks for securing business, social networks among black Chicago lawyers are an important source of business and career advancement. Wilkins found that black lawyers in Chicago took advantage of their ties to rising [black] political power to further their individual careers and their collective advancement. [T]he history of the plaintiffs' bar, like the history of the black bar, is a story about the central role that social networks and local political power play in the making of a subprofession.

Despite a powerful desire for status in the mainstream legal profession, these plaintiffs' lawyers have not sought to draw on the credentials and powerful professional networks that come from elite law schools. In fact, the plaintiffs' bar thrives in part because it has managed to resist some of the hierarchies embedded more generally in the profession. The plaintiffs' bar has made a virtue out of its own relative marginality. Rather than deny their working-class heritage and lack of connection to the elite law schools, they celebrate their differences. In doing so, they position themselves as uniquely qualified to serve their "disadvantaged" clients, creating both a market niche and a professional niche that at once defines and protects their place in the system.

While the unique professional ideology of the plaintiffs' bar solidifies and protects their market niche, the focus of Chicago plaintiffs' lawyers on local law schools, working-class backgrounds, and local philanthropy perpetuates the relatively lower status of the plaintiffs' bar and reinforces the dominant position of the corporate bar. [D]espite increasing numbers of bar presidents and ever more impressive philanthropy, the plaintiffs' bar cannot come close to matching the prestige of the corporate bar—which, after all, defined the rules.

NOTES ON PARIKH AND GARTH

1. **Social Class and Stratification of the Bar.** Note the relationship between socioeconomic background, religion, ethnicity, and practice setting described in this excerpt. In what ways did Corboy's social background affect where Corboy went to law school and what his job opportunities were? To what extent do you observe similar phenomena in your law school experience or that of your friends?

2. **Legal Education and Stratification of the Bar.** How did legal education contribute to the stratification within the profession described in the Corboy article? Until the 1960s, elite colleges and universities maintained quotas on the number of Jews they would admit, typically capping enrollment at about 10 percent, and they refused to admit or only reluctantly admitted other racial, religious, and ethnic groups. To what extent do you think that America's education system might continue to affect the social composition of the legal profession?

3. **Then and Now?** If a study were to be done today of the urban bar in the largest metropolitan area near you, what do you imagine it would show regarding stratification? Being Catholic or Jewish is much less likely to predict career trajectory today than in the 1940s and 1950s when Corboy began his career. In their 1995 study of the Chicago bar, John Heinz and his co-authors found that religion and ethnicity played a much smaller part in the social structure of the bar than they did in the mid-1970s. On this point, it may be worth noting that six members of the U.S. Supreme Court are Catholic and the other three are Jews. The Heinz *et al.* research suggests that the axes of stratification in the Chicago bar have shifted from religion and ethnicity to gender and minority status.[1]

* * *

---

[1] JOHN HEINZ, ROBERT NELSON, REBECCA SANDEFUR AND EDWARD LAUMANN, URBAN LAWYERS: THE NEW SOCIAL STRUCTURE OF THE BAR (2005). Other studies of solo and small firm lawyers and plaintiffs' lawyers have also found a predominance of white men, but many such studies were conducted in the Northeast and the Upper Midwest. *See* Herbert Kritzer, *The Fracturing Legal Profession: The Case of Plaintiffs' Personal Injury Lawyers*, 8 INT'L J. LEGAL PROF. 225 (2001) (Wisconsin); Jerry Van Hoy, *Markets and Contingency: How Client Markets Influence the Work of Plaintiffs' Personal Injury Lawyers*, 6 INT'L J. LEGAL PROF. 345 (1999) (Indiana); Sara Parikh, *How the Spider Catches the Fly: Referral Networks in the Plaintiffs' Personal Injury Bar*, 5 N.Y.L.SCH. L. REV.243 (2006/07) (Chicago).

Regional Variation. How would the story of solo and small firm and plaintiffs' practice, and of stratification, differ if scholars had studied the West? Professors Carroll Seron and Richard Abel discussed this issue at the West Coast Law & Society meeting in 2011. The following is an edited synthesis of notes of their comments (used with permission of Professors Abel and Seron):

> Immigration patterns differ radically. In the East Coast and Mid-West, the dominant waves were eastern and southern European immigrants in the late nineteenth and early twentieth centuries; the great northern migration of African Americans in the mid-twentieth century; and recent migrations from everywhere. On the West Coast the significant migrations were internal (from the East and mid-West), from Asia, and from Mexico and Central America. These migrations affect the demographics of both the legal profession and its clients. Most immigrant groups have established their own professional associations. Sentiment about immigration is stronger in the West and Southwest.

> To be sure, the urban centers of the West and Southwest developed their own entrenched elites, but they were always much more fluid and porous than the Northeast. How did the fluidity of status and class in the West shape the development of the profession? Is it only a story of institutionalization of eastern firms? What role did the different types of economy play? In the west, ranching and agriculture played a bigger role. LA became a center of the film and TV industry and many Jewish lawyers succeeded in it. While Jews were outsiders in some LA circles, they also had the space to develop their own, relatively important base of power—and, influence. In thinking about the structure of the legal profession in the West and Southwest, it evolves in a place where people came to get away from the entrenched hierarchies that they could not break into in the East or elsewhere in the world. To be sure, they met new and perhaps different forms of hierarchy, but they were also more fluid. There are reasons to believe that the particular stories vary by area, and that the story in Los Angeles was different from that in San Francisco or Portland or Phoenix.

> In thinking about solo and small-firm practice in the West and Southwest, I would think that its history would show one of ethnic enclaves, particularly within the individual-client hemisphere. But, is this sustained over generations, or is it an entry point? Does the West and Southwest actually lay the foundation for immigrants' leveraging law as a site for social mobility?

> Without romanticizing the West, perhaps its wedge of fluidity and its attraction to outsiders is a "model." Much scholarly research on the legal profession finds the cup half full—there's always a residual where the WASPs enjoy privileges even in this more fluid,

heterogeneous profession. But, the other way to think about this is that the cup is getting smaller and smaller—with fewer and fewer sites where this closed, homogeneous elite can go it alone. I'm not suggesting that we live in a world without elites, or inequalities— far from it; rather, we may be a bit too hung up on documenting the vestiges rather than the main events—the collaborations, mergers, and negotiations across elites to form new synergies and sites of power and influence.

One study that addresses an aspect of the void identified by Professors Seron and Abel is a survey of all Latino lawyers in Los Angeles County conducted in 2000 by Professor Cruz Reynoso. The survey found a smaller percentage of Latinos in solo practice in Los Angeles (35%) than the percentage of lawyers in solo practice statewide (53% of all private practitioners) or nationwide (47%), but that the percentage of Los Angeles Latinos in firms of 2–5 lawyers or 6–10 lawyers was roughly similar to that of lawyers nationwide and statewide. As with studies of lawyers in the East and Midwest, the survey found that law school was a path of upward mobility for many Los Angeles Latinos: 92% of the Latino lawyers surveyed were the first in their immediate family to go to law school, 78% were the first in their extended family, and half were the first in their immediate family to attend college. Just over half of survey respondents reported having attended a first tier law school, and another third reported having attended a second tier school.[2]

One study of 460 Texas plaintiffs' lawyers based on a survey conducted in 2006 found many similarities between plaintiffs' bar in Texas and Chicago. Although the authors did not discuss the ethnicity of the lawyers in their sample, they did observe generally that the Texas plaintiffs' bar resembles the plaintiffs' bar in other regions, and many scholars have noted that plaintiffs' lawyers are largely white, male, and educated at local or regional law schools. The authors continued:

> [P]laintiffs' lawyers constitute a distinct practice community in Texas and elsewhere. [T]hese lawyers are specialists. [O]ver one-third of the respondents are board certified in personal injury trial law and/or civil trial law. In contrast, only 4% of all Texas lawyers are certified in personal injury trial law and/or civil trial law.

> For most of our respondents, automobile accident cases account for the largest percentage of their caseloads, followed by medical malpractice, commercial litigation, and products liability. Most do not handle high-value cases—the typical case value is modest ($38,000 in 2006 dollars). In addition, the size of their practices is small. Thirty-seven percent of our respondents are solo practitioners, and another 48% work in firms of 2 to 5 lawyers. This means that 85% work in very small firms or as solos. The

---

[2] Cruz Reynoso, *A Survey of Latino Lawyers in Los Angeles County—Their Professional Lives and Opinions*, 38 UC DAVIS L. REV. 1563, 1593, 1626 (2005).

comparable figure for Texas lawyers generally is 60%. With the exception of the visible lawyers with high-volume or mass tort practices, Texas plaintiffs' lawyers also tend to have small staffs. This would be expected for practices relying on the contingency fee, which must keep overhead as low as possible.

[T]he predominant source of clients is some form of referral. [J]ust under three-quarters of their caseloads comes from referrals. Referrals from other lawyers are much more important for plaintiffs' lawyers than for lawyers generally, and this may reflect their status as specialists and their willingness to pay referral fees to the lawyers who refer cases to them. Referrals from clients are the most important source of business for lawyers generally, and they are the second-most important for plaintiffs' lawyers.

Three elements appear important in understanding the community's normative values. First is the commitment to public service or the public good—as the plaintiffs' lawyers define it. Related is the idea of actually trying cases. Last is the nature and substance of the solicitation techniques used. [T]he remarks of a younger lawyer in Houston [are illustrative of the commitment to the public good as these lawyers perceive it]: "Amongst plaintiffs' lawyers . . . you have true believers who are doing this because they really care, they love people, they want to work for people, they want to help people and that's why they got into this business in the first place. It wasn't just making money."[3]

Referral Networks and Referral Fees. Studies of the plaintiffs' bar note the significance of referrals to the operation of a plaintiffs' practice. Although at one point, elites in the organized bar considered it unseemly for one lawyer to pay another to refer a matter, the Model Rule 1.5 explicitly allows it so long as certain conditions are met.

Rule 1.5(e) and Referral Fees

A division of a fee between lawyers who are not in the same firm may be made only if: (1) the division is in proportion to the services performed by each lawyer or each lawyer assumes joint responsibility for the representation; (2) the client agrees in writing to the arrangement, including the share each lawyer will receive; and (3) the total fee is reasonable.

The justification typically offered for allowing referral fees is that it provides an incentive for lawyers to recognize their own limited expertise and to refer cases to lawyers whom they believe most capable of providing successful representation.

---

[3] Stephen Daniels & Joanne Martin, *Plaintiffs' Lawyers and the Tension Between Professional Norms and the Need to Generate Business*, in LAWYERS IN PRACTICE: ETHICAL DECISION MAKING IN CONTEXT 112–114 (Leslie C. Levin & Lynn Mather eds., 2012).

In her study of referral networks, Sara Parikh found that these networks are highly organized and are more likely to transfer cases from low-end, neighborhood practices that tap into ethnic or occupational niches to high-end personal injury lawyers than the reverse or than laterally within a sector. She also found that referral relationships reinforce and reproduce stratification within the profession, with high-end lawyers securing more high-value cases and low-end lawyers securing more low-value cases through the referral networks.[4] Parikh's study concluded that this referral network may be beneficial for lawyers as well as clients:

> Referring attorneys would benefit by securing fees in cases they referred out; recipients would benefit from the additional business; and consumers would benefit because they would be more likely to end up in qualified hands.

> [M]ost individual consumers are unaware of the different types of expertise within the legal profession. When a personal legal matter arises, individual consumers often turn to a lawyer they know who may or may not practice the kind of law specific to the case. Attorneys serving individual clients are frequently faced with cases that are outside of their expertise. The risk is that the attorney will take cases that he is unqualified to handle. Fee-splitting was designed to discourage this. The institutionalization of referral fees was thought to benefit the client, whose case would be more likely to end up in the hands of an attorney capable of managing the case. Most personal injury attorneys believe that the fee-splitting system does serve the client's best interest.[5]

The Role of Substantive Law in Defining Professional Identity. The Parikh & Garth article on the Chicago plaintiffs' bar notes the significance of so-called "tort reform" in constructing the identity of lawyers in that practice segment. Views about tort policy became a significant feature of the professional identity of plaintiffs' lawyers, as is explained in more detail in the following excerpt:

"THE IMPACT THAT IT HAS HAD IS BETWEEN PEOPLE'S EARS:" TORT REFORM, MASS CULTURE, AND PLAINTIFFS' LAWYERS

Stephen Daniels and Joanne Martin
50 DePaul Law Review 453 (2000)

[This article is based on a mail survey of Texas plaintiffs' lawyers done in 2000, with 552 useable responses; interviews with 96 plaintiffs'

---

[4] Sara Parikh, *How the Spider Catches the Fly: Referral Networks in the Plaintiffs' Personal Injury Bar*, 5 N.Y. L. SCH. L. REV. 243, 252 (2006/07).

[5] *Id.* at 261, 265.

lawyers in four major urban centers and a few small towns in Texas, done in the mid to late 1990s; and interviews with a small number of non-plaintiffs' lawyers, defense lawyers, and judges in Texas.]

Tort reform's vision of civil litigation is a part of contemporary American mass culture, competing with other images of the legal system for acceptance. The vision's basic or unifying theme is the idea of a system run amok, for which "we all pay the price." It is a vision full of evocative metaphors and threatening images. It describes a system where, among other things, the number of personal injury suits is significantly higher than in the past (the litigation explosion); where more people bring lawsuits than should (frivolous lawsuits); where the size of awards is increasing faster than inflation (skyrocketing awards); where the size of most awards is excessive (outrageous awards); where the logic of verdicts and awards is capricious (the lawsuit lottery); where the cost of lawsuits is too high and the delays too great (a wasteful, inefficient system); where there is no longer a fair balance between the injured person and the defendant (exploiting "deep pockets"); and ultimately a system where the cost to society is unacceptably high ("we all pay the price").

The vision is complex, including a set of reasons or causes for the system gone wrong that are also familiar: people can sue without risk, paying the lawyer only if they win (reflecting a lack of personal responsibility); people think they can make a lot of money (greed and getting something for nothing); laws make it too easy to sue (a lack of fairness); people know the insurance company will pay (greed combined with a lack of fairness); people believe that anyone suffering an injury should be compensated regardless of fault (again, the lack of fairness combined with a lack of responsibility); and lawyers are looking for big contingency fees (more greed).

Texas plaintiffs' lawyers fervently believe that tort reform's public relations campaigns have had a profound effect on the cultural environment surrounding civil litigation. The "common sense" view of these lawyers is that juries have changed as a result of those campaigns. In our survey, for instance, 84.2 percent of all respondents stated their view that juries today are less likely to decide for the plaintiff in a personal injury suit than five years ago; 70.8 percent said juries are less likely to award economic damages; and 89.4 percent said juries are less likely to award non-economic damages.

Changes in jury verdicts, real or perceived, reverberate throughout the civil litigation process and may affect lawyers' practices in a variety of ways. Local jury verdicts play an important role for plaintiffs' lawyers, as well as for defense lawyers and insurance adjusters, in establishing the context in which the vast majority of matters are settled by fixing the "going rates." Each of the participants in this process follow verdicts carefully in the jurisdictions in which they work, and most regularly read one or more of the local jury verdict reporters available in Texas.

Among the lawyers we interviewed, there is a widely shared conclusion that the impact of the reformers' public relations campaigns has fallen the heaviest on the typical plaintiffs' lawyers, the ones handling "bread and butter" cases (simple cases of lower value), rather than the lawyers handling larger, more complex matters.

"Bread and butter" practices tend to be built upon the frequently occurring, lower-value car wreck cases. Such lawyers depend on a reasonable return on these cases, including non-economic damages, for cash flow and for survival. Many lawyers say they are not getting a good return on these cases, especially when it comes to non-economic damages. "The cases aren't . . . don't settle for what they used to," said one lawyer in a frequently heard complaint. A Fort Worth lawyer whose practice relies heavily on car wreck cases summarized the situation bluntly: "Without cash flow coming in you can't pay your bills and you can't fund your cases . . . we are in a brutal process of some [lawyers] being weeded out—and I may be one of them."

Non-economic damages, of course, are one of the targets of the reformers. These damages are of vital importance to the "bread and butter" lawyers because they can make the difference between earning a profit on a typical case or failing to realize any gain. Without some amount of non-economic damages on these low-value cases, the lawyer may not be able to recover enough to pay the client's bills, collect all or even most of the fee, and recoup his or her out-of-pocket expenses (the lawyers almost always front the case's costs). Short-changing the client is not something most lawyers want to do in what is a very competitive market for clients, a market in which the primary way of attracting new business is still through word-of-mouth client referrals. In fact, a number of lawyers said that they would, and have, cut their fee in order to not short-change the client.

What have "bread and butter" lawyers done in reaction to what they see as an altered, harsher environment? Some lawyers, in response to the altered environment, have simply gone out of business or substantially re-oriented their practices away from a primary concern with plaintiffs' cases taken on a contingency fee basis. Downsizing is more common, and similar to lawyers leaving the practice area, it diminishes the available supply of legal services for potential litigants. Greater attention to screening is the third reaction to the altered environment by "bread and butter" lawyers. Since juries and insurance companies are tougher, a number of lawyers commented that they need to be more careful in the cases they choose. Lawyers are less willing to take cases with relatively low damages and primarily soft tissue injury.

Exit and downsizing diminish the available supply of legal services. The supply is further diminished in the efforts of these lawyers to stay financially solvent. As a result, the client with a small, but legitimate claim may not be able to find a competent attorney, or have his or her claim successfully settled.

In addition to paying more attention to the case, many lawyers also said they must now pay more attention to who they will take as a client. In the survey, "bread and butter" lawyers were asked if they would take the hypothetical $3,000 soft tissue case described earlier if the client is unemployed; 53.5 percent said they would take the client today, while 71.3 percent would have taken the client five years ago. If the client had been a personal injury plaintiff in the past, 47.0 percent would take the client today, while 68.2 percent would have taken the client five years ago. If the client has a criminal record, 38.1 percent would take the client today, while 57.4 percent would have taken the client five years ago.

Along with a greater emphasis on more careful screening comes a greater sensitivity as to how the cases lawyers do accept are to be handled. Some lawyers are responding to this risk by using mediation more than they did in the past. Mediation is also cheaper, meaning less of a problem for cash flow and overhead.

Diversifying a practice's mix of business or finding new substantive markets for contingency fee work is another response to the altered environment. This response may further diminish the supply of legal services for some injured people, while expanding the supply for others. Diversification is not something a lawyer does as a result of a new opportunity. Rather, diversification is often a result of necessity and involves moving to what are perceived as safer markets. One lawyer told us: "I know how to practice criminal law. I know how to do divorces. I don't want to do them, but to be a lawyer you might still have to. And I think a lot of personal injury lawyers are coming to that conclusion."

Lawyers who diversify, for the most part, want to move into non-contingency fee areas which mean little or no real litigation, and a relatively steady income stream, like simple divorces, wills, and bankruptcies, or any other matters that can be automated and handled by legal secretaries or paralegals.

NOTES ON TORT REFORM AND PLAINTIFFS' LAWYERS

1. *What Is the Impact of Tort Reform?* Daniels and Martin argue that the public relations campaigns that have taken the label of tort reform have affected both how the public perceives civil litigation and how plaintiffs' lawyers perceive themselves and their work. What are their arguments and findings on these issues? Do you find them compelling?

2. ***Local and Specialty Bar Associations.*** Parikh and Garth note the importance of involvement in organized bar association activities in Corboy's career and in the self-conception of elite plaintiffs' lawyers, and the Daniels & Martin study of the Texas plaintiffs' bar echoes this finding. A number of studies of bar associations, including the ABA, state and local bar associations (like the Associated Bar of the City of New York), and specialty bar associations like ATLA have documented their importance in the professional socialization of lawyers.[6] Why is membership in a local bar association and, especially, a specialty bar like ATLA (in the Corboy excerpt) so significant in the lives of these lawyers? Local and specialty bars, unlike the ABA or the state bar, do not have the influence (in the case of the ABA) or the power (in the case of the state bar) to propose or adopt regulations governing the profession, although they sometimes adopt their own specialized standards of practice and encourage their members to abide by them.[7]

3. ***Choosing Sides.*** Plaintiffs' lawyers specializing in tort are not unique in practicing consistently on one side of a particular type of dispute. In labor and employment, civil rights, some aspects of securities, consumer protection, environmental law, and other fields, lawyers also tend to specialize in representing either plaintiffs or defendants but not both. How do the lawyers develop a professional identity in relationship to the kinds of clients they represent and their views about desirable social and legal policy? In other practice areas, lawyers may switch from one "side" to another intermittently or frequently. For example, some lawyers represent both plaintiffs and defendants in intellectual property infringement cases. Do you think it is good or bad for society (or lawyers) that lawyers in some fields do not switch sides?

C. CONTINGENCY FEES AND FEE-SHIFTING STATUTES

One of the major differences among practice settings is in how lawyers get paid, and in how much. Apart from the realities of who has money to pay lawyers, the law of attorneys' fees has a great impact on the practices of lawyers. The American Rule, as it is known, is that each side in litigation pays its own fees. In England, and those countries following the English Rule, the loser pays the winner's attorneys' fees in litigation. Under the American Rule, in the absence of any legal right to recover attorneys' fees, lawyers and clients have developed the contingent fee agreement as a way to enable plaintiffs to vindicate their legal rights.

---

[6] *See,* e.g., Robert L. Nelson & David M. Trubek, *Arenas of Professionalism: The Professional Ideologies of Lawyers in Context*, in LAWYERS' IDEALS/LAWYERS' PRACTICES: TRANSFORMATIONS IN THE AMERICAN LEGAL PROFESSION 179, 185 (Robert L. Nelson et al. eds., 1992); Jack King, *Origins of the Organized Criminal Defense Bar: The National Association of Criminal Defense Lawyers—Part One*, THE CHAMPION, May/June 2008.

[7] *See,* e.g., THE AMERICAN ACADEMY OF MATRIMONIAL LAWYERS, BOUNDS OF ADVOCACY: AMERICAN ACADEMY OF MATRIMONIAL LAWYERS STANDARDS OF PRACTICE (2000).

Contingency Fees. Plaintiffs' lawyers are typically paid on contingency: that is, they get paid only if they recover money at trial or through settlement. They must count on winning or settling a case and taking a percentage of the recovery (often 25% if the matter settles before trial; 30–40% if the matter is tried to a jury; and 40–50% if the matter must be litigated through an appeal). Lawyers in private practice who represent large entities, like corporations, the government, and insurance companies, are typically compensated on an hourly basis or, especially recently, in fixed fee or "value-based" billing agreements. They typically can count on their clients having money to pay them, and when they litigate they are usually paid regardless of whether they win or lose at trial. Contingent fees are considered improper in some countries, reflecting a view that litigation is an evil that should not be incentivized through fee arrangements. In the United States, by contrast, many regard litigation as a mechanism to vindicate important rights and contingent fees as a way to achieve that.

A **contingency fee** agreement is one in which the amount of the fee is contingent on the outcome of the matter, typically on the plaintiff recovering money. Contingency fee agreements must be in writing, signed by the client, and state the method by which the fee is to be determined, including the percentage that accrues to the lawyer in the event of settlement, trial or appeal, and whether litigation and other expenses will be deducted from the recovery before or after the fee is calculated. Model Rule 1.5(c).

Fees may not be contingent upon the securing of a divorce or on the amount of alimony or child support or a property settlement. Contingent fees are also prohibited in criminal defense.

NOTES ON CONTINGENCY FEES

1.   *Who Should Pay Attorneys' Fees in Litigation?* What are the advantages and disadvantages of the American Rule as opposed to the English Rule?

2.   *Contingency Fees and the American Rule.* Why is the practice of contingency fee agreements a logical solution to some of the problems of the American Rule? What are the advantages and problems, for clients, for lawyers, and for the public, of contingency fee agreements?

* * *

Statutory Fee Shifting. You probably have deduced that the American Rule makes litigation unaffordable for any person who does not have the money to hire a lawyer unless the possible recovery in litigation is enough to cover the costs, and sometimes even meritorious cases do not offer the promise of sufficient recovery. For example, intentional discrimination in employment, education, voting, and housing is unlawful, but the economic damages, if they are calculable at all, are often too small to cover the cost of litigation. To address this problem, Congress and many legislatures have enacted fee-shifting statutes covering several categories of cases in which the likely recovery in a meritorious case may not be enough to cover the costs. Fee-shifting statutes are particularly common in civil rights, including employment and housing discrimination and government deprivations of rights to education, to vote, as well as in cases of police abuse, and under environmental protection and consumer protection statutes. The purposes of such statutes are both to provide an incentive to private persons to enforce the public policy reflected in the law (individual plaintiffs play the role of "private attorneys general") and to protect the poor and vulnerable from violations of their rights by enabling them to find lawyers to take their cases.

The calculation of fee awards under fee-shifting statutes and other rules providing for recovery of attorneys' fees (such as in class actions) are explained in the *Bluetooth* case excerpted below. Judicial review of fee awards under fee-shifting statutes and class action settlements are by far the most commonly enforced law governing attorneys' fees. However, fees are also regulated under state ethics rules, such as Model Rule 1.5. As we saw in Chapter 6, Model Rule 1.5 provides that a lawyer shall not charge "an unreasonable fee." Reasonableness is judged by a multi-factor inquiry that considers:

(1) The time and labor required, the novelty or difficulty, and the skill required by the case;

(2) Likelihood apparent to the client that the lawyer will not be able to work for others while handling the matter;

(3) The customary fee for similar services in the same locality;

(4) The amount involved and the results obtained;

(5) Time limitations imposed by the client or the circumstances;

(6) The nature and length of the attorney client relationship;

(7) The experience, reputation, and ability of the lawyer;

(8) Whether the fee is fixed or contingent.

Under Model Rule 1.5, a contingent fee might be unreasonable if either there is no risk of nonrecovery (for example, if an attorney charged a client a contingent fee to collect the life insurance proceeds from her recently deceased husband's policy and there was no doubt that the insurance company would pay), or where the recovery is likely to be so large that a contingent fee would exceed an appropriate level of compensation for the work and risk involved. Restatement (Third) of the Law Governing Lawyers § 35 comment *c*.

IN RE BLUETOOTH HEADSET PRODUCTS LIABILITY LITIGATION

United States Court of Appeals for the Ninth Circuit
654 F.3d 935 (9th Cir. 2011)

HAWKINS, SENIOR CIRCUIT JUDGE:

The settlement agreement approved in this products liability class action provides the class $100,000 in *cy pres* awards and zero dollars for economic injury, while setting aside up to $800,000 for class counsel and $12,000 for the class representatives—amounts which the [trial] court subsequently awarded in full in a separate order. William Brennan and other class members (collectively "Objectors") challenge the fairness and reasonableness of the settlement and appeal both the approval and fee orders, arguing the district court abused its discretion in failing to consider whether the gross disproportion between the class award and the negotiated fee award was reasonable.

Plaintiffs filed twenty-six putative class actions in courts around the country against Motorola, Inc., Plantronics, Inc., and GN Netcom, Inc. (collectively "defendants"), alleging defendants knowingly failed to disclose the potential risk of noise-induced hearing loss associated with extended use of their wireless Bluetooth headsets at high volumes, in violation of state consumer fraud protection and unfair business practice laws. The Judicial Panel on Multidistrict Litigation coordinated these cases in *In re Bluetooth Headset Products Liability Litigation* in the Central District of California.

Plaintiffs sought money damages on behalf of millions of individuals who had purchased Bluetooth headsets since June 30, 2002, purportedly in reliance on allegedly misleading representations about the safety and usability of the product. The complaint did not state a claim for personal injury but asserted economic injury, alleging plaintiffs would not have purchased their Bluetooth headsets but for defendants' willful false advertising. Plaintiffs sought actual damages in the amount paid for the product, which they claimed to be between $70 and $150 per headset, along with injunctive relief, restitution, punitive damages, attorneys' fees and costs.

Class counsel spent considerable time researching legal and industry standards on acceptable noise levels, surveying warnings on other audio devices, obtaining acoustic test results and other documents from defendants, and working with experts to review this data and evaluate the risk of noise-induced hearing loss. The parties voluntarily exchanged discovery and held at least three in-person meetings to discuss the merits of the litigation and discovery issues before participating in a formal mediation session.

Unable to reach a settlement at that time, defendants shortly thereafter filed a joint motion to dismiss on various grounds, insisting their products are safe and denying any wrongdoing on their part. The parties successfully participated in another mediation session and filed a proposed class action settlement agreement purporting to resolve all claims. [After considering the objections, the district court certified the class for settlement purposes only, pursuant to Federal Rule of Civil Procedure 23(b)(3), and approved the settlement agreement.] The district court later entered a separate order awarding $850,000 to class counsel for fees and costs and $12,000 to be distributed among the nine representative plaintiffs.

We review for abuse of discretion a district court's award of fees and costs to class counsel, as well as its method of calculation.

Objectors argue that the district court should not have approved as fair and reasonable a settlement agreement that, on its face, so disproportionately advances the interests of class counsel over those of the class itself. They further contend that class counsel should not have been awarded eight times the amount of the class recovery. While attorneys' fees and costs may be awarded in a certified class action where so authorized by law or the parties' agreement, Fed. R. Civ. P. 23(h), courts have an independent obligation to ensure that the award, like the settlement itself, is reasonable, even if the parties have already agreed to an amount.

We have approved two different methods for calculating a reasonable attorneys' fee depending on the circumstances. The "lodestar method" is appropriate in class actions brought under fee-shifting statutes (such as federal civil rights, securities, antitrust, copyright, and patent acts), where the relief sought—and obtained—is often primarily injunctive in nature and thus not easily monetized, but where the legislature has authorized the award of fees to ensure compensation for counsel undertaking socially beneficial litigation. The lodestar figure is calculated by multiplying the number of hours the prevailing party reasonably expended on the litigation (as supported by adequate documentation) by a reasonable hourly rate for the region and for the experience of the lawyer. Though the lodestar figure is presumptively reasonable, the court may adjust it upward or downward by an appropriate positive or negative multiplier reflecting a host of "reasonableness" factors, including the quality of representation, the benefit obtained for the class, the complexity and novelty of the issues presented, and the risk of nonpayment.

Where a settlement produces a common fund for the benefit of the entire class, courts have discretion to employ either the lodestar method or the percentage-of-recovery method. Because the benefit to the class is easily quantified in common-fund settlements, we have allowed courts to award attorneys a percentage of the common fund in lieu of the often more time-consuming task of calculating the lodestar. Applying this calculation method, courts typically calculate 25% of the fund as the "benchmark" for a reasonable fee award, providing adequate explanation in the record of any "special circumstances" justifying a departure.

Though courts have discretion to choose which calculation method they use, their discretion must be exercised so as to achieve a reasonable result. Thus, for example, where awarding 25% of a "mega-fund" would yield windfall profits for class counsel in light of the hours spent on the case, courts should adjust the bench-mark percentage or employ the lodestar method instead.

Absent any explanation from the district court, we are concerned that the amount awarded was 83.2% of the total amount defendants were willing to spend to settle the case, viewing the $800,000 allotment for attorneys' fees, the $12,000 allotment for an incentive award, the $100,000 *cy pres* award, and the $50,000 allotment for fees as a "constructive common fund." Twenty-five percent of this $962,000 fund, by contrast, would have yielded only $240,500 in attorneys' fees. Plaintiffs urge us to find that the fee award is justified because the injunctive relief confers a valuable benefit and was the primary objective of the lawsuit, but the district court did not make findings on the value of the injunctive relief, so we cannot evaluate whether it justifies an otherwise disproportionate award.

On remand, the district court may reach any number of conclusions: it may find the $800,000 attorneys' fee award reasonable in light of the hours reasonably expended and the results achieved, and re-approve both orders; it may determine the fee request is excessive but find no further evidence that class counsel betrayed class interests for their own benefit, and thus uphold the agreement while lowering the fee award; or it may find the fee request excessive and conclude that class counsel therefore negotiated an unreasonable settlement and direct the parties back to the negotiating table.

NOTES ON THE REGULATION OF FEES

1. ***Standards for Judicial Review of Contingency Fees or Fee Awards.*** When, if ever, should the organized bar (in the form of disciplinary proceedings) and/or courts (in the form of review of fee awards, as in the *Bluetooth* case) invalidate or modify fee agreements between clients and lawyers?

(a) Consider conflicts of interest. When do a lawyer and client have a conflict of interest as a result of a fee agreement? Don't the attorney and client *always* have some form of conflicting interests about how the lawyer gets paid, regardless of whether the billing is hourly, flat fee, or contingency? What is the basis for bar or court review of the agreement? What are the benefits and risks of outside review?

(b) Consider excessiveness. What fee is excessive? Why do contingency agreements pose a risk of an excessive fee?

(c) Consider informed client consent. Model Rule 1.5 requires fee agreements be "communicated to the client, preferably in writing." And when the fee is contingent, Model Rule 1.5(c) requires the agreement be in writing signed by the client; state the method by which the fee is computed, including the percentage; identify expenses to be deducted from the recovery and whether the deduction will be before or after the contingent fee percentage is computed; and identify expenses the client must pay regardless of whether the client prevails.

2. *What Is the Purpose of Each Factor?* Notice the similarities in the factors used by courts to evaluate the propriety of a fee award under a fee-shifting regime and the factors used under Model Rule 1.5 to consider the reasonableness of a fee agreement. What is the purpose of each of these factors?

3. *Is Cross-Subsidization Permissible?* Should lawyers be permitted to collect large fees in some cases to subsidize the costs of other cases? In considering the relationship between the fee in any given case and the recovery in that case, is it appropriate to consider how many other clients the lawyer represented in similar matters from whom the lawyer collected nothing? Is there a difference between subsidizing unsuccessful cases and subsidizing successful cases that produce too small a recovery to cover the litigation costs?

4. *Fee Provisions in Settlements.* Settlements can pose challenging conflicts of interest between plaintiffs' lawyers and their clients. The *Bluetooth* case involved settlement of a class action, in which courts are particularly concerned that lawyers for the class might negotiate a settlement that benefits the named plaintiffs and the lawyers but provides nothing for the other members of the class (as in the *Bluetooth* matter). In what respects is this troubling? Is it always wrong? What role should courts play in monitoring settlements containing fee agreements?

Settlements can also pose challenging conflicts of interest between plaintiffs' lawyers and their clients in civil rights cases. For example, a defendant may indicate willingness to settle but demand that the total settlement, including the attorneys' fees that the plaintiff is entitled to under a fee-shifting statute, be negotiated as a package, leaving the division of the amount to the plaintiffs and their lawyers. Some courts and disciplinary authorities initially banned the package negotiating tactic because it created a conflict between the lawyers and the plaintiffs. The Supreme Court rejected the idea that the tactic was impermissible, reasoning that defendants have an interest in knowing their total possible liability when settling a case.

Evans v. Jeff D., 475 U.S. 717 (1986). A difference between the *Jeff D.* scenario and the *Bluetooth* situation is that the conflict between the plaintiffs and their lawyers in *Jeff D.* was created by the defense lawyers' settlement offer; the conflict in *Bluetooth* was created (perhaps) by the plaintiffs' lawyers. Is that relevant?

PROBLEM 23–1

A lawyer represents a plaintiff grievously injured in an auto accident in a products liability action against the manufacturer of an SUV that rolled over as the vehicle rounded a tight turn. The manufacturer knew that the design of the vehicle posed a high risk of rollovers but decided not to modify the design because it decided it would be cheaper to pay the damages judgments than to modify the design late in the design process. To punish the manufacturer and deter similar conduct by it and other manufacturers in the future, the jury awarded $100 million in punitive damages because it determined that a large award was necessary to hurt the company's bottom line enough to deter future wrongdoing. The contingent fee agreement complied with the informed consent provisions of Model Rule 1.5. It provided for a low percentage (20%) if the recovery exceeded $10 million, but still the lawyer's fee was $20 million. Is the fee excessive? (In considering when a fee to a plaintiffs' lawyer for a high-value litigation is excessive, you might also consider what answer you gave to Problem 6–1 when we considered whether a lawyer who represented a start-up company could enforce an agreement with the client that the lawyer would be paid in shares of the company stock that later became worth many millions of dollars.)

D. SUMMARY

In this chapter, we studied the plaintiffs' bar. We considered similarities within the plaintiffs' bar across regions of the country and the possible regional and practice specialty variations among some sectors of the individual and small business client hemisphere. We saw how referral networks, contingency fee agreements, and fee-shifting statutes are very important to clients and lawyers in these practice sectors, and we studied the law governing these forms of fees.

CHAPTER 24

BOUTIQUES

■ ■ ■

A. INTRODUCTION

Boutiques, as explained in the first section of this chapter, are small law firms that represent large organizational clients, offer highly specialized services, and/or attract elite lawyers. Boutiques fit both in the world of small firms and in the world of large law firms because many boutiques compete with large firms in recruiting lawyers with elite credentials and for work from corporate clients. When boutiques serve large entities, they challenge the generalization that lawyers in small firms serve primarily individual clients and small businesses. When they attract lawyers with elite credentials, they defy the notion that those lawyers tend to work in large firms or in corporate counsel offices when they work in private practice. Thus, boutiques straddle the divide between what Heinz and Laumann once termed the two hemispheres of the bar. The bulk of this chapter explores how and why boutiques form thrive.

Lawyers do not agree on the definition of a boutique law firm and, in particular, on how boutiques differ from small firms. For purposes of the following discussion, we define a boutique as a small law firm that represents large organizational clients, provides highly specialized services, and/or recruits elite lawyers with offers of generous compensation or sophisticated legal work. Boutiques have lately become of interest to commentators and scholars because they challenge some of the conventional wisdom about the economic structure of law firms, and because they complicate the story about the relationship between practice setting, client type, and lawyers' status and prestige.

B. WHAT IS A BOUTIQUE?

The term boutique is used in myriad ways. Our working definition includes two elements that are common to most definitions used in academic and popular sources: specialization and size.[1] In one of the rare scholarly treatments of this practice setting, two scholars have defined boutiques as small, specialized firms that intentionally "cultivate their

---

[1]   Black's Law Dictionary defines "boutique": "[a] small specialty business; esp., a small law firm specializing in one particular aspect of law practice."

comparative advantage in selected specialties and suppress any push to more general coverage in order to maintain their attractiveness for referral work."[2]

Some boutiques represent some of the same large corporations that big firms represent, and they succeed in competing with large firms for business because they offer highly specialized services. Common areas of specialization include intellectual property, tax, employment, environmental, immigration, bankruptcy, and either trial or appellate work. Although many boutiques cater primarily to clients in the corporate hemisphere, some also serve individuals and small business clients. Some boutiques represent only individuals or nonprofit organizations (civil rights boutiques fit this description). Not every firm that we define as a boutique specializes. Some boutiques focus on criminal and civil litigation, which may include such a broad area of subject matters that it stretches the notion of specialization.[3] Conversely, not every small firm that specializes in a field of practice fits the conventional definition of a boutique. Small firms that specialize in areas of practice associated primarily with individual client service, such as small real estate transactions, family law, or plaintiffs' personal injury are rarely called boutiques.

Although boutique generally connotes small, there is no consensus among lawyers about how small a firm must be in order to be defined as a boutique. In 1993, when having 100 lawyers was enough to make a firm large, Caplin & Drysdale (then with 50 lawyers) was often called a boutique specializing in tax.[4] (It still specializes in tax, saying it offers "the know-how and experience to rival largest firms combined with the efficiency that characterize a legal boutique."[5]) Another large firm with a subject specialty is Frangomen, LLC, a corporate immigration firm with 300 lawyers in 39 offices in 15 countries. If the firm had 30 lawyers instead of 300, it likely would be called a boutique because it specializes in providing immigration services to corporate clients and the employees whom they seek to recruit across national borders. (The firm's website does not refer to the firm as a boutique).

To sociologists of the profession, and perhaps to law students too, one of the most intriguing aspects of boutiques is that they tend to regard themselves, and to be regarded by others, as elite firms. Firms that claim the term boutique tend to use boutique synonymously with "elite" to

---

[2]   MARC GALANTER & THOMAS PALAY, TOURNAMENT OF LAWYERS: THE TRANSFORMATION OF THE BIG LAW FIRM 125 (1991).

[3]   *Harlee & Bald, P.A.: A litigation boutique law firm*, SARASOTA MAGAZINE (June 22, 2003).

[4]   Larry Smith, *Tax Boutiques Maintain Independence As New Challenges Loom*, OF COUNSEL (Apr. 5, 1993), p.1.

[5]   "Message from the President," Our Firm, http://www.capdale.com/about.aspx.

describe themselves. What makes a social group elite and the production of hierarchy through the creation of social distinctions have long been fascinating to sociologists.[6] As you read this chapter, examine the value judgments implicit in how various lawyers and commentators use the term boutique.

In the readings that follow, we present information about how boutiques form, how they attract clients and lawyers, how they thrive, and how they fail. There is no substantial scholarly literature on boutiques. Therefore, the readings come from the legal press rather than from books or academic journal articles. (You may notice that, unlike academic sociological studies, these popular or legal press articles are based on unscientific samples of interviews and may be less empirically rigorous, more impressionistic, and thus less thorough or reliable as description.) The readings explain how the creation and survival of boutiques are influenced by conflicts of interest, client pressures on billing, and lawyers' concerns about life-style issues in large firms. As the readings suggest, boutiques may be especially well-positioned to benefit from the restructuring of the legal services market generated by the recession of 2008–2011. They typically charge lower rates than large firms, and they face fewer disqualifying conflicts of interest. Boutiques attract highly qualified lawyers who wish to develop and offer specialized expertise without working in large bureaucratically organized institutions. They also draw lawyers who are willing to sacrifice financial compensation for "life-style" benefits, such as more flexible work arrangements than are typically afforded in large firms. Some boutique firms are structured to allow lawyers to mesh client service with political activism. (We will return to the latter point when we consider "private public interest law firms" in Chapter 29.)

C. THE FORMATION AND SURVIVAL OF BOUTIQUES

One factor contributing to the emergence and prosperity of boutique firms is conflicts of interest. As we saw in Part IV, conflicts of interest rules complicate the ability of large firm practitioners to accept work. Large firms with multiple offices spread across many cities represent large corporations with multiple subsidiaries, and when (for example) the transactional lawyers in New York represent a large corporation, that firm's intellectual property lawyers in California or international commercial arbitration lawyers in Dubai are prohibited from handling matters for adversaries of the same company without client consent. It may be more profitable for the California lawyers to set up shop in a

---

[6]　　*See, e.g.,* PIERRE BOURDIEU, DISTINCTION: A SOCIAL CRITIQUE OF THE JUDGMENT OF TASTE (Richard Nice, trans., 1984).

smaller, boutique form so that they can accept the work that clients are trying to send. As an article in the legal press put it, without the conflict problems, "the clients can then hire the same people they would have chosen to hire at a larger firm, at a potentially lower rate. The draw: substantial savings, same people."[7] When a large law firm has a conflict of interest prohibiting it from representing a valued client, it may prefer to refer the matter to a boutique rather than to another large firm because the boutique will be less likely (because less able) to attempt to recruit the client to give all its legal work to the firm.[8]

Cost is another reason lawyers leave large firms to start boutique practices and large corporate clients hire boutique firms. Boutiques generally operate with lower overhead costs because they have smaller and less expensive offices and smaller administrative staffs. Boutiques, therefore, can charge less. When they can provide the same quality legal service at lower cost, corporate in house counsel, who are expected to control legal costs while producing good results for the corporation, find them an appealing choice.

> Boutiques can be unique service providers in that they typically have a specific expertise or focus in niche areas that enable them to offer specialized services to clients, along with a personal touch. IP boutiques were one of the first to become highly competitive among sophisticated consumers of legal services, competing with firms that were larger in headcount and geographic desirability. The complexities of intellectual property law and the attorneys' day-to-day focus on that subject matter gave those boutiques a competitive edge in their field. Similarly, attorneys practicing in environmental boutiques, immigration boutiques, and other specialty areas often focus their attention on the complexities of specific regulations and develop skill sets in areas that may not be available in many firms. In addition, because the focused practitioners have chosen a boutique for their practice, they may be able to offer their specialized services for a more competitive rate and innovative or flexible fee structure as they are not burdened by the overhead that comes with multiple offices, non-billing service staff such as recruiters and marketers, and other fixed costs that must be passed on to the client.[9]

---

[7] Debra Tsuchiyama Baker & David P. Young, *Unique Times for Boutiques*, 47 HOUSTON LAWYER 4 (Mar/Apr 2010).

[8] Larry Smith, *Orange County Debacle Raises Key Business Issues for Law Firms*, OF COUNSEL, July 17, 1995.

[9] Debra Tsuchiyama Baker & David P. Young, *Unique Times for Boutiques*, 47 HOUSTON LAWYER 4 (Mar/Apr 2010).

With lower fixed costs, boutiques can have more flexibility when it comes to billing arrangements. They can take on small matters at lower billing rates, which has advantages for lawyers who provide specialized representation to small clients unable to afford large firm fees. Lower billing rates also help junior lawyers who would like to develop their trial or other skills in small-dollar cases and would like to bring in their own business but are unlikely to be able to recruit Fortune 100 companies as clients. The ability to charge a lower hourly rate or a flat rate may enable boutiques to recruit very talented lawyers. For example, lawyers who want to try cases may find boutique litigation firms the most realistic opportunity to get into the courtroom and actually try cases before a jury, which is a relatively rare occurrence for lawyers at some of the nation's largest law firms. The billing rates of large firms make litigation through trial economically irrational for all but the so-called "bet the company" kind of case. When tens or hundreds of millions of dollars are at stake in litigation, clients may settle rather than gamble on a jury verdict. And when such high-dollar cases do go to trial, a client will typically allow only the most seasoned trial lawyer to stand up in court. Particularly for young lawyers who need to try cases to gain experience, a boutique may be the only path (other than going into government work) to gaining that experience. Boutiques also are able to negotiate fee arrangements quickly, which can help in the effort to retain a client who needs immediate legal assistance.[10]

Understanding the Boutique Law Firm

Boutiques that serve large corporate clients sometimes compete successfully against large firms. Factors that sometimes give boutiques advantages in this competition include fewer conflicts of interest, lower overhead costs, lower rates and greater flexibility in billing arrangements, and the ability to attract talented lawyers with specialized knowledge who want more autonomy than large law firms typically offer.

Some boutiques formed because lawyers sought more autonomy than they could find at large firms. The attractions of boutique practice are explained in the following profile of a San Diego litigation boutique:

ENTERPRISE: LAW, BOUTIQUE ALSO MEANS UNIQUE
Renee Beasley Jones
San Diego Business Journal, Nov. 25, 2002

More than 10 years ago, [Fred] Kosmo came to Wilson Petty from Gibson, Dunn & Crutcher LLP, a well known worldwide firm that boasts

---

[10] Heather Chambers, *Boutique Law Offices Appear More Charming*, SAN DIEGO BUS. J., Jan. 18, 2010.

of more than 800 attorneys. Like Kosmo, most of the 12 partners and associates at Wilson Petty came from heavyweights such as Gibson Dunn, Gray Cary and Luce Forward. At larger firms, working nights and weekends often equates with getting noticed, Kosmo said. Not at Wilson Petty. While the firm offers the chance to tackle high-profile cases found at national and international firms—clients include Johnson & Johnson, Ford Motor Co., Honda, University of California Board of Regents, Petco Animal Supplies Inc. and Mail Boxes Etc. the firm's philosophy sneers at the idea that quality defense comes from 80-hour workweeks. Of course, emergencies come up and long hours sometimes follow. Kosmo recently worked at home from 7:30 p.m. to 11:30 p.m. after putting in a full day. But it's the exception rather than the rule.

Wilson Petty, formed in 1991, breaks all gender and minority molds—locally and nationally. Of the firm's six partners, Kosmo is the lone male. "People joke with me about being the token male," he said with a grin. Of the firm's 12 lawyers, eight are female. Two Wilson Petty partners are black women, which makes the firm even more rare. Recent research from the National Association of Law Placement shows that minority attorneys account for only 3.5 percent of partners in the nation's major law firms. Nationally, women account for less than 15.8 percent of partners in those firms, the NALP reports. "It has amused me that there are segments of the San Diego legal community that have dubbed us 'the chick firm,'" said Regina Petty, one of the firm's partners. At one time, Wilson Petty partners sat down to discuss ways to change the "chick-firm" perception. They decided to let it stand. "If that's what they're thinking, that's OK," Petty said. "They're underestimating us, and we'll quietly walk away with all the clients we want." At Wilson Petty, gender never enters into hiring decisions, Petty said. Lawyers are invited to join the firm for two basic reasons. First, they must be topnotch litigators. Second, they must be good people.

The firm offers a wide range of legal expertise. Practice areas include real property, employment law, First Amendment litigation, and product liability and warranty. Wilson Petty has won notable cases, including a major victory for Johnson & Johnson in the well-publicized latex glove case. About six years ago, Petco retained Wilson Petty. The firm handles Petco's employment litigation nationwide. Other law firms provide other types of defense for the company. Several things make Wilson Petty a standout, said Paul Schmitt, vice president of human resources at Petco. The firm forges personal relationships with clients, Schmitt said. No customer service rep calls. "It's Claudette Wilson, whose name is on the door, who gets to know you, who becomes part of your organization," he said. When Schmitt calls Wilson Petty, he's forwarded directly to an attorney at least 80 percent of the time. When he leaves a voice-mail message, the call back comes fast. "We've worked with larger firms in the past and certainly bigger names. They lost our business because Wilson Petty had something to offer that they didn't match," Schmitt said. Whether Wilson Petty was a rare woman or minority-owned firm never entered into Petco's decision to retain its services. "That's gravy. That's nice. It's a nice plus," Schmitt said.

* * *

Some boutiques, such as intellectual property boutiques, formed because of changes in industry. Many intellectual property boutiques emerged in the 1980s and 1990s with the explosion of the technology and internet sectors of the economy. They could compete with large firms for clients who needed lawyers with technical backgrounds because intellectual property is a large and lucrative practice area and law firms with the right intellectual property expertise did not need to offer a full range of legal services in order to attract large corporate clients.[11] Patent litigation, for example, was regarded as so specialized that IP boutiques could be a successful niche practice without needing a broad array of expertise. Large law firms began to grow their IP practices by some combination of lateral hiring or merger with an IP boutique, but some IP boutiques thrive either because of their expertise or because small- and medium-sized firm clients do not need the full array of legal services and prefer the billing structure that boutiques offer.[12] As one news account described the emergence of IP boutiques,

> IP boutique firms have had a wonderful run because IP has been hot for a long time, but the market has changed dramatically, said Joel Henning, senior vice president and head of Hildebrandt International's Chicago office. Many IP boutiques relied on patent prosecution for profitability, and that could be a problem in today's market, Henning said. "Some general practice firms are getting out of patent prosecution all together," he said. "It is one of the areas of the law that is beginning, and I stress only beginning, to be outsourced overseas to India."

> A corporation's general counsel may outsource the company's patent prosecution, or the outside law firm may use offshore outsourcing, Henning said. These individuals from India speak good English, are well-trained in both the law and in a science or technical area, and have the overall skills to handle patent prosecution. Their work may then be reviewed for quality and consistency by either the corporation's inside counsel or by the outside firm. "IP litigation remains very hot but because it's

---

[11] Larry Smith, *IP Update: Outside, Inside Counsel in Tug of War as Profitability Soars*, OF COUNSEL, Mar. 18, 1991 (describing the growth in the amount of and profitability of IP work in the late 1980s and the competition between boutiques and large firms to attract clients).

[12] Olivia Clarke, *The IP World: A Place for Firms of All Sizes*, CHICAGO LAWYER, May 2008.

so hot, the good general practice firms with high-end litigators have been very, very savvy about competing with the IP boutique for the most profitable IP litigation," Henning said, "and they are increasingly successful at it."

Some boutique and general practice firms have found a way to work together. Large firms often recommend Davis McGrath when conflicts prevent them from handling the matter themselves, said Bill McGrath, name partner and associate director of John Marshall's Center for Intellectual Property Law. Davis McGrath, a 12-lawyer IP boutique firm that started in 1990, may work with a larger firm when the boutique has a particular expertise that the larger firm doesn't have. "They feel comfortable sending the matter to us," McGrath said. "We aren't going to walk away with the client, but we are providing excellent services." His firm has grown and become more sophisticated in terms of the type of clients it handles, but it wants to maintain a small-firm atmosphere, he said. "I don't want it to sound like partners at big firms don't pay attention to their clients, but in some ways, with a smaller firm, more senior partners are probably more accessible than they might be at a larger firm," McGrath said.

There will always be clients who decide to work with a firm that has the expertise, as opposed to a firm that is a one-stop shop. A news account quoted a partner at an 80-lawyer IP boutique firm as saying: "In whatever area you are working in, you have to have a deep expertise. If you are going to do biotechnology work, it is not enough that you have some people with some chemical background. You need to have people who are really knowledgeable in that area."[13] Boutique firms must communicate to clients and potential clients the importance of hiring lawyers who work with their specific problems, specific business or specific technology.

Some commentators believe that the increasing availability of high-end boutique practitioners is changing the way corporate clients structure their legal teams. One article in the legal press reported that in complex or unusual cases, a general counsel might choose to pair firms to obtain the necessary expertise. "For instance, environmental regulatory specialists may not have a significant record of courtroom trial experience and may not be familiar with the client's litigation style or risk tolerance. Another litigation boutique that has the requisite trial experience may lack the needed regulatory expertise."[14]

---

[13] Id.

[14] Debra Tsuchiyama Baker & David P. Young, *Unique Times for Boutiques*, 47 HOUSTON LAW. 4 (Mar/Apr 2010).

There may be as many stories of the founding, growth, and philosophy of boutique firms as there are boutiques. Many are founded by lawyers leaving large firms because of conflicts of interest and the desire for more flexibility. Boutiques often thrive and compete with large firms to attract large corporate clients by using alternative billing arrangements to attract clients. Boutiques often recruit lawyers for their specialized expertise. And many successful boutique firms confront the question whether to remain small and specialized or to grow to whatever size the business will support.

News accounts of Boies, Schiller & Flexner, which started as a boutique but grew rapidly, capture a number of the phenomena contributing to the founding and success of boutiques. In 2008, Boies, Schiller reported $3 million in profits per partner, which was the third-highest on the *American Lawyer* magazine's list of the 100 large law firms. Boies, Schiller, in a strategy unusual among elite corporate law firms, represents both plaintiffs and defendants. "Over the last five years, the firm says, 48 percent of its revenue has come from pure contingency fee cases and alternative fee arrangements. 'We are probably the largest, most diversified law firm that has a long history and extensive experience with alternative fee arrangements,' says Boies."[15] The firm was founded in 1997, when Boies left his equity partnership at the large New York law firm, Cravath, Swaine & Moore. He left because Cravath's biggest client at the time, Time Warner Inc., parent of the Atlanta Braves, objected to Boies's representation of the New York Yankees in a suit against Major League Baseball. Schiller had been a partner at a Washington, D.C. boutique which later merged with a large New York firm, and Schiller and Boies had been co-counsel on a case in the late 1980s. According to a new account,

> Boies set up an office in Armonk, New York, and Schiller opened one in Washington, D.C. Their initial budget was around $4 million. It was the perfect size. Or at least Boies thought so. He figured that he could avoid administrative headaches and take only the cases that interested him.

> But the firm proved to be a magnet for business. Clients like the Yankees, E.I. du Pont de Nemours and Company, Philip Morris International, Inc., and CBS Corporation, and new ones like Napster, Inc., and Calvin Klein, Inc., kept calling. Along the way, there was also that small government case against

---

[15] Andrew Longstreth, *Don't Bet Against the House: Big Wins on Contingency Cases Push Boies Schiller into the Am Law 100*, AM. LAW. (May 2009), p. 124. Reprinted and excerpted with permission from the May 2009 edition of The American Lawyer © 2009 ALM Media Properties, LLC. All rights reserved. Further duplication without permission is prohibited.

Microsoft Corporation and an election dispute between George W. Bush and Al Gore.[16]

The firm grew from 50 lawyers in 1999 to 250 lawyers and 32 equity partners in 2009. Through lateral hires and mergers, it opened offices scattered across the country from New Hampshire to California.

But while the firm has grown, the model has stayed roughly the same and proven remarkably durable. It was and remains built around the idea of representing a core group of clients who need high-end legal work on a regular basis. The firm is also highly selective about which clients it takes on. If a company is not likely to come to them for their biggest and most complicated pieces of litigation, the firm will often take a pass. To make sure that a new matter is worth it, Boies, Schiller charges new clients a minimum engagement fee, which has ranged from $250,000 to $5 million, on top of the time billed. (This does not apply to contingency cases.)

When they started out, Boies and Schiller had a business plan that called for 40 percent of the firm's time to be devoted to repeat clients; about 30 percent for one-off engagements; and about 30 percent allotted for plaintiffs class action suits, where the firm could reap 30 percent of a settlement or verdict. The firm never ended up devoting that much time to pure contingency fee cases, but the fees reaped from them have generally increased over the years.

Both Schiller and Boies had developed a taste for plaintiffs work before they started their firm. While at Cravath, Boies had represented the government against financier Michael Milken on partial contingency, and Schiller had taken on a company called Mc-Caw Cellular Communications, Inc., in a class action breach-of-contract suit. Having their own shop allowed them to be more aggressive in filing class actions. "The idea was that we wouldn't have to be as highly leveraged if we were able to achieve some premiums over the hourly rate through contingency cases and some of those one-shot matters," says partner William Isaacson, who came with Schiller from Kaye Scholer.

Today, the class action suit remains central to the firm's model and helps distinguish it from most of The Am Law 100. In the upper echelons of corporate defense firms, filing a class action is still considered taboo. And while some firms will take on a contingency fee case periodically, Boies, Schiller seeks out opportunities every year. The firm is currently acting as co-lead

---

[16] *Id.*

counsel in a securities fraud case against a Madoff "feeder" fund, an antitrust action against Chinese manufacturers of vitamin C, and a RICO suit against Amway Global. Filing the suits is partly philosophical. Seeing a case from a plaintiff's side, the Boies, Schiller lawyers argue, informs their work as defense lawyers. They can better size up a case from the start and know what costs will be involved. Then there's the potential economic upside. "The core clients keep the lights on, but the contingency fees provide a turbocharge to our revenues," says Boies, Schiller partner Richard Drubel, Jr., whose docket includes nearly 90 contingency fee cases.[17]

* * *

The survival of a boutique, like any other law firm, depends on the continuing ability of the firm to attract and retain clients. That, in turn, can depend on three factors. First there is the question of how they continue to compete with other firms for business. Second there is the temptation that many boutiques face to merge with a larger firm. Third is the question faced by all small firms: whether the firm can groom both the legal skills and the business development abilities of younger lawyers so that the firm survives the retirement of the core group of founding partners whose reputations made the firm a viable entity in the first place. As noted above in the discussion of Boies, Schiller, that firm initially prospered by its willingness to use alternative billing arrangements that large law firms would not consider. As large law firms began to abandon the exclusive reliance on hourly billing in favor of various value-based billing arrangements, the boutiques lost that competitive edge and had to find others. Similarly, many boutiques initially enjoyed a competitive edge because of their specialized expertise in, for example, tax or intellectual property, but large law firms then began to build their own departments with comparable expertise. Many boutiques then had to consider whether to merge with a larger firm or to find new subpractice areas to keep a step ahead of their large firm competitors.

According to a news account of the Washington, D.C. tax boutique Caplin & Drysdale, the firm responded to large law firms' development of tax departments to become even more specialized on particular aspects of tax practice. The partners believed large firms would not be able to provide clients the wide variety of specialized tax practitioners or as many well-connected insiders as Caplin & Drysdale employed.[18]

---

[17] *Id.*

[18] Larry Smith, *Tax Boutiques Maintain Independence as New Challenges Loom*, OF COUNSEL, April 5, 1993.

The survival of tax boutiques like Caplin & Drysdale in the face of aggressive expansion by the national firms has been to a certain extent a Washington, D.C. phenomenon. These boutiques have remained particularly important fixtures on the legal scene in D.C. because, obviously, many clients need savvy lobbyists working Congress and the bureaucracy (although Caplin says his own firm has not featured lobbying to the same extent as other prominent locals, like Miller & Chevalier). Lobbying attracts out-of-town firms to the Beltway and simultaneously helps many natives thrive. Despite formidable challenges from firms like Shearman & Sterling, these locals can still bank successfully on their reputations as insiders. Stuart Lewis, managing partner at Silverstein and Mullens, a prominent D.C. boutique, describes D.C. as a "right now" sort of market where the best lawyers get fast solutions to immediate problems. The established D.C. tax boutiques also have more solid ties, not only to Congress, but to the bureaucracy for handling administrative matters.

There's an even more important factor discouraging mergers: most good tax boutiques are extremely de-leveraged. Just about everyone interviewed comments that tax practice is intrinsically partner-intensive. According to Paul Hoffman, partner at the L.A. boutique Hoffman, Sabban & Watenmaker, the legal issues are often too esoteric to delegate; training journeymen lawyers would require enormous investments of otherwise billable time. Hoffman also echoes the other lawyers interviewed, who say that tax clients need lots of "handholding" by partners, and that they will typically demand lots of partner time. These mainstay clients are often prosperous closely-held businesses and/or wealthy individuals who aren't deterred by the rates charged by senior partners. Carr says those rates are, in fact, somewhat higher than at many other kinds of boutiques.

Fundamental cultural and economic differences thus discourage both the large and small firms from merging. Heldenbrand points out that a partner at a boutique who takes home $500,000 on a $1 million book of business will probably take home $400,000, or less, after shouldering his or her share of big firm overhead. "I've never been offered a deal that wasn't going to decrease the value of my practice," comments a partner at one L.A. boutique. Only if a merger were to open up long-term prospects with new clients would it make sense. The megafirms, meanwhile, certainly aren't enticed by clients who get upset when $300-an-hour partners don't personally "dot the i's" on every document. As Heldenbrand says, merging with the boutiques would only make sense for these larger firms if the acquired tax lawyers are able to service clients more efficiently than they themselves can with current staff, or by referring out the work.

Alan Olson concedes "some logic" to the argument that tax clients prefer de-leveraged firms. In fact, clients tell him, "I don't even want to see an associate!" Yet Olson also points out that the recession [of the early 1990s] has meant de-leveraging for the megafirms as well, and that McDermott has responded to clients' tax needs by adding on partners in Chicago. Eventually, big firm economics will likely necessitate a return to more leveraged staffing patterns; the marketing challenge at that point will be to show clients that "smart young lawyers" can do much of their tax work more cost efficiently than partners.

As another alternative to merging, many tax boutiques have, unlike, say, bankruptcy boutiques, grown over the years to become full-service firms themselves. One megafirm alumnus points out that some of the leading general service firms in L.A. did, in fact, begin life as tax boutiques. These include Kindel & Anderson, Irell & Manella, Tuttle & Taylor, and even Latham & Watkins. "As their clients grew, they grew too," he says. A few prominent boutiques in New York went the other direction and became exceedingly specialized.

As Lyles Carr points out, many tax boutiques have avoided diversifying, particularly into the corporate area, because they're afraid they might alienate referral sources. Goldberg agrees. As long as a tax boutique is just a tax boutique, the corporate firms referring work "know we won't steal their clients," he says. The 40-lawyer Roberts & Holland, which competes with some big firms for business while depending on others for referrals, can thus expect only "finite growth," although Goldberg won't venture a guess just how much growth is possible.[19]

NOTES ON BOUTIQUES

1. *The Attractions and Drawbacks of Boutiques.* What are the attractions of boutique firms for lawyers? For clients? What are the disadvantages of boutique firms for lawyers and for clients?

2. *Are Boutiques More Suited to Some Practice Areas than Others?* What types of law practice or legal specialty are most conducive to the boutique firm structure?

3. *Understanding Why Boutiques Are and Are Not Viable.* What common threads can you identify in why some boutiques thrive and why

---

[19] *Id.*

some either merge into another firm or go out of business? How are these phenomena similar to what occurs at other small firms? How do they differ?

D. SUMMARY

The notion that the private practice of law is divided into two worlds—one in which large law firms represent large organizational clients and the other in which small firms represent individuals and small businesses—remains a powerful heuristic for understanding the work lives of the three-quarters of American lawyers who are in private practice. Like every generalization, however, it has exceptions, and boutique law firms are one interesting, if somewhat ill-defined, exception. Many boutique law firms represent large corporate clients doing the sort of sophisticated intellectual property, tax, transactional, and litigation work performed by large law firms. In this chapter we considered why boutiques form, why they sometimes compete successfully in both the market to provide legal services and the market to hire lawyers, and why some consider boutiques particularly well-suited to thrive in the business environment that has challenged large law firms in the first decades of the twenty-first century.

SUBPART D

LAWYERS AND THE PRACTICE OF DISPUTE RESOLUTION

■ ■ ■

In this section, we examine lawyers in the practice of dispute resolution. The section is composed of three chapters: one examines lawyers and the practice of negotiation, one examines lawyers practicing as third party neutrals in alternative dispute resolution (ADR), and one studies judges. Negotiation is probably the most common of all lawyer behaviors; it is practiced by all lawyers in all kinds of practice settings. Negotiation is a skill that is taught in most law schools and is worthy of study by all lawyers. Our goal in this section is not to teach you to be skilled negotiator, but rather to teach you why negotiation presents an array of ethical challenges that form part of the canon of the law of legal ethics that we cover in this book. Additionally, some familiarity with the theory and practice of negotiation is important to understanding why many lawyers seek out other lawyers to mediate their negotiations and why mediation is a recognized form of legal practice that occurs in many practice settings. Lawyers work as mediators in large and small firms, where they combine mediation with client representation. Lawyers work in solo and very small firms where they practice only mediation. A federal government agency is dedicated entirely to providing mediation services. In academia, law professors combine mediation with teaching and scholarship. Lawyers also engage in dispute resolution as arbitrators and judges where they have the power to impose a resolution on parties to the dispute. Lawyers specializing in arbitration typically either work full-time as arbitrators or as academics who combine arbitration with teaching and scholarship, but some lawyers combine a part-time practice in arbitration and mediation with a part-time practice representing clients. The combined federal and state judiciaries are extremely large and diverse in their daily activities, their working conditions, and their membership.

What unites negotiation, third-party neutrals in ADR, and the judiciary is that in all three lawyers work as dispute resolvers rather than as advocates or counselors.

CHAPTER 25

NEGOTIATION

■ ■ ■

A. INTRODUCTION

No lawyer activity is more ubiquitous in every practice setting than negotiation. Although negotiation is not inherently a legal skill, all lawyers negotiate. Lawyers who specialize in litigation negotiate on behalf of clients to settle most of their cases. Real estate lawyers negotiate deals to sell or develop land. Environmental lawyers negotiate arrangements to protect or clean up land, water, and air. Criminal prosecutors and defense lawyers resolve the vast majority of their cases through plea negotiations. Corporate transactional lawyers negotiate the purchase, sale and merger of parts or all of companies, the financing of new ventures, and the bankruptcy or restructuring of failing ventures. Intellectual property lawyers negotiate rights to use information. Lawyers who specialize in family law negotiate property division and child custody at divorce. It is increasingly common among family law practitioners—and lawyers who specialize in other fields—to engage in a practice known as "collaborative lawyering" in which both clients and their lawyers agree that if they cannot reach a negotiated agreement the lawyers will withdraw and the clients must find other lawyers to litigate. Lawyers negotiate on their own behalf over their own terms of employment, and they negotiate with their employees. Lawyers negotiate leases on their office space, and they negotiate with expert witnesses, accountants, and others who provide services to firms.

Negotiation is not only ubiquitous but also conceptually important to our understanding of the role the legal profession plays in the implementation of law. Because all deals and most disputes are worked out through negotiation, it is the process through which law operates on the ground. Although most of your courses focus on how courts and agencies apply the law, in the real world law is interpreted and attains its practical meaning by parties through negotiation. Negotiation determines legal outcomes that affect clients and society at large, but it is also a process that vitally affects how lawyers regard their own success and happiness. Lawyers should and do evaluate themselves not only by *what* they achieve for their clients and themselves but *how* they achieve it. Importantly, negotiation occurs without supervision by clients, tribunals, regulatory bodies, or the public at large. Because it is unsupervised and is so important, lawyers exercise enormous discretion in choosing how they negotiate. To understand what the legal profession does, why, and whether it is ethical, therefore, we need to understand the practice of negotiation and the law and norms governing it.

In this chapter, we will survey the legal profession's practice of negotiation and the rules of professional conduct and other law governing lawyers in negotiation. We focus on two of the thorniest issues about the practice and ethics of negotiation: when is it permissible for lawyers to take advantage of a disparity of bargaining power, and what standards of candor do we expect of lawyers in negotiation?

B. THE LEGAL PROFESSION AND THE PRACTICE OF NEGOTIATION

Some negotiations are relatively simple, such as settling a lawsuit between two people alleging a single cause of action in which the defendant's liability is clear and the only issue to be resolved through negotiation is the damages defendant will pay. The negotiation is bilateral and focuses on a single issue. Some negotiations are hugely complex, involving multiple parties (multilateral negotiation) and multiple issues, some of which are economic and some of which are not. International treaty negotiations are an example. Land use and large real estate developments may fall into that category, as do complex corporate transactions, major legislative change, and the re-structuring of complex government programs or institutions like prison reform or school reform. Some negotiations resolve litigation (settlement negotiations) and some create a new relationship that is anticipated to continue into the future (transactional negotiations). Negotiations may involve issues that all parties may easily quantify in dollars (some transactions and some settlements) and some may involve little money but a great deal of emotion (family law). Some may involve the interests of third parties who are not represented in the negotiation (child custody, collective bargaining agreements between unions and employers, and land use issues). Each of these types of negotiation calls for some skills that are common to all negotiations and some that may be unique to that setting. And each presents lawyers with some common ethical issues and some that are unique to certain settings.

> **Every lawyer must make three interrelated choices when beginning a negotiation:**
>
> (1) How can I be most effective?
>
> (2) What do the rules allow me to do in this negotiation?
>
> (3) What style should I adopt and what strategy or approach to the negotiation should I take?

Law and the rules of ethics give lawyers enormous discretion in choosing an approach to negotiation. Outright lies and threats, and failing to correct a misrepresentation by the lawyer or the client, violate the Model Rules and can constitute fraud or extortion. Beyond, that, however, law constrains lawyers relatively little in negotiation. On this as on much else, lawyers' behavior is likely to be constrained by their conscience and by the norms of their practice setting and community more than it is by the rules of ethics. As with most other lawyer tasks, we leave to other courses to teach you the most effective strategies or techniques of negotiation.[1] We focus here on helping you see how practice settings shape lawyer behavior and we explore the ethical constraints shaping lawyers' choices. Because effective strategy and ethics are so often conflated in thinking about negotiation, however, we address strategy to the extent necessary to show that a considerable legal and other literature insists that it is not necessary to be unethical to be effective as a negotiator.

Choosing an Approach to Negotiation. A simple bilateral negotiation may usefully be considered as one or the other of two types, or more likely some combination: (1) competitive and distributive; or (2) collaborative and integrative. A competitive/distributive negotiation is one in which the parties are negotiating for the division of a fixed sum or thing. They are negotiating to divide a pie; nothing the parties can do in the negotiations will expand the size of the pie, and a gain for one party in the negotiation will be a loss for the other. A collaborative/integrative negotiation is one in which the parties aspire to expand the possibilities of joint gain by considering how they can expand the size of what each or both can recover, so that a gain for one does not necessarily entail a loss for the other. It might be, for example, that one party to the negotiation really doesn't care for pie but collects pie plates and is delighted to learn

---

[1]   Students intrigued by the techniques and strategy of negotiation who do not wish to wait for an upper-level negotiation course could consult the short and accessible summary of negotiation theory and strategy in MELISSA L. NELKIN, NEGOTIATION: THEORY AND PRACTICE, chapters 2 and 3 (2d ed. Lexis/Nexis, 2007) or X.M FRASCOGNA, JR. & H. LEE HETHERINGTON, THE LAWYER'S GUIDE TO NEGOTIATION (2d ed., ABA, 2009).

that this one is a valuable antique. In that context, the parties are both enriched when they realize that the pie plate is valuable.[2]

> A negotiation is **competitive** or **distributive** if the parties are negotiating to divide a fixed sum or thing, like dividing a pie. A negotiation is **collaborative** or **integrative** if the negotiation can expand the possibilities of joint gain by, for example, expanding the subject of negotiation so that a gain for one is not a loss for the other.

If a negotiation has the potential to be integrative or collaborative, the kinds of strategic behavior that many think is necessary for effective negotiation (lying, refraining from making the first offer, refusing to make a counteroffer in an attempt to make one party to bargain against herself) become counterproductive to both parties. Some negotiations have greater potential to be integrative than others.[3] Yet, in the end, most negotiations have some element of both. However much the parties collaborate to openly discuss the problem at hand and the possible solutions to it, their motivations for negotiating, and their interests in the matter, in the end they still have to decide what happens to the pie and the plate.

> **Strategic Behavior in Collaborative Negotiation**
>
> Strategic behavior by one or both parties who seek to maximize their individual gain in negotiation can thwart the potential for both parties to achieve even greater gains through collaborative or integrative negotiation.

Even in negotiations that have greater potential to be either integrative or distributive, lawyers face a range of choices about technique and approach and opportunities for strategic behavior. The lawyer for the pie plate collector, for example, has a choice once she learns that her client considers the plate valuable. Should she reveal that her client dislikes that kind of pie or that the plate is worth thousands of dollars? How much should she involve her client in the negotiations if she knows that the client is extremely angry at the other person? If she expects to negotiate frequently in the future with the other lawyer, how accommodating should she be both in the process and on the substance?

---

[2] Negotiation theorists distinguish between competitive and distributive by pointing out that competitive refers more to the process and distributive refers more to the nature of the deal that must be made. The distributive aspect of a negotiation is the aspect that divides up whatever the parties are negotiating about (e.g., dividing a pie). The parties could be more or less competitive or cooperative in negotiating the division. Similarly, the integrative aspect of a negotiation focuses on expanding or re-imagining the subject of the negotiation, and the parties could be more or less competitive or cooperative in discussing that.

[3] There is a huge literature on negotiation theory, and it is an oversimplification to suggest that negotiations are either distributive or integrative, but the dichotomy is useful for purposes of exploring the ethical issues in negotiation.

On the other hand, if the other lawyer behaves rudely or if she believes that the other lawyer is lying, how should she react?

A lawyer's choices about the approach to take to negotiation are influenced by her personality and her comfort with conflict, cooperation, and other behaviors or atmospheres in negotiation. Some of those qualities in lawyers are cultural, although what "culture" means in this context and how it operates to affect lawyers' negotiation styles is poorly understood.[4] Some people in some parts of the world prize speed in negotiations, while others insist upon a process of relationship-building before getting down to business. Some express certain things directly or bluntly, while others value finesse and indirection. A lawyer who believes that all Israelis or all Chinese negotiate in the same way as each other is likely to be embarrassed, surprised, and ineffective. Similarly, although a number of scholars have studied gender differences in negotiation styles in the United States and have identified some tendencies that are gender-linked, there is a wide range of difference among men and women in negotiating style.

In negotiation, as in every other aspect of practice, lawyers are deeply influenced by the norms and expectations of their practice setting. For junior lawyers especially, the expectations of their supervisors may lead them to be more or less aggressive, candid, or cooperative, and if they are taught to believe that most negotiations are distributive rather than integrative, they will tend to see negotiations in that light. Like anyone else, the lawyer will also consider the particular situation— whether she knows her negotiating partners, whether they are confrontational or cooperative, what is at stake, and the like. She will take all of these factors into account in deciding how to handle the ethical issues she confronts.

You may study these topics in detail in upper-level courses on negotiation. The purpose of this short summary is simply to disabuse you of the common misconception that there is one right style of negotiation or that all lawyers would or should approach the same negotiation in the same way.

Effectiveness in Negotiation. A common perception among law students and young lawyers is that one has to be aggressive or combative in order to be effective in negotiation. Many experienced lawyers insist that this is a misconception. A voluminous literature on the theory and practice of negotiation emphasizes that lawyers can be extremely effective in negotiation by being forthcoming with information, accommodating,

---

[4]   Students interested in reading some of the many works on culture and negotiation might consult: Kevin Avruch, *Culture and Negotiation Pedagogy*, 16 NEGOTIATION J. 377 (2000); RAYMOND COHEN, NEGOTIATING ACROSS CULTURES: INTERNATIONAL COMMUNICATION IN AN INTERDEPENDENT WORLD (rev. ed. 1997); Jayne Seminare Docherty, *Culture and Negotiation: Symmetrical Anthropology for Negotiators*, 87 MARQUETTE L. REV. 711 (2004).

and cooperative. On the other hand, both experienced lawyers and theorists of negotiation assert that negotiators can make gains for their position by engaging in certain forms of strategic behavior. We explore some of the empirical and theoretical literature below in order to show the range of thinking about ethics and effectiveness in negotiation.

Empirical studies of lawyer effectiveness in negotiation are relatively scarce, in part because negotiation often occurs in private. In an influential study of lawyer negotiation styles, Gerald Williams asked 1000 Phoenix, Arizona lawyers to evaluate the effectiveness of their negotiating partner or adversary in their recent negotiation experience. Williams found that 65% of lawyers used a cooperative approach and 24% used a competitive negotiation style.[5] While lawyers using both styles were rated as effective by their colleagues, a much greater percentage of those using a cooperative approach were rated as "effective" than those using a competitive style.[6]

Effective cooperative negotiators were described by their negotiating partners as being motivated to be ethical, to maximize the settlement for the client, to get a fair settlement, and to maintain a good relationship with the opponent. They were said to have accurately estimated the value of the case, to know the client's needs, to take a realistic opening position, to be willing to share information, and to be forthright, trustful, fair-minded, logical (not emotional), courteous, tactful, wise, careful, and not to use threats. Effective competitive negotiators were likewise said to know their clients' needs, to have maximized the settlement for the client, and to be prepared and astute, but in other respects competitive negotiators differed. They were said to have maximized the lawyer's own fee, to have outmaneuvered the opponent, to be tough, dominant, forceful, ambitious, arrogant, clever, and to have been careful about the timing and sequence of their actions. Ineffective cooperative negotiators were described in some favorable terms (honest, forthright, trustful, sincere) but were missing crucial qualities (being perceptive, reasonable, creative, or astute). Ineffective competitive negotiators tended to be described as having more negative traits, including being unreasonable, complaining, devious, obnoxious, and irritating.

A more recent empirical study replicated the 1976 Williams study by surveying approximately 750 Phoenix and Milwaukee lawyers and asked them to evaluate the effectiveness of their negotiating partner/adversary in a recent negotiation experience. The report of that study is excerpted here:

---

[5]   GERALD R. WILLIAMS, LEGAL NEGOTIATION AND SETTLEMENT 18 (1983).

[6]   Id. at 19.

SHATTERING NEGOTIATION MYTHS: EMPIRICAL EVIDENCE ON THE EFFECTIVENESS OF NEGOTIATION STYLE

Andrea Kupfer Schneider
7 Harvard Journal on Negotiation 143 (2002)

The data reported herein is based on a wide-ranging study that asked lawyers to evaluate the negotiation styles and the resulting effectiveness of other lawyers. First, the study shows that effective negotiators exhibit certain identifiable skills. For example, the research indicates that a negotiator who is assertive and empathetic is perceived as more effective. The study also reveals distinctive characteristics of ineffective negotiators, who are more likely to be stubborn, arrogant, and egotistical. Furthermore, when this adversarial negotiator is unethical, he is perceived as even less effective. Third, the study found that problem-solving behavior is perceived as highly effective.

Despite the public perception of lawyers, it appears that close to two-thirds of lawyers continue to engage in non-adversarial modes of communication and that these lawyers are perceived as highly effective by their peers.

Compared to the Williams study, the changes in the percentage of adversarial bargainers is striking. Twenty-five percent of competitive negotiators were seen as effective in the Williams study as compared to 9% in this study. Alternatively, only 33% of competitive negotiators were seen as ineffective in the Williams study while 53% were in this study.

In the Williams study, 73% of negotiators fell in the cooperative group and 27% were in the competitive group. In this study, only 64% of attorneys were clustered in the problem-solving group and 36% of attorneys were in the adversarial group. As the vast majority of those attorneys who were considered ineffective were also adversarial negotiators (90% of ineffective lawyers were adversarial), we can hypothesize that the increase in ineffective lawyers over twenty-five years from 12% to 22% comes from the increase in adversarial bargainers from 27% to 36%.

It looks like the gap between these styles is widening. While the problem-solving or cooperative group has remained much the same, the adversarial or competitive group seems to be growing more extreme and more negative. [A]s adversarial bargaining has become more extreme, it has also become far less effective.

* * *

One important question in assessing the effectiveness of different approaches to negotiation is how and why the process of negotiation affects the outcome. The negotiation process affects the lawyers involved, of course. People who are comfortable with conflict may find an aggressive negotiation to be fun, or at least not distressing. A competitive, scorched earth, no-holds-barred negotiation is miserable for anyone who does not thrive in that sort of environment. A lawyer who feels she must try to be cutthroat, duplicitous, or nasty in order to succeed in negotiation may not last long in practice, or at least a practice in which that is what is expected in negotiation. Conversely, a lawyer who feels that the negotiation process was reasonable, fair, engaging, and pleasant may thrive as a negotiator. But how does the process affect the outcome, and what benefits or costs do clients incur by different negotiating processes? The following excerpt attempts to assess the question whether the lawyers' perceptions of each other's behavior in the process affects the result.

JUST NEGOTIATION
Rebecca Hollander-Blumhoff
88 Washington University Law Review 381 (2010)

[In prior research,] Tyler and I examined the relationship between procedural justice and monetary outcome in two separate studies—one in which integrative potential was low (a largely zero-sum negotiation), and one in which the integrative potential was higher (there was opportunity for "expanding the negotiation pie"). In the low-integrative-potential negotiation, there was no relationship between procedural fairness and actual outcome; in the higher-integrative-potential negotiation, higher levels of procedural justice were significantly related to a more even distribution of the surplus that was created. This research suggests that there is no systematic relationship between fair treatment and outcome in a zero-sum setting: the feeling that one has been fairly treated during a negotiation has no connection to doing well or poorly on the substance of the negotiation. Fair treatment, then, does not appear systematically to "bamboozle" people into accepting poor outcomes, nor does fair treatment systematically seem to ensure a favorable outcome. In an integrative setting, fair treatments' effects on outcome are limited to the distribution of any surplus that is created, and these effects tend toward an equal distribution of that surplus.

Our findings suggest that the procedural justice experienced in the negotiation plays a significant role in shaping how individuals assess their negotiated outcomes, and, specifically for individuals in the role of lawyers, how they think about a recommendation to accept or reject a settlement. If, in fact, subjective experiences of fairness during negotiation play a significant role in shaping lawyers' recommendations about acceptance of settlement, this suggests that lawyers who engage in negotiations characterized by higher levels of procedural justice are more likely to recommend settlements to their clients. This finding would indicate that an attorney who treats opposing counsel in a manner that produces a subjective perception of fair process is more likely to reach an accepted settlement, all other things being equal, than one whose behavior gives rise to a perception of unfair treatment.

NOTES ON NEGOTIATION STYLES

1. ***Can All Negotiations Be Collaborative?*** Can any negotiation be made more integrative than distributive if one or both of the parties tries to make it so? If one party decides to make the negotiation more competitive, what can the other party do to resist?

2. ***What Influences the Choice of Negotiating Style?*** In your experience in negotiation, what influenced your decision about whether to be more or less forthcoming with information and accommodating of the people with whom you negotiated? How did their behavior influence yours? How do the studies excerpted above correspond (or not) to your own experiences of the process of negotiation?

3. ***Negotiating on Behalf of a Client.*** Some people believe that they should behave differently in negotiation when they are negotiating on behalf of some other person (as a lawyer does for a client) than when they are negotiating on their own behalf. Some find it liberating to have a "client" to represent because the negotiation feels less personal, and some find it oppressive because they feel constrained to be tougher than they would otherwise be. Do you think a lawyer should do for a client in negotiation things that she would not do on her own behalf?

* * *

C. THE LAW GOVERNING LAWYERS' CONDUCT IN NEGOTIATION

In addition to formulating a strategy and analyzing its possible effectiveness, a third crucial choice confronting a lawyer entering negotiation concerns ethics. What is permissible or impermissible for a lawyer to say or do in negotiation? Ethical questions, as we have seen throughout this book, involve at least two considerations for every lawyer: (1) What does the law require or allow? and (2) What is ethical? This section identifies the relevant law that constrains lawyers' conduct in negotiations and considers how lawyers should exercise the discretion that the law gives them.

There are at least three important sources of law governing what lawyers may do in negotiation. First, the law of contracts determines whether an agreement is enforceable. A contract is unenforceable if it was procured by fraud or misrepresentation or based on a material mistake. Second, criminal and tort law prohibit misrepresentation, and in extreme cases, making threats to obtain something of value in negotiation can constitute the crime of extortion. Third, both the Model Rules and particular ethics rules governing lawyers in specific practice situations regulate negotiation. As we will see below, however, the Model Rules leave a great deal of discretion to the lawyer to determine how to behave in negotiation. Model Rule 4.1 prohibits lawyers from making "a false statement of material fact or law" or failing "to disclose a material fact when disclosure is necessary to avoid assisting a criminal or fraudulent act by a client." We will discuss Model Rule 4.1, along with relevant principles of contract and tort law, below in the segment on candor in negotiations.

Duty to Convey Offer. We have already covered some of the pertinent Model Rules governing the lawyer-client relationship in negotiation. The client decides whether to settle or to plead guilty. Model Rule 1.2(a). If a client refuses to consider settling or pleading guilty, the lawyer cannot attempt to negotiate a settlement or plea agreement. But if a lawyer does have client authorization to try to negotiate a resolution, the Model Rules allow the lawyer to conduct the negotiations as she feels appropriate until the other side makes an offer. Under Model Rule 1.4(a)(1), the lawyer must keep the client informed and, in particular, the lawyer "must promptly inform the client of" the substance of any settlement offer or plea offer "unless the client has previously indicated that the proposal will be acceptable or unacceptable or has authorized the lawyer to accept or to reject the offer." Model Rule 1.4 Comment [2].

Beneath that simple rule lies a much more complex question for most lawyers about the optimal amount of lawyer-client interaction before and during negotiations. Some lawyers believe they should engage in significant counseling with their client before any negotiations with another party to identify the client's best alternatives to a negotiated agreement, various negotiation strategies and their likely outcomes, integrative solutions that would meet the client's and the other party's needs, how much negotiating authority the client should give the lawyer, and how that might affect the negotiation process.[7] Other lawyers prefer to leave clients out of the negotiations as much as possible. Whatever lawyers think desirable, some clients will have the power in the attorney-client relationship to demand that the lawyer negotiate in a particular fashion.

PROBLEM 25–1

Imagine a negotiation to settle a lawsuit arising out of a car accident in which the defendant was intoxicated at twice the legal limit for blood alcohol. The lawyer for the defendant offers to settle the case for ten percent of the amount of damages the plaintiff's lawyer believes the evidence shows that the plaintiff has suffered. The defendant's losses in the matter are covered by an

---

[7]   Donald G. Gifford, *The Synthesis of Legal Counseling and Negotiation Models: Preserving Client-Centered Advocacy in the Negotiation Context*, 34 UCLA L. REV. 811, 844 (1987).

insurance policy with a limit of three times what the defendant has offered, and the evidence shows that the defendant has, in addition, considerable personal wealth. The plaintiff's lawyer scoffs at the offer and says, "That's ridiculous and you know it. We've presented you medical bills for the injuries your client caused mine that are five times what you are offering. And that doesn't even include damages for pain and suffering or punitive damages. Make an offer that is worthy of my calling my client to discuss." If the plaintiff and his lawyer have had no conversations about what settlement offers the plaintiff will accept, has the plaintiff's lawyer violated Model Rules 1.2 and 1.4? (It would seem the lawyer has, because under Rule 1.2 the client decides whether to settle a matter and the Comment to Rule 1.4 requires the lawyer to "promptly inform the client" of settlement offers "unless the client has previously indicated that the proposal will be acceptable or unacceptable or has authorized the lawyer to accept or to reject the offer.") Why might the lawyer prefer to be able to flatly reject the offer rather than consult with the client about it? What if the plaintiff has told his lawyer that he will take a reasonable offer just to get the suit over with? Apart from what the Model Rules require, what should the plaintiff's lawyer consider in deciding what to say to his client about settlement offers that the lawyer deems unworthy of serious consideration?

D. UNEQUAL BARGAINING POWER

A classic hypothetical problem to consider the issue of unequal bargaining power in negotiation is the Ultimatum Game. Two people are offered $1000 to divide as they chose, but if they don't agree on the division, they will get nothing. How should we evaluate the fairness of the negotiations between them in the following scenarios?

1. They split it 50–50 or 60–40 or 90–10.

2. One is rich and the other is desperately poor. The rich person insists on a 90–10 split, pointing out that he can easily afford to walk away from the $900 if the other person does not agree. The poor person agrees because she needs the $100 to pay her rent tomorrow.

3. One knows an embarrassing secret about the other and threatens to disclose it.

4. One has a crush on the other and agrees to take a small share to avoid alienating the other, but the object of the affection is unaware of this. Alternatively, suppose the object of affection knows about the crush and the feeling isn't mutual, but the lawyer leads the other to believe the feeling is mutual.

As noted above in the introduction to this chapter, the Model Rules say nothing on the issue of the fairness of negotiations. In any unequal society, disparities of bargaining power occur, and we lack a moral consensus about which disparities are permissible to exploit. For lawyers engaged in negotiation, unequal bargaining power can be an especially vexing moral issue when the lawyer's own sense of a fair result differs from what the lawyer thinks she could negotiate for her client because of the other side's poor bargaining position. Does loyalty to her client compel her to strive for the maximum she can get? At one point, the ABA considered including in the Model Rules the statement: "In conducting negotiations, a lawyer shall be fair in dealing with other participants." Why do you imagine the ABA considered such a rule? Why do you imagine the ABA decided not to proceed? Do you agree with the ABA's choice? Could you devise a better approach?

In this section, we will consider three relatively clear outer boundaries on the ability of lawyers to exploit disparities in bargaining power: threatening criminal or other proceedings, extortion, and dealing with unrepresented persons. We will then examine the problem of disparate bargaining power in a few selected practice settings where the problem is especially salient.

Threatening Criminal or Other Proceedings. In some states, ethics rules prohibit a lawyer from making threats to report the opposing party or the opposing party's lawyer to gain strategic advantage. For example, California DR 5–100(A) provides: "A member [of the bar] shall not threaten to present criminal, administrative, or disciplinary charges to obtain an advantage in a civil action." The Model Rules, however, contain no such prohibition. ABA Formal Opinion 92–363 (July 6, 1992) decided that a lawyer may use the possibility of bringing criminal charges in negotiations in a civil case if both are well founded in fact and law, the lawyer does not suggest improper influence over the criminal process, and the threat would not constitute extortion under state law. Lawyers may also agree not to file criminal charges as part of civil settlement if that does not violate state law requiring reporting of crimes. On the other hand, ABA Formal Opinion 94–383 (1994) determined that a threat to file disciplinary charges to gain advantage in civil case may violate Model Rule 8.4 if it raises a question about adversary's honesty, trustworthiness, or fitness because reporting is mandatory, or if the misconduct is unrelated to civil claim, or if the charges not well founded in fact and law, or if the threat has no substantial purpose or effect other than to embarrass opposing counsel.

Extortion. A negotiator who contemplates using especially aggressive negotiating tactics to take advantage of the weak bargaining position of her adversary could cross the line from obnoxiousness to criminality. Obtaining an agreement by threat is the crime of extortion. More precisely, extortion is "the obtaining of property from another, with his consent, . . . induced by a wrongful use of force or fear." California

Penal Code § 518. See also Model Penal Code § 223.4 (defining theft by extortion as taking property by threatening to commit a criminal act, to inflict bodily injury, to reveal a secret tending to expose another to contempt or ridicule, or other forms of coercion). Your other courses may explore the nuances of criminal law that make the use of fear "wrongful" in a criminal sense. Suffice it to say here that a negotiation that seems exploitative may be illegal.

Transactions with Unrepresented Persons. Particularly in the solo and very small firm sector where many lawyers represent individuals or small businesses, a lawyer may negotiate with individuals or small businesses who cannot afford to hire counsel. The negotiation then pits a not-wealthy person represented by counsel against an even-less-wealthy unrepresented person. In this context, one of the ethical and practical dilemmas of unequal bargaining power confronting the lawyer is governed by the rule relating to dealing with unrepresented persons. Model Rule 4.3 and the lawyer's obligations when dealing with unrepresented persons are covered in Chapter 6. A lawyer negotiating on behalf of a client must be careful when negotiating with someone who is not represented by counsel to avoid giving legal advice and to be sure that the person understands the lawyer represents a client with adverse interests. The lawyer may, however, answer questions about the law and prepare legal documents that require the other party's signature.

Disparate Bargaining Power and the Problem of Third Party Interests. However painful it is for a lawyer to deal with a situation when her client is in a position to extract a one-sided deal from another because of disparities of bargaining power, lawyers can console themselves (if it is a consolation) that the problem is a part of living in a market economy where there are vast inequalities in wealth and power. The problem is even more acute, however, when the negotiations will affect the rights of third parties who are not represented in the negotiations.

Family law is the classic example of this dilemma. When a married couple with children divorces, the parents must negotiate a division of the family's assets, whether one parent will pay the other alimony, spousal support or child support, whether they will have joint legal and physical custody of the minor children and, if not, which one will have custody. The legal literature on the topic examines in detail what many family lawyers (and those who have experienced a messy divorce) know anecdotally: sometimes, an angry spouse will use a fight over child custody as a bargaining chip to extract a more favorable settlement of the financial terms.

The dilemma for the lawyer of the angry spouse is whether to participate in the client's strategy. The problem is complicated by the fact that people value money and child custody differently. Some parents would prefer, for whatever reasons, to spend less time with their children. Some would give up any amount of money in order not to lose custody of or time with their children. A classic article examines the ways that parties can use their legal entitlements strategically to gain advantage in negotiations by taking advantage of the other spouse's preferences.[8] A husband who knows his wife would sacrifice anything not to lose her children can threaten to contest her custody in order to force her to settle on less favorable monetary terms. For the husband's lawyer the ethical dilemma is especially acute if he knows that the husband does not really want to have sole custody of the children but has some factual and legal basis for challenging her custody.

Although the Model Rules do not speak directly to this dilemma, the ethical guidelines for family lawyers do. *The Bounds of Advocacy: Goals for Family Lawyers* (American Academy of Matrimonial Lawyers) Goal 6.1 states: "An attorney representing a parent should consider the welfare of, and seek to minimize the adverse impact of divorce on, the minor children." Goal 6.2 says: "An attorney should not permit a client to contest child custody, contact, or access for either financial leverage or vindictiveness." The Comment to 6.2 elaborates: "Tactics oriented toward asserting custody rights as leverage toward attaining some other, usually financial, goal are destructive. . . . [T]he lawyers should negotiate parenting issues based solely on considerations related to the child, then negotiate child support based on financial considerations. If despite the attorney's advice, the client persists, the attorney should seek to withdraw." Of course, not every lawyer is prepared to jeopardize his or her own livelihood by withdrawal, especially when the client is a major source of the lawyer's income or is in a position to affect the lawyer's reputation in the community.

PROBLEM 25–2

You represent the defendant, a small manufacturing corporation, in a suit brought by an environmental justice organization and several individuals. The suit alleges that your client is discharging pollutants into the groundwater surrounding its facility. The neighborhood surrounding the facility is a low-income area in which a number of very recent immigrants live. The CEO of your client suspects that several of the plaintiffs are undocumented immigrants and has suggested that in settlement negotiations, you should point out to the lawyers for the plaintiffs that many or most of their clients are undocumented immigrants and that it would be unfortunate if Immigration and Customs Enforcement (ICE) agents were to conduct a raid in the neighborhood. The CEO has suggested you say that, in

---

8   Robert H. Mnookin & Lewis Kornhauser, *Bargaining in the Shadow of the Law: The Case of Divorce*, 88 YALE LAW JOURNAL 950 (1979).

exchange for a favorable settlement, he would keep his suspicions to himself. You insist that you cannot threaten to call ICE in order to obtain a settlement, to which your client's CEO replies, "that may be, but you can't stop me from doing it, and I'd like you to tell the other side that I intend to do it." What should you do?

Read Model Rules 4.4 (a), 1.2(d), and 1.16(b)(4).

E. CANDOR AND TRUTHFULNESS IN NEGOTIATION

Sooner or later, every lawyer will confront the temptation to lie or to mislead by failing to disclose information in negotiation. Sometimes it will seem like a simple form of exaggeration or puffery ("this is great deal for you") and sometimes it will be an outright lie. Sometimes the lie might seem justifiable because the question it answers should never have been asked ("what is the minimum your client will accept to settle this claim?"). Lying in negotiation raises many issues for lawyers.

Model Rule 4.1: Truthfulness in Statements to Others

A lawyer shall not knowingly make a false statement of material fact or law to a third person or fail to disclose a material fact when disclosure is necessary to avoid assisting a criminal or fraudulent act by a client, unless disclosure is prohibited by Rule 1.6.

Model Rule 4.1 condemns lying and it requires disclosure of facts when nondisclosure would constitute assistance in a crime or fraud. But Comment [2] to the rule suggests a huge exception: "Whether a particular statement should be regarded as one of fact can depend on the circumstances. Under generally accepted conventions in negotiation, certain types of statements ordinarily are not taken as statements of material fact. Estimates of price or value placed on the subject of a transaction and a party's intentions as to an acceptable settlement of a claim are ordinarily in this category."

Does Model Rule 4.1 therefore really condemn lying, or does it only condemn those falsehoods that violate "generally accepted conventions in negotiation"? Which conventions are those? The Comment suggests estimates of value and negotiation positions are not generally regarded as statements of fact, but is that always so? If a property has been appraised or a used car has a book value, is that not a fact? More generally, does the Comment suggest that it's OK to lie only about the value of the subject of the transaction and one's client's willingness to settle, or are those only examples of a larger category of factual statements about which it is acceptable to lie? ABA Formal Opinion 06–439 (Apr. 12, 2006) will not reassure those who wish there were a higher ethical bar to lying. It states that it is not unusual for negotiators to make statements that are "less than entirely forthcoming." So long as such statements are the sort "upon which parties to negotiation ordinarily would not be expected justifiably to rely," such statements are acceptable forms of "posturing" or "puffing."

Critics have lambasted the Model Rule's exception, while some lawyers have insisted it is necessary because lying is inevitable. As the late judge Alvin Rubin said in an influential article, many lawyers contrast the willingness of lawyers to lie about a client's willingness to settle (because lawyers do not expect candor about negotiating strategy) with the clearly wrongful conduct of falsifying documents or making other false statements of fact. But to Rubin, the distinction is meaningless and the rule's tolerance of lying about settlement strategy opens a door to an "anything goes" attitude: "To most practitioners it appears that anything sanctioned by the rules of the game is appropriate. But gamesmanship is not ethics."[9] Other lawyers argue that negotiation is like playing poker. "Like a poker player, a negotiator hopes that his opponent will overestimate the value of his hand. Like the poker player, in a variety of ways he must facilitate his opponent's inaccurate assessment. The critical difference between those who are successful negotiators and those who are not lies in this capacity both to mislead and not to be misled."[10] The following excerpt summarizes other arguments for and against the Model Rule 4.1 approach:

DOING THE RIGHT THING: AN EMPIRICAL STUDY OF ATTORNEY NEGOTIATION ETHICS

Art Hinshaw & Jess K. Alberts
16 Harvard Journal on Negotiation 95 (2011)

[C]ritics contend that [Model] Rule [4.1]'s truthfulness standard is too low to provide any protection not already provided in the law and that it promotes deceptive negotiation practices. In contrast to what one would expect from an ethical standard purporting to regulate honesty, critics claim that the Rule encourages a shocking amount of deception. Critics question why an ethical standard was even enacted if it adopts an "anything short of fraud is acceptable" standard as the ethical floor. Lawyers are already required to comply with the lowest level of legally acceptable behavior, thus the Rule requires nothing more than the law already provides. Furthermore, this standard emphasizes an adversarial view of negotiation, promoting deceptive tactics just short of fraud as a means of preemptory self-defense. Finally, critics assert that if indeed most negotiators deceive those with whom they negotiate, that reality should not establish the practice as ethically appropriate behavior.

---

[9]   Alvin B. Rubin, *A Causerie on Lawyers' Ethics in Negotiation*, 35 LA. L. REV. 577 (1975).

[10]   James J. White, *Machiavelli and the Bar; Ethical Limits on Lying in Negotiation*, 1980 ABF RES. J. 926.

The Rule's supporters usually rely on one or more of three intertwined theories when responding to critics—the necessities of the adversarial process, the idiosyncratic nature of the negotiation process, and the futility of more rigorous rules. Proponents of adversarial necessity point out that as zealous advocates, lawyers must attempt to gain any advantage that best serves their clients' interests, particularly in negotiation. Thus, lawyers must be well-versed in several time-tested deceptive bargaining tactics. Additionally, the Rule's proponents point out that unlike any other lawyerly activity, negotiation has its own set of rules that legitimize deception short of fraud. As one prominent scholar has noted, "[t]o conceal one's true position, to mislead an opponent about one's true settling point, is the essence of negotiation." Thus, proscribing such tactics would bar lawyers from engaging in negotiation tactics that their clients legally use on a routine basis, thereby creating a disincentive to use lawyers when negotiating. Moreover, such bargaining already is common in legal negotiation; thus the Rule's defenders argue that any tougher standard would be futile because it would be routinely violated creating "a continuing hypocrisy" that could negatively impact other rules as well.

* * *

Game theorists who specialize in the theory of negotiation identify reasons why lying or dissembling can be strategically advantageous, at least in the short term. Consider the two people negotiating over how to divide the pie. The one who realizes that the pie plate is a valuable collector's item is better off not disclosing its value: "I tell you what, you take half the pie, and I'll take the other half home with me in the plate." If the other person also realizes the plate is valuable but thinks the first person does not, she too should lie, perhaps by insisting that she doesn't care for that type of pie but would be happy to have the plate because it has a decoration that has sentimental value for her. Is it really necessary to be a successful negotiator that one learn to mislead one's negotiating partners and to see through their lies? The following excerpt explains that although lying may be an effective strategy in the short term, it has serious costs:

THE ETHICS OF LYING IN NEGOTIATIONS

Gerald Wetlaufer
75 Iowa Law Review 1219 (1990)

The lies that we tell in the course of negotiations may have a number of different effects on the negotiation, on the parties, and on the larger community.

[An] important category of lies is comprised of those "distributive" lies by which the liar seeks to capture an advantage over the other party.

To illustrate the effect of these lies, let us assume that Mr. Seller is negotiating to sell a factory and that his reservation price is $900,000. Below that price, he is better off keeping the plant. After an extensive search, he has identified one, and only one, prospective purchaser. Her name is Ms. Buyer. Mr. Seller has estimated that her reservation price, the price above which she will not buy, is $1,200,000. Though he has no way of knowing for sure, you and I know that this estimate is exactly right. Mr. Seller's objective is to sell at the highest possible price, even if it means lying. In the course of several hours of bargaining, Mr. Seller has, through an outright lie about a competing bid, persuaded Ms. Buyer that he will not sell the property for anything less than $1,100,000, a figure that is $200,000 above his actual reservation price. The bargaining continues and eventually they split the difference between Mr. Seller's *perceived* reservation price ($1,100,000) and Ms. Buyer's *actual* reservation price ($1,200,000). With a price of $1,150,000, Ms. Buyer is happy because she believes she has captured exactly half of the available surplus. Mr. Seller is ecstatic, believing (correctly) that he has captured $250,000 of the $300,000 surplus and that his "winning margin" of $200,000 is attributable solely to his skills as a liar. Other distributive lies, such as lies about the mileage of a used car, may operate in slightly different ways, sometimes by altering the other party's assessment of its own reservation price. What these lies all have in common is that, if they are successful, the liar becomes richer in the degree to which the victim becomes poorer.

Distributive lies are not, however, always successful. There are, in fact, three ways they can misfire and cause injury to the *liar*. First, distributive lies may fail to deceive, either because they are never believed or because they are believed but then discovered. Lies that fail in this way may cause such damage to the relationship between the negotiators that the intended victim will be unwilling or unable to enter into what would otherwise be a mutually beneficial agreement. These lies may also create a short-term shift in bargaining power *away* from the liar and in favor of the intended victim. They may have adverse effects on the liar's credibility and effectiveness both in the remainder of the negotiation at hand and in future negotiations with this and other adversaries. They may also provoke defensive or retaliatory lying.

Distributive lies also may cause injury to the liar, and to the liar's victim, when they deceive the victim and thereby block the parties from reaching a beneficial agreement that otherwise would have been available. Assume for instance that Ms. Buyer is negotiating over the price of a car and that her reservation price is such that she will not pay more than $10,000. Further, she has estimated that Mr. Seller's reservation price is such that he will not accept less than $8500. Ms. Buyer has, by lying, persuaded Mr. Seller that her reservation price is

$9000–$1000 less than her actual reservation price. Her belief is that there is $1500 in surplus to be distributed between the parties, that she will by her lie capture $1000 of that surplus, and that she will then perhaps "split the difference" with regard to the remaining $500. Unfortunately, Ms. Buyer has misjudged Mr. Seller's reservation price. Instead of the $8500 that she had estimated, Mr. Seller's reservation price is actually $9300. There is still a $700 range, $9300 to $10,000, within which an agreement would leave *both* parties better off than they would be without an agreement. But having committed herself to her false reservation price ($9000), Ms. Buyer may now be unwilling or unable to make an offer *higher* than that amount. Consequently, the deal may be lost and her all-too-successful distributive lie will have deprived the liar and her victim of $700.

A nominally successful lie can also cause injury to the liar and the victim by causing them to reach an agreement that is less beneficial than it might otherwise have been. [W]hile lying may be the watchword in distributive bargaining, full and truthful disclosure is the key to identifying and exploiting opportunities for integrative bargaining. Thus certain kinds of lies, told to secure distributive (pie-splitting) advantages, may make it impossible for the parties to discover and exploit the integrative (pie-expanding) opportunities that may be available. For example, lies about our interest or priorities can *simultaneously* win the liar a larger share of the pie *and* blind both parties to those avenues by which the pie might have been expanded. In this way, a successful distributive lie may injure both the liar and his victim by causing them to reach an agreement that is less productive of *total* profit than might, but for the lie, have been the case.

Lying in negotiations may also cause injuries that are more general and far-reaching than the immediate effects upon the parties to the negotiation. Lies that are discovered may, for instance, cause persons other than the liar to engage in defensive lying either later in that same negotiation or in *other* negotiations. Such lies can diminish the level of trust and increase the frequency with which additional lies are told. As public trust declines, so does our ability to engage in effective communications and to make and exchange credible commitments, including the promises that underlie contracts. As these capacities decline, so does the efficiency with which we are, all of us, able to conduct our affairs. These discovered lies may, in addition, diminish the possibilities of ethical restraint, community and reciprocity.

Moreover, lies that are successful and undiscovered may lead to further lies by lowering the liar's barriers against lying and by empowering, at least in the mind of the liar, some justification for lying that is, on the merits, insufficient. As those justifications are empowered, the barriers against lying fall still further. Otherwise successful lies may also affect the liar's self-image and sense of personal integrity, as well as his trust in others. Thus, undiscovered lies, like discovered lies, may have adverse effects on a community's capacity for trust, efficiency, ethics, and reciprocity.

In the end, lying in negotiations can produce a wide range of possible effects. While the distribution of these effects is anything but symmetrical, they include both costs and benefits. Two things, though, are clear. The most important is that we cannot say as a general matter that honesty is the best policy for individual negotiators to pursue if by "best" we mean most effective or most profitable. In those bargaining situations which are at least in part distributive, a category which includes virtually all negotiations, lying is a coherent and often effective strategy. In those same circumstances, a policy of never lying may place a negotiator at a systematic and sometimes overwhelming disadvantage. Moreover, there are any number of lies, including those involving reservation prices and opinions, that are both useful and virtually undiscoverable. Accordingly, if the policy we pursue is one of honesty, we must do so for reasons other than profit and effectiveness. The second point is that one who lies in negotiations is in a position to capture almost all of the benefits of lying while suffering only a small portion of the costs and that, in the language of the economists, this state of affairs will lead, almost automatically, to an overproduction of lies.

NOTES ON LYING IN NEGOTIATION

1. ***When, If Ever, Is It Legally Permissible to Lie?*** Consider the arguments for and against the Model Rule 4.1 approach and the Comment [2] exception for lies that are acceptable according to "generally accepted conventions in negotiations." Which do you find the most persuasive or the most appealing?

2. ***Does Rule 4.1 Allow Lies that Rule 8.4 Condemns?*** Rule 8.4(c) generally prohibits lawyers "to engage in conduct involving dishonesty, fraud, deceit or misrepresentation. Can you reconcile Model Rule 4.1's Comment [2] with Model Rule 8.4(c)?

3. ***Is Lying Legally Permissible If It Helps the Client?*** In determining the scope of the generally accepted lies alluded to in Comment [2], should it matter whether lying is effective? It is sometimes argued that lying is not merely acceptable under the Model Rules, but a lawyer is obligated by the duty of loyalty to lie on behalf of the client if it will serve the client's interest. How would you respond to that argument?

4. ***Does Lying Beget More Lying?*** One study of the effects of lying in negotiation documented the effect of lying on other lawyers' willingness to be candid. The authors asked a sample of more than 700 lawyers how they would handle a hypothetical case in which they represent a man suing his ex-girlfriend for intentionally infecting him with a deadly sexually transmitted

disease without telling him that she knew she was infected. Just before settlement negotiations, the hypothetical client informs the lawyer that he is not in fact infected but wants to pursue the suit anyway to punish the ex-girlfriend for her recklessness and seek recompense for the harm she caused in making him afraid he had it. Thirty percent of the respondents indicated they would agree to participate in the client's plan and fail to disclose that the client had no basis for claim. Of those who agreed with the client's request, most said they did so because of the professional rules of conduct regarding client confidences and because they considered it up to the client to make such decisions. (You should know by now that the survey respondents were wrong about both of those principles.) Those who agreed to the client's request tended to expect that other lawyers would agree with the client's request. That is, lawyers who were willing to mislead their opponent about a material fact in negotiation believed that other lawyers would do the same thing in their circumstances.[11] In other words, lying begets lying.

5. **If Candor to an Adversary Is Not Required, Why Is Candor to a Court?** The contrast between Model Rule 4.1's tolerance for a certain amount of lying in negotiation and Model Rule 3.3(b)'s strict requirement of candor to the tribunal strikes some observers as especially troubling, if not downright hypocritical. If some lies are acceptable in negotiations as a form of puffery, why is it not acceptable to exaggerate the strength of precedent in support of one's case or fail to disclose adverse facts when asked about them by the court? Can you reconcile these two positions?

* * *

The Risks of Lying in Negotiation

- A settlement agreement procured by misrepresentation may be voidable under the law of contracts.

- Misrepresentations or nondisclosure of material facts may constitute fraud under the law of torts, or even a criminal fraud.

- The duty of candor to the tribunal under Rule 3.3 can apply to settlement negotiations when the court must approve the terms of the settlement.

Lying in negotiation poses risks of legal liability. A client is not well served by a lawyer's deception about the contract the client hired the lawyer to negotiate if the contract is either invalidated or rewritten on less favorable terms. A settlement agreement based on a material misstatement may violate Model Rule 3.3(b)'s requirement of candor to the tribunal if the settlement agreement must be approved by a court (some but not all settlements of litigation must be approved by the court)

---

[11] Art Hinshaw & Jess K. Alberts, *Doing the Right Thing: An Empirical Study of Attorney Negotiation Ethics*, 16 HARV. J. NEGOTIATION 95 (2011).

because Rule 3.3 includes fraudulent conduct in settlement agreements. A misrepresentation or a failure to disclose information necessary to correct the other party's misapprehension may invalidate the settlement agreement as a matter of contract law and may also be a tort. The Restatement (Second) of Contracts § 153 provides that mistake of fact is grounds for voiding contract if "the other party had reason to know of the mistake or his fault caused the mistake." The contract is not voidable, however, even if the other party knew of the mistake, if the party who is harmed by the mistake "is aware, at the time the contract is made, that he has only limited knowledge with respect to the facts to which the mistake relates but treats his limited knowledge as sufficient." *Id.* § 154. Unless a lawyer is confident that the party who is ignorant of the mistake and stands to lose from it is aware of his own limited knowledge, it is risky to not correct the mistake. A person's non-disclosure of a fact known to him is not always equivalent to an affirmative misstatement, but it is when he knows that disclosure of the fact is necessary to prevent some previous assertion from being a misrepresentation (this is also required under Comment [1] to Model Rule 4.1) or from being fraudulent or material, or when he knows that disclosure of the fact would correct a mistake of the other party as to a basic assumption on which that party is making the contract and if non-disclosure of the fact amounts to a failure to act in good faith and in accordance with reasonable standards of fair dealing. Restatement (Second) of Contracts § 161. In addition, there is a duty to disclose where he knows that disclosure of the fact would correct a mistake of the other party as to the contents or effect of a written term of the agreement or where the other person is entitled to know the fact because of a relation of trust and confidence between them. *Id.* Moreover, under the law of torts, a lawyer's misleading statement or omission may amount to fraud. A fraudulent misrepresentation is (1) intentional misrepresentation to induce an action or inaction; (2) reasonable reliance on the misrepresentation; and (3) resulting damages. Restatement (Second) of Torts § 525, 526, 531 (1977). Misrepresentations can also occur through omissions that are the equivalent of affirmative false statements, particularly when one has made a representation about a fact and remains silent after learning that fact is not true. *Id.* § 531. In sum, a party's false statement or failure to disclose information about a material term of the contract may enable the other party to void the contract entirely or to ask the court to rewrite the contract.

A Taxonomy of Untruths

The Model Rule 4.1 prohibition on misstating "material" facts and the Comment [2] exceptions for misstatements that are permissible under "generally accepted conventions in negotiation" reflect a view that some lies more egregious than others. As you consider which forms of deception are or should be legally permissible, consider:

a. Legal context

    1. plea bargaining versus settlement of a civil suit

    2. misleading statements to regulatory body vs. others

    3. misleading statements to investors vs. others

b. Social context: a one-shot business transaction (e.g. sale of a car or piece of land) versus an ongoing business transaction

c. Misleading the adversary about a point of law as opposed to the facts

d. Misleading statements made by the lawyer versus those made by client

e. Failing to correct a misimpression the lawyer created versus failing to correct a misimpression that the lawyer had no role in creating versus failing to update another about a change in circumstances

f. Misleading an adversary about the substance of the transaction versus the client's position

The following cases illustrate a range of circumstances in which courts have found lawyers violated various laws by being dishonest in negotiation. Pay close attention to the fact that many of these cases are reported because the lawyers thought they could get away with a lie and they didn't. In each case, note the legal duties the court found the lawyer to have violated by lying and also consider whether the lie violated Model Rule 4.1.

1. ***Misstating a Fact***. Lawyer for an insurance company misstated the policy limit on a homeowner's insurance policy to plaintiff's lawyer when negotiating settlement of a claim for injuries in a house fire. Plaintiff's lawyer recommended that his client settle for the policy limit of $100,000, in reliance on defense lawyer's statement. In fact, the policy limit was $300,000. Plaintiff sues defense counsel for misrepresentation. *Fire Insurance Exchange v. Bell*, 643 N.E.2d 310 (Ind. 1994) (court rejected defense arguments that no one can rely on what lawyer said in settlement negotiations and that plaintiff's lawyer should have gotten the policy in discovery and learned policy limits himself).

2.   ***Making Allegations Without Knowledge***. Rodney Sweetland, a lawyer, sued a large bank on behalf of a dozen people alleging that the bank had improperly sold their credit reports to third parties. In pretrial discovery, the bank requested Sweetland and the plaintiffs to identify the employees who had allegedly sold the credit reports, but Sweetland refused, asserting attorney-client privilege. Sweetland offered to settle the case for $75,000 per plaintiff and to reveal the names of the bank employees who had sold the credit reports. After the court rejected the claim of attorney-client privilege, it transpired that neither the plaintiffs nor Sweetland knew the name(s) of the allegedly errant bank employee(s). The bank sought sanctions against Sweetland for making false assertions in pleadings and in discovery, including in the settlement letter. What result? *Ausherman v. Bank of America*, 212 F. Supp. 2d 435 (D. Md. 2002) (upholding sanctions under Fed. R. Civ. P. 37(b) for false statements in settlement offer).

3.   ***Failing to Disclose the Death of the Plaintiff***. Lawyer represents plaintiff in a suit for personal injuries. Just before settlement negotiations, plaintiff dies of the injuries. Must plaintiff's lawyer inform defense counsel that plaintiff has died? Would it matter whether plaintiff's estate is entitled under the substantive law to recover the full extent of damages after plaintiff's death or, on the other hand, as in a suit for libel, a cause of action terminates upon the death of the plaintiff? ABA Formal Opinion 95–397 (Sept. 18, 1995) (lawyer must voluntarily disclose client's death even though law does not normally require lawyer to volunteer adverse facts in negotiation); *Virzi v. Grand Trunk Warehouse and Cold Storage Co.*, 571 F. Supp. 507 (E.D. Mich. 1983) (setting aside settlement); *Kentucky Bar Ass'n v. Geisler*, 938 S.W.2d 578 (Ky. 1997) (ordering public reprimand of lawyer); *People v. Jones*, 375 N.E.2d 41 (N.Y. 1978) (prosecutor has no duty to reveal victim's death and did not make any affirmative misrepresentation about victim's status).

4.   ***Failing to Disclose a Client's Immigration Status***. You represent a young family in suit arising out of a car accident. The parents survived but were severely injured. Their infant child, who was not riding in an infant car seat, was killed. After your clients' deposition, in which they came across as very compelling witnesses, you learned that your clients are undocumented immigrants—a fact which did not emerge at the deposition and of which you think the defense is unaware—and they insist they are unwilling to risk drawing attention to themselves by testifying at trial. In settlement negotiations, must you mention that your clients have instructed you to take any amount, no matter how small, to avoid going to trial? What if the defense asks you point blank about your

clients' immigration status and its impact on their willingness to testify?[12]

5. ***Failing to Correct Another Party's Misunderstanding.*** Larry Lawyer represents Ella, one of four adult children of a wealthy woman who died leaving a substantial amount of money and a large house. Ella is the executor of the estate (meaning Ella is responsible for managing the property until it is divided up among the heirs). The four children negotiated an agreement dividing the estate into what three of them thought was four equal shares, with Ella getting the house where she had lived with their mother. In the negotiations, the other 3 children assumed (wrongly) that the mother's house was part of the estate, when in fact a separate legal document left the house to Ella alone. Larry and Ella knew this, and neither said anything about it. Indeed, Larry said nothing at the entire negotiation, but merely drafted the settlement agreement at the end. As a consequence, Ella got the house plus one quarter of the rest of the estate, instead of having the house count as part of her one-quarter. See *In re Potts*, 158 P.3d 418 (Mont. 2007) (upholding bar discipline of lawyer). Did he violate an ethical duty?

6. ***Failing to Disclose the Existence of Insurance.*** Medina was injured in a traffic accident and retained an attorney, Ernest Addison, to represent him. As a result of the accident, Medina was hospitalized and incurred expenses there totaling approximately $125,000. The defendants responsible for the car accident were insured by State Farm Automobile Insurance Company, with a policy limit of $100,000, by Sea Insurance Company, Ltd., with an umbrella liability policy having a limit of $1 million, and by Allstate Insurance Company, with a policy having a limit of $50,000. Addison met with the business manager for the hospital to arrange for payment of Medina's hospital expenses from the proceeds of the insurance policies. Addison became aware at this meeting that the business manager was under the false impression that State Farm and Allstate were the only two companies whose policies covered the accident. Addison negotiated for a release of the hospital's lien without disclosing the existence of the third policy. The hospital agreed to release the lien in exchange for $45,000 of the State Farm settlement of $100,000, and an additional $15,000 if and when Medina settled with Allstate, plus another $5,000 if the settlement proceeds from Allstate exceeded $40,000. Did Addison have either a legal or an ethical duty to disclose the existence of the third policy with the $1 million limit? See *State ex rel. Nebraska State Bar Ass'n v. Addison*, 412 N.W.2d 855 (Neb. 1987) (noting that hospital

---

[12] This hypothetical is based on a well-known negotiation exercise found in the TEACHER'S MANUAL TO DEBORAH RHODE AND DAVID LUBAN, LEGAL ETHICS (5th ed. 2009). They attribute the problem to Henry Hecht; it appeared originally in the AMERICAN BAR ASSOCIATION CONSORTIUM FOR PROFESSIONAL EDUCATION AND THE AMERICAN BAR ASSOCIATION CENTER FOR PROFESSIONAL RESPONSIBILITY, DILEMMAS IN LEGAL ETHICS (1977).

asserted release was not binding and upholding 6-month suspension of Addison from practice of law).

F. SUMMARY

In this chapter we introduced the wide range of situations in which lawyers are called upon to negotiate and the variety of approaches that the law allows lawyers to take to negotiation. We sampled the literature on effectiveness in negotiation and saw that many different styles of negotiation are effective and legally permissible. We then studied constellations of legal and ethical issues surrounding two classic negotiation dilemmas: the problem of unequal bargaining power and the problem of candor. Model Rule 4.1 prohibits lawyers from knowingly making false statements of material fact or law or failing to disclose material facts when disclosure is necessary to avoid assisting a criminal or fraudulent act by a client, and lawyers and their clients face possible criminal or civil liability if they mislead or threaten in negotiations.

CHAPTER 26

LAWYERS AS THIRD-PARTY NEUTRALS: MEDIATION AND ARBITRATION

■ ■ ■

A. INTRODUCTION

In this chapter we examine the role that lawyers play when they act as third party neutrals who facilitate the resolution of disputes rather than as advocates representing one party to a transaction or a dispute. We focus on work as a third party neutral and leave to courses in alternative dispute resolution (ADR) to teach you how to represent clients in these types of processes. After surveying the variety of types of ADR, and the sources of regulation of lawyers' work as third party neutrals, we study two of the principal forms of ADR: mediation and arbitration. We also consider some of the principal legal and ethical issues facing lawyers who work as mediators and arbitrators.

Alternative dispute resolution (ADR) is a term that refers loosely to any form of dispute resolution other than a decision by a court. ADR is very common in every sort of legal practice. Ethics rules in some states encourage lawyers to advise clients about the use of ADR, and comment [5] to Model Rule 2.1 says that "it may be necessary under Rule 1.4 [governing the lawyer's obligation to communicate with clients] to inform the client of forms of dispute resolution that might constitute reasonable alternatives to litigation." ADR includes processes of varying degrees of formality, including the following:

Organizational Dispute Resolution. An organization (such as a corporation's human resources department or an online retailer like Amazon.com or service provider like Paypal.com) may allow or require community members, employees, or consumers to present disputes to a third party and receive some form of assistance in resolution. In some organizations, if the informal dispute resolution system does not produce agreement, the parties will be required to resolve it through arbitration. (The next time you visit a website, click on the Terms of Service link and see what dispute resolution system you have "agreed to" by visiting the page.) Some large organizations employ an ombudsperson to investigate and resolve disputes or problems within the organization. For example, an employee who believes that someone within an organization is engaged in unethical or illegal behavior can report the problem to the ombudsperson who is empowered to investigate and, depending on the organization, to issue a report or to resolve the complaint.

Mediation. Parties to a dispute or negotiating a transaction choose a third person as a mediator to assist them in negotiating a resolution. The mediator has no power to impose a solution, but only facilitates the parties' negotiations with the goal of helping them agree to a solution. Mediation can be very casual (any third party, not necessarily a lawyer, can help the parties negotiate a solution) or very formal (a lawyer trained as a mediator convenes and structures a meeting or series of meetings that results in a formal, written agreement). While mediators often emphasize voluntary participation as a cornerstone of mediation philosophy, in fact, participation in mediation is not always voluntary. Most states have enacted laws requiring or strongly encouraging mediation (often known as court-annexed mediation) as part of the pretrial process in certain kinds of cases (often in family law), and sometimes mediation is required by courts as a part of the pretrial process in any civil case.

Arbitration. Parties to a dispute choose (or may be assigned) a third person to decide their dispute. Arbitration is used to resolve disputes that would otherwise be litigated. Parties to commercial contracts, especially international contracts, have long agreed to arbitrate disputes arising under their agreements. Unions and the companies that employ unionized workers have long used arbitration to resolve all disputes arising out of their collective bargaining agreements. Since 1990, large employers have often required all employees to agree as a condition of employment to arbitrate all disputes arising out of the employment relationship, and many health care practices require all patients to agree to arbitrate all disputes. Arbitration is also used to resolve negotiating disputes.

Private Adjudication. Parties to a dispute agree to litigate their dispute before a judge hired and paid by them, rather than assigned and paid for by the government. Typically, private adjudication is very similar in process to adjudication in a court, and the judge is often a retired judge. The difference is that the parties do not use the court building or resources and therefore do not have to wait for a trial date, and the parties can adopt the rules of procedure that they wish. Unlike arbitration, however, the judge's decision is appealable.

Mini-Trial or Summary Jury Trial. Parties to litigation agree to present all or part of their case to a mock jury or to a neutral third party acting as a judge to render a decision. The process is not binding on the parties, but rather is to give them an idea of how an actual judge or jury would respond to the parties' evidence and arguments. The parties then use that information in settlement negotiations or to prepare a trial strategy.

B. WHAT ROLES DO LAWYERS PLAY IN ADR?

Lawyers work as third-party neutrals, and they represent clients in ADR proceedings. Employment as a third-party neutral has emerged since the 1980s as an appealing career, or career phase, for many lawyers. The U.S. Bureau of Labor Statistics estimated that 9,400 people were employed full time as mediators, arbitrators and conciliators in the U.S. in 2010.[1]

Some lawyers are employed in-house by corporations or organizations that maintain large internal dispute resolution programs. Some work as solo practitioners offering their service as a mediator or arbitrator. Some are employed by or contract with private organizations that offer ADR services: JAMS (www.jamsadr.com) and AAA (www.adr.org) are two of the best known such organizations in the private sector. JAMS and AAA offer the services of neutrals as well as rules of procedure for different kinds of ADR. For a fee (or, in qualifying cases through their foundations, pro bono) JAMS and AAA offer a package of services to resolve disputes through arbitration, mediation, or some other ADR process. Each of them employs or has as affiliates hundreds of lawyers and retired judges across (and outside) the U.S. with training and experience as arbitrators and mediators. Each of them offers various rules of procedure for conducting different kinds of ADR, ranging from specialized rules for arbitrating employment or insurance or commercial contract disputes, to simple and relatively inexpensive online mediations for small-dollar disputes (or disputes in which the disputants are able or willing to spend only a few hundred dollars for mediation). In the federal government, the Federal Mediation and Conciliation Service (www.fmcs.gov) employs trained mediators to facilitate resolution of a variety of disputes, mainly but not exclusively in the labor-management area, and it maintains a referral list of arbitrators.

---

[1] Bureau of Labor Statistics, U.S. Department of Labor, *Occupational Outlook Handbook, 2012–13 Edition*, Judges, Mediators, and Hearing Officers, on the Internet at http://www.bls.gov/ooh/legal/judges-mediators-and-hearing-officers.htm.

> **A lawyer may perform one or more of three roles of third party neutral:**
>
>   *Facilitator*—The neutral assists the parties to negotiate. She helps them articulate their needs (or interests or demands); she suggests alternatives, encourages them to see the dispute in a new light or from the other side's point of view, and attempts to reduce the risk that anger or intransigence will prevent the parties from reaching a mutually satisfactory agreement.
>
>   *Evaluator*—The neutral offers his assessment of the case. In some types of mediation, the parties expect the mediator to offer his own analysis of their arguments or positions or his own assessment of how a judge or jury is likely to perceive them.
>
>   *Decisionmaker*—The neutral is employed to decide the matter. This is what arbitrators and private judges do.

Lawyers involved in ADR, both as third party neutrals and as those who represent clients in ADR, strenuously debate the proper mix of these roles generally, and their merits in addressing particular kinds of disputes. Some of these debates are considered below.

C. HOW IS THE LEGAL PRACTICE OF ADR REGULATED?

The plethora of organizations providing ADR services or requiring or encouraging the use of ADR and the wide range of different types of ADR make it impossible to describe succinctly the regulation of the lawyer's roles in it. And because some types of ADR are performed by lawyers as well as nonlawyers (e.g., family therapists conduct mediation, and managers serve as company ombudspersons), different sources of professional regulation apply to those performing the same service.

1. ***The Law Governing Lawyers***. When lawyers represent clients in ADR, regardless of the type, the same rules and norms that govern their conduct in any other setting apply, including the Model Rules, malpractice liability, and the norms of their practice setting. In addition, many dispute resolution service providers, such as AAA and JAMS, have rules of procedure that regulate the behavior of parties and their representatives, just as courts have rules of procedure to govern lawyers' conduct of cases.

2. ***Some Rules of Professional Conduct Apply Only to Lawyers Representing Clients***. Lawyers working as third party neutrals are governed by the rules of professional conduct adopted by the state in which they practice, just as are lawyers practicing in any other sector of the profession. However, some rules of professional conduct may apply

only to lawyers representing clients. With two exceptions, the Model Rules do not speak to the specific ethical or other issues that are unique to practice as a third party neutral. The text of the Model Rules even leaves some doubt as to which ones apply to lawyers working as third party neutrals, for most of them speak in terms of "representing" a "client." Third party neutrals <u>have</u> clients—those who hire them to resolve their disputes—but they do not <u>represent</u> clients. The Preamble to the Model Rules acknowledges that a lawyer may work in a "nonrepresentational role" as a third party neutral, and cautions that some Model Rules apply to lawyers "even when they are acting in a nonprofessional capacity." Although the particulars of what the Model Rules require may differ for third party neutrals and for lawyers representing clients, the major principles do not.

The two Model Rules that address the role of lawyers as third party neutrals focus on clarifying the lawyer's role and conflicts of interest. Model Rule 2.4(b) requires a lawyer serving as a third-party neutral to "inform unrepresented parties that the lawyer is not representing them. When the lawyer knows or reasonably should know that a party does not understand the lawyer's role in the matter, the lawyer shall explain the difference between the lawyer's role as a third-party neutral and a lawyer's role as one who represents a client."

Model Rule 1.12 governs post-ADR conflicts of interest. A former mediator, arbitrator or judge in a matter cannot represent one of the parties in the same matter without written informed consent. The law firm is conflicted too, though screening is allowed.

3. ***Rules of Court.*** Virtually every state that requires mediation or arbitration annexed to court adjudication has promulgated rules of conduct governing those who serve as mediators, arbitrators, or other third-party neutrals under those systems.[2]

4. ***ADR Service Providers Promulgate Their Own Rules.*** Many dispute resolution service providers (like JAMS and AAA) have adopted their own requirements of conduct for third party neutrals providing services under their auspices.

5. ***Codes of Conduct of Professional Associations of Mediators and Arbitrators.*** Because the Model Rules of Professional Conduct have almost nothing specific to say about the conduct of lawyers working as third party neutrals, the ABA, the National Arbitration Association, and other professional organizations of third party neutrals have promulgated various codes of conduct applicable to particular types of third party neutral practice.

---

[2] Rules governing mediation in all 50 states are compiled in the appendix to SARAH R. COLE *ET AL.*, MEDIATION: LAW, POLICY & PRACTICE (2011–2012).

6. *The Uniform Mediation Act and Other State Law*. In addition to codes of conduct, some organizations have promulgated model rules of procedure or model laws that contain provisions governing the conduct of third party neutrals. For example, the National Conference of Commissioners on Uniform State Laws has promulgated a Uniform Mediation Act. Ten states and the District of Columbia have enacted the Uniform Mediation Act.[3] Some states have enacted legislation empowering courts to promulgate codes of conduct for mediators and arbitrators and have made compliance with such codes mandatory for third party neutrals.[4]

7. *Employment Contracts*. Third party neutrals are typically hired by contract with the parties. As in any other professional-client relationship, the client(s) can insist on certain contract terms.

8. *Market and Peer Group Controls*. Most mediators and arbitrators are chosen on a case-by-case basis by parties or their lawyers. To attract future clients, third party neutrals must be perceived as providing a valuable service. Those who work as solo practitioners or in small firms must market their services and develop a reputation through word-of-mouth or client referral. Those who work as employees of organizations or as contractors who are part of a referral network must conform to the demands and expectations of the organization.

The labor market for third party neutrals affects the conditions of work for them, but may also powerfully affect the results of the process for those who rely on them. Arbitrators, mediators, private judges, or any other third party neutral who routinely works for one party may come to depend on that party for their livelihood. We consider this possible source of bias in some detail below.

D. MEDIATION

Mediation takes a wide variety of forms. Mediators sometimes facilitate business transactions, and often resolve disputes either before the parties have framed them as a possible law suit or after both have retained counsel and filed suit. Mediation is required by courts in some civil cases in an effort to encourage settlement. Mediation is required by statute in some kinds of disputes (such as labor-management disputes in the railroad and airline industries and in some employment discrimination suits).

---

[3] *See* www.uniformlaws.org for the current status of enactment.

[4] *See, e.g.*, Cal. Code Civ. Pro. § 1281.85 (requiring arbitrators to adhere to Ethics Standards for Neutral Arbitrators); www.courts.ca.gov/documents/ethics_standards_neutral_arbitrators.pdf.

> **Mediation Is Facilitated Negotiation**
>
> The core concept of mediation is **party self-determination**. The parties themselves decide what their dispute is about, what their needs or interests are, and whether or how to resolve the dispute through mediation. The application of law to fact does not alone resolve the dispute; rather, the parties decide what values or principles will guide them and work out their own resolution. **The mediator is a neutral facilitator** who helps the parties agree but does not take sides or impose her views.

Mediation is thought to be an antidote to destructive strategic behavior in negotiation by reducing opportunities to engage in it. Mediation does so in several ways: (1) It recognizes the full range of party interests, values, and priorities (not just money or the governing law); (2) It manages emotional and relational issues in a "safe" place where the parties can discuss their feelings, gain respect, offer and accept apologies, and share information; (3) It reduces the potential for conflicting interests between lawyer and client by encouraging the client to be involved in the statement of priorities and resolution of the dispute; (4) Mediation reduces the risks associated with honest disclosure of information so as to enable both sides to gain mutually optimal settlements that would not be possible if neither side trusted the other enough to disclose information that would lead to a settlement; (5) It improves communication and preparation by both lawyers and clients by forcing them to focus on the dispute and carve out time in their busy schedules to resolve it; (6) It reduces cognitive barriers to settlement by forcing parties to see the matter from the perspective of others.[5] After describing the mediation process and the role of the mediator, we will consider the circumstances in which mediation can address the problems of self-interested, strategic, and potentially destructive behavior that can occur in unfacilitated negotiation, and when it cannot.

1. A TYPICAL MEDIATION

Mediation can take many forms, and can last anywhere from a few hours to many days, but a typical mediation might go something like this. Mediators generally prefer that the parties be present, not just their lawyers. Indeed, some mediation experts insist that without parties there, it's not really mediation because it's not party self-determination. In some cases neither side is represented by counsel. Mediators often resist having only one party be represented by counsel, and law in some states regulates when counsel can and cannot be present in mediation.[6] Court-

---

[5] See COLE, *ET AL.*, MEDIATION: LAW, POLICY & PRACTICE at 51–60.

[6] *See, e.g.,* Cal. Fam. Code § 3182(a) (mediator may exclude attorney from participating); Wis. Stat. § 767.405(10) (permitting mediator to include counsel).

annexed settlement mediations generally deem it crucial that each party have at least one person present who has full settlement authority. Many court programs and provider organizations require that the attorneys provide to the mediator in advance a short confidential mediation statement. The statement summarizes the issues involved (legal and otherwise) and indicates what the attorney and client are looking for.

At the beginning of the mediation session, the mediator generally provides an explanation of the mediation process, and the parties agree to the procedures and the extent of confidentiality of mediation communications. The mediator generally asks each or all parties—both the clients and their attorneys—to take turns providing a brief overview of the dispute and what they want to say about it. Mediators encourage the parties to speak in addition to their attorneys. By having the parties present during the mediation, the parties obtain a better understanding of the other parties' interests and positions. Mediators insist that this process creates a better understanding between the parties.

The mediator often suggests an individual caucus with each party separately. Whatever is said during the caucus is confidential, and is not repeated to the other side, unless consent is obtained, although the mediator is free to use the information provided in an effort to nudge the parties toward agreement. After a caucus with all sides, the mediator generally meets with everyone together again. Often the mediator will encourage brainstorming of ideas for resolution and discussion of several options for resolution.

During this discussion, the mediator may be more or less aggressive in suggesting options and possible outcomes, and in assessing each party's statements. In evaluative mediation, the parties expect the mediator to offer her perspective on the parties' statements or asserted desires. (In mediation, it's often frowned upon to refer to the parties' positions; parties have perceptions, concerns, and interests, but they are not supposed to have positions or make arguments.). In facilitative or transformative mediation, the parties' expectations about whether the mediator will state her own assessment may be less clear. Facilitative mediation aids the parties to reach their own agreement, and transformative mediation aspires to help parties transform their relationship (and, perhaps, themselves). Mediators debate when one or another of these approaches is more appropriate. Whatever mediators think, attorneys who represent parties in mediation, at least in some cases, often want evaluation.[7] Yet in some states and in some mediation programs, mediators are strongly discouraged from evaluating a case or

---

[7]   ABA Section of Dispute Resolution, Task Force on Improving Mediation Quality, Final Report 2006–2008, available at www.abanet.org/dispute.

offering their opinions on it, even when specifically requested to do so by a party or an attorney.[8]

The role of mediators as evaluators and the proper mix of party discussion in joint session and separate caucuses are hot topics among mediators, as is the role of lawyer representatives in mediation. Some scholars lament that the increasingly widespread use of court-annexed mediation has fundamentally changed the nature of mediation, and not for the better.[9] In essence, the critique is that the mediator has become more like a settlement facilitator.[10]

Whatever mix of party- and lawyer-control and individual and joint sessions, eventually the parties decide whether they have reached agreement or if they need more time. Ideally, the mediation ends (whether after one session lasting a few hours, or multiple sessions over days or weeks), when an agreement is reached. The mediator usually requires the agreement to be reduced to writing and signed by all parties. Sometimes the mediator will draft all or portions of the agreement, but sometimes the mediator will avoid doing so.

2. THE MEDIATOR'S ROLE

Many mediators speak in rather glowing terms about the mediation process and about their role in it. Surveys of mediators and lawyers who represent clients in mediation have found that the mediators are more likely than the lawyers to value what some call the "softer" side of the process—articulating feelings, believing one has been heard, healing or preserving relationships, and the like.[11] Some speak in lofty terms about the skilled mediator's capacity to bring happiness to unhappy people, to transform relationships, to bring peace to families and communities, and to promote democracy and justice by empowering individuals to resolve their own disputes, to create their own norms to govern their relationships. Some assert that mediation may be the only form of dispute resolution capable of making people better people and promoting moral

---

[8] In North Carolina, for example, the Standards of Conduct for all mediators certified by the state Dispute Resolution Commission or who are conducting court-annexed mediation provide:

A mediator shall not impose his/her opinion about the merits of the dispute or about the acceptability of any proposed option for settlement. A mediator should resist giving his/her opinions about the dispute and options for settlement even when he/she is requested to do so by a party or attorney.

North Carolina Supreme Court, Standards of Professional Conduct for Mediators, Preamble §V(C) (2006), *available at* http://www.nccourts.org/Courts/CRS/Councils/DRC/Documents/Standards_030110.pdf.

[9] Nancy A. Welsh, *Making Deals in Court-Connected Mediation: What's Justice Got to Do With It?*, 79 WASH. U. L.Q. 787, 789–793 (2001).

[10] James J. Alfini, *Mediation as a Calling: Addressing the Disconnect Between Mediation Ethics and the Practices of Lawyer Mediators.* 49 S. TEX. L. REV. 829, 834 (2008).

[11] ABA Task Force on Mediation Quality, at 8.

growth.[12] Mediators typically contrast their perspective on mediation as a process—it is more likely than negotiation or adjudication to produce creative solutions to problems and to expand rather than just divide the settlement pie—with lawyers' tendency to focus only on the results— whether the mediation produced a good settlement for the client, and whether the client is happy with the results.

Some criticisms of mediation are similar to criticisms of other forms of dispute resolution, including litigation. In short, the criticism is that mediation rarely succeeds in its most transformative aspirations. It suppresses conflict rather than defusing or resolving it, and it produces compromise in cases in which there should be none.[13] An important critique of mediation in cases in which there has been domestic violence asserts that mediation sacrifices the right to be free from violence to the "interests" or "needs" of batterers to explain away violence as simply anger or overreaction to the victims' poor housekeeping or unwillingness to do what they want.[14] How we assess the success of the mediation as a process or in its results might depend on the underlying facts.

NOTES ON MEDIATION

1. **_Enthusiasm About Mediation._** All lawyers are prone to a certain amount of hyperbole about the importance of their role, but the tone and the substance of the praise of mediation are particularly glowing. Why do many find it such an appealing form of practice?

2. **_How Strictly Should Mediation Be Regulated?_** A longstanding debate about mediation concerns whether or how strictly law should regulate who may be a mediator. In some states, one critic complained, "there are stiffer requirements to become a hair stylist than there are to become a mediator."[15] Enacting legislation to establish qualification, licensing and disciplinary standards for mediators as for other professions can be controversial because, as the former executive director of the Society of Professionals in Dispute Resolution said, "There are many paths to competence, such as life skills and on-the-job experience, as well as professional training. . . . Just because [people have] a professional degree doesn't mean that they're going to be good mediators."[16]

As with every other aspect of the regulation of the legal profession, there is a tension between stiff regulation in an effort to ensure quality and allowing greater access to the practice. Greater regulation of the

---

[12] Sara Cobb, *Creating Sacred Space: Toward a Second-Generation Dispute Resolution Practice*, 28 FORDHAM URB. L. J. 1017, 1017 (2001).

[13] An early and still influential critique of ADR exploring these ideas is Owen Fiss, *Against Settlement*, 93 YALE L.J. 1073 (1984).

[14] *See* Trina Grillo, *The Mediation Alternative: Process Dangers for Women*, 100 YALE L.J. 1545 (1991).

[15] Richard C. Reuben, *The Lawyer Turns Peacemaker*, ABA J. (August 1996), at 54.

[16] *Id.*

qualifications of mediators will also operate as a barrier to entry to the occupation. This tension has remained acute over the decades, as illustrated in the Final Report of the ABA Section of Dispute Resolution Task Force on Improving Mediation Quality, which recognized the importance of mediator knowledge and skill but took no position on how mediators ought to be trained, and no position on mediator credentialing or regulation.

E. LEGAL AND ETHICAL ISSUES FOR MEDIATORS

1. CONFIDENTIALITY

Under most state laws governing mediation, almost everything that is said and done during the mediation remains confidential in most circumstances. Confidentiality stems from the same policy that underlies the settled rule that settlement negotiations are generally not admissible in evidence: to use a settlement offer or a statement in mediation to prove, for example, that the defendant in an auto accident case admitted he was negligent, would discourage people from discussing settlement or mediating disputes.[17] The confidentiality of mediation is protected both by a privilege—which, like attorney-client privilege, is a rule of evidence enforced by tribunals[18]—and by a mediator's duty of confidentiality—which, like the lawyer's duty of confidentiality, is an ethical principle applicable in all contexts, except that mediators are not subject to loss of a license for violating the duty because mediators are generally not separately licensed. The proper scope of confidentiality for mediation is hotly contested among mediators and others.

RINAKER V. SUPERIOR COURT
California Court of Appeal
74 Cal. Rptr. 2d 464 (1998)

In this juvenile delinquency proceeding, the minors, Christopher G. and Huy D., are charged by the People of California with committing vandalism during an incident in which the minors allegedly threw rocks at Arsenio Torres's car.

The incident also was the basis of a civil harassment action brought by Torres against the minors. After Torres obtained a temporary restraining order against them, the minors participated with Torres in

---

[17] The nuances of the law governing confidentiality in mediation are discussed in SARAH R. COLE, ET AL., MEDIATION: LAW, POLICY & PRACTICE, chapter 8.

[18] In federal courts, Federal Rule of Evidence 408 prohibits admission in evidence of settlement offers and responses and also "conduct or statements made in compromise negotiations" to prove liability or to impeach a witness through a prior inconsistent statement. The rule allows use of such evidence, however, for other purposes, including to prove an effort to obstruct a criminal investigation or prosecution or to prove some other wrongful conduct such as threats, extortion, assault, or harassment.

mediation conducted by petitioner Kristen Rinaker in an effort to resolve the civil harassment action.

Rinaker is a volunteer mediator affiliated with the Mediation Center of San Joaquin County (the Center), a community-based, nonprofit corporation. Among other things, the Center provides mediation support services to respondent Superior Court of San Joaquin County, which encourages parties to civil harassment actions to resolve their differences through mediation.

According to Rinaker, the participation by such parties in mediation is voluntary. Those who elect to participate must agree that statements made in mediation are confidential and that mediators will not testify regarding mediation proceedings. Mediation proceedings are not conducted under oath, do not follow traditional rules of evidence, and are not limited to developing the facts. Rather, mediators are instructed to "draw out the parties' subjective perceptions of, and feelings about, the events that have brought them into conflict" and to encourage parties "to verbally acknowledge the other's point of view, whether they come to share that point of view or not."

Following mediation, the court entered an order in the civil harassment action, directing the minors to stay away from Torres's properties and stating: "All parties to be respectful of each other. No parties will make accusations against each other without evidence."

Thereafter, the minors served Rinaker with a subpoena to appear and testify in the juvenile delinquency proceeding being prosecuted against them. Rinaker balked, and the minors filed a "motion to compel witness to testify."

The minors claimed that, during mediation of the civil harassment action, Torres had "admitted to all present, including the mediator, that he did not actually see who threw the rocks at his car." Asserting they would seek to introduce Rinaker's testimony to that effect only if Torres should testify otherwise on direct examination during the juvenile delinquency proceeding, the minors argued their rights to due process of law and a fair trial would be compromised if Rinaker were not compelled to testify.

Rinaker opposed the motion, arguing that statements made during the mediation are privileged under [California Evidence Code] section 1119 and protected from disclosure by the right of privacy embodied in article I, section 1 of the California Constitution. Rinaker further suggested that, even if statements during mediation are admissible in a subsequent juvenile delinquency proceeding, by voluntarily agreeing to participate in confidential mediation, the minors waived any right to compel her testimony.

Section 1119 states: "Except as otherwise provided in this chapter: (a) No evidence of anything said or any admission made for the purpose of, in the course of, or pursuant to, a mediation or a mediation consultation is admissible or subject to discovery, and disclosure of the evidence shall not be compelled, in any arbitration, administrative adjudication, *civil action, or other noncriminal proceeding* in which, pursuant to law, testimony can be compelled to be given. (b) No writing . . . that is prepared for the purpose of, in the course of, or pursuant to, a mediation or a mediation consultation is admissible or subject to discovery, and disclosure of the writing shall not be compelled, in any arbitration, administrative adjudication, *civil action, or other noncriminal proceeding* in which, pursuant to law, testimony can be compelled to be given. (c) All communications, negotiations, or settlement discussions by and between participants in the course of mediation or a mediation consultation shall remain confidential."[3]

Because a juvenile delinquency proceeding is a civil action, it comes within the plain language of section 1119. Had the Legislature intended to exclude juvenile delinquency proceedings from the scope of the statute, it knew how to say so as it did, for example, with mediation in a civil proceeding involving child custody or visitation (see fn. 3, *ante*).

The confidentiality provision of section 1119 must yield if it conflicts with the minors' constitutional right to effective impeachment of an adverse witness in this juvenile delinquency proceeding.

In the context of criminal proceedings, the constitutional right of an accused to confront and cross-examine a prosecution witness includes the right to impeach, i.e., discredit, the witness with evidence of his or her inconsistent statements.

Likewise, due process of law entitles juveniles to certain fundamental protections of the Bill of Rights in proceedings that may result in confinement or other sanctions, whether the state labels these proceedings "criminal" or "civil."

According to Rinaker, voluntary mediation of civil harassment disputes was specifically designed to relieve crowded court calendars and to divert potentially explosive harassment cases to a forum where peaceful resolutions are likely. Without confidentiality, mediations would be subject to all kinds of manipulation and abuse. The heart of the mediation exchange typically involves concessions, waivers, confusions, misstatements, confessions, implications, angry words, insults . . . the list could go on. The very atmosphere that serves to promote resolution in mediation would quickly become a trap for the unwary if proceedings

---

[3] The confidentiality provided by section 1119 may be waived, and the section does not apply to mediation in a family conciliation court proceeding, mediation of child custody and visitation, or a mandatory settlement conference.

were not kept confidential. Warnings would need to be given; protections would need to be devised. Parties would need the advice of counsel to participate in mediations. The costs and complexity of the process might soon rival those of a litigation, thus nullifying a large advantage of community mediation, its accessibility to ranks of the public who are sometimes excluded from more expensive dispute resolution opportunities.

The minors concede mediation serves an important function. Therefore, they do not seek a blanket policy allowing statements made in mediation to be automatically admissible in juvenile delinquency proceedings. Rather, they assert the confidentiality provision of section 1119 must yield when it conflicts with the constitutional right to impeach a witness in a juvenile delinquency proceeding.

The minors' position finds support in California case law addressing other statutes which exclude or limit evidence on public policy grounds. For example, a criminal defendant's constitutional right to cross-examine and impeach witnesses prevails over the statutory psychotherapist-patient privilege. Similarly, courts in civil cases have allowed impeachment with evidence ordinarily excluded on public policy grounds. [The court cited cases allowing, to impeach a witness, use of evidence of subsequent repairs (which is inadmissible to prove negligence) and evidence of insurance (which is inadmissible to prove wrongdoing).]

That section 1119 serves an important public purpose in promoting the settlement of legal disputes through confidential mediation rather than litigation does not justify the preclusion of effective impeachment of a prosecution witness in a juvenile delinquency proceeding with statements the witness made during mediation. When balanced against the competing goals of preventing perjury and preserving the integrity of the truth-seeking process of trial in a juvenile delinquency proceeding, the promotion of settlements must yield to the constitutional right to effective impeachment.[5]

We find no merit in Rinaker's claim that an order compelling her to give such testimony treads impermissibly upon the right of privacy guaranteed by article 1, section 1 of the California Constitution.*

According to Rinaker, two privacy rights are threatened by the proposed disclosure of Torres's statements in mediation: Torres's

---

[5] We are not unsympathetic to Rinaker's concern that unpaid mediators, like her, "would hesitate to volunteer their time so freely if, solely as a result of conducting a mediation, they might be required to become witnesses in later litigation involving disputants." This legitimate concern, however, does not override the greater public interest of preventing perjury and preserving the integrity of the truth-seeking process of trial in a juvenile delinquency proceeding.

* [Eds: Article I, section 1 of the California Constitution provides: "All people are by nature free and independent and have inalienable rights. Among these are enjoying and defending life and liberty, acquiring, possessing, and protecting property, and pursuing and obtaining safety, happiness, and privacy."]

expectation that one's revelations will not be repeated, and Rinaker's expectation that one will not be compelled to breach an entrusted confidence.

It has long been established that, when balanced against the competing goals of preventing perjury and preserving the integrity of the truth-seeking process of trial in a juvenile delinquency proceeding, the interest in promoting settlements (in this case through confidential mediation of Torres's civil harassment action against the minors) must yield to the constitutional right to effective impeachment.

Thus, neither Rinaker nor Torres had a reasonable expectation that any statements made by Torres during confidential mediation concerning the rock-throwing incident which were inconsistent with other statements he made about the minors' involvement in the incident would remain private if he later were called as a witness to testify against the minors in a juvenile delinquency proceeding. Cf. *Garstang v. Superior Court* (1995) 39 Cal.App.4th 526, 532–537 (held that the right of privacy barred the plaintiff in a civil action for slander and intentional infliction of emotional distress from obtaining the disclosure of statements made during an educational institution's confidential ombudsman process for informally resolving employee and student "conflicts, disputes and grievances").

Here, the record indicates that, based upon an incident in which the minors allegedly threw rocks at his car, Torres filed a petition to obtain a temporary restraining order and enjoin the minors from harassing him. The record does not include the petition; however, because Torres obtained a temporary restraining order and the matter went to mediation, we presume he filed an affidavit identifying the minors as the culprits in the rock-throwing incident. Thus, we presume that, in agreeing to confidential mediation as defendants in the civil harassment action, the minors believed Torres would inform the mediator that they were responsible for the rock-throwing.

Without knowing that Torres would make inconsistent statements during mediation concerning their alleged involvement in the rock-throwing incident, the minors had no knowledge of facts giving rise to their constitutional right to effective impeachment during the subsequent juvenile delinquency proceeding. Accordingly, when they voluntarily agreed to participate in confidential mediation in an effort to settle the civil harassment action against them, the minors did not knowingly and intelligently waive their right to use any inconsistent statements made by Torres during mediation to impeach his testimony in a subsequent juvenile delinquency proceeding because that right was not known to them under the facts at the time they agreed to mediation.

NOTES ON RINAKER

1. **Confidentiality of Mediation.** The confidentiality of mediation varies, depending on state law. The Uniform Mediation Act (UMA) empowers parties to mediation and the mediator to refuse to disclose and to prevent others from disclosing a mediation communication. The privilege can be waived through a written or electronic record of an oral waiver during the proceedings. There are no implied waivers. The UMA excepts from the privilege: criminal acts or attempts or efforts to conceal them; threats to commit crimes of violence or to inflict bodily harm; an agreement signed by all the parties to the agreement; use of evidence to prove or disprove a claim of professional misconduct by the mediator or by a party or its representative; and evidence of abuse, neglect, or exploitation of a child "in a proceeding where a child or adult protective agency is a party." Some state mediation privilege laws do not contain explicit exceptions to confidentiality but instead treat it as a qualified privilege that can be overcome by a showing of need.

California is one of few states to impose a broad rule of confidentiality on mediation through Evidence Code § 1119, the provision construed in *Rinaker*.

2. **Why Do Mediators Favor Confidentiality?** Why do you imagine Rinaker resisted testifying? What are the harms to mediators or to mediation as a process when mediators are later compelled to testify about what the parties said or did?

3. **Should Mediation Be Confidential?** What do you see as the advantages and disadvantages of the court's rule? Could you devise a better rule that allows some later use of evidence of mediation without too much? Why do you suppose the California legislature made the confidentiality of mediation absolute with the exceptions identified in footnote 3 of the court's opinion? Given that the Legislature had identified those specific exceptions but had not included one applicable on the facts of *Rinaker*, should the court create additional exceptions? How broadly should the *Rinaker* exception apply? Should it allow impeachment only in juvenile delinquency proceedings? What about in other civil actions where a great deal is at stake? In *Olam v. Congress Mortgage Co.*, 68 F. Supp. 2d 1110 (N.D. Cal. 1999), a woman whose home was in foreclosure participated in a mediation which resulted in a settlement agreement that was signed by the parties and contemplated a later drafting of a formal agreement. She later refused to sign the formal agreement relinquishing her home, insisting that during the 15-hour mediation session, in which both sides were represented by counsel, she had sat by herself in a conference room, was ill and fainted several times, was not involved in the negotiations, was afraid to ask questions, and did not understand the agreement that had been reached. The bank insisted the woman was fabricating her story about the mediation and sought to compel the mediator to testify. On what basis could or should the mediator be compelled to testify? (The court ordered the mediator to testify. The mediator's account did not support the plaintiff's.)

2. CANDOR OF PARTIES AND MEDIATOR

Just as in unassisted negotiation, parties have incentives to lie or to mislead by omission in mediation. When mediation works as it is intended, proponents of mediation insist, the parties do not lie or mislead because they both realize that they will gain the most by being honest. The challenge for a mediator is to convince both parties that they have the most to gain by honesty, to detect when one party is not being candid, and to induce that party to be candid or to let the other party know that the expectation of candor is not being honored by both sides.

What should a mediator do when she suspects one party is lying? Can or should the mediator maintain neutrality? The law of many jurisdictions creates an exception to the rule of mediation confidentiality when any party to the mediation, or the mediator, is engaged in professional misconduct, criminal behavior, or fraud. Other than terminating the mediation and signaling that the mediator will reveal one party's abuse of the process, are there other things that a mediator could do to nip dishonesty in the bud?

The success of mediation, measured both by the process and by the results, is generally thought to depend quite significantly on the skills of the mediator. A skillful mediator is supposed to be able to detect when the parties are lying and to induce them to be candid, to elicit creative solutions to negotiating impasses, to know when to push the parties to agree and when to declare a recess or to terminate the mediation entirely.

3. DISPARITIES OF BARGAINING POWER

Mediation is supposed to address the disparities of bargaining power that plague negotiation and litigation by stripping away the advantages possessed by those who can afford to hire the best lawyers and spend the most money preparing for a negotiation or litigation. The parties themselves come to the mediation and, when it works as intended, speak honestly about their wants, needs, and fears. The advantage the law may give one side in terms of substantive rights—the shadow of the law—is supposed to fade away and the parties meet as equals to brainstorm creative mutually beneficial approaches to their dispute.

There is a tension between party self-determination and disparities of bargaining power. A mediator determined to let the parties work out their own resolution, and to stay strictly neutral about what happens, risks allowing a party with greater bargaining power to exploit the less-powerful party. In some types of mediations, mediators insist they should not attempt to balance disparities of bargaining power or even to consider it as a relevant factor. An example of this is mediation of negotiating disputes in unionized industries. If the labor or product market conditions are such that either the union or the employer is in a position to force the other side to accept major concessions, mediators say they are not in a position to intervene. On the other hand, in marital dissolution mediations in which one spouse has power and the other does not, many mediators say they should attempt to keep disparities of bargaining power from affecting the resolution.

F. ARBITRATION

What Is Arbitration?

Arbitration is a process in which disputants agree to have a third party, or a panel of third parties, resolve their bargaining dispute or a dispute that would otherwise be litigated.

A TYPICAL ARBITRATION

Arbitration has a long and uncontroversial history of use by sophisticated contracting parties, such as large companies doing business across national borders, who seek an expert to resolve their disputes free from the possible bias of one contracting party's national courts and to obtain a judgment that may be more easily enforceable in courts around the world than a court judgment.[19] It is also the preferred method of dispute resolution under collective bargaining agreements in unionized workplaces because neither unions nor employers have trusted courts to quickly, cheaply, and sensibly resolve disputes arising under their agreements.

Since the mid-1980s, a widespread and highly controversial use of arbitration has emerged in consumer and individual employment contracts. Unlike commercial or union arbitration agreements, which are bilateral agreements freely negotiated by sophisticated contracting parties engaged in ongoing relationships, arbitration agreements imposed on consumers and individual employees are drafted by sophisticated company lawyers and imposed on consumers and employees without negotiation. Some of these agreements, predictably, are one-sided, favoring the corporation in matters of substance, procedure and remedies. As we will see, company-imposed and controlled arbitration can create ethical dilemmas for arbitrators. Mandatory pre-dispute arbitration agreements are now ubiquitous in employment and consumer relationships. One 2004 study estimated that one-third of the average

---

[19] Indeed, international commercial arbitration is a growth area for American lawyers as "a growing number of companies involved in international projects are choosing to arbitrate big-money disputes." Because millions or billions of dollars are at stake in many international arbitrations, large law firms have found it a lucrative practice area. Elizabeth Olson, *Growth in Global Disputes Brings Big Paychecks for Law Firms*, N.Y. TIMES, Aug. 27, 2013, B1. One lawyer at a large firm estimated the annual revenues generated by the firm's international arbitration practice had increased tenfold between 1997 and 2002. Martha Neil, *Small World, Big Business*, ABA J. (Sept. 2002), p. 28.

person's transactions were covered by such agreements,[20] and that percentage has probably grown with the increasing number of consumer transactions that occur online.

Arbitration can be almost as formal as adjudication in court. In some arbitrations, especially those that resolve statutory or other claims not limited to those based solely on the contract between the parties, the parties can obtain pretrial discovery of the facts, make motions to dismiss or for summary judgment, conduct hearings in which the rules of evidence apply, and appeal adverse rulings to an appellate panel or to a court. In such arbitrations, the arbitrator(s) are likely to be lawyers or retired judges, and are expected to act exactly as a judge would in following the law and writing an opinion finding facts and making determinations of law. As many companies have insisted that all their employees agree to arbitrate all statutory, tort, contract, and other common law claims arising out of employment, arbitrations have become more like these private trials in order that the arbitration agreement not be deemed to operate as a waiver of substantive statutory or common law legal rights.

Arbitration can also be quite informal: there may be no in-person hearing, the arbitrator is not expected to decide the case based on external law, the rules of evidence do not apply, and the arbitrator is not expected to issue a written decision other than a simple statement of who wins.

The role of the arbitrator thus varies widely depending on the type of arbitration. Arbitrators are typically chosen for some combination of their judgment and their expertise. While there has been little controversy over the selection of arbitrators in commercial and labor-management arbitration, the selection of arbitrators for consumer and individual employee arbitration has generated criticism. Large companies that draft and administer arbitration programs for thousands of consumers or employees quickly learn which arbitrators tend to rule for the company and which for the employee and, as repeat players, will select those who tend to be favorable to the company. Individual consumers or employees do not have the advantage of experience in selecting arbitrators.

Just as party-determination is the most important tenet of mediation, the primacy of the contract is the most important tenet of arbitration. The arbitrator is a creature of contract and can do only that which contract empowers him to do.

---

[20] Linda J. Demaine & Deborah R. Hensler, *Volunteering" to Arbitrate Through Predispute Arbitration Clauses: The Average Consumer's Experience*, LAW & CONTEMP. PROBS., Winter/Spring 2004, at 55 (the study focused on "important purchases" (such as automobiles), ongoing contracts (such as telephone service), and contracts that had a potentially large impact (such as health care services)).

In some cases the parties agree on a single arbitrator, while in others each party chooses an arbitrator and the two arbitrators together choose a third. Arbitration usually has some characteristics of a trial. The parties may write pre- or post-arbitration briefs framing the legal and factual issues and stating their position on each. The parties make opening statements and then offer evidence through the introduction of documents and the testimony of witnesses. Each side can cross-examine the other's witnesses. The parties make closing arguments. The arbitrator(s) usually do not decide the issue on the spot but instead take some number of days (with the maximum often dictated by the contract), to issue an award (or decision). Sometimes the arbitrator's award will simply state the conclusion: whether the claimant or respondent wins and if the claimant wins, what the remedy will be. Sometimes the award will state reasons. The contract that provides for arbitration will determine whether the arbitrator's award will be confidential (as is typically required in consumer and individual employment arbitration agreements drafted unilaterally by companies) or will be reported in the compendia of arbitration decisions (as is typically the case in unionized labor-management collective bargaining agreements and some international commercial contracts).

A number of empirical studies of arbitration awards have been conducted. Some studies find plaintiffs are less likely to win and, when they do win, recover less than in court.[21]

Like mediators, arbitrators are regulated by a wide variety of organizations. Although arbitrators are not separately licensed, many aspire to enhance their marketability by joining membership organizations like the National Association of Arbitrators, which imposes conditions on members such as that they only conduct arbitrations that meet the minimum fairness standards known as the "due process protocols." As with mediators, there may be a tension between the desire to ensure that arbitrators have particular sorts of education, training, and experience and the desire to ensure a diverse pool of arbitrators. In *Smith v. American Arbitration Association*, 233 F.3d 502 (7th Cir. 2000), a woman involved in an arbitration sued the arbitration provider because there was only one woman in the AAA's entire pool of arbitrators, and that one woman had been struck by the other party in the arbitration. The court rejected the contention that the all-male pool violated the equal

---

[21] Alexander J.S. Colvin, *Empirical Research on Employment Arbitration: Clarity Amidst the Sound and Fury?* 11 EMPLOYEE RTS. & EMP. POL'Y J. 405 (2007). Another important survey of the empirical studies of employment arbitration is David Sherwyn, Samuel Estreicher & Michael Heise, *Assessing the Case for Employment Arbitration: A New Path for Empirical Research*, 57 STAN. L. REV. 1557 (2005). The authors urge that any assessment of arbitration as compared to litigation should analyze how cases are resolved before a final determination as well as how arbitrators and courts ultimately decide those that reach final decision. They believe that comparing pre-decision resolutions shows that arbitration has considerable advantages as compared to litigation, in terms of the speed and affordability of settlements.

protection rights of litigants compelled to arbitrate because arbitration is a private system that does not implicate the state action necessary to trigger equal protection scrutiny.

G. LEGAL AND ETHICAL ISSUES FOR ARBITRATORS

One of the most challenging issues for lawyers working as arbitrators is whether arbitration processes are fair to those who use them. When an arbitration process is designed and negotiated by two parties of equal sophistication and bargaining power, as in commercial or labor-management arbitration, there may be only small risk that the process would be systematically unfair to one side. Some lawyers complain, indeed, about too much even-handedness: "My experience is that arbitrators usually just want to 'split the baby' in order to make both parties happy—or at least to try to avoid alienating either party to remain on 'the list' for future business."[22] When an arbitration process is designed by a sophisticated party and imposed without negotiation in an adhesion contract on another, there is a risk of systematic unfairness to the party that does not design the process. That risk may be exacerbated if the party that created the system uses it repeatedly against individuals who use it only once.

A major concern about the fairness of arbitration concerns this so-called repeat player effect. It is summarized as follows:

> Unlike judges, arbitrators get paid only when selected to arbitrate a dispute. This economic reality of arbitration has given rise to fears of "repeat-arbitrator bias"-the view that arbitrators will decide cases in favor of the repeat player, which is the party more likely to be in a position to appoint the arbitrator to serve again. In consumer arbitration, consumers are unlikely to be repeat players (although their attorneys may be). Thus, the fear is that arbitrators will tend to favor businesses in the hopes of being selected for future cases more frequently. More broadly, commentators have expressed concerns about what might be called "repeat-player bias" (rather than repeat-arbitrator bias)—bias that results from businesses structuring the dispute resolution process in their favor.

> Several factors may reduce the likelihood or consequences of repeat-arbitrator or repeat-player bias. First, arbitration providers, as well as individual arbitrators, may seek to maintain a reputation for fair and unbiased decision making. Such reputational constraints may reduce the risk that repeat-

---

[22] Richard C. Reuben, *The Lawyer Turns Peacemaker*, ABA J. (August 1996), at 54 (quoting a risk manager for a city).

> arbitrator or repeat-player bias will occur. Second, even if arbitrators and arbitration providers have an incentive to make decisions that businesses want, it is not necessarily the case that those decisions will be unfavorable to consumers.
>
> In the employment context, although several studies have identified a repeat-player effect, they have not found evidence of repeat-player bias. For example, employees win less often against repeat businesses—businesses that arbitrate on a repeat basis—than against non-repeat businesses. This repeat-player effect might be due to repeat-arbitrator or repeat-player bias, but it might also be due to better screening of cases by repeat businesses, who are more accustomed to dealing with disputes than non-repeat businesses. If repeat businesses are more likely to settle weak claims than non-repeat businesses, they will have a higher win rate in cases that go to an award than non-repeat businesses.[23]

The authors of that study found some evidence of a repeat player effect in its sample of 301 consumer arbitrations conducted under the auspices of the AAA, but found it was probably due to better case screening by the repeat player rather than to arbitrator bias. A larger study of arbitration in employment cases found strong evidence of a repeat player effect.[24]

A Harvard Law Review survey of developments in the use of arbitration by corporate plaintiffs seeking to collect debts from consumer defendants found evidence of repeat-player bias in the processes of the National Arbitration Forum (NAF), a corporation that provided arbitration services to creditors, especially credit card companies.[25] After a front-page *Wall Street Journal* article on NAF and a lawsuit brought by the Minnesota Attorney General accusing NAF of a variety of improprieties in its consumer debt collection arbitration business in which arbitrators were controlled by the debt collectors and ruled for them over 95% of the time, NAF ended its consumer debt arbitration business.[26]

A study of securities arbitration attempted to discern whether arbitrators may be influenced by the fact that many of them do not work

---

[23] Christopher R. Drahozal & Samantha Zyontz, *An Empirical Study of AAA Consumer Arbitrations*, 25 OHIO J. DISPUTE RESOLUTION 843, 857–860 (2010).

[24] Alexander J.S. Colvin, *An Empirical Study of Employment Arbitration: Case Outcomes and Processes*, 8 J. EMPIRICAL LEG. STUD. 1 (2011).

[25] *Developments in the Law—Access to Courts, Mandatory Arbitration Clauses: Proposals for Reform of Consumer-Defendant Arbitration*, 122 HARV. L. REV. 1170 (2009). The Public Citizen report is *How Credit Card Companies Ensnare Consumers* (Sept. 2007), available at http://www.citizen.org/publications/release.cfm? ID=7545.

[26] The NAF story is recounted, along with other concerns about bias of third-party neutrals who are "embedded" in company-controlled ADR processes, in Nancy A. Welsh, *What Is (Im)Partial Enough in a World of Embedded Neutrals?* 52 ARIZ. L. REV. 395 (2010).

full-time as arbitrators. Many work part-time as arbitrators and part-time as lawyers representing parties in the securities industry. The study found that what the lawyer did for a living besides work as an arbitrator had an effect. Attorney-arbitrators who had represented brokerage firms in other securities cases were significantly less generous to plaintiffs in arbitration awards. Attorneys who represent investors in arbitration proceedings were not more generous when they serve as arbitrators, nor were arbitrators who represent both investors and brokerage houses.[27]

Whatever may be the case about the extent of the problem, it presents ethical challenges for arbitrators who may become biased by the circumstances of their hiring and for arbitrators who confront instances in which one party is attempting to use the process to disadvantage the other. The following case is an example:

ENGALLA V. PERMANENTE MEDICAL GROUP, INC.

California Supreme Court
938 P.2d 903 (1998)

MOSK, JUSTICE:

Plaintiffs are family members and representatives of the estate of Wilfredo Engalla. Engalla was enrolled, through his place of employment, in a health plan operated by the Permanente Medical Group, Inc., Kaiser Foundation Hospitals, and the Kaiser Foundation Health Plan (hereafter Kaiser).

[Over several years, Kaiser doctors allegedly negligently misdiagnosed Engalla's lung cancer as allergies until the cancer was so advanced that it was inoperable. Engalla brought a claim against Kaiser for medical malpractice.] According to the terms of Kaiser's Group Medical and Hospital Services Agreement, [the claim] was submitted to arbitration. After attempting unsuccessfully to conclude the arbitration prior to Engalla's death, the Engallas filed a malpractice action against Kaiser in superior court, and Kaiser filed a petition to compel arbitration. In opposing the petition, plaintiffs claimed that Kaiser's self-administered arbitration system was corrupt or biased in a number of respects and that Kaiser engaged in a course of dilatory conduct in order to postpone Engalla's arbitration hearing until after his death, which should be grounds for refusing to enforce the arbitration agreement.

The arbitration program is designed, written, mandated and administered by Kaiser. In regard to the latter, Kaiser collects funds from claimants and holds and disburses them as necessary to pay the neutral arbitrator and expenses approved by him or her. It monitors

---

[27] Stephen J. Choi, Jill E. Fisch & A.C. Pritchard, *Attorneys As Arbitrators*, 39 J. LEGAL STUDIES 109, 111–12 (2010).

administrative matters pertinent to the progress of each case including, for example, the identity and dates of appointment of arbitrators. It does not, however, employ or contract with any independent person or entity to provide such administrative services, or any oversight or evaluation of the arbitration program or its performance. Rather, administrative functions are performed by outside counsel retained to defend Kaiser in an adversarial capacity.

[Engalla's lawyer, Mr. Rand, made a demand for arbitration in late May in which he explained the nature of the claim, advised Kaiser of Engalla's terminal condition, and appealed to Kaiser to expedite the adjudication of the claim.]

After hearing nothing for two weeks, Rand again wrote to Kaiser, repeated his agreement to arbitrate, and stressed the fact that "Mr. Engalla has very little time left in his life and I again urge you to assist me in expediting this matter for that reason." Several days later, Kaiser's in-house counsel, Cynthia Shiffrin, whose responsibility it was to monitor the Engallas' file, responded to the claim by acknowledging receipt and providing a copy of the arbitration provision per Rand's request. In turn, she requested $150, as required by the arbitration provision, as a deposit for half the expenses of the arbitration. Rand mailed the check the same day he received Shiffrin's letter. Shiffrin also expressed her willingness to comply with the request to avoid delay, noting that she had arranged for "expedited copies" of Engalla's medical records, and promising that outside counsel would contact Rand "in the near future with Kaiser's designation of an arbitrator."

[The California Supreme Court then summarized the plaintiff's unsuccessful efforts over the ensuing five months to prod Kaiser's lawyers to select its arbitrator, commence discovery, and conduct the hearing. First, Kaiser's outside counsel, Willis F. McComas, refused to designate Kaiser's arbitrator until the plaintiff had first chosen his. Although Rand objected to this staggered disclosure as not authorized by the arbitration agreement, he eventually capitulated and named his choice. Kaiser's lawyer still delayed for another month before naming its arbitrator and then named one without first ascertaining whether he was available. It turned out that Kaiser's arbitrator was unavailable for four months, and further delays ensued as plaintiff urged Kaiser to appoint a substitute.

Then, the Court explained, Kaiser caused additional delays in the selection of the third arbitrator. According to the contract, the two party arbitrators were to select a neutral arbitrator, but "in reality the selection is made by defense counsel after consultation with the Kaiser medical-legal department. Kaiser has never relinquished control over this selection decision. Indeed, in this case, [Ney, Kaiser's lawyer] instructed

[Molligan, the arbitrator Kaiser had chosen] on who should be proposed and who was unacceptable" as a third, supposedly neutral, arbitrator.]

On August 30, having still heard nothing about the third arbitrator, Rand wrote to Judicial Arbitration and Mediation Services (JAMS) Judge Daniel Weinstein requesting proposals for judges who could be available for a hearing date "within the next several weeks."

On September 3, Ney [Kaiser's lawyer] wrote to Molligan [the arbitrator Kaiser had chosen], rejecting as unacceptable Judge Francis Mayer, one of the "neutrals" Molligan had suggested. Apparently, this veto was exercised pursuant to McComas's instructions. Ney expressed doubts about the availability of Molligan's other two choices—retired Judge Fannin or Weinstein, although he had not checked with either judge—and pressed instead for one of his own choices. On September 5, while Molligan was out of town, Rand agreed to one of the suggestions, Judge Robert Cooney, on the condition that "he can be available to commence this matter this month." If he was not available, Rand suggested two JAMS judges he knew to be available in September. Rand wrote to McComas again on September 18 and 25, literally begging for responses to his many suggestions for expediting the arbitration process.

Despite this additional prompting, McComas did not respond for almost three weeks and, when he finally wrote to Rand on September 24, he expressed uncertainty as to whether Judge Cooney had been agreed upon. Rand immediately responded on September 26 that Judge Cooney had been accepted and that he was only waiting for confirmation that the judge would be available "in the very near future." Apparently, because Kaiser holds itself out as the program administrator, collects and disburses arbitrator fees and had, in fact, proposed Judge Cooney, Rand assumed Kaiser would handle the formal retention of Judge Cooney and pay a deposit on his fees. Kaiser takes the position that it is the claimant's burden to move the case along, including making arrangements with the neutral arbitrator.

After almost two more weeks, McComas wrote again on October 7, this time claiming that "[t]o this date, neither you nor your clients have agreed to the appointment of a neutral arbitrator" because "[y]ou apparently agreed to Judge Cooney with an unrealistic condition."[5] Rand responded on October 16, stating, "I am incredulous that you are *still* asking that we agree to the appointment of the neutral arbitrator. We have repeatedly informed you that we will agree to your suggestion of

---

[5]   The Engallas claim that McComas dissembled on September 24 and October 7 when he expressed uncertainty about Judge Cooney's availability and the plaintiffs' agreement to appointment of the retired judge. They argue that, by that time, McComas had not even contacted Judge Cooney to determine his availability, and that, in fact, Judge Cooney was available during September and October to preside over the hearing. They conclude that, by initially feigning uncertainty about whether Engalla had agreed to Judge Cooney's appointment, McComas managed to delay the appointment for over six weeks.

Judge Cooney. Why do you continue to insist that we have not agreed? My only reservation was and still is a question concerning availability." On October 18, Rand again wrote that he was "still waiting to hear from you concerning the final retention of Judge Cooney. I had promised him that he would be hearing from you when I advised him that we had agreed to his appointment."

Finally, on October 22, McComas wrote to say that he understood the Engallas had agreed to retain Judge Cooney as the neutral arbitrator, conditioned upon his availability, and that he had, therefore, instructed Ney to complete the retainer. By this time, 144 days—almost 3 months more than the 60 days for the selection of the arbitrators represented in the Service Agreement—had elapsed since the initial service of the claim. Engalla died the next day.

Statistically, delays occur in 99 percent of all Kaiser medical malpractice arbitrations. An independent statistical analysis of Kaiser-provided data of arbitration between 1984 and 1986 reveals that in only 1 percent of all Kaiser cases is a neutral arbitrator appointed within the 60–day period provided by the arbitration provision. Only 3 percent of cases see a neutral arbitrator appointed within 180 days. On average, it has taken 674 days for the appointment of a neutral arbitrator. For claimants whose cases were resolved by settlement or after a hearing, the time required to appoint a neutral arbitrator consumed more than half the total time for resolution. Furthermore, because the arbitration provision of the Service Agreement does not clearly establish a time frame for a hearing (it must be within a "reasonable time" after appointment of the neutral arbitrator), and because Kaiser claims it has no obligation to participate in a hearing until it deems itself ready, there tend to be significant additional delays after appointment of the neutral arbitrator. Thus, on average, it takes 863 days—almost 2 1/2 years—to reach a hearing in a Kaiser arbitration.

Immediately upon learning of Engalla's death on October 23, Rand notified McComas of that fact and asked him to stipulate that Kaiser would not capitalize on the delays that had plagued the arbitration. [Under California law, the death of the plaintiff in a medical malpractice suits limits the noneconomic damages that may be recovered to $250,000 instead of the $500,000 cap that would apply if the plaintiff were still alive.] Rand's request for a stipulation to override the effect of [the damages cap] was refused. At that point, Rand notified McComas that the Engallas refused to continue with the arbitration.

The Engallas argue that Kaiser's various dilatory actions constituted a waiver of its right to compel arbitration.

We conclude that the evidence of Kaiser's course of delay, reviewed extensively above, which was arguably unreasonable or undertaken in bad faith, may provide sufficient grounds for a trier of fact to conclude that Kaiser has in fact waived its arbitration agreement.

We emphasize, that the delay must be substantial, unreasonable, and in spite of the claimant's own reasonable diligence. When delay in choosing arbitrators is the result of reasonable and good faith disagreements between the parties, the remedy for such delay is a petition to the court to choose arbitrators, rather than evasion of the contractual agreement to arbitrate. In this case, there is ample evidence that the claimant was diligent in seeking Kaiser's cooperation, and instead suffered from Kaiser's delay, a delay which was unreasonable or in bad faith. We leave it to the trial court to determine on remand whether waiver of the right to compel arbitration has in fact occurred.

NOTES ON ENGALLA

1. *The Strategic Use of Delay.* Why do you suppose that Kaiser drafted an arbitration agreement providing deadlines for the selection of arbitrators and the conduct of hearings that it failed to observe in 99 percent of cases? Your course on procedure may discuss the strategic use of delay in litigation. Defining when the strategic use of delay is illegal has been a challenging task for courts and commentators, in part because reasonable minds differ as to when delay may be appropriate or justifiable. But at least when lawyers litigate in court, a judge who believes that a litigant is using delay to harass or to thwart the substantive rights of the other has an arsenal of tools—including discovery sanctions, attorney discipline, and contempt orders—to punish and deter it. In arbitration, as this case illustrates, there is often no one empowered to do anything about it. What reforms to arbitration process would address this problem?

2. *Discipline for Lawyers and Arbitrators?* The *Engalla* case raises, but does not decide, issues relating both to the conduct of Kaiser's lawyers and the conduct of the arbitrator nominated by Kaiser. Do you think either behaved inappropriately? In what respects? Would Model Rule 8.4 (which prohibits lawyers from engaging in conduct "prejudicial to the administration of justice") cover what either Kaiser's lawyers or its arbitrator did? If lawyer discipline is not a solution, what is?

3. *How Should Arbitrators Be Selected?* Why do arbitration agreements often provide that each party chooses one arbitrator (referred to in the case as the "party arbitrators") and the two arbitrators choose a third (the "neutral arbitrator")? Should an arbitrator nominated by one party agree to allow the party that nominated him or her to dictate who the arbitrator should nominate or veto as the third arbitrator? Why might an arbitrator agree to cooperate in that way?

4. *Independent v. Embedded Arbitration.* What measures could be taken, and by whom, to prevent the kind of situation that occurred in Engalla? Should courts or legislatures limit the ability of companies to create

and manage their own arbitration systems, as Kaiser did, and instead require them to use systems maintained by independent entities (like the AAA)? Should the ability of companies to design and maintain their own systems be limited at least when arbitrations involve consumers or individual employees, which is when the arbitration agreements are unilaterally drafted and imposed in adhesion contracts? What are the advantages and disadvantages of "embedded" mediation and arbitration programs as opposed to those that are maintained by independent entities like AAA and JAMS? Should there be some form of discipline or liability for arbitrators when they are involved in proceedings that lack fundamental fairness?

H. SUMMARY

In this chapter we examined the roles of lawyers as mediators who facilitate the resolution of disputes and as arbitrators who are empowered by contracts to decide disputes. We considered the strengths and limitations of the principal sources of regulation of lawyers' work as third party neutrals. The law governing lawyers, including the Model Rules and malpractice law, covers some work as a third party neutral, and some states have enacted statutes regulating the conduct of ADR. The rules of procedure of ADR service providers regulate the behavior of parties and their representatives, and courts have rules of procedure to govern lawyers' conduct in court-annexed ADR. Third party neutrals are typically hired by contract with the parties. As in any other professional-client relationship, the client(s) can insist on certain contract terms. Any third party neutral who routinely works for one party may come to depend on that party for their livelihood, which can present difficult ethical issues for the third-party neutral and can have a significant impact on the results of matters they handle.

CHAPTER 27

JUDGES

■ ■ ■

A. INTRODUCTION

In this chapter we consider the judiciary as a sector of the legal profession, examining how judges are selected, the demographics of the judiciary, and the variation among judicial posts. We introduce the ABA Code of Judicial Conduct, which is to judges what the Model Rules are to lawyers. We then examine two issues in the legal regulation of judicial behavior: the disqualification or recusal of judges and judicial elections.

B. THE JUDICIARY AS A PRACTICE SECTOR

There are approximately 33,400 judges working today in the United States: 1,769 federal judges and 31,657 state judges. In addition, many thousands more federal and state officers serve as administrative law judges employed by agencies to hear cases involving the agency.[1]

The mechanics of judicial selection differ between federal and state courts and among states. The U.S. Constitution provides that federal judges are appointed by the President "with the advice and consent of the Senate." Typically, when the President is a member of the same party as the Senators from a state, the President gives great weight to the Senators' recommendations, especially for the district courts. When the President is of a different party, the White House assumes responsibility for identifying potential nominees. States use a number of different mechanisms. In the early nineteenth century, states generally selected judges in the same way as the federal government through executive appointment. In the mid- and late-nineteenth century, many states switched to an elected judiciary, and many states still elect some or most of their judges. Since then, many states have returned to an appointment system for some judges (typically the high court) or to a hybrid system. The best known hybrid system is known as the Missouri Plan (also used in California, Virginia, and Maine). Under it, the governor appoints judges from a list of nominees submitted by a nominating commission. Judges thus appointed serve a term and must stand for a retention

---

[1] Data on the size and composition of the federal and state judiciaries are compiled by the Judicial Conference of the United States, see www.uscourts.gov, and the National Center for State Courts, Court Statistics Project, see www.courtstatistics.org.

election. In some states (notably, in Texas and several other Deep South states and in Ohio, Pennsylvania, Illinois and Michigan), judicial elections are regular partisan elections like any other in which judges run as identified Democrats, Republicans, or Independents. In some states (in the Pacific Northwest, the upper Midwest, and a few Southern states), judicial elections are nonpartisan and judges do not identify their party affiliation.

The demographics of the judiciary have changed over time in some respects and in other respects little has changed. The justices on the U.S. Supreme Court are, and always have been, elites. The current justices attended elite universities (almost exclusively Harvard, Yale, and Princeton). They practiced law in elite jobs. On all federal courts since 1980, the number of women and people of color has grown, but other demographic features of the federal judiciary as a whole (age at appointment, prior experience as a state judge) have not changed dramatically over the course of American history.[2] One study did find a change in vocational background since 1950 mainly at the district court level: a steady decline in the proportion of judges appointed directly from private practice and a corresponding increase in state judges and U.S. magistrate and bankruptcy judges.[3] Presidents Bush and Clinton appointed far more former prosecutors and law firm partners than public defenders and public interest lawyers. Diversifying the federal bench in terms of race, ethnicity and gender (as recent presidents have done to a greater degree than ever before) did not dramatically diversify the bench in socioeconomic status (federal judges tend to be reasonably well-to-do before joining the bench).[4]

A study of the demographics of the trial bench in all 50 states in 1979 and in 2004 found a statistically significant increase in the number of women, but relatively small changes in prior occupation. Nineteen percent had been prosecutors in both 1979 and 2004, whereas only about two percent had been public defenders. Forty and 47 percent (in 1979 and 2004, respectively) had been in private practice. Four percent had been public officials, and over 27 and 20 percent (in 1979 and 2004, respectively) had been judges.[5] A huge cottage industry has arisen among political scientists and law professors since the 1980s attempting to explain influences on judicial behavior and debating the question whether

---

[2] Monique Renee Fournet, Kyle C. Kopko, Dana Wittmer & Lawrence Baum, *Evolution of Judicial Careers in the Federal Courts, 1789–2008,"* 92 JUDICATURE 62–74 (2009).

[3] Russell Wheeler, *Changing Backgrounds of U.S. District Judges: Likely Causes and Possible Implications*, 93 JUDICATURE 140 (2010).

[4] Theresa M. Beiner, *How the Contentious Nature of Federal Judicial Appointments Affects Diversity on the Bench*, 39 U. RICHMOND L. REV. 849 (2005).

[5] Erin J. Williamson, *Demographic Snapshot of State Trial Court Judges: 1979 and 2004*, American University (unpublished, n.d.).

or how prior work experience, race, gender, political affiliation, or other characteristics of judges affect their decisions.[6]

What judges do on a daily basis is almost as varied as what lawyers do. The United States Supreme Court justices decide only about 75 cases a year based on briefing and argument, and they have four law clerks each to help them do it. They and their clerks sift through thousands of petitions for certiorari to determine which 75 cases they will hear and decide. State supreme courts likewise control most of their own docket (though many decide more than 75 cases annually). Every other court must decide all cases filed (except those that settle). An appellate judge's job is intellectual and solitary, mainly involving reading and writing. Appellate judges are seen by the public at work only during oral argument, but their work product is highly visible and read with great care by the litigants and the bar. At the other end of the deliberativeness spectrum would be the job of a state trial judge in a busy court, such as a family court or juvenile court, where some judges remark that the job involves as much social work as it does law. The judge has no law clerks to help her with her work. Seldom are the litigants represented by a lawyer. The caseload can be overwhelming and the amount of time a judge can devote to each case may be small—minutes or, at most, a few hours. The job involves little research or writing, but a great deal of interaction with litigants all day long and ruling on their disputes (or parts of them) on the spot. Some state trial courts of general jurisdiction publish some of their opinions (as in New York); some publish no opinions (as in most California trial courts).

C. AN OVERVIEW OF THE REGULATION OF JUDICIAL CONDUCT

A thorough account of the regulation of judicial behavior is far too ambitious a project for a survey course on the legal profession; it could be a course unto itself. This is simply a short survey of some of the major principles and a slightly closer look at two issues that are especially salient to lawyers and to the public: the disqualification of judges and the regulation of judicial election campaigns.

The ABA has promulgated and periodically revises a code of conduct for judges just as it does for lawyers. Most states and the federal courts have adopted codes of judicial ethics based on the ABA Code, just as they have adopted codes of lawyers' professional ethics based on the Model Rules. The first version was the Canons of Judicial Ethics, which the ABA

---

[6] One study, for example, found that judges who had formerly worked as criminal defense lawyers were more likely to accept challenges to the federal sentencing guidelines than were judges who formerly worked as prosecutors. Gregory C. Sisk, Michael Heise & Andrew P. Morriss, *Charting the Influences on the Judicial Mind: An Empirical Study of Judicial Reasoning*, 37 N.Y. U. L. REV. 1377 (1998).

adopted in 1924 and replaced in 1972 with a Code of Judicial Ethics. The ABA substantially revised the Code of Judicial Ethics in 1990, and most states revised their own codes accordingly. The ABA revised the Code again in 2007 (changing its name to the Code of Judicial Conduct), but not all states have revised their judicial codes in response. The Judicial Conference of the United States, which has administrative responsibility for the federal courts other than the Supreme Court, last revised the ethics code for federal judges in 2009, but its code is based on the 1990 ABA Code, not the 2007 version. The U.S. Supreme Court has never adopted the Code of Judicial Conduct for itself.[7]

The Code of Judicial Conduct

Like the Model Rules, the Code of Judicial Conduct is promulgated by the ABA and does not become a binding source of law until it is enacted by a state or federal judiciary. In one version or another, it has been adopted by all states and by the federal courts except the Supreme Court.

Canon 1: A judge shall uphold and promote the independence, integrity, and impartiality of the judiciary, and shall avoid impropriety and the appearance of impropriety.

Canon 2: A judge shall perform the duties of judicial office impartially, competently, and diligently.

Canon 3: A judge shall conduct the judge's personal and extrajudicial activities to minimize the risk of conflict with the obligations of judicial office.

Canon 4: A judge or candidate for judicial office shall not engage in political or campaign activity that is inconsistent with the independence, integrity, or impartiality of the judiciary.

The Code of Judicial Conduct, like the Model Rules, is a compendium of nearly 30 separate rules. The Code is divided into four Canons, each of which contains many detailed rules on the theme articulated in general terms by the Canon. Canon 1 states the general principle that judges must "uphold and promote the independence, integrity, and impartiality of the judiciary, and shall avoid impropriety and the appearance of impropriety." The crucial concept here is that judges are required to avoid "the appearance of impropriety" as well as actual impropriety; an earlier version of the code governing lawyers required them to avoid the appearance of impropriety, but that standard was abandoned for lawyers while it was retained for judges.

---

[7] See James Alfini, *Supreme Court Ethics: The Need for Greater Transparency and Accountability*, 21 PROF. LAW. 2 (2012).

Canon 2 requires impartiality, competence and diligence. This Canon encompasses rules stating general precepts about impartiality, competence, civility, and diligence, and specific rules banning ex parte communications, prohibiting judges from making public statements about pending or impending cases, and requiring judges to recuse themselves in any case in which their impartiality "might reasonably be questioned." We will examine some (but not all) of the specifics of the recusal rule below.

Canon 3 requires judges to conduct their "personal and extrajudicial activities to minimize the risk of conflict with the obligations of judicial office." There are highly detailed rules under this Canon regulating membership in private organizations, management of the judge's and her family's investments, outside employment (which is banned), acceptance of honoraria for speaking or teaching (allowed but must be reported), acceptance of gifts and travel expenses (regulated and generally must be reported except for small things).

Finally, Canon 4 provides that "a judge or candidate for judicial office shall not engage in political or campaign activity that is inconsistent with the independence, integrity, or impartiality of the judiciary." Like the other Canons, this one contains several detailed rules regulating both sitting judges and judicial election campaigns. We examine some of the rules below.

Judges who violate the Code are subject to discipline. Under many state codes, discipline can be as minor as a reprimand or as severe as removal from office, but federal judges can only be removed by impeachment.

With judges as with lawyers, laws and norms other than the code of ethics govern their conduct. For federal judges, the Constitution allows removal from office only for "high crimes and misdemeanors" as determined through impeachment, which requires a vote by the House of Representatives and a trial and conviction by the Senate. Only a handful of federal judges have been impeached in American history. State judges can be removed by impeachment if they have life tenure, through election if not, and through discipline. State and federal statutes regulate the behavior of state and federal judges, respectively. The range of state statutes is too great to canvass here. For federal judges, a principal statute regulating disqualification is 28 U.S.C. § 455, which is discussed below.

D. RECUSAL AND DISQUALIFICATION

The Code of Judicial Conduct requires judges to recuse (or disqualify) themselves "in any proceeding in which the judge's impartiality might reasonably be questioned, including but not limited to" specified circumstances, such as when the judge "has a personal bias or prejudice concerning a party or a party's lawyer, or personal knowledge of facts that are in dispute in the proceeding," or a member of the judge's family is a party, or a lawyer, or is likely to be a material witness, or a party or a party's lawyer has made significant contributions to the judge's election campaign, or the judge or a member of the judge's family has an interest (financial or otherwise) that "could be substantially affected by the outcome of the proceeding." Rule 2.11. Comment [1] to the rule states that "Under this Rule, a judge is disqualified whenever the judge's impartiality might reasonably be questioned," regardless of whether any of the specific grounds for disqualification apply.

Disqualification of federal judges is, in addition, covered by a statute, 28 U.S.C. § 455. For the Supreme Court, the statute is all that applies. Section 455 is substantially the same as Rule 2.11, and indeed it was patterned after the 1972 version of the Code of Judicial Conduct.

Finally, in a few extreme cases, courts have ruled that a judge's bias deprives a litigant of due process.[8] The *Caperton* case discussed below addresses due process as a basis for disqualification.

One basis for seeking disqualification is bias, or the appearance of bias. The following matter explores that:

CHENEY V. U.S. DISTRICT COURT FOR DISTRICT OF COLUMBIA

542 U.S. 367 (2004)

[A few days after assuming office, President George W. Bush assigned Vice President Dick Cheney, who had been a high-ranking executive in an oil and energy company when he was not working in the government, to chair the National Energy Policy Development Group (NEPDG or Group) to develop a national energy policy. After several months, the NEPDG published a report. A citizen group and an environmental organization sued, alleging that the NEPDG had failed to comply with the procedural and disclosure requirements of the Federal Advisory Committee Act (FACA or Act), which was enacted to monitor the committees established to advise officers and agencies in the executive branch. FACA imposes a variety of open-meeting and disclosure requirements on groups that meet the definition of an "advisory committee." The environmental and citizen group plaintiffs alleged that "non-federal employees," including "private lobbyists," "regularly

---

[8] Aetna Life Ins. Co. v. Lavoie, 475 U.S. 813 (1986) (state supreme court justice who cast deciding vote and wrote opinion for court in 5–4 decision was a plaintiff in another suit raising the same issue as the case decided and would stand to benefit financially from the ruling); Bracy v. Gramley, 520 U.S. 899 (1997) (judge who was later convicted of taking bribes may have been biased against defendant who did not offer a bribe).

attended and fully participated in non-public meetings," which meant that the Group was not entitled to the statutory exemption from the open-meeting and disclosure requirements. The defendants sought an order protecting them from having to produce documents in pretrial discovery. The district court denied the protective order. The court of appeals similarly refused the protective order.

By the time the case reached the United States Supreme Court, it became publicly known that Justice Scalia had gone duck hunting in Louisiana with Vice President Cheney. One of the plaintiffs in the litigation, the Sierra Club, then filed a motion in the Supreme Court asking Justice Scalia to recuse himself from deciding the case because Vice President Cheney was a defendant. Justice Scalia denied the motion in the following order.]

Memorandum of JUSTICE SCALIA.

For five years or so, I have been going to Louisiana during the Court's long December-January recess, to the duck-hunting camp of a friend whom I met through two hunting companions from Baton Rouge, one a dentist and the other a worker in the field of handicapped rehabilitation.

During my December 2002 visit, I learned that [my Louisiana host] Mr. Carline was an admirer of Vice President Cheney. Knowing that the Vice President, with whom I am well acquainted (from our years serving together in the Ford administration), is an enthusiastic duck hunter, I asked whether Mr. Carline would like to invite him to our next year's hunt. The answer was yes. The Vice President said that if he did go, I would be welcome to fly down to Louisiana with him. (Because of national security requirements, of course, he must fly in a Government plane.) The trip was set long before the Court granted certiorari in the present case, and indeed before the petition for certiorari had even been filed.

[Justice Scalia described the trip and explained he and Vice President Cheney joined 11 other hunters, were never alone together, and never mentioned this case.]

Let me respond, at the outset, to Sierra Club's suggestion that I should "resolve any doubts in favor of recusal." That might be sound advice if I were sitting on a Court of Appeals. There, my place would be taken by another judge, and the case would proceed normally. On the Supreme Court, however, the consequence is different: The Court proceeds with eight Justices, raising the possibility that, by reason of a tie vote, it will find itself unable to resolve the significant legal issue presented by the case. Thus, as Justices stated in their 1993 Statement of Recusal Policy: "We do not think it would serve the public interest to go beyond the requirements of the statute, and to recuse ourselves, out of an excess of caution, whenever a relative is a partner in the firm before us or acted as a lawyer at an earlier stage. Even one unnecessary recusal impairs the functioning of the Court." Moreover, granting the motion is (insofar as the outcome of the particular case is concerned) effectively the same as casting a vote against the petitioner. The petitioner needs five votes to overturn the judgment below, and it makes no difference whether the needed fifth vote is missing because it has been cast for the other side, or because it has not been cast at all.

Even so, recusal is the course I must take—and will take—when, on the basis of established principles and practices, I have said or done something which requires that course. I have recused for such a reason this very Term. I believe, however, that established principles and practices do not require (and thus do not permit) recusal in the present case.

My recusal is required if, by reason of the actions described above, my "impartiality might reasonably be questioned." 28 U.S.C. § 455(a). Why would that result follow from my being in a sizable group of persons, in a hunting camp with the Vice President, where I never hunted with him in the same blind or had other opportunity for private conversation? The only possibility is that it would suggest I am a friend of his. But while friendship is a ground for recusal of a Justice where the personal fortune or the personal freedom of the friend is at issue, it has traditionally *not* been a ground for recusal where *official action* is at issue, no matter how important the official action was to the ambitions or the reputation of the Government officer.

A rule that required Members of this Court to remove themselves from cases in which the official actions of friends were at issue would be utterly disabling. Many Justices have reached this Court precisely because they were friends of the incumbent President or other senior officials—and from the earliest days down to modern times Justices have had close personal relationships with the President and other officers of the Executive. [Justice Scalia described dinner parties and poker games involving Presidents and Supreme Court Justices from John Quincy Adams through Harry Truman.] A no-friends rule would have disqualified much of the Court in *Youngstown Sheet & Tube Co. v. Sawyer,* 343 U.S. 579 (1952), the case that challenged President Truman's seizure of the steel mills. Most of the Justices knew Truman well, and four had been appointed by him.

It is said, however, that this case is different because the federal officer (Vice President Cheney) is actually a *named party*. That is by no means a rarity. At the beginning of the current Term, there were before the Court (excluding habeas actions) no fewer than 83 cases in which high-level federal Executive officers were named in their official capacity—more than 1 in every 10 federal civil cases then pending.

Regardless of whom they name, such suits, when the officer is the plaintiff, seek relief not for him personally but for the Government; and, when the officer is the defendant, seek relief not against him personally, but against the Government.

Richard Cheney's name appears in this suit only because he was the head of a Government committee that allegedly did not comply with the Federal Advisory Committee Act (FACA), and because he may, by reason of his office, have custody of some or all of the Government documents that the plaintiffs seek. Cheney is represented here, not by his personal attorney, but by the United States Department of Justice in the person of the Solicitor General. And the courts at all levels have referred to his arguments as (what they are) the arguments of "the government."

The recusal motion, however, asserts the following: "Because his own conduct is central to this case, the Vice President's reputation and his integrity are on the line."

I think not. Certainly as far as the legal issues immediately presented to me are concerned, this *is* "a run-of-the-mill legal dispute about an administrative decision." I am asked to determine what powers the District Court possessed under FACA, and whether the Court of Appeals should have asserted mandamus or appellate jurisdiction over the District Court. Nothing this Court says on those subjects will have any bearing upon the reputation and integrity of Richard Cheney. Moreover, even if this Court allows discovery to proceed in the District Court, the issue that would ultimately present itself *still* would have no bearing upon the reputation and integrity of Richard Cheney. That issue would be, quite simply, whether some private individuals were *de facto* members of the National Energy Policy Development Group (NEPDG). It matters not whether they were caused to be so by Cheney or someone else, or whether Cheney was even aware of their *de facto* status; if they *were de facto* members, then (according to D.C. Circuit law) the records and minutes of NEPDG must be made public.

To be sure, there could be political consequences from disclosure of the fact (if it be so) that the Vice President favored business interests, and especially a sector of business with which he was formerly connected. But political consequences are not my concern, and the possibility of them does not convert an official suit into a private one. That possibility exists to a greater or lesser degree in virtually all suits involving agency action. To expect judges to take account of political consequences—and to assess the high or low degree of them—is to ask judges to do precisely what they should not do. It seems to me quite wrong (and quite impossible) to make recusal depend upon what degree of political damage a particular case can be expected to inflict.

The recusal motion claims that the fact that "Justice Scalia [was] the Vice President's guest on Air Force Two on the flight down to Louisiana" means that I "accepted a sizable gift from a party in a pending case," a gift "measured in the thousands of dollars."

Let me speak first to the value, though that is not the principal point. Our flight down cost the Government nothing, since space-available was the condition of our invitation. And, though our flight down on the Vice President's plane was indeed free, since we were not returning with him we purchased (because they were least expensive) round-trip tickets that cost precisely what we would have paid if we had gone both down and back on commercial flights. In other words, none of us saved a cent by flying on the Vice President's plane.

The principal point, however, is that social courtesies, provided at Government expense by officials whose only business before the Court is business in their official capacity, have not hitherto been thought prohibited. Members of Congress and others are frequently invited to accompany Executive Branch officials on Government planes, where space is available. I daresay that, at a hypothetical charity auction, much more would be bid for dinner for two at the White House than for a one-way flight to Louisiana on the Vice President's jet. Justices accept the former with regularity. While this matter was pending, Justices and their spouses were invited (*all* of them, I believe) to a December 11, 2003, Christmas reception at the residence of the Vice President—which included an opportunity for a photograph with the Vice President and Mrs. Cheney. Several of the Justices attended, and in doing so they were fully in accord with the proprieties.

[Justice Scalia's memorandum then offered two examples of prior instances in which Supreme Court justices accepted invitations from executive branch officials to vacation with them while cases were pending against the official in his official capacity. Justice Byron White went on a skiing vacation in Colorado with Attorney General Robert Kennedy and his family while there were pending before the Court at least two cases in which Robert Kennedy, in his official capacity as Attorney General, was a party. Justice Robert Jackson spent the weekend at the home of a third person in Charlottesville, Virginia and rode back and forth with President Roosevelt while an important case about the scope of federal power was pending.]

I see nothing wrong about Justice White's and Justice Jackson's socializing—including vacationing and accepting rides—with their friends. Nor, seemingly, did anyone else at the time. If friendship is basis for recusal (as it assuredly is when friends are sued personally) then activity which suggests close friendship must be avoided. But if friendship is *no* basis for recusal (as it is not in official-capacity suits) social contacts that do no more than evidence that friendship suggest no impropriety whatever.

Of course it can be claimed (as some editorials have claimed) that "times have changed," and what was once considered proper—even as recently as Byron White's day—is no longer so. That may be true with regard to the earlier rare phenomenon of a Supreme Court Justice's serving as advisor and confidant to the President—though that activity, so incompatible with the separation of powers, was not widely known when it was occurring, and can hardly be said to have been generally approved before it was properly abandoned. But the well-known and constant practice of Justices' enjoying friendship and social intercourse with Members of Congress and officers of the Executive Branch has *not* been abandoned, and ought not to be.

[The Court later decided the case in an opinion by Justice Kennedy. Justice Scalia concurred in part and dissented in part. By a vote of 7–2, the Court vacated the lower court decision refusing to protect the defendants from having to comply with discovery requests and remanded to the lower court to determine whether the Vice President and the other government defendants would be able to protect their interest in confidentiality by asserting executive privilege in response to particular discovery requests.]

NOTES ON CHENEY

1. ***Family But Not Friends?*** Both Rule 2.11 and 28 U.S.C. § 455 provide for judicial recusal or disqualification based on relatively slight forms of interest, including if a relative of the judge or her spouse is or represents a party to the proceeding. Yet, other than the general impartiality standard, they do not provide for recusal in cases of personal friendship. Why not? Justice Scalia asserts that requiring recusal in cases involving friends would be problematic because Supreme Court justices are often close friends with high-level executive branch officials: "Many Justices have reached this Court precisely because they were friends of the incumbent President or other senior officials." Does this suggest that personal friendship is not an influence or that it would simply be unadministrable to require disqualification? In some cases, judges have been disqualified based on their friendship with litigants, or even their friendship with friends of litigants. In *United States v. Tucker*, 78 F.3d 1313 (8th Cir. 1996), on motion of Independent Counsel Kenneth Starr, a district judge was removed from trial of former Arkansas governor Jim Guy Tucker because the district judge was acquainted with Bill and Hillary Rodham Clinton, had been a guest at the White House, and the case against Governor Tucker involved matters related to the investigation of the Clintons.

2. ***When Is a Government Official Really the Litigant?*** The suit challenging the activities of the Group was animated by the concern that

Dick Cheney's longstanding and close financial and personal ties with Halliburton, a huge energy company, and George W. Bush's own pre-government work as an oil company executive, had led the administration to hand over the making of national energy policy to a group of energy company executives and lobbyists. Are you persuaded by Scalia's characterization of the suit as having nothing to do with Cheney's own reputation? If the complaint had specifically alleged that the Vice President's own interests had driven the operations of the Group, would the basis for Scalia's decision change?

3.   *Who Should Decide on Recusal?* Should judges rule on their own recusal motions? As you see, in the U.S. Supreme Court, the justices do, and there is no further review. In lower federal courts, judges typically rule on their own motions initially, but they may step aside to allow the chief judge of the court to rule, as in note 5 below, and in any event, the ruling on the motion can be appealed.

4.   *The Rule of Necessity.* Comment [3] to Rule 2.11 says recusal is not required when no other judge is available to decide the case, either because all judges have an interest or the matter requires immediate judicial action, such as a temporary restraining order. In matters that require immediate action, "the judge must disclose on the record the basis for possible disqualification and make reasonable efforts to transfer the matter to another judge as soon as practicable." In *United States v. Will*, 449 U.S. 200 (1980), several district judges sued to receive a pay raise on the theory that inflation had reduced their pay in violation of the constitution. Because all federal judges would be affected by the ruling and therefore all would be recused, the Supreme Court ruled that recusal was unnecessary.

5.   *When Does a Judge Have a Personal Interest in the Litigation?* What kinds of personal interests in a matter should be the basis for disqualification? In *Perry v. Schwarzenegger*, 790 F. Supp. 2d 1119 (N.D. Cal. 2011), litigants defending Proposition 8, California's ban on same-sex marriage, asserted that the district judge must be recused because he was in a longstanding same sex relationship and would therefore personally benefit from his ruling allowing same sex couples to marry. The chief judge of the district ruled on the recusal motion and rejected it: "to base a recusal standard on future subjective intent to take advantage of constitutional rights is to create an inadministrable test." Should it matter whether the judge announced a desire or intention to marry as a result of the ruling?

6.   *Recusal Based on Extrajudicial Statements.* Another basis for seeking recusal is that the judge previously made statements about a matter suggesting that the judge would not approach the matter impartially. Rule 2.10 of the Code of Judicial Conduct prohibits judges from making "any public statement that might reasonably be expected to affect the outcome or impair the fairness of a matter pending or impending in any court." Rule 2.10(E), however, does permit a judge to "respond directly or through a third party to allegations in the media or elsewhere concerning the judge's conduct

in a matter." Rule 2.11 provides that recusal based on extrajudicial statements is appropriate when: "The judge, while a judge or a judicial candidate, has made a public statement, other than in a court proceeding, judicial decision, or opinion, that commits or appears to commit the judge to reach a particular result or rule in a particular way in the proceeding or controversy." Rule 2.11(a)(5). Consider the following situations:

(a) In a high-profile and controversial case, plaintiffs accused the judge of hypocrisy in making an important pretrial ruling because she had ruled differently on a similar issue in another case. The newspaper reported the plaintiffs' allegations of hypocrisy and described the judge's ruling inaccurately. The judge wrote to the newspaper, with copies to the parties, enclosing her order and correcting the newspaper's description of the ruling. The reporter telephoned the judge for comment and then ran a story quoting the judge explaining the difference between the two cases. The plaintiffs moved to disqualify the judge on the basis of her statements to the press. The court of appeals ordered recusal because a reasonable person could have interpreted the judge's remarks about the factual differences in the case "as doing more than correcting those misimpressions and creating an appearance of partiality." Do you agree? *In re Boston's Children First*, 239 F.3d 59, 244 F.3d 164 (1st Cir. 2001).

(b) An 18-year-old pleaded guilty to theft and was sentenced to probation. Two days after the sentencing hearing, the defendant robbed and killed a student at the local university. The local news reported the sensational murder extensively, and many criticized the judge for allowing the defendant (who had a criminal history) to be released on probation. The judge is running for re-election and her opponent has accused the judge of being soft on crime and has insinuated that the judge is to be blamed for the death of the student. The judge seeks your advice about whether or how she can explain to the public that the record of the defendant's criminal history was sealed and not available to her because his offenses had been committed as a juvenile and, in any event, the state's computerized criminal records are badly outmoded and almost impossible for judges to search.[9]

(c) You have been appointed by the State Supreme Court to serve on a commission to consider revisions to the Code of Judicial Conduct to allow judges to speak publicly about rulings in certain cases. What would you recommend about what judges should be allowed to say and in what form?

---

[9] *See http://www.dukechronicle.com/article/2-indicted-carson-case-monday;* Anne Blythe, *Chapel Hill Murder Case Forced Probation Reforms*, NEWS & OBSERVER, Dec. 1, 2011, http://www.newsobserver.com/2011/12/01/1681954/murder-case-forced-reforms.html: Eli Saunders, *This Year's Willie Horton?,* TIME MAGAZINE (Nov. 25, 2007) (Gov. Mitt Romney, running for president in 2008, called for resignation of a Massachusetts judge who had ordered a man to be released from state penitentiary and six months later the man committed a double murder); Denise Lavoie, *State's High Court to Consider Allowing Judges to Speak Out*, BOSTON GLOBE (Jan. 29, 2008).

E. JUDICIAL ELECTORAL CAMPAIGNS

As noted above, many states require judges to run for election and/or re-election. In this section we consider two sets of issues arising out of judicial elections: (1) regulation of monetary contributions to campaigns; and (2) regulation of statements by candidates for judicial office. The amount of money spent on judicial elections has increased substantially in the first decade of the 21st century, and the increase has been especially marked in states with partisan judicial elections.[10] The Code of Judicial Conduct contains some rules regulating both campaign contributions and campaign speech. In extreme cases, as we will see in the *Caperton* case below, campaign contributions compromise judicial impartiality to the point that disqualification is required by the constitutional due process guarantee. While both the Code of Judicial Conduct and the due process clause of the federal constitution require certain protections against judicial bias, efforts to police judicial elections in the name of protecting impartiality generate problems of their own. Legal regulation of campaign contributions or expenditures or judicial campaign statements potentially violates the free speech protections of federal and state constitutions, as illustrated by the second case excerpted below.

CAPERTON V. A.T. MASSEY COAL CO.
United States Supreme Court
556 U.S. 868 (2009)

JUSTICE KENNEDY delivered the opinion of the Court.

[In 2002, a West Virginia jury returned a $50 million verdict against A.T. Massey Coal Co. and its affiliates and in favor of Caperton.] Don Blankenship is Massey's chairman, chief executive officer, and president. After the verdict but before the appeal, West Virginia held its 2004 judicial elections. Knowing the Supreme Court of Appeals of West Virginia would consider the appeal in the case, Blankenship decided to support an attorney who sought to replace Justice McGraw. Justice McGraw was a candidate for reelection to that court. The attorney who sought to replace him was Brent Benjamin.

In addition to contributing the $1,000 statutory maximum to Benjamin's campaign committee, Blankenship donated almost $2.5 million to "And For The Sake Of The Kids," a political organization formed under 26 U.S.C. § 527. The § 527 organization opposed McGraw and supported Benjamin. Blankenship's donations accounted for more than two-thirds of the total funds it raised. Blankenship spent, in

---

[10] *See, e.g.,* Joanna Shepherd, *Justice At Risk: An Empirical Analysis of Campaign Contributions and Judicial Decisions* (American Constitution Society, June 2013), and sources cited therein.

addition, just over $500,000 on independent expenditures—for direct mailings and letters soliciting donations as well as television and newspaper advertisements—"to support Brent Benjamin." Blankenship's $3 million in contributions were more than the total amount spent by all other Benjamin supporters and three times the amount spent by Benjamin's own committee.

Benjamin won. He received 382,036 votes (53.3%), and McGraw received 334,301 votes (46.7%).

In October 2005, before Massey filed its petition for appeal in West Virginia's highest court, Caperton moved to disqualify now-Justice Benjamin under the Due Process Clause and the West Virginia Code of Judicial Conduct, based on the conflict caused by Blankenship's campaign involvement. Justice Benjamin denied the motion in April 2006.

[In November 2007 the West Virginia Supreme Court, in a 3–2 split, reversed the $50 million verdict against Massey. Justice Benjamin joined the majority opinion.]

Caperton sought rehearing, and the parties moved for disqualification of three of the five justices who decided the appeal. Photos had surfaced of Justice Maynard [who had joined the majority] vacationing with Blankenship in the French Riviera while the case was pending. Justice Maynard granted Caperton's recusal motion. On the other side Justice Starcher granted Massey's recusal motion, apparently based on his public criticism of Blankenship's role in the 2004 elections. In his recusal memorandum Justice Starcher urged Justice Benjamin to recuse himself as well. He noted that "Blankenship's bestowal of his personal wealth, political tactics, and 'friendship' have created a cancer in the affairs of this Court." Justice Benjamin declined Justice Starcher's suggestion and denied Caperton's recusal motion.

The court granted rehearing. Justice Benjamin, now in the capacity of acting chief justice, selected Judges Cookman and Fox to replace the recused justices. Caperton moved a third time for disqualification. Justice Benjamin again refused to withdraw.

In April 2008 a divided court again reversed the jury verdict, and again it was a 3-to-2 decision. Justice Davis filed a modified version of his [sic—eds: Justice Davis is a woman] prior opinion, repeating the two earlier holdings. She was joined by Justice Benjamin and Judge Fox. Justice Albright, joined by Judge Cookman, dissented.

It is axiomatic that a fair trial in a fair tribunal is a basic requirement of due process. As the Court has recognized, however, most matters relating to judicial disqualification do not rise to a constitutional level.

The Court has identified instances which, as an objective matter, require recusal. [The Court then discussed two cases finding a due process violation based on a judge's actual or perceived bias. One involved a local court where the judge received a salary supplement from criminal fines assessed in case of a conviction but not in the case of acquittal. The other involved a local judge who, under state law, acted in the role of a one-person grand jury and called the defendant to testify. Then, finding the defendant to have testified falsely, he charged the defendant with perjury and tried him on the perjury charge.]

Based on the principles described in these cases we turn to the issue before us.

Caperton contends that Blankenship's pivotal role in getting Justice Benjamin elected created a constitutionally intolerable probability of actual bias. Though not a bribe or criminal influence, Justice Benjamin would nevertheless feel a debt of gratitude to Blankenship for his extraordinary efforts to get him elected.

[The Court then discussed the difficulty of discerning whether a judge is actually biased against or in favor of a litigant.]

The difficulties of inquiring into actual bias, and the fact that the inquiry is often a private one, simply underscore the need for objective rules. Otherwise there may be no adequate protection against a judge who simply misreads or misapprehends the real motives at work in deciding the case.

We turn to the influence at issue in this case. Not every campaign contribution by a litigant or attorney creates a probability of bias that requires a judge's recusal, but this is an exceptional case. We conclude that there is a serious risk of actual bias—based on objective and reasonable perceptions—when a person with a personal stake in a particular case had a significant and disproportionate influence in placing the judge on the case by raising funds or directing the judge's election campaign when the case was pending or imminent. The inquiry centers on the contribution's relative size in comparison to the total amount of money contributed to the campaign, the total amount spent in the election, and the apparent effect such contribution had on the outcome of the election.

Massey responds that Blankenship's support, while significant, did not cause Benjamin's victory. In the end the people of West Virginia elected him, and they did so based on many reasons other than Blankenship's efforts. Massey points out that every major state newspaper, but one, endorsed Benjamin. It also contends that then-Justice McGraw cost himself the election by giving a speech during the campaign, a speech the opposition seized upon for its own advantage.

Whether Blankenship's campaign contributions were a necessary and sufficient cause of Benjamin's victory is not the proper inquiry. Much like determining whether a judge is actually biased, proving what ultimately drives the electorate to choose a particular candidate is a difficult endeavor, not likely to lend itself to a certain conclusion. This is particularly true where, as here, there is no procedure for judicial factfinding and the sole trier of fact is the one accused of bias.

The temporal relationship between the campaign contributions, the justice's election, and the pendency of the case is also critical. It was reasonably foreseeable, when the campaign contributions were made, that the pending case would be before the newly elected justice. So it became at once apparent that, absent recusal, Justice Benjamin would review a judgment that cost his biggest donor's company $50 million. Although there is no allegation of a quid pro quo agreement, the fact remains that Blankenship's extraordinary contributions were made at a time when he had a vested stake in the outcome.

One must also take into account the judicial reforms the States have implemented to eliminate even the appearance of partiality. Almost every State—West Virginia included—has adopted the American Bar Association's objective standard: "A judge shall avoid impropriety and the appearance of impropriety." ABA Annotated Model Code of Judicial Conduct, Canon 2 (2004).

The West Virginia Code of Judicial Conduct also requires a judge to "disqualify himself or herself in a proceeding in which the judge's impartiality might reasonably be questioned." Canon 3E(1); see also 28 U.S.C. § 455(a) ("Any justice, judge, or magistrate judge of the United States shall disqualify himself in any proceeding in which his impartiality might reasonably be questioned").

The Due Process Clause demarks only the outer boundaries of judicial disqualifications. Congress and the states, of course, remain free to impose more rigorous standards for judicial disqualification than those we find mandated here today. Because the codes of judicial conduct provide more protection than due process requires, most disputes over disqualification will be resolved without resort to the Constitution. Application of the constitutional standard implicated in this case will thus be confined to rare instances.

CHIEF JUSTICE ROBERTS, with whom JUSTICE SCALIA, JUSTICE THOMAS, and JUSTICE ALITO join, dissenting.

Until today, we have recognized exactly two situations in which the Federal Due Process Clause requires disqualification of a judge: when the judge has a financial interest in the outcome of the case, and when the judge is trying a defendant for certain criminal contempt. Vaguer notions of bias or the appearance of bias were never a basis for disqualification, either at common law or under our constitutional precedents. Those issues were instead addressed by legislation or court rules.

Today, however, the Court enlists the Due Process Clause to overturn a judge's failure to recuse because of a "probability of bias." Unlike the established grounds for disqualification, a "probability of bias" cannot be defined in any limited way.

In any given case, there are a number of factors that could give rise to a "probability" or "appearance" of bias: friendship with a party or lawyer, prior employment experience, membership in clubs or associations, prior speeches and writings, religious affiliation, and countless other considerations. We have never held that the Due Process Clause requires recusal for any of these reasons, even though they could be viewed as presenting a "probability of bias." Many state statutes require recusal based on a probability or appearance of bias, but that alone would not be sufficient basis for imposing a constitutional requirement under the Due Process Clause.

But there are other fundamental questions as well. With little help from the majority, courts will now have to determine:

1. How much money is too much money? What level of contribution or expenditure gives rise to a "probability of bias"?

2. How do we determine whether a given expenditure is "disproportionate"? Disproportionate to what?

3. Are independent, non-coordinated expenditures treated the same as direct contributions to a candidate's campaign? What about contributions to independent outside groups supporting a candidate?

4. Does it matter whether the litigant has contributed to other candidates or made large expenditures in connection with other elections?

5. Does the amount at issue in the case matter? What if this case were an employment dispute with only $10,000 at stake? What if the plaintiffs only sought non-monetary relief such as an injunction or declaratory judgment?

[The dissent then listed, in another 35 numbered paragraphs, questions that it considered to have been left unanswered by the majority opinion. Among the questions raised were whether the judge's vote must be outcome determinative in order for his non-recusal to violate due process and what remedies would be appropriate.]

And why is the Court so convinced that this is an extreme case? It is true that Don Blankenship spent a large amount of money in connection with this election. But this point cannot be emphasized strongly enough: Other than a $1,000 direct contribution from Blankenship, Justice Benjamin and his campaign had no control over how this money was spent.

It is also far from clear that Blankenship's expenditures affected the outcome of this election. Justice Benjamin won by a comfortable 7-point margin (53.3% to 46.7%). Many observers believed that Justice Benjamin's opponent doomed his candidacy by giving a well-publicized speech that made several curious allegations; this speech was described in the local media as "deeply disturbing" and worse. Justice Benjamin just might have won because the voters of West Virginia thought he would be a better judge than his opponent.

NOTES ON CAPERTON

1. *How Much Is Too Much?* Under what circumstances should judicial campaign contributions by litigants be a basis for recusal? The Model Code of Judicial Conduct contains the following provision on recusal based on campaign contributions: "(4) The judge knows or learns by means of a timely motion that a party, a party's lawyer, or the law firm of a party's lawyer has within the previous [insert number] year[s] made aggregate contributions to the judge's campaign in an amount that is greater than $[insert amount] for an individual or $[insert amount] for an entity." Rule 2.11(A)(4). Rule 4.4 permits judges to form campaign committees and instructs judges to direct the committee "to solicit and accept only such campaign contributions as are reasonable, in any event not to exceed, in the aggregate, $[insert amount] from any individual or $[insert amount] from any entity or organization; [and] not to solicit or accept contributions for a candidate's current campaign more than [insert amount of time] before the applicable primary election, caucus, or general or retention election, nor more than [insert number] days after the last election in which the candidate participated." How would you determine what amounts to fill in where the ABA left blanks? What light does *Caperton* shed on that question?

2. *What Else Determines the Permissibility of Campaign Contributions?* How would you answer the questions posed by Chief Justice Roberts in dissent? Do you think the questions need to be answered in the abstract either by the Code of Judicial Conduct or as a matter of due process? Could they be resolved on a case-by-case basis? What facts or circumstances would be relevant to deciding the propriety of judicial campaign contributions? What would be the disadvantage of a case-by-case approach?

3. *Why Was* Caperton *a Due Process Case Rather than a Code of Judicial Conduct Case?* The U.S. Supreme Court addressed the recusal as a matter of due process because no other theory was available. The West Virginia bar and the West Virginia Supreme Court enforce the Code in West Virginia; the U.S. Supreme Court had no authority to overturn the state supreme court's determination about the violations of state law.

4. ***Are Contributions to Judicial Elections Protected Speech Under the First Amendment?*** In *Citizens United v. Federal Election Commission*, 558 U.S. 310 (2010), the Court struck down a federal statute restricting expenditures by the same kind of independent committee that made the expenditures on behalf of Justice Benjamin on the ground that the statute restricted speech protected by the First Amendment. *Caperton* was decided before *Citizens United* and, therefore, the Court did not have to distinguish the two cases. Is there a basis for distinguishing contributions to or expenditures by judicial election campaigns from those of campaigns for other elected offices?

In the case and notes that follow, we consider the impact of the First Amendment's free speech clause on the efforts to restrict campaign statements in judicial elections.

REPUBLICAN PARTY OF MINNESOTA V. WHITE
United States Supreme Court
536 U.S. 765 (2002)

JUSTICE SCALIA delivered the opinion of the Court.

The question presented in this case is whether the First Amendment permits the Minnesota Supreme Court to prohibit candidates for judicial election in that State from announcing their views on disputed legal and political issues.

Since Minnesota's admission to the Union in 1858, the State's Constitution has provided for the selection of all state judges by popular election. Since 1912, those elections have been nonpartisan. Since 1974, they have been subject to a legal restriction which states that a "candidate for a judicial office, including an incumbent judge," shall not "announce his or her views on disputed legal or political issues." Minn.Code of Judicial Conduct, Canon 5(A)(3)(d)(i) (2000). This prohibition, promulgated by the Minnesota Supreme Court and based on Canon 7(B) of the 1972 American Bar Association (ABA) Model Code of Judicial Conduct, is known as the "announce clause." Incumbent judges who violate it are subject to discipline, including removal, censure, civil penalties, and suspension without pay. Lawyers who run for judicial office also must comply with the announce clause. Minn. Rule of Professional Conduct 8.2(b) (2002) ("A lawyer who is a candidate for judicial office shall comply with the applicable provisions of the Code of Judicial Conduct"). Those who violate it are subject to, inter alia, disbarment, suspension, and probation. Rule 8.4(a); Minn. Rules on Lawyers Professional Responsibility 8–14, 15(a) (2002).

[Gregory Wersal, a candidate to be associate justice of the Minnesota Supreme Court sought an advisory opinion from the Lawyers Board [the state disciplinary agency]] with regard to whether it planned to enforce the announce clause. The Lawyers Board responded equivocally, stating that, although it had significant doubts about the constitutionality of the provision, it was unable to answer his question because he had not submitted a list of the announcements he wished to make.

Shortly thereafter, Wersal filed this lawsuit seeking a declaration that the announce clause violates the First Amendment.

We know that "announc[ing] . . . views" on an issue covers much more than promising to decide an issue a particular way. The prohibition extends to the candidate's mere statement of his current position, even if he does not bind himself to maintain that position after election. All the parties agree this is the case, because the Minnesota Code contains a so-called "pledges or promises" clause, which separately prohibits judicial candidates from making "pledges or promises of conduct in office other than the faithful and impartial performance of the duties of the office," a prohibition that is not challenged here and on which we express no view.

[R]espondents acknowledged at oral argument that statements critical of past judicial decisions are not permissible if the candidate also states that he is against stare decisis. Thus, candidates must choose between stating their views critical of past decisions and stating their views in opposition to stare decisis. Or, to look at it more concretely, they may state their view that prior decisions were erroneous only if they do not assert that they, if elected, have any power to eliminate erroneous decisions.

Respondents contend that this still leaves plenty of topics for discussion on the campaign trail. These include a candidate's "character," "education," "work habits," and "how [he] would handle administrative duties if elected." Indeed, the Judicial Board has printed a list of preapproved questions which judicial candidates are allowed to answer. These include how the candidate feels about cameras in the courtroom, how he would go about reducing the caseload, how the costs of judicial administration can be reduced, and how he proposes to ensure that minorities and women are treated more fairly by the court system.

One meaning of "impartiality" in the judicial context—and of course its root meaning—is the lack of bias for or against either party to the proceeding. Impartiality in this sense guarantees a party that the judge who hears his case will apply the law to him in the same way he applies it to any other party.

We think it plain that the announce clause is not narrowly tailored to serve impartiality (or the appearance of impartiality) in this sense. To be sure, when a case arises that turns on a legal issue on which the judge (as a candidate) had taken a particular stand, the party taking the opposite stand is likely to lose. But not because of any bias against that party, or favoritism toward the other party. Any party taking that position is just as likely to lose. The judge is applying the law (as he sees it) evenhandedly.

It is perhaps possible to use the term "impartiality" in the judicial context to mean lack of preconception in favor of or against a particular legal view. A judge's lack of predisposition regarding the relevant legal issues in a case has never been thought a necessary component of equal justice, and with good reason. For one thing, it is virtually impossible to find a judge who does not have preconceptions about the law. Since most Justices come to this bench no earlier than their middle years, it would be unusual if they had not by that time formulated at least some tentative notions that would influence them in their interpretation of the sweeping clauses of the Constitution and their interaction with one another. Indeed, even if it were possible to select judges who did not have preconceived views on legal issues, it would hardly be desirable to do so.

A third possible meaning of "impartiality" might be described as open-mindedness. This quality in a judge demands, not that he have no preconceptions on legal issues, but that he be willing to consider views that oppose his preconceptions, and remain open to persuasion, when the issues arise in a pending case. It may well be that impartiality in this sense, and the appearance of it, are desirable in the judiciary, but we need not pursue that inquiry, since we do not believe the Minnesota Supreme Court adopted the announce clause for that purpose.

Respondents argue that the announce clause serves the interest in open-mindedness, or at least in the appearance of openmindedness, because it relieves a judge from pressure to rule a certain way in order to maintain consistency with statements the judge has previously made. The problem is, however, that statements in election campaigns are such an infinitesimal portion of the public commitments to legal positions that judges (or judges-to-be) undertake, that this object of the prohibition is implausible. Before they arrive on the bench (whether by election or otherwise) judges have often committed themselves on legal issues that they must later rule upon. [The opinion notes examples, including that Justice Hugo Black participated in several cases construing and deciding the constitutionality of the Fair Labor Standards Act, even though as a Senator he had been one of its principal authors.] Most frequently, of course, that prior expression will have occurred in ruling on an earlier case. But judges often state their views on disputed legal issues outside the context of adjudication—in classes that they conduct, and in books and speeches.

The short of the matter is this: In Minnesota, a candidate for judicial office may not say "I think it is constitutional for the legislature to prohibit same-sex marriages." He may say the very same thing, however, up until the very day before he declares himself a candidate, and may say it repeatedly (until litigation is pending) after he is elected. As a means of pursuing the objective of open-mindedness that respondents now articulate, the announce clause is so woefully underinclusive as to render belief in that purpose a challenge to the credulous.

We know of no restrictions upon statements that could be made by judicial candidates (including judges) throughout the 19th and the first quarter of the 20th century. Indeed, judicial elections were generally partisan during this period, the movement toward nonpartisan judicial elections not even beginning until the 1870's. Thus, not only were judicial candidates (including judges) discussing disputed legal and political issues on the campaign trail, but they were touting party affiliations and angling for party nominations all the while.

There is an obvious tension between the article of Minnesota's popularly approved Constitution which provides that judges shall be elected, and the Minnesota Supreme Court's announce clause which places most subjects of interest to the voters off limits. The disparity is perhaps unsurprising, since the ABA, which originated the announce clause, has long been an opponent of judicial elections. That opposition may be well taken (it certainly had the support of the Founders of the Federal Government), but the First Amendment does not permit it to achieve its goal by leaving the principle of elections in place while preventing candidates from discussing what the elections are about.

JUSTICE O'CONNOR, concurring.

I join the opinion of the Court but write separately to express my concerns about judicial elections generally. I am concerned that, even aside from what judicial candidates may say while campaigning, the very practice of electing judges undermines [judicial impartiality].

We of course want judges to be impartial, in the sense of being free from any personal stake in the outcome of the cases to which they are assigned. But if judges are subject to regular elections they are likely to feel that they have at least some personal stake in the outcome of every publicized case. Elected judges cannot help being aware that if the public is not satisfied with the outcome of a particular case, it could hurt their reelection prospects. See [Julian] Eule, *Crocodiles in the Bathtub: State Courts, Voter Initiatives and the Threat of Electoral Reprisal*, 65 U. COLO. L.REV. 733, 739 (1994) (quoting former California Supreme Court Justice Otto Kaus' statement that ignoring the political consequences of visible decisions is " 'like ignoring a crocodile in your bathtub' ").

Minnesota has chosen to select its judges through contested popular elections instead of through an appointment system or a combined appointment and retention election system along the lines of the Missouri Plan. In doing so the State has voluntarily taken on the risks to judicial bias described above. As a result, the State's claim that it needs to significantly restrict judges' speech in order to protect judicial impartiality is particularly troubling. If the State has a problem with judicial impartiality, it is largely one the State brought upon itself by continuing the practice of popularly electing judges.

JUSTICE GINSBURG, with whom JUSTICE STEVENS, JUSTICE SOUTER, and JUSTICE BREYER join, dissenting.

I would differentiate elections for political offices, in which the First Amendment holds full sway, from elections designed to select those whose office it is to administer justice without respect to persons.

Legislative and executive officials serve in representative capacities. They are agents of the people; their primary function is to advance the interests of their constituencies. Candidates for political offices, in keeping with their representative role, must be left free to inform the electorate of their positions on specific issues. Armed with such information, the individual voter will be equipped to cast her ballot intelligently, to vote for the candidate committed to positions the voter approves.

Judges, however, are not political actors. They do not sit as representatives of particular persons, communities, or parties; they serve no faction or constituency. They must strive to do what is legally right, all the more so when the result is not the one "the home crowd" wants. Even when they develop common law or give concrete meaning to constitutional text, judges act only in the context of individual cases, the outcome of which cannot depend on the will of the public.

Prohibiting a judicial candidate from pledging or promising certain results if elected directly promotes the State's interest in preserving public faith in the bench. The perception of that unseemly quid pro quo— a judicial candidate's promises on issues in return for the electorate's votes at the polls—inevitably diminishes the public's faith in the ability of judges to administer the law without regard to personal or political self-interest.

NOTES ON REPUBLICAN PARTY OF MINNESOTA V. WHITE

1. **Should Judges Be Elected?** Justice O'Connor's concurring opinion argues that the difficult problems in regulating judicial election campaigns illuminate a fundamental tension between judicial impartiality and electoral accountability. Having considered the difficulties of regulating both campaign contributions and campaign statements, consider the advantages of electing judges and the advantages of the Article III appointment and life-tenure model. Which model is better and why?

2. **Do Judicial Elections Systematically Skew Results in Certain Types of Cases?** One study has shown that in states in which the high court judges are elected and in which they must decide capital cases, "stronger

public support for the death penalty produces significantly more conservative judges, and these conservative judges are more likely to uphold capital convictions."[11] Is that a good or a bad thing? What light, if any, should evidence like that shed on the question whether judges should be elected or appointed?

3. ***Should Elected Judges Be Permitted to Say More than Appointed Judges?*** What statements by judges running for election or re-election should be a basis for discipline or recusal? Does your answer depend on how you feel about judges feeling accountable to voters?

4. ***Should Judicial Elections Be Nonpartisan?*** Many states, including Montana, require that judicial elections be nonpartisan and prohibit candidates for judicial office from indicating party affiliation. Montana prohibits any political party to "endorse, contribute to, or make an expenditure to support or oppose a judicial candidate." Mont. Code Ann. § 13–35–231. Is Montana's law unconstitutional? *See Sanders County Republican Election Committee v. Bullock*, 698 F.3d 731 (9th Cir., 2012) (enjoining enforcement of Montana statute). Is there a distinction between prohibiting party endorsements and prohibiting expenditures or contributions?

5. ***Are Judges Different?*** Should the free speech rights of judges in electoral campaigns differ from the free speech rights of other candidates for elective office? If not, which provisions of the Code of Judicial Conduct and 28 U.S.C. § 455 do you deem vulnerable to a free speech challenge?

PROBLEM 27–1

A blue ribbon commission has sought your advice on whether ethics rules should prohibit judges from ruling on cases in which their views are likely to be affected by fear of well-organized and well-funded campaigns to remove them from office based on their votes in controversial cases. They offer you the following examples from recent experience and ask whether there are any regulatory measures that could ensure an appropriate level of political accountability, free speech in election campaigns, and yet preserve an appropriate degree of judicial independence:

(a) Three justices on the Iowa Supreme Court were voted out of office after voting with the other four members of the court unanimously to strike down the state's prohibition on same-sex marriage.[12]

(b) Justice Penny J. White was voted off the Tennessee Supreme Court in 1997 after she joined the court majority to affirm a rape and murder

---

[11] Paul Brace & Brent D. Boyea, *State Public Opinion, the Death Penalty, and the Practice of Electing Judges*, 52 AM. J. POL. SCI. 360, 370 (2008).

[12] Grant Schulte, *Iowans Dismiss Three Justices*, DES MOINES REGISTER (Nov. 3, 2010). A national organization that played a significant role in funding the campaign against the three targeted another justice who joined the opinion in November 2012, as well as three justices on the Florida Supreme Court. John Eligon, *Iowa Justice Who Ruled for Gay Marriage Faces Test that Peers Failed*, N.Y. TIMES (Oct. 23, 2012), p. A14; Lizette Alvarez, *Republican Party Aims to Remake Florida Supreme Court*, N.Y. TIMES (October 3, 2012), A20.

conviction but reverse a death sentence. At the time of the election, the Republican governor of Tennessee stated that he hoped the prospect of being voted out of a job would prompt judges to think carefully before deciding cases.

(c)   Justice Deborah Agosti of the Nevada Supreme Court was targeted for recall in 2003 after she wrote the opinion of the court holding that the Nevada constitutional provision requiring adequate expenditures for public education took precedence over another Nevada constitutional provision relating to taxes. Although she narrowly survived the recall vote, she concluded that she would not win re-election and decided not to run.

(d)   Judge Harold Baer of the U.S. District Court changed his ruling on a motion to suppress evidence in a case involving suspected drug dealers after the case made headlines and President Bill Clinton, who had appointed Baer to the court, demanded that Baer resign from the bench. *United States v. Bayless*, 913 F. Supp. 232, 921 F. Supp. 211 (S.D.N.Y. 1996).

F. SUMMARY

In this chapter, we saw that the Code of Judicial Conduct, which has been adopted by all states and by all federal courts except the Supreme Court generally requires judges to uphold the independence, integrity, and impartiality of the judiciary, and to avoid impropriety and the appearance of impropriety. The rules of judicial conduct are typically enforced by the judge recusing himself or by a party making a motion for disqualification, but in extreme cases judges are subject to discipline, including removal from office. Specific prohibitions include limits on gifts and campaign contributions and avoiding presiding over cases in which a member of the judge's family or a company in which the judge has a significant financial interest is a party or represents a party. In addition, judges are prohibited from making extrajudicial statements if doing so will compromise the judge's impartiality. Some of these regulations, especially those governing campaign contributions and extrajudicial statements, are difficult to implement in a state that requires judges to stand for election.

SUBPART E

PUBLIC INTEREST PRACTICE

■ ■ ■

We turn now to the last unit in our survey of the various types of practice settings in which American lawyers work—"public interest practice." As we'll see, the term "public interest law" is used in a variety of different ways, not all of them consistent with one another. For purposes of organizing the following discussion, we use "public interest practice" to refer to organizations and nonprofit groups receiving government or philanthropic subsidies whose purpose is either to serve people who cannot otherwise afford legal services or to pursue some vision of the public good.

We begin this unit with an examination of lawyers who work in legal services programs designed to address the legal needs of poor people (Chapter 28). The next chapter (Chapter 29) considers lawyers who work for nonprofit public interest law organizations. Chapter 30 considers several particularly thorny ethical issues for public interest lawyers who seek to achieve collective benefits for many people rather than just particular individual clients.

CHAPTER 28

LEGAL SERVICES

■ ■ ■

A. INTRODUCTION

Topic Overview and Chapter Organization

This chapter examines the sector of the profession that provides civil legal assistance to those unable to afford a lawyer. We study the legal regulation imposed by Congress through the Legal Services Corporation's strict limits on what law offices that receive LSC funding can do and whom they can represent. We then examine the work of legal services lawyers, with particular emphasis on the way in which their work is affected by the pervasive problem of scarce legal resources. We study a variety of innovative methods legal aid lawyers have adopted to provide adequate representation to underserved clients. Lastly, we consider the debate spawned by empirical work attempting to assess the impact of subsidized legal services for clients.

The U.S. Constitution provides a right to appointed counsel in criminal cases in which the defendant faces the possibility of incarceration because, as the Supreme Court explained, the principle that "every defendant stands equal before the law cannot be realized if the poor man charged with a crime has to face his accusers without a lawyer to assist him." *Gideon v. Wainwright*, 372 U.S. 335, 344 (1963). The constitutional right to counsel in criminal cases obligated every state to set up a system of lawyers to provide criminal defense to indigent persons, thus making indigent criminal defense a recognized practice setting.

In contrast, there is no constitutional right to counsel in civil cases. The Court held in *Lassiter v. Department of Social Services,* 452 U.S. 18 (1981), that a state did not violate the constitutional guarantee of due process when it imposed what many would consider the most grievous possible harm on a civil litigant—taking a child away from his mother—without providing a lawyer to represent her in the proceeding to terminate parental rights. Because there is no constitutional right to counsel in civil cases, the ability of poor people to obtain legal representation depends on an assortment of state and federal statutes and private charity. The organization and funding of legal services to the poor in civil cases varies from one area of law to another, one city to another, and one state to another. We will study the problems of access to justice in greater detail in Part VI of this book. Here we focus on the sector of the profession that provides civil legal assistance to those unable to afford a lawyer.

Early programs to provide legal assistance to the poor began in the late nineteenth century with funding from private charity and local governments. Like many forms of poor relief, these efforts were aimed at undercutting support for socialism and anarchism, to create social stability, not social change. Legal aid societies were terribly underfunded compared to the need.[1] By one estimate, in 1963, all the civil legal services programs in the U.S. combined had only 400 lawyers nationwide and a budget that was less than two-tenths of one percent of the nation's total annual expenditure on legal services.[2]

The War on Poverty launched by the Johnson Administration in 1964 led to a substantial infusion of federal money and attention to the need for legal services for the poor. In 1965, the Office of Economic Opportunity began providing federal funds to civil legal services programs and attracted talented, ambitious young lawyers to OEO-funded legal aid programs. The social and legal change agenda of these legal services lawyers reflected the progressive agendas of the civil rights and welfare rights movements. Civil legal services to the poor became a way for idealistic lawyers to promote social change by trying to empower impoverished communities and eradicate pervasive inequality.

With the election of Richard Nixon in 1968, the conservative backlash against the social movements of the 1960s found a powerful ally in government. The Nixon Administration tried to eliminate the OEO funding of legal services for the poor, but Congress ended up institutionalizing it in 1974 by creating the Legal Services Corporation (LSC) as a private, non-profit corporation to administer federal funding for legal aid to the poor. Because the Legal Services Corporation was essentially born from an effort to kill anything like it, the statute that created it contained restrictions on what the federal funds could be used for. It prohibited LSC-funded attorneys from lobbying and political organizing or from handling what were then particularly controversial matters, including school desegregation cases, cases challenging the military draft, and cases protecting abortion rights. Nevertheless, the Legal Services Corporation expanded civil legal assistance for the poor

---

[1] An influential 1919 Reginald Heber Smith study, *Justice and the Poor*, and studies conducted by the American Bar Association and others over the course of the mid-twentieth century, documented the need for legal services. EARL JOHNSON, JR., JUSTICE AND REFORM: THE FORMATIVE YEARS OF THE AMERICAN LEGAL SERVICE PROGRAM (1974); REGINALD HEBER SMITH, JUSTICE AND THE POOR (1919, repr. ed. 1972).

[2] JOHNSON, JUSTICE AND REFORM, at 6–9.

from a primarily urban phenomenon to a nationwide program with offices scattered across every state.

Meanwhile, philanthropic organizations, most notably the Ford Foundation, began to provide significant funding for legal services as part of a broader effort to address poverty and social injustice. Legal services organizations established with foundation funding in the late 1960s and early 1970s provided legal representation on a range of issues, including workplace discrimination, welfare rights, affordable housing, consumer protection, and environmental justice. Later, the agenda broadened to include immigrant rights, wage theft, homelessness, and HIV/AIDS, among other issues. Although the Ford Foundation ceased being a significant funder of legal services to the poor by the 1980s, many of the organizations founded in the 1960s and 1970s survived based on some mixture of philanthropy, federal, state, local, and bar association funding, and attorneys' fees awarded under fee-shifting statutes.[3]

Today, civil legal assistance is provided by a number of different programs. Legal aid offices, organized civil pro bono programs, judicare programs (which offer publicly-funded legal services for low-income persons with certain types of problems), and law school clinical programs all provide representation. Other programs provide only information; these include telephone hotlines delivering specific legal advice or general legal information; courthouse lawyer-for-a-day programs; staffed assistance centers or computer kiosks in courthouses that assist *pro se* civil litigants; and court websites that provide court forms and/or information about using the courts.[4] The Legal Services Corporation is the largest single funder, but overall more funds come from other sources, including state and local governments, the private bar, private foundations, and IOLTA programs (which are explained below). Moreover, every state and most localities have organized pro bono programs run by bar associations, legal aid organizations, or independent nonprofits.[5]

The need for subsidized legal services in civil cases for those who cannot afford lawyers far outstrips the supply of lawyers who provide such service. Unlike public defender offices, which are constitutionally required to provide representation to all eligible criminal defendants, legal services offices can and do turn away huge numbers of eligible people who seek representation. Perhaps the single most significant challenge facing lawyers practicing in this sector of the profession, as well

---

[3] For a recent, comprehensive history of civil legal aid in the United States, see EARL JOHNSON JR., TO ESTABLISH JUSTICE FOR ALL: THE PAST AND FUTURE OF CIVIL LEGAL AID IN THE UNITED STATES (2014).

[4] Rebecca Sandefur & Aaron Smyth, *Access Across America: First Report of the Civil Justice Infrastructure Mapping Project* (Oct. 11, 2011), at 11.

[5] Alan W. Houseman, *The Future of Civil Legal Aid: A National Perspective*, 10 U. D.C. L. REV. 35 (2007).

as one of the most significant challenges facing courts and other institutions that administer the law, is managing the dearth of legal representation for those in need. Some believe the magnitude of the problem is staggering:

> Law is a $100 billion per year industry. Of that $100 billion, however, less than $1 billion is dedicated to delivering legal services to low-income Americans. Put in terms of people rather than dollars, there is about one lawyer for every 240 nonpoor Americans, but only one lawyer for every 9,000 Americans whose low income would qualify them for legal aid. Forty-five million Americans qualify for civil legal aid, and they are served by a mere 4,000 legal-aid lawyers plus an estimated 1,000 to 2,000 additional poor people's lawyers. To put in perspective what those numbers mean, the American Bar Association's Comprehensive Legal Needs Study found that every year about half of low-income people face legal needs—that is, "situations, events, or difficulties any member of the household faced . . . that raised legal issues." That amounts to 4,500 cases a year for each lawyer—90 a week, 18 a day. Obviously, no lawyer can handle a caseload that large. Even supposing that a lawyer could handle one case a day—itself an incredible assumption—the result would be that 95% of low-income people's legal needs remain unaddressed.[6]

As we will see in Part VI of this book, others question whether the unmet legal needs of poor people are as large as the excerpt above suggests.

B. FUNDING OF LEGAL SERVICES

Funding for Legal Services

Lawyers who work full time providing legal services for the poor are funded by four principal sources: (1) The Legal Services Corporation provides federal funds to legal services offices; (2) Governments and bar associations provide funds for particular types of legal services as parts of other social welfare programs (such as to address homelessness, domestic violence, problems of veterans, elderly or disabled people, and public health issues); (3) States provide funding through the Interest on Lawyer Trust Accounts (IOLTA) program; (4) Private philanthropy funds some offices, or provides funding to support a lawyer in an office.

In addition, law school clinical programs are an important source of legal services, and many legal services offices operate networks of lawyers in private practice who provide pro bono legal service.

---

[6] David Luban, *Taking Out the Adversary: The Assault on Progressive Public-Interest Lawyers*, 91 CAL. L. REV. 209 (2003).

Funding for indigent civil legal services has frequently been attacked by those who oppose the aims of legal services programs, just as have welfare and other forms of financial support for the poor, disabled, and elderly. The following excerpt describes some of the principal sources of funding, and recent challenges to their continued existence.

TAKING OUT THE ADVERSARY: THE ASSAULT ON PROGRESSIVE PUBLIC-INTEREST LAWYERS

David Luban
91 California Law Review 209 (2003)

The 1996 Legal Services Corporation Restrictions. The single biggest source of funding for poor people's lawyers is the Legal Services Corporation.* [T]his budget fund[s] [about] one underpaid legal-services lawyer per 10,000 poor people.

Restrictions on the use of LSC funding have always existed. From the beginning of the program, Congress prohibited LSC recipients from using their federal funds on volatile political issues like abortion, school desegregation, and the military draft. LSC lawyers could still advocate on these issues provided they did not use federal funds to do so.

In 1996, however, Congress enacted restrictions on legal-services lawyers that went much further. Not only do they prohibit LSC recipients from taking on certain issues, but they also forbid them from representing entire classes of clients. These include whole classes of aliens, many of whom are legal. The new regulations likewise prohibit the representation of all incarcerated people, including those not convicted of a crime, and those whose cases have nothing to do with why they are in jail, as, for example, in parental-rights lawsuits. The restrictions also prevent LSC attorneys from using specific procedural devices or arguments. They cannot attempt to influence rulemaking or lawmaking, participate in class actions, request attorney's fees under applicable statutes, challenge any welfare reform, or defend anyone charged with a drug offense in a public-housing eviction proceeding. Furthermore, LSC grant recipients must file statements revealing the identity of their clients and stating the facts of the case, and these statements must be made available "to any Federal department or agency that is auditing or monitoring the activities of the Corporation or of the recipient."

Perhaps the most devastating regulation, however, is Congress's prohibition on LSC recipients using their nonfederal funds for these prohibited activities. This requirement had a drastic effect. A legal-aid office could no longer accept an LSC grant if it did any prohibited legal

---

*   [Eds: the budget for the Legal Services Corporation in fiscal year 2014 was $365 million. Data on funding levels for the LSC since its founding may be found at http://www.lsc.gov/congress/funding/funding-history.]

work. This provision forced legal-services providers to split into separate organizations with separate offices, one receiving federal funds and abiding by the restrictions, the other maintaining its freedom of action at the cost of its LSC grant. The result was bifurcated organizations substantially weaker than the initial organization. Some organizations had to purchase duplicate computer systems and hire duplicate staff. Some locales could afford only a restricted office, so that clients with the "wrong" cases were forced to travel hundreds of miles to find counsel or, more realistically, do without. In hundreds of ongoing cases, restricted LSC lawyers had to withdraw.

Opponents of progressive lawyers quickly took advantage of the regulations. For example, when the restrictions went into effect, New York legal-services lawyer David Udell was helping to monitor an already-settled class action against a federal agency. The LSC threatened that if he continued to participate in the case, it would defund every legal-services lawyer in New York City and fire every employee. The LSC backed down when Udell filed a constitutional challenge to the restrictions, in the form of a motion to withdraw conditional on the restrictions being upheld. But later, when Udell informed the monitoring court that the defendant had violated the settlement, "[t]he defendant's counsel (a lawyer in the federal programs branch of the Department of Justice) reported my action to LSC. LSC then declared that my letter to the court was 'adversarial' and ordered me off the case on pain of defunding all legal services programs in New York City, even though the merits of the underlying case had been resolved years earlier." Again, Udell backed the Corporation down through legal action, and the LSC contented itself with merely docking his pay for going to court against it. Udell fared less well in another class action, when the LSC ordered him out but the judge ordered him to stay in the case while at the same time refusing to prevent LSC from taking disciplinary action against Udell or other legal-services lawyers in New York. Udell had no recourse but to work on a part-time basis and handle the class action, during his off hours, for no pay. Although this example makes the LSC seem like the heavy, the LSC was only doing what Congress wanted it to do.

The Challenges to IOLTA Programs. IOLTA programs provide the second biggest source of funds for legal-aid lawyers, after the LSC. Lawyers are required to maintain trust accounts for client money that they hold. When the amount is large, or held for a significant time period, attorneys open an interest-bearing savings account in the client's behalf, but when the amount of money the lawyer holds for clients is small, or the money is held for a short period of time only, the administrative cost of getting the interest to clients would devour the interest and might actually cost the client money. In such cases, the attorney deposits client funds in a demand account, that is, an account from which funds may be obtained on demand. Until 1980, banking law prohibited interest payments on demand accounts. In 1980, Congress amended the law to permit interest-bearing demand accounts, but only for "funds in which the entire beneficial interest is held by one or more individuals or by an organization which is operated primarily for religious, philanthropic, charitable, educational, political, or other similar purposes and which is not operated for profit." States responded to the new law by creating IOLTA programs: nonprofit foundations to fund low-income legal services, financed by the interest on lawyer's demand trust accounts. Lawyers participating in IOLTA programs pool client funds that are too small or held for too short a time to generate collectible interest for the client in an IOLTA account, where the interest goes to the nonprofit foundation funding low-income legal services. Client funds that are capable of generating collectible interest for the client—that is, interest that would not be devoured by the transaction costs of getting it to the client—must still be deposited into a separate savings account for the client, not into the IOLTA account.

The idea was ingenious. The clients could not get the interest on small or short-term lawyer-held funds because transaction costs would gobble it up. Because no one else could get the interest either, it all went to the banks by default. As one Texas judge quipped, IOLTA takes from the banks and gives to the poor. IOLTA programs generated more than $125 million a year for indigent legal services in 2001. Almost all were enacted by the states' highest courts under their rulemaking authority. All fifty states and the District of Columbia have IOLTA plans, and half of them are mandatory.

[Professor Luban explained in some detail that IOLTA faced constitutional challenges from conservative activists who objected to the using interest on trust fund accounts to fund legal services programs. The Supreme Court upheld the IOLTA system against the argument that the use of interest constituted an unconstitutional taking of private property, reasoning that absent the program no one would receive the interest anyway. *Brown v. Legal Foundation of Washington*, 538 U.S. 216 (2003).]

<u>Law School Clinics and the Battle of New Orleans</u>. Today, American law schools offer clinics in more than 130 different subject areas, staffed by more than 1,400 clinical instructors.[**]

Civil and criminal litigation clinics form the backbone of clinical education in the United States, and they typically provide one-client-at-a-

---

[**] [Eds: A 2007 survey showed that law school clinic students provide approximately 2.4 million hours of free legal services to 120,000 clients each year. DAVID A. SANTACROCE & ROBERT R. KUEHN, CENTER FOR THE STUDY OF APPLIED LEGAL EDUCATION, REPORT OF THE 2007–2008 SURVEY 19–20, *available at* http://www.csale.org/files/CSALE.07-08.Survey.Report.pdf. The attacks on clinics described by Professor Luban continued after his article was written. *See* Robert R. Kuehn & Peter A. Joy, *"Kneecapping" Academic Freedom*, 69 ACADEME (2010), available at http://www.aaup.org/AAUP/pubsres/academe/2010/ND/feat/kueh.htm.]

time, more-or-less routine, direct client representation. Clinical education also includes street-law programs, entrepreneurial clinics with business clients, and externships. While nothing in principle prevents conservatives from starting clinics devoted to issues they favor, for example, crime victims' rights or small business deregulation clinics, it has rarely come to pass, although the [Washington Legal Foundation (WLF)] started an Economic Freedom Law Clinic at George Mason Law School, which takes a "pro-free enterprise, limited government, and economic freedom perspective." The perception of a leftward tilt makes law school clinics a natural target for adversaries of progressive public-interest law.

The principal lightning rod has been environmental-law clinics, which sometimes take anti-development stances that put them at odds with business interests. [The article recounts efforts in the 1980s, 1990s and 2000s, to eliminate environmental law clinics at the University of Oregon, the University of West Virginia, the University of Wyoming, the University of Pittsburgh, and Tulane University. Some of the efforts succeeded.]

* * *

The 1996 Restrictions on Legal Services Corporation Funding

The efforts to eliminate LSC and federal funding for legal services for the poor recurred over the years. After 1979, the LSC never again achieved a level of funding (measured in real dollars) that it had in the 1970s. In real dollars, the LSC budget in 2009 was less than half of what it was in 1979. Although each effort to entirely eliminate the program failed, many of them succeeded in adding to the list of matters that LSC-funded lawyers cannot handle.

As noted by Professor Luban, the largest set of restrictions was enacted in 1996 when Congress enacted the Omnibus Consolidated Rescissions and Appropriations Act (OCRAA), P.L. 104–134 (1996), which contained the following list of restrictions:

SEC. 504. (a) None of the funds appropriated in this Act to the Legal Services Corporation may be used to provide financial assistance to any person or entity (which may be referred to in this section as a "recipient")—

(1) that [advocates or opposes any electoral redistricting plan];

(2) that attempts to influence the issuance, amendment, or revocation of any executive order, regulation, or other statement of general applicability and future effect by any Federal, State, or local agency;

(3) that attempts to influence any part of any adjudicatory proceeding of any Federal, State, or local agency if such part of the proceeding is designed for the formulation or modification of any agency policy of general applicability and future effect;

(4) that attempts to influence the passage or defeat of any legislation, constitutional amendment, referendum, initiative, or any similar procedure of the Congress or a State or local legislative body;

(5) that attempts to influence the conduct of oversight proceedings of the [Legal Services] Corporation or any person or entity receiving financial assistance provided by the Corporation;

(7) that initiates or participates in a class action suit;

(8) that files a complaint or otherwise initiates or participates in litigation [in which any plaintiff is identified by a pseudonym, such as Jane Doe. This provision also requires each plaintiff to sign a statement of facts on which the complaint is based and requires that the statement be provided to any federal agency "monitoring the activities of the [Legal Services] Corporation or of the recipient"];

(11)* that provides legal assistance for or on behalf of any alien, unless the alien is lawfully admitted for permanent residence; [or] is married to a United States citizen or is a parent or an unmarried child under the age of 21 years of such a citizen; [or] is lawfully present in the United States as a result of withholding of deportation; [or has been granted political asylum];

(12) that supports or conducts a training program for the purpose of advocating a particular public policy or encouraging a political activity;

(14) that participates in any litigation with respect to abortion;

(15) that participates in any litigation on behalf of a person incarcerated in a Federal, State, or local prison;

(16) that initiates legal representation or participates in any other way, in litigation, lobbying, or rulemaking, involving an effort to reform a Federal or State welfare system, except that this paragraph shall not be construed to preclude a recipient from representing an individual eligible client who is seeking specific relief from a welfare agency if such relief does not involve an effort to amend or otherwise challenge existing law in effect on the date of the initiation of the representation;

---

*   [Eds: Numbers 9, 10 and 13 deliberately omitted.]

(17) that defends a person in a proceeding to evict the person from a public housing project if—

(A) the person has been charged with the illegal sale or distribution of a controlled substance; and

(B) the eviction proceeding is brought by a public housing agency because the illegal drug activity of the person threatens the health or safety of another tenant residing in the public housing project or employee of the public housing agency.

OCRAA provided for regular audits of all LSC-funded offices to ensure compliance with the restrictions.

As noted in Professor Luban's article, the 1996 OCRAA restrictions not only prohibited the use of LSC funds to engage in prohibited activities, but also prohibited any entity that received such funds to use *other funds* to support the activity. As a consequence, any office receiving LSC funds either had to cease the activity or give up all LSC funds. Many legal services offices that received LSC funds decided to split into two entirely separate organizations: one continued as an LSC-funded organization and gave up all matters prohibited by the restrictions; the other would rely on private philanthropy, IOLTA funds, and attorneys' fees and would handle matters that LSC prohibits.

NOTES ON RESTRICTIONS ON LEGAL SERVICES WORK

1. *What Can LSC-Funded Law Offices Not Do?* Examine each one of the numbered paragraphs in section 504 of OCRAA. What types of legal representation does it prohibit? What are the arguments for and against prohibiting recipients of federal funds from providing that type of legal representation using private funds?

2. *Do You Think the LSC Restrictions Violate the Model Rules?* Do any of the OCRAA restrictions raise ethical issues under the Model Rules? Consider the following:

Model Rule 1.1 requires lawyers to provide "competent representation," including "the legal knowledge, skill, thoroughness and preparation reasonably necessary for the representation."

Model Rule 1.2 provides that "a lawyer may limit the scope of representation if the limitation is reasonable under the circumstances and the client gives informed consent."

Model Rule 1.4 requires lawyers to consult with clients about the representation and, in particular, about "any relevant limitation on the lawyer's conduct when the lawyer knows that the client expects assistance not permitted by . . . other law."

Model Rule 1.6 requires lawyers to guard the confidentiality of "information relating to the representation of a client," except, among other exceptions, "to comply with other law."

Model Rule 1.8(f) provides that a "lawyer shall not accept compensation for representing a client from one other than the client unless the client gives informed consent and there is no interference with the lawyer's independence of professional judgment or with the lawyer-client relationship." As we saw in Part II, this rule requires lawyers to serve their client's interests even when a third party is paying for the representation.

Model Rule 5.4(c) provides that a "lawyer shall not permit a person who employs or pays the lawyer to render legal services for another to direct or regulate the lawyer's professional judgment in rendering such legal services."

3. ***The ABA's View of the LSC Restrictions.*** The ABA issued a Formal Opinion (96–399) on the OCRAA restrictions. The Opinion is critical of the restrictions but does not quite condemn them as forcing lawyers to violate the Model Rules.

The Opinion considered the hardest ethical dilemma to be the one that confronted those lawyers who already represent clients who become ineligible for representation under the OCRAA restrictions. Some legal services lawyers would be confronted with choosing "between their obligations to ineligible clients and their obligations to eligible clients who will not be served if LSC funding is lost. Where retaining an ineligible client or representation would deprive the office of a substantial amount of funding, a legal services lawyer may, but is not required to, withdraw from the prohibited representation under Model Rule 1.16(b)(5)." In a footnote discussing the trade-off between continued representation of existing clients and the loss of LSC funding, the Opinion noted: "Although a lawyer's obligation to remain professionally independent forbids a lawyer to drop an existing client merely because a funding source does not like that client, a lawyer's obligation to provide competent representation may require a lawyer to drop the same client if the retention of the matter would prevent the lawyer from serving other existing clients. The end result for the client would be the same, but the ethical implications would not. The ethical issue is not whether the lawyer decides to withdraw from some matters, but what considerations—convenience or duty to other existing clients—motivate the lawyer's decisions." Do you agree with the Opinion's analysis? As a legal services lawyer, what would you choose?

The choice between abandoning an existing client and loss of LSC funds did not disappear after the early period of adjustment to the new restrictions. Even if an office determined prospectively not to undertake representation of noncitizens, those incarcerated, or those charged with eviction for drug-related offenses, a client's circumstances could change such that he would suddenly become ineligible. In analyzing how to handle such clients, the Opinion concluded:

A legal services lawyer may ask an existing client to agree prospectively to abide by the funding restrictions on what matters the lawyer may handle and what means may be used, as long as the lawyer does not believe that such restrictions will adversely affect the representation. However, a legal services lawyer may not ask a client to consent to limitations on the scope of representation that would in her judgment effectively preclude her from providing competent representation. A fortiori, a legal services lawyer cannot ask an existing client to agree to the future termination of her representation in the event that client becomes ineligible because, for example, of a change in immigration status or incarceration. If such a change in eligibility occurs, however, the lawyer may withdraw under Rule 1.16(b)(5) after balancing the interests of that client against the interests of those existing clients who will not be served if funding is lost.

Do you find the Opinion satisfactory on this point?

The restrictions were challenged, and all but one were upheld by the court of appeals. The government sought Supreme Court review.

LEGAL SERVICES CORP. v. VELAZQUEZ

United States Supreme Court
531 U.S. 533 (2001)

KENNEDY, J:

This suit requires us to decide whether one of the conditions imposed by Congress on the use of LSC funds violates the First Amendment rights of LSC grantees and their clients. [T]he restriction prohibits legal representation funded by recipients of LSC moneys if the representation involves an effort to amend or otherwise challenge existing welfare law. As interpreted by the LSC and by the Government, the restriction prevents an attorney from arguing to a court that a state statute conflicts with a federal statute or that either a state or federal statute by its terms or in its application is violative of the United States Constitution.

The United States and LSC rely on *Rust v. Sullivan,* 500 U.S. 173 (1991), as support for the LSC program restrictions. In *Rust,* Congress established program clinics to provide subsidies for doctors to advise patients on a variety of family planning topics. Congress did not consider abortion to be within its family planning objectives, however, and it forbade doctors employed by the program from discussing abortion with their patients. Recipients of funds under Title X of the Public Health Service Act challenged the Act's restriction that provided that none of the Title X funds appropriated for family planning services could be used in programs where abortion is a method of family planning. The recipients argued that the regulations constituted impermissible viewpoint discrimination favoring an antiabortion position over a pro-abortion approach in the sphere of family planning.

We upheld the law, reasoning that Congress had not discriminated against viewpoints on abortion, but had merely chosen to fund one activity to the exclusion of the other. Title X did not single out a particular idea for suppression because it was dangerous or disfavored; rather, Congress prohibited Title X doctors from counseling that was outside the scope of the project.

The advice from the attorney to the client and the advocacy by the attorney to the courts cannot be classified as governmental speech even under a generous understanding of the concept. In this vital respect this suit is distinguishable from *Rust*.

LSC has advised us, furthermore, that upon determining a question of statutory validity is present in any anticipated or pending case or controversy, the LSC-funded attorney must cease the representation at once. This is true whether the validity issue becomes apparent during initial attorney-client consultations or in the midst of litigation proceedings. A disturbing example of the restriction was discussed during oral argument before the Court. [A]s the LSC advised the Court, if, during litigation, a judge were to ask an LSC attorney whether there was a constitutional concern, the LSC attorney simply could not answer.

An informed, independent judiciary presumes an informed, independent bar. Under § 504(a)(16), however, cases would be presented by LSC attorneys who could not advise the courts of serious questions of statutory validity. The disability is inconsistent with the proposition that attorneys should present all the reasonable and well-grounded arguments necessary for proper resolution of the case. By seeking to prohibit the analysis of certain legal issues and to truncate presentation to the courts, the enactment under review prohibits speech and expression upon which courts must depend for the proper exercise of the judicial power. Congress cannot wrest the law from the Constitution which is its source.

• The restriction imposed by the statute here threatens severe impairment of the judicial function. Section 504(a)(16) sifts out cases presenting constitutional challenges in order to insulate the Government's laws from judicial inquiry. If the restriction on speech and legal advice were to stand, the result would be two tiers of cases. In cases where LSC counsel were attorneys of record, there would be lingering doubt whether the truncated representation had resulted in complete analysis of the case, full advice to the client, and proper presentation to the court. A scheme so inconsistent with accepted separation-of-powers principles is an insufficient basis to sustain or uphold the restriction on speech.

The restriction on speech is even more problematic because in cases where the attorney withdraws from a representation, the client is unlikely to find other counsel. The explicit premise for providing LSC attorneys is the necessity to make available representation to persons financially unable to afford legal assistance. There often will be no alternative source for the client to receive vital information respecting constitutional and statutory rights bearing upon claimed benefits. Thus, with respect to the litigation services Congress has funded, there is no alternative channel for expression of the advocacy Congress seeks to restrict. This is in stark contrast to *Rust*. There, a patient could receive the approved Title X family planning counseling funded by the Government and later could consult an affiliate or independent organization to receive abortion counseling. Unlike indigent clients who seek LSC representation, the patient in *Rust* was not required to forfeit the Government-funded advice when she also received abortion counseling through alternative channels. Because LSC attorneys must withdraw whenever a question of a welfare statute's validity arises, an individual could not obtain joint representation so that the constitutional challenge would be presented by a non-LSC attorney, and other, permitted, arguments advanced by LSC counsel.

Congress was not required to fund an LSC attorney to represent indigent clients; and when it did so, it was not required to fund the whole range of legal representations or relationships. The LSC and the United States, however, in effect ask us to permit Congress to define the scope of the litigation it funds to exclude certain vital theories and ideas.

For the reasons we have set forth, the funding condition is invalid.

[Dissenting opinion omitted.]

NOTES ON VELAZQUEZ

1. ***Who Should Decide Priorities?*** Should the goals and policies of legal services programs be set by lawyers, clients, or governmental actors (including, but not limited to, when government is the source of funding)? In particular, should Congress or legal services lawyers decide on priorities? Does your answer depend on the nature of the issue involved?

2. ***Is Limiting Legal Advice Different from Limiting Medical Advice?*** The Court majority insisted that the LSC restriction on lawyers is different from the restriction on doctors and health care professionals providing advice and services at issue in *Rust v. Sullivan*. The four dissenting justices in *Velazquez* found the distinction insignificant (but would have upheld the restriction on lawyers). In what respect is limiting the advice lawyers can give clients and the types of representation they can provide different from limiting the advice and care that doctors can provide? Is it just that courts depend on lawyers giving clients good advice but no one but patients and their family and friends depends on doctors giving good advice?

3. ***What Does*** Velazquez ***Suggest About the Other LSC Restrictions?*** Because the legal services lawyers chose not to appeal the lower court decision upholding the restrictions, the Court did not have occasion to rule on the other restrictions. Does its reasoning suggest that the Court might find other restrictions problematic?

4. ***Limiting Goals Versus Limiting Methods.*** Are restrictions on issue agendas (e.g., limitations on cases on abortion, compulsory military service, or school desegregation) more or less legitimate than restrictions on how cases can be handled (e.g., no class actions, no Doe plaintiffs)?

C. THE WORK OF LEGAL SERVICES LAWYERS

Topic Overview

In the remaining two sections of this chapter, we examine the work of poverty lawyers through the lens of the dominant problem many face: a scarcity of resources relative to the number of people who need and qualify for subsidized legal services. We will study the dearth of affordable legal services available to persons of modest means in some detail in Part VI of this book. Here we examine how the inadequate number of lawyers relative to the need for legal services affects the work lives of legal services lawyers. We will explore how they envision their work and assess their success, the techniques they adopt to address scarcity, and critical perspectives on whether legal services programs ameliorate the problems that lawyers aspire to solve.

Given the scarce resources, how should offices handle client intake? Should resources be focused on particular issues (e.g. housing) to the exclusion of others (e.g. domestic violence)? Should prospective clients with complex matters be turned away because their cases will take too many resources, or should those with simple matters be turned away because they are more likely to work them out on their own?

The dearth of resources in the face of the never-ending stream of problems creates a variety of quotidian problems for legal services lawyers as well. Forming an effective lawyer-client relationship across linguistic, cultural, and socioeconomic differences is challenging in any circumstance. The difficulties are exacerbated by the need to define the scope of the representation when a single client faces a multitude of legal problems (for example, domestic violence, consumer debt, and impending eviction) and the lawyer may be able or willing to handle only some.

The ABA Formal Opinion 96–399 cautions lawyers about the importance of clarifying the scope of representation: "Before accepting a new client a legal services lawyer subject to LSC funding restrictions must inform the client about all of the restrictions that apply because that lawyer is funded by the LSC, must inform the client that such restrictions would not apply if the lawyer were not funded by the LSC, and must carefully screen the client to ensure that the representation will not endanger funding. A legal services lawyer must inform her new clients that they must maintain their eligibility (i.e., avoid incarceration and maintain an acceptable immigration status) in order to continue the representation. With regard to the restrictions on what matters may be pursued and what means may be used, the lawyer may ask a new client to consent to those restrictions if the lawyer believes that the representation would not be adversely affected by the limitation." As a practical matter, how would you handle the initial interview with a client when you must explain the legal and other limitations on what you can do for the client?

A number of studies based on in-depth interviews with legal services lawyers explore how legal services lawyers adapt to the challenges of their work. In the first study, an ethnography of Chicago legal aid lawyers published in 1982, the scholar Jack Katz found

> However important as a political or moral issue, poverty is presented to legal assistance offices in a stream of individual problems. So long as he or she is poor, a person's civil conduct will rarely affect the interests of more than a small circle of others.

> There is typically no elaborate social network attending problems when they are presented to legal assistance lawyers. The poor seek out lawyers for assistance with personal troubles which are often in or near a crisis state: having been denied public aid, having received an eviction notice, having had utilities shut off, having had a violent domestic argument. In such a practice, it is unusually difficult to treat problems as of far-reaching significance.

> Poor clients may insist their problems are of unsurpassed importance, and their lawyers may agree; but the latter will not be urged to that opinion by adverse parties and opposing counsel. Typical adversaries for legal assistance lawyers include other poor people, as for example, in domestic relations conflicts; small real estate owners, as in disputes between tenants and resident landlords; and the lower echelons of workers in public-aid bureaucracies, retail stores, and debt-collection agencies. A poor person usually will have a great deal to lose from litigation but not enough to make it worthwhile for an adversary to expend substantial legal resources to take it from him.

> Because poverty is taken as a reason for routine treatment by adversaries, opposing counsel, and even courts, it is reasonable for the poor themselves, who live constantly in this

environment, not to expect more than summary service from legal assistance lawyers. The statement by clients "I only came here because I couldn't afford a real lawyer" has become a stock and somewhat bitter joke among legal assistance lawyers.[7]

An ethnography of Chicago legal aid lawyers published in 2011 found no change in many of the same phenomena that Katz found in 1982.[8] One thing, however, had changed: lawyers were less convinced of their ability to do something significant about the problems their clients faced because of the 1996 LSC restrictions on filing impact litigation or engaging in lobbying or other systematic approaches to address the structural causes of the problems of poverty.

> [Our] findings differ significantly from Katz's conclusions about lawyers' motivations. Katz's lawyers tolerated difficulties at work because of their access to litigation. Present-day legal aid lawyers, limited to individual cases, lack the ability to construct their feelings of professional significance around impact litigation.

> For legal aid lawyers today, the realization that they will not be able to effect the change they had envisioned is often connected to turning down large numbers of qualified clients. Rejecting clients is particularly taxing for these lawyers because legal aid offices tend to be the client's last resort.

> The interviewees reported that sustaining empathetic attitudes toward their clients was challenging within the constraints of their practice. Many newcomers discover that their dedication to social justice does not translate into actual compassion for their clients, who at times fail to measure up to their idea of a perfect client. Because most attorneys have middle-class backgrounds and only indirect knowledge of the poor, many find it hard to remain understanding and appreciative of their clients who may not have a middle-class sensibility when it comes to keeping appointments or following up with lawyers' requests.

> At the same time, our interviewees agreed that too much empathy can also be debilitating for lawyers. Several shared stories about their colleagues who got so caught up in caring for their clients that they could no longer do their best as attorneys.

> What do present-day legal aid attorneys do to maintain positive professional identities and mitigate their

---

[7]   JACK KATZ, POOR PEOPLE'S LAWYERS IN TRANSITION (1982).

[8]   Marina Zaloznaya & Laura Beth Nielsen, *Mechanisms and Consequences of Professional Marginality: The Case of Poverty Lawyers Revisited*, 36 LAW & SOC. INQUIRY 919 (2011).

marginalization in a context in which impact litigation is no longer accessible? About half of the attorneys who had been in practice for more than three years made their peace with the routine character of their work by finding other benefits in legal aid practice. The emphasis on lifestyle advantages associated with working in legal aid, such as not having to bill hours, spending time at home with families, and maintaining hobbies. These respondents saw their positive impact on individuals' lives an added benefit of the job.

More than half of long-term lawyers, however, held onto the idea of making a positive difference in a world riddled with inequalities. [They frame] the importance of legal aid in terms of helping specific individuals rather than bringing about abstract socioeconomic justice. Their stories were ones of initial disappointment and eventual realization that their work was just as, if not more, important than effecting large-scale change through litigation.[9]

Another in-depth study of legal services lawyers and their clients found that both lawyers and clients found deep satisfaction in their professional work and interaction. One lawyer said, "I mean, am I changing the world? No. But the revolution still isn't happening and at some basic level this office, legal aid programs, and myself personally make a difference in people's lives. I love this job, this is a great job. And we do make a difference, both individually and on issues that affect our client population. And *but for* the work we did, things would be considerably worse for our clients." A client in the same study said, "I guess without legal service I wouldn't be sitting here. So I'm really grateful for that. That was like a load of pressure—you can't imagine—off of me. I couldn't deal with anything else until, you know, until that assurance. I needed a lawyer, somebody to represent me or to speak for me."[10]

NOTES ON THE WORK OF LEGAL SERVICES LAWYERS

1. *What Is the Role of the Poverty Lawyer?* Notice the extent to which the studies above reflect a range of opinions on whether the role of a lawyer for the poor should be more in the nature of social work or legal work, community organizer or service provider, reformer or revolutionary. How do you imagine the aspirations and disappointments of legal services lawyers are reflected in their evolving conception of their role?

---

[9] *Id.*

[10] COREY S. SHDAIMAH, NEGOTIATING JUSTICE: PROGRESSIVE LAWYERING, LOW-INCOME CLIENTS, AND THE QUEST FOR SOCIAL CHANGE 45–46, 67 (2009).

2. ***Would Changes in the Structure and Funding of Legal Services Make a Difference?*** To what extent do you believe that the challenges of legal services practice described in the excerpts above are inherent in the nature of a poverty law practice, and to what extent do you believe that changes in the structure and funding of legal services could ameliorate them?

3. ***Is It Poverty or Is It Law?*** Some challenges encountered by legal services lawyers are also encountered by those in other professions whose job it is to work with people whose problems may be caused or exacerbated by poverty. Those professions include teachers, social workers, health care practitioners, and clergy. Are there aspects of being a lawyer that make it more difficult to find satisfaction in working in poor communities as compared to other professions' experience? What could lawyers learn from other professions about these issues?

* * *

The scarcity of funds to support civil legal assistance for the poor has spawned a number of powerful critiques of the work of legal services lawyers. One concerns the process by which legal services lawyers decide whom to represent and whom to turn away, and what representation to provide for those clients whom the lawyer does undertake to represent. At the broadest level, some have argued that, by choice or by circumstances, legal services lawyers have become fundamentally conservative, putting band-aids on festering social wounds. They settle for results that are inadequate even to ameliorate client problems, let alone solve them. They are isolated from client communities, and therefore lack a guiding vision and expertise about how to conduct client matters and address client needs. They miss opportunities to work with nonlawyers in a multidisciplinary way to solve social problems. They are not properly accountable to their clients because the clients are not paying their fees or sufficiently involved in decision-making about the work. The critique and prescription for better legal service have not fundamentally changed since the following article was published in 1970:

PRACTICING LAW FOR POOR PEOPLE
Stephen Wexler
79 Yale Law Journal 1049 (1970)

Poverty will not be stopped by people who are not poor. If poverty is stopped, it will be stopped by poor people. And poor people can stop poverty only if they work at it together. The lawyer who wants to serve poor people must put his skills to the task of helping poor people organize themselves. This is not the traditional use of a lawyer's skills; in many ways it violates some of the basic tenets of the profession.

If all the lawyers in the country worked full time, they could not deal with even the articulated legal problems of the poor. And even if somehow lawyers could deal with those articulated problems, they would not change very much the tangle of unarticulated legal troubles in which poor people live. In this setting the object of practicing poverty law must be to organize poor people, rather than to solve their legal problems. The proper job for a poor people's lawyer is helping poor people to organize themselves to change things so that either no one is poor or (less radically) so that poverty does not entail misery.

Two major touchstones of traditional legal practice—the solving of legal problems and the one-to-one relationship between attorney and client—are either not relevant to poor people or harmful to them. Traditional practice hurts poor people by isolating them from each other, and fails to meet their need for a lawyer by completely misunderstanding that need. The lawyer for poor individuals is likely, whether he wins cases or not, to leave his clients precisely where he found them, except that they will have developed a dependency on his skills to smooth out the roughest spots in their lives.

If organizing is the object of a poverty practice, what are the methods for achieving that object? One method by which an existing organization can be strengthened is for a lawyer to refuse to handle matters for individuals not in the organization.

Selection of clients is only the first step; the cornerstone of a practice is the kind of service a lawyer provides for his clients. The hallmark of an effective poor people's practice is that the lawyer does not do anything for his clients that they can do or be taught to do for themselves.

* * *

Lawyers and community organizers have explored a number of ways to be effective in their shared effort to address social problems. The following essay is by a lawyer with practice experience as both a legal services lawyer and a lawyer for other organizations.

LAW AND ORGANIZING FROM THE PERSPECTIVE OF ORGANIZERS: FINDING A SHARED THEORY OF SOCIAL CHANGE

Betty Hung
1 Los Angeles Public Interest Law Journal 4 (2009)

[L]egal strategies, when pursued in combination with and in support of grassroots organizing campaigns, are more effective than legal strategies alone in both empowering communities and achieving social justice goals. In practice, however, tensions between lawyers and organizers persist and, at times, hinder campaigns for social justice. Rather than building the power of marginalized communities, lawyers tend to create dependency on lawyers and legal strategies without altering structural inequalities and the status quo.

The key to effective partnerships in social justice movements is a shared theory of social change based on the primacy of affected community members. Community members—not lawyers or organizers— should lead and be at the center of efforts seeking to improve their lives. Organizers and lawyers can and should find common ground as facilitators, supporters, and allies of affected community members.

According to organizers, the decision to involve lawyers in their organizing campaigns is contextual and based on strategic considerations, namely whether legal strategies can help to advance a campaign. [O]rganizers uniformly [say] that they view legal strategies, including litigation, legal community education, and legislative advocacy, as just one of multiple components that comprise a campaign.

The key strategic questions that organizers consider in deliberating whether to involve lawyers include: Will legal tactics put *pressure* on the organizing targets? Will legal tactics help to enhance the *legitimacy* of the grievances against the target? Will lawyers and legal tactics provide *support for organizers* by defending them from attacks, providing them with legal guidance, or helping to build trust and credibility with members? Will lawyers and legal tactics provide *support for members* by defending them from attacks, educating them about their legal rights, or providing support through direct legal services? Will legal tactics generate *publicity* and *public support* that will put pressure on the targets and cultivate allies, alliances, and support for the campaign? Will legal support help to *institutionalize* and *enforce* hard fought victories?

[Organizers are dismayed that] lawyers—even those who profess to value the primary role of community organizing in social justice struggles—privilege litigation and other legal strategies at the expense of organizing. They also [say] lawyers often do not communicate effectively with clients or organizers about the status of legal advocacy. Organizers commented that members who have pending cases often complain that attorneys do not keep them updated about their cases and/or that they did not understand fully what the attorneys told them. The members, who sometimes are intimidated by the attorneys, will then ask the organizers, whom they trust, to explain what is going on with their cases. All too often, however, organizers feel that the lawyers have not apprised them of the status of the case. When organizers ask the attorneys, often on behalf of the members/clients, for updates on the legal advocacy, they are told that attorney-client privilege prevents disclosure of such information. The result is that organizers and members both feel disempowered.

In essence, affected community members—not lawyers or organizers—should be in the lead and at the center of campaigns for social justice. In my experience, two additional factors are essential to achieve authentic relationships of trust and solidarity. First, there must be an understanding and appreciation of the particular experiences, skills, and knowledge that each person—whether an organizer, lawyer, or community member—brings to the table. It entails recognition that multiple strategies—organizing, legal, research, media, alliance building—are necessary to challenge existing institutions and power structures and to shift power to the hands of those who are marginalized. Organizing, like lawyering, is a skilled profession and craft and should be valued. Most importantly, community members themselves are the "experts" on the conditions in which they live and work and, with their first hand knowledge and experience, possess wisdom and insight into what type of social transformation is necessary and the best means to get there. In offering and honoring their respective knowledge, experience, and skills, community members, organizers, and lawyers can establish relationships based on equality and mutual respect.

Second, there is a human dimension to movement building that is integral to developing trust. In my years of working with garment workers, immigrant youth, taxi drivers, and car wash workers, a fundamental lesson I have learned is to approach and respect community members first and foremost as human beings and partners in a shared struggle for social change. People are not simply "clients" or "members" to be organized, but rather individuals with their own histories and hopes for achieving a measure of justice. Trust is built when community members feel that a relationship with lawyers or organizers is not about expediency or utilitarianism in achieving campaign goals, but is based on true solidarity and friendship.

NOTES ON WEXLER AND HUNG

1. **What Should Poverty Lawyers Aspire to Do?** Are you persuaded by Wexler's account of the nature of poverty law practice? Are you persuaded by his critique of how lawyers are trained to think about problems? Do you agree with his proposal? Is Hung's approach a good response to his critique?

2. **Who Should Decide?** What are the advantages and disadvantages of relying on the judgments of legal services lawyers in determining what will most benefit the client population? Does your answer to this question, informed by Wexler's and Hung's arguments, suggest you might revise your answer to the question we considered above about whether Congress, legal services program boards of directors, individual legal services lawyers, or clients should decide how to allocate scarce resources? How would a client-directed process of priority setting be implemented?

3. ***Can an LSC-Funded Lawyer Be an Effective Organizer?*** If an LSC-funded lawyer were convinced by Wexler and Hung arguments, would the OCRAA restrictions pose an obstacle to implementing their suggestions?

* * *

A distinctive innovation in legal services practice has been to re-imagine the nature of the attorney-client relationship to enable lawyers to help clients without investing much time or other resources. Many legal aid programs throughout the country operate self-help programs independently or in conjunction with courts. These websites and kiosks with touch-screen computers provide pro se litigants and others needing legal assistance with pleadings and access to other legal services, such as help with filing for the Earned Income Tax Credit. The programs are explained by the former head of the Legal Services Corporation:

> Some programs provide only access to information about the law, legal rights, and the legal process. Other programs actually provide individualized legal advice and often provide also legal assistance in drafting documents and advice about how to pursue cases.

> A critical part of expanding access has focused on a range of limited legal assistance initiatives to provide less than extended representation to clients who either do not need such extended representation in order to solve their legal problems or live in areas without access to lawyers or entities available to provide extended representation. Many legal aid programs now operate legal hotlines, which enable low-income persons who believe they have a legal problem to speak by telephone to a skilled attorney or paralegal and receive advice and brief service. Legal hotlines may provide answers to clients' legal questions, analysis of clients' legal problems, and advice on solving those problems so that the client can resolve the problem with the information from phone consultation.[11]

Is the emphasis on self-help a necessary evil of scarce resources or, instead, a step toward enabling clients to achieve the kind of self-reliance that Wexler called for? Should the goal of every legal aid lawyer be to provide the most thorough and comprehensive service possible? Should legal services lawyers aspire to provide the same "no stone left unturned" standard of service that corporate clients demand (and pay for) from their lawyers?

---

[11] Alan W. Houseman, *The Future of Civil Legal Aid: A National Perspective*, 10 UNIV. D.C. L. REV. 35 (2007).

D. THE IMPACT OF LEGAL SERVICES PROGRAMS

The political controversy about legal aid to the poor, combined with the constant threat of drastic cuts in government and private funding, have produced a longstanding debate over the impact and value of subsidized legal services. Moreover, the need to triage cases and turn away thousands or tens of thousands of eligible prospective clients every year has prompted legal services lawyers to think about how to allocate their scarce time and resources.

A fundamental premise of free legal services to poor people is that legal assistance will leave the client better off than if the client had no lawyer. Although the Supreme Court in *Lassiter* rejected the contention that a lawyer is necessary to ensure due process of law in civil cases, lawyers tend to believe that it makes a difference whether you have a lawyer. In a world of scarce resources, however, it is important to think about where having a lawyer makes the most difference.

Does Legal Assistance Matter?

Empirical studies of legal assistance programs reach contrasting conclusions about whether people who are represented by lawyers get better results than those who represent themselves. What light do the following studies shed on the goals and methods of legal aid programs?

Two studies of random samples of people needing legal assistance in prevention of eviction found legal representation made a positive difference. One tested the effect of providing legal representation to low-income tenants in New York City's Housing Court.[12] Almost all landlords in Housing Court are represented by lawyers, but the vast majority of tenants are not. The study was a randomized experiment involving a treatment group of legal aid-eligible tenants that was targeted to receive legal counsel through a pro bono project and a control group that was not. The study found that the tenants with legal representation experienced significantly more beneficial outcomes than their counterparts who did not have legal representation, independent of the merits of the case. The study also found that giving tenants lawyers imposed only modest time delays or other administrative burdens on the court system and may even have been more efficient for the courts. Although judgments were issued against 52% of those without assistance, only approximately 32% of those with assistance had judgments against them. Similar differences appear in the percentage of warrants for eviction and the percentage of stipulations for rent abatements and repairs. The cases in which the tenant received legal assistance took longer to resolve (about 111 days

---

[12] Carroll Seron, Gregg Van Ryzin, Martin Frankel, & Jean Kovath, *The Impact of Legal Counsel on Outcomes for Poor Tenants in New York City's Housing Court: Results of a Randomized Experiment*, 35 LAW & SOCIETY REV. 419 (2003).

compared to 82 days), but the cases with lawyers did not generate significantly more court appearances or motions than those in which the litigant did not receive legal assistance. Because the study randomly assigned lawyers, these differences in outcomes can be attributed solely to the presence of legal counsel and are independent of the merits of the case. The presence of an attorney at the tenant's side may actually enhance court efficiency by reducing the number of motions, particularly post-judgment motions.[13] Another more recent study of people facing eviction reached similar conclusions: Those who were represented by a lawyer avoided eviction, paid less back rent, and did better on other outcome measures and without significant cost to the court system, although their cases did take somewhat longer to resolve.[14]

These studies did not directly answer the question of what specifically the lawyers did that produced the positive results. However, the lawyers interviewed in the first study identified four tasks that lawyers do that typically make a difference: (1) determining what rent is owed; (2) negotiating a reasonable time period for payment when money is owed; (3) negotiating or litigating when, e.g., the housing agency has not issued the full amount of arrears, has issued them to the wrong landlord, or when the client qualifies for a special grant to cover rent; and, (4) obtaining abatements of rent when repairs were not completed in a timely manner.[15]

A third study suggests that the type of proceeding and the type of legal assistance may matter to whether legal representation produces better outcomes for clients than clients achieve proceeding pro se. This study assessed the effectiveness of assistance from the Harvard Legal Aid Bureau (HLAB), a clinical program at Harvard Law School, in filing appeals of denials of unemployment benefits in the Massachusetts Unemployment Appeals Bureau.[16] On average, 76% of claimants who received an offer of representation prevailed in their first-level appeals, while 72% of those who did not receive an offer prevailed. This difference is not statistically significant. Cases in which the claimant received an offer of legal assistance took a statistically significant 16 days longer to resolve than those not receiving an offer of assistance.

These studies suggest a number of factors may explain when legal representation makes a difference to client outcomes. One concerns the nature of the proceeding. In a process in which the judge or arbiter

---

[13] Id.

[14] D. James Greiner, Cassandra Wolos Pattanayak, & Jonathan Hennessey, *The Limits of Unbundled Legal Assistance: A Randomized Study in a Massachusetts District Court and Prospects for the Future*, 126 HARV. L. REV. 901 (2013).

[15] Id.

[16] D. James Greiner & Cassandra Wolos Pattanayak, *Randomized Evaluation in Legal Assistance: What Difference Does Representation (Offer and Actual Use) Make?*, 121 YALE L.J. 2118 (2012).

shoulders the burden of ensuring that all relevant documentary and witness evidence is gathered and considered (as in the Massachusetts Unemployment Appeals Bureau), having a lawyer may not make as much of a difference as a lawyer makes in a traditional court system. Second, when the process and legal standards are relatively simple, litigants may be able to represent themselves reasonably effectively. Third, where a legal process or legal rules are complex, it may matter whether the litigant is represented by an expert in the law as opposed to a law student. Fourth, it appears that lawyers make more of a difference after cases are screened at the intake stage through providing information and requiring prospective clients to take initial steps to determine whether they need legal assistance.

NOTES ON THE IMPACT OF LEGAL ASSISTANCE

1. ***What Explains the Different Findings?*** Why do you suppose that two studies found that lawyers helped clients in housing court and the other found that lawyers did not clearly help clients in unemployment appeals? Might it be that housing court procedures are more complex and therefore require a lawyer and unemployment appeals do not? Might it be that negotiating with landlords for a good resolution is harder without a lawyer than is negotiating for unemployment insurance benefits? What else might explain the difference?

2. ***Policy Implications.*** What are the policy implications of these studies? If reducing complexity of law and procedure reduces the need for lawyers, should courts and advocates for the poor aim to reduce complexity? If screening cases at the intake stage leads to better results for those litigants who proceed past the intake stage, what should legal services lawyers do? What other policies would you recommend in light of these studies?

E. SUMMARY

In this chapter, we studied the nature, regulation, and funding of civil legal services programs, with particular emphasis on the limits imposed by Congress through the Legal Services Corporation on what law offices that receive LSC funding can do and who they can represent. We examined the work of legal services lawyers, and a variety of philosophies lawyers have about how to provide the best quality legal service and to empower clients to address the legal problems they face. We considered the way in which legal services work is affected by the pervasive problem of too many prospective clients relative to the available legal resources, and we surveyed some of the approaches legal aid lawyers have adopted to deal with the shortage of resources and to provide adequate representation to underserved clients. Lastly, we considered empirical studies of the impact of subsidized legal services for clients.

CHAPTER 29

PUBLIC INTEREST LAW

■ ■ ■

A. INTRODUCTION

This chapter examines lawyers who work in what are commonly called public interest law organizations, defined here as nonprofit organizations that seek to serve disadvantaged constituencies and/or some vision of the public good. As we'll see throughout the following materials, the definition of public interest law has been the subject of a good deal of controversy over several decades, and the term continues to be used in a variety of ways that are not entirely consistent. We explore these definitional issues and why they matter. We also consider how and why this form of practice emerged, how it relates to larger political struggles over social change and the roles of lawyers in such efforts, and the connection between this form of practice and access to justice.

This chapter begins by considering the definition of public interest law, the concept's malleability, and how, over the past several decades, the term has been applied to a broad set of strategies and causes. We compare the term "public interest lawyer" with a related and overlapping concept of "cause lawyer" and explore the relationship between cause lawyering and conventional practice. We then consider some criticisms of public interest law leveled by critics from the political left and right.

B. WHAT IS PUBLIC INTEREST LAW?

The term public interest law is used in many different ways. As one scholar has noted, "Today, people use the term 'public interest' law as a gloss for a wide range of sometimes contradictory lawyering categories":

> Some people define "public interest" law as lawyering for the poor. Some define it as "cause" lawyering. Others think of it as lawyering specifically with a left wing or politically progressive agenda. Still others define the term as encompassing jobs in the public and nonprofit sectors. This last definition equates "public interest" law with law practiced in organizational forms in which

lawyers do not take fees for their legal services from their clients.[1]

In the materials that follow, we will try to distinguish among these various definitions of public interest law and explain how definitional issues relate to fundamental questions about the roles of lawyers in society and the moral content of lawyers' work.

The following excerpt sketches the early history of the term's use and some criticisms of the concept's premises:

DEFINING PUBLIC INTEREST LAWYERING
Alan Chen and Scott Cummings
Public Interest Lawyering: A Contemporary Perspective (2012)

For at least the last century, lawyers have sought to deploy their legal skill to advance the interests of individual clients or social groups deemed less powerful: legal aid lawyers from the early twentieth century who dispensed free legal services to aid the urban poor; so-called "country lawyers" who provided professional charity in order to help their less fortunate neighbors; and activist lawyers who defended war protesters, labor organizers, and racial minorities suffering discrimination.

Yet it was not until the 1960s that the term "public interest law" was coined in a self-conscious effort to describe a nascent movement to use legal advocacy, primarily litigation, to advance a liberal political agenda associated primarily with the protection and expansion of rights for racial minorities, the poor, women, and other disadvantaged groups, while also providing collective goods, like a clean environment. At the outset of the U.S. public interest law movement, its definition was sometimes couched in the language of market failure. In a classic study from the 1970s, public interest law was defined as "activity that (1) is undertaken by an organization in the voluntary sector; (2) provides fuller representation of underrepresented interests (would produce external benefits if successful); and (3) involves the use of law instruments, primarily litigation." The study drew upon economic analysis to elaborate the concept of "external benefits," which was grounded in efficiency—putting productive resources "to their most 'valuable' uses"—and equity—ensuring that the distribution of the resulting goods and services was fair. The central claim was that public interest law was activity that "if it is successful, will bring about significant external gross benefits to some persons; that is, the activity provides more complete representation for some interest that is underrepresented in the sense that the interest has

---

[1]   Susan D. Carle, *Re-Valuing Lawyering for Middle-Income Clients,* 70 FORDHAM L. REV. 719, 729–30 (2001).

not been fully transmitted through either the private market or governmental channels."[2]

It was this notion of "underrepresentation" that informed other definitional efforts. For Gordon Harrison and Sanford Jaffe, the Ford Foundation program officers who designed and executed the foundation's initial PIL [Public Interest Law] funding initiative (and one of the first to use the term), public interest law was "the representation of the underrepresented in American society."[3] This included both the provision of lawyers to "poor or otherwise deprived individuals who are unable to hire counsel," as well as legal actions in the defense of "broad collective interests"—such as on behalf of "consumer protection and environmental quality"—"for the benefit of large classes of people" who could not individually afford the cost of mounting lawsuits and who could not easily organize collectively to advance their political interests. Nan Aron, writing about public interest law at the end of the 1980s, articulated a similar position:

> Public interest law is the name given to efforts to *provide legal representation to interests that historically have been unrepresented or underrepresented* in the legal process. Philosophically, public interest law rests on the assumption that many significant segments of society are not adequately represented in the courts, Congress, or the administrative agencies because they are either too poor or too diffuse to obtain legal representation in the marketplace.[4]

The classic definition, rooted in underrepresentation, came under attack from two directions. Beginning in the 1970s, and gaining momentum in the 1980s, the emergent conservative movement took issue with both the efficiency and equity rationales for public interest law. In terms of efficiency, conservatives argued that it was not obvious that regulation benefitted society at large, rather than simply making distributional choices. Thus, environmental regulation could have the effect of reducing jobs, or consumer regulation might increase prices. Without aggregating individual preferences for a clean environment and jobs, for consumer safety and low prices, it was not clear *ex ante* what the optimal social welfare function was. The concept of equity was indeterminate as well. What qualified as an underrepresented group? Conservatives argued that the concept of underrepresentation was politically contingent and changed over time. Whether or not one agreed

---

[2] Burton A. Weisbrod, *Conceptual Perspective on the Public Interest: An Economic Analysis, in* PUBLIC INTEREST LAW: AN ECONOMIC AND INSTITUTIONAL ANALYSIS 10–12, 22 (Burton A. Weisbrod, Joel F. Handler & Neil K. Komesar et al. eds., 1978).

[3] Gordon Harrison & Sanford M. Jaffe, *Public Interest Law Firms: New Voices for New Constituencies*, 58 A.B.A. J. 459, 459 (1972).

[4] NAN ARON, LIBERTY AND JUSTICE FOR ALL: PUBLIC INTEREST LAW IN THE 1980S AND BEYOND 3 (1989) (emphasis added).

with the conservative framing, it highlighted a fundamental tension in equity conceptions of public interest law: on contested issues of public policy, one group's benefit could be construed as another's burden.

As conservatives challenged the meaning of public interest law from the right, critics on the left challenged its practice—and offered new theories to supplant what many viewed as the outmoded and politically ineffective model of litigation-centered reform embodied in the conventional definition of public interest law. Beginning in the 1980s, new theories emerged with an impressive array of new labels: community lawyering, critical lawyering, facilitative lawyering, political lawyering, progressive lawyering, rebellious lawyering, third dimensional lawyering, law and organizing, and legal pragmatism—to name some of the most prominent. Although these theories varied considerably, they shared the concern that rights-based efforts, by themselves, were inadequate to the task of radical social transformation. All of these efforts rested upon a liberal discomfort with lawyer-led strategies that undercut genuine participatory democracy and risked inflicting a double-marginalization on clients: disempowered by society and then by the very lawyers who purported to act on their behalf. This critique of "lawyer domination" was the foundation for the most powerful left critique of public interest law— one that corresponded to the right-wing attack on public interest law as democratically unaccountable.

Despite all the critiques of its political and conceptual coherence, the use of "public interest" as a rubric for a distinctive, equality-enhancing form of lawyering has shown great resilience. Although it is unavoidably contested, public interest law remains the term-of-choice for U.S. practitioners, and has taken root in emerging democracies around the world.

NOTES ON CHEN AND CUMMINGS

1. *What Is the Public Interest?* Is a public interest lawyer one who represents the public's interest? Would it be possible for everyone to agree on what types of lawyers' work benefit the public as a whole? Do questions about what serves the public interest inevitably generate conflict among competing visions of the public good? If a public interest lawyer is not a lawyer who advocates for the public good, what is she?

2. *The Underrepresentation Rationale.* Most definitions of public interest law incorporate the idea of serving interests that are underrepresented in the private market for legal services or in the political process. What exactly does it mean to be underrepresented? The Chen and Cummings excerpt identifies two ways in which a group or cause might be underrepresented: 1) because they are too poor to afford counsel, or 2) because they are too diffuse to organize effectively to pursue their collective interests. People who do not have enough money to hire lawyers clearly meet

the first part of this definition. What types of interests and groups qualify under the second part? This rationale has been sometimes been invoked to cover consumer and environmental advocacy within the definition of public interest law. Does it matter that these two groups cut across socio-economic lines and include some wealthy people?

3. ***Does It Matter Why Interests Are Underrepresented?*** Do lawyers who represent groups that find it difficult to find representation because their views or conduct are abhorrent—such as Nazis, pedophiles, terrorists, and serial killers—fall within a definition of public interest law that turns on underrepresentation?[5] If not why not? Does your answer depend on the type of work performed for the client?

4. ***Can Public Interest Lawyers Oppose One Another?*** Is it problematic that "underrepresented" interests might sometimes come into conflict with one another? When that happens, are both sets of opposing advocates still public interest lawyers?

5. ***"Private Public Interest Law"?*** Can a lawyer who collects fees for her services be a public interest lawyer? If not, why not? If so, under what circumstances? Notice that the Weisbrod definition quoted at the beginning of the Chen & Cummings excerpt specifies that public interest law is by definition in the "voluntary" (nonprofit) sector. However, not all definitions of public interest law include that criterion. Some lawyers in private practice claim that their firms prioritize service to underrepresented constituencies over profitability and therefore that deserve the public interest law label. Such firms, sometimes called "private public interest law firms," generally rely on fees awarded pursuant to fee-shifting statutes rather than charitable donations to keep their practices afloat.[6]

6. ***Are Some Plaintiffs' Lawyers Public Interest Lawyers?*** Some plaintiffs' lawyers challenge corporate practices on behalf of large, disorganized and diffuse groups of accident victims, consumers, and investors who could not individually afford the cost of pursuing lawsuits. The clients in these lawsuits therefore appear to fit the second part of the concept of underrepresentation described in the Chen & Cummings excerpt. Moreover, the plaintiffs' lawyers in these lawsuits typically view themselves as advocates for the little guy. But contingency fee arrangements and fee shifting statutes sometimes make it possible for entrepreneurial plaintiffs' lawyers to earn very large fees for such work. Are these lawyers public interest lawyers? If not, why not?

* * *

---

[5] This question comes from ALAN K. CHEN & SCOTT L. CUMMINGS, PUBLIC INTEREST LAWYERING: A CONTEMPORARY PERSPECTIVE 14 (2013).

[6] For a discussion of this model, see Scott Cummings & Ann Southworth, *Between Profit and Principle: The Private Public Interest Law Firm*, in PRIVATE LAWYERS AND THE PUBLIC INTEREST: THE EVOLVING ROLE OF PRO BONO IN THE LEGAL PROFESSION (Robert Granfield & Lynn Mather, eds, 2009).

The following excerpt explains how advocates associated with conservative and libertarian causes adapted the form and rhetoric of public interest law to advance their own public policy objectives, many of which the founders of the public interest law movement in the late 1960s and early 1970s would have opposed. The article explores how lawyers of the political left and right now battle one another in the courts, legislatures, and media—while all claiming to do so under the banner of public interest law.

CONSERVATIVE LAWYERS AND THE CONTEST OVER THE MEANING OF "PUBLIC INTEREST LAW"

Ann Southworth
52 U.C.L.A. Law Review 1223 (2005)

The term "public interest law" first appeared in the late 1960s and initially was associated almost exclusively with liberal causes. When conservative public interest lawyers declared their entrance into the political scene in the mid-1970s, their critics portrayed them as cheeky challengers of left legal activists, not the same breed of professional. Since then, however, conservative and libertarian legal advocacy groups have multiplied, and the idea that these organizations and their lawyers might be similar in important respects to those of the liberal public interest law movement has gained currency. Conservative and libertarian lawyers created a vibrant, highly differentiated field of conservative legal advocacy organizations modeled on liberal public interest law firms (PILFs) and generated substantial competition among legal advocacy groups of the left and right over the meaning of "public interest law."

The creation of conservative PILFs during the past three decades was just one part of a larger phenomenon of conservative institution building that began around the time of Barry Goldwater's failed 1964 presidential bid. That campaign was "the first political expression of a rising conservative movement" that had intellectual roots in the work of traditionalists, classical liberal economists, and anticommunists. Despite substantial contradictions among these intellectual currents, they came together in opposition to the liberal establishment, which conservatives blamed for Goldwater's overwhelming defeat. This powerful coalition of religious conservatives, libertarians, business interests, and nationalists united behind the task of building a conservative infrastructure—a "counter-establishment"—to help win hearts and minds for conservative ideas.

Lawyers were particularly interesting participants in the creation of this organizational field, not only because they initiated the enterprises and recruited patrons, but also because they had a distinctive stake in its success. The liberal public interest law movement of the 1960s and 1970s fundamentally challenged traditional conceptions of law and the role of lawyers in its operation. The very label, "public interest lawyer," asserted moral superiority over attorneys who represented private clients— particularly corporate clients—in conventional practices. Moreover, the moral activism that the new public interest lawyers posed as the alternative to conventional value-neutral practice norms supported causes that many conservatives did not favor. Conservative public interest law groups would vindicate the notion that conservatives, like liberals, could field a cadre of principled crusaders. Although the contest took the shape of investment in organizations, it also was a war of ideas about what types of practice were legitimate and what constituted worthy public service.

The conservative public interest law movement was a direct response to the creation of public interest law organizations in the late 1960s and 1970s and to the legal and social changes these groups helped produce. The success of these organizations presented an obvious counterstrategy for conservatives: to beat liberals at their own game by creating public interest law groups to speak for competing values and constituencies. They adopted the organizational form and rhetoric of public interest law to serve sometimes conflicting causes of the conservative movement.

Public interest law organizations claimed to represent people whose interests were so diffuse that they fell outside the marketplace for legal services. Although there was considerable disagreement about the meaning and theoretical justification for this organizational form, public interest lawyers generally asserted that new types of organizations and lawyers were necessary to respond to the deficiencies of pluralism by representing groups whose interests were underrepresented in administrative agencies and courts. Public interest law groups would open administrative agencies' procedures to participation by the citizens they were supposed to benefit. They would expand the repertoire of citizen activists to include direct and significant participation in the central decision making processes of corporations and government bureaucracies, with recourse to administrative hearings and courts when such access was denied.

Dozens of public interest law organizations were created in the late 1960s and early 1970s to pursue social change through courts, legislatures, and administrative agencies. By 1976, there were over ninety such organizations employing over 600 attorneys, many of them supported by the Ford Foundation. Public interest law groups achieved highly publicized successes, benefit[ting] from a receptive judiciary during the Warren era and from loosening standards regarding standing, ripeness, sovereign immunity, and private rights of action.

Galvanized by the achievements of this new breed of lawyers and their organizations, some conservatives responded by attacking the premises of the movement. Some asserted that public interest law groups undermined democratic processes by replacing the decisions of elected officials with edicts from the courts, and some, including many religious conservatives, rejected the rights discourse of the new public interest litigation. However, conservatives also sought to create their own organizations with similar form and opposing mission. The organizational counterattack began with business-oriented groups. Christian evangelicals, whose ambivalence about engaging with secular law delayed their participation in legal rights advocacy, took up the challenge soon thereafter.

The field of conservative public interest law is now quite well developed, with distinct constituencies of conservatives represented by different organizations and lawyers. Where there once were a few regional conservative organizations representing the business perspective on regulatory matters, there now are dozens of groups, including some libertarian organizations that attempt to distance themselves from large business interests. The views of Christian evangelicals are now advocated by many groups representing particular interests, differentiated along theological lines and by issue. In addition to the conservative groups that were established in the 1970s, there now are newer specialized legal advocacy groups focusing on affirmative action, home schooling, pornography, property rights, school vouchers, tort reform, and gun ownership. Organizations also distinguish themselves from one another according to the types of strategies pursued—for example, direct representation versus amicus participation, grassroots activism versus insider networking, and research targeted at Congress and the media versus scholarly publications directed primarily at professors and judges. Conservative and libertarian PILFs sometimes oppose one another and occasionally even form alliances with liberal PILFs.

During the past three decades, as conservatives have deployed an organizational model born of liberal legal activism to pursue different social and political goals, they have unsettled conventions and assumptions about public interest practice, increased competition in the courts, agencies, and legislatures, and gained the upper hand in public policy debates. In the late 1960s, the public interest law movement was almost synonymous with left legal activism. Today dozens of conservative and libertarian organizations call themselves "public interest law" groups. Of the fifty-three organizations that described themselves using the words "public interest law" or "public interest legal" in briefs filed in the U.S. Supreme Court from 2000 through 2004, twenty-one were conservative or libertarian. In accordance with the prescription [of one conservative strategist during the early 1980s], conservative and libertarian groups have "challenged the moral monopoly . . . enjoyed by traditional public interest lawyers and their allies"[7] and stripped the term "public interest law" of its exclusively left-oriented connotations.

This competition between PILFs of the left and right has made public policy formation more complicated and antagonistic and has contributed to acrimony over judicial nominations. It also has laid bare an essential truth about public interest law—that advocates for [nonprofit] law reform organizations, all viewing themselves as public interest lawyers, may disagree fundamentally about what the public interest requires.

NOTES ON SOUTHWORTH

1. **Do Conservative Groups Fit the Definition of Public Interest Law?** Is Southworth correct to characterize religious conservative and libertarian organizations as public interest law groups for causes of the political right? If not, how would you distinguish them from organizations that you do think qualify as public interest law groups?

2. **Subsequent Research on the Use of "Public Interest Law" in Supreme Court Briefs**. In a follow-up study of discourse around public interest law, Southworth again examined how various organizations use the phrase "public interest law" or "public interest legal" to describe themselves in U.S. Supreme Court briefs. She found that from 1970 through 2011, 1281 briefs were submitted by organizations that called themselves "public interest law/legal" organizations Of those 1281 briefs, 812—almost two-thirds—were filed by groups that pursued conservative and libertarian missions.[8]

Does that finding suggest that conservative and libertarian groups think it's important to be regarded as public interest law groups by the Court and other potential audiences for their briefs, including, perhaps, their own members and supporters? If so, why?

3. **Does the Label Matter?** Southworth describes this struggle over use of the phrase "public interest law" as a "frame contest" with significant consequences:

> The contest over the meaning of public interest law is symbolically important because the phrase conveys approval; the organizations, activities, and lawyers associated with the term are understood to enhance access to justice, or to advance some other vision of the public good. This struggle over discourse also carries direct and practical implications because financial benefits—such as law school scholarship eligibility, summer funding, loan forgiveness, and pro bono credit—sometimes turn

---

[7]　See Michael Horowitz, The Public Interest Law Movement: An Analysis With Special Reference to the Role and Practices of Conservative Public Interest Law Firms 1 (n.d.) (unpublished memorandum) (on file with authors).

[8]　Ann Southworth, *What is Public Interest Law? Empirical Perspectives on an Old Question*, 62 DEPAUL L. REV. 493 (2013).

on the definition of public interest law. Thus, how the phrase is used and defined is integrally related to the allocation of some types of legitimacy and resources within the American legal profession. Moreover, this contest over framing may have significant consequences for judicial decision making and public policy formation to the extent that public interest law organizations and lawyers exercise special influence tied to their perceived status as champions of underrepresented constituencies . . .

The phrase "public interest law" may once have been understood to apply to a relatively small number of organizations and lawyers serving a limited set of constituencies, but [it] is now used to describe a much larger set of groups, advocates, and policy agendas. These "public interest law/legal" organizations take opposing sides of nearly every divisive social and economic issue of our time; they advocate for gun control as well as gun rights, for environmental protection and property rights, for stronger protections for organized labor and for the "right to work," for pro-choice and pro-life positions, and for diversity initiatives and the end of affirmative action. All of these groups claim the special professional legitimacy that the "public interest law" label confers.

In the article's conclusion, Southworth suggests that the term "public interest law," as it is used in briefs, the press, and popular discourse, may "obscure[ ] more than it reveals about the relative disadvantage of the clients represented and how policies pursued under its banner relate to the public good."[9] Do you agree or disagree? Why?

C. WHAT IS A CAUSE LAWYER?

The next excerpt explains why some scholars have rejected the term public interest lawyer in favor of "cause lawyer"—a concept that focuses less on the notion of the underrepresentation of the interests served and more on the lawyer's motivation. This excerpt also examines what some people find attractive about cause lawyering and how it differs from conventional practice.

---

[9] Ann Southworth, *What is Public Interest Law? Empirical Perspectives on an Old Question*, 62 DEPAUL L. REV. 493, 516 (2013).

PROFESSIONAL AND POLITICAL PERSPECTIVES
Stuart A. Scheingold & Austin Sarat
Something to Believe In (2004)[10]

At gatherings of lawyers, talk of alienation and anxiety about their work is frequently present. Worries about increased commercialism, complaints about the costs of their work to family, and stories about the strains of having to provide services to clients whose goals are incompatible with the lawyer's personal moral commitments abound.

But alienation and anxiety about the nature of lawyering work do not affect all lawyers equally. For those whose idea and practice of lawyering involves service to a cause, many of the symptoms of alienation and anxiety are absent. This is not to suggest that such lawyers have no worries about their work. That is surely not the case. It is to suggest, however, that what William Simon says about lawyering in general— namely that "no social role encourages such ambitious moral aspirations as the lawyer's, and no social role so consistently disappoints the aspirations it encourages"—is markedly less true of those lawyers whose practices are devoted to the realization of their own moral aspirations.

Moral and political commitment, the defining attributes of cause lawyers are, for most of their peers, relegated to the margins of their professional lives. Conventional or client lawyering involves the deployment of a set of technical skills on behalf of ends determined by the client, not the lawyer. Lawyering, in this conception, is neither a domain for moral or political advocacy nor a place to express the lawyer's beliefs about the way society should be organized, disputes resolved, and values expressed.

For cause lawyers, such objectives move from the margins to the center of their professional lives. Lawyering is for them attractive precisely because it is a deeply moral or political activity, a kind of work that encourages pursuit of their vision of the right, the good, or the just. Cause lawyers have *something to believe* in and bring their beliefs to bear in their work lives. In this sense, they are neither alienated from their work nor anxious about the separation of role from person.

On the Definition of Cause Lawyering. Scholarship on cause lawyering is plagued by definitional and conceptual challenges. Indeed it is not possible to provide a single cross-culturally valid definition of cause lawyering. As a result, cause lawyering is a disputed and evolving concept, one that requires researchers to attend to the complex political and professional terrain on which it occurs. At its core, cause lawyering is about using legal skills to pursue ends and ideals that transcend client service—be those ideals social, cultural, political, economic or, indeed,

---

legal. Yet cause lawyers are associated with many different causes, function with varying resources and degrees of legitimacy, deploy a wide variety of strategies, and seek extraordinarily diverse goals.

Included under the umbrella of cause lawyering are such polar ideological opposites as poverty and property rights lawyers, feminist and right-to-life lawyers, as well as such disparate pursuits as human rights, environmental, civil liberties, and critical lawyering. Cause lawyering is found in the full range of professional venues: large and small private firms, salaried practice in national and transnational nongovernmental organizations, and government and privately funded lawyering. For better or for worse, this tremendous variation is the hallmark of cause lawyering. Indeed, the term *cause lawyering* conveys a core of meaning which is valid within a wide range of historical and cultural contexts while at the same time being sufficiently inclusive to accommodate a variety of forms.

Definitionally, cause lawyering is associated with both intent and behavior. Serving a cause by accident does not, in our judgment, qualify as cause lawyering. On the other hand, there is evidence that the accidental can be transformed into the intentional when a lawyer's ideals are awakened by service undertaken for other reasons. Thus, clinical activities in law school, which may be undertaken solely to escape the classroom and gain practical experience, can lead students to cause lawyering because they put students in touch with the problems of marginalized elements of the population. In other words, commitment to a cause can just as easily be a consequence of representation undertaken for different reasons as the other way around. Nor does cause lawyering preclude mixed motives.

Still, whether pure or impure, whether before or after the fact, we deem political or moral commitment an essential and distinguishing feature of cause lawyering. Lawyers are drawn to causes by a search for something in which to believe or as an outlet to express their already formed beliefs. Although cause lawyering is in general a low status and poorly paid professional activity, it does provide what conventional legal ethics deny—the opportunity to harmonize personal conviction and professional life.

One of the most noteworthy things that has emerged from the recent spate of research on cause lawyering in the United States and elsewhere is just how widespread cause lawyering has become. In the United States, cause lawyering has flourished at least since the 1960s. This has been due in large part to the successes of the civil rights movement and to the work of a number of well-established social advocacy organizations like the NAACP Legal Defense Fund, the Environmental Defense Fund, the Center for Constitutional Rights, and many others. The emergence of cause lawyering elsewhere in the world can be traced to a combination of factors, including the spread of written constitutions and constitutional courts, the neoliberal values driving globalization, and the development of transnational human rights networks.

It is thus important to appreciate at the outset just how protean and heterogeneous an enterprise cause lawyering is—an enterprise which grows and reinvents itself in confrontations with a vast array of challenges. Nonetheless, there are recurrent themes and patterns that enable us to bring some order to this apparent chaos while at the same time illuminating the loci of cause lawyering within the legal profession.

Both the variations within cause lawyering and its underlying unity emerge as one considers its goals and strategies. In terms of goals, cause lawyers array themselves along a left-right political continuum. With respect to strategy, the choice tends to be more dichotomous-that is between legal and political strategies. While each of these elements of cause lawyering will be treated separately, we see them as interdependent and will indicate how and why this is the case.

What we call cause lawyering is often referred to as public interest lawyering within the legal profession and among academics. However, we prefer *cause lawyering* because it is an inclusive term. It conveys a determination to take sides in political and moral struggle without making distinctions between worthy and unworthy causes. Conversely, to talk about public interest lawyering is to take on irresolvable disputes about what is, or is not, in the public interest. Whether the pursuit of any particular cause advances the public interest is very much in the eye of the beholder.

Invocations of the public interest have a long history in the literature of reform. Muckrakers from time immemorial have railed against the special interests in the name of the public and its interest. But what is the public interest and how is it defined?

The public interest is a notoriously slippery concept, which generally does little or no analytic work. According to one scholar, "The public interest may be described as the aggregate of common interests, including the common interest in seeing that there is fair play among private interests. The public interest is not the mere sum of the special interests, and it is certainly not the sum of the organized special interests. Nor is it an automatic consequence of the struggle of the special interests." In this conception, discovering the public interest is a "value neutral technical process".

Unfortunately, as David Truman long ago observed, such appeals "do not describe any actual or possible political situation within a complex modem nation. We do not need to account for a totally inclusive interest, because one does not exist." The public interest neither identifies any interest, nor can it point the way toward policy or reform. Instead, the primary function of the concept in our language is to convey approval or commendation. It serves as a symbol to legitimize the acts of any group that can successfully identify itself with it in the public mind. For cause lawyers, the way to justice is the way of politics, a way that names and defends interests with particularity and acknowledges the conflicts and costs which the pursuit of those interests necessarily entails. This assertive engagement in the contentious issues of public life is one way in which lawyering provides something to believe in.

[B]oth cause lawyers and conventional practitioners see themselves as divided by, and united in, a professional project which provides a public good. This ethical discourse over the nature of legal professionalism and its contribution to society is captured in the contrasting answers of conventional and cause lawyers to one deceptively simple ethical question. Should lawyering be driven primarily by client service, or are lawyers entitled, even obligated, to serve objectives that transcend service to clients?

Cause lawyers identify explicitly, and without apologies, with the latter possibility. In so doing, they distinguish themselves from, and put themselves ethically at odds with, the vast majority of lawyers, who see their primary professional responsibility as providing high-quality service to individuals and organizations without being substantively committed to the ends of those clients. Of course, cause lawyers also serve their clients but tend to see client service as a means to their moral and political ends. Accordingly, conventional practitioners are likely to view cause lawyering as ethically suspect at best. In sharp contrast, cause lawyers believe that they are responding to higher ethical standards. Cause lawyering thus stands in an ambiguous relationship to the professional project of the organized bar.

Cause Lawyers and the Legal Profession. It is important to acknowledge that both cause and conventional lawyers have ideals, that conventional lawyers are not simply cynical maximizers of their own wealth and status, and that cause lawyers are not simply altruistic and self-abnegating. However, the ideals of conventional and cause lawyering are dramatically different. According to the ethical codes of the legal profession here and in some other countries, it is the essential duty of lawyers to provide vigorous and skillful representation. Irrespective of whether lawyers approve of a client's moral stance, they are supposed to provide zealous advocacy on the client's behalf.

Conventional lawyers are not, therefore, supposed to have any qualms about switching sides or representing clients whose values and behavior are reprehensible to them. The prevailing codes of professional ethics expressly allow lawyers to represent clients without endorsing their views or goals. The rules allow the sale of legal expertise without requiring a lawyer to take into account any of the moral or political implications of their representation. Indeed, to do so is a point of professional pride and a demonstration of professional responsibility. British barristers are, thus, readily prepared to both prosecute and defend in criminal cases—in accordance with the "cab-rank" rule. Similarly, the noted American "litigator" David Boies probably considers it a hallmark of his professionalism to have successfully represented IBM in an antitrust suit brought by the U.S. Justice Department and subsequently to have represented the Justice Department in an antitrust suit brought against Microsoft. More broadly, politically liberal U.S. lawyers, including Boies, think nothing of working on behalf of corporations, on the one hand, and serving liberal causes or serving in Democratic administrations on the other. Conventional practitioners would see anyone who characterizes this flexibility as inconsistent or cynical as confusing professional ethics with personal morality.

Cause lawyers reject this way of thinking about the professional project. They expressly seek clients with whom they agree and causes in which they believe. Not only are they eager to take sides in social conflict and to identify themselves with the sides they take, but they are determined to construct their legal practice around this taking of sides. They deny that their effectiveness will be put at risk by the values they share with their clients. Indeed, cause lawyers often argue that the more closely they identify with their clients' values, the better advocates they will be. Shared values, according to this perspective, are conducive to a deeper understanding that will enable them to engage in context-sensitive advocacy.

Cause lawyers tend to transform the nature of legal advocacy, becoming advocates not only, or primarily, for their clients but for causes and, one might say, for their own beliefs. In thus reversing the priorities of the organized legal profession and in staking out the moral high ground, cause lawyers challenge their professional community.

<u>Convergence Between Conventional and Cause Lawyering</u>. At first glance, it might therefore seem that cause and conventional lawyers inhabit entirely different and mutually antagonistic professional worlds. Yet there are points of convergence and overlap that blur the widely acknowledged distinctions between them. Many so-called conventional lawyers tend to represent primarily, perhaps exclusively, those with whom they agree. This certainly seems to be the case with many, perhaps most, lawyers who represent corporations. Consider also personal injury lawyers in the United States. They are divided between a plaintiffs' bar and a defense bar. The plaintiffs' bar represents almost exclusively individuals or classes of individuals who have been injured—whether as consumers, workers, victims of police abuse, or the like. Conversely, the

defense bar represents only the targets of such suits—typically business corporations and insurance companies. Thus, these and many other conventional practitioners certainly fail to convey the requisite sense of neutrality called for by the ideology of advocacy. However, many of these conventional practitioners would deny what cause lawyers proudly proclaim—that they are self-consciously choosing sides in basic social conflicts.

Consider also that many cause lawyers use conventional legal practices to finance low-fee or no-fee representation of causes in which they believe. Similarly, lawyers in conventional corporate practice frequently set aside a portion of their time to provide pro bono advocacy for a variety of causes to which they are committed. Although cause and conventional lawyers are marching to distinctly different ethical drummers, there is often substantial convergence and overlap in the ways that they practice law.

In addition, there is a long-standing tradition, going back at least to de Tocqueville, of viewing conventional legal practice as a bulwark of civil society and liberal democracy. Accordingly, the profession has regularly represented itself as providing a public good in return, some have argued, for an official entitlement to monopolize the provision of legal services. To our way of thinking, it is not important whether this broader vision of professional responsibility is attributable to a strategic quid pro quo or to taking seriously the conception of the legal profession as a foundational social institution. Either way, conventional lawyers in general and the organized profession in particular clearly take comfort from a belief that the whole of their enterprise of client representation is somehow bigger and more beneficent than the sum of its parts.

This widely proclaimed conception of lawyering as a higher calling leads to convergence between some types of conventional practice and cause lawyering. The result is, on the one hand, to add to the complexity of disentangling cause and conventional lawyering. Nonetheless, we will argue that there is a meaningful distinction—albeit with some contestable conceptual terrain at the point of convergence. To think of law as a higher calling leads almost inevitably to some receptivity to cause lawyering among conventional practitioners. The extent of convergence and receptivity depends not only on the way in which cause lawyering is practiced [but also on] how conventional lawyers interpret their own higher calling.

NOTES ON SCHEINGOLD & SARAT

1. *Public Interest Lawyer v. Cause Lawyer.* Why do Scheingold & Sarat find the concepts of public interest law and public interest lawyering problematic? Why do they prefer the concept of cause lawyering? How do they define the term?

2. ***Cause Lawyer v. Conventional Lawyer.*** How is a cause lawyer different from a "conventional" lawyer? What do Scheingold & Sarat mean by insisting that "political or moral commitment is an essential and distinguishing feature of cause lawyering"?

3. ***Convergence and Overlap.*** Do cause lawyering and conventional lawyering sometimes converge and overlap in practice? If corporate lawyers and plaintiffs' lawyers generally agree with and are comfortable representing their clients, are they really conventional lawyers? If cause lawyers take some cases that they do not find particularly compelling in order to finance their work on causes about which they care much more, are they nevertheless cause lawyers? Are lawyers in private practice who do significant amounts of pro bono work for causes they believe in better described as conventional lawyers or part-time cause lawyers? Is a lawyer who works in a nonprofit organization but does not feel particularly committed to the organization's mission a cause lawyer or a conventional lawyer? What, if anything, turns on the answers to these questions?

4. ***Lawyer Alienation.*** Scheingold and Sarat assert that cause lawyers rarely express alienation from their work and that they differ from conventional lawyers in this regard. If Scheingold and Sarat are correct, what accounts for this? Based on what you have read about the many sectors of legal practice thus far, why do some lawyers feel alienated from their work and why do Scheingold and Sarat believe cause lawyers do not? Under what circumstances do you think conventional lawyers are likely to feel alienated, or not?

D. CRITIQUES OF PUBLIC INTEREST LAW

As the excerpts in parts B and C of this chapter point out, critiques of public interest law come from both the political right and left. From the right, critics have charged that several ideas at the heart of the definition of public interest law—especially the notion of the public interest and the concept of underrepresentation—are hopelessly vague and that powerful institutions, such as law schools, the media, the organized bar, groups that fund scholarships, and other philanthropic interests tend to interpret those mushy terms to favor liberal/progressive causes. According to conservative critics, public interest lawyers' agendas sometimes harm their intended beneficiaries and divert resources from much needed individual client service. From the left, critics have asserted that public interest lawyers tend to overestimate the efficacy of law, to favor litigation over other more promising strategies, to usurp clients' decisionmaking roles, and to undermine progressive movements.

The following excerpt comes from the political left, from a lawyer who is sympathetic with the core goals of the public interest law movement but critical of some aspects of its rhetoric and priorities. The critique is dated in some respects, but it raises several enduring questions—about the consequences of the emergence of public interest law as a specialized practice type; about relative priorities among causes encompassed under the public interest law umbrella; and about public interest lawyers' accountability to the constituents they claim to represent. We take up the last of these issues in more depth in Chapter 30.

BEYOND ENTHUSIASM AND COMMITMENT
Kenney Hegland
13 Arizona Law Review 805 (1971)

The basic goal of the public interest law movement is to assure adequate representation of currently unrepresented or underrepresented interests and peoples. Democratic theory and the adversary system require that all be heard. All are not. Thus, the large "public interest" umbrella encompasses such diverse interests as racial equality, consumer protection, poverty and ecology.

While agreeing totally that a vast amount of legal talent must be shifted to the unrepresented, this article questions whether the public interest firm, as presently conceived, can accomplish this goal.

The solution [to the problem of inadequate access to legal services for the poor] advocated by the public interest movement, is to have more attorneys represent the poor and, similarly, blacks, consumers and ecologists. Given the vast numbers of unrepresented individuals and the magnitude of their interests (racial equality, consumer protection, poverty and ecology), the public interest movement simply cannot succeed by the infusion of small bands of dedicated attorneys. What is needed is the active support and involvement of the private bar.

Viewed from the perspective of allocation, what of the sign on the door, "Public Interest Law Firm"? The assertion, represented both by the sign and much of the rhetoric of the movement, that there are two kinds of practitioners—public interest practitioners ("good guys") and other practitioners ("bad guys")—is bad politics. It undercuts the goal of representation of the unrepresented by alienating the "bad guys" so that they will not support, help or even possibly become "good guys." The danger with the assertion that there are two kinds of legal practice—public interest and private interest—is that the public interest law firm may become the institutionalized conscience of the bar. For the traditional practitioner, justice may become, even more than it is today, "someone else's" problem.

Further, the sign on the door, "Public Interest Law Firm," clouds the basic issues and hence prevents the movement from allocating help on a "greatest need" basis. The public interest law movement is the assertion of special interests which are currently slighted or ignored by decision makers in defining the "public interest." Recognition that public interest law firms are really asserting special interests underscores the fact that there will be conflicts between public interest firms. The clearest example is the conflict between ecology firms and poverty firms. Insistence on strict conservation measures will raise the cost of low cost housing; curtailment of pollution causing power generation will mean that many poor families will go without heat.

[T]here is a more subtle competition between various public interests. The basic thrust of the public interest movement is to represent people who currently do not have legal representatives. Given the fact that legal manpower is a scarce commodity, it should be allocated to those interests which have least chance of success without it. As the politically powerful—the upper and middle classes—cannot escape breathing smog and drinking impure water, the ecology movement can be expected to achieve its goal (if it is achievable at all) politically, without massive legal help. Indeed, the executive and legislative branches of government are expressly designed to respond to majority movements, which the ecology movement is fast becoming. Compare the "political muscle" of the black welfare recipient. The fight against poverty cannot be won without attorneys whereas the fight against pollution may be. This should be remembered by law students planning their careers and by practitioners desiring to participate in "public interest" work.

By definition, the public interest law firm begins with a concept of the public interest and fashions its clients around that. This reverses the traditional process where attorneys begin with clients and then fashion a concept of the public interest to correspond to the interests of their clients. This is not to say, as is frequently alleged, that public interest law firms use their clients as pawns. There is enough "lawyer" in public interest practitioners to prevent them from sacrificing a client's interests on the altar of the higher good. A more accurate view of public interest clients is that they are "tickets"—without which the firm could not play the law game.

By viewing clients as tickets rather than as individuals, the lawyer becomes a planner rather than an advocate. The planner begins with a nebulous class, such as blacks, consumers, the poor, and then generalizes and distills the interests of that class, projects goals and finally adopt strategies. The advocate, on the other hand, begins with specific individuals or specific groups within the generalized class and thereafter simply acts as their advocate, allowing them to define their interests, formulate their goals, and adopt methods of achieving them.

The shift from advocacy to planning has been justified on the basis that it is the best way to allocate limited legal manpower; there are just too many blacks, too many poor people, too many consumers to treat them as individuals. To maximize the effectiveness of the limited number of attorneys involved, it is reasoned, they must focus on issues common to the generalized class rather than on problems of individuals or specific groups within the generalized class. This reasoning, for example, leads many legal services programs to reject service cases, such as divorce and bankruptcy, in favor of law reform—a focused attack on statutes which adversely affect the generalized class of poor persons.

While the allocation analysis seems to demand the new role, there are dangers when lawyers become planners rather than advocates. Immediately, there arises the problem of accountability. How can one assume that these new planners truly represent the interests of blacks, consumers or the poor? Once the attorney breaks the moorings of a specific client's interests, how can he be held accountable? How can the attorney be sure of the correctness of his concept of the interests of a generalized class of people such as the poor?

NOTES ON HEGLAND

1. *Good Guys v. Bad Guys.* Hegland claims that the rhetoric of the public interest movement suggests that "there are two kinds of practitioners—public interest practitioners ('good guys') and other practitioners ('bad guys')" and that drawing this distinction is "bad politics." Based on what you have learned thus far about the legal profession—drawing on either your observations before coming to law school or what you've learned since you arrived—is Hegland's observation true today? In other words, do lawyers who work in public interest organizations today tend to function as "the institutionalized conscience of the bar"? Does the existence of a sector of practice dedicated to public interest law discourage other lawyers from thinking about how their work relates to the public good? If so, is that problematic?

2. *Why Does the Label Matter?* Recall Southworth's observation that conservative and libertarian groups have actively claimed the "public interest law" label. Why is that status helpful for public policy advocates? Might the reasons relate to assumptions (to borrow Hegland's argument) about what types of lawyers are viewed as "good guys" and which ones are viewed as "bad guys"? Who is the audience for claims about whether certain work is public interest work, and how does the audience for such claims matter?

3. *Relative Need.* Do you agree with Hegland's argument that the concept of public interest law tends to divert attention from the relative need of various underrepresented interests? In particular, do you think he is right that it draws attention away from what he thinks should be the highest priority—meeting the legal needs of the poor?

4. *Does Definitional Ambiguity Matter?* Do you see any similarities between Scheingold & Sarat's reasons for rejecting the term public interest lawyer in favor of cause lawyer and Hegland's unease with the concept of public interest law?

5. *Accountability.* The last section of the Hegland excerpt raises the issue of how lawyers who seek to serve broad constituencies rather than, or in addition to, particular clients (whether individuals, groups or organizations) can be held accountable to the broader constituencies they seek to serve. Are you persuaded by his argument? What, if anything, is problematic about the practice? We take up the issue of lawyer accountability in public interest practice in more detail in Chapter 30.

E. SUMMARY

This chapter examined lawyers who work in "public interest law" organizations. It addressed definitional controversies surrounding this type of practice and related questions about what makes this sector distinctive, attractive, and sometimes controversial. We explored how public interest practice has grown over the past several decades and how persistent disagreement among advocates of the political left and right about what exactly "counts" as public interest law relates to the white hat status that public interest law enjoys in the courts and other arenas in which law and public policy are made. We examined a concept of the "cause lawyer" and its relationship to public interest law and conventional lawyering. Finally, we briefly addressed several common critiques of public interest law.

CHAPTER 30

ISSUES OF ACCOUNTABILITY IN PUBLIC INTEREST PRACTICE

Cause Lawyers

• • •

A. INTRODUCTION

This chapter explores issues of accountability in public interest practice. When public interest lawyers seek to serve causes or constituencies in addition to individual clients, questions arise about how the people whom the lawyers purport to represent can ensure that the lawyers are responsive to their needs and preferences. As we saw in Chapters 5 and 6, issues about lawyer power vis-à-vis clients can be worrisome when clients are poor and/or vulnerable in other respects. But they also can be problematic when the represented constituency or cause is disorganized and/or diffuse. As noted in Chapter 29, concerns about the accountability of public interest lawyers have been raised by critics on both sides of the political spectrum. They implicate conflicts of interest (involving tensions among the priorities of lawyers, clients, and causes), and as well as the allocation of decisionmaking authority between lawyers and clients.

The first excerpt in this chapter considers the responsibilities of lawyers who handle class actions for injunctive relief on behalf of large plaintiff classes. The second excerpt examines the responsibilities of lawyers who pursue precedents that would benefit large categories of people but where the actual client is an individual whose interests diverge from the cause that the litigation is designed to advance. The third excerpt explores the variety of ethical issues that arise in the representation of collective interests, and how service to organizations with well-defined governance structures sometimes minimizes the issues of accountability that confront lawyers who handle class actions and impact litigation on behalf of individuals.

B. INSTITUTIONAL REFORM CLASS ACTIONS

The following excerpt, Derrick Bell's classic "Serving Two Masters," raises questions about the conduct of civil rights lawyers in connection with the campaign to achieve racial balance in public schools. At the start of the campaign, the lawyers and most parents of children in the schools that were the subject of the litigation shared the view that integration was the key to improving educational opportunity for their children. Over time, however, many parents became doubtful that complete integration—and the racial tension, long bus rides, and white flight associated with school integration—was the best approach. NAACP lawyers opposed compromise desegregation plans that community leaders and school officials had negotiated to settle class action lawsuits in several cities because the plans concentrated on improving predominantly black schools rather than bussing white students into black schools to achieve full integration. Bell criticized the lawyers who opposed those compromise plans. He argued that the lawyers' commitment to maximum desegregation led them to disregard the wishes of parents who questioned the price of pursuing full integration and who placed a higher priority on securing better educational opportunities for their children.

The class action device used in the NAACP's school desegregation campaign is a procedural mechanism for litigating on behalf of large groups of people who have suffered common injury. Rule 23 of the Federal Rules of Civil Procedure allows representatives to sue on behalf of all members of a class if: "(1) the class is so numerous that joinder of all members is impracticable; (2) there are questions of law or fact common to the class; (3) the claims or defenses of the representative parties are typical of the claims or defenses of the class; and (4) the representative parties will fairly and adequately protect the interests of the class." Rule 23(a). There are several types of class actions, including suits for damages (common in personal injury and consumer litigation brought by lawyers in the private plaintiffs' bar) and institutional reform class actions (sometimes pursued by public interest lawyers, such as the NAACP lawyers considered in Bell's article). A court order approving or "certifying" a class action determines that the criteria for proceeding as a class have been met and that the lawyer representing the class fairly and adequately represents the interests of class members. A judgment in a class action will bind all members of the class and very likely prevent them from pursuing individual claims on the same subject. That raises the question whether it is fair to allow lawyers for the class and the class representatives to define the goals and tactics of the class. Attorneys' fees may sometimes be awarded to class counsel, which raises the possibility that lawyers will be motivated by their own pecuniary interests rather than the interest of serving the class members.

Professional responsibility issues relating to class action litigation are so numerous that they are the subject of entire textbooks and law school classes, and we will not try to canvass all those issues here. Bell's article highlights two issues that sometimes arise in institutional reform class actions: conflicts of interest among members of a plaintiff class (in this case, conflicts between the interests of parents who wanted complete integration and those who preferred to focus on improving predominantly black schools) and conflicts between class lawyers' ideological commitments and their clients' preferences.

As you saw in Chapter 10, a lawyer is prohibited from representing a client if one of two types of conflicts of interest exists: 1) if the client's interests are "directly adverse" to those of another client, or 2) if there is a "significant risk" that a representation will be "materially limited" by a lawyer's obligation to another client or the lawyer's own interests. If either of these types of conflicts exists, the lawyer may proceed only with informed consent. In class actions, conflicts of interest can be particularly problematic because, by definition, large numbers of people nominally represented by class counsel are not before the court and therefore are not in a position to monitor the lawyer's actions on their behalf. Although class actions do not receive any special attention in the Model Rules, a good deal of commentary suggests that a lawyer for a class has especially strong duties to identify conflicts of interest within a represented class, to apprise the judge of conflicts that arise during the course of the representation, and to assist in taking corrective measures, including supporting the appointment of another lawyer to represent dissenting members of a class. But the lawyer has strong disincentives to identify and remedy conflicts where doing so threatens to derail litigation in which the lawyer and his employer have invested a good deal of time and resources, where the appointment of additional counsel is likely to complicate negotiations, and where opposing counsel may take advantage of the surfacing of such conflicts to argue that the class should be "decertified" and that no attorneys' fees should be awarded to class counsel.

Bell argues that those kinds of disincentives arose in the school desegregation litigation. He asserts that civil rights lawyers' "single-minded commitment" to maximum integration led them to disregard both conflicts among the parents they represented and conflicts between the lawyers' commitment to full integration and their obligations to the plaintiff class.

SERVING TWO MASTERS: INTEGRATION IDEALS AND CLIENT INTERESTS IN SCHOOL DESEGREGATION LITIGATION
Derrick A. Bell Jr.
85 Yale Law Journal 470 (1976)

Largely through the efforts of civil rights lawyers, most courts have come to construe *Brown v. Board of Education* as mandating "equal educational opportunities" through school desegregation plans aimed at achieving racial balance, whether or not those plans will improve the education received by the children affected. To the extent that "instructional profit"* accurately defines the school priorities of black parents in Boston and elsewhere, questions of professional responsibility are raised that can no longer be ignored:

How should the term "client" be defined in school desegregation cases that are litigated for decades, determine critically important constitutional rights for thousands of minority children, and usually involve major restructuring of a public school system? How should civil rights attorneys represent the often diverse interests of clients and class in school suits? Do they owe any special obligation to class members who emphasize educational quality and who probably cannot obtain counsel to advocate their divergent views? Do the political, organizational, and even philosophical complexities of school desegregation litigation justify a higher standard of professional responsibility on the part of civil rights lawyers to their clients, or more diligent oversight of the lawyer-client relationship by the bench and bar?

This article will review the development of school desegregation litigation and the unique lawyer-client relationship that has evolved out of it. It will not be the first such inquiry. During the era of "massive resistance," southern states charged that this relationship violated professional canons of conduct. A majority of the Supreme Court rejected those challenges, creating in the process constitutional protection for conduct that, under other circumstances, would contravene basic precepts of professional behavior.** The potential for ethical problems in these constitutionally protected lawyer-client relationships was recognized by the American Bar Association Code of Professional Responsibility, but it is difficult to provide standards for the attorney and protection for the client where the source of the conflict is the attorney's ideals. The magnitude of the difficulty is more accurately gauged in a much older code that warns: "No servant can serve two masters: for either he will hate the one, and love the other; or else he will hold to one, and despise the other."

<u>Lawyer-Client Conflicts: Sources and Rationale</u>. Having convinced themselves that *Brown* stands for desegregation and not education, the established civil rights organizations steadfastly refuse to recognize reverses in the school desegregation campaign. Why have [civil rights lawyers] been so unwilling to recognize the increasing futility of "total desegregation," and, more important, the increasing number of defections within the black community?

---

    *   [Eds.: By "instructional profit," Bell meant educational quality.]

    **   [Eds.: This refers to the Supreme Court's decision in *NAACP v. Button*, 371 U.S. 415 (1963), which held that the First Amendment prohibits states from preventing the NAACP from soliciting clients for its national litigation campaigns. Some southern states had argued that soliciting clients for these purposes constituted unprofessional conduct.]

[Here Bell argues that civil rights lawyers have seen school integration as a major test of the country's continued commitment to civil rights progress and therefore have been reluctant to consider any retreat from that goal. He also argues that civil rights attorneys have been responsive to the supporters of the organizations that employ them—primarily middle class blacks and whites who believe strongly in integration.]

Client-Counsel Merger. The position of the established civil rights groups obviates any need to determine whether a continued policy of maximum racial balance conforms with the wishes of even a minority of the class. This position represents an extraordinary view of the lawyer's role. Not only does it assume a perpetual retainer authorizing a lifelong effort to obtain racially balanced schools; it also fails to reflect any significant change in representational policy from a decade ago, when virtually all blacks assumed that integration was the best means of achieving a quality education for black children, to the present time, when many black parents are disenchanted with the educational results of integration.

This malady may afflict many idealistic lawyers who seek, through the class action device, to bring about judicial intervention affecting large segments of the community. The class action provides the vehicle for bringing about a major advance toward an idealistic goal. At the same time, prosecuting and winning the big case provides strong reinforcement of the attorney's sense of his or her abilities and professionalism. The psychological motivations which influence the lawyer in taking on "a fiercer dragon" through the class action may also underlie the tendency to direct the suit toward the goals of the lawyer rather than the client.

The questions of legal ethics raised by the lawyer-client relationship in civil rights litigation are not new. The Supreme Court's 1963 treatment of these questions in *NAACP v. Button*, however, needs to be examined in light of the emergence of lawyer-client conflicts which are far more serious than the premature speculations of a segregationist legislature.

The Court deemed NAACP's litigation activities "a form of political expression" protected by the First Amendment. Justice Brennan conceded that Virginia had a valid interest in regulating the traditionally illegal practices of barratry, maintenance, and champerty, but noted that the malicious intent which constituted the essence of these common law offenses was absent here. He also reasoned that because the NAACP's efforts served the public rather than a private interest, and because no monetary stakes were involved, "there is no danger that the attorney will desert or subvert the paramount interests of his client to enrich himself or an outside sponsor. And the aims and interests of NAACP have not been shown to conflict with those of its members and nonmember Negro litigants."

Joined by Justices Clark and Stewart, Justice Harlan expressed the view that the Virginia statute was valid. In support of his conclusion, Harlan carefully reviewed the record and found that NAACP policy required what he considered serious departures from ethical professional conduct. First, NAACP attorneys were required to follow policy directives promulgated by the National Board of Directors or lose their right to compensation. Second, these directives to staff lawyers covered many subjects relating to the form and substance of litigation. Third, the NAACP not only advocated litigation and waited for prospective litigants to come forward; in several instances and particularly in school cases, "specific directions were given as to the types of prospective plaintiffs to be sought, and staff lawyers brought blank forms to meetings for the purpose of obtaining signatures authorizing the prosecution of litigation in the name of the signer." Fourth, the retainer forms signed by prospective litigants sometimes did not contain the names of the attorneys retained, and often when the forms specified certain attorneys as counsel, additional attorneys were brought into the action without the plaintiff's consent. Justice Harlan observed that several named plaintiffs had testified that they had no personal dealings with the lawyers handling their cases and were not aware until long after the event that suits had been filed in their names. Taken together, Harlan felt these incidents justified the corrective measures taken by the State of Virginia.

Justice Harlan was not impressed by the fact that the suits were not brought for pecuniary gain. The NAACP attorneys did not donate their services, and the litigating activities did not fall into the accepted category of aid to indigents. But he deemed more important than the avoidance of improper pecuniary gain the concern shared by the profession, courts, and legislatures that outside influences not interfere with the uniquely personal relationship between lawyer and client. In Justice Harlan's view, when an attorney is employed by an association or corporation to represent a client, two problems arise:

> The lawyer becomes subject to the control of a body that is not itself a litigant and that, unlike the lawyers it employs, is not subject to strict professional discipline as an officer of the court. In addition, the lawyer necessarily finds himself with a divided allegiance—to his employer and to his client—which may prevent full compliance with his basic professional obligations.

He conceded that "[t]he NAACP may be no more than the sum of the efforts and views infused in it by its members" but added a prophetic warning that "the totality of the separate interests of the members and

others whose causes the petitioner champions, even in the field of race
relations, may far exceed in scope and variety that body's views of policy,
as embodied in litigating strategy and tactics."

Justice Harlan recognized that it might be in the association's
interest to maintain an all-out, frontal attack on segregation, even
sacrificing small points in some cases for the major points that might win
other cases. But he foresaw that

> it is not impossible that after authorizing action in his behalf, a
> Negro parent, concerned that a continued frontal attack could
> result in schools closed for years, might prefer to wait with his
> fellows a longer time for good-faith efforts by the local school
> board than is permitted by the centrally determined policy of the
> NAACP. Or he might see a greater prospect of success through
> discussions with local school authorities than through the
> litigation deemed necessary by the Association. The parent, of
> course, is free to withdraw his authorization, but is his lawyer,
> retained and paid by petitioner and subject to its directions on
> matters of policy, able to advise the parent with that undivided
> allegiance that is the hallmark of the attorney- client relation? I
> am afraid not.

NAACP v. Button in Retrospect. As the majority [in _Button_] found,
the NAACP did not "solicit" litigants but rather systematically advised
black parents of their rights under _Brown_ and collected retainer
signatures of those willing to join the proposed suits. The litigation was
designed to serve the public interest rather than to enrich the litigators.
Not all the plaintiffs were indigent, but few could afford to finance
litigation intended to change the deep-seated racial policies of public
school systems.

On the other hand, Justice Harlan was certainly correct in
suggesting that the retainer process was often performed in a perfunctory
manner and that plaintiffs had little contact with their attorneys.
Plaintiffs frequently learned that suit had been filed and kept abreast of
its progress through the public media. Although a plaintiff could
withdraw from the suit at any time, he could not influence the primary
goals of the litigation. Except in rare instances, policy decisions were
made by the attorneys, often in conjunction with the organizational
leadership and without consultation with the client.

The _Button_ majority obviously felt that the potential for abuse of
clients' rights in this procedure was overshadowed by the fact that
Virginia enacted the statute to protect the citadel of segregation rather
than the sanctity of the lawyer-client relationship. As the majority
pointed out, litigation was the only means by which blacks throughout
the South could effectuate the school desegregation mandate of _Brown_.

The theoretical possibility of abuse of client rights seemed a rather slender risk when compared with the real threat to integration posed by this most dangerous weapon in Virginia's arsenal of "massive resistance." Most legal commentators reacted favorably to the majority's decision for precisely this reason. Justice Harlan was criticized by these writers for refusing to recognize the motivation for Virginia's sudden interest in the procedures by which the NAACP obtained and represented school desegregation plaintiffs.

Nevertheless, a few contemporary commentators found cause for sober reflection in Harlan's dissent. And even those writers who viewed the decision as necessary to protect the NAACP conceded that the majority had paid too little attention to Justice Harlan's conflict-of-interest concerns. Current ABA standards thus appear to conform with *Button* and its progeny in permitting the representation typically provided by civil rights groups. They are a serious attempt to come to grips with and provide specific guidance on the issues of outside influence and client primacy that so concerned Justice Harlan. But they provide little help where, as in school desegregation litigation, the influence of attorney and organization are mutually supportive, and both are so committed to what they perceive as the long-range good of their clients that they do not sense the growing conflict between those goals and the client's current interests. Given the cries of protest and the charges of racially motivated persecution that would probably greet any ABA effort to address this problem more specifically, it is not surprising that the conflict—which in any event will neither embarrass the profession ethically nor threaten it economically—has not received a high priority for further attention.

Idealism, though perhaps rarer than greed, is harder to control. Justice Harlan accurately prophesied the excesses of derailed benevolence, but a retreat from the group representational concepts set out in *Button* would be a disaster, not an improvement. State legislatures are less likely than the ABA to draft standards that effectively guide practitioners and protect clients. Even well-intentioned and carefully drawn standards might hinder rather than facilitate the always difficult task of achieving social change through legal action. And too stringent rules could encourage officials in some states to institute groundless disciplinary proceedings against lawyers in school cases, which in many areas are hardly more popular today than they were during the massive resistance era.

Client involvement in school litigation is more likely to increase if civil rights lawyers themselves come to realize that the special status accorded them by the courts and the bar demands in return an extraordinary display of ethical sensitivity and self-restraint. The "divided allegiance" between client and employer which Justice Harlan feared would interfere with the civil rights lawyer's "full compliance with his basic professional obligation" has developed in a far more idealistic and thus a far more dangerous form. For it is more the civil rights lawyers' commitment to an integrated society than any policy directives or pressures from their employers which leads to their assumptions of client acceptance and their condemnations of all dissent.

NOTES ON BELL

1. *What Conflicts?* What conflicts of interest does Bell identify in the school desegregation litigation? Are some of them conflicts among members of the plaintiff class? Are some of them conflicts between clients (members of the class) and the cause that the public interest organization that employs the lawyer seeks to advance (desegregation)? Which of these types of conflicts are implicated in Bell's assertion that "[i]dealism, though perhaps rarer than greed, is harder to control"? What exactly does he think can be dangerous about lawyer idealism?

2. *What Should the Rules Say?* Are additional legal restrictions advisable to ensure that lawyers avoid the types of conflicts that Bell identifies? As noted above, the conflict of interest rules already require lawyers to identify and respond to conflicts of interest among clients and between clients and the lawyers' own interests, including ideological interests. Another ethics rule, MR 5.4(c), provides that a lawyer shall not permit a person who employs the lawyer to render legal services for another to "direct or regulate the lawyer's professional judgment" in providing those services. What problems do these rules fail to address? Would you favor any additional changes in the rules of civil procedure or ethics rules?

One commentator has argued that procedural reforms might help ameliorate the problems highlighted in Bell's article. Deborah Rhode has advocated requiring class counsel to document what measures they take to communicate with and respond to concerns of members of the plaintiff class. She argues that "[r]equiring attorneys to record contacts with the class and perceptions of conflict would, if nothing else, narrow their capacity for self-delusion about whose views they were or were not representing."[1] Do you think she is right? What would be the disadvantages of such a rule change?

3. *Ethical Sensitivity and Self-Restraint.* Notice that Bell does not advocate restricting class action litigation or changing the ethics rules. Instead, he urges judges to carefully monitor class actions to ensure that the interests of class members are adequately protected, and he calls on civil rights lawyers to exercise "ethical sensitivity and self-restraint." What would the latter part of Bell's prescription mean in practice? Would it require lawyers to regularly canvass the views and preferences of members of a plaintiff class? How might lawyers go about discerning the interests and preferences of the members of a large plaintiff class? Would it sometimes

---

[1]   Deborah L. Rhode, *Conflicts in Class Actions*, 34 STAN. L. REV. 1183 (1982).

require lawyers to acknowledged dissent within the plaintiff class and support the appointment of separate counsel to represent dissenting class members, even if those steps might jeopardize the litigation strategy?

C. LAW REFORM ON BEHALF OF INDIVIDUAL CLIENTS

Some types of law reform pursued by public interest lawyers proceed on behalf of individual clients rather than classes of affected people. The following excerpt considers the responsibilities of lawyers in reform litigation on behalf of individual clients whose interests diverge from those of the cause. The lawyer and client at the heart of the controversy analyzed in this article are not particularly famous, but the litigation that brought them together—*Roe v. Wade*—certainly is.

OF CAUSES AND CLIENTS: TWO TALES OF *ROE V. WADE*
Kevin C. McMunigal
47 Hastings Law Journal 779 (1996)

Consider the following situation. It is the late 1960s and criminal statutes prohibiting abortion are common throughout the country. A lawyer wants to challenge the constitutionality of one such statute and interviews a pregnant woman to be the plaintiff in the case. The lawyer is bright, idealistic, and committed to the cause of women's reproductive choice. Having had an illegal abortion herself, she is working without pay and determined to change the law limiting access to abortion. The would-be plaintiff is unsophisticated, nearly destitute, and neither aware of nor committed to any cause. Having once before given a child up for adoption, she is desperate to abort her current pregnancy. Finding a plaintiff has not been easy, and the lawyer feels this woman meets her criteria: she is pregnant, wants an abortion, and is too poor to travel to a state where abortion is legal.

There is one complication: the young woman says she was raped. This allegation confronts the lawyer with a strategic choice. The criminal statute in question has no rape exemption, so she could rely on the rape allegation and argue that the statute is unconstitutional because of its failure to exempt rape victims. Or she could ignore the rape allegation in favor of a broad challenge to the statute's general prohibition of abortion.

Which strategy is the lawyer to choose? The narrower strategy probably has a greater chance for success, at least in the abstract. Of all aspects of the criminalization of abortion, banning abortion in rape cases is perhaps the least popular and most difficult to defend. Thus, it may be the statute's most vulnerable point. Higher likelihood of success on the merits may also speed resolution of the case and increase the availability of injunctive relief in the trial court. Because the prospective plaintiff is already pregnant, she must prevail and probably also obtain injunctive relief in the trial court in a matter of months to have any hope of aborting her pregnancy.

The lawyer, though, has concerns about the rape allegation. The woman states that she failed to report the rape and there were no corroborating witnesses. Weakness on the rape allegation might undermine the entire case. In addition, the broad strategy would advance the cause of reproductive choice more significantly than the rape strategy, appealing to the lawyer's sense of responsibility to a broad female constituency dedicated to expanding abortion rights and to women in the future who will seek to abort pregnancies not resulting from rape.

May the lawyer agree to represent the woman but reject using the rape allegation? If so, on what ground? Suspected falsity? Inadequate proof? Because it would be in the woman's best interest or because the broader challenge would better serve the abortion rights cause?

We rarely have access to detailed accounts of public interest litigation from both the lawyer's and the client's perspectives. Two recent books on *Roe v. Wade*, however, give us both the lawyer's and the client's stories of that case. Sarah Weddington, the most celebrated of the *Roe* lawyers, provides a lawyer's account. Norma McCorvey, the individual plaintiff fictitiously named "Jane Roe," writes from a client's perspective.

As the autobiographical portions of their books indicate, Weddington and McCorvey brought to the *Roe* case some common experiences and interests. Each knew first-hand what it was like to experience an unplanned pregnancy and to be desperate for an abortion but unable to obtain one because of the Texas criminal ban on abortion. Weddington and McCorvey each had an interest in having the Texas abortion statute abrogated and each needed the other to accomplish this end. Unlike some lawyers and clients in public interest practice, no barriers of sex or race divided them.

But their experiences and interests also diverged significantly. Weddington was well educated, politically aware and committed, while McCorvey was poorly educated, and neither politically aware nor committed. Weddington was interested in making history, changing the law to "somehow, someday free women from the horrors of illegal abortion." McCorvey, by contrast, was simply "at the end of [her] rope," interested in terminating the pregnancy that was the source of her current dilemma.

In more abstract terms, their relationship reflected a tension between McCorvey's present individual interest in obtaining an abortion and the future collective interests of other women in greater access to abortion. In a legal system in which individual cases both resolve present disputes and generate future legal norms, any case may be subject to such a tension between the present individual interests of parties affected by the case as a dispute resolution mechanism and the future collective interests of those affected by the case as a precedent. In *Roe*, this tension was particularly acute. McCorvey was desperate and had no one other than her lawyer to look out for her interests. At the same time, the case also held the potential to dramatically advance the emotionally charged collective interests animating the abortion rights cause, to undo in one bold stroke a century of restrictive abortion legislation.

How, then, did this mix of similar and dissimilar interests play itself out in the *Roe* case?

The Rape Allegation. McCorvey in her first meeting with Weddington claimed that her pregnancy resulted from rape. More than ten years later, McCorvey would admit in an interview with Carl Rowan that this claim was false. But in 1970 and for years thereafter, McCorvey maintained that she had been raped. Weddington chose not to use the allegation.

When Weddington met McCorvey in 1970, abortion rights activists in the United States were pursuing two distinct strategies in attacking the criminal prohibition of abortion. The nature of each is critical to appreciating Weddington's response to McCorvey's rape claim. A reform strategy sought to liberalize the law of abortion by decriminalizing certain categories of abortion, such as those of pregnancies resulting from rape or incest, but otherwise left the criminal ban on abortion intact. An abolition strategy sought complete repeal of criminal abortion laws, including liberalized statutes such as those advocated by the reform strategy. Exemplified by the American Law Institute's Model Penal Code abortion provision, the reform strategy had succeeded in a number of states and was gaining momentum at the time Weddington met McCorvey in early 1970. The abolition strategy, by contrast, supported by groups such as the National Organization for Women, had met with little success in state legislatures in the late 1960s. In 1973, the abolitionist strategy ultimately prevailed in *Roe*, which invalidated restrictive abortion statutes, and in its companion case, *Doe v. Bolton*, which invalidated liberalized abortion statutes.

McCorvey's rape claim, then, had strategic significance because it raised the possibility for Weddington of choosing either a reform or an abolition strategy in pursuing *Roe*. Weddington was clearly cognizant of both strategies. In 1970, both reform and abolition strategies were being actively pursued by abortion reformers around the United States. Indeed, Weddington describes herself as "moderating a conflict among pro-choice forces" in Texas in 1970 about whether to back reform or abolition legislation, describing the dispute between reform and abolition strategies as a "conflict between what was possible and what was ideal."

How should Weddington have handled this choice? Was she required to reject the rape allegation because of suspected falsity? If Weddington had known McCorvey was lying, she would have been required to reject the allegation. Because she did not know McCorvey was lying, she was not barred on that ground from using the allegation. Neither suspected falsity nor lack of corroboration required Weddington to reject McCorvey's rape claim.

What decision was best for McCorvey? A reform strategy relying on the rape allegation probably had the better chance of success, as Weddington's own description of reform legislation as representing the "possible" and abolition the "ideal" suggests. Higher likelihood of success on the merits would have increased the chances of a speedier resolution and obtaining injunctive relief, both significant for McCorvey's chances for obtaining an abortion since she was already pregnant. But there were also significant risks associated with use of the rape allegation. If proof of the rape allegation was weak and its truth suspect, it might provide the opposing side a point of vulnerability for attacking and undermining the plaintiff's entire case. In other words, lack of credibility on that one issue might result in loss of credibility and sympathy on other factual and legal issues. It also might raise a contested factual issue which could delay resolution of the case and thus decrease McCorvey's chances for obtaining an abortion.

What decision on the rape allegation was best for the abortion rights cause? This is not an easy question to answer. The advantages and disadvantages of both the reform and abolition strategies were widely debated at the time by abortion reformers. Some favored an incremental approach of attempting to liberalize abortions laws, while others favored the more ambitious strategy of seeking complete abolition. The suspected falsity of the rape claim weighed against its use. If it was later exposed as false, it could cause a public relations nightmare for the abortion rights cause.

Weddington and her co-counsel Linda Coffee, who was present at Weddington's first meeting with McCorvey, opted not to rely on McCorvey's rape claim. They chose instead an abolition strategy. Weddington offers the following justification for the decision not to rely on the rape claim:

> As the conversation continued, Jane Roe asked if it would help if she had been raped. We said no; the Texas law had no exception for rape. It was just as illegal for a doctor to do an abortion for someone who had been raped as it was in any other situation. I did ask, "Were there any witnesses? Was there a police report? Is there any way that we could prove a rape occurred?" Her answer in each instance was no.

Neither Linda nor I questioned her further about how she had gotten pregnant. I was not going to allege something in the complaint that I could not back up with proof. Also, we did not want the Texas law changed only to allow abortion in cases of rape. We wanted a decision that abortion was covered by the right of privacy. After all, the women coming to the referral project were there as a result of a wide variety of circumstances. Our principles were not based on how conception occurred.

Though rejection of McCorvey's rape claim may well have been appropriate, this justification is problematic for several reasons. Weddington fails to confront directly the strategic significance of the decision being made or even to mention the possibility of a reform strategy. Nor does she mention the interests of her client, McCorvey, or how Weddington's decision about the rape allegation and choice of strategy might affect her client's interests.

The third justification offered by Weddington for rejecting the rape raises several problems. First, to whom is Weddington referring when she uses the words "we" and "our"? She might simply mean the lawyers, herself and [her co-counsel] Linda Coffee. Or she might be referring to the lawyers' broader constituency, supporters of the abortion rights cause, such as the abortion referral project volunteers who first suggested bringing a test case to challenge the Texas abortion statute. In either case, the assumption underlying this reference to the desires and principles of the lawyers or their constituency as a justification for rejection of the rape allegation is at odds with basic conflict of interest norms governing lawyers. Neither the interests of the lawyer nor the interests of third parties are permitted to influence the judgment of a lawyer in representing a client. Rather, only the interests of the client are to guide the lawyer.

McCorvey appears not to have been informed by Weddington about her decision not to use the rape allegation and consequently agonized for years over her false claim of rape. It seems that whatever might have been in McCorvey's best interest at the time the case was filed, McCorvey, in retrospect, seems relieved that the rape allegation was never used.

Two Tales of Roe v. Wade. For Weddington, the story of *Roe v. Wade* is first and foremost a story of law reform in the service of the collective interests of women. In this story, the idea of service to an individual client has no particular significance. Weddington at the end of her book, for example, states that "the story of *Roe* is the story of the women of this country and their continuing efforts to push back the barriers that have limited their decisions and circumscribed their freedoms" Significantly, McCorvey as an individual is not mentioned. Rather, the protagonists of Weddington's story are women as a group, and the story's drama arises from the conflict between two large interest groups—the abortion rights cause and the anti-abortion movement.

[Surprisingly] McCorvey in her book ultimately describes the process of being reshaped through the *Roe* case as an experience of empowerment and liberation, rather than one of disempowerment and subjugation. She states at the end of her book, for example, "without Jane Roe, without a cause to fight for and a purpose for living, the original Norma would never have survived." However, McCorvey's realignment on the abortion issue and her baptism by the national director of Operation Rescue, the militant anti-abortion group, roughly a year after publishing her book, make the transformatory experience she describes in that book look more like another example of her tendency to allow others to dominate her.

A recurring problem in the regulation of lawyers is how to deal with incentives that tempt a lawyer to behave improperly. Concern with this problem is common in any agency relationship. Legal and ethical rules governing lawyers often focus on risks to a client from economic incentives that may affect her lawyer, while ignoring risks from noneconomic incentives such as the lawyer's ideals. [T]he Model Rules, reflecting the pecuniary-nonpecuniary distinction found in the Supreme Court's solicitation cases, prohibit a lawyer from soliciting a potential client in person "when a significant motive for the lawyer's doing so is the lawyer's pecuniary gain." Here, again, financial motives are viewed as dangerous, rendering such solicitation "fraught with the possibility of undue influence, intimidation, and overreaching." Nonpecuniary motives such as idealism, by contrast, are seen as benign. Accordingly, public interest lawyers driven by ideals rather than dollars are exempted by the Model Rules from the personal solicitation prohibition on the ground that "[t]here is far less likelihood that a lawyer would engage in abusive practices against an individual where the lawyer is motivated by considerations other than the lawyer's pecuniary gain."[2]

Weddington's and McCorvey's stories prompt us to examine closely the assumptions that underlie this view. They provide a powerful illustration of how a lawyer's ideals may be a potent threat to a client's interests and support Derrick Bell's observation that "[i]dealism, though perhaps rarer than greed, is harder to control."[3]

NOTES ON MCMUNIGAL

1. *Who Speaks for Causes and Constituencies?* When lawyers seek to represent causes or constituencies as well as individuals and organizations, who "speaks" for the causes or constituencies? If the lawyer

---

[2] Model Rule 7.3 cmt. 4 (emphasis added).

[3] Derrick A. Bell Jr., *Serving Two Masters: Integration Ideals and Client Interests In School Desegregation Litigation,* 85 YALE L. J. 470 (1976).

herself decides what is in the interests of the cause or constituency, what steps can she take to ensure that her judgments about the interests and preferences of the client are consistent with her client's interests and preferences?

2.   ***Is It Permissible to Consider the Impact of Precedent?*** Was it necessarily wrong for Weddington to consider the interests of women who would be affected by the precedent in *Roe v. Wade?* If not, how might she have better reconciled her clear duty to protect McCorvey's interests with her desire to advance to cause of abortion rights?

3.   ***What Changes, If Any, Would You Suggest?*** Does current law provide enough guidance to lawyers about how to manage the issues of accountability raised in the McMunigal excerpt? If not, what changes would you suggest? Would you advocate modifying any of the ethics rules—e.g., Rule 1.7 (examined in Chapter 10), 1.8 (Chapter 6), or 7.3 (Chapter 22)—to take into greater account how ideological as well as pecuniary motives can threaten a lawyer's commitment to clients' interests? If not, why not?

D. VARIATIONS IN PROBLEMS OF ACCOUNTABILITY

The following article, based on a study of civil rights and poverty lawyers in Chicago, explores variation in the types of issues of accountability these lawyer encounter, and it considers how some lawyers attempt to minimize and manage the kinds of conflicts of interest identified by Bell and McMunigal.

COLLECTIVE REPRESENTATION FOR THE DISADVANTAGED: VARIATIONS IN PROBLEMS OF ACCOUNTABILITY
Ann Southworth
67 Fordham Law Review 2449 (1999)

Critics of civil rights and poverty lawyers sometimes suggest that lawyers who venture away from individual representation to pursue collective ends for disadvantaged clients risk betraying members of the groups they purport to serve. Inherent in collective work, some say, is the opportunity and temptation for lawyers to gloss over deep conflicts within represented groups and to substitute their own understanding of the collective good for the client's actual preferences. This Article draws on an empirical study of civil rights and poverty lawyers to identify variations in accountability problems that lawyers confront in representing groups and to suggest that these problems are much less pressing in some types of collective representation than in others.

Lawyers serving poor people have been attracted to collective approaches to stretch resources, to increase their clients' leverage with third-parties, and to help clients build alliances. Aggregating claims sometimes increases access to the legal system for individuals who otherwise would be unable to find representation. Achieving systemic change benefiting large numbers of people often is more efficient than seeking redress for each of many aggrieved individuals. Moreover, claims that might alone seem trivial to a defendant or a policymaker acquire greater significance when asserted on behalf of groups. In projects not involving litigation, groups sometimes can obtain collective goods that they would be unable to secure individually. Helping groups of people form and sustain organizations and pursue collective projects through those organizations enables disadvantaged clients to achieve common ends and build political power.

Collective representation takes various forms. A lawyer representing one person may pursue a precedent or an injunction affecting many people. In such actions, the client is the individual, but the lawyer may regard her work as directed toward social change for a constituency. Lawyers may represent individuals who together pursue a common objective in litigation or legislative advocacy without identifying themselves as a group for any other purpose. Clients and their lawyers may seek remedies on behalf of a plaintiff class. Groups also may form organizations which themselves launch projects, including litigation, on behalf of the organization itself or its members.

Lawyers in all types of collective representation face ethical dilemmas regarding their clients' identities and conflicts within the groups they represent, but civil rights and poverty lawyers' ethical predicaments in collective practice have received particularly critical scrutiny. When public interest lawyers pursue law reform litigation on behalf of individuals, do they owe exclusive fealty to the individual client or may they properly seek to benefit third parties as well? If lawyers seek to represent a constituency or a cause rather than just an individual client, who speaks for that constituency or cause? How should conflicts between the individual and the constituency, or within that constituency, be resolved? When law reform litigation produces precedents affecting persons who are not parties, does the lawyer owe any duty to those affected nonparties? When asked to represent a group, how should a lawyer discern the interests and preferences of that group when it lacks formal decisionmaking procedures? In injunctive class actions, how should the lawyer discern the interests of class members and how should she respond to conflicts within the class?

Current ethics doctrine does not adequately address how lawyers should manage these issues of client autonomy and conflicts of interests in representing groups. Most provisions of the Model Rules of Professional Conduct simply assume that the client is an individual. The rules of ethics require loyalty to individual clients and prohibit lawyers from allowing other interests, including their own, to interfere with their duties to those individuals. A lawyer may represent multiple individuals if she reasonably believes that the representation of those individuals will not be adversely affected and the clients consent to her representing them all, but the clients in such representation remain the individuals rather than the group and the rules generally discourage joint representation. Where the client is an organization, the Model Rules of Professional Conduct, adopted by most states, squeeze organizations into the individual representation model by adopting the "entity theory" of representation, whereby lawyers are to treat the entity, rather than any of its particular members or constituencies, as the client. Under this approach, lawyers generally look to the officers of an organization for guidance about the client's interests and wishes. The Model Rules do not differentiate among types of organizations, and they hardly even mention class actions.

This Article argues for an approach to defining lawyers' ethical obligations when representing groups that recognizes differences, not only between individual and collective representation, but also among different types of collective representation. Although there may be certain common benefits in all forms of collective representation, these types of lawyering differ in important respects—particularly in terms of lawyers' power vis-à-vis clients, the reliability of the decision-making methods employed by groups, and members' opportunities to exit. While injunctive class action litigation almost always raises difficult problems of accountability, and while law reform litigation on behalf of individuals frequently does as well, these issues are far less prominent in the representation of organizations whose internal governance structures generate decisions on behalf of the group. The more individual clients are able to hold accountable the groups in which they participate and the lawyers who represent them, the less we need to worry about lawyers' power to suppress conflict and to speak for those groups.

[We should also pay close] attention to attractive aspects of lawyers' roles in building institutions serving disadvantaged people and [avoid] treating all collective work as threatening to individual client autonomy. In this study, lawyering for organizations was more common than class action litigation, and lawyers for organizations generally said that their clients participated more actively in setting goals and strategy than did clients who were individuals or plaintiff classes. Lawyers who represented organizations also often reported that they facilitated the groups' organizing efforts and improved organizational operations. Far from threatening poor people's capacities to organize, the lawyers in this study who represented organizations appeared to contribute toward that end. The data described here suggest that lawyers sometimes can help poor clients build and sustain institutions (and thereby build and consolidate power) without usurping the client group's prerogative to define goals.

I. Comparing Forms of Collective Representation

In 1993 and 1994, I conducted interviews with sixty-nine lawyers who worked on civil rights and poverty issues in Chicago to learn about their work and relationships with clients. [The study included lawyers in several different practice settings, including legal services, grass-roots clinics, civil rights firms, law firms not primarily devoted to civil rights, law school clinics, and advocacy organizations.] Many of the clients described by lawyers in this study were groups rather than individuals, and, therefore, this study invites attention to differences among these types of group representation.

[C]ollective work constituted over two-thirds of the 197 matters described by lawyers in this study. In thirty-seven matters on behalf of individuals, lawyers said that law reform was one of the purposes of the representation. Lawyers reported that plaintiff classes were their clients in thirty-six matters. In sixty-four matters, lawyers described the client as an organization. [These organizations included 16 advocacy organizations, 10 service organizations, 20 economic development organizations, 2 church-related organizations, 5 for-profit entities, 4 tenant organizations, and 7 coalitions, committees, and councils.] This latter category comprised primarily formal organizations but also several groups whose structure and processes were just beginning to take shape.

Even if the composition of collective representation in this study differs from the makeup of civil rights and poverty practice elsewhere in the United States, it calls into question the view that collective work in civil rights and poverty practice proceeds primarily through class action litigation, and it allows comparison among different types of group representation. In this study, work on behalf of organizations formed a much more prominent part of the collective dimension of civil rights lawyering than class actions did. The class actions described here were almost exclusively injunctive class actions rather than small-claims damages actions, and the classes were mostly unorganized groups. Lawyers' reports about their roles in setting strategy and about what their work achieved also indicate significant differences in clients' decision-making functions and benefits achieved by types of collective representation. They suggest that organizations generally may be better able than plaintiff classes and individuals to work with lawyers without surrendering control over their purposes. They also show that organizations often pursue objectives as to which the class action and law reform types of collective representation are irrelevant.

Client Autonomy. Where the clients were organizations, lawyers were more likely to report that the client controlled the decisions about strategy than they were in any other type of client representation. Lawyers representing individuals in law reform litigation and lawyers handling class actions generally reported that they played more significant roles than did lawyers representing organizations or individuals where there was no law reform component.

These differences in lawyers' accounts of their roles in setting strategy were consistent with these lawyers' narrative observations. Lawyers for individuals often indicated that their clients looked to them as experts who would tell them what to do, and lawyers who represented individuals in law reform cases sometimes indicated that their strategy choices were influenced by law reform implications. Lawyers for plaintiff classes typically reported that they set strategy largely on their own. Lawyers for organizations generally described their roles more narrowly. One lawyer observed, in characteristic fashion, "my job is to define the parameters." As to another matter, this lawyer stated, "I don't think I played a significant role at all; I was a sounding board, not a catalyst." Lawyers who represented established organizations commonly reported that their clients had formulated their essential strategy before coming to the lawyer and that the lawyer helped them refine and execute their plans.

This study did not gather information necessary to explain these reported differences in lawyers' roles by client type, but one might reasonably conclude that structural attributes of these different types of representation help explain those variations. The prominent role in setting strategy described by lawyers in class actions is consistent with scholarship analyzing accountability problems in class actions. Plaintiff classes ordinarily are unorganized groups who do not exist before or after the suit. In this study, for example, plaintiff classes included inmates confined to segregation in the Illinois prisons, mothers of children on AFDC, and children in Illinois state mental institutions. Class representatives typically lack any direct accountability to the class members they represent. Moreover, class actions lack formal procedural mechanisms for assessing preferences of class members or for holding accountable the attorneys who represent them. All but one of the class actions in this study were injunctive class actions, in which members of the class are not even entitled to notice of the action. Although courts are required to monitor the representation at the class certification and settlement phases of the litigation, they often exercise little independent scrutiny. As one lawyer in my study noted, "the court never says, '[W]hat does your client think about that, Mr. [X]?'"

The influential roles of lawyers for individuals in this study are consistent with other empirical evidence demonstrating that lawyers typically exercise substantial control in service to poor individuals and in "personal plight" practice. Those who have tried to account for these

relatively high levels of control by lawyers representing poor individuals
have cited, on the one hand, clients' lack of confidence, sophistication, and
financial leverage and, on the other, lawyers' interest in using scarce
resources efficiently, their perception that clients rely on them to set
strategy, and, sometimes, their sense that poor pay and working
conditions entitle them to depart from conventional client-centered
norms.

A variety of reasons might explain why lawyers in this study
reported that organizations played more significant roles in setting
strategy than plaintiff classes did. Most obviously, organizations, unlike
plaintiff classes, are capable of resolving internal disputes and generating
strategy choices. Whereas classes ordinarily do not endure beyond the
suit, organizations exist before and after the representation and they
have extra-litigation mechanisms for ensuring that the organizations'
leaders represent the interests of members. Unlike individual members of
a class, who generally are stuck with the position taken on behalf of the
class in injunctive class actions, individuals who are disgruntled by the
collective stance selected by an organization ordinarily may leave the
group. Organizations that fail to adequately represent the views and
interests of their members risk losing their members' support. Thus,
lawyers generally may defer to the group's decision-making procedures
because they ordinarily reflect choices by individual members to commit
themselves to the group. Moreover, groups that are sufficiently well-
organized to present themselves as organizations may be better
positioned than poor individuals to insist on calling the shots vis-à-vis
their lawyers.

II. Lessons for Lawyers' Ethics

Just as our procedural rules governing class actions may reflect
ambivalence about when to allow collective litigation to proceed in our
resolutely individualistic legal system, current ethics doctrine offers
scattered bits of guidance about how lawyers should approach certain
types of collective representation without embracing any overarching
theory for managing problems of conflicts and accountability in collective
work. The rules generally assume that the client is an individual without
squarely acknowledging that, more often than not, lawyers represent
groups rather than individuals. Moreover, under current doctrine,
deciding whether to characterize one's representation as individual
representation, organizational representation, or class representation, is
pivotal; it leads to strikingly different guidelines for interacting with
clients. If one represents several individuals, the rules generally provide
that the lawyer owes a duty of loyalty and confidentiality to each of them
as individuals and that any conflict among them requires the lawyer to
withdraw from the representation of all. If the client is an organization,
whether formal or not, the lawyer is charged with representing that

organization rather than any of its constituents, and conflicts within the entity generally are to be resolved by reference to the organization's internal structure. Where the organizational structure is clear, this doctrine offers relatively simple answers about how lawyers should discern the client's interests and preferences; ordinarily, the lawyer looks to the officers for answers. Ethics doctrine, however, offers little guidance about representing groups that are just beginning to take shape and groups whose decision making processes fail to protect those whom the organization is designed to serve. In matters where the client organization lacks reliable internal governance procedures, lawyers are left to the ambiguous application of the "entity" theory to a group whose interests may be difficult to discern, whose constituencies may have conflicting interests, and/or whose members cannot agree, or have not yet agreed, on mechanisms for resolving disagreements. In the area of representation most plagued by conflicts and accountability problems—injunctive class actions—the Model Code and the Model Rules have virtually nothing to say.

This Article does not attempt to develop any uniform set of rules regarding conflicts and accountability issues in the many different circumstances in which lawyers represent groups. To the contrary, it argues in favor of an approach that is sensitive to the actual practice contexts in which lawyers work and to the pressures and constraints that influence lawyer behavior. Here I sketch a general framework for assessing conflicts and accountability in the various types of collective work that lawyers pursue for poor people.

Requiring lawyers to be accountable to clients and to respond to conflicts within groups may require different approaches for different types of collective representation, because the opportunities, pressures, and constraints of these various types of practice vary significantly. This study illustrates that, even within civil rights and poverty practice, groups differ substantially in their accountability to their own members and in their lawyers' power with respect to the groups. In law reform work on behalf of individuals, clients often have little leverage with lawyers who wish to pursue the cause at the expense of the client. Moreover, the constituencies on behalf of whom lawyers seek to change the law generally have no way of registering their preferences because they lack any formal relationship with the lawyer. In large injunctive class action litigation, the absence of formal mechanisms for discerning the preferences of class members and the inadequacy of current procedures for protecting the interests of dissenters give lawyers enormous power and responsibility to define the client's interests and to set strategy. As one lawyer in my sample observed, "It's very easy to lose touch with your clients, and then you become your client. [I]t's very easy to fall into this practice of not talking to clients and then just making all the decisions for clients." Lawyers who represent groups that are just taking shape and selecting methods for making decisions engage in a delicate task, because these clients often depend heavily on their lawyers' advice and because such fledgling organizations may be vulnerable to hijacking by willful leaders. Lawyers who represent groups whose decision-making structures give real voice to their members' deliberations and guidance to their lawyers about how to implement their collective purposes have less opportunity and justification for substituting their own goals and strategies. Even when those processes are not perfectly democratic, decisions generated by those procedures generally reflect arrangements agreed upon by participants in the group.

Any move toward clarifying lawyers' obligations in collective practice should take into account structural differences in various types of collective representation. With respect to another set of ethical issues—external questions about how lawyers should balance their responsibilities to clients against their responsibilities to third parties and the public—William Simon advocates a model of ethics according to which lawyers "attempt to reconcile the conflicting legal values implicated directly in the client's claim or goal." One of the variables he asks lawyers to consider is whether procedural mechanisms available for evaluating the client's proposed course of conduct are reliable: "[T]he more reliable the relevant procedures and institutions, the less direct responsibility the lawyer need assume for the substantive justice of the resolution; the less reliable the procedures and institutions, the more direct responsibility she need assume for substantive justice." Applying a similar criterion to an internal question about lawyer accountability—how to assess the client's interest and how to balance the interests of conflicting constituencies within the group—lawyers' ethics should consider the reliability of the procedures by which decisions will be made for the group, or in the case of formal organizations, for the natural persons who are the group's beneficiaries. The more reliable the decision-making structures and opportunities for exit by individual members, the less direct responsibility the lawyer should bear for discerning the interests and preferences of the group's members and responding to evidence of dissent within the group.

Applying this framework to the types of collective representation illustrated in this study yields the following basic guidelines for assessing clients' interests and resolving conflicts. Lawyers representing individuals in law reform litigation should be permitted to represent individuals whose interests and preferences coincide with their own law reform commitments, but they generally should serve their clients' ends at the expense of law reform if those purposes diverge, and they should not purport to represent the constituency of affected persons, who have no recourse against the lawyer. [Several lawyers in this study acknowledged that they had faced conflicts between their own law reform commitments and their clients' preferences, but all of those who indicated that they had such conflicts said that they resolved the conflict in favor of the client.] In class actions, lawyers should exercise ethical sensitivity in discharging their largely unconstrained role as class counsel. They should attempt to understand and to represent the interests of the members of the class and be attentive to conflicts within the class. Lawyers representing organizations whose decision-making structures are well-defined and from which members can easily exit generally may defer to decisions generated by those processes, except where they believe that those who speak for the organization are abusing the trust of the organization's intended beneficiaries. Organizations of poor people, no less than corporations, generally should benefit from the presumption that the entity, rather than its individual members, is the client. In groups without any formal decision-making apparatus, lawyers should help clients develop democratic processes for generating decisions.

This focus on the structure of relationships between lawyers and groups and between groups and their members in civil rights and poverty practice highlights how organizations sometimes can function as mediating institutions through which lawyers facilitate collective action without attempting to define clients' interests. Scholars have written extensively during recent years about the virtues of voluntary organizations. Commentators from both the left and the right embrace community organizations as vehicles for delivering social services and structuring civic life. A large body of recent research suggests that participation in local organizations powerfully improves communities' prospects for bettering schools, reducing crime, and promoting economic development. Proponents of organizations also applaud the ways in which collective processes shape individual participants' perceptions of their own interests and distill them through the lens of collective goals.

This [study] adds one more item to the list of organizations' virtues. Unlike class actions and law reform litigation, which impose few structural constraints on lawyers' conduct, organizations generally have internal mechanisms for resolving conflict and generating decisions binding on their lawyers. Unlike the members of injunctive plaintiff class actions and beneficiaries of reform litigation, who may constitute a group only in the limited sense that they share certain attributes as victims, members of small organizations share voluntary bonds; they generally have chosen to join groups and to participate as members. Class action lawsuits and law reform litigation on behalf of individuals have the advantage of allowing the enforcement of collective rights without the hard work of organizing. Indeed, it may be almost impossible to organize some of the disparate groups whose interests these devices sometimes promote. Nevertheless, organizations can protect dissenters and generate consensus in ways that class actions and impact litigation on behalf of individuals cannot.

Conclusion. Lawyers for poor people often serve groups rather than individuals. Yet, our conceptions of ethical lawyering draw primarily from models of service to individuals. Critics of lawyers for poor people often equate collective representation with class action litigation and other types of impact litigation as to which structural attributes of the groups represented and their relationships with their lawyers create serious problems of conflicts and accountability. This Article illustrates that collective representation for poor people often takes the form of representing organizations, where conflicts and lawyer accountability issues generally are much less worrisome and where the goals pursued may differ from those ordinarily sought through law reform work. Any move toward revising ethics doctrine to acknowledge that lawyers routinely serve groups rather than individuals should be sensitive to these important differences in types of collective representation. In a time when critics often suggest that lawyers threaten client autonomy whenever they depart from the most humble types of individual client service, we should avoid discouraging lawyers from helping clients build organizations and institutions serving clients' collective as well as individual needs.

NOTES ON SOUTHWORTH

1. **What Variation?** What are the basic differences in issues of accountability presented by the various types of collective representation in which public interest/cause lawyers engage?

2. **How Can a Lawyer Discern the Preferences of a Large Group?** In situations where a lawyer represents large groups (classes, informal groups, constituencies) that lack formal internal decision-making procedures, how should she discern the interests and preferences of the group? What specific measures should the lawyer take to ensure that she is speaking for the client(s)?

3. **Lawyer Accountability in the Representation of Organizations.** How, if at all, does the representation of organizations ameliorate the accountability problems presented in other types of collective representation? Do the issues of accountability actually disappear, or are they just defined away by the "single entity" notion embodied in Rule 1.13, which disguises conflict by treating disparate and sometimes conflicting constituents of an organization as one?

E. SUMMARY

This chapter has examined issues of accountability that arise when the intended beneficiaries of the lawyer's work are large constituencies rather than individual clients. We explored several high profile instances in which critics have argued that lawyers employed by public interest organizations have been insufficiently responsive to the needs and preferences of their clients. Derrick Bell's critique of civil rights lawyers' handling of school desegregation litigation in the 1970s asserted that those lawyers' commitment to the cause of integration led them to disregard the needs and preferences of some members of the plaintiff class—parents who wished to focus on improving predominantly black schools rather than continuing to fight for complete integration. His critique raised questions about how lawyers handling injunctive class actions should respond to dissent within a plaintiff class and how they should manage conflicts between class members' preferences and the mission of the organization that employs the lawyers. A case study of interactions between the lawyer and client in *Roe v. Wade* highlighted questions about how lawyers should manage tensions between the interests of the lawyer's individual client, the lawyer's ideological commitments, and the larger constituency that might be affected by a precedent. This chapter also considered more broadly the various types of collective representation in which public interest lawyers engage and variations in issues of accountability that arise in these types of representation. We explored whether the Model Rules' emphasis on individual client representation, and its neglect of group representation, leave lawyers with inadequate guidance about how to handle thorny issues of accountability in their work on behalf of groups and constituencies.

PART VI

CHALLENGES AND OPPORTUNITIES FOR THE PROFESSION IN THE 21ST CENTURY

■ ■ ■

The sixth and final Part of this book steps back—from questions about the various practice contexts in which lawyers work, the work they perform, and the ethical issues they confront in each of those arenas (the focus of Part V)—to explore big-picture questions about problems and opportunities for the American legal profession as a whole. The purpose of this Part is to prepare you to develop informed views on an interesting set of policy questions with major implications for lawyers and the public.

We begin with three chapters on access to legal services: the cost of legal services, unauthorized practice and innovation in legal services delivery, and pro bono. We then address questions of diversity in the profession, including the experience of racial and ethnic minorities and people with disabilities, and issues relating to gender and sexual orientation. Next we consider the consequences of the nationalization and globalization of the legal services market, as well as some legal and practical challenges posed by multi-disciplinary and transnational practice. We then consider legal education, bar admission, and discipline. The two final chapters may be of especially great relevance to your happiness in the profession: one reviews the literature on lawyer satisfaction, and the last reflects broadly on the future of the legal profession and your place within it.

CHAPTER 31

THE MARKET FOR LEGAL SERVICES

■ ■ ■

A. INTRODUCTION

This chapter is the first of three that consider issues of access to legal services. In Chapter 28, we examined legal assistance programs, where lawyers serve some of those who cannot afford to hire lawyers. That chapter also briefly reviewed available research on the legal needs of ordinary Americans. But we have not previously considered the larger questions of how the market for legal services operates, how well it works for various types of clients, who is permitted to provide legal services, and the organized bar's positions on these issues. The next several chapters explore those topics.

The ideal of equality before the law, or equality under law, is a fundamental political commitment and legitimating principle of the American system of government, reflected in the inscription over the main entrance to the United States Supreme Court building: "Equal Justice Under Law." Our legal system is complex, and navigating the system and gaining access to the machinery of law often requires assistance from someone with legal training. Therefore, whether people find equal justice under law may turn on the availability of affordable legal services.

Discussions about access to legal services are often intertwined with controversies over whether existing legal rules and procedures are too complex and whether our society relies excessively on law, lawyers, and litigation. These are topics of hot debate in American political life, and they reflect hard trade-offs. For now, we sidestep questions about the role of the courts in our society, the relationship between law and other mechanisms of social control, and whether the complexity of our legal system is a vice or virtue. Our focus here is on the availability and distribution of legal services and their implications for the justice system.

This chapter examines how the market for legal services operates. Much as lawyers may like to think of themselves as a profession that functions apart from markets, legal services in this country are distributed almost entirely through market mechanisms. Moreover, the market for legal services profoundly affects how our legal system and economy function, and it is shaped fundamentally by rules governing who can provide legal services. Understanding how this market works and its effects on the civil justice system is critical to debates about whether lawyers should continue to hold almost exclusive regulatory control over the provision of legal services.

The first excerpt in this chapter, by law professor and economist Gillian Hadfield, argues that the market for lawyers is imperfectly competitive and that lawyers' market power drives up the cost of legal services and makes them unaffordable for most individual consumers. We then consider the views of sociologist Rebecca Sandefur, who challenges the premise that cost is a major impediment to ordinary Americans' use of lawyers and suggests alternative explanations for why people often do not "take their problems to law." The third excerpt, also by Hadfield, notes that issues of access are not just about obtaining legal services to manage crises after the fact; also implicated are ex ante (before-the-fact) legal services—e.g., advice and assistance on loan agreements, insurance coverage, employment options, health care, and legal issues relating to family relationships. Her article raises troubling questions about whether lawyer control over the provision of legal services impedes ordinary households' access to the assistance they need to navigate the "law-thick" world in which we live.

B. THE COST OF LEGAL SERVICES

THE PRICE OF LAW: HOW THE MARKET FOR LAWYERS DISTORTS THE JUSTICE SYSTEM

Gillian K. Hadfield
98 Michigan Law Review 953 (2000)

Why do lawyers cost so much? Conventional popular culture has one suggestion: lawyers are an avaricious lot who will bleed you dry. Conventional economics has another: legal training is expensive. And conventional professional wisdom has another: lawyers enjoy a state-granted monopoly over which they control entry for the purposes of protecting the public. None of these is particularly compelling. While each seems to hold some grain of truth, each also raises more questions than it answers. How is it that the profession has come to be dominated by vice? Why is law so complicated that legal training is so expensive? Is the public better off with inexpensive low quality legal advice or high quality legal advice it cannot afford?

[In this article] I catalogue features of the market for lawyers and legal services that can be expected to cause the market to deviate from the conditions of perfect competition.

Complexity: The Cost of Complex Reasoning and Process. Lawyers are expensive, in the first instance, when what they do is complex and requires sophisticated and careful reasoning and the exercise of thoughtful judgment.

This account of the high price of lawyers appears quite benign, the product of competitive market forces: price equals cost. And indeed the fact of legal complexity and the cost of legal training plainly are a basis for legal expense in many cases. There are a few pieces of the complexity argument that we need to examine more closely, however, in order to see the problem with a straightforward claim that the cost of lawyers is simply the result of competitive market mechanisms and hence, in a sense, just a fact of economic life.

The hours required to resolve a legal matter are not fixed by abstract and immutable principles of justice. They are determined by procedures and reasoning requirements established and implemented by members of the profession (lawyers and judges and legislators) in an antagonistic, interactive process. From an economic point of view it then makes sense to ask whether the amount of time required to resolve a matter—essentially the complexity of the relevant law and procedure—is optimal: is the value obtained by an increase in complexity justified by the cost of increased lawyer time? This question has to be asked not only of a particular case, but, more importantly, of the system as a whole.

Credence Goods: The Role of Uncertainty. Economists refer to a good as a credence good if it is provided by an expert who also determines the buyer's needs. Buyers of credence goods are unable to assess how much of the good or service they need; nor can they assess whether or not the service was performed or how well. This puts buyers at risk of opportunistic behavior on the part of sellers: they may be sold too much of a service or billed for services not performed or performed poorly.

Legal services are credence goods. The sheer complexity of law makes it difficult for clients to judge the service they are receiving. Law is not merely complex. It is so complex that it is also highly ambiguous and unpredictable.

The process of resolving anything other than a routine legal matter involves many cumulative effects resulting from a cascade of judgments, large and small—what evidence to produce, how to craft pleadings or contractual language, what tone of voice to adopt in testimony or argument or negotiation, how cooperative or combative to be in response to other parties, how quickly to push for a decision, how much to spend on research or outside experts, and so on.

As a result of this sensitivity to detail and differences, law is also highly unpredictable. This makes it extremely difficult for anyone, including other lawyers, to judge whether the time spent on a case was honestly and carefully determined—whether the work performed on a case was the result of care and skill. As a consequence, the market for legal services is even more fundamentally disrupted than is ordinarily the case for credence goods. There is no way for ordinary competitive mechanisms to operate effectively when it is difficult to assess and therefore compare the services offered by competing providers.

Winner-Take-All: The Tournament of Superstars. It might seem that the difficulty of attributing legal outcomes to the quality of lawyering and so differentiating among lawyers would lead to a situation in which clients, recognizing the difficulties, are willing to pay only small premiums for lawyers they believe to be "better." If that were the case, high prices could be undercut by lawyers clients believed to be slightly less good but considerably cheaper. But the market for lawyers does not work this way.

Legal work is conducted in a tournament-style setting. What this means is that the impact of a lawyer on a legal outcome is a function not of the absolute quality of the lawyer, but of the lawyer's quality relative to the lawyers on the other side. Having a lawyer who is marginally better pays off disproportionately. Conversely, entrusting your case to a lawyer who is likely to be outperformed, even if only slightly, can cost you the case. As a result, the difference in value between a lawyer who is good and one who is marginally better can be very large. Clients are therefore (rationally) willing to pay a lot for a little.

Monopoly. The commonly recognized source of [lawyers'] monopoly power is artificial barriers to entry to the practice of law: state prohibition of the practice of law by nonlawyers and limitations on the number of people admitted to law schools and the bar. [Another] less recognized but probably more important source of the power to extract rents[*] is the state's monopoly on coercive dispute resolution—only dispute resolution through the public courts can force the other party to the table.

In light of its monopoly over coercive dispute resolution, the unified and importantly homogeneous nature of the legal profession takes on tremendous importance. The profession defines and reproduces itself. It establishes entry requirements that homogenize the reasoning processes and to some extent the values of its members—judges, lawyers, even many legislators. [D]ramatic responses to the perceptions, needs, and constraints of those who require dispute resolution services are unlikely to come from within the profession.

The Unified Profession. Although there are systematic differences among lawyers, and plenty of specialization and socioeconomic barriers affecting the distribution of lawyers across the corporate and personal spheres, we nonetheless have a single "legal system." Seen from a market perspective, this means that individuals and entities are pitted against

---

[*]   [Eds.: Economic rents are the additional profits that the monopolist can extract on account of its market position.]

one another in competition for access to legal resources. If we divide the world into personal and business clients, it is immediately evident that these client groups fundamentally differ in terms of their command of wealth. It is the wealth of the business client group that ultimately determines pricing in the market(s) for lawyers. Driven by corporate demand, backed by corporate wealth, the legal system prices itself out of the reach of all individuals except those with a claim on corporate wealth.

A market that puts individual clients in a bidding competition with corporate clients therefore necessarily ends up serving predominantly corporate clients at a price determined by corporate pre-tax wealth. This is a price that is systematically out of the reach of individuals. The only exceptions are individuals who have claims on aggregated wealth which can be accessed to pay lawyers, such as the victims of torts committed by corporate or insured tortfeasors, or shareholders with the right to maintain a derivative action against corporate managers.

The separate client groups that emerge in the market for lawyers represent fundamentally different goals for the legal system. Individuals invoke those parts of the legal system concerned with individual rights, personal dispute resolution, democratic governance, and social control. Business clients invoke those parts of the legal system concerned with management of the economy and corporate relationships—policing market conduct, regulating the production and distribution of goods and services by businesses, and resolving disputes between market competitors and contracting partners.

[I]t is important to emphasize that governance of the economy is a legitimate and necessary role for a legal system. The problem with the market for lawyers, however, is that this role squeezes out the other legitimate, and arguably primary, roles for law. The question for reform, then, is likely to be how the legal system might be restructured so as to reconcile the achievement of economic goals with more fundamental justice goals.

NOTES ON THE PRICE OF LAW

1. ***Imperfect Competition in the Legal Services Market.*** In what ways, and to what extent, do structural attributes of the U.S. market for legal services cause it to deviate from conditions of perfect competition?

2. ***Credence Goods.*** What is a credence good and why does Hadfield think that legal services fall within the definition? Based on what you have learned thus far in law school, do you think she is right?

3. ***Complexity and Monopoly.*** How do the complexity of law and the legal profession's monopoly over coercive dispute resolution affect the cost of legal services? Are you persuaded by Hadfield's account on these points? To the extent that these features of our system are undesirable, what reforms

might address the problem and what would be the disadvantages of such reforms?

4. **Competition Between Corporate Clients and Individual Clients.** How do corporate clients drive up the cost of legal services, according to Hadfield? Do you find her argument persuasive?

5. **Legal Training.** Hadfield draws attention to the fact that all lawyers in the U.S. are trained and licensed under a single model: three years of general law school education followed by a bar exam. How might this aspect of our legal system—its reliance on one unified set of educational and licensing requirements for lawyers serving all types of clients—bear on the cost of legal services? Would you favor disaggregating the legal profession into different tracks with different training requirements for lawyers serving different types of clients? What would be the advantages and disadvantages of such a change? We return to this issue in Chapter 35, on legal education.

C. OTHER INFLUENCES ON ORDINARY AMERICANS' USE OF LEGAL SERVICES

Hadfield's economic analysis in "The Price of Law" considers how imperfect competition in the market for legal services affects the cost of those services. In her account, the cost of legal services is a major barrier to access to legal services for all but corporations and very wealthy individuals. The following article questions Hadfield's assumption that cost is the primary impediment to ordinary Americans' use of lawyers.

MONEY ISN'T EVERYTHING: UNDERSTANDING MODERATE
INCOME HOUSEHOLDS' USE OF LAWYERS' SERVICES

Rebecca L. Sandefur
Middle Income Access to Justice (eds. Michael Trebilcock, Anthony Duggan,
Lorne Sossin & Michael Trebilcock, University of Toronto Press 2012)

Public Experience with Civil Justice Problems in the United States. In contemporary market democracies, law reaches deeply into many aspects of daily life. Civil justice problems are common and widespread. Though such problems come in many different forms that affect different aspects of people's lives and concern different kinds of relationships, they share a certain important quality: they are problems that have civil legal aspects, raise civil legal issues and have consequences shaped by civil law, even though the people who experience them may never think of them as "legal" and may never attempt to use law to try to resolve them.

For many people living in market democracies, such troubles emerge at the intersection of civil law and everyday adversity. For example, conservative estimates suggest that more than 100 million Americans are currently living in households that are experiencing at least one civil justice problem involving key areas of contemporary life such as livelihood, shelter, employment, health care, the intergenerational conservation of property, intimate relationships, and the care and support of dependent children and adults. [M]ost of these justice problems never make it to law: they are not taken to lawyers for advice or representation, nor do people pursue them in court.

A predominant account of why Americans do not take their problems to law features cost—not the cost of the civil justice system itself, which Americans have in a sense already paid for with their taxes, but the direct costs of using the system, particularly the cost of lawyers' services.

The Cost of Lawyers' Services. A quick glance at the disparity between the average lawyer's earnings and the average American's earnings reveals some of the basis for the perception that lawyers' services are priced out of the reach of many ordinary people. In 2009, the median annual earnings of American lawyers were $113,240. Compare that with median income for an American household in the same year, $49,777, and one sees that a single lawyer, on average, earns more than twice as much in a year as an entire American household, many of which include more than one earner. Lawyers do make a lot of money, at least on average and in relative terms.

However, when we examine not lawyers' earnings but what people pay lawyers, we learn quickly that we do not know a great deal about the costs of personal legal services—the kind that might be purchased by middle income folks when they face a divorce, or need to settle an estate, or have a problem with their employer, or experience identity theft, for example. No major contemporary survey asks Americans how much they paid for lawyers' services to handle a specific justice problem; nor do any of the recent social scientific surveys of lawyers ask attorneys or firms how much they charged for a case or consultation or body of work.

The information that does exist about what lawyers charge and what people pay for common legal services is thin, but it suggests that the costs of legal services vary greatly, from sums that would be affordable out-of-pocket for many moderate income households to sums that are potentially ruinous. A small body of work examines lawyers who work on contingent fee arrangements in tort cases, such as medical malpractice and auto accidents. Much of this work explores how lawyers secure clients, select cases, and allocate their work effort. When it explores lawyers' fees, the typical finding is that the effective hourly rates charged by contingent fee attorneys are, on average, modest: the mean effective hourly rate lawyers' received for contingent fee service circa 1980 was $47 per hour. These studies are informative, but they tend to focus more on lawyers than on consumers. They also provide information about only one group of justice problems. Some common justice problems, like divorce and child support, may not be served through contingent fee arrangements.[1] Other justice problems involve stakes that are too small to support contingent fee legal services, or appear to attorneys to have too low a likelihood of success to justify the costs of pursuing a case. In general, contingent fees are not practical for contractual work in which no money changes hands, such as writing a will or renegotiating the terms of a lease, or for preventative legal advice.

Information more to the point comes from a smattering of sources that survey lawyers about what they charge for specific services or ask consumers about what they actually paid. [A] survey, conducted in 1987 and 1988, inquired into lawyers' typical charges for specific legal services as part of their applications to participate in a group legal services plan. The quantities reported are the average full retail cost that lawyers reported in the survey, which I am terming a "Rack rate" in recognition of the fact that many clients will pay less.

The second source of cost information, which I am terming the Anecdata Cost, comes from a website, Cost Helper, that receives cost estimates for selected services from consumers and providers who visit the site. This information is "anecdata" because it is a sample of convenience, reflecting the reports of people who happened to post to the website. Anecdata give us a glimpse of some people's experiences, but give us no information about how representative those experiences are. Nevertheless, CostHelper is a contemporary source, and produces estimates that are on par with the inflation-adjusted estimates based on the 1987–88 survey of attorneys.

[S]ome kinds of basic, transactional legal services appear to be relatively affordable. Based on the attorney survey, real estate settlements cost in at a Rack Rate of around $1,000, depending on one's assumptions about inflation. Anecdata suggest that residential contract review may cost a couple of hundred dollars. A simple will has an average Rack Rate cost of $139 to $201, depending on assumptions about inflation, and an Anecdata Cost range of $150 to $600 or more. To put these amounts in perspective, in 2009 American households spent an average of about $2,600 on eating out in restaurants, and an additional about $2,700 on various forms of entertainment. Given these expenditures, we can surmise that many households probably could have afforded the costs of, for example, a simple will. On the other hand, some kinds of personal legal services are more expensive. The notable example is divorce. Especially when substantial litigation is involved, as in the case of contested divorces, legal services can be quite costly, running into the tens of thousands of dollars. To put the costs of contested divorce into

---

[1] Model Rule 1.5(d) provides that a lawyer may not enter into a contingent fee arrangement in divorce and criminal defense matters.

perspective, consider that, for what an American might pay in legal fees for a contested divorce, he or she could alternatively buy a new car.

[Sandefur also reports additional findings from the Civil Litigation Research Project (CLRP), a landmark study of public civil disputing behavior.] Among its data sources, CLRP included a sample of law suits and lawyers involved in what project authors termed "ordinary litigation." [These data include] legal services purchased by businesses as well as individuals; and focus[ ] on that rarified subset of justice problems that become cases filed with courts. We might expect that justice problems that become lawsuits are among the most complex, protracted and costly in terms of the consumption of lawyers' services. In a majority of these cases (59%), depending upon assumptions about inflation, total lawyers' fees were less than $3,500 to $5000 in current dollars, while a small number of cases were quite costly, leading to tens of thousands of dollars in lawyers' fees.

Taken together, the available data reveal that some legal services, in particular contested divorces, may cost tens of thousands of dollars. Other legal work, such as writing a simple will or settling the sale of a house, may cost as little as a few hundred dollars.

The little we know about the costs of legal services to ordinary Americans suggests that these costs vary from affordable to expensive. What we know about consumer satisfaction with legal fees suggests that when Americans purchase lawyers' services, they are often content with what they had to pay. Taken together, these two findings suggest that other factors besides money must be at play when people who are facing justice problems consider what to do about them. Indeed, when we turn to people's own accounts of why they do not turn to lawyers for their justice problems, cost plays a role, but it is not the predominant reason that people report for not taking their civil justice problems to lawyers.

The Social Construction of Legality. Among the most important reasons that people do not take their problems to lawyers is the fact that they do not think of those problems as legal. The legal nature of any given civil justice problem is not a self-evident fact, but is socially constructed. When confronted with a specific situation, the characterization of that situation as a legal problem reflects both how people think about and what people do about their own troubles, as well as the interactions they have with the friends, neighbors, family members and service providers to whom they may bring their troubles.

When Americans are asked not about their use of law, but simply about their experiences with justice problems, it becomes quickly evident that they often do not think of their justice problems in legal terms. In some of my own recent work, I invited randomly selected low- and moderate-income Americans living in two middle-sized cities in the US

Midwest to attend focus group meetings where they could discuss their experiences with "challenges facing American families today." The group meetings lasted one and half to two hours, and took place on weekday evenings in locations that were easily accessible by either car or public transportation, such as community centers and libraries. The groups were income stratified, so that people discussed these challenges in a context where other participants faced similar general economic circumstances and were eligible for similar kinds of charitable and public services.

People face many different kinds of problems and challenges; my interest was in those that might have civil legal aspects. Therefore, to help focus the participants' thinking on common justice problems, they were handed a card that listed some common kinds of challenges, all of which can involve civil justice problems. In the meetings, the first exercise was to go around the room and invite each participant to tell a story about his or her own experiences with a problem like the kinds listed on the card. [A]lmost all of the problems they described were civil justice problems in the sense that they had justiciable, or legally actionable, aspects.

One quality common to many participants' accounts of their experiences with civil justice problems was alegality: people described their experiences with problems that had clear legal aspects, raised obvious legal issues, and often had routes to remedy provided by formal law, but they did so in terms that made no reference to law, lawyers or courts.

There are clear legal aspects in the situation [one] person described. [S]he wanted to make a claim for the death benefits to which her child would be entitled under the federal Social Security program, a publicly subsidized life insurance program that pays survivors' benefits to the minor children of decedents who had been employed in eligible occupations and made tax contributions into the system before death. In order to secure these benefits, petitioners must go through a formal process that requires properly filling out specific forms and submitting documents in support of the application. In this case, a successful application would require providing evidence establishing the paternity of the child. It appears that this person's initial application was denied, which means that, in order to pursue her claim, she would have had to file a formal appeal asking for a reconsideration of her file, leading perhaps eventually an administrative hearing.

But despite law being "all over" her situation, she never mentions law, lawyers or attorneys in her account. On the other hand, among the most common words in her account is "help." This focus on help, but not specifically legal help, was also a common quality of people's stories about their experiences with their civil justice problems. People wanted help with their problems, but it was often not legal help that they described wishing for or turning to.

The pattern of alegality that I found in my study of public experience with civil justice problems is consistent with findings from studies of rights consciousness. The work seeks evidence of how people understand their legal rights when confronted with different kinds of situations that are formally governed by those rights. What I am terming alegality, the absence of thinking in terms of law or rights, turns out to appear in people's experiences with a wide variety of kinds of justice problems, including those involving family relationships, personal injury, invasions of privacy, street harassment, and employment and working conditions.

A pattern of pervasive alegality is consistent with behaviors of people who report in response to their justice problems in U.S. surveys. Among moderate income households in the 1992 ABA survey, law "was not considered at all" for the majority—60 percent—of civil justice problems experienced.

If we take people's behavior as indicative of what is shaping their thinking, we can infer an important factor that shapes the social construction of legality: the institutions of remedy that are available to people facing civil justice problems. Institutions of remedy provide ways of understanding civil justice problems, tools for handling them, and established, regularized routes to their resolution. Law is one such institution of remedy, but people regularly handle their problems in other ways, for instance by turning to other kinds of third parties for assistance. For some civil justice problems in the US context, however, there are few alternative routes to resolution besides law. Divorce is a prime example of this. While one can quit a job without going to court, it is not possible to formally dissolve a marriage or authoritatively assign custody of dependent children without a legal process. It is not surprising, therefore, that the category of civil justice problem most likely to involve lawyers is—family and domestic matters. In the 1992 ABA survey of moderate income households, 63% of justice problems involving family and domestic matters involved consultation with a lawyer, by comparison with 28% of civil justice problems overall.

One way to try to change how people think about their justice problems would be through campaigns of public legal education, in an effort to encourage people to think of certain kind of problems as legal problems and to go to attorneys for advice about them. An alternative or complementary strategy might be to ask people about the kinds of help they would like with their own justice problems and then develop services that meet people's own perceived needs—even if those services turn out not to be traditional legal services. In the US context, it is likely that providing some of the kinds of services that the public might envision as helpful would require changes in the regulation of lawyers' monopoly.

Policies that would address only the costs of legal services also do nothing to assist middle income people with another problem they face when they want to use lawyers, the problem of selecting a specific provider. Even in a context like the United States, where lawyer advertising has long been permitted and where bar-sponsored lawyer referral services have existed in many communities, members of the public seeking attorneys appear to eschew these impersonal sources in favor of information that comes with a personal warrant, whether from their own experience or the recommendation of someone they know. Expanding access to matching institutions that provide some kind of warrant of quality for providers, such as group legal services plans with performance assessments of serving attorneys, might be one mechanism that would assist people in selecting attorneys.

NOTES ON SANDEFUR

1.   *Why Don't Americans Take Their Problems to Law?* According to Sandefur, what factors influence whether moderate income people use lawyers? In what ways does her account of the significance of the cost of legal services differ from Hadfield's?

2.   *Why Worry?* Should we be concerned by Sandefur's finding that many Americans do not view their civil justice problems as legal problems and that they often do not turn to law to resolve those problems? If so, why?

3.   *Revisiting Lawyers' Monopoly on the Provision of Legal Services.* Do you agree with Sandefur that responding effectively to Americans' perceived needs with respect to civil justice problems might involve abandoning lawyers' monopoly on the provision of legal services?

4.   *Reconciling Sandefur and Hadfield.* Do Sandefur and Hadfield disagree fundamentally about the relationship between the cost of legal services and access to justice, or do they disagree mainly about emphasis?

D. EX ANTE LEGAL SERVICES

Discussions about access to legal services tend to focus clients' needs for representation during crisis situations—for example, providing criminal defense, preventing the client's eviction from housing, or seeking compensation for personal injury. The following excerpt explores a broader array of services that bear on whether ordinary Americans are able to organize their personal relationships and market interactions in ways that take full account of the law. It explores how ex ante (before the fact) advice can help ordinary citizens manage their lives in accordance with law and legality.

HIGHER DEMAND, LOWER SUPPLY? A COMPARATIVE ASSESSMENT OF THE LEGAL RESOURCE LANDSCAPE FOR ORDINARY AMERICANS

Gillian K. Hadfield
37 Fordham Urban Law Journal 129 (2010)

Systematic efforts to assess how well the legal markets and institutions that American lawyers (together with the judiciary) claim they have exclusive authority to structure, serve, and regulate are few and far between. Not only are there few studies of the performance of the legal system for non-corporate clients, those that exist are almost uniformly focused on the delivery of legal services to the poor as a form of charity or welfare assistance. While obviously of high significance, assessing only this segment of legal markets is a bit like assessing the performance of the U.S. health care system by asking only how well Medicaid and free clinics work. It treats the issues of access and cost for citizens as if they were entirely questions of the appropriate levels of charity (pro bono) and welfare spending.

But the vitality of a market democracy premised on the rule of law depends on more than minimal provision for those in desperate need at poverty levels of income. And it depends on more than the quality and cost of services available to corporate and other large entities. It depends on the success with which law manages to serve in fact—not merely on the books—as the fundamental organizing principle of the institutions and relationships of the ordinary citizen. Is law routinely available, for example, to consult before deciding how to choose between market options, or to evaluate how one has been treated in a relationship governed by legal principles? Or is law merely alive in moments of crisis? We know that even in those moments of crisis—the impending loss of a relationship with one's child, the loss of one's home to foreclosure, bankruptcy in the face of impossible medical bills, or grievous injury in an accident—our legal system is not committed (as it is somewhat half-heartedly committed in the case of a felony charge) to ensuring that an individual is fully able to participate in the systems that will manage this crisis. But what of the everyday life that falls short of crisis, that sets the path on which a crisis may occur or may be averted?

We live in an everyday world that is, in fact, flooded with law—how our children are supposed to be treated in school, what lenders are supposed to tell us when they sell us a mortgage, when our employers can and cannot change our conditions of work or pay, what is fair play in consumer markets, and so on. Every time we sign a document, click a box that says "I Agree," enter a retail shop, or get on a local bus we navigate a world that is defined by legal obligations and rights and, importantly, one that assumes that the ordinary citizen who moves in this world is doing so as a functioning, choosing, legal agent. Should that citizen end up in a

852
CHALLENGES AND OPPORTUNITIES FOR THE
PROFESSION IN THE 21ST CENTURY   PT. VI

crisis that requires more active use or response to the legal system—filing or responding to a lawsuit or enforcement action—she will inevitably be treated as if she functioned with this kind of legal agency on the path that brought her to this point: bound by the contracts she "agreed" to or the risks she was given "notice" of or the legal consequences of the actions she took in caring for her children.

We know that in the corporate client world, this is how the relationship with the legal system operates. Most corporate work is before-the-fact, everyday advice on what contracts to sign, which regulations apply, how conduct is likely to be interpreted by enforcement authorities or, in the event of litigation, what the options are for modifying the extent of legal liability, how to manage a dispute before it becomes a lawsuit, and so on. But for ordinary citizens in the U.S there is almost no functioning legal system in this ex ante sphere. This has implications not only for the probability of a crisis down the road that the legal system will have to address—with or without legal services made available to the individual in crisis—but, fundamentally, for the extent to which it is realistic to look at our elaborate legal and regulatory structures as effective organizing principles for everyday relationships. That can have implications far beyond the consequences for a single individual, reaching into the efficacy of our legal systems and the rule of law as a whole.

Consider the recent economic crisis. Among the many interacting factors that led to the collapse of the sub-prime mortgage markets—and the banking system that was heavily invested in securities collateralized by sub-prime mortgages—were the sub-prime mortgage agreements entered into by millions of ordinary Americans. [Other scholars have] documented the complexity of these mortgages, particularly refinancing agreements, and the utter failure of these markets to do what competitive markets are supposed to do, namely to match buyers' demands with sellers' offers. It is almost impossible to determine the true cost of these complex contracts and equally difficult for an ordinary homeowner with sub-prime credit to either evaluate what they are taking on or to compare across competitive providers. As a result, markets failed: people took on risk and obligations they could not afford and competition was ineffective in weeding out excessive or even abusive contract terms. This is market failure on a massive scale with enormous consequences for the entire economy, and is traceable to legal failure. That failure arose from reliance on complex legal rules which purportedly govern the relationship between lender and borrower on paper, but which in fact are largely ineffective on the ground, because of the complete absence in the individual consumer market of the kind of upfront contract review and advice that is routinely obtained in legal markets for corporate clients. Systemic failure of our ex ante legal advice markets for ordinary citizens has now precipitated millions of crises for individual homeowners and borrowers, with huge demands for back-end legal assistance in renegotiation of mortgages and management of foreclosure and bankruptcy processes. We can expect that few of those individual crises for ordinary people will be managed with legal assistance. As a result, the foundation on which our complex financial institutions and systems are built—globally—may well rest on a fundamentally lawless and unpredictable footing.

But concretely, we can say little about just how lawless this footing might be. Empirically, we lack any real data on the quantity or quality of legal services available to ordinary individuals, although casually most of us in the profession know that the bulk of civil legal services, and especially ex ante advisory services, are ultimately provided to corporations rather than ordinary folks. Indeed, we could say that the utter lack of attention to the size and vitality of the legal markets serving ordinary individuals in the conduct of their everyday lives in a law-thick world is itself testament to how the profession has defined these markets out of existence. We can look—and in what follows I will try to give some sense of what we will find—but for the most part there is nothing there.

To give some sense of just what is missing, after reviewing the few existing—and well-worn—legal needs studies, I provide some tidbits of data that might shed some light on the size of the U.S. legal markets serving non-corporate clients. The methodology here is not to look at individuals and count up, but rather to look for the macro indicators of the extent to which resources across the economy as a whole are devoted to providing legal inputs to ordinary citizens for civil matters. In doing so, I hope to broaden the focus beyond the existing studies which focus largely on the poor in particular moments of legal crisis and dispute. The goal is to try to get a handle on the health of the legal markets serving ordinary citizens as a whole. The paucity and unreliability of the data, however, make this an exercise in questions, not answers.

In 1993, the ABA conducted a study, published in 1994, assessing the legal needs of the poor (defined as those living at or below 125% of the poverty line), and of those with moderate income (those with incomes falling in the middle 60% of the income distribution). The study defined "legal needs" as problems or disputes that households had encountered, such as sub-standard housing, job loss, or divorce, and that could be addressed through the civil legal system. With few exceptions (review of documents for a real estate transaction, for example) the focus of the study was on ex post dispute resolution and the nature of the legal assistance that might be offered.

The study found that approximately 50% of households (47% of poor households and 52% of moderate-income households) were experiencing one or more legal needs at the time of the survey. Of those with legal needs, 37% of the poor sought assistance from a third-party for resolution of the problem, 29% from a specifically legal third party such as a lawyer (21%) or other from a non-legal third party (8%). Among moderate-income households, assistance from a third-party was sought with 51% of problems, 39% from a specifically legal source (lawyers 28%, other legal/judicial 12%).

Although the ABA opted not to update the 1994 Legal Needs studies, the Legal Services Corporation ("LSC") in 2005 published a study drawing on nine state surveys, assessing the incidence of legal needs among the poor and the experience in LSC-funded programs with unmet demand for legal aid and the number of legal aid lawyers. If anything, these studies suggest the situation is worse. LSC-funded programs reported that, as a result of resource limitations, they were only able to serve half of the poor who sought assistance. The number of legal aid attorneys providing civil legal services was calculated to be 6,581, a little over one-half of one percent of all U.S. lawyers.

The legal needs surveys give us a close-to-the-ground look at the legal problems encountered by ordinary Americans, albeit with a heavy focus on poor Americans. As we have seen, these surveys suggest that "law" plays a very small role in the everyday handling of potentially justiciable problems in the U.S. Put differently, the vast majority of the legal problems faced by (particularly poor) Americans fall outside of the "rule of law," with high proportions of people—many more than in the U.K., for example—simply accepting a result determined not by law but by the play of markets, power, organizations, wealth, politics, and other dynamics in our complex society.

As we know, however, the normative power of the existing focus on the legal needs of the poor is largely constrained to a humanitarian concern of wealth redistribution and fairness towards the most disadvantaged. But is there a deeper threat to the structure of a democratic society—especially one that purports to organize its relationships on the basis of law and legality—suggested by the finding that Americans are far more likely than those in [some other countries examined in the article] to "do nothing" in response to the legally cognizable difficulties they face? That they are far less likely to seek out others in their community capable of helping them to align their experiences with those contemplated by the laws and procedures that stack up in the voluminous legal materials of regulation, case law, statutes, and constitutions? Is there a paradox lurking here that in the system of adversarial legalism that [is] distinctive of the "American way of law" (to be contrasted with the greater reliance on bureaucratic means of policy making and implementation found in Europe), law is in practice less a salient part of everyday life in the U.S. than elsewhere?

In this section, I review some indicators—incomplete at best—of the overall extent to which the U.S. devotes resources at a macro level to the delivery of legality. I hope to move the emphasis away from the provision of legal support to the poor in ex post crisis and towards the systemic everyday use of law in fact by ordinary citizens throughout the income spectrum.

In 2005, legal services provided by private practitioners generated $180.9 billion in gross domestic product in the United States; total receipts for law firms totaled $221.6 billion. Neither figure counts legal services provided within corporations, government, legal aid providers, or other private associations, which account for 18% of all lawyers. If we "gross up" these numbers to value the contributions of lawyers in these other settings, the total size of the legal services sector in the United States is thus roughly $226 billion in GDP terms and $277 billion in expenditures on legal services.

Of the roughly $277 billion spent on legal services, approximately 31% is consumed by individuals as part of personal consumption expenditures ($85.6 billion in 2005). Another 1% ($2.8 billion) can be attributed to services provided by legal aid lawyers and public defenders. Some share, but it is not possible to easily say how much, of the expenditure on government lawyers other than legal aid and public defenders may be attributable to providing services to individual Americans; in some sense, one could classify all of those expenditures (approximately $22 billion or 8%) as being on behalf of ordinary citizens. This suggests that at most 40% of legal services are serving the needs of individual citizens as opposed to corporations and businesses.

These figures comport with data from the only U.S. study addressing the allocation of legal effort across different types of matters and clients. The Chicago Lawyers' Survey, first conducted in 1975 and updated in 1995, estimated that Chicago lawyers devoted 29% of total effort to services for individual or small business clients with an additional 6% serving organizations such as unions, environmental plaintiffs, state administrative agencies or municipalities for a total of 35%; this is a decrease from 45% in 1975.

In the abstract and in isolation it is difficult to say whether this share of legal services devoted to ordinary citizens' interests is enough. Of course, the ordinary citizen benefits from the operation of well-regulated and efficient markets and thus from the availability of legal services to corporate entities as well. To put further perspective on these numbers, I have therefore calculated what the personal share of the legal services market represents in terms of available legal effort and how this has changed over the last few decades.

In 1990, total expenditures by households on legal services were $62.2 billion in 2000 dollars. At that time, the average hourly rate for lawyers in small firms (less than 20 lawyers, where we find most of the lawyers providing services to individuals) was roughly (very roughly!) $157 in 2000 dollars. Based on the total U.S. population for that year, this implies an average of 1.6 hours per person for the year or 4.15 hours per average household. Conducting the same calculation for 2005 (total expenditures of $67.4 billion in 2000 dollars, an average hourly rate of $182 for small-firm lawyers) yields an average of 1.3 hours per person or 3.34 hours per household, a decline of 20%. As a rough calculation, using the ABA 1994 Legal Needs estimates of numbers of problems per household in a given year (1.0) and a straight average of the number of problems per household reported by the state surveys (2.0) for 2005 this suggests that in 1990 American households were able on average to draw on approximately 4 hours of legal time to address a legal problem and in 2005 they were able to draw on 1 hour and 40 minutes of legal time to address a problem.

These are startlingly low numbers, and they reflect only the corner of the legal landscape that involves a crisis such as a dispute over employment, a foreclosure, a denial of health care, or the risk of injury to or a diminished relationship with a child. They exclude the demand for legal assistance before problems arise, such as legal advice in assessing a complex mortgage offer, employment options, insurance coverage, or the potential for conduct to influence custody of a child. Suppose that for every dispute-related need there is an ex ante advice-related need (as appears to be the case for large corporations), meaning that there are twice as many legal needs as those measured by studies asking only about dispute-related needs. This would then imply that the average household is able to draw on less than an hour's worth of legal advice or assistance in dealing with the points at which their everyday lives intersect with the legal system.

The access problems in the U.S. legal system are largely conceptualized by the profession as problems of the ethical commitments of individual lawyers to assist the poor and the failure of federal and state bodies to provide adequate levels of funding to legal aid agencies and the courts. The first conceptualization fails, I believe, to come to grips with the dimensions of the problem, which cannot be solved with an increase in pro bono efforts, as welcome as such an increase would be. Pro bono currently accounts for at most 1–2% of legal effort in the country; even if every lawyer in the country did 100 more hours a year of pro bono work, this would amount to an extra thirty minutes per U.S. person a year, or about an hour per dispute-related (potentially litigation-related) problem per household. This does not even begin to address the realistic demands that ordinary households have for ex ante assistance with navigating the law-thick world in which they live, some of which could indeed reduce the need for ex post legal representation in litigation and crisis. The problem is not a problem of the ethical commitment of lawyers to help the poor. Nor is an increase in public legal aid likely to make a substantial impact. The cost of even that extra hour per dispute-related problem per household would be on the order of $20 billion annually at a market rate of $200 per hour. That would entail a twenty-fold increase in current U.S. levels of public and private (charitable) legal aid funding. Again, more legal aid funding would be welcome and is clearly called for, but it cannot make a serious dent in the nature of the problem.

Those concerned with access to justice have long emphasized how the extreme approach to unauthorized practice of law in the United States drastically curtails the potential for ordinary folks to obtain assistance with their law-related needs and problems. The regulatory problem, however, goes beyond a straightforward restriction on supply. The more fundamental problem with the existing regulatory structure is traceable to the fact that the American legal profession is a politically unaccountable regulator. Many critics of the bar's self-regulation have decried the tendency for the bar to put professional self-interest ahead of public interest. But this is what one would predict given that the bar is not a politically accountable policymaker. Even if the bar's narrow focus on ethical duties that govern attorney-client relationships were, as it likely often is, a well-intentioned execution of the norms that are absorbed through the process of legal training, rather than craven self-interest, the fact remains that like anybody it responds to its constituencies. The bar has by and large steered utterly clear of the idea that it is responsible—politically responsible—for the system-wide cost and complexity of the legal system, far beyond the ethical call to help the poor and perform pro bono work. It requires a political process to shift perceptions—much as perceptions about the federal government's responsibility for high gas prices or stock market failures are molded not in the abstract but in the crucible of political contest and public debate. The public does not hear policy positions from the policymaker—the bar— and does not vote or otherwise express its views on how the policymaker is executing on policy.

Because the bar, together with the state judiciaries, asserts exclusive policy authority in this field but is not in fact a politically accountable policymaking body, there is effectively no mechanism for policy change. There is nowhere to address policy proposals and no process for influencing policy adoption. The process is a wholly closed shop. That this does not seem an extraordinary way for an advanced market democracy to make economic and social policy is itself a consequence of the framing that results from the bar's assertion of authority. The bar bases its role on its expertise in the attorney-client relationship—and it styles its regulatory functions as the promulgation and enforcement of ethical standards. There are indeed ethical demands on lawyers and their professional bodies. But this defines out of the frame the fundamentally economic character of the market regulation the bar and judiciary control.

The problem we face in the American legal system is not a problem of how to increase pro bono or legal aid (although we should do that too), which are ultimately mere drops in the bucket on the order of a few percentage points of total legal effort and resources. Rather, the problem is one of urgent need for structural reform in the regulatory and policy/funding system responsible for the critical infrastructure of market democracy, particularly one that draws as heavily as the American system does on law and legalism to structure economic, political, and social relationships.

NOTES ON *EX ANTE LEGAL SERVICES*

1. *Are Ex Ante Services Important?* Why do ordinary Americans need access to ex ante legal advice and planning services? What is the relationship, if any, between access to such services and the operation of American democracy and the rule of law?

2. *Self-Regulation.* Hadfield is highly critical of the bar's control over the regulation of lawyers and the delivery of legal services in this country. Recall the discussion in Chapter 2 about the reasons that the legal profession offers to justify self-regulation—that the specialized knowledge that lawyers possess means that they should be governed only by others trained and immersed in the same activity and that they can be trusted to transcend their own self-interest in order to protect the interests of both clients and the public good. Is Hadfield's cynicism about self-regulation justified or misplaced?

3. *What Would Change?* If the organized bar were more directly politically accountable to the American public, what changes do you think would result? Keep this question in mind as we turn to our next topic— unauthorized practice and innovation in the delivery of legal services.

E. SUMMARY

This chapter examined the market for legal services. It considered how structural features of the market affect the cost of legal services and how factors other than cost influence the likelihood that ordinary Americans will seek lawyers' assistance with their problems. We considered the mechanisms by which citizens find lawyers (or do not) during times of crisis. But we also explored a type of legal services not typically contemplated in most discussions of access to justice issues—ex ante advice to help ordinary citizens align their social, political and economic arrangements with law so as to avoid trouble. This chapter raised questions about whether the market for legal services meets the needs of ordinary Americans, and, if not, what responses might be called for. We explore those options in the following two chapters.

CHAPTER 32

UNAUTHORIZED PRACTICE AND NON-LAWYER INVOLVEMENT IN THE PROVISION OF LEGAL SERVICES

■ ■ ■

A. INTRODUCTION

Many types of work that are arguably legal in nature can be performed only by a lawyer in the United States. Individuals are allowed to handle their own legal problems by representing themselves in civil and criminal cases (appearing "pro se") and writing their own wills. In most other respects, however, lawyers enjoy a monopoly on the provision of legal services. This monopoly is protected through unauthorized practice restrictions—prohibitions on the provision of legal services by anyone not licensed to practice law. Indeed, practicing law without a license is a crime in most states. In addition, non-lawyers are prohibited from participating in the financing, ownership, or management of a business engaged in the practice of law. This chapter examines what it means to "practice law" and the impact of statutes in virtually all jurisdictions that prohibit nonlawyers from engaging in the practice of law. It considers whether and under what circumstances restrictions on unauthorized practice are justified in order to protect the legal system and consumers. We next review innovations in the delivery of legal services designed to expand access through means other than the two primary strategies supported by the organized bar—increased funding for legal services for the poor (discussed in Chapter 28) and greater support for private bar pro bono (Chapter 33). Some of those innovations involve participation by non-lawyers and thereby violate current rules restricting who may provide legal services and what form legal practice can take. Finally, we consider the wisdom of allowing business models that might make it possible to deliver legal services more efficiently and cheaply but would require outside nonlawyer investment.

B. WHAT IS THE UNAUTHORIZED PRACTICE OF LAW?

Until the Great Depression, the practice of law was thought to be appearing in court on behalf of another person, and so nonlawyers could provide services in connection with business transactions, real estate acquisition, and other out-of-court situations. But in the 1930s, the bar began taking a much more aggressive stance toward defining services that only lawyers should be allowed to provide and in policing the boundaries of "the practice of law." It negotiated agreements with other service providers to distinguish tasks that would be limited to lawyers only and those that competitors could offer without being charged with unauthorized practice. In the 1970s, fears about antitrust liability led the bar to abandon these agreements with other occupational competitors, but unauthorized practice restrictions remain in place in all states.

Until recently, the ABA did not attempt to offer a uniform definition of the practice of law for purposes of identifying the parameters of unauthorized practice. In 2002, however, the ABA Board of Governors established a Task Force on the Model Definition of the Practice of Law to examine the issue. In 2003, the Task Force proposed that every state and territory adopt a definition of the practice of law and that its definition should include "the basic premise that the practice of law is the application of legal principles and judgment to the circumstances or objectives of another person or entity." It further proposed that each state should "determine who may provide services that are included within the state's or territory's definition of the practice of law and under what circumstances, based upon the potential harm and benefit to the public." The proposal generated a good deal of negative commentary, including a joint statement from the Department of Justice and the Federal Trade Commission on the proposal's anticompetitive effects. The Task Force then decided to leave it to states to adopt their own definitions, but it advised that such definitions should follow the broad outlines of the ABA's proposal.

There remains a good deal of variation in how states define the practice of law, but the definitions are generally quite broad and vague. Georgia's, for example, includes "the giving of any legal advice."[1] Nebraska defines the practice of law as "the application of legal principles and judgment with regard to the circumstances or objectives of another entity or person which require the knowledge, judgment, and skill of a person trained as a lawyer."[2] In Florida, the definition "includes the

---

[1]   Code of Georgia Annotated Title 15. Courts Chapter 19. Attorneys Article 3. Regulation of Practice of Law, § 5–19–50.

[2]   The statute goes on to say that the practice of law includes, but is not limited to, the following: "(A) Giving advice or counsel to another entity or person as to the legal rights of that entity or person or the legal rights of others for compensation, direct or indirect, where a relationship of trust or reliance exists between the party giving such advice or counsel and the party to whom it is given; (B) Selection, drafting, or completion, for another entity or person, of legal documents which affect the legal rights of the entity or person; (C) Representation of another entity or person in a court, in a formal administrative adjudicative proceeding or other formal dispute resolution process, or in an administrative adjudicative proceeding in which legal pleadings are filed or a record is established as the basis for judicial review; (D) Negotiation of legal rights or responsibilities on behalf of another entity or person; (E) Holding oneself out to

giving of legal advice and counsel to others as to their rights and obligations under the law and the preparation of legal instruments, including contracts, by which legal rights are either obtained, secured or given away."[3] Similarly, Iowa case law provides that the practice of law "includes, but is not limited to, representing another before the courts; giving of legal advice and counsel to others relating to their rights and obligations under the law; and preparation or approval of the use of legal instruments by which legal rights of others are either obtained, secured or transferred even if such matters never become the subject of a court proceeding."[4] In California, a statute makes unauthorized practice of law a crime but does not define the practice of law.[5] Cases define it broadly to include giving legal advice and preparing legal instruments.[6]

Under some of these expansive (and sometimes circular) definitions, a great deal of everyday conduct by other occupational groups and ordinary citizens seems to run afoul of unauthorized practice restrictions. Is a police officer practicing law when he gives Miranda warnings? Are credit counselors engaging in the practice of law when they help consumers negotiate payment plans with their creditors? Are realtors practicing law when they explain the terms of an agreement to sell a house or explain the nature of a mortgage? Are tenants' associations engaging in the practice of law when they inform renters of their legal rights and responsibilities? Are any of you subject to prosecution under unauthorized practice laws when you respond to questions from friends and family about what you've learned in law school that might affect their lives? Do these statutes reach everyday citizens trying to help each other navigate our law-rich world—for example, a father advising his child on the consequences of signing a contract?

Unauthorized practice of law statutes have been applied to a broad range of non-lawyer service providers. Most commonly, the statutes have been used to close down the operations of secretaries and paralegals who charge fees to help people fill out forms. For example, in *Florida Bar v. Brumbaugh*, the court enjoined a former legal secretary from helping couples fill out necessary forms to obtain amicable no-fault divorces.[7] She had served hundreds of customers without complaint, and the bar presented no evidence that her services were less competent than those

---

another as being entitled to practice law as defined herein." Nebraska Supreme Court Rules, Section 3–1001.

[3]   State ex rel. The Florida Bar v. Sperry, 140 So.2d 587, 591 (1962), vacated on other grounds, 373 U.S. 379 (1963).

[4]   Committee on Professional Ethics & Conduct v. Baker, 492 N.W.2d 695, 700 (Iowa 1992); Iowa Code of Prof'l Responsibility EC 3–5.

[5]   Cal. Bus. & Prof. Code §§ 6125–6126.

[6]   *See, e.g.,* Birbrower, Montalbano, Condon & Frank v. Superior Court, 17 Cal. 4th 119, 128 (1998).

[7]   Florida Bar v. Brumbaugh, 355 So. 2d 1186 (Fla. 1978).

provided by licensed lawyers. It found that she could legally sell forms and type up instruments completed by clients but that she could not correct any errors in the selection or preparation of legal forms or provide any assistance in filling them out. In a similar case, the Florida Supreme Court ordered jail time for a former legal secretary who violated a court order enjoining her from helping couples obtain simple no-fault divorces.[8] The defendant never served jail time for practicing without a license, but only because Florida's governor intervened. More recently, the Kentucky Supreme Court imposed a $5,000 fine against a woman who continued to prepare documents in uncontested divorce cases after receiving a warning letter from the Kentucky Bar Association. She was also ordered to pay costs and fees incurred by the bar association in bringing the action.[9] Similarly, the Supreme Court of Delaware found that special education consultants who represented parents in administrative hearings in which parents attempted to require schools to provide services for students with special education needs under the Individuals with Disabilities Education Act (IDEA) were engaged in the unauthorized practice of law.[10]

Interactive Software. Interactive software has also drawn unauthorized practice charges. A case in Texas involved Parsons Technology, a company that published and sold a computer software program called Quicken Family Lawyer, which provided various types of legal forms (e.g., employment agreements, real estate leases, premarital agreements, and will forms) along with instructions about how to fill them out. The program included a disclaimer indicating that users of the forms should understand that their particular circumstances should be taken into account in determining whether any particular form would meet their needs, and therefore that it might be advisable to seek the assistance of a lawyer. When the Texas Unauthorized Practice of Law Committee sued to enjoin the sale of the software in Texas, Parsons argued that its product did not violate the Texas unauthorized practice of law statute because it involved no personal contact. Alternatively, Parsons argued that the statute should be declared invalid because it violated Parsons' speech rights and was unconstitutionally vague. In *Unauthorized Practice of Law Committee v. Parsons Technology, Inc.,* a federal district court found that Parsons had violated the statute and that the statute was constitutional. The Texas legislature thereafter amended that state's unauthorized practice statute to provide that the practice of law does not include "computer software, or similar products . . . [that] clearly and conspicuously state that . . . [they] are not a substitute for the

---

[8] Florida v. Furman, 451 So.2d 808 (Fla. 1984).

[9] Kentucky Bar Association v. Tarpinian, 337 S.W.3d 627 (2011).

[10] In re Arons, 756 A.2d 867 (2000).

advice of an attorney." Thereafter, the Fifth Circuit vacated the injunction against the distribution of Quicken Family Lawyer.[11]

Interactive Websites. How do unauthorized practice of law statutes apply to interactive websites? In *In Re Reynoso*, 477 F.3d 1117 (9th Cir. 2007), the Ninth Circuit Court of Appeals held that Frankfort Digital Services, the seller of web-based software that prepares bankruptcy petitions, had engaged in the unauthorized practice of law. One of the websites, "Ziinet Bankruptcy Engine," stated that "Ziinet is an expert system and knows the law. Unlike most bankruptcy programs which are little more than customized word processors the Ziinet engine is an *expert* system. It knows bankruptcy laws right down to those applicable to the state in which you live. Now you no longer need to spend weeks studying bankruptcy laws." The site stated that its services were comparable to those of a "top-notch bankruptcy lawyer." It also offered access to a "Bankruptcy Vault" that included information about "stealth techniques" and "loopholes" that would enable customers to hide a bankruptcy from credit bureaus and help them retain property. The court held that Frankfort violated California's unauthorized practice statute because it went well beyond providing secretarial services and instead held itself out as holding legal expertise.

LegalZoom, a popular self-help website established in 2000, has tangled repeatedly with state bar organizations over whether the company is violating unauthorized practice rules. In 2011, after the North Carolina bar issued a cease and desist letter that accused the company of offering unauthorized legal advice to customers, LegalZoom sued the bar, alleging that it was unlawfully trying to prevent the company from offering its products to North Carolina residents. In September of 2012, North Carolina answered the complaint and filed a counterclaim against LegalZoom, arguing that its self-help legal document preparation services—"Legal Advantage Plus" and "Business Advantage Plus"—constitute unauthorized practice.[12] LegalZoom has also skirmished with bar authorities and private plaintiffs in many other states, including South Carolina, Alabama, Arkansas, California, Missouri, Ohio, Pennsylvania, Connecticut, North Carolina, and Washington.[13] Despite these legal troubles, the company currently does business in all 50 states and the District of Columbia, and in 2012 it announced that it had formed a partnership with QualitySolicitors, a U.K.-based legal services

---

[11] Unauthorized Practice of Law Committee v. Parsons Technology, Inc., 179 F.3d 956 (5th Cir. 1999).

[12] *See* Phillip Bantz, *N.C. State Bar Answers LegalZoom's Complaint, Files Counterclaim*, N.C. WEEKLY, Sept. 28, 2012.

[13] *See* Thomas Spahn, *Commentary: Battle Over Divorce Forms: Defining the Contours of Unauthorized Practice of Law*, LAWYERS WEEKLY USA, July 17, 2012; Janson v. LegalZoom.com, Inc., 802 F.Supp.2d 1053 (W.D. Mo. 2011); Connecticut Bar Ass'n Unauthorized Practice of Law Comm. Informal Op. 2008-01 (2008); Pennsylvania Bar Ass'n Unauthorized Practice of Law Comm. Formal Op. 2010–01 (2010).

company.[14] In January 2014, LegalZoom declared its intention to sell $200 million of its outstanding equity to a company backed by a European private equity firm.[15] LegalZoom's competitors in the market for large-scale web-based consumer-oriented platforms include RocketLawyer, USLegal, LawPivot, Nolo, LegalForce/Trademarkia, SmartLegalForms, and LawDepot.[16]

C. DO UNAUTHORIZED PRACTICE RESTRICTIONS PROTECT THE PUBLIC?

The bar has long maintained that unauthorized practice restrictions protect consumers against the harm that unqualified and unscrupulous service providers might cause. But many critics of the profession charge that current unauthorized practice restrictions serve primarily to protect the profession's occupational interests and that regulations less restrictive than outright bans on non-lawyer services would better protect consumers. Some say that concerns about protecting individuals from incompetent or unscrupulous service by non-lawyer providers could be met through some a combination of registration and certification requirements, mandatory malpractice insurance, and minimum ethical standards.[17]

In opposition to the ABA's proposed Model Definition of the Practice of Law, the Department of Justice and the Federal Trade Commission submitted comments urging the ABA not to adopt the proposed definition because it was "overbroad and could restrain competition between lawyers and non-lawyers to provide similar services to American consumers":

> [W]e urge the Task Force to consider carefully what specific harms the Model Definition is designed to address, whether the Definition is appropriately tailored to addressing those harms, and whether the elimination of any such harms would outweigh the reduction in lawyer-non-lawyer competition that could occur if any state adopted the proposed Model Definition. [T]he proposed Model Definition [does not] provide a clear articulation of the harms the Definition seeks to address. [It] notes only in general terms that "The primary consideration in defining the practice of law is the protection of the public."

---

[14] Lucy Burton, *LegalZoom to Tie Up With QualitySolicitors for British Launch*, THE LAWYER, Sept. 20, 2012.

[15] Jennifer Smith, *LegalZoom Plans to Pull Its IPO, Sell Stake to Permira*, WALL ST. J., Jan. 7, 2014.

[16] See Gillian Hadfield, *The Cost of Law: Promoting Access to Justice Through the (Un)Corporate Practice of Law*, INT'L REV. LAW & ECON. (2013).

[17] See DEBORAH L. RHODE, ACCESS TO JUSTICE 87–91 (2004); Deborah L. Rhode, *Access to Justice: Connecting Principles to Practice*, 17 GEO. J. LEGAL ETHICS 369 (2004).

The DOJ and the FTC recognize that there are circumstances requiring the knowledge and skill of a person trained in the law, and acknowledge the legitimacy of the Task Force's efforts to protect consumers in such situations. Nonetheless, the DOJ and the FTC believe that consumers generally benefit from lawyer-non-lawyer competition in the provision of certain services.

Some consumer advocates offered similar objections. The director of the legal reform group HALT, for example, argued that the ABA's proposed model definition of the practice of law "poses a major threat to the rights of millions of American consumers who choose to handle their routine legal tasks with the help of non-lawyer resources, such as document preparers, independent paralegals, title agents, independent insurance adjusters, even self-help books and software. The ABA proposal would largely stymie much-needed efforts to increase accessibility to our civil justice system through the expansion of such non-lawyer services."[18] HALT argued that the concept of unauthorized practice should be limited to fraudulent practice—holding oneself out as a lawyer when one is not.

Some proponents of expanded access to non-lawyer services argue in favor of allowing the development of various types of legal services providers to serve consumers with varied types of needs. Reform advocates often draw comparisons to developments in medicine, where pressure to reduce costs and expand coverage has led to extensive diversification and experimentation. According to this view, paralegals operating independently from lawyers could provide some types of routine legal services, much as nurse practitioners provide a cost-effective alternative to doctors for some types of basic medical care. Legislatures in several states, including California and Arizona, have taken small steps in this direction by making it legal for non-lawyers to prepare certain types of legal documents.[19] In 2012, Washington State's supreme court approved a rule allowing licensed legal technicians to help civil litigants navigate the court system—helping them select and complete forms, inform clients of procedures and deadlines, review and explain pleadings, and identify additional required documents.[20] Some advocates of regulatory reform would also liberalize lawyers' ethics rules to allow for the creation of high volume, low-cost options that either do not currently

---

[18] See James C. Turner, *Lawyer vs. Non-lawyer: ABA Chose Wrong Side in Drafting Unauthorized Practice Rule*, LEGAL TIMES, Feb. 3, 2003.

[19] In California, document preparers must be registered and bonded, while in Arizona they must be certified. See California Business and Professions Code Section 6400–6401.6; Arizona Code of Judicial Administration Section 7–208 (effective January 2003).

[20] Washington Courts, "Supreme Court Adopts Rule Authorizing Non-Lawyers to Assist in Certain Legal Matters," June 15, 2012, available at http://www.courts.wa.gov/newsinfo/?fa=news info.internetdetail&newsid=2136.

exist, or that operate under the shadow of threatened legal action by the bar because lawyers do not control all aspects of the services.

Here is one such argument in favor of a more liberal approach to non-lawyer provision of legal services, written by one of the leading advocates for expanding access:

ACCESS TO JUSTICE: CONNECTING PRINCIPLES TO PRACTICE
Deborah Rhode
17 Georgetown Journal of Legal Ethics 369 (2004)

The need for law without lawyers is by no means a new phenomenon. What is, however, new is the extent to which Americans are attempting to address their legal needs without professional assistance, and the increase in information and services available to help them. Eighteenth century litigants had to make do with a few manuals like *Every Man His Own Lawyer*. Today's consumer has thousands of options. Over the last several decades, the market for do-it-yourself legal materials has grown dramatically in response to broader social trends. Technological innovations have also expanded the services that individuals can obtain quickly and cheaply through the internet or computer software.

For obvious reasons, the organized bar has not welcomed these trends. In a purportedly selfless effort to "protect the public" from unauthorized practice of law, the profession has attempted to ban do-it-yourself kits, document preparation services, computer software, and interactive on-line information. The stated concern is that ignorant consumers will suffer from assistance offered by individuals who do not meet the competence and ethical standards established for licensed attorneys. The unstated concern is that the profession will suffer from unrestricted competition. Bar opposition has had diminishing success, but it continues to play an important role in restricting non-lawyer practitioners.

On the rare occasions when the public is consulted, it seems largely unsupportive of the protective efforts ostensibly launched in its behalf. In one ABA survey, over four-fifths of Americans agreed that many matters lawyers handled could be "done as well and less expensively by non-lawyers."

The public's support for greater access to lay legal services is well founded. Other nations generally permit non-lawyers to provide legal advice and assistance with routine documents, and no evidence suggests that their performance has been inadequate. In this country, the American Law Institute's *Restatement of the Law Governing Lawyers ("Restatement")* notes that "experience in several states with extensive non-lawyer provision of traditional legal services indicates no significant risk of harm to consumers . . ." So too, studies of lay specialists who provide legal representation in bankruptcy and administrative agency hearings find that they generally perform as well or better than attorneys. In the most systematic survey to date, a majority of states did not report unauthorized practice complaints from consumers; the vast majority came from lawyers and involved no claims of specific injury. Such findings should come as no surprise. Three years in law school and passage of a bar exam are neither necessary nor sufficient to ensure expertise in the areas where non-lawyer services flourish; lay specialists may be better able to provide cost-effective services than lawyers who practice in multiple fields.

This is not to discount the problems that can result from unqualified or unethical non-lawyer assistance. Some unlicensed practitioners, including disbarred attorneys, misrepresent their status and exploit vulnerable consumers. Immigrants are particularly common targets, both because they are often unfamiliar with the American legal system and because they are unlikely to approach law enforcement agencies to report abuses. However, the appropriate response to these problems is regulation, not prohibition. Consumers need an approach that balances their need for protection with their interests in competition and affordable services.

A preferable regulatory structure would provide both less and more protection—less for attorneys and more for consumers. Non-lawyers like accountants or real estate brokers who are already licensed by the state should be allowed to provide legal assistance related to their specialties. For currently unlicensed service providers, states should develop regulatory frameworks responsive to public needs, which may vary across different practice areas. Where the risk of injury is substantial, in contexts such as immigration, consumers may benefit from licensing systems that impose minimum qualifications and offer proactive enforcement. In other fields, it could be sufficient to register practitioners and permit voluntary certification of those who meet specified standards. States also could require all lay practitioners to carry malpractice insurance, and to observe basic ethical obligations governing confidentiality, competence, and conflicts of interest. Similar protections could extend to internet services. Enforcement, of course, poses substantial challenges, but the problems are not unique to lay legal assistance.

In general, an approach that seeks to regulate rather than preempt lay competition, would offer a number of advantages. Experience here and abroad suggests that increased competition between lawyers and non-lawyers is likely to result in lower prices, greater efficiency, and more consumer satisfaction. Regulating the activities of lay practitioners should help curb abuses that currently go unremedied, while encouraging innovative partnerships between lawyer and non-lawyer specialists.

NOTES ON THE CONSUMER PROTECTION RATIONALE
FOR UNAUTHORIZED PRACTICE RESTRICTIONS

1. ***Consumer Beware?*** Should consumers be allowed to take the risk of hiring a person who has not attended law school to perform services that are arguably "legal"? Or should the state protect consumers from making unwise decisions—at least in some circumstances? Under what conditions would you allow consumers to take the risk of hiring a nonlawyer to perform legal services?

2. ***Does the Type of Service Matter?*** Does your answer to the previous question depend upon whether the client wishes to use the services for in-court representation or for advising or transactional services? In a criminal matter, where the state arguably has an especially large stake in ensuring the fairness of the process, or in a civil matter? Does your answer depend on the complexity of the matter or the stakes involved? Does it matter whether the client can afford an attorney, or whether the state is prepared to provide free or subsidized counsel?

3. ***Regulatory Alternatives to Flat Bans.*** What measures, short of complete bans on lay competition, might answer potential concerns about unethical or incompetent service by non-lawyers? Would you favor the alternative regulatory measures advocated by Rhode in this excerpt?

* * *

Deregulation. Some critics have argued for more radical proposals that would not only allow for greater competition between lawyers and non-lawyers for out-of-court and relatively routine legal services, but also eliminate occupational licensing in law altogether. Consider the following argument in favor of completely deregulating legal services.[21]

FIRST THING WE DO, LET'S DEREGULATE ALL THE LAWYERS
Clifford Winston, Robert Crandall, Vikram Maheshri
Brookings Institution Press 2011

Lawyers are among the 20 percent of the U.S. labor force that is required to obtain a government license to practice a profession—a requirement that may not be justified because some legal services could be competently provided by persons who have not had a formal legal education and who have not passed a state bar examination to obtain a license. Even people who do have a legal education are prevented from taking a bar examination and practicing law in all but a few states unless they graduated from an ABA-accredited law school. And ABA regulations prevent licensed lawyers who work for firms that are not owned and managed by lawyers from providing legal services to parties outside their

---

[21] Clifford Winston and Robert Crandall, *Time to Deregulate the Practice of Law*, WALL ST. J., Aug. 22, 2011, A13.

firm. The ABA-imposed entry barriers are one important factor that unnecessarily raises the cost of legal services.

An underlying argument supporting occupational licensing in law is that a minimum level of intellectual ability or talent is required to be a competent practitioner; a licensing requirement therefore serves as a screening device to identify and weed out people who do not meet this standard of competence. However, the screening device also serves to prevent laypeople who could compete effectively with licensed lawyers from doing so legally. Further, some talented people are undoubtedly discouraged from entering the legal profession because they chafe at the expense and opportunity costs of a three-year course of study that can easily exceed $150,000 and are uninterested in working long hours as an associate lawyer in a big firm to recoup those expenses.

We recognize that specific legal training may be essential for providing certain legal services and that some unlicensed and untrained lawyers may not be able to perform certain complex legal services adequately, such as complex contracts and appellate litigation. But clients requiring more complex services are more likely to be sophisticated and therefore better able to determine a lawyer's quality without relying solely on an attorney's educational or bar examination history. Thus, given that substantial earnings premiums have been widespread and commonplace in the legal profession for decades, it is likely that eliminating the licensing requirement would allow a greater number of qualified participants to spur competition in the legal services market and reduce legal fees, creating substantial economic welfare gains.

Given the increasing ease with which information is transferred, we have good reason to believe that potential clients could privately assess—at least qualitatively—an attorney's quality level. Information culled from the Internet (along with other sources) about a lawyer's track record, level of experience, education, and certification status could serve to educate potential customers quickly and efficiently about that lawyer's credibility and competence. As in most other service industries, potential clients would likely be cautious about hiring someone to perform legal services who cannot provide assessments based on previous work or evidence of certification.

Even if lawyers had no licensure requirements, certification schemes could be used to help consumers find lawyers with certain desirable or unusual capabilities. For example, the National Board of Legal Specialty Certification provides certification for trial, civil, criminal, family, and Social Security disability lawyers. Of course, individuals claiming particular certification would be subject to general business laws that could result in their being charged with fraud if they were unable to prove certification claims. Over time, consumers would then determine whether one's education, examinations passed, and certification are in fact signals of greater ability and better service, and reward those accomplishments or ignore them accordingly. [Some researchers] have actually found in England and Wales that non-lawyers provided better legal service in civil matters such as welfare benefits, debt, housing, and employment than solo and small-firm practitioners provided.

Current licensure requirements may create only the perception of quality and increase the demand for credentialed lawyers even in situations where the credential does not add social value. [L]icensure may even create a false sense of security if consumers assume that state bar requirements and licensure mandates ensure a certain level of quality that does not really exist.

[T]he benefits from deregulating entry into the legal profession far outweigh any costs. By eliminating mandatory occupational licensing of lawyers in the United States and by forcing law firms to compete with suppliers of legal services that utilize alternative organizational forms, we would expect that competition in legal services would sharply increase, resulting in significantly greater variation in the price and quality of those services. Low-cost lawyers and non-lawyers would advertise their services, engage in aggressive price competition, and create a low-cost market centered on offering basic legal services that do not require extensive training to provide. Other lawyers (and law firms) would undoubtedly attempt to differentiate their services as "high quality" and try to maintain high prices, but most of those lawyers and their law firms would be forced to compete more intensely for clients.

NOTES ON DEREGULATION

1. *A Good Idea?* Would you favor deregulating the legal profession? What would be the potential costs and risks of such an approach? Would those costs and risks be likely to vary by the types of clients served? Would it be feasible to deregulate the practice of certain types of law, or at least lower the regulatory barriers to entry to certain types of practice?

2. *Can Consumers Adequately Evaluate Legal Services?* The authors claim that the increasing access to information via the Internet enables prospective consumers of legal services to adequately assess the quality of those services. Is it possible to square that claim with Hadfield's argument in Chapter 31 that lawyers' services are credence goods? If not, which argument do you find more convincing?

3. *Consequences for Vulnerable Populations.* Consider Rhode's argument about how unlicensed purveyors of legal services sometimes victimize unsophisticated consumers in immigrant communities. Would the kinds of voluntary certification systems and consumer research that Winston,

Crandall and Maheshri predict will flourish in a deregulated legal services sector adequately protect such consumers?

D. INNOVATIONS IN THE PROVISION OF LEGAL SERVICES TO INDIVIDUAL CLIENTS

A variety of efforts are now underway to improve access to affordable legal services for ordinary Americans. The following excerpt summarizes some of those developments: expanding the use of technology, especially web-based tools; simplifying judicial processes to make them easier for consumers to navigate and improving assistance to pro se litigants; allowing lawyers to offer "unbundled" (less than full) services; and encouraging innovations in employer-provided and privately marketed legal insurance programs.

The following excerpt explores such developments and the bar's position on these initiatives:

LEGAL SERVICES FOR ALL: IS THE PROFESSION READY?
Jeanne Charn
42 Loyola of Los Angeles Law Review 1021 (2009)

The last fifteen years have seen an explosion of innovation from state courts, the private bar, and legal services providers. The driver of this creativity has been tireless local efforts to find new resources and new approaches to helping people who would otherwise be forced to navigate the legal system alone. Change has been powered by solo practitioners and small firms looking for new ways to attract clients and meet their needs; by legal aid lawyers, swamped with requests for help, experimenting with new ways to offer at least some assistance; and by lower trial court judges and administrators, overwhelmed by parties without lawyers, finding ways to assist rather than discourage self-represented litigants. In all of these efforts, it is difficult to overstate the role that technology has played and will continue to play in spurring innovation.

Of crucial importance, the bench and bar have been willing to accommodate changes that are evolving on the ground by modifying the profession's normative structures. As the pace of innovation grows, the bench and bar will continue to be challenged to re-examine core norms and practices and to make more dramatic changes.

Private Bar Innovations. The solo and small-firm bar is the main legal resource for middle-income people and serves two to three times more poor people than the not-for-profit, government-funded legal services offices. Forty years ago, resistance and even hostility to government-funded legal aid was the norm in this sector of the bar. In the intervening years, experience has persuaded most solo and small-firm lawyers that legal aid does not draw from their client base. Rather it helps those whom the market cannot serve. As a result, not only has resistance declined, but many solo and small-firm lawyers are now strong supporters of subsidized legal services.

These lawyers practice in challenging, highly competitive markets. Their efficiency and effectiveness in meeting the needs of low-and middle-income clients is critically important to the access agenda because subsidies are not needed when the market can provide good quality, affordable service. Fortunately, service innovations that attract new clients, increase client choice, and control costs are flourishing. Examples include a lawyer who offers "will parties" modeled after Tupperware parties, with price per simple will decreasing as attendees increase. A solo practitioner in North Carolina operates a virtual law office. She provides mainly transactional services to households and small businesses entirely online. The Legal Grind advertises "coffee, counsel & community" on its Web site. Customers can enjoy premium coffee or tea along with legal advice du jour. Lawyers with expertise in over twenty areas of personal legal services and more than ten areas of interest to small businesses are available at scheduled hours at the coffee shop. Legal Grind operates as a licensed lawyer referral service, and its founders are considering franchising the concept.

More broad-based changes are under way as well. Discrete task representation, also known as "unbundled legal services," has gained a great deal of attention, including attention in bar ethics opinions, where the trend is clearly in the direction of acceptance and accommodation. Discrete task representation breaks down lawyer services into tasks that a client can purchase a la carte. Services may be provided at a fixed price or at hourly rates. This flexibility gives clients a great deal of control over costs and greater knowledge about what they are purchasing. Both attorneys and clients report high satisfaction with services provided on these terms.

Collaborative lawyers seek to save clients money and emotional turmoil by offering clients the opportunity to commit up front to solve disputes through negotiation, mediation, or other interest-based, non-adversarial means. Clients who choose collaborative lawyers typically agree that litigation is off the table and that if they are unable to reach a resolution, the collaborative lawyer cannot represent either party in subsequent litigation. Family law disputes are particularly amenable to collaborative lawyering, but firms are experimenting with the approach in employment cases and some transactional matters. The ABA supports collaborative lawyering and has addressed its particular features in light of its model ethics rules.

The ABA Standing Committee on Delivery of Legal Services focuses on private bar innovations that serve low-and middle-income people. The Committee has posted on its Web site an intriguing catalogue of innovative and niche practices, as well as guides, reports, and best practices for hotlines, self-help services, and many other novel approaches to providing legal advice and assistance. Innovators are less imbued with traditional modes of providing service and, as a result, are more consumer-friendly and open to services that are less dependent on lawyers, such as unbundled service. Whether by intent or necessity, these innovators challenge professional norms and traditional understandings of what it means to practice law or for a client to "have a lawyer."

It is critical for the private bar to continue to attract consumers and to drive down costs of quality assistance. In a full-access delivery system, the private bar should provide as much service as possible before we turn to publicly subsidized assistance. We should take the point at which the market cannot offer good quality, affordable service as the definition of the place where full or partial government subsidies are necessary to assure access.

Technology as a Driver of Innovation. Technology is already playing an important role in assisting self-represented parties. LSC operates a highly successful competitive grant program that incentivizes technology-heavy innovation. The solo and small-firm bar is increasingly incorporating technology that achieves efficiencies and enables service innovations.

The ABA Standing Committee on Delivery of Legal Services has held a series of public hearings, available on the Committee's Web site, on innovative uses of technology in service delivery to low-and middle-income people. Innovators include an array of not-for-profits as well as private bar providers. The range and creativity of the innovations described in these hearings are enormous and point to the unlimited potential of technology to drive down the costs of service, support providers, and offer services directly to consumers.

Court Innovations. A revolution is under way in state trial courts dealing with housing, consumer, family, and similar everyday problems of low-and middle-income households. These courts have huge volumes of unrepresented litigants. Prior practice was to urge unrepresented parties to "get a lawyer." In the past decade, however, lower trial courts in state after state have fundamentally altered their processes, staffing, and self-conceptions to facilitate and, in many instances, welcome litigants without lawyers. Courts have developed and funded self-help centers to aid unrepresented parties, hired or recruited pro bono "lawyers of the day" to offer on-site advice to people appearing without counsel, simplified forms and posted them on court Web sites, and changed calendars to better accommodate the schedules of people who work.

In many states, broad-based reforms are now under way to improve access, including reengineering court procedures, maximizing use of technology, and creating a national, bench-led project aimed at preparing judges for effective management of courts in which most litigants do not have conventional full-service legal representation. These remarkable changes in the trial courts' functioning and self-perception greatly benefit litigants who do not have attorneys. They also benefit clients who are represented. Streamlined forms and procedures reduce complexity and thus the time and cost of legal representation.

As efficient, consumer-friendly, court-based, and court-supported self-help centers expand, they are likely to draw more middle-income users who will opt to self-represent or, more likely, will purchase lawyer assistance on a discrete-task basis. Thus, the private bar's unbundled legal services innovations will prosper concurrently with court reforms that welcome prepared, self-represented parties.

Court leaders recognize that many clients require more extensive representation, and as a result they have become strong supporters of funding for increased access to expert services and of expanded opportunities for limited lawyer assistance. The courts have also been eager to evaluate their self-help programs. Some courts have hired outside experts and routinely survey users. To date, user responses have been overwhelmingly positive. In all of these respects, state courts have become important new stakeholders, driving innovation and urging greater coordination among both not-for-profit and private bar providers. Moreover, state courts bring new resources, as well as prestige and credibility to the access to justice agenda.

Legal Services Innovations. Many LSC grantees and other not-for-profits have embraced hotlines and other sources of limited assistance. For example, LSC has initiated and sustained a competitive Technology Initiative Grants program that fosters new uses of technology in service delivery. Impressive inventories of service innovations are available on the Web sites of LSC, NLADA (National Legal Aid & Defender Association), and the ABA Standing Committee on Legal Aid and Indigent Defendants.

The Legal Aid Society of Orange County ("LASOC") is one of the most innovative providers of legal services in the country. The program's Web site identifies an array of services that include "a hotline intake system, self-help clinics, workshops, on-line court forms," and in-depth representation. Client eligibility is determined via the program hotline, the main access point for those seeking help. In addition, the program offers services that do not require eligibility screening, including a "Small

Claims Advisory Program, Legal Resolutions, and LASOC's Lawyer Referral Service."

The LASOC has full-time computer programmers on staff to update its highly effective I-CAN! online forms and Earned Income Tax Credit ("EITC") electronic filing software that allows users anywhere in the country to file for the EITC while at the same time filing their state and federal income tax returns. LASOC innovations are disseminated by LSC and have been adopted by many legal services providers.

Can the Legal Profession Meet the Challenges? The organized bench and bar's long-standing commitment to the goal of universal access is unlikely to be realized absent a cost-effective, well-managed, state-based, mixed-model system. That model will challenge the core values and practices of the bar in three main areas: its identity and guild interests, its ethical ideals and norms, and its pursuit of autonomy and independence. Below, I outline the nature of these challenges and gauge the bar's likely response.

All sectors of the bar will experience tensions between their guild interests and their commitment to assuring practical and effective universal access. The solo and small-firm bar will be challenged by new modes of service that decrease and, in some instances, eliminate lawyer involvement. This threatens the bar's interest in maintaining its monopoly and sources of revenue. However, in a full-service system, the solo and small-firm bar will be offered new opportunities—referral of clients whose needs match their expertise and Judicare contracts to serve fully or partially subsidized clients. These lawyers may find that, in a reformed legal aid system, they spend less time getting clients and more time providing income-generating service to clients who need their help.

The corporate bar has embraced pro bono for reasons of professional satisfaction and idealism, but also because it meets many firm needs such as training, recruitment and retention, positive public relations, and use of slack time in various departments. However, a full-access delivery system will challenge big firms to take on cases based more on delivery system needs and less on the preferences of firm attorneys. Firms should also absorb most of the infrastructure costs of training their lawyers for pro bono work and linking them to pro bono clients.

The legal services bar will be asked to cede some autonomy in case selection and modes of service, to accept new providers as co-equal partners, and to redefine their distinct contributions to the larger delivery system. Like the solo and small-firm bar, salaried legal aid lawyers should focus on matters that require their extensive professional training and expertise, and leave to lay advocates, and self-help and limited-assistance centers all matters that these service resources can handle appropriately.

Traditionally, courts have been passive, depending on lawyers to frame issues and move cases. Courts have viewed judges' time as their most precious resource and protected it at the expense of attorney and client time. As courts have become more proactive in the face of many parties appearing without representation, judges, clerks, and court administrators have had to redefine their roles and identities. They have begun to attend to the time constraints of litigants and their representatives. Many courts are successfully meeting this challenge by simplifying procedures, forms, and language wherever appropriate and, in the process, ceding some of the mystique of the black-robed judge on the high bench.

The bench and bar have struggled and will continue to struggle when their guild interests collide with the profession's aspirations and ideals. Tensions and, in some instances, resistance will no doubt continue as the pace of change accelerates. But I have great confidence that the bench and bar will, as they have to date, adapt and continue to lead efforts to create a legal services delivery system that truly serves all Americans.

NOTES ON CHARN

1. *Will the Organized Bar Support Innovation?* Charn identifies a number of reasons to be optimistic about of the willingness and ability of the bench and bar to expand access to legal services by providing innovative ways to deliver legal services other than through a traditional full-service lawyer-client relationship. On the other hand, some of the excerpts that precede Charn's excerpt offer reasons to be skeptical about the bar's support for innovation, and the title of Charn's article suggests her own doubts. Why do you think the bench and some segments of the bar have embraced (or at least tolerated) the reforms that Charn identifies while other segments of the bar have continued to insist on broad prohibitions on unauthorized practice?

2. *Far Enough?* Do the developments that Charn identifies in her article go far enough in addressing the need for legal services and the problems caused by the restrictions on unauthorized practice?

3. *A Bigger Role for For-Profit Enterprises?* Does Charn underestimate the role that large-scale for-profit businesses, including web-based enterprises, could play in making legal services more readily available to ordinary Americans? Or does she perhaps implicitly underestimate the willingness of the bar to experiment with such changes?

E. OUTSIDE OWNERSHIP OF LEGAL SERVICES PROVIDERS

Should Walmart and Target be allowed to hire lawyers to offer legal services in their stores, in much the same way as some of their stores currently hire nurses, pharmacists, ophthalmologists, and doctors to provide medical services in on-site clinics? Should law firms be allowed to seek outside investors in order to increase the size and efficiency of their operations?

Innovations such as these would require changes in the regulation of U.S. legal services markets by allowing non-lawyer ownership, or partial ownership, of organizations that provide legal services. England, Australia and Canada now allow such arrangements, but they are forbidden in the U.S. Most jurisdictions follow Rule 5.4, which provides that "a lawyer or law firm shall not share legal fees with a non-lawyer" except in certain limited circumstances; that a lawyer "shall not form a partnership with a non-lawyer if any of the activities of the partnership consist of the practice of law"; and that "a lawyer shall not practice with or in the form of a professional corporation or association authorized to practice law for a profit, if a non-lawyer owns any interest therein. . . ." These restrictions are premised on the idea that allowing a lawyer to practice or share fees with nonlawyers threatens the lawyer's ability to exercise professional independence. The only U.S. jurisdiction that allows any non-lawyer participation in the ownership of a for-profit entity providing legal services is the District of Columbia, which for over twenty years has permitted such non-lawyer participation provided that the non-lawyers are employees of the firm, the firm provides exclusively legal services, and the non-lawyers agree to be bound by lawyers' ethical obligations.[22]

Sharing Fees with Nonlawyers and Outside Ownership of Legal Services Providers

Rule 5.4 provides in part

- a lawyer or law firm may not share legal fees with a nonlawyer except in very limited circumstances

- lawyers may not form a partnership with a nonlawyer if any of the activities of the partnership consist of the practice of law

- a lawyer may not practice with or in the form of a for-profit entity to practice law if a nonlawyer owns any interest in the practice or is a director or officer of the entity.

In 2009, the ABA created a commission (known as the Ethics 20/20 Commission) to identify and offer solutions for a growing number of ethics issues arising from globalization and rapid changes in technology. One of the issues that the Commission initially identified as worthy of study was the possibility of permitting limited non-lawyer ownership of law firms. It

---

[22]   D.C. Rules of Professional Conduct, Rule 5.4.

considered several proposals that would have limited the percentage of non-lawyer ownership and required non-lawyer owners to comply with the Rules of Professional Conduct. A discussion paper on alternative practice structures circulated by the Commission cited evidence of substantial market demand for "legal services that firms with nonlawyer partners are well-positioned to provide." It offered as examples "firms that focus their practice on land use planning with engineers and architects; law firms with intellectual property practices with scientists and engineers; family law firms with social workers and financial planners on the client service team; and personal injury law firms with nurses and investigators participating in the evaluation of cases and assisting in the evaluation of evidence and development of strategy." The report also noted that there have been no disciplinary cases involving interference with lawyers' professional judgment by nonlawyers with ownership interests in District of Columbia firms and that "[t]here is simply no evidence that the perceived risk of interference has materialized."[23] Nevertheless, in April 2012, the Commission abandoned the proposal without issuing a report.

The current prohibitions have recently come under fire from organizations that aspire to develop business models premised on high volume and low costs. In 2011, for example, the law firm of Jacoby & Meyers filed a lawsuit seeking to overturn the ban on non-lawyer ownership of law firms in New York, New Jersey, and Connecticut. The firm argued that the ethics rule against outside ownership violates federal constitutional law and "perpetuates economic inequality" because smaller firms do not have the same access to capital markets that large firms do.[24] In 2012, a federal district court dismissed the case, but in 2013 the Court of Appeals for the Second Circuit remanded the case to the district court.[25]

Economist Gillian Hadfield, whose analyses of the legal services market we read in the previous chapter, has argued that the proposal considered by the Ethics 20/20 Commission (and ultimately abandoned by it) did not go far enough. She asserts that a much more fundamental loosening of restrictions on the permissible forms of practice is necessary to support the kinds of radical innovation required to bring ordinary Americans the legal help they need. Recall that Rule 5.4 prohibits not just outside investment in law firms, but also a variety of other ways in which lawyers might collaborate with other professionals or service providers to

---

[23] ABA Commission on Ethics 20/20, *Discussion Paper on Alternative Practice Structures*, Dec. 2, 2011, p. 2.

[24] Debra Cassens Weiss, *Jacoby & Meyers Sues to Overturn Bans on Nonlawyer Ownership of Law Firms*, ABA J., May 19, 2011.

[25] Jacoby & Meyers LLP, Presiding Justices of the First, Second, Third & Fourth Departments, Appellate Div. of Supreme Court of State of New York, 488 F. App's 526 (2d Cir. 2012), last amended Jan. 9, 2013.

provide legal services. According to Hadfield, the legal profession is due for the kind of major restructuring that medicine has undergone in recent decades, including "larger scale organizations and more creative financial and management relationships between those who provide legal expertise—lawyers—and those who provide many of the other components that go into ultimately delivering legal assistance to people."[26]

Meanwhile, the U.K. Parliament's passage of the Legal Services Act of 2007 has begun to significantly change how legal services are delivered and regulated in the U.K. The act allows law firms to seek outside investment and for companies that are not law firms to offer legal services. Proponents of the law assert that greater competition will drive down prices, create new means for delivering legal services, and improve access to the law. The first major retailer to enter the market was the Co-Operative Group supermarket chain, which operates a national network of supermarkets, banks, funeral services and pharmacies. In 2012, it announced plans to hire 3,000 lawyers to provide consumer legal services.[27] The first U.S. firm to take advantage of changes under the Legal Services Act is Jacoby & Meyers, which in 2013 announced plans to expand to Europe through a joint venture with a London-based firm, MJ Hudson.[28]

In 2007, the Australian law firm of Slater & Gordon was listed on the Australian Stock Exchange. The firm sees to serve "everyday people" in areas such as personal injury, medical malpractice, employment, workers' compensation, family law, wills, real estate, and class actions. It has 70 locations in Australia and 12 in the U.K. In May of 2013, it announced plans to raise $63 million to buy three U.K. law firms.[29]

NOTES ON OUTSIDE OWNERSHIP OF LEGAL SERVICES PROVIDERS

1. ***Would Americans Buy Legal Services from Walmart?*** One journalist has described a vision of what loosened restrictions might mean for U.S. consumers: "Imagine an afternoon trip to a Wal-Mart: You pick up socks, a flat-screen television and a microwave meal. After checking out, you stop in the photo studio at the front of the store for a family portrait, and then shift one booth over to a lawyer, who drafts your will or real estate contract."[30]

---

[26] Gillian Hadfield, *The Cost of Law: Promoting Access to Justice Through the (Un)Corporate Practice of Law*, INT'L REV. LAW & ECON. (2013).

[27] See Owen Bowcott, *Co-op to Hire 3,000 Lawyers in Challenge to High Street Solicitors*, THE GUARDIAN, May 28, 2012.

[28] Ashley Post, *Jacoby & Meyers to Expand in Europe*, INSIDE COUNSEL, Aug. 14, 2013.

[29] Martha Neil, *Australia's Publicly Traded Slater & Gordon Raising $64M to Buy More UK Personal Injury Firms*, A.B.A J., May 7, 2013.

[30] John Eligon, *Selling Pieces of Law Firms*, N.Y.TIMES, Oct. 29, 2011.

Do you think that American consumers would be willing to buy basic legal services through a retailer such as Walmart or Target? More generally, what effects do you think a liberalized rule on outside ownership of the providers of legal services would have on the delivery of legal services to ordinary Americans?

2. *A Threat to Professional Values?* Opponents of proposals to allow non-lawyers to invest in law firms argue that non-lawyer owners could influence lawyers' judgments or otherwise erode the profession's ethical obligations of client loyalty and confidentiality. Supporters of the rule change argue that lawyers in law firms already are subject to pressure to focus on profitability and that allowing non-lawyer participation in organizations that provide legal services would not change that fact. Moreover, they argue that non-lawyers in organizations that provide legal services could be required to obey the ethical rules that apply to lawyers, thereby ameliorating concerns about how non-lawyer investment might dilute lawyers' commitments to core professional values. Which set of arguments do you find more convincing?

3. *Relevance of these Issues to the Corporate Sector.* These materials have focused primarily on how restrictions on non-lawyer participation in the provision of legal services affect the individual client/small business sector. Chapter 34 considers how these rules—including restrictions on combining various types of expertise in "multi-disciplinary practice"—affect U.S. lawyers' ability to compete in the global market for corporate legal services.

F. SUMMARY

The chapter explored what it means to "practice law" and considered the vast reach of statutes that prohibit nonlawyers from engaging in the unauthorized practice of law. We addressed the policies that underlie those restrictions and whether and to what extent the restrictions further those purposes. We explored various proposed innovations in service delivery models for ordinary consumers and how some of these approaches conflict with current rules restricting who may provide legal services and what form legal practice can take. Finally, we considered whether corporations should be allowed to offer legal services, much as they now provide banking, real estate, accounting, and even medical services. Such enterprises run afoul of ethics rules that prohibit lawyers from sharing legal fees with nonlawyers and forming enterprises with them to deliver legal services.

CHAPTER 33

PRO BONO

■ ■ ■

A. INTRODUCTION

The American legal profession has a longstanding tradition of providing free or reduced price legal services *pro bono publico* ("for the public good"), or "pro bono," to poor people, nonprofit organizations, civic groups, neighbors, friends, relatives, or clients who have fallen on hard times. Two rationales are commonly cited in support of this practice, which many lawyers believe is an ethical obligation. One is that lawyers, as officers of the court, have a special responsibility for the administration of justice. Second, the profession's monopoly on the delivery of legal services is thought to entail a responsibility to distribute some of the monopoly profits to those unable to afford lawyers' services. Some people also note that pro bono service educates lawyers about the legal needs of the poor and thus makes them better informed about the ways in which the administration of justice falls short.[1]

Model Rule on Pro Bono Service

Rule 6.1 provides that

- Every lawyer has a professional obligation to provide legal services to those unable to pay

- Lawyers should provide at least 50 hours of pro bono service per year

- Most of that service should be provided without fee or expectation of a fee to people of limited means or to organizations serving people of limited means

---

The Model Rules recognize pro bono service as a professional obligation but not a mandatory duty. Rule 6.1 provides that "[e]very lawyer has a professional responsibility to provide legal services to those unable to pay" and that "[a] lawyer should aspire to render at least (50) hours of pro bono publico legal services per year." Rule 6.1(a) provides that a "substantial majority" of those hours should be provided without fee or expectation of fee to people of limited means or charitable, religious, civic, community, governmental and educational organizations serving

---

[1]   *See* GEOFFREY C. HAZARD, JR., ET AL, THE LAW AND ETHICS OF LAWYERING 982 (2010).

people of limited means. Rule 6.1(b) provides that a lawyer should contribute additional services through free or substantially reduced fee to individuals, groups or organizations seeking to secure or protect civil rights, civil liberties, or public rights, or to charitable, religious, civic, community, governmental and educational organizations, or through providing legal services at substantially reduced fee to people of limited means, or by working to improve the law, the legal system, or the legal profession.

As we'll see, lawyers' understanding and practice of pro bono—what it means, what form it should take, whether it should be required, etc.— vary by practice setting and lawyer characteristics. The first part of this chapter explores the role that pro bono plays in meeting the needs of people of limited means. It then addresses how pro bono is defined in different practice sectors, the extent to which various types of lawyers engage in it, and how lawyers' differing interests within the profession affect debates about how much pro bono lawyers should be expected to perform. Finally, we consider proposals to make pro bono mandatory.

B. PRO BONO'S ROLE IN PROVIDING ACCESS TO LEGAL SERVICES

The first two excerpts in this chapter examine the role that pro bono plays in responding to unmet legal needs in this country. The first excerpt considers how pro bono has come to be institutionalized in large law firms and the benefits and limitations of this model of pro bono service. The second excerpt considers how reliance on pro bono as a major component of civil legal assistance for the poor makes that system vulnerable—how the market for legal services can affect the type, quality and amount of pro bono legal services available to individuals and groups.

THE POLITICS OF PRO BONO
Scott L. Cummings
52 UCLA Law Review 1 (2004)

[In the late 1990s], a radical change [was] taking place in how pro bono services were being dispensed. Whereas pro bono had traditionally been provided informally—frequently by solo and small firm practitioners who conferred free services as a matter of individual largesse—by the end of the 1990s pro bono was regimented and organized, distributed through a network of structures designed to facilitate the mass provision of free services by law firm volunteers acting out of professional duty.

This transformation was apparent at multiple levels. The American Bar Association (ABA) campaigned to make "pro bono a priority," revising the ethical rules on pro bono service, challenging the nation's biggest law firms to step up their pro bono commitments, and supporting the development of a pro bono infrastructure in nonprofit groups, law firms, and law schools. Local bar associations, public interest organizations, and legal services groups expanded programs designed to link unrepresented clients with pro bono volunteers. Big law firms, in turn, augmented their own pro bono systems, creating new pro bono positions, developing innovative projects, and sending their associates to staff public interest organizations and poverty law clinics. Private foundations turned their attention to funding pro bono programs, new ranking systems emerged to track pro bono performance, and states experimented with pro bono reporting requirements. As pro bono infiltrated corporate legal departments and business law practice groups, penetrated small-town communities, and shot across national borders, its transformation could not be ignored. Once confined to the margins of professional practice, pro bono had become radically institutionalized, emerging as the dominant model of delivering free legal services.

Pro bono's institutionalization has depended critically on the rise of the big corporate law firm. Although small-scale practitioners have been important actors in the pro bono system, it has been big firms that have provided the resources and prestige to promote pro bono as a central professional goal. At one level, the big firm's organizational structure provides very practical advantages over smaller practice sites in delivering pro bono services. Since the pro bono model seeks to deploy large numbers of lawyers to provide free services, it relies heavily on the big firm as a mass supplier of pro bono personnel. In addition, because big firms are highly leveraged, they can generally absorb the costs associated with pro bono more readily than their smaller counterparts, which cannot afford to forgo significant amounts of billable work. Finally, big firms have the administrative capacity to coordinate large-scale pro bono efforts that small firms cannot match.

Yet the relationship between pro bono and big firms has not been one-sided, with pro bono programs merely the lucky recipients of big-firm largesse. Pro bono has also provided critical organizational benefits to big firms themselves. Law firms, like other organizational structures, adapt to the demands of their environments in order to gain economic resources. A key resource for big firms is talented lawyers. As part of the intense market competition to attract elite law school graduates, many of whom care deeply about pro bono opportunities, big firms have therefore designed pro bono programs to complement broader recruitment and retention plans.

The first wave of institutionalization occurred in the late 1960s, as rapid law firm growth increased demand for new associates at a time when the lure of exciting new opportunities within the public interest field was drawing the attention of elite law students away from commercial work. There was a widespread perception that elite graduates would not opt for big firms unless they developed programs that provided opportunities to engage in pro bono. As a result, the number of formalized pro bono programs expanded. Some firms assigned partners and committees to screen and coordinate pro bono cases, while others provided attorneys to staff legal services clinics. Particularly in the Washington, D.C. area, the ethos of public service was translated into a number of innovative pro bono programs. A few firms, notably Hogan & Hartson, established full-fledged public interest departments with dedicated staff devoted full-time to pro bono work. Other firms, like Covington & Burling, participated in "release-time" programs which provided full-time lawyers and support staff to maintain a local legal services office. Taking this model one step further, Baltimore-based Piper & Marbury established a branch office in a low-income community to provide pro bono services. Thus, at the height of the federal legal services era, pro bono emerged as an institutionally viable, if still underdeveloped, feature of big-firm practice.

It was not until the 1990s that pro bono became deeply embedded within the large law firm structure. Pro bono's assimilation to big-firm practice came at a time of heightened anxiety about the direction of the profession, which was undergoing a dramatic economic expansion. Indeed, the biggest and most profitable law firms grew even bigger and more profitable during the 1990s.

This growth corresponded to several changes in the internal structure of big firms. The rising volume of business meant that firms needed to hire aggressively. To lure new associates in an environment where increasing numbers of lawyers were defecting to take positions in start-up businesses, investment banks, and venture capital companies, firms significantly raised starting salaries. In order to pay for six-figure starting salaries, law firms raised billable rates and ratcheted up billable-hours expectations for firm associates. Whereas one survey placed the average yearly billable hours of associates in all firms at just over 1800 in the mid-1990s, by 1999, another survey reported that the average had climbed to over 2000.

At the height of the boom, these changes appeared to be taking their toll on big-firm pro bono. In 2000, a front-page article in the *New York Times* reported that law firms were "cutting back on free services for poor," noting that only eighteen of 100 firms surveyed in 1999 had met the ABA guideline of fifty hours of pro bono per attorney. *AmLaw*'s headline in its 2000 survey was "Eight Minutes," which was the number of minutes per day that the average attorney spent on pro bono work. The *National Law Journal* reported that pro bono work in big law firms declined from 2.6 percent of billable hours in 1999 to 2.5 percent in 2000, emphasizing that "based on a 2,000-billable-hour year and a billable rate of $175, the drop represents a thousand pro bono hours at a firm of 300 lawyers, the median number of attorneys at the 250 largest U.S. firms." In addition to decreasing numbers, there was evidence that some firms were also pulling back from pro bono in other ways. For example, San Francisco's Pillsbury Madison & Sutro revised its pro bono policy in response to associate pay increases. Under the newly instituted policy, the first twenty hours of pro bono work did not count toward an associate's required minimum of 1950 billable hours. Many other top firms followed suit, changing their policies to give less credit to pro bono work.

Yet this period of economic growth and competitive pressure, which made pro bono more difficult to perform, also had the effect of deepening its institutional structure within big firms, which moved to shore up their public image and gain a competitive edge in the recruiting wars. As the National Association for Law Placement (NALP)—which distributes a Directory of Legal Employers that is widely read by prospective firm associates—and law schools began publishing information about law firm pro bono activity, firms were forced to take seriously the importance of pro bono as a recruitment device. As a result, big firms began tracking their own pro bono activity, factoring pro bono into firm budgets, and marketing pro bono as part of their recruitment efforts.

The advent of pro bono reporting in the legal trade press accelerated this trend. The *American Lawyer* began reporting data on the pro bono activity of AmLaw 100 firms in 1992, which transformed the way big firms viewed their pro bono programs. Whereas previous discussions of pro bono mostly relied on impressionistic evidence, now fluctuations in pro bono among the elite firms could be tracked on a yearly basis. More importantly, firms were actually ranked based on pro bono performance, which meant not just that recruits could compare pro bono among firms with more precision, but also that firms could make up for weaknesses in other areas by scoring high on pro bono.

The "Law Firm Pro Bono Challenge," launched in 1993 by the ABA-sponsored Law Firm Pro Bono Project, raised the stakes by calling on big firms to contribute 3 to 5 percent of their billable hours to pro bono, and publicizing which firms succeeded in meeting the Challenge and which failed. The Challenge was designed to promote pro bono programs in large firms, requiring signatories to demonstrate their "institutional obligation to encourage and support" pro bono by "promulgating and maintaining a clearly articulated and understood firm policy" and using their "best efforts" to ensure compliance with the 3 to 5 percent goal. In its first two years, there were over 170 signatories to the Challenge, which included many of the nation's elite firms. By requiring specific pro bono commitments and tracking compliance, the Challenge established another public benchmark that became a means to evaluate the relative merits of different firms on the basis of pro bono activity.

The combination of these developments prompted many large firms to augment their pro bono programs as a way to appeal to interested law students, improve their rankings, and facilitate compliance with the Challenge. Firms increased their reliance on pro bono committees, hired full-time coordinators to expand pro bono dockets, formalized pro bono policies, and undertook large-scale pro bono projects. They also cemented relationships with legal services and public interest groups, launched new externship programs, and publicized pro bono achievements on web sites and in annual reports.

[P]rivate lawyers do a tremendous service representing individual poor clients in routine matters and lending their institutional resources to support the reform agendas of public interest groups. Their volunteer work ranges from the mundane to the transformative and includes matters of intense personal interest and immense social import. But the central dilemma of pro bono remains: A system that depends on private lawyers is ultimately beholden to their interests. This means not just that private lawyers will avoid categories of cases that threaten client interests, but also that they will take on pro bono cases for institutional reasons that are disconnected from the interests of the poor and underserved. This is most apparent in the use of pro bono for law firm associate training.

There are other drawbacks to the pro bono system. Pro bono lawyers do not invest heavily in gaining substantive expertise, getting to know the broader public interest field, or understanding the long-range goals of client groups. Particularly in contrast to the way big-firm lawyers seek to understand and vigorously advance the goals of their client community, the partiality and narrowness of pro bono representation is striking. And the disparity of the resources devoted to billable versus pro bono work—which, even at the most generous firm, rarely constitutes more than 5 percent of total hours—underscores the vast inequality in legal services that persists.

The story of pro bono is still being written. As trends of privatization, volunteerism, and globalization press forward, one can expect pro bono to be a growth industry in the years to come, not simply shaping the American system of free legal services, but informing the discussion about equal access to justice around the world. Questions about pro bono's effectiveness as a model for meeting the legal needs of poor and underserved groups will therefore take center stage. It is important that the advantages of pro bono—its decentralized structure, collaborative relationships, pragmatic alliances, and flexible approaches—receive full attention. Yet these advantages must be carefully weighed against the systemic challenges that pro bono poses: its refusal to take on corporate practice and its dilettantish approach to advancing the interests of marginalized groups. Instead of professional platitudes about the virtues of volunteerism, robust debate is therefore in order—debate that includes a full airing of both the promise and perils of pro bono, and provides a rigorous account of what equal access to justice looks like in practice. To avoid this debate invites the uncritical expansion of pro bono as a stop-gap measure rather than a thoughtful response to the dilemma of unequal legal representation. More fundamentally, the failure to confront pro bono's limitations risks privileging professional interests over concerns of social justice—promoting the image of equal access without the reality.

NOTES ON CUMMINGS

1. *Trends.* What trends have fostered the development and "institutionalization" of big firm pro bono?

2. *What Role Does Pro Bono Play?* In what ways has big firm pro bono contributed toward answering the problem of unequal access to justice in this country? What are the drawbacks of relying on large firm pro bono as a means for addressing this need? According to Cummings, how do the pro bono services that large firms provide compare with those supplied by small firms?

3. *Benefits for Firms.* What benefits do large law firms derive through pro bono service, according to Cummings?

LAWYERS' PRO BONO SERVICE AND AMERICAN-STYLE CIVIL LEGAL ASSISTANCE

Rebecca Sandefur
41 Law & Society Review 79 (2007)

A large, and perhaps increasing, share of the civil legal assistance available to indigent Americans reflects lawyers' work in organized civil pro bono programs. Reliance on lawyers' pro bono work renders the stock of legal assistance vulnerable to those factors affecting pro bono participation. Empirical analysis of state-to-state differences in lawyers' participation in organized civil pro bono programs reveals that this activity is sensitive to conditions in legal services markets.

Pro Bono and Professionalism. Legal aid scholars have long expressed concerns that strong connections to the market can corrupt or disable lawyers' charity as a means of facilitating the poor's use of law. Most often recognized have been positional conflicts of interest, which emerge from a lawyer's service to classes of clients whose interests may be opposed, such as landlords and tenants, unions and employers, or merchants and consumers.

Positional conflicts are likely to have their most pronounced effects on the distribution of pro bono effort across different types of legal work. In particular, lawyers appear hesitant to take on pro bono cases that place their firms in positions of conflict between the interests of classes of existing and potential paying clients and classes of pro bono clients. For example, a lawyer in a firm that does legal work for one major banking company may be presented with a potential pro bono client who is a consumer with a complaint against a different major banking company. The concern is that the lawyer, if he or she took the pro bono case, would not give zealous representation and incisive advice for fear of antagonizing the paying client, the bank.

Reliance on charity in a market context may also affect the sheer amount of available assistance, through market conditions' effect on the amount of pro bono performed. Two dynamics, one internal to the organizations in which lawyers work and one characterizing lawyers' relationship with other occupations, illustrate how this can occur. Most simply, lawyers must be able to afford to do pro bono. Work that is billed to a client for less than the cost of performing it must be cross-subsidized by other work if the firm or the lawyer is to survive in business. Lawyers choose which cases to take and which to decline based, at least in part, on the other actualized and potential sources of revenue in their "portfolio" of work, trying to balance risk and potential payoffs. Individual lawyers and law firms are likely make at least implicit and informal, if not explicit and highly rationalized, calculations about how much pro bono work they can afford to do.

More subtly, pro bono participation may reflect strategies of market closure and the dynamics of competition between law and other occupations. As in other professions, lawyers act collectively through professional associations and other means to try to ensure that they can make a good living, both by encouraging demand for their services and by restricting the supply of those services. One important way in which they achieve the latter goal is by protecting legal work from encroaching occupations. Pro bono service can be understood as an important element of boundary maintenance.

When lawyers fail to assist indigent clients with their justiciable problems, other occupations—document preparers, estate planners, financial advisors, social workers—can step in to provide services at fee levels (including no fee) that poor people can afford. Historically, competing occupations have sometimes defended their activities by arguing that the high cost of lawyers' services puts civil justice beyond the budget of many ordinary Americans. In response to these concerns, state legislatures have both entertained the possibility of legalizing currently unauthorized practice and have actually done so by recognizing non-attorney providers of limited services in areas of historically legal practice. These legislative actions infringe upon lawyers' powers of self-regulation by taking away some of their authority to define what they do as the practice of law.

<u>Market Conditions</u>. In the analyses here, I focus on those ways in which the market context may affect the amount, rather than the type, of pro bono service provided.

Some lawyers and state professions can more easily afford to provide free services to indigent people because they can subsidize the free services with income from paid work. By this logic, states in which the profession takes in more receipts per lawyer should exhibit higher rates of pro bono service than states in which lawyers bring in less money; one might term this the *cross-subsidy* hypothesis. Cross-subsidy can operate both at the individual level, as individual members of firms or solo practitioners make decisions about how much pro bono work they will do, and at the organizational level, through the presence of "organizational slack". Organizational slack comprises spare resources of funds, technology, skill, and personnel that can be reserved until pressure of work requires them or can be deployed in other activities, such as pro bono service. At the level of states, higher revenues to the legal profession may reflect not only a brisk market for legal services, but also the greater presence of the kinds of legal organizations that perform the most lucrative legal work and accumulate substantial organizational slack, large law firms.

The second way in which conditions in the markets for legal services may affect the amount of pro bono service is through jurisdictional conflicts. If lawyers' pro bono service reflects, in part, an attempt to maintain jurisdictional closure, we would expect states where the legal profession feels that some historically legal work is under threat from other occupations to exhibit higher levels of pro bono service than states in which the profession does not feel under threat; one might term this the *interoccupational competition* hypothesis.

[Sandefur then explained her methods for analyzing the relationship between pro bono service, average per lawyer revenues, and perceived threat of encroachment by other occupations.]

Analysis of the available data suggests that conditions in state legal services markets bear strong relationships to pro bono participation. Higher revenues per lawyer are associated with greater participation in organized civil pro bono programs, as is the perception that the state's legal profession is under threat from unauthorized practice by other occupations. Lawyers' participation in this public service activity appears highly sensitive to the dynamics of legal services markets.

NOTES ON SANDEFUR

1. ***Market Conditions and Pro Bono.*** As Sandefur observes, pro bono has become an essential part of "American style legal assistance." How do conditions in the market for legal services affect pro bono service?

2. ***Positional Conflicts.*** In Chapter 12, we noted that business and ideological conflicts sometimes interfere with law firms' willingness to provide pro bono service. Both the Cummings and Sandefur excerpts refer to conflict issues in their analyses of the limitations of pro bono. Here Cummings explains in more detail how conflicts of interest, and especially "positional conflicts," limit what types of pro bono work large firms pursue:

> Decisions about pro bono are always filtered through the lens of how they will affect the interests of commercial clients. As a threshold matter, pro bono requests are subject to the same screening process that applies to fee-generating cases. Under the Model Rules of Professional Conduct, a private lawyer is generally not permitted to take on a pro bono matter that is directly adverse to another client or materially limits the lawyer's ability to represent another client. In specific cases, these conflict rules can operate to preclude pro bono representation.

> Even when actual conflicts do not bar pro bono representation, the specter of so-called positional conflicts presents an additional hurdle. Positional conflicts arise when a lawyer advances an argument on behalf of one client that is directly contrary to, or has a detrimental impact on, the position advanced on behalf of a second client in a different case or matter. Existing ethical rules generally permit representation despite the existence of positional conflicts, stating that a conflict exists only "if there is a significant risk that a lawyer's action on behalf of one client will materially limit the lawyer's effectiveness in representing another client in a different case." [Rule 1.7 comment [24]] This creates a fairly high standard for refusing oppositional work, precluding a lawyer or her firm from asserting antagonistic positions for different clients "when a decision favoring one client will create a precedent likely to seriously weaken the position taken on behalf of the other client."

> Large commercial law firms in theory treat positional conflicts the same in the pro bono and billable context. However, despite the latitude for accepting oppositional cases under the ethical rules, positional conflicts pose unique barriers for pro bono cases. One reason is that pro bono cases frequently involve claims asserted against businesses, which constitute the economic lifeblood of the big commercial firm. Particularly as corporate clients become more aggressive about ensuring that law firms do not switch sides on important business matters, law firms are reluctant to accept pro bono cases that even appear to adopt antagonistic positions. Moreover, when a positional conflict does emerge, law firms are generally unwilling to sacrifice fee-generating cases for those undertaken for free. Firms therefore tend to take an expansive view of positional conflicts in the pro bono context, making cautious case

selection decisions that screen out potentially troublesome pro bono work.[2]

One consequence of law firms declining to take pro bono cases presenting positional conflicts is that the lawyers with the greatest expertise in particular areas—such as employment, consumer credit, or land use law—are the ones least likely to bring their expertise to bear on pro bono projects. This has consequences not only for pro bono clients, who lose the benefit of lawyer expertise, but also for lawyers who would like to use their expertise on pro bono matters as well as for paying clients.

C. WHO DOES PRO BONO, HOW MUCH, AND WHY?

There is plenty of anecdotal evidence that lawyers who participate in pro bono work generally derive satisfaction from doing it. Lawyers' motivations for doing pro bono work vary. Some say that that family background, personal experiences, or volunteer service before law school have shaped their commitment to public service or particular causes. Some report that pro bono provides a welcome diversion from commercial concerns. Some welcome the opportunity handle a small matter that makes an appreciable and immediate difference for an individual client that is hard to see in the large and complex matters they handle for corporate clients. Some cite professional benefits, including the opportunity to develop new skills and areas of expertise and to build ties in the community.

The following excerpts from two empirical studies—one quantitative and the other qualitative—shed additional light on why lawyers engage in pro bono service and how it relates to their career aspirations and daily practices. These studies also lend perspective to questions about the characteristics of lawyers who participate in pro bono and variations in how lawyers define the concept.

PRO BONO AS AN ELITE STRATEGY IN EARLY LAWYER CAREERS

Ronit Dinovitzer & Bryant G. Garth
Private Lawyers and the Public Interest: The Evolving Role of Pro Bono in the
Legal Profession (Robert Granfield & Lynn Mather eds. 2009)[3]

Pierre Bourdieu's 1998 lecture entitled "Is a Disinterested Act Possible?" provides a useful starting point to situate pro bono activity within the patterns of behavior of actors in the legal field. In contrast to the legal profession's largely promotional and selfless view of pro bono, Bourdieu indicates that actors may invest in such "disinterested" activity while doing so "in accordance with their interests". Activity in a

---

[2]   Scott L. Cummings, *The Politics of Pro Bono*, 52 U.C.L.A. L. REV. 1, 116–118 (2004).

[3]   By permission of Oxford University Press, USA.

particular field may be *at the same time* interested (as opposed to disinterested) *and* altruistic. Within a Bourdieusian framework, then, one does not merely counterpose altruism to selfishness. Indeed, participation in some realms of social life *requires* actors to engage in what are apparently gratuitous, unprofitable, and altruistic acts, and an actor who has internalized the rules of the game of the field will spontaneously orient his or her strategies according to these underlying stakes and principles.

[W]e wish to draw on this theoretical perspective to better understand pro bono work in the legal field. First, the legal field tends to be structured in order to reward those who work to sustain the legitimacy of the field as a whole. That means that pro bono generally helps to legitimate a system whereby the overwhelming amount of resources work to sustain corporate power and clients with substantial economic means. Second, we posit that there is a division of labor within the legal field such that elites take the lead in promoting the ideals of the profession while also reaping the profits that come from those ideals. They and their law firms, for example, compete to gain recognition for pro bono activity and public service. Third, the rank and file of the profession typically do not have quite the same orientation to those ideals, because ordinary practitioners have to survive and make a living. They need in the first place to build a demand for their services. They are judged within the profession as a whole, however, according to a definition of pro bono that makes more sense in legitimating legal services to large corporate entities. Fourth, the division of labor within the legal field tends to reinforce social advantage and disadvantage. The strategy of investment in professional virtues is relatively more available to those who are socialized in the virtues of *noblesse oblige* and are in a position to implement the strategy. Elite status is confirmed in part because of the enactment of legal virtue—and the apparent distance it provides from the pure commerce of providing legal services.

THE *AFTER THE JD* STUDY

This [paper] relies on the first wave of data from the *After the JD* (AJD) study, a national longitudinal survey of law graduates. The study is based on a sample representative of the national population of lawyers who were admitted to the bar in 2000 and who graduated from law school between June 1998 and July 2000.

<u>Analysis.</u> We begin by offering an overview of the patterns of pro bono work in the AJD sample. Table 6.1 outlines the distribution of pro bono by practice settings. It is not surprising to find that across the profession, lawyers working in legal services and nonprofits report the highest average hours of pro bono work (261 hours and 80 hours [per year], respectively), though the data suggest that some of these

respondents count their regular work hours as pro bono work. Among those working in private law firms, the highest number of pro bono hours—as expected—is found among those working in the largest firms of over 251 lawyers, with about 70 percent of these lawyers engaging in some pro bono work. In these largest corporate law firms, lawyers performed an average of 73 hours of pro bono work in a 12-month period, which is a full 26 hours more than the amount of pro bono work in the settings with the next highest averages (firms of 101–250 lawyers and solo practice). In private law firms we find that pro bono hours decline as firm size declines, though it flattens out among the smaller and larger firms of between 2 and 100 lawyers. Another constituency that reports fairly high levels of pro bono is solo practitioners, with almost 80 percent of these lawyers reporting that they do some pro bono work, and with the average solo practitioner engaging in 47 hours of pro bono service over 12 months.

TABLE 6.1 PRO BONO HOURS BY PRACTICE SETTING

	Pro Bono Hours (excluding zero)		Any or No Pro Bono	
	Mean	Median	Some pro bono	No pro bono
Solo	46.58	30	79.60%	20.40%
Private firm 2–20	30.29	20	56.00%	44.00%
Private firm 21–100	29.39	16	47.10%	52.90%
Private firm 101–250	47.29	25	62.50%	37.50%
Private firm 251+	73.27	40	69.80%	30.20%
Government	20.21	10	16.90%	83.10%
Legal services or PD	261.15	20	23.10%	76.90%
Public interest	28.51	20	21.30%	78.70%
Nonprofit or education	80.18	30	41.40%	58.60%
Business	21.32	20	50.50%	49.50%
Other	10	10	46.90%	53.10%

[T]here is a strong relationship between law school eliteness and the settings within which lawyers work, with graduates of the country's most elite law schools obtaining positions in large corporate law firms. As indicated in Table 6.2, the average hours of pro bono peak at 90 hours for graduates of top-ten schools and decline to a low of 31 hours for the *U.S. News* category of tier three graduates; the anomaly is that graduates of *U.S. News* fourth tier law schools engage in more pro bono work than their counterparts from schools ranked 41st to 100th. It may be that graduates of the fourth tier are more committed to pro bono work and will find ways to engage in public service even if their work settings do not explicitly promote or reward it. Alternatively, some may argue that this anomaly may be the result of market forces; fourth tier graduates may be relying on pro bono to account for unpaid client bills or to build up their client base, or perhaps they are not getting as much responsibility and client work as they would like in law firm settings.

The patterns of pro bono work by gender and race reveal some expected and some surprising patterns (Table 6.2): African American respondents engage in the most pro bono work per year (66 hours) and Hispanics (for no apparent reason) the least (37 hours), whereas women on average engage in about 4 more hours of pro bono work per year than men (48 vs. 44 hours). Because practice settings are such strong determinants of participation in pro bono work, we also stratified the race and gender results by practice settings. The data indicate that Black lawyers on average engage in more pro bono service, but only in particular settings; in larger law firms (and especially in the largest law firms), Black lawyers engage in more pro bono work than other lawyers (106 hours in firms of over 251 lawyers compared to 72 hours for white lawyers in these firms), but in small and solo practice the averages are much more similar. Stratifying by firm size also demonstrates that Hispanic lawyers report some of the highest pro bono hours in the largest law firms (76 hours), but that Hispanic respondents working outside of the largest firms report lower pro bono hours than the average lawyer. Thus the earlier finding of lower pro bono hours among Hispanic respondents seems to be due, in large part, to the settings within which they work. The data for women are much more consistent, with women reporting higher hours compared to men in all settings except for solo practice.

TABLE 6.2: PRO BONO HOURS BY LAW SCHOOL TIER, RACE, AND GENDER

| | Pro Bono Hours | | Any or No Pro Bono | |
	Mean	Median	Worked some pro bono	Worked no pro bono
LAW SCHOOL TIER				
Ranked 1–10	89.58	50	71.00%	29.00%
Ranked 11–20	59.33	40	68.30%	31.70%
Ranked 21–40	45.71	20	57.80%	42.20%
Ranked 41–100	37.17	20	60.60%	39.40%
Tier 3	31.42	20	55.40%	44.60%
Tier 4	41.3	20	54.70%	45.30%
RACE				
Black	65.7	30	71.40%	28.60%
Hispanic	36.91	20	50.30%	49.70%
Asian	51.06	30	51.90%	48.10%
White	45.22	20	61.00%	39.00%

GENDER

Female	48.25	25	60·70%	39.30%
Male	43.58	20	59.80%	40.20%

The patterns we identify above highlight stratification in pro bono service, with graduates of more elite law schools and corporate lawyers in the largest firms more likely to engage in pro bono work. These patterns are closely related to, and in part derive from, different orientations and dispositions toward engaging in pro bono work. As we show in Table 6.3, lawyers who perform the most pro bono work report that pro bono opportunities were an extremely important factor in their job choice: these lawyers report an average of 98.5 pro bono hours per year. In contrast, lawyers who rated pro bono as not at all important in their choice of first job reported an average of 34.5 pro bono hours. We also find that engaging in pro bono activities during law school is related to the number of pro bono hours lawyers perform once they are in the job market, with prior pro bono experience resulting in about 14 more hours of pro bono service per year. Finally, we analyze the patterns of pro bono based on respondents' ratings of their desire to help individuals as a goal in their decision to attend law school. The results in Table 6.3 indicate that although the average pro bono hours are almost identical regardless of their desire to help individuals, 67 percent of respondents who indicated a desire to help individuals engaged in some pro bono work compared to 52.5 percent of those whose desire to help individuals was rated as irrelevant.

TABLE 6.3 PRO BONO HOURS BY IMPORTANCE OF PRO BONO HOURS TO JOB CHOICE, ENGAGEMENT IN PRO BONO DURING LAW SCHOOL, AND DESIRE TO HELP INDIVIDUALS

	Pro Bono Hours (excluding zero)	Percent Reporting any Pro Bono
	Mean	
Pro bono not at all important in job choice	34.49	51.4%
Pro bono extremely important in job choice	98.53	93.1%
Did not engage in pro bono work in law school	40.32	55.4%
Performed pro bono work while in law school	54.2	71.3%

Desire to help individuals as a lawyer rated as "irrelevant"	48.04	52.5%
Desire to help individuals as a lawyer rated as "very important"	48.73	67.14%

Discussion and Conclusions. Our work is situated within a viewpoint that posits a division of labor within the legal field, with elites more likely than the rank and file of the profession both to promote the ideals of the profession and to reap the profits that come from those ideals; the elites are more likely to compete to gain recognition for pro bono activity and public service, and they are rewarded for it.

Our results provide support for this characterization of the legal profession. We find that although lawyers in large law firms engage in more pro bono work, not all large-firm lawyers equally perform this altruistic work. Indeed, our results suggest that elite law school graduates working in the largest corporate law firms engage in significantly more pro bono work than their peers—and this holds when controlling for a full range of factors including the incentives that law firms offer (e.g., counting pro bono work as billable time), work hours, and social background. We also find that engaging in pro bono work is related to lawyers' orientations toward legal practice. We find that individuals who rate pro bono work as an extremely important feature of their job engage in more pro bono hours, and we also demonstrate that elite law graduates are more likely than others to express this disposition.

Our work also explored the contention that there is a value to disinterestedness by investigating the relationship between pro bono work and job satisfaction. Again, our results suggest that engaging in pro bono work brings with it important symbolic and tangible capital for new lawyers. We find that engaging in some pro bono work versus none increases all forms of job satisfaction, but that increasing pro bono hours either decreases or has no effect on job satisfaction; this combination suggests that pro bono provides a symbolic form of capital that is divorced from how much pro bono work one actually does. The data also suggest that pro bono work likely functions in a more concrete way to increase lawyer satisfaction by offering new lawyers substantively interesting work and opportunities to engage with clients—features that are otherwise largely absent from their private law settings.

Our analysis is of course incomplete in some respects. [D]espite documenting the value of disinterestedness, we must clearly also acknowledge that pro bono work provides a good in and of itself, regardless of the secondary value that it might bring to the lawyers who provide it. Therefore, we are not arguing that pro bono work is all "shuck" simply because there is an interest in disinterestedness. What we are positing is that it is important to recognize the value of pro bono so that we can better understand positions of power within the legal profession and how that professional hierarchy is structured and maintained.

NOTES ON DINOVITZER & GARTH

1. ***Eliteness and Pro Bono Ideals.*** What is the relationship that the authors posit between eliteness in the legal profession and pro bono ideals? Does their theory seem plausible to you? Do their preliminary findings support it?

2. ***Your Experience.*** Do this study's findings about who participates in law firm pro bono square with what you've observed thus far in law school about who participates in law school pro bono programs? If not, what are the differences, and what factors might explain them?

3. ***Pro Bono in Law School and Beyond.*** What do you think explains the relationship between students' pro bono participation in law school and their pro bono participation once in practice?

PRO BONO AND LOW BONO IN THE SOLO AND SMALL FIRM LAW FIRM CONTEXT

Leslie C. Levin

Private Lawyers and the Public Interest: The Evolving Role of Pro Bono in the Legal Profession (Robert Granfield & Lynn Mather eds. 2009)[4]

Lawyers in solo and small (2–5 lawyer) firms, who comprise more than 60 percent of all private practitioners, contribute more time and in greater numbers to the pro bono legal representation of persons of limited means than any other group of lawyers. [But] solo and small firms differ significantly from larger firm settings with respect to the ways in which pro bono work is found and performed, the motivations and incentives for performing it, the types of work performed, and the supports available for this work.

Just a few examples of the differences suffice to make this point. In large law firms, pro bono has been thoroughly institutionalized. A lawyer or administrator runs the law firm's pro bono program. Matters are often selected that can be appropriately handled by junior attorneys and that will not create conflicts with corporate clients. Pro bono work performed by large firms is typically performed entirely for free and is supplied to entirely different clients than those ordinarily serviced by the firm. Firm lawyers may be given time off to work exclusively on pro bono matters while still receiving full compensation. They may devote enormous resources to a single case. Large law firms view their pro bono programs as critically important to recruitment of new associates and firm marketing. Consequently, some large firm lawyers feel direct pressure from their colleagues or their clients to perform pro bono work.

In contrast, lawyers in solo and small firms do not have the support staff or associates that are available to large firm lawyers to help them with pro bono work. Some of the pro bono work performed by solo and small-firm practitioners is received from referrals by organized pro bono programs designed to provide free legal services to the poor, but more often it comes through friends, family and existing clients. Because their compensation is very directly tied to what they earn on an hourly or flat-fee basis, every hour these practitioners spend performing pro bono work directly affects their monthly take-home income. Many consider themselves to be doing pro bono when they perform "low bono" work, which involves the provision of legal services at reduced rates to individuals, including regular clients, who cannot otherwise pay. Thus, the very meaning of pro bono in the solo and small firm context is different than in the large firm setting. Moreover, the firm cultures of solo and small firms, and the motivations of lawyers in such firms for taking pro bono cases, are often very different from those in large-firm practices. Pro bono is rarely important for small firm recruiting and may actually be discouraged by firm partners due to economic concerns.

It would be a mistake, however, to think of solo and small firm lawyers as a monolithic group, even in the context of pro bono. They vary considerably in the types of clients they represent, in their level of administrative support, and in their economic success. Some are essentially cause lawyers who deliberately choose to represent underserved populations. Other lawyers build practices serving middle class and wealthier clients in personal plight areas such as family, landlord-tenant or criminal law, which are areas in which underserved populations also need legal assistance. Still others represent organizations and work in the same practice areas found in large law firms. Solo and small firm lawyers do, however, share common concerns about bringing in new business and being able to service their clients' matters diligently and competently. Cash flow is also a constant concern, and can make it difficult for these lawyers to hire as much administrative support as they need. These concerns can raise special challenges when these lawyers contemplate taking on pro bono work.

The current ABA Model Rule 6.1(a) reflects the large-firm view of pro bono. It places the greatest emphasis on rendering the "substantial majority" of legal services "without fee or expectation of fee" to persons of limited means or to organizations in matters that are designed to address the needs of persons of limited means. Although Model Rule 6.1(b)(2) states that lawyers should provide "any additional services" through "delivery of legal services at substantially reduced fee to persons of limited means," the structure of Rule 6.1 conveys that this is a less valued and desirable method of rendering pro bono service.

Exploration of the different mechanisms through which solo and small firm lawyers deliver pro bono services can help to provide a deeper understanding of the meaning of "pro bono" in this practice setting.

Occasional Planned No-Fee Pro Bono. Lawyers in solo and small-firm practice, like large-firm lawyers, participate in formal bar, court or legal services pro bono programs in which individuals of limited means are referred to volunteer attorneys who provide their services free of charge. Some of the planned pro bono work also comes to solo and small firm lawyers through friends and family, or from individuals who simply walk in the door "and tug at your heartstrings." This may be especially common in rural areas, where lawyers personally know many of the people in the community.

Formal Reduced Fee Programs. Solo and small firm attorneys also provide reduced-fee services through formal programs designed to assist individuals of limited means. Reduced-fee programs take two forms. In the first, the lawyer receives the reduced fee from the government or a legal services organization and the lawyer provides legal representation without cost to the client. In the second, which is often run by a bar association, legal services organization, or other non-profit organization, the lawyer receives the reduced fee directly from the client. These programs are grouped together because they both result in lawyers being paid a reduced fee through a formal program that is designed to benefit low income clients. The programs are also explicitly recognized as pro bono activities under ABA Model Rule 6.1, although they are in a less preferred category than the provision of free legal services.

Perhaps the best-known example of a reduced-fee program in which the government pays the lawyer is court-appointed counsel for indigent clients in criminal cases. A few jurisdictions have also institutionalized judicare programs, which pay private attorneys a low hourly fee to provide legal services to low income individuals in civil cases.

Low Bono Law Practices. A third way in which solo and small firm lawyers deliver legal services to persons of limited means is through law practices that are consciously positioned to service low-income individuals. During the last dozen years, law schools and other groups have worked with solo and small-firm practitioners to organize and support "low bono" law firm practices that provide discounted fee work to clients and take on other cases that may produce revenue through fee-shifting statutes. For example, the Law School Consortium Project is a network of 16 law schools that helps solo and small-firm attorneys who are interested in serving low- and middle-income communities and in finding an economically viable way in which to do so. It created the Community Legal Resource Network, which includes about 800 solo and small-firm practitioners and provides support for these lawyers through mentoring, listservs, and discounted support services, such as electronic research and insurance.

Unplanned Pro Bono: Nonpayers Who Become Pro Bono Clients. When a lawyer has a client who can no longer afford to pay her fees, the lawyer may find herself providing free or reduced-fee legal work, but not always for those who are indigent and not in an entirely voluntary sense. In some cases, the lawyer may feel a desire or a moral commitment to continue to represent the client. In other cases, the lawyer may not feel such a desire or commitment, but cannot readily withdraw from representing a client, especially when litigation is ongoing. Social relations within small communities may also make withdrawal difficult. Ethical obligations to handle client matters competently may require lawyers to continue to perform some legal work, even when it becomes apparent that the client will be unable to pay.

Solo and small-firm lawyers who perform free or reduced-fee work under these circumstances sometimes view it as pro bono work, although it is not recognized as such under ABA Model Rule 6.1 (a), which only includes work undertaken without expectation of a fee. Not surprisingly, even though there may be some altruism involved in the continuing willingness to represent the client for little or no compensation, this type of work is often viewed as a failure of the lawyer's business management skills.

Implications and Ideas for Serving Persons of Limited Means. Model Rule 6.1, which was promulgated by the historically elite ABA, reflects the views and practices of the elite (corporate) segment of the profession, and not those of solo and small firm lawyers. [T]o the extent that the ABA's Model Rule 6.1 has come to reflect the dominant view of what pro bono means in practice, it minimizes the important contributions of solo and small-firm lawyers. It may actually operate to discourage some of the free and reduced-fee work that would otherwise be performed.

Redefining Pro Bono. In order to encourage more pro bono work by lawyers in solo and small law firms, their provision of free and reduced-fee services to certain individuals should be recognized as providing a valued service. This requires [several] changes in the ABA's current rule. First, the meaning of "persons of limited means" should be defined more expansively. The current definition excludes many individuals who genuinely cannot afford lawyers. Second, legal work for a substantially reduced fee should not be relegated to a secondary position in the Model Rules—or worse, excluded altogether from the definition of "pro bono" under some state bar rules. Treating free legal work as the most favored form of pro bono reinforces the status hierarchies in the profession and devalues a good deal of the work that solo and small firm lawyers perform for underserved populations. There is admittedly good reason to encourage "no fee" legal work by those who can perform it. But Model Rule 6.1 also conveys that no-fee pro bono is the "purest" form of pro bono, when in fact the "purity" of the motivations underlying no-fee pro bono work is debatable. Many large firm lawyers draw precisely the same salaries for their pro bono work as for their paying legal work, even if no fee is charged for the work performed for their pro bono client. In contrast, reduced-fee pro bono performed by solo and small-firm lawyers can require a significant sacrifice. To the extent that the Model Rules seek to convey the values of the profession, they should not communicate that the reduced-fee work of solo and small-firm lawyers is less highly valued than the no-fee work performed in large law firms.

NOTES ON LEVIN

1. **Parallel Universes.** In what ways is pro bono in solo and small firms different from pro bono in large firms? In particular, what are the differences in the types of work performed, the motivations and incentives for doing the work, and the supports available? What differences are there in how pro bono is defined?

2. **Varying Definitions of Pro Bono and Lawyers' Varied Interests.** How do disagreements among American lawyers over the definition of, and rules governing, pro bono reflect differences in the practices and interests of lawyers in different sectors of the profession?

D. MANDATORY PRO BONO

Over the years, some advocates of pro bono have argued that lawyers should be required to engage in pro bono as a condition for retaining their licenses to practice. Proponents of mandatory pro bono argue that lawyers, as trustees of the legal system and beneficiaries of a monopoly in the legal services market, owe the public such services. They further argue that imposing a mandatory requirement would inject sorely needed resources into legal assistance programs, and that it would help bring the legal profession's rhetoric into better alignment with its actual practices.[5] Some opponents assert that lawyers should not be required to provide their assistance involuntarily because the needs of the poor are a societal problem that society as a whole should find ways to address. Other opponents argue that mandatory pro bono would not meet its intended purposes because the political compromises that would be necessary to secure bar approval would likely broaden the scope of activities qualifying as pro bono so much that the resulting services would do little to address the needs of the indigent.[6] Some argue that requiring lawyers who are

---

[5] *See* DEBORAH L. RHODE, ACCESS TO JUSTICE 145–84 (2004).

[6] *See* Esther Lardent, *Mandatory Pro Bono in Civil Cases: The Wrong Answer to the Right Question*, 49 MD. L. REV. 78, 100–101 (1990).

unfamiliar with the problems of the poor to provide legal services to them is likely to result in the provision of low quality services.

NOTES ON MANDATORY PRO BONO

1. *A Good Idea?* Should all American lawyers engage in pro bono service? Should pro bono be mandatory—a condition of licensure? Do your answers depend on how pro bono is defined?

2. *Common Criticisms.* As noted above, critics of mandatory pro bono tend to suggest that while in principle lawyers are obliged to do pro bono, imposing a mandatory duty on them would be unfair, counterproductive, or impractical. Do you find these criticisms convincing?

3. *Divisions by Practice Type.* In a portion of the Levin piece not included in the excerpt above, she notes that solo and small-firm lawyers have strongly opposed mandatory pro bono and have seen it "as something that the elite of the bar was attempting to foist upon them." She also observed that the opposition was likely exacerbated by the fact that most mandatory pro bono proposals define pro bono as free legal services to individuals of limited means—and as not including the types of reduced-fee services that solo and small-firm practitioners often provide to their clients who are unable to pay.[7]

4. *New York's Rule.* New York recently adopted a new rule requiring recent law school graduates who apply for admission to the New York bar to demonstrate that they have performed 50 hours of pro bono service.[8] Qualifying pro bono work includes work performed in the service of low-income or disadvantaged individuals who cannot afford counsel, or involves the use of legal skills for an organization that qualifies as a tax-exempt charitable organization under the Internal Revenue Code, or for the benefit of the court system or government agencies or legislative bodies. A student's receipt of academic credit through law school clinics or externships does not disqualify the work.[9]

Do you support such a requirement? Should other states adopt it? What are the arguments for and against imposing such a requirement on new bar applicants but not existing members of the bar?

A California State Bar task force recently recommended adoption of a requirement of 50 hours of pro bono service prior to admission, or in the first year of practice, starting in 2016.

---

[7] Leslie C. Levin, *Pro Bono and Low Bono in the Solo and Small Law Firm Context,* in PRIVATE LAWYERS AND THE PUBLIC INTEREST: THE EVOLVING ROLE OF PRO BONO IN THE LEGAL PROFESSION (Robert Granfield & Lynn Mather eds. 2009).

[8] *See* Anne Barnard, *Top Judge Makes Free Legal Work Mandatory for Joining State Bar,* N.Y. TIMES, May 2, 2012.

[9] *See* New York State Bar Admission Pro Bono Requirement FAQs, Aug. 26, 2013, available at http://www.nycourts.gov/attorneys/probono/FAQsBarAdmission.pdf.

5. ***Reporting Hours.*** Some states, including Florida, Illinois, Maryland, Mississippi, and Nevada, require the reporting of pro bono hours but do not impose mandatory pro bono.[10]

E. SUMMARY

This chapter explored the concept of *pro bono publico* and its role in meeting unmet legal needs. It considered the benefits and limitations of reliance on large firm pro bono as a means of delivering legal services to poor and otherwise vulnerable individuals, and it investigated how and why lawyers in solo and small firm practices tend to define pro bono differently than lawyers in large firms. We also examined how lawyers' various understandings of pro bono relate to their career aspirations and daily practices. Finally, we addressed whether pro bono should be mandatory—a condition of licensure.

---

[10] *See* Kelly Carmody & Associates, Report Prepared for the Florida Supreme Court and the Florida Bar's Standing Committee on Pro Bono Legal Services, *Pro Bono: Looking Back, Moving Forward* (2008).

CHAPTER 34

PRACTICING ACROSS BORDERS AND BOUNDARIES

■ ■ ■

A. INTRODUCTION

Not so long ago, American lawyers served primarily local clients on local matters in local courts. It was unusual for lawyers to form partnerships with lawyers practicing outside the state where they lived and were licensed. Today, however, it is common for lawyers to serve clients on matters that span state and national borders and to have partners who practice half-way around the globe. Moreover, many large firm lawyers in the U.S. compete with foreign lawyers in an increasingly international legal services market. Pressure by corporate clients to unbundle legal services and to provide them "a la carte" has created new opportunities for various types of competing service providers. Those competitors include foreign lawyers, non-lawyer service providers (such as accountants), and entities that combine legal and other types of expertise into "multi-disciplinary practices" (MDPs)—a form of practice that is prohibited in most U.S. jurisdictions. Technology has facilitated cooperation and competition among lawyers and other service providers across state and national borders, as work can easily and instantaneously be transported via the Internet. Even cause lawyers are teaming up with one another across national borders to tackle social justice issues.

These changes in the geographic scope of lawyers' services, the types of service providers with whom lawyers compete in global markets, and the role of technology, have raised a host of practical and regulatory issues, which are the primary focus of this chapter. We first consider the issue of multijurisdictional practice—the question of whether and to what extent a lawyer may serve clients in a U.S. jurisdiction other than the one in which she is licensed and, when that occurs, which jurisdictions have authority to regulate and what law applies. We then examine the phenomena of unbundling, outsourcing and multidisciplinary practice. Finally, we consider circumstances in which U.S. lawyers, especially those serving corporate clients, compete in a global legal services market and interact with foreign-educated lawyers.

B. MULTIJURISDICTIONAL PRACTICE

Admission to the bar in one state does not permit a lawyer to practice law in another. Rather, American lawyers are subject to state-based admission and disciplinary processes. About half the states have reciprocity statutes allowing nonresidents to be admitted to the state's bar without having to pass the bar examination if the applicant's state also does so. But many states, including California, require all lawyers to take the state bar examination in order to practice there.

As we've already seen, unauthorized practice restrictions in every state prohibit non-lawyers from practicing law without a license. But those restrictions generally do not distinguish between lawyers and non-lawyers; a lawyer practicing law in a jurisdiction in which she is not licensed violates unauthorized practice restrictions, just as those without any legal training do. Model Rule 5.5 provides that "[a] lawyer shall not practice law in a jurisdiction in violation of the regulation of the legal profession in that jurisdiction, or assist another in doing so." Restrictions on out-of-state practice by lawyers licensed in another state are typically justified on the ground that competence to practice in one jurisdiction does not necessarily guarantee competence in another.

Unauthorized Practice of Law

- Rule 5.5(a) provides that a lawyer may practice law only in a jurisdiction in which the lawyer is authorized to practice and that a lawyer may not assist others to engage in unauthorized practice.

Lawyers admitted in one jurisdiction are sometimes allowed to participate in a specific litigation in another jurisdiction in which they are not licensed by permission of a court. A lawyer seeks permission by filing a motion to appear *pro hac vice* and to provide advice to the client in connection with that matter. Such motions are usually brought by a lawyer already admitted to the court for purposes of bringing a lawyer with special competence into the case.

There are no mechanisms comparable to *pro hac vice* motions to allow for lawyers who provide counseling and transactional services to move across state lines for limited purposes. Moreover, most transactional work takes place in settings that never come to the attention of the bar. As a consequence, while there is no process by which lawyers may obtain permission to provide transactional or counseling services in a jurisdiction to which they are not admitted, there is also no formal court or bar oversight of whether lawyers are doing so. (As we will see, however, a disgruntled client can raise the issue of unauthorized practice by refusing to pay the lawyer's bill or filing a complaint with the bar.) Some critics of restrictive reciprocity standards argue that the ready availability of information about the law of every state undercuts justifications for limiting transactional practice to in-state lawyers based in arguments about local competence.[1] As a practical matter, until very recently, business lawyers have paid little attention to unauthorized practice restrictions and freely competed with one another across state lines.

Birbrower **and Revised Rule 5.5.** The application of unauthorized practice statutes to lawyers engaged in out-of-state practice generated little controversy until the California Supreme Court ruled in *Birbrower v. Superior Court*, 17 Cal. 4th 119 (1998) that a New York law firm's $1 million fee agreement was unenforceable because the firm's lawyers had engaged in the unlicensed practice of law in California. The client, a California corporation, had retained the Birbrower firm to handle a dispute with another California corporation, and the lawyers traveled to California several times to confer with their clients and accountants, to meet with representatives of the other party to the dispute, and to interview potential arbitrators. After the parties settled, the client filed a malpractice action in California Superior Court, and the lawyers filed a counterclaim to recover their fees. The client moved for summary judgment on the ground that the fee agreement was unenforceable, and the trial court and California Supreme Court agreed. The court reasoned that because the New York lawyers had engaged in unauthorized practice, the California client had no obligation to pay for the services rendered.

Birbrower's holding that the lawyers had engaged in unauthorized practice was not particularly shocking; the client was a California corporation, the lawyers had spent substantial time working on the matter in California, and the contract that was the subject of the dispute was based on California law. But major national law firms were stunned by language in the opinion indicating the definition of law practice did not depend on finding any physical presence in the state: "Physical presence is one factor we may consider in deciding whether the unlicensed lawyer has violated [California's unauthorized practice statute], but it is by no means exclusive. . . . [O]ne may practice law in the state in violation of [the statute] although not physically present here by advising a California client on California law in connection with a California legal dispute by telephone, fax, computer, or other modern technological means." The Court emphasized that any exception to the prohibition on in-state practice by lawyers licensed elsewhere would have to be created

---

[1]   *See* Restatement Section 3 cmt. E ("Modern communications, including ready electronic communication to much of the law of every state, makes concern about a competent analysis of a distant state's law unfounded.").

by the California legislature. It found "irrelevant" whether or not the Birbrower lawyers were "in fact, competent to practice in California."

Although major law firms had previously crossed state lines without regard for unauthorized practice restrictions as necessary to address their clients' needs, *Birbrower* alerted firms that they were now vulnerable to nonpayment by their clients for services deemed to constitute unauthorized practice in another state, and perhaps also to discipline for unauthorized practice. The decision generated attention to the ways in which local regulatory control was at odds with the realities of multijurisdictional practice and to technology's role in revolutionizing what it means to "practice law in a state."

In 2000, soon after the *Birbrower* decision, the ABA established a Commission on Multijurisdictional Practice, which recommended amendments to Rule 5.5 to achieve a "proper balance between the interests of a state in protecting its residents and justice system . . . and the interests of clients in a national and international economy in the ability to employ or retain counsel of choice efficiently and economically."[2] The current version of Rule 5.5 provides that a lawyer may not "establish an office or other systematic and continuous presence" in a jurisdiction in which the lawyer is not licensed or "hold out to the public or otherwise represent that the lawyer is admitted to practice in that jurisdiction." However, the rule allows a lawyer to provide legal services "on a temporary basis" in a jurisdiction in which she is not admitted if the services meet one of the following conditions: 1) they are provided "in association" with a lawyer licensed in the jurisdiction who "actively participates" in the matter; 2) they are in or reasonably related to pending or potential litigation in which the lawyer is authorized or reasonably expects to be authorized to appear; 3) they are provided in an ADR proceeding and "arise out of or are reasonably related to" the lawyer's practice in the home jurisdiction; or 4) they "arise out of or are reasonably related to" the lawyer's practice in a jurisdiction in which the lawyer is admitted to practice. Rule 5.5 also allows for two types of lawyers to establish a "systematic and continuous" presence in a jurisdiction in which they are not licensed: 1) in-house corporate or government lawyers; and 2) lawyers providing services authorized by federal or other law—for example, lawyers licensed by the Patent & Trademark Office to practice patent law.

---

[2] American Bar Association, *Report of the Commission on Multijurisdictional Practice*, Aug. 2002, p. 5.

> **Multijurisdictional Practice**
>
> - Rule 5.5(b) provides that a lawyer who is not admitted to practice in a jurisdiction generally may not establish an office or other systematic and continuous presence in the jurisdiction for the practice of law or hold out to the public or otherwise represent that the lawyer is admitted to practice in that jurisdiction.
>
> - Rule 5.5(c) allows a lawyer to provide legal services "on a temporary basis" in a jurisdiction in which she is not admitted if the services meet one of the following conditions: 1) they are provided "in association" with a lawyer licensed in the jurisdiction who "actively participates" in the matter; 2) they are in or reasonably related to pending or potential litigation in which the lawyer is authorized or reasonably expects to be authorized to appear; 3) they are provided in an ADR proceeding and "arise out of or are reasonably related to" the lawyer's practice in the home jurisdiction; or 4) they "arise out of or are reasonably related to" the lawyer's practice in a jurisdiction in which the lawyer is admitted to practice.
>
> - Rule 5.5(d) creates two exceptions to the general prohibition on lawyers establishing a "systematic and continuous" presence in a jurisdiction in which they are not admitted: for 1) in-house corporate or government lawyers; and 2) lawyers providing services authorized by federal or other law or rule to be provided in the jurisdiction.

Although the revised version of Rule 5.5 loosens restrictions on multijurisdictional practices, it leaves largely untouched a system of state-by-state licensure based on geography. It also still relies on standards that turn on the sometimes perplexing question of whether a lawyer is providing legal services *in* a jurisdiction.

PROBLEM 34–1

Lawyer A previously practiced in a small firm in State A, where most of her work involved negotiating employment compensation packages for corporate executives. Over time, she developed a strong reputation and eventually decided that she could continue her practice without being associated with a firm. She is licensed in State A only, but her clients are located in major cities throughout the country. She keeps a small office in State A and travels to other states as necessary to meet with her clients. She also maintains a website through which prospective clients can review her expertise and credentials and contact her.

Is she engaged in the unauthorized practice of law when she serves out-of-state clients?

PROBLEM 34–2

Lawyer serves as in-house counsel at Behemoth Corporation in State A, where the corporation's headquarters are located. Lawyer is licensed to practice in State A but nowhere else. Behemoth transfers Lawyer to State B, where he continues to work as an in-house lawyer. He wants to avoid taking the State B bar, because the bar exam is no fun and because he expects to return to State A within a few years. Would it be problematic for him to continue to work for Behemoth in State B without being licensed to practice there?

Disciplinary Authority and Choice of Law. Multijurisdictional practice raises a host of jurisdictional and choice of law issues. If a lawyer practices in multiple jurisdictions, which jurisdiction has authority to discipline the lawyer and which jurisdiction's professional responsibility rules apply? At the time the ABA amended Rule 5.5 to address multijurisdictional practice, it also amended Rule 8.5, which governs which states have jurisdiction to discipline lawyers and what law applies when discipline involves a lawyer working in more than one state. The rule now specifies that a lawyer is subject to the disciplinary authority of a jurisdiction in which she is admitted to practice "regardless of where the lawyer's conduct occurs." In addition, a lawyer is subject to the disciplinary authority of a jurisdiction in which she is not licensed if she "provides or offers to provide any legal services" there. Thus, a lawyer may be subject to disciplinary authority of more than one jurisdiction.

Which jurisdiction's professional responsibility rules apply when a lawyer is subject to more than one set of rules with inconsistent requirements? For example, when lawyers from several jurisdictions are involved in negotiating a transaction as to which differing rules of confidentiality or conflicts of interest are implicated, which of those conflicting standards applies? Rule 8.5(b) provides that for matters in litigation, the rules of the jurisdiction in which the tribunal sits govern, unless the rules of that tribunal provide otherwise. For "any other conduct," the rules of the jurisdiction in which the lawyer's conduct occurred apply, unless the "predominant effect" of the lawyer's conduct is in a different jurisdiction, in which case the rules of that jurisdiction apply.

Disciplinary Authority

- Rule 8.5(a) provides that lawyers are subject to the disciplinary authority of the jurisdiction where they are admitted to practice, as well as any jurisdiction where they provide or offer to provide services.

Choice of Law

Rule 8.5(b) specifies which rules of professional conduct apply in any exercise of disciplinary authority:

- For conduct in connection with a matter pending before a tribunal, the rules of the jurisdiction in which the tribunal sits apply, unless the rules of the tribunal provide otherwise.

- For any other conduct, the rules of the jurisdiction in which the lawyer's conduct occurred apply, unless the predominant effect of the conduct is in a different jurisdiction, in which case the rules of that jurisdiction apply.

It is not always obvious how Rule 8.5(b)'s standard for conduct other than litigation applies. What does it mean for a lawyer's conduct to "occur" in a particular jurisdiction? If a lawyer licensed in New York gives advice by telephone to a client in Florida, which state's rules govern? Would the answer be the same if the lawyer licensed in New York provided the same advice to the client while the lawyer was physically present in Florida? What if a client who lives and works in Florida visits New York briefly for purposes of meeting the lawyer but the advice concerns conduct that will occur in Florida? And how should one determine the jurisdiction of the "predominant effect" of the lawyer's conduct? If a lawyer practicing in California learns from a corporate client's employee in New Mexico that the company, based in New Jersey but incorporated in Delaware, is about to release a dangerous product onto the market, which state's confidentiality rules would apply? Lawyers confronted with such difficult questions in applying the "predominant effect" standard might find some comfort in Rule 8.5b's partial safe-harbor provision: "A lawyer shall not be subject to discipline if the lawyer's conduct conforms to a rule of a jurisdiction in which a lawyer reasonably believes the predominant effect of the lawyer's conduct will occur."

PROBLEM 34–3

Lawyer is admitted to practice in State A, but he handles a contract negotiation for Client in State B. While there, he engages in some aggressive negotiating tactics, including misrepresenting an essential element of the agreement. The opposing party to the contract later sues Lawyer and his client for fraud and refers Lawyer to State B's disciplinary authority. Does State B have jurisdiction to discipline Lawyer? If so, which state's rules of professional conduct should apply?

The Katrina Rule. In 2007, in response to unauthorized practice issues arising from the dislocation of lawyers and clients after Hurricane Katrina, when many lawyers moved from Louisiana and Mississippi to neighboring states, and lawyers came from other states to help those in hard-hit areas, the ABA adopted the so-called "Katrina Rule." That rule authorizes out-of-state lawyers to provide pro bono services in a state in which there has been a disaster and allows lawyers from that state to conduct their home state practices in jurisdictions that have adopted the Katrina rule. As of the date this book went to press, 16 states had adopted the rule, 14 were considering the rule, 7 had rejected it, and one seemed unlikely to adopt it.

Virtual Law Firms. What does the current state-based regulatory system mean for lawyers who provide legal services? Are such practices even permitted? Virtual law firms deliver legal services to clients directly over the Internet and communicate with firm members and co-counsel through secure online interfaces. VLP Law Group, one of the first of these firms, was founded in 2008 by a group of lawyers who saw life-style and scheduling advantages in pooling their resources in a single firm while working remotely. VLP's 30-plus lawyers have no central office, but the firm claims that its "lean model" allows it to "provide sophisticated, focused services to our clients" at competitive rates. Another virtual firm, Axiom Law, does not call itself a law firm (perhaps because doing so would raise questions about the legality of the model), but it recruits lawyers from elite law schools who previously worked for major law firms. Axiom assembles teams of lawyers to handle discrete client matters, but these assignments often require greater skill, knowledge, and coordination than contract attorneys typically provide. The firm currently employs 1,000 lawyers in eleven offices in New York, San Francisco, London, Chicago, Los Angeles, Washington, D.C., Boston, Hong Kong, Atlanta, Gurgaon, India, Houston, Singapore and Belfast.[3] The claim that the organization is essentially a temp agency rather than a law firm allows it to raise capital in ways not permitted by law firms—that is, by allowing non-lawyers to participate in Axiom's ownership and management.[4]

If the lawyers who participate in these enterprises are located in different jurisdictions, and the firm itself does not have any physical location apart from the location of its lawyers, must they comply with the ethics rules in all the jurisdictions in which their lawyers are located and all places where their clients reside? Lawyers who seek to establish and maintain virtual firms face considerable uncertainty about the applicable rules and regulations.[5]

---

[3] *See* Axiom Law, HW, at http://www.axiomlaw.com/index.php/whoweare/hq.

[4] *See* Stephen Gillers, *A Profession, If You Can Keep It: How Information Technology and Fading Borders Are Reshaping the Law Marketplace and What We Should Do About It*, 63 HASTINGS L. J. 953 (2012).

[5] *See* Stephanie L. Kimbro, *Regulatory Barriers to the Growth of Multijurisdictional Virtual Law Firms and Potential First Steps To Their Removal*, 13 N.C. J. L. & TECH. ON. 165 (2012).

NOTES ON MULTIJURISDICTIONAL PRACTICE

1.   *What Is "Practicing In" a Jurisdiction?* In an age of geographic mobility and instant communication, what does it mean to "practice law in" a jurisdiction? Does a regulatory system that turns on geographic location make any sense? Would we be better off with a licensing regime modeled on the licensure of automobile drivers, who may freely cross state boundaries so long as they are duly licensed in one state?

2.   *Justifications for Excluding Lawyers Licensed in Other States.* Should unauthorized practice restrictions prevent lawyers who are licensed in one state from "practicing in" jurisdictions where they are not licensed? Do states have legitimate interests in such broad rules of exclusion? If so, what are they?

3.   *Unauthorized Practice as a Defense to Fee Claims.* Should the client in *Birbrower* have been allowed to invoke unauthorized practice as a reason to avoid paying legal fees?

4.   *National Standards.* Would you support proposals to replace the current state-by-state bar admissions process with a uniform national system? Why or why not? Alternatively, should we maintain state-by-state licensing for lawyers who practice in tribunals (for whom some understanding of local rules and practice may be essential), but leave lawyers who handle primarily advising and transactional work to compete freely with one another in a national market? Who would benefit and who would lose under each of these alternatives to the current system?

C. UNBUNDLING AND OUTSOURCING

The following two excerpts describe recent trends toward disaggregating legal services and outsourcing some of their components to lawyers and non-lawyers trained in other jurisdictions or abroad. As you read these materials, consider the advantages and disadvantages of these developments for consumers and providers of legal services. Please also consider how lawyers and legal educators in the U.S. should adapt to the forces that are driving these trends.

OUTSOURCING AND THE GLOBALIZING LEGAL PROFESSION

Jayanth K. Krishnan
48 William & Mary Law Review 2189 (2007)

It is difficult to say precisely when American law firms first began outsourcing legal work abroad. News accounts report that over a decade ago the Dallas litigation firm of Bickel & Brewer established a subsidiary in Hyderabad, India, named Imaging and Abstract International, "to scan, abstract and index documents." Throughout the next several years other American firms, as well as some British law firms, turned to cheaper labor markets to handle legal services.

India has received a large amount of attention by those engaged in American legal outsourcing. [There are] three primary business models of U.S. legal outsourcing to India.

The first model involves American corporations outsourcing their legal work to their subsidiaries, a practice which began in earnest in 2001. Among the first of the U.S. companies to start this trend was General Electric. By establishing an in-house legal office in India, staffed by Indian lawyers to handle issues relating to its plastics and consumer finance divisions, GE reportedly has saved over two million dollars. Similarly, DuPont Corporation's India office now hires in-house Indian lawyers to draft patent applications and conduct novelty searches to ensure that proposed innovations have not already been protected. In 2004, the megalegal publishing corporation, West, opened an office in Mumbai (Bombay) where Indian lawyers were hired to prepare synopses of unpublished American court rulings.

A second way that legal outsourcing has developed involves American businesses directly hiring Indian law firms. Nishith Desai Associates (NDA) is one of India's best known tax planning and business law firms. With offices in Mumbai, Bangalore, and now California and Singapore, NDA boasts a client list of over two dozen large, American-based corporations. Rather than relying on lawyers from the United States, these corporations outsource both litigation-related and transactional matters to this Indian firm.

Numerous Silicon Valley law firms have also been directly hiring Indians to write patent applications in order to satisfy the demands of cost-conscious clients. As one well-known San Francisco intellectual property lawyer stated, "I had reservations [about hiring foreign workers], and still do, about holding ourselves out to be the Wal-Mart of patent prosecution . . . [but] [t]he client is happy, and the patents are good, and we're profitable, so it's working out."

Aside from corporations establishing subsidiaries or directly hiring Indian law firms, third party niche vendors are becoming the most significant players in the legal outsourcing field. Sometimes referred to as legal processing outsourcing (LPO) companies, these third-party vendors serve as intermediaries between the American corporation or American law firm looking to outsource and Indians eager to do the work. Today there are several third-party vendors, with some even billing themselves as capable of having their foreign employees perform more than just basic office tasks.

For example, the Dallas-based Atlas Legal Research company highlights to its corporate and law firm clients that it has lawyers in Bangalore, India, who are experienced in writing "legal briefs for all kinds of cases-from dog bites and divorces to medical malpractice, trademark, and federal securities." Pangea3, another American third-party vendor started by two University of Pennsylvania Law School graduates, boasts that it is "the world's premier provider of legal outsourcing services." And Michigan-based Lexadigm advertises that its foreign lawyers "provide large-law-firm-quality work at literally one-third the price."

OfficeTiger, and other LPO firms like it, have a simple business plan to reduce costs. [For] tasks [that] can be performed by willing, qualified workers in India where wages are much lower, LPOs have been approaching American law firms and their clients in an effort to persuade them to outsource many of these services using a company like OfficeTiger as a conduit. One LPO executive, who asked that he and his company remain anonymous, reported that the salaries for his personnel in India range from $2500 per year to only as high as $35,000–$40,000 per year. Intellevate, another third-party vendor, also cites lower costs as a reason for sending work to India: "The prevailing wage in India is significantly less than in the US," its website states.

Various American corporations and American law firms have caught on to this trend as well. While filing complicated, high-tech patent applications can range from $8000 to $10,000 in the Midwest, and up to $12,000 in Silicon Valley, outsourcing this job to India costs between $5000 and $6000. Moreover, for other types of services, there are reports indicating that Indian lawyers who work as outsourced employees, at the high end, charge only twenty dollars an hour.

The low cost of labor, the surge in information technology, favorable macroeconomic policies, [and] the high quality of workers with advanced educations [make] India [a] fertile ground for American legal outsourcers.

Supply Chains and Porous Boundaries: The Disaggregation of Legal Services

Milton C. Regan, Jr. and Palmer T. Heenan
78 Fordham Law Review 2137 (2010)

An announcement on June 18, 2009, by global mining company Rio Tinto sent a powerful message to law firms that the world is changing. The company declared that it had entered into an agreement with legal process outsourcing (LPO) company CPA Global to perform legal work on a scale that would reduce Rio Tinto's annual legal expenses by an estimated twenty percent, or tens of millions of dollars. This work currently was being done by lawyers in the company's legal department. Traditionally, if a company's inside lawyers did not handle legal work, the company engaged an outside law firm to do much of it. Rio Tinto's managing attorney, Leah Cooper, however, explained that the company no longer wanted to pursue that option: "For a long time," she said, "we've been asking law firms to provide us with ways to better control and predict our costs, but at best they offered a discount or a cap in fees . . . . In the end, we decided to take the initiative ourselves."

A team of CPA lawyers in India will be dedicated to working for Rio Tinto, and Cooper has said that she wants them to function as does any other Rio Tinto office. At the time of the announcement, CPA had already completed forty projects for the company, including contract review, legal research and analysis, merger and acquisition due diligence work, and draft joint venture agreements. The majority of the work that the LPO will be performing is relatively routine, but Rio Tinto stresses that most of it "is not volume-based; it's day-to-day work that requires constant communication." Furthermore, the mining company wants CPA lawyers to take on more sophisticated and strategic work.

Rio Tinto's contract with CPA Global represents an initiative in which inside counsel is attempting to manage legal costs by expanding competition for corporate legal work beyond law firms. CPA Global will be doing millions of dollars' worth of work that law firm associates otherwise would be doing. Rio Tinto's standard for using CPA lawyers poses a direct threat to firms: "If you had a junior associate sitting next to you, would you hand the assignment to that junior associate? If the answer is "yes,' it can probably go to India." The competitive threat to law firms does not end there, however. Rio Tinto is not satisfied with limiting CPA Global to routine work; it wants the LPO increasingly to assume responsibility for more complex matters. As CPA does so, this will mean even less business for outside law firms. Rio Tinto stresses that it will still hire law firms for their "strategic expertise." As time goes on, and LPOs gain more sophisticated expertise, however, that may begin to encompass a smaller and smaller portion of work, which could spell trouble for many of today's large law firms.

To compete in this world, law firms will have to begin considering how they might engage in the same disaggregation process as their clients. That is, they will need to break work down into discrete units and determine who is the most cost-efficient provider of each component. In some cases, that provider may be outside the firm, and the firm will need to engage in outsourcing. Law firms thus might increasingly face the same decision that their corporate clients regularly confront: whether to produce all the goods or services they need inside the firm or contract to obtain them from third parties in the market.

If the legal services market so develops, that sector of the economy would come to mimic the way that production is organized in many other industries. Corporate outsourcing of legal work is an example of what many organizations—including law firms—have been doing for many years: outsourcing administrative and support services. Outside vendors now assume responsibility for human resources, accounting, and information technology functions for many economic enterprises. These are all activities that assist an organization in conducting its basic line of business, whether manufacturing automobiles or providing telecommunications service.

For law firms, however, providing legal services is their business. In economic terms, having a portion of that work done by people outside the firm constitutes outsourcing parts of its production operations to third parties. Widespread adoption of this practice by law firms therefore would correspond to corporations' increasing tendency to divide up the process of producing goods and services into discrete components and contracting with suppliers to provide them.

Legal services traditionally have been regarded as relatively "bundled," in the sense that they consist of tightly linked elements that cannot be easily separated. The underlying premise of this assumption is that someone with a distinct sense of legal judgment is necessary to understand how the various elements of a matter are linked together. The corollary is that persons without this perspective are likely to miss legally significant features of information.

Law firms, however, have been decomposing their work within the firm for quite some time. They delegate responsibility for discrete aspects of a case or a transaction to a variety of people, both lawyers and non-lawyers, in what we might think of as a supply chain. A major piece of litigation, for instance, involves a complex division of labor that includes preparation of and response to discovery requests; review of documents for responsiveness, relevance, significance, and privilege; preparation of deposition questions and digests of deposition testimony; briefings with experts; preparation of motions and pleadings; argument at trial; and numerous other tasks. Large transactions include people working on various aspects of due diligence, review of regulatory compliance, preparation of a multitude of interconnected documents, negotiation, and many other activities. This work may be divided among paralegals, staff attorneys, junior associates, senior associates, income partners, and equity partners.

Ideally, this division of labor reflects an effort to direct work to the least costly person who can perform it and to maximize use of the distinct set of skills that each person can deploy. Furthermore, the allocation of responsibility has shifted over time, as junior partners now do what senior partners used to, senior associates do work formerly done by junior partners, junior associates complete the tasks that used to be done by senior associates, paralegals take on responsibilities formerly borne by junior associates, and technology substitutes for some tasks paralegals used to do. Law firms also increasingly have begun to use contract lawyers as part of these teams. They have looked, in other words, to workers outside the firm so that they can use even lower-cost personnel to perform services, both to reduce costs to clients and to avoid high fixed overhead in the face of fluctuating demand.

The emergence of LPOs in recent years provides further evidence that such decomposition is feasible. Consider, for instance, the range of different activities in which CPA Global engages. It includes preparing summonses and complaints, interrogatories and requests for production of documents, motions, witness kits, timelines of events and exhibits, deposition summaries in various formats, memoranda of law, legal briefs, letters to third parties presenting a legal position, multijurisdictional surveys of laws, and annotated summaries of cases. Its document review and management services include analysis and identification of documents for due diligence purposes, materiality in litigation, and privilege in response to discovery requests. Contract management includes drafting, revising, summarizing, and analyzing contracts.

Pangea3, another major LPO, performs a similar range of tasks, which includes merger and acquisition due diligence reports on companies' potential or existing liabilities; drafting contracts such as nondisclosure agreements, vendor contracts, supply agreements, software license agreements, telecommunications service agreements, office leases, and internet, advertising, and media agreements; and litigation document organization and review.

Assuming that some decomposition of services is feasible, law firms must then determine which tasks are most suitable for completion by persons inside and outside the firm. That is, which resources are integral to the firm's performance of its core functions and which are not? In general terms, the basic function of law firms is to provide legal services, with specific firms defining their core functions in different ways depending upon the types of practices on which they focus. Law firms confront a threshold challenge, however: it is not entirely clear exactly what constitutes legal services. The organized bar has been notoriously unsuccessful in defining the practice of law in order to exclude non-lawyers from engaging in what lawyers traditionally have done. Other occupations increasingly are furnishing services that formerly were provided only by lawyers, such as tax advice, estate planning, organizing responses to requests for production of documents, litigation case assessment, and legal compliance monitoring. Legal process outsourcing companies are becoming involved in an expanding range of activities, which include legal research, contract analysis, preparation of questions for depositions and trial, and creation of legal documents.

The San Diego County Bar Association, for instance, has held that a firm in India was not practicing law in California when it took responsibility for conducting legal research, developing case strategy, preparing deposition outlines, and drafting correspondence, pleadings, and motions in an intellectual property dispute in San Diego Superior Court. The Bar Association noted that "when the client asked how the attorneys developed the theory on which summary judgment was granted, and had done the work so inexpensively, the attorney told him that virtually all of the work was done by India-based Legalworks." As long as the two-lawyer California law firm that engaged Legalworks retained control over the case and reviewed the draft work performed by the contractor, the Indian company was deemed to be assisting a California lawyer in practicing law in the state, not engaging in the practice of law itself.

The difficulty in defining law firm core functions raises a fundamental question: Why would a client engage a law firm rather than contract directly with LPOs or other specialized suppliers to obtain the services it needs? What do law firms offer that a client cannot obtain from a collection of providers who furnish particular types of services?

Law firms will need to articulate reasons why clients should turn to them rather than other professionals for such assistance. On a more general level, the continuing advance of disaggregation would create even more ambiguity about what skills distinguish lawyers from other occupations.

This trend reflects the maturation of the legal services sector into a highly competitive industry driven more forcefully than ever by pressures for efficiency. How law firms, clients, and organizations connected with this industry respond could shape not only the future of law firms, but of the legal profession itself.

NOTES ON KRISHNAN AND REGAN & HEENAN

1. ***Drivers of Outsourcing.*** What factors explain the growth in outsourcing of legal services from the U.S. to India and other low-cost countries? Note that some of the same outsourcing companies that have been sending work to India also have recently begun to hire lawyers in lower-cost areas of the U.S., such as Texas, West Virginia, North Dakota, and Kansas. A 2011 *N.Y. Times* story reported that Pangea3 had hired hundreds of American lawyers in Carrollton, Texas. The story also noted that many of Pangea3's competitors were also hiring steadily in depressed regions of the U.S.[6]

2. ***Unbundling.*** What economic forces are causing law firms to unbundle legal services? How does the challenge of identifying skills that differentiate lawyers from other types of service providers relate to the trends described in the Regan & Heenan excerpt?

---

[6]   *See* Heather Timmons, *Where Lawyers Find Work*, N.Y. TIMES, June 3, 2011, B1.

3. ***Outsourcing and Unauthorized Practice.*** Are foreign lawyers who handle work outsourced from U.S. firms engaging in the unauthorized practice of law? Are U.S. lawyers who handle outsourced work from firms in other U.S. jurisdictions engaging in the unauthorized practice of law? Do your answers to either of these questions turn on the nature of the services provided? The California Bar has opined that legal work is assistance rather than unauthorized practice if it is adequately supervised or reviewed by a lawyer admitted in California and if the California lawyer retains control of the case or matter. How should the bar decide how much supervision or control is enough?

4. ***Client Consent.*** Should law firms that outsource work to foreign lawyers or to lawyers working in other U.S. jurisdictions be required to notify clients of the outsourcing arrangements and obtain their consent? A formal opinion issued by the ABA in 2008 provides that outsourcing may be permissible as long as the following conditions are met: (1) the lawyer remains ultimately responsible for rendering competent legal services to the client; (2) the lawyer complies with Rule 5.1 (regarding the duties of lawyers who supervise other lawyers) and Rule 5.3 (requiring lawyers who have supervisory authority over non-lawyers to ensure that their conduct is compatible with the lawyers' professional obligations); (3) the lawyer makes appropriate disclosures to the client regarding the use of lawyers or non-lawyers outside of the lawyer's firm; and 4) the lawyer gains client consent if the lawyers or non-lawyers to whom work with be outsourced will have access to confidential information.[7] Does the ABA Opinion take the right approach?

PROBLEM 34–4

Law Firm, located in State A, is trying to respond to its clients' demands for lower fees. It has concluded that it can lower its prices by hiring Indian lawyers to do some types of work remotely from Mumbai. May the firm outsource the work to India? If so, under what circumstances? Alternatively, could it hire lawyers to work remotely from State B, which has been hit hard by the recession and where lawyers are willing to work for considerably lower salaries than lawyers in State A?

D. MULTIDISCIPLINARY PRACTICE

As we saw in Chapter 32, most U.S. jurisdictions forbid lawyers to join forces with other service providers, such as accountants, engineers, social workers, business consultants, and economists, to address clients' complex needs through multidisciplinary practices ("MDPs"). Most jurisdictions follow some version of Model Rule 5.4, which provides that "a lawyer or law firm shall not share legal fees with a non-lawyer" except in certain limited circumstances; that a lawyer "shall not form a

---

[7] ABA Formal Opinion 08-451, Lawyer's Obligations When Outsourcing Legal and Nonlegal Support Services (August 5, 2008).

partnership with a non-lawyer if any of the activities of the partnership consist of the practice of law"; and that "a lawyer shall not practice with or in the form of a professional corporation or association authorized to practice law for a profit, if a non-lawyer owns any interest therein." These restrictions are premised on the idea that allowing a lawyer to practice or share fees with non-lawyers threatens the lawyer's ability to exercise professional independence because the lawyer may be tempted to recommend the MDP's services to clients even if those services are of lower quality than available alternatives. Critics of MDPs also argue that these institutions are unlikely to honor other ethical rules that lawyers must obey (such as rules on conflicts of interests and confidentiality) and that they will exert pressure on lawyers to bend to MDPs' business imperatives. They also argue that mixing legal services with other types of services is likely to jeopardize application of the attorney-client privilege, which covers only communications between lawyers and clients (and their agents).

Large accounting firms have long employed lawyers as full-time employees to serve their clients, but they have taken the position that these lawyers are providing tax advice, not legal advice. (Accountants are authorized to provide tax advice and to advocate regarding tax matters before the Internal Revenue Service.) The distinction between tax advice and legal advice is indistinct in practice. But accounting firms have successfully maintained that this distinction allows them to escape the reach of unauthorized practice restrictions and rules prohibiting lawyers from sharing fees with nonlawyers and entering into law practice with them.

The ABA has more than once considered and rejected proposals to permit MDPs. The ABA Commission on Multidisciplinary Practice, established in 1998, proposed allowing some limited forms of MDPs. But in 2000 the ABA House of Delegates soundly defeated that proposal and instead urged states to reaffirm their commitment to enforce unauthorized practice restrictions and prohibitions on fee sharing. As discussed in Chapter 32, the Ethics 20/20 Commission considered a proposal to permit alternative practice structures, but it abandoned the proposal in 2012.

The United Kingdom and Australia now allow multidisciplinary practice arrangements. In the 2007 UK Legal Services Act, the United Kingdom authorized lawyers to engage in multidisciplinary practice and to work in law firms owned by non-lawyers. In 2012, the United Kingdom Solicitors Regulation Authority began issuing licenses for "alternative business structures." These are organizations that are more flexible than traditional law firms in the following respects: lawyers and non-lawyers can share the management and control of the business; the entity can allow external investment and ownership; and the organization can offer multiple services to clients, including legal services, from within the same entity. The Solicitors Regulation Authority already has issued dozens of licenses to alternative business structures.[8]

NOTES ON MULTIDISCIPLINARY PRACTICE

1. *A Good Idea?* Would you favor allowing non-lawyers to invest in legal businesses and permitting the creation of multidisciplinary practices (MDPs)? Why or why not? Are you persuaded by critics who warn that lawyers employed in firms partially owned by nonlawyers will be less likely than lawyers in private law firms to obey rules of professional conduct?

2. *Global Competition.* Do you agree with those who argue that the U.S. legal profession's strict limitations on fee sharing and permissible forms of practice put U.S. firms at a serious competitive disadvantage in the global market for legal services?

E. TRANSNATIONAL PRACTICE

Many American lawyers seek to serve foreign clients or to handle disputes and problems that have international implications. Similarly, foreign lawyers seek opportunities to practice within the United States and/or to give advice about U.S. law abroad.

In the corporate legal services market, global competition is commonplace. The global legal services market produced over $623 billion in revenues in 2011,[9] and it is projected to generate nearly $650 billion by 2015.[10] The United States International Trade Commission has estimated that the U.S. exported $7.5 billion in legal services in 2011.[11] Of the world's 100 highest grossing firms, 76 are headquartered in the U.S., and 14 are based in the U.K.[12]

As global firms pursue clients and business opportunities around the world, they sometimes encounter restrictive policies toward foreign lawyers. U.S. trained lawyers who seek to provide legal services overseas often face rules that sharply limit the practice of foreign firms. Some jurisdictions, such as Korea, Singapore, Malaysia and India, have recently liberalized access to their legal services markets by foreign lawyers, but bar associations in other countries, such as Brazil and Vietnam, have called for more restrictions on foreign law firms. Similarly, while most states in the U.S. allow lawyers who have been trained abroad

---

[8] *See* Solicitors Regulation Authority, Alternative Business Structures, Register of Licensed Bodies, http://www.sra.org.uk/absregister/.

[9] MarketLine, *Global Legal Services*, October 2012.

[10] *See* First Research, *Legal Services Industry Profile*, available at http://www.firstresearch.com/Industry-Research/Legal-Services.html.

[11] UNITED STATES INTERNATIONAL TRADE COMMISSION, RECENT TRENDS IN U.S. SERVICES TRADE, 2011 ANNUAL REPORT 5–7–5–10 (2013).

[12] *The 2012 Global 100*, AM. LAW., October 2012.

to practice as "foreign legal consultants" in the U.S. and to advise about the laws of their home country, non-U.S. lawyers still are subject to state-by-state regulation that restricts their access to the U.S. market.

Global law firms—firms with offices and lawyers stationed around the world—may be better positioned than domestic firms to take advantage of trends toward globalization of the economy. One such U.S. firm, Baker & McKenzie, has seventy-two offices in forty-five countries, including Indonesia, Malaysia, Vietnam, Bahrain, Kazakhstan and Azerbaijan.[13] Similarly, U.K.-based Clifford Chance has offices in 30 countries, including Ukraine, Qatar, and Morocco.[14] The notion that global law firms might hold advantages in competing for lucrative corporate legal work has fueled some international law firm mergers, as firms have tried to build a global presence across key markets. In 2012, for example, China's King & Wood merged with Australia's Mallesons Stephen Jaques into the firm of King & Wood Mallesons.[15] In 2013, King & Wood Mallesons merged with SJ Berwin, a UK firm with a strong European and Middle East practice, to form a 2700 lawyer firm.[16] The UK's Norton Rose merged with Australian, Canadian and South African firms before joining with U.S.-based Fulbright & Jaworski in 2013 to form Norton Rose & Fulbright, a 3800 lawyer firm.[17] Many recent mergers take the form of loose organizational structures called vereins, in which the merged entities remain financially independent.[18]

Transnational practice on behalf of large corporate clients receives more attention than cross-border practice for individual and small business clients, but the latter is common. The United States Census Bureau reported that virtually every state in the U.S. experienced a substantial increase in its foreign-born population between 1990 and 2000, and that all but five jurisdictions had at least a thirty-percent increase during that period. Foreign-born residents often have family law, inheritance or business relationships with their country of origin, and lawyers sometimes facilitate those interactions.[19] Thus, even within the individual client hemisphere, transnational practice has become a reality for many lawyers.

---

[13]   Baker & McKenzie, *Passionately Global*, http://www.bakermckenzie.com/.

[14]   Clifford Chance, *Locations*, http://www.cliffordchance.com/home.html.

[15]   Hildebrandt Consulting LLC, *2013 Client Advisory*, available at http://hildebrandt consult.com/uploads/Citi_Hildebrandt_2013_Client_Advisory.pdf.

[16]   Elizabeth Broomhall, *SJ Berwin-King & Wood Mallesons Merger Gets Green Light Creating $1 Billion Global Giant*, LEGALWEEK.COM, July 31, 2013.

[17]   Brian Baxter, *Report: Law Firm Mergers Poised for Record Year in 2013*, THE AM LAW DAILY, July 8, 2013, available at http://www.americanlawyer.com/PubArticleALD .jsp?id=1202609982829&Report_Law_Firm_Mergers_Poised_for_Record_Year_in_2013&sl return=20130829140204.

[18]   Chris Johnson, *Vereins: The New Structure for Global Firms*, AM. LAW., Mar. 7, 2013.

[19]   ABA SECTION OF LEGAL EDUCATION AND ADMISSIONS TO THE BAR, REPORT OF THE SPECIAL COMMITTEE ON INTERNATIONAL ISSUES 8 (JULY 2009).

Even public interest law is becoming more transnational. An American-born concept once largely confined to the United States has evolved into a more globalized set of institutions and practices.[20] For example, American lawyers have sued multinational corporations in the U.S. and other courts for human rights abuses. Public interest organizations have also worked with local grassroots groups to research, document, and expose legal and human rights violations and to seek redress from governments and corporations, often working in transnational fora governed by so-called soft law norms (quasi-legal international norms that lack legally binding force), as well as in domestic tribunals. Canvassing the rich emerging literature on these trends would take us far afield from the primary focus of this chapter—the practical and regulatory challenges of globalization for the American legal profession. Suffice it to say for our purposes that activist lawyers interested in promoting social justice in the global arena are crossing national borders, both literally and virtually, as never before.

Legal services are covered by a variety of international trade agreements, which seek to lower trade barriers by overriding national laws that restrict the import of goods and services. Indeed, the United States is subject to fifteen bilateral and regional trade agreements that apply to legal services.[21] The potential impact of these agreements on the United States legal services market and lawyer regulation is just beginning to be appreciated. International trade agreements may be implicated whenever a U.S. lawyer regulation affects foreign lawyers. For example, state rules that severely restrict admission and/or temporary practice by foreign lawyers might be deemed an illegitimate restraint on free trade in services under some of these agreements.[22]

NOTES ON TRANSNATIONAL PRACTICE

1. *Implications for Lawyer Regulation.* What are the implications of transnational practice for lawyer regulation? Would it be useful to have more uniform standards for admission and practice across national boundaries?

2. *Is Uniformity Attainable or Advisable?* What are the impediments to achieving uniformity in the regulation of lawyers across national borders? What would be the costs?

---

[20] *See* Scott L. Cummings and Louise G. Trubek, *Globalizing Public Interest Law*, 13 U.C.L.A. J. INT'L L. & FOR. AFF. 1 (2008).

[21] *See* Laurel S. Terry, *From GATS to APEC: The Impact of Trade Agreements on Legal Services*, 43 AKRON L. REV. 875, 877 (2010).

[22] *Id.*

PROBLEM 34–5

A major international law firm with an office in New York serves several clients that seek to invest in emerging markets, such as China, India, and Brazil. The firm would like to hire foreign lawyers from those countries to work in New York and advise clients on the laws of their home countries. May it do so? Alternatively, could the firm open offices in China, India and Brazil and send U.S.-trained lawyers to work there? What might be the legal and practical impediments to bringing lawyers trained and licensed in foreign countries to the firm's New York office or sending its American-trained and New York-licensed lawyers to foreign countries?

F. SUMMARY

This chapter has explored ways in which law practice has globalized over the past several decades, as U.S. lawyers seek to compete in markets that do not observe state and national boundaries. These changes have placed considerable strain on the American system of state-by-state licensing. The current ethics rules generally prohibit lawyers from practicing law in states where they are not licensed but allow lawyers some flexibility to provide services to clients there on a temporary basis. We considered whether the current regulatory scheme strikes the right balance between ensuring adequate regulatory oversight over lawyers and permitting them freedom to compete with one another and with non-U.S. based providers and giving clients choice in the selection of legal service providers. We also examined trends toward disaggregating legal services and outsourcing some of their components. We explored proposals that would allow U.S. lawyers to join with other service providers in multidisciplinary practices, and we considered the concerns that have thus far led to the defeat of such proposals. Finally, we examined how transnational practice has become a reality for many American lawyers—not just for those serving corporate clients but for those serving individuals as well.

CHAPTER 35

LEGAL EDUCATION

■ ■ ■

A. INTRODUCTION

Few topics covered in this book might be of greater immediate interest to you than this chapter, which surveys some of the most important issues about contemporary legal education. The chapter begins with a history of legal education and critiques of legal education; as you will see, many of the issues and proposals being debated today were debated a century ago. The chapter's treatment of the content of legal education focuses in particular on the contemporary curriculum with its mix of doctrinal, skills, clinical and interdisciplinary instruction. The chapter then examines contemporary debates over the content, pedagogy, length, and cost of legal education and considers some of the most significant proposals for reform. As you read the materials that follow, note the ways various interest groups in the organized bar influence the structure and content of legal education.

B. THE HISTORY OF LEGAL EDUCATION

Until the early twentieth century, many lawyers did not attend law school and had no college degree; most states did not even require lawyers to have graduated from high school. Although some lawyers attended law school, law schools were not affiliated with universities but instead were stand-alone proprietary schools. The majority of lawyers learned law the same way anyone learned a skill or a trade: by working as an apprentice under the supervision of one already practicing the trade. This was known as "reading the law," and it is still permitted in a few states (including California) as an alternative to attending law school, although the requirements of study and supervision have become much stricter.

Topic Overview

American legal education assumed its modern form in the early twentieth century as a result of the sustained effort of the American Bar Association and influential leaders of university-affiliated law schools, especially Harvard, to increase the academic rigor of legal education and the educational requirements to obtain admission to the bar. As you read about the history of legal education and the history of criticisms of it, notice how today's debates over legal education resemble those of the late nineteenth and early twentieth centuries.

One of the principal goals of the American Bar Association from its founding in 1878 was to enhance the stature and quality of the bar by requiring all lawyers to graduate from law school. In 1900, the American Bar Association Section on Legal Education created the Association of American Law Schools (AALS) to help improve and standardize legal education, a function the AALS still performs today. In 1921, the ABA adopted its first set of Standards for Legal Education and, shortly thereafter, issued its first list of law schools that met its standards. This was the beginning of the ABA's role as an accrediting agency for law schools, and its power increased over time as many states adopted rules allowing only graduates of ABA-accredited schools to be admitted to practice.

Although critics of contemporary American legal education charge it has changed too little in the last 100 years, legal education today is radically different from what it was for the first 100 years of American history, when there was little organized legal education. The current system was the product of a sustained reform effort waged by the American Bar Association and some influential law schools between 1870 and 1930. The distinctive features of legal education—3 years of university-based graduate education delivered by a full-time professoriate teaching a curriculum focused on legal doctrine and skills, with a sprinkling of theory, social science, and humanities—were once reforms to address perceived inadequacies of the haphazard legal education of the nineteenth century.

1. FOUNDATIONS OF CONTEMPORARY LEGAL EDUCATION

LAW SCHOOL: LEGAL EDUCATION IN AMERICA FROM THE 1850S TO THE 1980S
Robert B. Stevens
(University of North Carolina Press, 1983)[1]

Such success as American legal education had had before the Civil War had been achieved through proprietary schools [which were not affiliated with universities]. [In 1870, at the beginning of the deanship of Christopher Columbus Langdell, Harvard Law School] had no relation to Harvard College. During Langdell's deanship, which lasted until 1895, Harvard not only became the preeminent law school in the country, but institutionalized legal training was established as *de rigueur* for leaders of the profession. In addition to the development of a system of teaching that emphasized the analysis of appellate cases, it was Langdell's goal to turn the legal profession into a university-educated one—and not at the undergraduate level but at a level that required a three-year post-baccalaureate degree.

Harvard's innovations concerned not only its student body but also its faculty. James Barr Ames [appointed in 1873 as assistant professor of law] was the first of a new breed of academic lawyer, a law graduate with limited experience of practice who was appointed for his scholarly and teaching potential. Ames, a recent Harvard Law graduate who had scarcely practiced law, was exactly the type of professor Langdell demanded: "A teacher of law should be a person who accompanies his pupils on a road which is new to them, but with which he is well acquainted from having often traveled it before. What qualifies a person, therefore, to teach law, is not experience in the work of a lawyer's office, not experience in dealing with men, not experience in the trial or argument of cases, not experience, in short, in using law, but experience in learning law."

The case method proved to be a brilliant and effective vehicle for the "imaginative activity" of the law. Generations of law students were to be weaned on determining relevant facts, making arguments to a law professor masquerading as a court, and justifying or destroying judicial opinions in terms of legal "rightness" and, later, in terms of the nonlegal desirability of some principle or another. Practitioners had always had some doubts about the case method, both intellectually and politically. Even John Chipman Gray [a noted nineteenth-century legal scholar] was forced to admit that "given a dunce for a teacher, and a dunce for a

---

student, the study of cases would not be the surest mode to get into the Bar."

It was in this context that the 1891 report of the ABA Committee on Legal Education attacked the heart of the Harvard system. The report argued that the ideal work of the lawyer was to be done by knowing the rules and keeping clients out of court. Teaching decisions without systematically instilling rules led to the "great evil" manifested by young lawyers who were all too willing to litigate, did not restrain their clients, cited cases on both sides in their briefs, and left all responsibility to the court. As it turned out, the ABA meetings of 1891 and 1892 were the last serious doubts the legal establishment expressed about the case method. The fashionability of the Langdell system grew with remarkable rapidity. [In the 1890s, as graduates of Harvard Law School or faculty who had taught there took teaching jobs at law schools across the country, the case method was adopted at most university-affiliated law schools.]

The case method system held a trump card—finance. The method enabled the establishment of the large class. Although numbers fluctuated, Langdell in general managed Harvard with one professor for every 75 students; the case method combined with the Socratic method enabled classes to expand to the size of the largest lecture hall.

Part-time law schools opened up a whole new sector of the legal education market. The first of these was established in the 1860s for students who had full-time jobs. [I]n the late 1880s part-time law schools began to spring up in the cities with heavy immigrant populations. [I]mmigrant groups early saw the importance of both education and of law in America as well as the need and advantage of being a lawyer.

[Through the expansion of the number of law schools, it became] increasingly possible for white males, even poor immigrants, to qualify for the legal profession. The portals were far narrower for blacks and women. Although blacks seem to have entered the legal profession in this country sooner than women, their success was more limited. Already facing social ostracism, they fought white middle-class prejudice against blacks practicing law. The career of John Mercer Langston was exceptional. The son of a Virginia planter and a half-black, half-Indian slave, he entered Oberlin, one of four colleges in the country then admitting blacks, in 1849. He eventually went on to be the first dean of Howard Law School, which opened in 1868, and later acted as president of Howard University. Howard's Law School ought to have increased the number of black lawyers quickly, and for a while it did flourish because of the absence of admission requirements, a two-year program, and a reasonable supply of government clerks to fill its evening program. Then it fell on harder times. In 1877, the District [of Columbia, where Howard is located] moved to require three years of training for lawyers. In 1879, Congress announced that none of its appropriation might be used for Howard's professional schools. Census figures show that although black lawyers nationwide, at one point, outnumbered women lawyers, reaching 431 in 1890, the Jim Crow system took its toll. By 1900, their number was only 728, below that for women.

Despite the intimidation from the Supreme Court [which held in *Bradwell v. Illinois*, 83 U.S. 130 (1873), that states could exclude women from the practice of law], women fought for their right to be lawyers. As early as 1869 the University of Iowa admitted women law students. Michigan soon followed Iowa's lead and in 1872 Boston University Law School admitted women. In 1878 two women successfully sued to be admitted to the first class at Hastings Law School. The elite law schools, however, remained hostile. A Yale Law School alumnus opined in 1872, "In theory I am in favor of their studying law and practicing law, provided they are ugly." Overall, the census reported five women lawyers in the United States in 1870. As of 1880, it listed 75 and, by 1900, there were 1,010.

At its first meeting in 1879, the ABA Committee on Legal Education and Admissions to the Bar began the crusade for an expansive program of standardization. In 1896, the ABA approved the requirement of a high school diploma and two years of law study for bar admission. By 1897, the period of study required was lengthened to three years, with the hope that state legislatures would not only approve but also restrict the method of study to that of attending law school. In 1908, the association was discussing a requirement of two years of college before law school, although its official requirement was still a high school diploma (and would remain so until 1921).

By 1916, the AALS was prepared to debate a resolution not to recognize any night [law school courses] after 1920. It was in that debate that Eugene Gilmore, a law professor at Wisconsin, later to be president of the University of Iowa, announced: "the universities can turn out all the lawyers the country needs; we don't have to sit up nights to find ways for the poor boy to come to the Bar." The leaders of the bar shared the then current assumptions about the ethnic superiority of native white Americans. In 1909, the ABA adopted a requirement that lawyers had to be American citizens. A New York delegate defended the college requirement of prelaw training: it was "absolutely necessary" to have lawyers "able to read, write and talk the English language—not Bohemian, not Gaelic, not Yiddish, but English." In 1922, the Yale Board of Admissions was deeply concerned about "the Jewish problem." Dean Swan of the Yale Law School suggested to the state bar in 1923 that students with foreign parents should be required to remain longer in college than native-born Americans before being admitted to law school. At a Yale faculty meeting in the same year, Swan argued against using grades as the basis of limiting enrollment to the law school, because such a development would admit students of "foreign" rather than "old American" parentage, and Yale would become a school with an "inferior student body ethically and socially."

In 1923, the ABA issued its first list of approved schools. In 1924, the AALS established a requirement of one full-time teacher for each 100 students, tightened the definition of part-time education, and [revised requirements first set in1912 regarding the number of books a law library must contain.] ABA standards were met by only about half the country's law schools. [I]n 1927, of the 48 states and the District of Columbia, 32 still had no formal legal requirement for prelaw studies, and 11 required merely high school graduation or its equivalent. In 1927, none required attendance at law school.

[Over the course of the 1930s, states began to require two or three years of prelegal college education.] Increasingly, the states required law school training and required that training to be in ABA schools; and, increasingly, the students went to those schools.

NOTES ON LEGAL EDUCATION BEFORE 1940

1. *Why Require Graduation from Law School as a Condition of Admission to the Bar?* Today, about half the states (not including California and New York) restrict bar admission to graduates of law schools that are accredited by the American Bar Association. A tiny number of states (including California and New York) do not require law school graduation, but instead allow candidates for admission to "read the law" under the tutelage of a lawyer. Why did the ABA urge attendance at law school almost to the exclusion of apprenticeship in a law office as a way of training lawyers? Why require ABA accreditation? Which of the reasons motivating the ABA to accredit law schools in the early twentieth century remain valid today?

2. *The Case Method.* What do you think of the reasons why the case method and the Socratic method were adopted in law schools and rapidly became the norm?

3. *Part-Time Law School.* The ABA waged a long campaign against part-time law schools, including night schools, in the early twentieth century. Are there any legitimate reasons to restrict admission to the bar to those who study law full time? What is the connection between the elite bar's opposition to part-time law schools and its opposition to proprietary law schools? What echoes of the debate over university based "academic" study of law as opposed to trade-school based "practical" study of law can you see in legal education today?

4. *Should Law Be a Graduate Degree?* The United States is unusual in making law entirely a graduate degree; this was a result of the ABA's long campaign to reform legal education. Many countries are

transforming law from an undergraduate to a graduate degree. What are the arguments for law being a graduate or undergraduate degree?

5. *Why a Full-Time Law Faculty and Well-Stocked Library?* Why did the ABA and the AALS insist on a minimum number of full-time law faculty and a minimum number of volumes in the law library? What are the costs and benefits of these requirements? What are the tensions between law professors being members of university faculty and law professors being members of the profession, in terms of teaching and scholarship?

2. THE HISTORY OF CRITIQUES OF LEGAL EDUCATION

Although the appellate case method dominated elite legal education through the 1960s, it had critics beyond those in the practicing bar who, as noted in the Stevens excerpt, thought it trained lawyers to litigate rather than to advise clients how to avoid litigation. Another major criticism was leveled in the 1930s by the Legal Realists, who insisted that study of appellate cases did not effectively train lawyers to understand law as social policy and was intellectually impoverished because it neglected the insights of the social sciences. As legal historian Laura Kalman wrote in her classic history of Yale Law School, Legal Realism was "the most concerted attempt ever to challenge" the Harvard-Langdell model of legal education.[2] Although Legal Realism was a broad critique of law as well as legal education, it had more influence in changing legal education than it did in changing the way that lawyers practice or judges decide cases. Kalman explained:

> The realists' success in using the social sciences in the classroom was [slight]. On the one hand, the realists and almost everyone afterward changed the titles of their casebooks "from 'Cases on X' to 'Cases and Materials on Y.'" On the other, there was widespread agreement that with but few exceptions, realist casebooks made ineffective use of the social sciences and did not significantly depart from their precursors. They ensured that social science would be kept at its proper distance: "law and," with the "and" functioning to marginalize social science.
>
> In the end, realism changed the lives of teachers more than students. It made many elite law professors wonder whether they should move closer to the university. But that created a sense of unease. Torn between campus and the profession, [the law professor] was a victim of "intellectual schizophrenia," which had him "devoutly believing that he can be, at one and the same time, an authentic academic and a trainer of" practitioners.

---

[2] LAURA KALMAN, YALE LAW SCHOOL AND THE SIXTIES: REVOLT AND REVERBERATIONS (2005).

[T]he law teacher must continue training potential lawyers to pick apart cases. Since a good lawyer was supposed to be a jack-of-all trades, a good law teacher must fill whatever hole in the core curriculum arose, no matter how much time preparation consumed.[3]

The push to integrate the study of legal doctrine with the study of social sciences and the humanities continued throughout the twentieth century and had a significant long-term impact. Many law schools offer courses on law and economics, sociology, anthropology, history, philosophy, and literature. A substantial number of law professors have a PhD as well as a JD. In the 1980s, the formal study of law and economics became especially influential and pervasive at many law schools, particularly as the Olin Foundation gave large gifts to many law schools to hire faculty trained in economics and to support research on the economic analysis of law. Law and economics as a school of thought penetrated policymaking in the administrative, legislative, and judicial branches of government.

Besides the Legal Realists' attack in the 1930s on the intellectual poverty of the case method, a second strand of criticism of the structure and content of legal education gained traction in the progressive activism of the 1960s. Law student activists across the country lambasted the tension and tedium of the classroom, the failure of professors to provide meaningful feedback, the overwhelming importance of grades, and a curriculum that was focused on the legal issues of concern to business rather than on the problems of the poor. They also challenged the denial of admission to women and people of color and the absence of student involvement in important law school governance decisions, including faculty hiring, curriculum, and admissions.[4]

Student activists demanded and in many cases achieved changes in law school policies in the 1960s and 1970s. Schools changed admissions policies to allow women and people of color to matriculate in greater numbers. They allowed some student involvement in setting academic policy. Selection for law review was not based on first-year grades alone. Some courses were graded on something other than just a single final examination. Schools offered more courses to train students in skills like writing, negotiation, interviewing. They established law school clinics to enable students to develop practical legal skills and to provide legal services to poor people.

Criticism of the elitism, hierarchy, dearth of real-world training, and corporate focus of legal education, especially at elite law schools, continued through the 1970s and the 1980s and merged with criticism of

---

[3]   *Id.*

[4]   *Id.* at 11, 28.

American law more generally. The most influential strains of criticism were Critical Legal Studies (CLS) and, slightly later, Critical Race Studies (CRS). These intellectual movements encompassed widespread critiques of law and politics as well as legal education. Critical Race Studies (CRS), which remains influential in legal education, identifies ways in which law enables racial subordination and makes systematic racial inequalities seem normal or inevitable rather than the product of deliberate legal policies.

As applied to legal education, CLS produced a pithy indictment of legal education authored by Duncan Kennedy, a professor at Harvard Law School, who originally published the critique in 1983 as a pamphlet addressed to first year law students. In *Legal Education and the Reproduction of Hierarchy: A Polemic Against the System*, Kennedy excoriated law schools for squelching the public service aspirations of entering first year law students and channeling them into large firm corporate practice. He also criticized law schools for fomenting competition among law students, and for the content and pedagogy of the curriculum:

> The classroom is hierarchical with a vengeance, the teacher receiving a high degree of deference and arousing fears that remind one of high school rather than college. [Class discussion] is a demand for a pseudo-participation in which you struggle desperately, in front of a large audience, to read a mind determined to elude you.

> The actual intellectual content of the law seems to consist of learning rules, what they are and why they have to be the way they are, while rooting for the occasional judge who seems willing to make them marginally more humane. The basic experience is of a double surrender: to a passivizing classroom experience and to a passive attitude toward the content of the legal system.

> Law students learn skills, to do a list of simple but important things. They learn to retain large numbers of rules organized into categorical systems. They learn "issue spotting," which means identifying the ways in which the rules are ambiguous, in conflict, or have a gap when applied to particular fact situations. They learn elementary case analysis. And they learn a list of balanced, formulaic, pro/con policy arguments that lawyers use in arguing that a given rule should apply to a situation, in spite of a gap, conflict or ambiguity, or that a given case should be extended or narrowed. These are arguments like "the need for certainty," and "the need for flexibility;" "the need

to promote competition," and the "need to encourage production by letting producers keep the rewards of their labor."

The intellectual core of the ideology is the distinction between law and policy. Teachers convince students that legal reasoning exists, and is different from policy analysis, by bullying them into accepting as valid in particular cases arguments about legal correctness that are circular, question-begging, incoherent, or so vague as to be meaningless.

[The first year curriculum of] contracts, torts, property, criminal law and civil procedure [teaches students] the ground-rules of late nineteenth century laissez-faire capitalism. Teachers teach them as though they had an inner logic, as an exercise in legal reasoning with policy playing a relatively minor role.

This whole body of implicit messages is nonsense. Legal reasoning is not distinct, <u>as a method for reaching correct results</u>, from ethical and political discourse in general (i.e., from policy analysis). There is never a "correct legal solution" that is other than the correct ethical and political solution to that legal problem.

Law schools channel their students into jobs in the hierarchy of the bar according to their own standing in the hierarchy of schools. Students confronted with the choice of what to do after they graduate experience themselves as largely helpless: they have no "real" alternatives to taking a job in one of the conventional firms that hires from their school. Partly, faculties generate this sense of student helplessness by propagating myths about the character of the different kinds of practice. They extol the forms that are accessible to their students; they subtly denigrate or express envy about the jobs that will be beyond their students' reach; they dismiss as ethically and socially suspect the jobs their students won't have to take.

The actual capacities of lawyers have real social value; they are difficult to acquire; and one can't practice law effectively without them. But they are nowhere near as inaccessible as they are made to seem by the mystique of legal education. By mystifying them, law schools make it seem necessary to restrict them to a small group, presumed to be super-talented. That, in turn, makes it seem necessary to divide the labor in the joint enterprise of providing legal services so that most of the participants (secretaries, paralegals, office assistants, court clerks, janitors, marshals, and so on) are firmly and permanently excluded from doing the things that are most challenging and rewarding within the overall activity. Once they have devalued everyone else on "professional" grounds, it also seems natural for those who have gone to law school to specialize in the most desirable tasks, while controlling the whole show and reaping the lion's share of the rewards.

Beginning in the late 1970s, a different set of criticisms of legal education came from the conservative movement, which claimed that law schools were bastions of liberal legal orthodoxy. In the early 1980s, the Federalist Society for Law and Public Policy was founded by law students at Yale and the University of Chicago and sponsored by conservative and libertarian faculty, including Robert Bork and now U.S. Supreme Court Justice Antonin Scalia. The founders sought to create a forum for conservative law students to debate, make connections with conservative lawyers and judges, and "proclaim the virtues of individual freedom and of limited government."[5]

C. CONTENT AND PEDAGOGY

The curricula at most law schools are strikingly similar in content and pedagogy. The vast majority of law schools offer first-year courses in civil procedure, contracts, torts, property, criminal law, constitutional law, and legal research and writing. At most schools, the upper-level curriculum includes few mandatory courses beyond an upper level writing requirement and some sort of additional professional skills training and professional responsibility course as mandated by the ABA.[6] Eighty-five percent of law schools surveyed by the ABA in 2010 regularly offered in-house live-client clinical opportunities, and 30 percent offered off-site, live-client opportunities.[7]

---

[5] *Preface,* 6 Harv. J.L. & Pub. Pol'y, at iii, iii–iv (1982). For more on the founding and current operations of the Federalist Society, see ANN SOUTHWORTH, LAWYERS OF THE RIGHT: PROFESSIONALIZING THE CONSERVATIVE COALITION 116–117, 131–141 (2008); STEVEN TELES, THE RISE OF THE CONSERVATIVE LAW MOVEMENT: THE BATTLE FOR CONTROL OF THE LAW 135–151 (2008).

[6] ABA Standard 302(a) mandates that each student must receive substantial instruction in "(1) the substantive law generally . . . ; (2) legal analysis and reasoning, legal research, problem solving and oral communication; (3) writing in a legal context, including at least one rigorous writing experience in the first year and at least one additional writing experience after the first year; (4) other professional skills generally regarded as necessary . . . ; (5) the history, goals, structure, values, rules, and responsibilities of the legal profession and its members."

[7] ABA SECTION OF LEGAL EDUCATION AND ADMISSIONS TO THE BAR, A SURVEY OF LAW SCHOOL CURRICULA: 2002–2010 (2012).

Topic Overview

Law schools nationwide typically require the same first year courses, and the upper level curriculum typically consists of a mix of courses teaching surveys of legal doctrine in a wide variety of subject matters in the lecture-discussion format of the first year, smaller courses offering advanced treatments of doctrine and comparative, theoretical, or interdisciplinary perspectives on law, and an array of courses teaching skills. Most schools also offer an array of experiential learning opportunities, ranging from live client clinics supervised by law school faculty to externships in law offices. The number of classroom hours and a few elements of the content of the curriculum are dictated by the American Bar Association as part of the accreditation process and by the state bar in each state as a requirement for admission to the bar. The bulk of the curriculum is determined by the judgment of each faculty about what lawyers should know and, at some schools, by the content of the state bar examination.

Some critics suggest that the curriculum at most law schools better prepares students for corporate practice than for service to individuals and small business clients. The emphasis on appellate opinions and legal memo and brief writing is said not to reflect the work that lawyers typically do for individual clients and not to train lawyers to meet the legal needs as to which there is the largest unmet demand, such as divorces, landlord-tenant matters, immigration issues, and personal bankruptcy.[8] Critics also urge law schools to train students in marketing and law office management so they can launch or work in solo or small practices.[9]

If law schools tend to focus more on preparing students for service to large organizations than to individuals and small businesses, that phenomenon may be driven in part by the perspectives of faculty, who are overwhelmingly graduates of elite law schools.[10] Faculties are said have little understanding of the legal needs of individuals and small business and to set curricula based on their own experiences in corporate and elite government practice settings and as students at schools that primarily train lawyers for those types of practice.

---

[8] Deborah L. Rhode, *Legal Education: Rethinking the Problem, Reimagining the Reforms*, 40 PEPPERDINE L. REV. 437, 447–48 (2013).

[9] See William Hornsby, *Challenging the Academy to a Dual (Perspective): The Need to Embrace Lawyering for Personal Legal Services*, 70 MD. L. REV. 420, 437 (2011); Randolph J. Jonakait, *The Two Hemispheres of Legal Education and the Rise and Fall of Local Law Schools*, 51 N.Y.L. SCH. 864, 889–96 2006/07.

[10] *See* Brian Leiter, *Where Current Faculty Went to Law School*, http://www.leiterrankings. com/jobs/2009job_teaching.shtml (last visited October 10, 2013) (finding that of all tenured and tenure-track faculty at American law schools in 2008, two-thirds had graduated from law schools ranked in top 20).

A major debate over legal education concerns the relative emphasis on so-called "academic" or "doctrinal" courses (typically taught in a discussion format) and so-called "skills" or "clinical" courses. This debate dates back to the nineteenth century and the efforts of elite schools and the ABA to improve the stature (and, they thought, the quality) of the bar by increasing the academic rigor of legal education and downplaying the traditional emphasis on learning through apprenticeship. Recently, however, the debate on experiential education has been framed in terms of whether law students get their money's worth if they do not learn what lawyers really do, particularly as large law firms find that their clients resist paying for the work of first year associates.[11]

Although the ABA waged a long campaign to emphasize doctrinal teaching in the late nineteenth and early twentieth century, recently both the ABA and other influential commentators on legal education have urged greater emphasis on teaching skills and ethics through actual or simulated experiential or clinical instruction and skills training. Two of the most influential proposals for reform in legal education were the ABA's MacCrate Report of 1992 and the Carnegie Report of 2007.[12] Both faulted excessive reliance on the case method and lecture-discussion classroom instruction on doctrine. The Carnegie Report identified what it termed "two major limitations on legal education." First, "[m]ost law schools give only casual attention to teaching students how to use legal thinking in the complexity of actual law practice." Second, "[l]aw schools fail to complement the focus on skill in legal analyses with effective support for developing ethical and social skills. Students need opportunities to learn about, reflect on and practice the responsibilities of legal professionals. Despite progress in making legal ethics a part of the curriculum, law schools rarely pay consistent attention to the social and cultural contexts of legal institutions and the varied forms of legal practice."

Both the Carnegie Report and the MacCrate Report called for greater emphasis on clinical education. Clinical and some other faculty and deans, with some but not unqualified support of the AALS, embraced the MacCrate Report and issued calls for every law school to provide a faculty-supervised direct client representation clinical experience. Some

---

[11] As part of a series of influential articles highly critical of legal education, one article excoriated law schools for failing to teach knowledge and skills essential in the first year of practice even at large firms. David Segal, *What They Don't Teach Law Students: Lawyering*, N.Y. TIMES (Nov. 19, 2011). Other articles in the same series criticized the cost of legal education, an issue we address below in section D.

[12] SECTION ON LEGAL EDUCATION AND ADMISSION TO THE BAR, LEGAL EDUCATION AND PROFESSIONAL DEVELOPMENT—AN EDUCATIONAL CONTINUUM: REPORT OF THE TASK FORCE ON LAW SCHOOLS AND THE PROFESSION, NARROWING THE GAP (1992) (known as the MacCrate Report, after one of its authors); WILLIAM M. SULLIVAN, ET AL., EDUCATING LAWYERS: PREPARATION FOR THE PROFESSION OF LAW (Carnegie Foundation 2007) (known as the Carnegie Report).

deans caution that adopting faculty-supervised, in-house, direct client representation clinical experiences for every law student would be prohibitively expensive.[13] As a matter of pedagogy, some faculty believe that simulated exercises are better for students because they allow instruction in a wider range of skills and are better for clients, who should not run the risk of having students learn at their expense.

Many critics of legal education have urged law schools to emulate the model of medical education in which the first two years are classroom instruction and the third and fourth years are spent rotating through various real-world practice settings. Unlike medical schools, which are affiliated with or run hospitals and outpatient medical clinics, law schools do not operate substantial legal services offices and would therefore depend on persons other than faculty to train students in real-world practice settings. Moreover, medical care is funded by an elaborate mix of insurance, private, and public funding. In contrast, there is almost no public funding for legal services, and there is thus no obvious way to compensate lawyers whose job it is to train fledgling lawyers.

NOTES ON THE LAW SCHOOL CURRICULUM

1. *The Evolution of Classroom and Experiential Instruction.* The Stevens excerpt on legal education before the 1960s and the MacCrate Report reveal that the views of ABA leaders have evolved over the course of a century as to what skills, knowledge, and aptitudes law school should cultivate. What are those changes and what accounts for them?

2. *What Should Be Emphasized?* There is a long history to the debate over whether legal education should emphasize vocational education or academic graduate training, and to some extent the debate presents a false dichotomy, as legal education can include both vocational and academic components. Nevertheless, when resources are finite, priorities must be identified. How would you approach that issue?

3. *The Role of Cost.* In light of the Stevens excerpt recounting the financial advantages of classroom lecture-discussion, a response to the MacCrate Report that involves a dramatic increase in resources for clinical education would require the money to come from somewhere. Given that a dramatic increase in the cost of legal education to finance more clinical teaching is unlikely, what would you recommend to the dean and faculty of your law school about how to reallocate resources to implement your preferred vision of legal education?

---

[13] *See* Russell Engler, *The MacCrate Report Turns 10: Assessing Its Impact and Identifying Gaps We Should Seek to Narrow*, 8 CLINICAL L. REV. 109, 113–123 (2002) (describing the discussions among law faculty in the wake of the MacCrate Report).

D. CONTEMPORARY DEBATES OVER LEGAL EDUCATION

1. RANKINGS AND STRATIFICATION

Some critics contend that ABA accreditation requirements and ferocious competition to succeed in the *U.S. News* rankings discourage experimentation and divert law schools from meeting law students' diverse expectations.[14] Some accreditation requirements, such as those that require support for faculty scholarship may serve the needs of some types of students more than others. The *U.S. News* ranking system, which powerfully influences students' school choices[15] and some employers' hiring decisions,[16] drives many resource allocation decisions by faculty and law school administrators. It leads law schools to give high priority to the academic reputations of their faculty and to the school's reputation with lawyers and judges because that is the most heavily weighted criterion in the ranking formula. The method used to measure law schools' reputations is deeply flawed; it rests entirely on a survey that goes to unnamed legal professionals, and the response rate to the survey is exceedingly low.[17] The rankings race also leads law schools to shift scholarship money from students most in need to those with the highest LSAT scores and median GPAs, because those scores also figure prominently in the rankings.[18] Critics argue that all of these factors tend to work against students who aspire to serve low and moderate income clients because they drive up the cost of tuition and reduce the availability of need-based financial aid. On the other hand, the pursuit of rankings may benefit students in some ways. *U.S. News* ranks schools based in part on the percentage of the graduating class that has employment in a job requiring a JD, which encourages schools to help their graduates find jobs at graduation. The ranking formula also encourages schools to maintain a low student-faculty ratio (recall Harvard's was 75 to 1 in the nineteenth century; elite schools now maintain a 12-1 student-faculty ratio).

---

[14] Deborah L. Rhode, *Legal Education: Rethinking the Problem, Reimagining the Reforms,* 40 PEPPERDINE L. REV. 437, 447–48 (2013).

[15] Michael Sauder & Ryon Lancaster, *Do Rankings Matter? The Effects of U.S. News and World Report Rankings on the Admissions Process of Law Schools,* 40 LAW & SOC'Y REV. 40 (2006).

[16] *Law Schools Report: Our Annual Survey of the Law Schools that NLJ 250 Law Firms Relied on the Most to Fill Their First-Year Associate Classes,* NAT'L L. J., Feb. 28, 2011.

[17] STEVEN HARPER, THE LAWYER BUBBLE: A PROFESSION IN CRISIS 17–18 (2013).

[18] *See* William D. Henderson & Andrew P. Morris, *Student Quality as Measured by LSAT Scores: Migration Patterns in the U.S. News Rankings Era,* 81 IND. L.J. 183 (2006).

2. COST

Few issues in contemporary legal education have garnered more public attention than its cost, especially since 2009, as the recession dimmed job prospects.[19] To understand the many issues associated with the cost of legal education, consider the elements of a law school budget. A realistic estimate of the annual budget of a small (approximately 500 students) moderately elite law school is about $30 million. Of that, approximately two-thirds is the cost of faculty and staff salaries and benefits (about $10 million is spent annually on faculty salaries and benefits and about $9 million is spent on staff and administration, including library staff). Depending on the school, the other $10 million of the annual budget is spent on the library collection and information technology ($1.5 million), operations ($4 million), and scholarships ($5.5 million).

Where does the $30 million a year come from? The vast majority of law schools depend on student tuition; only a few have endowments and receive charitable giving in amounts large enough to free them from dependence on tuition. At one point, state universities received public funding to subsidize low tuition for students enrolled in all degree programs, but many states ceased significant subsidies for their public law schools in the 1990s. Tuition at elite state university law schools approaches tuition at private universities, although many state law schools remain committed to a lower-cost model of legal education.

Even at state universities that still enjoy public funding for legal education, and especially at all other schools, the major source of revenue is tuition. Not every student pays the full tuition. Many law schools offer scholarships to recruit students with particular credentials, including high undergraduate GPA or LSAT scores or other indicators of talent or promise for professional success. Critics assert that law schools offer too few need-based scholarships and too many "merit-based" scholarships in order to attract students with high grades and LSAT scores to boost their *US News* ranking and academic profile. These critics argue that students with less sought-after credentials pay full tuition (typically with money financed by loans) while students with valued credentials pay less than the full tuition, with the result that some students subsidize the legal education of others. If financial aid were strictly need-based, the wealthier students would subsidize the education of poorer students; if it is largely merit-based, the students with less valued credentials subsidize the education of those with more valued credentials.

Those students without wealth sufficient to afford tuition borrow money. Hence, most law schools are quite dependent on the availability of

---

[19] David Segal, *Is Law School a Losing Game?* N.Y. TIMES (Jan. 8, 2011); David Segal, *Law School Economics: Ka-Ching!* N.Y. TIMES (July 16, 2011).

student loans. As you may know, law students are eligible in most cases to borrow the full cost of tuition and living expenses in some combination of federally subsidized and unsubsidized loans, depending on financial need. Educational loan programs were a reform effort of the 1960s intended to make elite college and graduate and professional education financially accessible to all students. Defenders of readily available student loans argue that they enable any student with the academic qualifications to attend even the most elite and expensive university. Critics argue that liberal loan programs have fueled a rapid increase in the cost of elite and nonelite education and have made students and schools insensitive to whether the benefits of education are justified by the cost.

As the amount of debt incurred by students rose with the increase of tuition, some began to worry that graduates who did not obtain high-paying large law firm jobs would be unable to pay their debt and would be deterred from choosing jobs most suited to their interests or to social needs and perhaps even from enrolling in law school at all. Some federal student loans are eligible for the Income Based Repayment (IBR) program in which borrowers with lower incomes after law school pay less than the ordinary monthly repayment amount. The IBR amount is capped at 15 percent of the borrower's "discretionary income," a term of art defined in the program. After 25 years of payment on the reduced IBR schedule, the remaining balance may be forgiven. In addition, under the federal IBR program, after 10 uninterrupted years of employment in qualifying public service employment and steady repayment under the IBR, debtors in qualified public service employment may have the balance of their debt forgiven. Some law schools have created loan repayment assistance programs (LRAPs) which subsidize the loan payments of alumni who take qualifying low-income public interest jobs. The IBR and most LRAP programs cover all of a borrower's educational debt, not just law school debt. Those schools that maintain LRAP programs to cover the educational debt not covered by the federal IBR program typically fund such programs out of their operating budgets, which effectively means that the charitable contributions of alumni and the tuition payments of current students subsidize the educational costs of past students who have taken public interest jobs. LRAP programs tend to be more generous at schools with substantial numbers of alumni in highly-paid law firm and corporate jobs.

One of the most influential contemporary criticisms of American legal education focuses on the high cost of full-time law faculties.

FAILING LAW SCHOOLS

Brian Tamanaha
(University of Chicago Press, 2012)[20]

Law faculties have been growing for some time now owing to a combination of factors: to handle larger numbers of students, to make up for reduced teaching loads, to add more scholars, to add clinical and legal writing teachers, and to lower faculty-student ratios (a factor on *US News* rankings). AALS tallied 7,421 full-time law faculty in 1990–91. The number has increased every year since, reaching 10,965 in 2008–09. Student-faculty ratios have plummeted as a result. At the largest law schools, the ratio was cut almost in half, from 27.3 students per faculty in 1989–90, to 15.3 in 2009–10; at midsized schools over this period it dropped from 25 to 14.4.

Although it is frequently suggested that this reduction is beneficial to students, and it does result in more seminars with smaller enrollments, the reality is that students do not necessarily gain more interaction with professors from having more of them around. Student face time takes away from scholarship, which is what professors are rewarded for.

Law professors *do not* teach in legal studies departments but in law schools. That is why persistent complaints arise about the excessive academic orientation of the faculty. Law professors—and the PhDs on law faculties—are paid substantially more than they would earn had they worked in legal studies departments. Students matriculate to gain entry to the practice of law and expect to learn the skills that will enable them to succeed as lawyers. It is questionable whether a professor with little or no practice experience is ideally suited to train students for legal practice.

Law schools are financially trapped by what they have become: top-heavy institutions with scholars teaching few classes (writing a lot) and clinicians teaching few students. The perpetual "more" of recent decades—creating more time for writing, hiring more scholars and more skills-training teachers, and spreading more money around—severely constrains law schools going forward.

Taking the entire span from 1985 through 2009, resident tuition at public law schools increased by a staggering 820 percent—from $2,006 to $18,472 (nonresident tuition increased by 543 percent, from $4,724 to $30,413)—while tuition at private law schools went up by 375 percent—from $7,526 to $35,743. These increases far outstripped the rate of inflation.

Student debt has ballooned in conjunction with tuition. The average combined debt (undergraduate and law school) of law school graduates in

---

the mid-1980s was $15,676. The average debt of law graduates was $47,000 in 1999. In 2010, average law school debt alone was $68,827 for graduates from public schools and $106,249 at private schools. Average college debt for graduates of the class of 2010 was $25,250.

Students from elite law schools have a solid chance of securing corporate law jobs that pay a salary sufficient to comfortably manage $120,000 debt. Top-fifteen law schools send 30–60 percent or more of their graduates to NLJ 250 firms each year. But the percentage of graduates securing these positions rapidly falls the further down the law school ranking one goes.

Starting pay for new law graduates falls into a distinctive pattern called a bimodal distribution, with two earnings clusters separated by a large gap of about $100,000. For the class of 2010, nearly half of law graduates earned between $40,000 and $65,000. Among those who reported their salaries, nearly 20 percent of law graduates earned around $160,000. [A]bout one-third of law graduates in the past decade have not obtained jobs as lawyers, and this is disproportionately the case at the lowest-ranked law schools.

Law schools have raised their tuition to obscene levels because they can. Elite law schools charge $10,000 to $15,000 higher than nonelite schools do because demand for their credentials is greater. But even nonelite schools can charge hefty tuition because demand for law degrees is strong enough to support it.

Taken in isolation, what [elite] schools have done can be justified. Yale and Harvard distribute financial aid on an exclusively need basis, which in effect makes the students from higher socioeconomic classes help defray the costs of those from lower (in contrast to the reverse-Robin Hood merit scholarship arrangement at virtually all other law schools in which the bottom half of the class subsidizes the top.)

The wisdom of the members of the bar who a century ago argued on behalf of a differentiated system of legal education—wanting to allow research-oriented law schools to coexist alongside law schools that focus on training good lawyers at a reasonable cost—has been confirmed by subsequent events. Unfortunately, they lost the battle to elite legal educators who imposed their standard on all. The research brand of law schools became the model imposed and enforced through AALS and ABA standards.

Affordability and elite status are mutually exclusive under current circumstances. [A law school that aspired to be] an excellent law school that trains top quality lawyers at an *affordable price* would [adopt a different model].

What might that [look] like? For starters, [it] would have to sell the vision of affordable excellence, recruiting top faculty who were willing to accept less pay (more in line with professors in other departments) to make that vision a reality; professors would have practice experience as well as [be] excellent scholars; they would teach two classes a semester, leaving ample time to write; the entering class would be capped at two hundred students; the third year would entail externships in excellent public-service work settings; tuition would be set below $20,000; there would be no merit scholarships; [the endowment would be used for] need-based scholarships, supplemented by fund raising. [If such a school existed at an elite university], quality students would [enroll]. And graduates would leave law school with manageable debt levels that would enable them to eschew the corporate law route if they so desired. This would have been the ideal law school for the twenty-first century. The only problematic element in an otherwise realistic plan would [be] recruiting enough top professors who would teach four courses and accept lower pay.

NOTES ON THE COST OF LEGAL EDUCATION

1. ***Can Law Schools That Cut Costs Compete for Faculty and Students?*** Professor Tamanaha suggests that the ideal law school would pay faculty and staff substantially less than is current practice, have a smaller faculty who teach more classes and more students, and would recruit good students by charging lower tuition. If, as is the case, labor costs are between two-thirds and three-quarters of the cost of operating a law school, the main way in which the cost of operating a law school could be reduced would be a drastic cut in salaries and benefits. A 50 percent cut in faculty salaries and benefits will reduce the budget (and, therefore, tuition) by about a third. Do you think that a law school could cut faculty and staff salaries by half, increase teaching loads, and still recruit top faculty? If not, would it nevertheless be better for students if a school followed his model? Would some students choose to attend such a school if it were one-third less expensive than other schools to which they were admitted?

2. ***Law School Debt and Law Graduates' Salaries.*** Tamanaha cites statistics on the correlation between the cost of tuition and law graduates' salaries in their first positions after law school, and he suggests that only those who begin in corporate law firms will be able to manage their debt. But many law graduates who begin their careers in large law firms leave after just a few years, and some lawyers who begin in small and medium firms move into large firms. Moreover, data from the *After the JD* study show that the salaries of lawyers in solo and medium firms and in government practice rose substantially between three and seven years after graduation; many of these lawyers are doing quite well financially.[21] These

---

[21] The American Bar Foundation and the NALP Foundation for Law Career Research and Education, *After the JD II: Second Results from a National Study of Legal Careers* (2009).

findings may suggest that Tamanaha's focus on the match between debt and law school rank and first jobs following graduation may yield misleading conclusions about whether law school is a good investment for those who cannot gain admission to elite schools.[22]

3. ***Rates of Repayment of Educational Debt.*** The *After the JD* study has gathered data about debt, including all educational debt—not just law school loans. At Wave 2 of the *AJD* project, 35.2 percent of respondents had paid off their educational loans. Among respondents working in private practice, those in large law firms were most likely to have no debt remaining—38 percent as compared with one-third in other private practice settings.[23] But respondents working in federal government settings, public interest jobs, and business were as likely as those in large firms to have no remaining debt by Wave 2, either because they benefited from loan forgiveness or family resources, or because they lived frugally.[24] By 2012, when Wave 3 of the data collection occurred, 47.6 percent of respondents had paid off their educational debt.

The *After the JD* study also finds uneven patterns of debt load and debt repayment by racial/ethnic identity. At Wave 2, African-Americans and Hispanic law graduates had substantially more debt remaining ($70,000 and $62,000) respectively) than Asian ($54,000) or white law graduates ($54,000). At Wave 3, African-Americans still had a median of $69,000 in educational debt, compared with $50,000 for whites and Hispanics and $40,000 for Asians.[25]

4. ***Imagine You Are the Dean.*** Suppose the dean and the faculty at your school wish to adopt Professor Tamanaha's proposals to reduce tuition to less than half of current levels. In effect, they have decided to cut the budget of your law school in half. They have sought your advice about how to accomplish that goal. Consider each of the following options, and consider whether your law school or a small group of schools could implement the change without a substantial number of other schools doing likewise: (a) cutting faculty and staff salaries by well over one-half (which will reduce the budget only by one-third); (b) shrinking the number of full-time faculty, including by firing both tenured and untenured faculty, and staffing the curriculum through reliance on adjunct faculty, increasing class size and/or teaching loads; (c) reducing the staff (which would reduce the budget only by a fraction, as most staff salaries are not large); (d) eliminating student

---

[22] *See* Ronit Dinovitzer, Bryant Garth & Joyce S. Sterling, *Buyers' Remorse? An Empirical Assessment of the Desirability of a Lawyer Career*, unpublished manuscript, available at http:// papers.ssrn.com/sol3/papers.cfm?abstract_id=2309587.

[23] RONIT DINOVITZER, ROBERT L. NELSON, GABRIELLE PLICKERT, REBECCA SANDEFUR & JOYCE STERLING AFTER THE JD II: RESULTS FROM A NATIONAL STUDY OF LEGAL CAREERS 80–83 (2009).

[24] Ronit Dinovitzer, Bryant Garth & Joyce Sterling, *Buyers' Remorse? An Empirical Assessment of the Desirability of a Lawyer Career,* 63 J. LEGAL EDUC. 211, 218 (2013).

[25] *10 Interesting Stats from the After the JD Survey*, ABA NEWS ARCHIVES, available at http://www.americanbar.org/news/abanews/aba-news-archives/2014/02/10_interesting_stats. html.

financial assistance (which, as you recall from the description of the hypothetical law school budget, is about one-sixth of the annual spending); (e) reducing expenditures for other operations, including maintenance of the building, all student organizations, and the library collection.

5. ***What Is the Purpose of a LRAP Program?*** As noted above, LRAP programs are a form of subsidy from students and alumni who take high-paying jobs to those who do not, and from students with little educational debt to those with large debt. They tend to be generous only at schools in which a significant percentage of the graduating class take jobs at the high end of the bimodal income distribution. Why do law schools that can adopt such programs have them? What is the purpose of an LRAP? Given that purpose, should undergraduate debt be covered?

3. SHOULD LAW SCHOOL BE TWO YEARS OR THREE?

As noted above, the ABA adopted a new set of accreditation requirements in 1921 to address anxieties about the character and competence of lawyers who were graduating from part-time law schools in the early 1900s. Among the new standards was a mandate that law students must complete three years of full-time study or devote the equivalent number of hours to study through part-time schooling.[26] Most university-affiliated law schools already had adopted a three-year requirement, but it was inconsistent with many of the programs that served working people.[27] In acrimonious ABA meetings that preceded adoption of the three-year requirement, advocates for increased admissions standards railed against the threat posed by uneducated foreigners, while advocates for night law schools argued against restrictions that would inhibit mobility for students from working-class families.

In adopting the three-year requirement, the ABA rejected recommendations of a Carnegie Commission report authored by Alfred Z. Reed (the "Reed Report'), which concluded that differences in law schools' educational programs were inevitable and reflected the fact that different types of law schools served "radically different types of practitioners."[28] It asserted that full-time university-affiliated law schools were necessary to provide the rigorous and broad legal education required for the lawyers who would become society's leaders, while two-year and part-time programs were adequate for most practitioners and would ensure that law schools "shall be kept accessible to Lincoln's plain people."[29] The ABA

---

[26] *Report of the Special Committee to the Section of Legal Education and Admissions to the Bar of the American Bar Association*, ANNUAL REPORT OF THE ABA 679, 687–88 (1921).

[27] JEROLD S. AUERBACH, UNEQUAL JUSTICE 118-19 (1976).

[28] *Id.* at 111 (quoting the Reed report).

[29] ALFRED Z. REED, TRAINING FOR THE PUBLIC PROFESSION OF THE LAW 290 (1921).

rejected the Reed Report's reasoning and recommendations, instead adopting unitary standards for all lawyers.

Proposals to abandon the three-year requirement have surfaced periodically since the 1920s. In 1971, a study by legal educators concluded that the third year of law school was unnecessary as long as certain essential courses were included in the two-year option. The study recommended that law school be available to those who had completed three years of undergraduate study and that the third year of law school should be eliminated as a requirement but made available for those who wanted to specialize.[30] The Carnegie Commission issued a similar recommendation the following year.

Calls to reexamine the three-year requirement have reemerged recently in connection with critiques of the high costs of legal education. Advocates of rule change have argued that allowing law students to sit for the bar exam after two years of law school rather than three would enable more students to afford to pursue careers in service to low or moderate-income Americans, while three year programs would continue to attract students who believe that the additional training and specialization would give them sharper skills and better preparation for the real-world challenges of practice and the job market.[31]

In *Failing Law Schools,* the book excerpted above, Professor Tamanaha outlines the argument in favor of two-year law school programs:

> The bar's position a century ago made consummate sense: two years of book learning followed by a one-year apprenticeship, then admission to the bar. The Carrington Report of four decades ago, which proposed three years of an undergraduate education followed by two years of law school, was also sensible.

> The essential change could be achieved in a stroke. The current ABA-imposed minimum of 1,120 classroom hours can be reduced by a third, instead mandating 747 hours of instruction.

> Some degree programs will be two years, others will remain at three, with clinical components; some will be heavily doctrinal, others will be skills oriented. One-year degrees (the current LLM) will be widely available for an additional year of specialization in a chosen subject. Schools will offer two-year and three-year program options for students, incentivizing schools to create a third year that adds significant value.

---

[30] The Carrington Report, reprinted as app. A in HERBERT L. PACKER AND THOMAS EHRLICH, NEW DIRECTIONS IN LEGAL EDUCATION 93 (1972).

[31] *See* Samuel Estreicher, *The Roosevelt-Cardozo Way: The Case for Bar Eligibility After Two Years of Law School*, 15 N.Y.U. J. L & PUB. POL'Y 599 (2012).

Differentiation across the market for legal education—currently suppressed by ABA standards—would arise. The law school parallel—in program and pricing—of vocational colleges and community colleges will come into existence, many of two-year duration. Prospective students will be able to pick the legal education program they want at a price they can afford. A law graduate who wishes to engage in a local practice need not acquire, or pay for, the same education as a graduate aiming for corporate legal practice. This is not the race to the bottom prophesied by AALS. It simply recognized that every law school need not be a Ritz-Carlton. A Holiday Inn-type law school would provide a fine education for many, adequate for the type of legal practice they will undertake.[32]

NOTES ON TWO YEARS V. THREE YEARS

1. *Competence.* Some critics of proposals to allow students to sit for the bar after two years of law school argue that it would glut the market with attorneys who do not have the skills and training that they need to practice competently. Are they right? Are proposals to reduce law school to two years in tension with the demand that law schools produce practice-ready graduates?

2. *Must We Choose?* Do we need to choose between a two and three year model, or could these different types of legal education programs co-exist? Tamanaha suggests that we should let students choose what type of training they will receive. What are the advantages and disadvantages of insisting on a unitary standard?

3. *A Third Year Apprenticeship?* Tamanaha argues that even if law schools do not change to a two year model, they should devote the third year to apprenticeships:

> Law schools can place students on a wholesale basis in already-existing practice settings (law firms, governments legal offices, courthouses, etc.), as many law schools already do through "externship" programs. A more ambitious program would involve the participation by law schools, in partnership with government-funded agencies, with the delivery of legal services to the middle class and poor at low cost. Under currently existing "hybrid" programs, a clinical professor has an office at the practice setting and works with the students on location. If understaffed legal services offices were offered the full-time assistance of the third-year class of local law schools, that would help fill unmet legal needs while the students get useful training. Privately financed, privately run versions of low-cost legal services are also possible, in conjunction with law schools, in areas like immigration services, tax

---

[32] BRIAN Z. TAMANAHA, FAILING LAW SCHOOLS 173–174 (2012).

services, employment problems, and a variety of other common tasks on which third year students can hone their practice skills.

Whichever the external setting, students would work as lawyers at an office earning basic wages (which would require a rule change in order to implement)—reviving a form of apprenticeship. Think of the lawyer equivalent of residency programs for graduates out of medical school. Law school staff and attorneys in the office would maintain oversight and provide advice, but students would handle much of the work themselves. Many third-year students already work part-time in law offices—this would amount to an institutionalized version of that. The responsibility of the law school would be to secure placement opportunities in practice settings while running a supplemental education component on the side. Tuition for the third year can be reduced to a level commensurate with the extent of the outplacement and supervision services provided by the school.

What practical or other obstacles do you see to adoption of the third-year apprenticeship model? How could the obstacles be overcome?

4. ***President Obama Joins the Debate.*** During the summer of 2013, in a question-and-answer session on higher education, President Obama endorsed cutting the classroom component of law school from three to two years and having students devote the final year of law school to work experience.[33] His comment generated strong responses. Yale Law School's Bruce Ackerman, for example, asserted that the third year is "not an expensive frill but a crucial resource in training lawyers for 21st-century challenges." He argued that legal decisions rest on economics, statistics, psychology, and other social sciences, and that law schools must prepare students to handle relevant insights from those other disciplines. President Obama's "cost-cutting" measure, Ackerman insisted, would "impoverish American public life" and "push legal education back more than 75 years":

> The predictable outcome will be massive professional retreat. Increasingly, lawyers will become secondary figures who prepare the way for "experts" to present the crucial arguments before administrative agencies, courts and legislatures. Decision-makers with two-year law degrees will proceed to rubber-stamp the expert testimony that seems most impressive because they aren't prepared to test it in a serious way.[34]

Do you agree with Professor Ackerman's predictions? How do you suppose President (and former University of Chicago Law School Senior Lecturer) Obama would respond?

---

[33] See Peter Lattman, *Obama Says Law School Should Be Two, Not Three, Years,* N.Y. TIMES, Aug. 23, 2013.

[34] Bruce Ackerman, *Why Legal Education Should Last for Three Years,* WASH. POST, Sept. 6, 2013.

4. TOO MANY LAWYERS?

Some say that the U.S. already has plenty of lawyers and that too many law graduates have recently flooded a saturated market.[35] Others cite evidence of unmet legal needs of low-income and moderate-income individuals and argue that the problem is not too many lawyers but rather that legal education is not producing legal services providers with the right kind of training at the right price.[36]

The following two excerpts illustrate these two perspectives. The first focuses on the mismatch between the number of law school graduates and the number of available law jobs as defined by the U.S. Department of Labor Statistics. The second excerpt rejects the notion that law schools should restrict access to legal training and expertise, and it also questions what counts as a law job.

POP GOES THE LAW

Steven J. Harper
Chronicle of Higher Education (March 11, 2013)

The Law School Admission Council recently reported[37] that applications were heading toward a 30-year low. Since 2004 the number of law school applicants has dropped from almost 100,000 to 54,000.

Good thing, too. That loud pop you're hearing is the bursting of the law bubble—firms, schools, and disillusioned lawyers paying for decades of greed and grandiosity. Like the dot-com, real-estate, and financial bubbles that preceded it, the law bubble is bursting painfully. But now is the time to consider the causes, take steps to soften the impact, and figure out how to keep it from happening again.

The popular explanation for the recent application plummet is that information about the profession's darker side, including the recession's exacerbation of the attorney glut, has finally started reaching prospective law students. Let's hope so. Marginal candidates and those choosing law school by default might be opting out, and the law-school market may finally be heading toward self-correction.

Still, the bubble has been huge, and the correction will need to be, too. There were 68,000 applicants to the fall of 2012 entering class, while the total number of new, full-time jobs requiring a law degree is 25,000 a year and falling.

---

[35] *See*, e.g., Eric Posner, *The Real Problem with Law Schools: They Train Too Many Lawyers*, SLATE, Apr. 2, 2013.

[36] *See* Deborah Rhode, *Legal Education: Rethinking the Problem, Reimaging the Reforms*, 40 PEPPERDINE L. REV. 437, 445 (2013).

[37] http://www.nytimes.com/2013/01/31/education/law-schools-applications-fall-as-costs-rise-and-jobs-are-cut.html?_r=1&

For full-time, long-term jobs that require passing the bar, only a dozen law schools out of 200 reported employment rates exceeding 80 percent nine months after graduation. Considering the investment in money, time, and brainpower that law school requires (not to mention the promises that law schools make to prospective students), something's gotta give, and maybe it finally has.

DOING GOOD INSTEAD OF DOING WELL? WHAT LAWYERS COULD BE DOING IN A WORLD OF "TOO MANY" LAWYERS

Carrie Menkel-Meadow
Oñati Socio-Legal Series (2013)

For some time now I have found the question, "are there too many lawyers" somewhat off putting, if not downright offensive. Who is asking that question to suggest that we restrict access to a legal education and/or to the legal profession itself? There are a lot of people wanting to study law. Whether that study of law immediately results in employment in a high-paying large law firm or should result in any particular form of employment is a different question. Law is a general first degree in much of the world, so might it be in the United States. But even if it is an expensive graduate degree, as long as there is truthful disclosure of employment data and people can make informed choices about what they want to study, I can see the value of a law degree far exceeding immediate employment pay-offs. Other commentators have suggested that if we simply stop thinking of law as a special "profession," but simply as a field of expertise, subject to the same vagaries of any other employment, with some specialized knowledge (and some ethical rules), the practice of law might more honestly face up to its modern economic challenges and begin to adapt, respond and perhaps innovate, as other fields of work have had to do.

[L]aw study may be an entry "portal" into a large number of other kinds of work—business, politics (either as a candidate or in the new profession of political consulting), policy work, government (non or quasi-legal work), NGO advocacy in both legal and non-legal settings, community, labor or other interest group organizing work, creative work (start-ups of many kinds, including scientific, educational, economic and entertainment), real estate work, education (teaching others about the law, whether lay people or other law students), deal making and social entrepreneurship, and peace work (whether legal mediation or non-legal international or domestic), which is hardly exclusive of all the possible jobs and tasks that someone with a law degree might perform. With some knowledge of the law all of these jobs and others we cannot even imagine at the moment are likely to be performed with a better sense of justice, equity, logic and rule-based accountability.

[I]f there are "too" many or just "many" lawyers, maybe some reallocation might actually provide for some better distribution of lawyers to those who are currently underserved. Or, the many lawyers might "redeploy" their legal skills in different, more socially useful ways. If the legal profession were subject to regular market forces, an oversupply of lawyers should lead to a lowering of price and to reallocation of services. [P]erhaps if "too" many lawyers are trained in the same way there might be some competition or reconfiguration of how legal education is delivered. [S]ome schools are offering more diversified legal education with the hope of making more "practice-ready" lawyers or training lawyers to do different things. Perhaps it is time to return to the ill-fated Reed Report on legal education and recognize that American legal education might be diversified, sectored and specialized. Some might study law to practice, others to train their minds in "legal thought" (logic, order, both inductive and deductive reasoning), others as an overlay on some other field (science, economics, business), and others just to become educated citizens of their countries or the world. [Finally], some might use law study to change the way we think about the world. Entrepreneurial (socially, legally and economically) new lawyers might just adapt, reconfigure and reconceive the work that lawyers do and see that there is more that people with legal education can do, not just for personal gain, but for the global society in which we live. With other ways to practice law (more conflict resolution, more diversity of the individual and organizational client base, with different forms of practice, and more sites and locations of legal issues, some policy based, some law-making, some transactional, some dispute resolving), there should be both more and different work for those who call themselves lawyers. The question then might be, not "are there too many lawyers?," but are lawyers being socially productive and what are they doing? There is no one "right" way to practice law, as there most certainly is no one way to achieve social justice.

NOTES ON THE "TOO MANY LAWYERS" QUESTION

1. **What Is a Law Job?** Harper uses Department of Labor Statistics data on positions requiring a JD as his measure of whether law schools are producing the right number of lawyers. The *U.S. News* formula for rankings treats jobs requiring a JD differently than other jobs when calculating the employment rate of law graduates. Recall Lawrence Friedman's observation in Chapter 2 that American lawyers prospered throughout the 19th century because "the profession was exceedingly nimble at finding new kinds of work and new ways to do it." Is trying to identifying the right number of lawyers a useful exercise? If so, how does one specify what constitutes a law job?

2. **Is It Good That Law School Applications Are Declining?** Harper cites dramatic declines in the numbers of LSAT test-takers and law school applicants as evidence that many fewer people are finding law school

an attractive choice. Indeed, more recent data suggests that the decline in the number of LSAT takers and law school applicants has continued.[38] Do you agree with Harper that these are good developments? If so, why?

3. ***Access to the Profession.*** One professor and former law school dean worries that the latest wave of crisis rhetoric about the profession will dissuade students who cannot gain admission to elite law schools from attending law school at all. He argues that the result may be that they miss the opportunity to make a worthwhile investment that would pay large dividends over the course of a career and that the profession will lose the diversity that comes from admitting students from less privileged backgrounds.[39] Which should worry us more—that some students will assume substantially more educational debt than they can handle or that they will forgo a career that requires expensive training but may yield long-term individual and societal benefits?

5. LAW SCHOOL ADMISSIONS

As you are no doubt aware, a major contemporary debate about legal education concerns admission criteria. Critics of admissions policies argue that heavy reliance on undergraduate grades and LSAT scores has a disparate impact on the basis of race and socioeconomic class and may not accurately screen for all the qualities that make for professional competence. Defenders of reliance on undergraduate GPA (UGPA) and LSAT scores emphasize the correlation between them and first-year law school grades, the correlation between UGPA and overall law school performance, and the correlation between first-year law school grades and bar passage. They posit that grades and test scores measure skills and aptitudes that lawyers need.[40] Much of the debate over admissions policy has focused on whether the predictive value of UGPA and LSAT is justified given the adverse impact of these numerical measures on the racial and socioeconomic diversity of law school admittees. In doctrinal terms, the issue is whether consideration of race in admissions constitutes unlawful race discrimination, and the use of race remains controversial and legally vulnerable even in those states that have not banned it outright for public universities. *Grutter v. Bollinger,* 539 U.S.

---

[38] *See* Jacob Gershman, *Number of LSAT Test Takers in June Falls to 14-Year Low,* WSJ LAW BLOG, July 11, 2014.

[39] *See* Bryant Garth, *Crises, Crisis Rhetoric, and Competition in Legal Education: A Sociological Perspective on the (Latest) Crisis of the Legal Profession and Legal Education,* STAN. L. & POL'Y REV. 503 (2013).

[40] The literature on law school admissions policies is substantial. One qualified defense of the reliance on grades and test scores is an empirical study of every graduating class at the law school at Brigham Young University. It found that the correlation between LSAT and first-year law school grades is stronger than the correlation between undergraduate GPA and first year law school grades; the correlation between undergraduate GPA and law school GPA is stronger than the correlation between LSAT and law school GPA, but overall concluded that the undergraduate grades and GPA are not strong predictors of academic success in law school. David A. Thomas, *Predicting Law School Academic Performance from LSAT Scores and Undergraduate Grade Point Averages: A Comprehensive Study,* 35 ARIZ. ST. L. J. 1007 (2003).

306 (2003) (upholding the use of race as a factor in law school admissions decisions); *Fisher v. University of Texas,* 631 F.3d 213 (5th Cir. 2011) (upholding the use of race in undergraduate admissions), *vacated,* 133 S. Ct. 2411 (2013) (holding that the Fifth Circuit erred in not applying strict scrutiny and remanding for further consideration).

Two professors at UC Berkeley conducted a large-scale empirical study to determine whether measurable qualities other than UGPA and LSAT might be more effective in predicting lawyer effectiveness. Professors Marjorie M. Shultz and Sheldon Zedeck surveyed and interviewed hundreds of lawyers, clients, judges, and law professors to identify 26 factors that are important to lawyer effectiveness.[41] The authors then devised and validated instruments to measure these professional performance factors and developed new tests that correlated with the large majority of the 26 factors conducive to lawyering effectiveness. The authors collected measures of prior academic achievement for 1,148 lawyers. The authors then asked supervisors, peers, and participants themselves to evaluate participants' professional performance on the effectiveness factor scales. The authors compared the evaluations of professional performance with the data on the participants' academic achievement and with their scores on the authors' tests. The authors found their tests predicted lawyer performance better than the LSAT, UGPA, or Index (which is a composite of UGPA and LSAT). By contrast, most of the 26 factors identified by attorneys as important to lawyer performance were not well predicted by the LSAT, UGPA, or Index score. In addition, unlike the LSAT, the authors' measures showed few racial or gender subgroup differences. The authors suggested a law school might use performance-predictive measures like those they studied in addition to or in lieu of UGPA and LSAT.

NOTES ON LAW SCHOOL ADMISSIONS

1. ***Should Law Schools Adopt New Criteria for Admission?*** The Shultz and Zedeck study suggests that law schools should modify their admissions criteria in order to screen for additional aptitudes or forms of intelligence that law school admissions criteria currently do not systematically consider. Are you persuaded?

2. ***What Might Happen if One Did?*** If a law school decided in principle to abandon reliance on LSAT/UGPA, what obstacles do you perceive to the adoption of a proposal like the Shultz and Zedeck one? How might those obstacles be overcome?

---

[41] Marjorie M. Shultz & Sheldon Zedeck, *Predicting Lawyer Effectiveness: Broadening the Basis for Law School Admissions Decisions,* 36 LAW & SOC. INQUIRY 620 (2011).

E. PROPOSALS FOR REFORM

In 2013, the ABA Task Force on the Future of Legal Education issued a report recommending substantial changes in the American legal education system. Among its primary observations, conclusions, and recommendations were these:

- A fundamental tension underlies the current problems in legal education. On the one hand, lawyers play a central role in the "effective functioning of ordered society" and therefore society "has a deep interest in the competence of lawyers, in their availability to serve society and clients, and their values." On the other hand, unlike medical training, which is subsidized by state and federal governments, lawyer training is delivered primarily through private markets. Therefore, it should be responsive to the preferences of law students, who have a legitimate interest in ensuring that they receive an education that will equip them to make a living and repay their loans.

- The system through which law school education is funded should be revamped: "Schools announce standard tuition rates, and then chase students with high LSAT scores by offering substantial discounts without much regard to financial need. Other students receive little if any benefit from discounting and must rely mainly on borrowing to finance their education. The net result is that students whose credentials (and likely job prospects) are the weakest incur large debt to sustain the school budget and enable higher credentialed students to attend at little cost." The Task Force recommended that a commission be established to recommend reforms regarding law school pricing and financing.

- Legal education is too standardized, and some ABA accreditation requirements add expense without ensuring commensurate value. Several of the accreditation standards should be revised or repealed, including those governing the proportion of courses that must be taught by full-time faculty, tenure and security of employment for faculty, the amount of required instruction time, and physical facilities. The ABA should expand opportunities for law schools to vary from accreditation requirements in order to pursue experiments in legal education.

- Law schools should devote more attention to skills training and experiential learning.

- State supreme courts and regulators of lawyers and law practice should consider reducing the amount of law study required for eligibility to sit for the bar examination or to be admitted to practice.

- States should create additional frameworks for licensing providers of legal services, such as licensing limited practitioners or authorizing bar admission for people whose bar preparation is not in the traditional three year classroom mold.[42]

NOTES ON THE ABA TASK FORCE RECOMMENDATIONS

1. *Are You in Favor?* Would you support some or all of the changes proposed by the ABA Task Force? Which of them do you think are likely to gain sufficient support to have a reasonable possibility of eventual adoption? What obstacles stand in the way of the successful adoption of whatever recommendations you support?

2. *Resistance from Some Law Professors.* Some law faculty were not pleased with the Task Force's recommendation to diminish the role of full-time faculty and change the tenure rule. More than 500 law professors signed a letter objecting to the elimination of tenure as an accreditation requirement.[43] The letter argued that the elimination of the requirement would threaten academic freedom, discourage dissenting voices in legal education, and impede efforts to recruit and retain minority law professors.[44]

3. *Legal Education Reform By the States.* A number of states, including New York and California, are currently considering whether changes in legal education might help ensure that law graduates are competent to practice law before they are admitted to the bar.[45] A State Bar of California Task Force recently recommended a pre-bar admission competency training requirement that could be fulfilled either by taking 15 units of practice-based, experiential course work designed to develop practice competency or 15 units of a bar-approved externship, clerkship or apprenticeship any time during or after completion of law school. It also recommended an additional competency training requirement of 50 hours of pro bono service.[46]

---

[42] See Working Paper, American Bar Association Task Force on the Future of Legal Education (2013).

[43] See Mark Hansen, *500 Law Profs Urge ABA Legal Ed Council to Keep Faculty Tenure as an Accreditation Requirement*, ABA J., Oct. 22, 2013.

[44] Letter to Judge Oliver, Council Chairperson, Section on Legal Education and Admissions to the Bar, Oct. 8, 2013.

[45] See New York State Bar Association Report of the Task Force on the Future of Legal Education (April 2, 2011); State Bar of California, Task Force on Admissions Regulation Reform: Phase 1 Final Report (June 24, 2013).

[46] State Bar of California, Task Force on Admissions Regulation Reform: Phase 1 Final Report (June 24, 2013)

F. SUMMARY

This chapter showed that the content and style of teaching in American law schools was the product of a series of reform efforts beginning at Harvard Law School in the 1870s, continuing through a sustained effort of the ABA and elites in the organized bar through the 1930s, and the efforts of student activists of the 1960s. Each of these reform efforts resulted in aspects of legal education that have been the subject of controversy today. The use of full-time faculty with relatively little law practice experience and who are oriented toward and rewarded for their scholarship and ability as classroom teachers was considered necessary to increase the intellectual and social credibility of law as a profession rather than as a trade. The 3-year requirement for a JD degree was the result of a long campaign to increase the quality and social standing of the bar. The increase since the 1970s in the number of experiential and skills courses in law schools was likewise the product of a longstanding reform effort aimed at improving the practice readiness of law graduates. The hierarchy among law schools, which bears on the contemporary debates over the cost of legal education, how law schools can best serve their students, and whether legal education adequately trains students to serve the right sort of clients, has its roots in the late-nineteenth century efforts of university-affiliated law schools to distinguish themselves from proprietary schools. Some of the most hotly-contested contemporary issues—the cost of law school, the role of debt in financing higher education, and admissions criteria—have their roots in earlier reform efforts that attempted to improve the quality of education and increase the stature of the bar, to make high-quality education affordable to those without family money, and to ensure that law graduates reflect the racial, ethnic, and socioeconomic diversity of the American population.

CHAPTER 36

BAR ADMISSION AND DISCIPLINE AND THE LAW OF MALPRACTICE

■ ■ ■

A. INTRODUCTION

A distinctive feature of the legal profession, one cherished by lawyers, is the power of self-regulation. Lawyers, through the bar association of each state and with the permission of the state legislature and high court, determine the criteria and administer the processes for granting and revoking licenses to practice law. The power to admit to practice, to discipline, and to disbar (and to collect dues to fund these operations) are the only coercive powers of the organized bar; all else the bar does is voluntary.

In Chapter 35 and over the course of law school, you see how the bar's control over admission to practice affects law schools, ranging from admissions criteria to curriculum. Once a lawyer is admitted to practice, the norms of the institutions within which lawyers practice, peer pressure, and client expectations may be more significant than the bar's influence for most lawyers most of the time. But while the threat of bar discipline may not concern most lawyers in their daily practices, the bar's standards influence the norms of the institutions in which lawyers work. Bar rules guide law office practices on conflicts of interest, confidentiality of client information, and client funds. Bar disciplinary rules also affect the law of malpractice, which prompts malpractice insurers to impose conditions on issuing policies, which affects law office management. Courts, not the state bar, create and enforce malpractice law, but they often look to the disciplinary rules in defining lawyers' standards of conduct. Finally, the bar's standards and processes for admission and discipline are significant for the profession's legitimacy and its ongoing efforts to protect the prerogatives of self-regulation.

This chapter first covers the requirements for admission to the bar, especially the bar exam and the Multistate Professional Responsibility Exam, and demonstrating good moral character. The chapter then examines the standards and processes for bar discipline and the tort law governing lawyer malpractice.

B. ADMISSION TO THE BAR

Topic Overview

Standards for admission to the bar emphasize two qualifications: competence and trustworthiness. Competence is measured typically by educational requirements—a college degree and a JD—and passage of two examinations (the bar exam and the Multistate Professional Responsibility Examination (MPRE)). Trustworthiness is determined by an assessment of the candidate's background as a way of determining moral character. In the name of ensuring competence and trustworthiness of the profession, most states require satisfactory completion of three requirements to be admitted to practice: (1) law school graduation; (2) passing the bar examination and the MPRE; and (3) demonstrating good moral character and fitness to practice law. Although these requirements are widespread, controversy exists about their implementation.

As explained in Chapter 35, today's requirements for admission to practice were not established until the 1930s. Until the early twentieth century, many lawyers had no college degree, and most states did not even require lawyers to have graduated from high school. Most lawyers learned law the same way anyone learned a skill or a trade: by working as an apprentice under the supervision of one already practicing the trade. This was known as "reading the law," and it is still permitted in a few states (including California) as an alternative to attending law school, although the requirements of study and supervision have been made much stricter.

The history of legal education, bar examinations, and the requirement of demonstrating good moral character reveals that they were not always used, or intended, solely to protect consumers from corrupt or demonstrably incompetent lawyers. They were also used to ensure that the right sort of people (as defined by those running the universities and the organized bar) became lawyers.

1. BAR EXAMINATION

Bar examinations were rare until the late nineteenth century. States (either through a court or through individual lawyers appointed by the court) typically administered a short oral examination for admission to the bar. The oral examinations did not ask a standard set of questions; both the questions and the grades were left to the discretion of the examiner. In the middle and late nineteenth century, states began using written bar examinations, and by the early twentieth century most states required lawyers to pass a written bar exam. Today, almost all states require anyone not admitted to the bar in another state to pass a written examination.

Between the late 1880s and the early 1920s, the ABA waged a successful campaign to persuade states to require the bar examination. All states except Wisconsin and New Hampshire now require candidates to pass the bar examination, and almost all states (except Maryland and Wisconsin) also require the Multistate Professional Responsibility Examination (MPRE).[1] Graduates of Wisconsin's two law schools (at the University of Wisconsin at Madison and at Marquette University in Milwaukee) and graduates of an honors program at the University of New Hampshire law school enjoy the "diploma privilege"; the JD diploma from an in-state school entitles them to join the state bar without sitting for the bar exam. If they choose to practice outside the state in which they attended law school, they must take the bar exam.

The Bar Exam and the MPRE

Almost every state requires prospective lawyers to pass the bar examination and the MPRE. These tests include nationally-standardized multiple-choice tests on several areas of law, including contracts, torts, property, constitutional law, evidence, criminal law and procedure, civil procedure, and professional responsibility. The essay portions of the bar exam cover some of these topics as well as state law. The state law topics vary from state to state. Major criticisms of the bar exam and the MPRE focus on whether the tests measure competence and whether other devices would better assess skills needed in law practice.

The bar exam consists of multiple elements. In most states, it includes one day (six hours) of multiple choice questions known as the Multistate Bar Exam (MBE), which is the same test across the country. The MBE tests knowledge of certain subjects of federal law (such as constitutional law, evidence, and civil and criminal procedure) as well as general common law doctrine (such as contracts, torts, and property) not specific to any particular state. Every state requires completion of at least a second day of examination (California requires a full third day and several other states require half a third day). The additional day(s) of examination consist of various types of essay questions. Beyond the subjects on the MBE, states test a variety of law on the essay questions, including substantive and procedural law that is unique to the state (such as family law, state evidence and civil procedure, oil and gas law, and so forth). Many states also include, as part of the essay portion of the bar exam, a "performance" or "practical" test in which candidates are given a

---

[1]   The National Conference of Bar Examiners maintains a website explaining the MBE and MPRE and tracking which states require them: www.ncbex.org.

library of materials and asked to write some legal document, such as a contract, a client letter, or an analytic or persuasive memorandum.

The Multistate Professional Responsibility Examination (MPRE) is a two-hour, 60-question multiple choice test on the rules of legal and judicial ethics that, in most states, can be taken any time after the first year of law school. (This book covers most of the law tested on the MPRE, but it does not attempt to be a prep course for the MPRE; any student planning to take the MPRE should study for it as one would for any other nationally standardized test.) The MPRE was first administered in 1980 and spread rapidly in the decade thereafter.[2]

A number of challenges have been made to various aspects of the bar examination and the MPRE. Although court challenges to the bar examination have almost uniformly failed, debate continues about whether the bar is an effective screening device and about how to make it more effective. The materials that follow focus on the major debates about the bar examination.

2. DOES THE BAR EXAM MEASURE COMPETENCE?

Two principal criticisms of the bar exam as a measure of competence are made. The first focuses on the substance of what is tested. The criticism is that a one-size-fits-all test of wide array of subjects is a poor fit for the specialized nature of today's law practice; in other words, it tests both too much and too little. Knowledge of the minutia of future interests in real property, for example, will never be used by lawyers specializing in criminal prosecution or defense. Conversely, the relatively superficial level at which knowledge of criminal law and criminal procedure are tested on the bar exam do not measure whether a law graduate is competent to begin trying or defending felonies.

The second common criticism of the bar exam is that it does not measure competence at the skills that lawyers need. Answering a series of multiple choice questions or writing a short essay spotting the issues in a hypothetical set of facts does not indicate whether a lawyer can negotiate and write a contract, interview or cross-examine a witness, draft a complaint, formulate a discovery plan, or persuade a client or a witness to be candid, design an efficient strategy to solve a legal problem, woo a prospective client, or run a successful law office. As the MacCrate Report said, "the traditional bar exam does nothing to encourage law schools to teach and law students to acquire many of the fundamental lawyering skills. [T]he examination influences law schools, in developing their curricula, to overemphasize courses in the substantive areas of law

---

[2]   The history of the MPRE, and of the standardization of bar examinations, is recounted in Paul T. Hayden, *Putting Ethics to the (Nationally Standardized) Test: The Origins of the MPRE,* 71 FORDHAM L. REV. 1299 (2003).

covered by the examination at the expense of courses in the area of lawyering skills."[3] This criticism is similar to the criticism made of law schools for relying heavily on the LSAT in the admissions process: both the LSAT and the bar exam measure certain cognitive skills that do not necessarily correlate with or predict lawyer competence.

Criticism of the MPRE as a device for measuring ethical competence is similar. It tests knowledge of rules rather than judgment. Reliance on a standardized test measuring knowledge of rules encourages law schools to teach to the standardized test rather than to teach the skills or to cultivate the habits and attributes that lawyers should have. Some have complained that the MPRE has actually undermined the teaching of professional ethics in law school by encouraging schools to treat ethics as nothing more than a set of technical rules to be learned. Professional ethics, critics assert, should be taught as a matter of professional identity and values, judgment, problem-solving, and introspection about how lawyers should behave. The dispute over the desirability of the MPRE surfaces in debates in some states over whether to raise the minimum passing score on the MPRE. Some insist that raising the score would protect consumers of legal services. Others argue it would exacerbate the tendency of law schools to focus on the minutia of ethics rules rather than on ethics, and it would do nothing to make lawyers more ethical.[4]

3. IS THE BAR EXAM SUFFICIENTLY JOB-RELATED TO JUSTIFY WHATEVER DISCRIMINATORY IMPACT IT HAS ON CERTAIN POPULATIONS?

A common criticism of the LSAT, the bar exam, and even the MPRE is that they, like many standardized pencil-and-paper tests, disparately affect people of certain races and socioeconomic backgrounds, particularly Blacks, Latinos, Native Americans, and some Asians.[5] Controversy about the racial and socioeconomic impact of the bar exam is affected by the fact that, unlike the organizations that administer the SAT, LSAT and other high-stakes standardized admissions tests, many state bars do not report aggregate data of bar exam pass rates by race, ethnicity, or other demographic factors. One state that does report bar passage statistics by race and ethnicity (California) indicates that a higher percentage of white

---

[3] MacCrate Report at 278.

[4] California debated this. *Bar Gets Tougher on Ethics Exam*, CAL. BAR J., Jan. 2006, at 1.

[5] William C. Kidder, *The Bar Examination and the Dream Deferred: A Critical Analysis of the MBE, Social Closure and Racial and Ethnic Stratification*, 29 LAW & SOC. INQUIRY 547 (2004); Kristin Booth Glen, *When and Where We Enter: Rethinking Admission to the Legal Profession*, 102 COLUM. L. REV. 1696 (2002); LINDA F. WIGHTMAN, LAW SCHOOL ADMISSION COUNCIL NATIONAL LONGITUDINAL BAR PASSAGE STUDY (1998).

bar exam takers pass than do Asian, black, Latino, or other minority takers.[6]

Assessing whether the bar exam measures competence and its discriminatory impact is justified is complicated by the fact that bar examiners are not transparent in explaining their reasoning for setting the minimum passing score. Analysis of efforts to raise bar exam passing scores in Florida, Illinois, Minnesota, New York, Ohio, Pennsylvania, and Texas noted that many of the states that attempted to raise the passing score have relatively large numbers of lawyers. "Several common themes emerged in the bar exam controversies: (1) each proposal drew heated opposition from law schools and civil rights organizations; (2) in each case, concerns were raised about the potential disparate impact on students of color; (3) the methods used to study and set the new passing standard were called into question; and (4) there was major debate about the relationship between the bar exam and competency to practice law, including skepticism about what truly motivated bar examiners to recommend raising the bar."[7] Critics point out that the selection of a minimum passing score is somewhat arbitrary, and that bar exam graders do not consistently apply a uniform set of standards in grading answers, such that two graders might disagree about whether a particular question or examination merits a passing score.[8] In one case, a disappointed bar applicant challenged the Arizona Board of Bar Examiner's practice of setting the passing score after the exams were graded as an illegal anticompetitive effort to restrict the number of licensed lawyers. The Supreme Court rejected the contention, reasoning: "By its very nature, grading examinations does not necessarily separate the competent from the incompetent or—except very roughly—identify those qualified to practice and those not qualified. At best, a bar examination can identify those applicants who are more qualified to practice than those less qualified." *Hoover v. Ronwin,* 466 U.S. 558, 578 n.31 (1984).

Bar examinations have also been criticized for their effect on law school curricula and on how people prepare for the bar. Conventional methods of preparation for the bar exam are asserted to be both unproductive and unfair. Some law schools (typically those whose

---

[6] On the July 2012 California Bar Exam, the pass rates of first-time takers were 74.7% for whites, 44.4% for blacks, 57.4% for Hispanics, 63.6% for Asians, and 54.5% for the category "Other Minorities." http://admissions.calbar.ca.gov/Portals/4/documents/gbx/JULY2012STATS. 122112_R.pdf. These pass rates are roughly similar to those reported for the July 2011 bar, the July 2010 bar, and before.

[7] Kidder, *The Bar Examination and the Dream Deferred,* 29 LAW & SOC. INQUIRY at 547–548.

[8] Andrea Curcio, *A Better Bar: Why and How the Existing Bar Should Change,* 81 NEB. L. REV. 363 (2002); DEBORAH L. RHODE, IN THE INTERESTS OF JUSTICE: REFORMING THE LEGAL PROFESSION 51–52 (2000); Michael J. Thomas, *The American Lawyer's Next Hurdle: The State-Based Bar Examination System,* 24 J. LEGAL PROF. 235 (2000).

graduates pass the bar exam at a relatively low rate) encourage or require their students to take a course on every subject tested on the bar exam, or encourage or require their faculty to use assessment devices that mimic the bar exam (such as closed book, time-pressured, essay and multiple choice exams) rather than other assessment devices that might better measure the knowledge or skills necessary in practice. Critics insist that these practices deprive law students of opportunities to learn skills or professionally useful knowledge in law school and have the same racially disparate impact that other high-stakes tests have. Another criticism of bar exam preparation focuses on the prevalence of expensive commercial bar review courses after an expensive legal education. In addition, as any recent bar exam taker will tell you in excruciating detail, spending six to eight weeks doing nothing but cramming for the bar exam is often a mind-numbing and anxiety-inducing rite of passage that is available only to those with enough resources to devote to full-time study and it may have no useful purpose other than simply gaining admission to the bar.

As noted above in Chapter 35, alternatives to the bar exam have been proposed that would measure competence through observed demonstration of practice skills in a real-world setting.

NOTES ON BAR EXAMINATIONS

1. *The Purpose of Examinations.* What is the purpose of the bar exam and the MPRE? Do they serve their purposes? Would another type of device serve the same purposes?

2. *What Should be Tested?* What subjects should be tested on the bar exam or the MPRE?

3. *In the Real World.* What are the practical obstacles to replacing examinations with an alternative measure of competence?

4. *The Diploma Privilege.* What are the advantages and disadvantages of a system like Wisconsin's, in which graduates of approved law schools in the state may be admitted to practice without taking the bar exam? Why did the ABA oppose the diploma privilege? Could or should the diploma privilege be implemented in a state like California, which has a large number of law schools of varying degrees of selectivity? One solution to that problem might be to extend the diploma privilege only to graduates of some law schools, or only to some graduates of law schools. Would such a limit be desirable? If a state were to extend the diploma privilege only to some graduates of a law school, how should it define who is eligible? Grades? Courses taken? Something else?

5. *Practice-Based Ways to Assess Competence.* An approach currently implemented only in New Hampshire, which has only one law school, extends the diploma privilege only to some graduates of the law

school, and even then requires that candidates must take prescribed courses in substance and skills and complete a series of written exercises that are reviewed by the bar examiners. Similar proposals have been made to allow candidates to demonstrate competence through something like a Public Service Alternative Bar Exam that would measure competence in the ten core skills proposed in the MacCrate Report by having candidates work as lawyers in a court system supervised by law school clinical faculty.[9]

4. MORAL CHARACTER AND FITNESS TO PRACTICE

The third requirement for admission to the bar is demonstrating good moral character and fitness to practice law. Typically, this requirement is satisfied by a candidate filling out a lengthy statement regarding his or her past and providing a list of references. The law school from which the candidate graduated fills out a form indicating that the person has obtained a JD and disclosing whether the law school is aware of anything in the candidate's record that would render him or her unfit to practice law. The bar examiner in the state sends a form to each of the candidate's past employers as well as all of the candidate's listed references asking brief questions about whether the reference is aware of any reason why the candidate should not be admitted to practice.

The moral character questionnaire demands full disclosure, and applicants may be denied admission for failing to make full disclosure. Model Rule 8.1 prohibits applicants for admission to the bar from knowingly making a false statement of material fact or failing to disclose a fact necessary to correct a factual misapprehension, or knowingly failing to respond to a lawful demand for information from an admission or disciplinary authority. Some applicants to the bar find the requirement of full disclosure to be offensive, especially when the information not disclosed would not be disqualifying.

A second hurdle for many applicants has to do with which aspects of their past conduct may be grounds for the bar to determine they lack good moral character or fitness for the practice of law. Currently, the Code of Recommended Standards for Bar Examiners, adopted by the ABA, the National Conference of Bar Examiners, and the AALS, identify a number of relevant factors.

---

[9]   Kristin Booth Glen, *When and Where We Enter: Rethinking Admission to the Legal Profession*, 102 COLUM. L. REV. 1696, 1720–1722 (2002).

Moral Character and Fitness

Standard of Character and Fitness. A lawyer should be one whose record of conduct justifies the trust of clients, adversaries, courts, and others with respect to the professional duties owed to them. A record manifesting a significant deficiency in the honesty, trustworthiness, diligence, or reliability of an applicant may constitute a basis for denial of admission.

Relevant Conduct. The revelation or discovery of any of the following should be treated as cause for further inquiry before the bar examining authority decides whether the applicant possesses the character and fitness to practice law:

- unlawful conduct
- academic misconduct
- making of false statements, including omissions
- misconduct in employment
- acts involving dishonesty, fraud, deceit, or misrepresentation
- abuse of legal process
- neglect of financial responsibilities
- neglect of professional obligations
- violation of an order of a court
- evidence of mental or emotional instability
- evidence of drug or alcohol dependency
- denial of admission to the bar in another jurisdiction on character and fitness grounds
- disciplinary action by a lawyer disciplinary agency or other professional disciplinary agency of any jurisdiction[10]

What bar committees have found disqualifying over the years has varied, as the following examples suggest. As you consider the examples, attempt to develop your own definition of what constitutes good moral character and fitness to practice law and what conduct (if any) you consider disqualifying. Consider whether conduct is disqualifying because it predicts future behavior as a lawyer, because it creates an appearance to the public that the lawyer (or the bar generally) is not to be trusted, or for some other reason. Assume that in each case, the applicant took and passed the MPRE and the bar examination.

---

[10] http://www.ncbex.org/assets/media_files/Comp-Guide/CompGuide.pdf

5. CRIMINAL RECORD

PROBLEM 36–1

A was convicted of felony murder when his accomplice in a drug deal shot another man. A did not pull the trigger, but he had worked as a drug courier and dealer for five years from the age of 13 until he was arrested and imprisoned for the shooting at age 18. He served 18 years in prison. He was a model prisoner, completing college while incarcerated, and he married a woman with whom he corresponded while in prison. Upon release from prison, he worked for three years with a non-profit organization devoted to rehabilitating former drug offenders and prisoners. He then attended law school and graduated with a solid academic record and no reports of any misconduct. *In the Matter of Hamm*, 123 P.3d 652 (Ariz. 2005).

PROBLEM 36–2

B served 18 years in prison as a model prisoner for stabbing his girlfriend to death. His record prior to prison showed he had been arrested multiple times for domestic violence. After being released from prison, he worked in odd jobs in construction, landscaping, and for a moving company. While in law school, B's girlfriend called the police one night to complain that he threatened to hit her. The police report indicates that when the police went to B's apartment, the girlfriend said she had overreacted and declined to press charges.

PROBLEM 36–3

While in law school, C was arrested three times while engaged in protest activities. In the first case, the charges were dropped, in the second case C pleaded no contest and paid a $300 fine, and in the third case C was convicted upon a guilty plea and sentenced to 100 hours of community service. Should it matter what C was protesting? Would your assessment change depending on whether C was charged with trespass, resisting arrest, refusing to follow a police order to disperse a protest being conducted without a permit, assault, or something else?

6. ACADEMIC MISCONDUCT

PROBLEM 36–4

D, a third year law student, plagiarized a substantial portion of his law review note. When law review staffers spotted the plagiarism while cite-checking the note, the law review editor questioned D about the plagiarism. D originally denied plagiarism, but admitted it when the editor showed him the similarities between his note and several sources. D explained that he must have forgotten which of his research notes were his own writing and which were cut and pasted from other sources.

PROBLEM 36–5

E, a first-year law student, neglected to hand in a major assignment in the first-year legal research and writing course. When the professor informed E that he would fail the course because she had not received the paper, E claimed the professor had lost the paper. E complained to another professor that the legal writing professor had a personal grudge against him because E was an outspoken member of a student organization that had been highly critical of the school's hiring and admissions policies. Finally, the dean of students reached an agreement with E that, if E could show that a draft of the paper was on his computer, the school would give E a passing grade in the legal research and writing course. E initially claimed that his computer had crashed, but finally admitted that he had never written the paper because he felt overwhelmed by law school.

PROBLEM 36–6

A form letter used by the bar admissions committees in many states asks the following questions in seeking law school deans' certification of the character and fitness of their graduates. Consider, as you decide what kinds of information law schools provide to bar admissions committees, whether schools should report uncorroborated allegations of academic misconduct. "(1) Does the applicant's record raise questions regarding the applicant's character or indicate a lack of integrity or trustworthiness? (2) Has the applicant engaged in any behavior, whether or not it was made part of the applicant's record, that reflects unfavorably on his or her character or fitness to practice law? (3) Is there any additional information of which you are aware that might impact the Board's determination of this person's character and fitness?"

7. EMPLOYMENT OR FINANCIAL RECORD

PROBLEM 36–7

While a young writer for a national magazine, F fabricated dozens of articles before finally being caught and fired from his job. He enrolled in law school, graduated, and moved to New York, where he underwent psychotherapy and passed the New York bar exam, but withdrew his application for admission when he learned he would be denied on moral grounds. He moved to California and found a job as a clerk in a law firm. He passed the California bar exam and applied for admission. At an evidentiary hearing on his application, many witnesses, including his law professors and the California lawyers for whom he worked, described him as reformed, but some of his editors from his career as a journalist described him as manipulative. The hearing officer ruled for F. The state bar appealed to the California Supreme Court. How should the Court rule?[11]

PROBLEM 36–8

G graduated from law school at the age of 47. In law school and before, G accumulated $170,000 in student loans. In addition, G owes another $30,000 on four different credit cards. Many of his credit card debts are past due. G has been slow to produce all his credit card records for the bar admission committee, and he incorrectly told the committee that none of his credit card debts were past due. He also was delinquent in paying taxes in several different years. He blamed some of the problem on his ex-wife, who failed to pay taxes on her accounting business during some of the years in question, and some on his own misunderstandings about his obligations to pay payroll taxes on his house-painting business. He truthfully informed the committee that he had resolved his tax problems except a deficiency of $1,500 owed to the state and $350 to the IRS. *In re Application of Stewart*, 860 N.E.2d 729 (Ohio 2006).

8. MEMBERSHIP IN ORGANIZATIONS OR ADHERENCE TO IDEAS

PROBLEM 36–9

Schware was denied admission to the New Mexico bar because he had previously been a member of the Communist Party and had participated in several strikes in which strikers and those attempting to suppress the strikes committed acts of violence. Schware left the Party in 1940, served in the U.S. Army during WWII, and graduated from law school in 1953. *Schware v. Board of Bar Examiners*, 353 U.S. 232 (1957) (reversing denial of admission). Would your answer change if Schware were a member of Al Qaeda?

PROBLEM 36–10

Konigsberg and Anastaplo were denied admission to the California and Illinois bars, respectively, because each refused to state whether he was or had ever been a member of the Communist Party or any other organization advocating the violent overthrow of the United States government. Noting that past membership in the Communist Party was not alone grounds for denial of admission, each argued that refusal to answer questions about membership in the Party were likewise not grounds for denial. The U.S. Supreme Court disagreed. *Konigsberg v. State Bar of California*, 366 U.S. 36 (1961); *In re Anastaplo*, 366 U.S. 82 (1961). Anastaplo went on to a

---

[11] Maura Dolan, *Stephen Glass' Fragile Dream*, L.A. TIMES, July 4, 2012, A1. The California Supreme Court ruled unanimously that the candidate could not be admitted to the bar because he had engaged in a pattern of deceit and had failed to prove he had been sufficiently rehabilitated. Maura Dolan, *Stephen Glass, Ex-Journalist Who Fabricated Stories, Can't Be a Lawyer*, L.A. TIMES, Jan. 27, 2014.

distinguished academic career.[12] Would your change if they were members Al Qaeda?

PROBLEM 36–11

Hale was denied admission to the Illinois and Montana bars because he was a leader of a white supremacist organization. Hale ran the organization's web site, which made a variety of hateful statements about blacks, Jews, and "other mud races." The bar argued that Hale's views would lead to disciplinable conduct even if simply holding the views themselves is not a basis for denying admission. *Hale v. Committee of Character and Fitness of the Illinois Bar*, 723 N.E.2d 206 (1999) (denying review of Illinois Supreme Court's character and fitness committee decision), *cert. denied*, 530 U.S. 1261 (2000).[13]

9. MENTAL OR PHYSICAL HEALTH OR SUBSTANCE ABUSE

Most state bar admissions committees ask questions about mental health and drug and alcohol abuse. The ABA-approved Code identifies "evidence of mental or emotional instability" or "evidence of drug or alcohol dependency" as proper subjects of inquiry. Prior to the 1980s, most states did not inquire about mental health or substance abuse on bar admission applications. States then began to inquire broadly into applicants' mental health and substance abuse at any point in time, typically asking whether the applicant had "ever had" or "been treated for" mental illness or substance abuse. After the effective date of the Americans With Disabilities Act of 1990, which prohibits disability discrimination in employment and licensing, states narrowed their inquiries to focus on severe mental health issues, hospitalizations, or conditions that would currently interfere with the practice of law.[14] Consider these scenarios:

PROBLEM 36–12

You are the dean of students at a law school. H, a second year law student, seeks your advice on whether to seek treatment for her drinking. H has always had a solid academic and employment record, but she worries that her family history of alcoholism makes her at risk for it too. She has

---

[12] *See* George Anastaplo, *Lawyers, First Principles, and Contemporary Challenges: Explorations*, 19 N. ILL. L. REV. 353 (1999).

[13] Hale was later convicted of soliciting an undercover FBI agent to kill a federal judge who had ruled against Hale's organization in a trademark dispute over the name of the organization. United States v. Hale, 448 F.3d 971 (7th Cir. 2006). Does knowing this fact about Hale change your answer to the question of whether, in principle, a white supremacist should be denied admission to the bar? Why or why not?

[14] *See* John Bauer, *The Character of the Questions and the Fitness of the Process*, 49 U.C.L.A. L. REV. 93 (2001) (analyzing whether the open-ended inquiries into mental health violate the Americans With Disabilities Act).

noticed that she has begun drinking too much when she goes out with friends on Thursday, Friday and Saturday nights. She says she was treated for use of illegal narcotics when she was in high school and has not used drugs in the ten years since. When you point out that the bar admissions committee in your state asks about treatments for substance abuse within the past two years and that answering yes to the question about treatment requires the applicant to disclose *all* her medical, psychiatric, and substance abuse treatment records for her lifetime, H says she'll decline to seek treatment now and will try to quit drinking on her own. What advice should you give H?

PROBLEM 36–13

J has applied for admission to the bar and has disclosed that he was convicted eight years ago, during his senior year in college, of assault arising out of a fist-fight, and two years ago, during his first year in law school, of driving under the influence of alcohol. Explaining his criminal record, J says he suffers from bipolar disorder, and at the time of both incidents he had ceased taking medication which controls his symptoms. J's psychiatric records reveal that he was diagnosed with bipolar disorder as a teen and that every few years since then he has stopped taking medication because he felt the condition was under control and he hates the side effects of the medication. J's current psychiatrist reports that J still dislikes the side effects and remains resistant to the idea of taking medication for the rest of his life, although J does admit that he probably needs to. J did not disclose the bipolar disorder in answer to the application question inquiring whether the applicant "currently has a condition that would affect your ability to practice law." The admission committee decided to deny admission on the grounds that J cannot be trusted to take his medication and failed to disclose a condition that would affect his ability to practice law. You are a member of the state Supreme Court and have been presented with plausible arguments that the Americans with Disabilities Act (ADA), the federal statute that prohibits some forms of disability discrimination, does not make it illegal to deny a license to an applicant on these facts. Therefore, setting aside the question whether the ADA would prohibit denial of a license, how would you rule on J's appeal?

10. RETHINKING REQUIREMENTS FOR BAR ADMISSION

The three requirements for admission to the bar—obtaining a JD, passing the bar exam and MPRE, and demonstrating good moral character—are nearly universal among states, but each of them has been criticized. The moral character requirement has also been sharply criticized as biased, arbitrary, and ineffective in protecting clients.[15] Should states abandon the requirement of demonstrating good moral

---

[15] See Deborah L. Rhode, *Moral Character as a Professional Credential*, 94 YALE L.J. 491 (1984).

character, or at least sharply narrow the grounds for denial of admission? If they were to do so, should the bar devote the resources it now spends screening the moral character of applicants to more vigorous enforcement of the ethics rules? What other admissions requirements, if any, should states impose?

As noted in Chapter 33, New York will soon require that applicants for admission to the bar demonstrate that they have performed 50 hours of law-related pro bono work under the supervision of a law professor or a licensed attorney during law school, and a California State Bar task force has proposed a similar requirement.[16] Work in a law school clinic for which the student received academic credit satisfies the requirement. New York does not require lawyers already admitted to practice in New York, or those admitted elsewhere seeking admission in New York, to satisfy the pro bono requirement. What are the justifications for requiring applicants to the bar to perform pro bono work? Should one think of it as a way to demonstrate competence (as might be suggested by the rule allowing clinic work performed for academic credit) or is it a way to demonstrate moral character? Is there any justification for requiring pro bono work of applicants but not of current bar members? Is limiting the pro bono requirement to applicants justified by the administrative concern that it is easier to monitor and enforce compliance among applicants than it is among all lawyers admitted to practice in New York?

If the pro bono requirement is motivated by the concern that the bar exam does not sufficiently test skills and that an additional requirement is necessary to ensure competence, perhaps requiring 50 hours of pro bono is not enough. Should states require applicants for admission to the bar to have completed a clinic during law school, in order to demonstrate that the prospective lawyer has developed some level of proficiency in representing clients? Should states require applicants to have completed a certain number of courses teaching legal skills, such as interviewing, counseling, negotiation, drafting, trial practice, or appellate advocacy?

C. DISCIPLINE

Topic Overview

Lawyer discipline tends to focus on two kinds of transgressions: incompetence and poor moral character, both of which are grounds for discipline, just as they are grounds for denial of admission to the bar. Many of the same policy and legal issues arise in disciplining lawyers on these bases as arise in denying admission, although sometimes the bar will deny admission for conduct that likely would not be the basis of

---

[16] http://www.nycourts.gov/attorneys/probono/FAQsBarAdmission.pdf; http://www.calbar journal.com/October2012/TopHeadlines/TH2.aspx.

discipline and, occasionally, may impose at least mild discipline for conduct that would not prevent admission. This section examines the processes of bar discipline and the sanctions imposed when lawyers are found to have violated the standards.

Bar associations in every state exercise power, typically delegated by the courts or the legislature or both, to discipline lawyers, including by revoking their license to practice law. Bar disciplinary proceedings are quasi-criminal in nature and, therefore, must comply with the constitutional requirements that those charged be accorded due process of law. Due process includes notice of the charges, the opportunity to present and to confront evidence and witnesses and to cross-examine witnesses, and the right to make arguments. Lawyers may not be disciplined for invoking the constitutional privilege against self-incrimination.

The Model Rules and comparable state rules of professional conduct are the primary, but not exclusive, basis for professional discipline. Model Rule 8.4 defines professional misconduct to include "to attempt to violate the Rules of Professional Conduct, or knowingly assist or induce another to do so," as well as "a criminal act that reflects adversely on the lawyer's honesty, trustworthiness or fitness as a lawyer," "conduct involving dishonesty, fraud, deceit or misrepresentation," or conduct "prejudicial to the administration of justice," among other things.

Bar Discipline

Bar associations in every state exercise power to discipline lawyers. Possible discipline includes a public or private reprimand, temporary suspension, or permanent revocation of the license to practice law. The basis for discipline includes violation of the rules of professional conduct, criminal or civil conduct that casts doubt on the lawyer's honesty, trustworthiness, or fitness as a lawyer, or conduct prejudicial to the administration of justice. The state bar in each state administers the disciplinary system, which includes a mechanism for clients, lawyers, judges, or a member of the public to report on lawyer misconduct, a process for investigating such complaints, a formal hearing on the complaint at which the accused lawyer and the state bar (acting as a form of prosecutor) present evidence and argument to a hearing officer, and a process for appealing the hearing officer's findings and recommended discipline to the state high court.

Bar discipline ranges from a figurative slap on the wrist (such as a private reprimand that is placed in a file but not reported to the public) to various forms of public discipline, including a public reprimand, or temporary or permanent suspension of the license (disbarment). Bars do not have the authority to impose fines or to order lawyers to pay compensation to victims of wrongful conduct. Criminal prosecution and civil liability (such as for malpractice) are the only way to punish offenders or to secure compensation for victims. However, bar disciplinary bodies have sometimes negotiated settlements of disciplinary proceedings in which the lawyer(s) pay a fine or perform some form community or pro bono legal service as a condition of imposition of a lesser punishment than disbarment. For example President Bill Clinton agreed to a $25,000 fine and a five year suspension in lieu of disbarment as punishment for lying under oath about his sexual relationship with Monica Lewinsky. Alston & Bird and its client, DuPont company, settled a criminal investigation relating to concealment of documents in a suit over a contaminated fungicide by each paying $2.5 million to various Georgia law schools to endow a chair in professional ethics, $1 million to endow an annual symposium on legal ethics, and $250,000 to support work by the Georgia bar's commission on professionalism.[17]

Each year, bar disciplinary agencies receive approximately 120,000 complaints against lawyers. (There are almost 1.3 million lawyers in the U.S.) In 2011, states disciplined a total of about 6,000 lawyers.[18] Bar disciplinary authorities dismiss about 90 percent of complaints without investigation or explanation because the bar decides it lacks probable cause to pursue the matter or lacks jurisdiction over the conduct alleged. About four percent of complaints result in some sort of discipline, but either a public or a private reprimand is the only discipline imposed in most cases that are investigated. Less than one percent of investigated complaints result in disbarment. There is a wide variation among states in the frequency with which severe sanctions such as disbarment or a long suspension are imposed. In 2011, for example, in California (which had 175,572 lawyers), 19,197 complaints were received by the state bar disciplinary agency. 944 resulted in a public sanction. 273 lawyers were disbarred and 854 were suspended. In Florida (which had 83,558 lawyers), 9,829 complaints were received. 380 resulted in public sanctions. 103 lawyers were disbarred and 142 were suspended. In Arkansas (which had 8,654 lawyers), 735 complaints were filed; 54 lawyers were publicly sanctioned, 11 were disbarred and 3 were suspended.[19]

If 90 percent of complaints about lawyers are never investigated, and only 4 percent of complaints result in discipline of any sort, we should wonder why. Data are lacking about reasons for the disparity between the

---

[17] Milo Geyelin, *DuPont and Atlanta Firm Agree to Pay Nearly 13 Million in Benlate Matter,* WALL ST. J., Jan. 4, 1999, at A18.

[18] American Bar Association Center for Professional Responsibility Standing Committee on Professional Discipline, 2011 Survey on Lawyer Discipline Systems, chart II (May 2013) (reporting 2011 data).

[19] *Id.; see generally* DEBORAH L. RHODE, IN THE INTERESTS OF JUSTICE: REFORMING THE LEGAL PROFESSION 159 (2000) (discussing the bar discipline system).

number of complaints filed and the number of investigations and sanctions. However, a leading scholar on the history and sociology of bar discipline has shown a long history of bar reluctance to discipline lawyers, ineptitude and indifference in the management of the disciplinary process, apparently inexplicable failures to discipline lawyers for egregious violations of fundamental ethics rules (such as stealing money from clients), and ineffectual efforts at reform.[20]

The most common grounds for discipline are neglect of client matters, misappropriation of client funds, and failure to communicate with clients. The most common complaint against lawyers concerns the fees charged, but lawyers are rarely disciplined for their fees. Another major controversy over bar discipline has to do with which lawyers are disciplined. Solo practitioners and lawyers in very small firms account for the overwhelming majority of discipline cases, which may reflect a larger number of egregious ethics rules violations as well as the limited resources given to disciplinary agencies to investigate and prove the kinds of violations that may occur at larger law offices.

Trying to understand why lawyers engage in ethical misconduct is a difficult task. Professor Richard Abel wrote two lengthy books on New York and California lawyer discipline and read hundreds of discipline cases during the research.[21] In the cases he chose for close study, the lawyers protested their innocence to the end, even in cases in which it was clear that they had transgressed fundamental rules of ethics and criminal law. They regarded themselves as victims of an unfair system, not as criminals. Among the experienced lawyers he profiled, "[e]thical misconduct is *learned* behavior, it is not the product of ignorance,"[22] and the misconduct reflected "greed more than need. None of the lawyers suffered the kind of poverty we associate with street crime. None was a substance abuser." However, among all lawyers disciplined, substance abuse is often a factor. Abel also found in his sample that the misconduct was habitual; it was not simply a momentary lapse of judgment brought on by personal life stress.[23]

1. COMPETENCE

As we saw above, Model Rule 1.1 requires that lawyers practice competently and Model Rule 1.3 requires that a lawyer "act with reasonable diligence and promptness in representing a client." In theory,

---

[20] *See* RICHARD L. ABEL, LAWYERS ON TRIAL: UNDERSTANDING ETHICAL MISCONDUCT 6–60 (2010) (recounting the history of California State Bar disciplinary system and recurring criticisms of it).

[21] *Id.*; RICHARD L. ABEL, LAWYERS IN THE DOCK: LEARNING FROM ATTORNEY DISCIPLINARY PROCEEDINGS (2008).

[22] ABEL, LAWYERS ON TRIAL at 461.

[23] *Id.* at 461–464.

therefore, incompetence of any sort is a basis for discipline. The problem, of course, is defining what level of competence is minimally necessary. Lawyers, being human, make mistakes, and it is difficult to determine which mistakes should be the basis for deciding a lawyer is so incompetent as to deserve discipline. Comment [1] to Model Rule 1.1 recognizes the difficulty of determining competence; it points out that one should consider "the relative complexity and specialized nature of the matter, the lawyer's general experience, the lawyer's training and experience in the field in question, the preparation and study the lawyer is able to give the matter and whether it is feasible to refer the matter to, or associate or consult with, a lawyer of established competence in the field in question." The comment recognizes that in some cases, "the required proficiency is that of a general practitioner," but that in others "[e]xpertise in a particular field of law may be required."

What circumstances are relevant to the imposition of discipline on the grounds of incompetence? For example, should youth and inexperience of a lawyer excuse or mitigate a failure? Should a crushing workload? Should a lawyer's personal problems (such as the lawyer's physical illness, a death or serious illness in the family, or relationship trauma)? Should substance abuse? Should mental illness, including depression, bipolar disorder, and so on? Moreover, consider the purposes of bar discipline, perhaps by analogy to the purposes of criminal punishment. Should bar discipline aspire primarily to protect consumers by removing lawyers from practice? Should it aim for rehabilitation? Should bar disciplinary rules aim to protect the bar's reputation by expressing moral condemnation of certain behavior? Are some of these purposes of discipline more relevant to bar discipline aimed at incompetence as opposed to bar discipline aimed at moral fitness? We consider discipline based on lack of good character and moral fitness next.

2. CHARACTER

Model Rule 8.4 defines the conduct that may lead to discipline on character grounds quite broadly. Not only does it include violation of any of the Model Rules, it also includes any criminal act "that reflects adversely on the lawyer's honesty, trustworthiness or fitness as a lawyer," and "conduct involving dishonesty, fraud, deceit or misrepresentation," or "prejudicial to the administration of justice." Comment [2] to Rule 8.4 notes that, although lawyers are "personally answerable to the entire criminal law, a lawyer should be professionally answerable only for offenses that indicate lack of those characteristics relevant to law practice." The comment suggests that some matters of "personal morality, such as adultery and comparable offenses," are not relevant to law practice. The relevance line can be difficult to draw and may depend on one's perspective.

President Bill Clinton was sued for sexual harassment by Paula Jones. At a pretrial deposition, Jones's lawyers asked Clinton about other incidents of inappropriate sexual conduct with employees or staffers and, in particular, whether he and Monica Lewinsky, a White House intern, had ever engaged in sexual relations. Clinton denied under oath that he had sexual relations with Ms. Lewinsky. The federal judge found that Clinton's statement was false and referred the matter to the Arkansas Supreme Court Committee on Professional conduct. A panel of the committee found that Clinton's statements violated Arkansas Rules 8.4(c) and 8.4(d), which are identical to Model Rules 8.4(c) and (d) and prohibit conduct "involving dishonesty, fraud, deceit or misrepresentation" and conduct "prejudicial to the administration of justice." (The panel recommended disbarment, but Clinton reached an agreement with the Arkansas Bar in which he admitted knowingly making false statements that were prejudicial to the administration of justice, paid a $25,000 fine, and acceded to suspension of his law license for five years.) Given the extraordinary publicity that attached to the allegations of his sexual relationships, some thought that perjury to spare his wife and daughter the humiliation of a public admission of an extramarital affair may have technically been a crime but was nevertheless an act of decency and discretion, since refusing to answer a question about his sexual relationships was not an option. Others thought they showed a pattern of duplicity.

Similar differences of opinion might arise about other forms of misconduct that might variously be described as evidencing disrespect for the law or as reflecting poor behavior unrelated to fitness to practice law. One could devise a long list of examples of conduct that might or might not reflect on a lawyer's fitness to practice law. Consider, for example, these examples of misconduct:

(1) A lawyer accumulated a large numbers of unpaid parking tickets or repeated traffic tickets for driving in excess of the speed limit.

(2) A lawyer failed to pay her personal income taxes, saying that she was extraordinarily busy at tax time and that she thought her spouse had handled the taxes that year.

(3) A lawyer is convicted of assault of his spouse or intimate partner.

(4) A lawyer is convicted of assault arising out of a fist-fight in a bar or in the parking lot of a sporting event.

(5) A lawyer filed a personal bankruptcy that is later determined to have been done for the purposes of avoiding paying child support to her former spouse after a long and exceedingly bitter divorce proceeding.

(6)   A lawyer is convicted of growing marijuana in the back yard of his home.

(7)   A lawyer pleads guilty to leaving the scene of an accident in which he accidentally drove his car into a bicyclist, fatally injuring the cyclist. The lawyer said he panicked.

Many of the same kinds of conduct that would be grounds for denial of admission are theoretically grounds for discipline as well. In practice, however, as a leading expert on the profession observed, there is a double standard; the bar may deny admission for the same types of conduct for which it would not discipline lawyers.[24] Is there a basis in principle for holding applicants to the bar to a higher standard of character than practicing lawyers?

An interesting question confronts bar disciplinary authorities who believe that lawyers who engaged in fraudulent or other conduct that is clearly grounds for discipline will face criminal charges. As a practical matter, if a lawyer is a target of a criminal investigation, the bar likely will defer action until the resolution of the criminal proceeding. If the lawyer is convicted of a crime, revocation of his law license may be accomplished with a minimal expenditure of bar resources, as the lawyer may resign or be disbarred summarily.

3.   ENFORCEMENT

Bar discipline relies on two sources to learn about lawyer misconduct: reporting by other lawyers and client complaints. Of these, reporting by other lawyers is more likely to prompt investigation. Only a small fraction of disciplinary complaints come from lawyers, but these are more likely than complaints from clients or nonlawyers to be investigated.[25] Ethics rules in many states follow Model Rule 8.3 in requiring lawyers to report misconduct, deeming it an essential aspect of self-regulation of the legal profession. The comments to Rule 8.3 take a slightly ambivalent position about whether lawyers are obligated to report all misconduct they witness. On the one hand, Comment [1] insists that "[a]n apparently isolated violation may indicate a pattern of misconduct that only a disciplinary investigation can uncover," and that "[r]eporting a violation is especially important where the victim is unlikely to uncover the offense." On the other, Comment [3] notes that "[i]f a lawyer were obliged to report every violation of the Rules, the failure to report any violation would itself be a professional offense," so

---

[24] Deborah L. Rhode, *Moral Character as a Professional Credential*, 94 YALE L.J. 491 (1984).

[25] Studies estimate ten percent of complaints come from lawyers; one study found that only four percent of California State Bar disciplinary complaints are made by lawyers. *See* RICHARD L. ABEL, LAWYERS ON TRIAL: UNDERSTANDING ETHICAL MISCONDUCT 466 (2010).

the obligation to report is limited "to those offenses that a self-regulating profession must vigorously endeavor to prevent."

Not every state makes reporting mandatory. California and Massachusetts, for example, do not require lawyers to report other lawyers' misconduct. What legitimate (or illegitimate) reasons might prompt a lawyer to decline to report another lawyer's misconduct?

Bar disciplinary proceedings are governed by constitutional due process standards. The lawyer accused of a disciplinary violation is entitled to notice of the charges against him, the right to present evidence and argument, and the right to confront and cross-examine evidence and witnesses against him.

4.   DISCIPLINE OF LAW FIRMS

Bar disciplinary agencies have almost always targeted individual lawyers, and have seldom prosecuted law firms either directly, for breaching the ethics rules binding on firms, or vicariously, holding the firm accountable for the actions of its employees or partners. As one scholar noted, the focus on individuals probably results from the disciplinary system's tie to licensing (issued to individuals) and to the development of bar discipline during the long era in which most lawyers practiced solo. This scholar called for discipline of law firms, both because many ethical lapses are encouraged by firm policy (which would be an appropriate case for vicarious liability) or are committed jointly by a number of lawyers in the firm, each of whom will attempt to shift responsibility onto others, such that it would be unfair to pin on one or two people the blame for misconduct committed or encouraged by many.[26] Some states (including New York and New Jersey) do extend to law firms the same prohibitions on unethical conduct that apply to individual lawyers. Thus far, efforts to amend the Model Rules to do so have failed.

Many have called for law firms to adopt some form of peer review that has long been the norm in medicine.[27] In hospitals, for example, doctors examine the records of morbidity and mortality for the entire hospital or a segment of it in order to identify problems and fix them prospectively, and some law firms have begun to implement such programs.[28] Law firms already review partners and associates at least annually to set compensation. Peer review to ensure ethics compliance in a law firm might consist of interviewing partners, associates, and clients, as well as examining compliance with firm policies on conflicts checks,

---

[26]   Ted Schneyer, *Professional Discipline for Law Firms?* 77 CORNELL L. REV. 1 (1992).

[27]   *See, e.g.,* RICHARD L. ABEL, LAWYERS IN THE DOCK: LEARNING FROM ATTORNEY DISCIPLINARY PROCEEDINGS 525 (2008)

[28]   Susan Saab Fortney, *Are Law Firm Partners Islands Unto Themselves? An Empirical Study of Law Firm Peer Review and Culture*, 10 GEO. J. LEGAL ETHICS 271 (1996).

content of engagement letters, and the appropriate use of opinion letters.[29]

Others have argued that law firm management should play a more substantial role in ensuring that a firm's lawyers comply with ethical obligations. Management systems can detect common violations, such as neglecting client matters, misappropriating client funds, and engaging in conflicts of interest.[30] Many law firms have adopted such compliance systems as an element of their strategies for managing risk.[31]

NOTES ON BAR DISCIPLINE

1. ***Who Should the Bar Target for Discipline?*** How should bar disciplinary authorities identify priorities, given scarce resources? Should they focus on egregious cases? Easy to prove cases? Cases indicating corruption, as opposed to incompetence? (There is strong evidence that state bars already do the latter, as recent studies of large numbers of New York and California discipline cases show that the overwhelming majority of cases involve unethical conduct rather than simple incompetence.[32])

2. ***Peer Review?*** Why have law firms been slow to adopt a peer review system that is common in medicine? Would it be a good idea to require it?

3. ***Discipline of Public Officials.*** However challenging it is to draw the line between personal and professional misconduct in the case of lawyers who are private citizens, the challenges are often greater when lawyers serve in public office. In each of the following cases, decide whether bar discipline is appropriate, and if so, what sanction to impose:

(a) Marc Dann served 17 months as Attorney General of Ohio before resigning in 2008. Prior to his 2008 resignation, he announced that he had an extramarital affair with a 28-year-old staffer. In 2009, he was convicted of using campaign funds for personal use and of falsifying financial statements, both misdemeanors. In 2004, Dann was reprimanded for being insufficiently prepared in a matter.[33]

(b) Richard Nixon resigned from the California Bar after he resigned the presidency in 1974. The New York bar refused to

---

[29] *Id.*

[30] Theodore Schneyer, *On Further Reflection: How "Professional Self-Regulation" Should Provide Compliance with Broad Ethical Duties of law Firm Management*, 53 ARIZ. L. REV. 577 (2011); Elizabeth Chambliss & David B. Wilkins, *The Emerging Role of Ethics Advisors, General Counsel, and Other Compliance Specialists in Large Law Firms* , 44 ARIZ. L. REV. 559 (2002).

[31] Elizabeth Chambliss, *New Sources of Managerial Authority in Law Firms*, 22 GEO. J. LEGAL ETHICS 63 (2009).

[32] *See* RICHARD L. ABEL, LAWYERS ON TRIAL: UNDERSTANDING ETHICAL MISCONDUCT (2010) (study of California lawyer discipline); RICHARD L. ABEL, LAWYERS IN THE DOCK: LEARNING FROM ATTORNEY DISCIPLINARY PROCEEDINGS (2008) (study of New York lawyer discipline).

[33] *See* Leigh Jones, *Former Ohio AG Loses Law License for Six Months*, NAT'L L. J., Nov. 20, 2012.

accept his resignation unless he admitted that he could not defend himself against a charge of obstruction of justice. Nixon declined and so New York proceeded to disbar him; he did not contest the proceeding and was disbarred in New York in 1976.

(c) Eliot Spitzer, while Attorney General and, later, Governor of New York, traveled to Washington, D.C. to have sex with prostitutes and took some efforts to disguise the purposes of his visits to the city and to hide the transfer of money to pay the prostitutes. Frequenting a prostitute is a misdemeanor in the District of Columbia and in New York, and the effort to hide the payments is a federal crime punishable by five years in prison.[34]

(d) D, an elected official, pleads no contest to soliciting a sexual relationship with another man in an airport restroom. D insists he entered the no contest plea only to avoid a media frenzy and that in fact he was asking for the person in the next stall to pass him toilet paper.

PROBLEM 36–14

A law firm of with 25 lawyers has outsourced some routine legal work to India. The law firm advised the client in its boilerplate retainer agreement that it might to outsource work to India, and the client's CEO did not object when he signed the agreement. The law firm told the client that outsourcing would save the client money. The legal work proves to be seriously inadequate, resulting in the failure of the transaction on which the legal work was performed and litigation against the client. The client complains to the law firm, which insists that the fault was the shoddy work done in India and poor supervision by the legal process outsourcing (LPO) company which the firm had hired to handle the outsourcing. The client reports the law firm to the state bar for discipline. What should the state bar consider in deciding on discipline?

D. MALPRACTICE

Lawyers' mistakes and ethical failings jeopardize clients' and third-parties' rights in many different contexts. For example, the lawyer who represented the car accident victim David Spaulding should have requested the medical evidence possessed by the defendants in *Spaulding v. Zimmerman* before settling the case, because then he would have known of the aortal aneurysm that David's own doctor failed to diagnose. Lawyers who fail to conduct adequate legal research commit malpractice if they file a suit or negotiate a contract that turns out to be unsupported by law, and therefore fails, when a viable theory would have been available. Lawyers who fail to keep track of deadlines commit malpractice

---

[34] Sewell Chan, *Could Spitzer Lose His Law License?* N.Y. TIMES, Mar. 13, 2008.

when they let the statute of limitations run out on a claim. The list goes on and on. Here we consider the remedies available to compensate clients for the harms caused by lawyers. Thus far we have seen that a lawyer's failing may be grounds for bar discipline of the lawyer, which will harm the lawyer but will not rectify the harm to the client. In egregious cases, a lawyer may be criminally prosecuted, but convicting the lawyer does not compensate the client for its losses. The lawyer's failing may be grounds for setting aside the results of the representation (such as vacating a conviction based on ineffective assistance of counsel), but even that does not fully compensate the client. In this segment we look briefly at one area of law that aims to compensate clients and some third parties for the harm done by lawyers: tort law causes of action for malpractice and breach of fiduciary duty.

Malpractice and Breach of Fiduciary Duty

Malpractice is a specialized application of the tort of negligence. A lawyer owes a duty of care to clients. When the lawyer's conduct falls below the standard of care required of lawyers in the jurisdiction, and the conduct is the but for and proximate cause of damage to a client, the client can sue the lawyer for damages.[35] A violation of the Model Rules is not by itself proof of malpractice, but it is often considered by courts to be evidence of a violation of the standard of care.

A breach of fiduciary duty claim punishes self-interested behavior of one who, as a fiduciary, should act in the interest of someone else. A lawyer is a fiduciary for his or her clients. A lawyer who steals money from a client or who has an egregious conflict of interest breaches a fiduciary duty.

One of the challenges facing the plaintiff in a legal malpractice case is proving that the lawyer's negligence caused the harm. For example, a lawyer who neglects to file a complaint before the expiration of the statute of limitations clearly commits malpractice. But whether the plaintiff lost money because of it would depend on whether the plaintiff would ultimately have succeeded in the litigation, which can be difficult to prove. The challenges of proving that malpractice harmed the client may be even greater in transactional matters where the value of the transaction the lawyer actually negotiated and the value of the one the disgruntled client-plaintiff wishes the lawyer had negotiated may be difficult to discern.

A negligence theory of malpractice is not the only basis for holding lawyers civilly liable to clients for damages caused by misconduct. Lawyers are sometimes sued for breach of fiduciary duty, which is a different claim. A fiduciary duty prohibits self-interested behavior by one

---

[35] Restatement of Law Governing Lawyers § 48.

who, as a fiduciary, should act in the interest of someone else. A lawyer who wrongful uses money from a client account or who has an egregious conflict of interest violates a fiduciary duty. A lawyer who acts as an escrow agent, holding money in a transaction between a client and a third party, can be liable to both the client and the third party if the lawyer absconds with or loses the money.

The Model Rules explicitly disclaim any intent to define competence for purposes of malpractice liability. Comment [20] on the Scope of the Model Rules states: "Violation of a Rule should not itself give rise to a cause of action against a lawyer nor should it create any presumption in such a case that a legal duty has been breached. The Rules are designed to provide guidance to lawyers and to provide a structure for regulating conduct through disciplinary agencies. They are not designed to be a basis for civil liability." However, the same Comment also recognizes that "since the Rules do establish standards of conduct by lawyers, a lawyer's violation of a Rule may be evidence of breach of the applicable standard of conduct."

Whether breach of a disciplinary rule constitutes malpractice is generally a matter of common sense. A lawyer who violates Rule 7.3 by soliciting a prospective client in person at the scene of an accident but who provides excellent representation to the improperly solicited client has not committed malpractice even though she violated a disciplinary rule. However, a lawyer who fails to advise a client about an important change in the law relevant to a transaction on which the lawyer is advising the client probably violates Rules 1.1 and 1.3 and commits malpractice if the legal change adversely affects the transaction and the client would and could have altered the transaction so as to avoid the problem.

Which standard should courts use in judging a lawyer's conduct: the standard of a general practitioner, or the standard of a specialist? Should it matter whether the professional is in a geographic area where there are many specialists or in a remote area where there are none? Or does the nationwide availability of online research and telephonic communication mean that any professional can easily find the expertise necessary? This is an issue that arises too in medicine: should a doctor treating a patient for a highly specialized condition be judged by the standard of care applicable to a specialist or the generalist, and the standard in that specific geographic area, or the state, or the nation? In legal malpractice actions, courts tend to hold lawyers to a statewide standard of care on the theory that lawyers are regulated at the state level and can obtain expertise by research. Moreover, because plaintiffs must prove the existence of the standard of care through expert testimony of one with expertise in the relevant community, requiring a plaintiff to prove the standard of care in a locality would require him to find a lawyer familiar with the local standards, which can be difficult in a small and closely-knit legal community where lawyers would be reluctant to testify against each other.

A lawyer's tort liability for misfeasance or malfeasance is not limited to clients. When a lawyer hurts a third party while representing a client, the third party may have a cause of action for damages against the lawyer when it is clear that the lawyer's services were intended to protect or to benefit the third party and where liability to the third party will not undermine the lawyer's relationship with the client. The Restatement of the Law Governing Lawyers § 51 identifies a number of circumstances when third parties may recover from the lawyer for harms. One is where the nonclient has been invited to rely on the lawyer's services and has reasonably relied (as where a lawyer provides a legal opinion about a transaction). Another is where the lawyer knows that a client intends that one of the primary objectives of the representation will be to benefit the nonclient (as where a lawyer drafts a will). A third is where the lawyer provides legal services to a client who has certain legal obligations to a third party related to the representation (as where the client is a trustee).

There are other circumstances where a lawyer's breach of duty may harm a third party but the third party may have no remedy for the harm. For example, in *Spaulding v. Zimmerman,* the defendants' lawyer may have made a mistake in failing to seek the clients' permission to inform David of his condition, but then as now, that decision was not actionable malpractice or the basis for professional discipline because the opposing counsel owed David no duty to provide the information. To take another example, when a lawyer for a corporation breaches the ethical duty of Model Rule 1.13(f) by failing to give an *Upjohn* warning to a corporate employee, the employee may mistakenly believe that what he or she tells the lawyer is confidential. The information the employee reveals is covered by the corporation's attorney-client privilege and the duty of confidentiality the lawyer owes the corporation, but the corporation is free to waive the privilege and use the information in whatever way it chooses. The corporation could provide the information to the police or prosecutors or could fire the employee. If the employee reveals compromising information that leads to the employee's criminal conviction or civil judgment, the employee has been harmed by the lawyer's wrongful conduct but likely has no effective remedy against the lawyer or anyone else.

Damages for malpractice are the same as tort damages generally. The plaintiff may recover economic damages proximately caused by the lawyer's breach of duty, as well as noneconomic damages (for emotional distress), especially where economic damages do not accurately reflect the plaintiff's harm. Punitive damages are available when the lawyer's conduct was intentional or reckless, or outrageous or in wanton disregard of the client's rights. *See* Restatement (Third) of the Law Governing Lawyers § 53.

Malpractice insurers may be an important source of regulation of those lawyers who obtain insurance. Insurers may require lawyers to adhere to certain office policies with respect to calendars (to avoid missing statutes of limitations and filing deadlines), engagement and termination of representation letters (to avoid giving clients the impression that the lawyer is handling a matter when the lawyer is not), and conflicts of interest (to avoid disqualification motions).

Many lawyers carry malpractice insurance, although some studies suggest that most do not. One study of a sample of 12,000 California lawyers found that in 1988 only 17 percent carried malpractice insurance.[36] For lawyers in small and not terribly profitable practices, malpractice insurance premiums may seem unduly expensive; the lawyers may conclude that the risk of liability is low and that disgruntled clients would be reluctant to sue because the lawyers have too few assets from which to collect a judgment. Uncollectible malpractice judgments present a regulatory problem for the bar because clients harmed by lawyer malpractice will receive no compensation, which removes the incentive to pursue unethical lawyers. Oregon is the only state that compels lawyers to obtain malpractice insurance, and many state bars have strenuously resisted requiring malpractice insurance, although a few other states require lawyers to disclose to clients whether they have malpractice insurance. Many states decline to require malpractice insurance because few carriers offer it and premiums can be quite high. Oregon has created a scheme that does not depend on private insurance.

NOTES ON MALPRACTICE

1. ***Should the Bar Do More to Ensure That Clients Are Compensated for Lawyer Mistakes and Misdeeds?*** What, if anything, should state bar associations do to ensure recovery for clients harmed by malpractice by uninsured lawyers? Recall from Chapter 32 on unauthorized practice that some in the organized bar have claimed that prohibitions on nonlawyers providing legal services are justified by the asserted fact that only lawyers carry malpractice insurance. If a significant number of lawyers do not, does that weaken this argument in favor of the lawyers' monopoly?

2. ***Should the Bar Encourage the Filing of More Complaints?*** If some failings in the malpractice and disciplinary process are the result of too few complaints by lawyers and judges, who are considered (at least by the bar) as the most reliable complainants, what could be done to encourage more reporting of unethical conduct?

---

[36] *See* RICHARD L. ABEL, LAWYERS ON TRIAL: UNDERSTANDING ETHICAL MISCONDUCT 468 (2010).

3. *The Relationship Between Discipline and Malpractice in Protecting Clients.* In allocating scarce resources, should bar disciplinary authorities consider the likelihood that a client or third party harmed by lawyer misconduct will bring and prevail in a malpractice action?

E. SUMMARY

This chapter examined the almost universal requirements for admission to the bar: obtaining a JD degree, passing the bar examination and the MPRE, and demonstrating good moral character. As to each of these three, the chapter considered the most commonly asserted justifications for the requirement—ensuring the competence and trustworthiness of lawyers and protecting their reputation—and also considered whether the requirement adequately serves the justification and whether alternatives might be preferable on the grounds of efficacy or fairness. Many have called for reconsideration of requirements for admission to practice to increase focus on practical skills rather than knowledge. The chapter also examined bar discipline. We identified the grounds on which lawyers can be disciplined, the principal grounds on which lawyers are in fact disciplined, the disciplinary process, and the penalties imposed. Bar discipline is designed to serve the goals of prevention and deterrence, not compensation of clients or third parties who are harmed by lawyer misfeasance or malfeasance. We considered whether the bar disciplinary system adequately protects clients and whether alternative mechanisms might better ensure competence and trustworthiness. Finally, the chapter briefly covered the law of attorney malpractice and breach of fiduciary duty, which are the primary legal theories under which clients or third parties may recover from lawyers who cause them harm. In all but one state, lawyers are not required to carry malpractice insurance and many lawyers do not.

CHAPTER 37

DIVERSITY OF THE LEGAL PROFESSION

■ ■ ■

A. INTRODUCTION TO THE DIVERSITY OF THE LEGAL PROFESSION

Although the American legal profession today includes people of almost every identity group or demographic characteristic in the national adult population, for much of American history the organized bar excluded all but white, Protestant, native-born men from the practice of law. While explicit exclusionary practices are now illegal, the profession remains less diverse than the general population. According to the ABA 2012 report on lawyer demographics (see Chapter 2), among the 1.2 million lawyers in America in 2005, men outnumbered women by 7 to 3. In 2010, 88 percent of lawyers identified as non-Hispanic white, 4.8% as non-Hispanic black, 3.7% as Hispanic, and 3.4% as non-Hispanic Asian-Pacific American. In contrast, according to 2010 Census data, 72% of the population identifies as white (by race), 83% identify as non-Hispanic (by ethnicity), and 50.8% of the population is female.[1] Of course, everyone fits into more than one demographic group, and the clarity we gain by examining the data on identity groups separately comes at the cost of obscuring the ways in which the intersection of multiple identities influences the experience of lawyers.

The demographics of the legal profession may change, however, as today's law students begin their careers. In 2012, 47% of the 146,288 J.D. students were female and 24.5% identified as a racial or ethnic minority.

> ### Topic Overview and Chapter Organization
>
> After surveying the data on the demographic composition of the legal profession with respect to race, ethnicity, gender, sexual orientation, and disabilities, this chapter considers why some groups are underrepresented and whether diversity is beneficial for lawyers, clients, and the public. We then examine laws and policies that prohibit discrimination and promote diversity.

---

[1] *See* http://www.census.gov/2010census/data/; http://www.census.gov/prod/cen2010/briefs/c2010br-03.pdf.

B. RACE AND ETHNICITY

The data on the legal profession noted above show underrepresentation of some groups but reveal nothing about the distribution of identity groups within the profession. Data on particular practice settings show a starker pattern of underrepresentation in some settings and overrepresentation in others. One annual survey of the racial and ethnic diversity of law firms is conducted by the *American Lawyer* magazine and published under the title "Diversity Scorecard." It asks the nation's largest law firms to report the percentage of minority attorneys at the firm. "Minorities" is typically defined to include both race and ethnicity, and as such includes what are typically considered racial groups (e.g., blacks, Native Hawai'ians), nonracial ethnicities (e.g., Latinos), and traits that may include multiple races and ethnicities (e.g., Asians). The *American Lawyer* "Diversity Scorecard" for 2012 reported that minorities constituted 13.6 percent of attorneys at large firms in 2011, compared to 13.9 percent in 2010. *American Lawyer* attributed the drop to two "tweaks" in the survey methodology. First, in collecting data for 2011, the survey for the first time asked firms to calculate full-time equivalent (FTE) numbers for the entire calendar year rather than a head-count. The FTE calculation means that part-time attorneys are prorated in the statistics. According to the magazine, this change "also means that the number of minority associates may have dropped at firms where the new class of associates starts in September, because those incoming associates now count for a quarter of what they once did. And this in turn may have caused some firms to perform less well under our new methodology because an incoming class of associates is often the most diverse group of attorneys in a firm." The other reason for the slight decrease in minority lawyers is that more firms responded to the survey in 2011 (233 as compared to 194 in 2010), and many of the new respondent firms have fewer minorities.

Although the overall percentage of minority attorneys at the large firms surveyed by *American Lawyer* dipped slightly, as did the percentage of minority partners (6.9 percent in 2011, compared to 7.0 in 2010), firms reported that minority partner promotions rose in 2011, increasing to 14.7 percent of all promotions from 14.4 percent in 2010. In addition, 16.4 percent of all lateral hires were minorities in 2011, compared to 11.4 percent in 2010.

NALP (an organization formerly the National Association for Law Placement but now known just as NALP) also releases an annual report on the representation of people of color in the legal profession. It includes data on a larger range of employers than the *American Lawyer* because it includes small and mid-size firms. An excerpt of its report on 2011 data follows.

WOMEN AND MINORITIES IN LAW FIRMS
NALP Bulletin, January 2012

While the representation of minorities as a whole among associates increased in 2011 after sliding in 2010, representation of women among associates declined a bit again for the second year in a row. Aggregate statistics about the representation of women and minority lawyers at law firms do not tell the whole story, however. For instance, among all employers listed in the 2011–2012 *NALP Directory of Legal Employers*, just 6.56% of partners were minorities and 2.04% of partners were minority women, and yet many offices report no minority partners at all. And in fact, although the most recent information suggests that the temporary setback for minority representation among associates as a whole has been reversed—rising from 19.53% in 2010 to 19.90% in 2011 after declining from 19.67% in 2009—a more detailed look reveals that that the bounce-back can be attributed entirely to an increase in Asian associates. Finally, the representation of minorities by specific race and ethnicity varies considerably by size of law firm and geography.

Among partners overall, Asians are somewhat more prevalent than either Black or Hispanic partners. (The term *minorities* as used here includes lawyers identified as Black, Hispanic, Native American, Asian, Native Hawaiian/Pacific Islander, and multi-racial. The very few Native American, Native Hawaiian, and multi-racial lawyers are not reported out separately.) Differences are evident, however, when comparing firms of differing sizes. For example, the presence of Black and Hispanic partners generally increases with firm size, whereas Asian partners are most prevalent at smaller and the largest firms. Percentages of female minority partners are generally highest in the largest firms, although for Asian women percentages at the smallest and largest firms are nearly identical.

At the city level, the presence of Black partners is highest in Atlanta, followed by Richmond and Detroit, both of which are much smaller than Atlanta in terms of partner counts. The presence of Black female partners exceeds 1% in just nine cities: Atlanta, Detroit, Ft. Lauderdale/West Palm Beach, Miami, Nashville, Raleigh, Tampa, Washington, DC, and Wilmington. Except for Atlanta, Washington, DC, and Miami, total partner counts in these cities are a few hundred or less. Black partners account for less than 0.5% of partners in Grand Rapids, Minneapolis, Orlando, Orange County, CA, and San Diego. Over half of minority partners in Austin, Miami, Minneapolis, Orlando, Phoenix, and Tampa are Hispanic. In each of these cities except Orlando, the presence of female Hispanic partners is also at or above average. Conversely, in 7 of 44 cities, fewer than 0.5% of partners are Hispanic. Asian partners are most common in the Los Angeles and Orange County, CA, areas, and in the San Francisco and San Jose areas. Asian women are most frequent in these same cities.

Among associates, Asians account for almost half of all minority associates at the national level, and in the largest firms. Comparing these 2011 figures with those from 2010 shows that the increase in minority representation from 19.53% in 2010 to 19.90% in 2011 is attributable to an increase among Asians, whose representation increased from 9.39% to 9.65%. The percentage of Black associates actually declined a bit, from 4.36% in 2010 to 4.29% in 2011, compared to 4.66% in 2009. Representation of Hispanics was essentially unchanged, at 3.83% in 2011, compared with 3.81% in 2010—and still lower than the 3.89% in 2009.

As is the case with partners, cities vary a great deal on these measures. For example, Black associates are most common in Atlanta, followed by Indianapolis, Charlotte, and Nashville, all cities with far fewer associates than Atlanta. In each of these cities Blacks account for over half of minority associates. The percentage of Black female associates was also highest in these cities, along with Washington, DC. Every city reported at least some Black associates and Black female associates. The pattern for Hispanic associates is similar to that at the partner level, with representation highest by far in Miami, followed by Austin, Ft. Lauderdale/West Palm Beach, and Orlando. Percentage representation was less than 1% in a few cities. The leading cities for Asian associates—both overall and for women specifically—are San Jose, followed by San Francisco, the Los Angeles and Orange County areas, New York City, and Seattle. Every city reported at least some Asian associates.

NOTES ON RACIAL AND ETHNIC DEMOGRAPHICS OF THE PROFESSION

1. ***Contrasting Large Law Firms with Other Practice Settings.*** Contrast the demographic data on the race and ethnicity of all American lawyers in the Introduction to this chapter, and in the table in Chapter 2, with the data in the NALP report and the *American Lawyer* "Diversity Scorecard" above. Notice that racial and ethnic minorities are even more underrepresented in large law firms than in the profession at large. Recall, too, Professor Reynoso's study of Latino lawyers in Los Angeles (discussed in Chapter 23), in which he found that Latinos are underrepresented in solo practice but overrepresented in small firm practice. What patterns do you observe in the data on the representation of racial and ethnic groups in the profession? What do you think might account for those patterns?

2. ***Selection Bias.*** Data on race and ethnicity usually rely on self-identification by survey respondents. The *American Lawyer* "Diversity Scorecard" is compiled from responses by law firms, which may in turn

depend on what the person who fills out the form surmises about the racial or ethnic identity of lawyers in the firm.

3.   ***Gaps in Data.*** The data reported above, drawn from the ABA, the U.S. Census, *American Lawyer*, and NALP do not report every racial or ethnic group that might be of interest. For example, they do not report information on some ethnicities or national origin groups, such as Arabs or Africans, and they do not disaggregate some racial, ethnic, or national origin groups (such as southeast Asians, or people with origins in the Indian subcontinent, or European or Middle-Eastern minority groups such as Armenians). What information do you wish these surveys provided? Are there categories that you think are missing?

C. GENDER AND SEXUAL ORIENTATION

Topic Overview

Data show that although women have constituted between 40 and 50 percent of law students since the 1980s, they are more likely than men to leave the profession, and they are underrepresented within law firm partnerships and overrepresented in public interest and nonprofit organizations. Women who work full-time as lawyers earn approximately 13% less than similarly situated male lawyers. This section explores the nature and reasons for the gendered career patterns. This section also explores the rapid increase in the number of lawyers who identify as LGBT and the possible reasons for it.

---

1. GENDER

Women constituted only 3 percent of law school classes in 1947 and in 1972, but they began entering law school in significant numbers in the mid-1970s. Women constituted about 40 percent of all law students beginning in the mid-1980s, and reached parity with men for the first time in the class that entered law school in 1993. Women have earned approximately 50 percent of JDs since the early 2000s.[2] Women are more likely to leave law practice and "their exits begin early and accelerate over time."[3] Women are underrepresented in positions of power and elite compensation, including in equity partnerships in large law firms, as general counsel of Fortune 500 companies, and in top positions in government. For example, although women have constituted somewhere between 40% and 45% of first-year associates at large law firms since the 1990s, they are only 19% of partners in law firms in the NALP Directory of Legal Employers, 16% of equity partners and 6% of managing

---

[2]   Joyce S. Sterling & Nancy Reichman, *Navigating the Gap: Reflections on 20 Years Researching Gender Disparities in the Legal Profession*, 8 FLA. INT'L L. REV. 515 (2013).

[3]   Id. at 516.

partners.[4] In 2012, only 52.3 percent of women surveyed in the *After the JD* (AJD) study who were working in law firms were partners, compared with 68.8 percent of male respondents working in law firms. Among those who were partners, 65.5 percent of men were equity partners, compared with 53 percent of women.[5]

These gendered career patterns do not simply reflect the experience of women who first entered the profession in the 1970s and 1980s. Rather, the pattern of women and men pursuing different careers continues with younger lawyers. As shown in the first wave of the AJD study, which surveyed a nationwide sample of nearly 4000 lawyers who first joined the bar in 2000 about their experience two or three years into practice, women were much better represented in government and public interest jobs than in private practice. For example, women were 42% of federal government lawyers and 53% of state and local government lawyers. They were overrepresented in public interest and nonprofit organizations, where they constitute nearly three-quarters of lawyers. About a third of solo practitioners in this cohort were women.[6]

All three waves of the AJD study also found that women are paid less than their male peers in all legal labor markets for all jobs across the country. The first wave of the AJD study found that after only two or three years in practice, the average full-time woman lawyer earned 5.2% less than the average full-time man. After seven years of practice, the difference increased to approximately 13% for full-time lawyers.[7] The third wave, which reports data gathered in 2012 and therefore describes lawyers twelve years into practice, found the pay gap had grown even more. Female respondents working full time earned 80 percent of the pay reported by their male counterparts. The most dramatic gap occurred between women and men working in business in a capacity other than as a lawyer; women made 67 percent of the pay reported by men.[8] Scholars

---

[4] *See* id. at 517; *NALP, Press Release: Representation of Women Among Associates Continues to Fall, Even as Minority Associates Make Gains* (Dec. 13, 2012); *NALP, Women and Minorities at Law Firms by Race and Ethnicity—An Update* (April 2013).

[5] "10 Interesting Stats from the After the JD Survey," ABA NEWS ARCHIVES, available at http://www.americanbar.org/news/abanews/aba-news-archives/2014/02/10_interesting_stats. html.

[6] Gita Z. Wilder, *Women in the Profession: Findings from the First Wave of the After the JD Study* (NALP 2007); AFTER THE JD III: THIRD RESULTS FROM A NATIONAL STUDY OF LEGAL CAREERS (2014).

[7] RONIT DINOVITZER, BRYANT GARTH, RICHARD SANDER, JOYCE STERLING & GITA WILDER, AFTER THE JD: THE FIRST RESULTS OF A NATIONAL STUDY OF LEGAL CAREERS (2004) (After the JD Wave I); RONIT DINOVITZER, ROBERT L. NELSON, GABRIELLE PLICKERT, REBECCA SANDEFUR & JOYCE STERLING, AFTER THE JD: SECOND RESULTS FROM A NATIONAL STUDY OF LEGAL CAREERS 67 (2009) (After the JD Wave II); Ronit Dinovitzer, Nancy Reichman & Joyce Sterling, *The Differential Valuation of Women's Work: A New Look at the Gender Gap in Lawyer's Incomes*, 88 SOC. FORCES 819 (2009).

[8] "10 Interesting Stats from the After the JD Survey," ABA News Archives, available at http://www.americanbar.org/news/abanews/aba-news-archives/2014/02/10_interesting_stats. html.

who analyzed the first two waves of AJD data determined that only 15% of the salary gap could be explained by different work experience, work settings, or other endowments of the lawyers, and attributed 75% of the gap to women being rewarded less than men for their endowments, although the reasons for the different valuation were unexplained.[9]

WOMEN IN THE LEGAL PROFESSION

Fiona Kay and Elizabeth Gorman
4 American Review of Law & Social Science 299 (2008)*

To what extent does sex segregation exist within the legal profession? Overall, women are somewhat more likely than men to be found in less remunerative and prestigious practice settings. In 2000, women were more likely than men to be found in solo practice (38% versus 35%), government (10% versus 7%), education (3% versus 1%), and legal aid or public defender offices (1.7% versus 0.7%). Women and men were about equally likely to work for corporations as in-house counsel (9% versus 8%). Female lawyers were less likely than male lawyers to work in law firms of 2 to 50 lawyers (27% versus 36%), equally likely to work in firms of 51 to 100 lawyers (4% of both women and men), and more likely than men to hold jobs in firms of over 100 lawyers—the best-paying and most prestigious category of firms (16.2% versus 13.6%).

In the *After the J.D.* sample of more than 4500 new lawyers surveyed two to three years after their bar passage in 2000, the proportions of female and male lawyers are similar across all firm size categories (2007). [Later data show that beginning in 2010 and through 2012, the percentage of women law firm associates fell slightly, from 45.4% in 2010 to 45.05% in 2012.]

Numerous studies suggest that in recent years overt discrimination has receded, while more subtle and structural discrimination persists (1995, 1996). However, some research finds pregnant female litigators still face overt discrimination (2001), and women are often excluded from mentorship (2005) and opportunities to work on challenging files (1995; 2003, 2005; 2006; 1995).

In addition, sexual harassment continues (2001, 1998, 2001). 26% of male lawyers in private practice reported observing sexual harassment of female lawyers, while 66% of female lawyers reported observing sexual harassment of female colleagues (1998). Furthermore, nearly 50% of the female lawyers working in corporate or public agency settings reported

---

[9] Dinovitzer, Reichman & Sterling, *Differential Valuation of Women's Work*, 88 SOC. FORCES at 836.

* [Eds: This article is a survey of the literature. We have omitted the author names in the citations in parentheses, but have retained the dates so that readers may consider whether the passage of time since the publication of the cited works may affect whether similar findings would be made if the studies were conducted today.]

having experienced or observed one or more of five types of sexual harassment by male superiors, colleagues, or clients during the two years prior to the survey (1998).

How do women lawyers fare when it comes to promotion and upward mobility? Women are clearly underrepresented in partnership positions. In 2007, women represented 45% of associates but only 18.3% of partners in large U.S. law firms. Women's presence among firm partners has increased over time—they represented only 12.3% of partners in 1993—but the pace of change has been slow.

What explains women's generally lower rates of attaining high-ranking legal positions? [W]omen's law school performance is similar to or better than that of men. Moreover, among Chicago lawyers who entered practice after 1970, neither class rank nor law school prestige influenced the probability of holding a senior position in either a firm or nonfirm setting, net of years of experience (2000), so neither factor could explain the gender gap. Some studies find that women work fewer hours than men (2000, 2001, 1999), but others find no gender difference in working hours (1998, 2005). The impact of hours worked on promotion prospects is also unclear. In the Chicago sample, hours worked per week were positively associated with being a law firm partner (2000). However, hours worked were negatively associated with senior positions in nonfirm settings. Women are more likely to take parental leaves (1998, 2004). However, because the number of fathers who take parental leaves is too small to produce meaningful results, it is impossible to disentangle the human capital effects of parental leaves from their likely reinforcement of decision-makers' gender biases.

An alternative possibility is that women lack the social networks and cultural dispositions that are crucial for forming and maintaining relationships with clients and other lawyers. Indeed, Kay & Hagan (1998) found, in a 1990 survey, that women scored lower than men on measures of both social capital (professional activities, association memberships, client origination, and representation of corporate clients) and cultural capital (disposition to share firm values versus valuing goals outside the firm). Inclusion of the social and cultural capital measures explained approximately one-third of the impact of gender on lawyers' partnership promotion chances, net of marital and parental status, hours and weeks worked, leaves taken, and urban location; a significant gender gap remained. In a second survey of the same sample six years later (in 1996), association memberships and representing institutional clients continued to explain part of the gender gap in the probability of partnership (1999).

[R]esearch suggests that firms hold men and women to different standards in evaluating their skills, social networks, and cultural dispositions. Thus, among University of Michigan graduates, Noonan &

Corcoran (2004) observed a stronger positive effect of law school grades on promotion for women than for men. Similarly, hours worked per week, disposition toward firm culture, number of professional activities, and client origination improved women's partnership prospects but had no effects for men (1998). This did not mean that women were better rewarded than men; men with low scores on social and cultural attributes still had better partnership chances than did women with exceptionally high scores. Thus, Kay & Hagan's results suggest that women had to demonstrate their affinity with firm culture and their ability to form valuable social ties, whereas men's capacities in these areas were taken for granted. In addition, children have a positive impact on men's promotion chances but none on women's (2000, 1998, 2004), suggesting that firms interpret parenthood as signaling stability and work commitment for men but not for women.

Studies suggest that gender bias plays a lesser role when firm decision-makers are female, when they are influenced by female clients, and when they have worked in environments where female leadership is institutionalized. Thus, Gorman's (2006) study of 1450 promotion events in 503 large firms showed that firms are more likely to promote women when they already have a larger proportion of women among existing partners. Beckman & Phillips (2005), who analyzed longitudinal data on 200 large law firms, observed that the number of female partners grew faster in firms that represent corporate clients with women in leadership positions. In a longitudinal study of Silicon Valley firms, Phillips (2005) found that new firms were quicker to select a first female partner when their founders had left parent firms with more female partners or where women had served as partners for longer periods of time.

Studies of lawyers' earnings generally report that women earn substantially less than men. Women's earnings are, on average, 52% to 64% of men's earnings, and the magnitude of that gap declines yet remains resiliently significant when law school status, academic distinction, labor supply, practice setting, specialization, hours worked, family situation, and measures of social capital (e.g., family background and social networks) are controlled (1995, 1990, 2003, 1997, 1995b, 1993, 2001, 1993).

[M]ost studies reveal that women and men are surprisingly similar in their levels of job satisfaction (1989; 2007; 1999, 2005; 1999; 1996). Several explanations have been offered for the paradox of why women have equal job satisfaction despite inferior jobs in terms of pay, levels of authority, and mobility prospects. The most common explanation centers on differential values. The argument is that women and men have different values and therefore care about different things in their jobs; women's work satisfaction is determined more by subjective, or intrinsic, work characteristics, for example, perceived autonomy and variety, than by objective, or extrinsic, features such as salary and promotions. Women may use different reference groups in assessing their satisfaction, comparing themselves only with other women or with women who stay at home. As a result, women may approach their work lives with lower expectations or a lower sense of personal entitlement, making satisfaction easier to achieve.

The assumption of reduced career commitment among women lawyers who are also parents has been challenged empirically. Wallace (2004) analyzed interview data with lawyers who were mothers and a large-scale survey of lawyers in Calgary, Alberta. Wallace found that women lawyers who are mothers exhibited higher levels of career commitment than other women practicing law, controlling for hours worked, alternative work arrangements, leaves taken, law experience, earnings, and work settings. Wallace suggested a selection process may be at work whereby less-committed women may have left law to raise their family or pursue other career avenues.

Research reveals that women are overrepresented in the exodus from law (1989, 1989a, 1992). [Studies based on more recent data on the attrition of women from law practice also found that women were more likely than men to leave law practice at all career stages, and to leave law firms to practice in nonprofits, small firms, and businesses. For example, 40% of women who graduated from law school in the early 1980s had left law by the early 2000s, primarily to begin new careers in business or nonprofits. One study noted that the youngest women lawyers in the sample had generally not left law practice to raise children full-time, but had instead left large firms to move to different types of law practice settings.*]

NOTES ON GENDER AND THE PROFESSION

1. **What Has Changed?** Examine the gender differences in the legal profession as summarized by Kay and Gorman. Which do you think persist today and which do you think have changed or will change shortly? Why?

2. **Have Women Changed the Practice of Law?** Chapter 4 explored the question whether women might bring a different sensibility than men do to the practice of law. Kay and Gorman refer to this hypothesis (which was advanced by many feminist legal scholars and lawyers in the 1980s). Do you find the hypothesis plausible?

3. **What Is the Outsider Experience?** In contrast to racial and ethnic minorities, women are more likely to have close connections to people of wealth and power. Yet the rates of attrition from large law firms remain

---

* [Eds. These studies are summarized in Sterling & Reichman, *Navigating the Gap*, 8 FLA. INT'L L. REV. at 13.]

comparably high for women and for people of color. What causes attrition? Is attrition a problem? For whom?

2. GENDER AND SEXUAL IDENTITY

Few aspects of the legal profession have changed as rapidly and recently as the treatment of lawyers who are openly lesbian, gay, bisexual or transgendered. Reflecting broad and rapid change in social attitudes toward LGBT people, lawyers have become aware of the presence of gender and sexual minorities in the profession. According to the Human Rights Campaign's 2013 Corporate Equality Index, for example, 99% of the respondents to its survey of Fortune 1000 corporations prohibit discrimination in employment on the basis of sexual orientation (up from 62% in 2002), 89% offer domestic partner health care benefits, and 84% prohibit discrimination on the basis of gender identity (up from 3% in 2002). Employment discrimination on the basis of sexual orientation remains legal in most states, however. Therefore, to the extent that employment policies of legal employers have changed, they have changed because of evolving social norms, not because of legal requirement.

There is significant geographic variation in the number of lawyers who publicly identify themselves as LGBT, which suggests that lawyers may feel more comfortable being out of the closet in some areas than others. Moreover, the number of lawyers who identify as LGBT in the NALP study excerpted below is less than the estimated number of LGBT people in the population as a whole, which suggests either that a disproportionate number of LGBT people choose not to become lawyers or that they are reluctant to identify themselves once they do enter the profession. Surveys report varying levels of discrimination in the general population. A 2008 study revealed that 37 percent of lesbians and gays reported having experienced workplace harassment and 12 percent had been fired because of their sexual orientation. In 2011, the largest survey to date of transgender persons found that 90 percent had experienced workplace harassment or had taken steps to avoid it and 47 percent had experienced discrimination on the basis of gender status in hiring, promotion, or termination of employment.[10]

MOST FIRMS COLLECT LGBT LAWYER INFORMATION, LGBT REPRESENTATION STEADY
NALP Bulletin, December 2011

The overall percentage of openly gay, lesbian, bisexual, and transgender (LGBT) lawyers reported in the NALP Directory of Legal

---

[10] Jennifer C. Pizer, et al., *Evidence of Persistent and Pervasive Workplace Discrimination Against LGBT People: The Need for Federal Legislation Prohibiting Discrimination and Providing for Equal Employment Benefits*, 45 LOY. L.A. L. REV. 715 (2012).

Employers (NDLE) in 2011 remained unchanged compared to 2010. A small increase in the percentage for associates was offset by a decrease at the partner level. Almost half (49%) of offices reported at least one LGBT lawyer.

The numbers remain relatively small, and because the total number of lawyers included in this analysis is somewhat smaller compared with 2010, the overall count of 2,087 LGBT lawyers is lower than it was in 2010. Nonetheless, the numbers have grown. In the 2002–2003 NDLE, the number of openly gay lawyers reported was just over 1,100, less than 1% of the total lawyers represented. Last year in 2010, those numbers stood at 2,137 and 1.88%. The 2,087 openly LGBT lawyers reported in the 2011–2012 NDLE also account for 1.88% of the total lawyers represented.

The presence of LGBT lawyers continues to be highest among associates, at 2.43%, and is up a bit from the figure of 2.35% reported in 2010. Openly LGBT associates are also better represented at large law firms, with firms of 701+ lawyers reporting 2.90% openly LGBT associates. Similarly, openly LGBT partners are best represented at the nation's largest firms, with firms of 701+ lawyers reporting 2.05% openly LGBT partners, compared with 1.44% among partners overall. An increase in openly LGBT partners in firms of 100 or fewer lawyers from 0.63% in 2009 to 1.17% in 2010 was notable last year. Although the current figure of 1.13% is a small decrease, the increase from 2009 has been largely sustained for two years.

Perhaps not surprisingly, there are wide geographic disparities in these numbers, and in fact about 60% of the reported openly LGBT lawyers are accounted for by just four cities: New York City, Washington, DC, Los Angeles, and San Francisco. The percentage of openly LGBT lawyers in these cities is correspondingly higher—almost 3% overall (and 5% in San Francisco specifically) compared with the 1.88% nationwide figure. In these same four cities, the percentage of openly LGBT summer associates is also higher, about 3.4% compared with 2.75% nationwide.

It is also the case that the percentage of offices reporting LGBT counts has remained at about 88% for the past three years, and is lower than the 92% that reported this information in 2007. This change may reflect more deliberate use of the "unknown" and "not collected" reporting options in the directory's demographic grid. Since 2006, employers have been required to fill out all portions of the grid with a number, which can be zero, or with either NC or UNK if the information was not collected or is unknown. However, the default entry is zero and must be actively changed to reflect "not collected" or "unknown." Thus, reported counts of zero do not unambiguously mean zero, and it may be the case that the prevalence of "unknown" or "not collected" is better reported rather than actually higher.

Nonetheless, it is clear that the percentage of LGBT lawy
two most recent years is higher than ever before. NALP
collecting demographic information on LGBT lawyers since 199
that time, the number of firms that give their LGBT la
opportunity to self-identify has risen to almost 90%. This year, a
offices/firms reporting counts, almost half reported at least or
LGBT lawyer and 13% of offices reporting a summer 2011 prog
reporting demographics reported at least one openly LGBT summer
associate. And, based on the figures for summer associates, the numbers
appear poised to increase, particularly at the largest firms.

NOTES ON THE DEMOGRAPHICS OF LGBT LAWYERS

1. **What Accounts for the Patterns?** The studies reported above
identify growth and geographic variation in the number of LGBT lawyers.
There are no studies of attrition comparable to the well-documented attrition
of women and racial minorities. What do you think are the major issues with
respect to equality for LGBT lawyers?

2. **Disaggregating the Group.** Legal and policy discussions with
respect to identity traits tend to identify categories (e.g., Black, LGBT,
Jewish) and treat them as monolithic, overlooking the variations within the
group and the intersections among different identities. To some extent, the
studies excerpted and described in this chapter and in Chapter 4 fall into this
pattern. To what extent do you think the experiences of lawyers vary within
these groups and when one considers intersections among them?

D. LAWYERS WITH DISABILITIES

In contrast to the abundant data on the experiences of racial and
ethnic minorities in the legal profession, much less is known about the
experiences of people with disabilities.[11] We do not even know precisely
how many people with disabilities are lawyers or law students. The ABA
reported in 2009 that only 3 states collected information on lawyers with
disabilities, and a 2011 NALP survey found that 18 percent of offices
surveyed did not collect data on lawyers with disabilities. Moreover,
disabilities are probably underreported in the profession. Of the
approximately 110,000 lawyers across 1,243 law offices for whom
disability information was reported in the 2009–2010 *NALP Directory of
Legal Employers*, just 255, or 0.23%, were identified as having a
disability. In contrast, a 2011 ABA survey of its members found 4.5%
reported having a disability—down from 6.87% in 2010; 6.76% in 2009;
6.69% in 2008; and 7.18% in 2007.[12] The Bureau of Labor Statistics

---

[11] A helpful resource is Adeen Postar, *Selective Bibliography Relating to Law Students and Lawyers With Disabilities*, 19 AM. U. J. GENDER SOC. POL'Y & L. 1237 (2011).

[12] ABA Commission on Disability Rights, Goal III Report 7 (ABA 2012). The report did not indicate why the number of lawyers reported having a disability abruptly fell by a third in one

reported that in 2011, 2.6% of persons employed in the legal profession had a disability.

Even less is known about the types of disabilities that lawyers have, or whether there is a pattern in where lawyers with disabilities work. According to NALP, the number of lawyers who are reported as having disabilities does not seem to vary in any systematic way either by firm size or by associate/partner status, but NALP did not report data showing the types of disabilities.[13] Although some data suggest that lawyers with disabilities are more likely to work in government, public interest, and small firm settings, anecdotal evidence suggests that lawyers with a variety of conditions work in a broad range of jobs in the profession. Lawyers with disabilities have reached the pinnacles of challenge and prestige in the profession, including positions as federal and state appellate judges, general counsel for organizations, U.S. Supreme Court law clerks, and equity partners in all forms of private practice.[14] One study of lawyers with hearing impairments found they are "large firm litigators, prosecutors, public interest lawyers, transactional/tax lawyers, solo practitioners, government lawyers, public defenders, small firm general practitioners, in-house counsel, law professors, and judges."[15]

NOTES ON THE DEMOGRAPHICS OF LAWYERS WITH DISABILITIES

1. ***Are Disabilities Under-Reported?*** The NALP study found a very small number of summer associates reported having disabilities, far less than one would predict given the number of people with reported disabilities in the profession and in law schools. Why do you suppose law students are so hesitant to reveal they have disabilities during a summer job?

2. ***Definitions of Disability.*** Although disability is a technical term of art in any statute that regulates the treatment of people with disabilities, in colloquial usage its meaning may vary and may have changed over time as some conditions (e.g., mood disorders, autism-spectrum conditions) have become better understood, more common, or more culturally salient. To what extent does an absence of consensus on what it means to have a disability affect both what the data show about the experience of lawyers with disabilities and policies that might address their underrepresentation in the profession?

---

year. Because this is a survey of ABA members (not lawyers generally), and the survey methodology is not reported, it is difficult to assess the reliability of the data.

[13] NALP Bulletin, Dec. 2009, *available at* http://www.nalp.org/dec09disabled.

[14] *See, e.g.,* Second National Conference on the Employment of Lawyers With Disabilities (ABA 2009).

[15] John F. Stanton, *Breaking the Sound Barrier: How the Americans with Disabilities Act and Technology Have Enabled Deaf Lawyers to Succeed*, 45 VAL. U. L. REV. 1185 (2011).

E. UNDERSTANDING THE REASONS FOR THE DEMOGRAPHICS

A number of scholars have attempted to explain why some people are underrepresented in law as compared to the general population or, more specifically, as compared to their representation in law schools. This section explores the literature and other sources analyzing the reasons why the legal profession does not represent the diversity of identity groups in American society.

1. WHY ARE SOME RACES AND ETHNICITIES UNDERREPRESENTED IN THE PROFESSION?

EXPERIENCING DISCRIMINATION: RACE AND RETENTION IN AMERICA'S LARGEST LAW FIRMS

Monique R. Payne-Pikus, John Hagan, Robert L. Nelson
44 Law & Society Review 553 (2010)

Even though women and minorities now enter America's largest law firms in growing numbers, relatively few are retained through the first decade of practice to join these firms as partners. Women today are roughly equal to men among entering associates in large firms, but they constitute only about 17 percent of partners. African and Hispanic Americans each form about 5 percent of entering associates, but neither group forms more than 1 percent of partners. So neither women nor minorities are well integrated into America's largest and most elite law firms. White males still make up more than 80 percent of the partners in these "white shoe" firms. We know more about the slightly longer-term experiences of women than about the more recent experiences of minorities, but the experiences in large law firms of women and minorities bear notable similarities and can help us understand the fate of both groups as institutionally predictable.

Becker's human capital theory is an important academic account of resistance to both women and minority lawyers.[*] The emphasis of Becker's theory is on the efficient development of human capital. His gender theory is grounded in the assumption that women lawyers' capitalization is compromised by a split in their specialized commitments to the spheres of work and family. Women are thus assumed to invest less and to be less committed to their legal careers because they also invest heavily in their families.

Recent research finds that although women lawyers fear the consequences of having children for their occupational careers, they

---

[*]   [Eds: See GARY S. BECKER, HUMAN CAPITAL (1964), and Gary S. Becker, *Human Capital, Effort, and the Sexual Division of Labor*, 3 J. LAB. ECON. 533–58 (1985).]

nonetheless still are opting in to the practice of law in numbers similar to men. Neither research on women generally nor research on women lawyers specifically indicates that women differ significantly from men in their long-term commitment to their careers. Young women leave law firms in greater numbers than men and they do not yet attain partnerships in equal proportion to men, but these numbers are still changing and there is little evidence that gender differences in outcomes result from the free and efficient choices of women to opt out of their investments and commitments to the legal profession.

Racial and ethnic minorities have only recently gained entrance in notable numbers to large firms, and their lower levels of advancement to partnership relative to entry suggest that today they experience an even more skeptical reception than women. To explain this, Beckerian human capital theory substitutes an emphasis on racial differences in legal learning for the emphasis on gender differences in family/work specialization. Thus in this human capital race theory of law firms, hiring preferences linked to affirmative action and resulting lowered requirements of academic achievement replace personal family preferences as the root causal force. Human capital theory asserts that as a result of affirmative action policies young minority lawyers who are hired by large U.S. law firms arrive with a human capital intellectual deficit.

Like the response to specialization decisions of young women, lower law school grades of minority law students entering firm practice are thought to be portentous. Human capital theory assumes that partners will socialize and mentor only those associates they presume to be most intellectually gifted.

Partner contact and mentoring is increasingly recognized as a key process and source of dissatisfaction and departures from law firms, especially for African American lawyers. In contrast with human capital theory, an institutional discrimination theory suggests that disparity in social contacts with partners and mentoring experiences with partners, rather than disparities in merit and performance, can explain the "paradox" of high rates of minority lawyers' dissatisfaction and departures after being hired into large law firms. If demonstrated to occur, this discrimination in partner contact and mentoring net of merit and performance would make racial/ethnic differences in attrition easily understandable. Given the reduced institutional investment of firms in human capital transmission to minority associates through mentoring, and given a subsequent declining return to minority associates (i.e., on their prior investment in the reputational capital of the law degrees they have already received) in the form of new skills, it would simply be institutionally predictable rather than paradoxical for these minority associates to leave firms in search of better career opportunities.

Partner contact and mentoring is a key way of transmitting knowledge and demonstrating the firm's investment and long-term valuing of recruited workers. Partner mentorship further provides sponsorship and visibility and may thereby improve prospects for advancement. Partner mentors can also provide access to challenging work assignments that can demonstrate the potential of an individual and provide opportunities for growth. Partner mentors may also help mentees if they are treated unfairly and provide emotional support in times of stress as well as feelings of acceptance, friendship, and support.

Research confirms the concern that racial/ethnic minorities are less likely to be mentored. This lack of mentoring is not because of a lack of interest on the part of minorities. Almost half of the women lawyers studied by Simpson (1996) reported that they did not receive the training and challenging cases needed to develop their legal skills. Similarly a study by the American Bar Association of minority women lawyers found that 67.3 percent desired more and better mentoring by senior attorneys (Chanen 2006:36).

Wilkins and Gulati (1996) conducted an in-depth qualitative study of African American associates in large law firms. They maintain that racial/ethnic differences in treatment may be systemic within large law firms. They argue that while the "superstar" associates of any ethnicity will receive mentoring and training, racial/ethnic differences emerge when the "average" associate, the bulk of the cohort, is considered. They maintain that "average" whites are more likely to be mentored then "average" African Americans. Once African Americans realize they are not receiving the training needed to become partner, they decide to leave earlier in the process, while they still have some market value. The authors go on to argue that firms can do this because there are a limited number of partnerships available and so they are not adversely affected if preference is given to mediocre whites instead of African Americans because the entire group cannot become partner.

In contrast, Sander (2006) argues that African American associates are less likely to be mentored because of their differences in human capital. If Sander's human capital-based argument is accurate, then one would expect mentoring and training to matter less in explaining disparities in retention outcomes once "merit" is controlled for. If Wilkins and Gulati (1996) and institutional discrimination theory [are] correct, one would expect mentoring to continue to impact attrition even when "merit" is controlled for.

It is this debate between stereotype and institutional discrimination that we address in our analyses. We find, using the same data Sander considered, that institutional discrimination is a better predictor of minority attrition.

Cross-tabulations of the race/ethnicity of associates with key variables indicate that white associates consistently differ from minority group associates in large firms. Thus the reports of law school grade point averages (GPA) confirm the influence of affirmative action based racial/ethnic hiring preferences emphasized in the human capital merit performance theory. While approximately half of white associates (49.1 percent) in large firms report average marks between 3.5 and 4.0, about one fourth of African American (23.3 percent) and less than one-third (28.6 percent) of Hispanic associates report receiving these top-tier grades. This difference is especially noteworthy given the finding that minorities are more likely to attend top 20 law schools (60.0 percent of African Americans and 57.1 percent of Hispanics vs. 38.5 percent of whites), which on average give higher grades. However, it is still unclear what role these law school credentials play in lawyer retention and satisfaction.

More than half of the white associates in large firms report joining partners for meals (54.4 percent), while just more than one-quarter of African American (26.7 percent) but more than half of the Hispanic associates (57.1 percent) do so. Once more, less than half of the white associates (47.3 percent) desire more and/or better mentoring by partners, compared to more than two-thirds of African American (70.0 percent) and Hispanic (71.4 percent) associates. Both theories predict resulting disparities in outcomes such as plans to leave the firms and work satisfaction. So it is perhaps unsurprising that about one-fourth of white associates (23.0 percent) plan to leave in the next year, while in contrast half of African American (50.0 percent) and Hispanic (53.6 percent) associates are so inclined.

Several measures of in-firm merit and performance reveal much smaller differences than are reflected in law school grades between groups. White associates in large firms score slightly higher than African American associates and about the same as Hispanic associates on a four-level measure of taking leadership on legal matters versus doing routine legal work. Of course, this could reflect differences in work assignments rather than initiative. Meanwhile, African American (41.688) and Hispanic (42.825) associates score slightly higher than white associates (40.796) in hours billed per week. This could, in part, be due to the large number of minority lawyers in the four major cities, where lawyers work more hours on average. There is a notable difference in perceptions of discrimination in these large firms, with African Americans and Hispanics [reporting more discrimination and] whites [reporting the least]. Finally, African American associates score lowest on a 17-item scale of work satisfaction, while Hispanic associates report higher satisfaction than African American associates but lower satisfaction than white associates.

Sander (2006) [argued] that the lower law school grades of minority associates can account for what he regards as a racial paradox: namely, that minority associates plan to leave law firms soon after they are recruited into them. His reasoning is that lower law school grades are a merit-based predictor of poorer performance in early law firm careers and that this performance difference leads to minority associates leaving these firms. Yet Sander does not take the next step of demonstrating that there is a relationship between lower law school grades or performance in early law firm careers and plans to leave firms, or that such relationships can account for the more frequent "paradoxical" reports of African American and Hispanic compared with white associates' plans to leave these firms. [The authors of this study argue that the data show that African American and Hispanic law firm associates are more dissatisfied with their work *because* they believe they are not mentored adequately and do not have access to the best work, and that is why they are more likely than white associates to leave law firms.]

Prior research in a variety of subfields has reported a gradient in African and Hispanic American experiences of discrimination, with African American experiences being more acute in practice and perception. Similarly, although our research finds that both African and Hispanic American associates are more likely than others to plan to leave the large firms into which they are recruited, this disparity is stronger for African than for Hispanic American associates; and while African American associates also are significantly more likely than others to express work dissatisfaction in large law firms, this is not so clearly true of Hispanic associates. In general, the pattern of our results is more consistently predictable for young African than Hispanic American lawyers.

While the burden of effort to integrate American law firms has focused on recruitment of new associates into large firms, our research suggests that problems are not confined to recruitment policies but rather extend to the practices of partners with regard to minority lawyers once they are employed. Affirmative action mandates with regard to partner contact and mentoring of minority associates may be essential to achieve an effective racial integration of the upper reaches of the legal profession.

NOTES ON PAYNE-PICUS, HAGAN & NELSON

1. **What Explains Attrition?** What are the various factors that are suggested to account for the attrition of minority lawyers from law firms and other practice settings? Which seem most plausible to you and why? To what extent are the experiences of some races and ethnicities likely to be different from those of others?

2. **The Racial Paradox Hypothesis.** As the authors note, recent studies of the experiences of racial minorities in the legal profession

conducted by Professor Richard Sander concluded that the affirmative action by law schools and law firms actually hurts minorities by recruiting them into environments in which they do not thrive. This is the racial paradox hypothesis: affirmative action paradoxically winds up hurting the very people it is intended to help.[16] In particular, Sander argued in the *Stanford Law Review* article that affirmative action in law school admissions hurts minority students by placing them in academic competition with students who are more likely to succeed than they are, which results in minority students getting lower grades than they would have received if they had gone to a less selective law school, which in turn harms their chances to thrive in the profession. In the *North Carolina Law Review* article on the experiences of minority lawyers in large law firms, Sander argued that the deleterious effects of affirmative action continue in law firms as senior lawyers believe that minority lawyers are less qualified and therefore invest less effort in mentoring them. Sander's research prompted a large number of studies and articles in response; most of the responses, including the one excerpted above, focused on the core questions in Sander's research: whether affirmative action is good for minorities and what accounts for the underrepresentation of minorities in large law firms.

2.   GENDER AND THE NORMS OF TIME AND WORK

Both anecdotal reports and research data indicate that women are more likely to leave the practice of law than are men. Many surmise that this difference is attributable to gendered patterns in family responsibility. Moreover, women lawyers are less likely than their nonlawyer age peers to be married and to have children. In this section we explore these phenomena. In the process, we consider both the larger issue of norms about working time in the legal profession (and in elite occupations more generally) and the narrow question whether time norms explain the attrition of women lawyers. We also examine the question whether issues about working time, part-time work and work-life balance *should* be considered a gender issue.

THE PART-TIME PARADOX: TIME NORMS, PROFESSIONAL LIVES, FAMILY, AND GENDER

Cynthia Fuchs Epstein, Carroll Seron, Bonnie Olensky, and Robert Sauté
(Routledge 1999)

The legal profession, like other social groups, places values on the use of time, and lawyers have feelings about time that are socially patterned.

Professional work typically entails workdays and workweeks that spill over into what others might regard as personal or "after-hours" time.

---

[16]   Richard H. Sander, *A Systemic Analysis of Affirmative Action in American Law Schools*, 57 STAN. L. REV. 367–483 (2004); Richard H. Sander, *The Racial Paradox of the Corporate Law Firm*, 54 N. C. L. REV. 1755–822 (2006).

Indeed, for the physician, lawyer, soldier or minister, there has long been an expectation that they will not be clock watchers and will not allow competing demands from other spheres of life to undermine their professional work. In the course of professional socialization, doctors and lawyers usually acquire motivation for hard and demanding work, and become embedded in a professional environment where devotion to task is rewarded by upward mobility while ordinary effort is punished with stagnation, diminished rank, or lesser remuneration.

In law, where work may be evaluated both objectively (measured by cases won and value of deals closed), or subjectively (assessment of a person's "ideas"), hours worked serve as both objective and subjective evaluations, translating into a proxy for dedication and excellence.

Lawyers' human capital is the coin of their professional success. Their reputation for service and quality is a key component, along with training and experience in practicing law—skill, craft, and shrewdness; a passion for winning; and an attractive personal style. A reputation for availability is also part of the attorney's "symbolic capital." [R]ound-the-clock availability is no longer regarded as a gesture made only in cases of last-minute deadlines or emergencies—a theoretical promise of being "on duty" all the time. High-profile clients expect immediate and constant responsiveness.

Time has become objectified and more visible with stricter documentation of billable hours through computerized accounting system. The number of hours is not, however, the only dimension of time monitoring. *When* people work and *where* they work are also noticed and provide an overall cast to the social perception of a lawyer's time at work. [W]ork at home may have multiple consequences for lawyers; it permits flexibility, but it also removes the lawyer from visibility.

Law, as well as other occupational communities, is bound by mystiques about the distinctive and unique feats performed by its members. In law, part of the mystique is communicated by stories about arduous and long hours on cases, tales that bolster a sense of professional community. Yet, time heroics were in the past regarded as appropriate to professional youth. As part of the socially expected duration of stages in a professional career, round-the-clock service was expected to ease off; senior partners in large firms looked to a time when advanced status would permit them to slow down and enjoy the fruits of years of dedicated labor. More recently, however, attorneys report that this perquisite of seniority is disappearing. [P]artners of all ranks are called on to continue to work at a very demanding pace.

No matter where they work, most of the lawyers we studied who work fewer hours than their peers are *de facto* deviants from established guidelines for work time. They challenge the standard indicators of excellence and do not engage in practices believed to create much profit for their institutions. Even as organizations appear to grant these new demands, they define those who take them as deviants; only some part-timers avoid the stigma of difference. In the invidious comparison with full-time lawyers, the part-timer is often seen as less dedicated and less professional—a "time deviant." We use the term "stigma" here in its sociological sense to convey the way in which "otherness" is determined by social definition. Stigma, as Erving Goffman (1963) pointed out, has to do with relationships, not attributes. Stigma serves to place a boundary around the "normal." What is at issue is deviation from the norm.

Describing this study, the author asked [a law professor who was also a consultant for a major New York law firm] about the feasibility of part-time work in the New York firm. "Impossible," he asserted without hesitation. "But don't you work part-time for the firm?" she asked. "That's different," he said. "I provide expertise they need." "But couldn't a woman who wanted to limit her hours also provide expertise on a part-time basis as you do?" "I don't think we are getting anywhere with this conversation," the professor snapped.

[C]areer progression is a fairly modern phenomenon. Because it is a contemporary ideal and because career progression in law is linked to professionalization, not moving ahead puts one at risk of being labeled deviant. Mobility is a good indicator of the regard with which lawyers are held and of their integration within the profession. About 60 percent of a nationally representative sample of attorneys surveyed by the American Bar Association believed that reduced-hour or part-time employment limited opportunities for advancement including partnership. [A] part-time associate [said], "I'm not sure I have a career. I have a job. A career has a future and a path. I'm not sure I have a path." Not only are these professionals' ambitions downscaled, but their willingness to pursue challenging work and responsibility has been damaged by the frustration of performing work with uncertain levels of backup and lack of recognition. Although many part-time lawyers claim to have phases when they work considerably more than their agreed hours, they often feel that if they do not watch the boundaries, the firm or legal department for which they work would violate them. Hence, part-time attorneys face ambivalence about how much responsibility they wish to have. On the one hand, many express a desire to be assigned to meaty cases—the interesting ones with high visibility. At the same time they know that taking them may cause them to work beyond their desired schedule and may not lead to increased recognition or status.

Despite the obstacles, some structural and cultural conditions and strategic choices support mobility. Searching for patterns in the careers of part-time lawyers who attained some type of mobility we found these: Firms that are innovative in other spheres seem more receptive to reduced hours. For example, in California's Silicon Valley, five successful women partners in high-tech law firms of more than 100 attorneys [had worked part time]. (Part-time meant 8 a.m. to 6 p.m. five days a week). Firms that do not have constant quick-turnaround pressures also are more receptive to part-timers' advancement. The cultivation of legal specialties creates a pathway to lateral and upward mobility, providing an extra element of human capital that enhances the value of part-timers and cancels some of the stigma attached to reduced hours.

NOTES ON THE PART-TIME PARADOX

1. ***Time and Devotion.*** Could you envision the legal profession altering the norms of devotion to client and craft, at least as measured by time? Which aspects of the norms of devotion to client and craft do you find admirable and which do you think are undesirable, or at least dispensable?

2. ***The Billable Hour.*** Do you think that the reliance of many law firms, especially big firms, on hourly billing might help explain why private practice tends to demand time commitment? Critics of hourly billing say that it discourages efficiency and leads lawyers to measure each other's contributions to the firm in terms of the numbers of hours they bill and, in the case of partners, in terms of junior lawyers' hours for which partners claim billing credit.

Some of the newer firms mentioned in Chapters 24 and 34 have abandoned hourly fees in favor of flat fees and various types of "value-based" fee arrangements that take into account the quality of the work and/or outcomes for clients. These firms assert that their reliance on alternative billing methods reduces pressure to bill long hours and enables them to attract talented lawyers who want to avoid the billable hour rat-race.[17]

3. ***Are Norms About Working Time a Gender Issue?*** In what ways is part-time work a gender issue? In what ways is it not? Does considering part-time work as an issue of gender equality make the reforms you would like to see on that point more or less likely to occur?

4. ***The Having It All Debate.*** In the legal profession as in many other elite jobs, women lag behind men in almost every measure of professional attainment. A lively and sometimes acrimonious debate has raged for at least a generation about whether the gender gap is due to women choosing less demanding jobs in order to balance work and family and, if so, whether those choices are cause for concern. One articulation of the problem is that women need to "lean in" and challenge themselves to lead and to show others that women can be leaders.[18] Another is that women "can't have it all," except for those who are wealthy, powerful, and/or have partners who are

---

[17] *See* STEVEN J. HARPER, THE LAWYER BUBBLE: A PROFESSION IN CRISIS 77–79, 171–75, 191–92 (2013).

[18] SHERYL SANDBERG, LEAN IN: WOMEN, WORK, AND THE WILL TO LEAD (2013).

willing to sacrifice their own professional advancement to care for family.[19] Another framing of the problem challenges the notion that women's choices to prefer family over career explain the gender gap and insists that framing the issue as one of choice is wrong.[20] What do you think?

3. GENDER AND SEXUAL IDENTITY AND THE NORMS OF THE PROFESSION

Among the issues you might consider on the experience of LGBT people in the profession are two that we have considered with respect to women and other minorities: do LGBT lawyers think about legal issues differently such that their open presence in the profession has had or will have an impact on the law? And, if LGBT people are underrepresented in the profession as compared to the general population, what accounts for it? Is it bias, and, if so, what forms do bias take? Both of those issues are raised implicitly in the following case. Recall from Chapter 27 that the Code of Judicial Conduct, like the statute that regulates recusal of federal judges, requires judges to recuse themselves "in any proceeding in which the judge's impartiality might reasonably be questioned," such as when the judge "has a personal bias or prejudice concerning a party or a party's lawyer, or the judge has an interest (financial or otherwise) that "could be substantially affected by the outcome of the proceeding." Rule 2.11; 28 U.S.C. § 455.

PERRY V. SCHWARZENEGGER

U.S. District Court, Northern District of California
790 F. Supp. 2d 1119 (2011)*

JAMES WARE, CHIEF JUDGE.

Plaintiffs in this case are same-sex couples who claim that a California constitutional provision that redefined marriage in California solely to encompass a union between one man and one woman violated their rights under the federal Constitution. Defendant-Intervenors were

---

[19] See Anne-Marie Slaughter, *Why Women Still Can't Have It All*, THE ATLANTIC (June 13, 2012) (Princeton professor who left a high-level government job to spend more time with her children explains that women cannot "have it all at the same time" because of "the way America's economy and society are currently structured").

[20] See Nicole Buonocore Porter, *The Blame Game: How the Rhetoric of Choice Blames the Achievement Gap on Women*, 8 FLA. INT'L U. L. REV. 447 (2013).

* [Eds: This ruling, along with the judgment entered by Judge Walker on the merits of the challenge to Proposition 8 (a ballot initiative which banned same sex marriage in California), was affirmed by the Ninth Circuit. *Perry v. Brown*, 671 F.3d 1052 (9th Cir. 2012). The Supreme Court granted review on the merits but not on the ruling on recusal, and held that the proponents of Proposition 8 did not have standing to appeal the district court's order holding unconstitutional the Proposition 8 ban on same-sex marriage. *Hollingsworth v. Perry*, 133 S. Ct. 2642 (2013). Because the State of California refused to defend the constitutionality of Proposition 8, the effect of the Supreme Court's decision was to reinstate the district court ruling that a ban on same sex marriage unconstitutionally discriminated against same-sex people. This cleared the way for California to grant marriage licenses to same sex couples.]

allowed to intervene to advance an argument that the California constitutional provision did not violate the federal Constitution. After a court trial, Judge Walker entered judgment for Plaintiffs and enjoined enforcement of the state constitution against them. Defendant-Intervenors appealed. After he had retired, and while the appeal was pending, a newspaper article reported that Judge Walker shared that he is gay and that he was in a same-sex relationship at the time when he was presiding over this case. Defendant-Intervenors brought this Motion to vacate the Judgment.

Defendant-Intervenors contend that Judge Walker should be disqualified because his same-sex relationship gave him a markedly greater interest in a case challenging restrictions on same-sex marriage than the interest held by the general public. The Court rejects this argument on two readily apparent grounds. First, it is inconsistent with the general principles of constitutional adjudication to presume that a member of a minority group reaps a greater benefit from application of the substantive protections of our Constitution than would a member of the majority. The fact that this is a case challenging a law on equal protection and due process grounds being prosecuted by members of a minority group does not mean that members of the minority group have a greater interest in equal protection and due process than the rest of society. [W]e all have an equal stake in a case that challenges the constitutionality of a restriction on a fundamental right. [E]njoining enforcement of [an unconstitutional] law is a public good that benefits all in our society equally. The single characteristic that Judge Walker shares with the Plaintiffs, albeit one that might not have been shared with the majority of Californians, gave him no greater interest in a proper decision on the merits than would exist for any other judge or citizen.

Second, disqualifying Judge Walker based on an inference that he intended to take advantage of a future legal benefit made available by constitutional protections would result in an unworkable standard for disqualification. Under such a standard, disqualification would be based on assumptions about the amorphous personal feelings of judges in regards to such intimate and shifting matters as future desire to undergo an abortion, to send a child to a particular university or to engage in family planning. So too here, a test inquiring into the presiding judge's desire to enter into the institution of marriage with a member of the same sex, now or in the future, would require reliance upon similarly elusive factors. Given Section 455(b)(4)'s requirement that non-pecuniary interests must be "substantially affected" to require recusal, recusal could turn on whether a judge "fervently" intended to marry a same-sex partner versus merely "lukewarmly" intended to marry, determination that could only be reached through undependable and invasive self-reports. The Ninth Circuit has recognized the inherent unworkability of such a subjective recusal standard. *Feminist Women's Health Center v. Codispoti,* 69 F.3d 399, 400 (9th Cir. 1995). In holding that recusal was not warranted in an action brought by an abortion clinic against protestors of the clinic where one of the presiding panel judges belonged to the Catholic faith, the court acknowledged that any test where recusal would turn on whether the judge's religious beliefs were "fervently-held" or "lukewarmly maintained" would collapse under such amorphous, unworkable distinctions.

To hold otherwise, and require recusal merely based on the fact that the presiding judge is engaged in a long-term same-sex relationship, is to place an inordinate burden on minority judges. Such a standard would, in essence, infer subjective future intent on the basis of a judge's membership in a particular class.

NOTES ON GENDER AND SEXUAL IDENTITY AND PROFESSIONAL NORMS

1. ***Does Identity Affect the Ways That Lawyers and Judges Reason?*** Some critics of the defenders of Proposition 8 asserted that the motion to recuse Judge Walker itself was animated by bias because it assumed that only heterosexuals or people who disclaim any desire to marry a person of the same sex are unbiased on the issue of a constitutional right to same sex marriage. Do you agree? Does one's sexual orientation affect how one is likely to regard marriage equality? Under what circumstances does believing that a judge's membership in a particular group will affect how he or she approaches a case reveal bias of the person who questions the judge's impartiality? A gay Florida state trial judge recounted an episode in which a public defender representing a man accused of beating a patron of a gay nightclub asked the judge whether he could be fair. "I looked at him and I said, 'Well, let me ask you a question. If I were a black judge and this had to do with a racial issue, would you ask the black judge the same question? Or if it was a rape case, would you ask a woman judge the same question? I suspect the answers to those questions are no. So, why are you asking me that question to begin with?"[21] Did the public defender's query about the judge's impartiality reflect homophobia or something else? (It may have been a tactical blunder to voice the doubts.)

2. ***Why Does Diversity Matter?*** In this chapter and the preceding one, much of the data about inequality focuses on the prospects of minorities in large law firms and some other elite jobs in the profession, including in high-level corporate counsel and judicial, executive, and legislative government positions. Why does it matter whether racial, religious, and ethnic minorities, women, people with disabilities, and LGBT people attain or thrive in elite positions in the legal profession?

---

[21] Siobhan Morrissey, *Overlooked No Longer: A New ABA Commission Will Address Sexual Orientation and Gender Identity Issues in the Legal Profession,* A.B.A. J., Dec. 2007, at 62.

3.   *Professional Norms and Identity Performance.* To
that professional norms demand particular gendered or cultural
behavior or attire, should lawyers be expected to abandon nonce
aspects of their identity performance? You may have received exp
implicit messages from friends, mentors, or your law school administra
faculty regarding appropriate professional behavior. That advice some
includes guidance about how to dress for a job interview or for work on be
of clients and how to respond to questions or to behave in various socia
business situations. And that guidance often explicitly or implicit
encourages adherence to gendered and culturally specific expectations. It
may be in suggestions about business attire, such as clothes, jewelry, or
hairstyle, or it may be in terms of describing one's personal life and situation.
Some lawyers insist that lawyers have a duty to their clients to behave in
whatever way is necessary (within reason) to be effective in representation,
and that can include adherence to gendered norms about professional attire.
Others believe employment discrimination laws do (or should) prohibit legal
employers from demanding adherence to some gendered or culturally specific
norms of grooming and attire. What do you think?

4.   PEOPLE WITH DISABILITIES AND CONCEPTIONS OF THE LAWYER

The reasons that persons with disabilities are underrepresented in
law compared to the general population may be similar to the reasons for
the underrepresentation of some racial and ethnic groups, although they
may also differ. One reason may be that some people with particularly
severe disabilities are underrepresented among the population of persons
who possess the educational prerequisites to become a lawyer. Cornell
University's Employment and Disability Institute—using data from the
American Community Survey (ACS), an annual survey that is sent to
about 3 million households—reports that 12.2% of working-age persons
with disabilities hold a bachelor's degree or higher, compared to 30.8% of
non-disabled persons. Yet the percentage of lawyers with disabilities is
small even compared to the population of persons with disabilities who
are highly educated. A second factor—one which distinguishes the bar's
treatment of race and gender from its treatment of disabilities—is that
many state bars explicitly exclude people with some disabilities from the
practice of law, or make it more difficult for them to obtain a license. (See
Chapter 36.)

A third factor, reported anecdotally by many lawyers, is explicit or
implicit bias and the lack of encouragement or mentoring. Some disabled
lawyers report having been discouraged from pursuing a career in law.
For example, Professor Paul Miller, a 1986 Harvard Law School graduate
with achondroplasia (dwarfism) who eventually became a noted civil
rights lawyer, a Commissioner of the Equal Employment Opportunity
Commission, a law professor, and an advisor to Presidents Clinton and

Obama, had terrible difficulties finding a job when he graduated from Harvard. One of the dozens of rejection letters he received after interviewing at law firms informed him that clients would see the firm that hired him as a "circus freak show."[22] One small national qualitative study of lawyers with disabilities reported a number of common experiences.[23] Aspiring lawyers with disabilities were ignored, treated as fragile, or discouraged from pursuing the rigors of a career at a large law firm. Some had difficulties convincing senior lawyers that they were capable of doing the work. "[T]he daily struggle of managing other people's reactions to and stereotypes about disability can become a job in itself."[24] As one blind lawyer, Kareem Dale, said:

> I started my legal career in 1999 at a large Chicago law firm. I practiced in the litigation department for seven years, where there were some great attorneys, who gave me an opportunity as a person with a disability when many others would not give me that opportunity. People there mentored me on a daily basis, and without their mentoring, I probably would never have made it through. For all of those things, I am immensely grateful. However, what I came to learn is that a few good people do not necessarily dictate what the institution itself is doing in employing lawyers with disability. What happens a lot of times, as many of you all know, whether you are employers of lawyers or whether you are attorneys yourselves, is that the law firm is a unique structure. You have partners who run their own business; they have their own little company within the law firm itself. If partners have a great deal of business, they can dictate which lawyers are going to be on their cases. So you have these mini law firms throughout the individual firms.
>
> As I stayed at the firm, I came to learn is that it was extraordinarily difficult, being a person with a disability, trying to grow with the rest of my mates who had started when I started. There still exists in our society a systemic discrimination against people with disabilities, and it's not necessarily from bad intent. As we all know, it has a lot to do with pure lack of knowledge or a lack of understanding about how a lawyer with a disability can get the job done. "I don't know how Kareem can view 10,000 documents, so I won't staff him on my case, because I know the person down the hall can read that many documents."

---

[22] Dennis Hevasi, *Paul S. Miller, Advocate for the Disabled, Dies at 49*, N.Y. TIMES, Oct. 21, 2010, at A37.

[23] Carrie Griffin Basas, *The New Boys: Women With Disabilities in the Legal Profession*, 25 BERKELEY J. GENDER L. & JUSTICE 32 (2010).

[24] *Id.* at 57.

Despite the fact that I got good reviews, it became a challenge on a daily basis to excel at a law firm because of that lack of knowledge, and it became a struggle, as I'm sure many of the blind attorneys in this room can attest. Most partners don't know that you can have a screen reader to read your e-mail or a screen reader so that you can read your memos and make sure they're formatted correctly, or if you do a document review, your reader will be there and you'll be able to talk to your reader about what is there. Or you can scan the documents and read them off Adobe or any number of mechanisms to get the work done. But as I always said to the partners in my firm, you need not worry about how I get it done. You only need to worry about is it getting done, because the buck always stops with the attorney. As people with disabilities, we know that that's the way we want it. We want the buck to stop with us. And we want people to know that we will get the job done, no matter what. That is the ultimate bottom line.[25]

NOTES ON UNDERSTANDING THE UNDERREPRESENTATION OF LAWYERS WITH DISABILITIES

1. ***Diversity Within the Group.*** Some disabilities are easily perceived by other people and others are not. To what extent are both demographic data and the experiences of lawyers with disabilities affected by the choice not to reveal a disability?

2. ***Understanding Institutional Behavior.*** Kareem Dale pointed out in the excerpt above that his experience of working at a large law firm was that it was really a federation of mini law firms. What light does that shed on the nature of discrimination? Bear this in mind when you read Section G of this chapter on the application of employment discrimination law in law firms.

F. EVALUATING THE ARGUMENTS FOR DIVERSITY

As you surely know from your experiences in higher education and in life more generally, underlying the debate over the reasons for the underrepresentation of some groups in certain segments of society is a significant disagreement over whether or to what extent we as a society *should* aspire to having a world in which the demographics of any particular institution reflect the demographics of the general population. In other words, why should we care if able-bodied white men are overrepresented in some sectors of life? This is part of the debate over the

---

[25] Remarks of Kareem A. Dale, Second National Conference on the Employment of Lawyers With Disabilities (ABA 2009).

existence and nature of discrimination and the value of affirmative action. Here we focus on one part of that larger debate: to what extent does diversity of the legal profession matter? What are the arguments for and against efforts to remedy the underrepresentation of certain groups in certain sectors of law practice? The article excerpted below addresses that issue in a specific practice context: major law firms. It focuses in particular on the question whether diversity is good or bad for law firms and their clients (as opposed to whether it is good or bad for the lawyers who are the intended beneficiaries of policies to promote diversity).

GOOD BUSINESS: A MARKET-BASED ARGUMENT FOR LAW FIRM DIVERSITY

Douglas E. Brayley & Eric S. Nguyen
34 Journal of the Legal Profession 1 (2009)

The increasingly intense discussion about law firm diversity pits those making rights-based arguments against those who argue that firms are simply businesses with no less—and no greater—obligation than other businesses to promote diversity. Those who hope for a more integrated bar are often at odds with those who focus primarily on the bottom line. Scholars have not yet produced a rigorous empirical analysis of the relationship between diversity and profitability at law firms. This article fills that important gap in the literature by analyzing detailed data on the racial diversity and financial performance of the country's 200 largest law firms. The data demonstrate that highly diverse firms generate greater revenue per lawyer and turn higher profits per partner.

Many observers recognize that corporate clients have increasingly pressured firms to demonstrate a commitment to diversity. Many major corporate purchasers of legal services now explicitly require their law firms to show a commitment to diversity and some, including Wal-Mart, have withdrawn work from firms who failed to live up to diversity standards. This client-based pressure to diversify is felt particularly strongly at large firms that cater to the largest national and international companies. Scholars have not, however, presented empirical evidence to demonstrate that corporate clients' demands for law firm diversity have any measurable impact on a firm's behavior or its bottom line. Furthermore, not all observers are convinced that such client-based arguments for law firm diversity are compelling.

Others argue that law students and young lawyers increasingly prefer diversity in the workplace. The recent effort by a group of Stanford law students—Building a Better Legal Profession—to influence law firms by releasing "diversity rankings" suggests that today's young lawyers do indeed care about their future employers' commitment to diversity. In a business that depends on the regular inflow of talent from top law schools, law firms may be sensitive to student preferences. Similarly, diversity advocates argue that law firms should work to improve their retention of female and racial minority associates because attrition costs firms between $200,000 and $500,000 per associate, including lost revenues, lost training expenses, lost institutional knowledge, and replacement costs. However, diversity advocates have not shown empirical evidence that a firm's commitment to diversity affects law students' career choices or associate attrition rates. Furthermore, large law firms are built on attrition and depend on promoting only a small proportion of each incoming class of associates to partner. So long as the associates work hard and bill hours while they remain at the firm, and so long as a few acceptable candidates for partnership remain, high attrition rates may not particularly concern a firm's management.

This article relies on data reported for 2007 from *The American Lawyer* for the 200 highest-grossing law firms, the so-called AmLaw 200. The primary measure of diversity is the aggregate diversity ranking reported by *The American Lawyer* for 2006. The rankings are based on the percentage of a firm's attorneys—both partners and associates—who are black, Asian, Latino, mixed, or from otherwise underrepresented minorities. [We] compare highly diverse firms with the rest of the AmLaw 200. Throughout this article, the phrase "highly diverse firms" refers to the 50 most diverse firms in the AmLaw 200. Highly diverse firms have anywhere from 22 to 294 minority attorneys, representing between 15 percent and 25 percent of their attorneys. Among other firms, minority representation may be as low as four percent of all attorneys.

[O]n average, firms in the top quartile of diversity scores have higher profits per partner (PPP) and generate more revenue per lawyer (RPL) than the rest of the AmLaw 200. As with the relationship between diversity and firm size, this analysis does not show a necessary link between diversity and financial success: the firms with the lowest and highest PPP and RPL in the AmLaw 200 are not in the top quartile of diversity scores. Because this analysis does not control for other variables that could be driving these differences in PPP and RPL, a regression analysis is necessary to isolate the effect of diversity. Diverse firms may perform better simply because they have more lawyers working longer hours in bigger cities. [The authors then attempt to isolate the effect of diversity by controlling for hours worked and a firm's size and location.]

As expected, firms with an office in a major market and attorneys who work a higher number of hours each week are likely to generate greater revenue per lawyer. City and hours worked also matter. Even controlling for these factors, the AmLaw diversity rank had a strongly significant effect on a firm's revenue per lawyer. In other words, for two firms in the same city, working the same number of hours, with the same number of lawyers, differences in diversity are significantly correlated with differences in financial performance.

The models assume that causation runs in only one direction: greater diversity allows firms to generate higher revenue. In reality, the causation may also run in the opposite direction: higher revenue allows firms to make themselves more diverse. As a result, it is difficult to conclude that diversity itself causes higher revenue.

[T]he results [of our analysis] provide a market-based justification for firms to turn greater attention to minority hiring. According to the model, a firm ranked in the top quarter in the diversity rankings will generate more than $100,000 of additional profit per partner than a peer firm of the same size in the same city, with the same hours and leverage but a diversity ranking in the bottom quarter of firms.

[T]hese results demonstrate empirically that diversity, revenue, and profitability are inextricably linked. They do not prove which way causation runs. Indeed, causation probably runs in both directions.

There are at least three possible explanations for the correlation between firm diversity and financial performance. First, diverse firms may perform better because large corporate clients have begun to send their business to firms with better representation of racial minorities and women. Second, diverse firms may be more productive, especially because they can recruit and retain top legal talent. Third, causation may run in the opposite direction, with financially successful firms able to devote greater resources to diversity programs.

Client demand may drive part of the diversity-profitability relationship. As corporate clients demand that their matters be staffed with a diverse set of attorneys, firms with a demonstrable commitment to diversity are more successful in bringing in new business and retaining existing clients. Strong anecdotal evidence supports this theory. A number of major American companies have begun to demand publicly that law firms pay more attention to issues of diversity. In 2004, Sara Lee general counsel Roderick Palmore issued "A Call to Action: Diversity in the Legal Profession," in which signatory companies promised "to end or limit ... relationships with firms whose performance consistently evidences a lack of meaningful interest in being diverse." Since the Call was issued, about 90 companies have signed on.

The list of Call to Action signatory companies provides a tool with which to analyze the client-demand hypothesis. We compared the list of signatory companies with two databases compiled by American Lawyer Media that list which large law firms represent which corporate clients. After eliminating duplicate entries, we ranked law firms based on the number of signatory companies they represent.

Of the five firms with the most Call to Action signatory clients, four [are] in the top quartile of diversity. Of the top 11 firms, seven [are in the top quartile of] diversity and all but one are above the median. Of the top

20 firms, nine are in the top diversity quartile and 16 have above-median diversity scores. This ranking thus suggests that the Call to Action signatories are indeed using some of their market power to choose firms with good diversity records.

A second possible explanation for the correlation is that diverse law firms produce legal services at higher quality or more efficiently. Two specific mechanisms may be at work. First, associates may be more satisfied with their work when they are surrounded by a more heterogeneous group of coworkers. Satisfaction in turn increases the ability to retain good lawyers, helping the firm both keep a productive worker and avoid the expense of recruiting a replacement. The data provide only weak support for this theory. Second, diverse firms may be able to recruit better talent if students at highly ranked law schools consider firm demographics and diversity efforts when deciding on a place to work. Indeed, BBLP is premised partly on a hope that firms will respond to student demand for diversity. The data we analyzed, however, do not provide support for this theory.

If associates are more satisfied working in a heterogeneous environment, reported associate satisfaction should correlate with diversity scores after controlling for other relevant variables. We tested the effect of the AmLaw diversity rankings on two dependent variables. In none of these models does greater diversity correlate significantly with midlevel associate satisfaction. Instead, satisfaction appears to be a product of more conventional explanations.* For example, associates are significantly more satisfied at less leveraged firms. Associates are happy when the firm turns higher profits—but they are even happier when leverage is low and the associates thus have a greater chance of eventually sharing in those profits.

Attorneys satisfied with their salaries and workplace diversity were likely to be planning to stay longer. The same attorneys were more likely to say they were satisfied to have become lawyers. These findings provide some support, but only weak support, for the theory that diverse workplaces improve attorney satisfaction. The most important limitation on the model is that the key explanatory variable is satisfaction with workplace diversity, not the level of workplace diversity itself. As a result, the precise finding is that lawyers satisfied with diversity in the workplace are likely to stay longer—not that lawyers in more diverse workplaces are likely to stay longer.

---

* [Eds: Brayley & Nguyen rely on a 2007 survey conducted by *American Lawyer* magazine of midlevel associates at law firms. As explored in detail in Chapter 38, lawyer satisfaction is a difficult phenomenon to define and measure, and surveys of lawyer satisfaction may understate or significantly overstate levels of satisfaction. Even where satisfaction is defined and accurately measured, it is difficult to draw conclusions about what causes satisfaction.]

[D]ata on associate satisfaction and law student preferences provide little evidence to support the idea that diverse firms are more profitable because they can draw and retain better lawyers. If diversity pushes revenue and profits, it is likely because clients—not young lawyers—demand it.

NOTES ON THE ARGUMENTS FOR DIVERSITY

1. *The Call to Action.* The Brayley & Nguyen article refers to the "Call to Action," an influential and high-profile 2005 effort of corporate in-house counsel to persuade law firms to hire more lawyers of color. Similar efforts have been made since. In 2010, for example, general counsel of a number of large corporations pledged to direct $30 million in legal work to law firms owned by minorities and women.[26] Why do corporate counsel care about the race, gender, and ethnicity of the lawyers in the law firms they hire?

2. *Debating the Business Case for Affirmative Action.* Brayley and Nguyen's argument that diversity is beneficial to law firms and clients from a business standpoint echoes a long-term debate over the strategic costs and benefits of defending affirmative action policies by appealing to the instrumental benefits of diversity for institutions rather than the intrinsic justice of equal representation or the benefits (or harms) to those affected by affirmative action policies. One scholar summarized the debate, as applied to law firms, this way:

> [T]he advancement of the "business case for diversity," while well-reasoned and well-intended, has backfired, ending up weakening and eroding the meaning of diversity. Meant to enhance the normative case for diversity with utilitarian grounds, and motivate large law firms and other legal employers to pursue diversity vigorously, it led to debates over the instrumental value of diversity, increasingly overlooking other compelling grounds for it. Indeed, we have been down that road before. As Deborah Malamud points out, when William Julius Wilson argued that race-based affirmative action benefits the black middle class and not the "truly disadvantaged" members of the black community, he meant to foster discourse about additional means to aid disadvantaged blacks, and surely did not mean for his work to be used by opponents of race-based affirmative action. Similarly, advocates of the "business case for diversity" likely did not mean to weaken diversity by undermining its normative justifications, but opponents of diversity initiatives have seized the opportunity to reframe and focus attention on the (admittedly often questionable) instrumental grounds for diversity. Indeed, David Wilkins, who has written extensively about the "business case for diversity," has astutely

---

[26] Zach Lowe, *Major Companies Pledge $30 Million to Minority and Women Owned Law Firms*, AM. LAW. (Mar. 5, 2010).

cautioned against both an uncritical adoption of it and against abandoning other justifications for diversity: "given the limitations with self-interested justifications for client participation in programs to increase law firm diversity, advocates for those programs would be well advised not to give up on . . . 'normative diversity arguments.'"[27]

If one were not persuaded by Brayley and Nguyen's data and analysis on the benefits of diversity for large law firms and their clients, would their normative claims be undermined, in your judgment? If so, why? If not, do you think there is a better case to be made for or against law firm efforts to promote diversity?

3. ***Satisfaction as a Measure of Business Success?*** Brayley and Nguyen find little evidence to support the common argument that diversity benefits law firms because associates at diverse firms are more satisfied with their work lives and therefore diverse firms are more able to recruit and retain talent than less diverse firms. Chapter 38 addresses the lively scholarly debate about how properly to measure lawyer satisfaction; many frequently cited measures of lawyer satisfaction lack social science rigor and may be unreliable. Why might lawyer satisfaction be correlated, or not, with diversity? Is the satisfaction of large law firm associates a good justification for the efforts of such firms to promote diversity?

G. LAW AND POLICIES PROHIBITING DISCRIMINATION AND PROMOTING DIVERSITY

One hypothesis explaining the underrepresentation of some groups in law firms as compared to their representation in law schools is discrimination in hiring and promotion. As noted above, for much of American history, legal employers of all types overtly discriminated on the basis of race, religion, ethnicity, gender, sexual orientation and disability. Discrimination in hiring and promotion on all of those bases except sexual orientation is now illegal under federal law, and it has been for many years. Title VII of the Civil Rights Act has prohibited discrimination on the basis of race, religion, gender, and national origin since 1965.[28] The Americans with Disabilities Act, in effect since 1991, prohibits discrimination on the basis of disability and requires employers to make reasonable accommodations for the known disabilities of

---

[27] Eli Wald, *A Primer on Diversity, Discrimination, and Equality in the Legal Profession or Who Is Responsible for Pursuing Diversity and Why*, 24 GEO. J. LEGAL ETHICS 1079, 1081–82 (2011). The scholars whom Professor Wald cited in this excerpt are: Deborah C. Malamud, *Affirmative Action, Diversity, and the Black Middle Class*, 68 U. COLO. L. REV. 939 (1997); WILLIAM JULIUS WILSON, THE TRULY DISADVANTAGED: THE INNER CITY, THE UNDERCLASS AND PUBLIC POLICY (1990); David B. Wilkins, *From "Separate Is Inherently Unequal" to "Diversity is Good For Business": The Rise of Market-Based Diversity Arguments and the Fate of the Black Corporate Bar*, 117 HARV. L. REV. 1548 (2004).

[28] 42 U.S.C. § 2000e-2.

employees if doing so will not cause undue hardship to the employer.[29] Many states also prohibit discrimination on the basis of race, gender, national origin, religion and disability, and a few states prohibit discrimination on the basis of sexual orientation and gender identity.[30]

Why Have Employment Discrimination Laws Not Led to a More Diverse Profession?

Discrimination in employment on the basis of race, gender, national origin, and disability has long been unlawful. Is underrepresentation attributable to unlawful discrimination? If so, why? If not, what else is at work here?

In this section we briefly consider a large and complicated issue concerning compliance with laws prohibiting employment discrimination. Most law schools offer one or more courses devoted entirely to the law of employment discrimination. Our purpose here is simply to raise the question whether or to what extent employment discrimination law addresses whatever diversity issues the profession faces. As you read the following case, consider the practical challenges faced by a law firm associate who encounters overt or subtle forms of discrimination. Consider, too, the practical challenges facing law firm management. Given what you learned about the internal and external labor markets for law firm associates and partners in Chapter 15, what can or should a firm do to prevent or remedy conduct by partners or senior associates that leads to higher levels of attrition of minority, female, or other underrepresented lawyers?

HASAN V. FOLEY & LARDNER LLP

United States Court of Appeals for the Seventh Circuit
552 F.3d 520 (7th Cir. 2009)

RIPPLE, CIRCUIT JUDGE.

Zafar Hasan, a Muslim of Indian descent and a former associate at the law firm Foley & Lardner LLP ("Foley"), brought this action claiming that Foley had terminated his employment after the terrorist attacks of September 11, 2001, because of his religion, race, national origin and color. The district court granted Foley's motion for summary judgment. Mr. Hasan now appeals. For the reasons set forth in this opinion, we reverse the judgment of the district court and remand the case for further proceedings.

---

[29]   42 U.S.C. § 12112.

[30]   *See, e.g.,* California Gov't Code § 12940(a) (prohibiting employment discrimination on the basis of "race, religious creed, color, national origin, ancestry, physical disability, mental disability, medical condition, marital status, sex, age, or sexual orientation").

Foley invited Mr. Hasan to join the Business Law Department in its Chicago office in October 2000. At first, Foley was pleased with Mr. Hasan's performance.[1] In a June 2001 evaluation, department chair Edwin Mason and partner Robert Vechiola described Mr. Hasan's performance: "Zafar has a great attitude and is eager to learn. He has good business sense and a great deal of maturity for his age." The partners also noted, though, that Mr. Hasan needed to pay more attention to detail, develop his substantive skills and submit more polished work to his supervisors. Six months later, a group of four partners evaluated Mr. Hasan's work for the period between March 15 and September 15, 2001. The partners praised Mr. Hasan as "a hard worker" with a "great attitude" and commented that he managed clients and co-workers exceptionally well. Although the partners repeated their criticisms of Mr. Hasan's drafting skills, efficiency and attention to detail, all of the partners agreed that he was "on track for advancement" and generally exceeded or met the firm's expectations. Mr. Hasan was assigned to work on a large transaction for Foley's client, GMAC, and maintained high billable hours through the late summer of 2001. As of September 30, 2001, Mr. Hasan had billed 2,467.5 hours, the highest in his practice group. He also had received praise from both GMAC and his supervising partner for his work on the transaction.

Mr. Hasan and Foley agree that matters changed after the terrorist attacks of September 11, 2001. On the day of the attacks, another Foley attorney heard George Simon, a partner on the firm's Management and Compensation Committees, opine that "those people don't belong here . . . they should kick them all out." The other attorney understood Mr. Simon to be talking about Muslims. Mr. Hasan responded to the events of September 11 by publishing articles and appearing on television to publicize his view of Islam as a peaceful religion. According to Mr. Hasan, when he posted copies of some of his articles on his office door, Foley partner Doug Hagerman warned him to be "careful" and "not to upset any sacred cows." Hagerman asked, "Are you sure you want to have those [articles] up here?"

In late 2001, one of Mr. Hasan's supervising partners, Bryan Jung, received an e-mail from GMAC's in-house counsel complaining that Foley had overbilled the project Mr. Hasan had worked on and had provided insufficient and "sloppy" documents. After investigating the complaint, however, Jung concluded that the problems identified by the client might not have been anyone's fault but instead stemmed from communication

---

[1] At the beginning of this litigation, Foley maintained that Mr. Hasan's evaluations had been destroyed and that Mr. Hasan had been discharged for poor performance alone. Foley partners agreed in their depositions that Mr. Hasan's work always had been substandard. After Foley located the largely positive evaluations, the firm began to claim that Mr. Hasan had been fired because his work had declined and that they lacked work for all but the most talented associates in the department.

gaps among the large number of people working on the project. At the project's conclusion, GMAC told Mr. Hasan that Foley had done a "great job."

After September 11, Mr. Hasan's billable hours began to drop precipitously, while the average hours of other associates in his department increased. Mr. Hasan managed to find work with the firm's litigation group during December of that year, but, in 2002, he billed only 879 hours, the fewest hours billed by any associate in his department. Most of the department's associates were assigned to work on a second large project for GMAC, called "MINT." Mr. Hasan was not asked to work on MINT, even though he had requested more work. In fact, even when GMAC representatives asked Mr. Hasan to perform more work for them, Foley did not assign Mr. Hasan to the MINT project. Foley maintains that, although the MINT project occupied many associates, the Business Law Department lacked work generally and, consequently, it assigned what little work there was to its best associates and that Mr. Hasan did not fall into that category.

Mr. Hasan's May 2002 evaluation was less positive than his previous evaluations. His supervising partners stated that Mr. Hasan's technical skills were behind his class level. Partners also criticized Mr. Hasan's efficiency, observing that he billed more time than should have been necessary to complete projects. Mr. Hasan's evaluators did praise his intelligence, confidence and advocacy skills, but they warned Mr. Hasan that he would be "outplaced" if his performance did not improve by September. According to Mr. Hasan, Foley later revised the evaluation, adding that Mr. Hasan had failed to exercise tact with a client in December 2000, some eighteen months earlier. The firm also retracted its threat of "outplacement." Instead, it stated that it would simply place a warning in Mr. Hasan's file and evaluate his progress again in September.

Six partners evaluated Mr. Hasan's work in his next review. Most of the partners agreed that Mr. Hasan's work met or exceeded firm expectations. Peter Schaafsma, with whom Mr. Hasan had worked the most, reported that Mr. Hasan was "one of his corporate 'go to guys' " and was "a joy to work with." Todd Pfister, for whom Mr. Hasan had done little work, was not as positive: "For various reasons, a number of partners seem to have lost confidence in Zafar. As a result, his workload has diminished substantially and he is falling farther behind in his professional development." Pfister concluded that the firm needed to "address this situation promptly." A third partner, Robert Vechiola, mentioned Mr. Hasan's low hours but noted that Mr. Hasan was willing "to do anything to improve his hours, including relocating to another office and/or working with other departments." After Schaafsma submitted his glowing evaluation of Mr. Hasan's work, Mason (the department chair) told him that his praise was inconsistent with the other partners' assessments and asked him to explain his review. In his deposition, Schaafsma stated that he was surprised that other partners had given Mr. Hasan negative reviews and believed that Mason was trying to convince him to retract his praise for Mr. Hasan's work.

Mr. Hasan states that, in October 2002, Vechiola assured him, based on a conversation between Vechiola and Mason, that "there was no basis" for firing Mr. Hasan. Vechiola does not recall whether that conversation ever occurred. In any event, in October 2002, Mason chaired a meeting to evaluate the department's associates. Partner John Cleary attended the meeting and later testified that, at the meeting, Simon (the partner who made the "kicking out" comment on September 11) criticized Mr. Hasan's performance, even though Simon never had worked with Mr. Hasan. Ultimately the partners decided to terminate Mr. Hasan's employment. In a later conversation with Cleary, Vechiola described the meeting as a "sand nigger pile-on" and reported that, after Simon criticized Mr. Hasan, the rest of the partners joined in. Mr. Hasan says that Vechiola told him that it was "too bad that [Simon] and those guys took out their religious dispute in Israel on you and had you fired." Vechiola, however, does not recall having made that statement. Foley maintains that no partners participating in the decision to fire Mr. Hasan discussed Islam or September 11 during the meeting.

Mason informed Mr. Hasan in early December that Foley was terminating his employment because of "deficiencies in performance" and "a perception that he was behind the level of where he should be" professionally. Mason explained that the Business Law Department did not have enough work and that, because Mr. Hasan had "lost the confidence of a sufficient number of partners," the firm did not think it likely that Mr. Hasan would "receive enough work in the future." Mr. Hasan responded that Vechiola had told him there was no basis for firing him, but Mason explained that the partners had reached a different conclusion.

Foley permitted Mr. Hasan to remain at the firm for six months following his termination. Mr. Hasan claims that Pfister told him, in February 2003, that Simon previously (and unsuccessfully) had tried to derail the promotion of a pregnant associate eligible for partnership. According to Mr. Hasan, Pfister reported that Simon laughed when another partner told him that such action was inappropriate and that it was Pfister's opinion that Simon disregarded employment laws. Pfister told Mr. Hasan that Simon had "done the same thing" to Mr. Hasan that he had tried to do to the pregnant associate. Mr. Hasan ultimately left his employment with Foley on June 13, 2003.

During the time Mr. Hasan worked at Foley, the Business Law Department employed two other Muslim associates. Foley placed one of those associates on probation in May 2002 and then transferred her to the firm's litigation group in 2003. Foley terminated the other Muslim associate's employment shortly after Mr. Hasan left the firm. Foley notes that another Muslim lawyer has worked at the firm since 1996 and became a partner in 2006, but, at oral argument, Foley conceded that the Muslim partner was not in the Business Law Department.

About two weeks after Mr. Hasan left the firm, two Foley partners circulated a memo to the entire Chicago office in which they boasted that the firm's "financial picture is strong" and that "profits per equity partner" for 2002 exceeded the prior year's profits by twenty-five percent. At oral argument, Foley's attorney admitted that the firm had not fired any other associates in the Business Law Department for economic reasons. In the fall of 2002, the Business Law Department hired new associates from Foley's summer associate class to begin work in 2003.

Mr. Hasan submits that the facts in the record, while possibly weak proof of discrimination individually, together would allow a jury to infer that Foley terminated his employment because he is Muslim and of Indian descent.

[T]he district court concluded that Simon's comment that Muslims should be "kicked out" was not valid circumstantial evidence of discrimination because Simon was not Mr. Hasan's direct supervisor. [D]erogatory remarks are relevant if they are made by someone who provided input into the adverse employment decision. The record shows that Simon attended the meeting at which the partners decided to fire Mr. Hasan and that he participated in that decision. That others were also involved in making that decision does not make Simon's participation irrelevant. There is also evidence in the record that Simon's criticisms at that meeting incited anti-Muslim and racially charged commentary from other partners. Vechiola's description of the meeting as a "[racially tinged] pile on" suggests as much, as does Pfister's comment that Simon had targeted Mr. Hasan just as he had targeted another lawyer, albeit unsuccessfully. Viewing the facts in the light most favorable to Mr. Hasan, the record would allow the rational inference that Simon not only participated in the decision to fire Mr. Hasan but also may have instigated it.

The district court concluded that Simon's comment could not be evidence of discriminatory intent because he expressed his anti-Muslim sentiments on September 11, 2001, a year before Mr. Hasan was fired. The district court also believed that the fact that Mr. Hasan's hours fell after September 11 did not, on its own, raise any suspicions. Mr. Hasan's post-September 11 decrease in hours alone may not carry much meaning, but it gains substantial significance in the context of (1) partners' anti-Muslim comments, (2) their refusal to give him work even when he asked for it, (3) Mr. Hasan's good relationship with the department's primary client, (4) Mr. Hasan's previous positive performance reviews and (5) the fact that other associates had sufficient work and even increased their hours on average during the relevant period.

The district court also held that Mr. Hasan's evidence regarding Foley's treatment of other Muslims in the Business Law Department was irrelevant to his discrimination argument. Our precedents establish, however, that behavior toward or comments directed at other employees in the protected group is one type of circumstantial evidence that can support an inference of discrimination.

Finally, the record, viewed in the light most favorable to Mr. Hasan, supports neither of Foley's purported reasons for firing Mr. Hasan. Foley initially claimed that it fired Mr. Hasan for poor performance. With the exception of Schaafsma, who is no longer at the firm, Mr. Hasan's supervising partners all testified at their depositions that, at the time Mr. Hasan was fired, his work was uniformly unacceptable. However, after Foley located Mr. Hasan's work evaluations, which were mostly positive, the firm changed its tune, maintaining that it actually fired Mr. Hasan not because his work was unacceptable but because it only had enough work to keep the best associates in the department occupied. Moreover, Mason's attempt to convince Schaafsma to retract his praise for Mr. Hasan's work permits an inference that the Business Law Department intended to sabotage Mr. Hasan's evaluations. This contradictory evidence calls into question the credibility of the partners' deposition testimony; credibility determinations are reserved to the jury.

A reasonable jury could also find that Foley's alternative explanation—that it fired Mr. Hasan because the firm did not have enough work for all the associates in the Business Law Department—is pretextual as well. The record is inconsistent as to whether Foley fired any associates in the Business Law Department other than Mr. Hasan for lack of available work during the economic downturn, although, at argument, Foley's lawyer assured us that it had not. A jury could reasonably infer that Foley partners directed work towards other, non-Muslim associates in the Business Law Department in order to use Mr. Hasan's lack of work as a pretext to fire him. A jury could also conclude that the Business Law Department hired new associates because it actually had plenty of work. This issue cannot be resolved at summary judgment; a fact-finder must decide which interpretation of the record is correct.

NOTES ON HASAN V. FOLEY & LARDNER

1. *Understanding the Nature and Prevalence of Discrimination.* Suits successfully proving racial, ethnic, gender, disability, or religious employment discrimination by law firms and other legal employers are relatively rare. It may be that instances of unlawful discrimination are correspondingly rare, or it may be that discrimination is hard to prove. What light does *Hasan v. Foley & Lardner* shed on that question? To what extent do you think your own life experiences affect your perception of the prevalence of discrimination? To what extent do you think the life experiences of decision-makers—law firm partners, judges, and juries in litigated cases—affect how claims of discrimination are handled before and during litigation?

2. *Assessing the Effect of Law and Policy.* Is anti-discrimination law an effective way to address the issues described in this chapter? Consider whether the existence of such laws promotes efforts by employers to prevent discrimination and whether the threat of litigation deters illegal discrimination. Consider, too, the criticism that such laws make it unduly difficult for employers to fire or to pass over for promotion less-qualified candidates for fear of litigation.

3. *Disability Discrimination.* The federal Americans with Disabilities Act and its state law equivalents require not only that employers avoid unequal treatment of people with disabilities (just as Title VII prohibits unequal treatment on the basis of race, religion, gender and national origin), but also that employers make reasonable efforts to accommodate the known disabilities of workers when such accommodations are not an undue hardship and would enable disabled employees to perform the essential functions of the job. Reasonable accommodations may include altering physical spaces (by providing elevators and ramps rather than just stairs), providing or facilitating the use of devices (such as software to enable hearing-impaired or sight-impaired employees to absorb or convey information), or flexible work schedules.

H. SUMMARY

This chapter surveyed data on the demographics of the legal profession with respect to race and ethnicity, gender, gender identity and sexual orientation, and disability. It explored hypotheses explaining the demographics, and examined the effect of identities on career patterns, norms about devotion to work, and the relationship between sexual or gender identity and notions of professionalism. The chapter then considered different perspectives on whether diversity in law offices is intrinsically or instrumentally beneficial for lawyers, clients, and society at large. Finally, the chapter briefly considered how the laws that prohibit status-based employment discrimination apply to law firms.

CHAPTER 38

LAWYER SATISFACTION

■ ■ ■

A. INTRODUCTION

In the popular and legal press, one commonly hears that lawyers are miserable and that they generally regret their career choices. But is that true? Do lawyers typically regret the decision to attend law school or to enter the profession? What are the sources of satisfaction and dissatisfaction in lawyers' careers? Do they vary by types of practice? This chapter takes a close look at these questions and the best available research on these issues.

The first excerpt, by a law professor and former large firm lawyer, asserts that lawyers generally are unhappy, that lawyers in large law firms are the least happy of all lawyers, and that long hours and an excessive focus on money are at the root of the trouble. The remaining materials in this chapter examine the available evidence on lawyers' career satisfaction, raise questions about the empirical basis for the claim that lawyers as a group are dissatisfied, and disaggregate the issue into narrower questions for closer analysis.

B. ARE LAWYERS UNHAPPY?

On Being a Happy, Healthy, and Ethical Member of an Unhappy, Unhealthy, and Unethical Profession
Patrick J. Schiltz
52 Vanderbilt Law Review 871 (1999)

Dear Law Student:

I have good news and bad news. The bad news is that the profession that you are about to enter is one of the most unhappy and unhealthy on the face of the earth—and, in the view of many, one of the most unethical. The good news is that you can join this profession and still be happy, healthy, and ethical. I am writing to tell you how.

A study of California lawyers by the RAND Institute for Civil Justice found that only half say if they had to do it over, they would become lawyers. On the whole, California lawyers were reported to be "'profoundly pessimistic' about the state of the legal profession and its future." [A] nationwide poll of attorneys conducted by the National Law Journal found that less than a third of those surveyed were "very satisfied" with their careers.

For almost thirty years, the University of Michigan Law School has been surveying its former students five years after they graduate. Given the stellar reputation of their alma mater, Michigan graduates would presumably have more employment options available than graduates of most other law schools and thus would presumably be among the most satisfied practitioners in America. Yet the annual surveys have discovered surprisingly low levels of career satisfaction in general and a marked decline in career satisfaction over time, at least for lawyers in private practice.

The most comprehensive data on career satisfaction of lawyers were produced by three national surveys conducted under the auspices of the Young Lawyers Division of the American Bar Association ("ABA"). Taken together, the surveys show a substantial decline in the job satisfaction of attorneys. In 1984, 41% of lawyers said that they were "very satisfied" with their jobs; in 1990, only 33% of all lawyers surveyed were "very satisfied," a decline of one-fifth in just six years. At the same time, the number of lawyers who were "very dissatisfied" with their jobs rose from 3% in 1984 to 5% in 1990.*

[C]areer dissatisfaction is not distributed equally throughout the profession. Lawyers in some practice settings are happier than lawyers in others. And lawyers in large law firms are often among the least happy. This appears to be true for both associates and partners.

<u>Explaining the Unhappiness of Lawyers</u>. In every study of the career satisfaction of lawyers of which I am aware, in every book or article about the woes of the legal profession that I have read, and in every conversation about life as a practicing lawyer that I have heard, lawyers complain about the long hours they have to work. Without question, the single biggest complaint among attorneys is increasingly long workdays with decreasing time for personal and family life. Lawyers are complaining with increasing vehemence about living to work, rather than working to live—about being asked not to dedicate, but to sacrifice their lives to the firm.

[In the late 1960s], most partners billed between 1200 and 1400 hours per year and most associates between 1400 and 1600 hours. As late as the mid-1980s, even associates in large New York firms were often not

---

* [Eds.: More recent results of surveys of law graduates have been reported since this article was written. Readers curious about recent survey data on lawyer satisfaction and related topics may wish to consult RONIT DINOVITZER ET AL., AFTER THE JD II: SECOND RESULTS FROM A NATIONAL STUDY OF LEGAL CAREERS 27 (2009); John Monahan and Jeffrey Swanson, *Lawyers at Mid-Career: A 20-Year Longitudinal Study of Job Satisfaction*, 6 J. EMPIRICAL LEGAL STUDIES 451 (2009). Some findings from these studies are summarized at the end of this chapter.]

expected to bill more than 1800 hours annually. Today, many firms would consider these ranges acceptable only for partners or associates who had died midway through the year.

Workloads, like the job dissatisfaction to which they so closely relate, are not distributed equally throughout the profession. Generally speaking, lawyers in private practice work longer hours than those who work for corporations or for the government.

Why do lawyers work too much? In one sense, the answer is easy: It's the money, stupid. It begins with law students. The vast majority of law students—at least the vast majority of those attending the more prestigious schools (or getting good grades at the less prestigious schools)—want to work in big firms. And the reason they want to work in big firms is that big firms pay the most.

Of course, students deny this. Students—many of whom came to law school intending to do public interest work—don't like to admit that they've "sold out," so they come up with rationalizations, justifications, accounts, and disclaimers for seeking big firm jobs. They insist that the real reason they want to go to a big firm is the training, or the interesting and challenging work, or the chance to work with exceptionally talented colleagues, or the desire to "keep my doors open." They imply that the huge salaries are just an afterthought—mere icing on the cake. Or they reluctantly admit that, yes, they really are after the money, but they have no choice: Because of student loan debt, they must take a job that pays $80,000 per year. $60,000 per year just won't cut it.

Most of this is hogwash. As I will explain below, almost all of the purported non-monetary advantages of big firms either do not exist or are vastly overstated. Moreover, there are few lawyers who could not live comfortably on what most corporations or government agencies pay, whatever their student loan debt. Students are after the money, pure and simple. The hiring partner of any major firm will tell you that if his firm offers first year associates a salary of $69,000, and a competitor down the street offers them $72,000, those who have the choice will flock to the competitor—even if the competitor will require them to bill 200 hours more each year.

As the salaries of first year associates go up, the salaries of senior associates must rise to keep pace. After all, no sixth year associate wants to be paid less than a first year associate. And as the salaries of senior associates go up, the salaries of junior partners must rise to keep pace. After all, no junior partner wants to be paid less than a senior associate. And, of course, as the salaries of junior partners go up, so must the salaries of senior partners.

How do firms pay for this ever-spiraling increase in salaries? In reality, firms have only one option: They have to bill more hours. The market for lawyers' services has become intensely competitive. As the number of lawyers has soared, competition for clients has become ferocious. Clients insist on getting good work at low hourly rates. If clients do not get what they want, they will move their business to one of the thousands of other lawyers who are chomping at the bit to get it. Raising billing rates to pay for spiraling salaries is simply not much of an option for most firms. As a result, firms get the extra money to pay for the spiraling salaries in the only way they can: They bill more hours. Everyone has to work harder to pay for the higher salaries. And when salaries go up again, everyone has to work still harder.

I am leaving out one wrinkle—an important wrinkle that you should know about if you are contemplating joining a large law firm (or a firm that acts like a large law firm). The partners of a big firm have a third option for making more money. This option involves what big firm partners euphemistically refer to as "leverage." I like to call it "the skim." Richard Abel calls it "exploitation."* The person being exploited is you.

Basically, what happens is that big firms buy associates' time wholesale and sell it retail. Here is how it works: As a new associate in a large firm, you will be paid about one-third of what you bring into the firm. If you bill, say, 2000 hours at $100 per hour, you will generate $200,000 in revenue for your firm. About a third of that—$70,000 or so—will be paid to you. Another third will go toward paying the expenses of the firm. And the final third will go into the pockets of the firm's partners. Firms make money off associates. That is why it's in the interests of big firms to hire lots of associates and to make very few of them partners. The more associates there are, the more profits for the partners to split, and the fewer partners there are, the bigger each partner's share.

Money is at the root of virtually everything that lawyers don't like about their profession: the long hours, the commercialization, the tremendous pressure to attract and retain clients, the fiercely competitive marketplace, the lack of collegiality and loyalty among partners, the poor public image of the profession, and even the lack of civility. Almost every one of these problems would be eliminated or at least substantially reduced if lawyers were simply willing to make less money. Thousands of lawyers choose to give up a healthy, happy, well-balanced life for a less healthy, less happy life dominated by work. And they do so merely to be able to make seven or eight times the national median income instead of five or six times the national median income.

The Ethics of Lawyers. It is hard to practice law ethically. Complying with the formal rules is the easy part. The rules are not very specific, and they don't demand very much. Acting as an ethical lawyer in the broader,

---

*   [Eds: Richard Abel is prominent sociologist of the legal profession.]

non-formalistic sense is far more difficult. I have already given you some idea of why it is hard to practice law in a big firm (or any firm that emulates a big firm) and live a balanced life. But even practicing law ethically in the sense of being honest and fair and compassionate is difficult. To understand why, you need to understand what it is that you will do every day as a lawyer.

Here is the problem: After you start practicing law, nothing is likely to influence you more than the culture or house norms of the agency, department, or firm in which you work. If you are going into private practice—particularly private practice in a big firm—you are going to be immersed in a culture that is hostile to the values you now have. The system does not want you to apply the same values in the workplace that you do outside of work (unless you're rapaciously greedy outside of work); it wants you to replace those values with the system's values. The system is obsessed with money, and it wants you to be, too. The system wants you—it needs you—to play the game.

In a thousand ways, you will absorb big firm culture—a culture of long hours of toil inside the office and short hours of conspicuous consumption outside the office. You will work among lawyers who will talk about money constantly and who will be intensely curious about how much money other lawyers are making.

As the values of an attorney change, so, too, does her ability to practice law ethically. The process that I have described will obviously push a lawyer away from practicing law ethically in the broadest sense— that is, in the sense of leading a balanced life and meeting non-work-related responsibilities. When work becomes all-consuming, it consumes all. However, absorbing the values of big firm culture will also push a lawyer away from practicing law ethically in the narrower sense of being honest and fair and compassionate. In the highly competitive, money obsessed world of big firm practice, most of the new incentives for lawyers, such as attracting and retaining clients, push toward stretching ethical concerns to the limit.

Unethical lawyers do not start out being unethical; they start out just like you—as perfectly decent young men or women who have every intention of practicing law ethically. They do not become unethical overnight; they become unethical just as you will (if you become unethical)—a little bit at a time. And they do not become unethical by shredding incriminating documents or bribing jurors; they become unethical just as you are likely to—by cutting a corner here, by stretching the truth a bit there. [Here he argues that lawyers begin taking incremental unethical steps that eventually add up to a willingness to engage in serious misconduct—padding hours, cheating in discovery, encouraging witnesses to lie, mischaracterizing precedent in briefs, etc.]

On Being a Happy, Healthy, and Ethical Lawyer. I now want to give you some advice—advice about how you can be a happy, healthy, and ethical member of an unhappy, unhealthy, and unethical profession.

My "big picture" advice is simple: Don't get sucked into the game. Don't let money become the most important thing in your life. Don't fall into the trap of measuring your worth as an attorney—or as a human being—by how much money you make.

If you let your law firm or clients define success for you, they will define it in a way that is in their interest, not yours. It is important for them that your primary motivation be making money and that, no matter how much money you make, your primary motivation continue to be making money. If you end up as an unhappy or unethical attorney, money will most likely be at the root of your problem.

You cannot win the game. If you fall into the trap of measuring your worth by money, you will always feel inadequate. There will always be a firm paying more to its associates than yours. There will always be a firm with higher per-partner profits than yours. There will always be a lawyer at your firm making more money than you. No matter how hard you work, you will never be able to win the game. You will run faster and faster and faster, but there will always be a runner ahead of you, and the finish line will never quite come into view. That is why the game will make your clients and partners so rich and you so unhappy.

Law students and young lawyers have to stop seeing workaholism as "a badge of honor." They have to stop talking with admiration about lawyers who bill 2500 hours per year. Attorneys whose lives are consumed with work—who devote endless hours to making themselves and their clients wealthy, at the expense of just about everything else in their lives—are not heroes. And that is true whether the lawyers are workaholic because they truly enjoy their work or because they crave wealth or because they are terribly insecure. At best, these attorneys are people with questionable priorities. At worst, they are immoral. There are certainly better lawyers after which to pattern your professional life.

NOTES ON SCHILTZ

1.   *Does This Portrait Fit What You Know About Large Firm Practice?* Are Schiltz's claims about the organizational cultures of big firms consistent with what you learned about these institutions in Chapter 15?

2.   *Law Students' Motivations and Concerns.* Schiltz asserts that most law students are strongly motivated to make money, to accept the highest paying jobs that they can find, and to overestimate the extent to which financial considerations must drive their career choices. Based on your own observations and impressions, does this claim ring true?

3. ***Corruption of Judgment Theory and Obedience and Conformity Norms.*** Is Schiltz's account of how "perfectly decent young men [and] women" become unethical consistent with the social science research on obedience and conformity norms, described in Chapter 16? Based on what you know, does Schiltz underestimate the ability of young lawyers to resist what he views as the most pernicious aspects of big firm culture?

C. WHAT IS CAREER SATISFACTION AND HOW SHOULD WE MEASURE IT?

The next excerpt analyzes the research that Schiltz relies on but draws very different conclusions about lawyers' satisfaction with their work and career choices. It also puts a finer point on exactly what we mean by career satisfaction and how we should measure it.

CROSS-EXAMINING THE MYTH OF LAWYERS' MISERY
Kathleen E. Hull
52 Vanderbilt Law Review 971 (1999)

At first glance, the evidence on job satisfaction among lawyers may appear mixed, but upon closer inspection it becomes clear that the most valid, well-designed research has produced little if any support for the notion that lawyers are unhappy in their work. The studies cited by Schiltz range from trade journal surveys to more serious scholarly enterprises, and the significance we attach to their findings should be in direct proportion to the validity and reliability of the research techniques employed.

Some of these same studies cited by Schiltz produce findings that fail to support his contention that lawyers are largely unhappy in their work. For example, overall findings from the ABA surveys in 1984 and 1990 do not bolster a claim of widespread dissatisfaction in the profession. In the 1984 survey, 81% of respondents were either "somewhat satisfied" or "very satisfied" with their current job, whereas only 12% were "somewhat dissatisfied" and 3% were "very dissatisfied." In 1990, 76% were either "somewhat satisfied" or "very satisfied," while 14% were "somewhat dissatisfied" and 5% "very dissatisfied." These figures hardly suggest job dissatisfaction of crisis proportions in the law.

Other studies boasting higher response rates and sounder survey techniques provide further confirmation that rumors of lawyers' misery are greatly exaggerated. Chambers' 1989 study of University of Michigan law graduates, which achieved a 71% response rate surveying graduates five years after law school, found that 82% of female graduates and 83% of male graduates were "somewhat" or "quite" satisfied with their careers at the five-year mark. A follow-up survey showed little change in satisfaction levels over time.

Beyond his reliance on studies of dubious data quality and his relative inattention to some studies that produce findings of high satisfaction levels, there is also a conceptual difficulty embedded in Schiltz's discussion of the research on lawyers' satisfaction. Schiltz blends together a number of conceptually distinct findings under the general umbrella of "satisfaction." Asking people whether they hope to be in the same job at some future point in time, or asking them whether they would choose the same occupation if they had it to do over again, produces only indirect evidence at best regarding satisfaction with their current situation. People may hope to change jobs in the future even if they love their current work, possibly because they know a job change will be necessary to keep "moving up" (e.g., from firm practice to a judgeship) or because they hope to renegotiate the tradeoff between work and personal priorities in the future. These kinds of reasons for seeking a change do not necessarily prove that the current job produces unhappiness; they only demonstrate that people like (or sometimes need) change.

Relying on the American Bar Association surveys conducted in 1984 and 1990 and the unpublished Michigan data covering the years 1981 through 1996, Schiltz argues that there has been a "marked" and "substantial" decline in lawyers' job satisfaction in recent years. With regard to the ABA data, he points to the fact that 41% of respondents were "very satisfied" in 1984, compared to only 33% in 1990.

These figures are interesting, but we should not attach undue importance to them for at least two reasons. First, not all of the decline in the "very satisfied" category translated into increases in the proportion of "dissatisfied" or "very dissatisfied" lawyers. In fact, among the overall sample, the proportion who were "dissatisfied" rose modestly from 12% in 1984 to 14% in 1990, and the proportion "very dissatisfied" inched up from 3% in 1984 to 5% in 1990. In other words, only about half of the eight percentage-point decline in the "very satisfied" category is accounted for by increases in dissatisfied respondents. The other half is accounted for by similarly modest growth in the proportion of lawyers who were "satisfied" or merely "neutral."

Second, even given a moderate decline in average satisfaction between the two survey years, we must take into consideration the broader context of these surveys. In particular, this kind of short-term trend in job satisfaction might simply reflect the ups and downs of the legal profession's fortunes over time. Like any industry, the legal services industry experiences periods of boom and bust, often closely linked to the cycles of the larger economy. While the mid-1980s represented a "boom" time for lawyers, by the early 1990s the climate had changed [for the worse].

Other surveys with longitudinal data covering somewhat different time periods show satisfaction levels holding fairly steady across time. In short, there is no consistent body of evidence that lawyers' work satisfaction has been declining in recent years, and the two surveys that suggest such a decline may simply reflect a short-term downturn in the growth in the market for lawyers' services in the U.S.

The assertion that large-firm lawyers are significantly less satisfied than lawyers in other practice settings is central to Schiltz's broader arguments. But how solid is the evidence for this claim?

In data [from a rigorous study of Chicago lawyers], there are no significant differences in satisfaction by practice setting among practicing lawyers. Compared to lawyers in other settings, large-firm lawyers seem neither remarkably happy nor remarkably miserable. Only 39% of large-firm lawyers were "very satisfied," the lowest proportion for any practice setting. By contrast, 60% of public interest lawyers fell into this category, as did 51% of government lawyers, 50% of internal counsel lawyers, 47% of solo practitioners, 46% of small-firm lawyers, and 45% of medium-firm lawyers. But 47% of large-firm attorneys were "satisfied," the highest proportion for any practice setting. And only 2% of large-firm lawyers were "dissatisfied" or "very dissatisfied," compared to 11% of government lawyers, 9% of solo practitioners and small-firm lawyers, 7% of medium-firm lawyers and public interest lawyers, and 5% of internal counsel.

Specifically, large-firm lawyers are significantly more satisfied than other private-practice lawyers with their salaries, their chances for advancement, and the prestige of their organizations. On salary, for example, 73% of large-firm attorneys were either "satisfied" or "very satisfied," compared to 57% of medium and small-firm attorneys and 46% of solo practitioners.

But large-firm lawyers are significantly less satisfied with their control over the amount of work they must do and also with the policies and administration of their firms. Only 56% of large-firm lawyers were "satisfied" or "very satisfied" with control over amount of work, compared to 65% of medium-firm lawyers, 79% of small-firm lawyers and 74% of solo practitioners. Just 43% of large-firm lawyers reported satisfaction with the policies/administration of their firms, similar to the 42% of medium-firm lawyers, but lower than the 68% of small-firm lawyers who liked their firm's policies.

A different way to approach the question of whether the experience of large-firm employment drives lawyers to other settings is to look at the current position of all lawyers who started in large firms, regardless of whether they have made a job change. This approach arguably gives a more complete picture of lawyer retention in various practice settings, because it includes lawyers who start in a setting and remain in the setting by not changing jobs, as well as those who change jobs but remain in the same general setting. If we look at lawyers in the Chicago sample who have been out of law school for at least five years, we find that 63% of those who started in the large-firm setting are currently in that setting. Among those who started in solo practice or small-to-medium sized firms, 65% are currently in that same setting. By contrast, only 40% of those who began in government, public interest, or legal education currently work in those settings, and only 42% of those who began in internal counsel or nonlegal positions currently work in the same setting.

NOTES ON HULL

1. **What Do the Data Show?** According to Hull, what are the problems with the data upon which Schiltz relies in asserting that lawyers are unhappy, and what are the problems in how he interprets the available data?

2. **Elements of Career Satisfaction.** What are the various elements of career satisfaction identified by Hull? How do lawyers in different practice settings rank in terms of those elements of satisfaction?

D. COMPARATIVE PERSPECTIVES

The following excerpt draws attention to how lawyers compare with other occupational groups in terms of career satisfaction. It also calls into question whether firms are as similar to one another as Schiltz suggests.

THINKING ABOUT THE BUSINESS OF PRACTICING LAW
Michael J. Kelly
52 Vanderbilt Law Review 985 (1999)

The nagging question I have when confronted with all this evidence of discontent is to ask for some evaluative comparison. All the unhappiness data is solely confined to lawyers. If, for example, lawyers were not that much more unhappy than people inside their corporate clients, or physicians struggling with the transformation of the health care industry, would it worry us as much as it does Schiltz? And if we were to postulate that both law and medicine are undergoing significant change, would it not be entirely understandable that young people commencing their careers with expectations of a large degree of autonomy are distressed at the increasing "corporatization" or dominance by the organizations of practice in their professions?

The core of Schiltz's argument with which I most disagree is that large firms are all alike, or, to put it in its more modest, plausible, and compelling form, that big firms and big-firm lawyers are becoming more alike. I cannot disprove Schiltz's claims about the convergence occurring in large law firms. After all, there is evidence and intelligent speculation that supports it. Galanter and Palay's hypothesis, cited by Schiltz, is that in a culture that values autonomy, money is the one measure of the many goods of a practice upon which it is easiest to agree (or the least difficult to avoid) and therefore emerges as the prime focus of most partnership understandings. The vast majority of formulae or weighting systems for compensation in law firms reward those who strengthen the business and deploy to its full potential the firm's leverage by bringing in clients and servicing or retaining important clients.

So why am I so skeptical of the convergence thesis? One response is perhaps only temperamental: I am deeply suspicious of iron laws, particularly when it comes to organizations. Firms are human constructs. The character of an organization is determined by people, not solely by competitive pressures to which people respond. [O]rganizations develop different characters even in a situation of responding to the same economic pressures.

The advice Schiltz gives to law students, whether you agree with his diagnosis of large law firms or not, addresses thoughtfully the huge reality law graduates face—that the law firm is their profession and represents, enforces, and rewards the values that will determine the future of their career. I would encourage someone trying to learn about a firm to ask an interviewer to describe the leader of the firm. Is the leader the rainmaker extraordinaire, the most dominating personality, the most accomplished lawyer, someone with a sense of vision and direction for the firm, or someone with strong management skills? The person who heads the practice, at a time when organizational leadership is so critical to the future of law practice organizations, should speak volumes about the nature, let alone the future, of the firm. A riskier set of questions, probably best left to the time when an offer is in hand, could also be revealing. No firm of any size is likely to be free of conflict. Are people in the firm willing to discuss its internal conflicts, and describe how, if at all, they are resolved? Are people in the firm willing to talk about mistakes the firm has made? Current problems? Whether they do so and how they go about it would tell the questioner much about the self-confidence, character, and transparency (i.e., openness) of the organization.

Law is, and always has been, a business as well as a profession. Lawyers have, for most of American history, made good livings, and many have made fortunes. Once one escapes from the clutches of thinking of "profession" and "business" as dichotomies, and comes to terms with the fact that, whether we like it not, they are joined at the hip in private practice, a refreshing set of possibilities reveals itself. Virtually none of the criticisms or problems posed by Schiltz—imposed workaholic regimens, distorted compensation structures, unhappy professionals used and viewed in totally instrumental ways by management—are unique to large law firms or the private practice of law. [T]here is much to be gained by thinking of these organizations as businesses that may be profitable to their owners but have serious long-term problems. [T]hinking creatively about the business of private law practice could strongly—and realistically—support the enhancement of professional values. A sound business strategy entails a sustained and serious conversation that confronts the threats of drift and opportunism. Understanding the business better and taking creative action to improve the business may ultimately prove the most fruitful approach to developing happy, healthy, and ethical lawyers.

NOTES ON KELLY

1. *Law v. Medicine and Other Professions/Occupations.* Based on your experience, do you think that lawyers are more or less satisfied with their careers than doctors, business people, engineers, teachers, professional athletes, or car mechanics? Taking into account the different elements of career satisfaction identified by Hull, what would you expect to be the rewards and sources of dissatisfaction in these other professions and occupations?

2. *Common Ground and Disagreement.* What are the points of agreement and disagreement between Schiltz, Hull, and Kelly? How does Kelly's advice to law students differ from Schiltz's?

3. *Organizational Cultures.* Notice that Schiltz and Kelly agree that, for better or worse, the cultures of the organizations in which lawyers practice are likely to influence lawyers' lives, including their career satisfaction, much more than the rules of ethics and other activities of the organized bar. What aspects of organizational culture are most significant for lawyer satisfaction?

4. *Variation Among Firms.* Based on what you have learned thus far about large firms, do you think that Kelly is right to suggest that large firms differ substantially and that lawyers seeking satisfying careers in these institutions need to ask good questions in order to uncover important differences in institutional cultures? Or do you think that whatever variation exists among law firms is too insubstantial to matter?

5. *Reassessing Schiltz.* After having read Hull's and Kelly's critiques, which of Schiltz's claims do you find convincing and which do you question?

E. CAREER SATISFACTION, SOCIAL BACKGROUND, AND LAW SCHOOL HIERARCHY

Might lawyers' satisfaction with their careers vary by the lawyers' social backgrounds and law school? The following excerpt analyzes that issue, drawing from data on young lawyers gathered in the *After the JD* study.

LAWYER SATISFACTION IN THE PROCESS OF STRUCTURING LEGAL CAREERS

Ronit Dinovitzer and Bryant G. Garth
41 Law & Society Rev. 1 (2007)

Consistent with prior research, reported levels of job satisfaction in the AJD study are high: when asked to rate their satisfaction with 16 specific dimensions of their jobs, respondents consistently rate themselves as more satisfied than dissatisfied. In particular, lawyers express higher levels of satisfaction with their relationships with colleagues, their level of responsibility, the control over how they work, and the intellectual challenge of their work (all rated 5.39 or higher on a scale of 1–7), with somewhat lower ratings given to their performance evaluation process, the diversity of their workplace, and their opportunities for pro bono work (all rated 4.4/7 or lower). More strikingly, respondents' satisfaction with their career choice is very high: fully 79% of respondents report that they are extremely or moderately satisfied with their decision to become a lawyer. In contrast, however, when asked how long they plan to stay with their current employer, the data suggest a different pattern, with 44 percent of respondents expressing that they intend to be looking for a new job within two years—and almost one-quarter of these respondents express that they are already looking for a new position or plan to within one year.

These data present somewhat of a paradox: on the one hand, we find very high levels of reported satisfaction with the decision to become a lawyer, while on the other, we find fairly high levels of job mobility expectations, often taken as indicating lower levels of professional satisfaction. To get underneath this tension, we disaggregated these findings by the prestige of the law school attended by the respondents. [S]chools are a key site through which students acquire their professional expectations—schools thereby play a critical role in the reproduction of social stratification, with students not merely acquiring the skills they require for professional life, but [also] adapting to the dispositions necessary for the professional roles they are destined to take. This can be achieved because schools are themselves embedded in the reproduction of students' social origins: the prestige of the school that individuals attend is itself a function of their social class, so that in bestowing degrees and credentials, schools confirm and reaffirm students' anticipated status within the profession.

Our measure of the law school hierarchy is derived from the rankings published in the *U.S. News and World Report* for 2003; each school in the AJD data set was assigned its corresponding *U.S. News* score and was then placed into one of six major groupings: the top 10, top 11–20, top 21–40, top 41–100, schools in the third tier, and schools in the fourth tier. Analyses reveal that these rankings correlate well with the measures of lawyers' social background available in the AJD data. [S]tudents attending top 10 schools report fathers' occupational prestige scores that are significantly higher than those from the fourth-tier schools, with reports of fathers' occupational scores declining in a linear fashion along with law school tier. The data on fathers' educational attainment display a similar pattern: more than two-thirds of top 10 school graduates had fathers who had completed some graduate education, compared to one-third of fourth-tier graduates. The law school rankings also map directly onto the settings within which law graduates work, an indicator that the social hierarchies that led students into particular law schools will also continue to be reproduced in their professional careers. [M]ore than half of the graduates from top 10 schools work in the megafirms of more than 250 lawyers, compared to just 4 percent of fourth-tier graduates, who are instead working predominantly in small or solo practices. Even when they work in the public sector, graduates of elite schools are more likely to be working in the more prestigious federal government positions, while lower-tier graduates are more likely to work for state government.

Given these patterns, it is perhaps not surprising that measures of job satisfaction also track the hierarchy of law schools. While our initial examination of job satisfaction resulted in somewhat of a paradox, noting high levels of satisfaction at the same time as high job mobility intentions, examining these same measures by law school tier sheds considerable light on this disjuncture. [A]lmost 60 percent of top 10 graduates expect to leave their positions within two years, while only 27 percent report that they are extremely satisfied with their decision to become a lawyer. However, substantially fewer (41 percent) of the fourth-tier graduates intend to leave their employer within two years, while substantially more (43 percent) of these graduates are extremely satisfied with their decision to become a lawyer. These patterns suggest that there is in fact a convergence, rather than a divergence, between expressions of career satisfaction and job mobility intentions: the most elite students are the least satisfied with their career choice and the most likely to be thinking of leaving their employer, while lower-tier graduates express high levels of career satisfaction and high levels of commitment to their employer.

It may be, however, that this relationship between law school tier and job satisfaction has more to do with the practice settings in which these lawyers work, rather than being a direct consequence of the law schools they attended. After all, the most elite students are the most likely to be working in large corporate law firms, so their lack of satisfaction may be the result of where they work, rather than the dispositions they acquired in law school. To investigate this possibility, we restricted the sample to those respondents working in firms of more than 100 lawyers. The data confirm that even within these large law firms, the most elite graduates continue to express lower levels of career satisfaction than those from the fourth tier (26 percent of elites report extreme satisfaction, compared with almost half (49 percent) of those in the fourth tier). Similarly, we find that top 10 law school graduates are more likely to intend to leave their employer within two years, compared to their fourth-tier counterparts (59 versus 27 percent). These patterns suggest that the relatively lower satisfaction of elite graduates is not merely driven by their work settings, and that there is an independent relationship between law school tier and expressions of satisfaction that requires further investigation.

By incorporating patterns of social stratification into our analysis of satisfaction, we find that expressions of satisfaction map fairly clearly onto the hierarchy of law schools—and that attention to social hierarchies resolves the apparent tension between lawyers' career satisfaction and their mobility intentions.

Models of the Role of Satisfaction and Dissatisfaction. In this next section, we draw on in-depth interviews with AJD respondents in which they recount how they found their jobs, describe their practice settings and work life, and discuss their expectations for the future. These accounts reveal the ways in which individuals make meaning of their lives and find satisfaction in the positions that they occupy, while they also act as mechanisms through which stratification is reproduced and legitimated.

The discussion below constructs six major categories of lawyers, based on the tier of law school they attended. These groupings are intended to provide a first approximation of the kinds of people who graduate and make careers from the different law schools, building on the basic insight that the higher-ranked the law school, the more likely the graduates are to have come from privileged backgrounds—and it extends this insight by including a range of factors that grow out of, and are reinforced by, one's class position.

The Elites: Biding Time. Graduates from top 10 schools are overwhelmingly the children of advantage. In contrast to those who attended the lower-tier schools, their reasons for attending law school focused on the intellectual challenge of law school or developing a satisfying career—reasons that are less tied to lifestyle and financial success. At the same time, they are more likely than graduates of other tiers to have considered alternative lucrative and prestigious options, such as a career in investment banking. Their options in the legal field are plentiful, which is reflected in the number of job offers they received in the private sector; very few of them even sought positions in the public sector. Once on the job market, they were drawn to the four major metropolitan areas, to the large law firms (100+lawyers), and (compared to the sample as a whole) to public interest firms—which for them does not necessarily foreclose other options in private practice. They are on a fast track, and they are there by choice, which is reflected in their valuing prestige and mobility versus lifestyle in their choice of legal practice sector.

Graduates of top-tier schools have all the advantages, but the data suggest that they do not necessarily appreciate them. While they are significantly less likely to have already changed jobs, they are more likely to express plans to leave their employer in the relatively near future; when compared to their counterparts from all other tiers who are also working in large firms, we continue to find that they are more likely to express intentions to leave their employer. Their practice settings require them to put in significantly longer hours, which translates for them into much less satisfaction with their job setting. This sense of ambivalence about their job is paralleled by their ambivalence about their choice of career, reporting the lowest level of satisfaction with their decision to become a lawyer. This relative ambivalence is also seen in their involvement at work, with the elite students reporting less contact with partners, suggesting that they are not investing much in accumulating social capital where it requires the most effort. The combination of privileged position and relatively less satisfaction suggests that these top-tier graduates take for granted that they will be successful but at the same time that they also have some regret about other options they could have pursued, options they know may have been at least as satisfying. These elite graduates are ready and expect to move if and when something better comes up, but their relative lack of mobility to date suggests that the grumbling seen in plans to move does not necessarily lead to actual moves in the short term. At this stage of their career, they are still going through the motions that were planned for them by their enrollment in elite law schools.

Yet the path of the elite is not of one piece. [E]ven among the elites women and minorities continue to face obstacles. Thus while the elite credential bestows—and reaffirms—a successful trajectory for most graduates, it does not wholly overcome the well-established structures of inequality in the profession. These obstacles are not the focus of this article, but it is clear that the institutions of the legal profession are structured such that mastery of "the game" of success in the legal profession comes easier to elite white males.

The "Almost" Elites—Always in Second (Top 11–20). Across nearly all measures, graduates of schools ranking in the top 11–20 are "almost" identical to the elite students. The background of these respondents is clearly privileged, reporting significantly higher levels of occupational prestige and education for their fathers compared to respondents from all other schools, and they also have invested heavily in the private sector.

And while they are privileged compared to the average respondent, they are not given quite the same opportunities as the elite group, which is reflected in comparatively fewer offers, a lower likelihood of working in the largest law firms, somewhat lower salaries and hours worked, and more attention to salary as a factor in their choice of a position. Many of them also had to work harder to get their positions than those from the elite schools, suggesting that grades matter more as one moves down the law school hierarchy.

It is not surprising that those who worked harder to earn their positions are not as casual about leaving them. These graduates report a high rate of prior job stability, and they are not more likely than other graduates to express intentions to leave their job within two years. While they express the same relative dissatisfaction with aspects of large firm settings as the elite graduates, more of them are satisfied with their decision to become a lawyer (though they are still less satisfied than graduates of all other tiers). Their greater commitment to their jobs is also reflected in the fact that a larger percentage of these graduates network with partners, reflecting an effort to build relationships in their settings; we also see this commitment in their ratings of their opportunities for advancement, which are relatively high. In short, while the group is rather close to the elite in terms of where they work, they tend to be more grateful for the place they have found, sharing some of the characteristics of those from lower-ranked schools.

Between Elites and the Middle (Top 21–40). Graduates of law schools ranked 21–40 have social backgrounds similar to those of the groups described above. But the lines of demarcation become much stronger at this level. On almost every measure other than social class, graduates of top 21–40 schools are below those from top 20 schools: they received fewer job offers, a smaller proportion of them work in large firms, and they earn less. They also express sentiments that diverge from those of the elite: they are less likely, for example, to have gone to law school to "help" others. Grateful for the opportunities they have, when compared to graduates of the tiers above them, they are more committed to their employers, network more, and are more satisfied with their decision to become a lawyer. While still below the median for the sample, they are more likely than the elites to express a preference to work in settings that are identified with a better lifestyle than is found in the large corporate firms. Valuing "lifestyle," we see here and within the lower-ranking tiers, is not just a preference that some people express. It begins to come into play at this stage to help adjust law graduates to the fewer hours, less intense, and less prestigious work that is for the most part available to them. A law graduate who cannot gain access to the most elite positions tends, therefore, to find "lifestyle" reasons to accept that fate.

Happiness at the Top of the Middle (Top 41–100 Schools). Those who graduated from the top 41–100 schools come from less privileged backgrounds than those at the higher-ranking schools, and they understand law school as part of a project of upward mobility. When asked why they decided to go to law school, for example, they give somewhat higher than average ratings to careerist reasons. Their prospects are limited, with far fewer offers in the private sector and only 10 percent of these graduates making it to the larger firms (of at least 100 lawyers). These respondents give significantly higher ratings to lifestyle in their choice of practice setting, as could be expected, but they are still close enough to the top that they continue to emphasize the importance of prestige in their choices.

With law providing them with upward mobility, we find this group investing strongly in their career paths. A large proportion of these graduates expect to be staying with their current employer for more than two years. They know that law school made a difference in their career prospects, with more than one-third extremely satisfied with their decision to become a lawyer. They do not take for granted that they will have a successful career, working fairly long hours and working hard, even at networking. They are trying assiduously to learn the rules for advancement rather than relying on a feel for the game. The payoffs for these investments are also tangible: while their salaries are below the average in the sample, they are higher than those of graduates from the lower tiers, while their hours of work are no different than the average. Furthermore, their satisfaction with their job setting is higher than the average but their satisfaction with the power track is comparatively lower—at the same time, their position in the hierarchy means that they are still more satisfied with the power track than graduates of the tiers below them.* They know they have achieved upward mobility and are pleased, even though they do not have the same actual career prospects as those who start at the top.

The Third Tier—The Battle for Upward Mobility. In terms of socioeconomic background, law school for the third tier appears to represent an aspiration of upward mobility: more of these graduates report that they went to law school for careerist reasons, but they also went to law school to help others—perhaps because they remember where they came from. Their experience on the job market is fairly similar to those in the tier above them, but they tend to work predominantly in solo or small practice. Many of them justify that choice as a lifestyle decision, again reflecting their "choice" not to work in environments that were not in fact available to them.

---

*   [Eds. note: "power track satisfaction" consists of "satisfaction with compensation levels and satisfaction with opportunities for advancement."]

The experiences of this group also suggest a continuing struggle. They are less settled than other respondents, with a combination of high mobility in past employment and expected high mobility in the near future. Evidence of this struggle is also reflected in their ratings of their opportunities for advancement, which are the lowest of all groups. These low ratings reflect a very different strategy when compared with the low ratings reported by elite students, who take for granted that they will start and end at the top. Graduates of the third tier are working hard as they try to build their careers, working the same number of hours as those in the tiers above. The benefits do not come as easily to them, however, as they are earning less and express low levels of satisfaction with the power track. Yet the legal profession continues to offer them some satisfaction, particularly with their job setting, which they rate somewhat higher when compared with the average respondent. And for those who have made it into the largest firms the commitment is clear, with their expressions of intentions to leave their employer among the lowest for those working in large firms. Thus despite their lower pay and hard work, they are aware of their upward mobility, with more than a third reporting that they are extremely satisfied with their decision to become a lawyer.

The Fourth Tier: The Most Satisfied? Graduates of fourth-tier schools come from the least advantaged social backgrounds; their parents are the least educated and have the lowest occupational prestige scores in the sample. They are more likely than others to have considered starting their own business as an alternate career strategy, a dramatic contrast with the aspiration to work as an investment banker that was expressed by elite graduates. Moreover, the interviews again reveal the influence of a lifestyle preference for these graduates, who reject the long hours associated with working in a large law firm. At the same time, their experience on the job market suggests that they are fulfilling a particular market need—while fewer of them received more than two offers, their odds of receiving at least one offer is no different than the average. Their work settings are a stark contrast to the settings of the elite graduates: almost half of the fourth-tier graduates work in small or solo practice; they are also the least likely of all respondents to express that prestige and mobility were important in their choice of sector of practice. Perhaps this reflects the somewhat limited choices they faced in the job market.

Graduates of the fourth tier are working hard to make it. They work as hard as most other new lawyers (except for the elites)—yet they earn the least. They have experienced some instability already, with about 35 percent of this group having already changed jobs at least once. Their commitment is clear, however, with almost 60 percent intending to stay with their current employer longer than two years and expressing that they see some opportunities for advancement. Given that they are staying where they are, they report high levels of satisfaction with their job setting, the substance of their work, and the social index—again making virtues out of necessities. A higher percentage of these lawyers than any other group reports being extremely satisfied with their decision to become a lawyer. Thus despite the worse objective circumstances compared with graduates of other law school tiers, these graduates are well aware of the boost that the law degree gave to their careers. They believe that they are lucky, and that it makes little sense to want the professional rewards that are unattainable to them. They are therefore more or less pleased with where they are and plan to stay, especially if they are one of the few who made it to a large firm—if they can hang on to the position.

Mixing and Matching Careers and People: Social Class in Professional Sorting. At this early stage of lawyer careers, it is already clear how sentiments of satisfaction and dissatisfaction play into and legitimate the hierarchical structures of the legal profession. Those who can obtain the most prestigious and lucrative positions in large corporate law firms do so, they work long hours, and they internalize a relative dissatisfaction that encourages them to move. The relative unhappiness with the work and job setting in the large corporate law firms helps those from the lower-ranked schools—who typically are from relatively disadvantaged backgrounds—to feel pride in other choices. [T]he lower-ranked law schools themselves encourage students to make a professional virtue out of the careers that are available to their graduates. They emphasize values such as service to clients or the achievement of gaining access to the legal profession. In the meantime, the rite of passage of some tenure in large corporate law firms is so built into the elite opportunity structure that few from the top tiers of schools turn it down at the initial stages of their careers. The difficulties of that work are part of a process that makes it easier to accept the unequal access to high-paying and prestigious law jobs.

The relative lack of elite satisfaction, we note, also plays a role in the internal dynamics of the large corporate law firms. It is clear that the economics of the large law firm depend on relatively few associates making it to partner. Meanwhile, the long hours that associates work are essential to partner profits. Too many partners would depress those profits. This basic structure is the basis of Galanter and Palay's hypothesis of the "tournament of lawyers." It is difficult to administer a tournament, however, when there are too many contestants and the criteria for victory are not very precise. Our hypothesis is that relative dissatisfaction encourages attrition and makes the screening process far more manageable for law firm managers. While there is no detailed research about the partnership decision as such, it would be difficult for partners to make defensible decisions if all the associates sought to stay.

It is probably relatively easy to use evaluations to determine workplace success among associates, but difficult to determine who is so outstanding as to warrant partnership. The difficult lifestyle of the large law firm that encourages very high attrition makes this decision somewhat easier.

The patterns of expected mobility raise some cause for concern, however, when examined by race and gender. Our data indicate that women are more likely than men to be planning to leave their employers within one year and that minorities are also more likely to express these intentions. Law firms are under strong pressure to hire and retain more women and minorities, but the system of high attrition reaffirms the patterns of the large corporate law firm as still a white male institution. Minorities and women who choose to leave may believe that it is their own choice—perhaps for lifestyle reasons—but the cumulative impact and sentiments such as those just quoted suggest that the institutional dynamics of law firms are also part of this process.

<u>Conclusion</u>. The implications of the system of stratification documented in this article and in others are significant. We know for example, from the pathbreaking work of the Chicago Lawyers project, that the legal profession is divided into two hemispheres, with one sphere serving corporations and the other serving personal clients. It is clear from the AJD data that this segmentation of lawyers into separate spheres begins early in their careers, and that it is related to patterns of stratification. [T]op 10 law school graduates report, on average, that they spend 69 percent of their time serving corporate clients and 35 percent of their time representing personal clients or small businesses. The patterns almost reverse as we follow the hierarchy of law school tier, with average fourth-tier graduates devoting 28 percent of their time to representing corporate clients and 57 percent of their time to personal clients or small businesses. The direct correlation between law school tier and client type, and the step-graded pattern of this correlation, demonstrates that the system of stratification in the legal profession is even more complex than the two-hemispheres thesis suggests.

The streaming of top law graduates into the corporate sphere has long raised questions about the ways in which the resources of the legal profession are expended, and the patterns we document in this article call for further reflection on the implications of stratification for the legal field. With lawyers from lower-tier law schools not only accepting of their place in the profession's hierarchy, but also extolling its virtues by relying on the benefits of lifestyle, we find a continued convergence of elite lawyers and corporate clients that is reproduced through career preferences. [I]t is precisely this elite convergence that continues to provide law firms with their own status and underwrites their ability to retain and bill corporate clients. That this hierarchy is legitimated through individual career aspirations ensures that any change would be difficult to effect—and elite law schools, continuing to draw their students from predominantly privileged social origins, will continue to place their graduates in large, urban law firms generating wealth for corporate clients. This is a paradigm that some of these new elite lawyers may be challenging, as they look outside of the large law firms for opportunities. The implications of this challenge, however, remain unknown: while it may result in reform of law firms, it may instead work to their advantage by differentiating among elite students, with departures even extending the influence of firms and law schools beyond the legal field. Lawyer satisfaction, as a result, provides an early signal for how law's symbolic value may be remade—or reproduced—in the coming decades.

NOTES ON DINOVITZER & GARTH

1.   *The Research Findings.* What do the *After the JD* data suggest about overall levels of satisfaction with jobs and career choice among the lawyers who graduated from law school in 2000? What do they suggest about the relationship between social background and lawyer satisfaction?

2.   *Alternative Interpretations?* Are you persuaded by the notion that law graduates who cannot gain access to the most elite positions in the profession tend to find lifestyle reasons to accept that fate? Are there other explanations for their satisfaction that you find more convincing?

* * *

Recent Data on Lawyer Satisfaction. Recent research continues to show high levels of job satisfaction among lawyers. Data from Wave 2 of the *After the JD* Study (*After the JD II*), published in 2009, found that three-quarters of respondents were "extremely" or "moderately" satisfied with their decision to become a lawyer. Across 19 different measures of job satisfaction, respondents reported high levels of satisfaction. Moreover, on all but one of those 19 measures (the exception was "opportunity for advancement"), respondents reported higher levels of satisfaction in Wave 2 than in Wave 1 of the study. Overall career satisfaction was fairly stable across workplaces, but the sources of satisfaction varied by practice setting. Lawyers in megafirms reported the highest levels of "power track" satisfaction (opportunities for advancement and prestige) but the lowest levels of satisfaction with hours and control over their work. Lawyers in government expressed high levels of satisfaction with balance and control but less satisfaction with the power track. Lawyers in legal services and public interest jobs were most satisfied with the content of their work and the value of their work to society but least satisfied with the power track dimensions of their work. Consistent with the results of Wave 1 of the study, black and Hispanic respondents reported the highest levels of career satisfaction in Wave 2; fully 80 percent of black and Hispanic sample members said that they were moderately or extremely satisfied with their decision to become a lawyer. Overall, women were slightly less satisfied with their career choice than men; 74.1 percent of women were extremely to moderately satisfied with the decision to become a lawyer, as compared with 78.4 percent of men.[1]

A study of University of Virginia Law School graduates, based on survey data gathered in 2007 from the Class of 1990, found that 81.2 percent of respondents were "extremely" or "moderately" satisfied with their decision to become a lawyer, while over 81 percent said that they were satisfied with their job setting. The report found no significant gender differences in respondents' satisfaction with the decision to become a lawyer.[2]

The data collection for the *After the JD II* report and the study of University of Virginia Law School graduates took place before the financial crisis in the autumn of 2008. Would you expect current levels satisfaction among lawyers to be the same, higher, or lower than the levels reported in those studies?

Some have suggested that the combination of rising law school tuition, increased law school debt, and the most recent recession, have changed prospects for new law graduates fundamentally in ways that are likely to have far-reaching implications for lawyer satisfaction. In particular, critics have asserted that graduates of all but elite schools will regret the career choice because they will have difficulty finding jobs in large law firms and will be unable to repay their debt.[3] But participants in the *After the JD* research have argued that these predictions are not well-supported by the best available data. One article based on the *AJD2* data cited evidence that more than three-quarters of respondents in the study, irrespective of debt, expressed extreme or moderate satisfaction with the decision to become a lawyer. They also noted that while graduates of elite law schools were less likely to have debt seven years after law school than graduates of lower-ranked schools, graduates of lower-ranked law schools paid down their debt at a faster rate than graduates of elite schools. These scholars predicted that data on lawyer satisfaction for the period after the recession were likely to resemble data from the period before the recession.[4]

---

[1]   *See* RONIT DINOVITZER ET AL., AFTER THE JD II: SECOND RESULTS FROM A NATIONAL STUDY OF LEGAL CAREERS 48-51, 70, 76–77 (2009).

[2]   John Monahan and Jeffrey Swanson, *Lawyers at Mid-Career: a 20-Year Longitudinal Study of Job and Life Satisfaction*, 6 J. Empirical Legal Stud. 451 (2009).

[3]   *See, e.g.,* David Segal, *For Law Schools, a Price to Play the ABA's Way*, N.Y. TIMES, Dec. 17, 2011; BRIAN Z. TAMANAHA, FAILING LAW SCHOOLS (2012).

[4]   Ronit Dinovitzer, Bryant G. Garth & Joyce Sterling, *Buyers' Remorse? An Empirical Assessment of the Desirability of a Lawyer Career*, 63 J. LEGAL ED. 1, 5 (2013).

Results from the third wave of data collection for the *After the JD* study show that the high levels of career satisfaction reflected in earlier phases of this research continue. Thirteen years into their careers, most lawyers (76 percent) reported that they are moderately or extremely satisfied with their decisions to become a lawyer—a proportion that is virtually unchanged from prior waves of the survey. The more detailed measures of job satisfaction tell a similar story. Respondents report the lowest level of satisfaction with the performance evaluation process and the highest levels of satisfaction with the intellectual challenge, relationships with colleagues, control over how they work, substantive area of work, and level of responsibility. The respondents also reported high levels of satisfaction with the balance of personal life and work—5.4 on a 7 point scale, which is slightly higher than at Wave 2.

Overall career satisfaction in Wave 3 was high across workplaces, but lawyers in some practice areas were more satisfied with the decision to become a lawyer than others. The highest overall levels of satisfaction were in the public sector—legal services/public defender and public interest organizations—and in corporate counsel positions. Among lawyers in private practice, those in the largest firms and small firms expressed relatively high levels of satisfaction, while those in mid-sized firms (101–250 lawyers) reported the lowest levels of career satisfaction. As in previous waves of the *After the JD* research, lawyers in various types of practice settings ranked the components of job satisfaction differently. Lawyers in large firms scored well on the power track dimension of their work (compensation, opportunities for advancement, recognition of one's work, the performance evaluation process), but so did lawyers in firms of 2–20 lawyers. Large firms scored relatively poorly on the "job setting" dimension—control over hours worked, work relationships, and work/life balance. Legal services, public defender, and state government jobs scored well on social index and substance of work but received low scores on the power track dimension.[5]

F. SUMMARY

This chapter explored whether lawyers are satisfied with their careers. We began with an essay that boldly asserts that lawyers are unhappy. We then examined what career satisfaction *means* and how one might measure it. The best available empirical research on this topic suggests that career satisfaction varies by practice type and even within a practice settings. It also indicates that lawyers experience different types of career satisfaction, and that job satisfaction is best assessed by paying close attention to those various types of rewards. These elements of career

---

[5] Joyce Sterling, Robert Nelson, Bryant Garth, David Wilkins & Rebecca Sandefur, *After the JD Wave 3 Results,* presentation at the Law and Society Association Annual Meeting (May 29, 2014).

satisfaction include financial compensation, prestige, relationships with colleagues, levels of responsibility, control over work, intellectual challenge, a sense of the social value of one's work, and diversity of the workplace. Research from the *After the JD* study suggests that dimensions of job satisfaction are not distributed evenly across practice types and that lawyers' job satisfaction and social background are significantly related. Overall, the research presented in this chapter shows high levels of satisfaction among lawyers and raises questions about the common claim that lawyers are unhappy and that they regret their chosen careers.

CHAPTER 39

REFLECTIONS ON THE FUTURE OF THE LEGAL PROFESSION (AND YOUR PLACE WITHIN IT)

■ ■ ■

A. INTRODUCTION

In this final part of the book, we have examined a number of significant problems and opportunities facing the legal profession. They represent challenges for the society of which the profession is a part, for the profession, and for individual lawyers. You will almost surely have to confront many of these issues as you build your career. In this chapter, we ask you to reflect on those challenges and offer a few ideas about how you might navigate the interesting times that lie ahead for you and for the legal profession.

At the broadest level, the profession confronts difficulty in delivering services to all who need them. If law is to achieve the goals that legislatures, executive branch officials, and the judiciary have for it when they create law on behalf of the people, and if the rule of law is to be maintained in the daily lives of the governed and those who govern, people need access to legal services. In other words, legal services are often necessary to make law work in a complex and highly regulated society like ours. Lawyers enjoy considerable power and wealth by virtue of the fact that they have a monopoly on the practice of law and the power of self-regulation. A continuing failure to address access to justice may ultimately threaten both the profession's monopoly and its prerogatives of self-regulation.

Second, we have seen dramatic changes in the structure and organization of many forms of law practice, including (but not limited to) private practice in corporations, in law firms of all sizes, and in legal services for poor and middle-income Americans. In the Galanter and Henderson excerpt below, we consider changes in the structure of private law practice, especially (but not exclusively) the large law firm.

Third, there is reason to believe that the work of lawyers has changed dramatically in the last twenty years and will change more in the twenty to come. That is, we may be witnessing not only a transformation in the structure and organization of law practices, but

1061

also a transformation in the work of lawyers regardless of the type of organization in which they work. In the Richard Susskind excerpts below, we consider the changing nature of legal services.

Finally, and perhaps of most immediate interest to you, we ask you to reflect on the changes that you are undergoing on the path taking you into the legal profession. Law school is famous for its rigor (though many law students find the tales of its horrors to be a bit overblown, and we hope you too have been pleasantly surprised). Law school is also famous, for good reason, for changing the way you think. There is good and bad in teaching you to "think like a lawyer." The final excerpt asks you to reflect on the process of professional socialization. If you aspire to mindfulness as you reflect on the formation of your professional identity now, we hope you will retain that mindfulness as you go through your career and navigate all the large and small challenges you and our profession face.

B. CHANGES IN PRACTICE AND THE INFLUENCE OF MILLENIAL LAWYERS

THE ELASTIC TOURNAMENT: A SECOND TRANSFORMATION OF THE BIG LAW FIRM

Marc Galanter & William Henderson
60 Stanford Law Review 1867 (2008)

According to many human resource experts, the values and preferences of the next generation of lawyers, dubbed the Millennials, are on collision course with the work norms of large law firms. Millennials are defined as the generation born after 1980 who thus began graduating from high school before the year 2000. According to the standard educational timeline, the first wave began working as summer and entry-level associates during the last three to four years. The typical characterization of Millennial lawyers is that they demand a high level of racial and gender diversity within the firm's workforce, are unwilling to sacrifice life and family for work, believe that work should be fun, exciting, and high paying from day one, and are more than willing to frankly express these views to their employer.

[If demand for corporate legal services continues to rise, there could be] a generational "showdown" between entering associates and partners, [and] it is difficult to predict who will prevail or what a compromise might look like. Nonetheless, we cannot resist the urge to speculate.

An important data point is the recently formed Law Students Building a Better Legal Profession (BBLP), a grassroots student organization—formed in 2006 by students enrolled at Stanford Law School—that is urging change among the large law firms that its members may one day join. One of BBLP's key strategies is to compile information and rank large law firms on metrics that matter to the group, such as pro bono participation, firm transparency, billable hours, gender composition, diversity of the firm's partnership, and overall firm diversity along the lines of race, gender, and sexual orientation. Because these rankings are broken down at the major city level, students with multiple options will now have the information to make relatively targeted decisions. If the rankings take hold, firms that ignore BBLP's agenda will be at a considerable disadvantage in the market for associate talent. Hence, BBLP's describes its goals as "market-based workplace reforms."

Thus far, the group's success has been mixed. In April 2007, BBLP sent a letter to 100 of the nation's largest law firms urging them to adopt the group's recommendations. Although only six firms returned the communication, the group had in-person meetings with the managing partner of a national law firm, which in turn led to a pledge to support an initiative to support a project on attorney attrition.[3] More significantly, after extensive coverage in the mainstream media, the rankings generated enormous internet traffic, presumably from prospective law firm associates and law firm partners worried about how their firms fared. According to the group's founders, there is ample anecdotal evidence that students "crossed off firms from their interviews and callbacks by seeing that they were repeatedly at the bottom of our rankings."

Yet, in assessing the long term prospects of BBLP's program, the key analytical question is whether law firms managers have the power (a separate question from inclination) to accede to these demands. Unfortunately, we are skeptical. For example, one of BBLP's Principles is to replace an "hours culture" with a "quality culture" by scuttling the billable hour in favor of transactional billing and adopting balanced hours policies "that, without stigma, allow associates to work 80%, 70%, or 60% of fulltime hours for proportional pay" while keeping them on partnership track. From a purely economic perspective, a lawyer who works 70% of the typical full-time load is unlikely to deliver a pro rata return on his or her time because fixed overhead for office space and support staff is not thereby proportionately reduced. Certainly, the marginal profit is higher for the hours in excess of 2000 as opposed to 1400. From a partner perspective, staffing projects becomes more complicated and time-consuming. More significantly, there is overwhelming evidence that each partner's security in the firm depends upon client relationships in a fiercely competitive marketplace. Why would these folks want to confer partnership rewards on workers whose preferences would intensify that burden? Once again, there is no "firm" that can impose these lifestyle policies so long as it is made up of autonomous partners who can vote with their feet.

If the law firms and the Millennials are going to strike a deal, it is important to understand the associates' bargaining position. A law firm job can be evaluated along a variety of dimensions, including salary and bonus, working conditions, prestige, and value of future career options conferred by the skills and cachet an associate has acquired. Because elite law school graduates enjoy the most options, their career choices reveal information on the relative importance of these attributes. As an empirical matter, these employment patterns suggest that compensation, prestige, and outplacement options weigh more heavily with prospective associates than attributes like hours worked or family friendliness. Since better working conditions are already available at less elite firms in the Am Law 200, especially in smaller markets, what BBLP appears to be asking for is very high pay, very high prestige, location in a desirable urban market, excellent career options, reasonable promotion prospects, and sensible hours.

This is not necessarily a deal that the prestigious Wall Street firms need to accept. Rather than reducing their hours, which may prompt partner defections, they can rely on higher salaries and their marquee brand—a good that associates routinely trade on to build their resumes—to coax sufficient Millennials to join the firm. If firms at the top of the Vault rankings increase their starting salary another $20,000 and yet make no firm commitment toward BBLP's goals, what percentage of Millennials will go with the highest prestige job? For less profitable firms in the Am Law 200, with ratios of partner profits to associate pay below 4.0, each round of the salary wars prompts extremely difficult decisions. There is a strong perception among law firm partners that it is crucial to match the prevailing rate for associate pay because "otherwise, you are second-rate." Yet, unless the pay raise is self-funded through higher billable hour requirements (an outcome antithetical to BBLP's goals) or higher billing rates (something clients will resist), firms toward the bottom of the Am Law 200 will be more likely to lose key rainmaking partners to upstream rivals. Of course, this only exacerbates the separation dynamic we know is occurring between elite and semi-elite large law firms.

We foresee at least two responses by law firms that could fundamentally transform the structure, economics, and norms of large law firm practice. First, large law firms, particularly less elite firms under pressure from the salary wars, can bypass Millennials from elite law schools by slightly reducing their grade cutoffs for interviewing students from less prestigious regional law schools. In essence, these firms would be diluting the Cravath system, which aimed to hire the best students from the best law schools and give them the best training. Yet, there is empirical evidence that this may be a prudent strategy. According to a recent study by Ronit Dinovitzer and Bryant Garth, based on data from the After the JD Project, large law firm associates who graduated from less elite law schools are (a) more satisfied with their careers, and (b) express a lower likelihood of wanting to leave the firm. Because graduates of less elite law schools are less likely to come from families with professional or advantaged backgrounds, Dinovitzer and Garth suggest that large law firm employment delivers a much greater sense of accomplishment and mobility than that experienced by their counterparts from elite law schools. The second major transformation could be the emergence of a law firm that operates like a corporation, scuttling the promotion-to-partnership tournament and basing its hiring and promotion policies on each lawyer's marginal product. A firm operating on this model—once again, probably a semi-elite firm looking for refuge from the salary wars—would not be "selling" the elite credentials of its lawyers. Rather, it would be developing firm-specific capital by focusing on business processes that deliver high-quality legal services at a cost-effective and predictable price. Lawyers would be employees with salaries lower than their elite Wall Street counterparts; but they would also enjoy sensible hours that permit a better work-family balance—a combination of salary, prestige, and hours that is often found in in-house legal departments. Promotions would not be based on a multiyear tournament but on a lawyer's ability to profitably manage client matters, often taken a flat-fee basis or another nonhourly alternative. Demonstrated management and teamwork skills resulting in successful client engagements would carry more weight than Ivy League credentials. Further, a focus on job performance may be an ideal environment to develop the talents and abilities and women and minority attorneys, who have not fared well in a tracked and seeded promotion-to-partnership tournament.

Although general counsel may favor elite law firms for bet-the-company matters, this new business model could make substantial in-roads for higher volume, price-sensitive corporate work. And if nonlawyers could capitalize and share profits with law firms—an idea that is now a reality in Australia and coming soon to England—there would be ample funds to experiment with this new model. More importantly, the resulting business model would emphasize development of firm-specific capital, blunting the damage that could be done through lateral mobility and providing firm management with opportunities to develop secure and valuable niche markets.

NOTES ON CHANGES IN PRACTICE AND THE INFLUENCE OF MILLENNIALS

1. **The Generational Showdown.** Professors Galanter and Henderson published their analysis of the impact of Millennials just before the huge recession hit in 2009 and large law firms began laying off associates,

rescinding job offers to first-year associates, and/or postponing start dates by six to eighteen months. To what extent do you think the existence or outcome of a "generational showdown" between new law graduates and large law firms depends on whether law graduates feel they are facing a buyers' or a sellers' market for associates? If the "generational showdown" will occur if or when the demand for legal services returns to levels approaching those of 2008, what do you predict will result? What compromises do you think might be reached?

In the two years following the founding of Building a Better Legal Profession in 2007, the organization attracted a great deal of media attention,[1] spawned chapters at other law schools, and published a guide to law firms.[2] The group continues to maintain a database on law firm diversity, attrition, pro bono, and billable hours. However, it has received only a handful of media mentions since 2009.

2. ***How Do Millennials Really Think and How Will They Influence Practice and the Profession?*** Does Galanter and Henderson's description of the characteristics, values, and preferences of Millennial lawyers ring true? If not, how would you revise their description of Millennials and how would you modify their hypothesis about the likely impact of lawyers of your generation on the profession generally, or on law firms in particular?

3. ***A Corporate Model for Law Firms.*** Recent events suggest that Galanter and Henderson were correct in predicting that some law firms would modify or reduce their reliance on the promotion to partner up-or-out tournament in favor of a corporate model in which hiring and promotion practices are based on each lawyer's marginal product. While it is not (yet) the case that this new type of law firm has become prevalent, some firms are reconsidering their promotion practices, and some new types of law firms are emerging. For example, a new U.S. law firm created in 2010 called Clearspire looks substantially different than the traditional large firms with which it competes for corporate business. Clearspire claims to use the most advanced business practices and the most powerful technologies available to deliver legal services at substantially lower cost than conventional firms do. Clearwater does not bill by the hour and instead charges flat fees. Its overhead is low because it does not use fancy downtown office space, and it encourages its attorneys to work remotely. Similarly, Axiom Law matches lawyers hired on a temporary basis to work for clients, including almost half of the Fortune 100, for discrete projects at fixed rates. Its lawyers typically work at the clients' offices or from home. Axiom handles complex projects as well as piecemeal work, using teams of professionals including but not limited to lawyers. While Clearspire, Axiom, and other such emerging firms are not as profitable as major corporate firms and do not offer the same paths

---

[1] *See* Building a Better Legal Profession, Press Coverage, http://www.betterlegal profession.org/media.php (listing over 100 newspaper and magazine articles profiling the organization and its mission).

[2] BUILDING A BETTER LEGAL PROFESSION'S GUIDE TO LAW FIRMS (2009).

to lucrative partnerships, they nevertheless are growing fast and competing successfully with conventional large firms for some types of work.

What might be the advantages and disadvantages of the personnel practices of these new types of firms from the perspective of a new lawyer looking for career opportunities? What are the advantages and disadvantages from the standpoint of clients and the public?

4. ***Alternative Fee Arrangements.*** There has been a good deal of discussion in recent years about whether and to what extent hourly billing should give way to other fee arrangements. As discussed in Chapter 15, high hourly billable expectations pit the attorney's incentive to bill more time against the interest of clients, who must pay those bills. Reliance on billable hours as proxy for lawyer commitment to the firm encourages lawyers to "pad" client bills by inflating the time spent on client matters. In Chapter 37, we saw that high billable hour expectations drive some associates away from large firms and that women's attrition from these institutions is especially high. In 2008, Cravath, Swaine & Moore partner Evan Chesler argued that we should "kill the billable hour."[3] The hourly fee certainly is not dead, but many clients insist on alternative fee arrangements, such as hourly fees with caps, fixed fees, contingent fees, and base fees with bonuses tied to results.

5. ***Other Changes Afoot.*** In a series of lectures on the theme of "Legal Careers in the Global Age of More for Less," Professor David Wilkins argues that several major structural changes—the globalization of economic activity, the rise of information technology, and the blurring of 19th century categories of knowledge and organization—are fundamentally reshaping the market for legal services. He identifies several consequences of these structural changes. One is a reduction in the information asymmetry between buyers and sellers of legal services, which means that buyers (clients) can insist on the "unbundling" of services and control over what services lawyers perform and which to delegate to other types of service providers. Second, he predicts that competition will move away from reputation and credentials and toward valuation, assessed according to metrics determined by clients. He observes that these changes are putting substantial pressure on existing modes of practice and regulation.

According to Wilkins, lawyers who are not prepared for these challenges generally will not fare well, as clients insist on receiving "more for less" and as new types of service providers compete on price and efficiency. Wilkins also notes, however, that demand for legal services will be strong over the long term because clients and policymakers will continue to need lawyers to help them navigate an increasingly complex world.[4]

---

[3] Evan R. Chesler, *Kill the Billable Hour*, FORBES, Dec. 25, 2008.

[4] Slides for Wilkins's lectures on this topic are posted on the Harvard Program on the Legal Profession website, http://www.law.harvard.edu/programs/plp/pdf/wilkins_iba_slides.pdf.

C. THE FUTURE OF LEGAL SERVICES

Richard Susskind, British author of several major books on the legal profession, including *The Future of Lawyers,* and the apocalyptically titled *The End of Lawyers*, has gained a great deal of attention worldwide for his prediction that several powerful trends are revolutionizing the legal services industry. According to Susskind, the major drivers of this radical transformation are: 1) the "more for less" challenge—the expectation by clients of all types that lawyers deliver more legal services at less cost; 2) "liberalization," by which he means pressure to allow nonlawyers to compete directly with lawyers to deliver legal services; 3) the rapid growth of powerful information technologies, which will allow increasing amounts of legal work to be handled by advanced computer systems. He summarizes these trends and their implications in an excerpt from *The End of Lawyers*:

> Clients are requiring *more for less*. At the same time, new competitors are emerging. Liberalization of the legal market will bring external funding and a new wave of professional managers and investors who have no nostalgic commitment to traditional business models for law firms. To cap it all, a number of disruptive legal technologies are emerging which will directly challenge and sometimes even replace the traditional work of lawyers.
>
> I anticipate that the market is likely to respond in two ways to the changes just noted. First, new methods, systems, and processes will emerge to reduce the cost of undertaking routine legal work. This will extend well beyond the back-offices of legal businesses into the very heart of legal work. I expect there to be a strong pull by the market away from the delivery of legal advice on a bespoke basis [by which Susskind means individually tailored to the client's particular needs].
>
> The second response by the market will be for clients, in various ways, to share the costs of legal services. In-house lawyers will frequently work together and find ways of recycling legal work amongst themselves. In areas where their duplication of effort and expense is considerable, such as regulatory compliance, they will collaborate intensively and so spread the legal expense amongst their number. At the other end of the spectrum, citizens will have ready access to online legal guidance and to growing bodies of legal materials that are available on an open source basis.[5]

---

[5] RICHARD SUSSKIND, THE END OF LAWYERS: RETHINKING THE NATURE OF LEGAL SERVICES (2010).

Susskind argues that these three major drivers of change will produce a world that is substantially different from the world that lawyers confront today. He further predicts that the future for lawyers could be either "prosperous or disastrous," depending upon lawyers' attitudes and preparation for the dramatic and inevitable changes they will face:

> Lawyers who are unwilling to change their working practices and extend their range of services will struggle to survive. Meanwhile, those who embrace new technologies and novel ways of sourcing legal work are likely to trade successfully for many years, even if they are not occupied with the law jobs that most law schools currently anticipate for their graduates.

Susskind predicts that there will be fewer conventional lawyers in the future because clients will be unwilling to pay for expensive services that could be undertaken by less expert advisers supported by standard processes and sophisticated systems. He anticipates that there will remain "expert trusted advisors," who provide customized services to clients who have novel, complex or high value issues and who want personalized guidance. But he warns that the demand for expert trusted advisors will be limited and that lawyers who assume that all their clients' work will require such tailored treatment will do so at their peril. On the other hand, Susskind argues that there will be plenty of opportunity for lawyers who are flexible, open-minded and entrepreneurial, and he identifies a number of new types of jobs that will be available for those trained in law.

In his more recent book, *Tomorrow's Lawyers: An Introduction to Your Future,* Susskind elaborates on the types of new jobs he expects to be available for future lawyers. One of those jobs, according to Susskind, will be "the legal knowledge engineer," who analyzes, organizes, and distills huge quantities of legal materials and processes to be embedded in computer systems. This job will be more intellectually demanding than traditional legal work because it requires the ability to solve many problems, rather than simply respond to a particular issue or need. The second new law job, according to Susskind, will be the "legal technologist," who is trained and experienced in law as well as systems engineering and IT management. Legal technologists will handle the technical side of creating legal services systems. The third new role predicted by Susskind is the "legal hybrid," a lawyer with rigorous training in other disciplines, such as business, engineering, or science. Fourth, Susskind anticipates that there will be strong demand for "legal process analysts," who can analyze legal work, subdivide it into manageable chunks, and identify the appropriate supplier of each type of service. The fifth category, the "legal project manager," will follow up on the work of the legal process analyst by allocating the work to appropriate providers, ensuring that they complete it on time and on budget, control the quality of the work, and oversee its output and delivery. The sixth type of new job, the "ODR practitioner," will work in, and advise clients about, the new field of "on-line dispute resolution," in which experts in resolving disputes conduct their work largely or entirely through the Internet.[6] A seventh category, legal management consultants, will advise in-house legal departments on management challenges, such as strategy formulation, team building, and the introduction of information technology. Finally, Susskind predicts that "legal risk managers" will be needed to develop processes, techniques, and systems to help clients identify, assess, quantify, hedge, monitor and control the risks that they confront. Whereas conventional legal services are mostly reactive, in that they address questions and needs that clients have brought to their lawyers' attention, legal risk managers will be proactive, anticipating the needs of their clients and preempting legal problems.

Susskind asserts that these new jobs for tomorrow's lawyers will present a rich and exciting set of opportunities. But just as he predicts that the jobs of tomorrow will be in many ways different from the jobs of today, he also anticipates that many of the employers who will offer young lawyers these opportunities will not be conventional law firms but rather different types of businesses. Those businesses will include global accounting firms, major legal publishers, and legal process outsourcers (LPOs)—organizations that undertake routine and repetitive tasks such as document review in litigation and basic contract drafting. (As we saw in Chapter 34, LPOs have lately begun handling more challenging work as well.) The employers of young lawyers will also include "lawyer leasing agencies," such as Axiom, which assemble teams of lawyers to work on discrete projects on a temporary basis. They will include what Susskind calls "New-Look Law Firms," by which he means firms that eschew the old business models and pyramidic profit structure in favor of cost-containment, lower fees, and solid but not spectacular profits. Such firms include Clearspire (discussed above in the notes after the Galanter & Henderson excerpt) and the U.K.'s radiantlaw.com and Riverview Law. Other important sources for jobs in the future, Susskind predicts, will be online legal service providers, including not only large-scale businesses that produce legal documentation for complex deals, but also charitable organizations that try to increase access to justice through technology, as discussed in Chapter 32. Finally, Susskind predicts that legal management consulting businesses, which specialize in legal process analysis, legal project management, and legal risk management, will hire lawyers with expertise and experience in these fields.

---

[6] An example of such a firm is Cybersettle, an Internet company that uses double-blind bidding to help parties find a middle ground, primarily in connection with personal injury and insurance claims. *See* Clive Thompson, *Negotiating on the Internet Gets Lawyers' Egos Out of the Way*, LEGAL AFFAIRS, May/June 2004.

Susskind argues that these new types of employers, rather than conventional law firms, are likely to offer the greatest opportunities for new law graduates in the future. He also suggests that these employers may offer more vibrant and entrepreneurial environments than conventional firms and that they may be more open than conventional firms to young lawyers' ideas about how legal services might be improved.

NOTES ON SUSSKIND

1. **New Jobs for Lawyers.** List the types of new jobs that Susskind envisions for lawyers of the future and the tasks that he predicts will be performed by each. What are the catalysts of the changes he predicts? Do you think that the work of these new types of lawyers will be more or less plentiful, remunerative, or satisfying than the work of lawyers today?

2. **Tomorrow's Employers.** What are the attractions and downsides of working for the major types of employers that Susskind says will offer the primary opportunities for young lawyers in the future?

3. **Are the Predictions Plausible?** Do you think that Susskind's predictions are realistic? Are some more convincing than others? Which of the practice types/settings surveyed in Part V are likely to be most and least affected by the changes that Susskind anticipates?

4. **Who Will Benefit?** Would the realization of Susskind's predictions be good or bad from the standpoint of lawyers, clients, and/or the public?

D. CHARTING A CAREER

This book attempts to give you a good deal of information that we hope you will find useful as you prepare to launch your careers. It has offered historical perspectives, demographic information, portraits of various types of practice, ethics rules and other law governing lawyers, analyses of problems and opportunities for the profession as a whole, and, now, predictions about what the future holds for the profession. Sprinkled throughout are insights yielded by the *After the JD Study,* the first and only major longitudinal study of lawyers' careers. Along the way, we have tried to suggest how these materials might help you chart successful, rewarding, and responsible futures in law.

Many of the materials in this book suggest that lawyers will face huge changes and challenges in the years to come. The next two excerpts offer perspectives that might be relevant to how you approach these changes and challenges. In the first, Richard Susskind urges young lawyers to be benevolent custodians of the law. Borrowing wisdom from Wayne Gretzky, perhaps the greatest hockey player of all time, Susskind also advises young lawyers to "skate where the puck's going, not where it's been." The second set of excerpts, from Mark Twain's *Life on the Mississippi,* arguably have nothing whatsoever to do with the legal profession, but we hope that they may nevertheless prompt you to reflect on the process of preparing to enter the profession and what you hope to find once you get there.

TOMORROW'S LAWYERS: AN INTRODUCTION TO YOUR FUTURE
Richard Susskind
(Oxford Press 2013)

I implore you, tomorrow's lawyers, to take up the mantle of the benevolent custodians; to be honest with yourselves and with society about those areas of legal endeavor that genuinely must be preserved for lawyers in the interest of clients. Where, in all conscience, legal services can responsibly and reliably by offered by non-lawyers, celebrate access to justice and draw upon your creative and entrepreneurial talents to find other ways that your legal knowledge and experience can bring unique value to your clients.

As I often remind lawyers, the law is no more there to provide a living for lawyers than ill health exists to offer livelihood for doctors. It is not the purpose of law to keep lawyers in business. The purpose of law is to help to support society's needs of the law.

Alan Kay, a computer scientist from Silicon Valley, makes a different but related point. He once said that the "the best way to predict the future is to invent it." This is a powerful message for tomorrow's lawyers.

Here is the great excitement for tomorrow's lawyers. As never before, there is an opportunity to be involved in shaping the next generation of legal services. You will find most senior lawyers to be of little guidance in this quest. Your elders will tend to be cautious, protective, conservative, if not reactionary. They will resist change and will often want to hang on to their traditional ways of working, even if they are well past their sell-by date.

In truth, you are on your own. I urge you to forge new paths for the law, our most important social institution.

NOTES ON SUSSKIND

1.   **What Do Custodians of Law Do?** What does Susskind mean when he exhorts young lawyers to be benevolent custodians? How does Susskind's appeal to young lawyers to become benevolent custodians relate to other topics considered in this course, such as the regulation of the profession (Chapter 2), the lawyer's role (Chapter 3), the market for legal services (Chapter 31), unauthorized practice/nonlawyer services (Chapter 32), and pro bono (Chapter 33)?

2   **Will Senior Lawyers Help or Stand in the Way?** Do you accept Susskind's assertion that you will be "on your own" in forging a new future

for the profession? Might some of the oldsters offer wisdom, even if they cannot offer new ideas or technical know-how?

LIFE ON THE MISSISSIPPI
Mark Twain
(1883)

Now when I had mastered the language of this water and had come to know every trifling feature that bordered the great river as familiarly as I knew the letters of the alphabet, I had made a valuable acquisition. But I had lost something, too. I had lost something which could never be restored to me while I lived. All the grace, the beauty, the poetry had gone out of the majestic river! I still keep in mind a certain wonderful sunset which I witnessed when steamboating was new to me. A broad expanse of the river was turned to blood; in the middle distance the red hue brightened into gold, through which a solitary log came floating, black and conspicuous; in one place a long, slanting mark lay sparkling upon the water; in another the surface was broken by boiling, tumbling rings, that were as many-tinted as an opal; where the ruddy flush was faintest, was a smooth spot that was covered with graceful circles and radiating lines, ever so delicately traced; the shore on our left was densely wooded, and the sombre shadow that fell from this forest was broken in one place by a long, ruffled trail that shone like silver; and high above the forest wall a clean-stemmed dead tree waved a single leafy bough that glowed like a flame in the unobstructed splendor that was flowing from the sun. There were graceful curves, reflected images, woody heights, soft distances; and over the whole scene, far and near, the dissolving lights drifted steadily, enriching it, every passing moment, with new marvels of coloring.

I stood like one bewitched. I drank it in, in a speechless rapture. The world was new to me, and I had never seen anything like this at home. But as I have said, a day came when I began to cease from noting the glories and the charms which the moon and the sun and the twilight wrought upon the river's face; another day came when I ceased altogether to note them. Then, if that sunset scene had been repeated, I should have looked upon it without rapture, and should have commented upon it, inwardly, in this fashion: This sun means that we are going to have wind tomorrow; that floating log means that the river is rising, small thanks to it; that slanting mark on the water refers to a bluff reef which is going to kill somebody's steamboat one of these nights, if it keeps on stretching out like that; those tumbling "boils" show a dissolving bar and a changing channel there; the lines and circles in the slick water over yonder are a warning that that troublesome place is shoaling up dangerously; that silver streak in the shadow of the forest is the "break" from a new snag, and he has located himself in the very best place he could have found to fish for steamboats; that tall dead tree, with a single living branch, is not going to last long, and then how is a body ever going to get through this blind place at night without the friendly old landmark?

No, the romance and the beauty were all gone from the river. All the value any feature of it had for me now was the amount of usefulness it could furnish toward compassing the safe piloting of a steamboat. Since those days, I have pitied doctors from my heart. What does the lovely flush in a beauty's cheek mean to a doctor but a "break" that ripples above some deadly disease? Are not all her visible charms sown thick with what are to him the signs and symbols of hidden decay? Does he ever see her beauty at all, or doesn't he simply view her professionally, and comment upon her unwholesome condition all to himself? And doesn't he sometimes wonder whether he has gained most or lost most by learning his trade?

"I STOOD LIKE ONE BEWITCHED."

In my preceding chapters I have tried, by going into the minutiae of the science of piloting, to carry the reader step by step to a comprehension of what the science consists of; and at the same time I have tried to show him that it is a very curious and wonderful science, too, and very worthy of his attention. If I have seemed to love my subject, it is no surprising thing, for I loved the profession far better than any I have followed since, and I took a measureless pride in it. The reason is plain: a pilot, in those days, was the only unfettered and entirely independent human being that lived in the earth. Kings are but the hampered servants of parliament and people; parliaments sit in chains forged by their constituency; the editor of a newspaper cannot be independent, but must work with one hand tied behind him by party and patrons, and be content to utter only half or two thirds of his mind; no clergyman is a free man and may speak the whole truth, regardless of his parish's opinions; writers of all kinds are manacled servants of the public. We write frankly and fearlessly, but then we "modify" before we print. In truth, every man and woman and child has a master, and worries and frets in servitude; but in the day I write of, the Mississippi pilot had *none.* The captain could stand upon the hurricane deck, in the pomp of a very brief authority, and give him five or six orders while the vessel backed into the stream, and then that skipper's reign was over. The moment that the boat was under way in the river, she was under the sole and unquestioned control of the pilot. He could do with her exactly as he pleased, run her when and whither he chose, and tie her up to the bank whenever his judgment said that that course was best. His movements were entirely free; he consulted no one, he received commands from nobody, he promptly resented even the merest suggestions. Indeed, the law of the United States forbade him to listen to commands or suggestions, rightly considering that the pilot necessarily knew better how to handle the boat than anybody could tell him.

"VERY BRIEF AUTHORITY."

NOTES ON TWAIN

1.   *What's Gained and Lost.* Do these excerpts from Twain's *Life on the Mississippi* speak to your experience as a law student—about what you may feel you are gaining and losing in the process of becoming a lawyer and entering the profession?

2.   *Independence.* How do you think being a lawyer stacks up against being a river pilot in terms of independence or autonomy? What are the sources of constraint on lawyers' autonomy and whose interests do they serve? How do those sources of constraint vary by type of practice, and how are they likely to change in the future?

3.   *Navigating Your Career.* Does the idea of river piloting work as a metaphor for how you might be able to use what you've learned in this course to help you navigate successful and rewarding careers in law?

E. SUMMARY

This chapter has asked you to reflect on the future of the legal profession and what it holds for you. We considered the job market that Millennials will encounter and whether and how young lawyers are likely to influence law firms and other institutions that deliver legal services. We surveyed major drivers of change in the legal services industry, including client demands for more value for lower cost, the liberalization of controls over who can compete with lawyers in the legal services market, and technology. We explored predictions about what types of new positions are likely to be available for young lawyers in the coming years and what types of employers are likely to provide those jobs. We suggested perspectives that might bear on how you respond to the changing conditions in the legal services industry. Finally, we asked you to reflect on how your legal education and socialization into the legal profession might be changing your outlook on life and how knowledge about this changing profession might help you navigate the choices and challenges that lie ahead.

INDEX

References are to Pages